About the author

Respected wine critic and vigneron James Halliday has a career that spans over forty years, but he is most widely known for his witty and informative writing about wine. As one of the founders of Brokenwood in the Lower Hunter Valley, New South Wales, and thereafter founder of Coldstream Hills in the Yarra Valley, Victoria, James is an unmatched authority on every aspect of the wine industry, from the planting and pruning of vines through to the creation and marketing of the finished product. His winemaking has led him to sojourns in Bordeaux and Burgundy, and he is constantly in demand as a wine judge in Australia and overseas.

James has contributed to more than 56 books on wine since he began writing in 1979. His books have been translated into Japanese, French, German, Danish, Icelandic and Polish, and have been published in the UK, the US, as well as Australia. He is also the author of *James Halliday's Wine Atlas of Australia* and *The Australian Wine Encyclopedia*.

Wine zones and regions of Australia

NEW SOUTH WALES			
WINE ZONE		**WINE REGION**	
Big Rivers	(A)	Murray Darling	1
		Perricoota	2
		Riverina	3
		Swan Hill	4
Central Ranges	(B)	Cowra	5
		Mudgee	6
		Orange	7
Hunter Valley	(C)	Lower Hunter	8
		Upper Hunter	9
Northern Rivers	(D)	Hastings River	10
Northern Slopes	(E)	New England	11
South Coast	(F)	Shoalhaven Coast	12
		Southern Highlands	13
Southern New South Wales	(G)	Canberra District	14
		Gundagai	15
		Hilltops	16
		Tumbarumba	17
Western Plains	(H)		

SOUTH AUSTRALIA			
WINE ZONE		**WINE REGION**	
Adelaide Super Zone includes Mount Lofty Ranges, Fleurieu and Barossa wine regions			
Barossa		Barossa Valley	18
		Eden Valley	19
Fleurieu	(J)	Currency Creek	20
		Kangaroo Island	21
		Langhorne Creek	22
		McLaren Vale	23
		Southern Fleurieu	24
Mount Lofty Ranges		Adelaide Hills	25
		Adelaide Plains	26
		Clare Valley	27
Far North	(K)	Southern Flinders Ranges	28
Limestone Coast	(L)	Coonawarra	29
		Mount Benson	30
		Mount Gambier*	31
		Padthaway	32
		Robe	33
		Wrattonbully	34
Lower Murray	(M)	Riverland	35
The Peninsulas	(N)	Southern Eyre Peninsula*	36

VICTORIA			
WINE ZONE		**WINE REGION**	
Central Victoria	(P)	Bendigo	37
		Goulburn Valley	38
		Heathcote	39
		Strathbogie Ranges	40
Gippsland	(Q)	Upper Goulburn	41
		Alpine Valleys	42
North East Victoria	(R)	Beechworth	43
		Glenrowan	44
		King Valley	45
		Rutherglen	46
North West Victoria	(S)	Murray Darling	47
		Swan Hill	48
Port Phillip	(T)	Geelong	49
		Macedon Ranges	50
		Mornington Peninsula	51
		Sunbury	52
		Yarra Valley	53
Western Victoria	(U)	Ballarat*	54
		Grampians	55
		Henty	56
		Pyrenees	57

* Regions that have taken, or are likely to take, steps to secure registration.

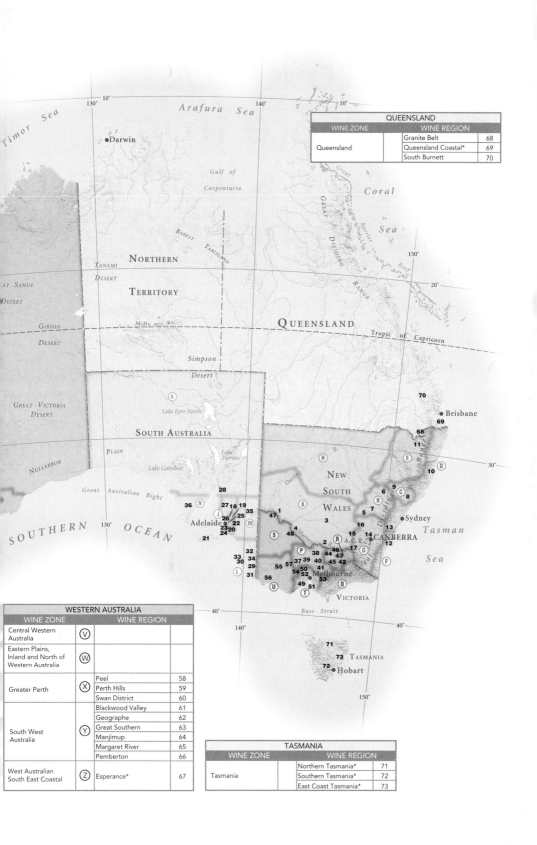

QUEENSLAND

WINE ZONE	WINE REGION	
Queensland	Granite Belt	68
	Queensland Coastal*	69
	South Burnett	70

WESTERN AUSTRALIA

WINE ZONE		WINE REGION	
Central Western Australia	Ⓥ		
Eastern Plains, Inland and North of Western Australia	Ⓦ		
Greater Perth	Ⓧ	Peel	58
		Perth Hills	59
		Swan District	60
South West Australia	Ⓨ	Blackwood Valley	61
		Geographe	62
		Great Southern	63
		Manjimup	64
		Margaret River	65
		Pemberton	66
West Australian South East Coastal	Ⓩ	Esperance*	67

TASMANIA

WINE ZONE	WINE REGION	
Tasmania	Northern Tasmania*	71
	Southern Tasmania*	72
	East Coast Tasmania*	73

James Halliday
Australian
Wine Companion

2010 Edition

Hardie Grant Books

MELBOURNE • LONDON

Published in 2009 by
Hardie Grant Books
85 High Street
Prahran, Victoria 3181, Australia
www.hardiegrant.com.au
www.hardiegrant.co.uk

The *Australian Wine Companion* is a joint venture between
James Halliday and Explore Australia Publishing Pty Ltd.

The map in this publication incorporates data copyright
© Commonwealth of Australia (Geoscience Australia) 2004.
Geoscience Australia has not evaluated the data as altered and incorporated
within this publication and therefore gives no warranty regarding accuracy,
completeness, currency or suitability for any particular purpose.

Australian wine zones and wine regions data copyright
© Australian Wine and Brandy Corporation, April 2005

ISBN 978 1 74066 754 8

Typeset by Megan Ellis
Printed and bound in Australia by McPherson's Printing Group

10 9 8 7 6 5 4 3 2 1

Contents

Introduction

The Australian wine industry is being buffeted by worldwide recession; by exchange rate fluctuations; by continuous sniping attacks from wine writers in our two major wine markets, the UK and the US, largely due to the contempt bred of familiarity; by the spectre of continuing surpluses; and the uncertainties of changed rainfall distribution, making the future of the Murray Darling almost impossible to predict.

Out of these and other issues, the view has emerged that the annual crush should be permanently reduced by up to 400 000 tonnes. One immediate problem is the starting figure. The plantings and production figures on page 48 graphically show the difficulty: in 'normal' vintages the yield is between 10.5 and 11 tonnes per hectare. So to decrease the 'normal' yield to 1 300 000 tonnes, 46 500 hectares have to be removed.

The consequence is obvious: give or take a few hectares, and you would be left with 127 200 hectares. If past history is any guide, one in every four vintages will provide a yield of less than 8 tonnes per hectare. This would result in a harvest of a fraction over 1 million tonnes, taking us back to where we were in 1999, unable to defend export markets, and paying too much for grapes, starting the cycle all over again.

However, the cure may be even worse than the foregoing would suggest. Since yield from the Riverina and the Murray Darling (often grouped as the Riverland) has historically been more stable than the non-irrigated regions, and has always contributed 60% or more of the annual vintage, it would seem logical to remove 45 000-plus hectares from the Riverland regions.

This would also fit with Australia's grand marketing plan of focusing on its high cost/high value (compared to the Riverland) regional wines from its high-profile cool to moderately cool regions spread across all states. Here the problem is the global recession, and the IMF prediction it will be unusually deep, unusually protracted, and have a slow and uneven recovery. Trying to build markets with higher priced wines will be very difficult, requiring more marketing dollars than are available.

So the Riverland regions are reprieved, and the axe falls on cool-climate areas. But what happens if the record low inflows into the Murray Darling turn out to be permanent (or at least common) due to climate change, rather than a drought, which has historical parallels (the Federation Drought and the Second World War Drought)? We have removed 45 000 hectares from cool regions, and suddenly find the Murray Darling's capacity has been permanently crippled. In this nightmare scenario, all of the massive gains the industry has made since 1985 will evaporate, and – in wine terms – we would be a Third World producer. Truly, damned if you do, and damned if you don't.

Australian vintage 2009: a snapshot

The story across South Australia, Victoria, Tasmania and, to a slightly lesser degree, New South Wales, has an eerie similarity as you move from region to region: a mild, indeed cool, growing season punctuated by between four and ten days of extreme heat from the end of January into the first week of February. Putting the Riverland and Riverina to one side, there was a constant refrain of significantly, frequently savagely, reduced yields. Curiously, the reduction in some instances was due to wet and cold weather at flowering; in other instances, the ongoing drought, but the net result was the same. Western Australia, too, had lower than average yields, but was unaffected by the heat; there, rain at inconvenient times increased disease pressure, pressure that the better growers were able to deal with. But right across Australia, early indications are of wines that will be of high to outstanding quality.

A state-by-state sprint around the regions comes up with the following.

SOUTH AUSTRALIA

Adelaide Hills Outstanding white and red wines; yields down 20% to 40%. **Barossa Valley** Shiraz, in particular, very good; down 35% to 40%. **Eden Valley** Good to very good, though not outstanding; down 30% to 40%. **Coonawarra** Latest and best harvest since '04; reds outstanding; down 20% to 50%. **McLaren Vale** Water and canopy management critically important; quality from poor to very good; down 15% to 50%, especially shiraz. **Padthaway** Not as good as Coonawarra; down 25% to 50%. **Murray Darling** Solid, full-flavoured whites; reds uneven; down 10%.

VICTORIA

Alpine Valley and **King Valley** No smoke taint; excellent flavour, balance and structure; yields down 20% to 50%. **Bendigo** Heat and drought affected quality except for old vine shiraz and cabernet; severely reduced. **Geelong** Grossly affected by heat; down by up to 65%. **Gippsland** Drought and heat led to small berries; some smoke taint, but also good wine; down 30%. **Grampians** Tiny berries and bunches, but no smoke taint; down 20%. **Henty** Handled heat very well but whites down 60% (frost) and reds down 60% (poor set). **Mornington Peninsula** A cool vintage overall, the heat wave causing some damage, though no smoke taint; yields down, especially pinot noir. **Murray Darling** Those with water and large canopies fared well; acceptable quality; moderate yields, down 10%. **Beechworth** Eight days over 40°C and some smoke taint; chardonnay down 50%. **Goulburn Valley** Great reds, good whites; down 40%. **Rutherglen** Heat and fire damage less impact than '08, but flavours modest; down 15% to 50%. **Pyrenees** Outstanding red vintage; no smoke; minimal effect from the heat wave; down somewhat. **Strathbogie Ranges** Shiraz and cabernet best performers; down 30%. **Sunbury** No smoke taint but heat shrivel demanded careful hand-picking; down 20%. **Upper Goulburn** Smoke taint concerns, but, if untainted, a very good red year; down significantly. **Macedon Ranges** Drought, rain during flowering and bird pressure; what remained was very good; down 50%. **Heathcote** Drought and heat, but no smoke taint issues, hand-picking and sorting tables; very good reds; down 15%. **Yarra Valley** Worst affected by heat, bushfires and smoke taint; yields down 30% to 100%.

NEW SOUTH WALES
Hunter Valley Semillon, as ever, very good; shiraz picked before mid-February rain quite good; yields down. **Cowra** Looking great until the heat; just okay; down 30%. **Canberra District** Outstanding vintage both white and reds; down 10%. **Mudgee** Outstanding reds; down 20%. **Orange** A memorable vintage for some, especially reds; whites good; down 10% to 50%. **Riverina** Fourteen days 40°C-plus; late-picked reds the best; new plantings offset yield loss. **Southern Highlands** Great vintage for all varieties; low yields.

WESTERN AUSTRALIA
Margaret River Excellent quality both white and reds; down 20% to 30%. **Great Southern** High quality despite rain late March/early April; below average yields. **Peel** As for much of Western Australia, powdery mildew a problem, but manageable. **Pemberton** Erratic weather patterns, but great sauvignon blanc. **Perth Hills** Very good quality; white yields down. **Swan Valley** High quality; down 15% to 25%.

TASMANIA
A cool and late vintage; slight hen and chicken fruit set, very high quality; down 20% to 50%.

QUEENSLAND
No fires, no heatwaves; an early start but delayed by mid-vintage rains; very good whites, variable reds.

OVERALL
At the time of going to print, unofficial but informed sources pointed to a harvest of 1.6 million tonnes; if this is correct, the Murray Darling has performed an (unwanted) miracle, and the Riverina has been well served by its effectively unrestricted water allocations for vineyards.

How to use the *Wine Companion*

The *Australian Wine Companion* is arranged with wineries in alphabetical order; the index lists the wineries by region, which adds a search facility. The entries should be self-explanatory, but here I will briefly take you through the information provided for each entry, using Tyrrell's as an example.

Wineries

Tyrrell's ★★★★★

Broke Road, Pokolbin, NSW 2321 **Region** Lower Hunter Valley
T (02) 4993 7000 **F** (02) 4998 7723 **www**.tyrrells.com.au **Open** 7 days 10-5
Winemaker Andrew Spinaze, Mark Richardson **Est.** 1858 **Cases** 500 000 **Vyds** 226 ha
One of the most successful family wineries, a humble operation for the first 110 years of its life which has grown out of all recognition over the past 40 years. In 2003 it cleared the decks by selling its Long Flat range of wines for an eight-figure sum, allowing it to focus on its premium, super-premium and ultra-premium wines: Vat 1 Semillon is one of the most dominant wines in the Australian show system, and Vat 47 Chardonnay is one of the pacesetters for this variety. It has an awesome portfolio of single-vineyard Semillons released when five–six years old. Exports to all major markets.

Winery name Tyrrell's

Although it might seem that stating the winery name is straightforward, this is not necessarily so. To avoid confusion, wherever possible, I use the name that appears most prominently on the wine label.

Winery rating ★★★★★

The effort to come up with a fair winery rating system continues. I looked at the ratings for this and the previous two years; if the wines tasted this year justified a higher rating than last year, the higher rating has been given. If, on the other hand, the wines are of lesser quality, I took into account the track record over the past two years (or longer where the winery is well known) and made a judgement call on whether it should retain its ranking, or be given a lesser one. If lesser, I have usually dropped the rating by only half a star where the prior record has been consistent. Where no wines were submitted by a well-rated winery which had a track record of providing samples, I used my discretion to roll over last year's rating.

There is another factor affecting winery ratings in this edition. While 2007 was an excellent vintage in WA, it was not so in Southeast Australia. The red wines, in particular, can be quite tough, and are ageing quickly. This is in sharp contrast to 2006, and (provided that grapes were picked before the heat) the 2008 vintage has been markedly superior. Thus it would be demonstrably unreasonable to downgrade a winery rating on the basis of one poor vintage.

While there are (only) 1467 wineries profiled in this edition there are a total of 2568 wineries to be found on www.winecompanion.com.au.

The precise meanings attached to the winery star rating is as follows; the percentage at the end of each rating is that of the total number of wineries in the *Wine Companion* database at the time of going to print.

★★★★★ Outstanding winery regularly producing wines of exemplary quality and typicity. Will have at least two wines rated at 94 points or above, and have had a five-star rating for the previous two years. 7%

★★★★★ Outstanding winery capable of producing wines of very high quality, and did so this year. Also will usually have at least two wines rated at 94 points or above. 7.5%

★★★★☆ Excellent winery able to produce wines of high to very high quality, knocking on the door of a 5-star rating. Will have one wine rated at 94 or above, and two (or more) at 90 or above; others 87 to 89. 10.5%

★★★★ Very good producer of wines with class and character. Will have two (or more) wines rated at 90 points or above (or possibly one at 94 and above). 12.5%

★★★☆ A solid, usually reliable maker of good, sometimes very good wines. Will have one wine at 90 points or above; others at 87 to 89. 7.5%

★★★ A typically good winery, but often has a few lesser wines. Will have wines at 87 to 89 points. 9.5%

★★☆ The ★★☆ and NR ratings appear in this book and www.wine
/NR/NX companion.com.au; the NX ratings only on the website. The ratings are given in a range of circumstances: where there have been no tastings in the past 12 months; where there have been tastings, but no wines scoring more than 86 points; and where the tastings have, for one reason or another, proved not to fairly reflect the reputation of a winery with a track record of success. 45.5%

Contact Details Broke Road, Pokolbin, NSW 2321 **T** (02) 4993 7000 **F** (02) 4998 7723

The details are usually those of the cellar door, or of the winery (when the wine is made under contract and is sold only through retail).

Region Lower Hunter Valley

A full list of zones, regions and subregions appears on pages 40 to 43. Occasionally you will see 'Various' as the region. This means the wine is made from purchased grapes, in someone else's winery.

www.tyrrells.com.au

An increasingly important reference point, often containing material not found (for space reasons) in this book.

Open 7 days 8.30–5

Although a winery might be listed as not open or open only on weekends, some may in fact be prepared to open by appointment. Many will, some won't; a telephone call will establish whether it is possible or not.

Winemaker Andrew Spinaze, Mark Richardson

In the large companies the winemaker is simply the head of a team; there may be many executive winemakers actually responsible for specific wines.

Est. 1858

This may be the year in which the land was purchased, the year grapes were first planted, the year of the first vintage, and so on. There may also be minor complications where there has been a change of ownership or break in production.

Vyds 226 ha

A new feature, showing the hectares of vineyard/s owned by the winery.

Cases 500 000

This figure (representing the number of cases produced each year) is merely an indication of the size of the operation. Some winery entries do not feature a production figure where the information considered to be confidential.

Summary One of the most successful family wineries, a humble operation for the first 110 years of its life which has grown out of all recognition over the past 40 years.

My summary of the winery. Little needs be said, except that I have tried to vary the subjects I discuss in this part of the winery entry.

New wineries

 The vine leaf symbol indicates the 148 wineries that are new entries in this year's *Wine Companion*.

Tasting notes

Ratings

94–100	🍷🍷🍷🍷🍷	**Outstanding.** Wines of the highest quality, usually with a distinguished pedigree.
90–93	🍷🍷🍷🍷🍷	**Highly recommended.** Wines of great quality, style and character, worthy of a place in any cellar.
87–89	🍷🍷🍷🍷	**Recommended.** Wines of above-average quality, fault-free, and with clear varietal expression.

In order to compress the amount of material in this year's *Wine Companion*, but also to preserve a like-on-like comparison with prior years, the 2.5- to 3.5-glass-rated wines will appear on www.winecompanion.com.au (2602 in all).

The additional ratings on www.winecompanion.com.au have the following meanings:

84–86   ♀♀♀♀   **Acceptable.** Wines of good commercial quality, free of any significant fault.

80–83   ♀♀♀   **Over to you.** Everyday wines, usually cheap and with little or no future, lacking character and flavour.

75–79   ♀♀♀   **Not recommended.** Wines with one or more significant winemaking faults.

♀♀♀♀♀ **Vat 1 Hunter Semillon 2005** Bright straw-green, it has a strikingly perfumed bouquet of grass, herbs and wild flowers, the palate charged with lemon juice and lemon zest flavours, crisp acid driving the long palate and lingering finish. Screwcap. 11.3% alc. **Rating** 96 **To** 2025 $55

The tasting note opens with the vintage of the wine tasted. This tasting note will have been made within the 12 months prior to publication. Even that is a long time, and during the life of this book the wine will almost certainly change. The price of the wine is listed where information is available. Notes for wines 94 points or over, for wines offering particularly good value, and for unusual wines, are printed in red.

To 2025

I have provided a (conservative) 'best by' date. Modern winemaking is such that, even if a wine has 10 or 20 years' future, during which it will gain greater complexity, it can be enjoyed at any time over the intervening months and years.

Screwcap

This is the closure used for this particular wine. The closures in use for the wines tasted are (in descending order): screwcap 79% (last year 68%), one-piece natural cork 14% (last year 17%), Diam 5% (last year 5%). The remaining 2% (in approximate order of importance) are ProCork, Twin Top, Crown Seal, Zork, Vino-Lok and Synthetic. I believe the percentage of screwcap will continue to rise.

11.3% alc.

I have endeavoured to always include this piece of information, which is in one sense self-explanatory. Recent changes to domestic and export labelling mean the stated alcohol will be within a maximum of 0.5% of that obtained by analysis. What is less obvious is the increasing concern of many Australian winemakers about the rise in levels of alcohol; much research and practical experiment are occurring. Reverse osmosis and yeast selection are two of the research fields of particular promise.

Winery of the year

Tyrrell's

As will always be the case, there were half a dozen wineries with equally strong claims to be accorded this accolade. Given the restrictions imposed by the climate and soil of the Hunter Valley, it might seem an unlikely environment to foster a winery with a range of wines, varieties and prices to edge out all others, as Tyrrell's has done. I hasten to add that it did not (in diving parlance) receive a 'degree of difficulty' bonus: the wines are what they are.

It is obvious the cornerstone of the Tyrrell's portfolio is Semillon, in turn that of the Hunter Valley as a whole. Tyrrell's' development of the range of Single Vineyard Semillons, some from very old plantings, has added a layer of character and choice unmatched by the other makers in the region. To back this up is Vat 1 Semillon, which has won more trophies and gold medals than any other Australian white wine.

There has been a similar enriching of the shiraz portfolio: the Single Vineyard Old Patch 1867 comes from the celebrated Stevens Vineyard; the Winemaker's Selection 4 Acres from the block on the right-hand side of the road as you drive up to the winery planted in 1879, the original planting was so close-spaced that in 1964 every second row was removed to allow tractors on to the vineyard.

Then, there is Vat 47 Chardonnay, the first quality chardonnay to be made in the 20th century, for long the pacesetter. The development of cool-climate regions, notably Margaret River and the Yarra Valley, and the arrival of the new Dijon clones from France, has meant the overall quality of Australian chardonnay has risen dramatically since 1971, the birth year of Vat 47. Notwithstanding this, Vat 47 still holds its head high, as does Tyrrell's Belford Single Vineyard Chardonnay.

Single vineyards and old vines are not enough, of course. The potential has to be realised in the winery, and this is achieved with seeming ease by the winemaking team headed by Andrew Spinaze. Here the credo is let the wines speak without interference or embroidery.

Next is the exceptional quality of the high volume Old Winery range with a RRP of $12, and a discount price well below that. Finally, there is the undoubted truth of Bruce Tyrrell's belief that, in his words: 'We are entering a golden age for Semillon.' It is a wine more prone to the vagaries of cork than any other, even low levels of sporadic oxidation wreaking havoc, let alone high levels or cork taint/TCA proper. The screwcap has ended all that, giving a guarantee that good semillon will cruise through its fifth, tenth, twentieth, even fiftieth, birthdays, changing as it does, gaining character and complexity, albeit losing primary fruit flavours and freshness. You can pick your moment to drink the wine, knowing there will be no nasty surprises waiting for you.

Best of the best of Australian wine

I make my usual disclaimer: while there were two periods of intense tasting activity in the 12 months during which the tasting notes for this edition were made, and while some wines were tasted more than once, an over-arching comparative tasting of all the best wines is simply not possible, however desirable it might be.

So the points for the individual wines scoring 94 or above stand uncorrected by the wisdom of hindsight. Nonetheless, the link between variety and region (or, if you prefer, between variety and terroir) is in most instances strikingly evident. It is for this reason that I have shown the region for each of the best wines. Medium and longer term prosperity will depend on a sense of place, of regional identity.

Brand Australia has been the foundation upon which the success of the past 20 years has been built, but all recognise the need to move on (once the recession relaxes its grip). While some naysayers may regard this as marketing rhetoric, the truth is that Australia is blessed with an unmatched range of terroir (including climate in that deceptively simple term), enabling it to make wines ranging from the uniquely complex fortified wines of Rutherglen (fashioned from frontignac and muscadelle, known locally as muscat and tokay), to the 100 Year Old Para Liqueur of Seppelt in the Barossa Valley, all the way through to the exceptional sparkling wines of Tasmania, grown in a climate every bit as cool as that of Champagne.

This is one of the principal reasons for the wines with the same points to be arranged by region, even though the main text is alpha-ordered. I should also point out that the cut-off for listing the wines of each variety differs considerably, depending on the strength of the class concerned.

Best of the best by variety

Riesling

An interesting spread of regions for the 96-point wines, pointing to the capacity Western Australia, Orange and Tasmania to compete. However, the overall dominance of the Clare and Eden valleys is blindingly obvious given the 95-point group.

RATING	WINE	REGION
96	2008 Leo Buring Leonay	Barossa Valley
96	2008 Grosset Polish Hill	Clare Valley
96	2008 Grosset Springvale Watervale	Clare Valley
96	2008 Leasingham Bin 7	Clare Valley
96	2007 Paulett Antonina Polish Hill River	Clare Valley
96	2005 Taylors St Andrews	Clare Valley
96	2008 Henschke Julius	Eden Valley
96	2003 Peter Lehmann Wigan	Eden Valley
96	2008 Duke's Vineyard	Great Southern
96	2008 Forest Hill Vineyard Block 1	Mount Barker
96	2008 Larry Cherubino The Yard Whispering Hill	Mount Barker
96	2008 Bloodwood	Orange
96	2007 Frogmore Creek	Southern Tasmania
95	2008 Coobara	Adelaide Hills
95	2008 Henschke Green's Hill Lenswood	Adelaide Hills
95	2001 Kersbrook Hill	Adelaide Hills
95	2004 Oranje Tractor	Albany
95	2008 Helm Classic Dry	Canberra District
95	2008 Ainsworth & Snelson Watervale	Clare Valley
95	2008 Crabtree Watervale	Clare Valley
95	2008 Jim Barry The Florita	Clare Valley
95	2008 Kilikanoon Mort's Reserve Watervale	Clare Valley
95	2008 KT & The Falcon Peglidis Vineyard Watervale	Clare Valley
95	2008 Leasingham Bin 8 KS	Clare Valley
95	2008 Leasingham Classic Clare	Clare Valley
95	2008 Little Brampton	Clare Valley
95	2007 Mitchell McNicol	Clare Valley
95	2008 O'Leary Walker Polish Hill River	Clare Valley
95	2008 Skillogalee Trevarrick	Clare Valley
95	2007 Tim Adams Reserve	Clare Valley
95	2008 Eden Road	Eden Valley
95	2008 Heggies Vineyard	Eden Valley
95	2008 Maverick Trial Hill	Eden Valley
95	2008 Penfolds Bin 51	Eden Valley

95	2008 Peter Lehmann	Eden Valley
95	2004 Peter Lehmann Wigan	Eden Valley
95	2008 Pewsey Vale Prima	Eden Valley
95	2008 The Colonial Estate Emissaire Reserve	Eden Valley
95	2002 Wolf Blass White Label Specially Aged	Eden Valley
95	2008 Frankland Estate Poison Hill Vineyard	Frankland River
95	2008 Frankland Estate Smith Cullam	Frankland River
95	2008 Houghton Wisdom	Frankland River
95	2008 Larry Cherubino The Yard Acacia Vineyard	Frankland River
95	2008 Amietta Vineyard	Geelong
95	2008 Crawford River	Henty
95	2008 Lethbridge Dr Nadeson Portland	Henty
95	2008 Paramoor	Macedon Ranges
95	2008 Goundrey Reserve	Mount Barker
95	2008 Josef Chromy	Northern Tasmania
95	2008 Abbey Creek Vineyard	Porongurup
95	2008 Duke's Vineyard Magpie Hill Reserve	Porongurup
95	2008 Frogmore Creek FGR	Southern Tasmania
95	2008 (Foster's) Heemskerk Coal River Valley	Southern Tasmania
95	2008 Kate Hill	Southern Tasmania
95	2008 Pressing Matters R139	Southern Tasmania
95	2008 Delatite Sylvia	Upper Goulburn

Chardonnay

I have discussed the chardonnay surplus at pages 46 to 48 (Plantings and Production); this list should put to rest any assertion that chardonnay is not the greatest white wine. It also underscores the magical union between the variety and the Margaret River. That said, Western Australia had much better growing seasons in 2007 and 2008 than the eastern states, so the statistical bias may be less marked once these vintages (and, perhaps, 2009) pass through the system.

RATING	WINE	REGION
97	2007 Marchand & Burch	Great Southern
97	2006 Leeuwin Estate Art Series	Margaret River
97	2007 Tuck's Ridge Buckle Vineyard	Mornington Peninsula
96	2006 Penfolds Yattarna	Adelaide Hills
96	2007 Petaluma Piccadilly Valley	Adelaide Hills
96	2007 Shaw & Smith M3 Vineyard	Adelaide Hills
96	2008 Shaw & Smith M3 Vineyard	Adelaide Hills
96	2007 Tapanappa Tiers Vineyard Piccadilly Valley	Adelaide Hills
96	2006 Tilbrook Lenswood Vineyard Reserve	Adelaide Hills
96	2006 Heggies Reserve	Eden Valley
96	2006 Bannockburn Vineyards	Geelong
96	2007 by Farr	Geelong
96	2007 Phillip Island Vineyard	Gippsland
96	2008 Marchand & Burch	Great Southern

96	2007 Tyrrell's Vat 47	Lower Hunter Valley
96	2007 Curly Flat	Macedon Ranges
96	2008 Brookland Valley	Margaret River
96	2008 Cape Mentelle	Margaret River
96	2006 Cullen Kevin John	Margaret River
96	2008 Hay Shed Hill	Margaret River
96	2007 McHenry Hohnen Rocky Road Vineyard	Margaret River
96	2007 Pierro	Margaret River
96	2007 Voyager Estate	Margaret River
96	2007 Woodlands Chloe Reserve	Margaret River
96	2007 Woodside Valley Estate Le Bas	Margaret River
96	2007 Kooyong Single Vineyard Selection Faultline	Mornington Peninsula
96	2007 Moorooduc Estate The Moorooduc	Mornington Peninsula
96	2007 Tuck's Ridge Turramurra Vineyard	Mornington Peninsula
96	2006 Dalwhinnie Moonambel	Pyrenees
96	2008 Galli Estate Artigiano	Sunbury
96	Barwang 842	Tumbarumba
96	2007 Domaine Chandon	Yarra Valley
96	2008 Oakridge 864	Yarra Valley
96	2007 PHI Lusatia Park Vineyard	Yarra Valley
96	2006 Sticks No. 29	Yarra Valley

Semillon

Little needs to be said, except to repeat Bruce Tyrrell's comment on the impact of screwcaps: 'Hunter Valley semillon is entering a golden age.' Thus, all but one of the 96-point semillons come from 2005 or are older. It also seems clear Peter Lehmann will remain a burr under the saddle of Hunter semillon-makers into the future.

RATING	WINE	REGION
96	2003 Brokenwood ILR Reserve	Lower Hunter Valley
96	2005 Tyrrell's Single Vineyard Stevens	Lower Hunter Valley
96	2005 Tyrrell's Vat 1	Lower Hunter Valley
96	2002 Tyrrell's Vat 1	Lower Hunter Valley
96	2005 Warraroong Estate	Lower Hunter Valley
96	2006 Warraroong Estate	Lower Hunter Valley
96	2004 Peter Lehmann Margaret	Barossa Valley
96	2005 Brookland Valley	Margaret River
95	2004 Brokenwood ILR Reserve	Lower Hunter Valley
95	2008 Capercaillie	Lower Hunter Valley
95	2008 Capercaillie The Creel	Lower Hunter Valley
95	2007 Keith Tulloch	Lower Hunter Valley
95	2003 Keith Tulloch Museum Release	Lower Hunter Valley
95	2004 Tatler Museum Release Nigel's	Lower Hunter Valley
95	2008 Tin Soldier	Lower Hunter Valley
95	2004 Tyrrell's Belford Reserve	Lower Hunter Valley
95	2003 Tyrrell's Museum Release Vat 1	Lower Hunter Valley

95	2003 Peter Lehmann Margaret	Barossa Valley
95	2008 Ashbrook Estate	Margaret River
95	2008 Vasse Felix	Margaret River

Sauvignon blanc

To the surprise of many observers – not the least myself – sauvignon blanc remains everyone's darling. More than this, Australia is holding its own against the might of Marlborough, keeping its share of the ever-increasing cake. It is little short of amazing that every one of these wines comes from cool regions; there are no climatic cuckoos here.

RATING	WINE	REGION
95	2008 Groom	Adelaide Hills
95	2008 Wirra Wirra Hiding Champion	Adelaide Hills
95	2008 Ashbrook Estate	Margaret River
95	2008 Howard Park	Margaret River
95	2008 Word of Mouth	Orange
94	2008 Barratt Piccadilly Valley	Adelaide Hills
94	2008 Geoff Weaver Lenswood	Adelaide Hills
94	2008 Nova Vita Firebird	Adelaide Hills
94	2008 Nova Vita Mad Russian	Adelaide Hills
94	2008 Riposte The Foil	Adelaide Hills
94	2008 The Lane Vineyard Block 10	Adelaide Hills
94	2008 Tomich Hill	Adelaide Hills
94	2008 Boynton's Feathertop Alpine Valleys	Alpine Valleys
94	2008 Brindabella Hills	Canberra District
94	2008 Alkoomi Black Label	Frankland River
94	2008 Scotchmans Hill	Geelong
94	2008 Harvey River Bridge Joseph River Estate Reserve	Geographe
94	2008 West Cape Howe	Great Southern
94	2007 Barwang Vineyard Tumbarumba	Hilltops
94	2008 Chalkers Crossing Tumbarumba	Hilltops
94	2008 Leeuwin Estate Art Series	Margaret River
94	2008 Stella Bella	Margaret River
94	2008 Watershed Senses	Margaret River
94	2008 Were Estate	Margaret River
94	2008 Taylors Jaraman	Margaret River/ Adelaide Hills
94	2008 Box Stallion	Mornington Peninsula
94	2008 Port Phillip Estate	Mornington Peninsula
94	2008 Yabby Lake Vineyard Red Claw	Mornington Peninsula
94	2008 Angullong	Orange
94	2008 Brangayne of Orange	Orange
94	2008 Logan	Orange
94	2008 Houghton Wisdom	Pemberton
94	2007 Houghton Wisdom	Pemberton

94	2008 Larry Cherubino	Pemberton
94	2008 Mount Trio Vineyard	Porongurup
94	2008 Limbic	Port Phillip Zone
94	2008 Bream Creek	Southern Tasmania
94	2008 Frogmore Creek	Southern Tasmania
94	2008 Home Hill	Southern Tasmania
94	2007 Roslyn Estate	Southern Tasmania
94	2008 Delatite	Upper Goulburn
94	2007 Gembrook Hill	Yarra Valley
94	2008 PHI Lusatia Park Vineyard Sauvignon	Yarra Valley

Sauvignon semillon blends

This is the fastest growing wine on the market (supported by varietal sauvignon blanc), and at the top end is the nigh-on exclusive preserve of the Margaret River in the super-premium wine segment. The maritime climate replicates that of Bordeaux, the Old World home of the blend (the percentage of muscadelle is rapidly decreasing in Bordeaux).

RATING	WINE	REGION
96	2008 Cullen Mangan Vineyard Sauvignon Blanc Semillon	Margaret River
96	2006 Stella Bella Suckfizzle Sauvignon Blanc Semillon	Margaret River
95	2008 Grosset Semillon Sauvignon Blanc	Clare Valley/ Adelaide Hills
95	2008 Cape Mentelle Sauvignon Blanc Semillon	Margaret River
95	2008 KarriBindi Semillon Sauvignon Blanc	Margaret River
95	2008 Lenton Brae Semillon Sauvignon Blanc	Margaret River
95	2008 Vasse Felix Sauvignon Blanc Semillon	Margaret River
95	2008 Voyager Estate Sauvignon Blanc Semillon	Margaret River
95	2008 Wise Eagle Bay Semillon Sauvignon Blanc	Margaret River
94	2008 Sorrenberg Sauvignon Blanc Semillon	Beechworth
94	2008 Harewood Estate Reserve Semillon Sauvignon Blanc	Great Southern
94	2008 Pepper Tree Semillon Sauvignon Blanc	Lower Hunter Valley
94	2008 Briarose Estate Sauvignon Blanc Semillon	Margaret River
94	2008 Cullen Sauvignon Blanc Semillon	Margaret River
94	2008 Eagle Vale Semillon Sauvignon Blanc	Margaret River
94	2008 Hay Shed Hill Block 1 Semillon Sauvignon Blanc	Margaret River
94	2008 Juniper Crossing River Semillon Sauvignon Blanc	Margaret River
94	2008 Leeuwin Estate Siblings Sauvignon Blanc Semillon	Margaret River
94	2008 Saracen Estates Sauvignon Blanc Semillon	Margaret River
94	2008 Thompson Estate Semillon Sauvignon Blanc	Margaret River
94	2008 Wills Domain Semillon Sauvignon Blanc	Margaret River
94	2008 wine by brad Semillon Sauvignon Blanc	Margaret River
94	2008 Fonty's Pool Single Vineyard Sauvignon Blanc Semillon	Pemberton
94	2008 Goona Warra Semillon Sauvignon Blanc	Sunbury
94	2005 Yarra Yarra Sauvignon Blanc Semillon	Yarra Valley

Other white wines

This group of wines shows that the 'alternative' varieties' Charge of the Light Brigade is yet to inflict many casualties on viognier, pinot gris, verdelho and gewurztraminer. The cause of the newer alternatives has not been helped by the embarrassing discovery that the CSIRO-supplied albarino is in fact savagnin, a gewurztraminer clone grown in the Jura region of France.

RATING	WINE	REGION
96	2008 Borrodell on the Mount Wine Makers Daughter Gewurztraminer	Orange
95	2008 Massena Vineyards The Surly Muse Viognier	Barossa Valley
95	2007 Yalumba The Virgilius Viognier	Eden Valley
95	2006 by Farr Viognier	Geelong
95	2008 Ashbrook Estate Verdelho	Margaret River
95	2007 Allies Saone Viognier	Mornington Peninsula
95	2008 Delatite Pinot Gris	Upper Goulburn
94	2008 Fox Gordon Abby Viognier	Adelaide Hills
94	2006 Heggies Vineyard Viognier	Eden Valley
94	2008 Mountadam Pinot Gris	Eden Valley
94	2008 Pewsey Vale Individual Vineyard Selection Gewurztraminer	Eden Valley
94	2007 Scotchmans Hill Cornelius Pinot Gris	Geelong
94	2008 Shadowfax Viognier	Geelong
94	2007 Harris River Estate Verdelho	Geographe
94	2008 Mount Langi Ghiran Cliff Edge Pinot Gris	Grampians
94	2008 Seppelt Drumborg Vineyard Pinot Gris	Grampians
94	2008 Dal Zotto Estate Arneis	King Valley
94	2008 Mr Riggs Wine Company Viognier	Adelaide Zone
94	2008 Prancing Horse Estate Pinot Gris	Macedon Ranges
94	2007 Moorooduc Estate Pinot Gris	Mornington Peninsula
94	2008 Paradigm Hill Pinot Gris	Mornington Peninsula
94	2007 Port Phillip Estate Quartier Arneis	Mornington Peninsula
94	2008 Scorpo Wines Pinot Gris	Mornington Peninsula
94	2008 Pipers Brook Vineyard Ninth Island Pinot Grigio	Northern Tasmania
94	2007 Tamar Ridge Research Series 81-1 Albarino	Northern Tasmania
94	2007 Tamar Ridge Research Series 83-1 Viognier	Northern Tasmania
94	2008 Millbrook Viognier	Perth Hills
94	2008 Millbrook LR Viognier	Perth Hills
94	2008 Craigow Gewurztraminer	Southern Tasmania
94	2008 Moondah Brook Verdelho	Swan Valley

Sparkling

The best sparkling wines are now solely sourced either from Tasmania or from the coolest sites in the southern parts of the mainland, with altitude playing a major role.

They are all fermented in the bottle, and most have had extended lees contact prior to disgorgement, giving them great complexity.

RATING	WINE	REGION
96	1998 Petaluma Croser Piccadilly Valley Pinot Noir Chardonnay	Adelaide Hills
96	1999 Granite Hills Knight Brut	Macedon Ranges
96	2003 Bay of Fires Arras Pinot Noir Chardonnay	Northern Tasmania
95	NV Hanging Rock Winery Reserve Cuvee (Late Disgorged)	Macedon Ranges
95	2003 (Pipers Brook) Kreglinger Vintage Brut Rose	Northern Tasmania
95	2005 Domaine Chandon Brut Rose Vintage	Yarra Valley
95	2005 Domaine Chandon Vintage Brut	Yarra Valley
95	2004 Yarrabank Cuvee	Yarra Valley
94	2004 Ashton Hills Blanc de Blancs	Adelaide Hills
94	2005 Petaluma Croser Piccadilly Valley Pinot Noir Chardonnay	Adelaide Hills
94	2004 Brown Brothers Patricia Pinot Noir Chardonnay Pinot Meunier Brut	King Valley
94	1991 Cope-Williams R.O.M.S.E.Y. Vintage Brut	Macedon Ranges
94	2003 Bay of Fires Pinot Noir Chardonnay	Northern Tasmania
94	2003 Ghost Rock Catherine Pinot Noir Chardonnay	Northern Tasmania
94	2001 Jansz Premium Vintage Late Disgorged	Northern Tasmania
94	NV Pirie Estate Non Vintage	Northern Tasmania
94	2004 Houghton Wisdom Chardonnay Pinot Noir	Pemberton
94	2003 Stefano Lubiana Vintage Brut	Southern Tasmania
94	2003 Dominique Portet Tasmanian Cuvee	Tasmania
94	NV Domaine Chandon Brut Rose Non Vintage	Yarra Valley
94	2004 Gembrook Hill Blanc de Blancs	Yarra Valley

I would like to make mention of a tiny group of wines, eagerly sought by the small percentage of wine drinkers who understand the peculiarities of the style and who, better still, are prepared to cellar them for a year or more, the longer the better. The Seppelt Show Reserve is missing only because it is not made every year.

RATING	WINE	REGION
95	2001 Peter Lehmann Black Queen Sparkling Shiraz	Barossa Valley
95	NV Primo Estate Joseph Sparkling Red	McLaren Vale
95	NV Rockford Black Shiraz	Barossa Valley
95	2006 Grampians Estate Black Sunday Friends Sparkling Shiraz	Grampians
94	2001 Houghton Museum Release Sparkling Shiraz	Swan Valley
94	NV Scarpantoni Estate Black Tempest	McLaren Vale

Sweet

Four barrel-fermented semillons and eight rieslings point the way for the future; moreover, there are many more semi-sweet rieslings made in the Mosel (Germany) fashion that are presently in no-mans-land, and ultimately may gain a category of their own. It's a happening scene in Australia in 2009–10.

RATING	WINE	REGION
96	2006 Brown Brothers Patricia Noble Riesling	King Valley
95	2008 Vasse Felix Cane Cut Semillon	Margaret River
95	2007 McWilliam's Limited Release Botrytis Semillon	Riverina
95	2008 macforbes RS37 Riesling	Strathbogie Ranges
94	2006 Hobbs of Barossa Ranges Semillon	Barossa Valley
94	2006 Hobbs of Barossa Ranges Viognier	Barossa Valley
94	2008 Primo Estate Joseph La Magia Botrytis Riesling Traminer	McLaren Vale
94	2008 Plantagenet Ringbark Riesling	Mount Barker
94	2007 Pirie Estate Clark's Botrytis Riesling	Northern Tasmania
94	2008 Bloodwood Silk Purse	Orange
94	2008 Craigow Iced Riesling	Southern Tasmania
94	2008 Pressing Matters R69 Riesling	Southern Tasmania
94	2007 Punt Road Botrytis Semillon	Yarra Valley

Rose

The number of roses on the market continues to grow, seemingly unabated and unstoppable. There are no rules: they can be bone-dry, slightly sweet, or very sweet. They can be and are made from almost any red variety, red blends or red and white blends. They may be a convenient way of concentrating the red wine left after the rose is run off (bleeding or saignee) from the fermenter shortly after the grapes are crushed, or made from the ground up using grapes and techniques specifically chosen for the purpose. The vast majority of wines fall in the former camp; those listed mainly come from the latter.

RATING	WINE	REGION
94	2008 Charles Melton Rose of Virginia	Barossa Valley
94	2008 Michael Hall Sang de Pigeon Shiraz Saignee	Barossa Valley
94	2008 Turkey Flat Rose	Barossa Valley
94	2008 Smallfry Cabernet Grenache Rose	Eden Valley
94	2008 Coriole Nebbiolo Rose	McLaren Vale
94	2008 Derwent Estate Rose	Southern Tasmania
94	2008 Domaine Chandon Pinot Noir Rose	Yarra Valley
94	2008 Yering Station ED Pinot Noir Rose	Yarra Valley

Pinot noir

Last year it was a three-way tie between the Mornington Peninsula, Tasmania and Yarra Valley; this year Mornington Peninsula has careered away with the honours, which is disconcerting for someone (like myself) who moved from Sydney to the Yarra Valley specifically to make pinot noir. The answer lies in part in the vintage comparison: Mornington Peninsula's winemakers rated 2007 9 out of 10; the Yarra Valley makers 7 out of 10 (as did Geelong and Tasmania). The fat lady is yet to sing.

RATING	WINE	REGION
97	2007 Tuck's Ridge Buckle Vineyard	Mornington Peninsula
96	2006 Bannockburn Stuart	Geelong
96	2007 by Farr Sangreal	Geelong
96	2007 Curlewis Reserve	Geelong
96	2007 Provenance	Geelong
96	2007 Bass Phillip The Estate	Gippsland
96	2007 Farr Rising Mornington	Mornington Peninsula
96	2007 Kooyong Single Vineyard Selection Ferrous	Mornington Peninsula
96	2007 Merricks Estate Close Planted	Mornington Peninsula
96	2007 Moorooduc Estate McIntyre Vineyard	Mornington Peninsula
96	2007 Paringa 'Estate'	Mornington Peninsula
96	2007 Paringa Estate Reserve Special Barrel Selection	Mornington Peninsula
96	2007 Scorpo	Mornington Peninsula
96	2007 Stonier	Mornington Peninsula
96	2007 Stonier Reserve	Mornington Peninsula
96	2007 Ten Minutes by Tractor 10X	Mornington Peninsula
96	2005 Laurel Bank	Southern Tasmania
96	2006 Punch Lance's Vineyard Close Planted	Yarra Valley
96	2006 Tarrawarra Estate MDB Yarra Valley	Yarra Valley
95	2007 Ashton Hills Estate	Adelaide Hills
95	2007 Tomboy Hill Smythes Creek	Ballarat
95	2006 Mt Terrible Jamieson	Central Victoria Zone
95	2002 Old Kent River	Frankland River
95	2007 by Farr Farrside	Geelong
95	2007 Curlewis	Geelong
95	2007 Caledonia Australis Reserve	Gippsland
95	2007 Phillip Island Vineyard	Gippsland
95	2006 Curly Flat	Macedon Ranges
95	2007 Allies	Mornington Peninsula
95	2007 Hurley Vineyard Garamond	Mornington Peninsula
95	2007 Kooyong Single Vineyard Selection Haven	Mornington Peninsula
95	2007 Kooyong Single Vineyard Selection Meres	Mornington Peninsula
95	2006 Merricks Estate Close Planted	Mornington Peninsula
95	2007 Paradigm Hill L'ami Sage	Mornington Peninsula
95	2007 Paradigm Hill Les Cinq	Mornington Peninsula
95	2008 Paringa Estate Peninsula	Mornington Peninsula
95	2007 Port Phillip Estate	Mornington Peninsula
95	2008 Scorpo Noirien	Mornington Peninsula
95	2006 Stonier KBS Vineyard	Mornington Peninsula
95	2006 Stonier Windmill Vineyard	Mornington Peninsula
95	2007 Ten Minutes by Tractor Wallis Vineyard	Mornington Peninsula
95	2008 Tollana Robinson Family Bin TR474	Mornington Peninsula
95	2006 Grey Sands	Northern Tasmania
95	2007 Tamar Ridge Kayena Vineyard	Northern Tasmania
95	2005 Bream Creek Reserve	Southern Tasmania

95	2006 Stefano Lubiana Estate	Southern Tasmania
95	2007 De Bortoli Estate Grown	Yarra Valley
95	2006 Tarrawarra Estate Reserve	Yarra Valley

Shiraz

The same tired old arguments that single-vineyard wines are inherently more interesting, and of higher quality, than vineyard or regional blends were trotted out when the glorious 2004 Grange was released. This means (by extension) that two of the 97-point wines and at least 14 of the 96-point wines did not deserve their places. Winemakers who have the opportunity to blend parcels do so because they believe they are making a better wine thanks to the well-known synergies that can (but not always will) come from blending.

RATING	WINE	REGION
98	2004 Penfolds Grange	South Australia
97	2006 Shaw & Smith	Adelaide Hills
97	2006 Penfolds Magill Estate	Adelaide Zone
97	2006 Trevor Jones Reserve Wild Witch	Barossa Valley
97	2006 Pikes The EWP Reserve	Clare Valley
97	2006 Wendouree	Clare Valley
97	2005 Wynns Coonawarra Estate Michael Limited Release	Coonawarra
97	1998 Brokenwood HBA	Hunter Valley/ McLaren Vale
97	2007 Dalwhinnie Moonambel	Pyrenees
96	2007 Shaw & Smith	Adelaide Hills
96	2004 Barossa Valley Estate E&E Black Pepper	Barossa Valley
96	2006 Charles Melton Grains of Paradise	Barossa Valley
96	2006 Dutschke Oscar Semmler Single Vineyard Reserve	Barossa Valley
96	2006 First Drop Fat of the Land Ebenezer Single Vineyard	Barossa Valley
96	2006 First Drop The Cream	Barossa Valley
96	2006 Gibson Barossavale Australian Old Vine Collection	Barossa Valley
96	2007 Glaetzer Amon-Ra Unfiltered	Barossa Valley
96	2004 Glen Eldon Black Springs Reserve	Barossa Valley
96	2007 Head The Brunette Single Vineyard	Barossa Valley
96	2006 Kalleske Johann Georg Old Vine	Barossa Valley
96	2006 Penfolds RWT	Barossa Valley
96	2004 Peter Lehmann Stonewell	Barossa Valley
96	2006 Peter Lehmann The 1885	Barossa Valley
96	2006 Teusner The Astral Series Riebke FG	Barossa Valley
96	2006 Torbreck The RunRig	Barossa Valley
96	2006 Torbreck The Factor	Barossa Valley
96	2006 Wolf Blass Platinum Label	Barossa Valley
96	2005 Yalumba The Octavius Old Vine	Barossa Valley
96	2008 Collector Reserve	Canberra District
96	2007 Collector Reserve	Canberra District
96	2006 Jim Barry The Armagh	Clare Valley

96	2006 Kilikanoon Attunga 1865	Clare Valley
96	2007 Leasingham Individual Vineyard Release Provis	Clare Valley
96	2006 Penna Lane The Willsmore	Clare Valley
96	2006 Gibson Barossavale Australian Old Vine Collection	Eden Valley
96	2005 Henschke Hill Of Grace	Eden Valley
96	2006 Henschke Mount Edelstone	Eden Valley
96	2006 Maverick Trial Hill	Eden Valley
96	2007 Poonawatta Estate The 1880	Eden Valley
96	2005 Poonawatta Estate The Centenarian Single Barrel Reserve	Eden Valley
96	2006 Yalumba Single Site Bartholomaeous Vineyard	Eden Valley
96	2006 Grampians Estate Black Sunday Friends Reserve	Grampians
96	2007 Mount Langi Ghiran Langi	Grampians
96	2006 Seppelt St Peters	Grampians
96	2007 Allies Garagiste Syrah	Heathcote
96	2007 Allies Stone Axe Vineyard	Heathcote
96	2004 Buckshot Vineyard	Heathcote
96	2006 Sanguine Estate D'Orsa	Heathcote
96	2006 Brokenwood Graveyard Vineyard	Lower Hunter Valley
96	2006 McWilliam's Mount Pleasant Maurice O'Shea	Lower Hunter Valley
96	2005 Tulloch Hector of Glen Elgin Limited Release	Lower Hunter Valley
96	2007 Tyrrell's Single Vineyard Old Patch 1867	Lower Hunter Valley
96	2007 Cape Mentelle	Margaret River
96	2005 Evans & Tate The Reserve	Margaret River
96	2006 Chapel Hill The Vicar	McLaren Vale
96	2006 Clarendon Hills Bakers Gully Syrah	McLaren Vale
96	2005 Clarendon Hills Piggott Range Syrah	McLaren Vale
96	2006 Coriole Lloyd Reserve	McLaren Vale
96	2006 Gemtree White Lees	McLaren Vale
96	2002 Geoff Merrill Henley	McLaren Vale
96	2004 Hardys Tintara Single Vineyard Upper Tintara	McLaren Vale
96	2007 Paringa Estate 'Estate'	Mornington Peninsula

Shiraz viognier

In best Australian Tall Poppy Syndrome fashion it has already become fashionable in some quarters to challenge the remarkable synergy obtained by co-fermenting around 5% of viognier with shiraz. The enhancement of colour, aroma and flavour is remarkable, as is the softening and smoothing of texture. Yes, it is not a panacea for lesser quality grapes and, yes, it is and should remain a subtext to the thrust of shiraz's flavour. Nonetheless, the wines in this group offer pleasure second to none. Overall, the blend works best in temperate to cool regions; the Barossa Valley is achieving its success through the force of numbers and the skills of the winemakers involved.

RATING	WINE	REGION
97	2008 Clonakilla	Canberra District
96	2007 Spinifex	Barossa Valley

96	2007 Pepper Tree The Gravels Single Vineyard Reserve	Wrattonbully
95	2006 Yalumba Hand Picked	Barossa Valley
95	2007 Lerida Estate Lake George	Canberra District
94	2005 Mount Torrens Vineyards Solstice	Adelaide Hills
94	2007 Yalumba Hand Picked	Barossa Valley
94	2007 Turner's Crossing	Bendigo
94	2007 Alkoomi Black Label	Frankland River
94	2007 Bellarine Estate Cellar Reserve	Geelong
94	2006 Syrahmi La La	Heathcote
94	2007 Amberley Estate	Margaret River
94	2006 McPherson Chapter Three	Nagambie Lakes
94	2007 Western Range Julimar	Perth Hills
94	2006 Salomon Estate Syrah Viognier	Southern Fleurieu
94	2006 Yarra Yarra Syrah Viognier	Yarra Valley
94	2006 Yarra Yering Dry Red No. 2	Yarra Valley
94	2007 Yering Station	Yarra Valley

Cabernet sauvignon

The affinity of cabernet sauvignon with a maritime climate is put beyond doubt by its home in Bordeaux's Medoc region. So it comes as no surprise to find that most (but not all) of Australia's top-quality cabernets come from regions with climates similar to Bordeaux (conspicuously Coonawarra and Margaret River) and/or are within 50 km of the sea with no intervening mountain range.

RATING	WINE	REGION
97	2007 Balnaves of Coonawarra The Tally Reserve	Coonawarra
97	2007 Forest Hill Vineyard	Great Southern
96	2006 Penfolds Bin 707	Barossa Valley
96	2006 Trevor Jones Wicked Witch Reserve Dry Grown	Barossa Valley
96	2005 Katnook Estate Odyssey	Coonawarra
96	2004 Murdock	Coonawarra
96	2006 Parker Coonawarra Estate Terra Rossa	Coonawarra
96	2002 Patrick T Museum Release Home Block	Coonawarra
96	2006 Yalumba The Menzies	Coonawarra
96	2004 Houghton Wisdom	Frankland River
96	2004 Brookland Valley Reserve	Margaret River
96	2003 Houghton Gladstones	Margaret River
96	2007 Saracen Estates Reserve	Margaret River
96	2007 Watershed Awakening	Margaret River
96	2005 Oakridge 864	Yarra Valley
96	2007 Seville Estate Old Vine Reserve	Yarra Valley
95	2005 Penfolds Bin 407	Barossa Valley
95	2005 Penfolds Bin 707	Barossa Valley
95	2006 Penfolds Cellar Reserve	Barossa Valley
95	2005 Jim Barry The PB	Clare Valley
95	2006 Mount Horrocks	Clare Valley

95	2006 O'Leary Walker	Clare Valley
95	2004 Skillogalee Trevarrick Single Contour	Clare Valley
95	2007 Balnaves of Coonawarra	Coonawarra
95	2006 Hollick Ravenswood	Coonawarra
95	2004 Katnook Estate Odyssey	Coonawarra
95	2006 Wynns Coonawarra Estate	Coonawarra
95	2007 Howard Park Scotsdale	Great Southern
95	2007 Capel Vale The Scholar	Margaret River
95	2007 Chapman Grove Atticus	Margaret River
95	2007 Deep Woods Estate Reserve	Margaret River
95	2007 Fraser Gallop Estate	Margaret River
95	2007 Jane Brook Estate Shovelgate Vineyard	Margaret River
95	2004 Leeuwin Estate Art Series	Margaret River
95	2005 Moss Wood	Margaret River
95	2007 Yalumba Ringbolt	Margaret River
95	2005 Howard Park Abercrombie	Margaret River/ Denmark
95	2006 Pirramimma	McLaren Vale
95	2006 Hardys Chateau Reynella Basket Pressed	McLaren Vale
95	2005 Goundrey Reserve	Mount Barker
95	2005 Plantagenet	Mount Barker
95	2005 Bream Creek	Southern Tasmania
95	2003 Domaine A	Southern Tasmania
95	2006 Pepper Tree Elderslee Road Single Vineyard Reserve	Wrattonbully
95	2007 De Bortoli Estate Grown	Yarra Valley
95	2006 Yering Station	Yarra Valley

Cabernet and family

This group revolves around the grapes of Bordeaux and primarily blends thereof, but with some single varieties, most notably merlot, the majority from moderately cool regions. Also included are the classic Australian cabernet and shiraz (or vice versa) blends.

RATING	WINE	REGION
96	2003 Chain of Ponds The Cachet Cabernet Sauvignon Shiraz Merlot	Adelaide
96	2006 Penfolds Bin 389 Cabernet Shiraz	Barossa Valley
96	2004 Peter Lehmann Mentor	Barossa Valley
96	2002 Yalumba The Reserve	Barossa Valley
96	2005 Tim Gramp Gilbert Valley Reserve Shiraz Cabernet	Mount Lofty Ranges
96	2001 Brand's Laira Eric's Blend	Coonawarra
96	2005 Lindemans Limestone Ridge	Coonawarra
96	2005 Majella The Malleea	Coonawarra
96	2006 Parker Coonawarra Estate Terra Rossa First Growth	Coonawarra
96	2006 Dominique Portet Andre Shiraz Cabernet Sauvignon	Heathcote/ Yarra Valley
96	2006 Bremerton Wines B.O.V.	Langhorne Creek

96	2007 Flametree Cabernet Merlot	Margaret River
96	2004 Voyager Estate Cabernet Sauvignon Merlot	Margaret River
96	2007 Woodlands Reserve de la Cave Merlot	Margaret River
96	2005 McWilliam's 1877 Cabernet Sauvignon Shiraz	Coonawarra (and other regions)
95	2002 Chain of Ponds The Cachet Cabernet Sauvignon Shiraz Merlot	Adelaide
95	2006 K1 by Geoff Hardy Tzimmukin	Adelaide Hills
95	2006 Grosset Gaia	Clare Valley
95	2006 Wynns Coonawarra Estate The Gables Cabernet Shiraz	Coonawarra
95	2006 Henschke Keyneton Estate Euphonium	Eden Valley
95	2005 Alkoomi Blackbutt	Frankland River
95	2007 Frankland Estate Smith Cullam Shiraz Cabernet	Frankland River
95	2007 Houghton Crofters Cabernet Malbec	Great Southern
95	2007 Celestial Bay Cabernet Shiraz	Margaret River
95	2005 Vasse Felix Heytesbury	Margaret River
95	2007 Woodlands Reserve de la Cave Cabernet Franc	Margaret River
95	2006 Primo Estate Joseph Moda Cabernet Sauvignon Merlot	McLaren Vale
95	2007 John Kosovich Wines Reserve Cabernet Malbec	Pemberton
95	2005 Tapanappa Whalebone Vineyard Merlot	Wrattonbully
95	Smith & Hooper Reserve Merlot	Wrattonbully
95	2006 Yarra Yering Merlot	Yarra Valley

Shiraz and family

A class utterly dominated by Rhône Valley blends of some or all of shiraz, grenache and mourvedre, a zinfandel, and a gamay a minor intrusion.

RATING	WINE	REGION
96	2006 Charles Melton Nine Popes	Barossa Valley
96	2007 Hewitson Old Garden Mourvedre	Barossa Valley
95	2006 Teusner The Astral Series Moppa Mataro	Barossa Valley
95	2007 Margan Family Limited Release Shiraz Mourvedre	Lower Hunter Valley
94	2006 Glen Eldon Wines Shiraz Mataro	Barossa Valley
94	2007 Groom Bush Block Zinfandel	Barossa Valley
94	2006 Kabminye Wines Carignan	Barossa Valley
94	2006 Landhaus Estate Shiraz Mourvedre	Barossa Valley
94	2006 Olssen Shiraz Mataro	Clare Valley
94	2007 Boireann Mourvedre Shiraz	Granite Belt
94	2006 Cassegrain Reserve Falerne Shiraz Merlot Tempranillo	Hastings River
94	2007 Springs Hill Vineyard Blewitt Springs Mourvedre	McLaren Vale
94	2007 Eldridge Estate of Red Hill Gamay	Mornington Peninsula
94	2004 Mitchelton Crescent Mourvedre Shiraz Grenache	Nagambie Lakes
94	2006 Hewitson Private Cellar Shiraz Mourvedre	Barossa Valley

Fortified wines

A relatively small but absolutely sensational group of wines, as quintessentially Australian as a Driza-Bone, and of unique style.

RATING	WINE	REGION
100	1908 Seppeltsfield 100 Year Old Para Liqueur	Barossa Valley
98	NV Chambers Rosewood Rare Muscat	Rutherglen
97	NV All Saints Estate Rare Muscat Museum Release	Rutherglen
97	NV All Saints Estate Rare Tokay (375 ml)	Rutherglen
97	NV Campbells Isabella Rare Tokay	Rutherglen
97	NV Chambers Rosewood Rare Muscadelle	Rutherglen
97	NV Morris Old Premium Rare Tokay	Rutherglen
97	NV Pfeiffer Wines Rare Tokay	Rutherglen
97	NV Seppeltsfield Rare Muscat	Rutherglen
97	NV Seppeltsfield Rare Tokay	Rutherglen
96	NV Seppeltsfield Rare Tawny DP90	Barossa Valley
96	NV Campbells Merchant Prince Rare Muscat	Rutherglen
96	NV Chambers Rosewood Special Tokay	Rutherglen
96	NV Morris Old Premium Tawny Port	Rutherglen
96	NV Pfeiffer Wines Rare Muscat	Rutherglen
96	NV Seppeltsfield Grand Tokay	Rutherglen

Best wineries of the regions

The nomination of the best wineries of the regions has evolved in two ways: five red stars for wineries with a particularly distinguished track record over the past three years, and five black stars for those who have been consistently at or near the top for this period. While I have deliberately refused to bind myself to this yardstick, the red-starred wineries have in almost all instances achieved five-star ratings for each of the past three years, and most of those with black stars have had maximum ratings in two of the past three years, including (importantly) this year.

ADELAIDE HILLS
Ashton Hills ★★★★★
Barratt ★★★★★
Bird in Hand ★★★★★
Chain of Ponds ★★★★★
Coobara Wines ★★★★★
Geoff Weaver ★★★★★
Honey Moon Vineyard ★★★★★
K1 by Geoff Hardy ★★★★★
Kersbrook Hill ★★★★★
Lobethal Road Wines ★★★★★
Mount Torrens Vineyards ★★★★★
Nova Vita Wines ★★★★★
Petaluma ★★★★★
Romney Park Wines ★★★★★
Setanta Wines ★★★★★
Shaw & Smith ★★★★★
The Lane Vineyard ★★★★★
Tilbrook ★★★★★

ADELAIDE ZONE
Penfolds Magill Estate ★★★★★

ALBANY
Oranje Tractor ★★★★★

BALLARAT
Tomboy Hill ★★★★★

BAROSSA VALLEY
Barossa Valley Estate ★★★★★

Cellarmasters ★★★★★
Charles Melton ★★★★★
Deisen ★★★★★
Dutschke Wines ★★★★★
Elderton ★★★★★
First Drop Wines ★★★★★
Gibson Barossavale/Loose End
  ★★★★★
Glaetzer Wines ★★★★★
Glen Eldon Wines ★★★★★
Grant Burge ★★★★★
Groom ★★★★★
Haan Wines ★★★★★
Hare's Chase ★★★★★
Head Wines ★★★★★
Hentley Farm Wines ★★★★★
Heritage Wines ★★★★★
Hobbs of Barossa Ranges ★★★★★
Jacob's Creek ★★★★★
John Duval Wines ★★★★★
Kaesler Wines ★★★★★
Kalleske ★★★★★
Kurtz Family Vineyards ★★★★★
Landhaus Estate ★★★★★
Langmeil Winery ★★★★★
Laughing Jack ★★★★★
Leo Buring ★★★★★
Massena Vineyards ★★★★★
Maverick Wines ★★★★★
Penfolds ★★★★★
Peter Lehmann ★★★★★

Quattro Mano ★★★★★
Rockford ★★★★★
Rohrlach Family Wines ★★★★★
Russell Wines ★★★★★
St Hallett ★★★★★
Saltram ★★★★★
Seabrook Wines ★★★★★
Seppeltsfield ★★★★★
Sheep's Back ★★★★★
Smallfry Wines ★★★★★
Sons of Eden ★★★★★
Spinifex ★★★★★
Teusner ★★★★★
The Colonial Estate ★★★★★
Thorn-Clarke Wines ★★★★★
Torbreck Vintners ★★★★★
Trevor Jones/Kellermeister ★★★★★
Turkey Flat ★★★★★
Two Hands Wines ★★★★★
Westlake Vineyards ★★★★★
Winter Creek Wine ★★★★★
Wolf Blass ★★★★★
Yalumba ★★★★★
Yelland & Papps ★★★★★

BAROSSA VALLEY/ADELAIDE HILLS
Fox Gordon ★★★★★

BEECHWORTH
Sorrenberg ★★★★★

BENDIGO
BlackJack Vineyards ★★★★★
Bress ★★★★★
Pondalowie Vineyards ★★★★★

CANBERRA DISTRICT
Brindabella Hills ★★★★★
Clonakilla ★★★★★
Collector Wines ★★★★★
Helm ★★★★★

CENTRAL VICTORIA ZONE
Mt Terrible ★★★★★
Tar & Roses/Trust ★★★★★

CENTRAL WESTERN AUSTRALIA ZONE
Across the Lake ★★★★★

CLARE VALLEY
Annie's Lane ★★★★★
Brian Barry Wines ★★★★★
Crabtree Watervale Wines ★★★★★
Gaelic Cemetery Wines ★★★★★
Grosset ★★★★★
Jim Barry Wines ★★★★★
Kilikanoon ★★★★★
Knappstein ★★★★★
KT & The Falcon ★★★★★
Leasingham ★★★★★
Mitchell ★★★★★
Mount Horrocks ★★★★★
O'Leary Walker Wines ★★★★★
Olssens of Watervale ★★★★★
Paulett ★★★★★
Pikes ★★★★★
Skillogalee ★★★★★
Taylors ★★★★★
Tim Adams ★★★★★
Wendouree ★★★★★
Wilson Vineyard ★★★★★

COONAWARRA
Balnaves of Coonawarra ★★★★★
Brand's Laira Coonawarra ★★★★★
Katnook Estate ★★★★★
Majella ★★★★★
Murdock ★★★★★
Parker Coonawarra Estate ★★★★★
Wynns Coonawarra Estate ★★★★★
Zema Estate ★★★★★

DENMARK
Harewood Estate ★★★★★
West Cape Howe Wines ★★★★★

EAST COAST TASMANIA
Freycinet ★★★★★
Kelvedon ★★★★★

EDEN VALLEY
Eden Springs ★★★★★
Flaxman Wines ★★★★★
Heggies Vineyard ★★★★★
Henschke ★★★★★
Pewsey Vale ★★★★★
Poonawatta Estate ★★★★★
Radford Wines ★★★★★

FLEURIEU ZONE
Springs Hill Vineyard ★★★★★

FRANKLAND RIVER
Alkoomi ★★★★★
Bobtail Ridge Wines ★★★★★
Ferngrove ★★★★★
Frankland Estate ★★★★★
Old Kent River ★★★★★

GEELONG
Bannockburn Vineyards ★★★★★
Bellarine Estate ★★★★★
by Farr ★★★★★
Clyde Park Vineyard ★★★★★
Curlewis Winery ★★★★★
Dinny Goonan Family Estate ★★★★★
Farr Rising ★★★★★
Lethbridge Wines ★★★★★
Scotchmans Hill ★★★★★
Shadowfax ★★★★★

GEOGRAPHE
Capel Vale ★★★★★
Harris River Estate ★★★★★
Willow Bridge Estate ★★★★★

GIPPSLAND
Bass Phillip ★★★★★
Bellvale Wines ★★★★★
Caledonia Australis ★★★★★
Phillip Island Vineyard ★★★★★

GLENROWAN
Baileys of Glenrowan ★★★★★

GRAMPIANS
Grampians Estate ★★★★★
Hyde Park Wines ★★★★★
Mount Langi Ghiran Vineyards
  ★★★★★
Seppelt ★★★★★
Westgate Vineyard ★★★★★

GRANITE BELT
Boireann ★★★★★

GREAT SOUTHERN
Forest Hill Vineyard ★★★★★
Marchand & Burch ★★★★★

HEATHCOTE
Buckshot Vineyard ★★★★★
Flynns Wines ★★★★★
Greenstone Vineyard ★★★★★
Jasper Hill ★★★★★
La Pleiade ★★★★★
Redesdale Estate Wines ★★★★★
Shelmerdine Vineyards ★★★★★
Stefani Estate ★★★★★

HENTY
Crawford River Wines ★★★★★

HILLTOPS
Barwang Vineyard ★★★★★
Chalkers Crossing ★★★★★

KANGAROO ISLAND
The Islander Estate Vineyards
  ★★★★★

KING VALLEY
Brown Brothers ★★★★★
Chrismont ★★★★★

LANGHORNE CREEK
Angas Plains Estate ★★★★★
Bremerton Wines ★★★★★
John's Blend ★★★★★

LOWER HUNTER VALLEY
Audrey Wilkinson Vineyard ★★★★★
Briar Ridge ★★★★★
Brokenwood ★★★★★
Capercaillie ★★★★★
Chateau Pâto ★★★★★
Chatto Wines ★★★★★
De Bortoli (Hunter Valley) ★★★★★
Keith Tulloch Wine ★★★★★
Lake's Folly ★★★★★
McGuigan Wines ★★★★★
McWilliam's Mount Pleasant ★★★★★
Margan Family ★★★★★
Meerea Park ★★★★★
Mistletoe Wines ★★★★★
Mount View Estate ★★★★★
Pepper Tree Wines ★★★★★
Tamburlaine ★★★★★
Tatler Wines ★★★★★
Tempus Two Wines ★★★★★
Thomas Wines ★★★★★
Tin Soldier Wine ★★★★★
Tower Estate ★★★★★
Tulloch ★★★★★
Tyrrell's ★★★★★
Warraroong Estate ★★★★★
Wyndham Estate ★★★★★

MACEDON RANGES
Curly Flat ★★★★★
Granite Hills ★★★★★
Hanging Rock Winery ★★★★★

MCLAREN VALE
Aramis Vineyards ★★★★★
Cape Barren Wines ★★★★★
Chapel Hill ★★★★★
Clarendon Hills ★★★★★
Coriole ★★★★★
d'Arenberg ★★★★★
Five Geese ★★★★★
Gemtree Vineyards ★★★★★
Geoff Merrill Wines ★★★★★
Hardys ★★★★★
Inkwell ★★★★★

Marius Wines ★★★★★
Maxwell Wines ★★★★★
Mitolo Wines ★★★★★
Mr Riggs Wine Company ★★★★★
Olivers Taranga Vineyards ★★★★★
Paxton ★★★★★
Primo Estate ★★★★★
Richard Hamilton ★★★★★
Scarpantoni Estate ★★★★★
Shingleback ★★★★★
Tintara ★★★★★
Wirra Wirra ★★★★★

MCLAREN VALE/FLEURIEU PENINSULA
Chateau Reynella ★★★★★

MARGARET RIVER
Ashbrook Estate ★★★★★
Briarose Estate ★★★★★
Brookland Valley ★★★★★
Brown Hill Estate ★★★★★
Cape Mentelle ★★★★★
Cape Naturaliste Vineyard ★★★★★
Celestial Bay ★★★★★
Chapman Grove Wines ★★★★★
Cullen Wines ★★★★★
Devil's Lair ★★★★★
Driftwood Estate ★★★★★
Edwards Wines ★★★★★
Evans & Tate ★★★★★
Evoi Wines ★★★★★
Flametree ★★★★★
Flying Fish Cove ★★★★★
Fraser Gallop Estate ★★★★★
Hay Shed Hill Wines ★★★★★
KarriBindi ★★★★★
Leeuwin Estate ★★★★★
Lenton Brae Wines ★★★★★
McHenry Hohnen Vintners ★★★★★
Moss Wood ★★★★★
Palmer Wines ★★★★★
Pierro ★★★★★
Redgate ★★★★★
Sandalford ★★★★★
Saracen Estates ★★★★★

Stella Bella Wines ★★★★★
Thompson Estate ★★★★★
Vasse Felix ★★★★★
Voyager Estate ★★★★★
Watershed Wines ★★★★★
Were Estate ★★★★★
Wills Domain ★★★★★
Windance Wines ★★★★★
Wise Wine ★★★★★
Woodlands ★★★★★

MARGARET RIVER/DENMARK
Howard Park ★★★★★

MORNINGTON PENINSULA
Allies Wines ★★★★★
Box Stallion ★★★★★
Darling Park ★★★★★
Eldridge Estate of Red Hill ★★★★★
Elgee Park ★★★★★
Hurley Vineyard ★★★★★
Kooyong ★★★★★
Main Ridge Estate ★★★★★
Merricks Estate ★★★★★
Montalto Vineyards ★★★★★
Moorooduc Estate ★★★★★
Paradigm Hill ★★★★★
Paringa Estate ★★★★★
Port Phillip Estate ★★★★★
Prancing Horse Estate ★★★★★
Red Hill Estate ★★★★★
Scorpo Wines ★★★★★
Seaforth Estate ★★★★★
Stonier Wines ★★★★★
Ten Minutes by Tractor ★★★★★
Tuck's Ridge ★★★★★
Willow Creek Vineyard ★★★★★
Yabby Lake Vineyard ★★★★★

MOUNT BARKER
Goundrey ★★★★★
Plantagenet ★★★★★
Poacher's Ridge Vineyard ★★★★★
3 Drops ★★★★★

MOUNT LOFTY RANGES ZONE
Michael Hall Wines ★★★★★

NAGAMBIE LAKES
Mitchelton ★★★★★
Tahbilk ★★★★★

NORTHERN TASMANIA
Barringwood Park ★★★★★
Bay of Fires ★★★★★
Grey Sands ★★★★★
Josef Chromy Wines ★★★★★
Pipers Brook Vineyard ★★★★★
Pirie Estate ★★★★★
Tamar Ridge ★★★★★

ORANGE
Bloodwood ★★★★★
Mayfield Vineyard ★★★★★
Printhie Wines ★★★★★
Word of Mouth Wines ★★★★★

PEMBERTON
Fonty's Pool Vineyards ★★★★★
Salitage ★★★★★
Truffle Hill Wines ★★★★★

PERTH HILLS
Millbrook Winery ★★★★★

PORONGURUP
Abbey Creek Vineyard ★★★★★
Castle Rock Estate ★★★★★
Duke's Vineyard ★★★★★

PORT PHILLIP ZONE
Kennedy & Wilson ★★★★★

PYRENEES
Dalwhinnie ★★★★★
Summerfield ★★★★★

RIVERINA
De Bortoli ★★★★★
McWilliam's ★★★★★
Nugan Estate ★★★★★

RUTHERGLEN
All Saints Estate ★★★★★
Buller (Rutherglen) ★★★★★
Campbells ★★★★★
Chambers Rosewood ★★★★★
Morris ★★★★★
Pfeiffer Wines ★★★★★
Stanton & Killeen Wines ★★★★★
Warrabilla ★★★★★

SOUTH AUSTRALIA
Tapanappa ★★★★★
Tollana ★★★★★

SOUTH WEST AUSTRALIA ZONE
Larry Cherubino Wines ★★★★★

SOUTHEAST AUSTRALIA
Hewitson ★★★★★

SOUTHERN TASMANIA
Bream Creek ★★★★★
Cape Bernier Vineyard ★★★★★
Craigow ★★★★★
Domaine A ★★★★★
Frogmore Creek ★★★★★
Kate Hill Wines ★★★★★
Laurel Bank ★★★★★
Pooley Wines ★★★★★
Pressing Matters ★★★★★
Stefano Lubiana ★★★★★

STRATHBOGIE RANGES
Plunkett Fowles ★★★★★

SUNBURY
Galli Estate ★★★★★
Goona Warra Vineyard ★★★★★

SWAN VALLEY
Faber Vineyard ★★★★★
Houghton ★★★★★
John Kosovich Wines ★★★★★

UPPER GOULBURN
Delatite ★★★★★

VARIOUS
Ainsworth & Snelson ★★★★★

YARRA VALLEY
Carlei Estate & Carlei Green Vineyards
★★★★★
De Bortoli (Victoria) ★★★★★
Domaine Chandon ★★★★★
Dominique Portet ★★★★★
Gembrook Hill ★★★★★
Giant Steps/Innocent Bystander
★★★★★
Hillcrest Vineyard ★★★★★
Hoddles Creek Estate ★★★★★
macforbes ★★★★★
Mount Mary ★★★★★
Oakridge ★★★★★
PHI ★★★★★
Punch ★★★★★
Seville Estate ★★★★★
Stuart Wines ★★★★★
Tarrawarra Estate ★★★★★
Toolangi Vineyards ★★★★★
Warramate ★★★★★
Wedgetail Estate ★★★★★
Yarra Burn ★★★★★
Yarra Yarra ★★★★★
Yarra Yering ★★★★★
Yarrabank ★★★★★
YarraLoch ★★★★★
Yering Station ★★★★★
Yeringberg ★★★★★

Ten of the best
new wineries

As ever, 10 of the best, not the best 10, chosen from a far-flung field stretching across all states (other than Queensland), with strong representation from Western Australia.

BOBTAIL RIDGE WINES Frankland River, WA / **PAGE 107**
June and Jeremy Roberts were among the early movers when they diversified their Frankland River grazing property by planting grapes in 1980. They fully intended to have wine made, but farming and family commitments meant 23 years passed before any Bobtail Ridge wines eventuated. Most of the grapes from the 11.4 hectares of vineyard are sold to Alkoomi, which doubles as a highly skilled winemaker.

FLAMETREE Margaret River, WA / **PAGE 242**
This is the newest of new winery ventures, a partnership between the Gordon and Towner families that resulted in the erection of a winery shortly prior to the 2007 vintage, the first (the partnership does not own any vineyards). The wines have had resounding success, the 2007 Cabernet Merlot winning multiple trophies at the WA Wine Show '08, the trophy for Best Cabernet Blend at the Margaret River Wine Show '08 and, the biggest prize of all, the Jimmy Watson Trophy, all in the same year. Jeremy Gordon's winemaking skills extend across the full range of Margaret River styles, and it is quite certain the Flametree name will continue to burn brightly in the years ahead.

HEAD WINES Barossa Valley, SA / **PAGE 294**
I would not normally include a 600-case production winery in this category, aware of the frustration that might follow if the wines are no longer available. However, Alex Head has started something special, after graduating with a degree in biochemistry from Sydney University in 1997, followed by retail and auction house experience while fitting in vintages with Tyrrell's, Torbreck, Laughing Jack and Cirillo Estate. His raison d'etre is Côte Rotie at the northern end of Rhône Valley, the imagery and styles of those wines evident in every facet of his initial releases.

HOBBS OF BAROSSA RANGES Barossa Valley, SA / **PAGE 307**
Greg and Allison Hobbs have pushed the envelope further than most newcomers would dream of, let alone attempt. They have 1 hectare of shiraz, planted in 1908, followed by further plantings of between 1 to 2 hectares in '88, '97 and 2004. Then they have a 0.5 hectare each of white frontignac (1940s) and semillon ('60s) and viognier ('88). Far from following the safe route and making conventional wines, they have obtained the services of Pete Schell to make an Amarone-style shiraz, and three super-luscious white wines from the three estate plantings made by cane-cutting and then further fruit desiccation on racks.

KENNEDY & WILSON Port Phillip Zone, Vic / **PAGE 348**

The partnership between brothers James and Peter Wilson, and Juliana Kennedy is almost certainly better known for its chocolate than for wine. But James Wilson has a masters degree in oenology from Adelaide University and is completing his PhD in that subject; brother Peter worked at Yarra Yering from 1986 to '96. Juliana, ex-CEO of a smartcard/SIM card company, describes herself as 'manager of the worldwide Kennedy and Wilson conglomerate'. The vineyard is near Kilmore, in the no-man's-land of Port Phillip Zone. The wines reflect the unambiguously cool climate.

LANDHAUS ESTATE Barossa Valley, SA / **PAGE 370**

The Jaunitis family (John, Barbara, and son Kane) acquired the Landhaus Estate wine business in 2002, followed by the purchase of the Landhaus Cottage and its 1-hectare vineyard. Bethany is the oldest German-established town in the Barossa, and the cottage was one of the first to be built. Kane worked vintages for Mitolo and Trevor Jones, also managing East End Cellars in Adelaide, a leading fine wine retailers. Every step they have taken since 2002 has been an unqualified success.

MARCHAND & BURCH Great Southern, WA / **PAGE 408**

This is a joint venture between Canadian-born and Burgundian-trained Pascal Marchand, and the Burch family of Howard Park. Chardonnay and Pinot Noir (and a little Shiraz) from the Frankland River/Margaret River regions of WA is to be followed by Gevrey Chambertin and Chambertin Clos de Beze from Burgundy. A thoroughly interesting business, with some inspired Chardonnays in its first releases.

MICHAEL HALL WINES Mount Lofty Ranges Zone, SA / **PAGE 418**

Michael Hall was a jewellery valuer for Sotheby's in Switzerland before coming to Australia in 2001 to pursue winemaking, a lifelong interest. He graduated dux of the wine science course at Charles Sturt University in '05, and along the way obtained vintage experience at Cullen, Giaconda, Henschke, Shaw & Smith, Coldstream Hills and Veritas; his Rhône Valley experience is equally impressive. He is winemaker at Rocland Estate and makes his own wines there, which are every bit as impressive as his CV suggests.

SONS OF EDEN Barossa Valley, SA / **PAGE 597**

This is substantial venture between winemaker Corey Ryan and viticulturist Simon Cowham. Corey has 22 vintages under his belt, starting as a winemaker with Henschke, then Rouge Homme and Penfolds Coonawarra, followed the Rhône Valley, and then becoming chief winemaker for Villa Maria Estates, NZ. Simon has an equally impressive career, covering every imaginable facet of the industry. With 52 hectares of estate vineyards to work with, they are making wines of exceptional quality.

SPRINGS HILL VINEYARD McLaren Vale, SA / **PAGE 602**

The origin of the business goes back to 1975, when brothers Anthony and Gary Whaite began the planting of cabernet sauvignon and shiraz. Over the years they have slowly extended the size of the vineyard to its present 17 hectares, adding merlot, mourvedre and grenache along the way. The vines are dry grown, and the winemaking involves traditional small batch techniques.

Ten dark horses

This is a highly subjective selection of 10 wineries that have excelled over the past 12 months. Thus they are not new wineries, nor 10 of the best (both covered elsewhere) but do have that little bit extra. Four come from Western Australia, three from South Australia, two from New South Wales and one from Victoria. Western Australia's strong performance reflects the excellent 2007 and 2008 vintages, far better than those of the east.

CHRISMONT King Valley, Vic / PAGE 165
Chrismont is a long-established King Valley producer owned by Arnie and Jo Pizzini. They focus on a full range of Italian varieties, winemaker Warren Proft teasing out the best features of these sometimes difficult varieties. The wines are all made from the 80 hectares of estate vineyards, and the current releases are of high quality and full of interest.

EDEN SPRINGS Eden Valley, SA / PAGE 222
Eden Springs is the venture of self-confessed wine lover Ray Gatt, who not only acquired the 20-hectare, 35-year-old Eden Springs Vineyard, but added the historic Siegersdorf Vineyard on the Barossa floor, and the neighbouring Graue Vineyard. High-quality contract winemaking has done the rest; the High Eden Riesling, Shiraz and Cabernet Sauvignon are all excellent. The prices are mouth-watering.

GLEN ELDON WINES Barossa Valley, SA / PAGE 269
Glen Eldon Wines is the venture of brothers Richard and Andrew Sheedy, and their wives Mary and Sue, who have acquired 30 hectares of high-quality Barossa vineyards, primarily planted to shiraz and cabernet sauvignon. Contract-grown grapes fill out the offering with Eden Valley Riesling, Barossa Viognier and other wines. The top-of-the-range Shirazs are expensive ($95 to $110), but there are three bargains (Shiraz, Shiraz Mataro and Cabernet Sauvignon) at $25 scoring 94 to 95 points.

HELM Canberra District, NSW / PAGE 298
Helm is the eponymous winery of Ken Helm, an indefatigable promoter of his wines and of the Canberra District generally, ever willing to appear on television or be interviewed on radio to discuss almost any subject, frequently with a sting in the tail. He has long focused on riesling, and was one of the key movers in establishing the International Riesling Competition staged in Canberra each year. It was thus wholly appropriate that his 2008 Classic Dry Riesling and Premium Riesling should both bring the trophies and gold medals he has long sought. You might think he will let the wines speak for themselves in the future, but I somehow doubt that.

ORANJE TRACTOR Albany, WA / PAGE 474
Oranje Tractor takes its name from the 1964 orange-coloured Fiat tractor purchased by Murray Gomm and Pamela Lincoln when they began the establishment of their

Albany vineyard in 1998. Their 3-hectare organic vineyard is planted mainly to riesling (the winery specialty) with some sauvignon blanc and a small amount of pinot noir. The remote location, and basically weekend opening times, mean they have limited quantities of vintages going back to 2003 on sale.

POACHER'S RIDGE VINEYARD Mount Barker, WA / PAGE 515

Poacher's Ridge Vineyard, established by Alex and Janet Taylor near Narrikup in Mount Barker, didn't produce its first commercial crop until 2004, but has been knocking on the 5-star door since that time, in no small measure on the back of the very successful Louis' Block Merlot; having said that, contract maker Rob Diletti is doing great things with the Vineyard's Riesling, Cabernet Sauvignon and Shiraz (as well as Merlot).

SMALLFRY WINES Barossa Valley, SA / PAGE 593

Smallfry Wines is the venture of Wayne Ahrens and partner Suzi Hilder, the latter the daughter of well-known Upper Hunter viticulturist Dick Hilder, Ahrens from a fifth-generation Barossa family. The majority of the grapes from the 27 hectares of their two vineyards are sold, a small amount retained to support the Smallfry label. The pick of the crop and skilled winemaking come up with the right answer.

WARRAROONG ESTATE Lower Hunter Valley, NSW / PAGE 682

Warraroong Estate dates back to 1978, when the vineyard was planted Peter Fraser and known as Fraser Vineyard. Now owned by Bob Bradley and Linda Abrahams, the skills of contract winemaker Andrew Thomas shine through on all the wines, none more so than the Semillon, with four vintages (2005–08 inclusive) now available for sale.

WATERSHED WINES Margaret River, WA / PAGE 684

Watershed Wines is, on any measure, a major success, its 187 hectares of vineyards producing 90 000 cases of high-quality wines for its investment syndicate owners. Relatively few of the investment scheme developments flourish, and this is an exception that proves the rule in no uncertain fashion. Senses Sauvignon Blanc and Cabernet Merlot (94 points each) are great value at around $24, Awakening Single Block Chardonnay ($40) and Wakening Cabernet Sauvignon ($55) are at another quality level (95 and 96 points respectively).

WILLS DOMAIN Margaret River, WA / PAGE 698

Wills Domain was purchased by Michelle and Darren Haunold in 2000, adding another chapter to a family history of winemaking stretching back to 1383 in modern day Austria. Prior to their purchase of the vineyard, which had been planted in 1985, the grapes were sold. Since 2001 the wines have been contract made, Darren Haunold's responsibility being the maintenance of the 21 hectares of estate plantings. That may not seem unusual, except that Darren Haunold lost the use of his legs in a car accident when he was 13, and does the work (including part of the pruning) from his wheelchair.

Special value wines

As always, these are lists of 10 of the best value wines, not the 10 best wines in each price category. There are literally dozens of wines with similar points and prices, and the choice is necessarily an arbitrary one. I have, however, attempted to give as much varietal and style choice as the limited numbers allow.

TEN OF THE BEST VALUE Whites $10 and under

89	2008 Possums Vineyard Two in the Pouch McLaren Vale Chardonnay Viognier	$6.50
89	2008 De Bortoli Sacred Hill Chardonnay	$7.50
89	2008 De Bortoli Sacred Hill Semillon Sauvignon Blanc	$7.50
89	2008 Oxford Landing Sauvignon Blanc	$8.95
90	2008 Lindemans Bin 95 Sauvignon Blanc	$8.99
88	2008 Arrowfield Estate Bowman's Crossing Semillon Sauvignon Blanc	$9
88	2008 Cheviot Bridge Long Flat Semillon Sauvignon Blanc	$9.95
90	2008 Oakover White Label Classic White	$10
89	2008 Deakin Estate Sauvignon Blanc	$10
88	2008 GISA Arc Semillon Sauvignon Blanc	$10

TEN OF THE BEST VALUE Reds $10 and under

90	2008 Possums Vineyard Two in the Pouch McLaren Vale Shiraz Cabernet Sauvignon	$6.50
90	2008 De Bortoli Sacred Hill Rose	$7.50
90	2008 Oxford Landing Cabernet Rose	$8.95
90	2007 Cheviot Bridge Long Flat Shiraz	$9.95
88	2008 Kirrihill Lizards of Oz Shiraz	$9.95
91	2005 Lindemans Reserve Coonawarra Cabernet Sauvignon	$9.99
90	2007 Deakin Estate Shiraz	$10
90	2007 Wombat Lodge Margaret River Cabernet Sauvignon Merlot Petit Verdot Malbec Cabernet Franc	$10
89	2005 Wombat Lodge South Point Margaret River Cabernet Sauvignon Merlot Shiraz	$10
88	2006 Warburn Estate Stephendale Winemakers Reserve Barossa Cabernet Sauvignon	$10

It is in these two groups that the effect of the wine surplus is most evident, forcing down the price (or upping the quality) of wines that would normally be far more expensive.

TEN OF THE BEST VALUE Whites $10–$15

93	2008 Piromit Pinot Grigio	$12.50
93	2008 Yalumba Y Series Viognier	$12.95
94	2008 Mount Eyre Hunter Valley Semillon	$13.95
94	2006 Chateau Francois Pokolbin Mallee Semillon	$14
94	2008 Hoddles Creek Estate Wickhams Road Gippsland Chardonnay	$14.99
95	2008 KarriBindi Semillon Sauvignon Blanc	$15
94	2005 Bobtail Ridge Frankland River Semillon	$15
94	2008 Goona Warra Sunbury Semillon Sauvignon Blanc	$15
94	2008 Jim Barry Watervale Riesling	$15
94	2008 Smallfry Barossa Semillon	$15

TEN OF THE BEST VALUE Reds $10–$15

93	2006 Andrew Peace Kentish Lane Langhorne Creek Cabernet Sauvignon	$12
91	2008 Yalumba Y Series Shiraz Viognier	$12.95
93	2008 Kingston Estate Cabernet Sauvignon	$12.99
90	2006 Mike Press Adelaide Hills Merlot	$12.99
92	2008 De Bortoli Windy Peak Yarra Valley Pinot Noir	$13
93	2007 Houghton Cabernet Sauvignon	$14
91	2008 Trentham Estate La Famiglia Sangiovese Rose	$14
92	2008 Hoddles Creek Estate Wickhams Road Yarra Valley Pinot Noir	$14.99
94	2007 Bobtail Ridge Frankland River Shiraz	$15
92	Jacob's Creek Three Vines Shiraz Grenache Sangiovese	$15

Australia's geographical indications

The process of formally mapping Australia's wine regions is all but complete, although will never come to a complete halt – for one thing, climate change is lurking in the wings. The division into states, zones, regions and subregions follows; those regions or subregions marked with an asterisk are not yet registered, and may never be, but are in common usage. In two instances I have gone beyond the likely finalisation: it makes no sense to me that the Hunter Valley should be a zone, the region Hunter, and then subregions which are all in the Lower Hunter Valley. I have elected to stick with the traditional division between the Upper Hunter Valley on the one hand, and the Lower on the other.

I am also in front of the game with Tasmania, dividing it into Northern, Southern and East Coast, and, to a lesser degree, have anticipated that the Queensland Coastal region will seek recognition under this or some similar name.

An intriguing addition is the proposed Orange Foothills GI, not a subregion of Orange, but a region in its own right.

State/Zone	Region	Subregion
NEW SOUTH WALES		
Big Rivers	Murray Darling Perricoota Riverina Swan Hill	
Central Ranges	Cowra Mudgee Orange Orange Foothills★	
Hunter Valley	Hunter Lower Hunter Valley★	Broke Fordwich Mount View★ Pokolbin★
	Upper Hunter Valley★	
Northern Rivers	Hastings River	

State/Zone	Region	Subregion
Northern Slopes	New England	
South Coast	Shoalhaven Coast Southern Highlands	
Southern New South Wales	Canberra District Gundagai Hilltops Tumbarumba	
Western Plains		

SOUTH AUSTRALIA

Adelaide (Super Zone, includes Mount Lofty Ranges, Fleurieu and Barossa)		
Barossa	Barossa Valley Eden Valley	High Eden
Far North	Southern Flinders Ranges	
Fleurieu	Currency Creek Kangaroo Island Langhorne Creek McLaren Vale Southern Fleurieu	
Limestone Coast	Coonawarra Mount Benson Mount Gambier★ Padthaway Robe Wrattonbully	
Lower Murray	Riverland	
Mount Lofty Ranges	Adelaide Hills	Lenswood Piccadilly Valley
	Adelaide Plains Clare Valley	Polish Hill River★ Watervale★
The Peninsulas	Southern Eyre Peninsula★	

State/Zone	Region	Subregion
VICTORIA		
Central Victoria	Bendigo Goulburn Valley Heathcote Strathbogie Ranges Upper Goulburn	Nagambie Lakes
Gippsland		
North East Victoria	Alpine Valleys Beechworth Glenrowan King Valley Rutherglen	
North West Victoria	Murray Darling Swan Hill	
Port Phillip	Geelong Macedon Ranges Mornington Peninsula Sunbury Yarra Valley	
Western Victoria	Ballarat★ Grampians Henty Pyrenees	Great Western
WESTERN AUSTRALIA		
Central Western Australia		
Eastern Plains, Inland and North of Western Australia		
Greater Perth	Peel Perth Hills Swan District	Swan Valley

State/Zone	Region	Subregion
South West Australia	Blackwood Valley	
	Geographe	
	Great Southern	Albany
		Denmark
		Frankland River
		Mount Barker
		Porongurup
	Manjimup	
	Margaret River	
	Pemberton	
West Australian South East Coastal	Esperance★	

QUEENSLAND

Queensland	Granite Belt	
	Queensland Coastal★	
	South Burnett	
	Darling Downs★	

TASMANIA

Tasmania	Northern Tasmania★	
	Southern Tasmania★	
	East Coast Tasmania★	

AUSTRALIAN CAPITAL TERRITORY

NORTHERN TERRITORY

Australian vintage charts

Each number represents a mark out of 10 for the quality of vintages in each region.

red wine   white wine

2005	2006	2007	2008

NSW

Lower Hunter Valley

2005	2006	2007	2008
7	6	8	2
9	7	10	7

Upper Hunter Valley

| 7 | 6 | 7 | 2 |
| 9 | 7 | 8 | 6 |

Mudgee

| 7 | 8 | 5 | 8 |
| 9 | 7 | 7 | 7 |

Cowra

| 7 | 6 | 7 | 9 |
| 8 | 6 | 6 | 7 |

Orange

| 8 | 9 | 6 | 8 |
| 9 | 8 | 7 | 7 |

Riverina

| 6 | 6 | 7 | 7 |
| 6 | 7 | 7 | 8 |

Canberra District

| 9 | 8 | 8 | 8 |
| 9 | 9 | 8 | 9 |

Southern Highlands

| 8 | 8 | 3 | 9 |
| 9 | 8 | 5 | 8 |

Perricoota

| 9 | 7 | 7 | 8 |
| 6 | 8 | 9 | 8 |

Gundagai

| 9 | 8 | 6 | 6 |
| 8 | 7 | 7 | 7 |

Hilltops

| 9 | 10 | 6 | 9 |
| 8 | 9 | 6 | 8 |

2005	2006	2007	2008

Tumbarumba

| 7 | 7 | 7 | 7 |
| 9 | 9 | 9 | 9 |

Hastings River

| 9 | 6 | 8 | 5 |
| 9 | 7 | 7 | 8 |

Shoalhaven

| 9 | 7 | 4 | 7 |
| 8 | 8 | 4 | 7 |

VIC

Yarra Valley

| 9 | 9 | 7 | 7 |
| 9 | 9 | 8 | 7 |

Mornington Peninsula

| 9 | 9 | 9 | 9 |
| 7 | 8 | 8 | 8 |

Geelong

| 8 | 8 | 7 | 7 |
| 7 | 8 | 7 | 7 |

Macedon Ranges

| 7 | 9 | 8 | 7 |
| 8 | 8 | 8 | 7 |

Sunbury

| 7 | 8 | 8 | 8 |
| 8 | 7 | 7 | 7 |

Grampians

| 10 | 8 | 8 | 7 |
| 9 | 8 | 7 | 7 |

Pyrenees

| 10 | 9 | 8 | 8 |
| 9 | 8 | 7 | 8 |

Henty

| 9 | 8 | 4 | 9 |
| 8 | 9 | 8 | 8 |

2005	2006	2007	2008

Bendigo

| 8 | 8 | 6 | 8 |
| 7 | 8 | 7 | 8 |

Heathcote

| 8 | 9 | 7 | 9 |
| 9 | 7 | 6 | 7 |

Goulburn Valley

| 8 | 9 | 8 | 8 |
| 8 | 8 | 7 | 9 |

Upper Goulburn

| 9 | 8 | ** | 7 |
| 9 | 8 | 4 | 8 |

Strathbogie Ranges

| 9 | 7 | ** | 8 |
| 8 | 8 | 7 | 7 |

Glenrowan & Rutherglen

| 7 | 7 | ** | 7 |
| 7 | 7 | ** | 6 |

King Valley

| 7 | 8 | ** | 7 |
| 9 | 7 | ** | 9 |

Alpine Valleys

| 8 | 8 | ** | 7 |
| 10 | 7 | ** | 7 |

Beechworth

| 8 | 8 | ** | 7 |
| 8 | 7 | ** | 6 |

Gippsland

| 9 | 9 | 9 | 8 |
| 9 | 8 | 8 | 7 |

Murray Darling

| 8 | 8 | 8 | 8 |
| 8 | 9 | 8 | 8 |

SA

	2005	2006	2007	2008
Barossa Valley	7	10	7	8
	8	7	6	7
Eden Valley	8	7	8	7
	9	8	7	8
Clare Valley	9	8	7	6
	9	7	6	8
Adelaide Hills	7	7	8	7
	8	9	6	7
Adelaide Plains	8	7	8	8
	9	8	7	7
Coonawarra	8	7	7	9
	7	6	7	7
Padthaway	8	8	8	6
	7	7	7	6
Mount Benson & Robe	8	7	7	8
	9	7	7	8
Wrattonbully	8	9	6	7
	8	7	6	8
McLaren Vale	8	8	7	7
	8	7	6	7

	2005	2006	2007	2008
Southern Fleurieu	8	8	8	8
	8	8	8	7
Langhorne Creek	9	8	8	8
	8	9	8	8
Kangaroo Island	8	8	7	8
	8	7	8	8
Riverland	8	9	8	6
	9	8	9	8

WA

	2005	2006	2007	2008
Margaret River	9	7	8	9
	9	9	8	9
Great Southern	9	6	8	8
	9	8	9	8
Manjimup	7	6	8	8
	9	8	9	9
Pemberton	9	6	9	8
	9	8	9	9
Geographe	7	6	8	8
	8	8	9	7
Swan District	9	7	8	8
	8	8	7	8

	2005	2006	2007	2008
Peel	10	9	9	8
	10	9	9	5
Perth Hills	10	8	8	7
	9	7	7	8

QLD

	2005	2006	2007	2008
Granite Belt	9	8	8	6
	9	7	7	8
South Burnett	9	7	8	6
	10	8	8	7

TAS

	2005	2006	2007	2008
Northern Tasmania	10	8	7	8
	9	7	8	7
Southern Tasmania	10	9	7	7
	9	8	8	7

★★ Frost and bushfire smoke taint precludes ratings; virtually no wine made in these regions.

Plantings and production

The plantings and production figures on page 48 shed minimal light on the appropriate responses to the supply and demand problems the industry faces. With the exception of sauvignon blanc and, to a lesser degree, shiraz, over the past four vintages plantings have either stalled or declined slightly, cabernet sauvignon in the latter category. Mourvedre shows the most dramatic decline in percentage terms, down 20%.

History is interesting, mainly because it shows how dramatic the contrast is of the changes that have occurred over the last two decades. Momentarily going back a further 10 years to 1980, bottled wine sales of riesling exceeded those of all other white wines combined.

Coming forward to 1990, you find that cabernet sauvignon, with 368 hectares in bearing and 934 hectares coming into bearing, looked certain to overtake shiraz, which had 4711 hectares in bearing, and 399 hectares to come into bearing. The rate of increase of cabernet plantings was significantly greater than shiraz, hence the belief. In fact, shiraz has continued to grow and there is no chance that cabernet will ever again challenge its primacy.

Merlot had a mere 318 hectares in bearing, albeit with 191 hectares coming into bearing. Throughout the rest of the 1990s its planting continued to increase at a furious rate; of the 8575 hectares planted by 2000, 5390 hectares were in bearing, 3185 hectares still to come into bearing. However, in the colloquial, by 2002 it had shot its bolt.

Unsurprisingly, pinot noir has come from a base of 801 hectares in bearing, 328 hectares yet to come into bearing in 1990. A detailed examination of the plantings on a region-by-region basis (unfortunately, not readily available) would doubtless show removals of pinot noir from warm areas, and off-setting plantings in cool regions. Merlot may have lost its lustre, but pinot noir has not. Its limiting factor is appropriately cool growing conditions.

The omnibus of other red varieties has remained static, and if you compare the 2004 plantings of the trendy new red varieties with those of 2008 in the table below, it's not hard to see why there has been no upwards movement in this category.

Coming back to the white varieties, the two big movers are sauvignon blanc and pinot gris, the percentage increase of the latter far in excess of that of sauvignon blanc. Were it not for the Kiwi factor, one would unhesitatingly put money on the back of sauvignon blanc rather than pinot gris. The former can be made with or without barrel fermentation, and with or without the incorporation of a significant amount of semillon, again with a choice of fermentation methods. The options for pinot gris, by contrast, are much more limited, and the inherent blandness of the taste of pinot gris suggests that once another generation comes along, there will be fewer buyers. The Kiwi factor, and Australia's spirited reply, means much more sauvignon blanc coming through the supply chain. How much more can we drink?

The wild card with semillon and riesling is the advent of screwcaps, and the progressive discovery by those who, deliberately or accidentally, cellar these wines for an extended period of time, and find that they have vinous magic.

Which leaves chardonnay, the leviathan that provides half the total white grape crush, and which – from numerous anecdotal reports – has the largest surplus. Despite the anything-but-chardonnay (ABC) club, it is also the foremost member of the always-brings-cash club (the other ABC club). Its problem is notwithstanding that while it makes the greatest white wines in the world, it is so flexible and eager to please that it is prostituted to make some of the worst – or, if not worst, unwanted – wines in the world. And, of course, everything in between.

If 10 000 of the 50 000 tonnes target were to be chardonnay, it would reduce its plantings by one third, and here the one certainty emerges. The moment it is removed, vignerons will realise the terrible mistake they have made, and hasten to replant it. When this happens, hope the new French (Dijon) clones will be selected, and the right (cool) regions chosen.

	2004	2005	2007	2008
CHARDONNAY				
hectares	28,008	30,507	32,151	31,564
tonnes	311,273	378,287	366,936	428,082
RIESLING				
hectares	4,255	4,326	4,432	4,400
tonnes	36,404	41,237	31,002	39,305
SAUVIGNON BLANC				
hectares	3,425	4,152	5,545	6,404
tonnes	39,774	38,355	36,515	62,420
SEMILLON				
hectares	6,278	6,282	6,752	6,716
tonnes	99,237	96,727	75,170	100,031
OTHER WHITE				
hectares	23,925	23,365	24,303	23,109
tonnes	266,794	253,837	192,026	223,075
TOTAL WHITE				
hectares	65,891	68,632	73,183	72,193
tonnes	753,482	808,443	701,649	852,913
CABERNET SAUVIGNON				
hectares	29,313	28,621	27,909	27,553
tonnes	319,955	284,062	183,052	258,066
GRENACHE				
hectares	2,292	2,097	2,011	2,011
tonnes	24,987	25,418	15,602	19,755
MOURVEDRE				
hectares	1,040	963	794	785
tonnes	13,992	10,149	6,596	8,401
MERLOT				
hectares	10,804	10,816	10,790	10,764
tonnes	123,944	132,586	90,461	125,285
PINOT NOIR				
hectares	4,424	4,231	4,393	4,490
tonnes	41,690	36,887	26,251	43,923
SHIRAZ				
hectares	39,182	40,508	43,417	43,977
tonnes	436,691	415,421	283,741	441,950
OTHER RED				
hectares	11,235	10,797	11,309	10,902
tonnes	101,816	105,460	63,339	86,741
TOTAL RED				
hectares	98,290	98,033	100,623	100,482
tonnes	1,063,075	1,009,983	669,042	984,121
TOTAL GRAPES				
hectares	164,181	166,665	173,776	172,675
tonnes	1,816,556	1,818,426	1,370,690	1,837,034
PERCENTAGE (TONNES)				
White	41.48%	44.46%	51.18%	46.43%
Red	58.52%	55.54%	48.82%	53.57%
YIELD PER HECTARE (TONNES/HECTARE)				
	10.91	10.55	7.88	10.63

Acknowledgements

It is, I suppose, inevitable that the production of a book such as this should involve many people in a long chain of events, some seemingly trivial, others of fundamental importance.

The starting point is the making of the thousands of bottles of wine that Ben Edwards and I taste each year, and the end point is the appearance of the book on retailers' shelves across Australia in August 2009.

My foremost thanks must go to the winemakers for sending the wines to me at their cost and, in particular, those who treat submission dates as serious deadlines rather than an approximate wish list on my part. Those who ignored the deadlines are increasingly likely to fall on their own sword as the competition for space in the book intensifies.

Next are those responsible for getting the wine to me, whether by the excellent parcel delivery service of Australia Post, by courier or by hand delivery. I am reliant on the goodwill and tolerance of many people involved in what may seem as a warped version of trivial pursuits as the wines are received; placed in bins; in due course fork-lifted up one storey and removed from those bins; unpacked; listed; entered into the database, with precise names cross-checked, alcohol, price, and closure type recorded; tasting sheets printed for the day's tasting of 150 wines, initially arranged by producer, but the re-sorted by variety; moved on to a long tasting bench; opened; poured at the same pace as I taste; the Riedel glasses returned to washing racks; washed, rinsed and dried (my task each day); the tasting notes dictated; the database now returning the notes to a winery-by-winery sequence; proofed by me (and at least three others at subsequent stages before going to print).

In the meantime, my office team of Paula Grey and Beth Anthony has been busy chasing up new, missing or inconsistent details regarding the wineries, and many of the wines, with special emphasis on new wineries.

Then there is the ever-patient, but deadline-conscious, team at Hardie Grant, working on the cover design (surely brilliant), page design, paper type and two-colour printing, which give rise to galley pages for proofreading again and again.

To my team of Ben Edwards, Paula Grey, Beth Anthony; Bev and Chris Bailey (Coldstream Post Office); Pam Holmes (and others at Coldstream Hills); John Cook (programmer); and the Hardie Grant team led by believer-in-chief Sandy Grant, along with Jasmin Chua (senior editor), Megan Ellis (typesetter) and Nada Backovic (cover designer), my heartfelt thanks. This is as much their book as it is mine.

Australian wineries and wines

Abbey Creek Vineyard ★★★★★

2388 Porongurup Road, Porongurup, WA 6324 **Region** Porongurup
T (08) 9853 1044 **F** (08) 9454 5501 **Open** By appt
Winemaker Castle Rock Estate (Robert Diletti) **Est.** 1990 **Cases** 1000 **Vyds** 1.6 ha
This is the family business of Mike and Mary Dilworth, the name comes from a winter creek running alongside the vineyard and a view of The Abbey in the Stirling Range. The vineyard is equally split between riesling, pinot noir, sauvignon blanc and cabernet sauvignon planted in 1990 and '93. The rieslings have had significant show success.

☆☆☆☆☆ **Porongurup Riesling 2008** A highly fragrant bouquet with lime and apple blossom aromas, plus an unusual touch of nettle; it has great focus, intensity and length, the finish clear and crisp. Screwcap. 12.5% alc. **Rating** 95 **To** 2020 $18
Porongurup Riesling 2007 Still very pale; has an abundance of lime-accented fruit on both bouquet and palate, the finish long and sustained. Screwcap. 13% alc. **Rating** 94 **To** 2017 $18

☆☆☆☆☆ **Porongurup Sauvignon Blanc 2008** Fragrant pea pod, grass and citrus aromas intermingle, and also largely define the palate, other than a touch of passionfruit. Screwcap. 13% alc. **Rating** 93 **To** 2012 $20

Abercorn

Cassilis Road, Mudgee, NSW 2850 **Region** Mudgee
T 1800 000 959 **www**.abercornwine.com.au **Open** Thurs–Mon 10.30–4.30
Winemaker Tim Stevens **Est.** 1996 **Cases** 3000 **Vyds** 8.14 ha
Tim Stevens is a busy man. In 1996 he acquired the then 25-year-old Abercorn Vineyard, and in late 2005 purchased the very well known adjacent Huntington Estate. He has developed his skills as a winemaker, enabling him to keep the style of the Abercorn and Huntington wines quite distinct. He describes Abercorn as the 'modern, smooth, regional style', with the A Reserve and the Growers Revenge leading the way.

☆☆☆☆☆ **Growers Revenge 2006** A rich, quite luscious, but relatively soft wine, with ample blackcurrant and blackberry fruit, plus licorice and spice, to go the distance, supported by fine tannins. Cabernet Sauvignon/Shiraz/Merlot. Screwcap. 13.9% alc. **Rating** 92 **To** 2021 $40

☆☆☆☆ **A Reserve Mudgee Shiraz 2005** Slightly diffuse colour, although the hue is good; distinctly savoury, light- to medium-bodied shiraz with a lemony twist on the finish partly balanced by oak. Screwcap. 14.2% alc. **Rating** 88 **To** 2014 $40
Mudgee Cabernet Merlot 2005 A soft, medium-bodied wine with some oak sweetness and gentle tannins, now close to its peak. Screwcap. 13.8% alc. **Rating** 87 **To** 2010 $20

Across the Lake ★★★★★

79 Mt Shadforth Road, Denmark, WA 6333 **Region** Central Western Australia Zone
T (08) 9848 1838 **www**.acrossthelakewines.com.au **Open** By appt
Winemaker The Vintage Wineworx (Greg Jones) **Est.** 1999 **Cases** 400
The Taylor family has been farming (wheat and sheep) for over 40 years at Lake Grace; a small diversification into grapegrowing started as a hobby, but has developed into more than that with 2 ha of shiraz. They were motivated to support their friend Bill (WJ) Walker, who had started growing shiraz three years previously, and has since produced a gold medal–winning wine. Having learnt which soils are suitable, the Taylors intend to increase their plantings.

☆☆☆☆☆ **Shiraz 2007** Classic Côte Rôtie style; leather, licorice and spice; tremendous intensity and thrust; great texture; excellent Shiraz from the remote Central Western Australia Zone. Gold WA Wine Show '08. Screwcap. 13.9% alc. **Rating** 95 **To** 2017 $25

Ada River

2330 Main Road, Neerim South, Vic 3831 **Region** Gippsland
T (03) 5628 1661 **F** (03) 5628 1661 **Open** W'ends & public hols 10–6
Winemaker Peter Kelliher **Est.** 1983 **Cases** 1500 **Vyds** 10 ha
The Kelliher family first planted vines on their dairy farm at Neerim South in 1983, extending
the vineyard in '89 and increasing plantings further by establishing the nearby Manilla Vineyard
in '94. Until 2000, Ada River leased a Yarra Valley vineyard; it has relinquished that lease and in
its place established a vineyard at Heathcote in conjunction with a local grower.

🍷🍷🍷🍷   **Heathcote Shiraz 2007** Bright colour; oaky bouquet, with bay leaf supporting
the blueberry fruit; dense and rich, the alcohol is noticeable, giving plenty of
warmth to the finish. Screwcap. 14.6% alc. **Rating** 87 **To** 2012 $25

Adinfern Estate

Bussell Highway, Cowaramup, WA 6284 **Region** Margaret River
T (08) 9755 5272 **F** (08) 9755 5206 **www**.adinfern.com **Open** 7 days 11–5.30
Winemaker Merv Smith, Matt Thomas **Est.** 1996 **Cases** 3500 **Vyds** 24.7 ha
Merv and Jan Smith have farmed their property as a fine wool and lamb producer for over
30 years, but in 1996 diversified with the development of a vineyard planted to sauvignon
blanc, semillon, cabernet sauvignon, chardonnay, malbec, shiraz and pinot noir. One hundred
tonnes of grapes are sold to other makers, 25 retained for Adinfern Estate. Exports to
Singapore and Hong Kong.

🍷🍷🍷🍷   **Margaret River Sauvignon Blanc 2008** Clean and varietal, with nettle,
gooseberry and some tropical notes; fresh and lively on the finish. Screwcap.
13% alc. **Rating** 89 **To** 2011 $20

Affleck

154 Millynn Road, Bungendore, NSW 2621 **Region** Canberra District
T (02) 6236 9276 **www**.affleck.com.au **Open** Fri–Tues 9–5 (closed June–Aug)
Winemaker Ian Hendry **Est.** 1976 **Cases** 5000 **Vyds** 2.5 ha
The cellar door and mail-order price list says that the wines are 'grown, produced and bottled
on the estate by Ian and Susie Hendry with much dedicated help from family and friends'.

🍷🍷🍷🍷   **Canberra District Sauvignon Blanc 2008** Gentle tropical fruits ranging
through passionfruit to pineapple, and a sweet, but balanced, finish. Screwcap.
12% alc. **Rating** 88 **To** 2010 $15

Ainsworth & Snelson

22 Gourlay Street, St Kilda East, Vic 3183 **Region** Various
T (03) 9530 3333 **F** (03) 9530 3446 **www**.ainsworthandsnelson.com **Open** Not
Winemaker Brett Snelson **Est.** 2002 **Cases** 5000
Brett Snelson and Gregg Ainsworth take a handcrafted regional approach to the production
of their wines. They use traditional techniques that allow the emphasis to remain on terroir,
sourcing grapes from the Clare Valley, Yarra Valley, Barossa and Coonawarra. Brett Snelson
keeps his winemaking skills sharp with an annual vintage in Roussillon. Exports to the UK,
France, Denmark, Norway, Hong Kong and Singapore.

🍷🍷🍷🍷🍷   **Watervale Riesling 2008** Green-straw; a wonderful bouquet flooded with
citrus blossom aromas, then a palate that opens with the same expressive fruit
before tightening up with excellent acidity on the finish. Great wine, great value;
350 cases made. Screwcap. 13.5% alc. **Rating** 95 **To** 2020 $22
Barossa Valley Shiraz 2005 Retains good hue; a fragrant bouquet, then a
pleasantly structured palate, with juicy fruit on the mid-palate, fine, savoury
tannins on the long finish. Screwcap. 15% alc. **Rating** 94 **To** 2020 $28

ȲȲȲȲȲ Yarra Valley Chardonnay 2006 An elegant wine, the bouquet showing some barrel ferment inputs, but the palate is fruit-driven, and has good thrust through to the finish. Screwcap. 13.5% alc. **Rating** 90 **To** 2014 $28

Albert River Wines ★★☆

869 Mundoolun Connection Road, Tamborine, Qld 4270 **Region** Queensland Coastal **T** (07) 5543 6622 **www**.albertriverwines.com.au **Open** Sun–Tues 9–4, Wed–Sat 9–8 **Winemaker** Peter Scudamore-Smith MW (Contract) **Est.** 1998 **Cases** 3000 **Vyds** 3.6 ha Albert River is one of the high-profile wineries in the Gold Coast hinterland. David and Janette Bladin, with a combined 30 years' experience in tourism and hospitality, have acquired and relocated two of Qld's most historic buildings, Tamborine House and Auchenflower House. The winery itself is housed in a newly constructed annex to Auchenflower House; the Bladins have established a vineyard on the property, and have another 50 ha under contract. All of its distribution is through cellar door, mail order and local restaurants. Exports to Japan.

Alkoomi ★★★★★

Wingebellup Road, Frankland River, WA 6396 **Region** Frankland River **T** (08) 9855 2229 **F** (08) 9855 2284 **www**.alkoomiwines.com.au **Open** 7 days 10–5 **Winemaker** Stephen Craig, Merv Lange **Est.** 1971 **Cases** 90 000 **Vyds** 103.5 ha For those who see the wineries of WA as suffering from the tyranny of distance, this most remote of all wineries shows there is no tyranny after all. It is a story of unqualified success due to sheer hard work, and no doubt to Merv and Judy Lange's aversion to borrowing a single dollar from the bank. The substantial production is entirely drawn from the ever-expanding estate vineyards – now over 100 ha. Wine quality across the range is impeccable, always with precisely defined varietal character. Exports to all major markets.

ȲȲȲȲȲ Blackbutt 2005 Good colour and intensity; a classic Bordeaux-style blend of Cabernet Sauvignon/Malbec/Cabernet Franc/Merlot, intense and uncompromising, which will mature over many years, never losing its birthright. Diam. 13.5% alc. **Rating** 95 **To** 2025 $63.60
Black Label Frankland River Sauvignon Blanc 2008 Restrained, yet pure, varietal bouquet, with fresh tropical fruit and zesty citrus flavours drawing out on the palate; quite long, and surprisingly generous with an attractive liveliness on the finish. Screwcap. 12.5% alc. **Rating** 94 **To** 2012 $20.50
Black Label Frankland River Chardonnay 2007 Finely crafted and structured; oak seamlessly integrated through the long palate and finish; grapefruit and nectarine the primary flavour drivers. Screwcap. 14% alc. **Rating** 94 **To** 2017 $22.30
Black Label Frankland River Shiraz Viognier 2007 A nice blend of spice and floral aromatics; blue and red fruits are evident, with very attractive violet and apricot kernel characters; medium-bodied with fine tannins, plenty of flavour and a long, savoury, mineral finish. Screwcap. 14% alc. **Rating** 94 **To** 2015 $20.50

ȲȲȲȲȲ Black Label Frankland River Riesling 2008 Fine and focused lime fruit, with a gentle mineral undertone; persistent carry of fruit from start to finish, showing delicacy and understated power. Screwcap. 12% alc. **Rating** 93 **To** 2016 $20.50
Wandoo Frankland River Semillon 2005 Pale straw-green; a complex wine, yet still in the first phase of its development; faint touches of cashew and contrasting mineral notes, honey still to come. Screwcap. 12% alc. **Rating** 93 **To** 2020 $34.80
White Label Frankland River Semillon Sauvignon Blanc 2008 Semillon drives the grassy, lemony bouquet and palate, which has considerable generosity and length. Screwcap. 12.5% alc. **Rating** 92 **To** 2012 $15.89
White Label Shiraz 2007 Strong, clear colour; refreshing cool-grown, fruit-driven medium-bodied shiraz with blackberry and spice flavours, fine tannins and minimal oak. Well-priced. Screwcap. 13.5% alc. **Rating** 90 **To** 2015 $15.89

ΨΨΨΨ **White Label Unwooded Chardonnay 2008** Fresh but fairly neutral fruit flavours; light stone fruit and citrus, and a clean finish. Screwcap. 13.5% alc. **Rating** 88 **To** 2012 $15.89

Jarrah Frankland River Shiraz 2005 Spicy peppery cool-climate shiraz which, however, lacks the density of colour and flavour expected from Alkoomi; partially redeemed by its length. Cork. 13.5% alc. **Rating** 88 **To** 2014 $44.70

Black Label Frankland River Cabernet Sauvignon 2006 Fresh and light, some minty/leafy nuances to the red and black fruits of both bouquet and palate; doesn't have enough structure. Screwcap. 13.5% alc. **Rating** 88 **To** 2011 $22.34

Frankland River Cabernet Merlot 2007 A strongly savoury second label wine, which nonetheless has a sufficient core of blackcurrant fruit and supporting tannins. Screwcap. 14.5% alc. **Rating** 87 **To** 2013 $15.90

All Saints Estate

All Saints Road, Wahgunyah, Vic 3687 **Region** Rutherglen
T (02) 6035 2222 **F** (02) 6035 2200 **www**.allsaintswine.com.au **Open** Mon–Sat 9–5.30, Sun 10–5.30
Winemaker Dan Crane **Est.** 1864 **Cases** 40 000 **Vyds** 39.77 ha
The winery rating reflects the fortified wines, but the table wines are more than adequate. The Terrace restaurant makes this a most enjoyable stop for any visitor to the northeast. The faux castle, modelled on a Scottish castle beloved of the founder, is classified by the Historic Buildings Council. All Saints and St Leonards are owned and managed by fourth-generation Brown family members, Eliza, Angela and Nicholas. Eliza is an energetic and highly intelligent leader, wise beyond her years, and highly regarded by the wine industry. Exports to the US.

ΨΨΨΨΨ **Rare Rutherglen Tokay NV** Dark olive mahogany; a sumptuous palate based on 50-year-old solera; another level of complexity altogether, again with a rich tapestry of rancio followed by a drying finish. Vino-Lok. 18% alc. **Rating** 97 **To** 2010 $110

Rare Rutherglen Muscat Museum Release NV Deep mahogany-brown, and the olive rim of extreme age; a highly fragrant bouquet with the immediate rapier of raisin fruit; the wine explodes in the mouth, with a Joseph's coat of vibrant flavours of Christmas pudding (and accompanying hard sauce), fleeting hints of fernet branca, then spiced cake, but throughout a vivid, lively vibrancy and freshness. From a solera established in 1920; All Saints say it is beyond Rare. Sold in the ultimate luxury pack. **Rating** 97 **To** 2010 $1000

Grand Rutherglen Tokay NV The next step in a clear flavour progression, much darker and headed towards olive-brown; great concentration, tea leaf, some burnt toffee and cake; material up to 25 years old. Vino-Lok. 18% alc. **Rating** 95 **To** 2010 $65

Grand Rutherglen Muscat NV Brown hues now dominant; extremely rich, luscious and viscous burnt toffee and spice; mouthfilling; long finish. Vino-Lok. 18% alc. **Rating** 94 **To** 2010 $65

ΨΨΨΨΨ **Classic Rutherglen Tokay NV** Bright golden brown; is indeed classic tokay, with tea leaf, Christmas cake and toffee flavours, then a long, dry finish. Vino-Lok. 18% alc. **Rating** 93 **To** 2010 $31

Classic Rutherglen Muscat NV Pale reddish-brown; clear-cut raisined muscat with notes of glace fruit and treacle; very good balance and length. Vino-Lok. 18% alc. **Rating** 93 **To** 2010 $31

ΨΨΨΨ **Riesling 2008** Lean, crisp and dry, with a vibrant core of apple and lime; shows restraint and good texture, with a fine line right through to the finish. Screwcap. 12.5% alc. **Rating** 89 **To** 2014 $20

Family Cellar Rutherglen Chardonnay 2007 Quite smoky and toasty, with plenty of oak framing the ripe peach fruit; the palate is very toasty and rich, with a strong nutty personality, and lots of toast on the finish. Screwcap. 13.5% alc. **Rating** 87 **To** 2012 $30

Allandale

132 Lovedale Road, Lovedale, NSW 2321 **Region** Lower Hunter Valley
T (02) 4990 4526 **www**.allandalewinery.com.au **Open** Mon–Sat 9–5, Sun 10–5
Winemaker Bill Sneddon **Est.** 1978 **Cases** 20 000 **Vyds** 6.47 ha
Owners Wally and Judith Atallah have overseen the growth of Allandale from a small cellar
door operation to a sound business. Allandale has developed a reputation for its chardonnay,
but offers a broad range of wines of consistently good quality, including red wines variously
sourced from the Hilltops, Orange and Mudgee. Exports to the UK, the US and other major
markets.

Matthew Hunter Valley Shiraz 2007 Bright, clear crimson-purple; a high-
flavoured and lively wine, with intense blackberry and plum fruit offset by
very well integrated American oak and balanced acidity; excellent development
potential. Value+. Screwcap. 14% alc. **Rating** 94 **To** 2022 $26

Allies Wines ★★★★★

15 Hume Road, Somers, Vic 3927 (postal) **Region** Mornington Peninsula
T 0439 370 530 **F** (03) 5983 1523 **www**.allies.com.au **Open** Not
Winemaker Barney Flanders, David Chapman **Est.** 2003 **Cases** 1200
Barney Flanders and David Chapman call Allies a collaboration; both come from a restaurant
background dating back many years, Barney on the floor and David in the kitchen. In 1997
they turned their sights to wine; Barney graduated from CSU with a wine science degree in
'99, and has since worked in the Mornington Peninsula, Yarra Valley, Trentino, Sonoma and
Côte Rôtie. David left the restaurant scene in 2004 and is studying wine science at CSU. They
own no vineyards and have made wine from various vineyard sources in various regions, but
in '06 took on the management of the 20-ha Merricks Grove Vineyard in Merricks North,
which will supply the core of the material for their Pinot Noir and Chardonnay. At the top
end of those releases come the limited-production Garagiste-branded wines.

Garagiste Heathcote Syrah 2007 Purple-crimson, clear; vibrant plum aroma
and flavour, exceptional thrust on the palate aided by fine-grained tannins and
perfectly judged oak. Screwcap. 13.6% alc. **Rating** 96 **To** 2020 $44
Stone Axe Vineyard Heathcote Shiraz 2007 Brightly coloured; a highly
fragrant bouquet of spice and plum, then an intense and complex palate showing
the unusual (but rewarding) decision to include 50% whole bunches; the finish is
exceptionally long. Screwcap. 13.4% alc. **Rating** 96 **To** 2020 $25
Garagiste Mornington Peninsula Chardonnay 2007 A very elegant wine,
the fruit flavours intense yet fine, offering nectarine, white peach and grapefruit,
barrel ferment–oak inputs sotto voce. Screwcap. 13% alc. **Rating** 95 **To** 2014 $44
Saone Mornington Peninsula Viognier 2007 Bright straw-green; emphatic
varietal aromas of apricot and spice are achieved without any phenolic thickness
on the vibrant palate; orange and apricot flavours are backed by very good acidity
and length. Screwcap. 13.5% alc. **Rating** 95 **To** 2012 $27
Mornington Peninsula Pinot Noir 2007 Fragrant and strikingly pure plum
and rose petal aromas are followed by a similarly pure and delicious palate, the long
finish supported by superfine tannins. Screwcap. 13.2% alc. **Rating** 95 **To** 2015 $28

Alta Wines

PO Box 395, Stirling, SA 5152 **Region** Adelaide Hills
T (08) 8124 9041 **F** (08) 8370 8840 **www**.altavineyards.com.au **Open** Not
Winemaker Sarah Fletcher **Est.** NA **Cases** 16 000 **Vyds** 23 ha
Sarah Fletcher came to Alta with an impressive winemaking background: a degree from
Roseworthy, and thereafter seven years working for Orlando Wyndham. She came face to
face with grapes from all over Australia, and developed a particular regard for those coming
from the Adelaide Hills. The range has been extended with varieties suited to the cool climate
of the Adelaide Hills. Exports to the UK, Canada and Hong Kong.

ΨΨΨΨ♀ **Adelaide Hills Sauvignon Blanc 2008** Both the spotlessly clean bouquet and palate are driven by fresh cut grass, herb and mineral notes, opening into a hint of the tropics on the finish. Screwcap. 13% alc. **Rating** 90 **To** 2010 $22

ΨΨΨΨ **Adelaide Hills Pinot Grigio 2008** A fragrant bouquet of pear and blossom is followed by a brisk, minerally palate. Screwcap. 13% alc. **Rating** 89 **To** 2010 $23
Adelaide Hills Pinot Noir 2007 A fragrant, spicy, savoury style, with good length and balance; the flavours are just a little austere, perhaps. Screwcap. 13.5% alc. **Rating** 89 **To** 2012 $28

Amadio Wines   ★★★★☆

461 Payneham Road, Felixstow, SA 5070 **Region** Adelaide Hills
T (08) 8337 5144 **F** (08) 8336 2462 **www**.amadiowines.com.au **Open** Not
Winemaker Danniel Amadio **Est.** 2004 **Cases** 75 000 **Vyds** 200 ha
Danniel Amadio says he has followed in the footsteps of his Italian grandfather, selling wine from his cellar (cantina) direct to the consumer, cutting out wholesale and distribution. He also draws upon the business of his parents, built not in Italy, but in Australia. Amadio Wines has substantial vineyards, primarily in the Adelaide Hills, and also small parcels of contract-grown grapes from Clare Valley, McLaren Vale and Langhorne Creek, covering just about every variety imaginable, and – naturally – with a very strong representation of Italian varieties. Exports to the US, Canada, Singapore, Hong Kong and China.

ΨΨΨΨ♀ **Block 2a Reserve Adelaide Hills Shiraz 2005** A harmonious array of black and red fruits plus a spicy veneer and undercoat of dark chocolate; good oak and tannin management. Cork. 14.5% alc. **Rating** 93 **To** 2017 $35
Sebastien's Adelaide Hills Cabernet Sauvignon 2005 Very good colour; the fruit flavours are still in a primary stage, with a mix of sweet blackcurrant, licorice and mocha, the ripe tannins in balance. Cork. 14% alc. **Rating** 93 **To** 2020 $35
Adelaide Hills Shiraz 2007 Strong crimson; powerful black fruits, spice and a touch of vanilla oak permeate the bouquet and the very long and forceful palate. Needs, and will repay, cellaring. Screwcap. 14% alc. **Rating** 91 **To** 2020 $20
McLaren Vale Cabernet Sauvignon 2006 An attractively savoury wine, without any overripe fruit or overt chocolate, the black fruits neatly trimmed by spicy tannins. Screwcap. 14.5% alc. **Rating** 90 **To** 2015 $20

ΨΨΨΨ **Misura Barossa Valley Shiraz Cabernet 2003** A tidemark of wine travel at the end of the cork; does have plenty going on, with mocha, vanilla and black fruits, but not clear why an '03 vintage wine should have been selected for late release. Cork. 14.5% alc. **Rating** 89 **To** 2013 $95
Adelaide Hills Sauvignon Blanc 2008 Light straw-green; cut grass and snow pea aromas are leavened by nuances of passionfruit/tropical flavours; however, needs more intensity. Screwcap. 13% alc. **Rating** 88 **To** 2010 $20
Adelaide Hills Pinot Grigio 2008 Plenty of character with pear and a little savoury, sulphide complexity; the palate has good weight, with a little savoury bitterness on the finish. Screwcap. 13% alc. **Rating** 88 **To** 2012 $21.99
Dog Leg Semillon Sauvignon Blanc 2008 Has as much varietal expression as one might hope for at this price point; driven by the grassy semillon, lifted by a touch of tropical fruit on the finish. Screwcap. 12.5% alc. **Rating** 87 **To** 2010 $12.99

Amarok Estate   ★★★☆

Lot 547 Caves Road, Wilyabrup, WA 6284 (postal) **Region** Margaret River
T (08) 9756 6888 **F** (08) 9756 6555 **www**.amarok.com.au **Open** Not
Winemaker David Crawford **Est.** 1999 **Cases** 2500 **Vyds** 21.3 ha
John and Libby Staley, with daughter, Megan, her husband, Shane, and youngest grandson, Lewis, have all had hands-on involvement in the establishment of vineyards – clearing bushland, rock picking, stick picking and planting, etc. The soils are gravelly loam over a clay granite base; the vineyard has a western aspect and is 5 km from the Indian Ocean. Plantings

include shiraz, cabernet sauvignon, merlot, semillon and sauvignon blanc. Exports to Hong Kong, Japan and Singapore.

ΨΨΨΨΨ **Platinum Release Margaret River Sauvignon Blanc 2007** Appealing wine, with gooseberry, passionfruit and citrus on both bouquet and palate; has balance and length, and a clean aftertaste. Screwcap. 13% alc. **Rating** 91 **To** 2012 $17.50

Amberley Estate   ★★★★☆

Thornton Road, Yallingup, WA 6282 **Region** Margaret River
T (08) 9750 1113 **F** (08) 9750 1155 **www.**amberleyestate.com.au **Open** 7 days 10–4.30
Winemaker Dan Stocker **Est.** 1986 **Cases** NFP **Vyds** 31 ha
Initial growth was based on its ultra-commercial, fairly sweet Chenin Blanc, which continues to provide the volume for the brand. However, the quality of all the other wines has risen markedly over recent years as the 31 ha of estate plantings have become fully mature. Now part of CWA following Constellation Wines' acquisition of Canadian winemaker Vincor, which had in turn acquired Amberley Estate in early 2004. Exports to the UK and the US.

ΨΨΨΨΨ **Margaret River Shiraz Viognier 2007** The usual good colour; an interesting wine, with particularly good texture from fine tannins running through the length of the palate, and adding to the bright red and black fruit flavours; great aftertaste. Screwcap. 13.5% alc. **Rating** 94 **To** 2017 $22.50

ΨΨΨΨΨ **Margaret River Semillon Sauvignon Blanc 2008** A green nettle and tropical fruit bouquet, with good definition; quite fleshy on the palate, taut acidity providing focus on the finish. Screwcap. 11.7% alc. **Rating** 92 **To** 2012 $22.50
First Selection Semillon 2004 Has complex structure and powerful flavours deriving from the barrel ferment and extended lees contact; does shorten somewhat on the finish. Screwcap. 13.5% alc. **Rating** 91 **To** 2014 $38
Margaret River Cabernet Merlot 2007 Slightly dull red-purple; cassis, bramble and blackcurrant aromas and flavours; well-balanced medium-bodied palate, with good structure and length. Screwcap. 13.5% alc. **Rating** 91 **To** 2016 $22.50

Amherst Winery   ★★★★☆

Talbot–Avoca Road, Amherst, Vic 3371 **Region** Pyrenees
T (03) 5463 2105 **www.**amherstwinery.com **Open** W'ends & public hols 10–5
Winemaker Paul Lesock, Adam Kerner **Est.** 1989 **Cases** 2500 **Vyds** 4.5 ha
Norman and Elizabeth Jones have planted vines on a property with an extraordinarily rich history, which is commemorated in the name Dunn's Paddock Shiraz. Samuel Knowles was a convict who arrived in Van Diemen's Land in 1838. He endured continuous punishment before fleeing to SA in 1846 and changing his name to Dunn. When, at the end of 1851, he married 18-year-old Mary Therese Taaffe in Adelaide, they walked from Adelaide to Amherst pushing a wheelbarrow carrying their belongings, arriving just before gold was discovered. The lease title of the property shows that Amherst Winery is sited on land once owned by Samuel Dunn. Exports to China.

ΨΨΨΨΨ **Pyrenees Shiraz 2007** Great colour; a dark and savoury bouquet with blackberry, roast meat and a little tar thrown into the mix; plenty of weight on the palate, and very attractive spice and acidity, then a quite silky finish. Screwcap. 13.5% alc. **Rating** 94 **To** 2016 $25

ΨΨΨΨΨ **Chinese Gardens Pyrenees Cabernet Sauvignon 2006** Good colour; a mix of ripe, almost fleshy, blackcurrant fruit, with cedar/vanilla oak and gently savoury tannins. Screwcap. 13.9% alc. **Rating** 91 **To** 2014 $28

ΨΨΨΨ **Daisy Creek Pyrenees Shiraz Cabernet 2007** Deeply coloured, with plenty of red berry fruits and a hint of florals; very toasty on the finish, but the quality of the fruit holds its own. Screwcap. 13.7% alc. **Rating** 88 **To** 2014 $16

Amicus ★★★★

Rifle Range Road, McLaren Vale, SA 5171 **Region** McLaren Vale
T 0411 411 511 **F** (08) 8299 9500 **www**.amicuswines.com.au **Open** Not
Winemaker Walter Clappis, Kimberly Clappis **Est.** 2002 **Cases** 1500
Amicus is a venture bred in the purple. Its owners are 30-year industry veteran (and former Ingoldby owner) Walter William Wilfred Clappis (he has always provided his name in full), wife Kerry, plus Amanda and Tony Vanstone and Robert and Diana Hill, known in an altogether different environment. The grapes come in part from the Clappis' McLaren Vale vineyard (run on biodynamic principles) and from grapes purchased from growers in Langhorne Creek.

♀♀♀♀♀ **Shiraz Cabernet Malbec 2005** Good colour; both the bouquet and palate are generously endowed with ripe black fruits, plum and chocolate; the tannins fine and soft, the positive oak contribution perfectly poised. Screwcap. 14% alc. **Rating** 93 **To** 2018 $28
Reserve Shiraz 2005 Hazy colour; a complex wine from start to finish, with fruit, dark chocolate, oak and tannins interwoven in a pattern formation, rather than seamless fusion. Difficult to rate. Cork. 14.5% alc. **Rating** 90 **To** 2015 $45

Amietta Vineyard ★★★★☆

30 Steddy Road, Lethbridge, Vic 3332 **Region** Geelong
T (03) 5281 7407 **F** (03) 5281 7427 **www**.amietta.com.au **Open** By appt
Winemaker Nicholas Clark, Janet Cockbill **Est.** 1995 **Cases** 450
Janet Cockbill and Nicholas Clark are multi-talented. Both are archaeologists, but Janet manages to combine part-time archaeology, part-time radiography at Geelong Hospital and part-time organic viticulture. Nicholas studied viticulture at CSU, and both he and Janet worked vintage at Michel Chapoutier's biodynamic Domaine des Béates in Provence in 2001. Plantings include lagrein and carmenere. Amietta is producing cameo wines of some beauty.

♀♀♀♀♀ **Geelong Riesling 2008** Very well made; vibrant lime, lemon, and green apple flavours; exceptionally good balance between fruit sweetness and acidity; even better length. Screwcap. 11.6% alc. **Rating** 95 **To** 2018 $27

♀♀♀♀♀ **Angel's Share Geelong Cabernet Carmenere 2006** Bright, light crimson hue; deliciously fresh cassis fruit is set among superfine tannins and subtle French oak. Little or no need for patience – what it has now may well be better than anything to follow in the future. Screwcap. 13.5% alc. **Rating** 91 **To** 2013 $35
Geelong Shiraz Lagrein 2006 Light red; a light-bodied, but aromatic and well-balanced wine, with floral characters throughout, finishing with a burst of spice. Screwcap. 13.8% alc. **Rating** 90 **To** 2015 $35

♀♀♀♀ **Geelong Shiraz 2006** A cool-grown, light-bodied shiraz with strong spicy/ peppery overtones to its red fruits; slightly reductive. Screwcap. 13.8% alc. **Rating** 88 **To** 2014 $35

Ammitzboll Wines ★★☆

PO Box 670, Bairnsdale, Vic 3875 **Region** Gippsland
T (03) 5156 4664 **F** (03) 5156 4164 **Open** Not
Winemaker Wendy Ammitzboll **Est.** 1995 **Cases** 400 **Vyds** 2 ha
Peter and Wendy Ammitzboll began planting their vineyard in 1995, completing it in 2004. Although the plantings were modest (1.2 ha of chardonnay, 0.6 ha of pinot noir and 0.2 ha of shiraz), their sole intention was to sell the grapes to one of the well-established wineries in the district. Realising there was a wine glut looming, they undertook several years of extension study at CSU, and embarked on winemaking of limited quantities. The Unwooded Chardonnay and Pinot Noir will be supplemented by a sparkling Pinot Chardonnay, Sparkling Rosé and Sparkling Shiraz.

Amulet Vineyard

Wangaratta Road, Beechworth, Vic 3747 **Region** Beechworth
T (03) 5727 0420 **www**.amuletwines.com.au **Open** Fri–Mon 10–5 or by appt
Winemaker Ben Clifton, Sue Thornton **Est.** 1997 **Cases** 1000 **Vyds** 6 ha
Sue and Eric Thornton have planted a patchwork quilt vineyard: sangiovese and pinot gris
1 ha each; the other varieties 0.5 ha or less, and in descending order of magnitude, are
barbera, shiraz, cabernet sauvignon, merlot, nebbiolo, orange muscat and pinot blanc. Amulet
is 11 km west of Beechworth, the vines are planted on gentle slopes at an elevation of 350 m.
Co-winemaker and son Ben Clifton is studying wine science at CSU. The cellar door enjoys
panoramic views, and wine sales are both by the glass and by the bottle.

ŸŸŸŸŸ **Le Braconnier 2004** A complex web of spice, black fruits, touches of cedar
and ripe tannins running the length of the palate; good oak adds another layer;
very well made. Shiraz/Merlot/Cabernet Sauvignon. Cork. 13% alc. **Rating** 94
To 2015 $48

ŸŸŸŸŸ **Beechworth Pinot Grigio 2006** Has more personality, presence and flavour
than most, partly due to positive bottle development; moves to dried pear flavours
in a savoury, minerally context. Screwcap. 14.5% alc. **Rating** 90 **To** 2010 $19
Beechworth Sangiovese Scelto 2004 Remarkably fresh colour; complex
aromas and flavours, with some spicy/minty/leafy notes before red cherry fruit
comes through to take command of a well-balanced palate, the tannins neatly
contained. Cork. 14.5% alc. **Rating** 90 **To** 2014 $30

Anderson

Lot 13 Chiltern Road, Rutherglen, Vic 3685 **Region** Rutherglen
T (02) 6032 8111 **F** (02) 6032 7151 **www**.andersonwinery.com.au **Open** 7 days 10–5
Winemaker Howard Anderson, Christobelle Anderson **Est.** 1992 **Cases** 2000 **Vyds** 8.8 ha
Having notched up a winemaking career spanning over 30 years, including a stint at Seppelt
(Great Western), Howard Anderson and family started their own winery, initially with a
particular focus on sparkling wine but now extending across all table wine styles. The original
estate plantings of shiraz, durif and petit verdot (6 ha) were expanded in 2007-08 with
tempranillo, saperavi, brown muscat, chenin blanc and viognier.

ŸŸŸŸŸ **Cellar Block Methode Champenoise Sparkling Shiraz 2002** A complex
and savoury wine, with fruit depth, richness of palate and fine palate structure;
well-handled level of sweetness. Cork. 14.5% alc. **Rating** 91 **To** 2012 $45

ŸŸŸŸ **Reserve Durif Shiraz 2006** Bright colour, and loaded with mulberry and
blackberry fruit; lots of flavour and good definition, if just a little simple. Screwcap.
14.5% alc. **Rating** 87 **To** 2014 $26
Reserve Petit Verdot 2005 Great colour; the wine has lots of fruit and fairly
good acidity, but needs more complexity for higher points. Cork. 15.5% alc.
Rating 87 **To** 2015 $29

Andrew Peace Wines

Murray Valley Highway, Piangil, Vic 3597 **Region** Swan Hill
T (03) 5030 5291 **www**.apwines.com **Open** Mon–Fri 8–5, Sat 12–4, Sun by appt
Winemaker Andrew Peace, Nina Viergutz **Est.** 1995 **Cases** 460 000 **Vyds** 100 ha
The Peace family has been a major Swan Hill grapegrower since 1980, moving into
winemaking with the opening of a $3 million winery in '96. The modestly priced wines are
aimed at supermarket-type outlets in Australia and exported to all major markets.

ŸŸŸŸŸ **Kentish Lane Langhorne Creek Cabernet Sauvignon 2006** Good
colour, still bright and deep; very attractive blend of blackcurrant, plum, chocolate
and mocha supported by fine, savoury tannins. Screwcap. 14% alc. **Rating** 93
To 2018 $12

Winemakers Choice Langhorne Creek Shiraz 2006 Good colour; offers the black cherry and plum fruit the Estate and Kentish Lane lack; the medium-bodied palate has the hallmark velvety softness of Langhorne Creek, but also finishes with authority. Screwcap. 14% alc. **Rating** 90 **To** 2014 $17

♥♥♥♥ **Winemakers Choice Langhorne Creek Cabernet Sauvignon 2006** Very much more savoury, more oaky and more tannic than Kentish Lane; for me, the balance of Kentish Lane is far better. Screwcap. 14% alc. **Rating** 89 **To** 2018 $17
Blue Sand Sauvignon Blanc 2008 Gentle tropical fruit aromas, then a lively, tangy, citrussy palate; good acidity adds to its length. Terrific value. Screwcap. 11% alc. **Rating** 87 **To** 2010 $10
Eighth Horse Shiraz 2008 Bright and juicy spiced blackberry bouquet; fleshy and fine on the finish. Bargain. Screwcap. 13.5% alc. **Rating** 87 **To** 2011 $9
Masterpeace Shiraz 2007 Light- to medium-bodied, with some savoury spicy overtones adding to the length and interest of the wine; fine tannins. Screwcap. 14% alc. **Rating** 87 **To** 2013 $12
Kentish Lane Langhorne Creek Shiraz 2006 Has a little more bite and fruit than the lesser-priced Estate version, with tangy notes on the finish giving length. Screwcap. 14% alc. **Rating** 87 **To** 2012 $12
Peace by Peace 2007 Unambiguously light-bodied, but does have fragrance and some nice red fruits; akin to a rose on steroids; serve slightly chilled. Shiraz/Cabernet Sauvignon/Grenache. Screwcap. 14% alc. **Rating** 87 **To** 2010 $10
Chardonnay Pinot 2008 Fresh and crisp, but inevitably without any chance to gain complexity; does have balance, and is not sweet. Cork. 12.5% alc. **Rating** 87 **To** 2010 $15

Angas Plains Estate   ★★★★★

Lot 52 Angas Plains Road, Langhorne Creek, SA 5255 **Region** Langhorne Creek
T (08) 8537 3159 www.angasplainswines.com.au **Open** W'ends & public hols 11–5
Winemaker Peter Douglas (Contract) **Est.** 2000 **Cases** 3000 **Vyds** 27 ha
Angas Plains Estate is a 10-min drive south of the historic town of Strathalbyn, on the banks of the Angas River. Owners Phillip and Judy Cross employ organic measures to tend their vineyard (shiraz, cabernet sauvignon and chardonnay). Exports to China.

♥♥♥♥♥ **Emily Cross Langhorne Creek Shiraz 2007** Crimson-purple; has the typical generosity of flavour and velvety texture of Langhorne Creek at its best; plum and blackberry are supported by good oak handling. Top outcome for the vintage. Screwcap. 14% alc. **Rating** 94 **To** 2020 $60
Special Reserve Langhorne Creek Cabernet Sauvignon 2006 Lovely wine; fragrant cassis and blackcurrant aromas are replayed on the supple, medium-bodied palate, joined by integrated new French oak (26 months in barrel) and soft tannins. Diam. 14% alc. **Rating** 94 **To** 2021 $29.95

♥♥♥♥♀ **PJ's Langhorne Creek Shiraz 2007** Bright, deep colour; a lively medium-bodied wine with an attractive display of red and black fruits, fine-grained tannins and well-integrated oak. Screwcap. 14% alc. **Rating** 90 **To** 2015 $25

Angove Family Winemakers   ★★★★

Bookmark Avenue, Renmark, SA 5341 **Region** South Australia
T (08) 8580 3100 www.angove.com.au **Open** Mon–Fri 9–5, w'ends 10–4
Winemaker Tony Ingle, Paul Kernich, Ben Horley, Alex Russell **Est.** 1886
Cases 1.5 million **Vyds** 480 ha
Exemplifies the economies of scale achievable in the Riverland without compromising potential quality. Very good technology provides wines that are never poor and sometimes exceed their theoretical station in life. The vineyard is currently being redeveloped with changes in the varietal mix. Angove's expansion into Padthaway, the Clare Valley, McLaren Vale and Coonawarra (these latter three via contract-grown fruit) has resulted in premium wines to back up its Riverland wines. Exports to all major markets.

ⓎⓎⓎⓎⓎ **Vineyard Select Coonawarra Cabernet Sauvignon 2006** Very correct varietal expression due to blackcurrant, and touches of sweet earth; excellent texture and mouthfeel; great value. Cork. 14.5% alc. **Rating** 92 **To** 2016 $19

Vineyard Select McLaren Vale Shiraz 2006 Attractive, well-balanced medium-bodied wine, with a pleasing touch of regional dark chocolate to the black fruits of the palate. Cork. 14% alc. **Rating** 90 **To** 2015 $19

Nine Vines Shiraz Viognier 2007 Light, bright crimson-purple; vibrantly fresh and juicy, the viognier component working to perfection. Great drink-now style, slightly chilled. Screwcap. 14% alc. **Rating** 90 **To** 2011 $14

ⓎⓎⓎⓎ **Vineyard Select Clare Valley Riesling 2008** Bright straw-green; an aromatic lime-accented bouquet promises a little more than the palate delivers, which is full of flavour, but low in acidity. Screwcap. 13% alc. **Rating** 89 **To** 2012 $16.40

Vineyard Select Adelaide Hills Sauvignon Blanc 2008 Somewhat marred by a sweaty/reductive edge to the bouquet, but does have an abundance of tropical fruit flavours. Screwcap. 13% alc. **Rating** 89 **To** 2012 $16.40

Vineyard Select Limestone Coast Chardonnay 2008 Fresh and lively, with some of the grapefruit typical of Padthaway, along with nectarine; nice balance and mouthfeel. Screwcap. 13.5% alc. **Rating** 89 **To** 2012 $16.40

Nine Vines Grenache Shiraz Rose 2008 Bright, light fuschia-purple; fresh cherry pop soda aroma and flavour offset by acidity; sweetness from fruit, not residual sugar. Screwcap. 12.5% alc. **Rating** 89 **To** 2009 $14

Vineyard Select McLaren Vale Shiraz 2007 Very good colour; a powerful and dense wine with blackberry, black cherry, licorice, dark chocolate, oak and tannins all competing for attention, tannins winning the day. Patience needed. Screwcap. 13.5% alc. **Rating** 89 **To** 2022 $19.70

Long Row Riesling 2008 Admirable wine at the price, obviously picked before the heat; has citrus blossom, herb and apple notes and good length. Origin not stated. Screwcap. 12.5% alc. **Rating** 88 **To** 2012 $9.75

Red Belly Black Shiraz 2007 Crimson-red; generously built and fruited, with appropriate tannins and a lick of vanilla oak. Honest wine, honest price. Screwcap. 14% alc. **Rating** 88 **To** 2012 $14.99

Organic Shiraz Cabernet 2007 A fragrant, light-bodied wine with juicy red and black fruits, no oak and minimal tannins; works well. Screwcap. 14% alc. **Rating** 88 **To** 2012 $13.95

Nine Vines Tempranillo Shiraz 2007 Interesting wine; some multidimensional flavours from the tempranillo running from preserved citrus in chocolate through to cherry and cassis. Screwcap. 13.5% alc. **Rating** 88 **To** 2010 $14

Long Row Shiraz 2007 A big mouthful of wine for a small price; solid black fruits and tannins make this a prime knockabout red. Screwcap. 14% alc. **Rating** 87 **To** 2012 $9.75

Organic Chardonnay 2008 While the bouquet is subdued, the palate has unexpected texture and length, with gently savoury nuances. Screwcap. 13.5% alc. **Rating** 87 **To** 2010 $13.95

Long Row Verdelho 2008 Clean, vibrant and slightly green-fruited bouquet; a little tart on the finish, but clean and good value for the money. Screwcap. 13.5% alc. **Rating** 87 **To** 2010 $9.99

Brightlands Cabernet Merlot 2007 A clean varietal wine; cassis and a touch of plum; medium-bodied with fine tannin on the finish. Screwcap. 14% alc. **Rating** 87 **To** 2012 $14.99

Angullong Wines ★★★★

Victoria Street, Millthorpe, NSW 2798 **Region** Orange
T (02) 6366 4300 **www**.angullong.com.au **Open** W'ends & public hols 11–5
Winemaker Jon Reynolds, Simon Thrushwood, Barry Kooij **Est.** 1998 **Cases** 5000
Vyds 216.7 ha
The Crossing family (Bill and Hatty, and third generation James and Ben) have owned a 2000-ha sheep and cattle station for over half a century. Located 40 km south of Orange,

overlooking the Belubula Valley, over 200 ha of vines have been planted since 1998. In all, there are 15 varieties, with shiraz, cabernet sauvignon and merlot leading the way. Most of the production is sold to Hunter Valley wineries. Exports to the EU.

ŦŦŦŦŦ **Orange Sauvignon Blanc 2008** A delicate, but pure, sauvignon blanc, the aromas and flavours ranging through passionfruit, gooseberry and grass; has excellent length and balance; prestigious Bert Bear Trophy Sydney Wine Show '09. Screwcap. 12.5% alc. **Rating** 94 **To** 2010 $14.99

ŦŦŦŦ **Fossil Hill Orange Viognier 2007** Very attractive, fresh style, with orange blossom aromas moving to apricot and citrus on the palate; clean, zesty finish. Screwcap. 12.5% alc. **Rating** 89 **To** 2010 $19.95

Angus the Bull ★★★

PO Box 611, Manly, NSW 1655 **Region** Southeastern Australia
T (02) 8966 9020 **F** (03) 9820 4677 **www**.angusthebull.com **Open** Not
Winemaker Hamish MacGowan **Est.** 2002 **Cases** 20 000
Hamish MacGowan has taken the virtual winery idea to its ultimate conclusion, with a single wine (Cabernet Sauvignon) designed to be drunk with premium red meat, or, more particularly, a perfectly cooked steak. Parcels of grapes are selected from regions across Victoria and SA each year, the multi regional–blend approach designed to minimise vintage variation.

ŦŦŦŦ **Cabernet Sauvignon 2007** Plenty of flavour in a somewhat rustic mould, ideal for a char-grilled rump steak. Screwcap. 14.5% alc. **Rating** 87 **To** 2011 $19.95

Angus Wines ★★★★

PO Box 383, Goolwa, SA 5214 **Region** Southern Fleurieu
T (08) 8555 2320 **F** (08) 8555 2323 **www**.anguswines.com.au **Open** Not
Winemaker Justin Lane, Angas Buchanan **Est.** 1995 **Cases** 300 **Vyds** 1.25 ha
Susan and Alistair Angus were pioneer viticulturists on Hindmarsh Island, and established 3.75 ha of shiraz and 1.25 ha of semillon. The wines were of consistently very good quality, but the dramatic reduction in water availability has meant they have had to remove all except 1.25 ha of shiraz. Part is bottled under the Angus Wines label; some is sold in bulk to other wineries. Every aspect of packaging and marketing the wine has a sophisticated touch. Exports to the UK.

ŦŦŦŦŦ **A3 Shiraz 2007** Dark black fruit, tar and fruitcake spice on the bouquet; dark and chewy on the palate, the tannin dominating; time is necessary. Screwcap. 14.5% alc. **Rating** 90 **To** 2018 $40

ŦŦŦŦ **A3 Shiraz 2006** A little jammy, with the alcohol pushing forward; a fruitcake and blackberry confiture palate; quite generous sweet fruit, and chewy tannins on the finish. Screwcap. 16% alc. **Rating** 88 **To** 2013 $40

Annie's Lane ★★★★★

Quelltaler Road, Watervale, SA 5452 **Region** Clare Valley
T (08) 8843 0003 **www**.annieslane.com.au **Open** Mon–Fri 8.30–5, w'ends 11–4
Winemaker Alex MacKenzie **Est.** 1851 **Cases** 230 000
The Clare Valley portfolio of Foster's, the name coming from Annie Weyman, a turn-of-the-century local identity. The brand consistently offers wines that over-deliver against their price points, with both wine show success and critical acclaim. Copper Trail is the flagship release, and there are some very worthy cellar door and on-premise wines. Exports to the UK, the US and Europe.

ŦŦŦŦŦ **Copper Trail Clare Valley Riesling 2007** Light straw-green; an immensely powerful bouquet of ripe citrus fruit, the palate a mirror image of the bouquet; has enough length to warrant immediate drinking, although will stay the course for a decade. Screwcap. 12% alc. **Rating** 94 **To** 2015 $36.99

Copper Trail Clare Valley Shiraz 2006 Is full-bodied, but not heavy; there are spice, earth and licorice notes to the core of blackberry fruit; has good tannin and barrel ferment–oak inputs. Screwcap. **Rating** 94 **To** 2026 $53.99

ΨΨΨΨΨ **Clare Valley Shiraz 2007** Ripe blue and blackberry bouquet, with a touch of spicy oak; medium-bodied and fresh palate, with well-balanced fruit and oak; spotlessly clean. Screwcap. 14.5% alc. **Rating** 91 **To** 2016 $19.99
Limited Release Clare Valley Sparkling Shiraz NV Sept '08 release; barrel-fermented and barrel-aged base wines across vintages with an average age of five years; spicy black fruits, but not heavy or sweet, the oak evident but not oppressive. Crown Seal. 14% alc. **Rating** 91 **To** 2014 $25

ΨΨΨΨ **Clare Valley Rose 2008** Pale bright fuschia-pink; light but fresh red berry fruits; not sweet. Screwcap. 12% alc. **Rating** 89 **To** 2010 $19.99
Chardonnay 2008 Bright colour; a toasty bouquet with the oak framing ripe nectarine fruit; the palate is fine, with a persistent toasty note that dominates the finish. Clare Valley/Adelaide Hills. Screwcap. 13% alc. **Rating** 88 **To** 2011 $19.99

Anniebrook

247 Wildwood Road, Carbunup River, WA 6280 **Region** Margaret River
T (08) 9755 1155 **F** (08) 9755 1138 **Open** Sat–Thurs 9.30–4.30
Winemaker James Pennington (Contract) **Est.** 1986 **Cases** 3000 **Vyds** 6.84 ha
A long time ago Wally Lewis (no relation to the celebrated rugby league player) and wife Dawn were third-generation graziers and sheep farmers. In 1985 they decided they had to find a much larger property further inland for their sheep farming, or radically change their existing business. They opted for the latter, simultaneously planting vines and flowers; they have planted shiraz, semillon, cabernet franc, chardonnay and sauvignon blanc, and 2 ha of flowers. For almost 20 years they sold the grapes to a nearby winemaker, but in 2006 took the plunge and contracted James Pennington to make the wines for them. Ambience and the Anniebrook River, which flows through the centre of the property, are ready attractions for cellar door visitors.

ΨΨΨΨ **Margaret River Cabernet Shiraz 2007** Not a common blend in Margaret River; but the spicy components give it status; medium-bodied, with a mix of black fruits; slightly short, but well priced. Screwcap. 14% alc. **Rating** 88 **To** 2014 $14
Golden Teardrop Margaret River Chardonnay 2008 Light-bodied, but has good typicity in a fresh, crisp nectarine and citrus spectrum. Screwcap. 13.5% alc. **Rating** 87 **To** 2011 $14

Anvers

Cnr Chalk Hill Road/Foggo Road, McLaren Vale, SA 5171 **Region** Adelaide Hills
T (08) 8323 9603 **F** (08) 8323 9502 **www.**anvers.com.au **Open** Not
Winemaker Kym Milne MW **Est.** 1998 **Cases** 10 000 **Vyds** 24.5 ha
Myriam and Wayne Keoghan established Anvers Wines with the emphasis on quality rather than quantity. The principal vineyard is in the Adelaide Hills at Kangarilla (16 ha of cabernet sauvignon, shiraz, chardonnay, sauvignon blanc and viognier), the second vineyard at McLaren Vale (shiraz, cabernet sauvignon). Winemaker Kym Milne has experience gained across many of the wine-producing countries in both northern and southern hemispheres. Exports to the UK and other major markets.

ΨΨΨΨΨ **Langhorne Creek Cabernet Sauvignon 2006** A pure, intense and focused cabernet, with strong blackcurrant fruit and ample but not excessive tannins, cedary French oak in the background. Carries its alcohol well. Multiple gold medals. Cork. 15% alc. **Rating** 94 **To** 2016 $28

ΨΨΨΨΨ **Adelaide Hills Fortified Shiraz 2007** Pleasingly dry, spicy style; good grapes, good winemaking. Cork. 18.5% alc. **Rating** 90 **To** 2014 $25

ΨΨΨΨ **Adelaide Hills Rose 2008** Clean, fresh and vibrant; a little short and simple on the finish. Screwcap. 13.5% alc. **Rating** 87 **To** 2011 $15

Arakoon

★★★★☆

229 Main Road, McLaren Vale, SA 5171 **Region** McLaren Vale
T (08) 8323 7339 **F** (02) 6566 6288 **www.**arakoonwines.com.au **Open** By appt
Winemaker Raymond Jones **Est.** 1999 **Cases** 3000
Ray and Patrik Jones' first venture into wine came to nothing: a 1990 proposal for a film about
the Australian wine industry with myself as anchorman. Five years too early, say the Joneses. In
1999 they took the plunge into making their own wine, and exporting it along with the wines
of others. As the quality of the wines has increased, so has the originally zany labelling been
replaced with simple, but elegant, labels. Exports to Sweden, Denmark, Germany, Singapore
and Malaysia.

♥♥♥♥♥ **Doyen Willunga Shiraz 2007** Bright colour; a focused black fruit bouquet,
with some charry oak and a floral hint; the palate is full-bodied, with a savoury
mineral edge to the fruit; good acid drive provides lightness and length on the
finish. Screwcap. 14.5% alc. **Rating** 94 **To** 2018 $45

♥♥♥♥♀ **Clarendon Shiraz 2007** Deep colour; dark personality of tar, confit blackberry,
fruitcake and a little bitter chocolate; warm-fruited and Christmas cakey on
the palate; there is a little heat on the chewy, oak-prevalent finish. Screwcap.
14.5% alc. **Rating** 90 **To** 2016 $32
Sellicks Beach Shiraz 2007 Fresh and bright blueberry and blackberry
bouquet with some fruitcake spice; juicy and vibrant, there is a savoury edge
that follows through on the finish, thus providing structure. Screwcap. 14.5% alc.
Rating 90 **To** 2014 $20

♥♥♥♥ **The Lighthouse McLaren Vale Cabernet Sauvignon 2006** Very developed
colour, as is the wine; soft chocolatey, early-drinking style. Screwcap. 14.5% alc.
Rating 87 **To** 2011 $20

Aramis Vineyards

★★★★★

PO Box 208, Marleston, SA 5033 **Region** McLaren Vale
T (08) 8238 0000 **F** (08) 8234 0485 **www.**aramisvineyards.com **Open** Not
Winemaker Scott Rawlinson **Est.** 1998 **Cases** NFP **Vyds** 25.6 ha
The estate vineyards have been planted to just two varieties: shiraz and cabernet sauvignon.
Viticulturist David Mills is a third-generation McLaren Vale resident and has been involved
in the establishment of the vineyards from the beginning. Winemaker Scott Rawlinson was
with Mildara Blass for eight years before joining the Aramis team under the direction of
owner Lee Flourentzou. Exports to the UK, the US, Canada, Germany, Denmark, Singapore
and Hong Kong.

♥♥♥♥♥ **The Governor McLaren Vale Syrah 2004** Attractive wine, with excellent
mouthfeel to the medium-bodied palate, and an array of red and black fruits
tinged with spice and dark chocolate; oak is evident, but very well integrated.
Cork. 14.5% alc. **Rating** 95 **To** 2015 $55
The Governor McLaren Vale Syrah 2006 Deep crimson; a rich bouquet full
of black fruits and oak, the flavours of the palate following suit, the finish with a
twist of spicy/savoury tannins. Cork. 14.5% alc. **Rating** 94 **To** 2020 $55
The Governor McLaren Vale Syrah 2005 Slightly more developed colour;
does have more movement in the mouth than the varietal and correspondingly
more length, but in the final analysis the price gap is greater than the quality gap.
Cork. 15% alc. **Rating** 94 **To** 2016 $55

♥♥♥♥♀ **Black Label McLaren Vale Shiraz 2005** Saturated colour; a richly textured,
plush and supple palate, replete with blackberry and dark chocolate fruit. Cork.
14.5% alc. **Rating** 93 **To** 2015 $24
McLaren Vale Shiraz Cabernet 2007 Deep colour; attractive blackberry/
blackcurrant fruits on the bouquet flow through to the juicy palate, which, while
full-flavoured, has a bright and lively finish. Value. Screwcap. 14.5% alc. **Rating** 92
To 2015 $18

♟♟♟♟ **Black Label McLaren Vale Shiraz 2006** Good colour; a fragrant black and red fruit bouquet, with similar flavours on the medium-bodied palate; good structure. Cork. 14.5% alc. **Rating** 89 **To** 2014 $24

Black Label McLaren Vale Cabernet Sauvignon 2006 A generously flavoured wine, with ripe blackcurrant fruit, positive oak and good tannin structure. Good outcome for the vintage. Cork. 14% alc. **Rating** 89 **To** 2016 $24

Black Label McLaren Vale Cabernet Sauvignon 2005 Firm blackcurrant fruit, with some briary/earthy overtones and a fractionally herbal finish. Cork. 14.5% alc. **Rating** 87 **To** 2014 $24

Arete Wines ★★★★

1 Banyan Court, Greenwith, SA 5125 (postal) **Region** Barossa Valley
T 0418 296 969 **F** (08) 8289 8470 **www**.aretewines.com.au **Open** Not
Winemaker Richard Bate **Est.** 2008 **Cases** 500

The name chosen by owner Richard Bate comes from Greek mythology, describing the aggregate of all the qualities of valour, virtue and excellence that make up good character. Having graduated with a bachelor of science (wine science major) degree from CSU, Richard worked at Barossa Valley Estate, then Saltram, Wolf Blass and Penfolds. His next move was to work for the Burgundian cooper François Frères distributing barrels within Australia, before venturing into the challenging world of the small winemaker. His intention is to make single vineyard wines wherever possible, with small quantities of each wine part of the strategy. Open fermentation of whole berries, basket-pressing and deliberately oxidative handling are all techniques he would have encountered at Penfolds. It is no surprise that the wines have incredible richness and depth.

♟♟♟♟♟ **Barossa Valley Shiraz 2008** Extraordinarily impenetrable purple-black colour; intense plum, prune and blackberry aromas and flavours, but no alcohol kick whatsoever; the tannins are soft, the oak merely a vehicle; 200 cases made. Screwcap. 14.5% alc. **Rating** 93 **To** 2013 $20

Arimia Margaret River ★★★★

Quininup Road, Wilyabrup, WA 6280 (postal) **Region** Margaret River
T (08) 9287 2411 **F** (08) 9287 2422 **www**.arimia.com.au **Open** By appt
Winemaker Mark Warren **Est.** 1998 **Cases** 6000

In 1997 Anne Spencer and Malcolm Washbourne purchased their 55-ha property overlooking the Indian Ocean, and its northern boundaries marked by the Cape Naturaliste National Park. Quininup Creek meanders through the property, providing the water source for its blue-green dam. The name is a combination of daughters Ariann and Mia. They have planted a 6-ha Joseph's coat array of varieties, the Short Story wines come from the traditional range of white varietals (semillon, sauvignon blanc, verdelho, chardonnay), the Full Story wines feature cabernet sauvignon, merlot, petit verdot, shiraz, grenache, mourvedre and zinfandel.

Arlewood Estate ★★★★

Cnr Bussell Highway/Calgardup Road, Forest Grove, WA 6286 **Region** Margaret River
T (08) 9755 6267 **F** (08) 9755 6267 **www**.arlewood.com.au **Open** By appt
Winemaker Bill Crappsley **Est.** 1988 **Cases** 6000 **Vyds** 9.7 ha

A series of events in 2007 have led to major changes in the Arlewood Estate structure. The Gosatti family sold the Harmans Road vineyard to Vasse Felix, but retained ownership of the brand and all stock. It will continue to have access to the cabernet sauvignon and merlot up to and including the 2009 vintage. In mid '08 Arlewood acquired the former Hesperos Estate vineyard, 10 km south of Margaret River, and Bill Crappsley, already a partner with the Gosattis in Plan B, became full-time winemaker for Arlewood and Plan B (see separate entry). Exports to the UK, the US, Switzerland, Singapore, Malaysia and Hong Kong.

♟♟♟♟ **Margaret River Cabernet Sauvignon 2007** Great colour; quite oaky, with essency cassis and black olive; oak dominates the palate, but there is a very concentrated and pure core of fruit that will find its way to the top in the future; needs time. Screwcap. 14.5% alc. **Rating** 90 **To** 2016 $40

ΨΨΨΨ   **Margaret River Shiraz 2006** Slightly green peppercorn bouquet with cranberry fruit and a touch of oak; cool, spicy and quite savoury. Screwcap. 14% alc. **Rating** 88 **To** 2012 $20
Single Vineyard Margaret River Cabernet Merlot 2006 Bright colour; a touch herbal, with cassis in the background; a little lean on the palate, but clean and fresh with good flavour. Screwcap. 13.5% alc. **Rating** 87 **To** 2014 $20

Arranmore Vineyard   ★★★☆

Rangeview Road, Carey Gully, SA 5144 **Region** Adelaide Hills
T (08) 8390 3034 www.arranmore.com.au **Open** W'ends & public hols 11–5
Winemaker John Venus **Est.** 1998 **Cases** 1000 **Vyds** 2 ha
One of the tiny operations that dot the landscape of the beautiful Adelaide Hills. At an altitude of around 550 m, the vineyard is planted to clonally selected pinot noir, chardonnay and sauvignon blanc.

ΨΨΨΨΨ   **PS Adelaide Hills Sparkling Red 2006** Although youthful and can never gain the lees complexity of the best examples, it does have good balance with fruit and dosage to give a long, clean finish. Cork. 13.5% alc. **Rating** 90 **To** 2014 $25

ΨΨΨΨ   **Special Reserve Black Pinot 2004** Diminished red hues; very earthy/foresty/savoury with a contrasting mint note; fair length and balance; 100 cases made. Screwcap. 13.2% alc. **Rating** 87 **To** 2011 $40

Arrowfield Estate

Golden Highway, Jerrys Plains, NSW 2330 **Region** Upper Hunter Valley
T (02) 6576 4041 **F** (02) 6576 4144 www.arrowfieldestate.com.au **Open** 7 days 10–5
Winemaker Barry Kooij, Adrianna Mansueto **Est.** 1968 **Cases** 80 000
Arrowfield continues in the ownership of the Inagaki family, which has been involved in the Japanese liquor industry for over a century. It has 47 ha of low-yielding, old vines in the Upper Hunter Valley, and also buys grapes from other parts of Australia, making varietal wines appropriate to those regions. In 2007 it merged with Mornington Peninsula winery Red Hill Estate, the merged group trading as InWine Group Australia, with Brenton Martin installed as CEO. Exports to all major markets.

ΨΨΨΨΨ   **Show Reserve Hunter Valley Semillon 2006** Still fresh and vibrant, with a faint touch of spritz lifting the palate; has extreme length, intense lemon and a touch of honey; delicious now, but with a long future. Screwcap. 10% alc. **Rating** 94 **To** 2020 $25

ΨΨΨΨΨ   **Cellar Door Release Riesling 2007** An aromatic bouquet with sweet citrus notes; the palate is firm and long, initially minerally but with fruit swelling on the finish. Orange. Screwcap. 12.5% alc. **Rating** 91 **To** 2017 $20
Cabernet Merlot 2006 Lively, tangy, spicy cool-grown style, although has no herbal or green characters; has considerable length, and good balance throughout. Orange. Screwcap. 14.5% alc. **Rating** 90 **To** 2015 $20

ΨΨΨΨ   **Semillon Sauvignon Blanc 2008** Well made, with plenty of presence and length; the tangy lemony finish, underwritten by good acidity, is the feature of the wine. Screwcap. 12% alc. **Rating** 89 **To** 2012 $20
Show Reserve Hunter Valley Chardonnay 2007 Nicely weighted fruit and oak on a medium-bodied palate with melon and peach fruit to the fore; ready now. Screwcap. 13.5% alc. **Rating** 89 **To** 2012 $25
Bowman's Crossing Semillon Sauvignon Blanc 2008 There can be no complaint at this price to a wine of unspecified origins that has lots of zesty lemon and passionfruit aromas and flavours, and a clean finish. Tip-top value. Screwcap. 11% alc. **Rating** 88 **To** 2010 $9
Unwooded Chardonnay 2007 A blend of Upper Hunter 'old vine' and Orange chardonnay that works well, the rich stone fruit mid-palate tightening up nicely on the finish. Screwcap. 13% alc. **Rating** 88 **To** 2012 $20

Sparkling Shiraz NV Base wines from Orange/Hunter Valley; of unstated age; somewhat simple, but well-balanced and has a clean, dry finish. Better than many. Crown Seal. 13.5% alc. **Rating** 88 **To** 2014 $35

Arundel   ★★★★☆

Arundel Farm Estate, PO Box 136, Keilor, Vic 3036 **Region** Sunbury
T (03) 9335 3422 **F** (03) 9335 4912 **www**.arundel.com.au **Open** Not
Winemaker Bianca Hayes, Mark Hayes **Est.** 1995 **Cases** 1000
Arundel was built around an acre of cabernet and shiraz planted in the 1970s but abandoned. When the Conwell family purchased the property in the early 1990s, the vineyard was resurrected and the first vintage was made by Rick Kinzbrunner in '95. Thereafter the cabernet was grafted over to shiraz, the block slowly increased to 1.6 ha, and an additional 4 ha of shiraz and 1.6 ha of viognier and marsanne planted.

♟♟♟♟ Shiraz 2007 Dense purple; black pepper and spice notes stand alongside the rich blackberry and licorice fruit on both bouquet and palate; medium- to full-bodied, with plenty of ripe tannins and good oak. Long life ahead. Cork. Rating 94 To 2020

♟♟♟♟♀ Shiraz 2006 Strong purple-crimson; spicy licorice, blackberry and a touch of pepper; still coming together, needs more time, but has all the makings. Cork. Rating 90 To 2016 $28

♟♟♟♟ Viognier 2007 Some colour development; has considerable texture and clear apricot/peach varietal fruit; catches slightly on the finish. Cork. Rating 89 To 2011 $28

Ashbrook Estate

379 Harmans Road, Wilyabrup via Cowaramup, WA 6284 **Region** Margaret River
T (08) 9755 6262 **F** (08) 9755 6290 **Open** 7 days 10–5
Winemaker Tony Devitt, Brian Devitt **Est.** 1975 **Cases** 13 000 **Vyds** 17.4 ha
A fastidious producer of consistently excellent estate-grown table wines that shuns publicity and the wine show system alike and is less well known than is deserved, selling much of its wine through the cellar door and by an understandably very loyal mailing list clientele. All the white wines are of the highest quality, year in, year out. Exports to the UK, Canada, Germany, India, Japan, Singapore and Hong Kong.

♟♟♟♟♟ Margaret River Semillon 2008 The alcohol would not be picked in a blind tasting; while the grassy/honeyed flavour is positive, the wine is light on its feet, the finish long, clean and balanced. Screwcap. 14% alc. Rating 95 To 2018 $22
Margaret River Sauvignon Blanc 2008 Offers a clean bouquet of gentle tropical fruits and touches of grass, then a long, focused palate with interwoven strands of gooseberry and acidity; very good mouthfeel and aftertaste. Screwcap. 14% alc. Rating 95 To 2011 $22
Margaret River Verdelho 2008 An aromatic tropical/banana bouquet, then a palate that opens as a reflection of the bouquet before quickly moving on to delicious lemony acidity, which gives great thrust to the mouthfeel. As good as they come. Screwcap. 14% alc. Rating 95 To 2013 $22
Margaret River Chardonnay 2007 Glowing green-yellow; showing the first signs of bottle development, white peach and barrel-ferment French oak equally balanced and integrated, cashew characters adding to the all-up flavour, and to the considerable length. Screwcap. 14.5% alc. Rating 94 To 2015 $32

♟♟♟♟♀ Margaret River Riesling 2008 A flowery and aromatic bouquet leads into a generously flavoured palate, with ripe citrus flavours; good length and balanced acidity. Screwcap. 13.5% alc. Rating 91 To 2013 $22

Ashton Hills ★★★★★

Tregarthen Road, Ashton, SA 5137 **Region** Adelaide Hills
T (08) 8390 1243 **F** (08) 8390 1243 **Open** W'ends & most public hols 11–5.30
Winemaker Stephen George **Est.** 1982 **Cases** 1500 **Vyds** 3 ha
Stephen George wears three winemaker hats: one for Ashton Hills, drawing upon an estate vineyard high in the Adelaide Hills; one for Galah Wines; and one for Wendouree. It would be hard to imagine three wineries with more diverse styles, from the elegance and finesse of Ashton Hills to the awesome power of Wendouree. The Riesling, Chardonnay and Pinot Noir have moved into the highest echelon.

ŶŶŶŶŶ **Estate Adelaide Hills Pinot Noir 2007** A voluminous, complex bouquet with varietal fruit and spicy/foresty nuances; has a long, immaculately balanced palate, the texture a special feature; excellent finish. Screwcap. 14% alc. **Rating** 95 To 2014 $49.50
Adelaide Hills Riesling 2008 Gently floral apple blossom aromas, then a finely structured palate with lime and green apple; long finish and excellent overall mouthfeel. Trophy Best Riesling Adelaide Hills Wine Show. Screwcap. 13% alc. **Rating** 94 To 2016 $30
Blanc de Blancs 2004 Bright green-straw; lively citrus and stone fruit with a touch of brioche/bread; fresh and lingering finish. Cork. 13.5% alc. **Rating** 94 To 2010 $33

ŶŶŶŶŶ **Reserve Adelaide Hills Pinot Noir 2007** Quite a warm personality of mulberry, clove and a little touch of game; the palate is quite firm and fine, with a slight brambly edge to the fruit; a touch of mint sitting on the top. Screwcap. 14% alc. **Rating** 92 To 2013 $55

Audrey Wilkinson Vineyard ★★★★★

Oakdale, De Beyers Road, Pokolbin, NSW 2320 **Region** Lower Hunter Valley
T (02) 4998 7411 **www**.audreywilkinson.com.au **Open** Mon–Fri 9–5, w'ends & public hols 9.30–5
Winemaker Jeff Byrne **Est.** 1999 **Cases** 15 000 **Vyds** 42.27 ha
One of the most historic properties in the Hunter Valley, set in a particularly beautiful location and with a very attractive cellar door. In 2004 it was acquired by Brian Agnew and family, and is no longer part of the Pepper Tree/James Fairfax wine group. The wines are made from estate-grown grapes, the lion's share to shiraz, the remainder (in descending order) to semillon, malbec, verdelho, tempranillo, merlot, cabernet sauvignon, muscat and traminer; the vines were planted between the 1970s and '90s. More recently, a small McLaren Vale vineyard of 3.45 ha, planted to merlot and shiraz, was acquired. Exports to NZ.

ŶŶŶŶŶ **Semillon 2008** Pale straw-green; has plenty to say on the bouquet, with lemon, spice and grass notes coming through on the long palate, which has abundant fruit weight. Screwcap. 11.5% alc. **Rating** 94 To 2018 $19.99
Museum Reserve Chardonnay 2006 An absolute powerhouse; incredibly rich, dense fruits on the palate make it a terrific example of the style; dried figs, tasty oak and fresh acidity, provide plenty of texture on the finish. Screwcap. 13.5% alc. **Rating** 94 To 2014 $35

ŶŶŶŶŶ **Museum Reserve Lake Shiraz 2007** Lively and bright purple hue; red fruits with a hint of earth and spice; quite plush and vibrant on the palate, with a dry savoury, dried herb complexity to the finish. Screwcap. 14% alc. **Rating** 93 To 2018 $50
Merlot 2006 The Hunter Valley can always spring surprises, and while merlot is not suited to the climate, wines such as this pop up from time to time. It has the texture and weight I want from merlot, the flavours a pleasing and correct mix of red berry fruits, black olive and spice. Screwcap. 14% alc. **Rating** 92 To 2014 $19.99

Museum Reserve Semillon 2008 A touch of green pea pod character, with focused lemon and straw on the bouquet; the palate shows good concentration and length, with strong potential for ageing. Screwcap. 11% alc. **Rating** 92 To 2020 $35

Hunter Valley Margaret River Semillon Sauvignon Blanc 2008 Strong pea pod aromas dominate a fresh, clean and varietal bouquet; the palate has lively acidity, with good flavour and purity of fruit on the finish. Screwcap. 10% alc. **Rating** 92 To 2014 $19.99

Hunter Valley Rose 2008 Vivid fuschia-crimson hue; bright cherry and raspberry fruit; dry style, impressive length and balance. Screwcap. 10.5% alc. **Rating** 92 To 2010 $19.99

Dessert Semillon 2007 Region of origin not specified; less rich than some, but equally better balanced than many, the acidity particularly good. Screwcap. 11.5% alc. **Rating** 92 To 2013 $25

Museum Reserve Culvert Shiraz 2005 Bright, fine and very even across the palate; red fruits intermingle with fresh leather and a little spice; an elegant style. Screwcap. 13.5% alc. **Rating** 91 To 2014 $35

Hunter Valley Shiraz 2007 A solid wine, neatly marrying regional and varietal characters, black fruits mingling with earthy notes; nice touch of oak and ripe tannins to close. Screwcap. 13.5% alc. **Rating** 90 To 2017 $19.99

Hunter Valley Chardonnay 2008 Pale colour, with spice and peach fruit aroma; lively and focused fruit with plenty of flavour, and an attractive, balanced finish. Screwcap. 12.5% alc. **Rating** 90 To 2014 $19.99

Tempranillo 2007 Quite a savoury dried earth, leather and dark cherry bouquet; the palate is rich and ripe with a softness to the finish that is gentle and appealing; more Hunter than Tempranillo? Screwcap. 14% alc. **Rating** 90 To 2013 $19.99

♟♟♟♟ **Hunter Valley Verdelho 2008** Clean and crisp nectarine fruit and vibrant acidity, provide a pure varietal expression; lively and crisp. Screwcap. 13% alc. **Rating** 89 To 2014 $19.99

Hunter Valley Shiraz 2006 Bright, clear colour; light- to medium-bodied; a mix of predominantly red fruits, with nuances of regional earth and leather; will mature quickly. Screwcap. 13.5% alc. **Rating** 89 To 2013 $19.99

Cabernet Merlot 2007 Light- to medium-bodied, with unexpected cassis flavours explained by a Padthaway component; fair length and balance. Screwcap. 14% alc. **Rating** 89 To 2015 $19.99

Pioneer Series Tempranillo 2007 Quite fragrant, with juicy berry fruit and a touch of American oak giving an adequate flavour dimension; for the wine student aka geek. Screwcap. 14% alc. **Rating** 88 To 2012 $25

Auldstone ★★★

Booths Road, Taminick via Glenrowan, Vic 3675 **Region** Glenrowan
T (03) 5766 2237 **www**.auldstone.com.au **Open** Thurs–Sat & school hols 9–5, Sun 10–5
Winemaker Michael Reid **Est.** 1987 **Cases** 2000
Michael and Nancy Reid have restored a century-old stone winery and have replanted the largely abandoned 26-ha vineyard around it. All the Auldstone varietal and fortified wines have won medals (usually bronze) in Australian wine shows. Exports to Singapore and China.

♟♟♟♟ **Liqueur Muscat NV** Highly perfumed with good aged material, and freshened quite well; a good example of the liqueur style. Cork. 18% alc. **Rating** 89 To 2010 $55

Austin's Wines ★★★★

870 Steiglitz Road, Sutherlands Creek, Vic 3331 **Region** Geelong
T (03) 5281 1799 **F** (03) 5281 1673 **www**.austinswines.com.au **Open** By appt
Winemaker Scott Ireland, Richard Austin **Est.** 1982 **Cases** 20 000 **Vyds** 61.5 ha
Pamela and Richard Austin have quietly built their business from a tiny base, and it has flourished. The vineyard has been progressively extended to over 60 ha, and production has

soared from 700 cases in 1998. Scott Ireland is now full-time resident winemaker in the capacious onsite winery, and the quality of the wines is admirable. Exports to the UK, the US and other major markets.

ΨΨΨΨΨ **Geelong Pinot Noir 2007** Good varietal character in aroma, flavour and texture; spicy/savoury nuances to the base of black cherry fruit; a long and balanced palate. Screwcap. 13.5% alc. **Rating** 92 **To** 2013 $27.50
Geelong Chardonnay 2007 A complex bouquet showing strong barrel-ferment inputs, the grapefruit and nectarine palate has good length and intensity, although still quite oaky. Screwcap. 13.5% alc. **Rating** 90 **To** 2014 $27.50
Six Foot Six Pinot Gris 2008 Pear drop aromas lead into a palate with very good texture and mouthfeel, especially at this alcohol level; a dry, but supple, finish to a good example of the variety. Screwcap. 12.5% alc. **Rating** 90 **To** 2012 $20

ΨΨΨΨ **Geelong Shiraz 2005** Spicy/briary aromas repeat on the light- to medium-bodied palate; cool-climate style, but needs more fruit concentration from the vineyard. Screwcap. 14.5% alc. **Rating** 87 **To** 2012 $27.50

Australian Domaine Wines   ★★★★☆

PO Box 13, Walkerville, SA 5081 **Region** South Australia
T (08) 8340 3807 **F** (08) 8346 3766 **www.**ausdomwines.com.au **Open** By appt
Winemaker Pikes (Neil Pike), Andrew Braithwaite **Est.** 1998 **Cases** 5000
Australian Domaine Wines is the reincarnation of Barletta Bros, who started their own brand business for leading Adelaide retailer Walkerville Cellars, which they then owned. The wines are made at Pikes using tanks and barrels owned by the Barlettas. Grapes are sourced from the Clare Valley, McLaren Vale and the Barossa Valley. Exports to the UK, the US and other major markets.

ΨΨΨΨΨ **Solitary Block Watervale Riesling 2008** Mineral and spice overtones to the bouquet; lively, crisp, precise and intense lime and mineral flavours; clean, dry, long finish. Great development prospects. Screwcap. 12% alc. **Rating** 94 **To** 2018 $20

ΨΨΨΨΨ **Solitary Block Kalimna Barossa Valley Shiraz 2006** Dense colour; rich and powerful, full-bodied wine with blackberry, licorice and plum-cake flavours. Impressive statement of variety and region. Cork. 15% alc. **Rating** 93 **To** 2020 $57
Solitary Block Marananga Barossa Valley Shiraz 2006 An even denser, fuller-bodied wine than the Kalimna, but not better – the alcohol catches up. Cork. 15.5% alc. **Rating** 92 **To** 2020 $87
The Hattrick 2005 The region expresses itself more clearly than any of the varietal components; a long and powerful palate with savoury dark chocolate elements, warming on the finish. Shiraz/Grenache. Cork. 15% alc. **Rating** 90 **To** 2015 $50

ΨΨΨΨ **Alliance Clare Valley Viognier 2008** Not particularly varietal on the bouquet, but more so on the fresh palate, which has length to the tropical/apricot fruit. Screwcap. 13% alc. **Rating** 89 **To** 2011 $16
Solitary Block The Juice 2007 Slight salmon; is in fact quite dry, despite mid-palate fruit sweetness in a red cherry/berry spectrum. Grenache Rose. Screwcap. 13% alc. **Rating** 88 **To** 2010 $20

Australian Old Vine Wine   ★★★☆

Farm 271, Rossetto Road, Beelbangera, NSW 2680 **Region** Riverina
T (02) 6963 5239 **F** (02) 6963 5239 **www.**australianoldvine.com.au **Open** 7 days 10–4
Winemaker Piromit Wines (Dom Piromalli) **Est.** 2002 **Cases** 2500 **Vyds** 18.3 ha
Elio and Marie Alban have registered the name Australian Old Vine Wine Pty Ltd for their business, designed to draw attention to their 7.6 ha of 50-year-old shiraz and 2.8 ha of 40-year-old cabernet sauvignon. Wines coming from the younger plantings (merlot, semillon, colombard and chambourcin) are released under the Australian Sovereign label. Ultimately, the plan is to buy grapes from old vineyards in the Barossa Valley and McLaren Vale for an Old Vine blend. Exports to Ireland, Germany, Russia and Poland.

ooooo **Alban Estate Semillon Botrytis 2007** Already deep gold in colour; very rich, high botrytis style with cumquat and preserved orange rind on a long finish. Screwcap. 11% alc. **Rating** 90 **To** 2011 $20

oooo **Alban Estate Limited Release Chambourcin 2007** Typical vivid colour; has the inherent limitations of chambourcin, but 12 months in barrel and appropriate winery adjustments have helped its cause considerably. Screwcap. 14% alc. **Rating** 87 **To** 2012 $15

Aventine Wines

86 Watters Road, Ballandean, Qld, 4382 **Region** Granite Belt
T 0409 270 389 www.aventinewines.com.au **Open** W'ends & public hols 9–5
Winemaker Jim Barnes **Est.** 1995 **Cases** 2000 **Vyds** 10 ha
The Aventine vineyard is situated at an elevation of 1000 m, on a north-facing hill high above the Ballandean Valley. The vines have established on shallow, weathered granite, with equal size plantings of chardonnay, shiraz, cabernet sauvignon and muscat. All the wines are made from estate-grown grapes.

Avenue Wines ★★★★

124 Seventh Avenue, Joslin, SA 5070 (postal) **Region** South Australia
T (08) 8362 4032 **F** (08) 8362 4032 www.avenuewines.com.au **Open** Not
Winemaker George Ochota **Est.** 2004 **Cases** 2000
The Ochota family established a vineyard in the Clare Valley in the 1960s, which eventually led to George Ochota becoming an amateur winemaker in the mid '90s; after winning numerous medals he decided it was time to take the plunge into commercial winemaking, buying grapes from the Clare Valley (including the former family vineyard), Langhorne Creek, McLaren Vale and Barossa.

ooooo **Grenache Shiraz Mourvedre 2007** Essency red fruit and a touch of spice; juicy, vibrant and fine on the finish; the wine exhibits good definition, depth of fruit and persistence on the finish. Screwcap. 15% alc. **Rating** 92 **To** 2015 $18
McLaren Vale Shiraz 2006 Good colour; mocha and blackberry bouquet with an attractive chocolate edge; medium-bodied and lithe, with an attractive tarry character to accentuate the dark fruit. Screwcap. 15% alc. **Rating** 91 **To** 2016 $20
Clare Valley Riesling 2008 Deep colour, vibrant hue; slate and lime bouquet; dry, focused and zesty lime juice palate; fresh and long. Screwcap. 11.5% alc. **Rating** 90 **To** 2014 $17

oooo **Barossa Valley Shiraz 2006** Warm-fruited with licorice, fruitcake and a touch of prune; medium-bodied with good texture and weight. Screwcap. 15% alc. **Rating** 89 **To** 2015 $20

B3 Wines

Light Pass Road, Barossa Valley, SA 5352 **Region** Barossa Valley
T (08) 8363 2211 **F** (08) 8363 2231 www.b3wines.com.au **Open** By appt
Winemaker Craig Stansborough **Est.** 2001 **Cases** NA
Peter, Michael and Richard Basedow are the three Brothers Basedow (as they call themselves), fifth-generation Barossans with distinguished forefathers. Grandfather Oscar Basedow established the Basedow winery (no longer in family ownership) in 1896, while Martin Basedow established the Roseworthy Agricultural College. Their father, John Oscar Basedow, died in the 1970s, having won the 1970 Jimmy Watson Trophy for his '69 Cabernet Sauvignon, a high point for the family. This is a virtual winery enterprise, grapes are purchased mainly from the Barossa Valley, Coonawarra, Adelaide Hills and Eden Valley. Exports to the US, Canada and Asia.

oooo **Eden Valley Riesling 2008** Lime blossom aromas precede a fruity, fleshy palate; drink now rather than later. Screwcap. 13.5% alc. **Rating** 89 **To** 2012 $18

Barossa Shiraz 2006 Very ripe fruit, showing some confit redcurrant and blackberry; loaded with sweet fruit on the palate and offset by fruitcake spice; rich, ripe and warm. Screwcap. 16% alc. **Rating** 89 **To** 2013 $18

Barossa Semillon 2007 Quite deep colour with vibrant green hue; straw, toast and a little honey on the bouquet; a quite generous palate, with cleansing acidity on the finish. Screwcap. 13% alc. **Rating** 88 **To** 2012 $14

Bacchus Hill ★★★

100 O'Connell Road, Bacchus Marsh, Vic 3340 **Region** Sunbury
T (03) 5367 8176 www.bacchushill.com.au **Open** W'ends 10–5, Mon–Fri by appt
Winemaker Bruno Tassone **Est.** 2000 **Cases** 2600 **Vyds** 15.5 ha
Bruno Tassone migrated from Italy when he was eight, and grew up watching his father carry on the Italian tradition of making wine for home consumption. Tassone, a lawyer, followed the same path before purchasing a 35-ha property with wife Jennifer. Here they have planted 2 ha each of riesling, semillon, sauvignon blanc, chardonnay, pinot noir, shiraz, cabernet sauvignon, 1 ha of chenin blanc and 0.5 ha of nebbiolo. A move to screwcaps would be of great advantage for the older wines. Exports to Canada.

 Le Repaire de Bacchus Riesling 2008 Deep colour; ripe stone fruit with a core of lemon; good acid, and a dry textural finish. Diam. 12.5% alc. **Rating** 88 **To** 2014 $22

Back Pocket ★★★

90 Savina Lane, Severnlea, Qld 4380 **Region** Granite Belt
T 0418 196 035 **F** (07) 4683 5184 www.backpocket.com.au **Open** Not
Winemaker Peter Scudamore-Smith MW (Contract) **Est.** 1997 **Cases** 600 **Vyds** 2 ha
Mal Baisden and Lel Doon purchased the 20-ha Back Pocket property in 1997, which had long been used for fruit growing, with a small patch of shiraz planted in the early '80s. It was progressively expanded to its present level: shiraz (0.7 ha), tempranillo (0.5 ha), fiano and graciano (0.4 ha each). The Old Savina Shiraz recognises the efforts of the Savina family who planted the shiraz; Arabia, a budget-priced shiraz; Castanets, 100% tempranillo; and Pickpocket, a rose produced from the juice run-off to concentrate the shiraz.

 Single Vineyard Pickpocket 2008 Lively red berry fruits, with just a little spice; a touch of sweetness works well with the fruit, concluding in a little dried herb savoury character. Shiraz Rose. Screwcap. 13.5% alc. **Rating** 88 **To** 2011 $19

Single Vineyard Arabia 2007 Clean and spicy blackberry fruit; a young and juicy, drink-early wine. Shiraz. Screwcap. 13% alc. **Rating** 87 **To** 2012 $17

Single Vineyard Old Savina Reserve Shiraz 2006 The 24 months the wine spent in French oak was too long for the tangy, spicy, herbal fruit. Interesting wine, nonetheless. Screwcap. 13% alc. **Rating** 87 **To** 2015 $24

Baddaginnie Run ★★★★

PO Box 579, North Melbourne, Vic 3051 **Region** Strathbogie Ranges
T (03) 9348 9310 **F** (03) 9348 9370 www.baddaginnierun.net.au **Open** Not
Winemaker Toby Barlow **Est.** 1996 **Cases** 2000 **Vyds** 24 ha
Winsome McCaughey and Professor Snow Barlow (Professor of Horticulture and Viticulture at the University of Melbourne) spend part of their week in the Strathbogie Ranges, and part in Melbourne. The business name, Seven Sisters Vineyard, reflects the seven generations of the McCaughey family associated with the land since 1870; Baddaginnie is the nearby township. The vineyard is one element in a restored valley landscape, 100 000 indigenous trees having been replanted. The wines are made by son Toby Barlow, former Mitchelton winemaker. Exports to Canada and China.

Strathbogie Ranges Shiraz 2007 Strong crimson-purple; has a most attractive juicy edge to the black cherry and plum fruit; the fresh finish is enhanced by good acidity and balanced French oak. Screwcap. 14% alc. **Rating** 93 **To** 2020 $24

Strathbogie Ranges Merlot 2004 This powerful and intense merlot was first tasted over three years ago, and has barely changed, still abounding with rich fruit, excellent colour and length of palate. Screwcap. 14.5% alc. **Rating** 92 **To** 2016 $28

 Strathbogie Ranges Rose 2008 Above-average fragrance, with small red berry fruits flowing into the palate, the small amount of sweetness balanced by acidity. Shiraz. Screwcap. 12.5% alc. **Rating** 89 **To** 2010 $18

Strathbogie Ranges Viognier 2008 One of the relatively rare viogniers which has some peach and apricot varietal aromas and flavours, but dodges the phenolic bullet. Screwcap. 14.5% alc. **Rating** 88 **To** 2010 $20

Badger's Brook ★★★☆

874 Maroondah Highway, Coldstream, Vic 3770 **Region** Yarra Valley
T (03) 5962 4130 **F** (03) 5962 4130 **www**.badgersbrook.com.au **Open** Wed–Sun 11–5
Winemaker Contract **Est.** 1993 **Cases** 2000
Situated next door to the well-known Rochford, it has 10 ha of vineyard, planted mainly to chardonnay, sauvignon blanc, pinot noir, shiraz and cabernet sauvignon, with a few rows each of viognier, roussanne, marsanne and tempranillo. All of the grapes are Yarra Valley sourced, including for the second Storm Ridge label. Now houses the smart brasserie restaurant Bella Vedere Cucina with well-known chef Gary Cooper in charge. Exports to Asia.

 Yarra Valley Shiraz Roussanne Marsanne 2006 Bright blue fruit bouquet with Asian spice to complement the fruit; medium-bodied and savoury, with some ironstone firmness showing on the finish. One for the Options Game. Screwcap. 13.5% alc. **Rating** 90 **To** 2014 $22

Storm Ridge Yarra Valley Shiraz 2006 Roasted charred meat and spicy black fruit on the bouquet; medium-bodied with a bit of tannin and plenty of red fruit on the finish. Screwcap. 13.5% alc. **Rating** 89 **To** 2014 $18

Storm Ridge Chardonnay Pinot Noir NV Clean and fresh citrus bouquet; chalky and crisp on the finish. Crown Seal. 13.5% alc. **Rating** 87 **To** 2012 $25

Bago Vineyards ★★☆

Milligans Road, Wauchope, NSW 2446 **Region** Hastings River
T (02) 6585 7099 **F** (02) 6585 7099 **www**.bagovineyards.com.au **Open** 7 days 11–5
Winemaker Jim Mobbs, Greg Hayward **Est.** 1985 **Cases** 5000 **Vyds** 10 ha
Jim and Kay Mobbs began planting the estate vineyards in 1985 with 1 ha of chardonnay, and have steadily expanded the plantings with a veritable Joseph's coat of varieties: chardonnay, together with verdelho, viognier, albarino, chanel paradisa, chambourcin, petit verdot, merlot, pinot noir and tannat.

Baie Wines ★★★

120 McDermott Road, Curlewis, Vic 3222 **Region** Geelong
T (03) 5257 1867 **F** (03) 5257 1867 **www**.baiewines.com.au **Open** W'ends 11–4
Winemaker Robin Brockett **Est.** 2000 **Cases** 1000 **Vyds** 6 ha
Baie Wines takes its name from the farming property Baie Park, owned by the Kuc family (headed by Anne and Peter) for over 30 years. It was not until 2000 that they established 2 ha each of sauvignon blanc, pinot gris and shiraz, the first vintage following in '06. The vineyard is planted on north-facing slopes running down to the shore of Port Phillip Bay, the maritime influence is profound. Peter almost single-handedly prunes the entire vineyard every year, and wife Anne is responsible for the meticulous vineyard upkeep. Son Simon manages the farm, and his wife Nadine is responsible for marketing.

 Bellarine Peninsula Pinot Gris 2008 Clean and bright pear and lemon bouquet; zesty, fresh and fine on the palate. Screwcap. 13% alc. **Rating** 87 **To** 2012 $20

Baileys of Glenrowan

Cnr Taminick Gap Road/Upper Taminick Road, Glenrowan, Vic 3675
Region Glenrowan
T (03) 5766 2392 **F** (03) 5766 2596 www.baileysofglenrowan.com.au **Open** 7 days 10–5
Winemaker Paul Dahlenburg **Est.** 1870 **Cases** 15 000 **Vyds** 143 ha

Just when it seemed that Baileys would remain one of the forgotten outposts of the Foster's
group, the reverse has occurred. Since 1998, Paul Dahlenburg has been in charge of Baileys
and has overseen an expansion in the vineyard and the construction of a 2000-tonne winery.
The cellar door has a heritage museum, winery-viewing deck, contemporary art gallery and
landscaped grounds, preserving much of the heritage value. Baileys has also picked up the pace
with its Muscat and Tokay, reintroducing the Winemaker's Selection at the top of the tree,
while continuing the larger-volume Founder series. In April 2009 Foster's announced the
winery, vineyards and the brand would be listed for sale as a going concern basis; until sold,
the winery will continue to operate as usual, and every effort made to protect the value of
what is an iconic brand. Exports to the UK and NZ.

ΨΨΨΨΨ **Winemaker's Selection Old Tokay NV** Obvious age showing from its
mahogany/olive-green colour; classic tea-leaf, butterscotch and malt flavours;
great harmony with the spirit; a long finish, at once sweet yet dry and spicy.
Cork. 16.5% alc. **Rating** 95 **To** 2010 $34.99
Winemaker's Selection Old Muscat NV Gloriously rich, luscious and
powerful; retains the essence of raisin muscat, but complexed by rancio and
oriental spices; again, perfect harmony with the fortifying spirit. Cork. 17% alc.
Rating 95 **To** 2010 $34.99
Founder Liqueur Muscat NV Intense, lively, grapey varietal character of raisins
and plum pudding; acidity gives more lift and intensifies the flavour, yet does not
bite; the volatile component of the acidity appears low. Cork. 17% alc. **Rating** 94
To 2010 $23.99

ΨΨΨΨΨ **Founder Liqueur Tokay NV** Moderate age; classic tea-leaf, butterscotch and
malt aromas and flavours; a lingering sweetness through the palate, then a final
farewell is (commendably) almost dry. Cork. 17% alc. **Rating** 93 **To** 2010 $23.99
Founder Tawny Port NV Tawny as it is made in Northeast Victoria, more
luscious and raisined than classic South Australian Tawnys. Clean, modern
packaging are a feature of the fortified range. **Rating** 92 **To** 2010

Baillieu Vineyard ★★★

Merricks General Store, 3458–3460 Frankston–Flinders Road, Merricks, Vic 3916
Region Mornington Peninsula
T (03) 5989 8088 **F** (03) 5989 7199 www.baillieuvineyard.com.au **Open** 7 days 9–5
Winemaker Balnarring Estate (Kathleen Quealy) **Est.** 1999 **Cases** 3000 **Vyds** 10 ha

Charlie and Samantha Baillieu re-established the former Foxwood Vineyard, growing
chardonnay, viognier, pinot gris, pinot noir and shiraz. The north-facing vineyard is part of the
64-ha Bulldog Run property owned by the Baillieus.

ΨΨΨΨ **Mornington Peninsula Pinot Gris 2008** A subdued bouquet and rather stolid
palate, but has flavour. Screwcap. 14% alc. **Rating** 87 **To** 2010 $22
Mornington Peninsula Pinot Noir 2007 Purple-crimson; has quite a firm
structure, but the mid-palate is curiously hollow; just enough plum and spice
flavours to score. Screwcap. 13.5% alc. **Rating** 87 **To** 2012 $25

Balgownie Estate ★★★★

Hermitage Road, Maiden Gully, Vic 3551 **Region** Bendigo
T (03) 5449 6222 **F** (03) 5449 6506 www.balgownieestate.com.au **Open** 7 days 11–5
Winemaker Mark Lane **Est.** 1969 **Cases** 10 000 **Vyds** 28.25 ha

Balgownie Estate continues to grow in the wake of its acquisition by the Forrester family. A $3 million winery upgrade coincided with a doubling of the size of the vineyard, and in 2004 Balgownie Estate opened a cellar door in the Yarra Valley (see separate entry). Mark Lane, Winestate Winemaker of the Year '08, has moved from Swings & Roundabouts to take up his position at Balgownie Estate. Exports to the UK, the US and other major markets.

The Goldfields Shiraz 2006 Bright crimson; both bouquet and palate are driven by intense spicy black fruits lifted by the small amount of co-fermented viognier. Screwcap. 14% alc. **Rating** 93 **To** 2016 $22.95

Bendigo Chardonnay 2006 The wine is developing at an impressive, leisurely pace; the tangy melon and citrus fruit has drive and thrust, the barrel ferment–oak inputs seen but not heard. Screwcap. 14% alc. **Rating** 91 **To** 2014 $29.95

The Goldfields Cabernet Merlot 2006 Bright colour, but surprisingly light-bodied for Bendigo, perhaps the reverse face of drought; red fruits with a savoury, herbal twist. Screwcap. 14% alc. **Rating** 88 **To** 2013 $22.95

Bendigo Cabernet Sauvignon 2006 Bright colour and hue; like the Cabernet Merlot, lighter than usual for Bendigo, earthy/savoury characters dominating the fruit. Screwcap. 14% alc. **Rating** 88 **To** 2015 $29.95

Balgownie Estate (Yarra Valley)   ★★★☆

Cnr Melba Highway/Gulf Road, Yarra Glen, Vic 3775 **Region** Yarra Valley
T (03) 9730 0700 **F** (03) 9730 2647 **www.**balgownieestate.com.au **Open** 7 days 10–5
Winemaker Mark Lane **Est.** 2004 **Cases** 3000 **Vyds** 7 ha
The Yarra Valley operation of Balgownie Estate neatly fits in with the Bendigo wines, each supporting the other. Winemaking to one side, Balgownie has the largest vineyard-based resort in the Yarra Valley, with 65 rooms and a limited number of spa suites. It specialises in catering for conferences and functions, and Rae's Restaurant is open for breakfast and lunch 7 days. Mark Lane, Winestate Winemaker of the Year '08, has moved from Swings & Roundabouts to take up his position at Balgownie Estate.

Pinot Noir 2007 Nice bright colour; fine and fragrant aromas, with red berry fruits supported by a delicate hint of spice; the palate is firmer than expected, and just a little firm on the finish. Screwcap. 13.5% alc. **Rating** 90 **To** 2014 $26.95

Chardonnay 2007 Quite a worked style, exhibiting plenty of oak, solids contact and lees stirring; dried figs and pears dominate, but the palate is a little heavy. Screwcap. 13.5% alc. **Rating** 87 **To** 2012 $26.95

Ballandean Estate   ★★★

Sundown Road, Ballandean, Qld 4382 **Region** Granite Belt
T (07) 4684 1226 **F** (07) 4684 1288 **www.**ballandeanestate.com **Open** 7 days 9–5
Winemaker Dylan Rhymer, Angelo Puglisi **Est.** 1970 **Cases** 15 000 **Vyds** 31.1 ha
The senior winery of the Granite Belt is owned by the ever-cheerful and charming, but appalling correspondent, Angelo Puglisi. The white wines are of diverse but interesting styles, the red wines smooth and usually well made. The estate speciality, Sylvaner Late Harvest, is a particularly interesting wine of great character and flavour if given 10 years' bottle age, but is only produced sporadically. Exports to Canada and Taiwan.

S.S.B. 2008 Pungent pea pod aroma, intermingling with zesty tropical fruit; very dry, with prominent acidity on the finish; slight CO_2 prickle. Semillon/Sauvignon Blanc. Screwcap. 12.4% alc. **Rating** 88 **To** 2011 $16.50

Late Harvest Sylvaner 2005 Obvious oak on the bouquet, with some mandarin; moderately sweet with cleansing acidity and reasonable length. Screwcap. 9% alc. **Rating** 88 **To** 2012 $18

Family Reserve Chardonnay 2007 Ripe grapefruit bouquet, quite toasty and rich; plenty of flavour, albeit with a slightly dry and grippy finish. Screwcap. 13.8% alc. **Rating** 87 **To** 2012 $22

Ballast Stone Estate Wines ★★★★

Myrtle Grove Road, Currency Creek, SA 5214 **Region** Currency Creek
T (08) 8555 4215 **F** (08) 8555 4216 **www.**ballaststonewines.com **Open** 7 days 10.30–5
Winemaker John Loxton **Est.** 2001 **Cases** 80 000 **Vyds** 410 ha
The Shaw family have been vintners for over 35 years, commencing plantings in McLaren
Vale in the early 1970s. Extensive vineyard holdings are now held in McLaren Vale (60 ha) and
Currency Creek (350 ha), with a modern winery in Currency Creek. The family produces
approximately 80 000 cases under the Ballast Stone Estate label as well as supplying others.
Exports to the UK, the US and other major markets.

ŢŢŢŢŢ **RMS McLaren Vale Cabernet Sauvignon 2004** An extremely potent and
powerful wine from 65-year-old McLaren Vale cabernet matured in French oak
for 32 months; black fruits, dark chocolate, lingering tannins and (obviously)
French oak all play a role. Cork. 14.5% alc. **Rating** 93 **To** 2019 $50
Emetior McLaren Vale Shiraz 2004 Some bottle-developed aromas starting
to appear, adding to the 30 months in French and American oak before bottling;
savoury notes are equally balanced by damson plum fruit, some chocolate and
spice. Cork doesn't inspire confidence. Cork. 15% alc. **Rating** 92 **To** 2015 $40
Currency Creek Chardonnay 2008 Bright straw-green; an attractive wine,
primarily driven by its grapefruit and nectarine flavours supported by just a touch
of French oak. Good value. Screwcap. 14% alc. **Rating** 90 **To** 2011 $15

ŢŢŢŢ **Currency Creek McLaren Vale Cabernet Sauvignon 2007** Quite complex,
with black fruits, mint, chocolate and vanilla all coming and going. Screwcap.
14% alc. **Rating** 87 **To** 2013 $20

Ballinaclash Wines ★★☆

Wombat Road, Young, NSW 2594 **Region** Hilltops
T 0418 271 770 **www.**ballinaclash.com.au **Open** Nov & Dec 7 days 8–5, or by appt
Winemaker Madrez Wine Services **Est.** 1997 **Cases** 500 **Vyds** 7 ha
In 1997 Peter and Cath Mullany began to diversify the cherry and stone fruit orchard set up
by Peter's father in 1965 by establishing a vineyard on part of the land. They now have 2 ha
each of shiraz and cabernet sauvignon, and 1.5 ha each of chardonnay and viognier. Selling all
their grapes to larger wine companies up to 2005, they moved to have a Cabernet Sauvignon
made, adding Chardonnay in '06, branching out to a Chardonnay Viognier and Shiraz in '07.
At their first-ever entry into a wine show in '08, their '07 Patrick Shiraz won the top gold
medal in its class at the Cowra National Wine Show, a dream start. As well as visiting the cellar
door, you can pick your own cherries, apricots, peaches, plums and strawberries in season.

Balnaves of Coonawarra ★★★★★

Main Road, Coonawarra, SA 5263 **Region** Coonawarra
T (08) 8737 2946 **www.**balnaves.com.au **Open** Mon–Fri 9–5, w'ends 12–5
Winemaker Pete Bissell **Est.** 1975 **Cases** 10 000 **Vyds** 51 ha
Grapegrower, viticultural consultant and vigneron, Doug Balnaves has over 50 ha of high-
quality estate vineyards. The wines are invariably excellent, often outstanding, notable for their
supple mouthfeel, varietal integrity, balance and length; the tannins are always fine and ripe,
the oak subtle and perfectly integrated. Coonawarra at its best. Winery of the Year 2008 Wine
Companion. Exports to the UK, The Netherlands, Germany, Denmark, Canada, Vietnam,
Japan and Hong Kong.

ŢŢŢŢŢ **The Tally Reserve Cabernet Sauvignon 2007** Power and grace; loaded with
sweet oak, the quality of fruit beneath is up to the task; layered cassis, redcurrant,
cedar and violet bouquet; great concentration of fruit on the palate, with a
refreshingly vibrant core of acid and pure fruit; lots of slippery fine-grained tannins
that counterpoint the vibrant and complex fruit with ease; wonderfully long and
satisfying. ProCork. 15% alc. **Rating** 97 **To** 2025 $95

Cabernet Sauvignon 2007 Intense Coonawarra fruit, with amazing purity and poise; polished cassis and redcurrant combine effortlessly with the fine oak framework; full-bodied, dark and dense, with layered fruit coursing along the palate, harmoniously mingling with the fine-grained tannins. ProCork. 14.5% alc. **Rating** 95 **To** 2020 $39

Cabernet Merlot 2007 Pure and fine redcurrant fruit aromas with cedary oak and a touch of cinnamon; the palate is seamless and the transition of fruit across the palate is integrated with the quite slippery fine-grained tannins; very long and very good value. Screwcap. 14.5% alc. **Rating** 94 **To** 2018 $26

ŶŶŶŶ♀ **The Blend 2007** Bright colour; restrained cassis and cedar bouquet, with a touch of mint in the background; more red fruit on the palate, plentiful fine and firm tannin, and a suggestion of Coonawarra mint on the finish. Value. Merlot/Cabernet Sauvignon. Screwcap. 14.5% alc. **Rating** 92 **To** 2016 $19

ŶŶŶŶ **Chardonnay 2007** Peach and dried fig bouquet; a rich, somewhat oaky palate, with plenty of ripe fruit lingering on the finish. Screwcap. 13% alc. **Rating** 89 **To** 2012 $30

Balthazar of the Barossa

PO Box 675, Nuriootpa, SA 5355 **Region** Barossa Valley
T (08) 8562 2949 **F** (08) 8562 2949 **www**.balthazarbarossa.com **Open** At the Small Winemakers Centre, Chateau Tanunda
Winemaker Anita Bowen **Est.** 1999 **Cases** 8000

Anita Bowen announced her occupation as 'a 40-something sex therapist with a 17-year involvement in the wine industry'. Anita undertook her first vintage at Mudgee, then McLaren Vale, and ultimately the Barossa; she worked at St Hallet while studying at Roseworthy College. A versatile lady, indeed. As to her wine, she says, 'Anyway, prepare a feast, pour yourself a glass (no chalices, please) of Balthazar and share it with your concubines. Who knows? It may help to lubricate thoughts, firm up ideas and get the creative juices flowing!' Exports to Canada, Malaysia, China and Singapore.

ŶŶŶŶŶ **Shiraz 2006** Deep and bright colour; the first impression of this wine is the oak, but underneath there is a brooding dark quality to the fruit; layered, complex and very polished bright red and black fruits come through on the palate, and the finish is long, even and generous. Screwcap. 15.5% alc. **Rating** 95 **To** 2025 $59

ŶŶŶŶ♀ **Ishtar Goddess White Viognier 2008** A little reductive on opening; good fruit intensity, with apricot and a hint of spice on the bouquet; the palate is full and rich, but avoids heaviness; exotic and well made. Screwcap. 14% alc. **Rating** 90 **To** 2012 $19.99

ŶŶŶŶ **Ishtar Grenache Shiraz Mourvedre 2006** Bright and juicy red fruits, with an element of whole-bunch spice and complexity; juicy and fine on the finish. Screwcap. 14% alc. **Rating** 89 **To** 2012 $19.99

Ishtar Adelaide Hills Pinot Grigio 2008 A hint of pink in the colour; aromas of pear and lemon, with a palate exhibiting quite pronounced acidity on the generous finish. Screwcap. 13.5% alc. **Rating** 88 **To** 2012 $19.99

Ishtar Adelaide Hills Sauvignon Blanc 2008 Gentle tropical fruit aromas, with a soft and easy palate in a similar fruit spectrum. Screwcap. 13.5% alc. **Rating** 87 **To** 2011 $19.99

Banderra Estate

Sandhills Road, Forbes, NSW 2871 **Region** Central Ranges Zone
T (02) 6852 1437 **F** (02) 6852 1437 **Open** Mon–Sat 9–5, Sun 12–5
Winemaker John Saleh, Chris Derrez (Contract) **Est.** 1920 **Cases** 350 **Vyds** 3 ha

Formerly Sand Hills Vineyard, Banderra Estate dates back to the 1920s, and the ownership of Jacques Jenet. The Salet family became owners a number of years ago and have re-established estate plantings of chardonnay, colombard, semillon, shiraz, merlot and cabernet sauvignon, with a little pinot noir and mataro. As well as at the historic cellar door, the wines will also be available at an outlet in the McFeeters Car Museum in Forbes.

ȲȲȲȲ **Chardonnay 2008** Neatly put together, with nectarine and melon fruit in an embrace of subtle oak giving some creamy/nutty characters. Screwcap. 13.5% alc. **Rating** 89 **To** 2014 $19

Sand Hills Vineyard Oloroso Cream Sherry NV The use of terminology such as this (Sherry) will finish before the end of '09 by agreement with the EU; this is certainly not Cream in style, and rather better than the name would suggest, a youthful cross of Amontillado and Oloroso (likewise headed for oblivion as names in Australia). Cork. 17.3% alc. **Rating** 87 **To** 2010 $15

Banks Thargo Wines   ★★★☆

Racecourse Road, Penola, SA 5277 (postal) **Region** Coonawarra
T (08) 8736 3313 **F** (08) 8737 3369 **Open** Not
Winemaker Banks Kidman, Jonathon Kidman **Est.** 1980 **Cases** 1500 **Vyds** 22 ha
The unusual name comes from family history. One branch of the Kidman family moved to the Mount Gambier district in 1858, but Thomas Kidman (who had been in the foster care of the Banks family from the age of 2–13) moved to Broken Hill/southwest Qld to work for the famous Kidman Bros pastoral interests. He 'retired' from the outback, and in 1919 bought this property. His second son was named Banks Thargomindah Kidman, and it was he and wife Genny who decided to diversify their grazing activities by planting vines in the 1980s: most is under contract, leaving 1 ha each of merlot and cabernet sauvignon for the Banks Thargo brand.

ȲȲȲȲȲ **Coonawarra Cabernet Sauvignon 2006** A deep bouquet, with a touch of mint complementing the cassis fruit well; the palate is rich and lively, and shows a nice balance of fruit, tannin and acid on the finish Screwcap. 15% alc. **Rating** 90 **To** 2014 $20

Bannockburn Vineyards   ★★★★★

Midland Highway, Bannockburn, Vic 3331 (postal) **Region** Geelong
T (03) 5281 1363 **F** (03) 5281 1349 **www**.bannockburnvineyards.com **Open** By appt
Winemaker Michael Glover **Est.** 1974 **Cases** 10 000
With the qualified exception of the Cabernet Merlot, which can be a little leafy and gamey, Bannockburn produces outstanding wines across the range, all with individuality, style, great complexity and depth of flavour. The low-yielding estate vineyards play their role. Winemaker Michael Glover is determined to enhance the reputation of Bannockburn. Exports to Canada, Dubai, Korea, China, Singapore and Hong Kong.

ȲȲȲȲȲ **Geelong Chardonnay 2006** A resplendently complex and rich bouquet is followed by a deeply textured palate; creamy/nutty nuances and lush white peach fruit, all counterbalanced by perfect acidity. Quality cork. 14% alc. **Rating** 96 **To** 2015 $51

Stuart Geelong Pinot 2006 While the style has similarities to the varietal, the wine announces itself from the word go, the bouquet and palate with intense spicy plum and black fruits, the finish expanding even further. Cork. 12.5% alc. **Rating** 96 **To** 2015 $67

Geelong Shiraz 2005 Impeccable cool Victorian shiraz; red fruits framed by an array of exotic spices; the key here is the texture, as it is silky and very supple, with attractive oak and fruit in complete harmony; has a distinctly European feel. Cork. 15% alc. **Rating** 95 **To** 2020 $49

Geelong Pinot Noir 2006 Developed colour; spicy nuances to the bouquet are repeated on the savoury/spicy palate, which leaves it to the aftertaste to proclaim its class. Cork. 12.5% alc. **Rating** 94 **To** 2013 $57

Serre Pinot Noir 2005 Some development in colour, which is quite light; spicy sous bois stem components sit alongside light, but ripe, fruit, the silky mouthfeel creeps up quietly; a wine requiring contemplation (and a knowledge of prior vintages). Cork. 13.5% alc. **Rating** 94 **To** 2013 $90

 Geelong Sauvignon Blanc 2007 A wine built around a powerful stony/ minerally frame, and an uncompromisingly dry finish. Cork. 14% alc. **Rating** 90 **To** 2012 $27
Geelong Saignee Rose 2006 Some salmon tinges to the colour; the low alcohol and punchy acidity define the flavour and mouthfeel of the dry palate. A cork for a rose is the ultimate defiance of the cork gods. 13% alc. **Rating** 90 **To** 2009 $21

Geelong Riesling 2007 The bouquet is all but non-existent, the strong suspicion being scalping by the cork; the generous palate in a spatlese style adds to the suspicion; a pity. 10.5% alc. **Rating** 88 **To** 2011 $25

Banrock Station ★★★

Holmes Road (off Sturt Highway), Kingston-on-Murray, SA 5331 **Region** Riverland
T (08) 8583 0299 **F** (08) 8583 0288 **www.**banrockstation.com **Open** 7 days 10–5
Winemaker Paul Burnett **Est.** 1994 **Cases** NFP **Vyds** 240 ha
The eco-friendly $1 million visitor centre at Banrock Station is a major tourist destination. Owned by Constellation, the Banrock Station property covers over 1700 ha, with 240 ha of vineyard and the remainder being a major wildlife and wetland preservation area. Recycling of all waste water and use of solar energy add to the preservation image. Each bottle of Banrock Station wine sold generates funds for wildlife preservation, with $5 million already contributed. The wines have consistently offered excellent value, even the more expensive alternative variety releases that have recently come onto the market. Exports to the UK, the US and Canada.

Mediterranean Collection Tempranillo 2007 Bright colour; slightly earthy bouquet with dark cherry fruit; fleshy and generous with some cinnamon spice and juicy fruit on the finish. Screwcap. 13.2% alc. **Rating** 88 **To** 2012 $15
Mediterranean Collection Montepulciano 2007 A savoury bouquet of bramble and dark cherry; the palate is juicy on entry, and tightens up with savoury tannin and an earthy character that works well with the fruit. Cork. 13.8% alc. **Rating** 88 **To** 2012 $15
Mediterranean Collection Vermentino 2008 Toasty and lifted fruit aromas; clean and well made, with cleansing acidity, and a little grip on the finish. Screwcap. 12.7% alc. **Rating** 87 **To** 2011 $15

Barambah ★★★☆

GPO Box 799, Brisbane, QLD 4001 **Region** South Burnett
T 1300 781 815 **F** 1300 138 949 **www.**barambah.com.au **Open** Not
Winemaker Peter Scudamore-Smith MW (Contract) **Est.** 1995 **Cases** 1000 **Vyds** 12 ha
Barambah has been purchased by Brisbane couple Jane and Steve Wilson. They live in a historic 19th-century West End home, but have owned a 1600-ha cattle property, Barambah Station, for the past seven years. This made them near-neighbours of Barambah, and they had ample opportunity to watch the development of the estate vineyard and the quality of its wines. When the opportunity came to purchase the winery and vineyard, they obtained consultancy advice from Peter Scudamore-Smith MW. His response was so positive they did not hesitate to buy the property.

 First Grid Chardonnay 2008 Very well made, the barrel ferment oak perfectly integrated and balanced with the stone fruit and melon flavours of the chardonnay; good length. Screwcap. 13% alc. **Rating** 92 **To** 2015 $24

First Grid Semillon 2008 Early picking has preserved green grassy aromas and flavours, allied with apple and a touch of gooseberry; perhaps a little too green, or the acid too evident. Screwcap. 10% alc. **Rating** 88 **To** 2015 $19

Baratto's

Vineyard 674–678, Hanwood, NSW 2680 **Region** Riverina
T (02) 6963 0171 **Open** Wed–Fr 10–5 or by appt
Winemaker Peter Baratto **Est.** 1975 **Cases** NA **Vyds** 15 ha
Baratto's is in many ways a throwback to the old days. Peter Baratto has 15 ha of vineyards and sells the wine in bulk or in 10 and 20 litre casks from the cellar door at old-time prices, from as little as a few dollars per litre. Exports to China.

Bare Rooted

101 Broome Street, Cottesloe, WA 6011 (postal) **Region** Margaret River
T 0409 291 415 **F** (08) 9385 3120 **www**.barerooted.com.au **Open** Not
Winemaker Rockfield Estate **Est.** 1996 **Cases** 200 **Vyds** 0.3 ha
Ross and Jeannine Ashton planted sauvignon blanc in 1996, on their 8-ha property, surrounded by groves and avenues of poplars, cork oaks, deciduous trees, conifers, olives and eucalypts; a small frog-filled dam overlooks the vineyard. The quirky name comes from the fact that when vine rootlings are planted, they are devoid of any soil around their roots and are in a dormant phase.

Barnadown Run

390 Cornella Road, Toolleen, Vic 3551 **Region** Heathcote
T (03) 5433 6376 **F** (03) 5433 6386 **www**.barnadownrun.com.au **Open** 7 days 10–5
Winemaker Andrew Millis **Est.** 1995 **Cases** 1500 **Vyds** 5 ha
Named after the original pastoral lease of which the vineyard forms part, established on the rich terra rossa soil for which Heathcote vineyards are famous. Owner Andrew Millis carries out both the viticulture and winemaking at the vineyard, which is planted to cabernet sauvignon, merlot, shiraz and viognier. Exports to Canada, Norway, Hong Kong, Singapore and China.

🍷🍷🍷🍷🍷 **Jean's Block Heathcote Shiraz 2005** Crunchy ripe blueberry fruit, with fine delineation and very attractive allspice aromas; the palate is incredibly bright, with ample levels of ripe fruit, spice, a touch of minerally complexity and a long, fleshy finish; big, but very well balanced. Cork. 15% alc. **Rating** 95 **To** 2018 $28

Barokes Wines

Suite 402, 111 Cecil Street, South Melbourne, Vic 3205 (postal) **Region** Various
T (03) 9675 4349 **F** (03) 9675 4594 **www**.wineinacan.com **Open** Not
Winemaker Steve Barics **Est.** 2003 **Cases** 150 000
Barokes Wines packages its wines in aluminium cans. The filling process is patented, and the wine has been in commercial production since 2003. The wines show normal maturation and none of the cans used since start-up shows signs of corrosion. Wines are supplied in bulk by large wineries in southeastern Australia, with Peter Scudamore-Smith acting as blending consultant. The wines are perfectly adequate for the market they serve, with remarkably even quality, and are prolific winners of bronze and silver medals at international wine shows. Exports to all major markets with increasing success, with production rising from 60 000 to 150 000 cases (24 cans per case).

Barossa Valley Estate
★★★★★

Seppeltsfield Road, Marananga, SA 5355 **Region** Barossa Valley
T (08) 8562 3599 **F** (08) 8562 4255 **www**.bve.com.au **Open** 7 days 10–4.30
Winemaker Stuart Bourne **Est.** 1985 **Cases** 80 000 **Vyds** 40.12 ha
Barossa Valley Estate is jointly owned by Constellation Wines Australia and Barossa Growers Holdings Limited, the latter representing the grower shareholders of the original co-operative. The 40 ha of vines directly owned by Barossa Valley Estate (shiraz, cabernet sauvignon, merlot, grenache, chardonnay and marsanne) contribute only a small part of the production; most of

the grapes come from the grower shareholders. Across the board, the wines are full flavoured and honest. E&E Black Pepper Shiraz is an upmarket label with a strong reputation and following; the Ebenezer range likewise. Exports to the UK, the US and other major markets.

♟♟♟♟♟ **E&E Black Pepper Shiraz 2004** An immaculate representation of pure Barossa power and grace; dark fruits are laced with red; the fruit on the palate is pure, bright, focused, and incredibly long and harmonious; made with precision, skill and great care. Cork. 15% alc. **Rating** 96 **To** 2024 $99
E&E Black Pepper Shiraz 2005 Retains good hue; a sumptuously rich and velvety wine that has waves of black fruits, chocolate and mocha supported by fine, ripe tannins and good oak – and nary a hint of pepper, black or otherwise. Cork. 15% alc. **Rating** 94 **To** 2020 $90
Ebenezer Cabernet Sauvignon 2004 Complex cabernet; dark chocolate and mocha wrap around a generous palate driven by quite luscious blackcurrant fruit; even better than the '05; good quality cork. 14% alc. **Rating** 94 **To** 2014 $30

♟♟♟♟♡ **E Minor Cabernet Merlot 2006** Deep colour; masses of blackberry fruit along with dark chocolate and a touch of licorice; a tribute to the '06 vintage and the winemaking. Tip-top value. Screwcap. 14% alc. **Rating** 93 **To** 2016 $17
Ebenezer Cabernet Sauvignon 2005 Holding purple hue; shows what can be achieved with Barossa cabernet if the alcohol is held in check; has good structure and clear varietal expression; stained cork an issue. 14.5% alc. **Rating** 93 **To** 2015 $30
Ebenezer Shiraz 2005 The colour is still bright, and the wine is developing slowly but impressively; there are notes of spice and licorice behind the blackberry fruit of the medium-bodied palate, which has a fresh finish. Cork. 14.5% alc. **Rating** 92 **To** 2020 $30
E&E Sparkling Shiraz 2004 A bold, juicy and complex wine, with flavours of plum, black cherry and vanilla; is not too sweet and oaky, will repay cellaring. Cork. 14% alc. **Rating** 92 **To** 2015 $50

♟♟♟♟ **E Minor Shiraz 2006** Generous, medium- to full-bodied wine, with blackberry and plum fruit backed by good tannins and subtle oak; pretty nifty for a second label. Value. Screwcap. 14% alc. **Rating** 89 **To** 2016 $17

Barratt ★★★★★

Uley Vineyard, Cornish Road, Summertown, SA 5141 **Region** Adelaide Hills
T (08) 8390 1788 **F** (08) 8390 1788 **www.**barrattwines.com.au **Open** Fri–Sun & most public hols 11.30–5 (closed Jun–Jul)
Winemaker Lindsay Barratt **Est.** 1993 **Cases** 2000 **Vyds** 8.4 ha
Lindsay and Carolyn Barratt own two vineyards at Summertown: Uley Vineyard and Bonython Vineyard. Part of the production is sold to other makers, the Barratt wines are made at the winery facility at the Adelaide Hills Business and Tourism Centre in Lobethal. Limited quantities are exported to the UK, Taiwan and Singapore.

♟♟♟♟♟ **Piccadilly Valley Adelaide Hills Sauvignon Blanc 2008** Bright and vibrant; delicious, juicy citrus flavours a welcome left-field play; the palate has great line and balance, the finish fresh. Screwcap. 13.5% alc. **Rating** 94 **To** 2011 $23
Piccadilly Valley Chardonnay 2007 A fine nectarine and gentle spice bouquet; elegant palate with tightly wound fruit, and vibrant acidity with grilled nuts on the long, fine and even finish. Screwcap. 13.5% alc. **Rating** 94 **To** 2013 $30
The Reserve Piccadilly Valley Pinot Noir 2007 More weight and power than The Bonython, with distinctly more plummy fruit; showing tar, earth, spice and dark fruits, the wine offers a fleshier and more substantial experience. ProCork. 14% alc. **Rating** 94 **To** 2014 $44

♟♟♟♟♡ **The Bonython Piccadilly Valley Pinot Noir 2007** Light colour; cherry, plum and gentle spice bouquet; light-bodied with focused sweet red fruit core, and an attractive silky finish. Screwcap. 14% alc. **Rating** 90 **To** 2012 $27

ΨΨΨΨ **Piccadilly Sunrise Rose 2008** Salmon pink; savoury red fruit bouquet, and a slight herbaceous edge; dry and quite linear on the palate, with the suggestion of red fruit lingering on the finish. Screwcap. 13% alc. **Rating** 88 **To** 2011 $21

Barretts Wines ★★★★

Portland-Nelson Highway, Portland, Vic 3305 **Region** Henty
T (03) 5526 5251 **Open** 7 days 11–5
Winemaker Rod Barrett **Est.** 1983 **Cases** 1000 **Vyds** 4.5 ha
Has a low profile, selling its wines locally, but deserves a far wider audience. The initial releases were made at Best's, but since 1992 all wines have been made on the property by Rod Barrett, emulating John Thomson at Crawford River Wines. The vineyard is planted to riesling (2 ha) and pinot noir (2.5 ha).

ΨΨΨΨΨ **Riesling 2008** Steely, pure lime juice bouquet; the palate displays a touch of green apple, and has a mineral personality; very dry and focused finish. Screwcap. 12.5% alc. **Rating** 92 **To** 2015 $20

Barrgowan Vineyard

30 Pax Parade, Curlewis, Vic 3222 **Region** Geelong
T (03) 5250 3861 **F** (03) 5250 3840 **www**.barrgowanvineyard.com.au **Open** By appt
Winemaker Dick Simonsen **Est.** 1998 **Cases** 150 **Vyds** 0.5 ha
Dick and Dib (Elizabeth) Simonsen began the planting of their shiraz (with five clones) in 1994, intending to simply make wine for their own consumption. With all five clones in full production, the Simonsens expect a maximum production of 200 cases, and accordingly release small quantities of Shiraz, which sell out quickly. The vines are hand-pruned, the grapes hand-picked, the must basket-pressed, and all wine movements are by gravity.

ΨΨΨΨΨ **Simonsens Bellarine Peninsula Shiraz 2007** Good depth to colour; warm spice, licorice and French oak nuances on the bouquet lead into a fleshy, medium- to full-bodied palate that has excellent balance and mouthfeel, and years in front of it. Cork. 13.4% alc. **Rating** 94 **To** 2020 $25

Barringwood Park

60 Gillams Road, Lower Barrington, Tas 7306 **Region** Northern Tasmania
T (03) 6492 3140 **F** (03) 6492 3360 **www**.barringwoodpark.com.au **Open** Jan & Feb 7 days, March–Dec Wed–Sun & public hols 10–5
Winemaker Tom Ravich (Contract) **Est.** 1993 **Cases** 1800 **Vyds** 5.2 ha
Judy and Ian Robinson operate a sawmill at Lower Barrington, 15 minutes south of Devonport on the main tourist trail to Cradle Mountain, and when they planted 500 vines in 1993 the aim was to do a bit of home winemaking. In a thoroughly familiar story, the urge to expand the vineyard and make wine on a commercial scale soon occurred, and they embarked on a six-year plan, planting 1 ha a year in the first four years and building the cellar and tasting rooms during the following two years. Another 1.2 ha has recently been planted, and I think I must acknowledge some responsibility for urging the Robinsons to do so.

ΨΨΨΨΨ **Forest Raven Pinot Noir 2007** Very good colour and clarity; a succulent ripe mix of plum and black cherry; good continuity and energy. Screwcap. 13.5% alc. **Rating** 94 **To** 2014 $29
Mill Block Pinot Noir 2007 Packed with ripe fruit flavour; has energy and length; good balance and acidity. Top gold medal Tas Wine Show '09. Screwcap. 13.5% alc. **Rating** 94 **To** 2015 $35

ΨΨΨΨΨ **Pinot Gris 2008** A flowery bouquet; plenty of fruit weight on the palate lengthened by acidity. Screwcap. 14.5% alc. **Rating** 90 **To** 2011 $27.50

ΨΨΨΨ **Schonburger 2008** An aromatic, grapey bouquet; good fresh fruit flavours on the palate that has length and balance. Screwcap. 12.1% alc. **Rating** 89 **To** 2012 $25

Barristers Block ★★★★

141 Onkaparinga Valley Road, Woodside, SA 5244 **Region** Adelaide Hills
T 0427 076 237 **F** (08) 8364 2930 **www.**barristersblock.com.au **Open** 7 days 10–5
Winemaker Richard Langford, Simon Greenleaf (Contract) **Est.** 2004 **Cases** 2500
Vyds 18 ha
Owner Jan Siemelink-Allen has had 20 years in the industry, and five years in SA's Supreme
Court in a successful battle to reclaim ownership of 10 ha of cabernet sauvignon and shiraz in
Wrattonbully after a joint venture collapsed; it is not hard to imagine the origin of the name.
In 2006 she and her family purchased an 8-ha vineyard planted to sauvignon blanc and pinot
noir near Woodside in the Adelaide Hills, adjoining Shaw & Smith's vineyard. As well as having
senior management positions, Jan is a member of the SA Premier's Wine Industry Advisory
Council; no rose-tinted spectacles here. Exports to the UK, Germany, Vietnam, Malaysia,
Hong Kong and Singapore.

 Adelaide Hills Sauvignon Blanc 2008 Pale colour; quite intense pungent
aromas of fresh cut grass and a touch of tropical fruit; clean and fresh, the palate
exhibits weight and texture that is tightened by good acidity on the finish.
Screwcap. 13% alc. **Rating** 91 **To** 2012 $21
Bully Barossa Wrattonbully Shiraz 2007 Blackberry, mulberry and fruitcake
spice bouquet; medium-bodied, fleshy and with a hint of tar providing complexity
and freshness to the finish. Screwcap. 15% alc. **Rating** 90 **To** 2015 $25

 Wrattonbully Cabernet Sauvignon 2006 A very minty bouquet, with ripe
cassis fruit beneath; dark and brooding, the alcohol at 15.5% sits apart from the
fruit and provides heat on the finish. Zork. **Rating** 87 **To** 2014 $25
Barossa Valley Sparkling GSM 2006 Quite juicy and varietal, with raspberry
fruit and a little spice; a drier style, with a bit of grip on the finish; should be
drunk in the short term. Cork. 14.5% alc. **Rating** 87 **To** 2012 $18.50

Barton Estate ★★★

2307 Barton Highway, Murrumbateman, NSW 2582 **Region** Canberra District
T (02) 6230 9553 **F** (02) 6230 9565 **www.**bartonestate.com.au **Open** Not
Winemaker Brindabella Hills, Kyeema Estate, Canberra Winemakers **Est.** 1997
Cases 900 **Vyds** 8 ha
Bob Furbank and wife Julie Chitty are both CSIRO plant biologists: he is a biochemist
(physiologist) and she is a specialist in plant tissue culture. In 1997 they acquired the 120-ha
property forming part of historic Jeir Station, and have since planted 15 grape varieties. The
most significant plantings to cabernet sauvignon, shiraz, merlot, riesling and chardonnay,
Joseph's coat completed with micro quantities of other varieties.

 Georgia Canberra Shiraz 2006 Spicy and savoury bouquet, some red fruit
and a prominent cinnamon character; medium-bodied and quite cool, with good
flavour and bright acidity to conclude. Screwcap. 13.5% alc. **Rating** 87 **To** 2014

Barton Vineyard ★★★★

2464 Macquarie Road, Campbell Town, Tas 7210 **Region** Northern Tasmania
T (03) 6398 5114 **www.**bartonvineyards.com **Open** Last Sunday each month or by appt
Winemaker Rebecca Wilson (pinot noir), Winemaking Tasmania (riesling and sparkling)
Est. 2001 **Cases** 350 **Vyds** 2 ha
This is the venture of Milly and Frank Youl. Frank is a sixth-generation Tasmanian with a
farming background, on a merino sheep stud; the property, long known as Barton, is adjacent
to the Macquarie River. After planting a few trial vines in 1987, the Youls finally took the
plunge (ignoring most advice) and planted pinot noir and riesling on a north-facing slope
in 2001. They have a small cottage for fly fishers near the Macquarie River, and I believe
I stayed in that cottage one year with fellow judges from the Tasmanian Wines Show. The
cottage brings the Youl family history full circle, as forebear James Youl introduced trout into
Australia.

ΨΨΨΨΨ **Riesling 2008** Pleasing style with nicely balanced line and tropical fruit nuances; has continuity and balance. Screwcap. **Rating** 90 **To** 2015 $22

Barwang Vineyard ★★★★★

Barwang Road, Young, NSW 2594 (postal) **Region** Hilltops
T (02) 6382 3594 **F** (02) 6382 2594 **www.**mcwilliams.com.au **Open** Not
Winemaker Andrew Higgins **Est.** 1969 **Cases** NFP **Vyds** 100 ha
Peter Robertson pioneered viticulture in the Young region when he planted his first vines in 1969 as part of a diversification program for his 400-ha grazing property. When McWilliam's acquired Barwang in 1989, the vineyard amounted to 13 ha; today the plantings are 100 ha. Wine quality has been exemplary from the word go: always elegant, restrained and deliberately understated, repaying extended cellaring. The Barwang label also takes in 100% Tumbarumba wines, as well as Hilltops/Tumbarumba blends.

ΨΨΨΨΨ **2006 Barwang Vineyard 842 Tumbarumba Chardonnay** Developing slowly but with extreme grace; driven by nectarine and grapefruit on both bouquet and palate, the French oak evident but balanced; has wonderful even flow through to a lingering finish. Screwcap. 13% alc. **Rating** 96 **To** 2020 $35
Tumbarumba Sauvignon Blanc 2007 A spotlessly clean bouquet, with nuances of passionfruit that intensify on the vibrant palate, and a lingering, fresh finish. Impressive. Screwcap. 11.5% alc. **Rating** 94 **To** 2010 $19.95
Tumbarumba Hilltops Chardonnay 2006 Bright, light straw-green; a brilliant wine at the price, with vibrant grapefruit and nectarine flavours; the oak has been well used as the final touch to a quality wine. Screwcap. 13% alc. **Rating** 94 **To** 2015 $19.99

ΨΨΨΨΨ **Reserve Tumbarumba Chardonnay 2006** Ripe peach and dried straw bouquet; focused citrus palate, with real depth to the fruit; long, toasty and fresh on the finish. Screwcap. 13% alc. **Rating** 92 **To** 2014 $19.99
Hilltops Shiraz 2007 Strong purple-red; a medium- to full-bodied wine with more weight and extract than most previous vintages; blackberry, licorice and spice are framed by powerful tannins. For the long haul, and a bargain. Screwcap. 14% alc. **Rating** 91 **To** 2022 $19.99
Hilltops Cabernet Sauvignon 2006 Good colour; like the Shiraz, has more tannins and extract than earlier vintages, but the black fruits and oak have the strength to carry the extract. Simply needs time. Screwcap. 14.5% alc. **Rating** 90 **To** 2020 $19.99

ΨΨΨΨ **Tumbarumba Pinot Gris 2008** Unusually tangy, citrussy overtones to the more usual pear and apple; good length and intensity. Screwcap. 14.5% alc. **Rating** 89 **To** 2010 $19.99

Barwick Wines ★★★★

Yelverton North Road, Dunsborough, WA 6281 **Region** Margaret River
T (08) 9755 7100 **F** (08) 9755 7133 **www.**barwickwines.com **Open** 7 days 11–4
Winemaker Nigel Ludlow **Est.** 1997 **Cases** 120 000 **Vyds** 194 ha
The production gives some guide to the size of the three estate vineyards. The first is the Dwalganup Vineyard in the Blackwood Valley region; the second is St John's Brook Vineyard in Margaret River; and the third is the Treenbrook Vineyard in Pemberton. Taken together, the three vineyard holdings place Barwick in the top 10 wine producers in WA. The wines are released under four labels: at the bottom, the Crush Label; next, the White Label estate range; next, the Black Label single-vineyard wines from any one of the three regions; and at the top The Collectables from small parcels of estate-grown grapes. Exports to the UK, the US and other major markets.

ΨΨΨΨΨ **Margaret River Sauvignon Blanc 2008** Good focus and intensity to the grass, herb and capsicum on both bouquet and palate; has good thrust through the long finish. Screwcap. 13% alc. **Rating** 93 **To** 2011 $19.95

Semillon Sauvignon Blanc 2008 Fragrant and juicy style; grass, lime and gooseberry aromas and flavours run seamlessly through the bouquet and well-balanced palate. Screwcap. 12% alc. **Rating** 90 **To** 2012 $14.95

Margaret River Shiraz Cabernet 2007 Well-made medium-bodied wine, with a lively mix of blackberry and blackcurrant fruit plus a dusting of spice and black pepper. Screwcap. 14% alc. **Rating** 90 **To** 2016 $19.95

ɧɧɧɧ **The Collectables Blackwood Shiraz 2005** Plenty of depth, structure and flavour but the line is broken; slightly sweet. Screwcap. 14.5% alc. **Rating** 89 **To** 2013 $35

Collectables Cabernet Sauvignon 2005 Aromatic and flavoursome; some green minty notes intrude slightly. Screwcap. 14% alc. **Rating** 87 **To** 2012 $35

Barwite Vineyards ★★★★☆

PO Box 542, Mansfield, Vic 3724 **Region** Upper Goulburn
T 0408 525 135 **F** (03) 5776 9800 **www**.barwitevineyards.com.au **Open** Not
Winemaker Delatite (Jane Donat) **Est.** 1997 **Cases** 1000
David Ritchie and a group of fellow grape and wine enthusiasts established their substantial vineyard in 1997 on a slope facing the mouth of the Broken River and thereon to Mt Stirling. Pinot noir (28 ha) and chardonnay (9 ha) were planted for Orlando, to be used in sparkling wine. Given the reputation of the region for the production of aromatic white wines, 4.5 ha of riesling were also planted, the intention being to sell the grapes. However, since 2003 some of the best parcels have been kept aside for the Barwite label.

ɧɧɧɧɧ **Upper Goulburn Riesling 2008** Fragrant citrus blossom and herb aromas lead into a focused and intense palate, with lime and lemon fruit fused with the acidity; lovely wine. Screwcap. 12% alc. **Rating** 94 **To** 2015 $16

ɧɧɧɧ꒤ **Upper Goulburn Chardonnay 2008** A tangy and fresh chardonnay reflecting its cool climate, the zesty finish long and satisfying. Altogether a high quality unoaked style. Value. Screwcap. 13% alc. **Rating** 90 **To** 2012 $16

ɧɧɧɧ **Upper Goulburn Pinot Noir 2006** From the Southern Alps near Mansfield; plunging open vats six times a day has over-extracted the wine, making it uncomfortably savoury; nonetheless, a bold effort, and the wine has length and varietal character. Screwcap. 14% alc. **Rating** 88 **To** 2011 $18

Barwon Ridge Wines ★★☆

50 McMullans Road, Barrabool, Vic 3221 **Region** Geelong
T 0418 324 632 **F** (03) 9882 4587 **www**.barwonridge.com.au **Open** By appt
Winemaker Geoff Anson, Ken King **Est.** 1999 **Cases** NA
This is the venture of Geoff and Joan Anson, and Ken King (who also owns Kings of Kangaroo Ground and manages the Eltham post office out of his winery). The partners have established 3.6 ha of pinot noir, shiraz, chardonnay, marsanne and cabernet sauvignon on the northern side of a ridge above the Barwon River, overlooking the You Yangs and ultimately the plains towards Port Phillip. Drought conditions since 1999, and limited access to water, has meant that many vines had to be replaced, and the vineyard has grown slowly. In the meantime limited quantities of grapes sourced from Geelong vineyards are being purchased, and the wines made at the Kangaroo Ground winery by the partners.

Basedow ★★☆

951 Bylong Valley Way, Baerami via Denman, NSW 2333 (postal) **Region** Barossa Valley
T 1300 887 966 **F** (02) 6574 5164 **www**.wineforlife.com.au **Open** Not
Winemaker Graeme Scott, Deane Rose, Tony Hewitt **Est.** 1896 **Cases** 25 000
An old and proud label, once particularly well known for its oak-matured Semillon, but which has changed hands on a number of occasions before passing into the ownership of James Estate in 2003. Continues making traditional styles, big in flavour, but not so much in finesse, the alcohol remaining relatively high.

Bass Fine Wines

★★★★☆

16 Goodman Court, Invermay, Launceston, Tas 7250 **Region** Northern Tasmania
T (03) 6331 0136 **F** (03) 6331 0136 **Open** Mon–Fri 9–5, w'ends 9–4
Winemaker Guy Wagner **Est.** 1999 **Cases** 3000
Owner/winemaker Guy Wagner has built the scope of his business over a period of 10 years, the greater expansion starting on 2007-08. He now makes wines for 17 small vineyards in Northern Tasmania in addition to his own wines; the 2008 crush was over 220 tonnes, with just one cellar hand to assist him. At the end of that year his partnership in the Rosevears winery ended, and a new winery was constructed prior to the 2009 vintage at Invermay, well inside the city of Launceston. The cellar door at this location has glass walls, allowing visitors to observe the workings of a small winery. Retail distribution in Tasmania, Vic, NSW and ACT. Exports to the US.

🍷🍷🍷🍷🍷 **Strait Chardonnay 2007** Bright green–yellow; a rich wine with layers of rounded fruit in a peach/melon spectrum; some struck match gives complexity. Gold medal Tas Wine Show '09. Screwcap. 13.5% alc. **Rating** 94 **To** 2015 $24

🍷🍷🍷🍷🍷 **Strait Pinot Noir 2008** Has generous plum/black cherry fruit supported by superfine tannins; good acidity and length. Screwcap. 13.5% alc. **Rating** 90 **To** 2014 $24

🍷🍷🍷🍷 **Strait Chardonnay 2008** Glowing yellow–green; full of peach flavour, but not quite enough focus or acidity. Screwcap. 13.5% alc. **Rating** 89 **To** 2013 $24
Riverview Pinot Noir 2007 Light crimson; light-bodied and lively red fruits with stemmy notes cutting across just a little too strongly. Screwcap. 13.5% alc. **Rating** 88 **To** 2012 $35

Bass Phillip

★★★★★

Tosch's Road, Leongatha South, Vic 3953 **Region** Gippsland
T (03) 5664 3341 **F** (03) 5664 3209 **Open** By appt
Winemaker Phillip Jones **Est.** 1979 **Cases** 1500
Phillip Jones retired from the Melbourne rat-race to handcraft tiny quantities of superlative Pinot Noir which, at its best, has no equal in Australia. Painstaking site selection, ultra-close vine spacing and the very, very cool climate of South Gippsland are the keys to the magic of Bass Phillip and its eerily Burgundian pinots. Tastings are sporadic and the rating is very much that of the best, not the lesser, wines.

🍷🍷🍷🍷🍷 **The Estate Pinot Noir 2007** An extremely complex and unusual wine from start to finish, with excellent mouthfeel and great length; a mix of *fraise du bois*, spice and plum; lingering aftertaste. Diam. 12.8% alc. **Rating** 96 **To** 2015 $70
Estate Chardonnay 2007 Fragrant nectarine blossom aromas lead into a supple and smooth palate with melon, nectarine and fig notes, the oak totally integrated; low alcohol gives the wine natural freshness and balance. Cork. 12.7% alc. **Rating** 95 **To** 2015 $45
Crown Prince Pinot Noir 2007 Colour not bright, but hue is good; not filtered; arresting smoky/stemmy bouquet; intense and very complex palate, with an array of ripe and sous bois flavours, although a fractionally bitter finish. Diam. 12.6% alc. **Rating** 94 **To** 2014 $52

Bass River Winery

★★★

1835 Dalyston Glen Forbes Road, Glen Forbes, Vic 3990 **Region** Gippsland
T (03) 5678 8252 **F** (03) 9462 2527 **www.**bassriverwinery.com **Open** Thurs–Tues 9–5
Winemaker Pasquale Butera, Frank Butera **Est.** 1999 **Cases** 400 **Vyds** 4 ha
The Butera family has established pinot noir (1 ha), chardonnay (0.75 ha), riesling, sauvignon blanc, pinot gris (0.5 ha each) and cabernet sauvignon (0.25 ha), with both the winemaking and viticulture handled by the father and son team of Pasquale and Frank. The small production is principally sold through the cellar door plus some retailers and restaurants in the South Gippsland area.

♟♟♟♟ **Rose 2008** Savoury dried red fruit bouquet with a meaty edge; a soft, dry palate with spicy mulberry fruit finish. Screwcap. 11.5% alc. **Rating** 87 **To** 2011 $18

Battle of Bosworth ★★★★☆

Edgehill Vineyards, Gaffney Road, Willunga, SA 5172 **Region** McLaren Vale
T (08) 8556 2441 **F** (08) 8556 4881 **www**.battleofbosworth.com.au **Open** By appt
Winemaker Joch Bosworth **Est.** 1996 **Cases** 5000 **Vyds** 77 ha
Battle of Bosworth is owned and run by Joch Bosworth (viticulture and winemaking) and partner Louise Hemsley-Smith (sales and marketing). The wines take their name from the Battle of Bosworth (which ended the War of the Roses), fought on Bosworth Field, Leicestershire in 1485. The vineyards were established in the early 1970s, by parents Peter and Anthea, in the foothills of the Mount Lofty Ranges in McLaren Vale. Conversion to organic viticulture began in 1995, with vines now 20 years and older fully certified A-grade organic by ACO. The label depicts the yellow soursob (*oxalis pes caprae*), hated by gardeners everywhere, but whose growth habits make it an ideal weapon with which to battle weeds in organic viticulture. Shiraz, cabernet sauvignon and chardonnay account for three-quarters of the plantings, with an additional nine varieties making up the numbers. Exports to the UK, the US and other major markets.

♟♟♟♟♟ **McLaren Vale Shiraz 2007** Bright colour; a serious bouquet of mocha, black fruit, tar and a good splash of well-handled oak; fresh and focused, with vibrant acid, plentiful tannins, and a positive step-up from previous vintages; proof that organic wine can be delicious, even in a tough vintage. Screwcap. 14.5% alc. **Rating** 95 **To** 2020 $24

♟♟♟♟♀ **McLaren Vale Shiraz Viognier 2007** Quite a dark and savoury bouquet, with black fruit supported by a touch of Provençale herbs; the palate is warm and chewy, with a vibrant acid backbone providing freshness on the finish. Screwcap. 14% alc. **Rating** 93 **To** 2014 $24
The War of the Rose 2008 Made in a dry style, but with plenty of red fruit flavour, and just a little savoury complexity; dry and long. Screwcap. 13% alc. **Rating** 90 **To** 2012 $18

♟♟♟♟ **Spring Seed Wine Co Four O'Clock McLaren Vale Chardonnay 2008** Six pickings over a 10-day period, one batch fermented oxidatively, reflect the effort to give this unwooded chardonnay more complexity than normal, and succeeds to a sufficient degree. Screwcap. 13.5% alc. **Rating** 87 **To** 2011 $15
McLaren Vale Cabernet Sauvignon 2007 Slightly soupy cabernet bouquet, with an amalgam of red and black fruits and a touch of shrivel on show; the palate is generous and quite tannic, with the firmness playing the winning hand at this point. Screwcap. 14% alc. **Rating** 87 **To** 2014 $24

🍇 Bawley Vale Estate ★★☆

226 Bawley Point Road, Bawley Point, NSW 2539 **Region** Shoalhaven Coast
T (02) 4457 2555 **F** (02) 4457 2649 **www**.bawleyvaleestate.com.au **Open** W'ends & public hols 11–4.30
Winemaker Crooked River Winery **Est.** 2003 **Cases** 2500 **Vyds** 2.4 ha
Bawley Vale Estate sits on 40 ha of prime south coast land acquired by Raymond and Loris McLoughlin in 2003. They have planted 0.7 ha of cabernet sauvignon, 0.4 ha each of verdelho, chardonnay and shiraz, 0.3 ha of chambourcin, 0.2 ha of arneis, plus small plantings of merlot, along with citrus and olive groves. The wines are sold through local restaurants and bottle shops and (of course) via the cellar door and website.

Bay of Fires ★★★★★

40 Baxters Road, Pipers River, Tas 7252 **Region** Northern Tasmania
T (03) 6382 7666 **F** (03) 6382 7027 **www**.bayoffireswines.com.au **Open** 7 days 10–5
Winemaker Fran Austin **Est.** 2001 **Cases** NFP

In 1994 Hardys purchased its first grapes from Tasmania with the aim of further developing and refining its sparkling wines, a process that quickly gave birth to Arras. The next stage was the inclusion of various parcels of chardonnay from Tasmania in the 1998 Eileen Hardy, then the development in '01 of the Bay of Fires brand, offering wines sourced from various parts of Tasmania. The winery was originally that of Rochecombe, then Ninth Island, and now, of course, Bay of Fires. Its potential has now been fully realised in the most impressive imaginable fashion. Exports to all major markets.

ŸŸŸŸŸ **Arras Pinot Noir Chardonnay 2003** Glowing yellow-green; it has exceptional intensity on the bouquet and palate alike; stone fruit, citrus and creamy brioche flavours flow seamlessly along the palate, the finish lingering for minutes. Cork. 13.1% alc. **Rating** 96 **To** 2015 $75
Riesling 2008 Sourced from a number of small vineyards; touches of herb with contrasting spicy notes running through the lime/citrus fruit core; has glorious length. Screwcap. 11.7% alc. **Rating** 94 **To** 2014 $36
Pinot Noir 2008 Good colour; clear varietal plum/black cherry fruit on the bouquet and palate given complexity by some barrel ferment characters. Gold medal Sydney Wine Show. Screwcap. 13.5% alc. **Rating** 94 **To** 2015 $38
Pinot Noir 2007 Has power but also vibrancy and thrust; good line to the cherry plum fruit; fine tannins on the finish. Gold medal Sydney Wine Show. Screwcap. 13.5% alc. **Rating** 94 **To** 2014 $38.50
Pinot Noir Chardonnay 2003 Pale bronze-salmon; very intense and long flavours; precise and zesty, with some positive aldehyde. Gold medal Tas Wine Show '09. Cork 13.4% alc. **Rating** 94 **To** 2013 $38.50

ŸŸŸŸŸ **Non Vintage Pinot Noir Chardonnay NV** Pale and bright; fine citrus fruit, and a touch brioche on the bouquet; fine bead, with a delicate mousse, chalky acidity and a focused finish. Cork. 12.6% alc. **Rating** 92 **To** 2014 $30
Pinot Gris 2008 Precise pinot gris flavours of pear, apple and a little spice; given no elaboration by oak or whatever else. A challenging price. Screwcap. 13.5% alc. **Rating** 90 **To** 2012 $36
Sparkling Rose NV Pale salmon blush; delicate red fruits, and pure citrus bouquet; quite fine on the palate, with a delicate bead, and a bit of grip to conclude; slightly savoury. Cork. 12.7% alc. **Rating** 90 **To** 2012 $30

Bay of Shoals   ★★★★☆

Cordes Road, Kingscote, Kangaroo Island, SA 5223 **Region** Kangaroo Island
T (08) 8553 0289 **F** (08) 8553 2081 **www**.bayofshoalswines.com.au **Open** 7 days 11–5
Winemaker Ruth Pledge **Est.** 1994 **Cases** NA **Vyds** 10 ha
John Willoughby's vineyard overlooks the Bay of Shoals, which is the northern boundary of Kingscote, Kangaroo Island's main town. Planting of the vineyard began in 1994 and it now comprises riesling, chardonnay, sauvignon blanc, cabernet sauvignon and shiraz. In addition, 460 olive trees have been planted to produce table olives.

ŸŸŸŸŸ **Kangaroo Island Chardonnay 2008** Very lively and juicy, with intense nectarine and grapefruit flavours backed by good acidity. Very good value. Screwcap. 13.2% alc. **Rating** 93 **To** 2015 $18
Kangaroo Island Shiraz 2007 Strong red-purple; has good mouthfeel and structure to the medium-bodied palate, with damson plum, blackberry and licorice fruit supported by supple tannins; good oak handling. Screwcap. 14.6% alc. **Rating** 92 **To** 2017 $20
Kangaroo Island Cabernet Sauvignon 2007 Ripe fruit introduces nuances of raspberry, blueberry and plum alongside more usual blackcurrant; good mouthfeel and soft tannins. Screwcap. 14.8% alc. **Rating** 90 **To** 2017 $20

ŸŸŸŸ **Island Blend 2007** Very rich and ripe flavours no surprise given the alcohol, ripe tannin likewise, vanillin oak ditto (85% new American oak). An unabashed Antipodean blend of Shiraz/Cabernet Sauvignon/Merlot. Screwcap. 15.5% alc. **Rating** 89 **To** 2017 $20

Kangaroo Island Riesling 2008 Lime and mineral bouquet; tight and linear palate, with quite accentuated lemon on the finish. Screwcap. 12.8% alc. **Rating** 87 To 2014 $18

Kangaroo Island Sauvignon Blanc 2008 An aromatic, rich and complex bouquet comes at the expense of freshness on the palate, which shows very ripe tropical fruit and minimal acidity. Will please some. Screwcap. 14% alc. **Rating** 87 To 2010 $18

Beckett's Flat

49 Beckett Road, Metricup, WA 6280 **Region** Margaret River
T (08) 9755 7402 **F** (08) 9755 7344 **www.**beckettsflat.com.au **Open** 7 days 10–6
Winemaker Belizar Ilic **Est.** 1992 **Cases** 8000 **Vyds** 13.6 ha
Belizar (Bill) and Noni Ilic opened Beckett's Flat in 1997. Situated just off the Bussell Highway, midway between Busselton and the Margaret River, it draws upon estate vineyards, first planted in 1992 (cabernet sauvignon, shiraz, sauvignon blanc, chardonnay, verdelho, semillon and merlot). The wines, which are made onsite, include a range of kosher wines under the Five Stones label. Exports to the US and Canada.

Belizar's Reserve Margaret River Chardonnay 2005 Showing a little toasty development, with grapefruit and a suggestion of grilled nuts; a lively palate, with plenty going on; the whole kitchen sink in the winemaker's armoury has been thrown at this wine, and it handles it well. Screwcap. 14% alc. **Rating** 92 To 2013 $25

Belizar's Reserve Justinian 2005 The bouquet has notes of leaf, cedar and cassis; the palate is dry and lean, showing persistent black fruit from start to finish. Merlot/Cabernet Sauvignon. Screwcap. 13.5% alc. **Rating** 89 **To** 2014 $29

Beckingham Wines

6–7/477 Warrigal Road, Moorabbin, Vic 3189 **Region** Mornington Peninsula
T 0400 192 264 **www.**beckinghamwines.com.au **Open** W'ends 10–5
Winemaker Peter Beckingham **Est.** 1998 **Cases** 4000 **Vyds** 3 ha
Peter Beckingham is a chemical engineer who has turned a hobby into a business, moving operations from the driveway of his house to a warehouse in Moorabbin. The situation of the winery may not be romantic, but it is eminently practical, and more than a few winemakers in California have adopted the same solution. His friends grow the grapes, and he makes the wine, both for himself and as a contract maker for others.

Beelgara

Farm 576 Rossetto Road, Beelbangera, NSW 2680 **Region** Riverina
T (02) 6966 0200 **www.**beelgara.com.au **Open** Mon–Sat 10–5, Sun 10–4
Winemaker Rod Hooper, Danny Toaldo, Sean Hampel **Est.** 1930 **Cases** 650 000
Beelgara Estate was formed in 2001 after the purchase of the 60-year-old Rossetto family winery by a group of growers, distributors and investors. The emphasis has changed significantly, with a concerted effort to go to the right region for each variety (in the Regional Reserve range), while still maintaining good value for money. Exports to the UK and other major markets.

Regional Reserve Clare Valley Shiraz 2006 Powerful, concentrated, chunky Clare shiraz, with a mix of blackberry, dark chocolate, licorice and vanilla; pleasantly fine tannins. Screwcap. 14.5% alc. **Rating** 92 To 2016 $19.95

Rascals Prayer Chardonnay 2008 Light straw-green; a fresh, light-bodied chardonnay, with some Adelaide Hills fruit and an airbrush of oak, and a somewhat surprising silver medal from the Adelaide Wine Show '08 to its credit. Screwcap. 12.5% alc. **Rating** 89 To 2010 $15

Regional Reserve Yarra Valley Chardonnay 2007 Light, fresh and clean, with hallmark Yarra Valley length; while not particularly complex, is well balanced. Screwcap. 12% alc. **Rating** 88 **To** 2011 $19.95

Winemakers Selection Adelaide Hills Sauvignon Blanc 2008 Has clear varietal expression, the aromas and flavours straddling grassy capsicum through to more tropical notes. Screwcap. 13% alc. **Rating** 87 **To** 2010 $16

Bianca Sun Dried Botrytis Semillon 2006 Incredibly sweet and concentrated with pure apricot marmalade character dominating from go to whoa; a little more acid would be better still. Cork. 11.5% alc. **Rating** 87 **To** 2015 $20

Belgravia Vineyards ★★★★

84 Byng Street, Orange, NSW 2800 **Region** Orange
T (02) 6361 4441 **www.**belgravia.com.au **Open** Sun–Thurs 10–8, Fri–Sat 10–late
Winemaker David Lowe, Jane Wilson (Contract) **Est.** 2003 **Cases** 6000
Belgravia is an 1800-ha mixed farming property (sheep, cattle and vines) 20 km north of Orange. There are now 190 ha of vineyard with 10 ha devoted to the Belgravia brand. In 2006 Belgravia opened its cellar door at the heritage-listed former Union Bank building in Orange, which also operates as a wine bar and restaurant. Exports to the UK and Denmark.

 Orange Sauvignon Blanc 2008 Well made, with an abundance of tropical fruit on both bouquet and palate, neatly offset by some grassy/capsicum nuances; good length. Screwcap. 13.9% alc. **Rating** 92 **To** 2010 $19.99

Orange Riesling 2008 Light lime blossom aromas; light but quite persistent and juicy lime and apple flavours; good development potential. Screwcap. 11.7% alc. **Rating** 91 **To** 2014 $19.95

Orange Pinot Gris 2008 Has above average aroma and flavour interest, with distinct dried fruit/pear flavours offset by good acidity. Screwcap. 13.5% alc. **Rating** 90 **To** 2010 $19.95

 Orange Gewurztraminer 2008 Typical of the majority of cool-grown gewurztraminers; a faint background of floral spice and lychee, and a clean finish. Screwcap. 13.9% alc. **Rating** 87 **To** 2012 $19.95

Bella Ridge Estate ★★☆

78 Campersic Road, Herne Hill, WA 6056 **Region** Swan District
T (08) 9250 4962 **F** (08) 9246 0244 **www.**bellaridge.com.au **Open** By appt
Winemaker Alon Arbel **Est.** 2003 **Cases** 3000 **Vyds** 8 ha
Alon Arbel came to WA from Israel in search of strong, easterly sea breezes to power his passion for windsurfing. Here he met wife-to-be, Jodi, and, after working overseas and travelling, they returned to Perth. A year out from completing a degree in engineering, Alon switched to Curtin University's oenology and viticulture course, which he duly completed. Entirely fortuitously, Jodi's parents, Frank and Lois, discovered a 10-ha property on the foothills of the Darling Scarp, with plantings dating back to 1966. The purchase of the property was a couple of months before commencement of the '04 vintage, by which time they had managed to erect a 30-tonne winery, crushing 20 tonnes of fruit for their own label and 10 tonnes for contract clients. Since then they have grafted the plantings to an ultra-eclectic mix, which includes the Japanese variety kyoho. Exports to Singapore.

Bellarine Estate ★★★★★

2270 Portarlington Road, Bellarine, Vic 3222 **Region** Geelong
T (03) 5259 3310 **F** (03) 5259 3393 **www.**bellarineestate.com.au **Open** 7 days 11–4
Winemaker Anthony Brain **Est.** 1995 **Cases** 6000 **Vyds** 12 ha
Important changes were made at Bellarine Estate prior to the 2007 vintage, with an onsite winery commissioned, and Anthony Brain (with extensive cool-climate winemaking experience) installed as winemaker. The vineyard is planted to chardonnay, pinot noir, shiraz, merlot, viognier and sauvignon blanc. The winery was opened in time for the 2007 vintage

and offers small-run bottling services for others. Julian's Restaurant is open for lunch seven days and dinner Fri/Sat evenings. Exports to the US.

🍷🍷🍷🍷🍷 **Two Wives Geelong Shiraz 2006** Dense, vivid colour momentarily stains the glass when swirled; layers of blackberry, licorice, stewed plum and spice fill the mouth and finish. Does carry its alcohol, but might have been even better with less. Screwcap. 14.8% alc. **Rating** 94 **To** 2020 $30

Cellar Reserve Geelong Shiraz Viognier 2007 Bright crimson-purple; a highly fragrant bouquet leads into a luscious and vibrant palate, the co-fermented viognier adding lift to the juicy, spicy red berry fruits; very good wine. Screwcap. 14.5% alc. **Rating** 94 **To** 2017 $36

🍷🍷🍷🍷 **Two Wives Geelong Shiraz 2007** Deep purple-crimson; spice and anise aromas are built into the medium-bodied palate, with plum and blackberry fruit; good length and balanced extract. Screwcap. 14.4% alc. **Rating** 92 **To** 2017 $30

Portarlington Ridge Geelong Pinot Noir 2006 Good colour retention; pure cherry and plum fruit on bouquet and palate; still tight and youthful thanks to almost citrussy acidity; needs yet more time. Value. Screwcap. 14.5% alc. **Rating** 90 **To** 2014 $17.50

James' Paddock Geelong Chardonnay 2007 A powerful and emphatic wine, with strong nectarine and white clingstone peach framed by positive, nutty French oak. Needs food to calm it down. Screwcap. 14.2% alc. **Rating** 90 **To** 2013 $28

OMK Geelong Viognier 2007 A well-made, powerful wine, with an array of blossom aromas and flavours moving through peach, spice and apricot; no shortage of flavour. Screwcap. 14.5% alc. **Rating** 90 **To** 2012 $26.50

Julian's Geelong Merlot 2006 Shows yet again the remarkable consistency of the Bellarine Estate house style, with emphatic, bright cassis/redcurrant fruit and a punchy finish. Screwcap. 14.3% alc. **Rating** 90 **To** 2014 $28

🍷🍷🍷🍷 **Phil's Fetish Geelong Pinot Noir 2007** Peculiar wine, the aroma and flavour suggestive of far riper grapes than the alcohol discloses; potent rhubarb characters throughout. Screwcap. 13.2% alc. **Rating** 88 **To** 2011 $32

Bellarmine Wines ★★★★☆

1 Balyan Retreat, Pemberton, WA 6260 (postal) **Region** Pemberton
T (08) 9844 9654 **F** (08) 9206 0270 **www**.bellarmine.com.au **Open** Not
Winemaker Dr Diane Miller **Est.** 2000 **Cases** 6000 **Vyds** 20 ha

This vineyard is owned by German residents Dr Willi and Gudrun Schumacher. Long-term wine lovers, the Schumachers decided to establish a vineyard and winery of their own, using Australia partly because of its stable political climate. The vineyard is planted to merlot, pinot noir, chardonnay, shiraz, riesling, sauvignon blanc and petit verdot. Following the departure of long-term winemaker Mike Bewsher, Diane Miller, previously head of the Vintage Wineworx contract winemaking facility, was appointed winemaker and operations manager. Exports to Germany.

🍷🍷🍷🍷🍷 **Pemberton Riesling 2008** Pale colour and vibrant hue; restrained green apple bouquet with a backbone of minerality; the palate is off-dry with pure fruit, focused acidity and an even Mosel-like slatey finish. Screwcap. 11.3% alc. **Rating** 94 **To** 2013 $18

🍷🍷🍷🍷 **Pemberton Riesling Dry 2008** Very pale straw-green; fragrant lime and apple bouquet; a delicate palate of good purity; time will build depth. Screwcap. 12.5% alc. **Rating** 93 **To** 2015 $18

Pemberton Sauvignon Blanc 2008 Tropical fruit and green nettle bouquet; ripe, generous, focused and lively on the finish; varietal with true focus. Screwcap. 12.5% alc. **Rating** 91 **To** 2012 $18

Pemberton Pinot Noir 2007 Clear and bright colour; while relatively light-bodied, has very good varietal fruit expression in a red and black cherry range; subtle oak and superfine tannins. Screwcap. 13.5% alc. **Rating** 91 **To** 2011 $20

Pemberton Riesling Auslese 2008 Good varietal definition, with a strong mineral core surrounding green apple and lime fruit; sweet, but with good texture; an interesting wine. Screwcap. 7% alc. **Rating** 90 **To** 2015 $17
Pemberton Shiraz 2007 Reductive on opening, but redcurrant and blueberry fruit showing with time; spicy on the palate, with savoury mineral characters; gravelly tannins prolong the tightly wound fruit on the finish. Screwcap. 14.5% alc. **Rating** 90 **To** 2014 $20

Bellbrae Estate   ★★★★

520 Great Ocean Road, Bellbrae, Vic 3228 **Region** Geelong
T (03) 5264 8480 **www.**bellbraeestate.com.au **Open** W'ends 11–5, 7 days (Jan)
Winemaker Matthew di Sciascio, Peter Flewellyn **Est.** 1999 **Cases** 2000 **Vyds** 4.02 ha
Bellbrae Estate (and the Longboard Wines brand) is the venture of friends Richard Macdougall and Matthew di Sciascio. Sharing a common love of wine, surf and coastal life, they decided to establish a vineyard and produce their own wine. In 1998 Richard purchased a small sheep grazing property with 8 ha of fertile, sheltered north-facing slopes on the Great Ocean Road near Bellbrae, and with Matthew's help as business associate, Bellbrae Estate was born. Since 2003 all the wines have been Geelong-sourced.

ŸŸŸŸŸ **Addiscott Geelong Pinot Noir 2007** Strong, clear and bright colour; abundant ripe pinot fruit aromas in a black cherry/plum spectrum are repeated on the generous palate. Screwcap. 13.5% alc. **Rating** 93 **To** 2014 $32
Longboard Geelong Pinot Noir 2007 Good hue and clarity; lighter than Addiscott, with more spicy/sappy/savoury nuances despite similar alcohol; interesting comparison; some might prefer this style. Screwcap. 13.5% alc. **Rating** 92 **To** 2013 $22

ŸŸŸŸ **Southside Geelong Sauvignon Blanc 2008** Clean aromas in a tropical/gooseberry spectrum; very tight minerally/citrussy palate with strong acidity and a dry finish. Screwcap. 12% alc. **Rating** 89 **To** 2012 $22
Longboard Geelong Semillon Sauvignon Blanc 2008 Clean, fresh and lively, with zesty lemony flavours on the well-balanced palate. Screwcap. 13% alc. **Rating** 89 **To** 2012 $18
Longboard Geelong Chardonnay 2008 Melon and pear bouquet; rich and ripe with depth to the mid-palate; very nutty on the finish. Screwcap. 13.5% alc. **Rating** 88 **To** 2012 $20

Bellvale Wines   ★★★★★

95 Forresters Lane, Berrys Creek, Vic 3953 **Region** Gippsland
T (03) 5668 8230 **F** (03) 5668 8230 **www.**bellvalewine.com.au **Open** By appt
Winemaker John Ellis **Est.** 1998 **Cases** 2500 **Vyds** 19 ha
John Ellis is the third under this name to be actively involved in the wine industry. His background as a former 747 pilot, and the knowledge he gained of Burgundy over many visits, sets him apart from the others. He has established pinot noir (10 ha), chardonnay (7 ha) and pinot gris (2 ha) on the red soils of a north-facing slope. He chose a density of 7150 vines per ha, following as far as possible the precepts of Burgundy, but limited by tractor size, which precludes narrower row spacing and even higher plant density. Exports to the UK, the US, Denmark, Singapore and Japan.

ŸŸŸŸŸ **Athena's Vineyard Gippsland Chardonnay 2007** A concentrated, rich and complex wine, with ripe stone fruit and melon dominant, the French oak (12 months) absorbed by the fruit. Has the viscosity of a Grand Cru Burgundy. Screwcap. 13% alc. **Rating** 94 **To** 2013 $35
The Quercus Vineyard Gippsland Pinot Noir 2007 Lively and bright; while the palate is light-bodied, it has excellent thrust and length, with strong spicy notes to its fragrant red fruits. Diam. 13% alc. **Rating** 94 **To** 2015 $35

Belvoir Park Estate

39 Belvoir Park Road, Big Hill, Vic 3453 **Region** Bendigo
T (03) 5435 3075 **www**.belvoirparkwines.com.au **Open** W'ends & public hols 11–5
Winemaker Ian Hall, Achilles Kalanis **Est.** 1997 **Cases** 1000 **Vyds** 3 ha
Ian and Julie Hall have established a boutique winery and vineyard on deep, granite-based soils
13 km south of Bendigo. Wines are crafted onsite using traditional techniques: hand-pruned
and hand-picked grapes, followed by small batch processing via open fermenters and a basket
press. The 2006 Symposiarch (a Shiraz Cabernet Merlot blend) is a powerful wine, but the
heavily stained Diam closure is very unusual and raised significant questions on heat exposure.
The winery rating of the two previous years has been retained.

Ben Potts Wines

Wellington Road, Langhorne Creek, SA 5255 **Region** Langhorne Creek
T (08) 8537 3029 **F** (08) 8537 3284 **www**.benpottswines.com.au **Open** 7 days 10–5
Winemaker Ben Potts **Est.** 2002 **Cases** 800
Ben Potts is the sixth generation to be involved in grapegrowing and winemaking in
Langhorne Creek, the first being Frank Potts, founder of Bleasdale Vineyards. Ben completed
the oenology degree at CSU, and ventured into winemaking on a commercial scale in
2002 (aged 25). Fiddle's Block Shiraz is named after great-grandfather Fiddle; Lenny's Block
Cabernet Sauvignon Malbec after grandfather Len; and Bill's Block Malbec after father Bill.
Exports to Switzerland, Hong Kong and Singapore.

ŸŸŸŸŸ **Fiddle's Block Langhorne Creek Shiraz 2005** Bright colour; alluring
blackberry fruit with a strong mineral core and a touch of tar; the palate is very
focused and the tannins quite plentiful and chewy; lively and very fresh for age;
one of the better 2005s around. Cork. 15% alc. **Rating** 95 **To** 2016 $32

ŸŸŸŸŸ **Lenny's Block Langhorne Creek Cabernet Sauvignon 2005** A warm, rich
and expressive bouquet of red and black fruit and mulled spices; the palate is hefty,
warm and long, with the acid and tannin bringing the fruit into line on the finish.
Cork. 15% alc. **Rating** 90 **To** 2014 $32

Ben's Run ★★★

PO Box 127, Broke, NSW 2330 **Region** Lower Hunter Valley
T (02) 6579 1310 **F** (02) 6579 1370 **www**.bensrun.com.au **Open** Not
Winemaker Pooles Rock (Patrick Auld, Usher Tinkler) **Est.** 1997 **Cases** 800 **Vyds** 3 ha
Ben's Run, say the owners, 'is named for our kelpie dog for graciously allowing part of his
retirement run to be converted into a showpiece shiraz-only vineyard'. Norman Marran was
a pioneer of the Australian cotton industry, with a distinguished career as a former director
of both the Australian Wheat Board and the Grains Research Corporation, and is currently
chairman of a leading food research company. Exports to the US, Japan and Singapore.

ŸŸŸŸ **Single Vineyard Hunter Valley Shiraz 2006** All savoury leather and spice with
some redcurrant fruit in the background; this follows on to the slightly chewy,
medium-bodied palate. Cork. 13.2% alc. **Rating** 87 **To** 2013 $20

Benarra Vineyards ★★★

PO Box 1081, Mt Gambier, SA 5290 **Region** Mount Gambier
T (08) 8738 9355 **F** (08) 8738 9355 **Open** Not
Winemaker Alana Ling Hill **Est.** 1998 **Cases** 400
Lisle Pudney has planted a substantial vineyard with the help of investors. In all there are over
26 ha of pinot noir and 4 ha each of sauvignon blanc and chardonnay, with another 40 ha to
be planted. The vineyard is 20 km from the Southern Ocean on ancient flint beds; a million-
year-old mollusc found on the property is depicted on the label of the Pinot Noir. Most of
the grapes are sold; a small portion is contract-made for the Benarra label, and is of good
quality and varietal character.

♀♀♀♀   **Flint Bed Pinot Noir 2008** A clean, crisp, but slightly closed bouquet leads into a palate with tropical fruits enhanced by a touch of residual sweetness. Screwcap. 12% alc. **Rating** 88 **To** 2011 $20

Bendbrook Wines ★★★

Section 19, Pound Road, Macclesfield, SA 5153 **Region** Adelaide Hills
T (08) 8388 9773 **F** (08) 8388 9373 **www.**bendbrookwines.com.au **Open** By appt
Winemaker Contract **Est.** 1998 **Cases** 2500 **Vyds** 5.5 ha
John and Margaret Struik have established their vineyard on either side of a significant bend in the Angas River that runs through the property, with cabernet sauvignon on one side and shiraz on the other. The name comes from the bend in question, which is indirectly responsible for the flood that occurs every 4–5 years. The Struiks have restored what was known as the Postmaster's Residence to be their home. Exports to Hong Kong.

♀♀♀♀   **Goat Track Shiraz 2007** A spicy/peppery bouquet changes gear on the medium-bodied palate with the arrival of plum and licorice to join the spicy characters of the bouquet; slightly jumpy tannins on the finish. Screwcap. 14% alc. **Rating** 89 **To** 2013 $28

Bended Knee Vineyard ★★★★

PO Box 334, Buninyong, Vic 3357 **Region** Ballarat
T (03) 5341 8437 **F** (03) 5341 8437 **www.**bendedknee.com.au **Open** Not
Winemaker Peter Roche **Est.** 1999 **Cases** 300 **Vyds** 1.2 ha
Peter and Pauline Roche have 0.5 ha each of chardonnay and pinot noir at moderately high density, and 0.2 ha of ultra-close-planted pinot noir at the equivalent of 9000 vines per ha. Here four clones have been used: 114, 115, G5V15 and 777. The Roches say, 'We are committed to sustainable viticulture and aim to leave the planet in better shape than we found it.' Ducks, guinea fowl and chooks are vineyard custodians, and all vine canopy management is done by hand, including pruning and picking. Although production is tiny, Bended Knee can be found at some of Melbourne's best restaurants.

♀♀♀♀♀   **Pinot Noir 2007** Vibrant colour; focused cherry, spice and a touch of ironstone; the palate exhibits fleshy red fruit, layers of Asian allspice and a firmness to the finish that complements the fruit well; very long and a little toasty on the finish. Screwcap. 12.5% alc. **Rating** 92 **To** 2013 $28

♀♀♀♀   **Chardonnay 2006** A big, toasty bouquet full of figs and straw; the palate has plenty of flavour, with the toasty fruit dominating; acidity freshens the wine on the finish, leaving a long and toasty finish. Screwcap. 12.7% alc. **Rating** 89 **To** 2012 $28

Bent Creek Vineyards ★★★★

Lot 10 Blewitt Springs Road, McLaren Flat, SA 5171 **Region** McLaren Vale
T (08) 8383 0414 **www.**bentcreekvineyards.com.au **Open** Sundays & public hols 11–5
Winemaker Peter Polson, Tim Geddes **Est.** 2001 **Cases** 7500
Peter Polson is now the sole owner of Bent Creek, which has acquired a second vineyard of 5 ha at McLaren Vale. As a parallel development, Tim Geddes is now assisting Peter in the winemaking.

♀♀♀♀♀   **Black Dog McLaren Vale Shiraz 2007** Dark and tarry with red fruit providing focus; the lively palate is concentrated and offers a fine underpinning of cranberry and leather on the finish. Screwcap. 14.5% alc. **Rating** 91 **To** 2014 $22
Reserve McLaren Vale Shiraz 2006 A wine to polarise opinions; those who accept the impact of the alcohol will find an abundance of black fruits, licorice and dark chocolate supported by fine tannins. Points are a deliberate compromise. Cork. 15.2% alc. **Rating** 90 **To** 2016 $39

Berton Vineyard ★★★

55 Mirroci Avenue, Yenda, NSW 2681 **Region** Riverina
T (02) 6968 1600 **www.**bertonvineyards.com.au **Open** Mon–Fri 10–4, Sat 11–4
Winemaker James Ceccato **Est.** 2001 **Cases** 15 000 **Vyds** 11 ha
The Berton Vineyard partners – Bob and Cherie Berton, Paul Bartholomaeus, James Ceccato and Jamie Bennett – have almost 100 years combined experience in winemaking, viticulture, finance, production and marketing. 1996 saw the acquisition of a 30-ha property in the Eden Valley and the planting of the first vines. It took two years for the dam to fill, and the vines struggled on the white rock soil, looking like little bonsais – hence the names of the estate-grown Bonsai Shiraz and White Rock varietals. The business also offers (in descending order of price) the cleverly labelled Head Over Heels range, the Hay Plains range and the Odd Socks range, all sourced from Riverina. Exports to the UK, the US and other major markets.

ΨΨΨΨ   **FoundStone Pinot Grigio 2008** Nectarine and lime bouquet; fresh and vibrant, with juicy fruit on the finish. Screwcap. 11.5% alc. **Rating** 87 **To** 2012 $10
Soldier Farms Big Rivers Old Vine Shiraz 2007 Bright colour; red fruits are framed by a little spice; medium-bodied with good texture and a lively finish. Screwcap. 14.5% alc. **Rating** 87 **To** 2012 $10
FoundStone Merlot 2008 A touch of reduction on the bouquet; plum and blackcurrant bouquet with a slight savoury edge; bright fruits on the palate; forward, easy drinking. Screwcap. 14.5% alc. **Rating** 87 **To** 2012 $10

Bethany Wines ★★★★☆

Bethany Road, Bethany via Tanunda, SA 5352 **Region** Barossa Valley
T (08) 8563 2086 **www.**bethany.com.au **Open** Mon–Sat 10–5, Sun 1–5
Winemaker Geoff Schrapel, Robert Schrapel **Est.** 1977 **Cases** 25 000 **Vyds** 32 ha
The Schrapel family has been growing grapes in the Barossa Valley for over 140 years, but the winery has only been in operation since 1977. Nestled high on a hillside on the site of an old bluestone quarry, Geoff and Rob Schrapel produce a range of consistently well-made and attractively packaged wines. They have vineyards in the Barossa Valley, the Eden Valley and (recently and interestingly) 2 ha each of chardonnay and cabernet sauvignon on Kangaroo Island. Exports to the UK, the US and other major markets.

ΨΨΨΨΨ   **Reserve Eden Valley Riesling 2008** Interesting contrast with the varietal; same alcohol and both are dry, but both the aromas and flavours of this wine are more fruity, in a classic Eden Valley lime/citrus framework. Screwcap. 10.5% alc. **Rating** 94 **To** 2020 $30

ΨΨΨΨ٩   **Barossa Chardonnay 2007** A generous peachy style, lifted and sustained by citrussy acidity on the finish; the Eden Valley component is a distinct plus. Screwcap. 13% alc. **Rating** 90 **To** 2013 $20

ΨΨΨΨ   **Eden Valley Riesling 2008** A fragrant bouquet with touches of herb, apple and lime, then a bracingly crisp palate with high acidity; deadset oyster wine. Screwcap. 10.5% alc. **Rating** 89 **To** 2016 $20
Barossa Semillon 2007 Bright golden-green; has good balance, and barrel ferment in older oak has added to the structure of the wine without making it unduly heavy or phenolic. Early maturing style. Screwcap. 12.5% alc. **Rating** 89 **To** 2013 $20
Barossa Cabernet Merlot 2006 Light- to medium-bodied, and in unusual style for the Barossa Valley, with a savoury elegance more typical of cooler climates; only for those who accept this style. Cork. 14% alc. **Rating** 89 **To** 2013 $28
Barossa Shiraz Cabernet 2006 Light- to medium-bodied, with gentle red and black fruits and appropriately fine tannins. Has it gone too far in the quest for lower alcohol? Screwcap. 13.5% alc. **Rating** 87 **To** 2014 $18

Bettenay's

Cnr Harmans South Road/Miamup Road, Wilyabrup, WA 6284 **Region** Margaret River
T (08) 9755 5539 **F** (08) 9755 5539 **www.**bettenaywines.com.au **Open** 7 days 11–5
Winemaker Greg Bettenay, Bryce Bettenay **Est.** 1989 **Cases** 5000 **Vyds** 11 ha
Relying upon advice from his soil scientist father in selecting the property, Greg Bettenay
began planting the vineyards in 1989, and now has cabernet sauvignon (4.5 ha), chardonnay,
sauvignon blanc, shiraz (1.5 ha each), semillon and merlot (1 ha each). The development also
extends to two cottages and a luxury treetop spa apartment known as The Lakeside Loft.
The third generation has joined the business in the form of son Bryce, bringing yet another
perspective to the winemaking.

ŶŶŶŶŶ **The Lost Plot Semillon Sauvignon Blanc 2008** Delicate, fresh and lively, with
tangy/citrussy aromas and flavours on the long, even palate; low alcohol a plus,
and will continue to develop on the back of the semillon. Screwcap. 12.5% alc.
Rating 93 **To** 2012 $22.50
Reserve Margaret River Chardonnay 2008 Excellent green-straw; has similar
flavours to the varietal, but with more depth and intensity, with slightly more
luscious fruit. Screwcap. 14% alc. **Rating** 93 **To** 2015 $32
Margaret River Merlot 2007 Good colour; has the weight, the structure and
the clear varietal expression expected of Margaret River; blackcurrant/cassis fruit
is complexed by black olive notes and fine tannins. Screwcap. 14% alc. **Rating** 92
To 2015 $35
Margaret River Chardonnay 2008 Attractive wine; stone fruit and grapefruit,
with some creamy/nutty/toasty notes in the background; good length and balance.
Screwcap. 14% alc. **Rating** 91 **To** 2014 $25

ŶŶŶŶ **Margaret River Cabernet Sauvignon 2007** A chunky, robust, full-bodied
cabernet, with plenty of black fruit flavours, but needed a much gentler touch in
the winery. Screwcap. 14% alc. **Rating** 87 **To** 2015 $35

Bidgeebong Wines

352 Byrnes Road, Wagga Wagga, NSW 2650 **Region** Gundagai
T (02) 6931 9955 **F** (02) 6931 9966 **www.**bidgeebong.com **Open** Mon–Fri 9–4
Winemaker Andrew Birks, Keiran Spencer **Est.** 2000 **Cases** 12 000
Encompasses what the founders refer to as the Bidgeebong triangle – between Young, Wagga
Wagga, Tumbarumba and Gundagai – which provides grapes for the Bidgeebong brand.
A winery was completed in 2002, and will eventually handle 2000 tonnes of grapes for
Bidgeebong's own needs, and those of other local growers and larger producers who purchase
grapes from the region. Exports to the UK, Canada, India, Singapore and China.

🌿 Big Brook Wines

PO Box 3024, Adelaide Terrace, Perth, WA 6832 **Region** Pemberton
T (08) 9776 1166 **F** (08) 9221 2990 **www.**bigbrookwines.com.au **Open** Not
Winemaker The Vintage Wineworx (Greg Jones) **Est.** 2008 **Cases** 3000 **Vyds** 11.6 ha
This is a family-owned winery established by the O'Toole family of Perth; while the
establishment date is 2008, the vineyard was then already 10 years old. Planted to sauvignon
blanc, chardonnay, merlot and cabernet sauvignon, it is adjacent to the Big Brook Forest from
which it takes its name. Throughout the year a brook runs through the vineyard and feeds the
dam, which has a population of the much-prized marron. It is seldom called on to provide
water for the vines, which are predominantly dry-grown.

ŶŶŶŶŶ **Pemberton Chardonnay 2008** Bright straw-green; an aromatic bouquet leads
into a light-bodied, but beautifully balanced, palate; barrel fermentation enhancing
both the structure and the nectarine/white peach citrus flavours. Gold medal
Perth Wine Show '08. Screwcap. 13.3% alc. **Rating** 94 **To** 2015 $21

ŶŶŶŶ **Pemberton Sauvignon Blanc Semillon 2008** One of those sauvignon blanc semillon blends that encourages you to gulp, rather than sip, its flavours so easy to like, especially when chilled. Screwcap. 12.2% alc. **Rating** 88 **To** 2010 $18
Pemberton Unoaked Chardonnay 2008 In the light, crisp crossover with sauvignon blanc territory; these characters give it the push that warmer-grown, unoaked chardonnays lack. Screwcap. 12.2% alc. **Rating** 88 **To** 2012 $17

big shed wines

1289 Malmsbury Road, Glenlyon, Vic 3461 **Region** Macedon Ranges
T (03) 5348 7825 **www**.bigshedwines.com.au **Open** 7 days, winter 10–6, summer 10–7
Winemaker Ken Jones, Miranda Jones **Est.** 1999 **Cases** 1200 **Vyds** 2 ha
Founder and winemaker Ken Jones was formerly a geneticist and molecular biologist at Edinburgh University, so the chemistry of winemaking comes easily. The estate-based wine comes from 2 ha of pinot noir (clones MV6 and D5V12), the other wines are made from purchased grapes grown in various parts of Central Victoria.

ŶŶŶŶ **Macedon Ranges Pinot Noir 2005** Bright raspberry and blackberry fruit; clean and juicy, but lacking a little complexity. Screwcap. 12.5% alc. **Rating** 87 **To** 2012 $27

Billanook Estate

280 Edward Road, Chirnside Park, Vic 3116 **Region** Yarra Valley
T (03) 9735 4484 **www**.billanookestate.com.au **Open** W'ends & public hols 10–6
Winemaker Domenic Bucci, John D'Aloisio **Est.** 1994 **Cases** 1200 **Vyds** 17 ha
The D'Aloisio family has been involved in the agricultural heritage of the Yarra Valley since the late 1960s, and in '94 planted the first vines on their 36-ha property. The vineyard is planted to cabernet sauvignon (5.9 ha), shiraz (3.3 ha), chardonnay (3.2 ha), sauvignon blanc (1.7 ha), pinot noir (1.4 ha) and merlot (1.1 ha). Most of the grapes are sold to various wineries in the Valley, leaving a small percentage for the Billanook Estate label.

ŶŶŶŶŶ **Yarra Valley Shiraz 2004** Strong crimson; very ripe black fruits on both the bouquet and opulent palate, which has touches of spice and licorice. An interesting wine that is still very young and juicy. Diam. 15% alc. **Rating** 91 **To** 2019 $22

ŶŶŶŶ **Yarra Valley Chardonnay 2004** Glowing yellow-green; so far, the cork has done its job (although slightly soggy) and the stone fruit, melon and fig fruit is still fresh. 14% alc. **Rating** 89 **To** 2012 $20
Yarra Valley Cabernet Sauvignon Merlot 2005 Very good colour; medium- to full-bodied, with layers of red and black fruits, and still needing more time to fully open up. Diam. 14% alc. **Rating** 89 **To** 2015 $20
Yarra Valley Sauvignon Blanc 2008 Bright light green; a spotlessly clean bouquet; a well-balanced palate turning around grassy/citrussy fruit. Diam. 13% alc. **Rating** 87 **To** 2010 $19
Yarra Valley Rose 2008 Well made; it balances a touch of sweetness with precisely judged acidity, although the fruit flavour is a little amorphous. Diam. 12% alc. **Rating** 87 **To** 2009 $16
Yarra Valley Pinot Noir 2004 Retains very good hue for a five-year-old pinot; the colour seems to have been achieved by high acidity/low pH, which nips the finish; unfortunately, the acid will remain as the fruit diminishes, so further cellaring will be counterproductive. Diam. 13.5% alc. **Rating** 87 **To** 2011 $22

Billy Pye Vineyard

PO Box 229, Ashton, SA 5137 **Region** Adelaide Hills
T (08) 8390 1332 **F** (08) 8390 3435 **Open** Not
Winemaker Colin Best, John Bowley **Est.** 1997 **Cases** 75 **Vyds** 2 ha
The history of Billy Pye Vineyard is fascinating, dating back to 1858 when William Grasby began establishing an apple orchard on a property near Balhannah on the upper reaches

of the Onkaparinga River. He died in 1899, the orchards inherited by his son Joseph. The neighbouring property on the southern side had been owned since 1868 by colourful local character WH (Billy) Pye, a surveyor and engineer. His property contained the largest hill in the area, known locally as Billy Pye Hill, where he built his house, and after he died in 1913, Joseph Grasby acquired the property. In 1997 Sandra Schubert, a fifth-generation Grasby, began to plant a vineyard on the northern slopes of Billy Pye Hill in partnership with John Bowley, leaving the top of the hill with the native vegetation Billy had loved. The grapes from the 1 ha of pinot noir and 0.8 ha of chardonnay are currently sold under contract, but the intention is to retain future vintages and make the wine at Leabrook. In the meantime the only wine from Billy Pye Vineyard is a red blend (Shiraz/Merlot) coming from a 0.25-ha planting. John Bowley and Colin Best, the latter the Leabrook winemaker, both studied civil engineering at Adelaide University, and worked together many years ago.

ΨΨΨΨΨ **Glengyle Red 2006** A very lively, spicy bouquet and palate, with red and black fruits contrasting with spicy brambly notes, the tannins fine, the oak subtle. Shiraz/Merlot/Cabernet Sauvignon. Screwcap. 14.5% alc. **Rating** 90 **To** 2016 $28

Bimbadgen Estate ★★★★

790 McDonalds Road, Pokolbin, NSW 2320 **Region** Lower Hunter Valley
T (02) 4998 7585 **F** (02) 4998 7732 **www**.bimbadgen.com.au **Open** 7 days 10–5
Winemaker Simon Thistlewood, Jane Hoppe **Est.** 1968 **Cases** 50 000
Established as McPherson Wines, then successively Tamalee, Sobels, Parker Wines and now Bimbadgen, this substantial winery has had what might be politely termed a turbulent history. It has over 50 ha of estate plantings, mostly with relatively old vines, supplemented by a separate estate vineyard at Yenda (19 ha) for the lower-priced Ridge series, and purchased grapes from various premium regions. Exports to all major markets.

ΨΨΨΨΨ **Estate Hunter Valley Semillon 2008** An intense, high-flavoured young semillon with lemon and lime juice flavours surprisingly close to young riesling; great length. Good now or later. Screwcap. 9.5% alc. **Rating** 93 **To** 2015 $20
Signature Palmers Lane Vineyard Shiraz 2006 One of those Hunter Valley shirazs that appears too light to age for decades, but will. The wine has strong savoury/earthy/leathery notes on the medium-bodied, but very long, sustained palate. Screwcap. 14% alc. **Rating** 93 **To** 2026 $55
Hunter Valley Orange Semillon Sauvignon Blanc 2008 Has abundant fruit on the bouquet and palate, the tropical/passionfruit of the sauvignon blanc balanced against the more grassy notes of semillon. Screwcap. 11% alc. **Rating** 92 **To** 2012 $24
Limited Release Pinot Gris 2008 A highly scented, floral bouquet, then a palate which almost inevitably doesn't quite live up to the bouquet; nonetheless, an impressive wine; from Orange and high-altitude vineyards in NSW and Vic. Screwcap. 13% alc. **Rating** 90 **To** 2011 $24

ΨΨΨΨ **Myall Road Botrytis Semillon 2007** Good level of botrytis with marmalade and creamed apricot on the bouquet; sweet and sugary on the finish. Screwcap. 11% alc. **Rating** 88 **To** 2012 $26
Fortified Verdelho NV Plenty of rancio, with attractive nutty and a slight toffee complexity; quite sweet and fresh on the finish. Screwcap. 18% alc. **Rating** 87 **To** 2012 $26

🌿 binbilla ★★★☆

Good Friday Gully Road, Maimuru, NSW 2594 (postal) **Region** Hilltops
T (02) 6383 3305 **F** (02) 6383 3237 **www**.binbillawines.com **Open** Not
Winemaker Andrew McEwin (Contract) **Est.** 2001 **Cases** 375 **Vyds** 7 ha
Gerard and Berenice Hines planted their vineyard in 2001, with 4 ha of cabernet sauvignon, 2 ha of shiraz and 1 ha of riesling, which produced the first wines in '04. The more recent grafting of some vines to viognier will see the release of a Shiraz Viognier from the 2009 vintage. The only wine that is not estate-grown is the Chardonnay, which is grown on a

nearby Hilltops vineyard. The quantity made will increase as the vines come into full bearing, but is unlikely to exceed 1000 cases a year, with limited retail and restaurant listings in Melbourne, Sydney and Brisbane.

ŶŶŶŶ♀ **Special Steps Cabernet Sauvignon 2005** Attractive light- to medium-bodied palate, with gently ripe cassis and blackcurrant fruit; fine tannins, good oak management. Screwcap. 13.8% alc. **Rating** 90 **To** 2014 $18

ŶŶŶŶ **Good Friday Gully Shiraz 2006** Light colour and light-bodied, utterly belying the alcohol; fresh spicy red fruits with slightly herbal overtones. Screwcap. 14.5% alc. **Rating** 87 **To** 2011 $18
Good Friday Gully Shiraz 2005 Slight reduction is evident on both bouquet and palate, giving a touch of bitterness to the black fruits of the light- to medium-bodied palate; however, has good length. Screwcap. 14.5% alc. **Rating** 87 **To** 2012 $18

Bird in Hand   ★★★★★

Bird in Hand Road, Woodside, SA 5244 **Region** Adelaide Hills
T (08) 8389 9488 **F** (08) 8389 9511 **www.**birdinhand.com.au **Open** 7 days 11–5
Winemaker Andrew Nugent, Kym Milne **Est.** 1997 **Cases** 60 000 **Vyds** 29 ha
This very successful business took its name from a 19th-century gold mine. It is the venture of the Nugent family, headed by Dr Michael Nugent; son Andrew is a Roseworthy graduate. The family also has a vineyard in the Clare Valley, the latter providing both riesling and shiraz (and olives from 100-year-old wild trees). In 2007 a state-of-the-art winery and a straw and mud barrel cellar were completed. The estate plantings (merlot, pinot noir, cabernet sauvignon, sauvignon blanc, riesling and shiraz) provide only part of the annual crush, the remainder coming from contract growers. Exports to the UK, the US and other major markets.

ŶŶŶŶŶ **Nest Egg Adelaide Hills Chardonnay 2008** Astute winemaking, the barrel ferment–oak inputs subservient to the tightly focused nectarine fruit, with mouth-watering grapefruit-accented acidity on the finish. Screwcap. 14.5% alc. **Rating** 95 **To** 2018 $60
Nest Egg Adelaide Hills Shiraz 2007 Vibrant colour; has a savoury, dried sage component framing the ample blackberry fruit of the bouquet; the palate is quite tightly wound and offers an array of flavours and textures from start to finish; will benefit from a little time. Screwcap. 14.5% alc. **Rating** 94 **To** 2020 $75

ŶŶŶŶ♀ **Two in the Bush Adelaide Hills Merlot Cabernet 2007** Fragrant and spotlessly clean; a very attractive mix of red cherry, cassis, plum and spice on both bouquet and the medium-bodied palate; silky tannins add length to an elegant and stylish wine. Screwcap. 14% alc. **Rating** 93 **To** 2013 $20
Adelaide Hills Sauvignon Blanc 2008 Has abundant tropical fruit on bouquet and palate alike, almost to a fault if that were possible; just a touch of thickness on the mid-palate. Screwcap. 13.5% alc. **Rating** 90 **To** 2010 $25
Adelaide Hills Chardonnay 2008 Bright green-straw; has classic Adelaide Hills fruit flavours with nectarine and a touch of citrus running through the long palate. Screwcap. 13.5% alc. **Rating** 90 **To** 2013 $25
Adelaide Hills Pinot Noir Rose 2008 Well made; clean and fresh strawberry-accented fruit; long palate, dry finish; fraction light-on. Screwcap. 12.5% alc. **Rating** 90 **To** 2010 $20
Mount Lofty Ranges Shiraz 2007 Bright colour; blueberry biscuit bouquet, with a touch of cinnamon; a warm palate, with blackberry confit and chewy tannins; rich and ripe. Screwcap. 14.5% alc. **Rating** 90 **To** 2016 $30
Joy 2006 Pale salmon; has been bottle-fermented, but is still youthful; a limited time on lees, no doubt; has length, and the spicy red fruit flavours are not compromised by sweetness. Cork. 13.5% alc. **Rating** 90 **To** 2012 $60

ŶŶŶŶ **Two in the Bush Adelaide Hills Semillon Sauvignon Blanc 2008** Bright green-straw; a powerful wine abounding with tropical and more citrussy flavours; broadens somewhat on the finish. Screwcap. 13.5% alc. **Rating** 89 **To** 2011 $20

Two in the Bush Mount Lofty Ranges Shiraz 2007 Deep purple-red; rich and luscious cool-climate fruit, with plum, licorice and spice; does shorten fractionally. Screwcap. 14.5% alc. **Rating** 89 **To** 2015 $20

Mount Lofty Ranges Merlot 2007 Good colour; damson plum and a little black olive, with soft and fleshy fruit. Screwcap. 14.5% alc. **Rating** 89 **To** 2014 $30

Two in the Bush Adelaide Hills Chardonnay 2008 Pleasant unwooded style, with enough energy to the fruit flavours to take it out of the bland, boring category. Screwcap. 13% alc. **Rating** 88 **To** 2011 $20

Clare Valley Riesling 2008 Deep colour; ripe Meyer lemon bouquet; rich, ripe and generous; good flavour, but lacks nerve. Screwcap. 13% alc. **Rating** 87 **To** 2013 $25

Adelaide Hills Sparkling Pinot Noir 2008 Pale pink; has an almost aggressively fruity bouquet, and a bright spicy/savoury/strawberry palate; dry finish. No hint of lees complexity, of course; may build fruit complexity on cork. 13% alc. **Rating** 87 **To** 2012 $25

Birthday Villa Vineyard ★★★

Lot 2, Campbell Street, Malmsbury Street, Vic 3446 **Region** Macedon Ranges
T (03) 5423 2789 **F** (03) 5423 2789 **www.**birthdayvilla.com.au **Open** By appt 10–5
Winemaker Greg Dedman (Contract) **Est.** 1968 **Cases** 300
The Birthday Villa name comes from the 19th-century Birthday Mine at nearby Drummond discovered on Queen Victoria's birthday. The 1.5 ha of traminer was planted in 1962, the 0.5 ha of cabernet sauvignon following later. The quality of the Gewurztraminer comes as no surprise; the very cool climate is suited to the variety. On the other hand, the Cabernet Sauvignon comes as a major surprise, although there are likely to be vintages where the variety will provide a major challenge as it struggles for ripeness.

♥♥♥♥ **Malmsbury Cabernet Sauvignon 2006** While the wine has low alcohol and minty/herbal notes, there is unexpected savoury blackcurrant fruit on the mid-palate. Screwcap. 12.6% alc. **Rating** 87 **To** 2013 $25

 # BK Wines ★★★★☆

34 Stopford Road, Hove, SA 5048 (postal) **Region** Adelaide Hills
T (08) 8296 9098 **F** (08) 8296 8580 **www.**bkwines.com.au **Open** Not
Winemaker Brendon Keys **Est.** 2007 **Cases** 200
BK Wines is owned by the Keys and Scott families. Brendon Keys came from NZ, and has worked in the US, Argentina, NZ and SA. BK Wines is an out-of-hours occupation; his main job is winemaker for Adelaide Hills Winery, which opened in November 2008. BK is thus a virtual winery, as it relies entirely on purchased grapes, and the wine is not made onsite.

♥♥♥♥♥ **La Bombe de Belle Piccadilly Valley Pinot Noir 2007** Vibrant colour; the bouquet shows gentle cherry and plum fruit, with a small touch of spice; good texture, with some fine and firm tannins providing a foil for the generous sweet fruit; persistent finish. Screwcap. 13.5% alc. **Rating** 91 **To** 2014 $35

♥♥♥♥ **Le Levrier Blanc Adelaide Hills Pinot Gris 2008** A rich example of gris, with candied fruits, a touch of pear and vibrant acidity on the finish; certainly made in the style of Alsace. Screwcap. 13.5% alc. **Rating** 89 **To** 2012 $23.50

Chou Chou Adelaide Hills Gewurztraminer 2008 Varietal lychee and rose petal bouquet; sweet and a little loose-knit on the palate, but is certainly an expression of the variety Screwcap. 12.5% alc. **Rating** 87 **To** 2012 $23.50

 # Black Spade Wines NR

Lot 51 Menge Road, Tanunda, SA 5352 **Region** Barossa Valley
T 0411 106 911 **www.**blackspade.com.au **Open** By appt
Winemaker Paul Judd **Est.** 2004 **Cases** 200 **Vyds** 0.5 ha
Black Spade Wines is the venture of Paul Judd, who has a micro-vineyard of 0.5 ha of cabernet sauvignon and mourvedre, supplemented by small quantities of shiraz purchased from Barossa

growers. The idea of making wine came from experience working with Bethany Wines and Rusden in the Barossa Valley, and Clos Du Bois in California although in no sense is this Judd's full-time occupation. A self-confessed card addict, even to the extent of games being played as the grapes go through the press, led to the adoption of the Black Spade name and wine label logo.

Blackbilly Wines

Kangarilla Road, McLaren Vale, SA 5171 **Region** McLaren Vale
T 0419 383 907 **F** (08) 8323 9747 **www**.blackbilly.com **Open** By appt
Winemaker Nick Haselgrove, Warren Randall **Est.** 2003 **Cases** 5000
Blackbilly has emerged from the numerous changes in the various Haselgrove wine interests. These days the people behind Blackbilly are Nick Haselgrove, Warren Randall, Warren Ward and Andrew Fletcher. Blackbilly is able to access the 400 ha of vines owned by Tinlins, along with smaller suppliers in McLaren Vale. Exports to all major markets.

ŦŦŦŦŢ **McLaren Vale Grenache Shiraz Mourvedre 2007** A very powerful, full-bodied wine with an array of tar, bitter chocolate and black fruit flavours, backed by full-throttle tannins; the top gold medal in its class at the Melbourne Wine Show '08 was surprising, but not as much as the fact that 64% is grenache. Screwcap. 14.5% alc. **Rating** 92 **To** 2022 $23

ŦŦŦŦ **McLaren Vale Shiraz 2007** Dense colour; a full-bodied wine with boatloads of blackberry, licorice, chocolate, plum and prune; obviously, will repay extended cellaring and will settle down well. Screwcap. 14% alc. **Rating** 89 **To** 2020 $23
Adelaide Hills Pinot Gris 2008 Has good balance and length, the pear and fruit flanked by lively, slightly citrussy, acidity; good length and balance. Screwcap. 13.5% alc. **Rating** 88 **To** 2010 $23
McLaren Vale Tempranillo 2007 A good example of the variety, with bright red fruits contrasting with a savoury/spicy edge, fine tannins unifying the parts. Screwcap. 14% alc. **Rating** 88 **To** 2012 $23
SB3 Sparkling Shiraz NV Rich black berry fruits more or less deal with the high dosage on a richly flavoured palate; minimal oak a plus. Cork. 13.5% alc. **Rating** 87 **To** 2012 $28

Blackboy Ridge Estate

PO Box 554, Donnybrook, WA 6239 **Region** Geographe
T (08) 9731 2233 **F** (08) 9731 2233 **www**.blackboyridge.com.au **Open** By appt
Winemaker David Crawford (Contract) **Est.** 1978 **Cases** 2300 **Vyds** 2.5 ha
The 22-ha property on which Blackboy Ridge Estate is established was partly cleared and planted to 2.5 ha of semillon, chenin blanc, shiraz and cabernet sauvignon in 1978. When current owners Adrian Jones and Jackie Barton purchased the property in 2000 the vines were already some of the oldest in the region. The vineyard and the owners' house are on gentle north-facing slopes, with extensive views over the Donnybrook area. A cellar door is planned for 2009.

ŦŦŦŦŦ **Barton Jones Shiraz 2007** Crimson-purple; blackberry and spice aromas are replicated on the medium-bodied palate, with excellent tannin structure and length. Fine example of cool-grown shiraz. Screwcap. 14.5% alc. **Rating** 94 **To** 2015 $20

ŦŦŦŦŢ **Barton Jones Cabernet Sauvignon 2007** Light, but vivid, crimson introduces a light- to medium-bodied palate, with fresh cassis and blackcurrant fruit and a juicy finish; no need for patience, although will hold. Screwcap. 13.5% alc. **Rating** 90 **To** 2014 $20

ŦŦŦŦ **Geographe Semillon 2007** Tight, crisp lemon mineral characters throughout; long, zesty finish. Years to go. Screwcap. 12% alc. **Rating** 88 **To** 2014 $16
Cabernet Shiraz 2007 Light- to medium-bodied; elegant, high-toned and charming; drink soon. Screwcap. 13.5% alc. **Rating** 88 **To** 2011 $16

Blackets/TK Wines   ★★★★

PO Box 5405, Sydney, NSW 2001 **Region** Adelaide Hills
T (02) 9232 5714 **F** (02) 9231 6660 **www**.blackets.com.au **Open** Not
Winemaker Tim Knappstein (contract) **Est.** 2007 **Cases** 2500 **Vyds** 27.54 ha
Sydney barrister Paul Blacket and wife Christine purchased the Lenswood Vineyard from
Tim and Annie Knappstein in 2004. Planting of the chardonnay, sauvignon blanc, semillon,
gewurztraminer and pinot noir had begun in 1981 and continued through to 2005, and has
been under the care of the same vineyard manager for the past 20 years. The Blackets also
acquire pinot noir and shiraz from a neighbouring high-altitude Adelaide Hills vineyard, with
an Eden Valley Riesling in the planning pipeline, plus shiraz and cabernet partly owned by
them with members of the Kilikanoon group and others. TK Wines is also owned by Paul
Blacket; production is now focused solely on the Lenswood vineyards.

🍷🍷🍷🍷🍷 **Blackets Adelaide Hills Shiraz 2007** Vibrant purple hue; blue fruits and strong
           spicy notes dominate the bouquet; dry and savoury on the palate, with a vibrant
           core of sweet fruit, and quite gravelly tannins. Screwcap. 14.5% alc. **Rating** 91
           To 2015 $28

🍷🍷🍷🍷 **Blackets Adelaide Hills Sauvignon Blanc 2008** A ripe tropical and fresh cut
          grass bouquet; a surprisingly rich palate, with depth but not quite enough acidity.
          Screwcap. 13.5% alc. **Rating** 89 **To** 2011 $22

Blackford Stable Wines   ★★★☆

PO Box 162, Charleston, SA 5244 **Region** Adelaide Hills
T (08) 8389 5312 **F** (08) 8389 5313 **www**.blackfordstable.com.au **Open** Not
Winemaker Nicky Cowper **Est.** 1998 **Cases** 200 **Vyds** 28.7 ha
Two odysseys lie entwined in the history of Blackford Stable. The first was that of Charles
Newman, who left his home in Blackford, Somerset, UK, in 1837, aged 16, to (successfully)
seek fame and fortune in Australia, and whose great-great-granddaughter and family live in
the Blackford homestead. The second odyssey was that of the Cowper family, whose 18-year-
old daughter Nicky moved from the beauty of NZ's southern Hawke's Bay region to begin
studies in oenology at the University of Adelaide's Waite Institute, convincing her parents to
follow her, and relocate permanently to Australia. A property they purchased is part of the
original Blackford estate, the stone stables are the embryonic home of Blackford Stable wines.
Parents Stephen and Angela have progressively planted 28 ha of chardonnay, sauvignon blanc,
semillon, riesling, pinot gris, merlot and cabernet sauvignon since 1998, selling most of the
grapes while daughter Nicky completed her studies and then worked vintages in the Barossa
Valley, Adelaide Hills, McLaren Vale, Vic, France, the US and South Africa.

🍷🍷🍷🍷🍷 **Adelaide Hills Cabernet Sauvignon 2005** Shows good varietal character in
           a blackcurrant spectrum, with attractive, slightly savoury, tannins aiding the length.
           Screwcap. 14.5% alc. **Rating** 91 **To** 2015 $22

🍷🍷🍷🍷 **Adelaide Hills Sauvignon Blanc 2007** Showing first signs of colour develop-
          ment; green pea and ripe citrus aromas, and a complex palate, with a mix of lemon
          rind and lemon tart, the 30% barrel ferment component adding texture without
          compromising the varietal fruit. Screwcap. 13.4% alc. **Rating** 88 **To** 2009 $16
          Adelaide Hills Sangiovese 2005 Strong colour for the variety; seems riper
          than the alcohol suggests, with slight confit/jam characters to the cherry fruit;
          tannins evident but acceptable. Screwcap. 13.5% alc. **Rating** 88 **To** 2012 $22
          Adelaide Hills Merlot 2005 Dense, dark colour; medium- to full-bodied red
          wine with good flesh and mouthfeel, but not enough varietal character. Screwcap.
          14.8% alc. **Rating** 87 **To** 2012 $22

BlackJack Vineyards   ★★★★★

Cnr Blackjack Road/Calder Highway, Harcourt, Vic 3453 **Region** Bendigo
T (03) 5474 2355 **www**.blackjackwines.com.au **Open** W'ends & public hols 11–5
Winemaker Ian McKenzie, Ken Pollock **Est.** 1987 **Cases** 2500

Established by the McKenzie and Pollock families on the site of an old apple and pear orchard in the Harcourt Valley and is best known for some very good Shirazs. Ian McKenzie, incidentally, is not to be confused with Ian McKenzie formerly of Seppelt (Great Western). A welcome return to top form. Exports to NZ.

♥♥♥♥♥ **Block 6 Bendigo Shiraz 2006** Slightly more complex aromas than the varietal, and despite much lower alcohol, has more texture, and attractive red and black berry fruits. Screwcap. 14% alc. **Rating** 94 **To** 2020 $35
Bendigo Cabernet Merlot 2006 Excellent hue and depth; some earthy edges to the bouquet; an extremely powerful palate, both deep and long, with lingering cassis and blackcurrant. Great future. Screwcap. 13.5% alc. **Rating** 94 **To** 2026 $25

♥♥♥♥♀ **Bendigo Shiraz 2006** A fragrant bouquet; denies its alcohol from the word go, featuring red fruits and shot through with spice, finishes with fine tannins. Screwcap. 15% alc. **Rating** 93 **To** 2018 $35
Chortle's Edge Bendigo Shiraz 2006 By far the most robust of the '06 BlackJack Shirazs, with abundant tannins and overall rustic notes; certainly has flavour. Screwcap. 14.5% alc. **Rating** 91 **To** 2014 $18

♥♥♥♥ **Major's Line Bendigo Shiraz 2006** Relatively light colour; light- to medium-bodied at best, with spicy fruit and a clean, fresh finish. Screwcap. 14.5% alc. **Rating** 88 **To** 2014 $25

Blackwood Wines ★★★

Kearney Street, Nannup, WA 6275 **Region** Blackwood Valley
T (08) 9756 0077 **F** (08) 9756 0089 www.blackwoodwines.com.au **Open** 7 days 10–4
Winemaker Stuart Pearce **Est.** 1996 **Cases** 15 000 **Vyds** 5 ha
Blackwood Wines draws upon estate plantings of chardonnay, merlot, chenin blanc and pinot noir, supplemented by contract-grown fruit that significantly broadens the product range. Redevelopment of the cellar door and winery is designed to see production increase significantly. Exports to the US, The Netherlands, United Arab Emirates, Hong Kong and Singapore.

♥♥♥♥ **Fishbone Classic White 2008** Fragrant, fresh and fruity, with a mix of multi-citrus and fruit salad flavours; attractive summer wine. Value. Semillon/Sauvignon Blanc/Chardonnay/Verdelho. Screwcap. 13% alc. **Rating** 89 **To** 2010 $15
Fishbone Margaret River Sauvignon Blanc Semillon 2008 Very grassy/lemony aromas and flavours with lingering acidity; oyster wine (or spicy Asian). Screwcap. 13% alc. **Rating** 87 **To** 2010 $20
Fishbone Merlot 2007 A fragrant bouquet, then a light, but fresh, red berry palate; unforced. Screwcap. 13.5% alc. **Rating** 87 **To** 2011 $15

Bleasdale Vineyards ★★★★☆

Wellington Road, Langhorne Creek, SA 5255 **Region** Langhorne Creek
T (08) 8537 3001 **F** (08) 8537 3224 www.bleasdale.com.au **Open** Mon–Sun 10–5
Winemaker Michael Potts, Paul Hotker, Ben Potts **Est.** 1850 **Cases** 100 000 **Vyds** 61 ha
This is one of the most historic wineries in Australia. Not so long prior to arrival of the 21st century, its vineyards were flooded every winter by diversion of the Bremer River, which provided moisture throughout the dry, cool growing season. In the new millennium, every drop of water is counted. The wines offer excellent value for money, all showing that particular softness which is the hallmark of Langhorne Creek. Exports to all major markets.

♥♥♥♥♥ **Generations Langhorne Creek Shiraz 2006** A dark and brooding personality of blackberry, mulberry and fruitcake, with a touch of tar for complexity; the palate is vibrant, but shows great depth and weight to the fruit; long, chewy and dense with a generous dollop of fruit that persists to the ultimate conclusion. Cork. 14.5% alc. **Rating** 94 **To** 2020 $38

ŢŢŢŢŢ Langhorne Creek Verdelho 2008 Lime and fresh quince on the bouquet; fresh
and vibrant fruit with tangy acidity and a clean focus to the conclusion. Screwcap.
13% alc. **Rating** 90 **To** 2012 $14
Langhorne Creek Malbec 2006 Dense and chewy with tobacco, blackberry
and a touch of mulberry; the palate is warm and generous, the tannins disappear
behind the ample fruit. Value. Screwcap. 14.5% alc. **Rating** 90 **To** 2014 $15
The Wise One Wood Matured Tawny NV Fruitcake aromas with attractive
nutty complexity; a soft touch of rancio and rather laid-back acidity makes
the wine a warm and friendly style for a cold winter's evening. Cork. 18% alc.
Rating 90 **To** 2010 $16

ŢŢŢŢ Bremerview Langhorne Creek Shiraz 2006 Red berry fruit, a touch of mint
and earth on the bouquet; the palate is warm and ample, with a slightly soft edge
to the conclusion. Screwcap. 14.5% alc. **Rating** 88 **To** 2012 $18
Langhorne Creek Sparkling Shiraz NV Blackberry fruit with just a touch
of fruitcake; nicely balanced sweetness, although a little on the high side. Cork.
13.5% alc. **Rating** 88 **To** 2012 $19
16 Year Old Blend Verdelho NV Nutty rancio characters dominate and push
the edge but don't quite go over; nutty, with a little floral complexity on the finish.
Cork. 19% alc. **Rating** 88 **To** 2010 $20

Blickling Estate ★★★★

Green Valley Road, Bendemeer, NSW 2355 **Region** New England
T (02) 6769 6659 **F** (02) 6769 6605 **www.**blickling.com.au **Open** 7 days 9–5
Winemaker First Creek Wines **Est.** 1999 **Cases** 4000 **Vyds** 10 ha
Rolf Blickling has established his vineyard (planted to riesling, chardonnay, sauvignon blanc,
pinot noir, cabernet sauvignon and shiraz) at an elevation of 950 m. Frosts in spring and April
underline how cool the climate is, necessitating careful site selection. The cellar door also
operates a lavender and eucalyptus oil distillery. This is the leader of the pack in New England,
perhaps in part due to skilled contract winemaking in the Hunter Valley.

ŢŢŢŢŢ Sauvignon Blanc 2008 The bouquet is fresh and clean, although relatively
subdued; the wine opens up with penetrating herb, grass and mineral flavours
on the long and dry palate; has plenty of thrust to the finish, and will be one of
those sauvignon blancs that thrive on 2–3 years bottle age. Screwcap. 13.2% alc.
Rating 92 **To** 2011 $22
Riesling 2008 Light straw-green; attractive lime, apple and herb varietal aromas;
then a crisp, firm and bone-dry palate, with a long, even finish; a certain austerity
will paradoxically underwrite its long-term development. Screwcap. 12% alc.
Rating 90 **To** 2013 $19

ŢŢŢŢ Rose 2008 Pale pink; made without fear or favour, bone dry and bracingly crisp,
but does have length and good balance; predominantly Cabernet Sauvignon, some
Shiraz. Screwcap. 13.3% alc. **Rating** 88 **To** 2010 $17

Blind Man's Bluff Vineyards

Lot 15 Bluff Road, Kenilworth, Qld 4574 **Region** Queensland Coastal
T (07) 5472 3168 **www.**blindmansbluff.com.au **Open** Wed–Sun 10–5
Winemaker Peter Scudamore-Smith MW (Contract) **Est.** 2001 **Cases** 500 **Vyds** 2.3 ha
Blind Man's Bluff Vineyards is situated 45 mins from Qld's Sunshine Coast. Noel Evans' dream
of establishing a vineyard, with his partner Tricia Toussaint and family members, turned into
reality in 2001 when the property was planted to chardonnay and shiraz. Various cellar door
activities have made the winery a state finalist for tourism.

Bloodwood

4 Griffin Road, Orange, NSW 2800 **Region** Orange
T (02) 6362 5631 **F** (02) 6361 1173 **www.**bloodwood.com.au **Open** By appt
Winemaker Stephen Doyle **Est.** 1983 **Cases** 4000 **Vyds** 8 ha

Rhonda and Stephen Doyle are two of the pioneers of the Orange district. The estate vineyards (chardonnay, riesling, merlot, cabernet sauvignon, shiraz, cabernet franc and malbec) are planted at an elevation of 810–860 m, which provides a reliably cool climate; frost can be an issue, but heat seldom is. The wines are sold mainly through the cellar door and by an energetic, humorous and informatively run mailing list (see, for example, the tasting note for Men In Tights). Has an impressive track record across the full gamut of varietal (and other) wine styles, especially Riesling, in a variety of styles; all of the wines have a particular elegance and grace. Very much part of the growing reputation of Orange. Exports to the UK.

ΨΨΨΨΨ **Riesling 2008** Fragrant spice, wild flower and apple aromas lead into an intense and lime juice palate, with immaculate balance and length. Screwcap. 12.5% alc. **Rating** 96 **To** 2020 $20
Silk Purse 2008 Very long and intense, with pure riesling fruit augmented, and not subverted, by botrytis; perfect balance of sweetness and acidity. Screwcap. 10.5% alc. **Rating** 94 **To** 2013 $25

ΨΨΨΨΩ **Chardonnay 2007** Has built-in complexity from the bouquet through to the finish; cashew and fig characters accompany the stone fruit at the core of the wine; the oak is well integrated. Screwcap. 13% alc. **Rating** 93 **To** 2013 $24
Big Men in Tights 2008 Big Men in Tights has been around as long as I can remember, originally made from malbec, now with an added dash of cabernet franc; it has generous red fruits and an unusually appealing spicy/savoury twist on the finish; now with a health warning 'traces of nuts may remain'. Screwcap. 13% alc. **Rating** 92 **To** 2010 $16
Cabernet Franc 2006 Bright crimson; has the fragrance that is prized in Bordeaux, and also the hint of tobacco leaf on the red fruits of the palate; good length and structure; a major surprise. Screwcap. 13.5% alc. **Rating** 92 **To** 2015 $25
Shiraz 2005 Still fresh and bright; a light- to medium-bodied wine reflecting its cool-grown origins with strong spicy overtones to its black cherry fruit; fine, slightly savoury tannins to conclude. Screwcap. 14% alc. **Rating** 90 **To** 2015 $24

Blue Metal Vineyard ★★★

Lot 18 Compton Park Road, Berrima, NSW 2577 **Region** Southern Highlands
T (02) 4877 1877 **www**.bluemetalvineyard.com **Open** Thurs–Mon 10–5 or by appt
Winemaker Jonathon Holgate, Nick Bulleid (Consultant) **Est.** 1999 **Cases** 2800 **Vyds** 11 ha
The Blue Metal Vineyard is situated on part of a cattle station at 790 m; the name comes from the rich red soil that overlies the cap of basalt rock. A wide range of grape varieties are planted, including sauvignon blanc, cabernet sauvignon, merlot, pinot gris, sangiovese and petit verdot. The wines have been very competently made. Exports to the UK.

ΨΨΨΨ **Lava One Botrytis Sauvignon Blanc 2007** Attractive apricot bouquet with a fresh pineapple fruit palate; lively and focused, and not too sweet. Screwcap. 12.5% alc. **Rating** 88 **To** 2014 $25
Signature Southern Highlands Pinot Gris 2008 Floral bouquet with a pure pear aroma; the palate is rich with good flavour; a little bitter twist provides freshness on the finish, with some heat from the alcohol in tow. Screwcap. 14.5% alc. **Rating** 87 **To** 2012 $25

Blue Poles Vineyard

PO Box 34, Mount Lawley, WA 6929 **Region** Margaret River
T (08) 9757 4382 **F** (08) 6210 1390 **www**.bluepolesvineyard.com.au **Open** Not
Winemaker Vasse River Wines (Sharna Kowalczuk) **Est.** 2001 **Cases** 750 **Vyds** 6.7 ha
Geologists Mark Gifford and Tim Markwell formed a joint venture to locate and develop Blue Poles Vineyard. Their search was unhurried, and contact with the University of Bordeaux (supplemented by extensive reading of technical literature) showed that a portion of the property included a block that mimicked some of the best vineyards in St Emilion and Pomerol, leading to the planting of merlot and cabernet franc in 2001. Further soil mapping and topography also identified blocks best suited to shiraz and Rhône Valley white

varietals, which were planted in 2003. The vineyard maintenance has proceeded with minimal irrigation, and no fertilisers.

Blue Pyrenees Estate   ★★★★

Vinoca Road, Avoca, Vic 3467 **Region** Pyrenees
T (03) 5465 1111 **F** (03) 5465 3529 **www**.bluepyrenees.com.au **Open** Mon–Fri 10–4.30, w'ends & public hols 10–5
Winemaker Andrew Koerner, Chris Smales **Est.** 1963 **Cases** 50 000 **Vyds** 170 ha
Forty years after Remy Cointreau established Blue Pyrenees Estate (then known as Chateau Remy), the business was sold to a small group of Sydney businessmen led by John Ellis (no relation to John Ellis of Hanging Rock). Former Rosemount senior winemaker Andrew Koerner heads the winery team. The core of the business is the very large estate plantings, most decades old, but with newer arrivals including viognier, petit verdot and pinot meunier. Exports to the UK, the US and other major markets.

ΨΨΨΨΩ **The Richardson Series Shiraz 2004** Good hue for age, still purple; attractive, spicy cedary aromas come through consistently on the palate, which has good texture, structure and length. Cork. 14.5% alc. **Rating** 93 **To** 2019 $49.95
The Richardson Series Cabernet Sauvignon 2004 Has strong Bordeaux overtones; it is finely structured and quite savoury, with as much earth and black olive as blackcurrant; within its parameters, an impressive wine. Cork. 14.5% alc. **Rating** 93 **To** 2017 $49.95
Estate Reserve Red 2004 The interplay of Cabernet (76%)/Shiraz (19%)/ Merlot (5%) gives a wine with fragrant fruit hovering between red and black on the medium-bodied palate. Show success in '08 no surprise. Cork. 14.5% alc. **Rating** 92 **To** 2014 $34.95
Reserve Shiraz 2005 Pleasant medium-bodied wine, with supple red and black fruits, mocha and cedar; the tannins are fine and soft. Screwcap. 14% alc. **Rating** 90 **To** 2015 $34.95
Merlot 2006 Good depth and density to the colour; has above-average weight and density, and tastes as if it may have had 15% cabernet added (which is perfectly legal); needs time for the tannins to soften. Screwcap. 14.5% alc. **Rating** 90 **To** 2016 $18.99
Midnight Cuvee 2002 Light straw-green; still very youthful, although age on lees not disclosed; largely chardonnay with a dash of pinot noir; good flavour and length. Diam. 11.5% alc. **Rating** 90 **To** 2014 $29.95

ΨΨΨΨ **Sparkling Shiraz 2004** Amazingly deep colour; methode champenoise from estate-grown grapes; spicy black fruits and a savoury finish. Can still improve. Diam. 14% alc. **Rating** 89 **To** 2014 $24.95
Sauvignon Blanc 2008 Interesting wine with an abundance of tropical fruit on both bouquet and palate; does trip over itself on the finish a little. Screwcap. 13% alc. **Rating** 87 **To** 2010 $17.95
Shiraz 2005 Light colour; medium-bodied wine with pleasant shiraz fruit but not much excitement. Screwcap. 14.5% alc. **Rating** 87 **To** 2013 $18

Blueberry Hill Vineyard   ★★★★

Cnr McDonalds Road/Coulson Road, Pokolbin, NSW 2320 **Region** Lower Hunter Valley
T (02) 4998 7295 **F** (02) 4998 7296 **www**.blueberryhill.com.au **Open** 7 days 10–5
Winemaker Monarch Winemaking Services **Est.** 1973 **Cases** 2000 **Vyds** 5.6 ha
Blueberry Hill Vineyard is part of the old McPherson Estate, with fully mature plantings of chardonnay, sauvignon blanc, shiraz, pinot noir, merlot and cabernet sauvignon. Part of the grape production is sold to other winemakers, part used for the extensive Blueberry Hill range.

ΨΨΨΨΩ **Sauvignon Blanc 2008** Although the label gives no clue, it has to be from a cool region, with classic passionfruit, gooseberry and kiwi fruit coursing through the long, well-balanced palate. Screwcap. 11.5% alc. **Rating** 92 **To** 2010 $25

Pinot Noir 2007 Wholly remarkable pinot from 100% estate-grown grapes, with far more varietal expression than usual from the Hunter Valley; attractive spicy nuances to the plum and cherry fruit; good balance and length. Screwcap. 14% alc. Rating 91 To 2012 $35

Bluestone Acres Vineyard ★★★

PO Box 206, Wandin North, Vic 3139 **Region** Yarra Valley
T (03) 5964 4909 **F** (03) 5964 3936 **www**.bluestoneacres.com.au **Open** Not
Winemaker Paul Evans **Est.** 2000 **Cases** 1000 **Vyds** 3.5 ha
Graeme and Isabel Ross have 1.3 ha of merlot, 1.2 ha of shiraz and 1 ha of sauvignon blanc on a north-facing slope. The soil is predominantly grey loam in the merlot and shiraz blocks, with a vein of volcanic red clay loam running through part of the shiraz and most of the sauvignon blanc block; a vein of basalt adds spice to the salt of the sauvignon blanc. Integrated pest management is used in the vineyard (no insecticides) and sprays are held to a minimum.

� **Yarra Valley Rose 2008** A merlot-based rose with sweet raspberry and strawberry fruit on the mid-palate before moving through to a balanced, dry finish. Screwcap. 12.3% alc. **Rating** 89 **To** 2010 $15
Yarra Valley Shiraz 2006 Light-bodied spice and herb nuances attest to the cool region (and site), black and red fruits emerging at the end of the palate and aftertaste; balanced oak a plus. Diam. 13.5% alc. **Rating** 88 **To** 2014 $23
Yarra Valley Sauvignon Blanc 2008 Despite low alcohol, has quite ripe tropical fruit balanced by touches of grass and asparagus; overall on the light side. Screwcap. 11.4% alc. **Rating** 87 **To** 2010 $18

Boat O'Craigo ★★★★

458 Maroondah Highway, Healesville, Vic 3777 **Region** Yarra Valley
T (03) 5962 6899 **www**.boatocraigo.com.au **Open** Thurs–Mon 10.30–5.30
Winemaker Al Fencaros, The Yarra Hill (Contract) **Est.** 1998 **Cases** 3500
Steve Graham purchased the property, which is now known as Boat O'Craigo (a tiny place in a Scottish valley where his ancestors lived), in 2003. It has two quite separate vineyards: a 12-ha hillside planting on one of the highest sites in the Yarra Valley, and 7.5 ha at Kangaroo Ground on the opposite side of the valley. Exports to China and Hong Kong.

♗♗♗♗♗ **Black Cameron Yarra Valley Shiraz 2006** Fragrant redcurrant, floral and spice bouquet; medium-bodied, with silky tannin and juicy red fruits that linger satisfyingly on the palate; poised and very good value. Screwcap. 14% alc. Rating 92 To 2015 $24
Healesville Yarra Valley Sauvignon Blanc 2008 Some matchstick complexity on the bouquet, with guava and fresh cut grass; quite rich and thickly textured, yet the finish is lively and lithe. Screwcap. 12.5% alc. **Rating** 90 **To** 2011 $18
Braveheart Yarra Valley Cabernet Merlot Cabernet Franc 2006 A black cherry and plum bouquet, with a touch of cedar; the palate is lively, and shows some black olive and brambly complexity; firm and dry on the finish. Diam. 13.6% alc. **Rating** 90 **To** 2014 $24

♗♗♗♗ **Dundee Yarra Valley Shiraz Viognier 2007** Bright colour; highly perfumed, with the apricot character from the viognier not fully integrating with the shiraz; medium bodied, cherry and plum with a little spice on the palate. Screwcap. 13.3% alc. **Rating** 89 **To** 2013 $24
Rob Roy Yarra Valley Pinot Noir 2007 Bright colour; waxy oak bouquet, with spiced cherry fruit; bright cherry fruit on the palate, with a toasty firm finish. Screwcap. 12.5% alc. **Rating** 88 **To** 2013 $24

🍇 Bobtail Ridge Wines ★★★★★

Lot 50 Yarnup Road, Frankland River, WA 6396 **Region** Frankland River
T (08) 9856 6289 **F** (08) 9856 6287 **www**.bobtailridge.com.au **Open** 7 days 10–4
Winemaker Alkoomi Wines **Est.** 1980 **Cases** 520 **Vyds** 11.4 ha

June and Jeremy Roberts were among the early movers in Frankland River, diversifying part of their property by planting vines with the intention of having the grapes vinified. Farming and family commitments delayed that process until 2003, when a Shiraz designed for easy drinking and short-term cellaring was made. In the meantime the plantings had been increased with 3.3 ha of riesling, 1.6 ha each of semillon, sauvignon blanc and cabernet sauvignon, 2.5 ha of shiraz and 0.8 ha of merlot. After some experimentation, they now make a Semillon, Riesling, Shiraz and Cabernet Merlot each year, the red wines matured in French oak. The family does all the vineyard work as part of its farming activities, using a minimal spraying program and hand-pruning the vines. The majority of the grapes are sold to Alkoomi, with only limited quantities vinified under the Bobtail Ridge label, which are consistently of excellent quality.

ΨΨΨΨΨ **Frankland River Riesling 2005** Bright, crisp and lively, a touch of CO_2 adding to the impact; a delicious combination of lime and green apple on the long finish. Screwcap. 12.5% alc. **Rating** 94 **To** 2015 $15
Frankland River Semillon 2008 Water white nine months from vintage; unusually aromatic and expressive grass and herb aromas followed by a vibrant palate with good thrust and length. Will age very well. Screwcap. 12% alc. **Rating** 94 **To** 2015 $15
Frankland River Semillon 2005 Bright straw-green; is precisely following the development path of quality semillon, adding the first hints of honey and toast to the base of citrus and herb fruit. Screwcap. 12% alc. **Rating** 94 **To** 2013 $15
Frankland River Semillon 2004 Consistent with the younger wines in terms of character and structure; here the toasty component is quite obvious although the grassy/citrussy/minerally finish and aftertaste is still fresh. Screwcap. 12% alc. **Rating** 94 **To** 2012 $15
Frankland River Shiraz 2007 Dense purple; full-bodied, very powerful and rich, with layers of blackberry, licorice and plum, ripe tannins embedded in the fruit. Needs a decade to reveal all. Screwcap. 14% alc. **Rating** 94 **To** 2027 $15

ΨΨΨΨΨ **Frankland River Semillon 2006** Bright, light straw-green; has verve and vitality, with wild herb, grass and citrus nuances; lancing acidity on the finish. Screwcap. 11.5% alc. **Rating** 93 **To** 2014 $15
Frankland River Cabernet Merlot 2007 More depth and structure than the Bobtail Shirazs; black fruits, cedar and savoury, but ripe, tannins run along medium- to full-bodied palate; long finish. Screwcap. 13% alc. **Rating** 91 **To** 2017 $15
Frankland River Riesling 2006 A complex, rich bouquet with some nuances possibly deriving from a touch of botrytis; the palate, too, is rich, but with energy and length. Screwcap. 11% alc. **Rating** 90 **To** 2014 $15
Frankland River Riesling 2004 Still a youthful green-straw colour, although there are some signs of development on the easygoing, lime-accented palate. Screwcap. 11% alc. **Rating** 90 **To** 2012 $15
Frankland River Shiraz 2004 Much riper fruit on the bouquet than the younger vintages, although the alcohol is the same, and there are elements of spice and pepper, and a savoury finish. Screwcap. 13.5% alc. **Rating** 90 **To** 2012 $15
Frankland River Cabernet Merlot 2005 Good weight and balance; predominantly blackcurrant with tannins on the back palate and finish; slightly furry/dusty. Screwcap. 13.5% alc. **Rating** 90 **To** 2015 $15

ΨΨΨΨ **Frankland River Shiraz 2006** A light- to medium-bodied strongly spicy/savoury wine with good balance and length, although robbed of greater fruit depth by the vintage. Screwcap. 13% alc. **Rating** 89 **To** 2013 $15
Frankland River Shiraz 2005 Bright hue; strongly spicy/peppery overtones to the red and black cherry fruit on both bouquet and palate; the tannins are slightly green, a pity. Screwcap. 13.5% alc. **Rating** 89 **To** 2013 $15
Frankland River Cabernet Merlot 2004 Holding youthful hue; lighter in body than the '05, but has length and attractive cassis and blackcurrant fruit. Screwcap. 13.5% alc. **Rating** 89 **To** 2014 $15

Frankland River Cabernet Merlot 2006 Light-bodied, fresh, predominantly red fruits; minimal tannins – but they are ripe – and oak. Screwcap. 12% alc. **Rating** 87 **To** 2012 $15

Bochara Wines

1099 Glenelg Highway, Hamilton, Vic 3300 **Region** Henty
T (03) 5571 9309 **F** (03) 5571 9309 **www**.bocharawine.com.au **Open** Fri–Sun 11–5, or by appt
Winemaker Martin Slocombe **Est.** 1998 **Cases** 1000 **Vyds** 2.2 ha
This is the small business of experienced winemaker Martin Slocombe and former Yalumba viticulturist Kylie McIntyre. They have established 1 ha each of pinot noir and sauvignon blanc and 0.2 ha of gewurztraminer, supplemented by grapes purchased from local growers. The modestly priced but well-made wines are principally sold through the cellar door on the property, a decrepit weatherboard shanty with one cold tap that has been transformed into a fully functional two-room tasting area, and through a number of local restaurants and bottle shops. The label design, incidentally, comes from a 1901 poster advertising the subdivision of the original Bochara property into smaller farms. Yet another to be decimated by the spring frosts of 2006, resulting in no wines from 2007. The 2008 vintage will flow through in the next edition. The rating has been maintained from the 2009 *Wine Companion*.

Boireann

26 Donnellys Castle Road, The Summit, Qld, 4377 **Region** Granite Belt
T (07) 4683 2194 **www**.boireannwinery.com.au **Open** 7 days 10–4.30
Winemaker Peter Stark **Est.** 1998 **Cases** 900 **Vyds** 1.6 ha
Peter and Therese Stark have a 10-ha property set amongst the great granite boulders and trees that are so much a part of the Granite Belt. They have planted no fewer than 11 varieties, including the four that go to make a Bordeaux-blend; shiraz and viognier; grenache and mourvedre providing a Rhône blend, and there will also be a straight merlot. Tannat (French) and barbera and nebbiolo (Italian) make up the viticultural League of Nations. Peter Stark is a winemaker of exceptional talent, producing cameo amounts of quite beautifully made red wines that are of a quality equal to Australia's best. The loss of the 2007 vintage to frost compelled Peter Stark to purchase grapes from other Granite Belt producers, demonstrating his exceptional winemaking skills.

ᵀᵀᵀᵀᵀ **Granite Belt Mourvedre Shiraz 2007** The blend, with 60% mourvedre, works exceptionally well; has structure from shiraz, the perfume and sweet berry fruit from the mourvedre; has personality, length and balance. Diam. 14.5% alc. **Rating** 94 **To** 2017
The Lurnea Granite Belt 2007 Excellent colour; a lovely wine with abundant red and black fruits with very good length and balance; the sure touch of finesse. Merlot (60%) ex–Golden Grove/Cabernet Franc ex–Masons Vineyard. Diam. 13.5% alc. **Rating** 94 **To** 2015
Granite Belt Cabernet Sauvignon 2007 Very good colour; a powerful wine, with classic cabernet structure and flavours, ranging through blackcurrant, cassis and black olive on the finish. Diam. 13.5% alc. **Rating** 94 **To** 2018

ᵀᵀᵀᵀᵀ **Granite Belt Shiraz 2007** A big wine, with lots of blackberry fruit and slightly chunky tannins; will evolve. Diam. 14% alc. **Rating** 92 **To** 2020
Mourvedre 2007 Typical varietal perfume; an elegant wine with sweet berry fruit, the tannins well controlled. Golden Grove. Diam. 15% alc. **Rating** 92 **To** 2014
Granite Belt Merlot 2007 Blackcurrant and black olive flavours on the palate have an obvious, albeit fine, tannin structure. Masons Vineyard. Diam. 13.5% alc. **Rating** 91 **To** 2013

ᵀᵀᵀᵀ **Granite Belt Barbera 2007** Ripe plummy fruit, with a slightly rustic mouthfeel, line not as seamless as usual. Golden Grove. Diam. 14% alc. **Rating** 89 **To** 2013

Borambola Wines

Sturt Highway, Wagga Wagga, NSW 2650 **Region** Gundagai
T (02) 6928 4210 **F** (02) 6928 4210 **www**.borambola.com **Open** 7 days 11–4 by appt
Winemaker Chris Derrez **Est.** 1995 **Cases** 3000 **Vyds** 9.16 ha
Borambola Homestead was built in the 1880s, and in the latter part of that century was the centre of a pastoral empire of 1.4 million ha, ownership of which passed to the McMullen family in 1992. It is situated in rolling foothills 25 km east of Wagga Wagga in the Gundagai region. The vineyards surround the homestead and include shiraz, cabernet sauvignon and chardonnay.

Borrodell on the Mount ★★★★☆

Lake Canobolas Road, Orange, NSW 2800 **Region** Orange
T (02) 6365 3425 **F** (02) 6365 3588 **www**.borrodell.com.au **Open** 7 days 10–5
Winemaker Chris Derrez, Lucy Maddox, Peter Logan, Phil Kerney **Est.** 1995
Cases 2000 **Vyds** 5.25 ha
Borry Gartrell and Gaye Stuart-Nairne have planted pinot noir, sauvignon blanc, pinot meunier, traminer and chardonnay adjacent to a cherry, plum and heritage apple orchard and truffiere. It is a 10-min drive from Orange, and adjacent to Lake Canobolas, at an altitude of 1000 m. The wines have been consistent medal winners at regional and small winemaker shows.

♀♀♀♀♀ **Wine Makers Daughter Orange Gewurztraminer 2008** Has an exceptionally fragrant and perfumed bouquet with an exotic array of spice and musk, baked apple and a hint of citrus, all of which come thundering through on the Alsatian-like palate. A wine in a hundred. Screwcap. 14.5% alc. **Rating** 95 To 2013 $22

♀♀♀♀♀ **Orange Chardonnay 2006** A smoky bacon edge to the bouquet is strange, as not much French oak was used, nor is it evident on the quite intense nectarine and grapefruit palate. Screwcap. 14.3% alc. **Rating** 90 **To** 2014 $20
Orange Pinot Noir 2006 Brightly hued; relatively light-bodied, and distinctly in the savoury/spicy spectrum, but has considerable thrust and energy to the long palate. Screwcap. 13.9% alc. **Rating** 90 **To** 2014 $27

♀♀♀♀ **Orange Sauvignon Blanc 2008** A slightly closed bouquet is followed by a palate that is also withdrawn; strange, for it's not reduction in the normal sense, and the underlying fruit is definitely there. Screwcap. 14.5% alc. **Rating** 88 To 2012 $20

Boston Bay Wines

Lincoln Highway, Port Lincoln, SA 5606 **Region** Southern Eyre Peninsula
T (08) 8684 3600 **www**.bostonbaywines.com.au **Open** Thurs–Mon 12–4
Winemaker David O'Leary, Nick Walker **Est.** 1984 **Cases** 4000 **Vyds** 6.87 ha
A strongly tourist-oriented operation that has extended the viticultural map in SA. It is situated on the same latitude as Adelaide, overlooking the Spencer Gulf at the southern tip of the Eyre Peninsula. Say proprietors Graham and Mary Ford, 'it is the only vineyard in the world to offer frequent sightings of whales at play in the waters at its foot'. White wines are the strength.

♀♀♀♀♀ **Riesling 2008** Focused lime fruit bouquet with a mere trace of mineral; the lime juice follows onto the palate, and provides a zesty, dry and focused finish. Screwcap. 11.8% alc. **Rating** 90 **To** 2015 $17
Chardonnay 2008 Restrained melon bouquet with a touch of citrus; quite focused showing mid-palate richness and vibrant acidity on the slightly lemony finish. Screwcap. 12.5% alc. **Rating** 90 **To** 2014 $17

Botobolar

89 Botobolar Road, Mudgee, NSW 2850 **Region** Mudgee
T (02) 6373 3850 **www**.botobolar.com **Open** Mon–Sat 10–5, Sun 10–3
Winemaker Kevin Karstrom **Est.** 1971 **Cases** 4000 **Vyds** 18 ha
One of the first (possibly the first) fully organic vineyards in Australia, with present owner
Kevin Karstrom continuing the practices established by founder Gil Wahlquist. Preservative-
free reds and low-preservative dry whites extend the organic practice of the vineyard to the
winery. Dry Red is consistently the best wine to appear under the Botobolar label, with gold-
medal success at the Mudgee Wine Show. Its preservative-free red wines are in the top echelon
of this class. Since 2008 the vineyard had been undergoing progressive retrellising that will lead
to a temporary reduction of production. Exports to Denmark and Japan.

 Merlot 2007 Deep colour; a full-bodied wine, but avoids excess tannins; there are
more black fruit flavours than red, and there isn't obvious varietal character, but at
this price it's hard to complain. Diam. 14% alc. **Rating** 88 **To** 2015 $15
Preservative Free Shiraz 2008 Fresh raspberry and cherry fruit aromas, a
touch of blackberry joining the party on the palate; well made, and protected by
the screwcap. Screwcap. 13% alc. **Rating** 87 **To** 2011 $16
KK's Choice Mudgee Shiraz 2005 Dense colour; bitter chocolate and
leather nuances to a full-bodied wine, the black fruit flavours yielding to very
powerful tannins that need to soften soon, but may not. Diam. 14% alc. **Rating** 87
To 2015 $18

Bowen Estate

Riddoch Highway, Coonawarra, SA 5263 **Region** Coonawarra
T (08) 8737 2229 **F** (08) 8737 2173 **Open** 7 days 10–5
Winemaker Doug Bowen, Emma Bowen **Est.** 1972 **Cases** 12 000 **Vyds** 32.4 ha
Bluff-faced regional veteran Doug Bowen, now with daughter Emma at his side in the winery,
presides over one of Coonawarra's landmarks. The 2006 reds mark a welcome return to top
form for this emblematic winery. Exports to the UK, the US, China, Japan and NZ.

Coonawarra Shiraz 2006 A welcome return to top form; touches of spice to
the black fruits of the bouquet, then a lively medium-bodied palate with ripples
of black fruits, spice and cedary oak; good tannins. Cork. 14.5% alc. **Rating** 94
To 2016 $29.80

Coonawarra Cabernet Sauvignon 2006 Full-bodied, with uncompromising
cabernet varietal fruit in regional mode: in other words, blackcurrant and earth on
a tightly wound palate. Great future. Cork. 14.5% alc. **Rating** 93 **To** 2021 $29.80

Coonawarra Chardonnay 2007 Gentle nectarine and grapefruit flavours
matched by subtle oak and balanced acidity; well made. Screwcap. 13.5% alc.
Rating 89 **To** 2012 $22.50

Box Stallion   ★★★★★

64 Tubbarubba Road, Merricks North, Vic 3926 **Region** Mornington Peninsula
T (03) 5989 7444 **F** (03) 5989 7688 **www**.boxstallion.com.au **Open** 7 days 11–5
Winemaker Alex White **Est.** 2001 **Cases** 9000 **Vyds** 16 ha
Box Stallion is the joint venture of Stephen Wharton, John Gillies and Garry Zerbe, who have
linked two vineyards at Bittern and Merricks North, with 16 ha of vines planted between
1997 and '03. What was once a thoroughbred stud has now become a vineyard, with the Red
Barn (in their words) 'now home to a stable of fine wines'. Exports to the US, Canada, Japan
and China.

Mornington Peninsula Sauvignon Blanc 2008 A fresh and clean bouquet
with gently tropical fruits, then a crisp, lively and immaculately balanced palate; this
is subtle rather than in-your-face, with good length and deserving its gold medals.
Screwcap. 13% alc. **Rating** 94 **To** 2010 $20

Mornington Peninsula Tempranillo 2006 A mix of bright fruits and darker, savoury nuances; has particularly good balance and mouthfeel, with a supple texture and good flavour. Very good tempranillo. Diam. 15% alc. **Rating** 94 To 2015 $40

 !!!!! Mornington Peninsula Gewurztraminer 2008 Rose petal, bath power and spice aromas lead into a relatively light but positively flavoured palate; good varietal expression. Screwcap. 13.1% alc. **Rating** 90 To 2013 $25
Red Barn Mornington Peninsula Chardonnay 2005 Still very youthful; obvious citrussy overlay to the stone fruit flavours courtesy of early picking, but has exemplary length in a quasi-Chablis mode, and a clean finish. Screwcap. 12.6% alc. **Rating** 90 To 2015 $20
The Enclosure Mornington Peninsula Chardonnay 2004 Very potent and funky, the fruit aromas and flavours bordering on the aggressive so intense are they; demands food, but will repay faith. Diam. 14% alc. **Rating** 90 To 2012 $25
Mornington Peninsula Dolcetto 2006 Light, but bright, fuschia-crimson; scented red fruits, then a mix of strawberry and morello cherry on the fine palate. Drink soon. Screwcap. 14.3% alc. **Rating** 90 To 2013 $20

!!!! The Enclosure Mornington Peninsula Pinot Noir 2006 Similar colour and savoury, spicy, forest floor flavours to Red Barn, but with a little more persistence and length. Diam. 14% alc. **Rating** 89 To 2010 $30
Mornington Peninsula Tempranillo 2005 Light-to medium-bodied weight; the fruit flavours range from citrus to strawberry to cherry; good length, though not much structure. Cork. 14.6% alc. **Rating** 89 To 2010 $40
Mornington Peninsula Arneis 2008 Quite fragrant lemon blossom and honeysuckle aromas; some hints of honeycomb on the palate; older vines giving more character than previously? Screwcap. 14.3% alc. **Rating** 87 To 2011 $20
Red Barn Mornington Peninsula Pinot Noir 2006 Light colour; simply too light, although it has pleasant sous bois savoury flavours and fair length. Diam. 14% alc. **Rating** 87 To 2009 $20

Boynton's Feathertop   ★★★★☆

Great Alpine Road, Porepunkah, Vic 3741 **Region** Alpine Valleys
T (03) 5756 2356 **F** (03) 5756 2610 **www**.boynton.com.au **Open** 7 days 10–5
Winemaker Kel Boynton **Est.** 1987 **Cases** 10 000 **Vyds** 18 ha
Kel Boynton has a beautiful vineyard, framed by Mt Feathertop rising above it. Overall, the red wines have always outshone the whites. The initial very strong American oak input has been softened in more recent vintages to give a better fruit/oak balance. The wines are released under the Boynton Reserve and Feathertop labels. The 2007 vintage, blitzed by drought and smoke taint, was a near-impossible challenge. Exports to Austria.

!!!!! Alpine Valleys Sauvignon Blanc 2008 The fragrant bouquet is bursting with passionfruit and tropical fruit, the well-balanced and focused palate providing more of the same. Excellent outcome. Screwcap. 13% alc. **Rating** 94 To 2011 $20

!!!!! Alpine Valleys Merlot 2006 Fragrant spice, cedar and tobacco aromas lead into an unexpectedly intense cassis-driven palate; impressive wine. Screwcap. 14% alc. **Rating** 93 To 2016 $25
Alpine Valleys Shiraz 2005 A fragrant bouquet of red fruits lifted by a splash of viognier, then a supple, smooth medium-bodied palate with fine, gently savoury, tannins on the finish. Screwcap. 14% alc. **Rating** 91 To 2014 $25

❧ Brackenwood Vineyard   ★★★★

Level 6, 431–439 King William Street, Adelaide, SA 5000 (postal) **Region** Adelaide Hills
T 0400 266 121 **F** (08) 8110 9889 **www**.brackenwoodvineyard.com.au **Open** Not
Winemaker Damon Nagel, Reg Wilkingson **Est.** 1999 **Cases** 1500 **Vyds** 6.4 ha

Brackenwood Vineyard is situated at the extreme southern end of the Adelaide Hills, skirted by the Old Victor Harbour Road. Damon Nagel has established 2.65 ha of shiraz, 1.7 ha of riesling, 1.3 ha of sauvignon blanc and 0.75 ha of chardonnay, and all wines are estate-grown. The wines are sold through an impressive list of Adelaide restaurants and speciality wine retailers.

ΨΨΨΨΨ **Adelaide Hills Sauvignon Blanc 2008** Offers a fragrant mix of herb, grass and gooseberry on the bouquet, augmented by a touch of passionfruit on the lively, clean and crisp palate. Value. Screwcap. 12.5% alc. **Rating** 93 **To** 2012 $19

MC Adelaide Hills Syrah 2008 Crimson; an aromatic bouquet with plum and blackberry to the fore; the well-balanced palate has the unmistakable footprint of partial carbonic maceration, which gives the tannins in particular a soft profile, the flavours spicy and lively. Value. Screwcap. 13% alc. **Rating** 93 **To** 2018 $19

Adelaide Hills Sparkling Shiraz 2005 Dense colour; despite bottle fermentation and some time on lees, is still very youthful, and will prosper for at least another five years, as the balance is good, the spicy fruit with good character. Crown Seal. 14% alc. **Rating** 91 **To** 2014 $24

Adelaide Hills Riesling 2008 Rich, ripe lime and tropical/passionfruit aromas and flavours; relatively early drinking the best course. Screwcap. 12% alc. **Rating** 90 **To** 2014 $19

RW Adelaide Hills Shiraz 2006 A largely successful attempt to create an Amarone-style wine, the bunches laid on straw mats for 88 days before crushing and fermentation; complex, slightly raisined flavours, and carries its alcohol with dignity; 375 ml. Vino-Lok. 15.5% alc. **Rating** 90 **To** 2013 $38

Reserve Adelaide Hills Shiraz 2005 Strong colour; a generous wine with a lush density of texture explained by the west-facing slope on which the grapes are grown; not typical Adelaide Hills, but no shortage of flavour, and a long life ahead. Screwcap. 14.5% alc. **Rating** 90 **To** 2020 $38

Adelaide Hills Botrytis Riesling 2006 Deep golden-yellow; extremely luscious and rich, into crystallised fruit territory, but with good acidity to balance, along with a touch of oak. Picked 21 May to 18 June. Screwcap. 10.5% alc. **Rating** 90 **To** 2012 $24

ΨΨΨΨ **Adelaide Hills Shiraz 2006** A highly aromatic and spicy bouquet is followed by a light-bodied palate with spicy overtones to the small berry fruits; no attempt to over-extract, but 22 months in French oak was a little too long. Screwcap. 14% alc. **Rating** 89 **To** 2013 $20

Adelaide Hills Pinot Noir 2007 Unusual colour, dark purple hue; a pinot of large proportions, with savoury black fruits on a solid, as yet slightly dumb, palate. Future development uncertain. Vino-Lok. 13.8% alc. **Rating** 88 **To** 2014 $32

Adelaide Hills Chardonnay 2007 A light- to medium-bodied chardonnay, fruit and French oak in harmony, although the overall flavour level is modest; apple and citrus are the main players. Vino-Lok. 13% alc. **Rating** 87 **To** 2012 $24

Braewattie   ★★★

351 Rochford Road, Rochford, Vic 3442 **Region** Macedon Ranges
T (03) 9818 5742 **F** (03) 9818 8361 **Open** By appt
Winemaker Jillian Ryan, Hanging Rock Winery **Est.** 1993 **Cases** 250 **Vyds** 5.5 ha
Maggi Ryan's great-grandfather acquired the Braewattie property in the 1880s, and it remained in the family until 1971. When the property came back on the market in 1990, Maggi and husband Des seized the opportunity to reclaim it, complete with a small existing planting of 300 pinot noir and chardonnay vines. Those plantings now extend to 4.4 ha of pinot noir and 1.1 ha of chardonnay; part of the production is sold and a small amount is contract-made. The Macedon Brut is a particularly good wine.

ΨΨΨΨ **Macedon Chardonnay 2006** Slow developing, aromatic, citrus-tinged style that has shrugged off the influence of barrel maturation; easy style to enjoy. Screwcap. 13% alc. **Rating** 89 **To** 2013 $20

Brand's Laira Coonawarra   ★★★★★

Riddoch Highway, Coonawarra, SA 5263 **Region** Coonawarra
T (08) 8736 3260 **www**.mcwilliams.com.au **Open** Mon–Fri 8–5, w'ends 10–4
Winemaker Peter Weinberg **Est.** 1966 **Cases** NFP **Vyds** 278 ha
Part of a substantial investment in Coonawarra by McWilliam's, which first acquired a 50%
interest from the Brand family, increased to 100%, and followed this with the purchase of
100 ha of additional vineyard land. Significantly increased production of the smooth wines for
which Brand's is known has followed. The estate plantings include the 100-year-old Stentiford
block.

ΨΨΨΨΨ **Eric's Blend 2001** The colour is still remarkably deep, the fruit still in the prime
of youth; an array of blackcurrant, blackberry and notes of licorice, earth and cedar
whispering in the background. Cabernet Sauvignon/Merlot/Shiraz. Cork. 14% alc.
Rating 96 **To** 2026 $74.99
Shiraz 2006 Bright colour; a touch of mint frames a focused core of red fruit;
the palate is quite dense but also with lightness from the red fruit and acid profile;
gently savoury on the finish. Screwcap. 14% alc. **Rating** 94 **To** 2016 $21.99
Stentiford's Old Vine Shiraz 2003 Retains good hue; has excellent structure,
silky tannins running through the length of the palate, caressing the spicy black
fruits, oak adding its support. Cork dictated by the heavy designer bottle. 15% alc.
Rating 94 **To** 2013 $74.99
Blockers Cabernet Sauvignon 2005 Some colour development; an appealing
mix of blackcurrant, mulberry and cedar/mocha oak on both bouquet and palate;
superfine tannins. Screwcap. 15.5% alc. **Rating** 94 **To** 2018 $24.99

ΨΨΨΨΩ **Chardonnay 2007** Pale straw-green; elegant light- to medium-bodied wine,
with stone fruit and citrus on the mid-palate, more savoury minerality on the
finish. Screwcap. 14% alc. **Rating** 93 **To** 2013 $21.99
Cabernet Merlot 2007 Fragrant cassis/red berry aromas lead into a medium-
bodied palate; powdery tannins appear early with some darker fruit flavours; fresh
acidity lengthens the palate. Screwcap. 14.5% alc. **Rating** 92 **To** 2017 $21.99

ΨΨΨΨ **Merlot 2006** Plums and spice with a touch of prune; the palate is quite soft and
full of sweet red fruit, and plenty of oak; soft and easy on the finish. Screwcap.
14.3% alc. **Rating** 89 **To** 2012 $24.99
Blockers Cabernet Sauvignon 2006 Quite dark colour and personality;
savoury tar and olive bouquet, with an underpinning of dark fruit; the palate is
dense, chewy and quite long. Screwcap. 14% alc. **Rating** 89 **To** 2014 $24.99

Brandy Creek Wines   ★★★☆

570 Buln Buln Road, Drouin East, Vic 3818 **Region** Gippsland
T (03) 5625 4498 **www**.brandycreekwines.com.au **Open** Thurs–Sun & public hols 10–5,
Fri–Sat nights
Winemaker Peter Beckingham (Contract) **Est.** 2005 **Cases** 2500 **Vyds** 3 ha
Marie McDonald and Rick Stockdale purchased the property on which they have since
established their vineyard, cellar door and café restaurant in 1997. Pinot gris, tempranillo and
pinot meunier has been progressively established, with other varieties purchased from local
growers. The café (and surrounding vineyard) is situated on a northeast-facing slope with
spectacular views out to the Baw Baw Ranges.

ΨΨΨΨΩ **Tempranillo 2007** Has positive varietal character, with juicy red berry fruits
and finely balanced acidity; a long palate and aftertaste are especially meritorious.
Screwcap. 15% alc. **Rating** 90 **To** 2013 $28

ΨΨΨΨ **Wooded Gippsland Chardonnay 2007** Has tangy/citrussy overtones to the
stone fruit on both bouquet and palate; the oak contribution is subtle. Screwcap.
13.5% alc. **Rating** 87 **To** 2012 $25

Brangayne of Orange

837 Pinnacle Road, Orange, NSW 2800 **Region** Orange
T (02) 6365 3229 **F** (02) 6365 3170 **www**.brangayne.com **Open** Mon–Fri 11–1, 2–4,
w'ends 10–5, or by appt
Winemaker Simon Gilbert **Est.** 1994 **Cases** 3000 **Vyds** 25.7 ha
Orchardists Don and Pamela Hoskins decided to diversify into grapegrowing in 1994 and
have progressively established high-quality vineyards. Right from the outset, Brangayne has
produced excellent wines across all mainstream varieties, remarkably ranging from Pinot Noir
to Cabernet Sauvignon. Son David has been managing the business since 2005. Exports to
the UK, Canada and Spain.

ΨΨΨΨΨ **Sauvignon Blanc 2008** A pungently varietal bouquet, with gooseberry kiwi
fruit and herbs, perilously close to sweaty/reductive, but the incisive palate throws
off that issue, so intense are the flavours. Not for everyone, perhaps. Screwcap.
12.5% alc. **Rating** 94 **To** 2011 $24

ΨΨΨΨΨ **Isolde Reserve Chardonnay 2006** Bright green-gold; complex, bottle-
developed wine, with layers of flavour; white peach, nectarine and some cashew
are framed by French oak, the acidity sufficient to reign the wine in. Screwcap.
14% alc. **Rating** 91 **To** 2013 $30

Brave Goose Vineyard

PO Box 633, Seymour, Vic 3660 **Region** Goulburn Valley
T (03) 5799 1229 **F** (03) 5799 0636 **www**.bravegoosevineyard.com.au **Open** By appt
Winemaker John Stocker, Don Lewis **Est.** 1988 **Cases** 400
Dr John Stocker and wife Joanne must be among the most highly qualified boutique vineyard
and winery operators in Australia. John Stocker is the former chief executive of CSIRO and
chairman of the Grape and Wine Research & Development Corporation for seven years, and
daughter Nina has completed the Roseworthy postgraduate oenology course. Moreover, they
established their first vineyard (while living in Switzerland) on the French/Swiss border in
the village of Flueh. On returning to Australia in 1987 they found a property on the inside
of the Great Dividing Range with north-facing slopes and shallow, weathered ironstone soils.
Here they have established 2.5 ha each of shiraz and cabernet sauvignon, and 0.5 ha each of
merlot and gamay, selling the majority of grapes from the 20-year-old vines, but making small
quantities of Cabernet Merlot, Merlot and Gamay. The brave goose in question was the sole
survivor of a flock put into the vineyard to repel cockatoos and foxes.

ΨΨΨΨΨ **Gamay 2008** Light crimson; an attractive tart edge to the light-bodied red fruit
flavours is present from the word go through to a bright finish; serve lightly chilled
with almost any food you choose. Cork. 12.5% alc. **Rating** 90 **To** 2010 $20

Braydun Hill Vineyard

38–40 Hepenstal Road, Hackham. SA 5163 **Region** McLaren Vale
T (08) 8382 3023 **www**.braydunhill.com.au **Open** Thurs–Sun & public hols 11–4
Winemaker Rebecca Kennedy **Est.** 2001 **Cases** 2500 **Vyds** 4.5 ha
It is hard to imagine there would be such an interesting (and inspiring) story behind a vineyard
planted between 1998 and 1999 by the husband and wife team of Tony Dunn and Carol
Bradley, wishing to get out of growing angora goats and into grapegrowing. The extension
of the business into winemaking was totally unplanned, forced on them by the liquidation of
Normans in late 2001. With humour, courage and perseverance, they have met obstacles and
setbacks which would have caused many to give up, and have produced wines since 2001
which leave no doubt this is a distinguished site capable of producing Shiraz of consistently
high quality. Exports to China, Taiwan and Singapore.

ΨΨΨΨΨ **Single Vineyard Premium McLaren Vale Shiraz 2007** Screams its varietal
origin, with dark chocolate wrapped around a core of supple black fruits; the
alcohol doesn't heat the wine unduly. Cork. 15.2% alc. **Rating** 90 **To** 2017 $35

Bream Creek

Marion Bay Road, Bream Creek, Tas 7175 **Region** Southern Tasmania
T (03) 6231 4646 **F** (03) 6231 4646 **www**.breamcreekvineyard.com.au **Open** At Potters
Croft, Dunalley, tel (03) 6253 5469
Winemaker Winemaking Tasmania (Julian Alcorso) **Est.** 1973 **Cases** 5000 **Vyds** 7.6 ha
Until 1990 the Bream Creek fruit was sold to Moorilla Estate, but since then the winery
has been independently owned and managed under the control of Fred Peacock, legendary
for the care he bestows on the vines under his direction. Peacock's skills have seen both an
increase in production and also outstanding wine quality across the range, headed by the Pinot
Noir. The list of trophies, gold, silver and bronze medals won extends for nine neatly-typed A4
pages. The Tamar Valley vineyard has been sold, allowing Fred Peacock to concentrate on the
southern vineyards, where he is still a consultant/manager of non-estate plantings. Exports to
Canada, Sweden Singapore and Indonesia.

ꝋꝋꝋꝋꝋ **Reserve Pinot Noir 2005** Bright and lively with red berries and five spice on
the bouquet; vibrant palate, with good acid, and a clean-fruited finish; velvety, long
and supple. Three trophies and six gold medals, including National and Adelaide
Wine Shows. Still available. Diam. **Rating** 95 **To** 2012 $34
Cabernet Sauvignon 2005 Great colour; vibrant and complex with redcurrant
and cassis framed by cedar and plentiful fine-grained tannins; long and fine. Still
available. Diam. **Rating** 95 **To** 2014 $24
Riesling 2007 Clean, crisp, minerally; good line, length and balance to a wine
with delicacy and finesse. Screwcap. 11.9% alc. **Rating** 94 **To** 2015 $21
Sauvignon Blanc 2008 An aromatic, flowery bouquet; passionfruit/tropical
fruit neatly tied up by good acidity, and a grassy note on the finish. Trophy and
gold medal Hobart International Wine Show '08. Screwcap. 12.5% alc. **Rating** 94
To 2010 $24

ꝋꝋꝋꝋꝋ **VGR Riesling 2008** Pleasantly ripe sweet lime juice flavours; has persistence and
length, and good balance. Drink now or later. Screwcap. 11.8% alc. **Rating** 90
To 2014 $21
Chardonnay 2007 Bright, light green-straw; fragrant blossom aromas; a lively
palate with brisk, citrussy acidity; good length. Screwcap. 12.7% alc. **Rating** 90
To 2015 $22
Pinot Noir 2007 Has plenty of quite sweet (not jammy) red fruits; a supple and
smooth palate, with good length. Screwcap. 13.5% alc. **Rating** 90 **To** 2014 $28
Reserve Pinot Noir 2006 A light- to medium-bodied wine with red cherry
fruit predominant, starting to mature well; good line, length and balance. Ten gold
medals. Screwcap. 13.9% alc. **Rating** 90 **To** 2014 $38

Bremerton Wines

Strathalbyn Road, Langhorne Creek, SA 5255 **Region** Langhorne Creek
T (08) 8537 3093 **F** (08) 8537 3109 **www**.bremerton.com.au **Open** 7 days 10–5
Winemaker Rebecca Willson **Est.** 1988 **Cases** 35 000 **Vyds** 100 ha
The Willsons have been grapegrowers in the Langhorne Creek region for some considerable
time but their dual business as grapegrowers and winemakers has expanded significantly. Their
vineyards have more than doubled (predominantly cabernet sauvignon, shiraz and merlot), as
has their production of wine. In 2004 sisters Rebecca and Lucy (marketing) took control of
the business, marking the event with (guess what) revamped label designs. Can fairly claim to
be the best producer in Langhorne Creek. Exports to all major markets.

ꝋꝋꝋꝋꝋ **B.O.V. 2006** A totally delicious array of black fruits complexed by splashes of
spice and dark chocolate, the tannins plush and soft, the palate long and satisfying.
High-quality 49 mm cork. Shiraz/Cabernet Sauvignon. 15% alc. **Rating** 96
To 2021 $75
Old Adam Shiraz 2006 Good colour; richly textured, with blackberry, plum and
licorice fruit in a medium- to full-bodied frame; has a long and sustained palate
with excellent balance; long (49 mm) cork. 15% alc. **Rating** 95 **To** 2016 $45

Selkirk Langhorne Creek Shiraz 2007 Purple-red; a complex bouquet of black fruits, licorice and spice, the palate taking these characters on to another dimension, with a touch of chocolate, ripe but soft tannins, and oak. Screwcap. 14.5% alc. **Rating** 94 **To** 2017 $24

Reserve Cabernet 2005 Elegant medium-bodied wine, with some cedary notes starting to make their appearance on a perfectly balanced palate, the oak integrated, the tannins fine. Quality cork. 15% alc. **Rating** 94 **To** 2015 $45

 TTTTT **Special Release Langhorne Creek Cabernet Sauvignon 2007** Has all the varietal aroma and flavour hallmarks expected of cabernet overlain with that special softness (in the best sense) of Langhorne Creek, and touches of chocolate and herb to add extra interest. Screwcap. 14.8% alc. **Rating** 92 **To** 2017 $24

Special Release Langhorne Creek Malbec 2007 Has the almost unreal depth of crimson-purple colour malbec can achieve, with lots of black fruits and Christmas pudding flavours, yet without much structure. Screwcap. 14.5% alc. **Rating** 90 **To** 2014 $24

TTTT **Tamblyn Langhorne Creek Cabernet Shiraz Malbec Merlot 2007** Good crimson colour; a powerful wine, slightly outside the normal supple Bremerton style; there is the full array of blackberry, blackcurrant, licorice and plum fruit girdled by positive tannins. Value, but patience needed. Screwcap. 14.5% alc. **Rating** 89 **To** 2017 $18

Bress ★★★★★

3894 Calder Highway, Harcourt, Vic 3453 **Region** Bendigo
T (03) 5474 2262 **www**.bress.com.au **Open** W'ends & public hols 11–5 or by appt
Winemaker Adam Marks **Est.** 2001 **Cases** 5000 **Vyds** 17.1 ha
Adam Marks has made wine in all parts of the world since 1991, and made the brave decision (during his honeymoon in 2000) to start his own business. Having initially scoured various regions of Australia for the varieties best suited to those regions, the focus has switched to three Central Victorian vineyards, in Bendigo, Macedon Ranges and Heathcote. The Harcourt Vineyard in Bendigo is planted to riesling (2 ha), shiraz (0.75 ha) and 2.15 ha of cabernet sauvignon and cabernet franc; the Macedon vineyard to chardonnay (3.8 ha), pinot noir (3.2 ha) and gewurztraminer (0.8 ha); and the Heathcote vineyard to shiraz (3.4 ha). Exports to the Maldives.

TTTTT **Gold Chook Macedon Chardonnay 2007** Bright straw-green; both the aroma and flavour attest to the cool climate, with nuances of lemon and herb, yet in no way pointing to unripe fruit; the delicate palate is very fresh, the oak a largely unseen hand. Screwcap. 13% alc. **Rating** 94 **To** 2015 $35

Unfiltered Heathcote Gold Chook Shiraz 2007 Has more weight, power and intensity than the Heathcote & Bendigo; the full-bodied palate is crammed with black fruits, tannins and oak, and will richly repay extended cellaring. Screwcap. 13.5% alc. **Rating** 94 **To** 2027 $40

TTTTT **Margaret River Semillon Sauvignon Blanc 2008** Lively and fresh; has a seductive blend of passionfruit/tropical fruit with an undercut of grass and mineral. Excellent unoaked style. Screwcap. 12.5% alc. **Rating** 93 **To** 2012 $20

Unfiltered Heathcote & Bendigo Shiraz 2007 Ripe blackberry, plum and black cherry fruit track through the bouquet and the soft, welcoming medium-bodied palate, the tannins fine and ripe, the oak restrained. Screwcap. 13.5% alc. **Rating** 93 **To** 2017 $20

Limited Release La Gallina Heathcote Tempranillo Syrah Garnacha 2008 An aromatic blend with echoes of Spain, although syrah is uncommon there; has evocative swells of spice, cinnamon and red fruits in a light- to medium-bodied frame, the tannins fine and ripe. Screwcap. 14.5% alc. **Rating** 93 **To** 2016 $22

Gold Chook Unfiltered Macedon Pinot Noir 2007 Spice, mint and also briar are the drivers of both bouquet and palate; good weight and texture. Screwcap. 13% alc. **Rating** 90 **To** 2012 $35

Briagolong Estate

Valencia-Briagolong Road, Briagolong, Vic 3860 **Region** Gippsland
T (03) 5147 2322 **F** (03) 5147 2341 **www.**briagolongestate.com.au **Open** By appt
Winemaker Gordon McIntosh **Est.** 1979 **Cases** 50 **Vyds** 2 ha
This is very much a weekend hobby for medical practitioner Gordon McIntosh, who invests his chardonnay and pinot noir with Burgundian complexity. He has made several decisions since 2003. First, having had his best vintage (1998) destroyed by TCA cork taint, he has moved to screwcaps. Next, he has introduced the Foothills of Gippsland range at a lower price point (but still estate-grown). Third, he has increased the price of the Estate Chardonnay and Pinot Noir, limited to exceptional barrels, which will not be released every year. Like many others in southern Vic, the 2007 vintage was ruined by smoke taint, and no wine will be released from this vintage; in the meantime, stocks of mature wines are being sold.

Brian Barry Wines

PO Box 128, Stepney, SA 5069 **Region** Clare Valley
T (08) 8363 6211 **F** (08) 8362 0498 **www.**brianbarrywines.com **Open** Not
Winemaker Brian Barry, Judson Barry **Est.** 1977 **Cases** 1500 **Vyds** 25.5 ha
Brian Barry is an industry veteran with a wealth of winemaking and show-judging experience. His is a vineyard-only operation (16 ha of riesling, 4 ha of cabernet sauvignon, 2 ha of shiraz, and lesser amounts of merlot and cabernet franc), with a significant part of the output sold as grapes to other wineries. The wines are made under contract at various wineries under Brian's supervision. As one would expect, the quality is reliably good. Exports to the UK and the US.

ŸŸŸŸŸ **Juds Hill Clare Valley Riesling 2008** Vibrant and tightly wound, with fresh lime juice, a strong element of talc, and a very dry finish; a pure style, strict and tight. Screwcap. 11% alc. **Rating** 94 **To** 2016 $22
Juds Hill Clare Valley Riesling 2007 Strong aromatics of lime juice, mineral and talc; good power and weight on the palate, with a long, persistent and very even finish; terrific line. Screwcap. 11% alc. **Rating** 94 **To** 2018 $22

ŸŸŸŸŸ **Juds Hill Vineyard Clare Valley Shiraz 2005** A savoury wine, with earth and mineral elements dominating the red fruit on the bouquet; the palate is fine and juicy, and yet a little tarry on the finish. Screwcap. 14% alc. **Rating** 93 **To** 2014 $35

Briar Ridge

Mount View Road, Mount View, NSW 2325 **Region** Lower Hunter Valley
T (02) 4990 3670 **F** (02) 4990 7802 **www.**briarridge.com.au **Open** 7 days 10–5
Winemaker Karl Stockhausen, Mark Woods **Est.** 1972 **Cases** 18 000 **Vyds** 39 ha
Semillon and Shiraz have been the most consistent performers, underlying the suitability of these varieties to the Hunter Valley. The Semillon, in particular, invariably shows intense fruit and cellars well. Briar Ridge has been a model of stability, and has the comfort of substantial estate vineyards from which it is able to select the best grapes. It also has not hesitated to venture into other regions, notably Orange. Exports to the US, Canada and China.

ŸŸŸŸŸ **Dairy Hill Single Vineyard Hunter Valley Shiraz 2007** An expressive bouquet of black fruit, licorice and spice aromas leads into a rich, soft but full-bodied palate; an instance of higher alcohol being beneficial; some similarities to 1965 Lindemans Shiraz when young. Screwcap. 15% alc. **Rating** 95 **To** 2027 $48
Cellar Reserve Hunter Valley Semillon 2008 Light, but fragrant, lemon blossom aromas, and a crisp and lively palate with grass, green apple and lemon notes, then bracing acidity to close. Screwcap. 10.5% alc. **Rating** 94 **To** 2018 $26
Signature Release Karl Stockhausen Hunter Valley Semillon 2008
A highly focused and intense palate with zesty lemon and mineral flavours intermingling through to the finish and aftertaste, the acidity very well balanced. Screwcap. 10% alc. **Rating** 94 **To** 2020 $26

Cellar Reserve Orange Chardonnay 2008 Fine and fresh; ranges across honeydew melon, stone fruit and grapefruit; 100% barrel fermentation in one-year-old French oak a total success. Screwcap. 14% alc. **Rating** 94 **To** 2014 $26

🍷🍷🍷🍷🍷 **Signature Release Karl Stockhausen Hunter Valley Shiraz 2007** Mainstream Hunter Valley characters of earth and sweet leather nuances behind the primary black fruit driver; good oak and tannins on the finish. Screwcap. 14% alc. **Rating** 93 **To** 2017 $29

Cellar Reserve Orange Shiraz 2007 Fragrant red fruits and spices on the bouquet move onto a more black fruit–accented palate, with substantial extract demanding patience; has overall balance, and will mature well. Screwcap. 14% alc. **Rating** 90 **To** 2020 $26

Cold Soaked Cabernet Sauvignon 2007 Good crimson-purple; solid blackcurrant and cassis fruit is indubitably varietal, backed by firm tannins and some oak. Screwcap. 14% alc. **Rating** 90 **To** 2020 $23

🍷🍷🍷🍷 **Homestead Verdelho 2008** Perfectly pitched at the cellar door, the touch of sweetness balanced by acidity, and giving the wine an extra degree of fruity appeal. Screwcap. 12.6% alc. **Rating** 88 **To** 2011 $21

Briarose Estate

Bussell Highway, Augusta, WA 6290 **Region** Margaret River
T (08) 9758 4160 **F** (08) 9758 4161 **www**.briarose.com.au **Open** 7 days 10–4.30
Winemaker The Vintage Wineworx (Greg Jones), Bill Crappsley (Consultant) **Est.** 1998
Cases 8000 **Vyds** 12.23 ha
Brian and Rosemary Webster began developing the estate plantings in 1998, which now comprise sauvignon blanc (2.33 ha), semillon (1.33 ha), cabernet sauvignon (6.6 ha), merlot (2.2 ha) and cabernet franc (1.1 ha). The winery is situated at the southern end of the Margaret River region, where the climate is distinctly cooler than that of northern Margaret River.

🍷🍷🍷🍷🍷 **Margaret River Sauvignon Blanc Semillon 2008** Strong herb and grass aromas, with citrus joining in on the long, focused and balanced palate; crisp finish. Gold WA Wine Show '08. Screwcap. 12% alc. **Rating** 94 **To** 2011 $27

Blackwood Cove 2007 Deep colour; dense, dark and full of earthy, savoury complexity; black olive and cedar intermingle with cassis and a suggestion of violets; full-bodied with abundant fine-grained tannins, vibrant acidity and ample fruit to weigh through the structure and oak that is evident. Cabernet Sauvignon/Merlot/Cabernet Franc. Screwcap. 14.8% alc. **Rating** 94 **To** 2016 $32

Margaret River Cabernet Franc 2007 A lively and lifted bouquet full of floral character, plum and a touch of cassis; the palate is very fleshy on the middle, but tightens up with ample fine-grained tannins, and really lively and fresh acidity; a very good example of the variety. Screwcap. 14.5% alc. **Rating** 94 **To** 2014 $26

🍷🍷🍷🍷🍷 **Margaret River Sauvignon Blanc 2008** Clean, well made in precise linear style; has length, and a crisp, zesty finish. Screwcap. 12.5% alc. **Rating** 91 **To** 2011 $25

Reserve Margaret River Merlot 2007 Good colour; attractive perfume of plum, olive and a little floral touch; the palate is generous and fine, with lively acidity framing the fruit on offer; quite persistent and generous on the finish. Screwcap. 14.5% alc. **Rating** 90 **To** 2014 $25

Reserve Margaret River Cabernet Sauvignon 2007 Attractive and pure cassis and red fruit on the bouquet; the palate is supple and generous, and has some complexity; a fleshy and fine finish. Screwcap. 14.5% alc. **Rating** 90 **To** 2014 $30

🍷🍷🍷🍷 **Margaret River Cabernet Merlot 2007** Bright colour; a slight herbal note dominates the bouquet, but cassis and cedar elements are there too; fine palate, albeit with an element of austerity. Screwcap. 14.8% alc. **Rating** 87 **To** 2013 $25

Brick Kiln ★★★★

PO Box 56, Glen Osmond, SA 5064 **Region** McLaren Vale
T (08) 8357 2561 **F** (08) 8357 3126 **www**.brickiln.com.au **Open** Not
Winemaker McLaren Vintners **Est.** 2001 **Cases** 1500 **Vyds** 8 ha
This is the venture of Malcolm and Alison Mackinnon, Garry and Nancy Watson, and Ian
and Pene Davey. They purchased the Nine Gums Vineyard in 2001, which had been planted
to shiraz in 1995–96. The majority of the grapes are sold, with a lesser portion contract-made
for the partners under the Brick Kiln label, which takes its name from the Brick Kiln Bridge
adjacent to the vineyard. Exports to the UK, Canada, Germany, China and Hong Kong.

ΨΨΨΨΫ McLaren Vale Shiraz 2007 Well made; the medium- to full-bodied palate
has a range of blackberry, licorice and dark chocolate flavours supported by fine,
ripe tannins and vanillin oak; carries its alcohol with ease. Screwcap. 14.8% alc.
Rating 90 **To** 2017 $25

✿ Brierley Wines NR

574 Rainbows Road, Childers, Qld 4660 **Region** Queensland Zone
T (07) 4126 1297 **www**.brierleywines.com **Open** Tues–Sun & school hols 10–4
Winemaker Luke Fitzpatrick **Est.** 1998 **Cases** 200 **Vyds** 2 ha
Tony and Sue Brierley have established 2 ha of chambourcin, which is fashioned into different
styles by contract-winemaker Luke Fitzpatrick, ranging from dry to sweet. The modest wine
list also includes a Semillon Chardonnay and a Fortified Tawny style.

Brimsmore Park Winery ★★★

40 Merricks Road, Merricks, Vic 3926 **Region** Mornington Peninsula
T (03) 5989 8164 **www**.brimsmore.com.au **Open** By appt
Winemaker Michael Darch **Est.** 1998 **Cases** 250 **Vyds** 2.8 ha
Michael and Sheila Darch began the establishment of Brimsmore Park in 1998. Situated on
the rolling hills of Merricks, it overlooks Western Port Bay and Phillip Island. The vineyard is
exclusively planted to pinot noir: MV6 for half of the vineyard, and the Dijon clones 114 and
115 (a quarter each). The benefits of concentrating on one variety are obvious, especially so
when that variety is pinot noir and the region is Mornington Peninsula.

ΨΨΨΨ Mornington Peninsula Pinot Noir 2005 More colour and weight than the
'06s, but still distinctly savoury/foresty/herbal overtones to the black fruits. Cork.
13% alc. **Rating** 87 **To** 2010 $18

Brindabella Hills ★★★★★

156 Woodgrove Close, via Hall, ACT 2618 **Region** Canberra District
T (02) 6230 2583 **www**.brindabellahills.com.au **Open** W'ends, public hols 10–5
Winemaker Dr Roger Harris, Brian Sinclair **Est.** 1986 **Cases** 2500 **Vyds** 5 ha
Distinguished research scientist Dr Roger Harris presides over Brindabella Hills, which
increasingly relies on estate-produced grapes, with small plantings of riesling, cabernet
sauvignon, shiraz, sauvignon blanc, merlot, chardonnay, cabernet franc and viognier. Wine
quality has been consistently impressive.

ΨΨΨΨΨ Canberra District Sauvignon Blanc 2008 A highly aromatic and fragrant
bouquet with an array of passionfruit and tropical notes; the palate is much the
same, a little more delicate and light than expected until it clicks in on the finish.
Great value. Screwcap. 11.9% alc. **Rating** 94 **To** 2012 $18
Canberra District Shiraz 2007 Strong crimson-purple; the classic, lifted
perfume of the bouquet immediately points to the co-fermentation of 3.3%
viognier, which also works its magic on the vibrant dark berry and plum fruit of
the palate; great drive and length. Screwcap. 14.5% alc. **Rating** 94 **To** 2017 $28

🍷🍷🍷🍷♀ **Canberra District Riesling 2008** Lime, leaf and blossom aromas, then a delightfully crisp palate with lime and green apple flavours; long finish. Screwcap. 11.8% alc. **Rating** 93 **To** 2018 $20
Aureus 2008 Interesting wine, five months French oak barrel fermentation/ maturation and 23% viognier has worked very well, the texture and flavour of chardonnay the main driver, but added to by the viognier and oak. Screwcap. 13.8% alc. **Rating** 91 **To** 2015 $25

🍷🍷🍷🍷 **Brio 2007** Light, bright crimson; the bouquet and entry into the palate offer cherry and sour cherry, but the wine thins out somewhat on the finish. Sangiovese. Screwcap. 12.6% alc. **Rating** 87 **To** 2013 $20

Brini Estate Wines

RSD 600 Blewitt Springs Road, McLaren Vale, SA 5171 (postal) **Region** McLaren Vale
T (08) 8383 0080 **F** (08) 8383 0104 **www.**briniwines.com.au **Open** Not
Winemaker Brian Light (Contract) **Est.** 2000 **Cases** 4000 **Vyds** 18 ha
The Brini family has been growing grapes in the Blewitt Springs area of McLaren Vale since 1953. In 2000 John and Marcello Brini established Brini Estate Wines to vinify a portion of the grape production; up to that time it had been sold to companies such as Penfolds, Rosemount Estate and d'Arenberg. The flagship Sebastian Shiraz is produced from dry-grown vines planted in 1947, the other wines from dry-grown vines planted in '64. Exports to the UK, Russia and Hong Kong.

🍷🍷🍷🍷🍷 **Sebastian McLaren Vale Shiraz 2006** Blackberry confiture, tar and fruitcake bouquet; the palate is dense with plenty of oak, but there is light from the acid to balance out the rich dark fruit. Screwcap. 14.5% alc. **Rating** 94 **To** 2016 $28

🍷🍷🍷🍷♀ **Limited Release Sebastian Shiraz 2006** Very concentrated, with masses of sweet fruit and dark chocolate aromas and flavours; the oak really dominates, so the assumption is for long cellaring before consumption; massively proportioned in every way. Screwcap. 15% alc. **Rating** 93 **To** 2018 $39

🍷🍷🍷🍷 **Blewitt Springs Shiraz 2006** Dark mocha fruit, with tar, blackberry and a touch of chocolate; thick and ample, with a bit of heat to the finish. Screwcap. 14.5% alc. **Rating** 87 **To** 2014 $18

Broke Estate/Ryan Family Wines

Wollombi Road, Broke, NSW 2330 **Region** Lower Hunter Valley
T (02) 6579 1065 **F** (02) 6579 1065 **www.**ryanwines.com.au **Open** Fri–Mon 11–5.30
Winemaker Matthew Ryan **Est.** 1988 **Cases** 2000 **Vyds** 19 ha
This is the flagship operation of the Ryan family, with largely mature vineyards, the lion's share to chardonnay, but also including meaningful plantings of semillon, sauvignon blanc, shiraz, merlot, barbera, cabernet franc and cabernet sauvignon.

Broke's Promise Wines

725 Milbrodale Road, Broke, NSW 2330 **Region** Lower Hunter Valley
T (02) 6579 1165 **F** (02) 9972 1619 **www.**brokespromise.com.au **Open** W'ends 10–5
Winemaker Margan Family **Est.** 1996 **Cases** 700 **Vyds** 3.3 ha
Joe and Carol Re purchased Broke's Promise in 2005 from Jane Marquard and Dennis Karp, and have continued the winemaking arrangements with Andrew Margan. The vineyard (chardonnay, barbera, verdelho, shiraz and semillon) is complemented by an olive grove and an art gallery.

🍷🍷🍷🍷♀ **Hunter Valley Barbera 2006** A very good example of the variety, with multi-spice and herb components on both bouquet and palate, which is not abrasive or tannic. Value. Screwcap. 14.5% alc. **Rating** 92 **To** 2015 $18

Broken Gate Wines

57 Rokeby Street, Collingwood, Vic 3066 **Region** Southeast Australia
T (03) 9417 5757 **F** (03) 8415 1991 www.brokengate.com.au **Open** Mon–Fri 8–5
Winemaker Josef Orbach **Est.** 2001 **Cases** 16 000
Broken Gate is a Melbourne-based multi-regional producer, specialising in cool-climate reds
and whites. Founder Josef Orbach lived and worked in the Clare Valley from 1994 to '98 at
Leasingham Wines, and is currently studying wine technology and viticulture at the University
of Melbourne. Exports (of the Side Gate brand) to China, Singapore and Thailand.

Brokenwood

401–427 McDonalds Road, Pokolbin, NSW 2321 **Region** Lower Hunter Valley
T (02) 4998 7559 **F** (02) 4998 7893 www.brokenwood.com.au **Open** 7 days 9.30–5
Winemaker Iain Riggs, PJ Charteris **Est.** 1970 **Cases** 100 000 **Vyds** 12.51 ha
Deservedly fashionable winery producing consistently excellent wines. Has kept Graveyard
Shiraz as its ultimate flagship wine, while extending its reach through many of the best eastern
regions for its broad selection of varietal wine styles. Its big-selling Hunter Semillon remains
alongside Graveyard, and there is then a range of wines coming from regions including
Orange, Central Ranges, Beechworth, McLaren Vale, Cowra and elsewhere. The two-storey
Albert Room tasting facility (named in honour of the late Tony Albert, one of the founders)
was opened in 2006. Exports to all major markets.

ŦŦŦŦŦ **HBA Hunter Valley McLaren Vale Shiraz 1998** Not released until 10 years
old, this 50/50 Hunter/McLaren blend was intended to mirror some of the great
regional blends of the 1940s, '50s and early '60s, and succeeds admirably. It has
quite brilliant texture and structure, and exceptional line and length. Now nearing
its plateau of perfection, cork permitting, it could easily live for another 20 years.
15% alc. **Rating** 97 **To** 2038 $200

ILR Reserve Semillon 2003 Still pale, but bright colour, with green tints; a wine
of extreme finesse, magically combining freshness and delicacy with clear varietal
expression ranging from nuances of honey and toast through to bright citrus, grass
and mineral notes. Screwcap. 11% alc. **Rating** 96 **To** 2023 $45

Graveyard Vineyard Hunter Valley Shiraz 2006 Strong purple-crimson;
has every bit of the intensity and structure expected of this wine, with a mix of
red cherry, blackberry, French oak and a lilting finish thanks to spot-on acidity.
Screwcap. 13.5% alc. **Rating** 96 **To** 2025 $125

ILR Reserve Semillon 2004 The bouquet has that slightly toasty aroma that
leads the uninitiated to conclude (wrongly) that the wine has seen oak, but the
palate is still vibrantly fresh, crisp and focused. Release Oct '09, and will live for
another 10 years minimum. Screwcap. 10.1% alc. **Rating** 95 **To** 2019 $45

Hunter Valley Semillon 2008 Crisp, fresh, zesty aromas and flavours, gaining
velocity on the back-palate and finish, with notes of lemon/lemon rind; lingering
aftertaste. Screwcap. 10% alc. **Rating** 94 **To** 2017 $20

Hunter Valley Shiraz 2007 A classy little brother to Graveyard Shiraz, with the
same vineyard origin; has great balance, texture and structure, with an interplay
between blackberry, sweet leather and earth. Screwcap. 13.5% alc. **Rating** 94
To 2020 $40

ŦŦŦŦŸ **Wade Block 2 Vineyard McLaren Vale Shiraz 2006** Shows more
development than the Graveyard, presumably higher pH from much higher
alcohol. The palate is trenchantly regional, with dark chocolate and luscious confit
plum. Screwcap. 15% alc. **Rating** 93 **To** 2016 $45

McLaren Vale Sangiovese 2007 As one might expect, a very well made wine,
with the accent on the cherry/sour cherry fruit rather than the tannins; a few
years will see it fully blossom. Screwcap. 14.5% alc. **Rating** 93 **To** 2014 $30

Indigo Vineyard Beechworth Viognier 2006 Moderately expressed varietal
character (pear and citrus) in a fresh, crisp wine (with good mouthfeel), deserving
the back label injunction to match it with seafood and sunshine. Screwcap.
14% alc. **Rating** 90 **To** 2011 $30

♟♟♟♟ **Cricket Pitch Sauvignon Blanc Semillon 2008** An easily assimilated style; the fruit aromas and flavours generous and balanced, barrel fermentation of a portion adding texture; the overall feel good. Screwcap. 12.5% alc. **Rating** 89 **To** 2011 $19
Beechworth Pinot Gris 2008 Pear, apple and stone fruit aromas and flavours have been preserved but not embroidered; is crisp, dry and has good length. Screwcap. 13.5% alc. **Rating** 89 **To** 2012 $25

Brook Eden Vineyard ★★★★

Adams Road, Lebrina, Tas 7254 **Region** Northern Tasmania
T (03) 6395 6244 **F** (03) 6395 6211 **www**.brookeden.com.au **Open** Thurs–Tues 11–5 Aug–June
Winemaker Winemaking Tasmania **Est.** 1988 **Cases** 1400 **Vyds** 2.25 ha
Peter McIntosh and Sue Stuart purchased Brook Eden from Sheila Bezemer in 2004. At 41° south and at an altitude of 160 m it is one of the coolest sites in Tasmania, and (in the words of the new owners) 'represents viticulture on the edge'. While the plantings remain small (1 ha pinot noir, 0.75 ha chardonnay and 0.25 ha each of riesling and pinot gris), yield has been significantly reduced, resulting in earlier picking and better quality grapes. Exports to Malaysia, Singapore and Hong Kong.

♟♟♟♟♑ **Riesling 2008** Somewhat shy bouquet; an attractive palate; with citrus and passionfruit flavours; good balance and acidity. Screwcap. 12.1% alc. **Rating** 92 **To** 2016 $25
Pinot Rose 2008 Vivid fuschia; very good mid-palate fruit ranging through cherry and strawberry; has good line and continuity. Screwcap. 12.5% alc. **Rating** 90 **To** 2010 $24
Friends Pinot Noir 2007 Bright colour; a fragrant and fresh bouquet; a firm palate with particularly good length, although the tannins do need to soften. **Rating** 90 **To** 2014

Brookland Valley ★★★★★

Caves Road, Wilyabrup, WA 6280 **Region** Margaret River
T (08) 9755 6042 **F** (08) 9755 6214 **www**.brooklandvalley.com.au **Open** 7 days 10–5
Winemaker Ross Pamment **Est.** 1984 **Cases** 130 000
Brookland Valley has an idyllic setting, plus its café and its Gallery of Wine Arts, which houses an eclectic collection of wine, food-related art and wine accessories. After acquiring a 50% share of Brookland Valley in 1997, Hardys moved to full ownership in 2004. The quality, and consistency, of the wines is awesome. Wine Companion Winery of the Year '09. Exports to the UK and the US.

♟♟♟♟♟ **Semillon 2005** Pale straw-green; very skilled and sophisticated winemaking, the barrel ferment in no way overplayed, the oak now both integrated and balanced, allowing the gently sweet lemon flavours of the palate free rein; long, balanced finish. Screwcap. 12% alc. **Rating** 96 **To** 2015 $38
Margaret River Chardonnay 2008 An immaculate array of stone and citrus fruit on display, with lightly toasted oak provides an attractive grilled nut bouquet, offset by a tightly wound core of fruit; the palate has refreshing acidity and glorious drive; fabulously long. Screwcap. 13.2% alc. **Rating** 96 **To** 2020 $38
Reserve Margaret River Cabernet Sauvignon 2004 Good colour; the bouquet has cassis fruit with a little leafy complexity; full-bodied, the palate shows the class of the wine, with a cascading array of black fruit and savoury complexity coming to the fore; incredibly long and intense with cool acidity providing focus on the finish. Cork. 14% alc. **Rating** 96 **To** 2020 $63
Verse 1 Margaret River Chardonnay 2007 Bright green-yellow; superfine but very intense and very long nectarine, white peach and grapefruit flavours are complexed by subtle oak, the wine in a Chablis mode. Screwcap. 13.5% alc. **Rating** 95 **To** 2016 $21
Margaret River Chardonnay 2004 Nice touch of funk, intense, long and focused palate. Has developed superbly. Cork. 13% alc. **Rating** 94 **To** 2012 $45

Verse 1 Margaret River Shiraz 2007 Dense crimson; an expressive and complex bouquet of plum, spice and blackberry leads into a luscious palate, redolent of black fruits; oak and tannins in balance. Gold medal National Wine Show '08. Screwcap. 14% alc. **Rating** 94 To 2020 $21

Verse 1 Margaret River Cabernet Merlot 2007 Bright red-purple; while only medium-bodied, has the strong structure of good Margaret River Bordeaux blends, with an array of black and red berry fruits; good oak and tannin support. Gold medal National Wine Show '08. Screwcap. 14% alc. **Rating** 94 To 2015 $21

 Verse 1 Margaret River Semillon Sauvignon Blanc 2008 Very pale straw-green; passionfruit and grassy aromas intertwine on the bouquet, with more citrussy notes appearing on the light-bodied palate, which has considerable length. Value. Screwcap. 12.5% alc. **Rating** 93 To 2012 $21

Merlot 2002 Combines fresh, small berry fruits with a well-judged web of fine tannins and French oak; a neat savoury twist on a long finish. Cork. 14.5% alc. **Rating** 92 To 2015 $38

 Verse 1 Margaret River Shiraz 2008 Cherry and strawberry fruit bouquet; fresh clean and well-defined palate; juicy and generous. Screwcap. 14.1% alc. **Rating** 88 To 2012 $21

Brookwood Estate ★★★

Treeton Road, Cowaramup, WA 6284 **Region** Margaret River
T (08) 9755 5604 **F** (08) 9755 5870 www.brookwood.com.au **Open** 7 days 11–5
Winemaker Bronnley Cahill **Est.** 1996 **Cases** 4000 **Vyds** 6.1 ha
Trevor and Lyn Mann began the development of their 50-ha property in 1996, and now have 1.3 ha each of semillon, sauvignon blanc and chenin blanc; 1.2 ha of shiraz and 1 ha of cabernet sauvignon. A winery was constructed in 1999 to accommodate the first vintage. Winemaking is now in the hands of Bronnley Cahill (Trevor and Lyn's daughter), with the experienced eye of Lyn in the background. Exports to Hong Kong.

 Margaret River Cabernet Sauvignon 2007 Powerful, black fruits but tannins are out of balance and may never soften sufficiently. Screwcap. 14% alc. **Rating** 87 To 2017 $39.95

Broomstick Estate ★★★

4 Frances Street, Mount Lawley, WA 6050 (postal) **Region** Margaret River
T (08) 9271 9594 **F** (08) 9271 9741 www.broomstick.com.au **Open** Not
Winemaker Mark Warren (Happs) **Est.** 1997 **Cases** 1000 **Vyds** 16.6 ha
The property that Robert Holloway and family purchased in 1993 on which the vineyard is now established was an operating dairy farm. In 1997, 5.5 ha of shiraz was planted. Over the following years 3.8 ha of merlot and then (in 2004) 5.3 ha of chardonnay and 2 ha of sauvignon blanc were added. The Holloways see themselves as grapegrowers first and foremost, but make a small amount of wine under the Broomstick Estate label. The name of the business derives from the vineyard's proximity to the town of Witchcliffe, or Witchy, as the locals call it. The label design reflects the association of witches with broomsticks and ravens.

Margaret River Shiraz 2007 A bright and juicy light- to medium-bodied wine from start to finish with cherry, raspberry and spice flavours; no need for patience. Screwcap. 13.8% alc. **Rating** 88 To 2013 $19.50

Brothers in Arms ★★★

PO Box 840, Langhorne Creek, SA 5255 **Region** Langhorne Creek
T (08) 83537 3182 **F** (08) 8537 3383 www.brothersinarms.com.au **Open** Not
Winemaker Justin Lane, Jim Urlwin **Est.** 1998 **Cases** 26 000 **Vyds** 300 ha
The Adams family has been growing grapes at Langhorne Creek since 1891, when the first vines at the famed Metala vineyards were planted. Guy Adams is the fifth generation to own and work the vineyard, and over the past 20 years has both improved the viticulture

and expanded the plantings. It was not until 1998 that they decided to hold back a small proportion of the production for vinification under the Brothers in Arms label, and now dedicate 50 ha to the Brothers in Arms wines (shiraz, cabernet sauvignon, malbec and petit verdot); the grapes from the remaining 250 ha are sold. Exports to the UK, the US and other major markets.

♟♟♟♟ **No. 6 Langhorne Creek Shiraz 2006** Good colour; pleasant medium-bodied wine with a mix of red and black fruits; appropriate tannins. Screwcap. 14.5% alc. **Rating** 88 **To** 2014 $22

Brown Brothers ★★★★★

Milawa-Bobinawarrah Road, Milawa, Vic 3678 **Region** King Valley
T (03) 5720 5500 **F** (03) 5720 5511 **www**.brownbrothers.com.au **Open** 7 days 9–5
Winemaker Wendy Cameron, Joel Tilbrook, Catherine Looney, Geoff Alexander, Chloe Earl **Est.** 1885 **Cases** 1.1 million **Vyds** 750 ha
Draws upon a considerable number of vineyards spread throughout a range of site climates, ranging from very warm to very cool. A relatively recent expansion into Heathcote has added significantly to its armoury. It is known for the diversity of varieties with which it works, and the wines represent good value for money. Deservedly one of the most successful family wineries – its cellar door receives the greatest number of visitors in Australia. Exports to all major markets.

♟♟♟♟♟ **Patricia Noble Riesling 2006** Bright gold; has an intensity of flavour that explains why it has such an armada of gold medals and trophies; the lower alcohol than traditional Australian styles (though not German) and citrussy acidity are the keys to a wonderful wine. Screwcap. 8.5% alc. **Rating** 96 **To** 2015 $34.95
Limited Release King Valley Chardonnay 2006 Fig and straw bouquet with a creamy dose of toasty oak; quite toasty and generous on the palate; there is real life and nerve to the finish; surprisingly long. Screwcap. 14% alc. **Rating** 94 **To** 2014 $29.90
Patricia Shiraz 2005 Supple and delicious; plum, spice, blackberry and mocha oak and fine, ripe tannins all coalesce. Cork. 14.5% alc. **Rating** 94 **To** 2015 $55.95
Patricia Pinot Noir Chardonnay Pinot Meunier Brut 2004 As ever, a very well-made, upper-echelon sparkling wine, with finesse and flavour; citrus, apple and stone fruit with some nutty/bready notes, and a fresh finish. Cork. 12% alc. **Rating** 94 **To** 2013 $39.95

♟♟♟♟♟ **Pinot Noir Chardonnay Pinot Meunier NV** Straw-green; has considerable complexity on bouquet and palate; some nutty brioche and good structure, finishing with energy; excellent length. Cork. 12.5% alc. **Rating** 93 **To** 2010 $23.50
Patricia Cabernet Sauvignon 2004 Even with five years' age, the fruit and tannins are still contesting primacy; happily, the contest is sufficiently even for it not to matter overmuch; good varietal black fruits have a nice burnish of cedary oak and tannins. Cork. 13.5% alc. **Rating** 92 **To** 2020 $55.95
Limited Release Heathcote Shiraz 2006 Blueberry fruit, bay leaf and a touch of earth; a rich and warm palate, with grainy tannins and a little spice contributed by the oak; has a generous, even and soft finish. Screwcap. 14.5% alc. **Rating** 91 **To** 2014 $29.90
Whitlands Sauvignon Blanc 2008 Cool nettle bouquet with a background murmur of tropical fruit; fresh cut grass on the palate, with focused acidity and good length. Screwcap. 13.5% alc. **Rating** 90 **To** 2011 $19
Limited Release King Valley Chardonnay 2005 Fresh and very lively, particularly given time in bottle; citrus and melon fruit are the drivers, but 40% mlf and French oak add support. Screwcap. 13.5% alc. **Rating** 90 **To** 2013 $20.90
Limited Release Heathcote Durif 2006 Incredible colour; deep and dark mocha fruit, laced with tar and blackberry confiture; deep and dense palate, with ample chewy, grainy tannins; quite bright despite its weight. Cork. 14.5% alc. **Rating** 90 **To** 2012 $21

King Valley Prosecco 2008 Clean and focused pear bouquet; the palate shows a touch of green apple; clean, fresh and crisp, with well-handled dosage, and cleansing chalky acidity. Cork. 12% alc. **Rating** 90 **To** 2011 $18.90

ΨΨΨΨ   Victoria Pinot Grigio 2008 Clean pear fruit aromas framed by an element of citrus; good depth and delineation of fruit for the variety, finishing very dry and with fine texture. Screwcap. 13% alc. **Rating** 88 **To** 2010 $18
Victoria Tempranillo 2006 Ripe cherry fruit, with a touch of bramble and spice; quite fleshy, and some roast meat savoury character on the palate; soft and ready to go. Screwcap. 13.5% alc. **Rating** 88 **To** 2011 $18
Victoria Cabernet Sauvignon 2006 Varietal cassis and cedar bouquet; chewy, firm and very dry on the finish. Needs time to soften. Screwcap. 14% alc. **Rating** 87 **To** 2013 $19
Moscato Rosa 2008 Skilfully made from grapes from all over Southeastern Australia; bright pink, with just a prickle of spritz, and a fairly dry finish. Muscat of Alexandria/Cienna (a cross between cabernet sauvignon/sumoll). Screwcap. 7% alc. **Rating** 87 **To** 2009 $16.50

Brown Hill Estate

Cnr Rosa Brook Road/Barrett Road, Rosa Brook, WA 6285 **Region** Margaret River
T (08) 9757 4003 **F** (08) 9757 4004 **www**.brownhillestate.com.au **Open** 7 days 10–5
Winemaker Nathan Bailey **Est.** 1995 **Cases** 3000 **Vyds** 22 ha
The Bailey family is involved in all stages of wine production with minimum outside help. Their stated aim is to produce top-quality wines at affordable prices, via uncompromising viticultural practices emphasising low yields per spot hectare. They have 7 ha each of shiraz and cabernet sauvignon, 4 ha of semillon and 2 ha each of sauvignon blanc and merlot, and by the standards of the Margaret River, the prices are indeed affordable.

ΨΨΨΨΨ   Fimiston Reserve Margaret River Shiraz 2007 Strikingly dense crimson; an equally dense, full-bodied palate with layers of blackberry, plum, licorice and vanilla, an appealing spicy, savoury edge tightening up the structure. Screwcap. 14.5% alc. **Rating** 94 **To** 2022 $30
Perseverance Margaret River Cabernet Merlot 2007 Ripe cassis and blackcurrant fruit is framed by quality oak and fine, ripe tannins; overall savoury fruit nuances. Screwcap. 14.2% alc. **Rating** 94 **To** 2017 $50

ΨΨΨΨΩ   Lakeview Margaret River Sauvignon Blanc Semillon 2008 The generous flavours are framed by good acidity and some minerality; the palate has clarity, thrust and good length. Value. Screwcap. 13.5% alc. **Rating** 93 **To** 2011 $17
Croesus Reserve Margaret River Merlot 2007 Strong colour; a very complex bouquet and palate, with a splendid array of fruitcake, plum, blackcurrant and spice flavours; fine tannins. Screwcap. 14% alc. **Rating** 93 **To** 2021 $35
Chaffers Margaret River Shiraz 2007 Deep crimson-purple; full-bodied black cherry, plum, spice and a hint of dark chocolate flavours are underpinned by persistent, but fine, tannins. Value. Screwcap. 14% alc. **Rating** 92 **To** 2017 $18
Charlotte Margaret River Sauvignon Blanc 2008 A fresh, clean and crisp bouquet leads into a lively palate with a mix of tropical fruits and more grassy components bolstered by fresh acidity. Value. Screwcap. 13.5% alc. **Rating** 91 **To** 2010 $17
Bill Bailey Margaret River Shiraz Cabernet 2007 Dense purple-red; an uncompromisingly full-bodied wine, with an aggressive bouquet and palate of unyielding black fruits. Needs time and vigorous decanting to unlock its secrets. Screwcap. 14.8% alc. **Rating** 90 **To** 2027 $45
Ivanhoe Reserve Margaret River Cabernet Sauvignon 2007 Deep colour; powerful but very austere, obviously reflecting the vineyard influence; built-in tannins run through the length of the palate. Screwcap. 14% alc. **Rating** 90 **To** 2017 $30

Brown Magpie Wines

125 Larcombes Road, Modewarre, Vic 3240 **Region** Geelong
T (03) 5261 3875 **F** (03) 5261 3875 **www.**brownmagpiewines.com **Open** 7 days 12–3
Winemaker Shane Breheny, Karen Coulston (Consultant) **Est.** 2000 **Cases** 5000
Shane and Loretta Breheny's 20-ha property is situated predominantly on a gentle, north-facing slope, with cypress trees on the western and southern borders providing protection against the wind. Over 2001 and '02, 9 ha of vines were planted, with pinot noir (5 ha) taking the lion's share, followed by pinot gris (2 ha), shiraz (1.5 ha) and 0.25 ha each of chardonnay and sauvignon blanc. Viticulture is Loretta Breheny's love; winemaking (and wine) is Shane's.

ÝÝÝÝÝ **Geelong Shiraz 2007** Excellent purple-crimson; bursting with spicy/tangy fruit on the palate, which has great thrust and persistence to the spicy/peppery black fruit and licorice flavours. Screwcap. 14% alc. **Rating** 94 **To** 2020 $27

ÝÝÝÝ¿ **Paraparap Geelong Pinot Noir 2006** Has more substance and flavour than the Breheny Vineyards, with spice and black cherry/plum fruit pushing through the support of oak and tannins. Screwcap. 14% alc. **Rating** 92 **To** 2015 $27
Geelong Pinot Grigio 2008 Fresh, lively and crisp, offering pear, apple and citrus aromas and flavours; has good length; correct grigio style; the two Brown Magpie wines deserve attention. Screwcap. 12.4% alc. **Rating** 90 **To** 2011 $22
Geelong Pinot Gris 2008 A serious and successful exercise in showing the difference between grigio and gris styles, even down to the shape and colour of the bottle; here in Alsace mode with rounded, mouthfilling luscious fruit. Screwcap. 14.5% alc. **Rating** 90 **To** 2013 $22
Breheny Vineyards Geelong Pinot Noir 2006 Fragrant and lively, with a mix of multi-spice and red cherry aromas that flow through into the light-bodied but long and well-balanced palate. Screwcap. 14% alc. **Rating** 90 **To** 2012 $22

ÝÝÝÝ **Geelong Late Harvest Pinot Gris 2008** Curiously, has a little more acidity and fruit freshness than the 'standard' pinot gris – confusing for the unwary. Screwcap. 13.5% alc. **Rating** 88 **To** 2010 $15

Buckshot Vineyard

PO Box 119, Coldstream, Vic 3770 **Region** Heathcote
T 0417 349 785 **www.**buckshotvineyard.com.au **Open** Not
Winemaker Rob Peebles **Est.** 1999 **Cases** 700 **Vyds** 3 ha
This is the venture of Meegan and Rob Peebles, which comes on the back of Rob's 15-plus-year involvement in the wine industry. That involvement included six vintages in Rutherglen starting in 1993, followed by 10 years at Domaine Chandon, squeezing in weekend work at Coldstream Hills' cellar door in '93. It is a tribute to the soils of Heathcote, and a long-time friendship with John and Jenny Davies, that sees the flagship Shiraz, and a smaller amount of Zinfandel (with some shiraz) coming from a 3-ha block, part of a 40-ha vineyard owned by the Davies just to the southwest of Colbinabbin. The wines are made by Rob at Domaine Chandon; 25% of the wine is exported to the UK and the US, with considerable success.

ÝÝÝÝÝ **Heathcote Shiraz 2004** Medium red-purple, virtually no change from the '05; bottle age has started to impart some really attractive spicy, savoury elements to accompany the luscious blackberry and licorice fruit. High-quality cork. 14.2% alc. **Rating** 96 **To** 2024 $29.95
Heathcote Shiraz 2006 Very good colour; a fragrant black fruit bouquet leads into a juicy, lush palate of blackberry, plum and licorice, gently savoury/spicy tannins and oak provide the counterpoints. Screwcap. 14.8% alc. **Rating** 95 **To** 2026 $31.95
Heathcote Shiraz 2005 Good colour; lifted, fragrant aromas lead into a potent wine with singular intensity on the palate, the flavours of blackberry, cherry and a dash of spice; the finish is long and even, bolstered by fine tannins and smoky oak. Cork. 14.5% alc. **Rating** 94 **To** 2020 $31.95

ŦŦŦŦŶ   **The Square Peg 2007** Bright colour; an interesting and particularly well
made wine, with attractive spicy, savoury overtones to the red cherry fruit; good
mouthfeel, balance and length – and even better aftertaste. Zinfandel/Shiraz.
Screwcap. 14.1% alc. **Rating** 92 **To** 2015
The Square Peg 2006 A Zinfandel (70%)/Shiraz (30%) from the big end of
town, like that of Lodi or the Sierra Nevadas; lusciously ripe and alcoholic, a
prerequisite for many aficionados, including Robert Parker Jr. Screwcap. 15.5% alc.
Rating 91 **To** 2016 $25.95

Buller (Rutherglen)   ★★★★★

Three Chain Road, Rutherglen, Vic 3685 **Region** Rutherglen
T (02) 6032 9660 **F** (02) 6032 8005 **www**.buller.com.au **Open** Mon–Sat 9–5, Sun 10–5
Winemaker Andrew Buller **Est.** 1921 **Cases** 4000
The Buller family is very well known and highly regarded in North East Victoria, and the
business benefits from vines that are now 80 years old. Limited releases of Calliope Shiraz and
Shiraz Mondeuse can also be good. The rating is given for the fortified wines, which appear
on www.winecompanion.com.au. Exports to the UK and the US.

ŦŦŦŦ   **Black Dog Creek King Valley Vermentino 2008** A clean and fresh bouquet,
then an equally fresh and lively palate with citrus and lychee flavours persisting
through the finish to the aftertaste. Holds considerable promise. Value. Screwcap.
13% alc. **Rating** 89 **To** 2010 $15

Bullock Creek Vineyard   ★★★★

111 Belvoir Park Road, Ravenswood North, Vic 3453 **Region** Bendigo
T (03) 5435 3207 **F** (03) 5435 3207 **Open** W'ends 11–6, or by appt
Winemaker Langanook (Matt Hunter), Bob Beischer **Est.** 1978 **Cases** 200
Bob and Margit Beischer purchased the well-established 2-ha vineyard (and surrounding
land) in 1998, initially selling the grapes to Bendigo TAFE, where Bob was undertaking
viticultural and winemaking studies, thus seeing their grapes vinified. The long-term plan
was to build their own winery, and this was completed for the 2006 vintage. Prolonged
drought has kept the yields very low. The estate-grown wines are released under the Bullock
Creek Vineyard label; the Bullock Creek Wines label is for those made incorporating some
locally grown grapes.

ŦŦŦŦŶ   **Marong Shiraz 2007** Bright purple-crimson hue; has luscious aromas and
flavours, and considerable drive and length, with just a touch of afterburn on the
finish courtesy of the alcohol. Screwcap. 15% alc. **Rating** 91 **To** 2017 $25

ŦŦŦŦ   **Bendigo Shiraz Cabernet 2007** Strong crimson-purple; a massive, full-
bodied wine that would have benefited from earlier picking or fining, or both.
Nonetheless, certainly makes its mark. Screwcap. 15% alc. **Rating** 89 **To** 2017 $20
Bendigo Cabernet Merlot 2006 Strong crimson-purple; the flavours are fully
ripe notwithstanding modest alcohol; cassis nuances drive the palate. Good value.
Screwcap. 13.5% alc. **Rating** 88 **To** 2014 $15

Bulong Estate   ★★★☆

70 Summerhill Road, Yarra Junction, Vic 3797 (postal) **Region** Yarra Valley
T (03) 5967 1358 **F** (03) 5967 1350 **www**.bulongestate.com **Open** 7 days 11–5
Winemaker Matt Carter **Est.** 1994 **Cases** 1000 **Vyds** 31 ha
Judy and Howard Carter's beautifully situated 45-ha property looks down into the valley
below and across to the nearby ranges, with Mt Donna Buang at their peak. Most of the grapes
from the immaculately tended vineyard are sold, with limited quantities made onsite for the
Bulong Estate label. The wines in the current release portfolio show confident winemaking
across the range.

ŦŦŦŦŶ   **Chardonnay 2007** Light-bodied, crisp and lively, in the new, early-picked
mode; delicate stone fruit and citrus is framed by quality oak characters on the
harmonious finish. Screwcap. 13% alc. **Rating** 92 **To** 2015 $24

🍷🍷🍷 **Sauvignon Blanc 2008** Delicate but correct, varietal expression of gooseberry and tropical fruits before finishing with a burst of citrussy acidity. Screwcap. 13% alc. **Rating** 89 **To** 2010 $19

Pinot Gris 2008 Faint bronze-pink; clear varietal character in the standard pear/ spice/apple spectrum; good length and balance. Screwcap. 14% alc. **Rating** 89 **To** 2011 $21

Cabernets 2006 Comes together well; inevitably, has spicy/savoury components but the main driver is cassis and raspberry fruit on the light- to medium-bodied palate. Screwcap. 13.5% alc. **Rating** 89 **To** 2015 $24

Cabernet Sauvignon 2005 Retains good hue; has juicy berry/cassis flavours, with some overtones of mint and leaf; not fully ripe. Cork. 13.5% alc. **Rating** 87 **To** 2014 $24

Bundaleer Wines

PO Box 41, Hove, SA 5048 **Region** Southern Flinders Ranges
T (08) 8296 1231 www.bundaleerwines.com.au **Open** At North Star Hotel, Melrose Wed–Sun 11–5
Winemaker Angela Meaney **Est.** 1998 **Cases** 3000 **Vyds** 7 ha
Bundaleer is a joint venture between third-generation farmer Des Meaney and manufacturing industry executive Graham Spurling (whose family originally came from the Southern Flinders Ranges). Planting of the vineyard (shiraz and cabernet sauvignon) began in 1998, the first vintage in 2001. It is situated in a region known as the Bundaleer Gardens, on the edge of the Bundaleer Forest, 200 km north of Adelaide. This should not be confused with the Bundaleer Shiraz brand made by Bindi. Exports to the UK and Hong Kong.

🍷🍷🍷🍷 **Clare Valley Riesling 2008** Lemon, lemon rind and blossom aromas lead into a juicy, citrus-tinged palate, which has good balance and length. Value. Screwcap. 12% alc. **Rating** 91 **To** 2014 $16

Southern Flinders Ranges Shiraz 2006 A light- to medium-bodied palate that reflects the good vintage and has developed nicely, with spicy/savoury overtones to the mix of licorice and blackberry fruit; good length. Screwcap. 14% alc. **Rating** 90 **To** 2015 $19

Southern Flinders Ranges Cabernet Sauvignon 2006 Attractive cedary notes are starting to develop in a supple medium-bodied wine; the flavours are primarily built around blackcurrant and a touch of chocolate, supported by fine tannins – and cedar. Screwcap. 14.5% alc. **Rating** 90 **To** 2016 $19

🍷🍷🍷 **Clare Valley Chardonnay 2008** The Clare Valley and chardonnay are generally acrimonious partners, but here an uneasy truce has been declared; the chardonnay actually showing pleasing stone fruit flavours and good length. Screwcap. 13.5% alc. **Rating** 87 **To** 2011 $16

Bundaleera Vineyard

449 Glenwood Road, Relbia, Tas 7258 (postal) **Region** Northern Tasmania
T (03) 6343 1231 **F** (03) 6343 1250 **Open** W'ends 10–5
Winemaker Pirie Consulting (Andrew Pirie) **Est.** 1996 **Cases** 1000
David (a consultant metallurgist in the mining industry) and Jan Jenkinson have established 2.5 ha of vines on a sunny, sheltered north to northeast slope in the North Esk Valley. The 12-ha property on which their house and vineyard are established gives them some protection from the urban sprawl of Launceston. Jan is the full-time viticulturist and gardener for the immaculately tended property.

🍷🍷🍷🍷 **Pinot Noir 2007** Fresh and lively, with splashes of leaf, mint and spice along with core of red fruits. Screwcap. 14.5% alc. **Rating** 89 **To** 2012 $28

Chardonnay 2008 Substantial oak input into a ripe, generous wine that needed a gentler hand in the winery. Screwcap. 13.4% alc. **Rating** 88 **To** 2012 $19.95

Bunnamagoo Estate

Bunnamagoo, Rockley, NSW 2795 (postal) **Region** Central Ranges Zone
T 1300 304 707 **F** (02) 6377 5231 **www**.bunnamagoowines.com.au **Open** Not
Winemaker Robert Black **Est.** 1995 **Cases** 14 000 **Vyds** 128 ha
Bunnamagoo Estate (on one of the first land grants in the region) is situated near the
historic town of Rockley. Here a 6-ha vineyard planted to chardonnay, merlot and cabernet
sauvignon has been established by Paspaley Pearls, a famous name in the Western Australian
pearl industry. Increased production has led to the building of a winery and cellar door in
Henry Lawson Drive, Mudgee (with 122 ha of vines), opening in 2009. Robert Black is
now full-time winemaker.

    1827 Handpicked Chardonnay 2007 A restrained bouquet with suggestions
of lemon and mineral; quite a fresh palate, understated and quite fine; lacks a little
punch. Cork. 13.5% alc. **Rating** 87 **To** 2013 $39.95

Burge Family Winemakers

Barossa Way, Lyndoch, SA 5351 **Region** Barossa Valley
T (08) 8524 4644 **F** (08) 8524 4444 **www**.burgefamily.com.au **Open** Fri, Sat, Mon 10–5
Winemaker Rick Burge **Est.** 1928 **Cases** 4000 **Vyds** 9.5 ha
Rick Burge and Burge Family Winemakers (not to be confused with Grant Burge, although
the families are related) has established itself as an icon producer of exceptionally rich, lush
and concentrated Barossa red wines. Rick Burge's sense of humour is evident in the Nice
Red (a Merlot/Cabernet made for those who come to the cellar door and ask, 'Do you have
a nice red?'). 2008 marked 80 years of continuous winemaking by three generations of the
family. Exports to the US and other major markets.

    G3 2007 Light, but bright hue; a fragrant and lively array to predominantly
red fruits, with a twist of savoury tannins on the other side. Shiraz/Mourvedre/
Grenache. Cork. 14.5% alc. **Rating** 91 **To** 2015 $42

    Olive Hill Barossa Valley Semillon 2008 Straw-green; generously flavoured
and well-structured with an abundance of ripe lemon and tropical fruits. Screwcap.
13% alc. **Rating** 89 **To** 2012 $22
Barossa Valley Shiraz Rose 2008 Remarkable crimson colour; awash with
cherry and raspberry fruit that continues through the length of the palate, but
should have yielded more to acidity on the finish. Screwcap. 13% alc. **Rating** 89
To 2010 $24

Burke & Wills Winery

3155 Burke & Wills Track, Mia Mia, Vic 3444 **Region** Heathcote
T (03) 5425 5400 **F** (03) 5425 5401 **www**.wineandmusic.net **Open** By appt
Winemaker Andrew Pattison **Est.** 2003 **Cases** 1500 **Vyds** 4 ha
After 18 years at Lancefield Winery in the Macedon Ranges, Andrew Pattison moved his
operation a few miles north in 2004 to set up Burke & Wills Winery at the southern edge of
Heathcote, continuing to produce wines from both regions. While establishing 1 ha of shiraz,
0.5 ha of gewurztraminer and 0.5 ha of merlot, malbec and petit verdot at Burke & Wills,
he still retains a 19-year-old vineyard at Malmsbury at the northern end of the Macedon
Ranges, with 1 ha of cabernet sauvignon, merlot, malbec, cabernet franc, and 0.5 ha each
of chardonnay and pinot noir. Additional grapes come from contract growers in Heathcote.
Exports to the UK.

    The James Fagan Edition Heathcote Shiraz 2006 Vibrant and pure red
and blue fruit bouquet; there is a supple finesse to the palate that exhibits a
touch of mint and cranberry fruit; the acidity is accentuated and frames the
fruit harmoniously. Screwcap. 14% alc. **Rating** 94 **To** 2015 $25

ΨΨΨΨ♀ **Pattison Family Reserve Macedon Ranges Pinot Noir 2006** Lifted and bright, red cherry bouquet; tightly wound and quite focused with an underpinning of dark mineral character; quite firm with good acid and length. Screwcap. 13% alc. **Rating** 90 **To** 2013 $25

ΨΨΨΨ **Heathcote Shiraz 2007** Ripe mulberry and blueberry fruit; warm and rich palate, with firm tannin and good acidity; a little confected on the finish. Screwcap. 14% alc. **Rating** 89 **To** 2013 $25
Pattison Family Reserve Macedon Ranges Cabernet Merlot 2006 Bright colour; jubey cassis fruit with a touch of cedary oak; plenty of sweet fruit on the palate, and a fresh savoury finish. Cork. 13% alc. **Rating** 89 **To** 2014 $25
Pattison Family Reserve Macedon Pinot Noir Chardonnay NV Lemon bouquet, with a taut and racy palate; quite chalky and very dry. Cork. 12.5% alc. **Rating** 87 **To** 2015 $28

by Farr   ★★★★★

PO Box 72, Bannockburn, Vic 3331 **Region** Geelong
T (03) 5281 1979 **F** (03) 5281 1433 www.byfarr.com.au **Open** Not
Winemaker Gary Farr, Nick Farr **Est.** 1999 **Cases** 3000
In 1994 Gary Farr and family planted 12 ha of clonally selected viognier, chardonnay, pinot noir and shiraz at a density of 7000 vines per ha on a north-facing hill directly opposite Bannockburn vineyards. The quality of the wines is exemplary, their character subtly different from those of Bannockburn itself due, in Farr's view, to the interaction of the terroir of the hill and the clonal selection. Exports to the UK, the US, India, Malaysia, Hong Kong and Singapore.

ΨΨΨΨΨ **Geelong Chardonnay 2007** Glowing yellow-green; has immaculate balance and texture and structure, with seamless fruit and oak running through the long palate; gains a second wind with the finish and aftertaste. Cork. 13.5% alc. **Rating** 96 **To** 2015 $55
Sangreal 2007 A highly charged, fragrant bouquet leads into a palate of compelling silk and velvet red fruit flavours rippling through to the very long finish; notes of spice and oak are there, of course, as are the tannins, but it's fruit foremost. Cork. 13.5% alc. **Rating** 96 **To** 2017 $65
Geelong Viognier 2006 Mouthfilling and rich, with exceptional texture for a viognier at this level of alcohol; peach, apricot and a touch of marzipan before great acidity on the finish, oak in restraint throughout. An elephant standing on a thimble. Cork. 13% alc. **Rating** 95 **To** 2014 $50
Farrside Pinot Noir 2007 The bouquet has strong red fruit, spice and oak aromas; the palate has that trademark Farr texture, tannins and cherry/plum fruit seamlessly welded on the very long, sustained palate. Cork. 13.5% alc. **Rating** 95 **To** 2016 $55

ΨΨΨΨ♀ **Tout Pres Pinot Noir 2007** Slightly funky/foresty aromas; palate has powerful structure and depth, but neither the finesse nor the length of the other wines; perhaps needs time to explain itself. Cork. 13.5% alc. **Rating** 91 **To** 2014 $110

Byrne & Smith Wines   ★★★

PO Box 640, Unley, SA 5061 **Region** South Australia
T (08) 8272 1900 **F** (08) 8272 1944 www.byrneandsmith.com.au **Open** Not
Winemaker Duane Coates (Contract) **Est.** 1999 **Cases** NFP
Byrne & Smith is a family-owned wine business directed by Rob Byrne, with brother Terry managing the vineyards. The Byrne family has been involved in the Australian wine industry for three generations, with shareholdings in vineyards spanning over 500 ha in SA's prime wine-producing regions. The wines are sourced from the best parcels of fruit off the various estates in Waikerie (Riverland) and Stanley Flat (Clare Valley). The vines vary from 15 to over 35 years of age; the wines are matured separately before blending prior to bottling with minimal filtration. The portfolio focuses around Antiquarian, Thomson Estate and Scotts Creek. Exports to the UK, the US, Canada, Germany and Denmark.

♥♥♥♥ **Antiquarian Clare Valley Shiraz 2006** Deep colour; a powerful wine, with strong black fruits, licorice and spice, and even more extract and tannins; in the final analysis comes together well, but needs patience. Diam. 14% alc. **Rating** 89 **To** 2016 $28

Cahills Wines

448–484 Booie Road, Kingaroy, Qld 4610 **Region** South Burnett
T (07) 4163 1563 **Open** 7 days 10–4
Winemaker Crane Winery (Bernie Cooper) **Est.** 1998 **Cases** 120 **Vyds** 1.2 ha
When Cindy and John Cahill purchased a former 66-ha dairy farm in 1996, they did so with the intention of planting a vineyard. John worked for Lindemans for 13 years in Sydney, Brisbane and Cairns, and developed marketing skills from this experience. Nonetheless, they have hastened slowly, planting shiraz (in 1998) and chardonnay (in 2000). They make the Shiraz onsite; the Unwooded Chardonnay is processed at Crane Winery.

Caledonia Australis

PO Box 626, North Melbourne, Vic 3051 **Region** Gippsland
T (03) 9329 5372 **F** (03) 9328 3111 **www.**caledoniaaustralis.com **Open** Not
Winemaker Martin Williams **Est.** 1995 **Cases** 7000 **Vyds** 16.18 ha
The reclusive Caledonia Australis is a Pinot Noir and Chardonnay specialist, with three separate vineyard locations. The vineyards are in the Leongatha area, on red, free-draining, high-ironstone soils, on a limestone or marl base, and the slopes are east- to northeast-facing. Small-batch winemaking has resulted in consistently high-quality wines. Exports to the US, Singapore, Hong Kong and Japan.

♥♥♥♥♥ **Reserve Pinot Noir 2007** Slightly deeper colour than the varietal; similar aromas and flavours, but with distinctly greater intensity and depth; seems slightly riper, although the alcohol is the same. Screwcap. 13% alc. **Rating** 95 **To** 2015 $48
Gippsland Pinot Noir 2007 Bright, clear red colour; fresh, clear and expressive cherry/plum aromas, and juicy/silky fruit in the same spectrum on the palate; long finish, immaculately made. Screwcap. 13% alc. **Rating** 94 **To** 2013 $29

♥♥♥♥♡ **Gippsland Chardonnay 2007** A complex bouquet with some Burgundian funky aromas leads into a racy, lean palate of admirable length. Screwcap. 13% alc. **Rating** 93 **To** 2014 $29
Reserve Chardonnay 2007 Ripe peach, pear and toasty oak on the bouquet; quite rich on entry, with grapefruit and cream and a bit of grip at the finish; slow developing, showing class and power. Screwcap. 14% alc. **Rating** 93 **To** 2014 $47.95
Gippsland Chardonnay 2006 Quite toasty bouquet, with lemon and fresh fig aromas; evenly posed on the palate, with really vibrant and focused fruit and acidity, which draws out a surprisingly long finish. Screwcap. 13.5% alc. **Rating** 93 **To** 2015 $26.40
Mount Macleod Chardonnay 2008 Peach, pear and spiced nectarine bouquet; citrus comes through on the palate, with vibrant acidity, and a little grip to conclude. Screwcap. 13% alc. **Rating** 91 **To** 2013 $20
Mount Macleod Pinot Noir 2008 Bright cherry fruit bouquet with a touch of sugar beet; light-bodied and focused, there is a savoury core to the light red fruits; fresh and focused on the finish. Screwcap. 13% alc. **Rating** 90 **To** 2014 $20

♥♥♥♥ **Mount Macleod Pinot Noir 2007** Neatly packaged and proportioned; a light-bodied pleasing mix of confit cherry fruit and some savoury/earthy notes. Screwcap. 13% alc. **Rating** 89 **To** 2012 $19.50

Cambewarra Estate

520 Illaroo Road, Cambewarra, NSW 2540 **Region** Shoalhaven Coast
T (02) 4446 0170 **www.**cambewarraestate.com.au **Open** Thurs–Sun, public & school hols 10–5
Winemaker Tamburlaine **Est.** 1991 **Cases** 3000

Louise Cole owns and runs Cambewarra Estate, near the Shoalhaven River on the central southern coast of NSW; the wines are made at Tamburlaine in the Hunter Valley. Cambewarra continues to produce attractive wines that have had significant success in wine shows, comprehensively emerging on top in the local (Kiama) wine show, where Keith Tulloch is chairman of judges.

ŸŸŸŸ **Louise Late Harvest Chardonnay 2008** Deep yellow-gold; luscious yellow peach fruit, the residual sweetness largely balance by crisp acidity. Screwcap. 8.7% alc. **Rating** 89 **To** 2010 $26
Louise Late Harvest Verdelho 2007 Some interesting aromatic flavours, ranging through citrus, apricot and pineapple; the wine is ideal for a fresh fruit match. 375 ml. Screwcap. 11.2% alc. **Rating** 88 **To** 2011 $30
Anniversary Late Harvest Chardonnay 2004 Brassy-gold; cumquat, mandarin and spice; a little more substance than the Louise Late Harvest Chardonnay, and a little more life; both very interesting wines, however. 375 ml. Screwcap. 9.8% alc. **Rating** 88 **To** 2010 $26
Louise Late Harvest Chardonnay 2005 Deep yellow-gold; has gained much complexity, but the fruit will soon start to dry out. 375 ml. Screwcap. 8.5% alc. **Rating** 87 **To** 2009 $26

Camp Road Estate   ★★★☆

165 Camp Road, Greta, NSW 2334 **Region** Lower Hunter Valley
T (02) 4938 6272 **F** (02) 4938 6004 **www.**camproadestate.com.au **Open** Not
Winemaker David Hook **Est.** 1998 **Cases** 1500 **Vyds** 5.1 ha
Duncan and Libby Thomson, cardiac surgeon and cardiac scrub nurse, respectively, say Heartland Vineyard is the result of a seachange that got a little out of hand. 'After looking one weekend at some property in the Hunter Valley to escape the Sydney rat-race, we stumbled upon the beautiful 90 acres that has become our vineyard.' They have built a rammed-earth house on the property, and the vineyard is now a little over 5 ha, with shiraz, semillon, merlot, barbera, verdelho and viognier. Stress returned to the seachange when a trademark dispute caused them to drop the Heartland Vineyard name and substitute Camp Road Estate.

ŸŸŸŸ **Verdelho 2008** Lively, clean and fresh, with a really pleasing mix of fruit salad and citrus flavours on a perfectly balanced palate. Great value. Screwcap. 13.5% alc. **Rating** 89 **To** 2011 $12
Viognier 2007 A bargain price for a viognier that has clear varietal character, particularly on the apricot-accented bouquet; the palate is a little tough, but that's viognier. Screwcap. 13.5% alc. **Rating** 88 **To** 2010 $12
Merlot 2007 An unexpectedly persuasive portrayal of merlot from a region that theoretically doesn't suit it; an abundance of flavour and particularly good length; clever winemaking. Great value. Screwcap. 13.5% alc. **Rating** 88 **To** 2010 $12
Shiraz Viognier 2007 Bright crimson; the influence of the 5% viognier is very obvious, teetering on the edge of too much so; however, full of life and great value. Screwcap. 15% alc. **Rating** 88 **To** 2013 $13

Campania Hills   ★★★☆

447 Native Corners Road, Campania, Tas 7026 **Region** Southern Tasmania
T (03) 6260 4387 **Open** By appt
Winemaker Winemaking Tasmania (Julian Alcorso) **Est.** 1994 **Cases** 500
This is the former Colmaur, purchased by Jeanette and Lindsay Kingston in 2005. They had just sold their business, built up over 22 years, and thought they were returning to country life and relaxation when they purchased the property, with 1.5 ha of vines equally split between pinot noir and chardonnay (plus 700 olive trees). Says Lindsay Kingston, somewhat wryly, 'We welcome visitors. The last lot stayed three hours.'

ŸŸŸŸŸ **Pinot Noir 2007** A Janus pinot; one face shows opulently ripe fruit with a hint of over-extraction; the other face has vibrancy and length. Screwcap. 13.5% alc. **Rating** 90 **To** 2013 $20

Campbells

★★★★★

Murray Valley Highway, Rutherglen, Vic 3685 **Region** Rutherglen
T (02) 6032 9458 **www**.campbellswines.com.au **Open** Mon–Sat 9–5, Sun 10–5
Winemaker Colin Campbell **Est.** 1870 **Cases** 40 000
A wide range of table and fortified wines of ascending quality and price, which are always honest. As so often happens in this part of the world, the fortified wines are the best, with the extremely elegant Isabella Rare Tokay and Merchant Prince Rare Muscat at the top of the tree; the winery rating is for the fortified wines. A feature of the Vintage Room at the cellar door is an extensive range of back vintage releases of small parcels of wine not available through any other outlet, other than to Cellar Club members. Exports to the UK, the US and other major markets.

ŸŸŸŸŸ **Isabella Rare Rutherglen Tokay NV** Very dark olive-brown; broodingly complex, deep and concentrated aromas, then layer upon layer of flavour in the mouth of almost syrupy consistency. Incredibly intense and complex, with the varietal tea-leaf/muscadelle fruit continuity. Cork. 18% alc. **Rating** 97 **To** 2010 $123.70
Merchant Prince Rare Rutherglen Muscat NV Dark brown, with olive-green on the rim; particularly fragrant, with essency/raisiny fruit; has an almost silky viscosity to the intense flavours that flood every corner of the mouth, but yet retains elegance. Cork. 18% alc. **Rating** 96 **To** 2010 $110
Grand Rutherglen Tokay NV Olive mahogany; much, much more complex than the Classic, with all the key varietal characteristics enhanced by rancio; the palate is very long, and has no stale characters whatsoever. Cork. 17.5% alc. **Rating** 94 **To** 2010 $73.10
Grand Rutherglen Muscat NV Full olive-brown; highly aromatic; a rich and complex palate is silky smooth, supple and long, the strong raisin fruit balanced by the clean, fresh, lingering acid (and spirit) cut on the finish. Cork. 17.5% alc. **Rating** 94 **To** 2010 $73.10

ŸŸŸŸŸ **The Barkly Rutherglen Durif 2006** Really bright colour, with an abundance of sweet fruit, and an almost honey-like nectar appeal; the palate is rich, ripe, full and, not surprisingly, quite generous and long; a good example of Durif done well. Cork. 14.5% alc. **Rating** 93 **To** 2016 $39.90
Classic Rutherglen Tokay NV Medium brown; has clear-cut varietal character on both the bouquet and palate, with tea-leaf, toffee and cake flavours; a delicious balance between youth and full maturity; doesn't cloy. Cork. 17.5% alc. **Rating** 93 **To** 2010 $41.90
Bobbie Burns Rutherglen Shiraz 2007 A well-crafted wine with a long history, which has moved with the times by reducing its alcohol; medium-bodied, with supple blackberry fruit and well-balanced and integrated oak, the tannins likewise ripe and balanced. Screwcap. 14.5% alc. **Rating** 92 **To** 2020 $22.50
Classic Rutherglen Muscat NV Spicy/raisiny complexity starting to build; a large increase in intensity and length over the Rutherglen Muscat. Cork. 17.5% alc. **Rating** 92 **To** 2010 $41.90
Rutherglen Tokay NV Bright, light golden-brown; classic mix of tea-leaf and butterscotch aromas lead into an elegant wine that dances in the mouth; has balance and length. Cork. 17.5% alc. **Rating** 92 **To** 2010 $18.80
Limited Release Rutherglen Durif 2006 An obvious and successful attempt to introduce an element of subtlety and finesse into a normally very robust wine, with sweet red and black fruits and fine tannins on a well-balanced palate. Screwcap. 14.5% alc. **Rating** 91 **To** 2014 $24.90
Rutherglen Muscat NV A complex and very luscious wine, which has some spicy elements, not unlike tokay, adding interest. Screwcap. 17.5% alc. **Rating** 90 **To** 2010 $18.80

ŸŸŸŸ **Rutherglen Shiraz Durif 2006** Good colour; achieves the richness and depth expected of the blend, yet is medium-bodied, and has light and shade to its texture. Will develop well. Screwcap. 14.5% alc. **Rating** 89 **To** 2015 $15.80
Rutherglen Shiraz Durif 2005 Good clean fruit, and a juicy personality; a little straightforward. Screwcap. 14.5% alc. **Rating** 87 **To** 2012 $15.80

Camyr Allyn Wines

Camyr Allyn North, Allyn River Road, East Gresford, NSW 2311 **Region** Upper Hunter Valley
T (02) 4938 9577 **www**.camyrallynwines.com.au **Open** Wed–Mon 10–5
Winemaker Geoff Broadfield **Est.** 1999 **Cases** 2500 **Vyds** 4.3 ha
John and Judy Evers purchased the Camyr Allyn North property in 1997 and immediately set about planting verdelho, shiraz and merlot. The wines are made by Hunter Valley veteran Geoff Broadfield. The promotion and packaging of the wines is innovative and stylish, centring around trout flies.

ŸŸŸŸ **Hunter Valley Verdelho 2008** Vibrant colour; nectarine and lime bouquet; dominated by the high acid profile, the palate is zesty and lively. Screwcap. 12.5% alc. **Rating** 88 **To** 2012 $20

Cannibal Creek Vineyard

260 Tynong North Road, Tynong North, Vic 3813 **Region** Gippsland
T (03) 5942 8380 **F** (03) 5942 8202 **www**.cannibalcreek.com.au **Open** 7 days 11–5
Winemaker Patrick Hardiker **Est.** 1997 **Cases** 2500 **Vyds** 5 ha
The Hardiker family moved to Tynong North in 1988, initially grazing beef cattle, but aware of the viticultural potential of the sandy clay loam and bleached subsurface soils weathered from the granite foothills of the Black Snake Ranges. Plantings began in 1997, using organically based cultivation methods; varieties include pinot noir, chardonnay, sauvignon blanc, merlot and cabernet sauvignon. The family decided to make their own wine, and a heritage-style shed built from locally milled timber was converted into a winery and cellar door. Exports to China.

ŸŸŸŸŸ **Sauvignon Blanc 2008** Restrained bouquet of flint and tropical fruit; zesty citrus fruit on the palate, with an attractive textural element; quite long and fine. Diam. 12.5% alc. **Rating** 93 **To** 2012 $24

ŸŸŸŸ **Pinot Noir 2006** Quite developed, but showing attractive game and spice on the bouquet; a touch of velvet supports the red fruit with aplomb. Diam. 13.5% alc. **Rating** 88 **To** 2011 $28

Canobolas-Smith

Boree Lane, off Cargo Road, Lidster via Orange, NSW 2800 **Region** Orange
T (02) 6365 6113 **www**.canobolassmithwines.com.au **Open** W'ends, public hols 11–5
Winemaker Murray Smith **Est.** 1986 **Cases** 2000
Canobolas-Smith is one of the leading Orange region wineries, and its three labels are particularly distinctive. Over the years it has produced some quite outstanding Chardonnays. Much of the wine is sold from the cellar door, which is well worth a visit. Exports to the US and Asia.

ŸŸŸŸŸ **Wild Yeast Chardonnay 2005** Bright, fresh and focused with grilled nuts supported by ripe nectarine fruit; quite weighty on entry, the palate freshens up and concludes with a slight Amaro-like bitterness, thus providing freshness. Screwcap. 14% alc. **Rating** 92 **To** 2014 $25

ŸŸŸŸ **Shine Reserve Chardonnay 2005** Ripe peach and plenty of toasty oak; oak also dominates the palate, but there is richness and fruit definition to enjoy. Screwcap. 14% alc. **Rating** 89 **To** 2013 $45

Canonbah Bridge

Merryanbone Station, Warren, NSW 2824 (postal) **Region** Western Plains Zone
T (02) 6833 9966 **F** (02) 6833 9980 **www**.canonbahbridge.com **Open** Not
Winemaker Shane McLaughlin, Hunter Wine Services (John Hordern) **Est.** 1999
Cases 25 000 **Vyds** 31 ha

Shane McLaughlin has established the Canonbah Bridge vineyard (shiraz, merlot, semillon, verdelho, mourvedre, grenache, tempranillo and chardonnay) on the very large Merryanbone Station, a Merino sheep stud that has been in the family for four generations. The wines are at three price points: at the bottom is Bottle Tree, from Southeastern Australia; then Ram's Leap (estate-grown); and at the top, Canonbah Bridge, either estate or estate/regional blends. Exports to the UK, the US and other major markets.

ŸŸŸŸ **Drought Reserve Western Plains Shiraz 2004** Developed colour; medium-bodied at best, but does have length and balance to the savoury fruits; fully priced, and then some. Cork. 14.5% alc. **Rating** 87 **To** 2012 $34.99
Western Plains McLaren Vale Shiraz Grenache Mourvedre 2005 As the blend would suggest, a distinctly savoury/earthy wine, which does, however, have good persistence and length. Screwcap. 14% alc. **Rating** 87 **To** 2012 $19.99

Cape Barren Wines   ★★★★★
Lot 20, Little Road, Willunga, SA 5172 **Region** McLaren Vale
T (08) 8556 4374 **F** (08) 8556 4364 **www.**capebarrenwines.com.au **Open** By appt
Winemaker Brian Light (Contract) **Est.** 1999 **Cases** 5000 **Vyds** 62 ha
Lifelong friends and vignerons Peter Matthews and Brian Ledgard joined forces in 1999 to create Cape Barren Wines. They have vineyards throughout the McLaren Vale region, the jewel in the crown being 4 ha of 70-year-old shiraz at Blewitt Springs, which provides the grapes for the Old Vine Shiraz. The McLaren Vale Grenache Shiraz Mourvedre and McLaren Vale Shiraz come from their other vineyards; most of the grapes are sold. Exports to the UK, the US and other major markets.

ŸŸŸŸŸ **Native Goose McLaren Vale Shiraz 2007** Full flavoured but elegant and supple, with delicious black and red cherry fruit, fine tannins and perfectly balanced oak. Value. Screwcap. 14.5% alc. **Rating** 94 **To** 2020 $23.50
Blewitt Springs Vineyard Reserve Release Old Vine McLaren Vale Shiraz 2005 Powerful and full-bodied, from 70-year-old vines; it avoids dead fruit characters, but has a luscious combination of blackberry, raspberry and dark chocolate fruits; balanced tannins and oak. Diam. 14.5% alc. **Rating** 94 **To** 2020 $34.95
Native Goose McLaren Vale GSM 2007 Good colour; vibrant raspberry fruit with a touch of garrigue and spice; fleshy and soft on entry, but tightens up on the finish to show the more serious side of the wine; very well made. Screwcap. 14.5% alc. **Rating** 94 **To** 2014 $23.50

Cape Bernier Vineyard   ★★★★★
230 Bream Creek Road, Bream Creek, Tas 7175 **Region** Southern Tasmania
T (03) 6253 5443 **F** (03) 6253 6087 **www.**capebernier.com.au **Open** 7 days 9–5 or by appt
Winemaker Winemaking Tasmania (Julian Alcorso) **Est.** 1999 **Cases** 750 **Vyds** 4 ha
Alastair Christie and family have established 2 ha of Dijon clone pinot noir, another 1.4 ha of chardonnay and 0.6 ha of pinot gris on a north-facing slope overlooking historic Marion Bay. The property is not far from the Bream Creek vineyard, and is one of several developments in the region changing the land use from dairy and beef cattle to wine production and tourism.

ŸŸŸŸŸ **Chardonnay 2007** Bright deep gold; pear, lemon and a gentle touch of oak on the bouquet; a fine acid profile frames the elegant fruit, and draws out the palate to a long and even finish. Dijon clones. Screwcap. 13.2% alc. **Rating** 94 **To** 2014 $22
Pinot Noir 2007 Good colour; vibrant spiced cherry fruit comes to the fore, with a well-handled delicate seasoning of oak; the palate is fresh, providing crunchy, young and well-defined fruit. Screwcap. 13.5% alc. **Rating** 94 **To** 2014 $27.50

ŸŸŸŸ **Pinot Gris 2008** Clean and fresh, with some complex charcuterie aromas supporting pear and spice; rich but fine, and the fresh acidity on the finish provides line and length. Screwcap. 13.5% alc. **Rating** 89 **To** 2012 $22

Cabernet Merlot 2007 A restrained and savoury style, with black olive and cedar dominating; the tannins are fine and the acid refreshing. Screwcap. 13.5% alc. **Rating** 88 **To** 2013 $21

Cape Grace ★★★★

Fifty One Road, Cowaramup, WA 6284 **Region** Margaret River
T (08) 9755 5669 **F** (08) 9755 5668 **www**.capegracewines.com.au **Open** 7 days 10–5
Winemaker Robert Karri-Davies, Mark Messenger (Consultant) **Est.** 1996 **Cases** 2000
Vyds 6.25 ha
Cape Grace Wines can trace its history back to 1875 when timber baron MC Davies settled at Karridale, building the Leeuwin lighthouse and founding the township of Margaret River; 120 years later, Robert and Karen Karri-Davies planted the vineyard to chardonnay, shiraz and cabernet sauvignon, with smaller amounts of merlot, semillon and chenin blanc. Robert is a self-taught viticulturist; Karen has over 15 years of international sales and marketing experience in the hospitality industry. Winemaking is carried out on the property; consultant Mark Messenger is a veteran of the Margaret River region. Exports to Singapore and Hong Kong.

♥♥♥♥♀ **Margaret River Chardonnay 2007** Deep colour; a worked style, with more of everything; very ripe melon, grapefruit and a fair amount of toasty oak; rich and oaky palate, with a strong grilled nut finish; plenty of power. Screwcap. 13.5% alc. **Rating** 91 **To** 2014 $38
Margaret River Cabernet Sauvignon 2007 Vibrant colour; oak dominates the red and black fruit bouquet; initially very firm and dry on the palate, the fruit makes its presence felt once the structure and the oak subside; very fresh. Screwcap. 14% alc. **Rating** 91 **To** 2018 $45
Margaret River Shiraz 2007 Pronounced pencilly oak on the bouquet with red fruits and a touch of cinnamon; the palate is firm, with the oak quite dominant; gravelly tannin and fresh acid prolong the finish. Screwcap. 13.5% alc. **Rating** 90 **To** 2016 $33

Cape Horn Vineyard ★★★☆

Stewarts Bridge Road, Echuca, Vic 3564 **Region** Goulburn Valley
T (03) 5480 6013 **F** (03) 5480 6013 **www**.capehornvineyard.com.au **Open** 7 days 11–5
Winemaker Ian Harrison, John Ellis (Contract) **Est.** 1993 **Cases** 3000 **Vyds** 11 ha
The unusual name comes from a bend in the Murray River considered by riverboat owners of the 19th century to resemble Cape Horn, which is depicted on the wine label. The property was acquired by Echuca GP Dr Sue Harrison and her schoolteacher husband Ian in 1993. Ian Harrison has progressively planted their 11-ha vineyard to chardonnay, shiraz, cabernet sauvignon, zinfandel, marsanne and durif.

♥♥♥♥♀ **Echuca Goulburn Valley Marsanne 2008** Unoaked, but has a considerable all-up volume of flavour; honeysuckle, citrus and even a touch of herb. Guaranteed to develop well. Screwcap. 13.1% alc. **Rating** 90 **To** 2014 $18

♥♥♥♥ **Echuca Goulburn Valley Shiraz 2007** Strong crimson–purple; despite moderate alcohol, has very good concentration and depth for a red wine from this region; blackberry and plum, with obvious, but not excessive, oak. Will develop. Screwcap. 13.5% alc. **Rating** 89 **To** 2017 $20
Echuca Goulburn Valley Durif 2006 Strong colour; deep, full-bodied wine with some savoury/spicy notes to the black fruits, the tannins holding the wine nicely. Screwcap. 14% alc. **Rating** 89 **To** 2013 $22
Echuca Goulburn Valley Cabernet Sauvignon 2005 Has retained excellent hue, reflecting the mouthfeel of what appears to be low pH; a tangy crisp wine with the characters one expects from cool climates. Screwcap. 14% alc. **Rating** 88 **To** 2016 $20
Echuca Sparkling Durif Shiraz 2004 Better than many cobbled together dry reds; nice spicy berry fruit components, and a balanced finish. Cork. 14% alc. **Rating** 88 **To** 2014 $28

Cape Jaffa Wines

Limestone Coast Road, Mount Benson via Robe, SA 5276 **Region** Mount Benson
T (08) 8768 5053 **F** (08) 8768 5040 **www**.capejaffawines.com.au **Open** 7 days 10–5
Winemaker Derek Hooper **Est.** 1993 **Cases** 30 000 **Vyds** 24.9 ha
Cape Jaffa was the first of the Mount Benson wineries and all of the production now comes
from the estate plantings, which include three major Bordeaux red varieties, plus shiraz,
chardonnay, sauvignon blanc, semillon and pinot gris. The winery (built of local rock) has
been designed to allow eventual expansion to 1000 tonnes, or 70 000 cases. In 2008 Cape
Jaffa became a fully certified biodynamic vineyard. Exports to the UK, Canada, Thailand,
Cambodia, Philippines, Hong Kong and Singapore.

ΥΥΥΥΥ **Siberia 2005** Only light- to medium-bodied, but has great drive and movement
in the mouth; spicy red and black cherry fruit with spicy notes and fine, savoury
tannins. Diam. 14% alc. **Rating** 93 **To** 2015 $34.95
Brocks Reef Shiraz Viognier 2006 Bright colour; lively, juicy, spicy wine,
the medium-bodied palate with unexpected energy and drive on the finish and
aftertaste. No need whatsoever for patience. Very good value. Screwcap. 14.5% alc.
Rating 90 **To** 2012 $16
La Lune Mount Benson Rose de Syrah 2008 A scented, floral bouquet, then
a full-flavoured, albeit dry, palate with notes of Turkish delight, roses and spice. The
most expensive square-shouldered bottle and cloth label ever devised for a rose.
Screwcap. 14% alc. **Rating** 90 **To** 2010 $25

ΥΥΥΥ **Sauvignon Blanc 2008** Green nettle and tropical fruit bouquet; a vibrant and
lively palate, with good weight and appealing freshness. Screwcap. 13.5% alc.
Rating 89 **To** 2011 $16
Limited Release Merlot 2005 Small, sweet red berry fruits are offset by
savoury, though fine, tannins; overall, good varietal expression. Screwcap. 14% alc.
Rating 89 **To** 2013 $25
La Lune Mount Benson Shiraz 2006 Light colour; pleasant light- to medium-
bodied wine, with red and black fruits and an overcoat of vanilla oak. Diam.
14% alc. **Rating** 88 **To** 2012 $45
La Lune Mount Benson Semillon Sauvignon Blanc 2007 Quite developed
colour; powerful structure, with a slightly bumpy finish. Cloth label a part of
biodynamic marketing strategy. Screwcap. 13% alc. **Rating** 87 **To** 2010 $40
Mount Benson Shiraz 2006 Good colour; black and red berry fruit; soft and
ample sweet fruit, with a touch of spicy oak at the fringe. Screwcap. 14.5% alc.
Rating 87 **To** 2012 $20
La Lune Cabernet 2006 Certified biodynamic on conversion, but really very
light-bodied, bordering on thin. Mind boggling price. Diam. 13% alc. **Rating** 87
To 2011 $45

Cape Mentelle

Wallcliffe Road, Margaret River, WA 6285 **Region** Margaret River
T (08) 9757 0888 **F** (08) 9757 3233 **www**.capementelle.com.au **Open** 7 days 10–4.30
Winemaker Robert Mann, Simon Burnell, Tim Lovett **Est.** 1970 **Cases** 90 000
Vyds 166 ha
Part of the LVMH (Louis Vuitton Möet Hennessy) group. Cape Mentelle is firing on all
cylinders with the winemaking team now fully capitalising on the extensive and largely
mature vineyards, and which obviate the need for contract-grown fruit. It is hard to say which
of the wines is best; the ranking, such as it is, varies from year to year. That said, Sauvignon
Blanc Semillon, Chardonnay, Shiraz and Cabernet Sauvignon lead the portfolio. Exports to
all major markets.

ΥΥΥΥΥ **Margaret River Chardonnay 2008** Brilliant green-gold; has exceptional
structure and mouthfeel; the citrus and nectarine fruit is vibrant, and there is a
streak of minerality running through the wine; oak is present, but is not at all
intrusive. Screwcap. 13% alc. **Rating** 96 **To** 2020 $42

Margaret River Shiraz 2007 Dense crimson-purple; spicy fruit aromas on the bouquet, then a voluptuous palate with multiple flavours of spice, licorice and both red and black fruits; exemplary oak and tannin support. Screwcap. 14% alc. **Rating** 96 **To** 2027 $39

Margaret River Sauvignon Blanc Semillon 2008 Has excellent juicy vinosity on the mid-palate, flavours of lemon, gooseberry and grass all intermingling, the touch of barrel ferment barely noticeable; excellent balance and length for short-term cellaring. Screwcap. 12.5% alc. **Rating** 95 **To** 2013 $27.50

Margaret River Chardonnay 2007 Pale colour; tight, austere, disciplined style in Chablis mode; needs more time but will develop well. Gold WA Wine Show '08. Screwcap. 13% alc. **Rating** 95 **To** 2013 $42

Margaret River Shiraz 2006 Bright colour; superior medium-bodied shiraz, with spicy black cherry fruits on a palate of excellent clarity; tannins and oak very well judged. Screwcap. 14% alc. **Rating** 94 **To** 2016 $39

Margaret River Cabernet Sauvignon 2006 Remarkable achievement for the vintage; medium-bodied cassis, blackcurrant; tannins fresh rather than green. Gold WA Wine Show '08. **Rating** 94 **To** 2016

Margaret River Cabernet Sauvignon 2005 Excellent colour; a fragrant, savoury medium-bodied wine, the bouquet and palate offering a seamless array of black fruits, earth, licorice and French oak; admirable texture, line and length. Screwcap. 14% alc. **Rating** 94 **To** 2030 $85

Margaret River Cabernet Sauvignon 2004 A delicious wine, flowing harmoniously across the tongue, yet with the structure expected of cabernet; the vibrant cassis and blackcurrant fruit produces the magic. Screwcap. 14.5% alc. **Rating** 94 **To** 2019 $84

ҰҰҰҰҰ **Wallcliffe Sauvignon Blanc Semillon 2007** Attractive, moderately complex bouquet; good flavour but needs more thrust through to the finish; patience may be rewarded. **Rating** 92 **To** 2014

Marmaduke 2007 Good hue; strikingly different spicy/savoury tobacco aromas lead into a strangely harmonious light- to medium-bodied palate that pulls all the strings together on a long, fine finish. Value plus. Drink sooner rather than later. Shiraz/Grenache/Mataro. Screwcap. 14% alc. **Rating** 91 **To** 2012 $19

Marmaduke 2006 Bright crimson-purple; fresh, juicy berry fruit flavours in a breezy red spectrum; top brasserie food style. Screwcap. 13.5% alc. **Rating** 91 **To** 2014 $19

Trinders Margaret River Cabernet Merlot 2007 A substantial wine, the medium- to full-bodied palate very much in the usual Trinders style; ripe tannins are woven through blackcurrant/cassis fruit, oak in balance. Screwcap. 14.5% alc. **Rating** 91 **To** 2022 $32

Trinders Margaret River Cabernet Merlot 2006 Seems always to have struggled for enough vinosity, but this goes close, with intensity and length to the tangy, savoury flavours typical of this wine. Screwcap. 14% alc. **Rating** 91 **To** 2016 $32

ҰҰҰҰ **Margaret River Zinfandel 2007** Desiccated blackberry bouquet, with a touch of sage and spice; rich, ripe and warm, the tannin outlasts the fruit. Screwcap. 15% alc. **Rating** 87 **To** 2012 $55

Cape Naturaliste Vineyard   ★★★★★

1 Coley Road (off Caves Road), Yallingup, WA 6282 **Region** Margaret River
T (08) 9755 2538 **www**.capenaturalistevineyard.com.au **Open** Wed–Mon 10.30–5
Winemaker Ian Bell, Barney Mitchell, Craig Brent-White **Est.** 1997 **Cases** 4000
Vyds 9 ha

Cape Naturaliste Vineyard has a long and varied history going back 150 years when it was a coach inn for travellers journeying between Perth and Margaret River. Later it became a dairy farm, and in 1970 a mining company purchased it, intending to extract the mineral sands. The government stepped in and declared it a national park, whereafter (in 1980) Craig Brent-White purchased the property. The vineyard is planted to cabernet sauvignon, shiraz, merlot, semillon and sauvignon blanc, and is run on an organic/biodynamic basis. The quality of the wines would suggest the effort is well worthwhile. Exports to Hong Kong and Singapore.

ΨΨΨΨΨ **Torpedo Rocks Margaret River Semillon 2007** Bright straw-green; barrel ferment and maturation in French oak has been handled with great skill, adding complexity without detracting from the tangy, grassy, minerally fruit. Screwcap. 12.5% alc. **Rating** 94 **To** 2015 $29
The House Block Margaret River Cabernet Sauvignon 2005 An absolutely correct rendition of a medium-bodied cabernet that has perfect length and balance; the low yield justified two years in French oak, which has fined the tannins and acted synergistically with the flavour. Screwcap. 14% alc. **Rating** 94 **To** 2020 $35

ΨΨΨΨ **Margaret River Sauvignon Blanc 2008** Solid wine; good structure but needs more aromatic lift to balance the oak. Screwcap. 12% alc. **Rating** 88 **To** 2010 $23
Margaret River Semillon Sauvignon Blanc 2008 A clean and fragrant bouquet, with gentle tropical/passionfruit aromas, leads into a light, easy palate without much focus; a gold medal at Rutherglen, a happy wine show hunting ground. Screwcap. 12% alc. **Rating** 88 **To** 2010 $23
Torpedo Rocks Margaret River Cabernet Merlot 2005 Despite the very low yield (3.5 tonnes per hectare), two years in French oak was a little over the top, but the wine does have some cassis and blackcurrant fruit cocooned within that oak. Screwcap. 14% alc. **Rating** 88 **To** 2014 $28

Cape Thomas Wines ★★★☆

Southern Ports Highway, Mount Benson, SA 5275 **Region** Mount Benson
T (08) 8768 6155 **F** (08) 8768 7264 **www.**capethomasvineyards.com.au **Open** 7 days 10–4.30 summer, reduced hours spring, closed June–Sept
Winemaker Contract **Est.** 2006 **Cases** 500 **Vyds** 16 ha
Cape Thomas vineyards are owned and operated by Maureen, Peter and Tom Andrews, the family having been farming in the district for 57 years. Peter was a student at Roseworthy Agricultural College in the early 1960s, but it was not until '95 that he fulfilled his long-held ambition to diversify into viticulture. Until 2004 all of the grapes were sold to Cellarmasters and Norfolk Rise, but since then wines have been made under the Cape Thomas label, the first release coming in '06. The wines are sold at the Mount Benson Wine & Tourism Centre (along with Guichen Bay Vineyards' wines), which is owned and operated by a community trust offering a range of facilities for visitors and community projects.

ΨΨΨΨΨ **The Captain Cabernet Sauvignon 2007** Bright colour; redcurrant and a touch of sage; medium-bodied, with moderate tannins and bright fruit; clean and focused on the finish. Screwcap. 13% alc. **Rating** 90 **To** 2014 $25

ΨΨΨΨ **The Matthew Reserve Shiraz 2007** Ripe red fruit, with a touch of porty sweet character on the bouquet; the palate is juicy, with sage and red fruit combining well. Screwcap. 14% alc. **Rating** 88 **To** 2013 $22

Capel Vale ★★★★★

Lot 5 Stirling Estate, Mallokup Road, Capel, WA 6271 **Region** Geographe
T (08) 9727 1986 **F** (08) 6364 4882 **www.**capelvale.com **Open** 7 days 10–4
Winemaker Ryan Carter, Justin Hearn **Est.** 1974 **Cases** 100 000 **Vyds** 165.27 ha
Capel Vale was established by Perth-based medical practitioner Dr Peter Pratten in 1974. The first vineyard adjacent to the winery was established on the banks of the quiet waters of Capel River. The very fertile soil gave rise to extravagant vine growth, providing 95% of the winery's intake until the mid-1980s. The viticultural empire has since been expanded, spreading across Capel (35.66 ha), Mount Barker (25.06 ha), Pemberton (76.65 ha) and Margaret River (27.9 ha), with 18 varieties planted; the most recent arrivals are petit verdot, sangiovese, tempranillo and nebbiolo. Production is in excess of 100 000 cases, and every aspect of the business is subject to the close scrutiny of Dr Peter Pratten. Exports to all major markets.

ŢŢŢŢŢ **The Scholar Margaret River Cabernet Sauvignon 2007** A cool herbaceous character sits atop an essency bouquet of cassis and cedar; plenty of oak, but the palate delivers a layered, dark and complex personality of bright fruit, florals and very ripe fine-grained tannin; while built for the long haul, is quite approachable. Screwcap. 15% alc. **Rating** 95 **To** 2018 $74.95

Regional Series Margaret River Chardonnay 2007 An alluring bouquet of nectarine, grapefruit and a gentle spicy note from well-handled oak; the palate is quite rich on entry and tightens up with vibrant and focused acidity; long, toasty and quite fine. Value. Screwcap. 13.5% alc. **Rating** 94 **To** 2015 $22.95

ŢŢŢŢŢ **Debut Sauvignon Blanc Semillon 2008** Clean, fresh passionfruit and gooseberry aromas; crisp, almost juicy fruit flavours; good length and balance. Screwcap. 12.5% alc. **Rating** 92 **To** 2011 $17.95

Debut Shiraz Rose 2008 Light crimson; manages to combine considerable red berry fruit flavours with a long, dry finish; a very good rose likely to suit all tastes. Screwcap. 13% alc. **Rating** 91 **To** 2009 $17.95

Regional Series Pemberton Chardonnay 2008 A nectarine and toasty oak bouquet; showing some struck match complexity; rich and generous palate, with a slightly creamy and spicy finish. Screwcap. 13.5% alc. **Rating** 91 **To** 2013 $22.95

Regional Series Margaret River Cabernet Sauvignon 2007 A powerful wine, with ripe blackcurrant and plum aromas and flavours; positive tannins offset any alcohol heat. Screwcap. 15% alc. **Rating** 91 **To** 2014 $22.95

Regional Series Pemberton Semillon Sauvignon Blanc 2008 The aromatic bouquet is strongly expressive of the semillon component, the palate likewise, with grassy/lemony components leading the way, fresh tropical characters in the farewell. Screwcap. 12% alc. **Rating** 90 **To** 2012 $22.95

Regional Series Margaret River Cabernet Merlot 2007 Strong colour; blackcurrant and mulberry fruit on bouquet and palate is strongly supported by ripe tannin and appropriate oak; very full mouthfeel; will live. Screwcap. 15% alc. **Rating** 90 **To** 2017 $22.95

ŢŢŢŢ **Regional Series Pemberton Sauvignon Blanc 2008** A fresh, crisp minerally bouquet introduces a light, tightly wound palate with nuances of kiwi fruit and herb. Screwcap. 12% alc. **Rating** 89 **To** 2010 $22.95

Regional Series Mount Barker Shiraz 2007 Has contrasting components of very ripe plum and prune on the one hand, savoury/earthy/spicy on the other; still needs to resolve itself. Screwcap. 15% alc. **Rating** 89 **To** 2016 $22.95

Whispering Hill Mount Barker Shiraz 2007 Fragrant, zesty, lively mouth-feel and thrust, but is as yet distinctly oaky. Screwcap. 14.5% alc. **Rating** 89 **To** 2015 $54.95

Sassy Sparkling 2006 Good flavour augmented by fairly high dosage; crowd-pleasing style. Crown Seal. 12.5% alc. **Rating** 89 **To** 2010 $26.95

Cellar Exclusive Geographe Sangiovese 2007 Good colour; dried herb bouquet with some dark cherry fruit on offer; the palate is dry and savoury, with a little sweet fruit on the finish. Screwcap. 15% alc. **Rating** 88 **To** 2012 $26.95

Debut Unwooded Chardonnay 2008 Peach and nectarine on quite a juicy and forward palate; clean and fresh. Screwcap. 13.5% alc. **Rating** 87 **To** 2011 $17.95

Debut Merlot 2007 Despite the alcohol, in a distinctive, albeit varietal, spectrum of earth, olive, stem and spice; for the purist. Screwcap. 15% alc. **Rating** 87 **To** 2013 $17.95

Cellar Exclusive Geographe Petit Verdot 2007 Deep colour; a backward bouquet with dark black fruit, and a certain element of tar; the palate is very tannic and dry, but shows despite its fruit concentration; will always be a dark wine. Screwcap. 14.5% alc. **Rating** 87 **To** 2014 $26.95

Capercaillie ★★★★★

4 Londons Road, Lovedale, NSW 2325 **Region** Lower Hunter Valley
T (02) 4990 2904 **www.**capercailliewine.com.au **Open** Mon–Sat 9–5, Sun 10–5
Winemaker Various **Est.** 1995 **Cases** 6000 **Vyds** 6.25 ha

A highly successful winery in terms of the quality of its wines, as well as their reach outwards from the Hunter Valley. The Capercaillie wines have always been particularly well made, with generous flavour. Following the example of Brokenwood, its fruit sources are spread across southeastern Australia, although the portfolio includes high-quality wines which are 100% Hunter Valley. The sudden death of owner Alasdair Sutherland, followed a year later by the departure of winemaker Daniel Binet, posed a major question mark over its future. Exports to the UK and Dubai.

** TTTTT The Creel Hunter Valley Semillon 2008** Clean, fragrant, ultra-varietal herb, lanolin and grass aromas, citrus appearing alongside the other components on the long palate. Screwcap. 10% alc. **Rating** 95 **To** 2020 $21

Hunter Valley Semillon 2008 A spotlessly clean bouquet is followed by a star-bright and pure palate with nuances of lemon, grass, herb and mineral; a feather-like but long finish. Screwcap. 10% alc. **Rating** 95 **To** 2023 $25

The Ghillie Hunter Valley Shiraz 2007 Relatively light colour; a classic Hunter style that, while seemingly light in body, will continue to develop over decades thanks to flawless balance and length. Screwcap. 14.5% alc. **Rating** 94 **To** 2027 $70

The Clan 2007 Delicious wine that has been woven into a seamless whole despite diverse components (four varieties from three regions); an overriding red fruit flavour to a complex and supple wine. Cabernet Sauvignon/Petit Verdot/ Merlot/Shiraz. Screwcap. 15% alc. **Rating** 94 **To** 2021 $30

TTTTℙ Cuillin Chardonnay 2008 Early picking due to rain threatening has been a bonus, giving the wine a racy, citrussy overtone to the nectarine and melon fruit, oak irrelevant. Screwcap. 13% alc. **Rating** 91 **To** 2014 $23

Dessert Style Gewurztraminer 2008 There isn't much gewurz varietal character to be seen, but this is a very good wine, perfect for fresh fruit or light cake-based desserts, or just for something chilled ice-cold on a hot day. Screwcap. 10% alc. **Rating** 91 **To** 2010 $18

Capital Wines   ★★★★☆

43 Shumack Street, Weetangera, ACT 2614 (postal) **Region** Canberra District
T 0407 913 912 **www**.kyeemawines.com.au **Open** Not
Winemaker Andrew McEwin **Est.** 1986 **Cases** 900 **Vyds** 4.5 ha

This is a newly constituted venture between Mark and Jenny Mooney (of the Royal Hotel at Gundaroo) and Andrew and Marion McEwin (of Kyeema Wines). They have joined to found Capital Wines, which purchased Kyeema wine and related contract winemaking in 2008. The new venture has seen the creation of a new series of wines (The Ministry Series) with clever graphic design, and generally invigorated marketing efforts. The estate vineyard is still an important source, but grape purchases and an expanded winery are also part of the new venture. Whether by coincidence, or not, the releases of the new wines are of impressive quality.

TTTTT Kyeema Vineyard Reserve Shiraz 2007 Excellent purple-crimson; all about controlled power, with beautifully balanced spicy/peppery fruit, oak and tannins; the wine is little more than medium-bodied, but has great length and persistence. Screwcap. 13.7% alc. **Rating** 95 **To** 2022 $52

TTTTℙ The Frontbencher Shiraz 2007 Crimson-purple; a wine with lots of energy to its display of spicy red and black fruits, with a savoury licorice twist on the finish. Clever label design and story. Screwcap. 14% alc. **Rating** 92 **To** 2017 $25

The Senator Chardonnay 2008 Elegant, crisp light-bodied wine, with white peach and grapefruit aromas and flavours, the touch of barrel-ferment oak carefully controlled so as not to overwhelm the delicate fruit. Screwcap. 12.3% alc. **Rating** 91 **To** 2014 $22

The Backbencher Merlot 2006 Yet another well-made wine in the Ministry Series releases; has unequivocal varietal character from the cassis fruit and spicy tannins. Screwcap. 13.5% alc. **Rating** 90 **To** 2014 $25

♟♟♟♟   **The Ambassador Tempranillo 2007** A wine with good focus and varietal expression; red berry fruits are foremost, with a strong spicy contribution; tannins are balanced, and the oak subtle. Screwcap. 13.2% alc. **Rating** 89 **To** 2013 $26.50

Capogreco Winery Estate   ★★★

3078 Riverside Avenue, South Mildura, Vic 3500 **Region** Murray Darling
T (03) 5022 1431 **F** (03) 5022 1431 **Open** Mon–Sat 10–5
Winemaker Bruno Capogreco, Domenico Capogreco **Est.** 1976 **Cases** NA **Vyds** 33 ha
Italian-owned and run, the wines are a blend of Italian and Australian Riverland influences. The estate has 13 ha of chardonnay, 14 ha of shiraz and 6 ha of cabernet sauvignon, but also purchases other varieties. Exports to the UK and Canada.

♟♟♟♟   **Reserve Nuovo Millennio Shiraz 2000** Is fully developed, but who would guess it had spent seven years in 2500-litre American oak casks before being bottled on 17 Dec '07? Has a mix of mocha and vanilla flavours, with no tannins to speak of. A worthy curio at a low price. Cork. 14% alc. **Rating** 87 **To** 2011 $20

Carbunup Crest   ★★★★

PO Box 235, Busselton, WA 6280 **Region** Margaret River
T (08) 9755 7775 **F** (08) 9754 2618 **www.carbunupcrest.com.au Open** Not
Winemaker Flying Fish Cove **Est.** 1998 **Cases** 4000 **Vyds** 10.5 ha
Carbunup Crest is owned by the Meares family, with Kris Meares managing the business. Initially it operated as a grapevine rootling nursery, but it has gradually converted to grapegrowing and winemaking. There are two vineyards in the Margaret River, at Metricup (cabernet sauvignon, merlot and semillon) and Cowaramup (sauvignon blanc, cabernet sauvignon and merlot). The dry-grown vines produced grapes with excellent flavour, excellence reflected in the wines. Exports to Japan and other parts of Asia.

♟♟♟♟♟   **Margaret River Semillon Sauvignon Blanc 2008** A lively and intense interplay between grassy/citrussy components on the one side, and gooseberry/passionfruit on the other. Screwcap. 12.2% alc. **Rating** 91 **To** 2012 $21.95
Margaret River Chardonnay 2007 A fragrant bouquet with a striking mix of tropical and citrus aromas moves into a delicate, finely flavoured palate, perhaps a little too fine. Screwcap. 13.6% alc. **Rating** 90 **To** 2016 $22.95

Cardinham Estate   ★★★★

Main North Road, Stanley Flat, SA 5453 **Region** Clare Valley
T (08) 8842 1944 **F** (08) 8842 1955 **Open** 7 days 10–5
Winemaker Scott Smith, Brett Stevens **Est.** 1981 **Cases** 5000
The Smith family has progressively increased the vineyard to its present level of 60 ha, the largest plantings being of cabernet sauvignon, shiraz and riesling. It entered into a grape supply contract with Wolf Blass, which led to an association with then Quelltaler winemaker Stephen John. The joint venture then formed has now terminated, and Cardinham is locating its 500-tonne winery on its Emerald Vineyard and using only estate-grown grapes. This has seen production rise, especially with the staples of Riesling, Cabernet Merlot and Stradbroke Shiraz. Exports to the US and Hong Kong.

♟♟♟♟♟   **Clare Valley Riesling 2008** Vibrant hue; pure lemon and apple blossom bouquet, with zesty lime fruit coming forward on the palate; clean, fresh, vibrant and poised on the finish. Value Screwcap. 11.7% alc. **Rating** 93 **To** 2014 $18
Alexandria 1860s Clare Valley Muscat NV Clean, lightly toasted almond bouquet, with a gentle touch of spice; quite generous and rich, with appealing finesse on the finish. Cork. 16% alc. **Rating** 90 **To** 2014 $35

♟♟♟♟   **Clare Valley Shiraz 2005** Lifted redcurrant and a touch of spice and game; medium-bodied, juicy and fine on the finish. Screwcap. 14% alc. **Rating** 88 **To** 2014 $25

Cargo Road Wines   ★★★☆

Cargo Road, Orange, NSW 2800 **Region** Orange
T (02) 6365 6100 **F** (02) 6365 6001 www.cargoroadwines.com.au **Open** W'ends &
public hols 11–5, or by appt
Winemaker James Sweetapple **Est.** 1984 **Cases** 3000
Originally called The Midas Tree, the vineyard was planted in 1984 by Roseworthy graduate
John Swanson, who established a 2.5-ha vineyard that included zinfandel – 15 years ahead of
his time. The property was acquired in 1997 by Charles Lane, James Sweetapple and Brian
Walters. Since then they have rejuvenated the original vineyard and planted more zinfandel,
sauvignon blanc and cabernet.

♥♥♥♥♀ **Orange Gewurztraminer 2008** Strong varietal musk and rose aromas lead into
a generous, but not too fat or oily, palate; a good example of the variety, made in a
dry, yet generous, mould. Screwcap. 14.5% alc. **Rating** 90 **To** 2012 $22

♥♥♥♥ **Orange Sauvignon Blanc 2008** Pale straw-green; light passionfruit aromas
lead directly into the palate, joined by gooseberry and apple; needs a touch more
acidity. Screwcap. 13% alc. **Rating** 88 **To** 2010 $22
Orange Riesling 2008 A ripe style, with candied orange and a reasonable
amount of residual sugar on the palate; generous and clean; a drink-early style.
Screwcap. 12.7% alc. **Rating** 87 **To** 2011 $25

Carilley Estate   ★★★

Lot 23 Hyem Road, Herne Hill, WA 6056 **Region** Swan Valley
T (08) 9296 6190 www.carilleyestate.com.au **Open** Thurs–Mon 10.30–5
Winemaker John Griffiths **Est.** 1985 **Cases** 1500 **Vyds** 4.2 ha
The Carija family has owned and operated vineyards in the Swan Valley since 1957,
culminating in the establishment of Carilley Estate in '85 by doctors Laura and Isavel Carija.
The 4.2-ha vineyard is planted to chardonnay, chenin blanc, viognier, shiraz, malbec, merlot
and grenache. Most of the grapes are sold, with a small proportion made under the Carilley
Estate label.

♥♥♥♥ **Fiona's Wish Sparkling Chardonnay NV** Aperitif style, lemon and apple
bouquet; light, fresh and crisp with refreshing acidity, and a fine dry finish. Cork.
12.6% alc. **Rating** 87 **To** 2012 $27

Carlei Estate & Carlei Green Vineyards ★★★★★

1 Albert Road, Upper Beaconsfield, Vic 3808 **Region** Yarra Valley
T (03) 5944 4599 **F** (03) 5944 4599 www.carlei.com.au **Open** W'ends by appt
Winemaker Sergio Carlei **Est.** 1994 **Cases** 10 000
Sergio Carlei has come a long way in a short time: graduating from home winemaking in a
suburban garage to his own (commercial) winery in Upper Beaconsfield; Carlei Estate falls
just within the boundaries of the Yarra Valley. Along the way Carlei acquired a Bachelor of
Wine Science from CSU, and established a 2.25-ha vineyard with organic and biodynamic
accreditation adjacent to the Upper Beaconsfield winery. His contract winemaking services
are now a major part of the business, and showcase his extremely impressive winemaking
talents. Exports to the US, Canada, China, Singapore and Malaysia.

♥♥♥♥♥ **Estate Sud Heathcote Shiraz 2006** A dark and solid wine, with tarry black
fruit and an ironstone character; the palate is very firm and savoury, but the fruit
weight carries it with ease; as with all of these Heathcote wines, the acidity and
tannin levels are quite pronounced but intrinsically in balance. Diam. 14.9% alc.
Rating 94 **To** 2018 $59
Ding an Sich Forties Old Block Heathcote Shiraz 2006 Vivid purple hue;
a highly expressive bouquet of blueberry, ironstone, plum and a touch of bay leaf;
medium-bodied with full impact, as focused acid and tannin take the abundant
fruit on a long journey across the palate; silky, juicy, long and fine, with an
engaging savoury finish. Diam. 14% alc. **Rating** 94 **To** 2020 $75

ΨΨΨΨΨ **Estate Nord Heathcote Shiraz 2006** Quite ripe and spicy red fruit; acid is accentuated with red fruit showing through on the palate; takes a little while to divulge its personality, but the flavours are long and generous in the end. Diam. 14.7% alc. **Rating** 93 **To** 2018 $59

Estate Tre Rossi 2006 An intriguing blend, with a spicy core of red and black fruit, framed by the pronounced acidity of the Italian varietals; there is a sharp edge to the palate that provides a lively sense of light and shade; long and brambly on the finish. Shiraz/Barbera/Nebbiolo. Diam. 14.7% alc. **Rating** 92 **To** 2014 $39

Green Vineyards Yarra Valley Pinot Noir 2006 Bright colour; a spicy bouquet with sage framing cool cherry fruit; texture is the key to the palate, with a silky presence and fine-grained tannins supporting the soft and fleshy fruit well. Screwcap. 13.5% alc. **Rating** 91 **To** 2013 $29

Green Vineyards Heathcote Shiraz 2006 Ripe morello cherry and blueberry bouquet; quite spicy and truly medium-bodied on the palate, with a fleshy and generous conclusion. Diam. 14.9% alc. **Rating** 91 **To** 2015 $29

ΨΨΨΨ **Estate Yarra Valley Chardonnay 2007** Quite developed for its age with a distinctly savoury personality; the palate shows ripe lemon and a whole lot of grilled nuts; on the finish, the acid is pronounced and quite fresh. Screwcap. 13% alc. **Rating** 89 **To** 2012 $49

Green Vineyards Cardinia Ranges Pinot Gris 2008 Pinking colour; ripe orange zest bouquet; fresh vibrant and generous on the finish. Screwcap. 13.5% alc. **Rating** 88 **To** 2012 $29

Green Vineyards Yarra Valley Chardonnay 2007 Deep colour; almost overripe on the bouquet with the fruit verging on tropical; one can't help but feel the wine has been worked quite hard, with a rich, and slightly heavy finish. Screwcap. 13.5% alc. **Rating** 87 **To** 2012 $29

Carrickalinga Creek Vineyard ★★★

Lot 10 Willson Drive, Normanville, SA 5204 **Region** Southern Fleurieu
T 0403 009 149 **www.**ccvineyard.com.au **Open** W'ends 11–5.30 (summer)
Winemaker Tim Geddes (Contract) **Est.** 2001 **Cases** 500 **Vyds** 3 ha
Tim Anstey and Helen Lacey acquired their north-sloping property 2 km from the St Vincent Gulf in the wake of Tim's retirement from university teaching. The choice of region was driven by Dr John Gladstones' enthusiasm for the mild, maritime climate of the lower Fleurieu Peninsula, for red grapes in particular. In 2001 they planted 1 ha each of shiraz and cabernet sauvignon, followed later by 0.7 ha of chardonnay and 0.3 ha of viognier. The purpose-built hillside cellar door has spectacular views of both the coast and surrounding hills. Tim Geddes calls the shots with the winemaking; Tim Anstey is 'cellar hand'.

ΨΨΨΨ **Chardonnay Viognier 2008** The 25% viognier component certainly makes its presence felt in a crisp, tangy wine reflecting its cool maritime location; good length and balance. Will develop well. Screwcap. 13% alc. **Rating** 87 **To** 2013 $15

Casa Freschi ★★★★

PO Box 45, Summertown, SA 5141 **Region** Langhorne Creek
T 0409 364 569 **F** (08) 8390 3232 **www.**casafreschi.com.au **Open** Not
Winemaker David Freschi **Est.** 1998 **Cases** 2000 **Vyds** 8 ha
David Freschi graduated with a degree in Oenology from Roseworthy College in 1991 and spent most of the decade working overseas in California, Italy and NZ. In 1998 he and his wife decided to trade in the corporate world for a small family-owned winemaking business, with a core of 2.5 ha of vines established by his parents in '72; an additional 2 ha of nebbiolo have now been planted adjacent to the original vineyard. Says David, 'The names of the wines were chosen to best express the personality of the wines grown in our vineyard, as well as to express our heritage.' A second 3.5-ha vineyard has subsequently been established in the Adelaide Hills. Exports to the US and Canada.

ȲȲȲȲȲ La Signora 2005 Elegant, medium-bodied wine with spicy/savoury elements driving the blend of Nebbiolo (85%)/Cabernet Sauvignon/Shiraz/Malbec; the seemingly small components other than nebbiolo in fact build the mouthfeel. One of the best nebbiolos (it could have been labelled as such) on the market. Cork. 14% alc. **Rating** 93 **To** 2015 $40

Profondo Grand 2005 Medium- to full-bodied; looks firmly towards Bordeaux, with earthy cedary overtones to the complex array of fruit flavours, which range from quite sweet to distinctly savoury. Cabernet Sauvignon/Shiraz/Malbec. Cork. 14% alc. **Rating** 93 **To** 2018 $60

ȲȲȲȲ La Signorina 2008 A blend of Pinot Gris/Chardonnay/Riesling/ Gewurztraminer, resulting in a wine that is all about texture; light and bright on the palate, there is a slippery nature to the finish that is easy and non-challenging. Screwcap. 13% alc. **Rating** 88 **To** 2014 $29

Cascabel

Rogers Road, Willunga, SA 5172 (postal) **Region** McLaren Vale
T (08) 8557 4434 **F** (08) 8557 4435 **Open** Not
Winemaker Susana Fernandez, Duncan Ferguson **Est.** 1997 **Cases** 2500
Cascabel's proprietors, Duncan Ferguson and Susana Fernandez, planted a 5-ha mosaic of southern Rhône and Spanish varieties. The choice of grapes reflects the winemaking experience of the proprietors in Australia, the Rhône Valley, Bordeaux, Italy, Germany and NZ – and also Susana's birthplace, Spain. Production has moved steadily towards the style of the Rhône Valley, Rioja and other parts of Spain. Exports to the UK, the US, Switzerland, Japan and Spain.

ȲȲȲȲȲ McLaren Vale Tempranillo Graciano 2006 A finely crafted wine, with texture and structure immediately evident; the spicy red fruits are complemented by well-integrated French oak; has real character and presence. Screwcap. 14.5% alc. **Rating** 94 **To** 2016 $46

ȲȲȲȲȲ McLaren Vale Roussanne Viognier 2008 The 50/50 blend is a synergistic one, the roussanne tempering the tendency of the viognier to lack structure and acidity, the viognier adding flavour to the normally reticent marsanne; will develop well. Screwcap. 13.5% alc. **Rating** 90 **To** 2014 $27

Tipico McLaren Vale Grenache Monastrell Shiraz 2006 Strongly regional; savoury dark chocolate and spice influences running through the intense, tightly focused medium-bodied palate. Screwcap. 14.5% alc. **Rating** 90 **To** 2015 $28

ȲȲȲȲ Eden Valley Riesling 2008 Generous wine; strong regional expression of sweet lime juice, tightened up neatly by mineral-accented acidity on the finish. Screwcap. 12% alc. **Rating** 89 **To** 2015 $22

Fleurieu Shiraz 2006 Quite developed colour; the spicy/earthy chocolate aromas and flavours seem more akin to McLaren Vale than the Fleurieu; pleasant wine, nonetheless. Screwcap. 14.5% alc. **Rating** 89 **To** 2014 $33

McLaren Vale Tempranillo 2008 Fragrant light-bodied wine, with a blend of red fruits, touches of citrus rind and fine tannins. Screwcap. 13.5% alc. **Rating** 88 **To** 2016 $21

McLaren Vale Monastrell 2006 Stridently earthy, vegetal and spicy; these are legitimate elements of mourvedre (which monastrell is) but they come as a shock to me; others may relate more easily. Screwcap. 15% alc. **Rating** 88 **To** 2013 $44

Casella Wines

Wakely Road, Yenda, NSW 2681 **Region** Riverina
T (02) 6961 3000 **F** (02) 6961 3099 **www**.casellawines.com.au **Open** Not
Winemaker Alan Kennett, Phillip Casella **Est.** 1969 **Cases** 12 million
A modern-day fairytale success story, transformed overnight from a substantial, successful but non-charismatic business making 650 000 cases in 2000. Its opportunity came when the US

distribution of Lindemans Bin 65 Chardonnay was taken away from WJ Deutsch & Sons, leaving a massive gap in its portfolio, which was filled by yellow tail. It built its US presence at a faster rate than any other brand in history. Exports to all major markets, and is now rapidly penetrating the UK market. It has been aided in all markets by making small batches (500 dozen or so) of Reserve and Limited Release wines, and by spreading its net for these across three states. Surprisingly, no update information received, nor representative samples.

Cassegrain

764 Fernbank Creek Road, Port Macquarie, NSW 2444 **Region** Hastings River
T (02) 6582 8377 **F** (02) 6582 8378 **www.**cassegrainwines.com.au **Open** 7 days 9–5
Winemaker John Cassegrain **Est.** 1980 **Cases** 60 000
The short-lived merger of Cassegrain and Simon Gilbert Wines (now Prince Hill Wines) has largely been unwound, although the Cassegrain winery production remains at a high level, with a wide range of Premium, Reserve and Limited Release labels. The winery has recently been upgraded, with the building of a temperature-controlled bottle-maturation facility. Exports to the UK and other major markets.

ΥΥΥΥΥ **Reserve Falerne Shiraz Merlot Tempranillo 2006** A very successful varietal and regional (New England/Hunter Valley) blend; the medium-bodied palate has exemplary texture and structure, the predominantly red fruits backed by spice and fine tannins, the oak well integrated. Cork. 14% alc. **Rating** 94 **To** 2016 $32

ΥΥΥΥΥ **Stone Circle Semillon Sauvignon Blanc 2008** Spotlessly clean and vibrant, partially a function of the low alcohol semillon component; gentle tropical and kiwi fruit nuances come from the sauvignon blanc; fades slightly on the finish. Screwcap. 11% alc. **Rating** 90 **To** 2012 $13.95

ΥΥΥΥ **Edition Noir Eden Valley Riesling 2008** Fragrant lemon, lemongrass and spice aromas; the palate heads off elsewhere, quite soft and fruit-ripe. Strange wine, but far from unpleasant. Screwcap. 13% alc. **Rating** 89 **To** 2014 $23.50
Semillon 2008 Fresh and crisp; an intensely grassy/lemony palate, bordering on sour lemon, but none the worse for that. A blend of Hastings River/New England grapes. The ultimate options game wine. Screwcap. 10.5% alc. **Rating** 89 **To** 2018 $18.95
Edition Noir Hunter Valley Shiraz 2007 Very deep colour for the Hunter Valley; unusually concentrated plum and blackberry fruit, with soft tannin and vanilla oak; the alcohol registers as sweetness on the finish, rather than heat. Worth cellaring. Screwcap. 15.5% alc. **Rating** 89 **To** 2017 $23.50
Stone Circle New England Shiraz 2007 Well made; lively, spicy, peppery red fruits drive the bouquet and light- to medium-bodied palate; is more vibrant than the varietal. Screwcap. 13.5% alc. **Rating** 88 **To** 2014 $16.95
Stone Circle Tumbarumba Chardonnay 2008 A tangy unoaked wine, with stone fruit and citrus flavours backed by firm acidity. Screwcap. 13.5% alc. **Rating** 87 **To** 2012 $16.95
Chardonnay 2008 A workmanlike wine from Tumbarumba/New England; ripe stone fruit flavours and a hint of oak. Screwcap. 14% alc. **Rating** 87 **To** 2012 $18.95
Verdelho 2008 A grassy style, with clean citrus fruit aroma and flavour; good texture, seemingly dry finish. Screwcap. 12.5% alc. **Rating** 87 **To** 2010 $16.95
Rose 2008 An aromatic and spicy bouquet; has good, tangy flavour and length, the finish dry. Cabernet sauvignon from New England. Screwcap. 13.5% alc. **Rating** 87 **To** 2010 $18.95
Edition Noir Tumbarumba Pinot Noir 2007 A very savoury rendition of pinot noir, with some sweeter fruit notes briefly appearing on the mid-palate. Screwcap. 13% alc. **Rating** 87 **To** 2011 $23.50
Shiraz 2007 A light- to medium-bodied spicy wine with a unique blend of New England/Coonawarra grapes; has more length than depth; early consumption. Screwcap. 14% alc. **Rating** 87 **To** 2013 $18.95

Castelli Estate ★★★★

88 Tweeddale Road, Applecross, WA 6153 (postal) **Region** Great Southern
T (08) 9364 0400 **F** (08) 9364 0444 **www**.castelliestate.com.au **Open** Not
Winemaker Mike Garland (Contract) **Est.** 2007 **Cases** 2250
Castelli Estate will cause many small winery owners to go green with envy. When Sam Castelli purchased the property in late 2004, he was intending to simply use it as a family holiday destination. But because there was a partly constructed winery he decided to complete the building work and lock the doors. However, wine was in his blood courtesy of his father, who owned a small vineyard in Italy's south. The temptation was too much, so in 2007 the winery was commissioned, with 20 tonnes of Great Southern fruit crushed under the Castelli label. In 2008 the amount increased to 30 tonnes, and '09 40 tonnes. There is room for expansion because the winery actually has a capacity of 500 tonnes, and the underground cellar is fully climate controlled. The grapes are contract-grown, shiraz and cabernet sauvignon come from Hadley Hall Vineyard in Frankland River; Olde Eastbrook Vineyard in Pemberton provides the chardonnay; and Whispering Hill Vineyard in Mount Barker provides the riesling.

ΨΨΨΨΩ **Pemberton Chardonnay 2008** Clean, crisp and fresh, the whole focus on the delicate citrus and stone fruit flavours, supported and lengthened by vibrant acidity on the finish. Screwcap. 13.6% alc. **Rating** 90 **To** 2015 $28
Cabernet Sauvignon 2007 Strongly varietal, with blackberry fruit and persistent but fine tannins; seems certain to develop well. Very sophisticated packaging. **Rating** 90 **To** 2013

ΨΨΨΨ **Frankland River Shiraz 2007** Bright purple-crimson; a fresh, light- to medium-bodied wine with spicy/peppery cool-grown characters to its red fruits; has good tannin texture, although is overall a little too oaky. Screwcap. 14.5% alc. **Rating** 89 **To** 2015 $28
Riesling 2007 Very crisp and fresh, highlighted by the continuing display of spritz and brisk acidity. Will be long-lived. Screwcap. 11.9% alc. **Rating** 88 **To** 2014 $20

Castle Lion Vineyard ★★★★

Mulberry on Swan, 34 Hamersley Road, Caversham, WA 6055 **Region** Peel
T (08) 9525 4097 **F** (08) 9526 2458 **www**.castlelion.com.au **Open** Wed–Sun 10–5
Winemaker Stuart Pierce **Est.** 2001 **Cases** 6000 **Vyds** 13.5 ha
This is the venture of the Avila family, with roots going back to the Castilla y Leon region of Spain, and the ancient city of Avila. Planting of the vineyard began in 2001 (shiraz, cabernet sauvignon and merlot) and the vines are grown organically, although not yet certified as such. The Semillon Sauvignon Blanc, with a string of silver medals to its credit, is made from purchased grapes, one suspects from the Margaret River or similar region.

ΨΨΨΨΩ **Sauvignon Blanc Semillon 2008** A spotlessly clean bouquet, both it and the palate with precise grassy/minerally characters; bright finish. Screwcap. 12.3% alc. **Rating** 90 **To** 2010 $15.99

Castle Rock Estate ★★★★★

Porongurup Road, Porongurup, WA 6324 **Region** Porongurup
T (08) 9853 1035 **F** (08) 9853 1010 **www**.castlerockestate.com.au **Open** Mon–Fri 10–4, w'ends & public hols 10–5
Winemaker Robert Diletti **Est.** 1983 **Cases** 3000
An exceptionally beautifully sited vineyard, winery and cellar door on a 55-ha property with sweeping vistas from the Porongurups, operated by the Diletti family. The standard of viticulture is very high, and the site itself ideally situated (quite apart from its beauty). The two-level winery, set on the natural slope, maximises gravity flow, in particular for crushed must feeding into the press. The Rieslings have always been elegant and have handsomely repaid time in bottle; the Pinot Noir is the most consistent performer in the region. Exports to Japan and Singapore.

ΨΨΨΨ Riesling 2008 Good balance, line and length in particular; lovely flavour and mouthfeel. Certain to develop superbly. Gold WA Wine Show '08. Screwcap. 12.5% alc. **Rating** 94 **To** 2018 $18
Riesling 2002 Great colour; soft lime juice; delicious. Gold WA Wine Show '08. Screwcap. 12.5% alc. **Rating** 94 **To** 2012 $28

ΨΨΨΨΩ Sauvignon Blanc 2008 Pronounced varietal aromas, with just a trace of sweatiness; crisp and bright palate, with some savoury/grassy notes; good length. Screwcap. 13% alc. **Rating** 90 **To** 2011 $19

Catherine Vale Vineyard ★★★

656 Milbrodale Road, Bulga, NSW 2330 **Region** Lower Hunter Valley
T (02) 6579 1334 **F** (02) 6579 1299 **www**.catherinevale.com.au **Open** W'ends & public hols 10–5, or by appt
Winemaker Hunter Wine Services (John Hordern) **Est.** 1994 **Cases** 1500 **Vyds** 4.45 ha
Former schoolteachers Bill and Wendy Lawson have established Catherine Vale as a not-so-idle retirement venture. The lion's share of the vineyard planting is of semillon and chardonnay, with smaller amounts of verdelho, arneis, dolcetto and barbera; part is sold to contract winemaker John Hordern. Exports to Japan.

ΨΨΨΨ Semillon 2007 Plenty of weight and structure, with some riper lemon flavours appearing; patience not required. Screwcap. 11.5% alc. **Rating** 88 **To** 2013 $14

Caught Redhanded ★★★☆

1 Esplanade, Sellicks Beach, SA 5174 **Region** Adelaide Zone
T 0419 252 967 **Open** Not
Winemaker Phil Rogers, Linda Domas (Consultant) **Est.** 2009 **Cases** 500
Phil Rogers, a casualty of the 2001 Ansett Airlines collapse, enrolled at the start of '02 in the Charles Sturt University Bachelor of Wine Science program, completing his first vintage in '03 at Rosemount in McLaren Vale. His practical training involved 12 months as the trainee winemaker under the direction of Adrian Drumm at the Charles Sturt winery, followed by vintage at Hardys Chateau Reynella, later in the same year making Brunello de Montalcino and Chianti Classico in Tuscany, then back to Wirra Wirra for the '06 and '07 vintages, and McLaren Vintners in '08. Unable to gain full-time employment with a suitable winery, Phil made his first two barrels of McLaren Vale Shiraz in '06 for friends, before moving into commercial production in '07 with more McLaren Vale Shiraz and the introduction of Adelaide Hills Shiraz. Aromatic whites followed in '08, and in '09 the portfolio was expanded to include very small quantities of Adelaide Hills Pinot Noir, Pinot Gris and Merlot; Langhorne Creek Cabernet Sauvignon and continuing Shiraz. This hectic pace was easy meat for someone who had spent the last four years of his career with Ansett in the high stress world of airline operations, dealing with bad weather, broken aircrafts, sick flight attendants and unpaid pilots.

ΨΨΨΨΩ Adelaide Hills Sauvignon Blanc 2008 Crisp, clean, zesty varietal aromas flow through with confidence onto the palate where some tropical notes join to add to the impact. Screwcap. 12.5% alc. **Rating** 92 **To** 2011 $25

ΨΨΨΨ Fleurieu Adelaide Hills Pinot Gris Sauvignon Blanc 2008 Here the sole function of the sauvignon blanc is to add flavour to the pinot gris and lengthen its palate – which it does. Screwcap. 13.5% alc. **Rating** 87 **To** 2010 $25
Adelaide Hills Sauvignon Blanc Chardonnay 2008 Presumably unoaked; the two varieties do work well together up to a certain point, the chardonnay altering the dynamics considerably. Screwcap. 14% alc. **Rating** 87 **To** 2011 $20

Celestial Bay ★★★★★

33 Welwyn Avenue, Manning, WA 6152 (postal) **Region** Margaret River
T (08) 9450 4191 **F** (08) 9313 1544 **www**.celestialbay.com.au **Open** Not
Winemaker Bernard Abbott **Est.** 1999 **Cases** 8000

Michael and Kim O'Brien had a background of farming in the Chittering Valley when they purchased their 104-ha property. It is very much a family enterprise, with son Aaron studying viticulture and oenology at Curtin University, and daughter Daneka involved in marketing and sales. Under the direction of vineyard manager Sam Juniper, 52 ha of vines have been rapidly planted. The plantings are totally logical: semillon, sauvignon blanc, chardonnay, shiraz, cabernet sauvignon, merlot, malbec and petit verdot. Winemaker Bernard Abbott celebrated his 24th Margaret River vintage in 2009. Exports to the UK, the US, Malaysia, Taiwan, China, Singapore and Hong Kong.

ŸŸŸŸŸ **Margaret River Cabernet Shiraz 2007** Dense purple-crimson; voluminous aromas of cassis, blackcurrant and blackberry; a totally delicious medium- to full-bodied palate tracks the bouquet, the oak and tannins in precisely calibrated support. Screwcap. 14.6% alc. **Rating** 95 **To** 2030 $30

Margaret River Cabernet Sauvignon 2007 Crimson-purple; excellent varietal character on bouquet and palate alike, the fruit picked at perfect ripeness; has abundant blackcurrant and cassis fruit, with a touch of black olive on the finish; the tannins are ripe, the oak well integrated. Screwcap. 14% alc. **Rating** 94 **To** 2022 $25

ŸŸŸŸ **Margaret River Semillon Sauvignon Blanc 2008** Has good depth to the fruit, the 45% sauvignon blanc making the major flavour contribution; does shorten somewhat. Screwcap. 13% alc. **Rating** 88 **To** 2010 $18

Margaret River Chardonnay 2008 A complex wine, with strong barrel ferment and oak maturation inputs on the bouquet and palate; stone fruit and melon lurk under the oak; will appeal to some. Screwcap. 14% alc. **Rating** 88 **To** 2015 $20

Goose Chase White Diamond 2008 Chardonnay/Semillon/Sauvignon Blanc come together well, with good synergy providing an easy-access style. Screwcap. 13.4% alc. **Rating** 87 **To** 2010 $15

Margaret River Shiraz 2007 Strong, healthy colour; a full-bodied wine, with far more weight than usual for Margaret River, the alcohol catching up early on the palate; best left to the Barossa Valley. Screwcap. 15.5% alc. **Rating** 87 **To** 2014 $25

Cellarmasters   ★★★★★

Cnr Barossa Valley Way/Siegersdorf Road, Tanunda, SA 5352 **Region** Barossa Valley
T (08) 8561 2200 **F** (08) 8561 2262 **www**.cellarmasters.com.au **Open** Not
Winemaker Mark Robertson (Chief), Nick Badrice, John Schwartzkopff, Neil Doddridge, Hamish Seabrook **Est.** 1982 **Cases** 730 000
Dorrien Estate is the physical base of the vast Cellarmasters network that, wearing its retailer's hat, is by far the largest direct-sale outlet in Australia. It buys substantial quantities of wine from other makers either in bulk or as cleanskin (unlabelled bottles), or with recognisable but subtly different labels of the producers concerned. It also makes wine on its own account at Dorrien Estate, many of which are quite excellent and of trophy quality. (Chateau Dorrien is an entirely unrelated business.) Purchased by private equity firm Archer Capital in 2007. Exports to the UK and NZ.

ŸŸŸŸŸ **Black Wattle Black Label Chardonnay 2006** Distinguished chardonnay with the depth of fruit most frequently encountered in Margaret River all the more remarkable at this moderate alcohol; white peach and nectarine are cradled in fine oak. Screwcap. 13% alc. **Rating** 95 **To** 2016 $53.99

Dorrien Estate Bin 1a Chardonnay 2006 Bright green-straw; made from Eden Valley/Robe grapes picked at perfect ripeness, welded by fruit flavours of nectarine and white peach rather than oak. Screwcap. 13% alc. **Rating** 94 **To** 2015 $35.99

Dorrien Estate Bin 1 Barossa Valley Shiraz 2006 A powerful, medium- to full-bodied wine, with abundant black fruits, tannins and oak all well integrated and balanced; branded bottle. Screwcap. 15% alc. **Rating** 94 **To** 2026 $41.99

ŶŶŶŶŶ Black Wattle Mount Benson Shiraz 2007 Inky purple; a full-bodied wine, with layers of blackberry and stewed plum flavours offset by oak and savoury tannins on the long finish. Screwcap. 14.5% alc. **Rating** 93 **To** 2022 $40.99
Dorrien Estate The Growers Barossa Valley Shiraz 2006 Leading vineyards and skilled winemaking result in a juicy, medium-bodied palate, with a full range of shiraz flavours not intimidated by the alcohol levels. Screwcap. 15% alc. **Rating** 93 **To** 2021 $24.99
Avon Brae New Eden Vineyards Shiraz 2006 Strong licorice and spice aromas, then a juicy palate with well-integrated, but very evident, oak; seductive style; expensive custom-made branded bottle. Screwcap. 14.5% alc. **Rating** 93 **To** 2021 $23.99
Dorrien Estate Bin 1 Barossa Valley Cabernet Sauvignon 2006 Dense, dark colour; potent, inky/earthy black fruits course through the bouquet and palate alike. A vin de garde begging for long cellaring. Screwcap. 14% alc. **Rating** 93 **To** 2026 $41.99
Black Wattle Mount Benson Chardonnay 2007 Well made; subtle barrel ferment inputs into a medium-bodied, stone fruit-flavoured palate; citrussy acidity to close. Screwcap. 14% alc. **Rating** 90 **To** 2013 $27.99

Centennial Vineyards ★★★★☆

'Woodside', Centennial Road, Bowral, NSW 2576 **Region** Southern Highlands
T (02) 4861 8700 **F** (02) 4681 8777 **www**.centennial.net.au **Open** 7 days 10–5
Winemaker Tony Cosgriff **Est.** 2002 **Cases** 10 000 **Vyds** 29 ha
Centennial Vineyards, a substantial development jointly owned by wine professional John Large and investor Mark Dowling, covers 133 ha of beautiful grazing land, with 29 ha planted to pinot noir, chardonnay, sauvignon blanc, tempranillo, pinot gris, albarino, riesling and pinot meunier. Production from the estate vineyards is supplemented by purchases of grapes from other regions, including Orange. The consistency of the quality of the wines is wholly commendable, reflecting the skilled touch of Tony Cosgriff in a region that often throws up climatic challenges. Exports to the US, Denmark, Singapore, China and Korea.

ŶŶŶŶŶ Woodside Single Vineyard Shiraz 2007 The single vineyard in question is in Orange, and the wine is of high quality, marrying spicy red fruit cool-climate characteristics with considerable, but balanced, tannins, which provide both texture and structure. Screwcap. 14.6% alc. **Rating** 94 **To** 2022 $23

ŶŶŶŶŶ Reserve Orange Chardonnay 2007 A complex bouquet attesting to barrel ferment and the powerful, very intense fruit of the palate ranging through ripe stone fruit, fig and cashew flavours. Screwcap. 14.2% alc. **Rating** 93 **To** 2017 $30
Reserve Single Vineyard Riesling 2008 Lemon, apple and orange zest on the bouquet; generous on entry, with ample exotic fruit on offer; a little sweetness draws out the even and fine finish. Screwcap. 10.4% alc. **Rating** 90 **To** 2015 $24.99
Reserve Limited Release Sauvignon Blanc 2008 A strongly pungent bouquet, with a smoky overtone to the fruit; clean gooseberry character on the palate, with a zesty, fine finish. Screwcap. 13.4% alc. **Rating** 90 **To** 2012 $24.99
Reserve Sangiovese 2007 Fresh and vibrant, cherry/sour cherry fruit with spicy nuances and a touch of citrus; convincing varietal expression. Screwcap. 14.5% alc. **Rating** 90 **To** 2012 $30
Pinot Noir Chardonnay NV Fine mousse; extremely crisp, low dosage, aperitif style, with citrus fruits dominant, extended lees contact showing in the fine mousse rather than flavour; time on cork will help. 11.5% alc. **Rating** 90 **To** 2012 $28
Finale Late Harvest Semillon 2006 Golden yellow; well made and balanced with cumquat and crystallised citrus fruit; cleansing finish. Riverina. Screwcap. 12% alc. **Rating** 90 **To** 2011 $23

ŶŶŶŶ Woodside Single Vineyard Verdelho 2008 Fresh cut grass and nectarine bouquet; lively and generous, with vibrant acidity on the finish. Screwcap. 13.6% alc. **Rating** 89 **To** 2011 $19.99

Woodside Single Vineyard Riesling 2008 A lean and chalky wine, with lemon and some mineral character coming to the fore; crisp and clean on the finish. Screwcap. 11% alc. **Rating** 88 **To** 2014 $19.99

Woodside Single Vineyard Sauvignon Blanc 2008 Green nettle bouquet; clean and fresh, and a little drier and more austere than the Reserve. Screwcap. 12.2% alc. **Rating** 88 **To** 2011 $21.99

Reserve Single Vineyard Barbera 2007 A nicely made, light- to medium-bodied wine; clean red cherry and spice fruit, but not a lot of structure – the fault of the variety, not the winemaker. Screwcap. 13.5% alc. **Rating** 88 **To** 2012 $28

Bong Bong Sauvignon Blanc Chardonnay 2008 The sauvignon dominates, with pungent fruit coming to the fore; generous on the palate from the chardonnay. Screwcap. 12.4% alc. **Rating** 87 **To** 2011 $17.99

Ceravolo Wines

Suite 16, 172 Glynburn Road, Tranmere, SA 5073 (postal) **Region** Adelaide Plains
T (08) 8336 4522 **F** (08) 8365 0538 **www**.ceravolo.com.au **Open** Not
Winemaker Colin Glaetzer, Ben Glaetzer (Contract) **Est.** 1985 **Cases** 20 000

Dentist turned vigneron and winemaker, Joe Ceravolo, and his wife, Heather, have been producing single-vineyard wines from their estate on the Adelaide Plains since 1999. Significant wine show success has added to the reputation of their brand, particularly with Shiraz, Petit Verdot, Merlot and Sangiovese. Their son Antony is now working with them to take their family business into the next generation. The Ceravolos are also establishing new vineyards around their home in the Adelaide Hills, focusing on cooler climate Italian varieties such as picolit and primitivo. Wines are released under Ceravolo, St Andrews Estate and export-only Red Earth labels. Exports to the UK, the US and other major markets.

ΨΨΨΨ **Adelaide Plains Sangiovese 2007** Bright, light crimson; quite why this environment should produce good sangiovese I don't know, but the wine has both typical sour cherry fruit and the expected tannins (the latter in balance). Screwcap. 13% alc. **Rating** 89 **To** 2013 $17.95

Adelaide Plains Cabernet Sauvignon 2007 A testament to the resilience and toughness of cabernet sauvignon; firm but attractive cassis blackcurrant fruit and appropriate tannins on the finish. Cork. 14% alc. **Rating** 88 **To** 2013 $20

Adelaide Plains Sangiovese Rose 2008 Pale blush; slightly savoury with some cherry fruit evident; a hint of sweetness, with red fruits on the palate, and a slightly drying finish. Screwcap. 12.5% alc. **Rating** 87 **To** 2012 $17.99

Adelaide Plains Shiraz 2006 Pleasant medium-bodied wine, albeit with a strong American/vanillin oak influence throughout that coats the fruit; soft tannins help. Cork. 14.5% alc. **Rating** 87 **To** 2011 $22

Chain of Ponds

Adelaide Road, Gumeracha, SA 5233 **Region** Adelaide Hills
T (08) 8389 1415 **F** (08) 8389 1877 **www**.chainofponds.com.au **Open** Mon–Fri
9.30–4.30, w'ends & public hols 10.30–4.30
Winemaker Greg Clack **Est.** 1993 **Cases** 30 000

The Chain of Ponds brand has been separated from the now sold 200 ha of vineyards which were among the largest in the Adelaide Hills. It now has contract growers throughout the Adelaide Hills for the Chain of Ponds label, two single vineyard reds from Kangaroo Island, and the Norello blends with a SA appellation. Exports to the UK, the US, Canada, Singapore, Vietnam, China and NZ.

ΨΨΨΨΨ **The Cachet Adelaide Cabernet Sauvignon Shiraz Merlot 2003** Full of succulent fruit, all the components coming together seamlessly; blackcurrant, blackberry, spice and licorice are interwoven with subtle French oak; great mouthfeel, and a triumph for the vintage. Cork. 14% alc. **Rating** 96 **To** 2018 $60

The Cachet Adelaide Cabernet Sauvignon Shiraz Merlot 2002 Excellent colour retention; the cooler vintage shows in the touches of herb and spice on the bouquet, in the savoury nuances and in the length of the wine; an exercise in synergistic blending. Adelaide Hills/Barossa Valley/McLaren Vale. Cork. 14% alc. **Rating** 95 **To** 2017 $60

The Amadeus Adelaide Hills Cabernet Sauvignon 2005 Good colour; luscious black fruit on both bouquet and palate, along with quality French oak and supple tannins; there is a special quality to the flavour not easy to pin down. Cork. 14% alc. **Rating** 94 **To** 2018 $33

♟♟♟♟♟ The Ledge Adelaide Hills Shiraz 2005 Good hue/clarity; warm spice overtones to the bouquet, allied with oak; the very long and well-balanced palate offers more of the same; lingering finish. Cork. 14% alc. **Rating** 93 **To** 2020 $33

Black Thursday Adelaide Hills Sauvignon Blanc 2008 A relatively subdued, although not reduced or sweaty, bouquet; a mix of tropical, gooseberry and asparagus fruit on the palate, which has good length. Screwcap. 12.5% alc. **Rating** 90 **To** 2012 $19

♟♟♟♟ Adelaide Hills Pinot Grigio 2007 Opens quietly with some mineral and spice, but swells on the back-palate and finish to provide satisfying flavour and mouthfeel. Screwcap. 13% alc. **Rating** 89 **To** 2010 $22

Novello Rosso Sangiovese Grenache 2008 Very pale, but bright colour; cleverly made juxtaposition of a little sweetness and fresh acidity, helped by low alcohol. Screwcap. 11.5% alc. **Rating** 88 **To** 2011 $15

Section 400 Adelaide Hills Pinot Noir 2008 Very good colour; an extremely foresty/briary/earthy, low pH pinot, the antithesis of dry red character; you have to question if and when any sweet pinot fruit will emerge. Screwcap. 13.5% alc. **Rating** 87 **To** 2013 $20

Novello Nero Sangiovese Barbera Grenache 2005 The savoury/sour cherry sangiovese component is the driver in this light-bodied, easy-access wine. Screwcap. 14% alc. **Rating** 87 **To** 2011 $15

Chalice Bridge Estate ★★★★☆

796 Rosa Glen Road, Margaret River, WA 6285 **Region** Margaret River
T (08) 9433 5200 **F** (08) 9433 5211 **www**.chalicebridge.com.au **Open** By appt
Winemaker Bob Cartwright (Consultant) **Est.** 1998 **Cases** 40 000
Planting of the vineyard began in 1998; there are now over 28 ha each of cabernet sauvignon and shiraz, 27 ha of chardonnay, 12.5 ha of semillon, 18 ha of sauvignon blanc and 7 ha of merlot; it is the second-largest single vineyard in Margaret River. The 2006 appointment of former Leeuwin Estate senior winemaker Bob Cartwright was major news, adding thrust to a growing business. Sensible pricing also helps. Listed for sale in April 2009 by specialist wine industry brokers and advisers Gaetjens Langley. Exports to the UK, the US and other major markets.

♟♟♟♟♟ Margaret River Chardonnay 2007 Combines restrained oak and fruit selection with remarkable intensity and length of the melon, grapefruit and stone fruit palate; excellent balance and length. Screwcap. 13.5% alc. **Rating** 94 **To** 2019 $26

♟♟♟♟♟ Margaret River Semillon Sauvignon Blanc 2008 Penetrating cut grass aromas lead into an incisive palate, with lemon and grapefruit flavours; the freshness is heightened by the low alcohol. Screwcap. 11.5% alc. **Rating** 92 **To** 2011 $19.95

♟♟♟♟ Margaret River Sauvignon Blanc 2008 Extremely pale colour; very delicate, although clean and fresh; light nuances of gooseberry and passionfruit; pleasant finish. Screwcap. 12% alc. **Rating** 89 **To** 2010 $19.95

Margaret River Shiraz 2006 Fine, bright and truly medium-bodied; hints of dried herbs and ironstone come through on the palate, and the high acid finish frames the red fruits well. Screwcap. 13.5% alc. **Rating** 89 **To** 2015 $25.95

Chalk Hill ★★★★

PO Box 205, McLaren Vale, SA 5171 **Region** McLaren Vale
T (08) 8556 2121 **F** (08) 8556 2221 **www**.chalkhill.com.au **Open** Not
Winemaker Emmanuelle Bekkers **Est.** 1973 **Cases** 35 000 **Vyds** 74.3 ha
The growth of Chalk Hill has accelerated after passing from parents John and Diana Harvey to grapegrowing sons Jock and Tom. Both are heavily involved in wine industry affairs in varying capacities (Tom was a participant in the second intake of the Wine Industry Future Leaders Program) and the business has strong links with Greening Australia. (Chalk Hill donates 25c for each bottle sold, the highest per-bottle donation in the Australian wine industry.) Further acquisitions mean the vineyards now span each subregion of McLaren Vale, and have been planted to both the exotic (albarino, barbera and sangiovese) and the mainstream (shiraz, cabernet sauvignon, grenache, chardonnay and cabernet franc). Exports to all major markets; exports to the US and Canada under the Wits End label.

♥♥♥♥♥ **The Procrastinator 2008** Good colour; bright fruit with a pleasant seasoning of spice and floral aromatics; the palate is fleshy and concentrated, with good texture and focused acidity cleaning up the finish. Cabernet Franc/Cabernet Sauvignon. Value. Screwcap. 14.5% alc. **Rating** 90 **To** 2014 $18
McLaren Vale Shiraz 2006 Roast meat and black fruits, with a touch of bitter chocolate; evidence of a little sulphidey complexity; the palate is thick and unctuous with upfront sweet fruit followed by a dark, tarry finish. Screwcap. 15% alc. **Rating** 90 **To** 2016 $20

♥♥♥♥ **Oxytocin McLaren Vale Grenache Rose 2008** Raspberry jube bouquet with a little spice; sweet on entry, there is a little grip that provides a dry and focused finish. Screwcap. 12.5% alc. **Rating** 87 **To** 2011 $20

Chalkers Crossing ★★★★★

285 Grenfell Road, Young, NSW 2594 **Region** Hilltops
T (02) 6382 6900 **F** (02) 6382 5068 **www**.chalkerscrossing.com.au **Open** Mon–Fri 9–5
Winemaker Celine Rousseau **Est.** 2000 **Cases** 7000 **Vyds** 10 ha
Owned and operated by Ted and Wendy Ambler, Chalkers Crossing's Rockleigh Vineyard was planted in 1997–98. It also purchases grapes from Tumbarumba and Gundagai. Winemaker Celine Rousseau was born in France's Loire Valley, trained in Bordeaux and has worked in Bordeaux, Champagne, Languedoc, Margaret River and the Perth Hills. This Flying Winemaker (now an Australian citizen) has exceptional skills and dedication. Exports to the UK, Ireland, Germany, Denmark, China, Hong Kong and Japan.

♥♥♥♥♥ **Hilltops Riesling 2008** A scented floral/blossom bouquet, then a deliciously rich palate made for early enjoyment. Trophy NSW Wine Award '08, and the price is, as ever, great value. Screwcap. 12.5% alc. **Rating** 94 **To** 2013 $18
Tumbarumba Sauvignon Blanc 2008 Bright colour; fresh lemon and tropical fruit bouquet with good focus; lively and fresh palate, with cleansing acidity and a long finish. Screwcap. 13% alc. **Rating** 94 **To** 2012 $18

♥♥♥♥♥ **Hilltops Semillon 2008** Focused lemon fruit with a little straw in support; the palate is finely textured, with a dry and taut, slightly chalky, aspect to the finish; very youthful with good ageing potential. Screwcap. 13% alc. **Rating** 93 **To** 2016 $18

Chalmers Wines ★★★☆

PO Box 2263, Mildura, Vic 3502 **Region** Murray Darling/Heathcote
T 0400 261 932 **F** (03) 5026 3228 **www**.chalmerswine.com.au **Open** Not
Winemaker Sandro Mosele (Contract) **Est.** 1989 **Cases** 4000 **Vyds** 10 ha
In March 2008, founders Bruce and Jenny Chalmers sold (to Macquarie Diversified Agriculture Fund) what was the largest vine nursery propagation business in Australia, plus 650 ha of planted vines, an additional 600 ha available for planting, plus 1500 ha of protected

forest along a 14-km Murray River frontage. The Chalmers have, however, kept the brands and the winemaking side of the business, with a medium-term grape-supply contract from Macquarie. The future home of Chalmers Wines is an 80-ha property on the Mt Camel Range, 50 km north of Heathcote. The east-facing, sloped block, running to the top of the ridge, is being planted to vermentino, fiano, aglianico, sagrantino, lagrein, nero d'Avola, sangiovese and shiraz. Exports to the UK and Denmark.

♥♥♥♥♀ **Chalmers Vermentino 2008** A fragrant and flowery bouquet leads into a fresh palate with apple and stone fruit flavours, then lemony acidity to close. Screwcap. 13% alc. **Rating** 90 **To** 2010 $22

♥♥♥♥ **Project Wine Fiano Greco di Tufo 2005** Still bright green-straw; impossible to know which variety contributes which flavours to the marriage of ripe citrus and pineapple; ready now. Diam. 13% alc. **Rating** 88 **To** 2010 $27
Chalmers Sagrantino 2005 The Italian tannins storm the palate from the first instance, taking no prisoners, leaving the bright red fruit in chains from which it may or may not break free. Diam. 14.5% alc. **Rating** 87 **To** 2014 $28

Chambers Rosewood ★★★★★

Barkly Street, Rutherglen, Vic 3685 **Region** Rutherglen
T (02) 6032 8641 **www**.chambersrosewood.com.au **Open** Mon–Sat 9–5, Sun 10–5
Winemaker Stephen Chambers **Est.** 1858 **Cases** 10 000 **Vyds** 50 ha
On the basis of these tasting notes, joyfully written after the Chambers family relented and sent samples of its greatest fortified wines, one is left with no option but to say Chambers Rare Muscat and Rare Muscadelle (or Topaque or Tokay, what's in a name?) are the greatest of all in the Rutherglen firmament. Exports to all major markets.

♥♥♥♥♥ **Rare Rutherglen Muscat NV** Beautifully fragrant, with a sense of true age, depth and power; floral on entry, the acidity is extraordinary and gives the wine amazing life and nerve; the layers of flavour are almost countless, and this wine is truly something that every wine lover must experience at least once in their lives; one sip was taken for this entire note and the flavour is still building. Thanks to the Chambers for sending these in this year. Cork. 18% alc. **Rating** 98 **To** 2010 $250
Rare Rutherglen Muscadelle NV Pure power and grace, showing surprising restraint and poise; heavily toasted nuts, and the essence of old, yet fresh material; prunes, fresh oak and very clean fortifying spirit provide the springboard for an experience that stays for minutes. Suggested to be enjoyed with food, but maybe best contemplated on its own. Cork. 18% alc. **Rating** 97 **To** 2010 $250
Special Rutherglen Tokay NV Attractive olive-green hue; explosive burnt toffee, ground grilled nuts, a touch of cold tea and plenty of bitter chocolate; the palate is layered, long, luscious and completely delicious, and the dark chocolate character holds on for the longest time; staggering complexity. Cork. 18% alc. **Rating** 96 **To** 2010 $100
Grand Rutherglen Muscat NV A very appealing balance between freshness and age, with touches of oak, bitter almonds, toffee and some lifted floral, musky notes; the palate is poised, weighty and shows a very pleasant burnt caramel character on the finish; delicious. Screwcap. 18% alc. **Rating** 95 **To** 2010 $50

♥♥♥♥♀ **Rutherglen Muscat NV** A flamboyant, highly perfumed liqueur apricot and toasted nut bouquet; very rich and sweet, but in great balance and harmony; long and the spirit cleans up the finish well. Screwcap. 18.5% alc. **Rating** 91 **To** 2010 $16

♥♥♥♥ **Rutherglen Muscadelle NV** Lightly sweet and honeyed with orange pith and very clean fortifying spirit; zesty for the style, offering an insight into young wines made in this manner. Screwcap. 18.5% alc. **Rating** 89 **To** 2012 $16
Anton Ruche Rutherglen Shiraz + Mondeuse 2005 Bright colour; a very concentrated wine that speaks loudly of its warm origins; blackberry, tar and a generous amount of sweet fruit at the core; handles the 16.1% alcohol well. Screwcap. **Rating** 88 **To** 2011 $16

Rutherglen Roussanne 2007 Deep colour; toast, honey and a touch of spice; assertive acid cleans up the warm fruit well. Screwcap. 11.5% alc. **Rating** 87 **To** 2013 $15

Chapel Hill ★★★★★

Chapel Hill Road, McLaren Vale, SA 5171 **Region** McLaren Vale
T (08) 8323 8429 **F** (08) 8323 9245 **www.**chapelhillwine.com.au **Open** 7 days 12–5
Winemaker Michael Fragos, Bryn Richards **Est.** 1979 **Cases** 60 000 **Vyds** 44 ha
A leading medium-sized winery in the region. In 2000 Chapel Hill was sold to the Swiss Thomas Schmidheiny group, which owns the respected Cuvaison winery in California as well as vineyards in Switzerland and Argentina. Wine quality is as good, if not better, than ever. Winemaker Michael Fragos was named Winemaker of the Year at London's International Wine & Spirit Competition 2008. The production comes from the estate plantings of shiraz, cabernet sauvignon, chardonnay, verdelho, albarino, sangiovese and merlot, together with purchased grapes. Exports to the UK, the US and other major markets.

ŸŸŸŸŸ **The Vicar McLaren Vale Shiraz 2006** Strong colour; a powerful and exact evocation of McLaren Vale terroir, with blackberry, licorice and dark chocolate flavours supported by perfectly weighted tannins and oak. Screwcap. 14.5% alc. **Rating** 96 **To** 2026 $60
The Vicar McLaren Vale Shiraz 2007 Has not dissimilar texture and weight to the standard shiraz but much greater intensity to the cascade of black fruits, which are beautifully tempered by savoury tannins to provide flavour and structural balance. Screwcap. 14.5% alc. **Rating** 95 **To** 2022 $60

ŸŸŸŸŸ **Bush Vine McLaren Vale Grenache 2007** Typical McLaren Vale grenache; deep in flavour and mouthfeel, and very aromatic without the least confection character; resonating black fruits through to the finish. Screwcap. 15% alc. **Rating** 92 **To** 2014 $30
McLaren Vale Shiraz 2007 Good colour; medium- to full-bodied wine with a mix of black and red berry fruits, chocolate and spice set in a framework of dusty/ mocha tannins. Screwcap. 14.5% alc. **Rating** 91 **To** 2017 $30
McLaren Vale Cabernet Sauvignon 2007 Dense crimson-purple; an equally dense, chewy, full-bodied palate with blackberry, dark chocolate and mocha all intermingling; the tannins, while substantial, are ripe. Screwcap. 14% alc. **Rating** 91 **To** 2016 $30
Il Vescovo McLaren Vale Albarino 2008 A good example of the variety; zesty citrus aromas, complemented by a palate that has weight, yet exhibits freshness and lively fruit on the finish. Screwcap. 13% alc. **Rating** 90 **To** 2012 $22
McLaren Vale Cabernet Sauvignon 2006 Blackcurrant and dark chocolate aromas are joined by slightly more savoury/earthy notes on the palate, with some sweet oak inputs on the finish. Screwcap. 14.5% alc. **Rating** 90 **To** 2014 $30

ŸŸŸŸ **Il Vescovo McLaren Vale Sangiovese Rose 2008** Dry and savoury, with a dried herb character framing the red fruits; good acidity, and an attractive bitterness on the finish works well. Screwcap. 13% alc. **Rating** 89 **To** 2012 $16
Fleurieu Verdelho 2008 Bright and zesty, with early-picked flavours suggesting lower alcohol than is the case; almost grainy texture and acidity. Very unusual cool-grown style. Screwcap. 13.5% alc. **Rating** 88 **To** 2012 $15
Il Vescovo Adelaide Hills Tempranillo 2007 A meaty bouquet of black fruits and a hint of fresh herbs; medium-bodied, fresh, vibrant and with quite refreshing acidity on the finish. Screwcap. 14% alc. **Rating** 88 **To** 2012 $22

Chaperon Wines

39 Main Street, Maldon, Vic 3463 **Region** Bendigo
T (03) 5475 1150 **www.**chaperon.com.au **Open** 7 days 10.30–5
Winemaker Russell Clarke **Est.** 1994 **Cases** 400 **Vyds** 4.5 ha

In 1856 English immigrant Edward Bond purchased land in the Maldon area, then an adjoining property in 1871. Here he established the 'Grange Hill' winery and vineyard, which flourished in the 1880s, leading to the establishment of a second winery and vineyard. It disappeared in the 20th century, but in 1994 Russell Clarke and Angelina Chaperon bought the property and began replanting the vineyard and restoring the old winery buildings. They have chosen to bypass irrigation and practise organic viticulture in growing 1.2 ha of bush vine grenache and mourvedre, and 1.8 ha of trellised shiraz, plus mourvedre and viognier. The cellar door, located in the township of Maldon, doubles as a specialist chocolate shop.

ȲȲȲȲ **Grenache Shiraz Mourvedre 2006** An aromatic bouquet and a palate that, while light-bodied, has good length and balance to the savoury fruit characters; the tannins fine. Drink asap. Screwcap. 14.5% alc. **Rating** 88 **To** 2011 $18
Grenache Mourvedre Rose 2008 Very pale pink; counter cultural, with pointed citrussy acidity on the long finish; some spicy notes mid-palate on the way through. Screwcap. 13% alc. **Rating** 87 **To** 2009 $16

Chapman Grove Wines   ★★★★★

PO Box 1460, Margaret River, WA 6285 **Region** Margaret River
T (08) 9757 7444 **F** (08) 9757 7477 **www.**chapmangrove.com.au **Open** Not
Winemaker Bruce Dukes (Contract) **Est.** 2005 **Cases** 5000 **Vyds** 32 ha
A very successful venture under the control of managing director Ron Fraser. The contract-made wines come from the extensive estate vineyards planted to chardonnay, semillon, sauvignon blanc, shiraz, cabernet sauvignon and merlot. The wines are released in three price ranges: at the bottom end, the Dreaming Dog red varietals and blends; in the middle, the standard Chapman Grove range; and, at the top, ultra-premium wines under the Atticus label. Exports to the UK, China and Singapore.

ȲȲȲȲȲ **Atticus Margaret River Chardonnay 2007** A complex wine with strong barrel ferment aromas on the bouquet; the fruit asserting itself on the long palate, with nectarine and white peach running alongside nutty/creamy notes, tied with bright acidity on the finish. Screwcap. 14% alc. **Rating** 95 **To** 2015 $55
Atticus Margaret River Cabernet Sauvignon 2007 High quality immediately obvious; great balance to the medium-bodied palate, with blackcurrant, mulberry and cassis seamlessly woven with French oak and supple tannins. Screwcap. 13% alc. **Rating** 95 **To** 2020 $55
Atticus Margaret River Shiraz 2007 Bright crimson; fragrant and vibrant spice and cherry aromas flow through onto the medium-bodied palate, with fine-grained tannins and French oak adding to complexity. Screwcap. 13.7% alc. **Rating** 94 **To** 2017 $55

ȲȲȲȲȳ **Margaret River Chardonnay 2006** Still youthful, early picking part of the story perhaps; tangy grapefruit and citrus rind characters, together with fresh acidity. Will develop slowly. Screwcap. 13.5% alc. **Rating** 92 **To** 2017 $25
Margaret River Chardonnay 2007 Bright straw-green; very good stone fruit drives both bouquet and palate with minimal oak impact into a strongly regional wine. Screwcap. 13.5% alc. **Rating** 91 **To** 2014 $25
Margaret River Semillon Sauvignon Blanc 2008 A mix of tropical and grassy fruit on both bouquet and palate, with good overall freshness. Screwcap. 12.5% alc. **Rating** 90 **To** 2011 $18.99

ȲȲȲȲ **Margaret River Rose 2008** Fresh, crisp, light red fruit aromas and flavours; dry finish. Screwcap. 13.3% alc. **Rating** 89 **To** 2010 $18.99

🍂 Charlatan Wines   ★★★★

Cnr Kangarilla Road/Foggo Road, McLaren Vale, SA 5171 **Region** McLaren Vale
T (08) 8386 3463 **Open** 7 days 10–4
Winemaker Chad Fenton-Smith **Est.** 2005 **Cases** 350

Chad Fenton-Smith has a particularly well developed sense of humour, something which may come in very handy in the industry's turbulent times of 2009 and beyond. His entry into winemaking just happened, the opportunity coming through contacts he had made in the water tank industry. His first vintage in 2005 was little more than a hobby: 360 bottles of Shiraz made from two rows of vines left over after a big producer had taken its required tonnes from the grapegrower concerned. Production soared to the heady heights of 700 bottles in 2006, and while it was maturing in oak Chad and his partner went to Samuel's Gorge, to spend an hour with winemaker Justin McNamee. After a few glasses of wine Chad decided to quit his job, head to Adelaide University to begin a Bachelor of Science in viticulture and oenology and endeavour to subsist on one-quarter of his previous income. His head is buzzing with ideas, which only the brave or the innocent would contemplate. And the name? Well, it was self-bestowed on someone selling wine made on a whim, and without any winemaking experience whatsoever.

ŸŸŸŸŸ **Tipsy Hill McLaren Vale Sangiovese 2008** Well, well. McLaren Vale shiraz is easy meat, sangiovese not; but this is a particularly good sangiovese with classic cherry and sour cherry fruit, tannins there as ever, but not green or harsh. Screwcap. 14.4% alc. **Rating** 93 **To** 2016 $18
McLaren Vale Shiraz 2006 Deep, bright colour; an extremely rich and ripe wine, full of confit black fruits and a regional spike of dark chocolate; impressive display of 'amateur' winemaking. ProCork. 15% alc. **Rating** 92 **To** 2020 $25

ŸŸŸŸ **McLaren Vale Shiraz 2005** This vintage was not in the class of the '04 (or '06); here the fruit has been picked a little too late, the oak a bit too obvious. Screwcap. 15.3% alc. **Rating** 89 **To** 2014

Charles Cimicky   ★★★★☆

Gomersal Road, Lyndoch, SA 5351 **Region** Barossa Valley
T (08) 8524 4025 **F** (08) 8524 4772 **Open** Tues–Sat 10.30–4.30
Winemaker Charles Cimicky **Est.** 1972 **Cases** 15 000
These wines are of very good quality, thanks to the sophisticated use of good oak in tandem with high-quality grapes. Historically, happy to keep an ultra-low profile and, though sporadically sending samples, is evidently not in the business of wasting wine on journalists. Exports to the UK, the US, Switzerland, Canada, Malaysia and Hong Kong.

ŸŸŸŸŸ **The Autograph Barossa Valley Shiraz 2006** Dense opaque crimson-purple; intense black fruits and licorice aromas and flavours, but the extract (and alcohol) has been tightly controlled. Cork. 14.5% alc. **Rating** 94 **To** 2016 $28

ŸŸŸŸŸ **Trumps Barossa Valley Shiraz 2007** Rich and ripe (but not overripe) plum and blackberry fruit, with a luscious lick of dark chocolate and a dash of oak, make this a must-drink (rather than sip) style. Screwcap. 14.5% alc. **Rating** 92 **To** 2020 $19

Charles Melton

Krondorf Road, Tanunda, SA 5352 **Region** Barossa Valley
T (08) 8563 3606 **F** (08) 8563 3422 **www**.charlesmeltonwines.com.au **Open** 7 days 11–5
Winemaker Charlie Melton, Nicola Robbins **Est.** 1984 **Cases** 15 000 **Vyds** 32.6 ha
Charlie Melton, one of the Barossa Valley's great characters, with wife Virginia by his side, makes some of the most eagerly sought à la mode wines in Australia. Inevitably, the Melton empire has continued to grow in response to the insatiable demand. There are now 7 ha at Lyndoch, 9 ha at Krondorf and 1.6 ha at Light Pass, the lion's share to shiraz and grenache, and a small planting of cabernet sauvignon. An additional 30-ha property has been purchased in High Eden, with 10 ha of shiraz planted in 2009, and a 5-ha field planting of grenache, shiraz, mataro, carignan, cinsaut, picpoul and bourboulenc to be planted in spring 2010. The expanded volume has had no adverse effect on the wonderfully rich, sweet and well-made wines. The original Krondorf village church (circa 1864) has been acquired and converted to guest accommodation. Exports to all major markets.

ŸŸŸŸŸ　Grains of Paradise Shiraz 2006 Deep colour; a delicious medium-bodied wine, effortless, achieving flavour, intensity and length; a supple and spicy finish completes the package. Screwcap. 14.5% alc. **Rating** 96 **To** 2025 $57.50

Nine Popes 2006 A synergistic blend (Shiraz/Grenache) with no confection characters whatsoever; has wonderful texture in the layers of black and red fruits, oak and tannins in a calibrated support role. Screwcap. 14.5% alc. **Rating** 96 **To** 2021 $57.50

Barossa Valley Rose of Virginia 2008 Brilliant pale crimson; typically delicious red fruit aromas and flavours; early picking and six-week cold fermentation has overridden vintage threat. Screwcap. 13% alc. **Rating** 94 **To** 2009 $23.50

Voices of Angels Shiraz 2006 An unusually fragrant wine, with some smoky barrel ferment aromas alongside red and black fruits; the medium-bodied palate shows French oak influence, and also some whole bunch fruit characters. Screwcap. 14.5% alc. **Rating** 94 **To** 2020 $57.50

Charles Sturt University Winery　★★★

McKeown Drive (off Coolamon Road), Wagga Wagga, NSW 2650 **Region** Big Rivers Zone **T** (02) 6933 2435 **www**.csu.edu.au/winery **Open** Mon–Fri 11–5, w'ends 11–4 **Winemaker** Andrew Drumm **Est.** 1977 **Cases** 15 000

A new $2.5 million commercial winery was opened in 2002, complementing the $1 million experimental winery opened in '01. The commercial winery was funded through the sale of wines produced under the CSU brand, which always offer exceptional value. Following the University's acquisition of the former University of Sydney campus in Orange, it now has 7.7 ha of estate plantings at Wagga Wagga and 17 ha of mature vineyards at Orange, the latter planted to chardonnay, sauvignon blanc, shiraz, cabernet sauvignon and merlot. Interestingly, this teaching facility is using screwcaps for all its wines, white and red, recalling its pioneering use in 1977. Moreover, since 2005 its sparkling wines have been released under crown seal.

ŸŸŸŸ　Chardonnay 2008 Has plenty of flavour and presence, with yellow peach fruit leading both bouquet and palate; easy-access style. Screwcap. 13% alc. **Rating** 88 **To** 2010 $14.30

Charlies Estate Wines　★★★

38 Swan Street, Henley Brook, WA 6055 **Region** Swan Valley **T** (08) 9296 3100 **www**.charliesestatewines.com.au **Open** 7 days 10–4.30 **Winemaker** Mark Sheppard **Est.** 1998 **Cases** 40 000 **Vyds** 29 ha

Charlies Estate is the new name and face for a long-established vineyard, gardens and winery site, originally Evans & Tate Gnangara and thereafter Swanbrook Estate. It is the venture of Carmelo Salpietro, and offers wines at five price levels: Charlies Origins as the entry point, the Today Range (from key WA regions), The Knotted Vine (limited release from select fruit parcels) and Charlies Origins Regional Selection Range (also limited release).

ŸŸŸŸ　Regional Selection Pemberton Sauvignon Blanc Semillon 2008 Very light, but attractive, varietal aromas and flavours, with citrussy overtones to the gentle tropical fruit. Screwcap. 11% alc. **Rating** 89 **To** 2010 $20

Charlies Origins Chardonnay 2006 Light straw-green; clean, crisp and fresh; light stone fruit and melon flavours with just an eyelash of French oak. Screwcap. 13% alc. **Rating** 89 **To** 2013 $18

Charlies Origins Semillon Sauvignon Blanc 2008 A complex wine, unexpectedly so given its relatively low alcohol; ripe tropical fruit, a touch of herb, grass and oak; the hint of sweetness on the finish is not needed. Screwcap. 11.7% alc. **Rating** 87 **To** 2010 $18

Charlies Origins Cabernet Merlot 2006 Bright colour; seems to have salvaged more from the wet vintage than many, with a twist of juicy fruit on the finish. Screwcap. 13.2% alc. **Rating** 87 **To** 2011 $18

Chartley Estate

38 Blackwood Hills Road, Rowella, Tas 7270 **Region** Northern Tasmania
T (03) 6394 7198 **F** (03) 6394 7598 **www.**chartleyestatevineyard.com.au **Open** Not
Winemaker Winemaking Tasmania (Julian Alcorso) **Est.** 2000 **Cases** 1250
The Kossman family began the establishment of 2 ha each of pinot gris, sauvignon blanc and
pinot noir, and 1 ha of riesling in 2000. Although the vines are still relatively young, some
attractive wines from each variety have been made. Exports to Taiwan.

ΨΨΨΨ   **Pinot Gris 2008** Bright pale blush pink; has plenty of musk and pear fruit, plus
good acidity. Cork. 13.1% alc. **Rating** 89 **To** 2010 $22.95

Chateau Dore

303 Mandurang Road, Mandurang, Vic 3551 **Region** Bendigo
T (03) 5439 5278 **Open** 7 days 10–5
Winemaker Ivan Grose **Est.** 1860 **Cases** 500 **Vyds** 3 ha
Has been in the ownership of the Grose family since 1860, with the winery buildings dating
back to 1860 and 1893. The vineyards comprise shiraz, chardonnay and cabernet sauvignon;
most of the shiraz grapes are sold. All wine is sold through the cellar door and function
centre.

ΨΨΨΨ   **Cabernet Sauvignon 2003** Holding colour well; by far the best of the Chateau
Dore releases, with savoury blackcurrant fruit on a light- to medium-bodied, well-
balanced palate. Screwcap. 13.5% alc. **Rating** 88 **To** 2014 $22

Chateau Dorrien

Cnr Seppeltsfield Road/Barossa Valley Way, Dorrien, SA 5352 **Region** Barossa Valley
T (08) 8562 2850 **F** (08) 8562 1416 **www.**chateaudorrien.com.au **Open** 7 days 10–5
Winemaker Fernando Martin, Ramon Martin **Est.** 1985 **Cases** 3500 **Vyds** 28 ha
The Martin family, headed by Fernando and Jeanette, purchased the old Dorrien winery from
the Seppelt family in 1984; in '90 the family purchased Twin Valley Estate and moved the
winemaking operations of Chateau Dorrien to the Twin Valley site. All the Chateau Dorrien
group wines are sold at Chateau Dorrien; Twin Valley is simply a production facility. In 2006
the Martin family purchased a 32-ha property at Myponga, with mature vineyards that now
provide the grapes for San Fernando Estate, as the new name of the vineyard.

ΨΨΨΨΨ   **Barossa Valley Shiraz 2006** Good colour; while the fruit is ripe and lush, it is
not porty or dead; there are layers of blackberry, plum, chocolate and mocha; oak
and tannins are in balance. Value. Diam. 14.7% alc. **Rating** 90 **To** 2016 $20

ΨΨΨΨ   **Cabernet Sauvignon 2005** A medium- to full-bodied wine with earthy/briary
overtones to the black fruits of the bouquet and palate alike. Will be durable, but
won't transform with age. Diam. 14% alc. **Rating** 88 **To** 2015 $20

Chateau Francois

Broke Road, Pokolbin, NSW 2321 **Region** Lower Hunter Valley
T (02) 4998 7548 **F** (02) 4998 7805 **Open** W'ends 9–5, or by appt
Winemaker Don Francois **Est.** 1969 **Cases** 200
I have known former NSW Director of Fisheries Dr Don Francois for almost as long as
I have been involved with wine, which is a very long time indeed. I remember his early
fermentations of sundry substances other than grapes (none of which, I hasten to add, were
the least bit illegal) in the copper bowl of an antiquated washing machine in his laundry. He
established Chateau Francois one year before Brokenwood, and our winemaking and fishing
paths have crossed many times since. Some years ago Don suffered a mild stroke, and no longer
speaks or writes with any fluency, but this has not stopped him from producing a range of
absolutely beautiful semillons that flourish marvellously with age. I should add that he is even
prouder of the distinguished career of his daughter, Rachel Francois, at the NSW bar. The
semillon vines are now 40 years old, producing exceptional wine year after year that is sold
for the proverbial song. Five-star value.

ŶŶŶŶŶ Pokolbin Mallee Semillon 2006 Delicious and classic semillon, as yet saying little on the bouquet, but with long, intense and precise fruit on the palate; great now or later style; great bargain. Screwcap. 11% alc. **Rating** 94 **To** 2020 $14

Chateau Leamon

5528 Calder Highway, Bendigo, Vic 3550 **Region** Bendigo
T (03) 5447 7995 www.chateauleamon.com.au **Open** Wed–Mon 11–5
Winemaker Ian Leamon **Est.** 1973 **Cases** 2000 **Vyds** 8 ha
One of the longest-established wineries in the region, with estate and locally grown shiraz and cabernet family grapes providing the excellent red wines. Ian Leamon is the second generation of the family to be involved, taking responsibility for winemaking in the 1980s. The estate-grown shiraz, cabernet merlot and semillon is supplemented by riesling from the Strathbogie Ranges. Exports to Canada and Singapore.

ŶŶŶŶŶ Reserve Bendigo Shiraz 2006 Good hue; considerably more fruit fragrance on the bouquet and power on the medium- to full-bodied palate; spice is present, but has a pure support role; fine and quality oak finish the wine. Screwcap. 13.5% alc. Rating 94 To 2020 $38

ŶŶŶŶŶ Bendigo Shiraz 2006 Spicy/peppery/cedary aromas flow through to the medium-bodied palate, with blackberry fruit joining the fray, supported by fine tannins giving a savoury finish. Screwcap. 14.3% alc. **Rating** 90 **To** 2016 $23

Chateau Mildura

191 Belar Avenue, Irymple, Vic 3498 **Region** Murray Darling
T (03) 5024 5901 **F** (03) 5024 5763 www.chateaumildura.com.au **Open** 7 days 10–4
Winemaker Neville Hudson **Est.** 1888 **Cases** 5000
The history of Chateau Mildura is inextricably bound up with that of winemaking along the Murray River in the northwest corner of Vic. The fathers of irrigation, the founders of Mildura and Renmark (across the border in SA), were the Chaffey Brothers, who built the triple-gable brick winery in 1892. The story of the Chaffeys is an epic one, marked by as many failures as successes. After table wine production ceased in 1910, the building was used for the production of brandy until the '50s. In 2002 it was sold by Beringer Blass to Lance Milne, a local fourth-generation horticulturist. He has incorporated a boutique winery in a small area of the building, the remainder of which will be opened as a museum dedicated to the Chaffeys and their pioneering work.

ŶŶŶŶ Psyche Smuggler Sauvignon Blanc 2006 Has hung on remarkably well; not overly varietal, but is fresh and has some light tropical fruit, the price especially attractive. Screwcap. 10.5% alc. **Rating** 87 **To** 2010 $12.50
Psyche Smuggler Chardonnay 2006 An impressive wine given its price and origin; ripe nectarine and melon fruits are the drivers; the mouthfeel is good, as is the length. Screwcap. 13% alc. **Rating** 87 **To** 2010 $12.50
Psyche Reserve Shiraz 2006 Light bodied, clean, fresh and well made in an overall somewhat austere style. Screwcap. 14% alc. **Rating** 87 **To** 2012 $19.95

Chateau Pâto

67 Thompsons Road, Pokolbin, NSW 2321 **Region** Lower Hunter Valley
T (02) 4998 7634 **F** (02) 4998 7860 **Open** By appt
Winemaker Nicholas Paterson **Est.** 1980 **Cases** 600 **Vyds** 5 ha
Nicholas Paterson took over responsibility for this tiny winery following the death of father David during the 1993 vintage. The winery has 2.5 ha of shiraz (the first plantings), with 0.5 ha each of chardonnay, marsanne, roussanne and viognier and mourvedre; most of the grapes are sold, with a tiny quantity of shiraz being made into a marvellous wine. David's legacy is being handsomely guarded.

ŶŶŶŶŶ **Hunter Wine Country DJP Shiraz 2007** Vibrant colour; a concentrated redcurrant, leather and spice bouquet with a generous amount of oak; medium-bodied with bright red fruit coming to the fore, then an even, slightly earthy, high-acid finish. Screwcap. 13.7% alc. **Rating** 94 **To** 2020 $50

Chateau Reynella ★★★★★

Reynell Road, Reynella, SA 5161 **Region** McLaren Vale/Fleurieu Peninsula
T (08) 8392 2300 **F** (08) 8392 2202 **Open** Mon–Sat 10–4
Winemaker Fiona McDonald **Est.** 1838 **Cases** NFP
John Reynell laid the foundations for Chateau Reynella in 1838; over the next 100 years the stone buildings and cellars, with patches of lawn and leafy gardens were constructed. Thomas Hardy's first job in SA was with Reynella, noting in his diary that he would be able to better himself soon. He did just that, becoming by far the largest producer in SA by the end of the 19th century; 150 or so years after Chateau Reynella's foundation CWA completed the circle by acquiring Chateau Reynella and making it corporate headquarters, while preserving the integrity of the Reynell brand in no uncertain fashion.

ŶŶŶŶŶ **Basket Pressed McLaren Vale Shiraz 2006** A powerhouse wine; incredible concentration and depth, with toasty oak, chocolate, and essency blackberry fruit; mocha comes through on the palate, and the wine represents the essence of the region; dark, dense chewy and generous, with light acidity freshening the finish. Cork. **Rating** 95 **To** 2025 $54

Basket Pressed McLaren Vale Cabernet Sauvignon 2006 A very expressive wine; cedar, black olive, cassis and seamless oak handling; full-bodied with nerve and drive, the core of fruit carries the firm texture and structure of the wine with ease; lovely precision. Cork. **Rating** 95 **To** 2020 $54

McLaren Vale Grenache 2006 Good colour; bright raspberry fruit bouquet, and some darker more savoury dried herb characters coming through; the palate is generous and sweet on entry, but tightens up with a fine mineral edge to conclude; long, juicy and satisfyingly savoury. Cork. **Rating** 94 **To** 2015 $36

Chateau Tanunda ★★★★

9 Basedow Road, Tanunda, SA 5352 **Region** Barossa Valley
T (08) 8563 3888 **F** (08) 8563 1422 **www**.chateautanunda.com **Open** 7 days 10–5
Winemaker Tim Smith **Est.** 1890 **Cases** 10 000 **Vyds** 6.4 ha
This is one of the most imposing winery buildings in the Barossa Valley, built from stone quarried at nearby Bethany in the late 1880s. It started life as a winery, then became a specialist brandy distillery until the death of the Australian brandy industry, whereafter it was simply used as storage cellars. It is now completely restored and converted to a major convention facility catering for groups of up to 400. The winemaking philosophy has been taken back to its roots, with small-batch processing. The large complex also houses a cellar door where the Chateau Tanunda wines are sold; Chateau Bistro and the Barossa Small Winemakers Centre offer wines made by small independent winemakers in the region. It is a sister winery to Cowra Estate, as both are owned by the Geber family. Exports to the UK, Germany Switzerland, Sweden, Denmark, Belgium and China.

ŶŶŶŶŶ **Terroirs of the Barossa Lyndoch Shiraz 2007** Quite a rich and very ripe blackberry and fruitcake bouquet pushing the ripeness envelope; some red fruit comes to the fore on the palate, with good weight and depth, but lacks just a little stuffing. Cork. 14% alc. **Rating** 92 **To** 2016 $48

Terroirs of the Barossa Greenock Shiraz 2006 A pungent, assertive bouquet and palate with strong licorice influences; has length and punch. Cork. 15% alc. **Rating** 91 **To** 2016 $45

The Chateau Barossa Valley Cabernet Sauvignon 2007 While the alcohol is the same as Barossa Tower, and the weight (medium-bodied) likewise, this wine has more cassis and blackcurrant fruit, and benefits from cedary French oak. Cork. 14.5% alc. **Rating** 91 **To** 2017 $28

The Chateau Eden Valley Riesling 2008 Orange and lime blossom aromas, the palate far riper than the alcohol would indicate, and with plenty of upfront flavour for early consumption; has good acidity to provide balance. Screwcap. 10.5% alc. **Rating** 90 **To** 2014 $20

The Chateau Barossa Valley Shiraz 2007 The bouquet shows restrained black fruit, mocha, bramble and spicy oak; medium-bodied with soft and quite fleshy fruit from start to finish; shows a little heat on the finish. Cork. 14.5% alc. **Rating** 90 **To** 2015 $28

Terroirs of the Barossa Ebenezer District Shiraz 2006 Medium- to full-bodied; fragrant aromas of black fruits and spice plus obvious vanilla oak; fine tannins on a notably long and fine finish; a little less oak would have made a better wine. Cork. 15% alc. **Rating** 90 **To** 2014 $45

Terroirs of the Barossa Lyndoch Shiraz 2006 Elements of prune, plum and dark chocolate are obvious, manages to partially carry its alcohol load; tannins help to counter the heat that might have otherwise marred the finish. Cork. 16% alc. **Rating** 90 **To** 2016 $45

The Chateau 100 Year Old Vines Shiraz 2006 Very ripe with a little desiccated fruit on the bouquet; the alcohol really dominates, but there is an abundance of sweet fruit there; a little freshness would not go astray. Cork. 15.5% alc. **Rating** 90 **To** 2016 $90

Botrytis Semillon 2006 Deep gold; the honeyed richness is neatly balanced by crisp acidity; has developed well, but don't delay. Advertiser Public Choice Award. Diam. 11% alc. **Rating** 90 **To** 2010 $20

ŸŸŸŸ **Grand Barossa Shiraz 2006** A medium-bodied wine with three distinct components: earthy/spicy overtones; sweet red and black fruits; and vanillin oak. They are in balance, and may knit together in the medium term. Cork. 14.5% alc. **Rating** 89 **To** 2016 $25

Grand Barossa Cabernet Sauvignon 2005 Pleasant, well-made and well-balanced wine, with enough varietal fruit, and has not been overworked in the winery. Cork. 14.5% alc. **Rating** 89 **To** 2014 $25

Barossa Tower Shiraz 2007 Good purple hue; a fragrant, spicy, fruit-driven bouquet leads into a tangy, medium-bodied palate with the fruit once again the driver. Screwcap. 14.5% alc. **Rating** 88 **To** 2013 $18

Barossa Tower Cabernet Sauvignon 2007 Savoury/foresty nuances to the blackcurrant fruit of the bouquet and palate are clearly varietal, and are balanced by some oak sweetening. Screwcap. 14.5% alc. **Rating** 88 **To** 2015 $18

Nightwatch Barossa Valley Sparkling Shiraz NV Has been well assembled, with attractive touches of spice and licorice to the base wine; is neither too sweet, nor too oaky. Cork. 13.5% alc. **Rating** 88 **To** 2013 $29.99

Chatsfield ★★★★

O'Neil Road, Mount Barker, WA 6324 **Region** Mount Barker
T (08) 9851 1704 **F** (08) 9851 2660 **www**.chatsfield.com.au **Open** By appt
Winemaker The Vintage Wineworx (Greg Jones) **Est.** 1976 **Cases** 2000
Irish-born medical practitioner Ken Lynch can be proud of his achievements at Chatsfield, as can most of the various contract winemakers who have taken the high-quality estate-grown material and made some impressive wines, notably the Riesling and spicy, licorice Shiraz. Exports to the UK.

ŸŸŸŸŸ **Mount Barker Shiraz 2007** Strong colour; a very intense wine, with almost piercing black cherry and blackberry fruit running through to a long finish and aftertaste. Sure to develop well. Screwcap. 14.5% alc. **Rating** 90 **To** 2017 $20

Chatto Wines ★★★★★

McDonalds Road, Pokolbin, NSW 2325 **Region** Lower Hunter Valley
T (02) 4998 7293 **F** (02) 4998 7294 **www**.firstcreekwines.com.au **Open** 7 days 9–5
Winemaker Jim Chatto **Est.** 2000 **Cases** 7000

Jim Chatto spent several years in Tasmania as the first winemaker at Rosevears Estate. He has since moved to the Hunter Valley but has used his Tasmanian contacts to buy small parcels of riesling and pinot noir. Possessed of a particularly good palate, he has made wines of excellent quality under the Chatto label. A star Len Evans Tutorial scholar and an up-and-coming wine show judge, he is chief winemaker for Pepper Tree Estate. Exports to the US and Canada.

Cherry Tree Hill   ★★★☆

Level 2, 90 New South Head Road, Edgecliff, NSW 2027 **Region** Southern Highlands
T (02) 9362 1811 **F** (02) 9362 1822 **Open** Not
Winemaker Anton Balog, Eddy Rossi (Contract) **Est.** 2000 **Cases** 4000 **Vyds** 14 ha
The Lorentz family, headed by Gabi Lorentz, began the establishment of the Cherry Tree Hill vineyard in 2000 with the planting of 3 ha each of cabernet sauvignon and riesling; 3 ha each of merlot and sauvignon blanc followed in '01, and, finally, 2 ha of chardonnay in '02. The inspiration was childhood trips on a horse and cart through his grandfather's vineyard in Hungary, and Gabi's son David completes the three-generation involvement as manager of the business.

ΨΨΨΨΨ **Cabernet Merlot 2006** Good colour; light- to medium-bodied, but has attractive, juicy ripe fruit elements in the mix of cassis and blackcurrant supported by fine tannins. Surprise packet. Screwcap. 13.2% alc. **Rating** 90 **To** 2014 $25

ΨΨΨΨ **Riesling 2005** Light, bright colour; the palate has great freshness and crispness with apple nuances and minerally acidity. Screwcap. 12.8% alc. **Rating** 87 **To** 2012 $16

Cheviot Bridge   ★★★★

9th Floor, 564 St Kilda Road, Melbourne, Vic 3004 (postal) **Region** Upper Goulburn
T (03) 8656 7000 **F** (03) 9510 3277 **www**.cheviotbridge.com.au **Open** Not
Winemaker Hugh Cuthbertson **Est.** 1998 **Cases** NFP
Cheviot Bridge brings together a highly experienced team of wine industry professionals and investors, who provided the $10 million-plus required to purchase the Long Flat range of wines from Tyrrell's in 2003. The bulk of the business activity is that of virtual winery, acquiring bulk and/or bottled wine from various third-party suppliers. The current releases are very meritorious, both in terms of quality and price. The brands include Cheviot Bridge Yea Valley, Cheviot Bridge CB, Kissing Bridge, Thirsty Lizard, Long Flat, The Long Flat Wine Co and Terrace Vale (see separate entry). Exports to all major markets.

ΨΨΨΨΨ **Cheviot Bridge Yea Valley Cabernet Sauvignon 2008** A substantial wine with an abundance of most attractive blackcurrant and cassis fruit supported by good oak and tannins. Screwcap. 13.5% alc. **Rating** 93 **To** 2020 $30
Cheviot Bridge Yea Valley Shiraz 2008 At the rich end of spectrum for cool-grown fruit, but does have spicy notes and good mouthfeel; lively finish. Screwcap. 13.5% alc. **Rating** 92 **To** 2018 $30
Bin Ends Adelaide Hills Chardonnay 2008 A surprise packet, with very good fruit focus and intensity on the long, sustained nectarine and white peach palate; probably no barrel involvement. Screwcap. 13% alc. **Rating** 90 **To** 2011 $10.99
Long Flat Destinations Yarra Valley Pinot Noir 2008 Slight haze; ripe redcurrant and dark cherry bouquet, with charry oak providing a bit of spice; the palate is quite fleshy, with a bit of grip on the finish and a lingering sense of oak. Diam. 14% alc. **Rating** 90 **To** 2013 $14.95
Long Flat Destinations Barossa Valley Shiraz 2008 Full-bodied ripe plum, prune and chocolate fruit; mouthfilling wine with soft tannins and good oak integration. Zork. 14.5% alc. **Rating** 90 **To** 2017 $14.95
Long Flat Shiraz 2007 Red and black fruit, with fruitcake spice; generous and slightly warm-fruited with an even and a surprisingly fine-tannin finish. Screwcap. 14% alc. **Rating** 90 **To** 2014 $9.95

Long Flat Destinations Adelaide Hills Sauvignon Blanc 2008 Slightly left field, with spicy quasi-oaky notes; has structural complexity thanks to a mineral spine and framework. Screwcap. 13% alc. **Rating** 89 **To** 2011 $14.99
Long Flat Cabernet Shiraz 2007 Cassis, blackberry and fruitcake; vibrant red fruit palate, with good acidity and fine-tannin profile. Screwcap. 14.5% alc. **Rating** 89 **To** 2014 $9.95
Long Flat Semillon Sauvignon Blanc 2008 Bright colour; straw, tropical fruit and a little honey on the bouquet; fleshy on entry, with focused acidity and fresh fruit to conclude. Screwcap. 11.5% alc. **Rating** 88 **To** 2011 $9.95
Long Flat Destinations Coonawarra Cabernet Sauvignon 2006 Bright colour; cassis and a touch of mint, with fine tannin and fleshy fruit on the finish. Screwcap. 14.5% alc. **Rating** 87 **To** 2012 $14.95

Chimes Estate

9 Bernard Street, Claremont, WA 6010 (postal) **Region** Margaret River
T 0412 550 995 **www.**chimesestate.com.au **Open** Not
Winemaker Fermoy Estate (Michael Kelly) **Est.** 2001 **Cases** 520 **Vyds** 7 ha
Chimes Estate founders, Philip and Margaret Thompson, live in Claremont, Perth, commuting to the vineyard, orchard and olive grove on weekends and holidays. The 30-ha property, situated 13 km northeast of the Margaret River township, is located in a valley surrounded by state forest and cattle farms. From 2001 to '06 they established 3 ha of cabernet sauvignon, 1.5 ha each of sauvignon blanc and semillon, and 1 ha of merlot (the two white varieties planted in '06, the reds in '01 and '02). Most of the grapes are sold, but the intention is to increase production with a Merlot as well as Sauvignon Blanc and Semillon-based wines.

Margaret River Cabernet Sauvignon 2007 Very light bright colour; lacks some fruit depth, although cleverly made, including subtle use of oak. Gold WA Wine Show '08. Screwcap. 14% alc. **Rating** 93 **To** 2012 $19.50
Margaret River Rose 2007 A Merlot (70%)/Cabernet (30%) blend offers red fruits on the bouquet and a gentle but dry palate that finishes well. Bargain. Screwcap. 13.5% alc. **Rating** 90 **To** 2010 $12

Chrismont ★★★★★

251 Upper King River Road, Cheshunt, Vic 3678 **Region** King Valley
T (03) 5729 8220 **F** (03) 5729 8253 **www.**chrismont.com.au **Open** 7 days 11–5
Winemaker Warren Proft **Est.** 1980 **Cases** 18 000 **Vyds** 80 ha
Arnold (Arnie) and Jo Pizzini's vineyards in the Whitfield area of the upper King Valley have been planted with riesling, sauvignon blanc, chardonnay, pinot gris, cabernet sauvignon, merlot, shiraz, barbera, marzemino and arneis. The La Zona range ties in the Italian heritage of the Pizzinis and is part of the intense interest in all things Italian. Exports to the US and Sweden.

Christina 2005 Bright straw-green; a very lively, very intense wine with great length and thrust in a citrus and stone fruit spectrum, the oak absorbed by the fruit. High-quality cork. Chardonnay. 14% alc. **Rating** 94 **To** 2015 $45
La Zona King Valley Sangiovese 2006 Bright red colour; lively, juicy cherry fruit charged with fine, ripe tannins on the long, harmonious palate. Screwcap. 14% alc. **Rating** 94 **To** 2016 $24

La Zona King Valley Rosato Mezzanotte 2008 Salmon-pink; has a burst of spice from the Sangiovese/Barbera/Marzemino used to make the wine; good balance, length and a dry finish. Screwcap. 12.5% alc. **Rating** 90 **To** 2009 $18
Arnaldo 2005 An extreme style that will polarise opinions: does the fruit manage to carry the pervasive, savoury tannins? Like many Italian reds, the true answer can only be given with the help of appropriate food. Sangiovese/Cabernet Sauvignon. Cork. 14% alc. **Rating** 90 **To** 2020 $60

La Zona King Valley Albarino 2008 Dry, fresh and chalky palate; while the fruit flavours tend to neutrality, the wine has balance, length and a clean finish, characters which (presumably) earned it a Gold medal Sydney International Wine Competition 2009. Screwcap. 12.5% alc. **Rating** 90 **To** 2012 $22

 King Valley Riesling 2008 Has an attractive combination of citrus and tropical fruit aromas and flavours; an each-way proposition for now or later drinking. Screwcap. 12% alc. **Rating** 89 **To** 2013 $16

La Zona King Valley Barbera 2006 Has a considerable volume of tarry/spicy/savoury black fruit flavours on the mid-palate, yet doesn't follow through on the finish. Screwcap. 14% alc. **Rating** 88 **To** 2014 $24

La Zona King Valley Pinot Grigio 2008 Seems to have a little more texture than most, although the flavours are in the usual spectrum of pear and apple. Screwcap. 12.5% alc. **Rating** 87 **To** 2010 $22

La Zona King Valley Arneis 2008 A generous wine full of pear fruit on the bouquet and palate; plenty of richness, and a touch of anise on the mid-palate provides interest. Screwcap. 12% alc. **Rating** 87 **To** 2012 $22

La Zona King Valley Prosecco NV A spicy, bony aperitif; deliberately made in a bone-dry fashion, taking its inspiration from Northern Italy. Crown Seal. 12.5% alc. **Rating** 87 **To** 2010 $26

Chudacud Estate ★★★

Lot 22 Wade Road, Boyup Brook, WA 6244 **Region** Blackwood Valley
T (08) 9764 4053 **Open** Wed–Thurs & public hols 10–5, Fri–Sat 7 pm–11 pm
Winemaker Ian Duncan, Jennifer Duncan **Est.** 2001 **Cases** NFP **Vyds** 1 ha

Jennifer Duncan explains the background to Chudacud in fine style. 'This was my husband's dream and my nightmare!!!! Anyone with the slightest notion that wandering through the vineyard hand-in-hand is romantic – think again. It's damn hard work, but I must admit when the cork comes out of the bottle it makes it all worthwhile.' To that I can only add 'Amen'. Their 1 ha of shiraz planted in 2001 (after moving from the city) makes them the smallest winery in the Blackwood Valley. However, given the absence of food in the Blackwood wine country, the Duncans have built a commercial kitchen consisting of six barbecues where patrons can choose from rump steak, lamb, fish or chicken and cook their own, accompanied by gourmet salad. It's an old idea, but one that works very well.

 Blackwood Valley Sauvignon Blanc 2008 Distinctly better than the Chudacud reds, with tropical/passionfruit flavours and a hint of sweetness not interfering too much. Screwcap. 12.6% alc. **Rating** 87 **To** 2010 $16

Churchview Estate ★★★★☆

Cnr Bussell Highway/Gale Road, Metricup, WA 6280 **Region** Margaret River
T (08) 9755 7200 **www**.churchview.com.au **Open** Mon–Sat 9.30–5.30
Winemaker Greg Garnish **Est.** 1998 **Cases** 20 000 **Vyds** 54 ha

The Fokkema family, headed by Spike Fokkema, immigrated from The Netherlands in the 1950s. Business success in the following decades led to the acquisition of the 100-ha Churchview Estate property in '97, and to the progressive establishment of substantial vineyards. Exports to the UK and other major markets.

Margaret River Sauvignon Blanc Semillon 2008 A tight, brisk and precise wine that has had gold medal success at lesser shows and its not hard to see why; it has good length to its grassy flavours, and a clean finish. Well priced. Screwcap. 12.5% alc. **Rating** 93 **To** 2012 $18.50

Margaret River Unwooded Chardonnay 2008 Some slightly funky aromas on the bouquet precede a palate of unusually bright and brilliant fruit for an unwooded chardonnay; great thrust to the citrus/grapefruit flavours on the finish. Screwcap. 13% alc. **Rating** 93 **To** 2012 $18.50

The Bartondale Reserve Margaret River Chardonnay 2007 Complex and rich, with ripe stone fruit, fig and melon flavours enhanced by some bottle age; good acidity heightens the finish. Screwcap. 14% alc. **Rating** 91 **To** 2013 $29.50

The Bartondale Reserve Margaret River Shiraz 2006 A relatively light-bodied wine with plenty of drive, but it's not immediately obvious why this wine is twice the price of the varietal; certainly a good outcome for a difficult vintage, but is that enough? Screwcap. 13.5% alc. **Rating** 90 **To** 2016 $36.50

Margaret River Cabernet Merlot 2006 Hints of earth, spice and leather on the bouquet lead into a light- to medium-bodied, but quite vibrantly flavoured, palate; good balance and length. Screwcap. 13.5% alc. **Rating** 90 **To** 2015 $18.50

ΨΨΨΨ **Margaret River Shiraz 2006** Bright red-purple; aromatic and spicy red fruits on the bouquet carry through onto the palate, which is markedly refreshing. Screwcap. 14% alc. **Rating** 89 **To** 2016 $18.50

Sunset Ridge Margaret River Classic White 2008 Lively, fresh and crisp, far better than either its label or price would suggest; citrus, grass and stone fruit (in that order) drive the palate to a long finish. Screwcap. 13.5% alc. **Rating** 88 **To** 2011 $12.50

Margaret River Cabernet Sauvignon 2006 A light- to medium-bodied cabernet, with a mix of spicy and savoury overtones to the cassis fruits reflecting the alcohol and vintage conditions. Clever winemaking for the best outcome. Screwcap. 13% alc. **Rating** 88 **To** 2013 $18.50

Ciavarella ★★★☆

Evans Lane, Oxley, Vic 3678 **Region** King Valley
T (03) 5727 3384 www.oxleyestate.com.au **Open** Mon–Sat 9–6, Sun 10–6
Winemaker Cyril Ciavarella, Tony Ciavarella **Est.** 1978 **Cases** 3000 **Vyds** 2 ha
Cyril and Jan Ciavarella's vineyard was begun in 1978, with plantings being extended over the years. One variety, aucerot, was first produced by Maurice O'Shea of McWilliam's Mount Pleasant 60 or more years ago; the Ciavarella vines have been grown from cuttings collected from an old Glenrowan vineyard before the parent plants were removed in the mid-1980s. Tony Ciavarella left a career in agricultural research in mid-2003 to join his parents at Ciavarella.

ΨΨΨΨΩ **Oxley Estate Chardonnay 2006** Still youthful and cool, with lemon fruit and just a hint of toast coming to the fore; tangy acidity provides a fresh and focused finish. Great value. Screwcap. 13.8% alc. **Rating** 92 **To** 2014 $19

ΨΨΨΨ **Oxley Estate Cabernet Merlot 2006** A juicy and vibrant blend, with mostly red fruit on offer; the palate is quite racy and the tannin fine and linear; well constructed. Screwcap. 14% alc. **Rating** 89 **To** 2014 $22

Oxley Estate White Port NV Toast and honey with a touch of nutty rancio complexity; finishes slightly fruity and is clean and vibrant. Screwcap. 18.7% alc. **Rating** 88 **To** 2010 $19

Oxley Estate Cabernet Sauvignon 2005 Cassis and black olive with a touch of earth; medium-bodied with good acidity and freshness on the finish. Screwcap. 14.8% alc. **Rating** 87 **To** 2012 $22

Cicada Wines ★★★

PO Box 808, Riverwood, NSW 2210 **Region** Various
T (02) 9594 4980 **F** (02) 9594 5290 www.cicadawines.com **Open** 7 days 10–5
Winemaker Bogong Estate, Sorby Adams Wines **Est.** 2005 **Cases** 10 000
Cicada Wines is a successful and broad-ranging virtual winery, created by a group of wine lovers and professionals. It sources wines from leading wine regions around Australia, picking and choosing from the best vintages in those regions. The aim is to supply wines that display distinct regional clarity and value for money.

ΨΨΨΨ **Cherry Nose Pinot Noir 2008** Clear colour; cherry and plum aromas lead into a palate that moves through the fruit to arrive at a savoury tannin-driven finish. Strongly suggests food. Screwcap. 13.5% alc. **Rating** 88 **To** 2013 $17.99

 **Cirillo Wines**   ★★★

PO Box 168, Nuriootpa, SA 5355 **Region** Barossa Valley
T 0408 803 447 **F** (08) 8562 1597 **Open** Not
Winemaker Marco Cirillo **Est.** 2003 **Cases** 400 **Vyds** 6 ha
In 1973 the Cirillo family acquired one of the oldest vineyards in Australia, situated in the
Light Pass district of the Barossa Valley where the soil is deep silt sand over limestone and clay.
This combination of free-draining top soil and water-holding subsoil has sustained the 3 ha
of grenache, along with 1 ha madeira (sic) and 0.5 ha of shiraz planted in 1850, the latter
complemented by 1 ha of shiraz and 0.5 ha of mourvedre planted in 1988. Most of the grapes
are sold to Torbreck, leaving only a small portion for Cirillo, which is open fermented, hand
plunged and basket pressed before spending 24 months in a mix of used French and American
oak hogsheads. Marco Cirillo makes no apology for the high acid and high alcohol style of the
Cirillo 1850 Grenache, which he believes will sustain the wine for 20-plus years.

▼▼▼▼   **1850s Old Vine Barossa Valley Grenache 2005** A strongly varietal bouquet
is followed by a palate that simply can't deal with the impact of the alcohol,
breaking the fruit line into pieces. Screwcap. 16% alc. **Rating** 88 **To** 2013 $50

Clair de Lune Vineyard   ★★★★

8805 South Gippsland Highway, Kardella South, Vic 3951 **Region** Gippsland
T (03) 5655 1032 **www.**clairdelune.com.au **Open** 7 days 11.30–5.30
Winemaker Brian Gaffy **Est.** 1997 **Cases** 500 **Vyds** 4 ha
Brian Gaffy married a successful 20-year career in civil engineering with a long-term
involvement in the Bundaburra Wine & Food Club in Melbourne. His interest in wine grew,
leading to studies at the Dookie Agricultural College, with particular input from Martin
Williams MW and Denise Miller. He has planted a vineyard on the rolling hills of the
Strzelecki Range to sauvignon blanc, chardonnay, pinot noir and a mixed block of shiraz/
merlot/cabernet.

▼▼▼▼▽   **South Gippsland Pinot Noir 2006** A strongly foresty/savoury mode, but
has very good texture, balance and length attested to by multiple trophies at the
Gippsland Wine Show '08. Cork. 12.5% alc. **Rating** 93 **To** 2013 $35
South Gippsland Pinot Noir 2007 Similar style to the '06, and should develop
well; the savoury/foresty edges to the fruit aid complexity and structure; good
balance and length. Diam. 13% alc. **Rating** 92 **To** 2013 $35
Sauvignon Blanc 2008 A restrained bouquet is followed by a super-vibrant,
mineral, herb and asparagus-accented palate, with sherbet-accented acidity on the
finish. Screwcap. 11.5% alc. **Rating** 90 **To** 2011 $25
South Gippsland Oaked Chardonnay 2007 Understated wine reflecting
early picking, and a sensible decision to keep oak inputs to a minimum; white
peach and citrus are the drivers. Screwcap. 12.5% alc. **Rating** 90 **To** 2014 $28

▼▼▼▼   **Quartet Rose 2008** Frizzante style with lots of CO_2 immediately evident;
allsorts blend adds to interest, as does the bone-dry finish. Pinot Noir/Shiraz/
Merlot/Cabernet Sauvignon. Screwcap. 12% alc. **Rating** 87 **To** 2010 $21

Clairault   ★★★★☆

3277 Caves Road, Wilyabrup, WA 6280 **Region** Margaret River
T (08) 9755 6225 **F** (08) 9755 6229 **www.**clairaultwines.com.au **Open** 7 days 10–5
Winemaker Will Shields **Est.** 1976 **Cases** 30 000 **Vyds** 45.72 ha
Bill and Ena Martin, with sons Conor, Brian and Shane, acquired Clairault several years ago
and have expanded the vineyards on the 120-ha property. The 12 ha of vines established by
the former owners (most now over 30 years old) have been supplemented by another 33 or so
ha of vines, with a ratio of roughly 70% red varieties to 30% white. Deeply concerned about
the environment and consumer health, Clairault has joined with ERA (Environmentally
Responsible Agriculture) to implement the elimination of chemical use and the introduction
of biological farming. Exports to the UK, the US and other major markets.

Estate Margaret River Chardonnay 2007 Very toasty bouquet, with grapefruit playing a supporting role; excellent depth of fruit and concentration, with the oak playing a dominant role; a little time will see the ample fruit come to the fore. Trophy winner. Screwcap. 13.5% alc. **Rating** 95 **To** 2015 $32

Margaret River Semillon Sauvignon Blanc 2008 Oak works wells as a subtext; has good line and length; herb, grass and mineral notes. Screwcap. 12% alc. **Rating** 93 **To** 2011 $18
Margaret River Sauvignon Blanc 2008 A restrained bouquet is followed by a far more expressive palate, with good structure for the mix of gooseberry, mineral and grass flavours. Screwcap. 12.5% alc. **Rating** 92 **To** 2011 $24
Estate Margaret River Cabernet Sauvignon 2006 Cassis fruit with a strong element of cigar box; good levels of juicy red fruits come to the fore on the palate, and the finish is firm, with well-handled oak. Screwcap. 13.5% alc. **Rating** 90 **To** 2015 $44

Margaret River Cabernet Merlot 2006 A cool expression with more cedar and slightly herbal notes than ripe fruit; quite fresh and fine. Screwcap. 13.5% alc. **Rating** 87 **To** 2013 $24
Margaret River Cabernet Sauvignon 2006 Cool and slightly herbaceous bouquet; good texture and quite linear red fruit and acidity, with fine tannin structure on the finish. Screwcap. 14% alc. **Rating** 87 **To** 2013 $24

Clancy Fuller   ★★★★

PO Box 34, Tanunda, SA 5352 **Region** Barossa Valley
T (08) 8563 0080 **F** (08) 8563 0080 **Open** Not
Winemaker Chris Ringland **Est.** 1996 **Cases** 550
This is the venture of industry veterans who should know better: Paul Clancy, long responsible for the Wine Industry Directory that sits in every winery office in Australia, and Peter Fuller, who has built up by far the largest public relations business for all sectors of the wine industry. They own 2 ha of dry-grown 120-year-old shiraz at Bethany, and 2 ha of shiraz and grenache at Jacob's Creek.

Silesian Barossa Shiraz 2006 While only light- to medium-bodied, has considerable elegance; the thrust of the fresh red and black fruits of the palate carries through to the lively finish. Screwcap. 14.5% alc. **Rating** 92 **To** 2015 $25

Two Little Dickie Birds Barossa Rose 2007 Equal amounts of mourvedre and grenache in a salmon-coloured wine, with cleverly counterpoised acidity and residual sugar. Screwcap. 13% alc. **Rating** 87 **To** 2008 $18.50

Clarendon Hills   ★★★★★

Brookmans Road, Blewitt Springs, SA 5171 **Region** McLaren Vale
T (08) 8364 1484 **F** (08) 8364 1484 **www**.clarendonhills.com.au **Open** By appt
Winemaker Roman Bratasiuk **Est.** 1989 **Cases** NA
Age and experience, it would seem, have mellowed Roman Bratasiuk – and the style of his wines. Once formidable and often rustic, they are now far more sculpted and smooth, at times bordering on downright elegance. Roman has taken another major step by purchasing a 160-ha property high in the hill country of Clarendon at an altitude close to that of the Adelaide Hills. Here he has established 14 ha under vine with single-stake trellising similar to that used on the steep slopes of Germany and Austria. He makes 18 different wines each year, and since 1998 these have been of exceptional consistency in quality, a tribute to the old vines from which the wines come. Exports to the UK, the US and other major markets.

Bakers Gully Syrah 2006 A medium-bodied wine, with fine, fresh, almost slippery/juicy red fruits the main game in the mouth, but with darker notes in the background; fine tannins and a super-long finish. Cork. 14.5% alc. **Rating** 96 **To** 2031 $80

Piggott Range Syrah 2005 What can only be described as a totally serious wine; extremely powerful, with multi-layered black fruits complexed by touches of earth and mineral; the tannins are perfectly balanced, the wine precisely where it should be. Cork. 14.5% alc. **Rating** 96 **To** 2030 $300

Romas Vineyard Old Vines Grenache 2006 A remarkable wine; the flavour echoes and ricochets around the mouth, building on the back-palate and finish; a wine of extraordinary thrust, but also polish. From 80-year-old vines, made without acid addition, fining or filtration. Cork. 14.5% alc. **Rating** 96 **To** 2025 $125

Clarendon Vineyard Old Vines Grenache 2005 Bright, clear purple-red; offers a rich tapestry of succulent fruit in a blood plum spectrum, the oak evident but not over the top, finishing with soft tannins. Cork. 14.5% alc. **Rating** 95 **To** 2020 $75

Brookman Vineyard Cabernet Sauvignon 1998 Part of the extensive museum reserves available from Clarendon Hills, it leaves all the Brookmans that preceded it, and several that followed, in the shade; fine, long and elegant, with wonderful cassis fruit on the mid-palate, and silky tannins on the finish. Here, too, the oak card has been well played, even if it is more evident than that of the younger wines. Cork. 14.5% alc. **Rating** 94 **To** 2018 $80

Claymore Wines ★★★★

Leasingham Road, Leasingham, SA 5452 **Region** Clare Valley
T (08) 8843 0200 **F** (08) 8843 0200 **www**.claymorewines.com.au **Open** 7 days 11–4
Winemaker David Mavor, Ben Jeanneret **Est.** 1998 **Cases** 10 000 **Vyds** 20 ha
Claymore Wines is the venture of two medical professionals imagining that it would lead the way to early retirement (which, of course, it did not). The starting date depends on which event you take: the first 4-ha vineyard at Leasingham purchased in 1991 (with 70-year-old grenache, riesling and shiraz); '96, when a 16-ha block at Penwortham was purchased and planted to shiraz, merlot and grenache; '97, when the first wines were made; or '98, when the first releases came onto the market; the labels are inspired by U2, Pink Floyd and Lou Reed. Exports to the US, Denmark, Malaysia, Taiwan, Singapore and Hong Kong.

ŸŸŸŸŸ **Dark Side of the Moon Clare Valley Shiraz 2006** A dark, concentrated and very serious wine; dark fruits, with a little spice and mint, are framed by pencilly oak; the palate is almost thick in texture on entry but, as it travels across the palate, life and lightness return and the overall impression is fine and complex. Screwcap. 14.5% alc. **Rating** 94 **To** 2020 $25

ŸŸŸŸ **Joshua Tree Clare Valley Riesling 2008** A lifted bouquet of lime, with a dominant talc-like aroma; the palate is fresh and linear, with lime juice and a little spice on the finish. Screwcap. 12% alc. **Rating** 89 **To** 2014 $18

Clearview Estate Mudgee ★★★

Cnr Sydney Road/Rocky Water Hole Road, Mudgee, NSW 2850 **Region** Mudgee
T (02) 6372 4546 **F** (02) 6372 7577 **www**.clearviewwines.com.au **Open** Mon & Fri 10–3 (Mar–Dec), w'ends 10–4, or by appt
Winemaker Robert Stein Vineyard **Est.** 1995 **Cases** 1000 **Vyds** 11 ha
Paul and Michelle Baguley acquired the vineyard from the founding Hickey family in 2006. Paul brings 10 years' experience as a viticulturist, and Paul and Michelle have introduced additional wine styles. Plantings include shiraz, chardonnay, cabernet sauvignon and semillon.

ŸŸŸŸ **Rocky Waterhole Cabernet Sauvignon 2008** Vivid crimson; has the fresh red and black fruits promised by the bouquet; delicious drink-now style; could even be served slightly chilled. Screwcap. 13.5% alc. **Rating** 88 **To** 2012 $18

Church Creek Chardonnay 2008 Toasty oak and cashew fruit; a little light on, but clean and well made. Screwcap. 13% alc. **Rating** 87 **To** 2012 $16

Clemens Hill

686 Richmond Road, Cambridge, Tas 7170 **Region** Southern Tasmania
T (03) 6248 5985 **F** (03) 6248 5985 **Open** By appt
Winemaker Winemaking Tasmania **Est.** 1994 **Cases** 1500
The Shepherd family acquired Clemens Hill in 2001 after selling their Rosabrook winery
in the Margaret River. They also have a shareholding in Winemaking Tasmania, the contract
winemaking facility run by Julian Alcorso, who makes the Clemens Hill wines. The estate
vineyards have now been increased to 3.8 ha (pinot noir and sauvignon blanc). Following
the death of Joan Shepherd in 2006, John took John Schuts, an assistant winemaker at Julian
Alcorso's Winemaking Tasmania, into partnership.

ΨΨΨΨΩ **Pinot Noir 2007** Good hue and depth; a very correct medium-bodied pinot
with all the flavours in a smooth palate; good length, albeit with a slightly oaky
finish. Screwcap. 13.5% alc. **Rating** 90 **To** 2013 $35.20

 # Clockwork Wines

8990 West Swan Road, West Swan, WA 6056 (postal) **Region** Swan Valley
T 0401 033 840 **www**.clockworkwines.com.au **Open** Not
Winemaker Rob Marshall **Est.** 2008 **Cases** 5000 **Vyds** 5 ha
This is a separate business to that of Oakover Wines, although both are owned by the Yukich
family. Grapes are sourced from around WA, with the majority coming from Margaret River,
but also from Geographe, Frankland River and the Clockwork Vineyard in the Swan Valley.
The 2007 Clockwork Cabernet Merlot, somewhat luckily, perhaps, found itself in the line
up for the Jimmy Watson Trophy at its first show entry, part of a dominant contingent from
Margaret River thanks to its great vintage, unlike that of the eastern states.

ΨΨΨΨΩ **Margaret River Cabernet Merlot 2007** At the savoury/minty end of the
spectrum but has not been over-extracted, and does show good varietal character.
Clever label design. Screwcap. 13.8% alc. **Rating** 90 **To** 2014 $14.99

ΨΨΨΨ **Geographe Sauvignon Blanc 2008** Relatively low alcohol and good acidity
lengthen the palate, which has pleasant tropical fruit; easy on the gums. Screwcap.
11.7% alc. **Rating** 88 **To** 2010 $14.99
Margaret River Shiraz 2007 A relatively light-bodied, cheerful and lively
shiraz with fresh red fruit flavours and a light dressing of spice. Screwcap. 14% alc.
Rating 87 **To** 2012 $14.99

Clonakilla

Crisps Lane, Murrumbateman, NSW 2582 **Region** Canberra District
T (02) 6227 5877 **F** (02) 6227 5871 **www**.clonakilla.com.au **Open** 7 days 10–5
Winemaker Tim Kirk **Est.** 1971 **Cases** 9000
The indefatigable Tim Kirk, with an inexhaustible thirst for knowledge, is the winemaker
and manager of this family winery founded by Tim's father, scientist Dr John Kirk. It is not
at all surprising that the quality of the wines is excellent, especially the Shiraz Viognier, which
has paved the way for numerous others to follow, but remains the best example in Australia.
Exports to all major markets.

ΨΨΨΨΨ **Canberra District Shiraz Viognier 2008** As expected the wine is young and
buoyant, with a highly fragrant perfume of red fruit, fresh blackberry, violets,
roast meat and a little tar; the palate reveals the true potential of this superb wine,
with a cascading array of flavours and thrillingly silky tannin, poised acidity and a
peacocks tail on the very long and precise palate. **Rating** 97 **To** 2025
O'Riada Canberra District Shiraz 2007 A fine and restrained bouquet of red
fruit, Asian spices and a touch of mineral complexity; the oak is barely evident
and the fruit concentration is undeniable, as on the palate, the wine is long,
luscious and finishes with slippery fine tannin and true restraint. Screwcap. 14% alc.
Rating 95 **To** 2016 $45

Hilltops Shiraz 2008 Dark shiraz fruit, with blackberry, roast meat and a gentle spice background; medium-bodied with serious intent, the tannins are ripe, the fruit juicy and the finish, long and savoury; lovely harmony. 14% alc. **Rating** 94 **To** 2015 $33

♀♀♀♀♀ **Canberra District Riesling 2008** A clean bouquet, with faint nuances of toast and spice that yield to ripe citrus fruit on the well-balanced palate. Screwcap. 12.5% alc. **Rating** 92 **To** 2016 $30

Clos Clare   ★★★★

Old Road, Watervale, SA 5452 **Region** Clare Valley
T (08) 8843 0161 **F** (08) 8843 0161 **Open** W'ends & public hols 10–5
Winemaker Sam Barry, Tom Barry **Est.** 1993 **Cases** 1200
Clos Clare was acquired by the Barry family in 2008. Riesling continues to be made from the 2-ha unirrigated section of the original Florita Vineyard (the major part of that vineyard was already in Barry ownership) and newly introduced red wines are coming from a 48-year-old vineyard beside the Armagh site.

♀♀♀♀♀ **Watervale Riesling 2008** Tightly wound, fresh lime juice, and a strong slatey personality; a dry palate, with fresh lime a counterpoint to the savoury minerality on the finish; should age well. Screwcap. 12.2% alc. **Rating** 93 **To** 2020 $22

Clovely Estate   ★★★★

Steinhardts Road, Moffatdale via Murgon, Qld 4605 **Region** South Burnett
T (07) 3876 3100 **F** (07) 3876 3500 **www.**clovely.com.au **Open** 7 days 10–5
Winemaker Luke Fitzpatrick **Est.** 1998 **Cases** 30 000 **Vyds** 174 ha
Clovely Estate has the largest vineyards in Qld having established 174 ha of immaculately maintained vines at two locations just to the east of Murgon in the Burnett Valley. There are 120 ha of red grapes (including 60 ha of shiraz) and 54 ha of white grapes. The attractively packaged wines are sold in five tiers: Double Pruned at the top; followed by Estate Reserve; Left Field, featuring alternative varieties and styles; then the White Label range, for everyday drinking, distributed through the Qld retail market; and at the bottom, First Picked, primarily designed for the export market (the UK, the US, Singapore, Taiwan and China) at low price points. The estate also has a second cellar door at 210 Musgrave Road, Red Hill.

♀♀♀♀♀ **Estate Reserve South Burnett Chardonnay 2007** A tangy and gently spicy bouquet flows seamlessly onto the palate, with nectarine fruit supported by touches of cashew and contrasting acidity; good balance and length. Screwcap. 13.7% alc. **Rating** 91 **To** 2014 $28
Double Pruned South Burnett Shiraz 2006 The double pruning technique has certainly worked to concentrate the fruit (and delay harvest for up to three months); the wine has savoury/spicy overtones to black fruits, more commonly associated with cooler climates. Twin top. 14.5% alc. **Rating** 90 **To** 2016 $60

♀♀♀♀ **Left Field South Burnett Barbera 2007** A wine with positive varietal expression throughout in both flavour and structure; spiced plum and dried herb are dominant, oak incidental. Screwcap. 13.5% alc. **Rating** 89 **To** 2013 $20
Estate Reserve South Burnett Verdelho 2008 Has attractive grainy/lemony nuances to add complexity to the fruit salad base; likewise has good length. A mystifying doubling of price compared to the varietal (86 points). Screwcap. 13% alc. **Rating** 88 **To** 2011 $28
South Burnett Rose 2007 Light pink; well made, showing sangiovese to full advantage in a rose context; light, spicy strawberry fruit flavours, with a subliminal touch of sweetness balanced by acidity. Screwcap. 13.5% alc. **Rating** 88 **To** 2009 $13
South Burnett Shiraz Merlot Cabernet 2005 A wine that over-delivers on its price, the abundant red and black fruits supported by spicy/savoury tannins; is developing with assurance. Screwcap. 14% alc. **Rating** 88 **To** 2012 $13

Left Field South Burnett Grenache Shiraz Mourvedre 2007 Has authentic varietal aromas, but, despite the alcohol, is tighter and more savoury than traditional SA blends. Nonetheless, interesting offer. Screwcap. 15% alc. **Rating** 87 **To** 2013 $20

Clown Fish   ★★★★☆

Garstone Road, Cowaramup, WA 6284 **Region** Margaret River
T (08) 9755 5195 **F** (08) 9755 9441 **www.**cowaramupwines.com.au **Open** By appt
Winemaker Naturaliste Vintners (Bruce Dukes) **Est.** 1996 **Cases** 3000 **Vyds** 17 ha
Russell and Marilyn Reynolds run a biodynamic vineyard with the aid of sons Cameron (viticulturist) and Anthony (assistant winemaker). Plantings began in 1996 and have been expanded to cover merlot, cabernet sauvignon, shiraz, semillon, chardonnay and sauvignon blanc. Notwithstanding low yields and the discipline that biodynamic grapegrowing entails, wine prices are modest.

ᵀᵀᵀᵀᵀ **Margaret River Chardonnay 2008** Super-elegant, intense grapefruit and nectarine; long palate with great line. Gold WA Wine Show '08. Screwcap. 13.5% alc. **Rating** 94 **To** 2014 $22.50

ᵀᵀᵀᵀ♀ **Margaret River Sauvignon Blanc Semillon 2008** Lively, fresh, crisp and focused, the low alcohol eminently suited to the blend; delicate, but fresh, passionfruit nuances lift the palate of a drink-me-quick style. Screwcap. 12% alc. **Rating** 90 **To** 2011 $19.95
Margaret River Shiraz 2007 Convincing purple-tinged colour; an aromatic, light- to medium-bodied wine with juicy black and red fruits, tannins and warm, spicy oak all contributing. Screwcap. 14% alc. **Rating** 90 **To** 2016 $22.50
Margaret River Merlot Cabernet 2007 Bright red-purple; fresh juicy red and black fruits on the medium-bodied palate, with just a touch of savoury tannin. Screwcap. 13% alc. **Rating** 90 **To** 2014 $19.95

Clyde Park Vineyard   ★★★★★

2490 Midland Highway, Bannockburn, Vic 3331 **Region** Geelong
T (03) 5281 7274 **www.**clydepark.com.au **Open** W'ends & public hols 11–5
Winemaker Simon Black, Terry Jongebloed **Est.** 1979 **Cases** 6000
Clyde Park Vineyard, established by Gary Farr but sold by him many years ago, has passed through several changes of ownership. Now owned by Terry Jongebloed and Sue Jongebloed-Dixon, it has significant mature plantings of pinot noir (3.4 ha), chardonnay (3.1 ha), sauvignon blanc (1.5 ha), shiraz (1.2 ha) and pinot gris (0.9 ha), and the quality of its wines is exemplary. Exports to the UK.

ᵀᵀᵀᵀᵀ **Reserve Chardonnay 2007** Has every bit as much flavour as the varietal, but with more finesse and length to the stone fruit flavour that ripples to the lingering finish. Screwcap. 13.5% alc. **Rating** 95 **To** 2020 $45
Pinot Noir 2007 Exceptionally deep, dark purple-red; strongly structured, but not extractive, dark fruit in a black fruit/plum spectrum; good length; preferred to the Reserve. Screwcap. 13.5% alc. **Rating** 94 **To** 2015 $30

ᵀᵀᵀᵀ♀ **Chardonnay 2007** Has remarkable depth and texture for a wine at this level of alcohol; succulent stone fruit and fig flavours; oak is evident but in balance. Screwcap. 13.5% alc. **Rating** 93 **To** 2017 $30
Reserve Pinot Noir 2007 Similar deep colour to the varietal; potent aromas; while the alcohol is the same, seems more complex and riper, although not necessarily better; overall more oak and extract; needs time. Screwcap. 13.5% alc. **Rating** 92 **To** 2013 $45

Coal Valley Vineyard

257 Richmond Road, Cambridge, Tas 7170 **Region** Southern Tasmania
T (03) 6248 5367 **www**.coalvalley.com.au **Open** Thurs–Sun 10–4 (closed Jul)
Winemaker Alain Rousseau, Todd Goebel **Est.** 1991 **Cases** 1000 **Vyds** 4.5 ha
Since acquiring Coal Valley Vineyard in 1999, Gill Christian and Todd Goebel have increased
the original 1-ha hobby vineyard to pinot noir (2.3 ha), riesling, cabernet sauvignon, merlot,
chardonnay and tempranillo. Todd makes the Cabernet Sauvignon onsite, and dreams of
making all the wines. More remarkable was Gill and Todd's concurrent lives: one in India,
the other in Tasmania (flying over six times a year), and digging 4000 holes for the new vine
plantings. Exports to Canada.

ΨΨΨΨΨ **Chardonnay 2008** Interesting wine, with well above average impact and
complexity coming as much from the fruit as the oak; nectarine, grapefruit zest
and mineral drive the palate. Screwcap. 13.5% alc. **Rating** 92 **To** 2015 $28

ΨΨΨΨ **Pinot Noir 2007** A ripe, somewhat meaty bouquet, then a solid, plummy palate
with adequate length. Screwcap. 13.5% alc. **Rating** 87 **To** 2012 $32

Cobaw Ridge ★★★★

31 Perc Boyers Lane, Pastoria, Vic 3444 **Region** Macedon Ranges
T (03) 5423 5227 **F** (03) 5423 5227 **www**.cobawridge.com.au **Open** Thurs–Mon 12–5
Winemaker Alan Cooper **Est.** 1985 **Cases** 1500 **Vyds** 6 ha
Nelly and Alan Cooper established Cobaw Ridge's vineyard at an altitude of 610 m in the hills
above Kyneton. The plantings of cabernet sauvignon have been removed and partially replaced
by lagrein, a variety that sent me scuttling to Jancis Robinson's seminal book on grape
varieties: it is a northeast Italian variety typically used to make delicate rose, but at Cobaw
Ridge it is made into an impressive full-bodied dry red. This success has prompted Alan
Cooper to remove 0.5 ha of chardonnay and plant vermentino in its place. The Coopers' son
Joshua, taking a circuitous route via Europe and elsewhere in Australia before commencing a
Wine Science degree at Adelaide University, will become the sixth generation of the family
on the land. Exports to the UK.

ΨΨΨΨΨ **Pinot Noir 2007** Strong colour; a complex bouquet of predominantly black
fruits plus notes of leather, charcuterie and spice; the palate is likewise powerful,
and very savoury; time to go. Diam. 13.5% alc. **Rating** 91 **To** 2015 $38
Shiraz Viognier 2007 Usual vibrant colour; a lifted, fragrant bouquet of red
berry fruits and spice, the medium-bodied palate all about flavour rather than
extract; good length and balance. Diam. 13% alc. **Rating** 91 **To** 2017 $40
Chardonnay 2007 Bright straw-green; a high-toned, pungent bouquet is
followed by a rather terse palate, the fruit and oak still coming to terms with each
other; however, has good potential. Diam. 13.5% alc. **Rating** 90 **To** 2014 $32
Lagrein 2007 Deep purple-crimson; in typical fashion, has intense black fruits on
the bouquet and likewise the palate, yet there is a curious lack of vinosity and line,
which becomes evident on the finish. Diam. 13% alc. **Rating** 90 **To** 2017 $40

Coffman & Lawson NR

5 Flemington Road, Lyneham, ACT 2602 **Region** Canberra District
T (02) 6241 1166 **www**.clwm.net.au **Open** Not
Winemaker Nick Spencer **Est.** 2000 **Cases** NFP
The freehold of the former Kamberra winery (built by Hardys prior to becoming part
of CWA) was acquired by Elvin Global, a Canberra-based investment and management
company. In a relatively short space of time, there were both ownership and management
changes leading to the formation of Coffman & Lawson. It has leased the 2200-tonne capacity
winery with the primary aim of providing contract winemaking services, but also making
wine on its own account from grapes supplied by a co-operative as and when the opportunity
arises. Whether these will be cleanskin, buyers-own-brand or under the Coffman & Lawson
brand remains to be seen. Winemaker Nick Spencer has an interesting CV that suggests there
should be no problem with the quality of the wines at their given price points.

Cofield Wines

Distillery Road, Wahgunyah, Vic 3687 **Region** Rutherglen
T (02) 6033 3798 **www**.cofieldwines.com.au **Open** Mon–Sat 9–5, Sun 10–5
Winemaker Damien Cofield, David Whyte **Est.** 1990 **Cases** 13 000 **Vyds** 15.4 ha
Sons Damien (winery) and Andrew (vineyard) have taken over responsibility for the business
from parents Max and Karen. Collectively, they have developed an impressively broad-based
product range with a strong cellar door sales base. The Pickled Sisters Café is open for lunch
Wed–Mon (tel 02 6033 2377). A 20-ha property at Rutherglen, purchased in 2007, has 5.3 ha
planted to shiraz, and planting of durif and sangiovese followed. Exports to China.

Quartz Vein Shiraz 2006 Deep colour; full-bodied waves of black fruits range
through plum, cherry, blackberry and dark chocolate supported by ripe tannins;
very good wine from a top vintage. Diam. 14.7% alc. **Rating** 94 **To** 2021 $35

Durif 2007 Typical dense colour; black fruits, bitter chocolate and anise run
through the primary river of luscious black fruits. Great value. Diam. 14.2% alc.
Rating 93 **To** 2022 $20
Quartz Vein Durif 2007 Even denser colour than that of the varietal; a massive
wine, throwing alcohol-derived sweetness against the savoury extract of the
Stygian black fruits; I prefer the slightly lower octane model. Diam. 15% alc.
Rating 92 **To** 2022 $35
Rutherglen Shiraz 2007 A powerful wine with an array of black fruits, licorice
and ripe tannin, which gains appeal and attention the more it is tasted. Good value.
Screwcap. 14.5% alc. **Rating** 90 **To** 2017 $20

Sangiovese 2007 Positive colour; plenty of sour cherry aroma and flavour, the
tannins waiting until the last moment to catch hold; a year or two and a dish of
pasta is all that is needed. Screwcap. 13.5% alc. **Rating** 89 **To** 2013 $20
Dry Chenin Blanc 2008 It's a sign of the times when it is necessary to spell
out 'dry' on the label; quite fruity, and although it may be dry, will cause as much
confusion as it is meant to dispel. Screwcap. 12% alc. **Rating** 87 **To** 2012 $18
The Fifth Son 2007 Has those particular Christmas pudding/Christmas cake
aromas of Northeast Victoria, before the palate delivers a wallop to the head thanks
to its monstrous tannins. Approach with extreme caution. Screwcap. 14% alc.
Rating 87 **To** 2022 $20

Coldstream Hills   NR

31 Maddens Lane, Coldstream, Vic 3770 **Region** Yarra Valley
T (03) 5964 9410 **F** (03) 5964 9389 **www**.coldstreamhills.com.au **Open** 7 days 10–5
Winemaker Andrew Fleming, Greg Jarratt, James Halliday (Consultant) **Est.** 1985
Cases NA **Vyds** 100 ha
Founded by the author, who continues to be involved as a consultant, but acquired by
Southcorp in mid-1996; thus it is now a small part of Foster's. Expansion plans already
underway have been maintained, with 100 ha of owned or managed estate vineyards as the
base. Chardonnay and Pinot Noir continue to be the principal focus; Merlot came on-stream
in 1997, Sauvignon Blanc around the same time, Viognier and Reserve Shiraz later still.
Vintage conditions permitting, Chardonnay, Pinot Noir and Cabernet Sauvignon are made in
both varietal and Reserve form, the latter in restricted quantities. In the 2007 and '08 calendar
years, the wines won 13 trophies, 21 gold, 20 silver and 52 bronze medals. Tasting notes are
written by Andrew Fleming. Exports to the UK, the US and Singapore.

Coldstream Hills Reserve Yarra Valley Chardonnay 2007 Attractive stone
fruit aromas of white peach and nectarine, with cool-climate citrus overtones, flow
into an elegant wine with balanced acidity, texture and length; white peach, citrus
and quince are complexed by cashew nut barrel ferment characters. Champion
Wine of Show, International Wine Challenge, NZ '09. Screwcap. 14% alc.
Rating NR **To** 2017 $55.99

Coldstream Hills Yarra Valley Pinot Noir 2008 In a year in which no Reserve Pinot Noir was made, this wine could well attract significant show success. It has excellent texture and structure, with pure cherry and plum fruit supported by a judicious amount of French oak and perfect tannins on the finish. Screwcap. 14% alc. **Rating** NR **To** 2016 $34.99

Coldstream Hills Reserve Yarra Valley Cabernet Sauvignon 2006 A rich and powerful bouquet with dark plum, black olive and blackcurrant characters evident; the palate is fleshy and concentrated, with integrated cedary oak and fine tannins. An excellent example of Yarra Valley cabernet from a warm vintage. Screwcap. 14% alc. **Rating** NR **To** 2020 $55.99

Coldstream Hills Pinot Noir Chardonnay 2004 An elegant style with balance and length; the palate exhibits pinot perfume and structure with fine lemony chardonnay acidity; yeast autolysis characters of brioche and dry biscuits give the wine additional complexity. A multi-trophy and gold medal winner. Cork. 11.5% alc. **Rating** NR **To** 2011 $31.99

Coldstream Hills Yarra Valley Sauvignon Blanc 2008 The bouquet shows fragrant gooseberry characters with underlying passionfruit and lychee aromas; passionfruit pulp and gooseberry dominate on the palate with hints of lemon peel in the background. Screwcap. 12.5% alc. **Rating** NR **To** 2010 $28.99

Coldstream Hills Yarra Valley Chardonnay 2008 Attractive characters of grapefruit and lemon pith with underlying quince and stone fruit drive the bouquet; the palate has exemplary texture, layering of flavours and length; citrus and stone fruit characters are evident, and are supported by subtle toasty oak and a hint of minerality. Screwcap. 13.5% alc. **Rating** NR **To** 2018 $28.99

Coldstream Hills Yarra Valley Merlot 2007 The palate is elegant and round, with good texture and length. The tannins are chalky and persistent, giving the wine structure, concentration and cellaring capability. Fruit characters of dark cherry and plum dominate, with black olive and Christmas cake spice also evident. Charry, toasty oak further enhances the palate, but does not dominate. Screwcap. 13.5% alc. **Rating** NR **To** 2017 $34.99

Coldstream Hills Reserve Yarra Valley Shiraz 2006 Fragrant aromas of rose petal and plums with black pepper and spice, lead into the medium-bodied palate, which has silky tannins and length to the dark plum and cherry flavours, the oak well-integrated and balanced. Screwcap. 14.5% alc. **Rating** NR **To** 2018 $39.99

Collector Wines ★★★★★

12 Bourke Street, Collector, NSW 2581 (postal) **Region** Canberra District
T (02) 6116 8722 **F** (02) 6247 7682 **www.**collectorwines.com.au **Open** Not
Winemaker Alex McKay **Est.** 2007 **Cases** 1500
Owner and winemaker Alex McKay makes two Canberra District Shirazs, the Marked Tree Red from parcels of shiraz from vineyards in and around Murrumbateman, and the Reserve from a single patch of mature shiraz grown on an elevated granite saddle near Murrumbateman.

ᵽᵽᵽᵽᵽ Reserve Shiraz 2008 Crimson-purple colour; has greater complexity and depth than Marked Tree, but similar impressive length; here blackberry and black cherry drive the wine, the tannins perfectly balanced. Release Dec '09. Screwcap. 13.5% alc. **Rating** 96 **To** 2023 $46.95

Reserve Shiraz 2007 Slightly deeper colour than Marked Tree, vibrant purple-crimson; a powerful, medium- to full-bodied palate fuses black fruits, spice and a touch of licorice in a seamless whole. Screwcap. 13.5% alc. **Rating** 96 **To** 2027 $46.96

Marked Tree Red Shiraz 2008 Attractive, lively medium-bodied wine; predominantly red fruits seamlessly merge with spice and a touch of pepper on the very long palate; good oak and tannin balance. Release Sept '09. Screwcap. 13.5% alc. **Rating** 95 **To** 2022 $26.95

Marked Tree Red Shiraz 2007 Excellent crimson-purple; a perfectly composed and balanced medium-bodied shiraz, the bouquet fragrant, the palate laden with black fruits and ripe tannins; outstanding length. Screwcap. 13.5% alc. **Rating** 95 **To** 2022 $26.95

Colvin Wines ★★★★

19 Boyle Street, Mosman, NSW 2088 (postal) **Region** Lower Hunter Valley
T (02) 9908 7886 **F** (02) 9908 7885 **www**.colvinwines.com.au **Open** Not
Winemaker Andrew Spinaze, Drayton's Family Wines, Phil Ryan (Contract) **Est.** 1999
Cases 500 **Vyds** 5.19 ha
In 1990 Sydney lawyer John Colvin and wife Robyn purchased the De Beyers Vineyard, which has a history going back to the second half of the 19th century. By 1967, when a syndicate headed by Douglas McGregor purchased 35 ha of the original vineyard site, no vines remained. The syndicate planted semillon on the alluvial soil of the creek flats and shiraz on the red clay hillsides. When the Colvins acquired the property the vineyard was in need of attention. Up to 1998 all the grapes were sold to Tyrrell's, but since '99 quantities have been made for the Colvin Wines label. These include Sangiovese, from a little over 1 ha of vines planted by John Colvin in 1996 because of his love of the wines of Tuscany.

ΨΨΨΨΨ **De Beyers Vineyard Hunter Valley Semillon 2006** Very attractive wine, starting down the road to full flavour development; lemon and a hint of white peach run through the supple palate; 100 cases released. Screwcap. 10.4% alc. **Rating** 92 **To** 2014 $35
De Beyers Vineyard Hunter Valley Shiraz 2005 There is a touch of reduction on the bouquet, which is presently holding back the fruit flavours, but the finesse and length of the palate shows the future is assured for what will be a very good wine. Screwcap. 13.5% alc. **Rating** 90 **To** 2020 $38

ΨΨΨΨ **De Beyers Vineyard Hunter Valley Sangiovese 2005** While there are reasons to choose the Colvin 2000 Sangiovese, there are more to support this wine, which has the sweet and sour cherry fruit of the variety without harsh tannins. Screwcap. 12.5% alc. **Rating** 89 **To** 2012 $34

Condo Wines NR

3 Ward Street, Torrensville, SA 5031 (postal) **Region** Riverland
T (08) 8443 7551 **F** (08) 8443 6489 **www**.condowines.com.au **Open** Not
Winemaker Jo Irvine, David Norman (Contract) **Est.** 1997 **Cases** 2500 **Vyds** 36.5 ha
The Condo family, headed by Frank Condo, purchased their Allawah property at Swan Reach on the Murray River in 1981, but it was not until the mid '90s that they established their vineyard, planted predominantly to cabernet sauvignon and shiraz, with small amounts of merlot and chardonnay. The winemaking is simple, designed to keep production costs to a minimum. The major focus of the business is on exports (Canada, Vietnam and China), price being the obvious attraction.

Constable Estate Vineyards ★★★★

205 Gillards Road, Cessnock, NSW 2320 **Region** Lower Hunter Valley
T (02) 4998 7887 **F** (02) 4998 6555 **www**.constablehershon.com.au **Open** 7 days 10–5
Winemaker Liz Jackson (Contract) **Est.** 1981 **Cases** 2000 **Vyds** 5.55 ha
The business was created by long-term friends David Constable and Michael Herson; one of its points of attraction is its spectacular formal gardens: the Rose, Knot and Herb, Secret and Sculpture. When Michael Herson died in 2007, David Constable purchased his interests in the property from his estate; he has since replanted half the vineyard, and is actively engaged in a program to increase the quality of the wines and the profile of the business. The varieties planted are cabernet sauvignon, verdelho, semillon, shiraz and chardonnay.

ⵎⵎⵎⵎⵎ **Shiraz 2006** Shows its regional origin from the word go, with some earthy/ leathery overtones to the medium-bodied palate, where plum and blackberry fruit moves more to centre stage; good balance and length. Screwcap. 13.7% alc. **Rating** 90 **To** 2016 $25
Hunter Valley Botrytis Semillon 2007 Complex wine, fermented in French oak and six months' maturation; has notes of honey, cumquat and vanilla balanced by good acidity. Screwcap. 11% alc. **Rating** 90 **To** 2012 $30

ⵎⵎⵎⵎ **Premium Hunter Valley Chardonnay 2007** Crisp, early-picked style with a mix of citrus and melon fruit; sensitive winemaking has prevented the French oak influence from interfering with the fruit. Overtones of Chablis. Screwcap. 12.5% alc. **Rating** 89 **To** 2014 $28.50

Coobara Wines   ★★★★★

PO Box 231, Birdwood, SA 5234 **Region** Adelaide Hills
T 0407 685 797 **F** (08) 8568 5069 **www**.coobarawines.com.au **Open** Wed–Sat 10–5, Sun & public hols 12–4
Winemaker David Cook, Mark Jamieson **Est.** 1992 **Cases** 2500 **Vyds** 12 ha
David Cook has worked in the wine industry for over 18 years, principally with Orlando but also with Jim Irvine, John Glaetzer and the late Neil Ashmead. As well as working full time for Orlando, he undertook oenology and viticulture courses, and – with support from his parents – planted 4 ha of cabernet sauvignon and merlot on the family property at Birdwood. In 1993 they purchased the adjoining property, planting 2 ha of riesling, and thereafter lifting the plantings of merlot and cabernet sauvignon to 4 ha each, plus 2.8 ha of shiraz and 0.5 ha of riesling. In 2003 David decided to commence wine production, a fortuitous decision given that the following year their long-term grape purchase contracts were not renewed. Coobara is an Aboriginal word meaning 'place of birds'.

ⵎⵎⵎⵎⵎ **Adelaide Hills Riesling 2008** Lovely fragrant lime and apple blossom aromas; early picking has resulted in a totally delicious marriage of finesse and flavour, and perfectly balanced acidity. Screwcap. 10.5% alc. **Rating** 95 **To** 2018 $20
Adelaide Hills Cabernet Merlot 2007 Very attractive bouquet of cassis, blackcurrant and spice followed by an equally appealing medium-bodied palate with a long, supple, gently spicy finish. Screwcap. 14% alc. **Rating** 94 **To** 2020 $22

ⵎⵎⵎⵎⵎ **Adelaide Hills Merlot 2007** Bright crimson; good cool-grown merlot, with a mix of red fruits/cassis and a savoury twist on the finish; light- to medium-bodied, but has enough depth and juicy fruit flavour. Screwcap. 14% alc. **Rating** 90 **To** 2015 $22

ⵎⵎⵎⵎ **Adelaide Hills Shiraz 2007** Spicy red berry aromas attest to the cool-grown origins, the light- to medium-bodied palate likewise, with fresh red berry fruits and subtle oak. Screwcap. 14% alc. **Rating** 89 **To** 2015 $25

Cooks Lot   ★★★

Cassilis Road, Mudgee, NSW 2850 **Region** Mudgee
T (02) 9550 3228 **F** (02) 9550 4390 **Open** Tues–Sat 10–5
Winemaker Duncan Cook, Ian McRae **Est.** 2002 **Cases** 4500 **Vyds** 1 ha
Duncan Cook runs a cellar door and café business at the Parklands Resort. He has a token planting, with most of the grapes purchased from growers in Mudgee and Orange; winemaking is at Miramar, and when Duncan has completed his oenology degree at CSU, plans to take over the winemaking role. The cellar door and café have artworks by Amber Subaki, an illustrator who specialises in nudes and portraits, and who designed the Cooks Lot label.

ⵎⵎⵎⵎ **Orange Pinot Gris 2008** A distinct bronze tinge suggests some extraction, as does the mouthfeel and flavour; honey, nougat and ripe pear flavours. Screwcap. 14% alc. **Rating** 88 **To** 2010 $18.99

Orange Sauvignon Blanc 2008 A generous wine from start to finish; ripe, tropical fruits, but needs more finesse and acidity. Screwcap. 13.4% alc. **Rating** 87 To 2010 $18.99

Coolangatta Estate   ★★★★☆

1335 Bolong Road, Shoalhaven Heads, NSW 2535 **Region** Shoalhaven Coast
T (02) 4448 7131 **F** (02) 4448 7997 **www**.coolangattaestate.com.au **Open** 7 days 10–5
Winemaker Tyrrell's **Est.** 1988 **Cases** 5000 **Vyds** 10.5 ha
Coolangatta Estate is part of a 150-ha resort with accommodation, restaurants, golf course, etc.; some of the oldest buildings were convict-built in 1822. It might be thought that the wines are tailored purely for the tourist market, but in fact the standard of viticulture is exceptionally high (immaculate Scott Henry trellising), and the contract winemaking is wholly professional. It has a habit of bobbing up with gold medals at Sydney and Canberra wine shows. Its 2001 Semillon was a prolific gold-medal winner up to '08, and the '05 looks as if it will follow in its elder brother's footsteps.

ŶŶŶŶŶ Aged Release Estate Grown Semillon 2003 Still as fresh as a daisy; bright acidity drives the palate through to a surging finish; difficult to see the end point for the wine, which will depend on the cork gods. 10.2% alc. **Rating** 94 **To** 2013 $27

ŶŶŶŶŶ Estate Grown Semillon 2008 Pale straw-green; very correct young semillon, with a vibrant palate and crisp acidity; lemon juice and cut grass sing on the back-palate and finish. All it needs is time, unless now with shellfish. Screwcap. 10.7% alc. **Rating** 93 **To** 2018 $19

ŶŶŶŶ Elizabeth Berry Cabernet Sauvignon 2007 Light, bright purple; aromatic, light-bodied juicy red fruits; well balanced; for immediate drinking. Screwcap. 13.5% alc. **Rating** 87 **To** 2010 $22
Estate Grown Tannat 2007 Strong colour; a variety known mainly for its all-powerful tannin, and this doesn't disappoint. There are, however, some sweet red fruit flavours that might justify cellaring the wine. Screwcap. 14% alc. **Rating** 87 To 2015 $25

Coombend Estate

Coombend via Swansea, Tas 7190 **Region** East Coast Tasmania
T (03) 6257 8881 **F** (03) 6257 8884 **Open** 7 days 10–5
Winemaker Tamar Ridge (Andrew Pirie) **Est.** 1985 **Cases** 3000
In 2005 Tamar Ridge acquired Coombend Estate, including all the assets and the business name. Tamar Ridge has immediately commenced the establishment of a large vineyard that will dwarf the existing 1.75 ha of cabernet sauvignon, 2.25 ha of sauvignon blanc, 0.5 ha of pinot noir and 0.3 ha of riesling. Exports to Sweden.

ŶŶŶŶŶ Pinot Noir 2006 Strong colour heralds a powerful wine with black plum fruits and a long, firm finish; will richly repay five years' cellaring. Screwcap. 13.5% alc. **Rating** 92 **To** 2014 $25
Sauvignon Blanc 2008 Strong varietal sauvignon, with a blend of tropical fruit and a touch of nettle; the palate is lean and focused, with traces of pungent fruit and mineral lingering on the finish. Screwcap. 13.5% alc. **Rating** 92 **To** 2012 $23

ŶŶŶŶ The Mail Run 2006 Solid medium-bodied palate; has depth; some pleasantly earthy/cedary characters developing. Cabernet Sauvignon/Merlot/Cabernet Franc. Screwcap. 14.5% alc. **Rating** 87 **To** 2013 $25

Cooyal Grove

Lot 9 Stoney Creek Road, Mudgee, NSW 2850 **Region** Mudgee
T (02) 6373 5337 **F** (02) 6373 5337 **Open** Not
Winemaker Michael Slater (Contract) **Est.** 1990 **Cases** 500 **Vyds** 3 ha

In 2002 the 10-ha Cooyal Grove property of vines, pistachio nut trees and olives was purchased by Sydney publican John Lenard, and Paul and Lydele Walker, a local Mudgee vigneron and his wife. The partners say, 'We have worked almost every weekend in the vineyard and grove, undertaking every task from planting, pruning, training, harvesting, bottling and labelling. Given that all of the partners are only 30 years old and not yet financially able to employ outside labour, we seem to call on every friend, relative and friend's relatives to assist. This has made for a feeling of building something from scratch which we are proud of.' The vineyards now include 0.5 ha each of chardonnay, semillon, sauvignon blanc, merlot, shiraz and cabernet sauvignon.

ΨΨΨΨΫ **Mudgee Semillon 2008** Tangy lemony fruit on a bright and zesty palate, with particularly good length; is one wine now, will become another in five years or so. Value. Screwcap. 10.5% alc. **Rating** 90 **To** 2017 $15

Cope-Williams ★★★★

221 Ochiltrees Road, Romsey, Vic 3434 **Region** Macedon Ranges
T (03) 5429 5595 **F** (03) 5429 6009 **www**.copewilliams.com.au **Open** By appt
Winemaker David Cowburn **Est.** 1977 **Cases** 3000 **Vyds** 6.5 ha
One of Macedon's pioneers, specialising in sparkling wines that are full flavoured but also producing excellent Chardonnay and Pinot Noir table wines in warmer vintages. A traditional 'English Green'–type cricket ground and Real Tennis complex are available for hire and are booked out most days from spring through until autumn. The facilities have been leased to an independent operator, which Gordon Cope-Williams says will allow him to concentrate on the estate vineyards (3 ha each of chardonnay and pinot noir and 0.5 ha of cabernet sauvignon) and the sparkling wines made from the chardonnay and pinot noir. Exports to Switzerland and NZ.

ΨΨΨΨΨ **R.O.M.S.E.Y. Vintage Brut 1991** Deep, vibrant gold; tiraged in '93, then given seven years on yeast lees before disgorgement, and another nine years on cork. Happily, still has good mousse, and fruit freshness thanks to 100% chardonnay base wine. 12% alc. **Rating** 94 **To** 2010 $50

ΨΨΨΨ **Chardonnay 2006** Developed straw colour; the palate, however, is crisp, minerally and lively, reflecting the low alcohol (and the very cool vineyard site). Screwcap. 12% alc. **Rating** 88 **To** 2012 $19
Cabernet Merlot 2002 Has had a leisurely journey (not bottled until '05) and has almost defeated the odds of the very cool site and low alcohol; the flavours are spicy/foresty/savoury, but there is also a gleam of red fruits. Screwcap. 12% alc. **Rating** 87 **To** 2012 $20

Coral Sea Wines   NR

PO Box 538, Bangalow, NSW 2479 **Region** South Australia
T 0417 010 066 **F** (02) 6687 2398 **www**.coralseawines.com **Open** Not
Winemaker Contract **Est.** 2005 **Cases** 6000
Coral Sea Wines is the virtual winery venture of John Cooley. The range of Semillon Sauvignon Blanc, Chardonnay, Merlot, Cabernet Merlot, Shiraz and Brut Cuvee comes from grapes 'grown in South Australia's premier warm climate regions'. The business donates an unspecified amount to the World Wildlife Fund's 'Save the Coral Sea Appeal', and are very modestly priced at $70 for a 6-pack delivered anywhere within Australia. Exports to the Pacific Islands.

Coriole ★★★★★

Chaffeys Road, McLaren Vale, SA 5171 **Region** McLaren Vale
T (08) 8323 8305 **www**.coriole.com **Open** Mon–Fri 10–5, w'ends & public hols 11–5
Winemaker Simon White **Est.** 1967 **Cases** 35 000 **Vyds** 50 ha
Justifiably best known for its Shiraz, which – in both the rare Lloyd Reserve and standard forms – is extremely impressive; it was also one of the first wineries to catch on to the

Italian fashion with Sangiovese, but its white varietal wines lose nothing by comparison. Also produces high-quality olive oil. Exports to all major markets.

ÝÝÝÝÝ **Lloyd Reserve McLaren Vale Shiraz 2006** A masterly display of McLaren Vale shiraz at its opulent best, flush with black fruits and dark chocolate with exceptionally fine tannins running through the back-palate and aftertaste. It deserves a high-quality cork or a Diam. Cork. 14.5% alc. **Rating** 96 **To** 2016 $70
McLaren Vale Nebbiolo Rose 2008 Vivid colour for the variety; strawberry, rose petal and cherry flavours run through the long, dry palate, which has excellent acidity. A rose with attitude. Screwcap. 12.5% alc. **Rating** 94 **To** 2010 $19
The Soloist Single Vineyard McLaren Vale Shiraz 2006 Vibrant crimson; an aromatic bouquet with licorice, dark chocolate, black fruits and oak all showing, and which are duly repeated on the finely structured palate, finishing with silky tannins. Screwcap. 14.5% alc. **Rating** 94 **To** 2021 $38
Mary Kathleen Reserve McLaren Vale Cabernet Merlot 2006
An imperious wine that is presently fending off all suitors for her affections, yet will reward those who persist. There are layers of blackcurrant, dark chocolate and cassis over a bed of ripe tannins, all locked in an embrace. Cork. 14% alc.
Rating 94 **To** 2019 $45

ÝÝÝÝÝ **Estate Grown McLaren Vale Shiraz 2006** Excellent colour; a luscious and rich palate, yet not jammy or alcoholic, the plush black fruits offset by balanced tannins and integrated oak. Screwcap. 14.5% alc. **Rating** 93 **To** 2021 $28
Museum Release McLaren Vale Shiraz 2001 An underrated vintage in much of SA; cedary spicy characters have joined the regional chocolate, the black fruits still securely in the mid-palate. Now or another five years. Cork. 14% alc.
Rating 92 **To** 2014 $30
Brunello Clone McLaren Vale Sangiovese 2006 'Brunello clone' shouts the bold black and white label. Coriole was one of the early movers with sangiovese, if not the first, but this clone is a recent arrival. It has good colour and, at least in this vintage, offers a balance of varietal fruit and tannins. Much promise. Screwcap. 13.5% alc. **Rating** 90 **To** 2014 $30
Adelaide Hills Nebbiolo 2007 The hardest road of all, a pinot noir with the tannins of a cabernet. This wine, in fact, goes close to achieving the impossible, the fruit light but vibrant, the tannins less than fearsome. Screwcap. 13.5% alc.
Rating 90 **To** 2014 $35

ÝÝÝÝ **Redstone McLaren Vale Shiraz 2006** A robust red; strong black fruits and tannins are locked in an Indian arm wrestle, which may never conclude as the strength of each is equal. Screwcap. 14.5% alc. **Rating** 89 **To** 2020 $18.50
McLaren Vale Sangiovese 2007 Light, slightly developed colour; cherry and spice before strongly savoury tannins on the finish take over proceedings. Screwcap. 14% alc. **Rating** 89 **To** 2011 $22
McLaren Vale Fiano 2008 Time will tell whether older vines will produce more distinctive flavours; at the moment it relies on texture, structure and balance. Screwcap. 12.5% alc. **Rating** 88 **To** 2012 $25
McLaren Vale Semillon Sauvignon Blanc 2008 An old hand with making white wines of this style, but McLaren Vale is not going to challenge Margaret River, now or ever; that said, has pleasant citrus and tropical fruit flavours. Screwcap. 13% alc. **Rating** 87 **To** 2010 $18.50
McLaren Vale Chenin Blanc 2008 Lively, ripe almost tropical fruit aromas; juicy, simple and clean, with good acidity on the finish. Screwcap. 13% alc.
Rating 87 **To** 2010 $15

Cosham ★★★★

101 Union Road, Carmel, WA 6076 **Region** Perth Hills
T (08) 9293 5424 **www**.coshamwines.com.au **Open** Fri–Sun & public hols 10–5
Winemaker Julie Smith, Anthony Sclanderi **Est.** 1989 **Cases** 800 **Vyds** 2.2 ha

Has grown significantly from its small base in recent years. The vineyard, planted on an old orchard, consists of chardonnay, pinot noir, cabernet sauvignon, merlot, shiraz, plus a couple of rows of petit verdot and cabernet franc, established between 1990 and '95. They grow in gravelly loam with some clay, but overall in a well-drained soil with good rainfall. The vineyard is managed organically, no synthetic chemicals for canopy management or weed control; and they are using Dacron collars around the trunks of the vines instead of insecticides to stop the damaging weevil infestations.

ŶŶŶŶŶ **Bickley Valley Chardonnay 2004** Very good; lovely harmonious wine, which has aged wonderfully well. Gold WA Wine Show '08. Screwcap. 13.2% alc. **Rating** 94 **To** 2012 $25

Cowra Estate   NR

Boorowa Road, Cowra, NSW 2794 **Region** Cowra
T (02) 9907 7735 **F** (02) 9907 7734 **Open** At The Quarry Restaurant Tues–Sun 10–4
Winemaker Tim Smith **Est.** 1973 **Cases** 5000 **Vyds** 73 ha
Cowra Estate was purchased from the family of founder Tony Gray by South African–born food and beverage entrepreneur John Geber in 1995. A vigorous promotional campaign has gained a higher domestic profile for the once export-oriented brand. John Geber is actively involved in the promotional effort and rightly proud of the wines. The Quarry Wine Cellars and Restaurant offer visitors a full range of Cowra Estate's wines, plus wines from other producers in the region. The Geber family, incidentally, also owns Chateau Tanunda in the Barossa Valley. Exports to Switzerland and Denmark.

Crabtree Watervale Wines

North Terrace, Watervale SA 5452 **Region** Clare Valley
T (08) 8843 0069 **www.**crabtreewines.com.au **Open** 7 days 10.30–4.50
Winemaker Kerri Thompson **Est.** 1979 **Cases** 5000 **Vyds** 13.2 ha
In October 2007 wine industry executives Richard Woods and Rasa Fabian purchased Crabtree and left Sydney corporate life for the ultimate seachange. Collectively, they have decades of sales and marketing experience, but this will be an entirely new world; both are adamant that Crabtree remain an estate brand, and therefore limited in volume. They have acquired a highly talented and very experienced winemaker in Kerri Thompson (see KT & The Falcon separate entry), particularly given that riesling (5.5 ha) is the leading estate-varietal wine.

ŶŶŶŶŶ **Riesling 2008** Clean, firm lemon and lime zest aromas, then a classic regional palate; picked 15 Feb and has excellent length and focus to the pure varietal fruit expression. Screwcap. 13% alc. **Rating** 95 **To** 2016 $22
Pomona Individual Block Watervale Riesling 2008 A less exuberant bouquet than its sister wine, but a beautifully precise palate, with crystalline acidity on the long, dry finish. Rheingau, not Moselle; 100 dozen made. Screwcap. 12% alc. **Rating** 94 **To** 2018 $30

ŶŶŶŶŶ **Picnic Hill Vineyard Shiraz 2006** A full-blooded (though medium-bodied) wine with delicious plum, black cherry and blackberry fruit, the palate having a juicy mouthfeel, the tannins ripe and fine. Screwcap. 14.5% alc. **Rating** 93 **To** 2018 $22
Hilltop Riesling 2008 An attractive early-drinking style, with an abundance of citrus and tropical/pineapple flavour, plus a subliminal touch of sweetness on the finish. Screwcap. 12.5% alc. **Rating** 90 **To** 2013 $22
Bay of Biscay Rose 2008 Bright, light fuschia; fragrant red cherry and raspberry fruit aromas flow into the palate, which is balanced by good acidity; from 62-year-old estate vines. Screwcap. 13% alc. **Rating** 90 **To** 2010 $22

ŶŶŶŶ **Three Sixty Degrees Shiraz Cabernet Sauvignon 2006** A very pleasant light- to medium-bodied wine with plum, blackberry and blackcurrant fruit flavours; for modest cellaring, but good now. Screwcap. 14.5% alc. **Rating** 88 **To** 2013 $22

Three Sixty Degrees Shiraz Cabernet Sauvignon 2005 A savoury/earthy style that nonetheless has good mouthfeel, texture and length, with a lively finish. Screwcap. 14% alc. **Rating** 88 **To** 2012 $20

Picnic Hill Vineyard Shiraz 2005 A supple, light- to medium-bodied wine, with pleasantly earthy overtones to its black fruits; has not been over-extracted or swamped in oak, but does have length. Screwcap. 14% alc. **Rating** 87 **To** 2012 $20

Clare Valley Muscat NV Caramel, toffee and mandarin aromas and flavours are held together by gentle fortifying spirit. Cork. 20% alc. **Rating** 87 **To** 2010 $22

Craig Avon Vineyard ★★★★

Craig Avon Lane, Merricks North, Vic 3926 **Region** Mornington Peninsula
T (03) 5989 7465 **F** (03) 5989 7615 **Open** By appt
Winemaker Ken Lang **Est.** 1986 **Cases** 900 **Vyds** 2 ha
The estate-grown wines are produced from 1.2 ha of chardonnay, and 0.4 ha each of pinot noir and cabernet sauvignon. They are competently made, clean and with pleasant fruit flavour. The wines are sold through the cellar door and by mailing list.

Chardonnay 2006 More mainstream than the '07, with pure and supple nectarine/melon driving the bouquet and palate, barrel ferment inputs well controlled. Screwcap. 14% alc. **Rating** 93 **To** 2016 $37

Reserve Chardonnay 2007 The bouquet is complex, with some funky white burgundy characters; the flavours with the herbal/cabbage edge consistent with the bouquet; a difficult message to deliver. Diam. 14% alc. **Rating** 91 **To** 2015 $38

Pinot Noir 2006 A potent, very foresty/briary wine that challenges rather than pleases. I'm not convinced that part may be due to the cork and the passage of time in bottle. Cork. 14% alc. **Rating** 89 **To** 2012 $35

Cabernet Sauvignon 2005 In the severe style the Mornington Peninsula dictates; although it avoids outright herbal/green tannins, this is not to say tannins don't impose themselves, for they do. Cork. 13.8% alc. **Rating** 87 **To** 2015 $36

Craigow ★★★★★

528 Richmond Road, Cambridge, Tas 7170 **Region** Southern Tasmania
T (03) 6248 5379 www.craigow.com.au **Open** 7 days Christmas to Easter (except public hols), or by appt
Winemaker Winemaking Tasmania (Julian Alcorso) **Est.** 1989 **Cases** 1500 **Vyds** 10 ha
Craigow has 5 ha of pinot noir and another 5 ha of riesling, chardonnay and gewurztraminer. Hobart surgeon Barry Edwards and wife Cathy have moved from being grapegrowers with only one wine to a portfolio of six wines, while continuing to sell most of their grapes. Craigow has an impressive museum release program; the best are outstanding, while others show the impact of sporadic bottle oxidation (a diminishing problem with each vintage now under screwcap). In 2008 Craigow won the Tasmanian Vineyard of the Award. There is a degree of poetic history: the first settler, who arrived in the 1820s, was a Scottish doctor (James Murdoch), who among other things grew opium poppies for medical use; by 1872 his descendants were making wine from grapes, gooseberries and cherries. There is some suggestion that the grapes, known then as black cluster, were in all probability, pinot noir.

Gewurztraminer 2008 Fragrant rose petal and lychee aromas and flavours; very good varietal character throughout; sweetness balanced by acidity. Screwcap. **Rating** 94 **To** 2013

Iced Riesling 2008 Pure lime and green apple bouquet; quite sweet with tightly focused acidity and a very attractive varietal riesling palate; long and fresh, and a long future ahead. Screwcap. 9% alc. **Rating** 94 **To** 2015

Pinot Noir 2007 Good colour; rich but succulent and smooth cherry, plum and spice; good balance and length; the only question is the amount of oak. Screwcap. 13.5% alc. **Rating** 89 **To** 2014

Craneford ★★★★

Moorundie Street, Truro, SA 5356 **Region** Barossa Valley
T (08) 8564 0003 **F** (08) 8564 0008 **www**.cranefordwines.com **Open** 7 days 10–5
Winemaker Carol Riebke, John Glaetzer (Consultant) **Est.** 1978 **Cases** 25 000
Since Craneford was founded in 1978 it has undergone a number of changes of both location
and ownership. The biggest change came in 2004 when the winery, by then housed in the
old country fire station building in Truro, was expanded and upgraded. In 2006 John Glaetzer
joined the team as consultant winemaker, with Carol Riebke the day-to-day winemaker.
Quality grapes are sourced from small growers. Exports to all major markets.

ΨΨΨΨΨ **Basket Pressed Barossa Valley Shiraz 2007** Multiple layers of blackberry,
plum, licorice and dark chocolate fruit supported by positive tannins and good
oak. Great effort from '07. Cork. 15% alc. **Rating** 92 **To** 2017 $26
Merlot 2007 Attractive redcurrant fruit runs through the long palate, which has a
particularly well-balanced finish. Cork. 13.5% alc. **Rating** 91 **To** 2017 $30.30
Quartet 2006 Considerably deeper, darker and riper flavours than the '07; some
vinous sleight of hand means that the alcohol is largely obscured by a good, full-
bodied palate and finish. Cabernet Sauvignon/Shiraz/Merlot/Grenache. Screwcap.
15.5% alc. **Rating** 91 **To** 2020 $22.35
Barossa Valley Cabernet Sauvignon 2007 While the colour is not
convincing, there are strong black fruit characters and an unexpected jab of dark
chocolate, improbably working well. Cork. 15% alc. **Rating** 90 **To** 2017 $26

ΨΨΨΨ **GSM 2007** While the fruit aromas and flavours have that distinctive sweet core,
and the alcohol adds to the sweetness on the finish, it is well balanced and has
plenty of character throughout. Cork. 15% alc. **Rating** 89 **To** 2014 $22.35
Quartet 2007 Good colour; has an attractive array of cassis and red berry fruits
on the light- to medium-bodied palate, which has ripe tannins and subtle oak.
Cork. 15% alc. **Rating** 89 **To** 2015 $22.35

Crawford River Wines ★★★★★

741 Hotspur Upper Road, Condah, Vic 3303 **Region** Henty
T (03) 5578 2267 **F** (03) 5578 2240 **www**.crawfordriverwines.com **Open** By appt
Winemaker John Thomson, Belinda Thomson **Est.** 1975 **Cases** 5000
Time flies, and it seems incredible that Crawford River has celebrated its 30th birthday. Once
a tiny outpost in a little-known wine region, Crawford River is now one of the foremost
producers of Riesling (and other excellent wines) thanks to the unremitting attention to detail
and skill of its founder and winemaker, John Thomson. His exceptionally talented and (dare
I say) attractive daughter Belinda has returned full time after completing her winemaking
degree and working along the way in Marlborough (NZ), Bordeaux, Ribera del Duero
(Spain), Bolgheri and Tuscany, and the Nahe (Germany), with Crawford River filling in the
gaps. Severe frosts in spring '06 led to secondary bud shoot, and thanks to skilled viticulture,
the small '07 crop ripened well, with only cabernet sauvignon lacking structure, hence the first
Crawford River rose. Exports to the UK, Ireland, Canada, Japan and South-East Asia.

ΨΨΨΨΨ **Riesling 2008** Pure lemon and lime with a touch of candied fruit complexity
on the bouquet; dry, linear and with a profound texture that carries the finish to
a long and very satisfactory conclusion, full of minerals and lemon fruit. Screwcap.
14% alc. **Rating** 95 **To** 2020 $33.50

ΨΨΨΨΨ **Cabernet Sauvignon 2004** Cool fruited with savoury black olive and cedar,
and a touch of leather from the development; firm, dry and quite structured, the
tannins are fine and draw the palate through to the savoury finish. Cork. 13.5% alc.
Rating 91 **To** 2015 $40.50
Sauvignon Blanc Semillon 2008 Lifted tropical fruit on the bouquet; the palate
is fresh, and offers a little sweetness to counterbalance the tangy acidity. Screwcap.
13% alc. **Rating** 90 **To** 2012 $24.50

Creed of Barossa

Lyndoch Hill Retreat, Cnr Barossa Valley Way/Hermann Thumm Drive, Lyndoch, SA 5351
Region Barossa Valley
T (08) 8524 4046 **F** (08) 8524 4046 **www**.creedwines.com **Open** 7 days 10–5
Winemaker Daniel Eggleton **Est.** 2005 **Cases** 10 000
This is the venture of luxuriantly bearded Mark Creed and business partner (and winemaker) Daniel Eggleton. Their first wine (an intriguing blend of shiraz, cabernet franc and viognier) was made in 2004, with a number of different Shirazs, Merlot, Cabernet Franc and a little Grenache in the pipeline. The partners also own a consulting wing, called C & E Dry Grown Projects Pty Ltd, to make wines for others, and to collaboratively market and distribute those wines. Prior to the 2007 vintage the partners built a small winery, and in mid-2008 moved the cellar door to the Lyndoch Hill Retreat complex, which includes a restaurant, accommodation, conference facilities and garden. Delayed bottling of the 2008 vintage wines has prevented tastings for this edition; the rating is that of last year. Exports to the UK, the US, Canada, Phillipines, Malaysia, China and NZ.

Crisford Winery

556 Hermitage Road, Pokolbin, NSW 2022 **Region** Lower Hunter Valley
T (02) 6574 7120 **Open** Not
Winemaker Neal Crisford **Est.** 1990 **Cases** 300 **Vyds** 2.5 ha
Carol and Neal Crisford have established a vineyard of merlot and cabernet franc. Neal produces educational videos on wine used in TAFE colleges and by other wine educators. The wine is sold through the Hunter Valley Wine Society.

ŸŸŸŸŸ **Hunter Valley Cabernet Franc Petit Verdot Merlot 2007** Bright, light crimson-purple; an ultra-fresh blend of red fruits, spotlessly clean; the light-bodied palate is fruit-driven, oak and tannins very much in the background. Screwcap. 13.1% alc. **Rating** 90 **To** 2014 $22.95

ŸŸŸŸ **Hunter Valley Mudgee Cabernet Franc Merlot 2006** Similar colour to the Cabernet Franc/Petit Verdot/Merlot; has more cedary/spicy and tobacco flavours; strange that the petit verdot makes such an impact. Screwcap. 13.1% alc. **Rating** 88 **To** 2013 $22.95

Crittenden Estate

25 Harrisons Road, Dromana, Vic 3936 **Region** Mornington Peninsula
T (03) 5981 8322 **F** (03) 5981 8366 **www**.crittendenwines.com.au **Open** 7 days 11–4
Winemaker Garry Crittenden, Rollo Crittenden **Est.** 2003 **Cases** 5000 **Vyds** 14 ha
The wheel of fortune has turned full circle with son Rollo Crittenden returning to the (new) family wine business established by father Garry in 2003. In so doing, both father and son have severed ties with Dromana Estate, the old family business. For good measure, winemaking will be moved to a new winery at Patterson Lakes.

ŸŸŸŸŸ **The Zumma Pinot Noir 2007** The massive, non-eco-friendly bottle does accurately foretell the high quality of this effortlessly bright and silky wine, which flows smoothly from start to finish. Screwcap. 13% alc. **Rating** 94 **To** 2015 $49

ŸŸŸŸŸ **Mornington Peninsula Pinot Noir 2007** Star-bright, light crimson; fragrant cherry and strawberry aromas repeated on the fore-palate, the wine surging on the crisp contrasting acidity of the finish. Screwcap. 13.5% alc. **Rating** 92 **To** 2015 $34
Mornington Peninsula Chardonnay 2007 Very much in traditional Mornington Peninsula style, the influence of partial mlf very evident; is a finely honed and balanced wine, but would have had more length in the absence of mlf. Screwcap. 13.5% alc. **Rating** 90 **To** 2014 $34
Los Hermanos Albarino 2008 Vibrant and zesty bouquet of lemon, spice and a touch of straw; the lively acidity dominates the palate, but the fruit stands up to it, and shines through on the light-bodied, long and zesty finish. Screwcap. 12.5% alc. **Rating** 90 **To** 2012 $28.50

ŢŢŢŢ Los Hermanos Tempranillo 2008 A deeply coloured example of the variety; medium- to full-bodied with generous, mouthfilling black fruits, and a savoury twist courtesy of the tannins. Could quite conceivably repay cellaring. Screwcap. 13.5% alc. **Rating** 89 **To** 2015
Mornington Peninsula Pinot Grigio 2008 Has textural complexity, achieved with the loss of some brightness to the fruit; nonetheless, interesting wine. Screwcap. 13% alc. **Rating** 87 **To** 2010 $30

Cullen Wines   ★★★★★

Caves Road, Cowaramup, WA 6284 **Region** Margaret River
T (08) 9755 5277 **F** (08) 9755 5550 **www.**cullenwines.com.au **Open** 7 days 10–4
Winemaker Vanya Cullen, Trevor Kent **Est.** 1971 **Cases** 20 000 **Vyds** 45 ha
One of the pioneers of Margaret River, which has always produced long-lived wines of highly individual style from the mature estate vineyards. The vineyard has progressed beyond organic to biodynamic certification and, subsequently, has become the first vineyard and winery in Australia to be certified carbon neutral. This requires the calculation of all of the carbon used and carbon dioxide emitted in the winery, and the carbon is then offset by the planting of new trees. Winemaking is now in the hands of Vanya Cullen, daughter of the founders; she is possessed of an extraordinarily good palate. It is impossible to single out any particular wine from the top echelon; all are superb. Exports to all major markets.

ŢŢŢŢŢ Mangan Vineyard Margaret River Sauvignon Blanc Semillon 2008 A magical combination of delicacy on the bouquet and explosive intensity on the racing palate; 28% barrel ferment has been absorbed into the wine; wild yeast. 70/30. Screwcap. 11.5% alc. **Rating** 96 **To** 2015 $35
Kevin John Margaret River Chardonnay 2006 Immaculately balanced and structured, the components of fruit and oak so seamless that the near-explosive velocity of the build up in intensity of white peach and grapefruit on the finish and aftertaste takes you by surprise. Screwcap. 13.5% alc. **Rating** 96 **To** 2021 $70
Mangan Margaret River Merlot Petit Verdot Malbec 2007 Strikingly dense colour; a roughly equal blend of the three varieties, deliciously opulent and velvety; has spent only four months in oak but is not callow or tannic; masterly winemaking. Screwcap. 14.5% alc. **Rating** 95 **To** 2022 $45
Margaret River Sauvignon Blanc Semillon 2008 Has every bit as much flavour as the Mangan, but the fruit is a little riper and more opulent, the 27% barrel ferment a little more obvious; that said, has great complexity and power; 81/19. Screwcap. 12.5% alc. **Rating** 94 **To** 2014 $35
Diana Madeline 2006 Bright hue, although not particularly deep; lighter fruit style than usual, albeit with normal tannin structure; needs three years before entering its plateau. Cabernet Sauvignon/Merlot/Petit Verdot/Cabernet Franc/ Malbec. Screwcap. 13% alc. **Rating** 94 **To** 2014 $105

ŢŢŢŢŢ Margaret River White 2008 The dominant Sauvignon Blanc/Semillon blend inevitably (and appropriately) results in a full-flavoured wine smoothed by a small amount of chardonnay and verdelho. Screwcap. 12.5% alc. **Rating** 90 **To** 2012 $19

Cumulus Wines

PO Box 41, Cudal, NSW 2864 **Region** Orange
T (02) 6390 7900 **F** (02) 6364 2388 **www.**cumuluswines.com.au **Open** During Orange Food Week (Apr) and Wine Week (Oct)
Winemaker Debbie Lauritz, Andrew Bilankij **Est.** 2004 **Cases** 200 000 **Vyds** 500 ha
Cumulus Wines was established in 2004, and is now majority owned by the Berardo Group of Portugal (which has numerous world-size wine investments in Portugal, Canada and Madeira). Over 500 ha of vineyards, planted in the late 1990s, focus on shiraz, cabernet sauvignon, chardonnay and merlot. The wines are released under three brands: Rolling, from the Central Ranges Zone; Climbing, solely from Orange fruit; and a third, yet to be named, super-premium from the best of the estate vineyard blocks. Exports to the UK, the US and other major markets.

♟♟♟♟♟ **Rolling Shiraz 2007** Strong crimson; has a supple, medium-bodied palate with an abundance of blackberry fruit well supported by ripe tannins and integrated oak; attractive wine. Great value. Screwcap. 13.5% alc. **Rating** 92 **To** 2017 $17
Climbing Orange Shiraz 2007 Vivid colour; dark plum, bramble and a little spice; medium-bodied, with clever use of oak; dry and a little savoury on the finish. Screwcap. 14% alc. **Rating** 90 **To** 2014 $20

♟♟♟♟ **Rolling Central Ranges Chardonnay 2008** Restrained white peach and melon bouquet; fine and focused, with an elegant interplay of oak and fruit; understated with generosity. Value. Screwcap. 12.5% alc. **Rating** 89 **To** 2012 $17
Climbing Orange Pinot Gris 2008 Slight bronzing; off-dry with candied orange and a touch of pear; fresh and flavoursome on the finish. Screwcap. 12% alc. **Rating** 88 **To** 2011 $20
Climbing Orange Cabernet Sauvignon 2007 Plum and cedar bouquet; soft and fleshy fruit, with good concentration and generous fruit weight. Screwcap. 13.5% alc. **Rating** 88 **To** 2013 $20

Cupitt's Winery   NR
60 Washburton Road, Milton, NSW 2539 **Region** Shoalhaven Coast
T (02) 4455 7888 **F** (02) 4455 7688 **www.**cupittwines.com.au **Open** Wed–Sun 10–5
Winemaker Rosie Cupitt **Est.** 2007 **Cases** 1200 **Vyds** 4 ha
Griff and Rosie Cupitt run what is effectively a combined winery and restaurant complex, taking full advantage of the location on the south coast of NSW. Rosie studied oenology at CSU and has more than a decade of vintage experience, taking in France and Italy; she also happens to be the Shoalhaven representative for Slow Food International. The Cupitts have 4 ha of vines centred on chambourcin and merlot, and buy viognier from Beechworth and Rutherglen, chardonnay and cabernet franc from the Southern Highlands, and cabernet sauvignon from Beechworth. A visit to the website is recommended.

Curlewis Winery   ★★★★★
55 Navarre Road, Curlewis, Vic 3222 **Region** Geelong
T (03) 5250 4567 **F** (03) 5250 4567 **www.**curlewiswinery.com.au **Open** By appt
Winemaker Rainer Breit **Est.** 1998 **Cases** 2500
Rainer Breit and partner Wendy Oliver purchased their property in 1996 with 1.6 ha of what were then 11-year-old pinot noir vines. Rainer, a self-taught winemaker, uses the full bag of pinot noir winemaking tricks: cold-soaking, hot-fermentation, post-ferment maceration, part inoculated and part wild yeast use, prolonged lees contact, and bottling the wine neither fined nor filtered. While Rainer and Wendy are self-confessed 'pinotphiles', they have planted a little chardonnay and buy a little locally grown shiraz and chardonnay. Exports to Canada, Sweden, Malaysia, Singapore and Hong Kong.

♟♟♟♟♟ **Reserve Geelong Pinot Noir 2007** Fractionally deeper colour; a particularly rich, velvety smooth pinot seemingly achieved without effort, and certainly without any alcohol push; will evolve for seven years or more; well worth all the patience at your command. Screwcap. 13% alc. **Rating** 96 **To** 2017 $70
Geelong Pinot Noir 2007 Deep, bright colour tinges of crimson-purple; here the depth of the plum and black cherry fruit needs less elaboration; has excellent balance, and just the right amount of oak and tannin support. Screwcap. 13% alc. **Rating** 95 **To** 2015 $42
Geelong Syrah 2007 Has an unusually fragrant bouquet of spice and floral red fruits; the palate moves well to the left, with strong savoury and spicy, licorice and black fruits joining the red notes of the bouquet. Screwcap. 13.5% alc. **Rating** 94 **To** 2022 $32

♟♟♟♟♟ **Bel Sel Geelong Pinot Noir 2007** Clear colour; shows the experience of winemaker Rainer Breit; an unambiguously good pinot at this price, with a complex array of flavours within a silky mid-palate and a textural, light tannin finish. Screwcap. 14% alc. **Rating** 93 **To** 2014 $26

Curly Flat   ★★★★★

263 Collivers Road, Lancefield, Vic 3435 **Region** Macedon Ranges
T (03) 5429 1956 **F** (03) 5429 2256 **www**.curlyflat.com **Open** W'ends 1–5 or by appt
Winemaker Phillip Moraghan, Matt Regan **Est.** 1991 **Cases** 5000
Phillip and Jeni Moraghan began developing Curly Flat in 1992, drawing in part on Phillip's
working experience in Switzerland in the late 1980s, and with a passing nod to Michael
Leunig. With ceaseless help and guidance from the late Laurie Williams (and others), the
Moraghans painstakingly established 8.5 ha of pinot noir, 3.5 ha of chardonnay and 0.7 ha of
pinot gris, and a multi-level, gravity-flow winery. Exports to the UK, Japan and Hong Kong.

▼▼▼▼▼ **Macedon Ranges Chardonnay 2007** Bright straw-green; a high-quality wine
that is at peace with its maker – and itself; the components are harmoniously
balanced, yet are quite vocal, notably the white peach, grapefruit and nectarine
flavours on the long palate. Screwcap. 13.6% alc. **Rating** 96 **To** 2017 $40
Macedon Ranges Pinot Noir 2006 In the mainstream of the Curly Flat
pinot style; supple, velvety red fruits open the story, and persist while complex
spicy/foresty notes whisper in the background. Pleasure now or later. Screwcap.
13.5% alc. **Rating** 95 **To** 2016 $46

▼▼▼▼▽ **Williams Crossing Chardonnay 2007** A vibrant, crisp and zesty wine, with a
strong citrus component running through its length, buttressing the nectarine fruit
and French oak. Bargain. Screwcap. 13.3% alc. **Rating** 93 **To** 2014 $20
Williams Crossing Pinot Noir 2007 Clear red; strong varietal expression, with
red fruits set against complexing stem and tannin notes on the finish; very good
length, likewise value. Screwcap. 13.5% alc. **Rating** 93 **To** 2014 $24
Macedon Ranges Pinot Grigio 2008 Straw-green, not common with pinot
grigio; winemaking inputs have given the wine more texture and structure than
usual, and the finish, while long, is bone dry. A serious wine. Screwcap. 11.7% alc.
Rating 93 **To** 2012 $24
Williams Crossing Pinot Noir 2006 Retains bright hue with no browning;
fragrant cherry aromas with an intriguing hint of peach lead into a light-bodied but
vibrant and long palate. Great value. Screwcap. 13.5% alc. **Rating** 93 **To** 2012 $22

Currency Creek Estate   ★★★

Winery Road, Currency Creek, SA 5214 **Region** Currency Creek
T (08) 8555 4069 **www**.currencycreekwines.com.au **Open** 7 days 10–5
Winemaker John Loxton **Est.** 1969 **Cases** 10 000 **Vyds** 65 ha
For over 35 years this family-owned vineyard and relatively low-profile winery has produced
some outstanding wood-matured whites and pleasant, soft reds selling at attractive prices.
Shiraz takes the lion's share of the plantings, then cabernet sauvignon, sauvignon blanc,
chardonnay, riesling and semillon. It will be apparent from this that the essential part of the
grape production is sold. Exports to the UK, the US and China.

▼▼▼▼ **The Black Swamp 2005** Wine names can be unappealing, and this beats NZ's
Muddy Water winery; the wine itself is black and tarry as befits its blend of
Cabernet Sauvignon/Merlot/Malbec/Petit Verdot. Screwcap. 14.5% alc. **Rating** 87
To 2015 $20

Cuttaway Hill   ★★★★

PO Box 630, Bowral, NSW 2576 **Region** Southern Highlands
T (02) 4871 1004 **F** (02) 4871 1005 **www**.cuttawayhillwines.com.au **Open** Not
Winemaker Monarch Winemaking Services **Est.** 1998 **Cases** 12 000 **Vyds** 23.5 ha
Owned by the O'Neil family, Cuttaway Hill is one of the largest vineyard properties in
the Southern Highlands, with three vineyard sites. The original Cuttaway Hill vineyard at
Mittagong has chardonnay, merlot, cabernet sauvignon and shiraz. The Allambie vineyard, on
the light sandy loam soils of Ninety Acre Hill, is planted to sauvignon blanc, pinot gris and
pinot noir. The third and newest vineyard, at Maytree, west of Moss Vale, in a relatively drier

and warmer meso-climate, has cabernet sauvignon, merlot and pinot noir (and a small amount of chardonnay). The standard of both viticulture (headed by Mark Bourne) and contract winemaking is evident in the quality of the wines, not to mention the growth in production and sales. Exports to the UK, the US, Canada, Sweden and China.

ΨΨΨΨ? **Southern Highlands Sauvignon Blanc 2008** Strong varietal, cut grass and herbaceous aromas; fresh, lively and fine on the palate, with good acidity and generous fruit weight on the finish. Screwcap. 13% alc. **Rating** 90 **To** 2013 $20
Southern Highlands Pinot Gris 2008 A true gris style, with ripe pear fruit, and a touch of spice for complexity; quite rich and unctuous, but with fresh lively acidity on the finish. Screwcap. 14.5% alc. **Rating** 90 **To** 2014 $25

Cypress Post   ★★★

PO Box 1124, Oxley, Qld 4075 **Region** Granite Belt
T (07) 3375 4083 **F** (07) 3375 4083 **www.**cypresspost.com.au **Open** Not
Winemaker Peter Scudamore-Smith MW (Contract) **Est.** 2000 **Cases** 300 **Vyds** 3.5 ha
The Olsen family – headed by doctors Michael (a consultant botanist) and Catherine – has a strong botanical and conservation background continuing over two generations. The property has been registered under the Land for Wildlife program and will continue to be run on these principles, blending science and caring for the future. Plantings include shiraz (2 ha), viognier, marsanne (1 ha each) and pinot gris (0.5 ha).

ΨΨΨΨ **6000 Granite Belt Shiraz Rose 2008** Light crimson; unusual style, with far more texture than normal; red berry fruits and a dry finish. Food-style rose. Screwcap. 13% alc. **Rating** 87 **To** 2009 $18.50

D'Angelo Estate   ★★★☆

41 Bayview Road, Officer, Vic 3809 **Region** Yarra Valley
T 0417 055 651 **F** (03) 5943 1032 **www.**dangelowines.com.au **Open** By appt
Winemaker Benny D'Angelo **Est.** 1994 **Cases** 5500 **Vyds** 15 ha
The business dates back to 1994 when Benny D'Angelo's father planted a small block of pinot noir for home winemaking. One thing led to another, with Benny taking over winemaking and doing well in amateur wine shows. This led to the planting of more pinot and some cabernet sauvignon. Expansion continued with the 2001 acquisition of a 4-ha site at Officer, which has been planted to six clones of pinot noir, and small parcels of cabernet sauvignon and shiraz. Grapes are also purchased from a wide range of vineyards stretching from Gippsland to Langhorne Creek.

ΨΨΨΨ? **Officer Sauvignon Blanc 2008** Bright, crisp and fresh, with good balance between grassy/herbal notes on the one side and more tropical fruit on the other. Screwcap. 12.8% alc. **Rating** 90 **To** 2010 $20

ΨΨΨΨ **Fugiastro Officer Pinot Noir 2006** Light colour; elegant light-bodied wine with quite vivid fruit on the mid-palate, before a spicy, gently savoury finish. Screwcap. 13.8% alc. **Rating** 89 **To** 2013 $25
Il Don 2005 The wine spent 30 months in new oak, mainly, if not entirely, American, and it is this that dominates the wine. Shiraz/Cabernet Sauvignon. Diam. 15% alc. **Rating** 89 **To** 2013 $50
Lady Chardonnay 2008 A quite complex, but soft, light- to medium-bodied wine, with creamy cashew notes to the stone fruit and melon of the palate. Screwcap. 13.8% alc. **Rating** 88 **To** 2011 $20
Officer Pinot Grigio 2008 Has authentic pinot grigio style, with nashi pear and apple aromas and flavours, together with a hint of musk. Screwcap. 13.2% alc. **Rating** 88 **To** 2010 $20
Fugiastro Yarra Valley Pinot Noir 2006 Very light colour; despite its marginally higher alcohol, which is adequate, has green stemmy notes throughout; does have length and the extract is not excessive. Screwcap. 14% alc. **Rating** 88 **To** 2012 $25

Gin Gin Bin Officer Blanc de Noir NV Fresh, crisp and very well balanced, particularly given its youth and pinot noir base; disgorged later than the previous release. Cork. 11.5% alc. **Rating** 88 **To** 2011 $20

d'Arenberg ★★★★★

Osborn Road, McLaren Vale, SA 5171 **Region** McLaren Vale
T (08) 8329 4888 **F** (08) 8323 9862 **www.**darenberg.com.au **Open** 7 days 10–5
Winemaker Chester Osborn, Jack Walton **Est.** 1912 **Cases** 250 000 **Vyds** 185.7 ha
Nothing, they say, succeeds like success. Few operations in Australia fit this dictum better than d'Arenberg, which has kept its almost 100-year-old heritage while moving into the 21st century with flair and elan. As at last count the d'Arenberg vineyards, at various locations, have 22 varieties planted (more than any other single producer), as well as 120 growers in McLaren Vale. There is no question that its past, present and future revolve around its considerable portfolio of richly robed red wines: shiraz, cabernet sauvignon and grenache being the cornerstones, but with over 20 varietal and/or blend labels spanning the gulf between roussanne and mourvedre. The quality of the wines is unimpeachable, the prices logical and fair. It has a profile in the both the UK and the US that far larger companies would love to have.

ŸŸŸŸŸ The Feral Fox Adelaide Hills Pinot Noir 2007 Bright colour; a fragrant bouquet, with strong sous bois and stem notes takes time to tell its tale; interesting palate, with similar tangy flavours; excellent length; best example to date. Screwcap. 14.5% alc. **Rating** 94 **To** 2015 $30
The Footbolt Shiraz 2006 Full-bodied, strongly regional style, without excess alcohol or any dead fruit; attractive mix of blackberry, dark chocolate and a touch of spicy/toasty oak; ripe tannins. Screwcap. 14.5% alc. **Rating** 94 **To** 2016 $19.95

ŸŸŸŸŸ The Custodian Grenache 2006 Clear colour; fragrant red berry aromas; has good structure and intensity; red and black berry fruits, some spice and chocolate nuances and fine tannins. Screwcap. 14.5% alc. **Rating** 93 **To** 2014 $19.95
The Dry Dam McLaren Vale Riesling 2008 A somewhat unlikely part of the new wave of rieslings with deliberate residual sugar and low alcohol: unlikely because of the region and because the wine is as good as it is. Drink while fresh. Screwcap. 11.5% alc. **Rating** 92 **To** 2013 $16.95
The Love Grass McLaren Vale Shiraz 2006 Dark chocolate and mulberry fruit bouquet; medium-bodied and quite tannic, but with ample sweet fruit to tidy it up; a solid, slightly savoury style. Screwcap. 14.5% alc. **Rating** 91 **To** 2014 $25
d'Arry's Original Shiraz Grenache 2006 The colour hue is good, but not as deep as expected from the vintage; the usual attractive medium-bodied palate offers a mix of blackberry, dark cherry and chocolate fruit, finishing with persistent tannins. Screwcap. 14.5% alc. **Rating** 91 **To** 2015 $19.95
The Broken Fishplate Adelaide Hills Sauvignon Blanc 2008 Full of character and flavour in a rich tropical fruit spectrum, finishing with bracing acidity. Screwcap. 13% alc. **Rating** 90 **To** 2010 $19

ŸŸŸŸ Nostalgia Rare NV Rich tawny/raisiny style, which despite its age doesn't show much rancio, simply because it is so luscious. Cork. 20% alc. **Rating** 89 **To** 2010 $32.95
The Stump Jump Riesling 2008 Bright lemon juice bouquet; soft, fleshy, clean and accessible palate; best enjoyed in its youth. Screwcap. 13% alc. **Rating** 88 **To** 2013 $11.95
The Stump Jump Sauvignon Blanc 2008 Ripe tropical bouquet with a slight pungent edge; good weight, crisp and well defined. Screwcap. 13% alc. **Rating** 88 **To** 2012 $11.95
The Laughing Magpie Shiraz Viognier 2007 A little too much viognier apricot; a wine with good flavour and very pronounced acidity; lacks balance. Screwcap. 14.5% alc. **Rating** 88 **To** 2013 $30

The Stump Jump Lightly Wooded Chardonnay 2008 Offers a very ripe bouquet of apricot, nectarine and a touch of spice; an intensely fruit sweet palate, provides generosity, if just a little one-dimensional. Screwcap. 13% alc. **Rating** 87 To 2012 $11.95

Dal Zotto Wines ★★★★☆

Main Road, Whitfield, Vic 3733 **Region** King Valley
T (03) 5729 8321 **F** (03) 5729 8490 **www.**dalzotto.com.au **Open** 7 days 10–5
Winemaker Otto Dal Zotto, Michael Dal Zotto **Est.** 1987 **Cases** 15 000 **Vyds** 48 ha
The Dal Zotto family is a King Valley institution; ex-tobacco growers, then contract grapegrowers and now primarily focused on their Dal Zotto Estate range. Led by Otto and Elena, and with sons Michael and Christian handling winemaking and sales/marketing, respectively, the family is producing increasing amounts of wine from its substantial estate vineyard. The cellar door is in the centre of Whitfield, and is also home to Rinaldo's Restaurant. Exports to the UK and China.

ΨΨΨΨΨ **King Valley Arneis 2008** Attractive pear flesh and mineral aromas fairly leap out on the bouquet; the palate is generous and maintains a slight Italian savoury twist to the fruit; fresh and vibrant acidity draws out the palate, showing how delicious this variety can be. Screwcap. 12.5% alc. **Rating** 94 To 2012 $22

ΨΨΨΨΨ **King Valley Puccini Prosecco 2008** Pale colour; bright pear flesh aromas with a touch of citrus; the palate is lively, fine and with a gentle touch of sugar, quite appealing; well balanced on the finish, it should be enjoyed in the full flush of youth. Diam. 11.5% alc. **Rating** 90 To 2011 $17.50
King Valley Pinot Grigio 2008 A strong savoury straw component works well with a touch of lemon and pear; the palate has good weight and texture, and the finish is dry and savoury. Screwcap. 12.5% alc. **Rating** 90 To 2012 $24.99
King Valley Rosata 2008 Bright pale pink; vibrant red berry fruit with a little savoury bramble on the side; the flavour is fresh and lively, the finish dry; good value and good fun. Screwcap. 12.5% alc. **Rating** 90 To 2012 $15
Contro Shiraz 2004 A robust, full-flavoured, indeed full-frontal, wine; licorice, dark chocolate and spice components very obvious, as are the tannins. Needs time. Cork. 14% alc. **Rating** 90 To 2014 $40

ΨΨΨΨ **King Valley Barbera 2006** Has good varietal expression, with notes of spice and herb to the black fruits, but shortens on the back-palate and finish. Screwcap. 13.5% alc. **Rating** 87 To 2013 $22

Dalfarras ★★★★

PO Box 123, Nagambie, Vic 3608 **Region** Nagambie Lakes
T (03) 5794 2637 **F** (03) 5794 2360 **Open** At Tahbilk
Winemaker Alister Purbrick, Alan George **Est.** 1991 **Cases** 10 000
The personal project of Alister Purbrick and artist wife Rosa (née Dalfarra), whose paintings adorn the labels of the wines. Alister, of course, is best known as winemaker at Tahbilk, the family winery and home, but this range of wines is intended to (in Alister's words) 'allow me to expand my winemaking horizons and mould wines in styles different from Tahbilk'. Exports to Sweden.

ΨΨΨΨΨ **Sauvignon Blanc 2008** Very good varietal character; the aromas and flavours run from grassy to tropical, but without any break in the line; a juicy mouthful and great value; seems cool-grown, no region of origin stated. Screwcap. 13% alc. **Rating** 91 To 2010 $15.95

ΨΨΨΨ **Marsanne Viognier 2008** Marsanne is definitely the big brother in this relationship, providing the structure and the vitality, but viognier does add a touch of fruit interest; development potential courtesy of the marsanne. Screwcap. 13.5% alc. **Rating** 88 To 2012 $15.95

Cabernet Sangiovese 2006 Relatively light-coloured; the tannins hit from the word go, presumably as much or more from the sangiovese as the cabernet; precise and long palate within that context. Screwcap. 14% alc. **Rating** 88 **To** 2014 $15.95

Dalrymple Estate ★★★★

1337 Pipers Brook Road, Pipers Brook, Tas 7254 **Region** Northern Tasmania
T (03) 6382 7222 **F** (03) 6382 7222 www.dalrymplevineyards.com.au **Open** 7 days 10–5
Winemaker Natalie Fryar **Est.** 1987 **Cases** 4000 **Vyds** 15 ha
Dalrymple Estate was established many years ago by the Mitchell and Sundstrup families; the vineyard and brand were acquired by Hill Smith Family Vineyards in late 2007. Plantings are split between pinot noir and sauvignon blanc, and the wine is made at Jansz Tasmania.

ꟼꟼꟼꟼ **Sauvignon Blanc 2008** Ample tropical and gooseberry fruit on both bouquet and palate; easy-access style for immediate drinking. Vino-Lok. 11.5% alc. **Rating** 87 **To** 2009 $24.95
Pinot Noir 2007 Red cherry, almost maraschino, flavours; light- medium-bodied, and has balance and length. Vino-Lok. 14% alc. **Rating** 87 **To** 2012 $29.95

Dalwhinnie ★★★★★

448 Taltarni Road, Moonambel, Vic 3478 **Region** Pyrenees
T (03) 5467 2388 **F** (03) 5467 2237 www.dalwhinnie.com.au **Open** 7 days 10–5
Winemaker David Jones, Gary Baldwin (Consultant) **Est.** 1976 **Cases** 4500
David and Jenny Jones are making wines with tremendous depth of fruit flavour, reflecting the relatively low-yielding but very well-maintained vineyards. It is hard to say whether the Chardonnay, the Cabernet Sauvignon or the Shiraz is the more distinguished. A further 8 ha of shiraz (with a little viognier) were planted in 1999 on a block acquired on Taltarni Road. A 50-tonne contemporary high-tech winery now allows the wines to be made onsite, with three single-vineyard Shirazs in the pipeline under the Eagles Series, South West Rocks and Goddess labels. On the other side of the ledger, the Pinot Noir has been discontinued. Exports to the UK and other major markets.

ꟼꟼꟼꟼꟼ **Moonambel Shiraz 2007** Brilliant crimson colour; a marvellous combination of elegance and intensity, the rippling red and black fruit flavours perfectly balanced by silky tannins and oak; extreme length and great balance. ProCork. 13.5% alc. **Rating** 97 **To** 2020 $55
Moonambel Chardonnay 2006 Bright, light colour; a particularly distinguished wine, at once complex yet seamless, the generosity of the fruit expressed more in structure than flavour, the oak perfectly integrated and balanced; has great line and length. ProCork. 13.1% alc. **Rating** 96 **To** 2020 $35

ꟼꟼꟼꟼꟼ **Moonambel Pinot 2007** Continues to surprise that Moonambel can produce fragrantly varietal pinot noir; early picking essential, and while the wine is strongly savoury, has good texture and length. ProCork. 13% alc. **Rating** 91 **To** 2012 $38
Moonambel Cabernet 2007 Slightly diffuse colour; the palate is on the austere side in terms of flavour even before the slightly dry tannins take hold of the finish; is this the drought speaking? ProCork. 13.5% alc. **Rating** 90 **To** 2017 $48

Darling Park ★★★★★

232 Red Hill Road, Red Hill, Vic 3937 **Region** Mornington Peninsula
T (03) 5989 2324 www.darlingparkwinery.com **Open** Fri–Mon 11–5 (7 days Jan)
Winemaker Judy Gifford **Est.** 1989 **Cases** 2000 **Vyds** 2.2 ha
Josh and Karen Liberman have energetically expanded the range of Darling Park's wines while maintaining a high-quality standard. The Art of Wine club offers back vintages, as well as previews of upcoming releases. Wine labels feature artworks from the owners' collections; artists include Sidney Nolan, Arthur Boyd, John Perceval and Charles Blackman. The most important source of grapes for the venture come from Hugh Robinson, who produces some

of the best grapes available for sale on the Mornington Peninsula. The arrangement with Darling Park is a permanent one, with purchase by area, rather than by tonnes of grapes produced.

🍷🍷🍷🍷🍷 **Reserve Chardonnay 2005** Fine, intense and tight, with a lovely framework of nectarine, melon and citrus fruit, the barrel ferment influence restrained; has very good mouthfeel and length. Screwcap. 13.5% alc. **Rating** 94 **To** 2013 $30
Shiraz 2006 Bright and lively, with a seductive and slightly aromatic array of spices to go with the core of red berry fruits; fine tannins and subtle oak; the touch of viognier works well. Screwcap. 14.5% alc. **Rating** 94 **To** 2016 $29

🍷🍷🍷🍷 **Pinot Gris 2008** Fragrant and flowery peach and pear blossom aromas, the texture of the palate bolstered by barrel fermentation of a component; quality gris. Screwcap. 13.5% alc. **Rating** 92 **To** 2011 $25
Cane Cut Pinot Gris 2008 This technique has resulted in more sweetness and richness than any other attempt with the variety. Honey, peach and spiced pear all coat the mouth, with enough acidity to give balance; full-on dessert wine. Screwcap. 12.5% alc. **Rating** 90 **To** 2013 $28

🍷🍷🍷🍷 **Pinot Gris Viognier 2008** A 50/50 blend in which the viognier provides most of the flavour, the pinot gris helps the elegant texture; works well. Screwcap. 13.5% alc. **Rating** 89 **To** 2010 $25
Pinot Noir 2007 Light, bright crimson-red; elegant, light-bodied style with plum and strawberry fruit on the well-balanced palate. Screwcap. 14.3% alc. **Rating** 89 **To** 2013 $30
Rose 2008 Light salmon-pink; a gently aromatic strawberry-accented bouquet and palate, with a crisp, dry finish. Well made. Screwcap. 13.5% alc. **Rating** 88 **To** 2010 $20

Darlington Vineyard ★★★

Holkam Court, Orford, Tas 7190 **Region** Southern Tasmania
T (03) 6257 1630 **F** (03) 6257 1630 **Open** Thurs–Mon 10–5
Winemaker Frogmore Creek **Est.** 1993 **Cases** 600
Peter and Margaret Hyland planted a little under 2 ha of vineyard in 1993, located on the Freycinet coast. The first wines were made from the 1999 vintage, forcing retired builder Peter Hyland to complete their home so that the small building in which they had been living could be converted into a cellar door. The vineyard looks out towards the settlement of Darlington on Maria Island, the site of Diego Bernacchi's attempt to establish a vineyard in the 1880s and lure investors by attaching artificial bunches of grapes to his vines.

🍷🍷🍷🍷 **TGR Riesling 2008** Pale, but bright green; subtle wine; light varietal expression, very well balanced. **Rating** 89 **To** 2012
Pinot Noir 2007 Light, bright colour; similarly light, breezy red fruits, but has good length, focus and balance; seduction, not rape. **Rating** 89 **To** 2013
Riesling 2008 Blossom/spice aromas; moderately sweet citrus flavours; good line/balance; finishes well. **Rating** 87 **To** 2014

David Hook Wines

Cnr Broke Road/Ekerts Road, Pokolbin, NSW 2320 **Region** Lower Hunter Valley
T (02) 4998 7121 **www**.davidhookwines.com.au **Open** 7 days 10–5
Winemaker David Hook **Est.** 1984 **Cases** 10 000 **Vyds** 8 ha
David Hook has over 20 years' experience as a winemaker for Tyrrell's and Lake's Folly, also doing the full Flying Winemaker bit with jobs in Bordeaux, the Rhône Valley, Spain, the US and Georgia. He and his family began establishing the vineyard in 1984. The estate-owned Pothana Vineyard has been in production for 25 years, and the wines made from it are given the 'Old Vines' banner. This vineyard is planted on the Belford Dome, an ancient geological formation that provides red clay soils over limestone on the slopes, and sandy loams along the creek flats; the former for red wines, the latter for white. Exports to the US and Japan.

ΨΨΨΨΩ **Pothana Vineyard Old Vines Belford Semillon 2008** A touch of green nettle complements the zesty lemon sherbet bouquet; tight and zesty on the palate; the indications are there for ageing potential, but with enough weight for some early drinking pleasure. Screwcap. 11% alc. **Rating** 91 **To** 2018 $25

ΨΨΨΨ **The Gorge Hunter Valley Shiraz 2007** Purple hues; potent black fruit and regional earth aromas; a very robust, rustic wine that demands time, and could well repay cellaring. Screwcap. 14% alc. **Rating** 88 **To** 2016 $18
Pothana Vineyard Old Vines Belford Shiraz 2007 Clean and juicy with a hint of spice and red fruit on the bouquet and palate; juicy and fine. Screwcap. 14% alc. **Rating** 87 **To** 2012 $40

Dawson's Patch   ★★★

71 Kallista-Emerald Road, The Patch, Vic 3792 (postal) **Region** Yarra Valley
T 0419 521 080 **www.**dawsonspatch.com.au **Open** Not
Winemaker Paul Evans (Contract) **Est.** 1996 **Cases** 500 **Vyds** 1.2 ha
James and Jody Dawson own and manage this vineyard at the southern end of the Yarra Valley, planted to chardonnay. The climate here is particularly cool, and the grapes do not normally ripen until late April. Jody has completed a degree in viticulture through CSU. The tiny hand-crafted production is sold through local restaurants and cellars in the Olinda/Emerald/Belgrave area.

ΨΨΨΨ **Yarra Valley Chardonnay 2006** Seems riper in flavour than the alcohol would suggest, with buttery yellow peach flavours, strongly mlf influenced (likewise oak). Diam. 13.5% alc. **Rating** 89 **To** 2013 $27

De Bortoli   ★★★★★

De Bortoli Road, Bilbul, NSW 2680 **Region** Riverina
T (02) 6966 0100 **www.**debortoli.com.au **Open** Mon–Sat 9–5, Sun 9–4
Winemaker Darren De Bortoli **Est.** 1928 **Cases** 3 million **Vyds** 300 ha
Famous among the cognoscenti for its superb Noble One, which in fact accounts for only a minute part of its total production, this winery turns around low-priced varietal and generic wines that are invariably competently made and equally invariably provide value for money. These come in part from estate vineyards, but mostly from contract-grown grapes. The rating is in part a reflection of the exceptional value for money offered across the range. Exports to all major markets.

ΨΨΨΨΨ **Black Noble NV** A unique wine, has fortified and long barrel-aged Noble One as its base; super intense, yet elegant, and shows no hint of volatile acidity; flavours of exotic spices and mandarin. Cork. 17.5% alc. **Rating** 94 **To** 2010 $34

ΨΨΨΨΩ **Old Boys 21 Years Old Tawny NV** High-quality tawny, with potent rancio; intense and long, with spiced biscuit and cake flavours; balanced acidity. Cork. 19% alc. **Rating** 92 **To** 2010 $42
Sacred Hill Rose 2008 Bright raspberry bouquet with a touch of bramble; clearly defined, fresh, crisp and lively; cleverly handled sweetness is barely noticeable on the finish. Exceptional value. Screwcap. 12.5% alc. **Rating** 90 **To** 2011 $7.50

ΨΨΨΨ **Deen De Bortoli Vat 2 Sauvignon Blanc 2008** Remarkable achievement for the region and price, with gooseberry; the special sauvignon blanc yeast developed by the AWRI may be an explanation; whatever, good wine and very good value. Screwcap. 12% alc. **Rating** 89 **To** 2010 $12.99
Sacred Hill Chardonnay 2008 Stone fruits and a touch of spice; clean, fresh, focused and zesty on the finish; outstanding value. Screwcap. 12.5% alc. **Rating** 89 **To** 2012 $7.50
Sacred Hill Semillon Sauvignon Blanc 2008 Crisp and lively, with authentic tropical kiwi fruit sauvignon blanc backing up the grassy/lemony semillon; soft acidity on a clean finish. Bargain. Screwcap. 11.5% alc. **Rating** 89 **To** 2010 $7.50

Sacred Hill Semillon Chardonnay 2008 Clean, fresh and flavoursome stone fruit bouquet; vibrant and focused on the finish, with a touch of sulphidey complexity for interest. Screwcap. 12% alc. **Rating** 88 **To** 2012 $7.50

Deen De Bortoli Vat 4 Petit Verdot 2007 Great colour and an abundance of juicy red fruits; quite toasty on the finish; a fun, easy-drinking barbecue wine. Screwcap. 14% alc. **Rating** 88 **To** 2011 $12.99

Deen De Bortoli Vat 1 Durif 2007 Deep colour and quite an elegant expression of this bold variety; dark chewy fruit is framed by a noticeable coat of charry oak. Screwcap. 14% alc. **Rating** 88 **To** 2012 $12.99

8 Year Old Tawny Port NV Good rancio and balance; spicy/biscuity aromas and flavours; not too sweet. Cork. 18.5% alc. **Rating** 88 **To** 2010 $23

Sacred Hill Riesling 2008 Ripe stone fruit bouquet, with a touch of spice; clean and zesty finish. Great Value. Screwcap. 13% alc. **Rating** 87 **To** 2012 $7.50

Sacred Hill Shiraz Cabernet 2008 Bright colour; a little reductive on opening, with juicy red fruits, and some savoury tannins to clean up. Screwcap. 14% alc. **Rating** 87 **To** 2012 $7.50

Sacred Hill Traminer Riesling 2008 A highly perfumed wine with rose petal and musk aromas; quite sweet on the palate, causing some heaviness on the finish; nonetheless, a good expression of the varieties. Screwcap. 12% alc. **Rating** 87 **To** 2009 $7.50

Deen De Bortoli Vat 8 Shiraz 2007 As always, over-delivers at its price point; bright plum and blackberry fruit, with a pleasing savoury twist on the finish. Screwcap. 14% alc. **Rating** 87 **To** 2010 $12.99

Emeri Chardonnay Pinot Noir NV Creamy lemon fruit bouquet; fresh chalky acid and clean fruit on the finish; well-handled dosage. Diam. 11.5% alc. **Rating** 87 **To** 2011 $13.99

Emeri Sparkling Shiraz NV Bright colour; vibrant juicy fruit, pure blackberry and spice; juicy and fun on the palate, with a fresh and slightly savoury finish. Diam. 13.5% alc. **Rating** 87 **To** 2012 $13.99

De Bortoli (Hunter Valley)   ★★★★★

532 Wine Country Drive, Pokolbin, NSW 2320 **Region** Lower Hunter Valley
T (02) 4993 8800 **F** (02) 4993 8899 **www.debortoli.com.au Open** 7 days 10–5
Winemaker Steve Webber **Est.** 2002 **Cases** 35 000 **Vyds** 35 ha
De Bortoli extended its wine empire in 2002 with the purchase of the former Wilderness Estate, giving it an immediate and significant presence in the Hunter Valley courtesy of the 26 ha of established vineyards; this was expanded significantly by the subsequent purchase of an adjoining 40-ha property. Exports to all major markets.

ᵡᵡᵡᵡᵡ **Murphy Vineyard Limited Release Semillon 2004** Elegant, with intense varietal aromas and flavours while retaining delicacy to the grass, lemon and honey-accented fruit; clean, crisp finish with balanced acidity. Screwcap. 12% alc. **Rating** 94 **To** 2019 $32

Wills Hill Vineyard Limited Release Shiraz 2007 A fresh and fragrant bouquet and palate, with particularly expressive cherry, plum and blackberry fruit, the tannins fine, the oak good. Screwcap. 13.5% alc. **Rating** 94 **To** 2021 $35

ᵡᵡᵡᵡ **Hunter Valley Semillon 2007** Fresh, lively style, which has barely developed in the first year of its life; needs more time; will improve. Screwcap. 11.5% alc. **Rating** 88 **To** 2015 $19.50

Hunter Valley Merlot 2007 Good colour; despite modest alcohol, has rich and ripe flavours in a redcurrant mode; pleasant wine, although not particularly regional. Screwcap. 13.5% alc. **Rating** 88 **To** 2014 $19.50

De Bortoli (Victoria)   ★★★★★

Pinnacle Lane, Dixons Creek, Vic 3775 **Region** Yarra Valley
T (03) 5965 2271 **F** (03) 5965 2464 **www.debortoli.com.au Open** 7 days 10–5
Winemaker Steve Webber **Est.** 1987 **Cases** 350 000 **Vyds** 228.86 ha

The quality arm of the bustling De Bortoli group, run by Leanne De Bortoli and husband Steve Webber, ex-Lindemans winemaker. The top label (De Bortoli), the second (Gulf Station) and the third label (Windy Peak) offer wines of consistently good quality and excellent value – the complex Chardonnay and the Pinot Noirs are usually of outstanding quality. The volume of production, by many times the largest in the Yarra Valley, simply underlines the quality/value for money ratio of the wines. This arm of the business has vineyards in the Yarra Valley, and in the King Valley. Viticultural resources to one side, Steve Webber was Gourmet Traveller Winemaker of the Year '07, recognition he thoroughly deserved. Exports to all major markets.

ŶŶŶŶŶ **Estate Grown Yarra Valley Pinot Noir 2007** Precise and pure varietal aromas with no one fruit character dominant; the palate is perfectly weighted and poised, with silky mouthfeel and great length. Screwcap. 13% alc. **Rating** 95 **To** 2015 $38
Estate Grown Yarra Valley Cabernet Sauvignon 2007 Excellent bright crimson-purple; deliciously fragrant aromas lead into a bell-clear varietal palate, with supple, silky mouthfeel and a long, harmonious finish; shows no green characters at all. Screwcap. 13% alc. **Rating** 95 **To** 2017 $35
Estate Yarra Valley Chardonnay 2007 A very complex bouquet, with some savoury elements, is followed by a tightly wound and focused palate; neither its intensity or length is compromised by its low alcohol. Screwcap. 12% alc. **Rating** 94 **To** 2018 $28

ŶŶŶŶŶ **Gulf Station Yarra Valley Sauvignon Blanc 2008** Minerally/chalky aromas lead into a sculpted palate of considerable length and complexity from fermentation in cask and tank, plus lees stirring. Screwcap. 12% alc. **Rating** 93 **To** 2012 $18
Yarra Valley Pinot Noir Rose 2008 Deliberately walks to the beat of a different drum; bone-dry, with a framework of chalky/spicy flavours on the long palate; despite its lightness, is a food style. Screwcap. 13% alc. **Rating** 93 **To** 2011 $22
Reserve EZ 2008 Austere, dry talc/mineral characters with connotations of Alsace; a highly cerebral wine that will pass over the heads of many tasters. May develop well. Gewurztraminer/Pinot Gris/Riesling. Screwcap. 13% alc. **Rating** 92 **To** 2014 $38
Windy Peak Yarra Valley Pinot Noir 2008 Brilliant colour; fragrant cherry aromas; fresh and bright cherry and plum varietal fruit on the light-bodied palate. Exceptional value; ready now. Screwcap. 13% alc. **Rating** 92 **To** 2011 $13
Yarra Valley Melba Reserve 2006 A savoury wine, with dark mocha and cassis fruit on the bouquet; the palate is very firm and unyielding, tannins dominate; very concentrated, but with a fine and complex European palate; more structure than fruit, but is built for the long haul. Cabernet Sauvignon/Merlot. Screwcap. 14% alc. **Rating** 92 **To** 2020 $55
Windy Peak Sauvignon Blanc Semillon 2008 Lively, bright and crisp, with a mix of gooseberry, grass and mineral aromas and flavours; long, clean, dry finish; very good value. Screwcap. 12% alc. **Rating** 90 **To** 2010 $13
Gulf Station Yarra Valley Chardonnay 2007 Typical subtlety and complexity; stone fruit and melon have a near-invisible oak frame; very good length and persistence. Screwcap. 12% alc. **Rating** 90 **To** 2013 $18
Rococco Yarra Valley Blanc de Blanc NV Fine elegant lemon fruit and green apple bouquet, with a fine bead and linear acidity; a nicely balanced wine, with a dry, even and attractive finish. Cork. 12% alc. **Rating** 90 **To** 2014 $21.99

ŶŶŶŶ **Gulf Station Yarra Valley Riesling 2008** Lime and lemon zest aromas; a faint hint of spice but none of reduction; delicate and very fresh; falls away fractionally on the finish. Screwcap. 13% alc. **Rating** 89 **To** 2014 $19
Windy Peak King Valley Pinot Grigio 2008 Has plenty of character; pear and mineral with a touch of straw on the finish give the wine an almost Italian feel and charm; made for food. Screwcap. 12.5% alc. **Rating** 89 **To** 2010 $13
Windy Peak Cabernet Merlot 2007 Has more structure and stuffing than others in this price range and varietal mix; abundant cassis and blackcurrant; needs time to fully evolve. Screwcap. 13% alc. **Rating** 89 **To** 2015 $13

Yarra Valley Melba Lucia 2006 A Eurocentric style; cherry fruit and a hint of cassis; strongly tannic on the palate, with a slight amaro bitterness to the finish. Cabernet Sauvignon/Merlot/Sangiovese/Petit Verdot. Screwcap. 14% alc. **Rating** 89 **To** 2014 $28

Windy Peak King Valley Sangiovese 2006 Shows clear varietal fruit with a mix of red and sour cherry flavours on its light-bodied palate; good lunch red. Screwcap. 13.5% alc. **Rating** 88 **To** 2010 $14.95

Windy Peak Chardonnay 2007 Assertive and complex wine with barrel ferment components rare at this price point; plenty of fruit, but short finish. Screwcap. 13% alc. **Rating** 87 **To** 2010 $13

Gulf Station Yarra Valley Pinot Grigio 2008 Almost devoid of colour; crisp and minerally, with subliminal notes of pear and green apple; a gently firm finish; part estate grown. Screwcap. 13.5% alc. **Rating** 87 **To** 2010 $19

De Iuliis   ★★★★☆

21 Broke Road, Pokolbin, NSW 2320 **Region** Lower Hunter Valley
T (02) 4993 8000 **F** (02) 4998 7168 **www**.dewine.com.au **Open** 7 days 10–5
Winemaker Michael De Iuliis **Est.** 1990 **Cases** 10 000
Three generations of the De Iuliis family have been involved in the establishment of their 45-ha vineyard. The family acquired the property in 1986 and planted the first vines in 1990, selling the grapes from the first few vintages to Tyrrell's but retaining increasing amounts for release under the De Iuliis label. Winemaker Michael De Iuliis has completed postgraduate studies in oenology at the Roseworthy campus of Adelaide University and was a Len Evans Tutorial scholar. He has lifted the quality of the wines into the highest echelon.

ᵠᵠᵠᵠᵠ Aged Release Hunter Valley Semillon 2002 Has developed considerable complexity to both structure and flavour; lemon, honey, toast and spice all coalesce. Cork. 11% alc. **Rating** 93 **To** 2012 $20

Show Reserve Hunter Valley Shiraz 2007 Ripe black fruit with prominent and highly polished oak on the bouquet; very dark and chewy palate, with an earthy undercurrent; the oak dominates at the moment, but there is a great deal of fruit to go the distance, Needs time. Screwcap. 14% alc. **Rating** 93 **To** 2018 $30

Charlie Hunter Valley Shiraz 2007 Good colour; ripe dark blackberry fruit, pushing ripeness but not overstepping the mark; tarry palate with some redcurrant and a touch of spice coming to the fore; big boned and well made. Screwcap. 14% alc. **Rating** 92 **To** 2016 $25

Hunter Valley Semillon 2008 Classic low-alcohol Hunter semillon; clean, crisp aromas still to fully evolve, but the palate shows much more character and flavour, verging citrus/tropical. Screwcap. 9.5% alc. **Rating** 91 **To** 2016 $16

Limited Release Hunter Valley Chardonnay 2007 Interesting savoury bouquet with smoky charcuterie and some fresh fig; plenty of sweet fruit and nutty complexity on the palate, offering cleansing acidity and a little grip on the finish; oak is a dominant feature. Screwcap. 13.5% alc. **Rating** 91 **To** 2013 $25

ᵠᵠᵠᵠ Show Reserve Hunter Valley Chardonnay 2008 Restrained bouquet of nectarine and straw; citrus on the palate, with fine acidity and a touch of nutty complexity on the finish. Screwcap. 12.5% alc. **Rating** 89 **To** 2012 $18

De Lisio Wines   ★★★★☆

Seaview Road, McLaren Vale, SA 5171 **Region** McLaren Vale
T (08) 8298 9040 **F** (08) 8298 9470 **Open** By appt
Winemaker Anthony De Lisio **Est.** 2002 **Cases** 6500
This is the venture of Anthony (Tony) and Krystina De Lisio, focused primarily on McLaren Vale Shiraz and Grenache, the exceptions being a Southern Fleurieu Pinot Grigio and a four-varietal blend red (Quarterback), which provide the major part of the volume of De Lisio Wines. Tony has many years experience as a viticulturist and vineyard manager in McLaren Vale, and has been able to source grapes grown just north of McLaren Vale township, at

Clarendon, Blewitt Springs, Kangarilla and McLaren Flat. The overall style of the wines is strongly oriented to the US, to which a significant part of the production is exported, along with Canada, Denmark, Singapore and China. The style is achieved through very ripe grapes from low-yielding, predominantly old vines, which are open-fermented and barrel-aged in predominantly French oak for up to 22 months.

ŸŸŸŸŸ **Catalyst McLaren Vale Shiraz Grenache 2005** Despite the alcohol and grenache, has a very attractive savoury, almost spicy edge to the well-balanced, medium-bodied palate; very good length. Cork. 15.5% alc. **Rating** 94 **To** 2015 $30

ŸŸŸŸŸ **Krystina McLaren Vale Shiraz 2005** Rich, powerful, glossy McLaren Vale style, with black fruits, licorice, dark chocolate and vanilla coalescing on the long palate. Stained cork a worry. 15% alc. **Rating** 93 **To** 2015 $40
McLaren Vale Shiraz 2006 The alcohol is immediately apparent but does not increase on the finish and aftertaste (as is common); glossy black fruits and a dusting of chocolate and licorice. Cork. 15.5% alc. **Rating** 91 **To** 2015 $65
Argento Southern Fleurieu Pinot Grigio 2008 Is not distinctively pinot grigio, but is fresh, vibrant and mouth-cleansing, with green apple/crunchy acidity. Screwcap. 13.5% alc. **Rating** 90 **To** 2010 $18

ŸŸŸŸ **McLaren Vale Grenache 2006** Has abundant flavour, but surely not necessary to have McLaren Vale grenache so ripe, the alcohol adding a sweet sugar coating. Cork. 16% alc. **Rating** 88 **To** 2013 $35

Dead Horse Hill ★★★★☆

Myola East Road, Toolleen, Vic 3551 **Region** Heathcote
T (03) 5433 6214 **F** (03) 5433 6164 **Open** By appt
Winemaker Jencie McRobert **Est.** 1994 **Cases** 500 **Vyds** 4 ha
Jencie McRobert (and husband Russell) 'did a deal with Dad' for approximately 65 ha of her parents' large sheep and wheat farm at Toolleen, 20 km north of Heathcote. It took a number of years for the dry-grown shiraz vines to achieve reasonable yields, but they are now yielding between 3.7 and 5 tonnes per ha of high-quality fruit. Jencie's introduction to wine came partly through the family dining table and partly from meeting Steve Webber, then working for Lindemans at Karadoc, when she was working in soil conservation and salinity management in the Mallee. She subsequently completed a course at CSU and makes the wine at De Bortoli in the Yarra Valley, with the odd bit of assistance from Webber.

Deakin Estate ★★★☆

Kulkyne Way, via Red Cliffs, Vic 3496 **Region** Murray Darling
T (03) 5029 1666 **F** (03) 5024 3316 **www.deakinestate.com.au Open** Not
Winemaker Dr Phil Spillman **Est.** 1980 **Cases** 400 000 **Vyds** 350 ha
Part of the Katnook Estate, Riddoch and Deakin Estate triumvirate, which constitutes the Wingara Wine Group, now fully owned by Freixenet of Spain. Deakin Estate draws from its own vineyards, making it largely self-sufficient, and produces wines of consistent quality and impressive value. Exports to all major markets.

ŸŸŸŸŸ **Shiraz 2007** What a surplus can do! Outstanding wine at the price; an excellent varietal fruit profile on the medium-bodied palate, supported by ripe tannins. Screwcap. 13.5% alc. **Rating** 90 **To** 2014 $10

ŸŸŸŸ **Sauvignon Blanc 2008** Impressive at the price; has fresh tropical fruit aromas, adding citrus/lemon flavours on the palate; not especially varietal, but well made. Screwcap. 11% alc. **Rating** 89 **To** 2010 $10
Crackerjack Chardonnay 2008 Bright straw-green; has impressive structure; oak infusion well handled; some cooler-grown fruit. Screwcap. 13.5% alc. **Rating** 88 **To** 2012 $15
Shiraz 2006 Good colour; black cherry aromas; light- to medium-bodied palate; has similar attractive fruit expression, but is distinctly short. Screwcap. 13.5% alc. **Rating** 87 **To** 2011 $10

Deep Woods Estate ★★★★☆

Commonage Road, Yallingup, WA 6282 **Region** Margaret River
T (08) 9756 6066 **www**.deepwoods.com.au **Open** Tues–Sun 11–5, 7 days during hols
Winemaker Travis Clydesdale **Est.** 1987 **Cases** 20 000
The Gould family acquired Deep Woods Estate in 1992, when the first plantings were four
years old. In 2005 the business was purchased by Perth businessman Peter Fogarty and family,
who also own Lake's Folly in the Hunter Valley, and Millbrook in the Perth Hills. The 32-ha
property has 16-ha plantings of cabernet sauvignon, shiraz, merlot, cabernet franc, chardonnay,
sauvignon blanc, semillon and verdelho. Vineyard and cellar door upgrades are underway.
Exports to Switzerland, Belgium, Denmark and Ireland.

ㅏㅏㅏㅏㅏ   **Reserve Margaret River Cabernet Sauvignon 2007** Well-made quality
cabernet; deeply structured black fruits in a tight frame of ripe tannins and quality
oak; finesse with power. Screwcap. 14% alc. **Rating** 95 **To** 2027 $35

ㅏㅏㅏㅏㅏ   **Reserve Chardonnay 2008** Very much in the modern style, with barrel ferment
inputs seamlessly folded into the nectarine and white peach fruit, finishing with
citrussy acidity. Screwcap. 13.5% alc. **Rating** 93 **To** 2016 $35
Margaret River Cabernet Sauvignon Merlot 2007 Rich black fruits and a
whisper of dark chocolate on the bouquet; a medium- to full-bodied palate with
blackcurrant, cedary French oak and firm tannins. Screwcap. 13.5% alc. **Rating** 93
To 2027 $27.95
Block 7 Margaret River Shiraz 2007 Rich and full-bodied wine, displaying
power way beyond its modest alcohol; red and black fruits and dusty tannins are
backed by obvious French oak. Screwcap. 13.5% alc. **Rating** 92 **To** 2020 $27.95
Margaret River Semillon Sauvignon Blanc 2008 Crisp, grassy semillon in
the ascendant on the bouquet, some tropical/passionfruit sauvignon blanc clicking
in on the palate, finishing with minerally acidity. Screwcap. 12.5% alc. **Rating** 90
To 2010 $19.95

ㅏㅏㅏㅏ   **Margaret River Verdelho 2008** A pleasant wine, but why perfectly good
Margaret River vineyards should be used to grow this (or chenin blanc) I don't
know – other than for cash flow benefits, of course. Screwcap. 12.5% alc.
Rating 87 **To** 2011 $19.95
Ebony Margaret River Cabernet Shiraz 2007 Plenty of depth and flavour to
its black fruits, but is a little short. Screwcap. 14% alc. **Rating** 87 **To** 2010 $14.90

Deetswood Wines

Washpool Creek Road, Tenterfield, NSW 2372 **Region** New England
T (02) 6736 1322 **www**.deetswoodwines.com.au **Open** Fri–Mon 10–5, or by appt
Winemaker Contract **Est.** 1996 **Cases** 2000 **Vyds** 2.4 ha
Deanne Eaton and Tim Condrick established their micro-vineyard in 1996, planting 2.4 ha of
semillon, chardonnay, pinot noir, shiraz, merlot, viognier and cabernet sauvignon. At the end
of the 19th century German immigrant Joe Nicoll planted vines here and made wines for
family use, and there is still one vine surviving on the site today from those original plantings.
The wines are normally consistent both in quality and style, offering further proof that this
is a very interesting area.

ㅏㅏㅏㅏㅏ   **Semillon 2008** Very pale colour; strong green–nettle bouquet with a touch of
lemon; the palate is focused and fresh, with good texture and crisp acidity on the
finish. Screwcap. 11.5% alc. **Rating** 92 **To** 2014 $20

Deisen ★★★★★

PO Box 61, Tanunda, SA 5352 **Region** Barossa Valley
T (08) 8563 2298 **F** (08) 8563 2298 **www**.deisen.com.au **Open** Not
Winemaker Sabine Deisen **Est.** 2001 **Cases** 1000
Deisen (owned by Sabine Deisen and Les Fensom) once again proves the old adage true that
nothing succeeds like success. In the first year, 3.5 tonnes of grapes produced five barrels of

Shiraz and two of Grenache. Since that time, production has grown slowly but steadily with bits and pieces of traditional winemaking equipment (small crushers, open tanks and hand-plunging, now housed in a slightly larger tin shed). The number of wines made and the tiny quantities of some (20 dozen is not uncommon) is staggering. The style of all the wines is remarkably similar: sweet and luscious fruit; soft, ripe tannins; and a warmth from the alcohol (toned down in recent releases). Exports to the US.

ŶŶŶŶŶ **Sweetheart Barossa Shiraz 2006** Slightly more aromatic and spicy on the bouquet than Backblock, and with more thrust on the palate, yet still well and truly in the family style. Quality cork. 15% alc. **Rating** 95 **To** 2021 $40
Backblock Barossa Shiraz 2006 In typical rich, dense Deisen style, with luscious black fruits, yet neither alcoholic nor in any way clumsy on the finish. High-quality cork, properly inserted. 15% alc. **Rating** 94 **To** 2018 $65
Barossa Shiraz 2005 Strong colour; full of flavour, albeit without any confit or dead fruit components; dark chocolate and mocha surround the black fruit flesh of the mid-palate. Cork. 14.8% alc. **Rating** 94 **To** 2015 $56

ŶŶŶŶŶ **Barossa GSM 2006** The wine has good structural integrity and a significantly wider spectrum of flavours, with red and black cherry, plus a touch of plum. Cork. 14.9% alc. **Rating** 91 **To** 2016 $40

ŶŶŶŶ **Barossa Late Grenache 2006** Most Barossa grenache and I have an uneasy relationship, and this is no exception; the confection characters are very strong, but there is little to balance the warm alcohol. Screwcap. 14.7% alc. **Rating** 87 **To** 2014 $37
Barossa Grenache 2005 Light colour; lots of sweet lolly fruit, but – as usual for Barossa grenache – no structure to speak of. I suppose it's a style issue, and others won't understand my grizzling. Cork. 15.5% alc. **Rating** 87 **To** 2012 $37

del Rios of Mt Anakie   ★★★★

2320 Ballan Road, Anakie, Vic 3221 **Region** Geelong
T (03) 9497 4644 **F** (03) 9499 9266 **www.**delrios.com.au **Open** W'ends 10–5
Winemaker Gus del Rio **Est.** 1996 **Cases** 5000
Gus del Rio, of Spanish heritage, established the 14-ha vineyard in 1996 on the slopes of Mt Anakie, northwest of Geelong (chardonnay, pinot noir, cabernet sauvignon, sauvignon blanc, shiraz, merlot and marsanne). The vines are hand-pruned, the fruit hand-picked and the wines are made onsite in the fully equipped winery, which includes a bottling and labelling line able to process over 150 tonnes.

ŶŶŶŶŶ **Geelong Sauvignon Blanc 2008** Pale with a vibrant hue; a ripe and complex bouquet of guava and gunflint; the palate reveals more tropical fruit and generous texture, leading to a dry, chalky and fine finish. Screwcap. 12.5% alc. **Rating** 92 **To** 2014 $18
Geelong Marsanne 2006 Exotic spiced honey bouquet, with some guava showing though on the finish; an interesting array of spices from cumin to cinnamon; good texture and fresh acidity cleans up the finish well. Screwcap. 13.5% alc. **Rating** 90 **To** 2012 $18

ŶŶŶŶ **Geelong Rose 2008** Bright colour; dry and savoury with cherry and sage on the bouquet and palate; good definition on the finish. Screwcap. 12.3% alc. **Rating** 88 **To** 2011 $16

Delamere Vineyard   ★★★

Bridport Road, Pipers Brook, Tas 7254 **Region** Northern Tasmania
T (03) 6382 7190 **F** (03) 6382 7250 **www.**delamerevineyards.com.au **Open** 7 days 10–5
Winemaker Shane Holloway **Est.** 1983 **Cases** 2500 **Vyds** 6.9 ha
Richie Richardson produces elegant, rather light-bodied wines that have a strong following. The Chardonnay has been most successful; a textured, complex, malolactic-influenced wine with a great, creamy mouthfeel.

ΥΥΥΥ **Blanc de Blancs 2004** Has attractive stone fruit flavours, but is not particularly complex. Cork. 13% alc. **Rating** 89 **To** 2013 $35
Pinot Noir 2007 Lively, bright and fresh spicy red fruits; good length, but is fractionally light on, especially given the oak level. Screwcap. 13% alc. **Rating** 88 **To** 2012 $27

Delatite ★★★★★

Stoneys Road, Mansfield, Vic 3722 **Region** Upper Goulburn
T (03) 5775 2922 **F** (03) 5775 2911 **www.**delatitewinery.com.au **Open** 7 days 11–5
Winemaker Andy Browning **Est.** 1982 **Cases** 18 000
With its sweeping views across to the snow-clad Alps, this is uncompromising cool-climate viticulture, and the wines naturally reflect that. Increasing vine age (much of the plantings are well over 20 years old), the adoption of organic (and partial biodynamic) viticulture seems also to have played a role in providing the red wines with more depth and texture; the white wines as good as ever. Exports to Denmark, China, Japan and Malaysia.

ΥΥΥΥΥ **Sylvia Riesling 2008** A delicious, fragrant bouquet leads into a Mosel Kabinett-style palate, distinctly off-dry; the sweetness is balanced by acidity, and lime juice flavours persist on the long finish. Screwcap. 10.5% alc. **Rating** 95 **To** 2013 $22
Upper Goulburn Pinot Gris 2008 Pale bright straw; spiced pear aromas lead into a pear and lemon juice palate, with arresting line and length. A seriously good pinot gris. Screwcap. 13% alc. **Rating** 95 **To** 2011 $22.90
Sauvignon Blanc 2008 Cleverly made, with several picking dates giving a complex array of flavours from grassy to tropical, which merge seamlessly on the generous, supple palate. Screwcap. 14% alc. **Rating** 94 **To** 2012 $22

ΥΥΥΥΥ **Catherine Gewurztraminer 2008** So delicious I couldn't help but swallow it; of spatlese sweetness; more lime juice than lychee or rose petal, but who cares? Will flourish in bottle. Screwcap. 10% alc. **Rating** 92 **To** 2013 $22
Dead Man's Hill Upper Goulburn Gewurztraminer 2008 Distinct, if initially delicate; rose blossom and spice aromas swell on revisiting the bouquet; the palate is strongly structured, bordering on Alsatian in texture, with crunchy acidity to close. Screwcap. 13% alc. **Rating** 91 **To** 2012 $24.90
Shiraz 2006 Spice and bramble aromas are reflected in the medium-bodied, welcoming, palate, which has fully ripened fruit, and none of the minty notes of a decade ago; arguably the good side of climate warming. Screwcap. 14.5% alc. **Rating** 90 **To** 2014 $27

ΥΥΥΥ **Dungeon Gully 2006** Bright colour; an effusive display of red fruit aromas and flavours; minimal tannins and structure; early-drinking style. Screwcap. 14% alc. **Rating** 88 **To** 2010 $22

Derwent Estate ★★★★☆

329 Lyell Highway, Granton, Tas 7070 **Region** Southern Tasmania
T (03) 6263 5802 **F** (03) 6263 5802 **www.**derwentestate.com.au **Open** 7 days 10–4
Dec–Jan, Mon–Fri 10–4 Feb–Easter
Winemaker Winemaking Tasmania (Julian Alcorso) **Est.** 1993 **Cases** 1800 **Vyds** 10 ha
The Hanigan family established Derwent Estate as part of a diversification program for their 400-ha mixed-farming property: 10 ha of vineyard have been planted since 1993 to riesling, pinot noir, chardonnay, cabernet sauvignon, sauvignon blanc and pinot gris.

ΥΥΥΥΥ **Rose 2008** Bright pink-fuschia; fresh strawberry fruit on the bouquet and palate; has good balance and length; and is not the least bit sweet. Gold medal Tas Wine Show '09. Screwcap. 13.5% alc. **Rating** 94 **To** 2010 $20

ΥΥΥΥΥ **Pinot Noir 2007** Quite deep colour; red fruits, spice and a touch of dark plum on the bouquet; the palate is quite dense, but is quite lively and fine on the finish; good tannins, and a savoury edge provides plenty of interest. Screwcap. 13.5% alc. **Rating** 93 **To** 2015 $29

Riesling 2008 A little reductive on opening; fine and steely fruit on the bouquet, with a linear, crisp lime juice palate, flowing through to a very dry and assertive finish; will reward cellaring. Screwcap. 11.8% alc. **Rating** 91 **To** 2020 $23
Chardonnay 2007 Green-straw; an intense, elegant wine with great thrust, energy and drive; stone fruit and grapefruit, plus harmonious oak. Screwcap. 12% alc. **Rating** 90 **To** 2014 $29

Deviation Road

214 Scott Creek Road, Longwood, SA 5153 **Region** Adelaide Hills
T (08) 8339 2633 **F** (08) 8331 1360 **www**.deviationroad.com **Open** Not
Winemaker Kate Laurie, Hamish Laurie **Est.** 1999 **Cases** 6600
Deviation Road was created in 1998 by Hamish Laurie, great-great-grandson of Mary Laurie, SA's first female winemaker. He initially joined with father Dr Chris Laurie in 1992 to help build the Hillstowe Wines business; the brand was sold to Banksia Wines in 2001, but the Laurie family retained the vineyard, which now supplies Deviation Road with its grapes. Wife Kate joined the business in 2001, having studied winemaking and viticulture in Champagne, then spending four years at her family's Stone Bridge winery in Manjimup. All the wines, except the Sangiovese (WA) and Riesling (other Adelaide Hills growers), come from the family vineyards, but only account for a small portion of the annual grape production of those vineyards. Exports to the UK, the US, Switzerland and Hong Kong.

ΨΨΨΨΨ **Reserve Adelaide Hills Shiraz 2007** Deep and vibrant colour; fragrant and fine with red and blue fruit, plenty of spice and fine-grained tannins on offer; long. silky and supple. Screwcap. 14% alc. **Rating** 94 **To** 2016 $34

ΨΨΨΨΨ **Reserve Adelaide Hills Chardonnay 2007** Nectarine and peach fruit dominates the bouquet, with a hint of toasty oak to complement; the palate is generous and rich, yet shows a zesty quality on the finish, providing light and shade. Screwcap. 14% alc. **Rating** 92 **To** 2015 $28

Devil's Lair

Rocky Road, Forest Grove via Margaret River, WA 6285 **Region** Margaret River
T (08) 9757 7573 **F** (08) 9757 7533 **www**.devils-lair.com **Open** Not
Winemaker Oliver Crawford, Charlotte Newton **Est.** 1981 **Cases** 220 000 **Vyds** 130 ha
Having rapidly carved out a high reputation for itself through a combination of clever packaging and impressive wine quality, Devil's Lair was acquired by Southcorp in 1996. The estate vineyards have been substantially increased since, now with sauvignon blanc, semillon, chardonnay, cabernet sauvignon, merlot, shiraz, cabernet franc and petit verdot, supplemented by grapes purchased from contract growers. An exceptionally successful business; production has increased from 40 000 to 220 000 cases, in no small measure due to its second label, Fifth Leg. Exports to the UK, the US and other major markets.

ΨΨΨΨΨ **Margaret River Chardonnay 2007** Bright, intense wine with very good thrust and drive; excellent fruit/oak integration; clean, vibrant finish. Gold WA Wine Show '08. **Rating** 94 **To** 2017 $44.99
Margaret River 2007 Strong red-purple; fragrant cedary/earthy aromas lead into a medium-bodied palate of lively, juicy cassis and blackcurrant fruits, the tannins fine and soft, the oak balanced. Cabernet Sauvignon/Merlot. Screwcap. 13.5% alc. **Rating** 94 **To** 2017 $60

ΨΨΨΨΨ **Margaret River 2006** A fresh bouquet of cassis, green olive and cedar; the palate is quite taut and finely poised, with plentiful fine-grained tannins providing a long, cool and savoury finish. Triumph for the vintage. Cabernet Sauvignon/Merlot. Screwcap. 13.5% alc. **Rating** 93 **To** 2016 $60.99
Fifth Leg Chardonnay 2007 Bright, pale straw-green; fresh, light-bodied but quite intense melon and stone fruit aromas and flavours, oak all but irrelevant; good length and balance. Screwcap. 13.5% alc. **Rating** 92 **To** 2012 $15.99

Margaret River Sauvignon Blanc 2008 Vibrant colour; guava and nettle bouquet; rich and ripe palate, with a food-friendly textural element that is most appealing. Screwcap. 13% alc. **Rating** 91 **To** 2012 $26.99

Dexter Wines   ★★★★☆

210 Foxeys Road, Merricks North, Vic 3926 (postal) **Region** Mornington Peninsula
T (03) 5989 7007 **F** (03) 5989 7009 www.dexterwines.com.au **Open** Not
Winemaker Tod Dexter **Est.** 2006 **Cases** 700 **Vyds** 7.1 ha
Tod Dexter was introduced to wine through a friendship between his parents and then leading Melbourne retailer Doug Crittenden. A skiing trip to the US indirectly led to Tod becoming an apprentice winemaker at Cakebread Cellars, a well-known Napa Valley winery, in 1979. After seven years he returned to Australia and the Mornington Peninsula, and began the establishment of a 7-ha vineyard planted to pinot noir and chardonnay. To keep the wolves from the door he became winemaker at Stonier, and leased his vineyard to Stonier, the grapes always used in the Stonier Reserve range. Having left Stonier to become Yabby Lake winemaker, and spurred on by turning 50 in 2006 (and at the urging of friends), he and wife Debbie decided to establish the Dexter label. Exports to the UK.

ΨΨΨΨΨ **Mornington Peninsula Chardonnay 2007** A finely crafted wine; a seamless fusion between nectarine, grapefruit and gently spicy French oak; impeccable line, length and bright acidity. Screwcap. 13% alc. **Rating** 94 **To** 2015 $38

ΨΨΨΨΨ **Mornington Peninsula Pinot Noir 2007** Excellent hue and clarity; a fragrant bouquet and elegant palate; quality pinot, but a little less oak might have produced an even better outcome. Screwcap. 13% alc. **Rating** 92 **To** 2014 $49

di Lusso Estate   ★★★★

Eurunderee Lane, Mudgee, NSW 2850 **Region** Mudgee
T (02) 6373 3125 **F** (02) 6373 3128 www.dilusso.com.au **Open** 7 days 10–5
Winemaker Julia Conchie, Robert Paul (Consultant) **Est.** 1998 **Cases** 4000 **Vyds** 6.5 ha
Rob Fairall and partner Luanne Hill have brought to fruition their vision to establish an Italian 'enoteca' operation, offering Italian varietal wines and foods. When they began to plant their vineyard in 1998, the Italian varietal craze was yet to gain serious traction. They now have a thoroughly impressive range of barbera, sangiovese, vermentino, aleatico, lagrein, greco di tufo, picolit and nebbiolo. The estate also produces olives for olive oil and table olives, and the range of both wine and food will increase over the years. The decision to focus on Italian varieties has been a major success, the quality of the wines, however, rather than passing popularity, the key to that success.

ΨΨΨΨΨ **Mudgee Sangiovese 2006** Excellent hue, still predominantly red-purple; lively, flavoursome and strongly varietal in a sour cherry/black cherry spectrum; good length with fine tannins. A very good sangiovese. Screwcap. 14.2% alc. **Rating** 93 **To** 2014 $23
Appassimento 2005 Glowing gold; a remarkable wine produced from semillon dried on racks for two months; singed honey, cumquat and an aftertaste vaguely reminiscent of wasabi; don't be put off. Cork. 12.2% alc. **Rating** 92 **To** 2011 $45
Pinot Grigio 2008 Clear-cut varietal flavours of pear and citrus/grapefruit acidity are enhanced by the seamless line of the wine. Screwcap. 11.5% alc. **Rating** 91 **To** 2012 $25
Picolit 2006 Rare in northern Italy, but even rarer in Australia; has developed really attractive ripe lime/citrus flavours, and looks as if it will long outlive the soggy cork. 10.5% alc. **Rating** 91 **To** 2010 $23

ΨΨΨΨ **Arneis 2008** A lively combination of herb, mineral, citrus zest and apple, with good line and continuity. Screwcap. 14.5% alc. **Rating** 88 **To** 2012 $23
Mudgee Aleatico 2006 Pronounced grapey aromas; strikingly flavoured as if it were lightly fortified; spicy red fruits from old vines. Challenging wine. Rose. Diam. 14.5% alc. **Rating** 88 **To** 2011 $23

il Palio 2006 Light, but vivid, crimson-red; sour cherry flavours predominate with a tangy savoury finish attesting to Sangiovese (50%) leading the band of Shiraz/Cabernet Sauvignon/Barbera bringing up the rear. Screwcap. 14.5% alc. Rating 88 To 2014 $23

Vino Rosato 2008 Crisp and fresh, with cleansing acidity running through the light cherry-accented fruit; dry, but not aggressively so. Lagrein. Screwcap. 11.9% alc. Rating 87 To 2010 $18

Di Stasio

Range Road, Coldstream, Vic 3770 **Region** Yarra Valley
T (03) 9525 3999 **F** (03) 9525 3815 **www**.distasio.com.au **Open** By appt, or at Cafe Di Stasio, 31 Fitzroy Street, St Kilda
Winemaker Rob Dolan, Kate Goodman (Contract) **Est.** 1995 **Cases** 850 **Vyds** 5.6 ha
Famous Melbourne restaurateur Rinaldo (Ronnie) Di Stasio bought a virgin bushland 32-ha hillside block in the Yarra Valley, adjacent to the Warramate Flora and Fauna Reserve, in 1994. He has established equal quantities of pinot noir and chardonnay, put in roads and dams, built a substantial house, and also an Allan Powell–designed monastery, complete with art gallery and tree-filled courtyard sitting like a church on top of the hill. Production has never been large; the wines are sold through Cafe Di Stasio in St Kilda, a Melbourne icon.

ꟼꟼꟼꟼꟼ Yarra Valley Chardonnay 2007 Ripe spiced pear and nectarine bouquet; medium-bodied with good texture and elegant fruit on the palate; pleasant lingering toasty notes to conclude. Screwcap. 13% alc. Rating 91 To 2013 $35

Diamond Creek Estate ★★★☆

Diamond Fields Road, Mittagong, NSW 2575 **Region** Southern Highlands
T (02) 4872 3311 **F** (02) 4872 3311 **www**.diamondcreekestate.com.au **Open** By appt
Winemaker Eddy Rossi **Est.** 1997 **Cases** 2500 **Vyds** 6 ha
Helen Hale purchased Diamond Creek Estate in late 2002, by which time the chardonnay, sauvignon blanc, riesling, pinot noir and cabernet sauvignon planted in 1997 by the prior owner had come into bearing. The vineyard is established at 680 m on rich basalt soil, the north-facing slope being relatively frost-free. Since Helen acquired the property, some of the grapes have been sold to Southern Highlands Winery, but most has been retained for release under the Diamond Creek Estate label: these include Riesling, Sauvignon Blanc, Pinot Noir, Cabernet Sauvignon and a highly successful Noble Diamond Botrytis Chardonnay.

ꟼꟼꟼꟼꟼ Chardonnay 2007 Impressive and elegant, the fine nectarine and melon fruit gently supported by subtle French oak; acidity a given at this alcohol level. A plus for the Southern Highlands. Screwcap. 12.2% alc. Rating 92 To 2013 $20

ꟼꟼꟼꟼ Sauvignon Blanc 2007 A clean, minerally bouquet, then a juicy, perfectly balanced palate, with passionfruit to the fore; crisp, clean finish. Well made. Screwcap. 12.5% alc. Rating 89 To 2010 $20

Diamond Island Wines ★★★

PO Box 56, Bicheno, Tas 7215 **Region** East Coast Tasmania
T 0409 003 988 **Open** Not
Winemaker Winemaking Tasmania (Julian Alcorso) **Est.** 2002 **Cases** 470 **Vyds** 2 ha
Owner Derek Freeman has planted pinot noir, and is the personal full-time viticulturist, helped out during peak periods by a part-time employee. It may not seem much, but successfully growing pinot noir (or any other variety, for that matter) in Tasmania requires an enormous degree of attention to debudding, leaf plucking, wire raising and (in the winter months) pruning. Not surprisingly, Freeman says he has no plans to extend the vineyard at the moment.

ꟼꟼꟼꟼ Bicheno Pinot Noir 2007 Very concentrated and powerful; confit plum/ black fruits; almost too much of a good thing. Screwcap. 13.4% alc. Rating 88 To 2015 $16

Diamond Valley Vineyards ★★★★☆

PO Box 5155, Wonga Park, Vic 3115 **Region** Yarra Valley
T (03) 9722 0840 **F** (03) 9722 2373 **www**.diamondvalley.com.au **Open** Not
Winemaker James Lance **Est.** 1976 **Cases** 7000
One of the Yarra Valley's finest producers of Pinot Noir and an early pacesetter for the variety, making wines of tremendous style and crystal-clear varietal character. They are not cabernet sauvignon look-alikes but true pinot noir, fragrant and intense. The Chardonnays show the same marriage of finesse and intensity, and the Cabernet family wines shine in the warmer vintages. In early 2005 the brand and wine stocks were acquired by Graeme Rathbone, the Lances continuing to own the vineyard and winery, and make the wine. Exports to the UK.

ȲȲȲȲȲ **Reserve Yarra Valley Viognier 2008** Good colour; varietal apricot kernel and spice bouquet; lively texture, with a little grip and generous levels of fruit; the oak is evident, but well handled and frames the opulence of the variety with distinction. Screwcap. 14% alc. **Rating** 90 **To** 2012
Reserve Yarra Valley Pinot Noir 2007 Bright colour; seductive cherry and plum fruit, framed by prominent smoky aromas; a fleshy palate, with a little firmness to the finish; certainly a wine of the vintage. Screwcap. 13% alc. **Rating** 90 **To** 2012

ȲȲȲȲ **Reserve Yarra Valley Shiraz 2006** Green pepper and red fruit bouquet; medium-bodied with fine tannin and cool acid structure; savoury, high acid finish. Screwcap. 14% alc. **Rating** 89 **To** 2014
Yarra Valley Pinot Noir 2007 Dark fruited, with dark plum and Asian spice coming to the fore on the bouquet; the palate dense, with good acidity and flavour persistence; chewy and slightly ashy on the finish. Screwcap. 13% alc. **Rating** 88 **To** 2012
Reserve Yarra Valley Chardonnay 2007 Deep colour; forward and quite toasty bouquet; pear and nectarine and a healthy dollop of oak; plenty of flavour, but shows a broken line. Screwcap. 13.5% alc. **Rating** 87 **To** 2012

Diggers Bluff ★★★★☆

PO Box 34, Tanunda, SA 5352 **Region** Barossa Valley
T 0458 233 065 **F** (08) 8563 1613 **www**.diggersbluff.com **Open** By appt
Winemaker Timothy O'Callaghan **Est.** 1998 **Cases** 3000 **Vyds** 1.9 ha
Timothy O'Callaghan explains that his family crest is an Irish hound standing under an oak tree; the Diggers Bluff label features his faithful hound Digger, under a Mallee tree. He is a third-generation O'Callaghan winemaker, and – reading his newsletter – it's not too hard to guess who the second generation is represented by. Diggers Bluff has cabernet sauvignon, shiraz, grenache, alicante and mataro, all old vines. Exports to the UK, the US, Canada, Singapore and Hong Kong.

ȲȲȲȲȲ **Watch Dog 2002** The stark difference between the '03 (hot, rainy) and the '02 (very cool) vintages is reflected in the two Watch Dogs; this wine is long and savoury, with pleasing earthy nuances to the mainframe of black fruits. Cabernet Sauvignon/Shiraz. Cork. 14.5% alc. **Rating** 94 **To** 2017 $40

ȲȲȲȲȲ **Top Dog 2006** Rich, full-bodied wine with an array of black fruits tweaked on the finish by fresh acidity; the oak impact is significant, but appropriate. Shiraz. Cork. 15% alc. **Rating** 92 **To** 2021 $55
Watch Dog 2003 Largely mature, with some confit fruit notes and the threat of a break in the line and structure of the palate; however, the length is still there, as is the finesse of the tannins. Cabernet Sauvignon/Shiraz. Cork. 14.5% alc. **Rating** 90 **To** 2013 $40

ȲȲȲȲ **Stray Dog 2006** A light- to medium-bodied, savoury, tangy version of Grenache/Shiraz/Mataro, which has good length and a spicy finish. Screwcap. 13.5% alc. **Rating** 89 **To** 2013 $19

DiGiorgio Family Wines

Riddoch Highway, Coonawarra, SA 5263 **Region** Coonawarra
T (08) 8736 3222 **F** (08) 8736 3233 **www**.digiorgio.com.au **Open** 7 days 10–5
Winemaker Peter Douglas, Vanessa Marsden **Est.** 1998 **Cases** 25 000 **Vyds** 207 ha
Stefano DiGiorgio emigrated from Abruzzi, Italy in 1952. Over the years, he and his family gradually expanded their holdings at Lucindale. In 1989 he began planting cabernet sauvignon (99 ha), chardonnay (10 ha), merlot (9 ha), shiraz (6 ha) and pinot noir (2 ha). In 2002 the family purchased the historic Rouge Homme winery, capable of crushing 10 000 tonnes of grapes a year, and its surrounding 13.5 ha of vines, from Southcorp. Since that time the Coonawarra plantings have been increased to 80 ha, the lion's share cabernet sauvignon. The enterprise is offering full winemaking services to vignerons in the Limestone Coast Zone. Exports to the UK and other major markets.

ΨΨΨΨΨ **Coonawarra Cabernet Sauvignon 2005** Combines freshness and vitality with generous blackcurrant and earthy fruit flavours; the tannin structure is excellent, as is the length of the palate. Cork. 14% alc. **Rating** 94 **To** 2020 $23

ΨΨΨΨΨ **Coonawarra Shiraz 2005** Strong colour; a lively wine, with a fragrant bouquet and palate; red and black fruits, earth, spice and licorice all join in the play on the long palate and finish; high-quality cork, perfectly inserted. 14% alc. **Rating** 93 **To** 2020 $23

Sterita Limestone Coast Cabernet Merlot 2006 A lively and attractive blend of juicy red and black fruits, with good structure and texture ex fine tannins, the finish sure and long. Value. Screwcap. 14% alc. **Rating** 90 **To** 2016 $15

ΨΨΨΨ **Sauvignon Blanc 2008** A well-made wine from Limestone Coast/Adelaide Hills; has good intensity and length to its gently tropical fruit flavours, and a clean finish. Screwcap. 13% alc. **Rating** 88 **To** 2010 $18

Emporio Coonawarra Merlot Cabernet Franc Cabernet Sauvignon 2005 A spicy/cedary/earthy bouquet sets the scene for the medium-bodied palate, with modest cassis and blackcurrant components; good balance. Cork. 13.5% alc. **Rating** 88 **To** 2014 $23

Lucindale Cabernet Sauvignon 2005 A light- to medium-bodied wine with earth, spice and cedar underlying the blackcurrant fruits, the tannins fine and balanced. Screwcap. 14% alc. **Rating** 88 **To** 2013 $20

Traditional Method Coonawarra Sparkling Pinot Noir 2007 Bright pale pink; very light strawberry flavours, with an unexpectedly dry finish, and hence length. Cork. 12.5% alc. **Rating** 87 **To** 2010 $23

Dindima Wines

Lot 22 Cargo Road, Orange, NSW 2800 **Region** Orange
T (02) 6365 3388 **F** (02) 6365 3096 **www**.dindima.com.au **Open** 7 days Jan, w'ends & public hols 10–5, or by appt
Winemaker James Bell **Est.** 2002 **Cases** 600 **Vyds** 4 ha
In late 2002 the Bell family acquired a property on the northern slopes of Mt Canobolas at an altitude of approximately 895 m. Prior to 1996 the property had been an orchard. With its redevelopment as a vineyard some of the original muscat vines were retained (now about 45 years old) and new plantings of semillon, merlot, shiraz and cabernet sauvignon occurred. In '05 a further planting of chardonnay was made and plans to add a similar amount of riesling are underway. This family team, led by son James, regards attention to detail in all areas of the winemaking process as essential; theirs is very much a hands-on operation, especially in relation to vineyard canopy management.

ΨΨΨΨΨ **Orange Shiraz 2005** Dark, deep purple; blackberry, licorice, dark chocolate and spice intermingle on the bouquet; the wine is still very youthful and powerful, not so much through tannins as the masses of peppery black fruit flavours. Multi-trophy winner. ProCork. 13% alc. **Rating** 94 **To** 2020 $35

Dinny Goonan Family Estate ★★★★★

880 Winchelsea–Deans Marsh Road, Bambra, Vic 3241 **Region** Geelong
T 0438 408 420 **F** (03) 5288 7100 **www**.dinnygoonan.com.au **Open** 7 days Jan, w'ends
& public hols Nov–Apr, or by appt
Winemaker Dinny Goonan **Est.** 2001 **Cases** 1000 **Vyds** 5.5 ha
The establishment of Dinny Goonan Family Estate dates back to the 1980s when Dinny and
Susan Goonan bought a 20-ha property near Bambra, in the hinterland of the Otway Coast.
Dinny had recently completed a viticulture diploma at CSU, and initially a wide range of
varieties were planted in what is now known as the Nursery block to establish those best
suited to the area. As these came into production Dinny headed back to CSU, where he
completed a wine science degree. Ultimately, it was decided to focus production on Shiraz and
Riesling, with more extensive planting of these varieties. In '07 a 'sticky' block was added.

ᵀᵀᵀᵀᵀ **Early Harvest Riesling 2008** The bouquet is quiet, but the burst of gloriously
sweet lime juice fruit on the palate is no real surprise given the low alcohol; acidity
on the finish plays an essential role. Screwcap. 8% alc. **Rating** 94 **To** 2018 $25
Shiraz 2006 Brilliantly clear crimson colour points to the vibrant, juicy red fruits
on both bouquet and palate; oak and tannins are in veiled support for a delicious
light- to medium-bodied wine. Screwcap. 14.5% alc. **Rating** 94 **To** 2018 $23

ᵀᵀᵀᵀᵧ **Riesling 2008** Bright light straw-green; firm, fresh, clean and crisp, with a
minerally framework for the citrus and green apple fruit flavours; like the Early
Harvest, well made. Screwcap. 11% alc. **Rating** 91 **To** 2016 $20

ᵀᵀᵀᵀ **Semillon Sauvignon 2008** Spotlessly clean and crisp, with grass, lemon and
mineral flavours; however, very light-bodied and a little short on the finish; may
develop with a few years in bottle. Screwcap. 12.5% alc. **Rating** 87 **To** 2012 $25
Cabernets 2006 The cool-grown antecedents are a little too obvious, the
cassis fruit nipped by leafy, green notes; does have length. Screwcap. 13.5% alc.
Rating 87 **To** 2013 $23

Disaster Bay Wines ★★★★

133 Oaklands Road, Pambula, NSW 2549 **Region** South Coast Zone
T (02) 6495 6869 **F** (02) 6495 6869 **www**.disasterbaywines.com **Open** Not
Winemaker Dean O'Reilly, Andrew McEwen **Est.** 2000 **Cases** 400 **Vyds** 1 ha
Dean O'Reilly has a 10-year background in the distribution of fine table wines, culminating
in employment by Möet Hennessy Australia. He has accumulated the UK-based WSET
Intermediate and Advanced Certificates, completed various other programs and competitions,
and has been associate judge and judge at various Canberra district events. He has also travelled
through the wine regions of NZ, Champagne, Bordeaux, Chablis, Piedmont and Tuscany. The
wines are made at Kyeema with Andrew McEwen overseeing Dean's apprenticeship; the
grapes come from the 1-ha block owned by Dean adjacent to the Pambula River.

ᵀᵀᵀᵀᵧ **SS City of Sydney 1862 Merlot Blend 2007** Lively, fresh, juicy and exuberant
cassis and blackcurrant fruit; commendable restraint in winemaking, allowing the
fruit free rein. Merlot/Cabernet Sauvignon/Malbec/Cabernet Franc/Petit Verdot.
Screwcap. 13% alc. **Rating** 90 **To** 2013 $19.99

Djinta Djinta Winery ★★★★

10 Stevens Road, Kardella South, Vic 3951 **Region** Gippsland
T (03) 5658 1163 **F** (03) 5658 1928 **www**.djintadjinta.com.au **Open** Wed–Sun 10–5
Winemaker Marcus Satchell **Est.** 1991 **Cases** 600
One of a group of wineries situated between Leongatha and Korumburra, the most famous
being Bass Phillip. Vines were first planted in 1986 but were largely neglected until Peter and
Helen Harley acquired the property in '91. They set about reviving the 2 ha of sauvignon
blanc and a little cabernet sauvignon, and planted an additional 3 ha of merlot, cabernet franc,
cabernet sauvignon, semillon, marsanne, roussanne and viognier. The first vintage was 1995,

and in late '04 the property was purchased by Alex and Eleonor Biro. Winemaker Marcus Satchell has eight years' experience in the Yarra Valley, and vintage experience with Bonnie Doon Vineyard in California.

ΥΥΥΥΩ   **Reserve South Gippsland Merlot 2006** Very light colour and relatively light-bodied; however, has surprising length and intensity to the red berry and spicy/savoury fruits, the berry components dominant. A wine that grows on retasting. Screwcap. 13% alc. **Rating** 91 **To** 2013 $31
South Gippsland Semillon 2007 Very well made, focusing entirely on the citrus and lemon aroma and flavour, which has good structure and length; will continue to develop depth. Screwcap. 11% alc. **Rating** 90 **To** 2014 $22
South Gippsland Sauvignon Blanc Semillon 2008 Well made, with maximum retention of varietal fruit from the 66/34 blend, stainless steel-fermented and early-bottled; harmonious citrus, grass and stone fruit flavours. Screwcap. 12% alc. **Rating** 90 **To** 2011 $21

ΥΥΥΥ   **Classique 2008** Marsanne (80%) and Roussanne (20%) are not, by nature, expressive varieties when young; this wine has the acidity and balance to sustain it as the years in the cellar will see it grow and flower. Screwcap. 12.9% alc. **Rating** 89 **To** 2015 $25
South Gippsland Cabernet Merlot 2007 Light bright hue; similar weight to the Merlot, but has less complexity, although more cassis/blackcurrant fruit; like the Merlot, has surprising length. Screwcap. 12.5% alc. **Rating** 89 **To** 2014 $22
Ruby Creek Reserve 2006 Although it is one of the more expensive Djinta Djinta wines, and while it shows clear varietal influences, doesn't have enough flesh on the mid- to back palate. Screwcap. 12.5% alc. **Rating** 88 **To** 2013 $35
Classique 2007 As if to prove the point for the '08 Classique, this wine is still painfully young, heightened, perhaps, by the lower alcohol and greener fruit flavours; nonetheless, this will also develop in bottle. Marsanne/Roussanne/Viognier. Screwcap. 11.5% alc. **Rating** 87 **To** 2013 $25

🍂 Doc Adams   ★★★

PO Box 651, Willunga, SA 5172 **Region** McLaren Vale
T (08) 8556 2111 **F** (08) 8556 4540 **www**.docadamswines.com.au **Open** Not
Winemaker Michael Brown **Est.** 2005 **Cases** 900 **Vyds** 20 ha
Doc Adams is a partnership between viticulturist Adam Jacobs and orthopaedic surgeon Dr Darren Waters (and their respective wives). Adam graduated from CSU with a degree in viticulture and has had over 20 years' experience as a consultant viticulturist, first in the Mornington Peninsula and then McLaren Vale, Coonawarra, Adelaide Hills and Langhorne Creek. Darren has grown low-yielding shiraz vines in McLaren Vale since 1998, using all of his time off from his surgical practice. The estate-grown Shiraz is open-fermented, and is matured in 80% new French and 20% new American oak for 18 months. The Pinot Gris comes from a single low-yielding Adelaide Hills vineyard; the wine is given 24 hours skin contact, which leads to the light-golden colour and palate richness.

ΥΥΥΥ   **McLaren Vale Shiraz 2006** Dark chocolate fruit, with blackberry and a chewy tar-like palate; quite dense and rich, with lively acidity on the finish. Zork. 15% alc. **Rating** 88 **To** 2014 $25

DogRock Winery   ★★★★☆

114 De Graves Road, Crowlands, Vic 3377 **Region** Pyrenees
T (03) 5354 9201 **www**.dogrock.com.au **Open** W'ends 11–5
Winemaker Allen Hart **Est.** 1999 **Cases** 400 **Vyds** 6.2 ha
This is the micro-venture (but with inbuilt future growth to something slightly larger) of Allen (winemaker) and Andrea (viticulturist) Hart. Having purchased the property in 1998, planting riesling, chardonnay, marsanne, shiraz, tempranillo and grenache began in 2000. Given Allen's post as research scientist/winemaker with Foster's, the attitude taken to winemaking

is unexpected. The estate-grown wines are made in a low-tech fashion, without gas cover or filtration. The one concession to technology, say the Harts, is that 'all wine will be sealed with a screwcap and no DogRock wine will ever be released under natural cork bark'.

ΨΨΨΨҸ Pedro's Pyrenees Sparkling Red 2007 A pure-fruited, focused and slightly spicy sparkling red; an attractive balance of flavour, texture and liveliness that persists from the bouquet to the finish; very well made and well handled level of sweetness, on the drier side. Crown Seal. 13.5% alc. **Rating** 93 **To** 2014 $32
Pyrenees Grenache 2008 Clean raspberry fruit aromas have a touch of spice and a little minerality; the palate is quite firm, displaying a warm core of red fruits that linger with a little spice. Screwcap. 14% alc. **Rating** 92 **To** 2014 $27

ΨΨΨΨ Pyrenees Riesling 2008 Mandarin and an element of slate are present on the bouquet; quite pleasant flavour development on the palate, with vibrant acidity and a slight oxidative, nutty finish. Screwcap. 12% alc. **Rating** 88 **To** 2013 $20

Domain Barossa

25 Murray Street, Tanunda, SA 5352 **Region** Barossa Valley
T (08) 8563 2170 **F** (08) 8563 2164 **www.**domainbarossa.com **Open** W'ends 11–5.30
Winemaker Todd Riethmuller **Est.** 2002 **Cases** 3000
Todd Riethmuller and family are long-term residents of the Barossa Valley and have the inside running, as it were, when it comes to buying grapes from local growers. Thus they have been able to dispense with the expensive and often frustrating business of having their own winery, yet can make wines of exceptional quality.

ΨΨΨΨΨ Ruth Miller Eden Valley Riesling 2008 Early picking and an appreciable amount of CO_2 result in a zesty, lively palate with a mix of fresh cut green apple and citrus flavours, then a star-bright finish. Gold medal Barossa Valley Wine Show '08. Screwcap. 11.5% alc. **Rating** 94 **To** 2018 $17

ΨΨΨΨ Toddler GSM 2008 Has more stuffing and structure than many from the Barossa Valley, most likely due to bottling within six months of a hot, early vintage. Screwcap. 15% alc. **Rating** 89 **To** 2012 $21
Chardonnay 2008 Early picking has provided good dividends; the wine is uncomplicated but fresh, with attractive stone fruit flavours. Screwcap. 12.5% alc. **Rating** 88 **To** 2012 $17

Domain Day

24 Queen Street, Williamstown, SA 5351 **Region** Barossa Valley
T (08) 8524 6224 **www.**domainday.com.au **Open** W'ends & public hols 10–5
Winemaker Robin Day **Est.** 2000 **Cases** 8000 **Vyds** 15.1 ha
This is a classic case of an old dog learning new tricks, and doing so with panache. Robin Day had a long and distinguished career as winemaker, chief winemaker, then technical director of Orlando; he participated in the management buy-out, and profited substantially from the on-sale to Pernod Ricard. He hastened slowly with the establishment of Domain Day, but there is nothing conservative about his approach in his vineyard at Mt Crawford, high in the hills (at 450 m) of the southeastern extremity of the Barossa Valley, two sides of the vineyard bordering the Eden Valley, and moving to positive biological controls. While the mainstream varieties are merlot, pinot noir and riesling, he has trawled Italy, France and Georgia for the other varieties: viognier, nebbiolo, sangiovese, saperavi, lagrein, garganega, sagrantino and nebbiolo. Robin Day says, 'Years of writing descriptions for back labels have left me convinced that this energy is more gainfully employed in growing grapes and making wine.' Robin provides tutored tastings in the vineyard showcasing alternative varieties (by appointment). Exports to the UK and Canada.

ΨΨΨΨҸ Mt Crawford Viognier 2006 Highly aromatic and perfumed bouquet, with apricot standing proud, and coming through with equal power on the palate; admirable varietal expression. Screwcap. 13.8% alc. **Rating** 93 **To** 2012 $20

One Serious Mt Crawford Riesling 2007 Flowery apple blossom, citrus and spice aromas; crisp, crunchy, minerally palate; restrained fruit but good length and focus. Screwcap. 12% alc. **Rating** 91 **To** 2015 $20

ΥΥΥΥ **Mt Crawford Garganega 2007** Apple, pear skin and spice aromas moving into lemon citrus flavours on the fresh and vibrant palate. Screwcap. 12.5% alc. **Rating** 89 **To** 2012 $20

One Serious Mt Crawford Pinot Noir 2005 Lifted bouquet of cherry and spiced plum; a touch of sage comes through on the palate, and the texture is lively through to the finish. Screwcap. 13% alc. **Rating** 88 **To** 2012 $28

Mt Crawford Lagrein 2005 Deep colour; bright spiced blueberry bouquet; plenty of flavour, with a chewy/tarry palate; juicy on the finish. Screwcap. 13.5% alc. **Rating** 88 **To** 2013 $28

Domaine A   ★★★★★

Tea Tree Road, Campania, Tas 7026 **Region** Southern Tasmania
T (03) 6260 4174 **www.**domaine-a.com.au **Open** Mon–Fri 9–4, w'ends by appt
Winemaker Peter Althaus **Est.** 1973 **Cases** 5000 **Vyds** 11.5 ha
The striking black label of the premium Domaine A wine, dominated by the single, multi-coloured 'A', signified the change of ownership from George Park to Swiss businessman Peter Althaus many years ago. The wines are made without compromise, and reflect the low yields from the immaculately tended vineyards. They represent aspects of both Old World and New World philosophies, techniques and styles. Exports to the UK, Denmark, Switzerland, Germany, France, Belgium, Canada, NZ, China, Japan and Singapore.

ΥΥΥΥΥ **Cabernet Sauvignon 2003** Right in the mainstream of the classically austere Domaine A style, with a degree of complexity and intensity within that austere exterior that is quite remarkable. A wine made with fastidious attention to detail and without compromise. Cork. 13.5% alc. **Rating** 95 **To** 2023 $65

Pinot Noir 2005 Good hue retention; aromas of plum and spice, then a light-to medium-bodied palate with very good structure and length, the flavours in a foresty/savoury/spicy spectrum. Cork. 13.5% alc. **Rating** 94 **To** 2014 $70

ΥΥΥΥΥ **Lady A Sauvignon Blanc 2007** A strong influence of oak with a pungent varietal bouquet of gooseberry and tropical fruit; the palate is dominated by oak and is built for the long haul; more exotic guava fruit comes through on the finish, the oak persistent. Cork. 13.5% alc. **Rating** 93 **To** 2014 $60

Stoney Vineyard Sauvignon Blanc 2008 A ripe lemon bouquet, with a complex mineral character; subtle flavours with good drive, and chalky acidity on the finish; a complex and fine wine. Diam. 14% alc. **Rating** 92 **To** 2014 $35

Stoney Vineyard Reserve Pinot Noir 2004 Deceptively light in colour and in its initial impact on the palate, but reveals great thrust and length to the spicy/earthy/foresty flavours. Cork. 13.5% alc. **Rating** 92 **To** 2013 $40

Stoney Vineyard Cabernet Sauvignon 2003 Slightly more developed colour than its big brother and with some French oak evident; cedary nuances and fine tannins make it more approachable now and over the next five or so years. Cork. 13.5% alc. **Rating** 91 **To** 2018 $26

ΥΥΥΥ **Stoney Vineyard Cabernet Sauvignon 2004** In the austere, earthy European style of Domaine A, with the structure for a long life on a path different to that taken by most Australian wines. Diam. 13.5% alc. **Rating** 89 **To** 2014 $26

Domaine Chandon   ★★★★★

Green Point, Maroondah Highway, Coldstream, Vic 3770 **Region** Yarra Valley
T (03) 9738 9200 **F** (03) 9738 9201 **www.**chandon.com.au **Open** 7 days 10.30–4.30
Winemaker Matt Steel, Glenn Thompson, Andrew Santarossa, Adam Keath **Est.** 1986
Cases 120 000 **Vyds** 78 ha

Established by Moet & Chandon, and one of the two most important wine facilities in the Yarra Valley; the tasting room has a national and international reputation having won a number of major tourism awards in recent years. The sparkling wine product range has evolved, and there has been increasing emphasis placed on the table wines, now released under the Domaine Chandon label. An energetic young winemaking team has maintained the high-quality standards set by ex-CEO and mentor Dr Tony Jordan, who continues to consult to the winery. Exports to all major markets.

ΨΨΨΨΨ **Yarra Valley Chardonnay 2007** Bright green-straw; a very fragrant bouquet leads into a totally delicious palate with a cascade of nectarine and white peach flavours; has great length and finesse. Screwcap. 13% alc. **Rating** 96 **To** 2020 $28

Yarra Valley Vintage Brut 2005 One of the best Vintage Bruts from Domaine Chandon for many years; delicious fruit flavours woven through touches of biscuit and brioche; lingering clean finish; perfect dosage. Cork. 12.5% alc. **Rating** 95 **To** 2010 $39

Brut Rose Vintage 2005 Pale salmon; delicious fresh and lively wine, which has a lovely mixture of small red fruits and citrus, the dancing finish and aftertaste zesty and dry. Diam. 12.5% alc. **Rating** 95 **To** 2011 $39.95

Barrel Selection Yarra Valley Chardonnay 2007 Pale colour; a tight and restrained citrus and stone fruit bouquet; elegantly structured on the palate, with a gently grilled nut core to the wine; persistent white pear on the finish. Screwcap. 13% alc. **Rating** 94 **To** 2014 $49.95

Pinot Noir Rose 2008 Pale bright pink; bell-clear strawberry, rose petal and red cherry aromas drive a classy rose; long, dry but balanced finish; at once hedonistic and serious. Screwcap. 12.5% alc. **Rating** 94 **To** 2010 $24

Yarra Valley Pinot Noir 2008 A fragrant, spicy bouquet leads into a relatively light-bodied palate, which, nonetheless, has striking length to the plum, spice and oak flavours; fine tannins strengthen the finish. Screwcap. 13% alc. **Rating** 94 **To** 2015 $33.95

Barrel Selection Pinot Noir 2006 Bright crimson-red hue; fragrant red fruits on the bouquet lead into a vibrant and fresh palate; the precise red cherry flavours with considerable length. Screwcap. 13% alc. **Rating** 94 **To** 2013 $50

Heathcote Shiraz 2006 Superb bright crimson-purple; succulent and supple, but not heavy or sweet, black cherry and plum fruit supported by fine, ripe tannins. Screwcap. 14.5% alc. **Rating** 94 **To** 2020 $32

Barrel Selection Yarra Valley Shiraz 2006 Bright colour; essency blackberry fruit/toasty oak aromas; sweet-fruited, with lots of peppery spice and bright red and black fruits on the palate; quite a bit of oak, but the fruit carries it with ease. Screwcap. 14% alc. **Rating** 94 **To** 2018 $49.95

Barrel Selection Yarra Valley Shiraz 2005 Super-bright, clean and focused red fruit and spice aromas; loads of sweet fruit with a strong mineral core running through to the finish; well crafted. Screwcap. 14.5% alc. **Rating** 94 **To** 2015 $54

Brut Rose Non Vintage NV Bright pink; fragrant red fruit aromas and flavours; very good, supple mouthfeel, yet not sweet; has admirable length. Cork. 12.5% alc. **Rating** 94 **To** 2010 $29

ΨΨΨΨΨ **Sauvignon Blanc 2008** Complex winemaking courtesy of cross-regional selection and a small percentage of barrel fermentation in older French oak barriques gives the wine a pleasing tropical overtone; the texture enhanced by the barrel ferment component. Screwcap. 12% alc. **Rating** 93 **To** 2011 $24

Barrel Selection Yarra Valley Chardonnay 2006 Very fine and focused with pear fruit aromas framed by very good oak; the elegance continues on the palate, with a fine, savoury and slightly nutty finish. Screwcap. 13% alc. **Rating** 93 **To** 2015 $46

Pinot Gris 2008 Pale colour; pear and grapefruit bouquet, a touch of candied orange in the background; very lively palate, with savoury texture and a very clean, fine and focused finish; very good flavour. Screwcap. 13.5% alc. **Rating** 93 **To** 2013 $26.95

Yarra Valley Vintage Brut 2006 Fresh and restrained lemon bouquet, with a hint of toasted brioche; chalky and fresh on the palate, the fruit exhibits drive and nerve; an aperitif style. Diam. 12.5% alc. **Rating** 93 **To** 2012 $39.95

Vintage Tasmanian Cuvee 2005 Brilliant straw-green; 50/50 Chardonnay/ Pinot Noir with 30 months on yeast lees; still very crisp and youthful, will improve. Diam. 12.5% alc. **Rating** 93 **To** 2015 $39.95

Brut Rose Vintage 2006 Delicately perfumed with a mere suggestion of red fruit framing the more prominent citrus aromas; the palate is fine, with good texture and lightness to the finish. Diam. 12.5% alc. **Rating** 92 **To** 2012 $39.95

Z*D Blanc de Blancs 2005 Very tight and fresh; all lemon fruit, with a fine and creamy mouthfeel on the mid-palate, then a dry, minerally finish. Should age well. Crown Seal. 12.5% alc. **Rating** 92 **To** 2020 $39.95

Blanc de Blancs 2005 Tight and fine lemon fruit, with a touch of toasty complexity; the palate is fine, fresh and quite long, with the chardonnay fruit drawing out the chalky finish. Diam. 12.5% alc. **Rating** 90 **To** 2015 $39.95

Cuvee Riche NV Off-dry green apple bouquet with an undercurrent of citrus and stone fruit; sweet on entry, the acid cleans up the sugar and leaves the fruit to linger harmoniously on the palate; a good example of the style. Diam. 12.5% alc. **Rating** 90 **To** 2013 $39.95

Domaine Epis

812 Black Forest Drive, Woodend, Vic 3442 **Region** Macedon Ranges
T (03) 5427 1204 **F** (03) 5427 1204 **Open** By appt
Winemaker Stuart Anderson **Est.** 1990 **Cases** NA

Three legends are involved in the Domaine Epis and Epis & Williams wines, two of them in their own lifetime. They are long-term Essendon guru and former player Alec Epis, who owns the two quite separate vineyards and brands; Stuart Anderson, who directs winemaking, with Alec doing all the hard work; and the late Laurie Williams, the father of viticulture in the Macedon region and the man who established the Flynn & Williams vineyard in 1976. Alec Epis purchased that vineyard from Laurie Williams in 1999, and as a mark of respect (and with Laurie's approval) continued to use his name, in conjunction with his own. The Cabernet Sauvignon comes from this vineyard, the Chardonnay and Pinot Noir from the vineyard at Woodend, where a small winery was built in 2002.

The Williams Vineyard 2007 A red to dark fruit bouquet, with a touch of sage and earth; truly medium-bodied with fleshy fruit and quite fine tannin structure; a touch of cold tea adds complexity to the finish. Cabernet Sauvignon/Merlot. Diam. 13% alc. **Rating** 93 **To** 2015 $35

Macedon Ranges Pinot Noir 2007 Bright cherry colour; distinctly menthol and red cherry bouquet with a little earthy complexity; quite generous red fruit on entry, the structure comes through and provides focus and firmness on the finish. Diam. 13% alc. **Rating** 92 **To** 2014 $60

Macedon Ranges Chardonnay 2007 Deep golden hue; a very complex bouquet, heading toward bitter almond and Meyer lemon; tighter on the palate, there is burnt butter complexity; good acid provides focus to the finish; not a style for everyone. Diam. 13% alc. **Rating** 89 **To** 2014 $40

Domaines Tatiarra

Suite 102, 832 High Street, East Kew, Vic 3102 (postal) **Region** Heathcote
T (03) 9249 9572 **F** (03) 9249 9538 **www**.cambrianshiraz.com **Open** Not
Winemaker Ben Riggs, Peter Flewellyn **Est.** 1991 **Cases** 2300 **Vyds** 13.4 ha

Domaines Tatiarra Limited is an unlisted public company, its core asset being a 60-ha property of Cambrian earth identified and developed by Bill Hepburn, who sold the project to the company in 1991. It will produce only one varietal wine: Shiraz. The majority of the wine will come from the Tatiarra (an Aboriginal word meaning 'beautiful country') property, but the Trademark Shiraz is an equal blend of McLaren Vale and Heathcote wine. The wines are made at the Pettavel Winery in Geelong, with Ben Riggs commuting between McLaren Vale and the winery as required. Exports to the UK, the US, Canada, Denmark, Switzerland and Singapore.

♀♀♀♀♀ **Trademark Heathcote McLaren Vale Shiraz 2007** Perhaps it's due to the McLaren Vale regional character, but the wine carries its alcohol much better than the 100% Heathcote wines, with savoury, spice and bitter chocolate characters cutting back the alcohol sweetness. Cork. 15.5% alc. **Rating 92 To** 2017 $60.65
Caravan of Dreams Heathcote Shiraz Pressings 2007 Dense colour; massive full-bodied wine with bitter chocolate and black fruits to burn – as does the alcohol. Nonetheless, will appeal to some. Cork. 15.5% alc. **Rating 90 To** 2017 $60.65

♀♀♀♀ **Culled Barrel Heathcote Shiraz 2007** Deep colour; very much in the Domaines Tatiarra style – the basis for culling the barrel not obvious. Screwcap. 15.5% alc. **Rating 88 To** 2022 $25
Cambrian Heathcote Shiraz 2007 Lashings of black fruit flavours, but the alcohol comes thundering over the top – a pity; time may help. Cork. 15.5% alc. **Rating 88 To** 2017 $44.70
Culled Barrel Heathcote Shiraz 2006 Bright and juicy red and blue fruits, with a little spice and some strong oak flavours pushing through on the finish; good fruit definition and weight on the finish. Screwcap. 15.5% alc. **Rating 88 To** 2015 $23
Caravan of Dreams Heathcote Shiraz Pressings 2006 Bright red and blue fruits, with a steely minerality at the core; quite juicy despite the pressings label, with a savoury medium-bodied finish. Cork. 15.5% alc. **Rating 88 To** 2016 $51
Trademark Heathcote McLaren Vale Shiraz 2006 A quite oaky bouquet, with some dried black fruit character coming to the fore; a rich, unctuous and dense almost jam-like quality dominates the finish. Cork. 15.5% alc. **Rating 87 To** 2013 $61

Dominique Portet ★★★★★

870–872 Maroondah Highway, Coldstream, Vic 3770 **Region** Yarra Valley
T (03) 5962 5760 **F** (03) 5962 4938 **www.**dominiqueportet.com **Open** 7 days 10–5
Winemaker Ben Portet **Est.** 2000 **Cases** 12 000 **Vyds** 4.3 ha
Dominique Portet was bred in the purple. He spent his early years at Chateau Lafite (where his father was regisseur) and was one of the very first Flying Winemakers, commuting to Clos du Val in the Napa Valley where his brother was winemaker. He then spent over 20 years as managing director of Taltarni, and the Clover Hill vineyard in Tasmania. After retiring from Taltarni, he moved to the Yarra Valley, a region he had been closely observing since the mid-1980s. In 2001 he found the site he had long looked for and in a twinkling of an eye built his winery and cellar door, planting a quixotic mix of viognier, sauvignon blanc and merlot next to the winery. Son Ben is now executive winemaker, leaving Dominique with a roving role as de facto consultant and brand marketer. Ben (28) has a winemaking CV of awesome scope, covering all parts of France, South Africa, California and four vintages at Petaluma. Exports to the UK, the US and other major markets.

♀♀♀♀♀ **Andre Heathcote Yarra Valley Shiraz Cabernet Sauvignon 2006** Extremely elegant and fragrant, with distinct French touches to its make-up; beautifully balanced and weighted, its blackberry/blackcurrant fruit is suspended in a gossamer web of fine tannins and French oak. Easily the best wine under the Dominique Portet label. Cork. 14% alc. **Rating 96 To** 2020 $120
Heathcote Shiraz 2006 Slight colour development; right in the mainstream of Heathcote shiraz style, with black fruits in abundance, gently savoury tannins providing a good contrast. Cork. 14% alc. **Rating 94 To** 2016 $45
Heathcote Cabernet Sauvignon 2006 Good colour; has elegant, gently sweet cassis-accented fruit on both the bouquet and the medium-bodied palate; fine tannins and quality oak complete a harmonious, quality wine. Cork. 14% alc. **Rating 94 To** 2015 $42

Tasmanian Cuvee 2003 Pale straw-gold; good mousse; super-elegant fine style, creamy/brioche lees notes woven through the finely delineated, citrussy fruit; restrained dosage. Cork. 12.5% alc. **Rating** 94 **To** 2010 $40

♟♟♟♟♟ Yarra Valley Brut Rose LD NV Bright blush-pink; attractive texture and structure, with distinct strawberry and stone fruit flavours; long, crisp finish. Pinot Noir/Chardonnay. Cork. 13% alc. **Rating** 92 **To** 2010 $25
Yarra Valley Cabernet Sauvignon 2006 Potent and savoury, with briary overtones to the black fruits and persistent tannins of the palate; will benefit from time in bottle. Cork. 14% alc. **Rating** 92 **To** 2016 $42
Fontaine Yarra Valley Rose 2008 Pale salmon-pink; highly structured style, with a strong mineral component along with spice, herb and red fruit mix. Screwcap. 14.5% alc. **Rating** 90 **To** 2011 $20

♟♟♟♟ Yarra Valley Sauvignon Blanc 2008 Spotlessly clean bouquet; very restrained varietal expression, possibly fermentation or maturation in old French oak; good structure and length. Diam. 13.5% alc. **Rating** 89 **To** 2011 $26
Yarra Valley Merlot 2005 While the tannins are not in themselves aggressive, they do stand out in what is a light-bodied wine in fruit terms; needs food to soften the impact. Screwcap. 14.5% alc. **Rating** 88 **To** 2012 $26

Donnelly River Wines

Lot 159 Vasse Highway, Pemberton, WA 6260 **Region** Pemberton
T (08) 9776 2052 **F** (08) 9776 2053 **Open** 7 days 9.30–4.30
Winemaker Blair Meiklejohn **Est.** 1986 **Cases** NA
Donnelly River Wines draws upon 16 ha of estate vineyards planted in 1986, and has performed consistently well with its Chardonnay. Exports to the UK, Denmark, Germany, Singapore, Malaysia and Japan.

♟♟♟♟   Mist 2007 Good texture and focus with plenty of mid-palate fruit, but does have a congested finish. Verdelho/Semillon/Sauvignon Blanc. **Rating** 89 **To** 2010
Sauvignon Blanc 2007 An abundance of varietal fruit still holding together well, with bright kiwi fruit flavours. **Rating** 88 **To** 2010

Donny Goodmac   NR

PO Box 467, Healesville, Vic 3777 **Region** Yarra Valley
T (03) 5962 6724 **F** (03) 5962 6724 **www.**donnygoodmac.com.au **Open** Not
Winemaker Kate Goodman **Est.** 2002 **Cases** 600
The improbable name is a typically whimsical invention of the three proprietors: Donny is contributed by Stuart Gregor, whose marketing and PR prowess has hitherto prevented an entry for the venture in the *Wine Companion*. Kate Goodman is the (genuinely) good part of the team, while Cameron MacKenzie is the 'mac'. Goodman and MacKenzie both work full-time at Punt Road, where Kate is chief winemaker. What started as a little bit of fun in 2002 (less than 50 cases made) has grown to the dizzy heights of 600 cases, utilising old vine shiraz from the Pyrenees, and chardonnay and cabernet sauvignon from a couple of old vineyards in the Coldstream area of the Yarra Valley.

Donovan Wines

RMB 2017 Pomonal Road, Stawell, Vic 3380 **Region** Grampians
T (03) 5358 2727 **F** (03) 5358 2727 **Open** Sat 10–5, Sun 12–5
Winemaker Paul Stephens **Est.** 1977 **Cases** 3000 **Vyds** 10.5 ha
Donovan Wines (with Peter Donovan as chief executive and James Donovan as viticulturist) has increased production, with two vineyards, one at Stawell, the other at Great Western. Limited distribution in Melbourne; most of the wine is sold by mail order with some bottle age.

ÝÝÝÝ° Reserve Shiraz 2005 An interesting blend of dark fruits, spice and florals; the palate is quite fine but very firm, and layers of flavour provide real interest from start to finish. Screwcap. 14% alc. **Rating** 90 **To** 2018 $25

ÝÝÝÝ Merlot 2006 Clean varietal fruit, with elements of plum, black olive and plenty of fine-grained tannins; simple but a good example of the variety in Australia. Screwcap. 13.5% alc. **Rating** 88 **To** 2014 $15

Dookie Campus Winery ★★★
Dookie-Nalinga Road, Dookie, Vic 3647 **Region** Goulburn Valley
T (03) 5833 9295 **F** (03) 5833 9296 **www**.dookie.unimelb.edu.au **Open** Mon–Fri 10–4
Winemaker Sam Scarpari **Est.** 1896 **Cases** 2500 **Vyds** 21.1 ha
Dookie has a long history of teaching winemaking and viticulture dating back to the end of the 19th century. These days it is part of the University of Melbourne, and as well as being a teaching winery acts as a contract winemaking facility for boutique winemakers. Its estate vineyards, on soil similar to that of Heathcote, are planted to shiraz, cabernet sauvignon, sauvignon blanc and semillon.

ÝÝÝÝ Federli Shiraz 2007 Dense purple; a no-holds-barred full-bodied wine with an abundance of licorice and spice overtones to the blackberry fruit at its core. Needs years and will improve. ProCork. 14.9% alc. **Rating** 89 **To** 2022 $36
360° Cabernet Sauvignon 2006 Pleasant medium-bodied wine, with blackcurrant fruit and touches of savoury/black olive in the background; good overall flavour and mouthfeel. Screwcap. 14% alc. **Rating** 88 **To** 2014 $14

Doonkuna Estate ★★★★
3182 Barton Highway, Murrumbateman, NSW 2582 **Region** Canberra District
T (02) 6227 5811 **F** (02) 6227 5085 **www**.doonkuna.com.au **Open** 7 days 10–4
Winemaker Bruce March **Est.** 1971 **Cases** 4000 **Vyds** 19.2 ha
Following the acquisition of Doonkuna by Barry and Maureen Moran in late 1996, the plantings have been increased to almost 20 ha, and include shiraz, chardonnay, cabernet sauvignon, sauvignon blanc, zinfandel, sangiovese, riesling, merlot and pinot noir. A wide range of vintages of many of the wines are available at cellar door at modest prices.

ÝÝÝÝ° Reserve Shiraz 2007 Much deeper colour than the Rising Ground; dramatically greater density and richness to the fruit, although not overripe; spicy blackberry and licorice; ripe tannins. Screwcap. 13.5% alc. **Rating** 91 **To** 2020 $50
Cian Methode Traditionnelle 2005 An attractive blend of Chardonnay (55%)/ Pinot Noir (45%) which has spent two years on yeast lees, and gained considerable complexity without compromising the fresh acidity on the finish. Cork. 12.9% alc. **Rating** 90 **To** 2012 $30

ÝÝÝÝ Riesling 2008 A rich and ripe wine, with an abundance of lime/citrus fruit but not quite enough acidity to energise the finish. Screwcap. 12.1% alc. **Rating** 88 **To** 2013 $24
Sauvignon Blanc 2008 Light straw-green; a mix of gooseberry, grass and asparagus aromas and flavours; falls slightly short. Screwcap. 13.9% alc. **Rating** 88 **To** 2010 $18
Shiraz 2004 Pleasant medium-bodied wine, developing well, the fruit and oak in good balance, the tannins soft. Screwcap. 13.7% alc. **Rating** 88 **To** 2013 $40
Late Harvest Semillon 2007 Rich gold colour; peachy flavours with crème caramel for good measure; has balance. Screwcap. 11% alc. **Rating** 88 **To** 2011 $16
Rising Ground Shiraz 2007 Clear crimson; a light- to medium-bodied palate with a mix of spice and berry fruit, and savoury tannins to close. Screwcap. 12.5% alc. **Rating** 87 **To** 2014 $18

Dos Rios

★★★☆

PO Box 343, Nyah, Vic 3594 **Region** Swan Hill
T (03) 5030 3005 **F** (03) 5030 3006 **www.**dosrios.com.au **Open** Fri–Mon 9–9
Winemaker Cobaw Ridge (Alan Cooper) **Est.** 2003 **Cases** 1000 **Vyds** 1.4 ha
Bruce Hall entered the wine business as a small contract grower for McGuigan Simeon Wines.
From this point on, the story goes in reverse: instead of McGuigan Simeon saying it no longer
required the grapes, it purchased the vineyard in 2003. In the meantime, Hall had hand-picked
the grapes left at the end of the rows after the mechanical harvester had passed through, and
had the wines made by Alan Cooper of Cobaw Ridge. In 2004 he purchased a small property
northwest of Swan Hill with plantings of 20-year-old shiraz, which has been extended by
small areas of viognier, tempranillo, verdelho and moscato giallo. Exports to Spain and Japan.

ŸŸŸŸŸ **Reserve Swan Hill Shiraz Viognier 2006** Excellent crimson colour and
the lifted aromas from the co-fermentation of shiraz and viognier; remarkably,
30 months in used barriques has not diminished the fresh fruit. Very good value.
Screwcap. 13.5% alc. **Rating** 90 **To** 2014 $20

ŸŸŸŸ **Swan Hill Lagrein 2007** Dense and inky purple; the palate is nowhere near as
full-bodied and powerful as the colour suggests, with notes of rhubarb, chocolate
and plum jam. Utterly individual. Screwcap. 14% alc. **Rating** 88 **To** 2015 $20
Swan Hill Shiraz 2006 Excellent crimson-purple; a lively palate with a near-
citrus edge to the flavours and the crisp finish. Screwcap. 13.5% alc. **Rating** 87
To 2014 $20
Swan Hill Tempranillo 2006 Has the vaguely citrussy notes of many Aus
tempranillos, aided by contrasting spicy notes. Screwcap. 13.5% alc. **Rating** 87
To 2016 $20

Dowie Doole

★★★★

Cnr McMurtrie Road/Main Road, McLaren Vale, SA 5171 **Region** McLaren Vale
T (08) 8323 8875 **F** (08) 8323 8895 **www.**dowiedoole.com **Open** 7 days 10–5
Winemaker Brian Light (Contract) **Est.** 1996 **Cases** 20 000 **Vyds** 43.04 ha
Dowie Doole has three vineyards owned by individual partners: California Road in McLaren
Vale, the so-called Home Block in the Adelaide Hills (sauvignon blanc), and Tintookie at
Blewitt Springs. Steadily increasing amounts of the grapes are being used for the Dowie Doole
wines. Exports to the UK, the US and other major markets.

ŸŸŸŸŸ **Reserve McLaren Vale Shiraz 2006** At no stage does this medium-bodied
wine show its alcohol, nor indeed does it signal McLaren Vale; an elegant
palate weaves together black fruits, quality oak and fine tannins. Diam. 15% alc.
Rating 93 **To** 2021 $50
McLaren Vale Shiraz 2007 Deep, but clear, purple-red; restrained alcohol allows
the full range of fruit expression, ranging through blackberry, plum, licorice, spice
and a dusting of chocolate. Screwcap. 14.5% alc. **Rating** 91 **To** 2016 $25
McLaren Vale Merlot 2007 Vibrant crimson-purple; very well made and
astutely picked; luscious but not jammy red fruits and a whisk of tannin support.
Screwcap. 13.5% alc. **Rating** 90 **To** 2014 $25
McLaren Vale Cabernet Sauvignon 2006 A fragrant bouquet, then a
restrained but well-balanced and textured palate with quite juicy cassis fruit and
fine tannins in support. Screwcap. 14% alc. **Rating** 90 **To** 2016 $25

ŸŸŸŸ **Tintookie McLaren Vale Chenin Blanc 2006** Barrel ferment and 70-year-
old vines are the basis for an apparently ambitious price; the wine is built for the
long haul and may repay a modest gamble, but it's not there yet. Cork. 11.5% alc.
Rating 89 **To** 2016 $32
McLaren Vale Merlot 2008 Picked before the heatwave; has good fruit flavour,
and the weight and structure expected of merlot; supple red fruits and a soft tannin
finish. Screwcap. 13.5% alc. **Rating** 89 **To** 2014 $21

Second Nature McLaren Vale Cabernet Shiraz Merlot 2007 Light- to medium-bodied, with gently sweet red and black fruits and fine, ripe tannins; easy-access style. Screwcap. 14% alc. **Rating** 87 **To** 2010 $19

Downing Estate Vineyard

19 Drummonds Lane, Heathcote, Vic 3523 **Region** Heathcote
T (03) 5433 3387 **www.**downingestate.com.au **Open** W'ends 11.30–4.30 or by appt
Winemaker Don Lewis **Est.** 1994 **Cases** 1000
Bob and Joy Downing purchased 24 ha of undulating land in 1994, and have since established a 9.5-ha dry-grown vineyard planted to shiraz (75%), cabernet sauvignon and merlot. At any one time, a number of vintages of each wine are available for sale. Exports to the UK and the US.

Heathcote Shiraz 2005 Good colour, although not brilliant; a lively wine, with almost juicy red berry fruit on the well-balanced, medium-bodied palate. Bears no resemblance to the wine tasted 12 months ago. Screwcap. 15% alc. **Rating** 94 **To** 2020 $39

Driftwood Estate ★★★★★

3314 Caves Road, Wilyabrup, WA 6282 **Region** Margaret River
T (08) 9755 6323 **F** (08) 9755 6343 **www.**driftwood-winery.com.au **Open** 7 days 10–5
Winemaker Andrew Spencer-Wright, Hugh Warren **Est.** 1989 **Cases** 25 000
Driftwood Estate is a well-established landmark on the Margaret River scene. Quite apart from offering a brasserie restaurant capable of seating 200 people (open seven days for lunch and dinner) and a mock Greek open-air theatre, its wines feature striking and stylish packaging and opulent flavours. The winery architecture is, it must be said, opulent rather than stylish. Exports to the UK, the US and Singapore.

Margaret River Shiraz Cabernet 2005 Medium-bodied; lively red fruits, plum, cherry ex-shiraz, darker fruits ex-cabernet, including tannins. Gold WA Wine Show '08. **Rating** 94 **To** 2015

Dromana Estate

555 Old Moorooduc Road, Tuerong, Vic 3933 **Region** Mornington Peninsula
T (03) 5974 4400 **F** (03) 5974 1155 **www.**dromanaestate.com.au **Open** Wed–Sun 11–5
Winemaker Duncan Buchanan **Est.** 1982 **Cases** 30 000 **Vyds** 53.9 ha
Since it was established by Garry Crittenden (who exited some years ago), Dromana Estate has always been near or at the cutting edge, both in marketing terms and in terms of development of new varietals, most obviously the Italian range under the 'i' label. The business is now majority-owned by investors; the capital provided has resulted in the Yarra Valley Hills and Mornington Estate wines coming under the Dromana Estate umbrella. Exports to the UK, Canada, Korea, Japan, Singapore and Hong Kong.

Mornington Peninsula Pinot Noir 2007 Attractive pinot in an overall spicy/foresty mode, with just enough red fruits to give flavour balance; good length. Screwcap. 13% alc. **Rating** 91 **To** 2012 $33
Mornington Estate Sauvignon Blanc 2008 Clean, fresh and crisp, with predominantly grassy, snow pea and herb characters complexed by partial barrel fermentation (with wild yeast); has a cleansing finish. Screwcap. 13.5% alc. **Rating** 90 **To** 2010 $22
i Mornington Peninsula Arneis 2008 A variety with plenty going for it; pear, apple and honeysuckle with a grainy acidity that adds to length and texture. Screwcap. 12.9% alc. **Rating** 90 **To** 2011 $22
i Heathcote Nebbiolo 2006 Excellent colour for nebbiolo; usually a masochistic variety for winemaker and consumer alike, but this fragrant wine has far more things right than wrong; all it really needs is the right food – Italian of course. Screwcap. 14% alc. **Rating** 90 **To** 2015 $22

ŢŢŢ   i Mornington Peninsula Pinot Grigio 2008 A pinot grigio with attitude thanks to its cool-grown origins; whether it's more grigio than gris is the question, but the finish is crisp and clean. Screwcap. 13% alc. **Rating** 89 **To** 2010 $22
i Heathcote Sangiovese 2006 Typical light red colour; an enticing floral bouquet and promising entry, but the finish is too lean for higher points – nearly, but not quite. Screwcap. 14% alc. **Rating** 88 **To** 2012 $22

Dryridge Estate   ★★★

The Six Foot Track, Megalong Valley, NSW 2785 **Region** Central Ranges Zone
T (02) 4787 5625 **F** (02) 4787 5626 **www.**dryridge.com.au **Open** Sun 11–4 or by appt
Winemaker Madrez Wine Services **Est.** 1999 **Cases** 500 **Vyds** 4.7 ha
Bob and Barbara Tyrrell (no relation to Tyrrell's of the Hunter Valley) have pioneered commercial viticulture in the Megalong Valley adjacent to the Blue Mountains National Park. They have 1.8 ha of riesling, 1.1 ha of shiraz and 0.9 ha of cabernet sauvignon, and a further 0.9 ha to be planted (possibly fiano) in due course. The vines are set on typically east-facing rolling hillsides with granitic-derived light, sandy clay loam soils of moderately low fertility. The first of two lodges on the vineyard has been opened, providing 4.5-star accommodation.

ŢŢŢŢ   Six Foot Track Blue Mountains Shiraz 2008 Cool fruit, a little mint, and some smoked meat aromas; the palate has prominent acidity, and a slight tarry edge that adds interest. Screwcap. 13.5% alc. **Rating** 89 **To** 2014 $23
Six Foot Track Blue Mountains Rose 2008 Ripe red cherry fruit and a little garden herb; quite dry, with cleansing acidity and lingering red fruits. Screwcap. 12.5% alc. **Rating** 88 **To** 2011 $19

Ducketts Mill   ★★★★

1678, Scotsdale Road, Denmark, WA 6333 **Region** Denmark
T (08) 9840 9844 **F** (08) 9840 9668 **www.**duckettsmillwines.com.au **Open** 7 days 10–5
Winemaker Harewood Estate (James Kellie) **Est.** 1997 **Cases** 1200 **Vyds** 8 ha
Ducketts Mill is a twin operation with Denmark Farmhouse Cheese, both owned and operated by Ross and Dallas Lewis. They have the only cheese factory in the Great Southern region, and rely on James Kellie to make the wines from the extensive estate plantings (riesling, chardonnay, merlot, cabernet franc, ruby cabernet and cabernet sauvignon). Part of the grapes are sold, part made into Riesling, Late Harvest Riesling, Merlot and Three Cabernets. The handmade cheeses make an even wider choice.

ŢŢŢŢ°   Denmark Riesling 2008 Floral citrus blossom and passionfruit aromas; nicely balanced palate courtesy of mineral/citrus acidity, although softer than some. Screwcap. 12.5% alc. **Rating** 90 **To** 2014 $16
Unwooded Chardonnay 2008 Very rich and complex, multi-fruit flavours, but too sweet for higher points. Screwcap. 13.5% alc. **Rating** 90 **To** 2010 $16

ŢŢŢŢ   Denmark Merlot 2007 Light but bright hue; offers a light-bodied mix of small red fruits and hints of olive, spice and snowpea; good varietal expression. Screwcap. 14% alc. **Rating** 87 **To** 2012 $16

Duke's Vineyard   ★★★★★

Porongurup Road, Porongurup, WA 6324 **Region** Porongurup
T (08) 9853 1107 **F** (08) 9853 1107 **www.**dukesvineyard.com **Open** 7 days 10–4.30
Winemaker The Vintage Wineworx (Greg Jones) **Est.** 1998 **Cases** 3000 **Vyds** 10 ha
When Hilde and Ian (Duke) Ranson sold their clothing manufacturing business in 1998, they were able to fulfil a long-held dream of establishing a vineyard in the Porongurup subregion of Great Southern with the acquisition of a 65-ha farm at the foot of the Porongurup Range. They planted shiraz and cabernet sauvignon (3 ha each) and riesling (4 ha). Hilde, a successful artist, designed the beautiful scalloped, glass-walled cellar door sales area with its mountain blue cladding. In the lead-up to the 2007 vintage the biggest bushfire ever seen in

the Porongurup Range led to the loss of the entire vintage due to smoke taint. The closure of the National Park to tourists through to November 2007 meant almost no cellar door trade right through to Jan '08. Exports to the UK.

ΨΨΨΨΨ **Great Southern Riesling 2008** Fragrant and flowery bouquet with enticing citrus blossom aromas and a hint of spice; wonderfully delicate lime juice palate with drive and great length; perfect balance. Screwcap. 10.5% alc. **Rating** 96 **To** 2018 $20

Magpie Hill Reserve Riesling 2008 Fragrant and flowery, but a little more complex than the varietal; while bone dry, has both depth and length with a strong substrate of minerally acidity. Deserves five years minimum to open up and reveal all it has to offer. Screwcap. 11% alc. **Rating** 95 **To** 2023 $30

Great Southern Shiraz 2007 Fragrant aromas of black cherry, spice and a touch of pepper come through effortlessly on the supple, silky medium-bodied palate; lovely example of cool-grown shiraz. Screwcap. 14% alc. **Rating** 94 **To** 2017 $24

Great Southern Cabernet Sauvignon 2007 Very good colour; classic cabernet varietal character from a moderately cool region; fragrant and fine, with redcurrant fruit, fine tannins and oak in a seamless stream. Great value. Screwcap. 13.4% alc. **Rating** 94 **To** 2020 $22

ΨΨΨΨΨ **Great Southern Autumn Riesling 2008** Mineral, citrus and apple flow along the palate, which is so perfectly balanced the residual sugar is barely detectable; the wine needs time to relax in bottle. Screwcap. 10.2% alc. **Rating** 92 **To** 2015 $20

ΨΨΨΨ **Great Southern Rose 2008** Pale, but bright, colour; plenty of sweet raspberry/ cassis fruit on the mid-palate, acidity to balance the finish. Cabernet Sauvignon. Screwcap. 12.9% alc. **Rating** 88 **To** 2010 $18

Dunn's Creek Estate ★★★

137 McIlroys Road, Red Hill, Vic 3937 **Region** Mornington Peninsula
T 0413 020 467 **F** (03) 5989 2011 **www**.dunnscreek.com.au **Open** By appt
Winemaker Sandro Mosele (Contract) **Est.** 2001 **Cases** 500 **Vyds** 3.5 ha
This is the retirement venture of Roger and Hannah Stuart-Andrews, a former professional couple whose love of Italian and Spanish wines led them to their eclectic choice of varieties. Thus they have planted barbera, arneis, albarino and pinot gris.

ΨΨΨΨ **Mornington Peninsula Arneis 2008** Scented apple blossom aromas and touches of spice; the palate is bulked up by a touch of sweetness that the wine would have been better without. Screwcap. 13% alc. **Rating** 88 **To** 2012 $25

Dutschke Wines ★★★★★

PO Box 107 Lyndoch, SA 5351 **Region** Barossa Valley
T (08) 8524 5485 **F** (08) 8524 5489 **www**.dutschkewines.com **Open** Not
Winemaker Wayne Dutschke **Est.** 1998 **Cases** 10 000 **Vyds** 17.5 ha
Wayne Dutschke spent over 20 years working in Australia and overseas for companies large and small before joining his uncle (and grapegrower) Ken Semmler to form Dutschke Wines. In addition to outstanding table wines, he has a yearly release of fortified wines (doubtless drawing on his time at Baileys of Glenrowan); these sell out overnight, and have received the usual stratospheric points from Robert Parker. Triumphed in the 2007 vintage. Exports to the UK, the US and other major markets.

ΨΨΨΨΨ **Oscar Semmler Single Vineyard Reserve Barossa Valley Shiraz 2006** Demonstrates the Barossa Valley's capacity to produce shiraz with enormous depth and length without dead fruit; just mouth-watering, velvety shiraz flavours, tannins and oak in the chorus. Screwcap. 14.8% alc. **Rating** 96 **To** 2025 $50

St Jakobi Single Vineyard Barossa Valley Shiraz 2007 A striking bouquet with an extra degree of fragrance, ranging through red and black fruits, the medium- to full-bodied palate with fine tannins and quality oak supporting the fruit. Screwcap. 14.8% alc. **Rating** 95 **To** 2027 $35

GHR Neighbours Barossa Valley Shiraz 2007 Deep, dense colour; a robust, full-bodied wine with multiple layers of black fruits, licorice and tannins; built to last, and isn't alcoholic. Screwcap. 14.7% alc. **Rating** 94 **To** 2027 $25

ￍￍￍￍￍ Single Barrel Barossa Valley Shiraz 2006 Perfectly proves the other side of the coin, although Wayne Dutschke (along with Robert Parker) does not agree, for this was his choice of the best barrel in the winery from 2006. For my taste, the alcohol and fruit ripeness are just too much, however much one must acknowledge the depth of flavour. Screwcap. 15.5% alc. **Rating** 93 **To** 2025 $75

ￍￍￍￍ Willow Bend Barossa Valley Shiraz Merlot Cabernet Sauvignon 2007 A wine that is in a different idiom to the Dutschke shirazs, more willowy and lighter-bodied, with a mix of savoury red fruits. Screwcap. 14.7% alc. **Rating** 89 **To** 2013 $22

Dyson Wines   ★★★

Sherriff Road, Maslin Beach, SA 5170 **Region** McLaren Vale
T (08) 8386 1092 **F** (08) 8327 0066 **www**.dysonwines.com **Open** 7 days 10–5
Winemaker Allan Dyson **Est.** 1976 **Cases** 2000
Allan Dyson, who described himself (a few years ago) as 'a young man of 50-odd years', has recently added to his 1.5 ha of viognier with 2.5 ha of cabernet sauvignon and 2 ha of chardonnay, and has absolutely no thoughts of slowing down or retiring. All wines are estate grown, made and bottled.

ￍￍￍￍ Viognier 2008 Mouthfilling wine that carries its alcohol well; a correct apricot-tinged bouquet, with peachy flavours joining on the palate. Cork. 14.2% alc. **Rating** 88 **To** 2010 $20

Grande Privilege Reserve Chardonnay 2006 Very rich and ripe mouthfilling tropical fruit flavours verging on canned; ready right now. Cork. 14.5% alc. **Rating** 87 **To** 2010 $20

Eagle Vale   ★★★★☆

7087 Caves Road, Margaret River, WA 6285 **Region** Margaret River
T (08) 9757 6477 **www**.eaglevalewine.com **Open** Mon–Fri 10–5, w'ends by appt
Winemaker Guy Gallienne **Est.** 1997 **Cases** 13 000 **Vyds** 10.7 ha
Eagle Vale is a joint venture between the property owners, Steve and Wendy Jacobs, and the operator/winemaking team of Guy, Chantal and Karl Gallienne. It is a united nations team: Steve Jacobs was born in Colorado and has business interests in Bali. The Galliennes come from the Loire Valley, although Guy secured his winemaking degree at Roseworthy College/ Adelaide University. The vineyard is managed on a low-impact basis, without pesticides (guinea fowls do the work) and with minimal irrigation. All the wines are made from estate-grown grapes. Exports to the UK, the US, Seychelles, China and Hong Kong.

ￍￍￍￍￍ Margaret River Semillon Sauvignon Blanc 2008 Tightly wound citrus bouquet with a hint of pea pod and straw; lively palate, with real focus and drive, and a generous core of sweet fruit; long and very even. Screwcap. 13% alc. **Rating** 94 **To** 2013 $20

ￍￍￍￍￍ Whispering Lake Single Vineyard Margaret River Sauvignon Blanc Fume 2007 Bright colour; a green nettle bouquet with a splash of tropical fruit; mostly vibrant fruit on the palate, with a touch of toasty oak showing through on the finish; long and textured. Screwcap. 13.5% alc. **Rating** 92 **To** 2012 $32

Margaret River Chardonnay 2008 Bright colour; clean, with good concentration and good texture; young and raw at this point in time, but indicates a promising future. Screwcap. 14% alc. **Rating** 90 **To** 2014 $22

Echo Ridge Wines NR

Lot 1 Oakey Creek Road, Pokolbin, NSW 2320 **Region** Lower Hunter Valley
T (02) 4998 6714 **www**.echoridgewines.com.au **Open** Sat 11–4, Sun 10–3
Winemaker Mark Woods **Est.** 2005 **Cases** 2000 **Vyds** 10.7 ha
When Greg and Anthony Ward purchased the 40-ha property now known as Echo Ridge, it already had well-established vines, together with a 3000-tree olive plantation. They secured Mark Woods (of Briar Ridge) as their contract winemaker, but have deliberately sold part of the grape production, limiting the amount of each wine released to a maximum of 500 cases. They have also built and opened a sophisticated cellar door, which came on-stream in 2009. The vineyard is planted to semillon, shiraz, verdelho, chardonnay and petit verdot.

Eden Hall ★★★★☆

36a Murray Street, Angaston, SA 5353 **Region** Eden Valley
T (08) 8562 4590 **F** (08) 8342 3950 **www**.edenhall.com.au **Open** 7 days 11–5
Winemaker Kym Teusner, Christa Deans (Contract) **Est.** 2002 **Cases** 2500 **Vyds** 32.3 ha
David and Mardi Hall purchased the historic Avon Brae property in 1996. The 120-ha property has been planted to cabernet sauvignon (the lion's share with 13 ha), riesling (9.24 ha), shiraz (5.75 ha) and smaller plantings of merlot and cabernet franc. The majority of the production is contracted to Yalumba, St Hallett and McGuigan Simeon, with 10% of the best grapes held back for the Eden Hall label. The Riesling, Shiraz Viognier and Cabernet Sauvignon are all excellent, the red wines outstanding. Exports to the US, Malaysia and Japan.

ȲȲȲȲȲ **CSV Cabernet Shiraz Viognier 2005** Typical maker's mark on the wine; fragrant aromas of fruit and cedary oak lifted by the viognier component; supple finish. Screwcap. 14.5% alc. **Rating** 93 **To** 2015 $38
Shiraz 2005 A big, rich, oaky wine, with mocha, fruitcake and plenty of sweet oak; supercharged, but well put together. Screwcap. 14.5% alc. **Rating** 92 **To** 2015 $44
Cabernet Sauvignon 2005 Slightly hazy colour; gently ripe red and black fruits wrapped in a spicy cocoon of French and American oak; appealing flavours and texture. Screwcap. 14.5% alc. **Rating** 92 **To** 2015 $38

Eden Road Wines ★★★★☆

Hamilton Road, Springton, SA 5235 **Region** Eden Valley
T (08) 8568 1766 **F** (08) 8568 1767 **www**.edenroadwines.com.au **Open** By appt
Winemaker Nick Spencer, Hamish Young **Est.** 2006 **Cases** 1000 **Vyds** 18.8 ha
Eden Road Wines acquired the heritage-listed Stonegarden vineyard and winery at Springton in 2006. The original vineyard was planted in 1858, and some time between then and 1871 the winery was built. The winery is being refurbished to allow the restricted quantities of the estate wines to be made onsite, although the Coffman & Lawson (formerly Kamberra – see separate entry) winery in the Canberra District may possibly be used in place of the old Eden Road winery, as Nick Spencer is winemaker for both businesses, and Canberra is a lot closer to Tumbarumba than the Eden Valley.

ȲȲȲȲȲ **Riesling 2008** Pure and focused lemon, lime and talc bouquet, with an edge of exotic spices; pure on the palate, with fresh lime juice and mineral complexity, balanced by generous texture and weight; razor-like precision on the finish. Screwcap. 12.5% alc. **Rating** 95 **To** 2016 $22

ȲȲȲȲȲ **The Long Road Clare Riesling 2008** Restrained bouquet, offering a strong talc. personality; accentuated acidity and tightly wound lime juice palate; lean and minerally on the finish. Screwcap. 12.5% alc. **Rating** 90 **To** 2015 $18
Tumbarumba Chardonnay 2008 Pear and nectarine, with spice from toasty oak; quite figgy on the palate, with texture provided by the winemaking; a worked style that maintains freshness. Screwcap. 12.5% alc. **Rating** 90 **To** 2013 $25
Tumbarumba Pinot Noir 2008 A generous and quite silky wine; plum, spice and some earth notes are supported by fresh tannin and focused acidity; a cool herb character lingers on the finish. Screwcap. 13.5% alc. **Rating** 90 **To** 2014 $30

ΨΨΨΨ **The Long Road Adelaide Hills Sauvignon Blanc 2008** A clean tropical fruit bouquet; quite sweet on the palate, cleaned up by the acidity. Screwcap. 12.5% alc. **Rating** 88 **To** 2011 $18
The Long Road Tumbarumba Pinot Noir 2008 Vibrant colour; cherry and plum with a touch of spice; quite generous palate, with a bit of grip for interest. Screwcap. 12.5% alc. **Rating** 88 **To** 2012 $18

Eden Springs   ★★★★★

Boehm Springs Road, Springton, SA 5235 **Region** Eden Valley
T (08) 8564 1166 **www**.edensprings.com.au **Open** At Taste Eden Valley
Winemaker Jo Irvine, David Norman (Contract) **Est.** 1972 **Cases** 2000 **Vyds** 57.27 ha
When you read the hyperbole that sometimes accompanies the acquisition of an existing wine business, about transforming it into a world-class operation, it is easy to sigh and move on. When self-confessed wine lover Ray Gatt acquired Eden Springs, he proceeded to translate words into deeds. As well as the 19.82-ha Eden Springs Vineyard, he also acquired the historic Siegersdorf Vineyard (22 ha) on the Barossa floor, and the neighbouring Graue Vineyard (15.2 ha). He then put contract winemakers Joanne Irvine and David Norman in charge, tapping into their long-established credentials. It was hardly surprising that a string of wine show medals should be bestowed on the wines, my personal appreciation of the wines also no surprise. Perhaps the most obvious feature is the exceptional value for money they represent. Exports to the UK, the US and other major markets.

ΨΨΨΨΨ **High Eden Riesling 2008** A mix of floral and spicy notes on the bouquet; an excellent palate, crisp and bright, with citrus and acid interwoven from the start to the long, clean, lingering finish. Great future. Screwcap. 11.5% alc. **Rating** 94 **To** 2018 $16.90
High Eden Riesling 2007 Has an intense and complex bouquet with strong spicy notes, almost into Gruner Veltliner pepper aromas; reverts to classic Eden Valley on the palate, with highly focused lime and acidity; deserves its distinguished show record. Great value. Screwcap. 11% alc. **Rating** 94 **To** 2016 $16.90
High Eden Cabernet Sauvignon 2006 Good colour; an exceptional vintage resulted in a refined and pure cabernet, with perfectly ripened fruit providing intense blackcurrant flavours; the tannin structure perfect; 432 cases made. Worth twice the price. Screwcap. 14% alc. **Rating** 94 **To** 2026 $19.90

ΨΨΨΨ **High Eden Shiraz 2006** A fragrant and spicy bouquet leads into a light- to medium-bodied palate, with dark berry, spice and vanilla oak all intermingling. Screwcap. 14.5% alc. **Rating** 89 **To** 2013 $19.90
High Eden Cabernet Sauvignon 2005 Cedary/earthy aromas on the bouquet, with some of the same on the palate; here, however, there are also some red fruits; the finish is long and sustained. Screwcap. 14.5% alc. **Rating** 89 **To** 2013 $19.90

Edwards Wines   ★★★★★

Cnr Caves Road/Ellensbrook Road, Cowaramup, WA 6284 **Region** Margaret River
T (08) 9755 5999 **F** (08) 9755 5988 **www**.edwardswines.com.au **Open** 7 days 10.30–5
Winemaker Michael Edwards **Est.** 1993 **Cases** 10 000 **Vyds** 25 ha
Edwards Wines is a family-owned and operated winery, brothers Michael (formerly a wine-maker at Voyager Estate) and Christo are the winemaker and viticulturist, respectively. The vineyard includes chardonnay, semillon, sauvignon blanc, shiraz, cabernet sauvignon and mer-lot. The consistency in the quality of the wines is admirable. Exports to all major markets.

ΨΨΨΨΨ **Margaret River Chardonnay 2007** Immaculately made; balanced oak, mlf, fruit all in total harmony; good length; seamless. Screwcap. 13.5% alc. **Rating** 94 **To** 2015 $32
Margaret River Shiraz 2007 Bright crimson-red; a lively and vibrant medium-bodied mix of red and black fruits supported by good oak and fine, supple tannins; has excellent length. Screwcap. 14% alc. **Rating** 94 **To** 2020 $30

ፕፕፕፕ Margaret River Semillon Sauvignon Blanc 2008 Semillon a major
contributor to both flavour and structure; lemon zest/lemon sherbet flavours move
through the long and positive palate. Screwcap. 13% alc. **Rating** 91 **To** 2011 $23
Tiger's Tale Margaret River Cabernet Merlot 2007 Fragrant; medium-
bodied red fruits and sweet oak; seductive style; with a sprig of herbs on the finish.
Screwcap. 14% alc. **Rating** 90 **To** 2012 $18
Margaret River Cabernet Sauvignon 2007 A touch of development in the
colour, with some vanilla and mocha nuances to the black fruits of the bouquet
and palate; good texture and structure are its main points. Screwcap. 14.2% alc.
Rating 90 **To** 2017 $32

ፕፕፕፕ Margaret River Sauvignon Blanc 2008 A grass and asparagus bouquet leads
into a firm palate with grass and gooseberry flavours intermingling; does shorten
slightly. Screwcap. 13.2% alc. **Rating** 89 **To** 2010 $23
Tiger's Tale Margaret River Semillon Sauvignon Blanc 2008 Similar
flavours to its bigger brother, but slightly less intensity and drive; still, a wine
with plenty of character. Screwcap. 13% alc. **Rating** 89 **To** 2010 $18

Eighteen Forty-Seven ★★★★☆

PO Box 918, Rowland Flat, SA 5352 **Region** Barossa Valley
T (08) 8524 5328 **F** (08) 8524 5329 www.eighteenfortyseven.com **Open** By appt
Winemaker Alex Peel, John Curnow **Est.** 1996 **Cases** 3000 **Vyds** 8.62 ha
A youthful John Curnow began his career over 30 years ago buying and selling wines from
all over the world. He then moved to Coca-Cola, becoming a senior executive or CEO in
Hungary, the Czech Republic, NZ, the US and Australia. In 1996 he and wife Sue began
Eighteen Forty-Seven, with two vineyards planted to shiraz, semillon, petit verdot and a little
sauvignon blanc. The name has a dual source: the original land grant of the Rowland Flat
property dates from 1847, and 1–8–47 is John's birth date. Until 2002 the grapes were sold
to other Barossa Valley producers, but in that vintage the first wines were made, and have had
much critical acclaim. Exports to the US, Germany, the Czech Republic and Hong Kong.

ፕፕፕፕ First Pick Shiraz 2006 Deep colour, good hue; a powerful, highly concentrated
and focused wine, with abundant blackberry fruit, but is not over-extracted. Cork.
14.6% alc. **Rating** 94 **To** 2020 $95

ፕፕፕፕ Pappy's Paddock Barossa Valley Shiraz 2006 Dense colour; a super-
powerful wine, the higher alcohol impact considerable, and as sometimes happens
seems to thin out the fruit. Cork. 15.5% alc. **Rating** 90 **To** 2015 $42
Home Block Barossa Valley Petit Verdot 2006 Typically dark colour; big,
dense inky/tarry overtones to the fruit, but the tannins are under control, so while
the wine is full-bodied, it has balance, with attractive bitter chocolate nuances.
Cork. 14.9% alc. **Rating** 90 **To** 2016 $42

Elderton ★★★★★

3–5 Tanunda Road, Nuriootpa, SA 5355 **Region** Barossa Valley
T (08) 8568 7878 **F** (08) 8568 7879 www.eldertonwines.com.au **Open** Mon–Fri 8.30–5,
w'ends & hols 11–4
Winemaker Richard Langford **Est.** 1984 **Cases** 32 000 **Vyds** 46 ha
The founding Ashmead family, with mother Lorraine supported by sons Allister and
Cameron, continues to impress with its wines. The original source was 30 ha of fully mature
shiraz, cabernet sauvignon and merlot on the Barossa floor, subsequently 16 ha of Eden
Valley vineyards (shiraz, cabernet sauvignon, chardonnay, zinfandel, merlot and roussanne)
were incorporated into the business. The Command Shiraz is justifiably regarded as its icon
wine; energetic promotion and marketing both in Australia and overseas is paying dividends.
Elderton has followed in the footsteps of Cullen by becoming carbon neutral. Exports to all
major markets.

ŸŸŸŸŸ **Neil Ashmead Grand Tourer Barossa Shiraz 2008** Vibrant colour; dark blackberry, tar and licorice aromas unite on the bouquet; the palate is fully loaded with sweet fruit, chewy tannin yet shows lightness on its feet through fine acid on the finish; playful packaging, but a serious wine. Screwcap. 14% alc. **Rating** 95 To 2020 $70

Command Single Vineyard Barossa Shiraz 2006 Good colour; quite a restrained and elegant bouquet, showing more red fruit than black, and a little fruitcake spice; the palate is fresh and vibrant with toasty oak seamlessly framing the fruit; a long and harmonious finish with chewy tannins and fresh acidity. Screwcap. 14.5% alc. **Rating** 94 To 2020 $90

ŸŸŸŸŸ **Ashmead Single Vineyard Barossa Cabernet Sauvignon 2006** An elegant, medium-bodied wine, with some regional dusty/earthy inputs adding to complexity; the French oak is well integrated with blackcurrant fruit and a clean finish. Screwcap. 14.5% alc. **Rating** 92 To 2020 $90

Barossa Cabernet Sauvignon 2006 Some leathery/earthy nuances on the bouquet diminish on the powerful palate, with strong blackcurrant fruit and a jab of dark chocolate. Built to last. Screwcap. 14.5% alc. **Rating** 91 To 2020 $26

Barossa Shiraz 2006 Retains bright hue; has good structure and length to its black fruits, which are framed by gentle vanillin oak. Screwcap. 14.5% alc. **Rating** 90 To 2015 $29

Command Single Vineyard Barossa Shiraz 2005 Lavish 34 months in American (dominant) and French oak has resulted in an army greatcoat of oak wrapped around the undeniably good fruit, the latter giving the palate length. Screwcap. 14.5% alc. **Rating** 90 To 2020 $95

Ashmead Single Vineyard Barossa Cabernet Sauvignon 2007 A cassis bouquet with plenty of toasty oak on offer; quite luscious on entry, with red fruits to provide light to the warm and ripe black fruit; quite oaky, but very long on the finish. Screwcap. 14.5% alc. **Rating** 90 To 2014 $90

Ode to Lorraine Barossa Cabernet Sauvignon Shiraz Merlot 2006 A soft red and black fruit bouquet, with Christmas cake spice on display; the palate is soft and fleshy on entry, with good texture, chewy tannin and oak providing length on the finish. Screwcap. 14.5% alc. **Rating** 90 To 2015 $40

Barossa Zinfandel 2007 Ultra-ripe bouquet of blue and black fruit confiture; the palate is juicy, warm, ripe and a little chocolatey; everything you expect from the variety. Screwcap. **Rating** 90 To 2012 $26.95

Riverina Botrytis Semillon (375 ml) 2007 Typical glowing gold; not as luscious as some, which is no bad thing; candy cumquat vanilla flavours. Screwcap. 10.5% alc. **Rating** 90 To 2010 $19.95

ŸŸŸŸ **Friends Vineyard Series Eden Valley Riesling 2008** Highly fragrant lime juice aromas; elegant and fine, but doesn't have the concentration the bouquet promises. Screwcap. 11% alc. **Rating** 89 To 2012 $18.95

Friends Vineyard Series Sauvignon Blanc Semillon 2008 Developed colour; abundant flavour from Adelaide Hills sauvignon blanc and Barossa semillon; fractionally thick finish. Screwcap. 12.5% alc. **Rating** 89 To 2010 $18.95

Friends Vineyard Series Shiraz 2006 Lively, fresh light- to medium-bodied wine, with uncomplicated cherry flavours. Screwcap. 14.5% alc. **Rating** 88 To 2010 $18.95

Friends Vineyard Series Cabernet Sauvignon 2006 Generous ladles of blackcurrant fruit, but needs more time for the built-in tannins to soften, as they will. Screwcap. 14.5% alc. **Rating** 88 To 2012 $18.95

Barossa Merlot 2006 A very chunky, clunky version of merlot; almost inevitable in the Barossa Valley, even in a vintage such as this. Screwcap. 14.5% alc. **Rating** 87 To 2013 $29

Eldridge Estate of Red Hill ★★★★★

120 Arthurs Seat Road, Red Hill, Vic 3937 **Region** Mornington Peninsula
T (03) 5989 2644 **www**.eldridge-estate.com.au **Open** Mon–Fri 12–4, w'ends & hols 11–5
Winemaker David Lloyd **Est.** 1985 **Cases** 1000 **Vyds** 3 ha
The Eldridge Estate vineyard was purchased by Wendy and David Lloyd in 1995. Major
retrellising work has been undertaken, changing to Scott Henry, and all the wines are estate-
grown and made. David has also planted several Dijon-selected pinot noir clones (114, 115
and 777) which have been contributing since 2004, likewise the Dijon chardonnay clone 96.
An interesting move has been the development of the Euroa Creeks range (Early Harvest
Shiraz, Shiraz and Reserve Shiraz), made from contract-grown grapes (a long-term contract)
at the northern end of Heathcote. An interesting grafting of the skills of a cool-climate pinot
noir grower and maker onto the far bigger wine base of Heathcote shiraz.

ŶŶŶŶŶ **Euroa Creeks Shiraz 2006** Supple and rich, with velvety mouthfeel to the
plum, blackberry, licorice and spice fruit; the tannins are perfectly ripe, adding
structure and length, the oak faultless. Screwcap. 14% alc. **Rating** 95 **To** 2020 $40
Gamay 2007 Truly varietal; red cherry fruits, with just a touch of blueberry and
spice; vibrant cleansing acidity, and a lovely sweet spot of red fruit, draws out the
harmonious finish. Screwcap. 14% alc. **Rating** 94 **To** 2012 $35
Clonal Blend Pinot Noir 2007 Clear crimson; a fragrant bouquet is followed
by a long palate with perfect tension between red fruits and more spicy/savoury
overtones to the fine tannins. Screwcap. 14% alc. **Rating** 94 **To** 2015 $75
Pinot Noir 2007 Bright colour; a restrained bouquet with Asian spices gracefully
complementing the cherry and plum fruit; the palate is firm and precise, the
quality of the fruit undeniable; long, silky and even with the oak just showing its
hand on the finish. Screwcap. 14% alc. **Rating** 94 **To** 2015 $48
Euroa Creeks Early Harvest Shiraz 2006 Excellent colour; an unusually
fragrant and elegant Heathcote wine; the fruit aromas and flavours run from black
cherry to plum to multi-spice; the tannins are very fine, oak subtle. Screwcap.
14% alc. **Rating** 94 **To** 2016 $28
Euroa Creeks Reserve Shiraz 2006 Immaculately made, but radically different
to the Early Harvest, moving into blackberry and licorice, with tannins more
prominent, although remaining in balance. Will be long lived. Screwcap. 14.5% alc.
Rating 94 **To** 2030 $55

ŶŶŶŶ♀ **Chardonnay 2007** Vibrant colour; grapefruit, nectarine and grilled cashew
bouquet; quite oaky on the palate, the underlying fruit comes through with ease,
and the texture brings the wine home with real strength. Screwcap. 14% alc.
Rating 93 **To** 2014 $40
Euroa Creeks Single Vineyard Reserve Shiraz 2006 Very concentrated
and highly structured, Italianate savoury tannins running through the length
of the opulently flavoured palate; needs time. Screwcap. 14.5% alc. **Rating** 93
To 2020 $55
North Patch Single Vineyard Chardonnay 2007 A fine and linear wine with
citrus fruit and plenty of toasty oak; medium-bodied with vibrant acidity and a
long nutty finish; just a little question on the level of oak for the fruit. Screwcap.
14% alc. **Rating** 92 **To** 2014 $30
Euroa Creeks Shiraz No Viognier 2006 Has distinctly less fruit and structure;
still very good, and still showing the underlying philosophy. Screwcap. 14.5% alc.
Rating 92 **To** 2015 $40
Euroa Creeks Shiraz Viognier 2006 Brightly coloured; the substantial
co-fermented viognier (8%) has an obvious impact, one aspect entirely unexpected
is the break in the line of the palate, leaving a gap before the tannins cut in. All in
all, over the top viognier. Screwcap. 14.5% alc. **Rating** 92 **To** 2016 $40
Single Clone Pinot Noir 2007 Clone MV6. A little more evolution here; slight
confiture to the cherry fruit, with a bit of spicy oak overlay; quite dry and firm,
with a touch of spicy stem character coming through on the finish. Screwcap.
14% alc. **Rating** 90 **To** 2014 $40

🍷🍷🍷🍷 **Fume Blanc 2008** Capsicum and a touch of tomato; the texture is quite interesting, but the fruit fails to persist on the finish. Screwcap. 13.5% alc. **Rating** 87 **To** 2012 **$**25

Eleven Paddocks ★★★★

PO Box 829, Macleod, Vic 3084 **Region** Pyrenees
T (03) 9458 4997 **F** (03) 9458 5075 **www**.elevenpaddocks.com.au **Open** Not
Winemaker Gabriel Horvat, Gary Mills **Est.** 2003 **Cases** 1200 **Vyds** 8.1 ha
Eleven partners, under the direction of managing partner Danny Gravell, purchased a small vineyard in 2002 in the foothills of the Pyrenees Ranges near Landsborough. The quality of the first vintage was sufficient to encourage the partners to increase planting to 4 ha of shiraz, 2 ha each of chardonnay and cabernet sauvignon and a dash of petit verdot.

🍷🍷🍷🍷🍷 **Shiraz 2008** Crimson-purple; a vibrant wine, with juicy, peppery red fruit flavours on the medium-bodied, long palate, finishing with an appealing spicy/savoury twist. Value. Screwcap. 13.7% alc. **Rating** 93 **To** 2018 **$**22
Chardonnay 2008 Attractive melon/nectarine/citrus on the bouquet and fresh palate alike, the oak influence subtle. Screwcap. 13.2% alc. **Rating** 90 **To** 2014 **$**18
The McKinlay Shiraz 2007 Licorice, spice and black fruits are the fruit core of a medium- to full-bodied wine; the ample, savoury tannins are ripe and balanced, the oak subtle. Screwcap. 14.8% alc. **Rating** 90 **To** 2017 **$**28

🍷🍷🍷🍷 **Shiraz 2007** A fragrant, medium-bodied junior brother to The McKinlay, with an uncommon juicy twang to the finish, black cherry joining in along the way. Screwcap. 14.3% alc. **Rating** 88 **To** 2016 **$**22

Elgee Park ★★★★★

Merricks General Store, 3458–3460 Frankston–Flinders Road, Merricks, Vic 3916
Region Mornington Peninsula
T (03) 5989 8088 **F** (03) 5989 7199 **www**.elgeeparkwines.com.au **Open** 7 days 9–5
Winemaker Geraldine McFaul, Kathleen Quealy (Contract) **Est.** 1972 **Cases** 1600
Vyds 4.5 ha
The pioneer of the Mornington Peninsula in its 20th-century rebirth, owned by Baillieu Myer and family. The vineyards are planted to riesling, chardonnay, viognier (some of the oldest vines in Australia), pinot gris, pinot noir, shiraz, merlot and cabernet sauvignon. The wines are made by Geraldine McFaul (Willow Creek), with the exception of Viognier and Pinot Gris, which are made by Kathleen Quealy (Balnarring Estate). Exports to China.

🍷🍷🍷🍷🍷 **Family Reserve Mornington Peninsula Chardonnay 2007** A fine and elegant wine, with white peach and citrus aromas and flavours supported by finely integrated oak; good length. Screwcap. 13.5% alc. **Rating** 94 **To** 2015 **$**35
Family Reserve Mornington Peninsula Pinot Noir 2007 Bright crimson-purple; lively and flavoursome, with an array of plum, cherry and spice flavours; excellent acidity helps drive the thrust and length of the palate. Screwcap. 13% alc. **Rating** 94 **To** 2014 **$**35

🍷🍷🍷🍷🍷 **Family Reserve Mornington Peninsula Viognier 2007** Restrained style overall, but is distinctly varietal with ripe apple and apricot flavours intermingling; clean acidity to close. Screwcap. 13.5% alc. **Rating** 91 **To** 2012 **$**35

Elgo Estate ★★★☆

2020 Upton Road, Upton Hill, via Longwood, Vic 3664 **Region** Strathbogie Ranges
T (03) 9328 3766 **F** (03) 9326 3358 **www**.elgoestate.com.au **Open** By appt
Winemaker Dennis Clarke, Craig Lewis **Est.** 1999 **Cases** 13 000 **Vyds** 54.6 ha
The Taresch family (originally from Germany) has an 890-ha grazing property, with three vineyards: Tarcombe Valley Vineyard (the warmest, planted to shiraz and cabernet); Lakeside Vineyard (planted in the 1970s with chardonnay, merlot and riesling); and the highest at

Upton Hill (pinot noir and sauvignon blanc). An adjacent winery was built in 2004. Most of the power for the winery comes from a 150 kW wind-powered turbine.

ᵧᵧᵧᵧᵧ Strathbogie Ranges Shiraz 2006 Strong colour; has all the medium-bodied components of spicy, gently ripe black fruits, oak and tannins in harmonious balance; good length and finish. Screwcap. 14% alc. **Rating** 90 **To** 2016 $25

ᵧᵧᵧᵧ Strathbogie Ranges Chardonnay 2005 Nutty/toasty bottle-developed characters now joining the stone fruit flavours in what is still a relatively light-bodied wine. Screwcap. 13.5% alc. **Rating** 88 **To** 2012 $21
Strathbogie Ranges Riesling 2008 Firm, dry style that has length and balance, but lacks intensity and varietal expression. May improve with cellaring. Screwcap. 13% alc. **Rating** 87 **To** 2013 $21
Strathbogie Ranges Sauvignon Blanc 2008 Grassy notes on the bouquet lead into a gentle palate mixing herb/grass/citrus and tropical notes in equal proportions. Screwcap. 13.5% alc. **Rating** 87 **To** 2010 $18
Strathbogie Ranges Cabernet Sauvignon 2005 A light- to medium-bodied blend of leafy/minty cabernet with some sweeter chocolate and vanilla notes; adequate length and balance, now ready for consumption. Screwcap. 14% alc. **Rating** 87 **To** 2011 $25

Ellender Estate

Leura Glen, 260 Green Gully Road, Glenlyon, Vic 3461 **Region** Macedon Ranges
T (03) 5348 7785 **www.**ellenderwines.com.au **Open** W'ends & public hols 11–5, or by appt
Winemaker Graham Ellender **Est.** 1996 **Cases** 1000 **Vyds** 4.15 ha
The Ellenders have established pinot noir (2.7 ha), chardonnay (0.9 ha), sauvignon blanc (0.4 ha) and pinot gris (0.4 ha). Wine style is now restricted to those varieties true to the ultra-cool climate of the Macedon Ranges: pinot noir, pinot rose, chardonnay and sparkling. Exports to the United Arab Emirates.

ᵧᵧᵧᵧᵧ Methode Champenoise Pinot Chardonnay NV Distinctly complex; attractive bready/brioche yeast lees characters under the fresh stone fruit flavours; a crisp, dry finish, balanced acidity. Cork. 12.7% alc. **Rating** 90 **To** 2012 $38

ᵧᵧᵧᵧ Rosetta Macedon Ranges Pinot Rose 2008 Pale pink; offers varietal strawberry fruit on the bouquet and palate, with a subliminal touch of sweetness aimed at the cellar door. Screwcap. 11% alc. **Rating** 87 **To** 2009 $24

Elmslie

Upper McEwans Road, Legana, Tas 7277 **Region** Northern Tasmania
T (03) 6330 1225 **F** (03) 6330 1625 **Open** By appt
Winemaker Bass Fine Wines (Guy Wagner) **Est.** 1972 **Cases** 600 **Vyds** 4 ha
The estate plantings are some of the oldest in Tasmania, led by 1.25 ha each of cabernet sauvignon and pinot nor, but also with chardonnay, sauvignon blanc and shiraz. Since Kevin French acquired the vineyard and appointed Guy Wagner as winemaker, quality has improved greatly, with further gains in sight. Wines are released under the 3 Mountain View label.

ᵧᵧᵧᵧᵧ 3 Mountain View Pinot Noir 2008 Deep colour; a rich bouquet and palate, with layers of dark plum fruit shot through with spice; fine tannins also add to a very good pinot. Screwcap. 13.2% alc. **Rating** 94 **To** 2015 $32
3 Mountain View Signature Cabernet Sauvignon 2006 Big wine, with black fruits and lots of cedar and vanilla oak tannins; not too hard or green, good colour. Screwcap. 13.6% alc. **Rating** 90 **To** 2016 $42
3 Mountain View Pinot Noir 2006 Very firm; very fresh; high acidity/low pH; will be long lived. Screwcap. 13.4% alc. **Rating** 89 **To** 2014 $32

Elmswood Estate   ★★★★

75 Monbulk-Seville Road, Wandin East, Vic 3139 **Region** Yarra Valley
T (03) 5964 3015 **F** (03) 5964 3405 **www**.elmswoodestate.com.au **Open** 7 days 10–5
Winemaker Paul Evans **Est.** 1981 **Cases** 3000
Elmswood Estate has 9.5 ha of vineyard, planted in 1981 on the red volcanic soils of the
far-southern side of the Yarra Valley. The cellar door offers spectacular views across the Upper
Yarra Valley to Mt Donna Buang and Warburton. Exports to China.

 Yarra Valley Cabernet Merlot 2007 Bright colour; very well made, with
precisely defined fruit flavours backed up by balanced, ripe tannins and good oak.
Diam. 14% alc. **Rating** 93 **To** 2017 $25
Yarra Valley Cabernet Sauvignon 2007 The tannins are much stronger
than those of the Cabernet Merlot and need to soften; however, there is enough
blackcurrant fruit to reassure that they (the tannins) will soften before the fruit
dies. Diam. 13.8% alc. **Rating** 90 **To** 2020 $35

 **Riesling 2008** A racy wine, with some stony/minerally overtones to the apple
and citrus fruit; good length. Diam. 12% alc. **Rating** 89 **To** 2013 $20
Yarra Valley Pinot Noir 2007 Light, but bright, colour; some briary/stemmy/
green nuances lurk in the wine, but there is a foundation of pinot fruit. Diam.
12.5% alc. **Rating** 89 **To** 2012 $28
Yarra Valley Unoaked Chardonnay 2008 Quite fragrant; has juicy citrussy
elements to the fruit that give the wine life and zest, essential for this style. Diam.
13.5% alc. **Rating** 88 **To** 2011 $20
Yarra Valley Merlot 2007 Good crimson hue; has an expressive bouquet with
cassis to the fore, gently spicy/savoury tannins giving it structure on the palate.
Diam. 13.5% alc. **Rating** 88 **To** 2013 $28

Eperosa   ★★★★☆

24 Maria Street, Tanunda, SA 5352 (postal) **Region** Barossa Valley
T (08) 8563 1576 **F** (08) 8563 1576 **www**.eperosa.com.au **Open** Not
Winemaker Brett Grocke **Est.** 2005 **Cases** 300
Eperosa owner Brett Grocke qualified as a viticulturist in 2001, and, through Grocke
Viticulture, consults and provides technical services to over 200 ha of vineyards spread across
the Barossa Valley, Eden Valley, Adelaide Hills, Riverland, Langhorne Creek and Hindmarsh
Valley. He is ideally placed to secure small parcels of grapes of the highest quality, and treats
these with traditional, no-frills winemaking methods: de-stemmed, macerated prior to
fermentation, open fermented, hand plunging, basket pressed, then 18 months in used French
oak barrels. The wines are of impeccable quality.

Totality 2005 Ripe wine, with overtones of caramel and spice to the lusciously
sweet fruit of the mid-palate; superfine tannins perfectly dry out the finish.
Mataro/Shiraz. Cork. 14.5% alc. **Rating** 94 **To** 2015 $38

Synthesis 2005 Good hue; while the mid-palate flavours are typical of Barossa
Valley blends of Grenache/Mourvedre/Shiraz, the wine has more structure than
most, with dark berry fruits on the back-palate. Screwcap. 14.5% alc. **Rating** 93
To 2017 $31
Elevation 2005 A contradictory wine, the colour, aroma and site (300 m) all
pointing to cool-grown elegance, the palate seriously fruit-sweet before fine, silky
tannins appear on the finish. Perfect cork closure. Shiraz. 15% alc. **Rating** 91
To 2015 $35

Eppalock Ridge   ★★★★

633 North Redesdale Road, Redesdale, Vic 3444 **Region** Heathcote
T (03) 5443 7841 **www**.eppalockridge.com **Open** By appt
Winemaker Rod Hourigan **Est.** 1979 **Cases** 1500

Sue and Rod Hourigan gave up their careers in fabric design and television production at the ABC in 1976 to chase their passion for fine wine. This took them first to McLaren Vale, Sue working in the celebrated Barn Restaurant, Rod starting at d'Arenberg; over the next three years both worked vintages at Pirramimma and Coriole while undertaking the first short course for winemakers at what is now CSU. After three hectic years they moved to Redesdale in 1979 and established Eppalock Ridge on a basalt hilltop overlooking Lake Eppalock. The 10 ha of shiraz, cabernet sauvignon, cabernet franc and merlot are capable of producing wines of high quality. Exports to the US and Canada.

ΨΨΨΨΨ **Heathcote Shiraz 2005** A full-flavoured, full-bodied rich wine that has everything going for it except its alcohol, which strikes on the back-palate and finish. The points are a compromise for a curate's egg. Screwcap. 16% alc. **Rating** 90 **To** 2020 $30

Epsilon

PO Box 244, Greenock, SA 5360 **Region** Barossa Valley
T (08) 8562 8494 **F** (08) 8562 8597 **www**.epsilonwines.com.au **Open** Not
Winemaker Aaron Southern, Dan Standish, Jaysen Collins (Contract) **Est.** 2004
Cases 2500 **Vyds** 22 ha
Epsilon (the fifth-brightest star in a constellation) takes its name from the five generations of the Kalleske family's involvement in Barossa Valley grapegrowing; Julie Southern is née Kalleske. She and husband Aaron bought back this part of the family farm in 1994, initially selling the grapes but in 2003 joined forces with close friends Dan Standish and Jaysen Collins to produce the Epsilon wines. Exports to the UK, the US and other major markets.

ΨΨΨΨΨ **Barossa Valley Shiraz 2007** Attractive wine from a challenging vintage; black cherry and plum fruit with perfectly integrated and balanced oak; overall extract tightly controlled. Screwcap. 14.5% alc. **Rating** 92 **To** 2016 $20
Barossa Valley Tempranillo Graciano 2007 Bright colour; totally delicious and star-bright red fruit flavours to a light- to medium-bodied wine that is content with its lot and hasn't been forced. Screwcap. 14% alc. **Rating** 91 **To** 2013 $25

Ernest Hill Wines ★★★

307 Wine Country Drive, Nulkaba, NSW 2325 **Region** Lower Hunter Valley
T (02) 4991 4418 **F** (02) 4991 7724 **www**.ernesthillwines.com.au **Open** 7 days 10–5
Winemaker Mark Woods **Est.** 1999 **Cases** 4000 **Vyds** 12 ha
The Wilson family has owned the Ernest Hill property since 1990; the vineyard has semillon (3 ha); shiraz (2.5 ha); chardonnay (2 ha); verdelho (1.5 ha); traminer, merlot (1 ha each); tempranillo and chambourcin (0.5 ha each). The business has had show success with the wines so far released.

ΨΨΨΨ **Alexander Chardonnay 2006** A hay/straw and ripe grapefruit bouquet; the palate is very toasty, but exhibits balance for all its depth. Diam. 13.6% alc. **Rating** 89 **To** 2013 $30
Maisie Evelyn Gewurztraminer 2008 Highly perfumed rose water bouquet; touch of CO_2 with good flavour and a clean finish. Screwcap. 12.4% alc. **Rating** 88 **To** 2012 $20
Rosalie Joan Verdelho 2008 Pale colour with ripe lime and orange fruit on the bouquet; the palate is a little sweet, but the acidity balances it with ease. Screwcap. 13.1% alc. **Rating** 87 **To** 2012 $20

`ese Vineyards

1013–1015 Tea Tree Road, Tea Tree, Tas 7017 **Region** Southern Tasmania
T 0417 319 875 **Open** By appt
Winemaker Winemaking Tasmania (Julian Alcorso) **Est.** 1994 **Cases** 3500 **Vyds** 3.5 ha
Elvio and Natalie Brianese are an architect and graphic designer couple whose extended family has centuries-old viticultural roots in the Veneto region of northern Italy. The Pinot Noir can be outstanding. Exports to China.

🍷🍷🍷🍷 **Sauvignon Blanc 2008** Pungent herbal/grassy aromas are followed by a palate with some tropical notes providing flavour balance. 13% alc. **Rating** 88 **To** 2012 $20

Eumundi Winery ★★★

310 Memorial Drive, Eumundi, Qld 4562 **Region** Queensland Coastal
T (07) 5442 7444 **F** (07) 5442 7455 **Open** Wed–Sun 11–5
Winemaker Gerry Humphrey, Andrew Hickinbotham (Contract) **Est.** 1994 **Cases** 5000
Eumundi Vineyard is set on 21 ha of river-front land in the beautiful Eumundi Valley, 12 km from Noosa Heads. The climate is hot, wet, humid and maritime, the only saving grace being the regular afternoon northeast sea breeze. It is a challenging environment for growing grapes: the owners, Robyn and Gerry Humphrey, have trialled 14 different grape varieties and three different trellis systems. Currently they have tempranillo, shiraz, chambourcin, petit verdot, mourvedre and verdelho. Plantings in 2001 included tannat, albarino and refosco, followed by albarino in '02, which gives some idea of their eclectic approach. The establishment of the vineyard was financed by the sale of a 19 m charter yacht that used to sail the oceans around northern Australia. Quite a change in lifestyle, but then Gerry Humphrey started his business life with a degree in veterinary science, a PhD in endocrinology, and ship's masters ticket for coastal freighters. In 2008 he finished his winemaking studies at CSU, with yet another degree.

🍷🍷🍷🍷 **Heart of Darkness Tannat 2007** Incredibly dense colour and purple black hue; as equally incredibly tannic as the colour and the reputation of the variety suggest; low alcohol doubly amazing. A ride on the wild side. Zork. 13% alc. **Rating** 87 **To** 2014 $20

Evans & Tate ★★★★★

Cnr Metricup Road/Caves Road, Wilyabrup, WA 6280 **Region** Margaret River
T (08) 9755 2199 **F** (08) 9755 4362 **www**.evansandtate.com.au **Open** 7 days 10.30–5
Winemaker Matthew Byrne **Est.** 1970 **Cases** 450 000
The 39-year history of Evans & Tate has been one of constant change and for decades expansion, moving to acquire large wineries in SA and NSW. For a series of reasons, nothing to do with the excellent quality of its Margaret River wines, the empire fell apart in 2005; however, it took an interminable time before McWilliam's (together with a syndicate of local growers) finalised its acquisition of Evans & Tate in December '07. Remarkably, wine quality was maintained through the turmoil. Exports to all major markets.

🍷🍷🍷🍷🍷 **The Reserve Margaret River Shiraz 2005** Received an extraordinary six trophies at the Sydney Wine Show '08, combining fragrant cool-climate fruit with impeccable texture and structure, French oak and fine tannins completing the picture. Screwcap. 14.5% alc. **Rating** 96 **To** 2020 $37
Stellar Ridge Vineyard Margaret River Chardonnay 2005 Exemplary complexity and vinosity; looking very good. Gold WA Wine Show '08. Screwcap. 14.5% alc. **Rating** 95 **To** 2012 $45
The Reserve Margaret River Chardonnay 2005 At the elegant end of the scale for Margaret River, with almost juicy white peach, melon and citrus fruit upfront, supported by acidity, oak in the background. Will be long lived. Screwcap. 14.5% alc. **Rating** 95 **To** 2015 $29.95
Classic White Aromatic; intense, citrussy/minerally acidity runs through a dynamic palate. Gold WA Wine Show '08. Screwcap. 12.5% alc. **Rating** 94 **To** 2012 $19.99
The Reserve Margaret River Cabernet Sauvignon 2005 An elegant, medium-bodied cabernet; not the style that normally garners gold medals, but this has three to its credit; a mix of blackcurrant, black olive and spice, it has impeccable length and balance. Screwcap. 14.5% alc. **Rating** 94 **To** 2020 $29.95
The Reserve Margaret River Cabernet Sauvignon 2004 Cedary/minty with distinct development; has very good length; now at or near its peak. Gold WA Wine Show '08. Screwcap. 14.4% alc. **Rating** 94 **To** 2011 $29.95

ŦŦŦŦℒ **Margaret River Chardonnay 2007** A powerful wine with ripe grapefruit on the bouquet and complex spicy character from the well-handled oak; very fine acidity draws the palate out to a long and even finish. Screwcap. 14% alc. Rating 93 To 2015 $23

Margaret River Sauvignon Blanc Semillon 2008 Zesty, lively, lemony/lemon bitters flavours; incisive and penetrating. Screwcap. 12% alc. **Rating** 93 To 2015 $22.99

X&Y Vineyards Margaret River Sauvignon Blanc 2007 A lively, fresh and attractive array of citrus, gooseberry and lychee aromas and flavours; clean finish. Screwcap. 13% alc. **Rating** 91 To 2010 $17.99

Gnangara Cabernet Sauvignon 2007 Bright colour; ripe redcurrant and cassis fruit; quite finely structured; vibrant acid coursing along the entire palate, supporting the fruit with ease. Screwcap. 14.5% alc. **Rating** 90 To 2014 $13.99

Margaret River Classic Shiraz Cabernet 2007 Lovely colour, with strong toasty oak at this stage; there is plenty of good fruit beneath, and the structure and fruit depth indicate a good future. Screwcap. 14.5% alc. **Rating** 90 To 2015 $18.99

ŦŦŦŦ **Gnangara Shiraz 2007** Spice and red fruit bouquet; juicy and focused palate, with gravelly tannin providing a refreshing conclusion. Screwcap. 14.5% alc. Rating 89 To 2014 $13.99

Margaret River Shiraz 2005 Ripe and bright, with a distinct savoury/mineral edge to the fruit; quite fine and juicy on the finish. Screwcap. 14% alc. **Rating** 89 To 2012 $23

Margaret River Sauvignon Blanc 2008 Light and crisp minerally/grassy style; has fair length, but not up to usual standard. Screwcap. 12.5% alc. **Rating** 88 To 2010 $22.99

Margaret River Classic Red 2007 A light- to medium-bodied spicy/savoury red, with good balance but not a lot of thrust or character. Screwcap. 14.5% alc. Rating 87 To 2011 $19.99

🍇 Even Keel Wines ★★★★

76 Arthurs Seat Road, Red Hill, Vic 3937 **Region** Southeastern Australia
T 0405 155 882 **www**.evenkeelwines.com **Open** Not
Winemaker Samuel Coverdale **Est.** 2006 **Cases** 1500 **Vyds** 4 ha
Based in the Mornington Peninsula, Sam Coverdale planted 4 ha of vineyards at Red Hill in 2008. However, he casts his net far and wide to select grape varieties that best represent their region; the subtext is wines that are balanced and elegant, but with the structure to allow them to continue to develop in bottle.

ŦŦŦŦℒ **Tumbarumba Chardonnay 2006** Pale green-straw; cool-grown fruit helps invest the wine with elegance captured by quality winemaking and use of French oak; delicious nectarine and citrus fruit on the long palate and finish. Screwcap. 13.6% alc. **Rating** 93 To 2014 $27

Orange Sauvignon Blanc 2007 Ever so faintly sweaty aromas well within varietal bounds; very pleasing passionfruit/tropical fruit flavours; ambitious price. Screwcap. 12.5% alc. **Rating** 90 To 2009 $27

Canberra District Shiraz Viognier 2006 Bright crimson-purple; perfumed fruit with some spicy notes; very firm tannins and positive acidity; needs time, but will handsomely repay it. Screwcap. 13.8% alc. **Rating** 90 To 2016 $30

ŦŦŦŦ **Clare Valley Riesling 2008** A substantial wine, true to its Clare Valley terroir; ripe citrus flavours and a firm finish. Screwcap. 13.5% alc. **Rating** 89 To 2016 $25.50

Evoi Wines

92 Dunsborough Lakes Drive, Dunsborough, WA 6281 (postal) **Region** Margaret River
T 0407 131 080 **F** (08) 9755 3742 **www**.evoiwines.com **Open** Not
Winemaker Nigel Ludlow **Est.** 2006 **Cases** 100

Nigel Ludlow has been winemaker at Barwick Wines since 2002, and previously winemaker at Selaks' winery in Marlborough, NZ. He had also been a Flying Winemaker, with vintages in Hungary, South Africa and Spain. He established Evoi Wines as a small add-on to his major role at Barwick; only two wines are released, Chardonnay and Cabernet Sauvignon. Exports to Hong Kong.

ŸŸŸŸŸ **Reserve Margaret River Chardonnay 2008** Bright straw-green; an extremely seductive style, with wild yeast fermentation and partial mlf in no way obscuring the nectarine and white peach fruit; the oak is likewise subtle, the powerful finish all about its essential fruit character. Screwcap. 13.5% alc. **Rating** 95 **To** 2015 $49

Eyre Creek   ★★★★

Main North Road, Auburn, SA 5451 **Region** Clare Valley
T 0418 818 400 **F** (08) 8849 2555 **www.**eyrecreekwines.com.au **Open** W'ends & public hols 10–5, Mon–Fri as per sign
Winemaker Stephen John, O'Leary Walker Wines **Est.** 1998 **Cases** 2000 **Vyds** 2.9 ha
John and Glenise Osborne, well-known Auburn hoteliers, established Eyre Creek in 1998. In 2008 they opened their cellar door, a renovated 100-year-old dairy, just north of Auburn. They grow dryland shiraz and grenache. Future plantings will include riesling, cabernet sauvignon and viognier. The production is sold at the cellar door, mail order and at selected bottle shops and restaurants in Adelaide and Sydney.

ŸŸŸŸŸ **Clare Valley Riesling 2008** Citrus aromas plus a faint touch of spice on the bouquet lead into a richly flavoured palate with ripe lime and lemon fruit; ready sooner than later. Screwcap. 12.5% alc. **Rating** 92 **To** 2013 $18
The Brookvale Clare Valley Shiraz 2006 A potent, full-bodied shiraz in classic Clare Valley style, with spice and licorice overtones to the supple black fruits; ripe tannins on the finish. Screwcap. 14% alc. **Rating** 90 **To** 2020 $25

ŸŸŸŸ **Semillon Sauvignon Blanc 2008** Early picking and brisk acidity works well to provide a light-bodied, fresh unpretentious wine. Screwcap. 12% alc. **Rating** 87 **To** 2010 $18

Faber Vineyard   ★★★★★

233 Haddrill Road, Baskerville, WA 6056 (postal) **Region** Swan Valley
T (08) 9296 0619 **F** (08) 9296 0681 **www.**fabervineyard.com.au **Open** Sun 10–4
Winemaker John Griffiths **Est.** 1997 **Cases** 2000 **Vyds** 4 ha
Former Houghton winemaker, now university lecturer and consultant, John Griffiths teamed with wife, Jane Micallef, to found Faber Vineyard. They have established shiraz, verdelho, brown muscat, chardonnay and petit verdot. Says John, 'It may be somewhat quixotic, but I'm a great fan of traditional warm-area Australian wine styles – those found in areas such as Rutherglen and the Barossa. Wines made in a relatively simple manner that reflect the concentrated ripe flavours one expects in these regions. And when one searches, some of these gems can be found from the Swan Valley.' Possessed of an excellent palate, and with an impeccable winemaking background, the quality of John's wines is guaranteed, although the rating is also quixotic. A new cellar door, billed as a 'cellar door with a difference', opened in 2008.

ŸŸŸŸŸ **Dwellingup Chardonnay 2008** A finely crafted, elegant and, if anything, understated chardonnay that has absorbed barrel ferment and 10 months in oak with nonchalant ease; gentle stone fruit, melon and creamy nuances run the length of the palate. Screwcap. 13.5% alc. **Rating** 94 **To** 2015 $32
Dwellingup Malbec 2007 Bright crimson; fresh and spicy aromas and flavours, with none of the jammy fruit often associated with malbec, nor the lack of mid-palate structure; has bright red fruit flavours and very good length. Diam. 13.8% alc. **Rating** 94 **To** 2016 $32

ΨΨΨΨΩ Frankland River Cabernet Sauvignon 2007 Purple-crimson; strong blackcurrant aromas lead into a full-bodied palate with similar fruit joined by French oak and very robust tannins; demands cellaring despite a dodgy wine-streaked cork. 14% alc. **Rating** 93 **To** 2025 $45

Riche Shiraz 2008 Strong crimson-purple; supple, black fruits on the generously endowed, medium-bodied palate, the tannins fine and the oak well-integrated. High-quality cork. 14.2% alc. **Rating** 90 **To** 2015 $28

Reserve Swan Valley Shiraz 2006 Attractive medium-bodied wine, with distinct fruit sweetness and some contrasting spicy/savoury notes; good tannins and oak. Cork. 14.5% alc. **Rating** 90 **To** 2016 $70

ΨΨΨΨ Petit Verdot 2008 The hue is good, although more diffuse than the best examples of Faber, but the upside is a more open and accessible medium-bodied palate, the tannins not aggressive. Cork. 14.2% alc. **Rating** 89 **To** 2014 $28

Shiraz Cabernet 2008 An attractive medium-bodied palate, with a mix of blackberry, blackcurrant and cherry, the tannins fine, the oak subtle. Easy style, best young. Screwcap. 14.2% alc. **Rating** 88 **To** 2012 $17.50

Fabric Wines NR

PO Box 302, Coonawarra, SA 5263 **Region** Limestone Coast Zone
T 0433 989 600 **F** (08) 8736 3090 **www.**fabricwines.com **Open** Not
Winemaker Alana Hill-Ling **Est.** 2007 **Cases** 700
Fabric Wines is the brainchild of Adelaide-born owner/winemaker Alana Hill-Ling. The inspiration for the brand came from a London wine bar and the theme of interwoven wines from Limestone Coast regions. In late 2008 she left the security of employment with Coonawarra Developments to work full-time on Fabric Wines.

Fairview Wines

422 Elderslie Road, Branxton, NSW 2335 **Region** Lower Hunter Valley
T (02) 4938 1116 **F** (02) 9383 8609 **www.**fairviewwines.com.au **Open** By appt
Winemaker Rhys Eather (Contract) **Est.** 1997 **Cases** 500 **Vyds** 2.5 ha
Greg and Elaine Searles purchased the property on which they have established Fairview Wines in 1997. For the previous 90 years it had sustained an orchard enterprise. The property currently comprises 2 ha of shiraz that consistently produces award winning wine and 0.5 ha of verdelho. Organic procedures are used wherever possible to produce the fruit, and minimal sulphites and preservatives are used in the winemaking process.

ΨΨΨΨ Hunter Valley Shiraz 2006 Deep colour; full-bodied wine, steeped with black fruits and aggressive tannins; the stained cork may not allow the 15 years' cellaring the wine needs to realise its full potential. 14.5% alc. **Rating** 89 **To** 2021 $35

Falls Wines

Belubula Way, Canowindra, NSW 2804 **Region** Cowra
T (02) 6344 1293 **F** (02) 6344 1290 **www.**fallswines.com **Open** 7 days 10–4
Winemaker Madrez Wine Services (Chris Derrez) **Est.** 1997 **Cases** 1500 **Vyds** 94 ha
Peter and Zoe Kennedy have established Falls Vineyard & Retreat (to give it its full name) on the outskirts of Canowindra. They have planted shiraz, chardonnay, merlot, cabernet sauvignon and semillon, with luxury B&B accommodation offering large spa baths, exercise facilities, fishing and a tennis court.

ΨΨΨΨΩ Semillon 2003 Has developed very well, with an aromatic bouquet of lemon, herb and a hint of honeysuckle, and the palate, while light, does not disappoint. Surprise packet. Screwcap. 12% alc. **Rating** 90 **To** 2012 $18.99

ΨΨΨΨ Fields of Gold Chardonnay 2003 Has aged impressively given the region; gently ripe stone fruit and integrated oak define a wine now at its best. Screwcap. 13.5% alc. **Rating** 89 **To** 2010 $18.99

Farmer's Daughter Wines ★★★

791 Cassilis Road, Mudgee, NSW 2850 **Region** Mudgee
T (02) 6373 3177 **F** (02) 6373 3759 www.farmersdaughterwines.com.au **Open** Mon–Fri
9–5, Sat 10–5, Sun 10–4
Winemaker Greg Silkman **Est.** 1995 **Cases** 8000 **Vyds** 20 ha
The intriguingly named Farmer's Daughter Wines is a family-owned vineyard, run by the
daughters of a feed-lot farmer. Much of the production from the vineyard, planted to shiraz
(9.5 ha), cabernet sauvignon (3.5 ha), chardonnay and merlot (3 ha each), and semillon (1 ha),
is sold to other makers, but increasing quantities are made for the Farmer's Daughter label.
Exports to the US, Canada and Vietnam.

ϙϙϙϙ   **Mudgee Cabernet Sauvignon 2007** Good colour; juicy and clean, with a
slightly essency cassis core of fruit; medium-bodied and a touch of leather on the
finish. Screwcap. 13.1% alc. **Rating** 88 **To** 2012 $20

Farr Rising ★★★★★

27 Maddens Road, Bannockburn, Vic 3331 **Region** Geelong
T (03) 5281 1733 **F** (03) 5281 1433 www.byfarr.com.au **Open** By appt
Winemaker Nicholas Farr **Est.** 2001 **Cases** 2000
Nicholas Farr is the son of Gary Farr, and with encouragement from his father he has
launched his own brand with conspicuous success. He learned his winemaking in France
and Australia, and has access to some excellent base material, hence the quality of the wines.
Exports to Denmark, Hong Kong and Japan.

ϙϙϙϙϙ   **Mornington Pinot Noir 2007** Excellent hue – more purple than red; intense
multilayered and multiflavoured fruits on both bouquet and palate; no question
about ripeness here, nor the extreme length of the wine. Cork. 13.5% alc.
Rating 96 **To** 2017 $38
Geelong Shiraz 2006 Excellent bright colour; spiced plum and blackberry
aromas, which come through strongly on the opulently textured palate; has
admirable tannin and oak components. Cork. 14.5% alc. **Rating** 95 **To** 2021 $33

ϙϙϙϙϙ   **Geelong Pinot Noir 2007** Complex spicy forest nuances to the predominantly
red fruits of the bouquet, then a carefully constructed, slightly tangy palate; even a
touch of mint, perhaps. Cork. 13% alc. **Rating** 93 **To** 2014 $38
Geelong Saignee 2008 Typically pale colour, but also typically with farr
more than usual structure and length to the spiced small red fruit flavours. Cork.
13.5% alc. **Rating** 92 **To** 2011 $21

Farrawell Wines ★★★★

60 Whalans Track, Lancefield, Vic 3435 **Region** Macedon Ranges
T (03) 5429 2020 www.farrawellwines.com.au **Open** 4th Sat of each month 1–5, or by appt
Winemaker Trefor Morgan, David Cowburn (Contract) **Est.** 2000 **Cases** 400 **Vyds** 2 ha
Farrawell had a dream start to its commercial life when its 2001 Chardonnay was awarded the
trophy for Best Chardonnay at the Macedon Ranges Wine Exhibition '03. Given that around
1 ha each of chardonnay and pinot noir, and a tiny planting of sauvignon blanc, are the sole
source of wines, production will always be limited. Trefor Morgan is the owner/winemaker
of Mount Charlie Winery, but was perhaps better known as a Professor of Physiology at
Melbourne University.

ϙϙϙϙϙ   **Macedon Ranges Chardonnay 2007** A fresh bouquet with anise and
grapefruit; a stony mineral palate, with toasted nuts and a touch of citrus on
the quite long and fine finish. Screwcap. 13.5% alc. **Rating** 92 **To** 2014 $22

Farrow & Jackson Wines ★★★★

PO Box 904, Moss Vale, NSW 2577 **Region** Southern Highlands
T (02) 4887 7077 **F** (02) 4887 7197 www.farrowandjackson.com.au **Open** Not
Winemaker Southern Highlands Wines (Eddy Rossi) **Est.** 1998 **Cases** 500 **Vyds** 1.5 ha

Brian and Maureen Farrow established 1.5 ha of chardonnay on their Maple Hill property near Fitzroy Falls in 1998. The vines are planted on a north-facing slope of typical, regional brown basalt loam over a clay base, which is well drained and thus able to deal with an annual rainfall of around 1200 mm.

ŸŸŸŸŸ **Maple Hill Southern Highlands Chardonnay 2006** Attractive wine benefiting from time in bottle; ripe fig and stone fruit flavours marry with balanced French oak on the long palate. Screwcap. 13% alc. **Rating** 91 **To** 2012 $20

Feehans Road Vineyard

50 Feehans Road, Mount Duneed, Vic 3216 **Region** Geelong
T (03) 5264 1706 **F** (03) 5264 1307 **www.**feehansroad.com.au **Open** W'ends 10–5
Winemaker Lethbridge Wines (Ray Nadeson) **Est.** 2000 **Cases** 300 **Vyds** 1.2 ha
Peter Logan's interest in viticulture dates back to a 10-week course run by Denise Miller (at Dixons Creek in the Yarra Valley) in the early 1990s. This led to further formal studies, and the planting of a 'classroom' vineyard of 500 chardonnay and shiraz vines. A move from Melbourne suburbia to the slopes of Mt Duneed led to the planting of a vineyard, and to the appointment of Ray Nadeson as winemaker.

ŸŸŸŸŸ **Geelong Shiraz 2007** Good colour, with some cracked pepper framing redcurrant and blackberry fruit; medium-bodied, spicy and fine on the silky textured finish. Screwcap. 13.5% alc. **Rating** 92 **To** 2014 $28

Feet First Wines

32 Parkinson Lane, Kardinya, WA 6163 (postal) **Region** Western Australia
T (08) 9314 7133 **F** (08) 9314 7134 **www.**feetfirstwines.com.au **Open** Not
Winemaker Contract **Est.** 2004 **Cases** 8000
This is the business of Ross and Ronnie (Veronica) Lawrence, who have been fine wine wholesalers in Perth since 1987, handling top-shelf Australian and imported wines. It is a virtual winery, with both grapegrowing and winemaking provided by contract, the aim being to produce easy-drinking, good-value wines under $20; the deliberately limited portfolio includes Semillon Sauvignon Blanc, Chardonnay and Cabernet Merlot.

ŸŸŸŸŸ **Cabernet Merlot 2008** Medium-bodied, but the considerable tannin structure needs to settle down for the full array of spicy black and red fruits to express themselves. Top value. Margaret River/Pemberton. Screwcap. 13.5% alc. **Rating** 90 **To** 2020 $16.40

ŸŸŸŸ **Semillon Sauvignon Blanc 2008** Bright pale straw-green; an attractive, crisp and lemon-accented wine that has good intensity and length, especially at this price. Will kick on for a year or two. Value. Frankland River/Pemberton. Screwcap. 11.5% alc. **Rating** 89 **To** 2011 $16.40
Chardonnay Pinot Noir NV Bottle-fermented, and though quite young does have good length and balance of citrussy flavours. Will improve on cork for a year or two. 12% alc. **Rating** 87 **To** 2011 $17.90

Fenwick Wines ★★★

180 Lings Road, Wallington, Vic 3221 **Region** Geelong
T (03) 5250 1943 **F** (03) 5250 1943 **www.**fenwickwines.com **Open** By appt
Winemaker Scotchmans Hill (Robin Brockett) **Est.** 1997 **Cases** 350 **Vyds** 5 ha
When, in 1988, Madeleine and Dr David Fenwick purchased a 20-ha property between Ocean Grove and Wallington, it was pure chance that it had first been settled by Fairfax Fenwick – no relative. The Fenwicks planted 2 ha of pinot noir in 1997 and have since added 2 ha of chardonnay and 1 ha of shiraz, and increased the pinot noir plantings slightly with three clones (114, 115 and MV6). The first five vintages were contracted to Scotchmans Hill, thereafter split between Scotchmans Hill and Fenwick Wines.

▼▼▼▼ **Geelong Pinot Noir 2007** Strong colour; robust wine, with plum and spice aromas leading into a potent palate, dark fruits with forest/briar dominant; good length. Needs time. Screwcap. 13.5% alc. **Rating** 89 **To** 2014 $25
Geelong Shiraz 2007 A fresh, spicy/peppery cool-climate shiraz, the palate no more than light- to medium-bodied, finishing with gently savoury tannins. Screwcap. 14% alc. **Rating** 89 **To** 2014 $25
Geelong Chardonnay 2007 Glowing yellow-green; the richness of the wine belies its moderate alcohol; sweeps through to an uncompromising finish. Screwcap. 13.5% alc. **Rating** 88 **To** 2012 $25

Fermoy Estate   ★★★★☆

Metricup Road, Wilyabrup, WA 6280 **Region** Margaret River
T (08) 9755 6285 **F** (08) 9755 6251 **www.**fermoy.com.au **Open** 7 days 11–4.30
Winemaker Michael Kelly **Est.** 1985 **Cases** 30 000
A long-established estate-based winery with 14 ha of semillon, sauvignon blanc, chardonnay, cabernet sauvignon and merlot. Notwithstanding its significant production, it is happy to keep a relatively low profile. Exports to Europe and Asia.

▼▼▼▼▼ **Margaret River Merlot 2007** Underlines the ability of Margaret River to produce powerful, but utterly correct merlot; blackcurrant and cassis strengthened and lengthened by black olive notes and lingering tannins. Diam. 14.5% alc. **Rating** 93 **To** 2017 $32
Margaret River Cabernet Sauvignon 2007 An elegant medium-bodied style, with cassis and blackcurrant fruit cradled by fine, ripe tannins and well-integrated French oak. Screwcap. 14% alc. **Rating** 93 **To** 2017 $29
Margaret River Chardonnay 2008 In the understated style of the estate, with stony components to the citrus and apple taking it firmly in the direction of Chablis. Will repay cellaring. Screwcap. 14% alc. **Rating** 91 **To** 2018 $29
Nebbiolo 2007 Remarkably good; has the autocratic varietal character expected with lingering, savoury tannins; cherry and rose petal. Cork. 13.5% alc. **Rating** 91 **To** 2014 $47

▼▼▼▼ **Margaret River Sauvignon Blanc 2008** A crisp, clean bouquet leads into a grassy/minerally palate with good length and balance, unadorned and pure. Screwcap. 12.5% alc. **Rating** 89 **To** 2011 $19
Margaret River Shiraz 2007 In the lighter, more elegant style for which Fermoy Estate is well known; obvious spicy/earthy/savoury overtones to the medium-bodied fruit. Screwcap. 14.5% alc. **Rating** 89 **To** 2014 $25

Fern Hill Estate   ★★★

2 Chalk Hill Road, McLaren Vale, SA 5171 **Region** McLaren Vale
T (08) 8323 9666 **F** (08) 8323 9600 **www.**wineforlife.com.au **Open** At Marienberg Limeburners Centre 7 days 10–5
Winemaker Graeme Scott, Deane Rose, Tony Hewitt **Est.** 1975 **Cases** 5000
Fern Hill Estate, along with Marienberg and Basedow, became part of the James Estate empire in 2003. A revamping of the packaging and labelling, plus acquisition of grapes from the Adelaide Hills to supplement that of McLaren Vale, has been accompanied by a move away from retail to restaurant/on-premises sales.

▼▼▼▼ **Adelaide Hills Viognier 2008** Apricot and a touch of honey; fresh and varietal, with good fruit definition. Screwcap. 13.5% alc. **Rating** 87 **To** 2011 $19

Fernfield Wines   ★★★★

Rushlea Road, Eden Valley, SA 5235 **Region** Eden Valley
T (08) 8564 1041 **F** (08) 8564 1041 **www.**fernfieldwines.com.au **Open** 7 days 10–5
Winemaker Bronwyn Lillecrapp, Shannon Plummer **Est.** 2002 **Cases** 2000 **Vyds** 27.8 ha

The establishment date of 2002 might, with a little poetic licence, be shown as 1864. Bryce Lillecrapp is the fifth generation of the Lillecrapp family, his great-great-great-grandfather bought land in the Eden Valley in 1864, subdividing it in 1866, establishing the township of Eden Valley and building the first house, Rushlea Homestead. Bryce restored this building and opened it in 1998 as a bicentennial project, now serving as Fernfield Wines' cellar door. He heads up Fernfield as grapegrower, with his wife Bronwyn chief winemaker, son Shannon cellar hand and assistant winemaker, and daughter Rebecca the wine marketer. While all members of the family have married grapegrowing and winemaking with other vocations, they have moved inexorably back to Fernfield, where they have vines dating back three generations of the family (riesling, pinot noir, shiraz, merlot, cabernet sauvignon, traminer and cabernet franc). In 2002 they built a winery, and keep part of the crop for the Fernfield label. Exports to Singapore.

ŶŶŶŶ⫯ **Pridmore Eden Valley Shiraz 2005** Excellent depth and hue; a sensuous wine with rolling velvety waves of flavour to the spicy blackberry and plum fruit; gives a strong clue to the direction the '06s will ultimately take, although the wine altogether needs more time. Great value. Cork. 15% alc. **Rating** 93 **To** 2021 $20
Pridmore Eden Valley Shiraz 2006 Is made using the same techniques as Footstompers, and has the same density of flavour, albeit with an additional twist of licorice and spice on the finish. Also cries out for time in bottle. Cork. 14.9% alc. **Rating** 90 **To** 2020 $20

ŶŶŶŶ **Triple C Eden Valley Cabernet Sauvignon 2006** A restrained style, falling short of austerity, but tight and pure; cassis/redcurrant fruit is supported by brisk acidity; excellent value, especially for the purist. Screwcap. 14.1% alc. **Rating** 89 **To** 2014 $15
Footstompers Eden Valley Shiraz 2005 An aromatic cedar and spice bouquet, then a rich, opulent palate, with black fruits to the fore before there is a twitch of heat to the finish. Cork. 15% alc. **Rating** 89 **To** 2021 $20
Footstompers Eden Valley Shiraz 2006 Curious that a hand-picked, open-fermented and basket-pressed, and French oak-matured Eden Valley shiraz doesn't have much thrust and energy; it has plenty of flavour, of course, and 10 years more in bottle may transform it. Cork. 15% alc. **Rating** 88 **To** 2020 $20
Eden Valley Merlot 2006 The grapes were a little too ripe, perhaps, but this is a lot better than many merlots twice its price. Screwcap. 14.6% alc. **Rating** 87 **To** 2012 $10

Ferngrove   ★★★★★
276 Ferngrove Road, Frankland River, WA 6396 **Region** Frankland River
T (08) 9855 2378 **www**.ferngrove.com.au **Open** Mon–Fri 10–4, w'ends by appt
Winemaker Kim Horton **Est.** 1997 **Cases** 50 000 **Vyds** 225 ha
After 90 years of family beef and dairy farming heritage, Murray Burton decided in 1997 to venture into premium grapegrowing and winemaking. Today the venture he founded has two large vineyards in Frankland River planted to the leading varieties, the lion's share to shiraz, cabernet sauvignon, chardonnay, sauvignon blanc, merlot and semillon, with a small but important planting of malbec. The operation centres around the Ferngrove Vineyard, where a large rammed-earth winery and tourist complex was built in 2000. Part of the vineyard production is sold as grapes, part as juice or must, part as finished wine, and the pick of the crop is made for the Ferngrove label. The consistency of its wines across a wide range of price points is wholly admirable. Acquired Killerby (Margaret River) in 2008. Exports to the UK, the US and other major markets.

ŶŶŶŶŶ **Diamond Frankland River Chardonnay 2007** Elegant, carefully crafted wine; nectarine and melon fruit is supported by some creamy cashew notes and perfectly integrated French oak; carries its alcohol without demur. Screwcap. 14.5% alc. **Rating** 94 **To** 2010 $23.95

Frankland River Shiraz 2007 Deep crimson-purple; highly aromatic and saturated with dark plum, blackberry and an array of spices, all making significant inputs to a medium- to full-bodied wine which will age superbly. Screwcap. 14% alc. **Rating** 94 **To** 2022 $18.95

The Stirlings Shiraz Cabernet Sauvignon 2005 Excellent concentration of dark berry fruits, with a little dried herb character adding complexity; ample levels of fruit, with plenty of fine-grained tannins providing structure. Cork. 14.5% alc. **Rating** 94 **To** 2020 $50

Majestic Frankland River Cabernet Sauvignon 2007 The bouquet has aromas of pure cassis, cedar and an attractive core of savoury black olive; the palate is quite firm and rugged, with toasty oak and plenty of tannin; good levels of sweet fruit eventually take over the structure. Screwcap. 14% alc. **Rating** 94 **To** 2016 $28

King Malbec 2007 Very good colour; good entry into the mouth, but then that slight dip in the mid-palate typical of malbec; it rises again, with glossy cherry fruit to the fore. Gold WA Wine Show '08. Screwcap. 14% alc. **Rating** 94 **To** 2015 $28.99

King Malbec 2006 Has far more texture and structure than most malbecs, and the black fruits and Christmas cake flavours avoid the jammy trap; well-deserved gold WA Wine Show '07. Screwcap. 14.5% alc. **Rating** 94 **To** 2014 $27

ŸŸŸŸŸ **Cossack Frankland River Riesling 2008** A clean bouquet is followed by a well-balanced palate, with ripe citrus/grapefruit flavours and good acidity; yet to display the quality of prior vintages. Screwcap. 12.5% alc. **Rating** 90 **To** 2014 $22

Frankland River Sauvignon Blanc 2008 Restrained but focused and clean aromas and flavours; a firm palate, with good length; nuances of gooseberry throughout. Screwcap. 13% alc. **Rating** 90 **To** 2010 $18.99

Symbols Frankland River Cabernet Merlot 2007 Bright crimson-purple; classic blackcurrant and cassis fruit flavours in a medium-bodied palate; punches well above its weight. Screwcap. 13.5% alc. **Rating** 90 **To** 2011 $15.95

ŸŸŸŸ **Leaping Lizard Unwooded Chardonnay 2008** Vibrant hue; a restrained melon and grapefruit bouquet; a generous palate, with good acidity; clean and fresh. Value. Screwcap. 14% alc. **Rating** 89 **To** 2011 $15

Leaping Lizard Shiraz 2007 Bright crimson; attractive medium-bodied wine, with spicy plum and blackberry fruit supported by precisely balanced tannins. Good value. Screwcap. 14.5% alc. **Rating** 89 **To** 2015 $14.99

Frankland River Chardonnay 2008 Restrained lemon fruit bouquet, with a slight mineral edge; fine, tight and savoury palate. Screwcap. 13.5% alc. **Rating** 89 **To** 2013 $18.99

Dragon Shiraz 2007 Supple and seductive; clever oak use; has good fruit in a red spectrum. Screwcap. 14.5% alc. **Rating** 89 **To** 2014 $28.99

Majestic Frankland River Cabernet Sauvignon 2006 A somewhat austere medium-bodied wine, with herbal/earthy overtones to the blackcurrant fruit; I'm not convinced the fruit ripened fully. Screwcap. 13.5% alc. **Rating** 89 **To** 2013 $27

Leaping Lizard Sauvignon Blanc 2008 Firm, herbal/mineral style; needs more fruit on the mid-palate, but does have some thrust on the finish. Screwcap. 13% alc. **Rating** 87 **To** 2010 $14.99

Leaping Lizard Semillon Sauvignon Blanc 2008 A fresh and very grassy style; crisp acidity adds to the length. Screwcap. 13% alc. **Rating** 87 **To** 2010 $14.99

Fighting Gully Road ★★★

319 Whorouly South Road, Whorouly South, Vic 3735 **Region** Beechworth
T (03) 5727 1434 **F** (03) 5727 1434 **Open** By appt
Winemaker Mark Walpole, Joel Pizzini **Est.** 1997 **Cases** 700 **Vyds** 8.3 ha
Mark Walpole (chief viticulturist for Brown Brothers) and partner Carolyn De Poi began the development of their Aquila Audax Vineyard in 1997, planting the first vines. It is situated between 530 and 580 m above sea level: the upper-eastern slopes are planted to pinot noir and the warmer western slopes to cabernet sauvignon; there are also small quantities of shiraz, tempranillo, sangiovese and merlot.

ŶŶŶŶ Aquila 2006 Deep colour; an interesting wine with inspiration drawn from Southern France; oxidative nutty aromas combine with estery banana; the palate is thickly textured, showing some grip and plenty of weight; quite unusual, but not unattractive. Chardonnay/Viognier/Petit Manseng. Diam. 13% alc. **Rating** 89 To 2013 $19.45

Tempranillo 2004 Dried leather and dark cherry bouquet with a little spice; medium-bodied and quite dry and savoury on the finish. Cork. 14% alc. **Rating** 89 **To** 2012 $26.35

Final Cut Wines

169 Denison Road, Dulwich Hill, NSW 2203 (postal) **Region** Barossa Valley
T (02) 9560 0012 **F** (02) 9560 0015 **www**.finalcutwines.com **Open** Not
Winemaker David Roe, Geoff Weaver (Contract) **Est.** 2004 **Cases** 3000
The names of the wines point to the involvement of owners David Roe and Les Lithgow in the film industry. Theirs is a virtual winery (likewise appropriate to the cinema), the wines made by the hugely experienced Geoff Weaver from high quality, contract-grown grapes. David becomes involved in vintage, but it is otherwise long-distance winemaking from the directors' studio in Sydney. It should come as no surprise to find the wines are of high quality. Exports to the US and Canada.

ŶŶŶŶŶ Take Two Barossa Valley Shiraz Cabernet 2006 Has some textural affinities with Montage Shiraz, but the one-third cabernet and Stonewell origin of both components adds another dimension of flavour into blackberry and cassis, with touches of licorice and dark chocolate for good measure. Screwcap. 15% alc. **Rating** 93 **To** 2021 $29

Montage Shiraz 2006 Medium-bodied, with good texture and structure to the blackberry, spice and dark chocolate fruit flavours; that texture underpins the finish of a deftly made wine. Screwcap. 14.5% alc. **Rating** 90 **To** 2015 $19

Fire Gully

Metricup Road, Wilyabrup, WA 6280 **Region** Margaret River
T (08) 9755 6220 **F** (08) 9755 6308 **Open** By appt
Winemaker Dr Michael Peterkin **Est.** 1998 **Cases** 5000 **Vyds** 13.3 ha
The Fire Gully vineyard has been established on what was first a dairy and then a beef farm. A 6-ha lake created in a gully ravaged by bushfires gave the property its name. In 1998 Mike Peterkin of Pierro purchased the property and manages the vineyard in conjunction with former owners Ellis and Margaret Butcher. He regards the Fire Gully wines as entirely separate from those of Pierro, being estate-grown: the vineyards are planted to cabernet sauvignon, merlot, shiraz, semillon, sauvignon blanc, chardonnay, viognier and chenin blanc, and have been increased by over 4 ha in recent years. Exports to all major markets.

ŶŶŶŶŶ Reserve Margaret River Shiraz 2005 Excellent crimson; distinguished wine, with juicy berry/cherry fruit and multi spice and pepper flavours on the long finish; French oak a garnish. Cork. 14% alc. **Rating** 94 **To** 2015 $41.90

ŶŶŶŶ Margaret River Cabernet Sauvignon Merlot 2005 Bright and clear colour; vibrant and fresh blackcurrant fruit, but not much depth or texture. Cork. 14.5% alc. **Rating** 89 **To** 2014 $23.90

No. 1 Reserve Margaret River Shiraz Blend 2005 Notes of mint and gum leaf on the bouquet translate into a light- to medium-bodied savoury palate that doesn't quite come together. Cork. 14% alc. **Rating** 88 **To** 2014 $41.90

Fireblock

St Vincent Street, Watervale, SA 5452 **Region** Clare Valley
T 0414 441 925 **F** (02) 9144 1925 **Open** Not
Winemaker O'Leary Walker **Est.** 1926 **Cases** 3000 **Vyds** 6 ha

Fireblock (formerly Old Station Vineyard) is owned by Alastair Gillespie and Bill and Noel Ireland, who purchased the 70-year-old vineyard in 1995. Watervale Riesling, Old Vine Shiraz and Old Vine Grenache are skilfully contract-made, winning trophies and gold medals at capital city wine shows. Exports to the US, Sweden and Malaysia.

????? **Watervale Riesling 2008** Some colour development; classic Watervale style, with toast, citrus and spice; has developed quickly. Screwcap. 12% alc. **Rating** 90 **To** 2014 $20

???? **Old Vine Clare Valley Shiraz 2006** Has a savoury red fruit bouquet, with a slight briny quality to the fruit; very firm and dry, with reasonable length and depth. Screwcap. 15.5% alc. **Rating** 87 **To** 2014 $20

First Creek Wines

Cnr McDonalds Road/Gillards Road, Pokolbin, NSW 2320 **Region** Lower Hunter Valley
T (02) 4998 7293 **F** (02) 4998 7294 **www**.firstcreekwines.com.au **Open** 7 days 10–4
Winemaker Greg Silkman, Liz Jackson, Ryan McCann, Damien Stevens **Est.** 1984
Cases 35 000
First Creek is the shop front of Monarch Winemaking Services, which has acquired the former Allanmere wine business and offers a complex range of wines under both the First Creek and the Allanmere labels. Meticulous winemaking results in quality wines both for the contract clients and for the own-business labels. First Creek may have lost the services of Jim Chatto (to Peppertree), but has secured an outstanding winemaker to take his place - Liz Jackson. Exports to the UK, the US and Canada.

????? **Winemaker's Reserve Hunter Valley Shiraz 2007** A supple and polished wine, with very good line and length to its plum and black cherry fruit; immaculate mouthfeel and length, oak well-balanced and integrated, Screwcap. **Rating** 94 **To** 2020 $42

????? **Hunter Valley Canberra District Semillon Sauvignon Blanc 2008** A synergistic blend, shaped primarily by Hunter Valley semillon, the sauvignon blanc adding a dimension of flavour to the long palate and clean finish, all in a herb/grass/citrus spectrum. Screwcap. 10.5% alc. **Rating** 92 **To** 2013 $22
Hunter Valley Verdelho 2008 Clear varietal expression throughout, with ripe fruit salad flavours that don't go over the top. Screwcap. 13% alc. **Rating** 90 **To** 2013 $22
Premium Hunter Valley Shiraz 2007 A strongly regional medium-bodied style, with plenty of energy and thrust to the earthy/leathery edges to the black fruits of the palate; good length. Screwcap. **Rating** 90 **To** 2015 $22
Premium Canberra District Shiraz Viognier 2006 Aromatic and lively red fruits as befits the co-fermented blend; while only light- to medium-bodied, has good length and balance. Screwcap. **Rating** 90 **To** 2013 $25

???? **Premium Hunter Valley Shiraz 2004** A savoury leather-bound style, with red fruit playing a supporting role; the palate is even and firm with true medium-bodied weight to the finish. Screwcap. 13.5% alc. **Rating** 89 **To** 2018 $22

First Drop Wines

PO Box 64, Williamstown, SA 5351 **Region** Barossa Valley
T 0420 971 209 **F** (08) 8389 7952 **www**.firstdropwines.com **Open** Not
Winemaker Matt Gant **Est.** 2005 **Cases** 3500
This is a virtual winery, with no vineyards and no winery of its own. What it does have are two owners with immaculate credentials to produce a diverse range of wines of significantly higher quality than those of many more conventional operations. Matt Gant was in his final year of a geography degree at the University of London in 1995 when lecturer Tim Unwin (a noted wine writer) contrived a course that involved tastings and ultimately a field trip of Burgundy and Champagne. Geography went out the window, and Matt did vintages in NZ,

Spain, Italy, Portugal, the US and finally Australia. Working at St Hallett he won the Wine Society's Young Winemaker of the Year Award in 2004, and the Young Gun Wine Award for First Drop in '07. John Retsas has an equally impressive CV, working at St Hallett and Chain of Ponds, and is now general manager of Schild Estate. First Drop's portfolio includes Arneis, Nebbiolo, Barbera and Montepulciano (all from the Adelaide Hills), Barossa Albarino and Trincadeira Rose, and a string of Barossa Shirazs ranging from $24 to $80 a bottle. Exports to the UK, the US, Canada, Germany and NZ.

ŸŸŸŸŸ **The Cream Barossa Valley Shiraz 2006** More is more, and in this case handled with great care; the fruit is actually fleshier and more restrained than the three single-vineyard wines; and while there is plenty of oak, it is barely noticeable with the lavish level of fruit; the tannins also take a back seat, but they are ample and very fine; in the end the wine is incredibly powerful but beautifully balanced. Cork. 15% alc. **Rating** 96 **To** 2025 $100
Fat of the Land Ebenezer Single Vineyard Barossa Valley Shiraz 2006 Bright and vivid purple hue; an impressive wine in all respects; dark and concentrated black fruit bouquet with mocha and cinnamon adding complexity; the most engaging aspect is the silky texture of the voluminous palate, and the lively red fruits that come to fore, drawing out a wonderfully long finish; quite approachable, yet has an undoubtedly long future ahead. Cork. 15% alc. **Rating** 96 **To** 2020 $75
Fat of the Land Seppeltsfield Single Vineyard Barossa Valley Shiraz 2006 Quite cool and lifted bouquet, with cranberry, blackberry and a distinct floral character; the palate is vibrant and fresh, showing anise, plenty of fruit, oak and gently chewy tannin profile; long and seamless finish. Cork. 15.5% alc. **Rating** 95 **To** 2020 $75
JR Gantos Quinta do sul McLaren Vale Cabernet Sauvignon Touriga Nacional 2006 Lifted blueberry fruit, spice and cassis combine to offer a seductive bouquet; the palate is very rich, but shows lightness and precision, with a vibrant and savoury finish; certainly an intriguing blend. Screwcap. 14.5% alc. **Rating** 94 **To** 2014 $36

ŸŸŸŸŸ **Fat of the Land Greenock Single Vineyard Shiraz 2006** Quite a dark personality on opening; all fruitcake, mocha and oak; the palate is also dense and quite chewy, showing some sage amid the fruit; a little backward, time will tell if there is more to be had. Cork. 15% alc. **Rating** 93 **To** 2018 $75
Mother's Milk Barossa Shiraz 2007 Fruitcake spice supports a pure core of plum and blackberry; the palate is generous and textured, with a bright and even red and black fruit finish. Screwcap. 13.5% alc. **Rating** 92 **To** 2015 $24
Two Percent Barossa Shiraz 2006 Strong, spicy elements in both bouquet and palate; good mouthfeel, silky smooth; good wine; 2% Albarino. Screwcap. 15% alc. **Rating** 92 **To** 2016 $42
Minchia Adelaide Hills Montepulciano 2006 A striking label for a striking wine; strong colour, and has masses of blackberry and plum fruit on a full, but supple, palate, tannins and oak are in sympathy with the fruit. Screwcap. 15% alc. **Rating** 92 **To** 2015 $36
Bella Coppia Adelaide Hills Arneis 2008 Offers a positive and fragrant bouquet with citrus rind/citrus zest aromas followed by a lively palate with good thrust. Watch this space. Screwcap. 13.5% alc. **Rating** 90 **To** 2011 $24
The Big Blind Adelaide Hills Nebbiolo Barbera 2007 A thoroughly challenging varietal blend that comes off well if you mentally substitute pinot noir for nebbiolo; light- to medium-bodied, with some spicy overtones to the fine, savoury fruits and lingering tannins. Fascinating label story. Screwcap. 14% alc. **Rating** 90 **To** 2015 $28

ŸŸŸŸ **Mother's Ruin McLaren Vale Cabernet Sauvignon 2007** A soft and approachable sweet-fruited wine; mostly red fruits with slightly drying tannin to clean up the finish. Screwcap. 13.5% alc. **Rating** 88 **To** 2012 $24

5 Blind Mice

PO Box 243, Basket Range, SA 5138 **Region** Adelaide Hills
T (08) 8390 0206 **F** (08) 8390 3693 **www**.5blindmice.com.au **Open** Not
Winemaker Jodie Armstrong, Hugh Armstrong **Est.** 2004 **Cases** 120
Owners Jodie and Hugh Armstrong say, 'What started out as an idea between friends and
family to make something for themselves to drink at home during the week has blossomed
into a quest for something to stand proudly on its own.' They purchase pinot noir from three
sites in the Adelaide Hills, the vines 15–16 years old. The wine is made in the boutique
contract winery Red Heads Studio in McLaren Vale, with Jodie and Hugh making the wine
under the eyes of Justin Lane and Adam Hooper, the winemakers at Red Heads.

Five Geese

RSD 587 Chapel Hill Road, Blewitt Springs, SA 5171 (postal) **Region** McLaren Vale
T (08) 8383 0576 **F** (08) 8383 0629 **www**.fivegeese.com.au **Open** Not
Winemaker Boar's Rock (Mike Farmilo) **Est.** 1999 **Cases** 1500 **Vyds** 26.6 ha
Sue Trott is passionate about her Five Geese wine, which is produced by Hillgrove Wines. The
wines come from vines planted in 1927 and '65. The grapes were sold for many years, but in
1999 Sue decided to create her own label and make a strictly limited amount of wine from
the pick of the vineyards. Exports to the UK, the US, Canada, Hong Kong and Singapore.

ᵀᵀᵀᵀᵀ **McLaren Vale Shiraz 2006** A delicious medium-bodied wine that shows fully
ripe fruit (though not jammy or dead) can be achieved in McLaren Vale; the
red fruit flavours lilt in the mouth, vanillin oak entirely in tune with the fruit.
Screwcap. 14.5% alc. **Rating** 94 **To** 2016 $24
Old Vine McLaren Vale Grenache Shiraz 2006 Bright, clear crimson; an
elegant and harmonious medium-bodied palate with a marvellously long and
persistent finish and aftertaste. Value. Diam. 14.5% alc. **Rating** 94 **To** 2015 $20

Five Sons Estate

85 Harrisons Road, Dromana, Vic 3936 **Region** Mornington Peninsula
T (03) 5987 3137 **F** (03) 5981 0572 **www**.fivesonsestate.com.au **Open** W'ends & public
hols 11–5, 7 days in Jan
Winemaker Rollo Crittenden (Contract) **Est.** 1998 **Cases** 3000 **Vyds** 18.82 ha
Bob and Sue Peime purchased the most historically significant viticultural holding in the
Mornington Peninsula in 1998. Development of the 68-ha property began in the early
1930s, and was sold to a member of the Seppelt family, who planted riesling in '48. Two years
later the property was sold to the Broadhurst family, close relatives of Doug Seabrook, who
persisted with growing and making riesling until a 1967 bushfire destroyed the vines. Since
1998 (in descending order) pinot noir, chardonnay, shiraz, pinot gris and cabernet sauvignon
have been planted.

ᵀᵀᵀᵀ **Mornington Peninsula Chardonnay 2006** Bright colour; cool nectarine fruit
with a little spice; elegant and poised, with fresh acidity on the finish. Screwcap.
13.6% alc. **Rating** 89 **To** 2012 $24

Flametree

Cnr Caves Road/Chain Avenue, Dunsborough, WA 6281 **Region** Margaret River
T (08) 9756 8577 **F** (08) 9756 8572 **www**.flametreewines.com **Open** 7 days 10–5
Winemaker Jeremy Gordon **Est.** 2007 **Cases** 7000
Flametree is a partnership between two families, the Gordons (Jeremy and Daniela) and
the Towners (John, Liz, Jeremy and Rob), which has come a very long way in a very short
time. The wines are made from grapes purchased from growers in the Margaret River and
Frankland River regions, and made in a state-of-the-art winery completed just in time for
the 2007 vintage. The success that has followed in the wake of the wines of that vintage is
extraordinary. Flametree won the trophy for Most Successful WA Winery under 300 tonnes
at the Perth Wine Show '08 on the back of gold medals for its '07 Cabernet Merlot, '07

Merlot, plus a silver for its '08 Sauvignon Blanc Semillon and a bronze for the '07 Shiraz. The Cabernet Merlot continued to shine: blitzing the field at the Qantas Wine Show of WA, winning multiple trophies; winning the Jimmy Watson Trophy; and winning the trophy of the Margaret River Wine Show for Best Cabernet Blend.

ΨΨΨΨΨ **Margaret River Cabernet Merlot 2007** Very good colour; serious medium- to full-bodied wine with excellent focus and balance; long cassis and blackcurrant fruit, the tannins persistent but very fine, the French oak perfectly integrated and balanced. Multi-trophy winner WA Wine Show '08; Jimmy Watson Trophy '08; Trophy Best Cabernet Blend Margaret River Wine Show '08. Screwcap. 14.5% alc. Rating 96 To 2022 $25
Margaret River Merlot 2007 Deep crimson-purple; the bouquet and full-bodied palate both have a range of fruits ranging from redcurrant through plum and mulberry; while concentrated, the wine is not extractive. Screwcap. 13.5% alc. Rating 94 To 2017 $22
Reserve Release Margaret River Cabernet Sauvignon 2007 Dense purple-crimson; has all the depth and concentration one could possibly wish for, oozing blackcurrant and licorice, the tannins and 18 months in French oak providing structural integrity. Screwcap. 14% alc. Rating 94 To 2020 $49

ΨΨΨΨΩ **Margaret River Sauvignon Blanc Semillon 2008** Fresh and very lively, with a rippling palate, the fruit flavours swelling on the finish. Screwcap. 12.5% alc. Rating 91 To 2010 $19
Margaret River Chardonnay 2007 Some depth to the colour, and abundant flavour, with grapefruit and riper fruit components supported by obvious French oak; more power than finesse. Screwcap. 13.5% alc. Rating 90 To 2011 $25
Frankland River Shiraz 2007 Strong colour; a fragrant, fruity bouquet with a luscious damson plum and cherry palate to match; good balance and length. Screwcap. 15.5% alc. Rating 90 To 2013 $25

ΨΨΨΨ **Margaret River Classic 2008** In the mainstream of classic style, the varied fruit components meshing well to provide an all-purpose wine, with gentle fruit and a dry finish. Sauvignon Blanc/Semillon/Chardonnay. Screwcap. 13.5% alc. Rating 89 To 2010 $15
Reserve Release Frankland River Shiraz 2007 Dense, opaque colour; hyper-ripe and concentrated; Frankland comes to the Barossa; the back label accurately describes stewed fruits, prunes and dates. Send to Robert Parker Jr forthwith. Screwcap. 15.5% alc. Rating 89 To 2027 $49

Flaxman Wines ★★★★★

Lot 535 Flaxmans Valley Road, Angaston, SA 5353 **Region** Eden Valley
T 0411 668 949 **F** (08) 8565 3299 **www**.flaxmanwines.com.au **Open** By appt
Winemaker Colin Sheppard **Est.** 2005 **Cases** 500 **Vyds** 2 ha
After visiting the Barossa Valley for over a decade, and working during vintage with Andrew Seppelt at Murray Street Vineyards, Melbourne residents Colin and Fiona Sheppard decided on a seachange, and found a small, old vineyard overlooking Flaxmans Valley. It consists of 1 ha of 40+-year-old riesling, 1 ha of 50+-year-old shiraz and a small planting of 40-plus-year-old semillon. The vines are dry-grown, hand-pruned and hand-picked, and treated – say the Sheppards – as their garden. Yields are restricted to under 4 tonnes per ha, and small amounts of locally grown grapes are also purchased.

ΨΨΨΨΨ **The Stranger Barossa Shiraz Cabernet 2007** Good crimson colour, although unfiltered; a lively mix of redcurrant and blackberry fruit, with considerable thrust to the palate, finishing with fine tannins; 170 dozen made. Gold Barossa Valley Wine Show '08. Screwcap. 14% alc. Rating 94 To 2017 $35
Shhh Eden Valley Cabernet 2006 Excellent colour; extremely intense and tightly focused blackcurrant fruit, still almost elemental; 30 dozen made from a single barrel hidden from the wife. Screwcap. 14.5% alc. Rating 94 To 2026 $35

ӯӯӯӯҭ Eden Valley Shiraz 2006 Has the fresh underlying acidity of the Eden Valley, which supports the medium-bodied, bright red and black fruits; fine-grained tannins also add; 60 dozen made. Screwcap. 14.5% alc. **Rating** 93 **To** 2020 $45
Eden Valley Riesling 2008 Floral/blossom aromas; considerable lime juice fruit richness on the palate, but avoids heaviness; good length. Screwcap. 12.5% alc. **Rating** 92 **To** 2016 $25
Eden Valley Dessert Semillon 2008 Yellow-gold; some beeswax notes to bouquet and palate, the latter with luscious tropical/banana fruit; 60 dozen made. Screwcap. 11% alc. **Rating** 90 **To** 2012 $20

Flinders Bay

Bussell Highway, Metricup, WA 6280 **Region** Margaret River
T (08) 9757 6281 **F** (08) 9757 6353 **Open** 7 days 10–4
Winemaker O'Leary Walker, Flying Fish Cove **Est.** 1995 **Cases** 10 000 **Vyds** 50 ha
A joint venture between Alastair Gillespie and Bill and Noel Ireland, the former a grapegrower and viticultural contractor in Margaret River for over 25 years, the latter two Sydney wine retailers for an even longer period. The wines are made from grapes grown on the Karridale Vineyard (planted between 1995 and '98), with the exception of a Verdelho, which is purchased from northern Margaret River. Part of the grape production is sold, and part made under the Flinders Bay and Dunsborough Hills brands. Exports to the US, Sweden, Malaysia and China.

ӯӯӯӯҭ Karri Grove Estate Margaret River Sauvignon Blanc Semillon 2008 Well put together with a subliminal touch of sweetness; balanced fruit and oak, but doesn't quite get there in terms of intensity. Gold WA Wine Show '08. **Rating** 93 **To** 2011 $18
Dunsborough Hills Margaret River Sauvignon Blanc Semillon 2008
Fractionally reduced bouquet does not impact on the palate, which is very bright and fresh, the semillon adding structure; good length; will develop. Screwcap. 12.5% alc. **Rating** 90 **To** 2012 $17.80

ӯӯӯӯ Margaret River Merlot 2007 Clear-cut red berry/cassis and snow pea aromas and flavours are 100% true to merlot; light- to medium-bodied, the slightly savoury but fine tannins are wholly appropriate. Screwcap. 14% alc. **Rating** 89 **To** 2014 $20
Karri Grove Estate Margaret River Cabernet Merlot 2007 A pretty wine; fresh red fruit aromas and flavours run the show, tannins and oak well into the background. Drink me now style. Screwcap. 14% alc. **Rating** 89 **To** 2010 $15
Dunsborough Hills Margaret River Chardonnay 2008 Vibrant hue; a stone fruit bouquet with a touch of spice from the oak; mid-weight, with tangy acid and a little phenolic grip on the finish. Screwcap. 13% alc. **Rating** 88 **To** 2012 $16
Margaret River Sauvignon Blanc Semillon 2008 Pale colour; quite a neutral bouquet with a touch of green nettle; some tropical fruit on the palate; straight forward. Screwcap. 12% alc. **Rating** 87 **To** 2012 $20
Karri Grove Estate Margaret River Sauvignon Blanc Semillon 2007
Slightly diffuse tropical fruit aromas flow through onto the soft passionfruit and gooseberry palate; good balance. Screwcap. 13% alc. **Rating** 87 **To** 2010 $15
Wongaburra Chenin Blanc 2008 Pale colour; a ripe apple bouquet with good fruit definition; a bit of sugar on the palate provides good weight and texture; juicy on the finish. Screwcap. 13% alc. **Rating** 87 **To** 2012 $10
Dunsborough Hills Margaret River Shiraz 2007 Quite spicy, with dark red fruit in support; good weight, clean and fresh; quite aggressively tannic on the finish. Screwcap. 14.5% alc. **Rating** 87 **To** 2014 $16
Karri Grove Estate Margaret River Shiraz 2006 Pleasant medium-bodied spicy shiraz that belies its alcohol, although there is nothing to be gained from extended cellaring. Screwcap. 15% alc. **Rating** 87 **To** 2010 $15
Margaret River Cabernet Sauvignon 2007 Has some fruit concentration and sweetness, with redcurrant the dominant force; good weight and texture, just a little one-dimensional. Screwcap. 14% alc. **Rating** 87 **To** 2014 $20

Fluted Cape Vineyard   ★★★★

128 Groombridge Road, Kettering, Tas 7155 **Region** Southern Tasmania
T (03) 6267 4262 **Open** 7 days 10–5
Winemaker Hood Wines **Est.** 1993 **Cases** 150
For many years Val Dell was the senior wildlife ranger on the central plateau of Tasmania, his wife Jan running the information centre at Liawenee. I met them there on trout fishing expeditions, staying in one of the park huts. They have now retired to the Huon Valley region, having established 0.25 ha each of pinot noir and chardonnay overlooking Kettering and Bruny Island, said to be a spectacularly beautiful site. The wines are made for them by Andrew Hood and are sold through the cellar door and Hartzview Cellars in Gardners Bay.

🍷🍷🍷🍷♀ **Pinot Noir 2007** Powerful wine; masses of black fruits and *sous bois*/forest floor notes; will develop in an intriguing fashion. Screwcap. 13.8% alc. **Rating** 92 To 2014
   Chardonnay 2008 Has quite intense nectarine and citrus on both bouquet and palate; good line, length and balance. Screwcap. 13.3% alc. **Rating** 91 **To** 2013

Flying Duck Wines   ★★★

3838 Wangaratta-Whitfield Road, King Valley, Vic 3678 **Region** King Valley
T (03) 9819 7787 **F** (03) 9819 7789 **www.**flyingduckwines.com.au **Open** By appt
Winemaker Trevor Knaggs, Dennis Clark **Est.** 1998 **Cases** 600 **Vyds** 3.6 ha
Wayne and Sally Burgoyne with John and Karen Butler purchased the three-year-old vineyard in 2001, with 2 ha of shiraz that had been planted by Paul Burgoyne (Wayne's cousin), who continues to be involved with the operation as viticulturist. Merlot (0.8 ha), viognier and sangiovese (0.4 ha each) have been progressively added.

🍷🍷🍷🍷 **King Valley Merlot 2006** Cedar and cassis fruit on the bouquet; with plenty of rich plummy fruit, very much on the full side. Screwcap. 14% alc. **Rating** 87 To 2012 $25

Flying Fish Cove   ★★★★★

Caves Road, Wilyabrup, WA 6284 **Region** Margaret River
T (08) 9755 6600 **F** (08) 9755 6788 **www.**flyingfishcove.com **Open** 7 days 11–5
Winemaker Damon Eastaugh, Liz Reed, Ryan Aggiss **Est.** 2000 **Cases** 16 000
A group of 20 shareholders acquired the 130-ha property on which the Flying Fish Cove winery was subsequently built. It has two strings to its bow: contract winemaking for others; and the development of three product ranges (Upstream, Prize Catch and Margaret River varietals), partly based on 25 ha of estate plantings, with another 10 ha planned. Exports to the US, Italy, West Indies, Indonesia, Singapore, Japan and Hong Kong.

🍷🍷🍷🍷🍷 **Wildberry Estate Shiraz 2007** Dense purple-crimson; an evocative bouquet ranging through cherry, plum, licorice and dark chocolate is augmented on the palate with excellent tannin management and oak integration. Screwcap. 14.5% alc. **Rating** 95 To 2022 $29
   Wildberry Estate Cabernet Sauvignon 2007 Good purple-red; blackcurrant and earth aromas lead into a succulently rich, ripe and juicy palate with sweet black and red fruit flavours over a more savoury/earthy underlay. Screwcap. 14.5% alc. **Rating** 94 To 2017 $29

🍷🍷🍷🍷♀ **Margaret River Shiraz 2007** Dense purple-red; rich, spicy blackberry fruit aromas lead into a saturated array of black fruit, licorice and spice flavours; fine tannins throughout. Screwcap. 14.5% alc. **Rating** 93 To 2017 $22
   Margaret River Cabernet Sauvignon Merlot 2007 Deep but clear crimson-purple; luscious black and redcurrant fruit bolstered by fine tannins and oak. Impressive at the full end of the spectrum. Screwcap. 14.5% alc. **Rating** 93 To 2022 $22

Upstream Reserve Chardonnay 2007 A savoury style, with melon and nectarine fruit; quite taut, with just a little green edge, which prolongs the fruit richness on the finish. Screwcap. 14% alc. **Rating** 92 **To** 2013 $29

ＹＹＹＹ **Margaret River Sauvignon Blanc Semillon 2008** The semillon makes its presence felt in the structure, and the lemon citrus nuances to the gooseberry fruit at the core of the wine. Screwcap. 13% alc. **Rating** 89 **To** 2012 $22

Flynns Wines   ★★★★★

Lot 5 Lewis Road, Heathcote, Vic 3523 **Region** Heathcote
T (03) 5433 6297 **F** (03) 5433 6297 **www.**flynnswines.com **Open** W'ends 11.30–5
Winemaker Greg Flynn, Natala Flynn **Est.** 1999 **Cases** 2000 **Vyds** 4.4 ha
The Flynn name has a long association with Heathcote. In the 1970s John Flynn and Laurie Williams established a 2-ha vineyard next door to Mount Ida Vineyard, on the rich, red Cambrian soil. It produced some spectacular wines before being sold in 1983. Greg and Natala Flynn (no relation to John Flynn) spent 18 months searching for their property, 13 km north of Heathcote on the same red Cambrian soil. They have established shiraz, sangiovese, verdelho, cabernet sauvignon and merlot. Greg is a Roseworthy marketing graduate, and has had 22 years working on the coalface of retail and wholesale businesses, interweaving eight years of vineyard and winemaking experience, supplemented by the two-year Bendigo TAFE winemaking course. Just for good measure, wife Natala joined Greg for the last eight years of vineyard and winemaking, and likewise completed the TAFE course.

ＹＹＹＹＹ **MC Heathcote Shiraz 2007** Has more briary/savoury elements than prior releases, giving it a certain gravitas; the palate is medium- to full-bodied, balancing blackberry, licorice, spice and pepper against savoury, lingering tannins. Screwcap. 14.2% alc. **Rating** 94 **To** 2027 $33
Heathcote Sangiovese 2006 This wine has interesting aromas of spice and leather alongside more traditional sour cherry/red cherry; the fruit flavours have similar nuances, the tannins nicely balanced and integrated. Australian sangiovese doesn't come much better than this. Screwcap. 13.7% alc. **Rating** 94 **To** 2015 $30

ＹＹＹＹＹ **MC Heathcote Shiraz 2006** Fragrant red and black fruit aromas are followed by an unexpectedly vociferous palate, tangy and quite tannic. MC stands for multi clone, not maceration carbonique. Screwcap. 15.3% alc. **Rating** 91 **To** 2020 $33

Fonty's Pool Vineyards   ★★★★★

Seven Day Road, Manjimup, WA 6258 **Region** Pemberton
T (08) 9777 0777 **F** (08) 9777 0788 **www.**fontyspoolwines.com.au **Open** 7 days 12–4
Winemaker Melanie Bowater, Bernie Stanlake **Est.** 1989 **Cases** 20 000 **Vyds** 69.42 ha
The Fonty's Pool vineyards are part of the original farm owned by pioneer settler Archie Fontanini, who was granted land by the government in 1907. In the early 1920s a large dam was created to provide water for the intensive vegetable farming that was part of the farming activities. The dam became known as Fonty's Pool, and to this day remains a famous local landmark and recreational facility. The first grapes were planted in 1989, and the vineyard is one of the region's largest, supplying grapes to a number of leading WA wineries. An increasing amount of the production is used for Fonty's Pool. Exports to all major markets.

ＹＹＹＹＹ **Single Vineyard Pemberton Sauvignon Blanc Semillon 2008** Bright floral aromas lead into a very intense palate, with a strong citrussy core thrusting through to the lingering finish; a wine of remarkable purity. Screwcap. 12% alc. **Rating** 94 **To** 2011 $19.80

ＹＹＹＹＹ **Single Vineyard Pemberton Pinot Noir 2008** A complex wine, with ripe cherry and plum fruit surrounded by spice and a touch of French oak; has good thrust and energy, likewise value. Screwcap. 13% alc. **Rating** 92 **To** 2014 $22
Single Vineyard Pemberton Shiraz 2007 Dense purple; inky black fruits on the bouquet lead into a full-bodied palate with layers of fruit and strong tannin; needs a decade. Screwcap. 14.5% alc. **Rating** 90 **To** 2020 $22

Pinot Noir Chardonnay 2006 Elegant sparkling wine; fine aromas and flavours of lime, green apple and redcurrant. Interesting suggestion to consume within 18 months of (an unspecified) release date. Cork. 12.5% alc. **Rating** 90 **To** 2012 $28

♈♈♈♈ **Pemberton Rose 2008** Bright small red fruits on a lively and pleasantly dry wine; good length. Screwcap. 13.5% alc. **Rating** 89 **To** 2010 $17

Forest Hill Vineyard ★★★★★

South Coast Highway, Denmark, WA 6333 **Region** Great Southern
T (08) 9848 2199 **F** (08) 9848 3199 **www**.foresthillwines.com.au **Open** 7 days 10–5
Winemaker Clémence Haselgrove **Est.** 1965 **Cases** 35 000 **Vyds** 95.75 ha
This family-owned business is one of the oldest 'new' winemaking operations in WA, and was the site for the first grape plantings in Great Southern in 1965. The Forest Hill brand became well known, aided by the fact that a 1975 Riesling made by Sandalford from Forest Hill grapes won nine trophies. In 1997 a program of renovation and expansion of the vineyards commenced; the quality of the wines made from the oldest vines on the property is awesome (released under the numbered vineyard block labels). Exports to the UK and China.

♈♈♈♈♈ **Great Southern Cabernet Sauvignon 2007** A nigh-on perfect evocation of medium-bodied cabernet, the aroma and flavours wonderfully pure, with pinpointed accuracy to the cassis and blackcurrant fruit, the tannins exact, the oak likewise. Screwcap. 14.5% alc. **Rating** 97 **To** 2022 $24
Block 1 Mount Barker Riesling 2008 Extremely pale; at once intense yet reticent to unfold; superfine and delicate, yet long; tracks the bouquet; a 20-year proposition, 5-year minimum. Screwcap. 12.8% alc. **Rating** 96 **To** 2028 $38
Block 8 Mount Barker Chardonnay 2007 A fragrant, multi-faceted bouquet, with an interplay between fruit and barrel ferment oak, leads into a vibrant palate of nectarine, apple and grapefruit, the finish long and highly focused. Screwcap. 13.5% alc. **Rating** 95 **To** 2020 $38
Great Southern Riesling 2008 Extremely pale; scented floral spice and crushed lime leaves; while delicate, is offering more fruit against a mineral backdrop; lemony acidity. Will develop very well. Screwcap. 11% alc. **Rating** 94 **To** 2018 $21
Great Southern Chardonnay 2006 Elegant, melon and white peach; smooth and supple; light- to medium-bodied; oak restrained; admirable length. Gold WA Wine Show '08. Screwcap. 13.8% alc. **Rating** 94 **To** 2016 $24
Great Southern Shiraz 2007 Has exceptional drive and thrust to the spicy, peppery mix of red and black fruits on the medium-bodied, intense palate; great length and poise. Screwcap. 14.5% alc. **Rating** 94 **To** 2020 $24
Great Southern Cabernet Sauvignon 2006 Clever use of oak adds texture and structure to blackcurrant fruit and ripe tannins. Rare achievement for the vintage. Gold WA Wine Show '08. Screwcap. 13.9% alc. **Rating** 94 **To** 2018 $24

♈♈♈♈♈ **Great Southern Chardonnay 2007** Very elegant and skilfully crafted wine, all the fruit and oak components balanced and integrated; light- to medium-bodied, the smooth nectarine and white peach fruit backed by subtle oak. Screwcap. 13.5% alc. **Rating** 93 **To** 2015 $24
Boobook Great Southern Cabernet Merlot 2007 Medium-bodied, bringing together spicy black and red fruits, fine tannins and cleansing acidity. Screwcap. 14.5% alc. **Rating** 90 **To** 2016 $19

Forester Estate ★★★★☆

1064 Wildwood Road, Yallingup, WA 6282 **Region** Margaret River
T (08) 9755 2788 **F** (08) 9755 2766 **www**.foresterestate.com.au **Open** By appt
Winemaker Kevin McKay, Michael Langridge **Est.** 2001 **Cases** 25 000 **Vyds** 51.5 ha
The Forester Estate business partners are Kevin McKay and Redmond Sweeny. Winemaker Michael Langridge has a Bachelor of Arts (Hons) in Psychology and a Bachelor of Applied Science (wine science, CSU). As Kevin McKay says, 'He is the most over-qualified forklift driver in Australia.' They have built and designed a 500-tonne winery, half devoted to

contract winemaking, the other half for the Forester label. The estate vineyards are planted to sauvignon blanc, semillon, cabernet sauvignon, petit verdot, merlot, shiraz, malbec and cabernet franc. Exports to Singapore, China and Japan.

ŸŸŸŸŸ **Home Block Margaret River Shiraz 2007** Bright colour; an attractive array of plum, black cherry and blackberry fruit on the medium- to full-bodied palate, with a dusting of spice and good oak. Screwcap. 14% alc. **Rating** 94 **To** 2020 $35

ŸŸŸŸŸ **Margaret River Cabernet Merlot 2007** Light but bright purple-crimson; attractive light-bodied wine, with cassis, redcurrant fruits and a hint of olive; the well-balanced palate has very good energy and thrust. Good value. Screwcap. 14% alc. **Rating** 90 **To** 2014 $20
Margaret River Sauvignon Blanc 2008 Fresh and clean aromas; nicely balanced palate with passionfruit and gooseberry flavours; the length is good, as is the balance. Screwcap. 13.5% alc. **Rating** 90 **To** 2009 $18

ŸŸŸŸ **Margaret River Semillon Sauvignon Blanc 2008** Well knit and balanced, the semillon providing the structure and length, the sauvignon blanc playing a minor role in a fresh wine. Screwcap. 13% alc. **Rating** 89 **To** 2013 $19.50
Margaret River Chardonnay 2007 Bells and whistles style, but not quite enough thrust or vibrancy; ripe, peachy fruit. Screwcap. 13.3% alc. **Rating** 89 **To** 2011 $28.50
Margaret River Chardonnay 2006 Well made and well balanced, but there is a slight edge of bitterness to the citrussy component of the fruit flavours that drive the wine. Diam. 13.5% alc. **Rating** 89 **To** 2012 $28
Margaret River Shiraz 2005 Lively light- to medium-bodied spicy red fruits; good balance thanks to fine tannins; no need to wait. Screwcap. 14% alc. **Rating** 89 **To** 2012 $19.50
Margaret River Cabernet Sauvignon 2007 A similar light-bodied style to the Cabernet Merlot, but one expects more of a Cabernet Sauvignon at this price; undoubtedly elegant and balanced, but equally undoubtedly needs more structure and depth. Screwcap. 14% alc. **Rating** 89 **To** 2014 $33

Foster e Rocco   NR

139 Williams Road, Myers Flat, Vic 3556 (postal) **Region** Heathcote
T 0407 057 471 **Open** Not
Winemaker Adam Foster, Lincoln Riley **Est.** 2008 **Cases** 350
Long-term sommeliers and friends, Adam Foster and Lincoln Riley, have established a business that has a very clear vision: food-friendly wine based on the versatility of sangiovese. They made their first wine at Syrahmi, building it from the ground up, with fermentation in both stainless steel and a mixture of older French oak barrels.

Foster's Group Limited   NR

77 Southbank Boulevard, Southbank, Vic 3006 **Region**
T 1300 651 650 **F** (03) 9633 2002 **www.**fosters.com.au **Open** Not
Winemaker Chris Hatcher **Est.** 2005 **Cases** 38.7 million **Vyds** 11 532 ha
Foster's Wine Estates has two main streams of brands: those it had prior to the amalgamation with Southcorp, and those that came with Southcorp. Alphabetically, in the former category are: Andrew Garrett, Annie's Lane, Baileys of Glenrowan, Cartwheel, Early Harvest, Eye Spy, Half Mile Creek, Ingoldby, Jamiesons Run, Maglieri Lambrusco, Maglieri of McLaren Vale, Metala, Mildara, Pepperjack, Saltram, Shadowood, St Huberts, T'Gallant, Wolf Blass, Yarra Ridge and Yellowglen. The Southcorp originated brands are: Coldstream Hills, Devil's Lair, Edwards & Chaffey, Fisher's Circle, Killawarra, Leo Buring, Lindemans, Minchinbury, Penfolds, Queen Adelaide, Rosemount Estate, Rouge Homme, Seaview, Seppelt, The Little Penguin, Tollana and Wynns Coonawarra Estate. Those that have dedicated vineyards wholly or partially within their control and/or have separate winemaking facilities will be found under their separate entries. Those brands without, as it were, an independent existence are covered within this entry. Heemskerk is a latter entry. Exports to all major markets. A winery rating in this context is not possible.

ΨΨΨΨΨ **Heemskerk Coal River Valley Riesling 2008** Has all the magical mix of finesse, delicacy and intensity of Tasmanian riesling; a flowery bouquet, then precise citrus and apple fruit followed by citrussy acidity on the finish. Will cellar superbly. Screwcap. 12.5% alc. **Rating** 95 **To** 2028 $40

ΨΨΨΨΨ **Heemskerk Coal River Valley Riesling 2007** Intriguing wine; fragrant and crisp, its aromas and flavours a cross between riesling and sauvignon blanc, perhaps due to maturation on lees in large old oak. Pushes the envelope with a vengeance. Screwcap. 12.5% alc. **Rating** 92 **To** 2013 $40
Heemskerk Coal River Valley Chardonnay 2007 Very restrained, giving only a glimpse of where it is headed; the fruit, oak and acidity are tightly welded together. You know it is all there, and it will reveal all in the future, but when remains the unanswered question. Screwcap. 13% alc. **Rating** 92 **To** 2020 $50
Heemskerk Lowestoft Vineyard Derwent Valley Pinot Noir 2007 Attractive wine; light- to medium-bodied, but with good line and length to the mix of cherry, plum and rhubarb fruit; has a fine skein of tannin and oak to add to texture and complexity. Screwcap. 14% alc. **Rating** 91 **To** 2013 $60
Heemskerk Coal River Valley Chardonnay 2006 A flowery, tangy bouquet is followed by an almost grassy/sauvignon palate, but with enough grapefruit and melon to satisfy. Screwcap. 13.5% alc. **Rating** 90 **To** 2012 $50

Four Winds Vineyard ★★★★

PO Box 131, Murrumbateman, NSW 2582 **Region** Canberra District
T (02) 6226 8182 **F** (02) 6226 8257 **www**.fourwindsvineyard.com.au **Open** Not
Winemaker Graeme Lunney **Est.** 1998 **Cases** 750 **Vyds** 13.6 ha
Graeme and Suzanne Lunney conceived the idea for Four Winds in 1997, planting the first vines in '98, moving to the property full-time in '99, and making the first vintage in 2000. Son Tom manages the day-to-day operations of the vineyard; daughter Sarah looks after events and promotions; and youngest daughter Jaime, complete with a degree in Forensic Biology, joins the party at the most busy times of the year. Graeme makes the wine, and Suzanne tends the gardens and the 100 rose bushes at the end of the vine rows.

ΨΨΨΨΨ **Alinga Canberra District Shiraz 2005** Has a cranberry and spiced pear bouquet, with cinnamon and a touch of leather coming to the fore; the palate shows intense redcurrant character, with a savoury/leathery note to the finish. Value. Screwcap. 14% alc. **Rating** 93 **To** 2016 $18
Alinga Canberra District Unwooded Chardonnay 2008 A ripe bouquet of nectarine and a touch of spice; the fruit is generous on the palate, and the acidity cleans it up, leaving a little toasty complexity to finish. Value. Screwcap. 13.2% alc. **Rating** 90 **To** 2013 $16

ΨΨΨΨ **Alinga Canberra District Riesling 2008** Pale colour; lime with a touch of mineral; attractive, soft palate, with a dry, even and fine finish. Screwcap. 12.2% alc. **Rating** 89 **To** 2014 $16

Fox Creek Wines ★★★★☆

Malpas Road, McLaren Vale, SA 5171 **Region** McLaren Vale
T (08) 8556 2403 **F** (08) 8556 2104 **www**.foxcreekwines.com **Open** 7 days 10–5
Winemaker Chris Dix, Scott Zrna **Est.** 1995 **Cases** 35 000 **Vyds** 25 ha
Fox Creek has made a major impact since coming on-stream late in 1995. It is the venture of the Watts family: Jim (a retired surgeon), wife Helen and son Paul (a viticulturist); and the Roberts family: John (a retired anaesthetist) and wife Lyn. Kristin McLarty (née Watts) is marketing manager and Paul Rogers (married to Georgy, née Watts) is general manager. Moves are afoot to introduce organic practices in the vineyards, with trials of an organically registered herbicide derived from pine oil for weed control. The wines have enjoyed considerable show success. Exports to all major markets.

ⵯⵯⵯⵯⵯ **Reserve McLaren Vale Shiraz 2006** Deeply coloured, with an abundance of sweet black fruit, chocolate and fruitcake spice; the palate is rich, ripe and warm, with a layered array of dark fruit, and spicy oak on the finish. Screwcap. 14.5% alc. **Rating** 94 **To** 2018 $70

ⵯⵯⵯⵯⵯ **JSM McLaren Vale Shiraz Cabernet Sauvignon Cabernet Franc 2006** A delicious fruit-forward wine combining red and black fruits seamlessly, with a strong floral component providing allure; the palate is also fine, and runs seamlessly from start to finish. Screwcap. 14.5% alc. **Rating** 92 **To** 2017 $22

JSM McLaren Vale Shiraz Cabernet Sauvignon Cabernet Franc 2007 Raspberry fruit comes to the fore, supported by a little spice and a touch of chocolate; the palate is fleshy, warm and even, with an attractive juicy quality to the fruit. Screwcap. 13.5% alc. **Rating** 91 **To** 2014 $22.50

McLaren Vale Shiraz Grenache Mourvedre 2007 Bright colour; a restrained bouquet, with a certain lift to the fruit; an amalgam of red and black fruit on the palate, with fine acidity and good focus to the finish. Value. Screwcap. 14% alc. **Rating** 90 **To** 2013 $17.50

Red Baron McLaren Vale Shiraz 2008 A ripe and oaky bouquet with ripe blackberry fruit and a touch of mocha; the palate is thickly textured with clever winemaking providing an attractive framework for the fruit. Screwcap. 14.5% alc. **Rating** 90 **To** 2014 $17.50

Red Baron McLaren Vale Shiraz 2007 Ripe, dark and full of mocha and fruitcake aromas; clean and well made, with a bright core of juicy black fruits on the medium-bodied palate; soft, supple and easy. Screwcap. 14.5% alc. **Rating** 90 **To** 2014 $17

ⵯⵯⵯⵯ **Duet McLaren Vale Cabernet Merlot 2006** Deep colour; good flavour of cassis and a touch of chocolate; fleshy mid-palate, with cleansing acidity; good focus. Screwcap. 14.5% alc. **Rating** 89 **To** 2014 $19

Reserve McLaren Vale Cabernet Sauvignon 2006 Good colour; an uncompromisingly savoury wine with earthy/savoury/bitter chocolate characters throughout; the tannins need to soften considerably. Cries out for time. Screwcap. 14.5% alc. **Rating** 89 **To** 2020 $39

McLaren Vale Verdelho 2008 Ripe and slightly tropical bouquet with a touch of cumquat; the palate is zesty and fresh, with generous levels of sweet fruit on the finish. Screwcap. 14% alc. **Rating** 88 **To** 2012 $17

Fox Gordon ★★★★★

PO Box Box 62, Kent Town, SA 5071 **Region** Barossa Valley/Adelaide Hills
T (08) 8361 8136 **F** (08) 8361 9521 **www.**foxgordon.com.au **Open** Not
Winemaker Natasha Mooney **Est.** 2000 **Cases** 3000
This is the venture of three very well known figures in the wine industry: Jane Gordon, Rachel Atkins (née Fox) and Natasha Mooney. Natasha (Tash) has had first-class experience in the Barossa Valley, particularly during her time as chief winemaker at Barossa Valley Estate. The partners wanted to produce high-quality wine, but only small quantities, which would allow them time to look after their children; the venture was planned in the shade of the wisteria tree in Tash's back garden. The grapes come from dry-grown vineyards farmed under biodiversity principles, which, says Tash, makes the winemaker's job easy. Classy packaging adds the final touch. Exports to the UK, the US, Canada, Germany, India and China.

ⵯⵯⵯⵯⵯ **Abby Adelaide Hills Viognier 2008** Unusually fragrant and utterly correct varietal aromas of pear and musk, which come through unsullied by phenolics on the palate. As good as they come. Screwcap. 13.5% alc. **Rating** 94 **To** 2012 $19.95

Eight Uncles Barossa Valley Shiraz 2005 Dark and compelling, with fruitcake spice, blackberry fruit, judicious oak handling and a lively personality; the palate is rich, dense and chewy, offering plenty of fruit and tannin for those who enjoy a plush ride with their shiraz. Screwcap. 14% alc. **Rating** 94 **To** 2020 $27.99

ᵠᵠᵠᵠᵠ By George Barossa Valley Adelaide Hills Cabernet Tempranillo 2005
Cassis and cherry fruit bouquet with an element of fresh herbs and spice; the
palate is generous and warm, and shows a nice synergy between these two varieties
and regions. Screwcap. 14% alc. **Rating** 92 **To** 2014 $22.99

ᵠᵠᵠᵠ Princess Adelaide Hills Fiano 2008 Not particularly expressive on the
bouquet; the palate offers honeysuckle and pear, with a faintly phenolic finish.
Screwcap. 13.5% alc. **Rating** 89 **To** 2012 $19.95

Foxeys Hangout
795 White Hill Road, Red Hill, Vic 3937 **Region** Mornington Peninsula
T (03) 5989 2022 **www.**foxeys-hangout.com.au **Open** W'ends & public hols 11–5
Winemaker Tony Lee, Michael Lee **Est.** 1998 **Cases** 5000 **Vyds** 3.5 ha
This is the venture of Tony Lee and journalist wife Cathy Gowdie. Cathy explains where it all
began in 1998. 'We were not obvious candidates for a seachange. When we talked of moving
to the country, friends pointed out that Tony and I were hardly back-to-nature types. "Do you
own a single pair of shoes without heels?" asked a friend. But at the end of a bleak winter, we
bought an old farmhouse on 10 daffodil-dotted acres at Red Hill and planted a vineyard.' They
planted pinot noir, chardonnay and pinot gris on the north-facing slopes of the old farm. The
name (and the catchy label) stems from the tale of two fox-hunters who began a competition
with each other in 1936, hanging their kills on the branches of an ancient eucalypt tree to
keep count. The corpses have gone, but not the nickname for the area.

ᵠᵠᵠᵠᵠ Reserve Mornington Peninsula Pinot Noir 2007 Dark fruited with a hint of
spicy stem character and toasty oak; a touch of mint comes through the saturated
dark fruits on the palate, and the sweet spot at the core of the wine is generous,
amply framed by the spice notes. Screwcap. 13.5% alc. **Rating** 94 **To** 2015 $50

ᵠᵠᵠᵠᵠ Mornington Peninsula Pinot Noir 2007 Dark and spicy, with plum, Asian
allspice and a touch of tar; real weight and depth, with a powerful palate, and
an attractive silky texture; long and generous. Screwcap. 13.5% alc. **Rating** 91
To 2013 $30
Mornington Peninsula Shiraz 2007 Bright and spicy aromas with dark plum
and cranberry fruit; the palate is medium-bodied and bright on the quite long and
even finish. Screwcap. 13.5% alc. **Rating** 90 **To** 2014 $25

ᵠᵠᵠᵠ Mornington Peninsula Chardonnay 2007 Deep colour; yellow nectarine and
a touch of spice; quite rich and oaky on the palate, with an oxidative nutty finish.
Screwcap. 13.5% alc. **Rating** 88 **To** 2011 $25
Late Harvest Pinot Gris 2008 Candied orange and spice aromas; very sweet,
and a little more acid would be good, but the persistent pear character on the
finish is attractive. Screwcap. 11.5% alc. **Rating** 88 **To** 2011 $25
White Fox Vermentino 2008 Clean lemon and dried straw bouquet; light,
fresh and crisp on the palate. Screwcap. 12.5% alc. **Rating** 87 **To** 2011 $20

Frankland Estate
Frankland Road, Frankland, WA 6396 **Region** Frankland River
T (08) 9855 1544 **F** (08) 9855 1549 **www.**franklandestate.com.au **Open** Mon–Fri 10–4,
public hols & w'ends by appt
Winemaker Barrie Smith, Judi Cullam **Est.** 1988 **Cases** 15 000 **Vyds** 34.5 ha
A significant Frankland River operation, situated on a large sheep property owned by Barrie
Smith and Judi Cullam. The vineyard has been established progressively since 1988; the recent
introduction of an array of single-vineyard Rieslings has been a highlight. The venture into the
single-vineyard wines is driven by Judi's conviction that terroir is of utmost importance, and
the soils are indeed different. The climate is not, and the difference between the wines is not
as clear-cut as theory might suggest. The Isolation Ridge Vineyard is now organically grown.
Frankland Estate has held several important International Riesling tastings and seminars over
recent years. Exports to the UK, the US and other major markets.

ŸŸŸŸŸ **Poison Hill Vineyard Riesling 2008** A little more Germanic in style, with talc. and river stone character coming to the fore; the palate offers an intriguing combination of apple, lemon and some slightly riper more exotic fruit character; the finish is fine and very long, and exhibits distinguished line. Screwcap. 12% alc. **Rating** 95 **To** 2016 $27
Smith Cullam Riesling 2008 Pale straw-green; superb fruit, with a beautiful balance between acidity and residual sugar; has very good length. Screwcap. 11% alc. **Rating** 95 **To** 2020 $45
Isolation Ridge Vineyard Shiraz 2007 Dense purple colour; a dark and brooding personality, showing tar, blackberry, ironstone and some pencilly oak; quite savoury on the palate, the tannin, fruit and oak are all in tune to high level intensity; long and very chewy on the finish, this wine demands time to fully integrate and reward. Screwcap. 14.3% alc. **Rating** 95 **To** 2016 $27
Smith Cullam Shiraz Cabernet 2007 A powerful medium- to full-bodied wine, with waves of black fruits, ripe, savoury tannins and good oak. One of the best Frankland Estate red wines made to date, and will age superbly. Screwcap. 14.5% alc. **Rating** 95 **To** 2027 $54
Olmo's Reward 2005 Some development, with the dark cassis fruit softening the earthy, savoury tones; the palate shows real depth of character, with cedar, black olive and plenty of sweet fruit on the mid-palate; generous yet firm, with a fine, long and engaging conclusion to the finish. Merlot/Cabernet Franc/Petit Verdot/Malbec/Cabernet Sauvignon. Screwcap. 14% alc. **Rating** 95 **To** 2020 $40
Isolation Ridge Vineyard Riesling 2008 A tightly wound bouquet of pure lemon fruit and a strong regional minerality; the palate is lean, racy and very dry, with mouth-puckering lemony acidity on the finish. Screwcap. 12% alc. **Rating** 94 **To** 2018 $27

ŸŸŸŸŸ **Cooladerra Vineyard Riesling 2008** Poised and quite polished lemon fruit with a little exotic character, showing more ripeness than usual; quite rich on entry, the palate tightens toward the finish, with a textured and minerally finish. Screwcap. 12.5% alc. **Rating** 92 **To** 2015 $27
Rocky Gully Riesling 2008 Pure lime and slate bouquet; linear palate, showing a little CO_2 petillance; dry, steely finish. Screwcap. 12% alc. **Rating** 90 **To** 2014 $18
Isolation Ridge Vineyard Shiraz 2006 A little reductive on opening; full of dark fruits and savoury roast meat aromas; quite a cool, high acid finish, with fine savoury tannin on the finish. Screwcap. 13.5% alc. **Rating** 90 **To** 2015 $27

ŸŸŸŸ **Rocky Gully Shiraz Viognier 2007** Reductive bouquet; blueberry and roast meat, with a little pepper thrown in for good measure; firm, dry and savoury, with a sweet core of red fruit on the finish. Screwcap. 14.5% alc. **Rating** 89 **To** 2014 $18
Isolation Ridge Vineyard Cabernet Sauvignon 2007 Densely coloured; very raw at this point, with charry oak sitting next to dark cassis fruit and a suggestion of violet; the palate is incredibly tannic, and one wonders if these tannins will ever soften. Screwcap. 14% alc. **Rating** 89 **To** 2015 $24
Isolation Ridge Vineyard Sauvignon Blanc 2008 Deep colour; pure passionfruit bouquet and flavour; just a little simple. Screwcap. 13% alc. **Rating** 87 **To** 2011 $27

Frankland Grange Wines

Lot 71 Frankland/Kojonup Road, Frankland, WA 6396 **Region** Frankland River
T (08) 9388 1288 **F** (08) 9388 1020 **Open** By appt
Winemaker Alkoomi (Michael Staniford) **Est.** 1995 **Cases** 1000
Frank Keet used cuttings from Alkoomi when he planted 2.5 ha of shiraz in 1995, followed by 1.5 ha of chardonnay (also locally sourced) in '98. Given the quality of fruit coming from the Frankland River subregion, it seems highly likely that the number of wine producers will steadily increase in the years ahead.

▼▼▼▼ **Unwooded Chardonnay 2007** Deep colour; green hue; restrained melon and grapefruit bouquet with a little smoky complexity; medium-bodied and fresh, with some grip on the finish. Screwcap. 13% alc. **Rating** 88 **To** 2012 $18

Fraser Gallop Estate ★★★★★

547 Metricup Road, Wilyabrup, WA 6280 **Region** Margaret River
T (08) 9755 7553 **F** (08) 9755 7443 **www.**frasergallopestate.com.au **Open** By appt
Winemaker Clive Otto **Est.** 1999 **Cases** 8000 **Vyds** 18.6 ha
Nigel Gallop began the development of the vineyard in 1999, planting cabernet sauvignon, semillon, petit verdot, cabernet franc, malbec, merlot and multi-clone chardonnay. The vines are dry-grown with modest yields, followed by kid-glove treatment in the winery. The first vintage was 2002, the wine being contract-made offsite, but with Clive Otto (formerly of Vasse Felix) on board, a 300-tonne winery was built onsite for the '08 vintage. As well as wines under the Fraser Gallop Estate label, limited amounts of contract wine are made for others. Exports to the UK, the US and Singapore.

▼▼▼▼▼ **Margaret River Cabernet Sauvignon 2007** A high-quality wine from the first whiff of the bouquet through to the long finish; the medium- to full-bodied palate has a tapestry of flavours from the base of Cabernet Sauvignon (88%)/Petit Verdot/Cabernet Franc/Malbec, all supported by persistent but ripe tannins, the oak absorbed by the fruit. Screwcap. 14.5% alc. **Rating** 95 **To** 2022 $30
Margaret River Cabernet Merlot 2007 Good depth and clarity to the colour; unsurprisingly driven by its almost succulent cabernet component (92%); seductive currant flavours framed by quality French oak and fine tannins. Bargain. Screwcap. 14.5% alc. **Rating** 94 **To** 2027 $20

▼▼▼▼▽ **Margaret River Chardonnay 2008** Straw-yellow; a complex wine, with nectarine and white peach fruit cradled by subtle French oak; has good length and balance. Screwcap. 13.5% alc. **Rating** 92 **To** 2014 $30
Margaret River Semillon Sauvignon Blanc 2008 Partial barrel ferment immediately obvious on the bouquet, but is well integrated on the crisp palate, which has good length. Screwcap. 12.2% alc. **Rating** 91 **To** 2012 $20

Freeman Vineyards ★★★★

101 Prunevale Road, Prunevale, NSW 2587 **Region** Hilltops
T (02) 6384 4299 **F** (02) 6384 4299 **www.**freemanvineyards.com.au **Open** By appt
Winemaker Dr Brian Freeman, Xanthe Freeman **Est.** 2000 **Cases** 2000 **Vyds** 44.3 ha
Dr Brian Freeman has spent much of his long life in research and education, in the latter role as head of CSU's viticulture and oenology campus. In 2004 he purchased the 30-year-old vineyard previously known as Demondrille. He has also established a vineyard next door, and in all has 14 varieties that range from staples such as shiraz, cabernet sauvignon, semillon and riesling through to the more exotic, trendy varieties such as tempranillo, and on to corvina and rondinella. He has had a long academic interest in the effect of partial drying of grapes on the tannins, and, living at Prunevale, was easily able to obtain a prune dehydrator to partially raisin the two varieties. Exports to Denmark.

▼▼▼▼▽ **Rondo Rose 2008** Has above-average fruit intensity; spiced red fruits run through to a quite powerful, dry finish. Screwcap. 14% alc. **Rating** 90 **To** 2010 $20
Rondinella Corvina Secco 2004 Attractive wine, with spicy cherry and plum aromas and earthy palate flavours; then moves into a warm savoury/spicy finish. Rack-dried grapes. Screwcap. 14.5% alc. **Rating** 90 **To** 2011 $30

🍇 Freshy Bay Wines ★★★★

PO Box 4170, Mosmam Park, WA 6012 **Region** South West Australia Zone
T (08) 9384 9916 **F** (08) 9284 5964 **www.**freshybay.com **Open** Not
Winemaker Simon Ding, Nigel Ludlow **Est.** 2000 **Cases** 1200

Freshy Bay Wines is owned by Colin and Judy Evans, its establishment part of a winding-down process from their prior professional careers. In 2000 they planted 2 ha of shiraz and produced five vintages from '03 to '07 inclusive, which enjoyed show success and critical acclaim. Finding the responsibility of caring for the vineyard too onerous, it was sold, and the business now operates as a virtual winery, chardonnay being purchased from growers in the Margaret River region.

ΨΨΨΨΨ **Margaret River Chardonnay 2007** A modestly priced wine that nonetheless shows Margaret River character; the fruit flavours are in a stone fruit and citrus spectrum, and with depth; the oak is subtle. A portion comes from Pemberton. Screwcap. 14% alc. **Rating** 90 **To** 2013 $16.50
Geographe Shiraz 2004 Retains good hue; a spicy/savoury wine with good intensity and length, the tannins ripe, the oak subtle. Screwcap. 14% alc. **Rating** 90 **To** 2013 $16.50

ΨΨΨΨ **Geographe Shiraz 2005** Spicy/savoury/earthy nuances to both bouquet and palate complement the medium-bodied black fruits running throughout. Screwcap. 14% alc. **Rating** 88 **To** 2015 $16.50

Freycinet   ★★★★★

15919 Tasman Highway via Bicheno, Tas 7215 **Region** East Coast Tasmania
T (03) 6257 8574 **www**.freycinetvineyard.com.au **Open** 7 days 9.30–4.30
Winemaker Claudio Radenti, Lindy Bull **Est.** 1980 **Cases** 5000 **Vyds** 9.08 ha
The Freycinet vineyards are beautifully situated on the sloping hillsides of a small valley. The soils are brown dermosol on top of jurassic dolerite, and the combination of aspect, slope, soil and heat summation produces red grapes with unusual depth of colour and ripe flavours. One of Australia's foremost producers of Pinot Noir, with a wholly enviable track record of consistency – rare in such a temperamental variety. The Radenti (sparkling), Riesling and Chardonnay are also wines of the highest quality. Exports to the UK and Sweden.

ΨΨΨΨΨ **Chardonnay 2007** Elegant, harmonious wine with very good line and length; nectarine and white peach; good oak and acidity. Screwcap. 13.5% alc. **Rating** 94 **To** 2014 $30

Frog Island   ★★★

PO Box 423, Kingston SE, SA 5275 **Region** Limestone Coast Zone
T (08) 8768 5190 **F** (08) 8768 5008 **www**.frogisland.com.au **Open** Not
Winemaker Sarah Squire **Est.** 2003 **Cases** 2000
Sarah Squire (née Fowler) has decided to do her own thing, with full support from father Ralph (see separate entry for Ralph Fowler Wines). The quixotic name is taken from a small locality inland from the seaside town of Robe, and the wine is deliberately made in a fresh, fruit-forward style. Exports to The Netherlands.

ΨΨΨΨ **Shiraz 2006** A medium- to full-bodied wine, with generous helpings of blackberry, licorice and spice fruit, balanced by neat acidity and subtle oak on the finish. Has cellar potential. Screwcap. 14.5% alc. **Rating** 89 **To** 2016 $20
Sparkling Red NV No clue given about age or time on lees, but has some flavour complexity and good balance. Cork. 13% alc. **Rating** 87 **To** 2011 $18

Frog Rock Wines   ★★★★

Edgell Lane, Mudgee, NSW 2850 **Region** Mudgee
T (02) 6372 2408 **F** (02) 6372 6924 **www**.frogrockwines.com **Open** 7 days 10–5
Winemaker David Lowe, Jane Wilson (Contract) **Est.** 1973 **Cases** 8000
Frog Rock is the former Tallara Vineyard, established over 30 years ago by leading Sydney chartered accountant Rick Turner. There are now 60 ha of vineyard, with 22 ha each of shiraz and cabernet sauvignon, and much smaller plantings of chardonnay, semillon, merlot, petit verdot and chambourcin. Exports to Canada, Singapore, Hong Kong and Fiji.

Y Y Y Y Y **Mudgee Petit Verdot 2006** Still deep purple; good example of a variety that does well in intermediate climates; abundant black fruits, but no harsh tannins. Screwcap. 14.5% alc. **Rating** 90 **To** 2016 $25

Sticky Frog 2007 Already deep golden-bronze; a rich wine abounding with cumquat, spice, honey and spice; not too sweet and is well balanced. Screwcap. 12.2% alc. **Rating** 90 **To** 2010 $25

Y Y Y Y **Mudgee Pinot Gris 2008** Gently ripe pear and apple fruit; well balanced, but is fully priced. Screwcap. 13.5% alc. **Rating** 87 **To** 2010 $25

Frogmore Creek ★★★★★

20 Denholms Road, Cambridge, Tas 7170 **Region** Southern Tasmania
T (03) 6248 5844 **F** (03) 6248 5855 **www.**frogmorecreek.com.au **Open** W'ends 10–5
Aug–Apr, w'ends 11–4 May–Jul
Winemaker Alain Rousseau, Nick Glaetzer, Andrew Hood (Consultant) **Est.** 1997
Cases 18000 **Vyds** 28.6 ha
Frogmore Creek is a Pacific Rim joint venture, the owners being Tony Scherer of Tasmania and Jack Kidwiler of California. The partners have developed an organically grown vineyard, and have acquired the Hood/Wellington wine business previously owned by Andrew Hood, who continues his involvement as a consultant. Winemaking has been consolidated at Cambridge, where the Frogmore Creek and 42° South brands are made, as well as a thriving contract winemaking business. Exports to the US, Japan, Indonesia and South Korea.

Y Y Y Y Y **Riesling 2007** Mineral, apple and herb aromas; very lively and crisp palate; a touch of CO_2 works well. Trophies (including Best Wine of Show, Tas Wine Show '09). Unrecognisable from the wine tasted a year earlier. Screwcap. 11.8% alc. **Rating** 96 **To** 2020 $24

FGR Riesling 2008 An aromatic, lime-rich bouquet, then a more delicate palate with counterpoints of spritz, sweet lime and crunchy acidity. Top gold medal Tas Wine Show '09. Screwcap. 8.5% alc. **Rating** 95 **To** 2016 $24

Chardonnay 2007 Abundant and rich stone fruit flavours, intense and not flabby; oak well balanced and integrated; very good mouthfeel and length. Gold medal Tas Wine Show '09. Screwcap. 13.5% alc. **Rating** 95 **To** 2016 $30

Chardonnay 2006 Light, bright colour; very attractive nectarine/white peach fruit and a touch of citrus; very good balance and mouthfeel. Nice. Top gold medal Tas Wine Show '09. Screwcap. 14% alc. **Rating** 95 **To** 2013 $30

Sauvignon Blanc 2008 Much more fragrant than 42° South, with passionfruit blossom aromas, then a beautifully poised and elegant palate marked by crisp, natural acidity. Value. Screwcap. 12.2% alc. **Rating** 94 **To** 2011 $26

42° S Pinot Noir 2007 Bright, light colour; a wine of exceptional precision and purity, with vibrant red cherry accented fruit; while the palate is not weighty, it has admirable length. Screwcap. 13% alc. **Rating** 94 **To** 2013 $26

Y Y Y Y Y **42° S Pinot Grigio 2008** Has voluminous varietal aromas of musk, pear and white peach, the ultra-crisp and fine palate driven by low alcohol, bright acidity and dry finish. Screwcap. 12% alc. **Rating** 92 **To** 2011 $24

42° S Riesling 2007 Fragrant; attractive gently tropical fruit; good balance and purity; precision and length; high acidity. **Rating** 91 **To** 2014

42° S Pinot Noir 2008 Quite fragrant and spicy; light- to medium-bodied; some whole bunch characters; attractive red fruits; has elegance. Screwcap. 14.1% alc. **Rating** 91 **To** 2013 $26

42° S Sauvignon Blanc 2008 A strongly minerally/slatey/grassy bouquet leads into a palate that progressively builds flavour, adding gooseberry, through its length. Screwcap. 12.5% alc. **Rating** 90 **To** 2010 $24

Reserve Pinot Noir 2007 Good clarity; bright, fresh elegant red fruits; has thrust and drive through to a long finish. Screwcap. 12.7% alc. **Rating** 90 **To** 2013 $60

42° S Pinot Noir 2006 Bright and clear colour; tangy fruit flavours have faint nuances of stem and mint to the core of red cherry fruit. Screwcap. 13.5% alc. **Rating** 90 **To** 2012 $26

ŸŸŸŸ   **42° S Gewurztraminer 2006** Bottle development has added some flavour and interest; lychee, straw and spice; good balance. Screwcap. 13% alc. **Rating** 89 To 2012 $20

Pinot Noir 2007 Quite intense and powerful; some savoury stemmy characters do intrude on the back-palate and finish, but add to the complexity of the wine. Screwcap. 13.5% alc. **Rating** 88 **To** 2012 $36

42° S Sparkling NV Very pale blush; delicate but has some drive; a dry style, with small red fruits/strawberries. Cork. 12.5% alc. **Rating** 88 **To** 2013 $28

Cuvee Evermore 2006 Very pale pink, delicate flavours, good balance and length. Cork. 12.9% alc. **Rating** 87 **To** 2012 $37.50

Gaelic Cemetery Wines   ★★★★★

PO Box 54, Sevenhill, SA 5453 **Region** Clare Valley
T (08) 8843 4370 **F** (08) 8843 4353 **www**.gaelic-cemeterywines.com **Open** Not
Winemaker Neil Pike, John Trotter **Est.** 2005 **Cases** 500 **Vyds** 6.5 ha
This is a joint venture between winemaker Neil Pike, viticulturist Andrew Pike and Adelaide retailers Mario and Ben Barletta. It hinges on a single vineyard owned by Grant Arnold, planted in 1996, adjacent to the historic cemetery of the region's Scottish pioneers. Situated in a secluded valley of the Clare hills, the low-cropping vineyard, say the partners 'is always one of the earliest ripening shiraz vineyards in the region and mystifyingly produces fruit with both natural pH and acid analyses that can only be described as beautiful numbers'. The result is hands-off winemaking and maturation for 24 months in new and used Burgundian barriques. Exports to the UK, the US, Singapore and NZ.

ŸŸŸŸŸ   **Clare Valley Shiraz 2006** Strong blackberry, prune and licorice aromas and flavours, with a spicy, fine tannin finish. Surprisingly, manages to more or less conceal its alcohol; 200 dozen made. Cork. 16% alc. **Rating** 94 **To** 2021 $120

Galafrey

Quangellup Road, Mount Barker, WA 6324 **Region** Mount Barker
T (08) 9851 2022 **F** (08) 9851 2324 **www**.galafreywines.com.au **Open** 7 days 10–5
Winemaker Kim Tyrer, Paul Nelson **Est.** 1977 **Cases** 8000 **Vyds** 13 ha
Relocated to a purpose-built but utilitarian winery after previously inhabiting the exotic surrounds of the old Albany wool store, Galafrey makes wines with plenty of robust, if not rustic, character, drawing grapes in the main from 13 ha of estate plantings. Following the death of husband/father/founder Ian Tyrer, Kim and Linda Tyrer have taken up the reins, announcing, 'There is girl power happening at Galafrey Wines!' There is a cornucopia of back vintages available, some superb and underpriced, at the cellar door. Exports to Singapore, China and Japan.

ŸŸŸŸŸ   **Dry Grown Mount Barker Shiraz 2005** Vibrant colour; rich and ripe with an abundance of red fruits and spice; medium-bodied with lively acidity and ripe, fine-grained tannins; a hint of complexing leather frames the bright fruit on the long and even conclusion. Screwcap. 12.5% alc. **Rating** 93 **To** 2016 $24

Mount Barker Merlot 2006 Good colour; quite a savoury bouquet with black olive and plum in evidence; quite firm on the palate, where a sweetness of fruit combines with cedary complexity; deliberate finesse and purpose; long and very dry finish. Screwcap. 13.5% alc. **Rating** 93 **To** 2015 $24

Gallagher Wines

2770 Dog Trap Road, Murrumbateman, NSW 2582 **Region** Canberra District
T (02) 6227 0555 **www**.gallagherwines.com.au **Open** W'ends & public hols 10–5
Winemaker Greg Gallagher **Est.** 1995 **Cases** 2500 **Vyds** 2 ha
Greg Gallagher was senior winemaker at Taltarni for 20 years, working with Dominique Portet. He began planning a change at much the same time as did Portet, and started establishing a small vineyard at Murrumbateman in 1995, now planted to 1 ha each of chardonnay and shiraz.

ŢŢŢŢŢ **Canberra District Riesling 2008** A spotlessly clean wine from start to finish, surprisingly generous given its low alcohol and dry finish. Screwcap. 11.9% alc. **Rating** 90 **To** 2015 $18

ŢŢŢŢ **Canberra District Blanc de Blanc 2006** Bottle-fermented and made from estate-grown fruit (unspecified varieties); offers a mix of citrus, pear and apple fruit on a pleasingly dry palate. Crown Seal. 13.2% alc. **Rating** 89 **To** 2010 $35

Galli Estate ★★★★★

1507 Melton Highway, Rockbank, Vic 3335 **Region** Sunbury
T (03) 9747 1444 **F** (03) 9747 1481 **www**.galliestate.com.au **Open** 7 days 11–5
Winemaker Stephen Phillips **Est.** 1997 **Cases** 25 000 **Vyds** 143 ha
Galli Estate, founded in 1997 by (the late) Lorenzo and Pam Galli, is located at Rockbank in Sunbury with 37 ha of vines (chardonnay, shiraz, pinot grigio, cabernet sauvignon and merlot) planted on rich red volcanic soil. There is a second Camelback Vineyard at Heathcote, with 106 ha planted to a mix of mainstream and Mediterranean varieties (shiraz, cabernet sauvignon, chardonnay, sangiovese, viognier, tempranillo, nebbiolo, merlot, grenache and petit verdot). All wines are estate-grown. Exports to the US, Canada, Denmark, Japan, Singapore, China and Hong Kong.

ŢŢŢŢŢ **Artigiano Sunbury Chardonnay 2008** Bright green-straw; super-elegant, but intense, the citrus and nectarine fruit seamlessly welded to subtle French oak; has great drive through the finish. Screwcap. 13.5% alc. **Rating** 96 **To** 2015 $30
Sunbury Lorenzo 2007 Similar deep crimson-purple; while the style is likewise similar, the wine has greater intensity than Artigiano, and carries its French oak with ease; has tremendous length. Shiraz. Screwcap. 14.4% alc. **Rating** 95 **To** 2022 $42

ŢŢŢŢŢ **Artigiano Sunbury Shiraz 2007** Deep crimson; has a plentiful array of blackberry, licorice and spice-accented fruit, the overall extract of fruit, oak and tannins precisely right. Screwcap. 14.4% alc. **Rating** 93 **To** 2017 $26
Heathcote Tempranillo Grenache Mourvedre 2007 Very different to the Sangiovese Shiraz, of course; here, dark plum, licorice and firm tannins drive a long, well-balanced palate, the tempranillo holding sway. Good value. Screwcap. 14% alc. **Rating** 92 **To** 2016 $20
Sunbury Chardonnay 2008 Slightly less intense and complex than Artigiano, but is another very elegant expression of chardonnay, with nectarine and stone fruit drawn together by citrussy acidity. Screwcap. 13% alc. **Rating** 92 **To** 2014 $20
Artigiano Sunbury Chardonnay 2007 Vibrant in colour and aroma, with stone fruits offset by a complex line of minerality; quite fleshy, with grilled nuts and toasty oak framing the finish. Screwcap. 14% alc. **Rating** 91 **To** 2014 $21.95
Artigiano Heathcote Viognier 2008 Pale straw-green; fragrant apple and apricot aromas; finds that tiny point of balance between flavour and finesse; also has good length. Screwcap. 14.4% alc. **Rating** 91 **To** 2012 $22
Victoria Cabernet Merlot 2007 Clear purple-red; attractive blackcurrant fruit and splashes of cassis and spice runs through the medium-bodied palate, ending with supple tannins. Good value. Screwcap. 13.1% alc. **Rating** 90 **To** 2015 $18
Sunbury Sauvignon Blanc 2008 Keeps the balance between touches of citrus and herb on the bouquet, and the more prominent tropical, passionfruit flavours of the back-palate and finish. Screwcap. 12.5% alc. **Rating** 90 **To** 2011 $18
Heathcote Shiraz Viognier 2007 A complex wine, both in terms of flavour and structure, ranging from spice, red berry and leather, with gently savoury notes on the finish. Screwcap. 14% alc. **Rating** 90 **To** 2013 $17.95

ŢŢŢŢ **Heathcote Sangiovese Shiraz 2007** Plenty of savoury, sour cherry flavour from the sangiovese, but the drying tannins need an Italian audience. Screwcap. 15% alc. **Rating** 88 **To** 2013 $20

Gapsted   ★★★★

Great Alpine Road, Gapsted, Vic 3737 **Region** Alpine Valleys
T (03) 5751 1383 **F** (03) 5751 1368 **www**.gapstedwines.com.au **Open** 7 days 10–5
Winemaker Michael Cope-Williams, Shayne Cunningham **Est.** 1997 **Cases** 158 000
Vyds 166 ha

Gapsted is the major brand of the Victorian Alps winery, which started life (and continues)
as large-scale contract winemaking facilities. However, the quality of the wines it made for
its own brand (Gapsted) has led to the expansion of production not only under that label,
but under a raft of cheaper, subsidiary labels including Tobacco Road, Coldstone, Buckland
Gap, Snowy Creek, Dividing Range, and doubtless others in the pipeline. Its vineyards extend
across the Alpine Valleys and (mostly) the King Valley. Its success can be gauged from the
increase in production to over 150 000 cases, albeit with a hiccup following the 2007 bushfires.
Exports to the UK and other major markets.

♟♟♟♟♟ **Ballerina Canopy King Valley Sauvignon Blanc 2008** A lifted, almost
scented, bouquet of tropical fruits is followed by gooseberry and citrus flavours on
the clean and lively palate. Screwcap. 12.5% alc. **Rating** 92 **To** 2012 $19
Limited Release King Valley Sangiovese 2006 A convincing varietal
example; while the aromas and flavours oscillate around cherry and small red
fruits, there are spices and other nuances hard to pin down; fine tannins to close.
Screwcap. 14% alc. **Rating** 90 **To** 2013 $27
Ballerina Canopy Durif 2006 An impressively complex full-bodied wine that
spent 30 months in oak in a largely successful attempt to soften the durif tannins;
you have to take your hat off to this indestructible variety, loaded with black fruits
as it is. Cork. 15% alc. **Rating** 90 **To** 2016 $30

♟♟♟♟ **Limited Release Pinot Gris 2007** Deep colour; very ripe pear and candied
fruit bouquet, supported by spice; quite rich and lively with an element of
tangerine on the finish. Screwcap. 14% alc. **Rating** 89 **To** 2011 $21
Ballerina Canopy Merlot 2005 Distinctly savoury overtones to both bouquet
and palate are well within varietal compass; silky tannins, moderate length.
Surprise Blue-Gold medal Sydney International Wine Competition '08. Screwcap.
14.5% alc. **Rating** 89 **To** 2013 $25
Limited Release Saperavi 2006 Great colour; spicy blackberry, clove and
cinnamon bouquet; medium-bodied with attractive juicy fruit and vibrant acidity;
quite a bit of oak. Screwcap. 13.5% alc. **Rating** 89 **To** 2012 $27
Valley Selection Riesling 2008 Distinctly spicy bouquet, then tropical/citrus
flavours; overall loose structure; early consumption. Screwcap. 12.5% alc. **Rating** 88
To 2013 $16
Tobacco Road Merlot 2007 Has good varietal character, the red and black
fruits offset by gently savoury tannins and touches of spice. Screwcap. 13.5% alc.
Rating 88 **To** 2015 $13
Valley Selection Cabernet Merlot 2006 Redcurrant and cedar bouquet;
bright and generous fruit, with drying, slightly dusty tannins. Screwcap. 14% alc.
Rating 88 **To** 2013 $16
Valley Selection Moscato 2008 Departs from the norm with minimal spritz;
made from the red clone of muscat a petits grains; intensely grapey and sweet;
could be diluted with soda water and ice to have a seriously low-alcohol wine.
Screwcap. 6.5% alc. **Rating** 87 **To** 2009 $16

Garbin Estate   ★★★

209 Toodyay Road, Middle Swan, WA 6056 **Region** Swan Valley
T (08) 9274 1747 **F** (08) 9274 1747 **Open** Tues–Sun & public hols 10.30–5.30
Winemaker Peter Garbin **Est.** 1956 **Cases** 4500 **Vyds** 2.42 ha

Duje Garbin, winemaker and fisherman from a small island near the Dalmatian coast in the
Adriatic Sea, migrated to WA in 1937; he purchased in '56 the Middle Swan property on

which Garbin Estate stands. When he retired in the early 1990s, son Peter took over what was a thoroughly traditional and small business, and embarked on a massive transition: a new cellar door and processing area, upgraded major plant and equipment, and the establishment of a vineyard in Gingin. A former design draughtsman, Peter is now full-time winemaker, backed up by his wife Katrina, assistant winemaker, and sons Joel and Adam.

ŶŶŶŶ   **Margaret River Swan District Sauvignon Blanc Semillon 2008** A green nettle and tropical fruit bouquet; clean and crisp on entry, with just a little extra weight developing on the finish. Screwcap. 12.1% alc. **Rating** 87 **To** 2012 $19

Gartelmann Hunter Estate   ★★★★

701 Lovedale Road, Lovedale, NSW 2321 **Region** Lower Hunter Valley
T (02) 4930 7113 **F** (02) 4930 7114 **www**.gartelmann.com.au **Open** 7 days 10–5
Winemaker Jorg Gartelmann, Liz Jackson **Est.** 1970 **Cases** 4500
In 1996 Jan and Jorg Gartelmann purchased what was previously the George Hunter Estate – 16 ha of mature vineyards, most established by Sydney restaurateur Oliver Shaul in '70. A major change in the business model resulted in the sale of the vineyards after the 2006 vintage, and the grapes are now sourced from other Hunter Valley vineyards, giving the business maximum flexibility. Exports to Germany.

ŶŶŶŶŶ   **Sparkling Shiraz 2007** Good concentration; a vinous bouquet of blackberry, redcurrant and spice; the palate walks the line of generosity and complexity well; clean, fresh, quite long on the finish. Crown Seal. 13% alc. **Rating** 93 **To** 2013 $35
Diedrich Shiraz 2007 Purple hue; dark and dense with tar, red and blue fruit on the bouquet; chewy on the palate, with lively acidity and solid mineral persistence on the finish. Screwcap. 13.5% alc. **Rating** 92 **To** 2016 $40

ŶŶŶŶ   **Chardonnay 2007** A toast and straw bouquet; quite figgy, and a little oxidative nutty character coming through on the palate; a rich style. Screwcap. 13.5% alc. **Rating** 87 **To** 2012 $30

Geddes Wines   ★★★☆

PO Box 227, McLaren Vale, SA 5171 **Region** McLaren Vale
T (08) 8323 8814 **F** (08) 8323 8814 **Open** Not
Winemaker Tim Geddes **Est.** 2004 **Cases** 1200
Owner/winemaker Tim and wife Amanda, a chef, bring considerable experience to the venture. Tim's started in Hawke's Bay, NZ, with three vintages as a cellar hand, which directly led to a move to Australia to complete the oenology degree at Adelaide University. Dual vintages in the Barossa and Hunter valleys were woven in between settling down in McLaren Vale, where he has been a contract winemaker for a number of clients since 2002. Tim's 2007 lease of a 500-tonne winery means even greater contract work, while he slowly builds the Seldom Inn range (made every vintage) and the Geddes label, which is only made in the best years. The long-term aim is to make 3000 cases, relying on the selection of small parcels of fruit from a number of selected McLaren Vale subregions. Exports to Canada.

ŶŶŶŶŶ   **Seldom Inn McLaren Vale Petit Verdot 2007** Bright, vibrant, fresh and focused with violets and plenty of ripe black fruit; the tannin works well with the ample fruit weight. Screwcap. 14.5% alc. **Rating** 90 **To** 2013 $22

ŶŶŶŶ   **Seldom Inn McLaren Vale Shiraz 2007** A rich, ripe and warm-fruited bouquet with a definite chocolate edge to the blackberry pastille fruit; quite intense black fruit on the palate, with a slightly tarry and quite dry finish. Screwcap. 14.5% alc. **Rating** 89 **To** 2014 $22
Seldom Inn McLaren Vale Grenache Shiraz Mataro 2007 A little volatile on opening, there is a core of sweet red fruit; while a little advanced for its age, the concentration is without question. Screwcap. 15% alc. **Rating** 87 **To** 2013 $22

Gelland Estate ★★★★

PO Box 1148, Mudgee, NSW 2850 **Region** Mudgee
T (02) 6373 5411 **www**.gellandestate.com.au **Open** Not
Winemaker Rhys Eather (Contract) **Est.** 1999 **Cases** 500 **Vyds** 6 ha
Warren and Stephanie Gelland moved from Sydney to Mudgee in 1998 'to start a family with room to move'. They had no background in viticulture, but friends who had previously made the same move and established a vineyard suggested that the Gellands follow suit, which they duly did by planting 4 ha of cabernet sauvignon and 2 ha of chardonnay. More recently they have purchased small parcels of shiraz and viognier from Mudgee vineyards to add a Cabernet Shiraz, Viognier Chardonnay and Cabernet Rose to the portfolio.

ΨΨΨΨΨ **Mudgee Chardonnay 2007** Restrained power, with attractive grapefruit and spice on the bouquet; the palate is tightly wound with persistent fresh fruit characters; a little toasty complexity, and slightly creamy texture, linger with the citrus fruit on the finish. Great value. Screwcap. 13.5% alc. **Rating** 93 **To** 2014 $18
Mudgee Viognier 2008 Pure apricot and spice varietal bouquet; quite fleshy on the palate, there is freshness and texture, and vibrancy to the finish, not showing any heaviness at all. Screwcap. 13% alc. **Rating** 90 **To** 2012 $18

Gembrook Hill

Launching Place Road, Gembrook, Vic 3783 **Region** Yarra Valley
T (03) 5968 1622 **F** (03) 5968 1699 **www**.gembrookhill.com.au **Open** By appt
Winemaker Timo Mayer, Andrew Marks **Est.** 1983 **Cases** 2500 **Vyds** 6 ha
The Gembrook Hill vineyard (sauvignon blanc, chardonnay, pinot noir and semillon) is situated on rich, red volcanic soils 2 km north of Gembrook in the coolest part of the Yarra Valley. The vines are not irrigated, with consequent natural vigour control, and low yields. Harvest usually spans mid-April, three weeks later than the traditional northern parts of the valley, and the style is consistently elegant. Exports to the UK, Denmark, Japan and Malaysia.

ΨΨΨΨΨ **Yarra Valley Sauvignon Blanc 2007** Still bright and fresh, with a balance of green pea, passionfruit and tropical flavours, the finish long and clean. Screwcap. 13% alc. **Rating** 94 **To** 2010 $35
Blanc de Blancs 2004 Bottle fermented; from estate-grown chardonnay and aged on lees for four years; deliciously fine, crisp and clean citrus/nectarine fruit and creamy yeast overtones. Cork. 12.5% alc. **Rating** 94 **To** 2012 $50

Gemtree Vineyards

PO Box 164, McLaren Vale, SA 5171 **Region** McLaren Vale
T (08) 8323 8199 **www**.gemtreevineyards.com.au **Open** 7 days 10–5 at Salopian Inn
Winemaker Mike Brown **Est.** 1998 **Cases** 30 000 **Vyds** 133.16 ha
The Buttery family, headed by Paul and Jill, and with the active involvement of Melissa as viticulturist, have been grapegrowers in McLaren Vale since 1980, when they purchased their first vineyard. Today the family owns a little over 130 ha of vines. The oldest block, of 25 ha on Tatachilla Road at McLaren Vale, was planted in 1970. Exports to the the UK, the US and other major markets.

ΨΨΨΨΨ **White Lees McLaren Vale Shiraz 2006** In Burgundy, lees from Grand Cru wines are sometimes used to 'enrich' lesser wines; here the lees from a white ferment were added to barrels of newly fermented, high-quality shiraz and stirred regularly for 28 months. This is a terrific wine; 300 dozen made. Screwcap. 14.5% alc. **Rating** 96 **To** 2021 $45
Obsidian McLaren Vale Shiraz 2005 Powerful, full-bodied McLaren Vale style from start to finish, but an impressive one; blackberry fruit and dark chocolate influences have provided the foundation for three years in French oak. Screwcap. 15% alc. **Rating** 94 **To** 2025 $50

ꚖꚖꚖꚖꚖ **Bloodstone McLaren Vale Shiraz Viognier 2007** The co-fermentation of 5% viognier lifts the mouthfeel of the wine without riding over its regional dark chocolate undertones; the two forces join together rather than fight, giving the wine good palate-feel and thrust; an adult Cherry Ripe. Screwcap. 14.5% alc. **Rating** 93 **To** 2017

Cadenzia McLaren Vale Grenache Tempranillo Shiraz 2007 Good colour; a medium-bodied, bright and vibrant wine, the left-field blend (expected of Cadenzia) working well; there is a distinct juicy red tang to the palate, contributed in part by the tempranillo; long finish. Screwcap. 15% alc. **Rating** 93 **To** 2016

Citrine McLaren Vale Chardonnay 2008 Shows sophisticated use of winemaker inputs; fresh and crisp, with oak perfectly integrated and balanced; long, clean finish; well-priced. Screwcap. 13% alc. **Rating** 92 **To** 2012 $15

Moonstone McLaren Vale Albarino 2008 Very interesting wine with citrus zest, apple and spice aromas, the flavours similar, and with above-average conviction, lemony acidity lengthening the finish. Screwcap. 13.5% alc. **Rating** 92 **To** 2011 $25

The Phantom McLaren Vale Petit Verdot 2007 Typical dense colour; brooding black fruits and dark chocolate in more or less equal proportions; the tannins have been very well controlled, and the wine is already drinkable, but has years to go. Screwcap. 14.5% alc. **Rating** 92 **To** 2022 $28

Tatty Road Cabernet Sauvignon Petit Verdot Merlot Cabernet Franc 2007 Great colour, with an abundance of juicy, ripe red fruits and a hint of mocha; deep and complex, with a little savoury twist to the finish of an otherwise sweet-fruited wine. Screwcap. 14.5% alc. **Rating** 90 **To** 2015 $18

ꚖꚖꚖꚖ **Bloodstone McLaren Vale Tempranillo 2007** Both bouquet and palate offer a contradictory mix of juicy fruits then strongly savoury, almost lemony, tannins. Screwcap. 14.5% alc. **Rating** 88 **To** 2013 $25

Gentle Annie ★★★

455 Nalinga Road, Dookie, Vic 3646 **Region** Central Victoria Zone
T (03) 5828 6333 **F** (03) 9602 1349 **www**.gentle-annie.com **Open** By appt
Winemaker David Hodgson, Tony Lacy **Est.** 1997 **Cases** 8000
Gentle Annie was established by Melbourne businessman Tony Cotter; wife Anne and five daughters assist with sales and marketing. The name Gentle Annie refers to an early settler renowned for her beauty and gentle temperament. The vineyard includes 4 ha of verdelho, 31 ha of shiraz and 23 ha of cabernet sauvignon planted on old volcanic ferrosol soils, similar to the red Cambrian loam at Heathcote. The winemaking team is headed by David Hodgson, who also heads up the Oenology faculty at Dookie College. The increasing production of Gentle Annie wines has a substantial export component.

ꚖꚖꚖꚖ **Reserve Shiraz 2004** Deep colour; a potent wine, with flavours welling up on the fore-palate, but somewhat spiky on the finish. Poor quality cork a potential issue. 14.4% alc. **Rating** 89 **To** 2014 $32

Reserve Cabernet 2004 The colour is fractionally lighter than that of the varietal wine, simply because it is also less extractive, allowing varietal fruit expression more play. Cork. 14.5% alc. **Rating** 89 **To** 2019 $27

Verdelho 2006 Good example of a bottle-matured verdelho that has honeyed overtones to the fruit salad fruit – and a German import back label. Screwcap. 13% alc. **Rating** 88 **To** 2010 $14

Cabernet Sauvignon 2004 Powerful black fruits, with strong earthy components on a rustic palate; still somewhat raw at five years old. Cork. 14.5% alc. **Rating** 88 **To** 2017 $20

Shiraz 2004 Similarly dense colour to the Reserve; while full flavoured, the rustic, rough edges are more obvious; unimpressive cork for a potentially long-lived wine. 14.5% alc. **Rating** 87 **To** 2014 $20

Geoff Merrill Wines ★★★★★

291 Pimpala Road, Woodcroft, SA 5162 **Region** McLaren Vale
T (08) 8381 6877 **www**.geoffmerrillwines.com **Open** Mon–Fri 10–5, w'ends 12–5
Winemaker Geoff Merrill, Scott Heidrich **Est.** 1980 **Cases** 80 000 **Vyds** 132 ha
If Geoff Merrill ever loses his impish sense of humour or his zest for life, high and not-so-high, we shall all be the poorer. The product range consists of three tiers: premium (varietal); Reserve, being the older (and best) wines, reflecting the desire for elegance and subtlety of this otherwise exuberant winemaker; and, at the top, Henley Shiraz. Mount Hurtle wines are sold exclusively through Vintage Cellars/Liquorland. Exports to all major markets.

ᵀᵀᵀᵀᵀ **Henley McLaren Vale Shiraz 2002** The best Henley yet; still youthful and tightly focused; cork permitting, has another 20 years in front of it; the intense black fruits are seamlessly interwoven with tannins and oak. 15.5% alc. **Rating** 96 To 2025 $150
Henley McLaren Vale Shiraz 2001 Expected colour development, but good clarity; soft, rich medium- to full-bodied wine; an array of spice, black fruits, dark chocolate and French oak flavours on an individual style in a battleship bottle. Cork. 14% alc. **Rating** 94 To 2016 $160
McLaren Vale Shiraz Grenache Mourvedre 2005 Excellent hue; has the authority, which McLaren Vale regularly gives good examples of this blend, and which the Barossa Valley does not; offers a bouquet of red fruits in a supple but focused palate. Screwcap. 14.5% alc. **Rating** 94 To 2015 $20

ᵀᵀᵀᵀᵀ **G&W Cabernet Sauvignon 2005** A generous and juicy wine, the rich, dark chocolate-accented McLaren Vale component balanced by Coonawarra red and blackcurrant fruit; good line and mouthfeel. Screwcap. 14.5% alc. **Rating** 93 To 2020 $25.50
McLaren Vale Grenache Rose 2008 Vivid light crimson-fuschia; good focus, length and drive to the red fruit flavours and underlying minerality; dry finish. Screwcap. 14% alc. **Rating** 92 To 2010 $19.50
Reserve Coonawarra McLaren Vale Cabernet Sauvignon 2003 Has matured impressively, the palate long and fine in an elegantly earthy spectrum. Coonawarra (53%)/McLaren Vale (47%). Cork. 14% alc. **Rating** 92 To 2014 $40
Reserve Chardonnay 2004 Glowing yellow-green; a fully mature blend of McLaren Vale (73%)/Coonawarra (27%); has abundant toasty flavour balanced and lengthened by good acidity. Good value for a wine ready and rearing to go. Screwcap. 13.5% alc. **Rating** 91 To 2010 $27

ᵀᵀᵀᵀ **Jacko's Blend McLaren Vale Shiraz 2005** Retains good hue and clarity; pleasantly balanced and flavoured wine, with red and black fruits, restrained oak and soft tannins. Screwcap. 14.5% alc. **Rating** 89 To 2012 $25.50
Wickham Park McLaren Vale Merlot 2005 A little lean, but showing true varietal character of black olive and dark fruits; the palate is quite dry and firm on the finish. Screwcap. 14.5% alc. **Rating** 89 To 2012 $25
Pimpala Vineyard Cabernet Merlot 2003 Almost stridently regional, so strong is the dark chocolate overlay to the blackcurrant fruit; oak also makes a statement. Curious wine. Cork. 14% alc. **Rating** 89 To 2013 $32
Wickham McLaren Vale Sauvignon Blanc 2008 Clean and fresh, with vibrant herbaceous, cut grass aromas; the palate is quite thick on entry but brightens up with good acidity on the finish. Screwcap. 13.5% alc. **Rating** 87 To 2012 $20
Wickham Park McLaren Vale Chardonnay 2006 Fermentation and brief (nine weeks) maturation in French oak has added as much to the texture as to the flavour of the wine; good acidity helps. Screwcap. 14.5% alc. **Rating** 87 To 2012 $20

Geoff Weaver

2 Gilpin Lane, Mitcham, SA 5062 (postal) **Region** Adelaide Hills
T (08) 8272 2105 **F** (08) 8271 0177 **www**.geoffweaver.com.au **Open** Not
Winemaker Geoff Weaver **Est.** 1982 **Cases** 3500 **Vyds** 12.3 ha

This is the full-time business of former Hardys chief winemaker Geoff Weaver. He draws upon a little over 12 ha of vineyard established between 1982 and '88, and invariably produces immaculate Riesling and Sauvignon Blanc, and one of the longest-lived Chardonnays to be found in Australia, with intense grapefruit and melon flavour. The beauty of the labels ranks supreme with Pipers Brook. Exports to Germany and Singapore.

🍷🍷🍷🍷🍷 **Lenswood Sauvignon Blanc 2008** Classic Geoff Weaver style, delicate yet intense, achieved by excellent estate-grown fruit picked at the right moment and attention to detail in the winery; will hold for several years. Screwcap. 13.5% alc. Rating 94 To 2010 $24

Gherardi

PO Box 53, Margaret River, WA 6285 **Region** Margaret River
T (08) 9757 3142 **F** (08) 9757 3180 **www.**gherardi.com.au **Open** Not
Winemaker Jurg Muggli, Simon Keall **Est.** 1998 **Cases** 800
Peter Gherardi is one of the most experienced viticulturists in WA, but has the habit of disappearing from time to time as he follows new paths. In 1979 he began the establishment of Freycinet Estate, while employed by the WA Dept of Agriculture as a viticulturist and oenologist (he already had a degree in Applied Science [Wine] at what is now known as Charles Sturt University). In 1991 he sold the winery and vineyard to Michael Wright; the much expanded operation is now Voyager Estate. Peter then became a viticultural consultant, but found time to work vintages in Bordeaux, Tuscany, Piedmont and Provence. Returning permanently to Australia, he became chief viticulturist at Xanadu Wines from 2001–05, also lecturing viticulture and oenology students at the Curtin University Margaret River campus. He bristles at the suggestion that his most recent venture is a hobby, even if it consumes weekends, weekdays given to his continuing role as a viticultural consultant. The ladybirds on the labels are a sign of a near chemical-free environment that has achieved a natural balance.

🍷🍷🍷🍷🍷 **Margaret River Viognier 2007** Immediately proclaims its variety, with abundant apricot aroma and flavour, yet avoids phenolics, the finish crisp and clear. The '05 and '04 demonstrate cellaring potential to four years. Screwcap. 14% alc. Rating 90 To 2011 $25

🍷🍷🍷🍷 **Margaret River Merlot 2005** Has retained a youthful hue, and the palate is as fresh as the colour promises, the low pH a function of the low alcohol; zippy finish, though not overly generous. Screwcap. 13% alc. Rating 87 To 2010 $15

Ghost Rock Vineyard

PO Box 311, Devonport, Tas 7310 **Region** Northern Tasmania
T (03) 6428 4005 **F** (03) 6428 4330 **www.**ghostrock.com.au **Open** Wed–Sun &
public hols 11–5 (7 days Jan–Feb)
Winemaker Tom Ravech (Contract) **Est.** 2001 **Cases** 1500 **Vyds** 8 ha
Cate and Colin Arnold purchased the former Patrick Creek Vineyard (planted in 1989) in 2001. They run a printing and design business in Devonport and were looking for a suitable site to establish a vineyard. The vineyard (2 ha each of chardonnay, pinot noir, sauvignon blanc and pinot gris) is planted on a northeasterly aspect on a sheltered slope. The increase in plantings (and consequent production) has allowed the Arnolds to supply markets throughout the mainland.

🍷🍷🍷🍷🍷 **Catherine Sparkling 2003** Pale green-straw; rounded mouthfeel with creamy brioche along with crisp fruit, and overall delicacy. Gold medal Tas Wine Show '09. Cork. 12.5% alc. Rating 94 To 2013 $39

🍷🍷🍷🍷🍷 **Pinot Gris 2008** Good varietal character on both bouquet and palate, the latter with length and balance. Screwcap. 13.5% alc. Rating 90 To 2011 $26

🍷🍷🍷🍷 **Sauvignon Blanc 2008** A restrained bouquet, but the palate has some attractive varietal characters in a citrus/herb/gooseberry spectrum. Screwcap. 13% alc. Rating 89 To 2010 $25

Giant Steps/Innocent Bystander   ★★★★★

336 Maroondah Highway, Healesville, Vic 3777 **Region** Yarra Valley
T (03) 5962 6111 **www**.giant-steps.com.au **Open** Mon–Fri 10–10, w'ends 8–10
Winemaker Phil Sexton, Steve Flamsteed, Dave Mackintosh **Est.** 1997 **Cases** 52 000
Vyds 30.41 ha

Phil Sexton made his first fortune as a pioneer micro-brewer, and invested part of that fortune in establishing Devil's Lair. Late in 1996 he sold Devil's Lair to Southcorp, which had purchased Coldstream Hills earlier that year. Two years later he purchased a hillside property less than 1 km from Coldstream Hills, and sharing the same geological structure and aspect. The name Giant Steps comes in part from his love of jazz and John Coltrane's album of that name, and in part from the rise and fall of the property across a series of ridges ranging from 120 m to 360 m. The vineyard is predominantly planted to pinot noir and chardonnay, but with significant quantities of cabernet sauvignon and merlot, plus small plantings of cabernet franc and petit verdot. It also leases Tarraford Vineyard, with 8.5 ha of vines up to 19 years old. Innocent Bystander contributes 40 000 cases to the overall production of the venture. Exports to the UK, the US and other major markets.

🍷🍷🍷🍷🍷 **Giant Steps Arthurs Creek Vineyard Yarra Valley Chardonnay 2008**
Glowing yellow-green; an extremely complex funky Burgundian bouquet, but the palate is decidedly elegant with delicate, nectarine and citrus fruit to the fore. Has a great future. Screwcap. 12.7% alc. **Rating** 94 **To** 2016 $39.95
Giant Steps Tarraford Vineyard Yarra Valley Chardonnay 2007 A quite shy and subdued bouquet, the palate definition is the strength of this wine; plenty of toasty oak with nectarines and pear flesh and lively acidity providing outstanding length and harmony. Screwcap. 13.5% alc. **Rating** 94 **To** 2017 $39.95
Giant Steps Sexton Vineyard Yarra Valley Chardonnay 2007 A very well made wine, with significant texture and structure; the palate has great drive and thrust, all the components tightly interwoven. Screwcap. 14% alc. **Rating** 94 **To** 2014 $34.95

🍷🍷🍷🍷🍷 **Giant Steps Gladysdale Vineyard Yarra Valley Pinot Noir 2008** Bright and clean hue; a gently spicy red fruit bouquet, the palate with red and black cherry fruit augmented by spicy/savoury notes on the long finish. Screwcap. 13.5% alc. **Rating** 93 **To** 2014 $39.95
Innocent Bystander Yarra Valley Pinot Noir 2008 Really bright colour and lovely vibrant fruit; young, juicy and lots of fun with a touch of spice playing support to delicious cherry fruit; certainly a wine to be enjoyed and not necessarily in moderation. Screwcap. 13.9% alc. **Rating** 92 **To** 2012 $19.95
Giant Steps Sexton Vineyard Yarra Valley Merlot 2007 A no-holds-barred Merlot from the big end of town, with deep colour, masses of cassis-accented fruit, and tannins worthy of a top quality, Right Bank Bordeaux. Screwcap. 14% alc. **Rating** 92 **To** 2020 $34.95
Innocent Bystander Yarra Valley Chardonnay 2007 Bright and lively pear fruit aroma with a gentle touch of spicy oak; clean and fresh with a fine hint of citrus lingering on the finish. Screwcap. 14% alc. **Rating** 90 **To** 2013 $19.95
Innocent Bystander Yarra Valley Pinot Gris 2008 Pear fruit and some complex candied orange zest aromas on the bouquet; generous and quite full, but finishes fine with fresh acidity and a lingering pear-flesh flavour. Screwcap. 13.5% alc. **Rating** 90 **To** 2012 $19.95
Innocent Bystander Yarra Valley Pinot Rose 2008 Pale bright fuschia; fragrant strawberry aroma and flavour are locked into a crisp, long and dry palate; all-purpose food style. Screwcap. 13% alc. **Rating** 90 **To** 2010 $19.95

Gibson Barossavale/Loose End   ★★★★★

Willows Road, Light Pass, SA 5355 **Region** Barossa Valley
T (08) 8562 3193 **F** (08) 8562 4490 **www**.gibsonwines.com.au **Open** 7 days 11–5
Winemaker Rob Gibson **Est.** 1996 **Cases** 12 000 **Vyds** 21 ha

Rob Gibson spent much of his working life as a senior viticulturist for Penfolds. While at Penfolds he was involved in research tracing the characters that particular parcels of grapes give to a wine, which left him with a passion for identifying and protecting what is left of the original vineyard plantings in wine regions around Australia. He has two vineyards in the Barossa Valley at Stockwell (shiraz, mataro and grenache) and Light Pass (merlot), and one in the Eden Valley (shiraz and riesling), and also purchases grapes from McLaren Vale. Loose End is an important 7000-case brand launched in 2007 offering wines at lower price points. Exports to the UK, the US and other major markets.

ΨΨΨΨΨ **Australian Old Vine Collection Barossa Shiraz 2006** A sophisticated and subtle expression of old vine shiraz, with texture, structure and length every bit as important as the gently earthy/spicy fruit flavours; its class also shines on its extreme length. High-quality cork. 14.5% alc. **Rating** 96 **To** 2026 $99
Australian Old Vine Collection Eden Valley Shiraz 2006 Like its Barossa twin, has very good colour, and shares its texture and structure; here, though, the blackberry and licorice fruit swells on the back-palate, denoting its somewhat cooler origins. High-quality cork. 14.5% alc. **Rating** 96 **To** 2020 $99
Australian Old Vine Collection McLaren Vale Grenache 2007 Good hue; a prime example of the superiority of McLaren Vale grenache over that of all other Australian regions, with delicious, fragrant, red and black fruits supported by fine, savoury tannins. Cork. 14.5% alc. **Rating** 95 **To** 2020 $99

ΨΨΨΨΨ **Loose End GSM 2006** A particularly impressive example of this blend at any price, let alone this; vibrantly spicy notes run through the red and black fruits at the core of the palate, the tannins exactly weighted. Partly a tribute to '06. Grenache/Shiraz/Merlot/Mataro. Screwcap. 14.5% alc. **Rating** 93 **To** 2016 $18
Isabelle Blend 2005 Good hue for age; an unusually successful blend of Merlot/Cabernet Sauvignon/Petit Verdot which belies its Barossa base,the red and blackcurrant flavours varietal, not regional, the length and balance good. Screwcap. 14.4% alc. **Rating** 92 **To** 2020 $27.50

ΨΨΨΨ **Loose End Riesling 2008** Pleasing tropical aromas and flavours, with a touch of passionfruit; early maturing style. Eden Valley. Screwcap. 11.2% alc. **Rating** 89 **To** 2012 $18
Loose End Shiraz 2007 Shiraz/Viognier blends (here 4%) seldom work as well in warmer regions as in cool regions; this is no exception, although it does have sweet fruit and supple mouthfeel. Screwcap. 14.5% alc. **Rating** 88 **To** 2013 $18
Sparkling Merlot NV I am too old fashioned to learn new tricks in the sparkling red game, but this does have fresh fruit, isn't sweet, and isn't phenolic. Cork. 13% alc. **Rating** 87 **To** 2010 $28

Gilberts ★★★★

RMB 438 Albany Highway, Kendenup via Mount Barker, WA 6323 **Region** Mount Barker **T** (08) 9851 4028 **F** (08) 9851 4021 **www.**gilbertwines.com.au **Open** Wed–Mon 10–5 **Winemaker** Plantagenet **Est.** 1980 **Cases** 4000 **Vyds** 14.5 ha
Once a part-time occupation for sheep and beef farmers Jim and Beverly Gilbert, but now a full-time and very successful one. The mature vineyard (shiraz, chardonnay, riesling and cabernet sauvignon), coupled with contract winemaking at Plantagenet, has long produced very high-class Riesling, and now also makes excellent Shiraz. In 2000 a new red wine was introduced into the range named the Three Devils Shiraz in honour of their then nine- to 14-year-old sons. Exports to Hong Kong and Switzerland.

ΨΨΨΨΨ **Mount Barker Riesling 2008** Cool lemon and lime bouquet; plenty of mineral on the palate, with a steely, dry and quite fine finish. Screwcap. 11.5% alc. **Rating** 90 **To** 2015 $17

ΨΨΨΨ **Alira 2008** Lightly sweet, with regional characters of lemon, flint and a touch of stone fruit; soft and fleshy, with true focus. Riesling. Screwcap. 11.5% alc. **Rating** 88 **To** 2013 $16

Three Devils Mount Barker Chardonnay 2008 Fresh and lively grapefruit bouquet; quite a juicy and vibrant palate; a forward style. Screwcap. 13.5% alc. **Rating** 88 **To** 2012 $18

Mount Barker Cabernet Shiraz 2007 Bright colour; fruitcake and redcurrant fruit bouquet; ample, juicy and vibrant on the finish. Screwcap. 14% alc. **Rating** 87 **To** 2012 $19

Gilead Estate   ★★★

1868 Wanneroo Road, Neerabup, WA 6031 **Region** Swan District
T (08) 9407 5076 **F** (08) 9407 5187 **Open** W'ends June–Sept or by appt
Winemaker Simon Gauntlett, Judith Gauntlett **Est.** 1995 **Cases** 500 **Vyds** 1.5 ha
The business was started by Judith and Gerry Gauntlett, who planted 1.5 ha of shiraz, cabernet sauvignon, cabernet franc and merlot on the Tuart sands of Wanneroo in 1990, making the first wine in '95. In the wake of Gerry's death, the family has continued the business. Appropriately, the name comes from the Balm of Gilead produced from trees on the hills northeast of Galilee in Biblical times, and was said to have had healing and purifying qualities. The small production is mainly sold by mail order.

♟♟♟♟   **Merlot 2007** Good colour; has the structure the Shiraz lacks, but needs time to fill out the curiously empty back-palate and finish. Diam. 13.7% alc. **Rating** 87 **To** 2013 $18

Gilligan   ★★★☆

PO Box 235, Willunga, SA 5172 **Region** McLaren Vale
T (08) 8323 8379 **F** (08) 8323 8379 **www**.gilligan.com.au **Open** Not
Winemaker Mark Day, Leigh Gilligan **Est.** 2001 **Cases** 1000 **Vyds** 5.6 ha
Leigh Gilligan is a 20-year marketing veteran, mostly with McLaren Vale wineries (including Wirra Wirra). The Gilligan family has 4 ha of shiraz and 0.4 ha each of grenache, mourvedre, marsanne and roussanne, selling part of the production. In 2001 they persuaded next-door neighbour Drew Noon to make a barrel of Shiraz, which they drank and gave away. Realising they needed more than one barrel, they moved to Maxwell Wines, with help from Maxwell winemaker Mark Day, and have now migrated to Mark's new Koltz Winery at Blewitt Springs. Exports to the UK, the US and other major markets.

♟♟♟♟   **McLaren Vale Shiraz Grenache Mourvedre 2007** Powerful McLaren Vale character, with black fruits, earth, tar and dark chocolate all contributing; the substantial tannins suggest a cautious approach. Screwcap. 14.5% alc. **Rating** 89 **To** 2017 $23

Gioiello Estate   ★★★☆

PO Box 250, Tullamarine, Vic 3043 **Region** Upper Goulburn
T 0437 240 502 **www**.gioiello.com.au **Open** Not
Winemaker Steve Flamsteed, Scott McCarthy (Contract) **Est.** 1987 **Cases** 5000
Vyds 9.09 ha
The Gioiello Estate vineyard was established by a Japanese company and originally known as Diawa Nar Darak. Planted between 1987 and '96, it accounts for fractionally more than 9 ha on a 400-ha property of rolling hills, pastures, bushland, river flats, natural water springs and billabongs. The wines produced were sold only in Japan, but the quality was demonstrated by the 1994 Daiwa Nar Darak Chardonnay, which won the George Mackey Award for Best Wine Exported from Australia in '95. It is now owned by the Schiavello family, which is contemplating increasing the plantings with Italian varieties such as nebbiolo and arneis. The gold medal won by the 2007 Reserve Chardonnay at the 18th Annual Concours des Vins du Victoria in November '08 proves the Mackey Award was no fluke.

♟♟♟♟♟ **Upper Goulburn Chardonnay 2008** A toasty bouquet of grilled nuts and ripe melon; the palate is quite rich, with generous texture and weight; toasty yet fine, on the finish. Screwcap. 13.8% alc. **Rating** 90 **To** 2013 $25

Reserve Upper Goulburn Merlot 2007 Spiced plum with a touch of mint; quite fresh and focused on the palate, with a little black olive framing the dark plummy fruit. ProCork. 14% alc. **Rating** 89 **To** 2014 $40
Reserve Upper Goulburn Chardonnay 2007 Ripe pear and nectarine bouquet, with spicy oak; a very rich palate, with a slight mineral edge; broken line and slightly bitter finish. Screwcap. 14.3% alc. **Rating** 88 **To** 2013 $40

Gipsie Jack Wine Co ★★★

Wellington Road, Langhorne Creek, SA 5255 **Region** Langhorne Creek
T (08) 8537 3029 **F** (08) 8537 3284 **www**.gipsiejack.com **Open** 7 days 10–5
Winemaker John Glaetzer, Ben Potts **Est.** 2004 **Cases** 12 000
One might have thought the partners of Gipsie Jack have enough wine on their plate already, but some just can't resist the temptation, it seems. The two in question are John Glaetzer and Ben Potts, who made a little over 500 cases from two growers in their inaugural vintage in 2004. The 2007 vintage produced 11 000 cases from 15 growers, and the intention is to increase the number of growers each year. Glaetzer and Potts say, 'We want to make this label fun, like in the "old days". No pretentiousness, no arrogance, not even a back label. A great wine at a great price, with no discounting.' Exports to Canada, Switzerland, Hong Kong and Singapore.

Langhorne Creek Shiraz 2006 Pleasant, quite savoury, medium-bodied wine, with both red and black fruits, and light tannins on the finish. Screwcap. 14.5% alc. **Rating** 88 **To** 2013 $18
Langhorne Creek Malbec 2006 Impenetrable colour; a very oaky bouquet with lifted black fruit and a touch of spice; big, rich and ripe, the wine travels along a single dimension, offering generosity on the journey. Screwcap. 14.5% alc. **Rating** 88 **To** 2014 $20

GISA ★★★☆

3 Hawke Street, Linden Park, SA 5065 **Region** South Australia
T (08) 8338 2123 **F** (08) 8338 2123 **www**.gisa.com.au **Open** Not
Winemaker Mat Henbest **Est.** 2006 **Cases** 3000
Matt and Lisa Henbest have chosen a clever name for their virtual winery – GISA standing for Geographic Indication South Australia – neatly covering the fact that their grapes come variously from the Adelaide Hills (Sauvignon Blanc), McLaren Vale (Shiraz Viognier) and Barossa Valley (Reserve Shiraz). It in turn reflects Matt's long apprenticeship in the wine industry, as a child living on his parent's vineyard, then working in retail trade while he pursued tertiary qualifications, and thereafter wholesaling wine to the retail and restaurant trade. He then moved to Haselgrove, where he spent five years working closely with the small winemaking team, refining his concept of style, and gaining experience on the other side of the fence of the marketing equation.

Ellipse Reserve Barossa Valley Shiraz 2006 Good colour; has appealing spice, licorice and pepper nuances to the black fruits, which are the foundation of the wine; good drive through to the finish. Screwcap. 14% alc. **Rating** 91 **To** 2020 $35

Round Barossa Valley Cabernet Sauvignon 2006 A well-balanced and structured wine, with clear varietal definition and pleasing mouthfeel. Drink now or at any time over the next five years. Screwcap. 14% alc. **Rating** 89 **To** 2013 $19
Arc Semillon Sauvignon Blanc 2008 Unspecified regional blend driven by semillon with a lemony cast; has good balance, length and overall flavour; a snitch at this price. Screwcap. 13% alc. **Rating** 88 **To** 2011 $10
Round Adelaide Hills Sauvignon Blanc 2008 While the aromas and flavours are subdued, the wine has good texture and structure, possibly from the small percentage of Adelaide Hills semillon; a grassy style, and may evolve in the short term. Screwcap. 12.5% alc. **Rating** 87 **To** 2010 $19
Round Barossa Valley Shiraz 2006 A fresh, spicy light-bodied shiraz, which has a small component of Kangaroo Island fruit; finishes with savoury tannins. Screwcap. 13.5% alc. **Rating** 87 **To** 2013 $19

Gisborne Peak   ★★★

69 Short Road, Gisborne South, Vic 3437 **Region** Macedon Ranges
T (03) 5428 2228 **F** (03) 5428 4816 **www**.gisbornepeakwines.com.au **Open** 7 days 11–5
Winemaker John Ellis **Est.** 1978 **Cases** 1800 **Vyds** 5 ha
Bob Nixon began the development of Gisborne Peak way back in 1978, planting his dream
vineyard row-by-row. (Bob is married to Barbara Nixon, founder of Victoria Winery Tours.)
The tasting room has wide shaded verandahs, plenty of windows and sweeping views. The
vineyard is planted to chardonnay, pinot noir, semillon, riesling and lagrein.

ΨΨΨΨ   **Mawarra Vineyard Unwooded Chardonnay 2008** Vibrant green hue; an
overlay of eucalypt dominates the citrus fruit on the bouquet; fresh and vibrant on
the palate, with lingering acidity and fresh fruit on the finish. Screwcap. 13.2% alc.
Rating 88 **To** 2013 $20

Glaetzer Wines

34 Barossa Valley Way, Tanunda, SA 5352 (postal) **Region** Barossa Valley
T (08) 8563 0288 **F** (08) 8563 0218 **www**.glaetzer.com **Open** Not
Winemaker Ben Glaetzer **Est.** 1996 **Cases** 15 000
Colin Glaetzer and son Ben are almost as well known in SA wine circles as Wolf Blass
winemaker John Glaetzer, Colin's twin brother. Glaetzer Wines purchases all its grapes from
the Ebenezer subregion of the Barossa Valley, principally from fifth-generation growers. Its
four wines (Amon-Ra Shiraz, Anaperenna Shiraz Cabernet Sauvignon, Bishop Shiraz and
Wallace Shiraz Grenache) are all made under contract at Barossa Vintners in what might be
termed a somewhat incestuous relationship because of the common links in ownership of the
very successful Barossa Vintners business. Exports to all major markets.

ΨΨΨΨΨ   **Amon-Ra Unfiltered Shiraz 2007** Vibrant colour; saturated black fruits,
fruitcake, licorice and an element of tar; terrific purity and drive, and despite
the power, the palate is lithe and supple; complex, compelling and certainly
representative of the very essence of the region. Cork. 14.5% alc. **Rating** 96
To 2025 $90
Bishop Barossa Valley Shiraz 2007 Bright colour; there is a fresh herb
undercurrent to the dark fruit bouquet, also set off by a touch of prune; the palate
is warm and thickly textured and offers a full array of sweet fruit, toasty oak and
firm tannin on the finish. Cork. 14.5% alc. **Rating** 94 **To** 2018 $35

ΨΨΨΨΥ   **Anaperenna 2007** Dark fruited and loaded with lavish toasty oak; hints of cedar
and quite firm, almost rugged tannin profile across the palate; a little time will
be necessary for full integration. Shiraz/Cabernet Sauvignon. Cork. 14.5% alc.
Rating 93 **To** 2020 $55

ΨΨΨΨ   **Wallace Barossa Valley Shiraz Grenache 2007** Dark and savoury bouquet,
with a mere suggestion of sweet fruit on board; the palate has dusty tannins and
plenty of fruit; quite a blocky style. Screwcap. 14.5% alc. **Rating** 89 **To** 2015 $20

Glandore Estate

1595 Broke Road, Pokolbin, NSW 2320 **Region** Lower Hunter Valley
T (02) 4998 7140 **F** (02) 4998 7142 **www**.glandorewines.com **Open** 7 days 10–5
Winemaker Duane Roy **Est.** 2004 **Cases** 4000 **Vyds** 8 ha
Glandore Estate is the reincarnation of the Brokenback Vineyard established as part of The
Rothbury Estate in the early 1970s, but it had an even longer history. It was purchased by
legendary grapegrowers Mick and Jack Phillips in the '30s, and given the Glandore name.
New owners David Madson, John Cambridge and Peter McBeath, who acquired the property
in 2004 (with existing chardonnay vines), have extended the plantings with albarino, semillon
and viognier.

ΨΨΨΨ   **Shiraz 2007** Bright colour; red fruits are framed by a touch of spice and earth;
the medium-bodied palate has good flavour, but ultimately lacks depth and
complexity. Screwcap. 13.8% alc. **Rating** 88 **To** 2014 $25

Glaymond/Tscharke Wines ★★★★☆

PO Box 657, Greenock, SA 5360 **Region** Barossa Valley
T 0438 628 178 **F** (08) 8562 4920 **www.**tscharke.com.au **Open** Not
Winemaker Damien Tscharke **Est.** 2001 **Cases** 4000 **Vyds** 23.1 ha
Damien Tscharke grew up in the Barossa Valley among the vineyards at Seppeltsfield and
Marananga. In 2001 he began the production of Glaymond, four estate-grown wines based
on what he calls the classic varieties (following the trend of having catchy, snappy names),
followed by wines under the Tscharke brand using the alternative varieties of tempranillo,
graciano, zinfandel, montepulciano and albarino. Like the Glaymond wines, these are estate-
grown, albeit in very limited quantities. Exports to the US and other major markets.

ǷǷǷǷǷ **Glaymond The Distance Barossa Valley Shiraz 2006** Very good colour; the
wine is at the opulent, baroque end of the spectrum, but does not suffer from that;
velvety depths of blackberry, blackcurrant and licorice are the drivers, tannins and
oak trailing along behind. Screwcap. 15% alc. **Rating** 94 **To** 2026 $32

ǷǷǷǷǷ **Glaymond El Abuelo Barossa Valley Grenache 2006** The argument for
high alcohol with grenache receives strong support from this robust wine, with
strong prune, licorice and black fruits alongside some red notes making a more
than satisfactory mouthful. Screwcap. 15.5% alc. **Rating** 92 **To** 2016 $28
Tscharke Only Son Barossa Valley Tempranillo Graciano 2006 Dense
purple, verging on black; the palate is equally profound, but is not extractive,
nor (obviously) alcoholic. Nonetheless, not to be undertaken lightly. Screwcap.
15.5% alc. **Rating** 92 **To** 2021 $24
Tscharke Girl Talk Barossa Valley Albarino 2008 Considerable depth to
the bright green-gold colour; there is equally positive and fragrant fruit on the
bouquet, and flavours on the palate reminiscent of custard apple with a dressing of
citrus. Screwcap. 13% alc. **Rating** 91 **To** 2011 $21
Tscharke The Curse Barossa Valley Zinfandel 2007 Zinfandel has many faces;
this is a legitimate expression of the ripe, full-bodied style admired by Robert Parker
Jnr; luscious black fruits and soft tannins. Screwcap. 15% alc. **Rating** 91 **To** 2015 $34
Glaymond Asif Barossa Valley Cabernet Sauvignon 2006 Dense inky
colour; full of hyper-ripe black fruits and dark chocolate; the only thing missing
is true varietal expression, which may be of no concern to some. Screwcap.
15.5% alc. **Rating** 90 **To** 2026 $32
Tscharke Vintage Fortified Touriga Nacional 2004 Impressive wine; good
texture and structure; spicy blackberry fruit, and a relatively dry (Portuguese style)
finish. Cork. 19.5% alc. **Rating** 90 **To** 2020 $30

ǷǷǷǷ **Glaymond Landrace Barossa Valley Shiraz Mataro 2006** While the alcohol
is very high, the bouquet sends out the right varietal signals with licorice, spice
and black fruits; the palate, however, wobbles a little under the burden. Curate's
egg. Screwcap. 15.5% alc. **Rating** 89 **To** 2020 $34

Glen Eldon Wines ★★★★★

Cnr Koch's Road/Nitschke Road, Krondorf, SA 5352 **Region** Barossa Valley
T (08) 8563 3226 **F** (08) 8563 8290 **www.**gleneldonwines.com.au **Open** Mon–Fri
8.30–5, w'ends by appt
Winemaker Richard Sheedy **Est.** 1997 **Cases** 6000 **Vyds** 30 ha
The Sheedy family – brothers Richard and Andrew, and wives Mary and Sue – have
established their base at the Glen Eldon property in the Eden Valley, which is the home of
Richard and Mary. The shiraz and cabernet sauvignon come from their vineyards in the
Barossa Valley; riesling, viognier and merlot from contract-grown fruit; the riesling from the
Eden Valley. Exports to the UK, the US, Canada, Switzerland and China.

ǷǷǷǷǷ **Black Springs Reserve Shiraz 2004** Excellent colour and clarity; although
only medium-bodied, has considerable intensity and complexity, with rippling
red and black fruits, and fine tannins on the long finish; the acidity, too, is perfect.
Cork. 14.5% alc. **Rating** 96 **To** 2019 $95

Black Lady Shiraz 2006 Dense, inky colour; mouthfilling, luscious plum, black cherry and chocolate; harmonious and supple tannins; intense and long; not the least heavy. Barossa/Heathcote. Cork. 14.5% alc. **Rating** 95 **To** 2017 $110

Dry Bore Barossa Shiraz 2005 Deep crimson; voluminous berry aromas lead into a sumptuous palate with blackberry and blood plum to the fore; tannins are ripe and fine, the oak well integrated. Screwcap. 14.5% alc. **Rating** 95 **To** 2020 $25

Barossa Shiraz Mataro 2006 Strong colour; full-bodied, and has good structure and intensity to the blackberry, licorice and dark chocolate flavours, with no confection characters whatsoever; great surge on the finish. Screwcap. 14.5% alc. **Rating** 94 **To** 2021 $25

Barossa Cabernet Sauvignon 2005 Excellent colour; a perfectly ripened wine, with strong blackcurrant, cassis and cedar flavours, the tannins lined up in precise support, oak likewise. Screwcap. 14.5% alc. **Rating** 94 **To** 2020 $25

ΥΥΥΥΩ **Eden Valley Riesling 2007** Crisp, youthful and tightly structured; spotlessly clean and pure, and has all the prerequisites for a long life; give it five years to blossom, which it will. Screwcap. 12.5% alc. **Rating** 91 **To** 2017 $16

Kicking Back Barossa Shiraz Cabernet 2006 Good hue and depth; substantial medium- to full-bodied wine, with a potent mix of blackberry, plum and blackcurrant; will develop; low price for a wine to be cellared. Screwcap. 14.5% alc. **Rating** 90 **To** 2018 $16

Barossa Merlot 2006 Has good varietal character, structure and weight, ranging through blackcurrant, cassis, herb and black olive, tannins and oak balanced. Screwcap. 14.5% alc. **Rating** 90 **To** 2016 $22

ΥΥΥΥ **Kicking Back Barossa Shiraz Mataro Grenache 2006** Spicy smoky mocha aromas are followed by a medium-bodied spicy palate, with a mix of savoury and red fruits. Screwcap. 14.5% alc. **Rating** 88 **To** 2012 $16

Barossa Viognier 2008 Abundant apricot and nougat flavours achieved at the expense of a heavy phenolic load; cake and eat it stuff. Screwcap. 14% alc. **Rating** 87 **To** 2012 $22

GlenAyr   ★★★☆

Back Tea Tree Road, Richmond, Tas 7025 **Region** Southern Tasmania
T (03) 6260 2388 **F** (03) 6260 2691 **Open** Mon–Fri 8–5
Winemaker Contract **Est.** 1975 **Cases** 500

The now fully mature Tolpuddle Vineyard, managed by Warren Schasser, who is completing a Bachelor of Applied Science (viticulture) at CSU, provides the grapes that go to make the GlenAyr wines. The major part of the grape production continues to be sold to Domaine Chandon and Hardys, with most going to make premium table wine, and a lesser amount to premium sparkling.

ΥΥΥΥΩ **Tolpuddle Vineyards Chardonnay 2006** Developing nicely; quite rich stone fruit and citrus; oak balanced. Screwcap. 13.9% alc. **Rating** 91 **To** 2012 $23

ΥΥΥΥ **Shiraz 2006** Spicy cool-grown style; not fleshy, but does create interest with its lively mouthfeel. Screwcap. 13.5% alc. **Rating** 89 **To** 2014 $25

Tolpuddle Cuvee 2006 Salmon verging on bronze; has considerable depth of spicy flavours, but thickens slightly on the finish. Cork. 12.5% alc. **Rating** 87 **To** 2013 $29

Glenguin Estate   ★★★★

Milbrodale Road, Broke, NSW 2330 **Region** Lower Hunter Valley
T (02) 6579 1009 **F** (02) 6579 1009 **www**.glenguinestate.com.au **Open** At The Boutique Wine Centre, Pokolbin
Winemaker Robin Tedder MW, Rhys Eather **Est.** 1993 **Cases** 5000 **Vyds** 13.5 ha

Glenguin Estate was established by the Tedder family, headed by Robin Tedder MW, close to Broke and adjacent to Wollombi Brook. Subsequently, a small plot of 50-year-old vines in Pokolbin was acquired. Both vineyards are run without the use of pesticides and with a permanent sod culture between vine rows. From time to time grapes are purchased from regions as diverse as Orange and the Adelaide Hills to supplement the estate-grown grapes. Exports to the UK, Hong Kong, Singapore and NZ.

ŸŸŸŸ♀ Ancestors Semillon 2008 Pale colour; a racy, pure lemon bouquet with a touch of fresh straw; light lemon palate with fine acidity and persistent line. Screwcap. 10% alc. **Rating** 93 **To** 2016 $25
Aristea Hunter Valley Shiraz 2006 Bright colour; very concentrated, with toasty oak, redcurrant fruit and a touch of leather on the bouquet; a firm and quite dry palate, with a savoury tar-like quality to the finish. Screwcap. 14.5% alc. **Rating** 92 **To** 2016 $60

ŸŸŸŸ Protos Chardonnay 2008 Peach and straw bouquet with a healthy dose of oak; creamy and a little spicy on the palate, with peach on the finish. Screwcap. 13% alc. **Rating** 89 **To** 2012 $30
Two Thousand Vines Viognier 2008 Bright colour; apricot and a touch of varietal spice; thickly textured, with cleansing acidity; well balanced. Screwcap. 13.5% alc. **Rating** 89 **To** 2011 $25

Glenmore ★★★

PO Box 201, Yallingup, WA 6282 **Region** Margaret River
T (08) 9755 2330 **F** (08) 9755 2331 **www**.glenmorewine.com.au **Open** Not
Winemaker Ian Bell **Est.** 1990 **Cases** 1500 **Vyds** 5 ha
Ian Bell started his career as a cellar and vineyard hand at Moss Wood; he was encouraged to study viticulture at the then Roseworthy College in 1987, and returned in '89 to work for Moss Wood. Between 1990 and '99 he established cabernet sauvignon (3.5 ha), merlot, petit verdot and malbec (0.5 ha each) on the Glenmore property, which has been in the family's ownership since 1895. Between 1997 and 2001 all of the grapes were sold to Moss Wood and made under the Glenmore Vineyard Cabernet Sauvignon label. Since then, Ian has developed the Glenmore label in its own right, but continues to sell grapes to Moss Wood, the wine now being called Amy's Vineyard, named after Ian's grandmother Amy Beers who owned and ran beef cattle into her eighties. Exports to the UK.

ŸŸŸŸ Margaret River Cabernet Sauvignon 2004 Bright colour; youthful bouquet of cassis and redcurrant; medium-bodied with firm tannin and a slight glossy edge to the fruit. Screwcap. 14% alc. **Rating** 87 **To** 2014 $40

Goaty Hill Wines

Auburn Road, Kayena, Tas 7270 **Region** Northern Tasmania
T (03) 6391 9090 **F** (03) 6391 9094 **www**.goatyhill.com **Open** 7 days 10–5 Sept to May, June–Aug by appt
Winemaker Fran Austin (Contract) **Est.** 1998 **Cases** 3000 **Vyds** 19.5 ha
The partners in Goaty Hill are six friends from two families who moved from Victoria to Tasmania and, they say, 'were determined to build something for the future while having fun'. The partners in question are Markus Maislinger, Natasha and Tony Nieuwhof, Kristine Grant, and Margaret and Bruce Grant, and in 1998 they began the planting of pinot noir, riesling, chardonnay and sauvignon blanc. Part of the grape production is sold to Bay of Fires and, in return, the highly talented Bay of Fires winemaker, Fran Austin, makes the Goaty Hill wines from that part of the annual crop retained by the partners. Goaty Hill's first wine show entries have yielded a string of medals.

ŸŸŸŸŸ Pinot Noir 2008 Brilliant clarity; spice and red fruit aromas, then a palate quivering with life and intensity; a long, fine finish with gossamer tannins. Screwcap. 12.8% alc. **Rating** 94 **To** 2015 $27.95

ŸŸŸŸ♀ Chardonnay 2008 The bouquet is complex, but it is the palate that defines the wine; crisp grapefruit and nectarine flavours are wrapped around livewire acidity. Screwcap. 12.6% alc. **Rating** 92 **To** 2015 $24.95

Pinot Noir 2007 Excellent colour and clarity; succulent and smooth varietal flavours; pure line and length Screwcap. 13.7% alc. **Rating** 90 **To** 2013 $27.95

ҰҰҰҰ **Riesling 2008** Bright green-straw; an interesting mix of lemon and lime aromas and flavours, the palate driven by the minerally acidity which so distinguishes Tasmanian riesling. Screwcap. 11% alc. **Rating** 89 **To** 2013 $19.95

Golden Grove Estate ★★★★☆

Sundown Road, Ballandean, Qld 4382 **Region** Granite Belt
T (07) 4684 1291 **F** (07) 4684 1247 **www**.goldengroveestate.com.au **Open** 7 days 9–4
Winemaker Raymond Costanzo **Est.** 1993 **Cases** 2500 **Vyds** 12.4 ha
Golden Grove Estate was established by Mario and Sebastiana Costanzo in 1946, producing stone fruits and table grapes for the fresh fruit market. The first wine grapes (shiraz) were planted in 1972, but it was not until '85, when ownership passed to son Sam and wife Grace, that the use of the property started to change. In 1993 chardonnay and merlot joined the shiraz, followed by cabernet sauvignon, sauvignon blanc and semillon. The baton has been passed down another generation to Ray Costanzo, who has lifted the quality of the wines remarkably, and has also planted tempranillo, durif, barbera, malbec, mourvedre, vermentino and nero d'Avola. Its trophies and gold medals from the Australian Small Winemakers Show '08 are to be taken seriously: this is a well-judged show with entries from all over Australia, and has been running for over 30 years.

ҰҰҰҰҰ **Granite Belt Shiraz 2007** Excellent hue; an altogether superior wine, with supple, but rich, red and black fruits; seamless tannins and oak, and a long finish. Oldest shiraz vines (45 years old) in the region. Trophy Best Qld Shiraz Australian Small Winemakers Show '08. Screwcap. 14.3% alc. **Rating** 94 **To** 2017 $35

ҰҰҰҰҰ **Granite Belt Sauvignon Blanc 2008** Clean, crisp, well-made wine with a mix of grassy/lemony and more tropical fruit; estate-grown. Trophy Best Qld White Wine Australian Small Winemakers Show '08. Screwcap. 12.3% alc. **Rating** 90 **To** 2010 $26

Accommodation Creek Mediterranean Red 2008 Very good colour; an innovative blend if ever there was one, and has been expertly made as a juicy, drink-soon style. Tempranillo/Durif/Barbera. Screwcap. 14.5% alc. **Rating** 90 **To** 2012 $18

Granite Belt Tempranillo 2007 Attractive light- to medium-bodied varietal wine, with red fruits and a touch of green leaf and mint on the long finish. Gold medal New England Wine Show '08. Screwcap. 13.5% alc. **Rating** 90 **To** 2012 $22

Granite Belt Durif 2007 Superb purple-crimson; bright, healthy, rich and chewy black fruits, but the tannins are not excessive. Gold medal Qld Wine Awards '08. Screwcap. 14.5% alc. **Rating** 90 **To** 2014 $28

Castalina 2008 Yet another expertly made wine; citrus and a touch of honey offset by crisp acidity. Semillon. Screwcap. 9.5% alc. **Rating** 90 **To** 2012 $18

Golders Vineyard ★★★★

Bridport Road, Pipers Brook, Tas 7254 **Region** Northern Tasmania
T (03) 6395 4142 **F** (03) 6395 4142 **Open** By appt
Winemaker Richard Crabtree **Est.** 1991 **Cases** 600
Richard Crabtree continues to make the Golders Vineyard wines at the Delamere winery as he has in the past. The 2.5-ha vineyard established by Crabtree has in fact been sold, and since 2006, grapes have been purchased from the nearby White Rock Vineyard.

ҰҰҰҰҰ **Chardonnay 2008** A fragrant and delicate bouquet but with more thrust and drive to the palate; a mix of grapefruit and nectarine running through to the long finish, acidity playing a major role. Screwcap. 13.4% alc. **Rating** 92 **To** 2016 $28

Golding Wines   ★★★★

Western Branch Road, Lobethal, SA 5241 **Region** Adelaide Hills
T (08) 8389 5120 **F** (08) 8389 5290 **www**.goldingwines.com.au **Open** 7 days 11–4
Winemaker Justin McNamee, Darren Golding **Est.** 2002 **Cases** 1500 **Vyds** 18.5 ha
The Golding family has lived in the Lobethal area of the Adelaide Hills for several generations, and has trimmed its once larger viticultural holdings to concentrate on their Western Branch Road vineyard, planted to sauvignon blanc, albarino, chardonnay, pinot gris and pinot noir. In 2002 the Golding Wines brand was created, the owners being Darren and Lucy Golding, together with Darren's parents, Connie and Greg. In 2006 Darren secured some Marlborough sauvignon blanc through his brother-in-law, who happens to be managing director of NZ's largest independent contract winemaking company. This has resulted in three wines: The Local (100% estate-grown); The Tourist (100% Marlborough); and The Leap (51% estate-grown/49% Marlborough). Exports to Singapore, Maldives and Malaysia.

ŶŶŶŶ̦ **The Leap Lenswood Marlborough Sauvignon Blanc 2008** Does have a certain degree of extra complexity over The Local and The Tourist, delicate tropical fruits with a substrate of citrussy/grassy notes, the structure and length good. Screwcap. 13.5% alc. **Rating** 91 **To** 2010 $23

ŶŶŶŶ **The Local Lenswood Sauvignon Blanc 2008** Some green hints to the colour; unambiguously tropical aromas and flavours, but the wine is light on its feet. Screwcap. 13.4% alc. **Rating** 89 **To** 2010 $20
The Tourist Marlborough Sauvignon Blanc 2008 Very pale colour; the least interesting of the Golding sauvignon blancs, quite light in flavour and body, although what is there is correct. Screwcap. 13.6% alc. **Rating** 88 **To** 2010 $20

Gomersal Wines   ★★★★☆

Lyndoch Road, Gomersal, SA 5352 **Region** Barossa Valley
T (08) 8563 3611 **F** (08) 8563 3776 **www**.gomersalwines.com.au **Open** 7 days 10–5
Winemaker Ben Glaetzer **Est.** 1887 **Cases** 5000 **Vyds** 20 ha
The 1887 establishment date has a degree of poetic licence. In 1887 Friedrich W Fromm planted the Wonganella Vineyards, following that with a winery on the edge of the Gomersal Creek in 1891, which remained in operation for 90 years, finally closing in 1983. In 2000 a group of friends 'with strong credentials in both the making and consumption end of the wine industry' bought the winery and re-established the vineyard, planting 17 ha of shiraz, 2 ha of mourvedre and 1 ha of grenache via terraced bush vines. The Riesling comes from purchased grapes, the Grenache Rose, Grenache Shiraz Mataro and Shiraz from the replanted vineyard. Exports to the US, Ireland and NZ.

ŶŶŶŶŶ **Barossa Valley Shiraz 2006** Bright colour; vibrant red and blackberry fruit with a touch of spice and sage; plenty of volume, but with lively acidity and good focus on the finish; very good value. Screwcap. 14.5% alc. **Rating** 94 **To** 2018 $25

ŶŶŶŶ **Barossa Valley GSM 2006** A savoury bouquet, with dried herbs and dark plum fruit; quite dark on the palate, with good weight and texture. Screwcap. 14.5% alc. **Rating** 89 **To** 2014 $50

 # Good Catholic Girl Wines   ★★★★☆

Box 526, Clare, SA 5453 **Region** Clare Valley
T 0419 822 909 **www**.goodcatholicgirl.com.au **Open** Not
Winemaker Julie Ann Barry **Est.** 2005 **Cases** 460 **Vyds** 1 ha
Good Catholic Girl is the venture of Julie Ann Barry, one of the many children of the late Jim Barry. She says, 'Having been born into a Catholic wine family, in vintage, my fate was sealed. My Limerick Vineyard was planted in the Armagh area of the Clare Valley in 1997, cuttings taken from my father's famed Armagh shiraz vines planted across the paddock.' The Shiraz is named the James Brazill, Jim Barry's Christian names. She takes up the story thus 'In 2008 I made my first Clare Valley Riesling "Teresa" named after my mother, who is the true

GCG (good catholic girl), and loves Clare Riesling, and who may in time consume my entire production of 108 dozen!' Exports to the US.

ΨΨΨΨΨ **Teresa Clare Valley Riesling 2008** Light straw-green; bright, lively and zesty, with lime juice tempered by a touch of minerally acidity; skilled viticultural and winemaking inputs. Screwcap. 12.9% alc. **Rating** 94 **To** 2020 $30

ΨΨΨΨΨ **The James Brazill Clare Valley Shiraz 2005** How much of the alcohol came from the grapes or 'Dad's treasured old port barrels' in which the wine was matured is not certain – probably the former, but you never know. Whatever, rich and succulent; 250 dozen made. Screwcap. 16.2% alc. **Rating** 90 **To** 2015 $30

ΨΨΨΨ **The James Brazill Clare Valley Shiraz 2006** Does show some overripe fruit characters that introduce a soft, confit element, attractive to some but not all consumers; vanilla oak adds to the impression. Screwcap. 15.5% alc. **Rating** 88 **To** 2014 $30

Goona Warra Vineyard ★★★★★

790 Sunbury Road, Sunbury, Vic 3429 **Region** Sunbury
T (03) 9740 7766 **F** (03) 9744 7648 www.goonawarra.com.au **Open** 7 days 10–5
Winemaker John Barnier, Adrian Sautolin **Est.** 1863 **Cases** 3000 **Vyds** 6.92 ha
A historic stone winery, originally established under this name by a 19th-century Victorian premier. A brief interlude as part of The Wine Investment Fund in 2001 is over, the Barniers having bought back the farm. Excellent tasting facilities, an outstanding venue for weddings and receptions, and lunch on Sunday. Exports to Canada, China, Taiwan and Korea.

ΨΨΨΨΨ **Sunbury Semillon Sauvignon Blanc 2008** Lively, crisp and fresh grassy semillon (65%) does lead the way, the sauvignon blanc adding a dimension to the flavour; has particularly impressive length. Value-plus. Diam. 12% alc. **Rating** 94 **To** 2011 $15
Sunbury Chardonnay 2008 Sophisticated winemaking knowing when to draw the line has resulted in a harmonious and finely etched wine with a creamy mid-palate emerging into a bright, fruit-driven finish. Screwcap. 13% alc. **Rating** 94 **To** 2015 $25

Goulburn Terrace ★★★

340 High Street, Nagambie, Vic 3608 **Region** Nagambie Lakes
T (03) 5794 2828 **F** (03) 5794 1854 www.goulburnterrace.com.au **Open** By appt
Winemaker Dr Mike Boudry, Greta Moon **Est.** 1993 **Cases** 1000 **Vyds** 7 ha
Dr Mike Boudry and Greta Moon have established their vineyard on the west bank of the Goulburn River, 8 km south of Lake Nagambie. Planting began in 1993: 2.2 ha of chardonnay on the alluvial soils (10 000 years old, adjacent to the river), and 2.3 ha of cabernet sauvignon on a gravelly rise based on 400-million-year-old Devonian rocks; 1.2 ha of shiraz and 1.1 ha of marsanne followed later. The wines are made in small volumes, with open fermentation and hand-plunging of the reds; all are basket-pressed. Exports to Canada and Japan.

ΨΨΨΨ **Chardonnay 2004** Has developed slowly and confidently, due in part to the restraint of the moderate alcohol, and to the balanced use of barrel ferment inputs; in its infancy; a maximum result. Cork. 13.5% alc. **Rating** 89 **To** 2012 $27

Goundrey ★★★★★

Muirs Highway, Mount Barker, WA 6324 **Region** Mount Barker
T (08) 9892 1777 **F** (08) 9851 1997 www.goundreywines.com.au **Open** Not
Winemaker Peter Dillon **Est.** 1976 **Cases** NFP
Goundrey is part of the CWA empire. In 2008 it was put on the market by CWA, together with its 237 ha of estate vineyards. In 2009 it was purchased by comparative minnow West Cape Howe. The Goundrey brand name has been retained by CWA, and significant quantities of wine will continue to be made from its WA base, with 100% of the Goundrey-grown

grapes sold back to CWA pursuant to an ongoing contract with West Cape Howe. Exports to all major markets.

🍷🍷🍷🍷🍷 **Reserve Riesling 2008** Fragrant citrus, passionfruit and lime; brilliant clarity of flavour; light but insistent long palate. Gold WA Wine Show '08. Screwcap. 12.7% alc. **Rating** 95 **To** 2015 $27.50
Reserve Cabernet Sauvignon 2005 Excellent colour and clarity; very elegant wine with perfect balance and mouthfeel; strong varietal character without excess tannins; good oak. Gold WA Wine Show '08. Cork. 13.7% alc. **Rating** 95 **To** 2020 $36

🍷🍷🍷🍷🍷 **G Sauvignon Blanc Semillon 2007** Tropical and stone fruits mingle together to produce a wine with considerable weight and intensity; the palate is rich, yet has lively acidity provided by the lingering semillon fruit. Screwcap. 13% alc. **Rating** 91 **To** 2012 $21.50
G Sauvignon Blanc Semillon 2008 Almost water-white; bright, zesty and crisp grass and herb aromas and flavour supported by minerally acidity on the palate. Screwcap. 13% alc. **Rating** 90 **To** 2012 $21.50
Cabernet Tempranillo 2007 Deep crimson-purple; a very interesting blend with a fresh array of cherry/red berry fruits, then firm tannins to finish. Should age well in the short term. Screwcap. 14% alc. **Rating** 90 **To** 2014 $21.50

Gracebrook Vineyards   ★★★

4446 Wangaratta-Whitfield Road, King Valley, Vic 3678 **Region** King Valley
T (03) 5729 3562 **F** (03) 5729 3684 **www**.gracebrook.com.au **Open** 7 days 10–5
Winemaker David Maples, King Valley Wines **Est.** 1989 **Cases** 5000 **Vyds** 34.1 ha
David and Rhonda Maples' vineyard is planted to merlot, shiraz, riesling, cabernet sauvignon, sangiovese, chardonnay, dolcetto, sagrantino and alborino, plus trial rows of moscato giallo, muscadelle, muscat blanc, cabernet franc and muscat rouge. Their cellar door, housed in stables built in the 1880s, has panoramic views of the King Valley and can cater for functions/weddings for up to 100 people.

🍷🍷🍷🍷 **King Valley Pinot Grigio 2008** White pear and a touch of spice; clean, fresh and lively finish; a good, food-friendly style. Screwcap. 13% alc. **Rating** 88 **To** 2011 $18
The Stables King Valley Chardonnay 2006 Pale colour; citrus bouquet, with a touch of chalk on the palate; clean and fresh on the finish. Screwcap. 13.5% alc. **Rating** 87 **To** 2012 $16

Gracedale Hills Estate   ★★★★

770 Healesville-Kooweerup Road, Healesville, Vic 3777 **Region** Yarra Valley
T (03) 5967 3403 **F** (03) 5967 3816 **www**.gracedalehills.com.au **Open** Not
Winemaker Gary Mills **Est.** 1996 **Cases** 950 **Vyds** 3.2 ha
Dr Richard Gutch established 1.2 ha of chardonnay and 2 ha of shiraz at a time when most would be retiring from active business, but it represents the culmination of a lifelong love of fine wine, and Richard has no hard feelings towards me – it was I who encouraged him, in the mid-1990s, to plant vines on the north-facing slopes of his property. Here, too, the grapes have been sold to others, but he now retains sufficient grapes to make around 900 cases a year. In 2007 a purpose-built gravity-feed winery was built to reduce the amount of travelling, handling and processing of the fruit for the estate-grown wines.

🍷🍷🍷🍷🍷 **Hill Paddock Yarra Valley Chardonnay 2007** A graciously complex wine that makes its point in a low-alcohol context, grapefruit and nectarine aromas and flavours uppermost, barrel ferment underneath. Screwcap. 13% alc. **Rating** 92 **To** 2014 $25

🍷🍷🍷🍷 **Hill Paddock Yarra Valley Shiraz 2007** A complex wine with distinct smoky overtones presumably from the bushfires; some will not find this a problem, but if smoke taint is present, it will intensify with time. Screwcap. 13.5% alc. **Rating** 87 **To** 2012 $28

Gralyn Estate   ★★★★☆

4145 Caves Road, Wilyabrup, WA 6280 **Region** Margaret River
T (08) 9755 6245 **F** (08) 9755 6136 **www**.gralyn.com.au **Open** 7 days 10.30–4.30
Winemaker Dr Bradley Hutton **Est.** 1975 **Cases** 3300 **Vyds** 4.5 ha
Under the eagle eye of Merilyn Hutton, Gralyn Estate has established a high reputation for
its wines. The primary focus is on the full-bodied red wines, which are made in a distinctively
different style than most from Margaret River, with an opulence reminiscent of some of the
bigger wines from McLaren Vale. The age of the vines (30+ years) and the site are significant
factors. Lesser amounts of chardonnay and fortified wines are also made.

♀♀♀♀♀ **Margaret River Cabernet Shiraz 2007** Leafy bouquet, with a strong varietal
cabernet personality; fleshy and fresh, the tannins are certainly ample and the finish
long and dry. Screwcap. 14.8% alc. **Rating** 91 **To** 2016 $100
Margaret River Cabernet Sauvignon 2006 A little vegetal on the bouquet,
but there are some attractive, if thin, cassis and slight leafy notes; the acidity is very
fresh, and the fruit sits well with the oak; the price may be a little challenging for
most consumers. Screwcap. 13% alc. **Rating** 90 **To** 2015 $100

Grampians Estate   ★★★★★

1477 Western Highway, Great Western, Vic 3377 **Region** Grampians
T (03) 5354 6245 **www**.grampiansestate.com.au **Open** At Garden Gully
Winemaker Hamish Seabrook, Don Rowe, Tom Guthrie **Est.** 1989 **Cases** 1200
Vyds 8.6 ha
Graziers Sarah and Tom Guthrie began their diversification into wine in 1989, but their core
business continues to be fat lamb and wool production. Both activities were ravaged by the
2006 bushfires, but each has recovered, that of their grapegrowing and winemaking rising like
a phoenix from the ashes. They have acquired the Garden Gully winery at Great Western,
giving them a cellar door presence and a vineyard of 2.4 ha of 60-year-old shiraz, and 3 ha of
45-year-old riesling vines. During 2008 Grampians Estate wines continued to excel, winning
seven trophies. A feature of the cellar door will be wine education sessions during school
holidays, and the cellar door will not only offer the full range of Grampians Estate wines but
specially chosen wines from smaller local boutique wineries.

♀♀♀♀♀ **Black Sunday Friends Reserve Shiraz 2006** In the genre of the '98
Bannockburn Shiraz; grapes from six Vic cool-climate regions, most from the
Grampians and Pyrenees; a wonderful tapestry of vibrant spices and black fruits;
marvellous thrust to the almost explosive finish. Screwcap. 14.8% alc. **Rating** 96
To 2021 $50
Black Sunday Friends Sparkling Shiraz 2006 An echo of the great Seppelt
sparkling shirazs of the '40s and '50s (with a leap of imagination, perhaps); this
wine has absolutely wonderful sweet shiraz fruit – not sugar sweetness – on the
finish, and will develop and change for up to 20 years if well cellared. Crown Seal.
14.6% alc. **Rating** 95 **To** 2025 $35
Streeton Reserve Shiraz 2007 Good colour; the first tiny estate production
(358 kg) since the '06 bushfires, augmented with grapes from local growers; has all
the elegance and length for which Grampians Estate is rightly famous. Screwcap.
14.5% alc. **Rating** 94 **To** 2022 $65

♀♀♀♀♀ **Kelly's Welcome Pinot Noir Chardonnay 2007** Hand-picked grapes from
the estate and from a small Romsey vineyard; although young, has good stone
fruit flavours and balance; will fill out in bottle. Crown Seal. 11.5% alc. **Rating** 90
To 2011 $35

Granite Hills

1481 Burke and Wills Track, Baynton, Vic 3444 **Region** Macedon Ranges
T (03) 5423 7273 **www**.granitehills.com.au **Open** Mon–Sat 10–6, Sun 11–6
Winemaker Llew Knight, Ian Gunter **Est.** 1970 **Cases** 7000 **Vyds** 11.5 ha

Granite Hills is one of the enduring classics, pioneering the successful growing of riesling and shiraz in an uncompromisingly cool climate. It is based on riesling, chardonnay, shiraz, cabernet sauvignon, cabernet franc, merlot and pinot noir (the last also used in its sparkling wine). After a quiet period in the 1990s, it has been reinvigorated, with its original two icons once again to the fore. The Rieslings age superbly, and the Shiraz is at the forefront of the cool-climate school in Australia. Exports to Canada, Germany, Mauritius, Hong Kong, Singapore and China.

ΨΨΨΨΨ **Knight Macedon Ranges Brut 1999** High-quality sparkling wine; a blend of barrel-fermented Chardonnay (80%)/Pinot Noir (20%), then blended with reserve wines before six years on yeast lees in bottle. Exceptionally fine, yet vividly flavoured, the balance perfect. Diam. 13% alc. **Rating** 96 **To** 2014 $35
Knight Macedon Ranges Riesling 2007 A floral, flinty bouquet, then a tightly structured, fine palate; apple, citrus and mineral notes provide a seamless core of a wine with a 20-year life. Screwcap. 13% alc. **Rating** 94 **To** 2029 $20

ΨΨΨΨΨ **Knight Macedon Ranges Pinot Noir 2005** Retains bright hue; clear varietal expression in both flavour and structure; spicy, foresty nuances dance around the red fruits in the centre of the palate; long finish. Screwcap. 14.5% alc. **Rating** 92 **To** 2013 $24
Knight Heathcote Merlot 2005 From the cool southern end of Heathcote, only 12 km north of Granite Hills; light- to medium-bodied, with spicy/savoury varietal fruit supported by fine tannins; belies its alcohol. Screwcap. 15% alc. **Rating** 90 **To** 2014 $24
Knight Macedon Ranges Late Harvest 2007 Given the low alcohol, one might have expected more sweetness and intensity, as it is, a gentle Kabinett style; will grow in bottle. Screwcap. 8% alc. **Rating** 90 **To** 2015 $15

ΨΨΨΨ **Knight Macedon Ranges Cabernet Sauvignon 2003** Notwithstanding the alcohol, hasn't fully ripened in flavour terms, with spice, leaf, mint and olive all running alongside blackcurrant flavours; further age not likely to assist. Screwcap. 15% alc. **Rating** 89 **To** 2013 $26

Grant Burge ★★★★★

Jacobs Creek, Barossa Valley, SA 5352 **Region** Barossa Valley
T (08) 8563 3700 **F** (08) 8563 2807 **www**.grantburgewines.com.au **Open** 7 days 10–5
Winemaker Grant Burge, Craig Stansborough **Est.** 1988 **Cases** 400 000 **Vyds** 440 ha
As one might expect, this very experienced industry veteran makes consistently good, full-flavoured and smooth wines based on the pick of the crop of his extensive vineyard holdings; the immaculately restored/rebuilt stone cellar door sales buildings are another attraction. The provocatively named The Holy Trinity joins Shadrach and Meshach at the top of the range. In 1999 Grant Burge repurchased the farm from Mildara Blass by acquiring the Krondorf winery in Tanunda (not the brand), in which he made his first fortune. He renamed it Barossa Vines and opened a cellar door offering casual food. A third cellar door (Illaparra) is open on Murray Street, Tanunda. Exports to all major markets.

ΨΨΨΨΨ **Filsell Barossa Valley Shiraz 2005** Deep, dark, brooding and absolutely jammed with fruit and personality; the palate is dense, the flavours compelling, and despite the obvious weight of the wine, the finish is poised, fresh and very long; often one of the best wines in the stable. Cork. 15% alc. **Rating** 95 **To** 2025 $34.95
Meshach 2004 Deeply coloured and brightly fruited; a big wine with dense fruit, mocha and blackberry, and a lively splash of attractive red fruits; the palate is dense, yet there is a suppleness that provides a fine and focused finish. Shiraz. Cork. 14.5% alc. **Rating** 95 **To** 2020 $120

ΨΨΨΨΨ **Thorn Eden Valley Riesling 2008** Voluminous lime juice aromas and flavours; good length, line and balance. Screwcap. 13% alc. **Rating** 93 **To** 2015 $20.58
Filsell Barossa Valley Shiraz 2006 Big, swarthy Barossa red, with strong blackberry and earth flavours, alcohol part of the mix, as are the tannins. Cork. 15% alc. **Rating** 93 **To** 2016 $37.72

Barossa Vines Shiraz 2006 Medium-bodied; effusive red and black fruit flavours supported by ripe tannins and restrained oak; attractive wine; good length. Screwcap. 14.5% alc. **Rating** 92 **To** 2015 $16.30

Nebuchadnezzar Shiraz Cabernet 2004 Densely concentrated, with a touch of cedar evident beneath the mocha and blackberry character displayed in abundance; rich, ripe and juicy supple finish that makes this wine suitable for drinking immediately. Cork. 13.5% alc. **Rating** 92 **To** 2016 $37.50

The Holy Trinity Grenache Shiraz Mourvedre 2003 Shows development, but with real character; red fruits framed by a lick of leather, dried herbs and ample sweet fruit on the finish. Cork. 14.5% alc. **Rating** 91 **To** 2013 $37.72

Shadrach Cabernet Sauvignon 2006 A brooding wine, full of rich, ripe and essency cassis fruit; fully proportioned on the palate, similar essency fruit carries right through to the dark, and quite tannic, finish. Cork. 14.5% alc. **Rating** 90 **To** 2016 $55

ₒₒₒₒ **Summers Eden Valley Adelaide Hills Chardonnay 2007** A big, rich toasty wine, pushing toward fresh figs and almonds; rich and deep on the palate, but a little heavy on the finish. Screwcap. 13.5% alc. **Rating** 89 **To** 2013 $24

Cameron Vale Cabernet Sauvignon 2006 Clear red-purple; has attractive juicy cassis/blackcurrant fruit on the mid-palate, but doesn't kick on through to the finish. Screwcap. 14.5% alc. **Rating** 89 **To** 2013 $24

Moscato 2008 Fresh and full of musk and grapey essence; vibrant and fun, to be enjoyed in its youth. Screwcap. 8.5% alc. **Rating** 89 **To** 2009 $15.95

Lily Farm Barossa Frontignan 2008 Fresh, spicy and lively, only moderately off-dry; summer special for casual drinking. Screwcap. 11.5% alc. **Rating** 88 **To** 2010 $17

Barossa Vines Cabernet Merlot 2007 Rich and ripe, with some attractive varietal cassis and cedar character on display; plenty of sweet fruit, if a little one-dimensional on the finish. Screwcap. 14.5% alc. **Rating** 87 **To** 2012 $16.30

Grassy Point Wines ★★★★

Coatsworth Farm, 145 Coatsworth Road, Portarlington, Vic 3223 **Region** Geelong
T 0409 429 608 **F** (03) 5251 3969 **www**.grassypointwines.com.au **Open** By appt
Winemaker Provenance (Scott Ireland) **Est.** 1997 **Cases** 800 **Vyds** 6.2 ha
Partners David Smith, Robert Bennett and Kerry Jones purchased this 32-ha undeveloped grazing property in 1997. Coatsworth Farm includes a vineyard (pinot noir, chardonnay, sauvignon blanc, shiraz and cabernet franc), South Devon beef cattle and Perendale/White Suffolk-cross lambs.

ₒₒₒₒₒ **Bellarine Peninsula Sauvignon Blanc 2008** Straddles both the grassy end of the spectrum and the more dominant tropical end, with passionfruit and ripe gooseberry fruit; clean, crisp finish. Screwcap. 12.2% alc. **Rating** 92 **To** 2011 $16

Bellarine Peninsula Pinot Noir 2007 Strong, bright hue; has red and black cherry fruit on bouquet and palate alike; plenty of weight on the palate to underwrite improvement in bottle for several years. Screwcap. 13.4% alc. **Rating** 92 **To** 2014 $20

 # Greedy Sheep ★★★☆

PO Box 530, Cowaramup, WA 6284 **Region** Margaret River
T (08) 9755 7428 **F** (08) 9463 1444 **www**.greedysheep.com.au **Open** Not
Winemaker Dave Johnson, Darren Guiney **Est.** 2008 **Cases** 4000 **Vyds** 6 ha
Mining engineer Darren Guiney and electrical engineer wife Bridget lived and worked all around Australia in remote locations, but in 2004 decided to end the nomadic life and find a place to settle permanently. Margaret River was an obvious choice, for it was there they were married in 1999. They purchased the property in 2004, which had been planted to cabernet sauvignon, merlot, cabernet franc and malbec in '99. It pays to have a sense of humour, for in January '05 1000 sheep found their way into the vineyard, eating everything green within

their reach, including unripe grapes, which must have challenged their digestion. Sauvignon blanc has been purchased from Bridget's twin sister's vineyard, a mere 3 km away, semillon from elsewhere. Exports to the UK.

🍷🍷🍷🍷🍷 **Rose 2008** Vivid, light crimson, the palate with really attractive cherry fruit, and a web of acidity providing both length and crispness. Screwcap. 13.5% alc. **Rating** 91 **To** 2010 **$**16

Greenstone Vineyard ★★★★★

319 Whorouly South Road, Whorouly South, Vic 3735 (postal) **Region** Heathcote
T (03) 5727 1434 **F** (03) 5727 1434 **www**.greenstoneofheathcote.com **Open** Not
Winemaker Sandro Mosele (Contract), Alberto Antonini **Est.** 2002 **Cases** 4500 **Vyds** 20 ha
This is one of the most interesting new ventures to emerge over the past few years, bringing together David Gleave MW, born and educated in Canada, now a long-term UK resident who manages an imported wine business and writes widely about the wines of Italy; Alberto Antonini, a graduate of the University of Florence, with postgraduate degrees from Bordeaux and University of California (Davis), and Italian Flying Winemaker; and Mark Walpole, a 20-year veteran with Brown Brothers and now manager of their 700 ha of vineyards. The partners have chosen what they consider an outstanding vineyard on the red soil of the Heathcote region, planted to 17 ha of shiraz, 2 ha of sangiovese and 1 ha of monastrell (mourvedre). Exports to the UK, the US and other major markets.

Greg Cooley Wines ★★★★

Lot 2 & 4 Seipelt Lane, Penwortham, SA 5453 (postal) **Region** Clare Valley
T (08) 8843 4284 **F** (08) 8843 4284 **www**.gregcooleywines.com.au **Open** Not
Winemaker Greg Cooley **Est.** 2002 **Cases** 1500
Greg Cooley says, 'I followed the traditional path to winemaking via accountancy, fraud squad, corporate investigations, running a Wendy's Supa Sundaes franchise and then selling residential property. I left the property market in Brisbane just as the boom started in 2001 and moved to the beautiful Clare just about when the wine glut started. Things didn't look overly promising when my first wine entered into the Clare Show in 2003. The Riesling came 97th of a total of 97, a platform on which I have since built, having sought loads of advice from local winemakers and subsequently winning a medal the following year.' He explains, 'All my wines are named after people who have been of influence to me in my 45 years and their influence is as varied as the wine styles – from pizza shop owners, to my greyhound's vet and, indeed, my recently departed greyhound Tigger.' I have to confess that I am taken by Greg's path to glory because my move through law to wine was punctuated by the part-ownership of two greyhounds that always wanted to run in the opposite direction to the rest of the field.

🍷🍷🍷🍷🍷 **Bennett and Byrne Reserve Clare Valley Shiraz 2006** Good colour; a rich and potent bouquet with black fruits and vanilla oak; the palate has similar flavours plus ripe tannins needing to soften. Screwcap. 15% alc. **Rating** 93 **To** 2021 **$**30

Day Day and Chippa Clare Valley Sangiovese 2007 Well made; has the requisite sour cherry fruit at its core, but avoids the pervasive tannins that can mar sangiovese; good length, balance and finish. Screwcap. 14.5% alc. **Rating** 91 **To** 2014 **$**20

Monica, Macca and Moo Clare Valley Shiraz 2006 Relatively speaking, has a greater impact from vanillin oak and tannins on the finish than Bennet and Byrne, but does have plenty of black fruits sandwiched on the mid-palate. Screwcap. 15% alc. **Rating** 90 **To** 2016 **$**20

Rehbein and Ryan Reserve Clare Valley Cabernet 2006 Good colour; a complex wine, with strong cedary/earthy overtones to the tarry black fruits on the medium- to full-bodied palate; ripe savoury tannins on the finish. Long-term development. Screwcap. 15% alc. **Rating** 90 **To** 2021 **$**30

🍷🍷🍷🍷 **Terry and Suzi Clare Valley Cabernet Shiraz 2005** Powerful, luscious and very ripe fruit; blackberry jam, dark chocolate, warm spices and a dollop of vanilla; the saving grace is the soft tannin. Screwcap. 15% alc. **Rating** 89 **To** 2013 **$**20

Dad and Meads Clare Valley Grenache Shiraz 2006 Struggles a bit under its load of alcohol, but is not defeated; offers warm spices and a splash of berry fruit and a low-tannin finish. Screwcap. 15.5% alc. **Rating** 88 **To** 2012 $20

The Barton Clare Valley Pinot Noir 2006 Deep purple; a pleasant medium-bodied red wine, with good balance between fruit and tannins, but not even a hint of pinot varietal character. Screwcap. 14.5% alc. **Rating** 87 **To** 2014 $20

Glyn and Pini Clare Valley Merlot 2007 Tries hard to hide its varietal origin, with dark fruits and drying tannins; however, there is a base of fruit to work from. Screwcap. 15% alc. **Rating** 87 **To** 2014 $20

Grey Sands

Cnr Kerrisons Road/Frankford Highway, Glengarry, Tas 7275 **Region** Northern Tasmania
T (03) 6396 1167 **www**.greysands.com.au **Open** By appt (open 2nd w'end Nov 9–5)
Winemaker Fran Austin, Bob Richter **Est.** 1989 **Cases** 1000 **Vyds** 3.5 ha
Bob and Rita Richter began the establishment of Grey Sands in 1989, slowly increasing the plantings to the present total. The ultra-high density of 8900 vines per ha reflects the experience gained by the Richters during a three-year stay in England, when they visited many vineyards across Europe; as well as Bob Richter's graduate diploma from Roseworthy College. Exports to Canada.

Pinot Noir 2006 Fragrant plum and cherry blossom aromas, clean and pure, the palate likewise. Has perfectly expressed varietal character on the palate; great line and length, and no green characters. Diam. 14% alc. **Rating** 95 **To** 2013 $40

Merlot 2005 Good crimson-red; a spotlessly clean wine, with bell-clear varietal fruit in a cassis redcurrant spectrum, and perfectly judged tannins and oak in support. Diam. 13.6% alc. **Rating** 94 **To** 2015 $35

Chardonnay Viognier 2007 Driven by the chardonnay, and to a lesser degree nutty oak and natural acidity, viognier adds more to complexity than flavour; obvious development potential. Screwcap. 13.8% alc. **Rating** 91 **To** 2015 $35

Pinot Gris 2007 Certainly offers more texture and flavour than many pinot gris, but the price is decidedly challenging; has varietally correct pear and apple flavours, and may develop well. Screwcap. 14% alc. **Rating** 89 **To** 2012 $35

Griffin Wines

Tynan Road, Kuitpo, SA 5172 **Region** Adelaide Hills
T (08) 8239 2545 **F** (08) 8388 3557 **www**.griffinwines.com **Open** Not
Winemaker Phil Christiansen, Shaw & Smith **Est.** 1997 **Cases** 2400 **Vyds** 26.16 ha
The Griffins (Trevor, Tim, Mark and Val) planted pinot noir, merlot, chardonnay, sauvignon blanc and shiraz in 1997, having owned the property for over 30 years. Situated 3 km from Kuitpo Hall, its 350 m elevation gives sweeping views over the valley below.

No. 5 Adelaide Hills Unwooded Chardonnay 2008 Very good unwooded style, with fresh nectarine, grapefruit and passionfruit flavours backed by balanced acidity. Screwcap. 13% alc. **Rating** 90 **To** 2013 $17

No. 1 Adelaide Hills Shiraz 2006 Elegant, fresh and spicy red fruit on the bouquet, with just a hint of oak; good depth and weight, with generous fruit and fine texture to the finish. Screwcap. 14.3% alc. **Rating** 90 **To** 2014 $23

No. 2 Adelaide Hills Sauvignon Blanc 2008 Clean and fresh with aromas of tropical fruits and fresh cut grass; soft and easy on the palate. Screwcap. 13% alc. **Rating** 89 **To** 2011 $19.50

Groom

28 Langmeil Road, Tanunda, SA 5352 (postal) **Region** Barossa Valley
T (08) 8563 1101 **F** (08) 8563 1102 **www**.groomwines.com **Open** Not
Winemaker Daryl Groom **Est.** 1997 **Cases** 5600 **Vyds** 29.6 ha

The full name of the business is Marschall Groom Cellars, a venture owned by David and Jeanette Marschall and their six children, and Daryl and Lisa Groom and their four children. Daryl was a highly regarded winemaker at Penfolds before he moved to Geyser Peak in California. Years of discussion between the families came to a head with the purchase of a 35-ha block of bare land near Kalimna, adjacent to Penfolds' 130-year-old Kalimna Vineyard. Shiraz was planted in 1997, giving its first vintage in '99, the wine blended with the output from two vineyards, one 100 years old, the other 50 years old. The next acquisition was an 8-ha vineyard at Lenswood in the Adelaide Hills, planted to sauvignon blanc. In 2000, 3.2 ha of zinfandel was planted on the Kalimna Bush Block, with the first vintage in '03. Not surprisingly, a substantial part of the production is exported to the US.

🍷🍷🍷🍷🍷 **Adelaide Hills Sauvignon Blanc 2008** The bouquet is good, but it is the great vibrancy, almost urgency, of the palate that gives this wine its quality and style, with a long, grainy finish. Screwcap. 12.9% alc. **Rating** 95 **To** 2011 $24
Barossa Valley Shiraz 2007 Against all the odds, has some spicy/savoury aromas expected from a cool vintage, not a hot one; supple, juicy black fruits and licorice on the palate follow down a similar path, fine tannin to close. Cork. 14.5% alc. **Rating** 94 **To** 2017 $48
Bush Block Barossa Valley Zinfandel 2007 An utterly distinctive bouquet of raspberries, spiced plum, cake and spice; terrific lift, life and thrust to the finish. Groom's Californian experience shines through. Cork. 14.5% alc. **Rating** 94 **To** 2015 $29

Grosset   ★★★★★

King Street, Auburn, SA 5451 **Region** Clare Valley
T (08) 8849 2175 **F** (08) 8849 2292 **www**.grosset.com.au **Open** Wed–Sun 10–5 from Sept for approx 6 weeks
Winemaker Jeffrey Grosset **Est.** 1981 **Cases** 10 000 **Vyds** 22 ha
Jeffrey Grosset has assumed the unchallenged mantle of Australia's foremost riesling maker in the wake of John Vickery stepping back to a consultancy role for Richmond Grove. Grosset's pre-eminence in riesling making is recognised both domestically and internationally; however, he merits equal recognition for the other wines in his portfolio: Semillon Sauvignon Blanc from Clare Valley/Adelaide Hills, Chardonnay and Pinot Noir from the Adelaide Hills; and Gaia, a Bordeaux blend from the Clare Valley. These are all benchmarks. His quietly spoken manner conceals a steely will, exemplified by his long and ultimately successful battle to prevent the use of 'riesling' on flagons and bottles as a generic description, rather than varietal, and his subsequent success in having the Clare Valley riesling makers migrate en masse to screwcaps, unleashing a torrent of change across Australia. Trial plantings (2 ha) of fiano aglianico, nero d'Avola and petit verdot suggest some new wines maybe gestating. Exports to all major markets.

🍷🍷🍷🍷🍷 **Springvale Watervale Riesling 2008** A slightly more effusive bouquet than the Polish Hill, the expressive lime juice fruit flavours likewise making this wine ready right from the word go, without compromising its ability to age. Screwcap. 13% alc. **Rating** 96 **To** 2020 $36
Polish Hill Riesling 2008 A spotlessly clean and pure bouquet foreshadows an immaculately crafted palate, with a mix of lime, green apple and mineral flavours; iron fist in a velvet glove. Screwcap. 13% alc. **Rating** 96 **To** 2028 $44
Clare Valley Adelaide Hills Semillon Sauvignon Blanc 2008 As ever, a totally delicious and beautifully moulded mouthful of wine, the two components seamlessly woven in a citrus/stone fruit web tied up with gentle acidity. Screwcap. 13% alc. **Rating** 95 **To** 2012 $32
Gaia 2006 Pristine colour; a complex and appealing mix of red and blackcurrant, black olive, a dash of herbs, and beautifully handled oak; the palate is surprisingly generous and open knit, but offers a long, fine, ample and seductive fine-grained tannin finish; beautiful balance, as befits the name. Screwcap. 14% alc. **Rating** 95 **To** 2020 $60

ŸŸŸŸŸ **Piccadilly Adelaide Hills Chardonnay 2007** A pronounced grilled nut aroma complements the fresh pear fruit on the bouquet; there is a little bit of grip to the palate, with more toasted, nutty complexity framing the gentle pear flavour; quite savoury on the finish. Screwcap. 13.5% alc. **Rating** 91 **To** 2013 $53

ŸŸŸŸ **Adelaide Hills Pinot Noir 2007** Clove, cinnamon and a touch of mint; quite dark-fruited, with lots of flavour, but moving toward dry red; finishes with a dried herb complexity. Screwcap. 14% alc. **Rating** 89 **To** 2011 $66

Grove Estate Wines ★★★★

Murringo Road, Young, NSW 2594 **Region** Hilltops
T (02) 6382 6999 **F** (02) 6382 4527 **www**.groveestate.com.au **Open** W'ends 10–5, or by appt
Winemaker Clonakilla (Tim Kirk), Long Rail Gully Wines (Richard Parker) **Est.** 1989
Cases 4000 **Vyds** 55 ha
The Grove Estate partners of Brian Mullany, John Kirkwood and Mark Flanders purchased the then unplanted property situated on volcanic red soils at an elevation of 530 m with the intention of producing premium cool-climate wine grapes for sale to other winemakers. Over the ensuing years plantings included cabernet sauvignon, shiraz, merlot, zinfandel, barbera, sangiovese, petit verdot, chardonnay, semillon and nebbiolo. In 1997 a decision was taken to retain a small amount of cabernet sauvignon and have it vinified under the Grove Estate label, and the winemaking gathered pace thereafter. In 2003 Tim Kirk of Clonakilla began to make the Grove Estate Shiraz, and oversaw the making of the other wines by Richard Parker at Long Rail Gully. Kirk not only sharply lifted the quality of the winemaking but was also responsible for improvements in the vineyard; Grove Estate hasn't looked back since.

ŸŸŸŸŸ **The Partners Hilltops Cabernet Sauvignon 2007** Vibrant colour; a complex bouquet of blackcurrant, redcurrant and a touch of violet; generous levels of fruit with firm drying and silky tannins, providing a harmonious, long and slightly savoury finish. Screwcap. 14.5% alc. **Rating** 92 **To** 2015 $30
Hilltops Zinfandel 2007 Sweet fruitcake bouquet with red berry fruit and mulled spices coming to the fore; rich, warm and generous, a well-handled example of this pleasurable variety. Screwcap. 14.5% alc. **Rating** 92 **To** 2014 $25
The Wombat Way Viognier 2007 Complex full-bodied wine reflecting both variety and winemaking; whole berry (not bunch) pressed to French oak, with native (wild) yeast fermentation and nine months on yeast lees; a definite touch of ginger on the aftertaste. Screwcap. 14.5% alc. **Rating** 91 **To** 2012 $20

ŸŸŸŸ **The Murringo Way Chardonnay 2007** Quite developed yellow-gold; a very rich wine with oak and quick bottle development, plus alcohol at the top end; a drink-now special. Screwcap. 14.5% alc. **Rating** 87 **To** 2009 $20

Growlers Gully ★★★☆

354 Shaws Road, Merton, Vic 3715 **Region** Upper Goulburn
T (03) 5778 9615 **www**.growlersguly.com.au **Open** W'ends & public hols 11–5, or by appt
Winemaker Les Oates **Est.** 1997 **Cases** NA **Vyds** 2.25 ha
Les and Wendy Oates have established the Growlers Gully vineyard (shiraz, cabernet sauvignon, viognier and sauvignon blanc) at an elevation of 375 m on fertile brown clay loam soil. A rammed-earth cellar door sales outlet offers light meals and barbecue facilities. No harvest in 2007 due to smoke taint, the '06 Shiraz is still available at cellar door.

ŸŸŸŸŸ **Upper Goulburn Shiraz 2006** Strong colour; a full, supple medium- to full-bodied palate with a blend of satsuma plum and blackberry, the tannins soft. A shiraz/pinot noir blend from Growlers Gully could be interesting. Diam. 13.9% alc. **Rating** 90 **To** 2012 $25

Guichen Bay Vineyards ★★★

PO Box 582, Newport, NSW 2106 **Region** Mount Benson
T (02) 9997 6677 **F** (02) 9997 6177 **www**.guichenbayvineyards.com.au **Open** At Mount
Benson Tourist & Wine Information Centre
Winemaker Simon Greenleaf (White), Mark Day (Red) **Est.** 2003 **Cases** 700 **Vyds** 120 ha
Guichen Bay Vineyards is one of three adjacent vineyards known collectively as the Mount
Benson Community Vineyards. Chardonnay, sauvignon blanc, shiraz, merlot and cabernet
sauvignon were planted between 1997 and 2001. While the major part of the production is
sold, the owners have obtained a producer's licence, and a small quantity of grapes is held back
and made by local winemakers under the Guichen Bay Vineyards label.

ΨΨΨΨ **Mount Benson Sauvignon Blanc 2008** A clean bouquet; potent tropical/
gooseberry fruit runs through the length of the palate, almost sweet on the finish,
but with balancing acidity. Screwcap. 12.7% alc. **Rating** 88 **To** 2010 $16.50

Haan Wines

Siegersdorf Road, Tanunda, SA 5352 **Region** Barossa Valley
T (08) 8562 4590 **F** (08) 8562 4590 **www**.haanwines.com.au **Open** Not
Winemaker Mark Jamieson (Contract) **Est.** 1993 **Cases** 4500 **Vyds** 16.3 ha
Hans and Fransien Haan established their business in 1993 when they acquired a vineyard
near Tanunda. The plantings are shiraz (5.3 ha), merlot (3.4 ha), cabernet sauvignon (3 ha),
viognier (2.4 ha), cabernet franc (1 ha) and malbec, petit verdot and semillon (0.4 ha each).
Oak undoubtedly plays a role in the shaping of the style of the Haan wines, but it is perfectly
integrated, and the wines have the fruit weight to carry the oak. Exports to the UK and other
major markets.

ΨΨΨΨΨ **Merlot Prestige 2006** Vibrant, fresh and focused cedar, black olive and plum
fruit; the palate is fine, with pronounced acidity lending an elegant framework to
the slightly spicy fruit. Cork. 14.5% alc. **Rating** 94 **To** 2014 $45
Wilhelmus 2006 Deeply coloured, this classic blend of the five Bordeaux
varieties is enticingly rich and spicy on opening, with the strictness of the cabernet
pulling the parts together with ease; very long, very generous and surprisingly
accessible at this point in time. Cork. 14.5% alc. **Rating** 94 **To** 2018 $49.95

ΨΨΨΨΨ **Barossa Valley Viognier Prestige 2008** Very ripe apricot fruit; pushing the
envelope; the richness and varietal expression on the palate is inevitably achieved
at the cost of some phenolic weight. Screwcap. 14% alc. **Rating** 90 **To** 2010 $35

Hahndorf Hill Winery ★★★☆

Lot 10 Pains Road, Hahndorf, SA 5245 **Region** Adelaide Hills
T (08) 8388 7512 **F** (08) 8388 7618 **www**.hahndorfhillwinery.com.au **Open** 7 days 10–5
Winemaker Geoff Weaver (Consultant) **Est.** 2002 **Cases** 5000 **Vyds** 6.3 ha
Larry Jacobs and Marc Dobson, both originally from South Africa, purchased Hahndorf Hill
Winery in 2002. Larry gave up a career in intensive-care medicine in 1988 when he purchased
an abandoned property in Stellenbosch, and established the near-iconic Mulderbosch Wines.
When Mulderbosch was purchased at the end of 1996, the pair migrated to Australia and
eventually found their way to Hahndorf Hill. In 2006, their investment in the winery and
cellar door was rewarded by induction into the South Australian Great Tourism Hall of Fame,
having won the award for Best Tourism Winery for three consecutive years. In 2007 they
began the process of converting the vineyard to biodynamic status, and they were one of the
first movers in implementing a carbon offset program. They have successfully imported three
clones of gruner veltliner from Austria, and their first vintage is expected in 2010; however,
they have been beaten to the punch by Lark Hill. Exports to the UK, Singapore and China.

ΨΨΨΨΨ **Adelaide Hills Sauvignon Blanc 2008** A pungent bouquet with a hint of
tropical fruit; the palate is full of sweet fruit, with a cleansing acid bite to the finish.
Screwcap. 13% alc. **Rating** 90 **To** 2011 $21

♟♟♟   **Adelaide Hills Pinot Grigio 2008** Ripe pear and a touch of spice on the bouquet; good concentration and texture, with a crisp and punchy finish to the palate. Screwcap. 12.5% alc. **Rating** 89 **To** 2011 $24

Hainault   ★★★☆

255 Walnut Road, Bickley, WA 6076 **Region** Perth Hills
T (08) 9293 8339 **www**.hainault.com.au **Open** W'ends & public hols 11–5, or by appt
Winemaker Tony Davis (Contract) **Est.** 1980 **Cases** NA
Lyn and Michael Sykes became the owners of Hainault in 2002, after previous owner Bill Mackey and wife Vicki headed off elsewhere. The 11 ha of close-planted vines are hand-pruned and hand-picked, and the pinot noir is very sensibly used to make a sparkling wine, rather than a table wine.

♟♟♟♟♀   **Classic White 2008** The blend works well, semillon providing the structure and length, chardonnay filling out the palate nicely with gently peachy fruit. Screwcap. 12.9% alc. **Rating** 90 **To** 2012 $18

Halifax Wines

Lot 501 Binney Road, McLaren Vale, Willunga, SA 5172 **Region** McLaren Vale
T (08) 8557 1000 **www**.halifaxwines.com.au **Open** W'ends 11–4 or by appt
Winemaker Peter Butcher **Est.** 2000 **Cases** 1000 **Vyds** 4 ha
Owned and operated by Elizabeth Tasker (background in advertising and marketing) and Peter Butcher (20+ years in the wine industry, in marketing, sales, distribution, education and winemaking). A passionate proponent of wine's 'sense of place', Peter has worked with some of Australia's most well-known winemakers – Jeffrey Grosset, Peter Leske, Mike Farmilo and Peter Gago – and has also been influenced by visits to France and Italy. Produces a single-vineyard Shiraz from estate plantings, supplemented by small quantities of grenache (50-year-old vines), cabernet sauvignon (40-year-old vines) and mourvedre. Exports to the US and Hong Kong.

♟♟♟♟♟   **McLaren Vale Shiraz 2006** Bright, clear crimson-purple; fragrant, fresh and very lively with a chorus of red and black fruits singing through the length of the palate; refined and elegant. Screwcap. 14% alc. **Rating** 94 **To** 2016 $30

♟♟♟♟♀   **McLaren Vale Shiraz 2007** A rich and luscious shiraz without the burden of excess alcohol; blackberry, plum and dark chocolate are supported by ripe but fine tannins, oak seen but not heard; 420 cases made. Screwcap. 14% alc. **Rating** 93 **To** 2015 $30

Hamelin Bay   ★★★★☆

McDonald Road, Karridale, WA 6288 **Region** Margaret River
T (08) 9758 6779 **F** (08) 9758 6779 **www**.hbwines.com.au **Open** 7 days 10–5
Winemaker Julian Scott **Est.** 1992 **Cases** 15 000
The 25-ha Hamelin Bay vineyard was established by the Drake-Brockman family. The initial releases were contract made, but a winery with cellar door sales facility was opened in 2000, which has enabled an increase in production. Exports to the UK, Canada, Malaysia and Singapore.

♟♟♟♟♟   **Five Ashes Reserve Margaret River Chardonnay 2007** Ultra sophisticated, understated style, intense but fine grapefruit and melon is held in a fine web of French oak and balanced acidity; very long finish. Screwcap. 14% alc. **Rating** 94 **To** 2015 $45

♟♟♟♟♀   **Margaret River Semillon Sauvignon Blanc 2008** Very pale; slightly green pea pod bouquet with a background of ripe citrus; the palate is fresh and lively, with mouth-watering acidity to clean up. Screwcap. 12% alc. **Rating** 92 **To** 2012 $22
Margaret River Sauvignon Blanc 2008 Light, clean, crisp and very dry, with bone-tingling acidity cleaning up the finish; a hot day outside beckons this wine. Screwcap. 12% alc. **Rating** 90 **To** 2011 $22

ȲȲȲȲ **Five Ashes Vineyard Margaret River Chardonnay 2007** More expressive, perhaps, than the Reserve, but without the finesse of that wine; oak more evident, the fruit flavours of nectarine and melon broader. Screwcap. 13.5% alc. **Rating** 89 **To** 2012 $28

Rampant White 2008 Bright and focused nectarine fruit, joined by a touch of pea pod on the bouquet; the palate is lively and fresh, with an even and juicy finish. Screwcap. 12% alc. **Rating** 89 **To** 2011 $19

Five Ashes Vineyard Margaret River Cabernet Sauvignon 2006 Distinctly tart and savoury, with some minty touches as well; laboured hard in a very difficult red year. Screwcap. 13.5% alc. **Rating** 88 **To** 2015 $29

Hanging Rock Winery ★★★★★

88 Jim Road, Newham, Vic 3442 **Region** Macedon Ranges
T (03) 5427 0542 **F** (03) 5427 0310 **www**.hangingrock.com.au **Open** 7 days 10–5
Winemaker John Ellis **Est.** 1982 **Cases** 40 000 **Vyds** 14.5 ha
The Macedon area has proved very marginal in spots, and the Hanging Rock vineyards, with their lovely vista towards the Rock, are no exception. John Ellis has thus elected to source additional grapes from various parts of Victoria to produce an interesting and diverse range of varietals at different price points. Exports to the UK, the US and other major markets.

ȲȲȲȲȲ **Macedon Cuvee (Late Disgorged) NV VII** Yellow-gold; extremely complex, with strong nutty/brioche characters ex lees; very low dosage ensures elegance along with powerful flavour; not the least acidic, and aldehydes just where they should be. Cork. 12% alc. **Rating** 95 **To** 2010 $115

Heathcote Shiraz 2005 Retains excellent hue, although not entirely clear; handles its alcohol with ease, awash with juicy black and red fruits through the vibrant thrust of the long palate. Diam. 15% alc. **Rating** 94 **To** 2020 $70

Reserve Heathcote Shiraz 2001 Retains remarkable crimson–purple hue; the wine is correspondingly fresh, with vibrant black and red cherry fruit and a lively finish. Bottle variation could be an issue. Cork. 14% alc. **Rating** 94 **To** 2015 $105

Reserve Heathcote Shiraz 2000 The colour is still bright; a complex web of aromas and flavours has developed, ranging through black fruits, licorice, spice and earth; the palate has excellent length. Cork. 14% alc. **Rating** 94 **To** 2015 $105

ȲȲȲȲȲ **Odd One Out Nebbiolo Rose 2008** Pale salmon; well made and structured; spicy cherry fruit on an elegant, balanced palate. Arguably, best use of nebbiolo (from Heathcote). Screwcap. 14% alc. **Rating** 92 **To** 2011 $20

Macedon Cuvee NV XII. Bright gleaming green-gold; minimal aldehydes; toasty dried fruit and brioche flavours before lingering searing acid on the finish. Cork. 12% alc. **Rating** 92 **To** 2013 $49

Macedon Brut Rose NV Salmon-pink; good mousse; has an extra dimension of flavour and structure; creamy, nutty red fruits; good length. Cork. 12.5% alc. **Rating** 92 **To** 2010 $27

ȲȲȲȲ **Kilfara Pinot Noir 2006** Strong colour; a powerfully structured wine, with plenty of flavour, but not the silky vinosity on the mid-palate needed for higher points. Screwcap. 13.5% alc. **Rating** 89 **To** 2013 $24

Cambrian Rise Heathcote Shiraz 2005 Powerful, medium- to full-bodied wine with considerable extract and savoury tannins; does need a touch more mid-palate fruit for higher points. Diam. 15% alc. **Rating** 89 **To** 2015 $27

Hanging Tree Wines ★★★

294 O'Connors Road, Pokolbin, NSW 2325 **Region** Lower Hunter Valley
T (02) 4998 6601 **www**.hangingtreewines.com.au **Open** Fri–Sun 11–5 or by appt
Winemaker Andrew Thomas (Contract) **Est.** 2003 **Cases** 2500 **Vyds** 2.8 ha
Hanging Tree Wines (which started life as the Van De Scheur Estate) has been developed into a luxury resort. The homestead has two master suites and two deluxe rooms; the verandahs have accommodated wedding parties for up to 102 seated guests. The wines, from the

estate plantings of semillon, chardonnay, shiraz and cabernet sauvignon, are made by leading contract-winemaker Andrew Thomas.

ŶŶŶŶ **Limited Release HVO Semillon Sauvignon Blanc 2008** This regional/varietal blend is now established and works well; semillon is the driving force, the sauvignon blanc kicking in on the back-palate and finish. Commendable wine. Hunter Valley/Orange. Screwcap. 12.4% alc. **Rating** 89 **To** 2012 $19
Limited Release Hunter Valley Shiraz 2005 Retains bright hue; a relatively light-bodied but fresh wine that has captured the essence of the fruit without forcing it to be what it is not; red and black cherry fruits do the talking. Cork. 13% alc. **Rating** 89 **To** 2014 $22
Limited Release Hunter Valley Cabernet 2007 Ripe, warm red fruit flavours on both bouquet and palate, but balanced in the mouth by acidity; well made. Cork. 13.8% alc. **Rating** 88 **To** 2015 $24
Dante's Fuego Hunter Valley Sparkling Shiraz 2004 Despite its age, very reluctant to remain in the bottle when opened; a distinctly savoury, regional style that scores for its fresh, dry finish. Base wine spent 10 months in oak. Cork. 13% alc. **Rating** 88 **To** 2012 $35
Limited Release Shirlot 2006 Very light colour, and structure to match; the flavours are attractive, and the wine is best regarded as a Beaujolais alternative. Shiraz blend. Screwcap. 13.8% alc. **Rating** 87 **To** 2012 $22

Hanson-Tarrahill Vineyard   ★★★

49 Cleveland Avenue, Lower Plenty, Vic 3093 (postal) **Region** Yarra Valley
T (03) 9439 7425 **F** (03) 9439 4217 **Open** Not
Winemaker Dr Ian Hanson **Est.** 1983 **Cases** 1000 **Vyds** 9.4 ha
Dental surgeon Ian Hanson planted his first vines in the late 1960s, close to the junction of the Yarra and Plenty Rivers; in '83 those plantings were extended (by 3000 vines), and in '88 the Tarrahill property at Yarra Glen was established with a further 4 ha. The varieties planted are (in descending order) pinot noir, cabernet sauvignon, shiraz, cabernet franc, chardonnay and viognier. Exports to the UK.

ŶŶŶŶ **Tarra's Block Yarra Valley Cabernet Franc Cabernet Sauvignon Shiraz 2007** Essency cassis fruit, and lifted aromatics hinting at florals; the palate is full-bodied with quite fine and lingering red and black fruit on the finish. Diam. 14% alc. **Rating** 88 **To** 2014 $20

Happs   ★★★★☆

575 Commonage Road, Dunsborough, WA 6281 **Region** Margaret River
T (08) 9755 3300 **F** (08) 9755 3846 **www.**happs.com.au **Open** 7 days 10–5
Winemaker Erl Happ, Mark Warren **Est.** 1978 **Cases** 20 000 **Vyds** 37 ha
One-time schoolteacher, potter and winemaker Erl Happ is now the patriarch of a three-generation family. More than anything, Erl has been a creator and experimenter, building the self-designed winery from mudbrick, concrete form and timber, and designing and making the first crusher. In 1994 he began an entirely new vineyard at Karridale, planted to no less than 28 different varieties, including some of the earliest plantings in Australia of tempranillo. The Three Hills label is made from varieties grown at the 30-ha Karridale vineyard. Erl passed on to son Myles a love of pottery, and Happs Pottery now has four potters, including Myles. Exports to Denmark, Netherlands, Malaysia Hong Kong, China and Japan.

ŶŶŶŶŶ **Three Hills Sangiovese 2007** Light, but good, hue; tangy and incisive, showing strong varietal character from the start to the finish, which is very long, and has quite delicious sour cherry fruit. Cork. 13.5% alc. **Rating** 94 **To** 2015 $36

ŶŶŶŶ♀ **Three Hills Petit Verdot 2007** Typical full bore: deep colour, full body, full extract, but at least it achieves full ripeness (it seldom does at home in Bordeaux). Cork. 15% alc. **Rating** 92 **To** 2017 $36

Margaret River Semillon Sauvignon Blanc 2008 Bright straw-green; the bouquet has grassy aromas backed by gooseberry characters amplified on the quite intense and long palate, which also has echoes of stone fruit. Well priced. Screwcap. 13% alc. **Rating** 90 **To** 2012 $16

Margaret River Chardonnay 2007 Smoky barrel ferment inputs on grapefruit and nectarine; still in compartments. Screwcap. 14% alc. **Rating** 90 **To** 2013 $20

ΨΨΨΨ **Three Hills Merlot 2007** Good colour; strong varietal expression might have been stronger still at more moderate alcohol levels; not clear why picking should have been so delayed; Ribena-like flavours with some black olive notes. Cork. 15.5% alc. **Rating** 89 **To** 2015 $36

Three Hills Nebbiolo 2007 From some of the oldest nebbiolo vines in commercial production, the red cherry fruit set against persistent, savoury tannins. Only for the addicted, or the brave. Cork. 13.8% alc. **Rating** 89 **To** 2015 $36

Three Hills Grenache 2007 Fragrant spicy red fruit aromas lead into a palate in two parts: first sweet fruit, then pronounced tannins. The tatty cork may prevent the wine reaching its potential. 14% alc. **Rating** 88 **To** 2015 $36

Three Hills Cabernet Franc 2007 Good colour and plenty of fragrant red berry fruits, but the tannins are bitter; curate's egg; prayer and time may help. Cork. 14% alc. **Rating** 87 **To** 2013 $36

Harcourt Valley Vineyards ★★★★☆

3339 Calder Highway, Harcourt, Vic 3453 **Region** Bendigo
T (03) 5474 2223 **www.**harcourtvalley.com.au **Open** 7 days 11–5 (11–6 during daylight saving)
Winemaker Kye Livingstone, Quinn Livingstone **Est.** 1976 **Cases** 2000 **Vyds** 4 ha
Established by Ray and Barbara Broughton, the vineyard was handed over to John and Barbara Livingstone in 1988. Barbara's Shiraz was created by Barbara Broughton, but with the arrival of the 'new' Barbara it lives on as the flagship of the vineyard. The Livingstones planted a further 2 ha of shiraz on north-facing slopes with the aid of two sons, who, says Barbara, then 'bolted, vowing never to have anything to do with vineyards, but having developed fine palates'. John Livingstone died in mid-2004, but Barbara continues her role of viticulturist; winemaking is now in the hands of sons Kye and Quinn (who have returned to the fold).

ΨΨΨΨΨ **Sightings Shiraz 2006** Spicy red fruits with an intriguing note of bramble; quite fine and evenly textured on the palate, the tannins are savoury and the acid bright. Value. Screwcap. 13.5% alc. **Rating** 92 **To** 2014 $20

Sightings Cabernet Sauvignon 2006 Black olive, bay leaf and redcurrant fruit; the palate is quite fine, with a generous splash of red fruit and a savoury underpinning of sage. Screwcap. 13.5% alc. **Rating** 90 **To** 2014 $20

ΨΨΨΨ **Bendigo Chardonnay 2008** Bright colour; savoury/nutty bouquet, with lemon and nectarine in support; fresh acidity, and a little grip on the finish. Screwcap. 12.5% alc. **Rating** 88 **To** 2011 $20

Hardys ★★★★★

Reynell Road, Reynella, SA 5161 **Region** McLaren Vale
T (08) 8392 2222 **F** (08) 8392 2202 **www.**hardys.com.au **Open** Mon–Fri 10–4.30, Sat 10–4, Sun 11–4, closed public hols
Winemaker Paul Lapsley (Chief) **Est.** 1853 **Cases** NFP
The 1992 merger of Thomas Hardy and the Berri Renmano group may well have had some elements of a forced marriage when it took place, but the merged group prospered mightily over the next 10 years. So successful was it that a further marriage followed in early 2003, with Constellation Wines of the US the groom, and BRL Hardy the bride, creating the largest wine group in the world (the Australian arm of the business is known as Constellation Wines Australia, or CWA). The Hardys wine brands are headed by Eileen Hardy Chardonnay, Shiraz and Pinot Noir; then the Sir James range of sparkling wines; next the newly introduced HRB Riesling, Chardonnay, Shiraz and Cabernet; then the expanded Oomoo range; and at the bottom of the price pyramid, the Chronicles wines. Exports to all major markets.

🍷🍷🍷🍷🍷 **Eileen Hardy Chardonnay 2006** Grace and power; great depth of melon and nectarine fruits and plenty of savoury, cashew notes; very good oak matches the fruit impeccably. Screwcap. 13.3% alc. **Rating** 95 **To** 2014 $70

HRB Riesling 2008 A blend of Tasmania (30%)/Clare Valley (70%); a highly expressive bouquet with ripe apple and spice aromas; the palate offers the juicy lime and apple flavours of Tasmania, and the minerally structure of the Clare Valley. Screwcap. 12.5% alc. **Rating** 94 **To** 2016 $30

HRB Chardonnay 2007 Predominantly a blend of Margaret River/Adelaide Hills material, with 5% from Pemberton; an elegant style that greatly appeals to me, with a marvellous end-palate and aftertaste. Screwcap. 13.5% alc. **Rating** 94 **To** 2014 $30

Eileen Hardy Pinot Noir 2008 Deep hue; complex plum and black cherry aromas give a hint of the power to come on the full-bodied (by pinot standards) palate. Imperious wine, demanding years of patience. Screwcap. 13.5% alc. **Rating** 94 **To** 2018 $85

🍷🍷🍷🍷🍷 **Oomoo McLaren Vale Shiraz 2007** Bright colour; vibrant red and blackberry fruitcake bouquet; quite juicy and light on its feet, with a tarry and quite chewy finish. Always value. Screwcap. 14.3% alc. **Rating** 90 **To** 2015 $18.50

HRB Shiraz 2006 A blend of Clare Valley (60%)/Adelaide Hills (40%) material; a vibrant and spicy entry courtesy of the Adelaide Hills component, then quite savoury tannins on the finish, provided by the Clare Valley portion. Cork. 14% alc. **Rating** 90 **To** 2013 $40

Chronicle No. 3 Butcher's Gold Shiraz Sangiovese 2007 Bright, clear colour; this is a wine with much more character than the others in the range, with cherry fruits, sour and sweet, dancing around each other to the tune of a persistent drum beat of fine tannins. Screwcap. 14% alc. **Rating** 90 **To** 2013 $16.99

Oomoo Clare Valley Sparkling Shiraz 2004 Dense and dark in colour; blackberry fruit framed by a touch of mint and an essency blackcurrant palate; finishes dry with refreshing acidity. Cork. 14% alc. **Rating** 90 **To** 2012 $18.50

🍷🍷🍷🍷 **HRB Cabernet Sauvignon 2006** A Coonawarra (90%)/Margaret River (10%) blend; a very savoury style with earthy notes from Coonawarra very much to the fore, and a touch of leaf, perhaps from the small Margaret River component. Not convincing. Cork. 13.5% alc. **Rating** 89 **To** 2014 $40

Oomoo Adelaide Hills Sauvignon Blanc 2008 Pungent green fruit and hints of some tropical aromas; tight and zesty on the palate. Screwcap. 13% alc. **Rating** 87 **To** 2011 $18.50

Nottage Hill Chardonnay 2008 Vibrant colour; toasty nectarine fruit bouquet; generous palate weight, with a fleshy finish. Screwcap. **Rating** 87 **To** 2011 $11

Chronicle No. 1 Twice Lost Shiraz Cabernet Rose 2008 Vivid fuschia-pink; a bright and juicy-fruity style, with cherry pop and raspberry flavours. Screwcap. 12.5% alc. **Rating** 87 **To** 2010 $16.99

Nottage Hill Cabernet Sauvignon Shiraz 2007 Strong toasty aromas dominate, and the palate is dried out and quite hard; clean and modern but needs more fruit to carry the winemaking. Screwcap. 13.5% alc. **Rating** 87 **To** 2012 $10.50

Hare's Chase   ★★★★★

PO Box 46, Melrose Park, SA 5039 **Region** Barossa Valley
T (08) 8277 3506 **F** (08) 8277 3543 **www.**hareschase.com **Open** Not
Winemaker Peter Taylor **Est.** 1998 **Cases** 5000 **Vyds** 16 ha

Hare's Chase is the creation of two families who own a 100-year-old vineyard in the Marananga Valley area of the Barossa Valley. The simple, functional winery sits at the top of a rocky hill in the centre of the vineyard, which has some of the best red soil available for dry-grown viticulture. The winemaking arm of the partnership is provided by Peter Taylor, now in charge of Foster's vineyards and grape suppliers worldwide. Exports to the US, Canada, Switzerland, Singapore and Hong Kong.

ΨΨΨΨΨ **Barossa Shiraz 2006** Good hue and clarity; an intense yet elegant wine, with perfectly balanced and integrated fruit, oak and tannins; has thrust to its finish and aftertaste. ProCork. 14.5% alc. **Rating** 94 **To** 2020 $25

Barossa Shiraz 2004 In the refined, elegant style of this winery; co-fermentation with a small amount of viognier has worked very well to lift the bouquet; the palate, too, has attractive cedary/spicy nuances. Cork. 14.5% alc. **Rating** 94 **To** 2014 $25

ΨΨΨΨΨ **Barossa Valley Tempranillo 2006** Aromatic, with a mix of cherry/berry/tangy characters, the tannins fine but sufficient to carry the wine on for some years. Screwcap. 14% alc. **Rating** 90 **To** 2014 $20

ΨΨΨΨ **The Springer Barossa Blend 2006** Vital colour; has rather more tannins than expected from a Shiraz/Merlot/Cabernet Franc blend, but does have length and is well priced. Screwcap. 14.5% alc. **Rating** 89 **To** 2014 $15

Harefield Ridge Wines   ★★★

562 Pattersons Road, Wagga Wagga, NSW 2650 **Region** Gundagai
T (02) 6921 3512 **www**.cottontailwines.com.au **Open** Thurs–Sun 10–6
Winemaker Chris Thomas, Gerry McCormick **Est.** 2002 **Cases** 1500 **Vyds** 4 ha
Wagga Wagga residents Gerry McCormick and partner Sue Limberger are the owners of a 40-ha property on undulating land on the southwest slopes of the Great Dividing Range. In 2002 they commissioned a detailed analysis of soil structure on the property, and after sampling 12 pits at various sites, their consultant confirmed that the decomposed granite soil had an ideal structure and neutral pH suited to the production of premium grapes. In October 2002 they entered into a handshake agreement with John Casella to buy the grapes from the shiraz and chardonnay vines, which were planted the following month. With only 2 ha of each variety planted, it was a drop in the ocean for Casella and yellowtail, and the partners now retain the grapes. While the wine is made at the Tumbarumba Grape Processors Factory by Chris Thomas (with assistance from Gerry) plans have been lodged with the council to build a winemaking facility at the Harefield property.

ΨΨΨΨ **Cottontail Shiraz 2007** While the flavours are ripe and the wine medium bodied at best, the alcohol is not oppressive; sweet red and black fruits on the mid-palate dry out pleasantly, with dusty tannins on the finish. Screwcap. 14.5% alc. **Rating** 89 **To** 2014 $18.50

Harewood Estate   ★★★★★

Scotsdale Road, Denmark, WA 6333 **Region** Denmark
T (08) 9840 9078 **F** (08) 9840 9053 **www**.harewoodestate.com.au **Open** 7 days 10–4
Winemaker James Kellie, Luke Hipper **Est.** 1988 **Cases** 7500 **Vyds** 10 ha
In 2003 James Kellie, for many years a winemaker with Howard Park, and responsible for the contract making of Harewood's wines since 1998, purchased the estate with his father and sister as partners. Events moved quickly thereafter: a 300-tonne winery was constructed, offering both contract winemaking services for the Great Southern region and the ability to expand the Harewood range to include subregional wines that demonstrate the differences in style across the region. Exports to the UK, Denmark, Hong Kong and Japan.

ΨΨΨΨΨ **Great Southern Riesling 2008** Pale colour; a tightly wound and expressive bouquet, showing lime, mineral and a touch of floral character; graceful and poised, with precise acidity and some green apple freshness on the finish. Screwcap. 12% alc. **Rating** 94 **To** 2018 $19.95

Reserve Great Southern Semillon Sauvignon Blanc 2008 Bright hue; vibrant and expressive bouquet of nettle and ripe tropical fruit; quite engaging palate, with good texture, purity and poise; dry and minerally and a very long finish. Screwcap. 13.5% alc. **Rating** 94 **To** 2012 $25

Great Southern Shiraz Cabernet 2005 Substantial, medium- to full-bodied; chewy, with lots of textured black fruits, some red; good length. Gold WA Wine Show '08. Screwcap. 14.5% alc. **Rating** 94 **To** 2017 $19.50

ŸŸŸŸ♀ **Frankland River Shiraz 2007** Essency blueberry and blackberry fruit, with a generous dollop of toasty new oak; blackberry pastille comes out on the palate, plenty of gravelly tannin on the finish. Screwcap. 15% alc. **Rating** 92 **To** 2015 $30
Great Southern Shiraz Cabernet 2007 Very good colour and clarity; medium-bodied; spicy overtones to the basket of black fruits. Screwcap. 14% alc. **Rating** 92 **To** 2019 $19.50
Denmark Chardonnay 2007 Spiced peach bouquet, with quite prominent toasty oak; ripe and sweet stone fruit palate, with a vibrant core of acidity; long, juicy and fine. Screwcap. 14.5% alc. **Rating** 91 **To** 2012 $27.50

ŸŸŸŸ **Denmark Pinot Noir 2007** Very developed colour; stalky notes give length, but needs more sweet fruit. Screwcap. 14% alc. **Rating** 87 **To** 2011 $19.50

Harmans Ridge Estate

Cnr Bussell Highway/Harmans Mill Road, Wilyabrup, WA 6284 **Region** Margaret River
T (08) 9755 7409 **F** (08) 9755 7400 **www**.harmansridge.com.au **Open** 7 days 10.30–5
Winemaker Paul Green **Est.** 1999 **Cases** 5000
Harmans Ridge Estate, with a crush capacity of 1600 tonnes, is primarily a contract maker for larger producers in the Margaret River region who do not have their own winery/winemaker. It does, however, have 2 ha of shiraz, and makes wines under the Harmans Ridge Estate label from grapes grown in Margaret River. Exports to the UK and the US.

ŸŸŸŸ♀ **Howling Wolves Semillon Sauvignon Blanc 2008** Neatly balanced; while the semillon provides the line and length, sauvignon blanc shows through strongly on the bouquet; good synergy. 12.5% alc. **Rating** 91 **To** 2011 $14

ŸŸŸŸ **Howling Wolves Small Batch Chardonnay 2007** Smoky barrel ferment aromas lead into a tight palate, with grapefruit and melon to the fore. May expand with age. 13.5% alc. **Rating** 89 **To** 2013 $25
Howling Wolves Verdelho 2008 Quite crisp and fresh with fractionally smoky overtones to the balanced palate; lively finish. 13% alc. **Rating** 87 **To** 2010 $14

Harrington Glen Estate ★★★★

88 Townsend Road, Glen Aplin, Qld 4381 **Region** Granite Belt
T (07) 4683 4388 **F** (07) 4683 4388 **Open** 7 days 10–4, Sat & public hols 10–5
Winemaker Stephen Oliver **Est.** 2003 **Cases** 800 **Vyds** 3.24 ha
The Ireland family planted cabernet sauvignon, shiraz, merlot and verdelho vines in 1997, with follow-on plantings of muscat and viognier. Red grapes not required for cellar door production are sold to local wine producers, and some white grapes are purchased from other Granite Belt grape producers.

ŸŸŸŸ♀ **Granite Belt Cabernet Sauvignon 2007** Gold medals in local derbies not surprising; has clear varietal expression courtesy of blackcurrant and cassis, and exemplary tannin structure. Screwcap. 13.9% alc. **Rating** 93 **To** 2017 $30
Granite Belt Shiraz 2006 Retains red-purple hues; the long, medium-bodied palate has plenty of spicy/savoury complexity; not hard to see why it has had show success. Screwcap. 14.6% alc. **Rating** 90 **To** 2016 $25
Granite Belt Merlot 2007 Crimson-red; the balance and structure are nigh on perfect; juicy black plum and black cherry fruit flavours are supported by fine tannins and good oak. Screwcap. 13.3% alc. **Rating** 90 **To** 2017 $25

Harris River Estate

Lot 1293 Harris River Road, Collie, WA 6225 **Region** Geographe
T (08) 9734 1555 **www**.harrisriverestate.com.au **Open** Thurs–Sun 11–3
Winemaker Jane Gilham **Est.** 2001 **Cases** 2000 **Vyds** 34 ha
In 2000 Karl and Lois Hillier (and their six children) purchased the Harris River property to run cattle and have a farm life for the family. When it was subsequently suggested the soils

were ideal for vineyards, the family quickly diversified into grapegrowing, and even more quickly formed a company owned by family and friends to fast-track the progressive planting of viognier, verdelho, chardonnay, shiraz, merlot and cabernet sauvignon. At the same time a 200-tonne winery, incorporated in a three-storey winery/cellar door/restaurant/function centre, swung into action in 2002. The arrival of winemaker Jane Gilham and viticulturist Ray Dennis has paid big dividends. Exports to Singapore.

ΨΨΨΨΨ **Chardonnay 2007** Very good balance and length; creamy cashew mlf inputs; restrained oak; flows well across the tongue. Gold WA Wine Show '08. Screwcap. 13.5% alc. **Rating** 94 **To** 2015 $20
Verdelho 2007 Excellent varietal example; positive fruit salad with a long, tangy citrussy palate and finish. Gold WA Wine Show '08. Screwcap. 13.3% alc. **Rating** 94 **To** 2012 $20

Hartley Estate

260 Chittering Valley Road, Lower Chittering, WA 6084 **Region** Perth Hills
T (08) 9481 4288 **F** (08) 9481 4291 **www.**hartleyestate.com.au **Open** By appt
Winemaker Western Range Wines **Est.** 1999 **Cases** 6000 **Vyds** 17.46 ha
While driving through the Chittering Valley one Sunday with his daughter Angela, reminiscing about the times he had spent there with his father Hartley, Bernie Stephens saw a 'For Sale' sign on the property, and later that day the contract for sale was signed. Planting of of vines began, with Cabernet Sauvignon and Shiraz released in 2003. They form part of the Generations Series, recognising the involvement of three generations of the family. The major part of the crop goes to Western Range Wines; the remainder is made for the Hartley Estate label. Extensive landscaping has been carried out throughout the property, featuring sculptures, bird life, wild flowers and a lake.

ΨΨΨΨΨ **Hannah's Hill Shiraz 2007** Bright colour; loaded with new oak, the fruit beneath is plump and shows raspberry, blackberry and some roast meat and tar character; the palate is generous and vibrant, with a restraint that provides a long and fine finish; the oak will resolve in time. Screwcap. 15% alc. **Rating** 94 **To** 2016 $65

ΨΨΨΨΨ **Cabernet Merlot 2007** Bright cassis, raspberry and cherry fruits on a light- to medium-bodied palate, with enough tannins on the finish to provide structure. Value. Screwcap. 14% alc. **Rating** 90 **To** 2014 $15

ΨΨΨΨ **Classic White 2008** Has enough tropical fruit salad generosity to please most palates in an informal setting, served ice cold. Screwcap. 13% alc. **Rating** 87 **To** 2010 $15

Hartz Barn Wines

1 Truro Road, Moculta, SA 5353 **Region** Eden Valley
T (08) 8563 9002 **F** (08) 8563 9002 **www.**hartzbarnwines.com.au **Open** By appt
Winemaker David Barnett **Est.** 1997 **Cases** 2600
Hartz Barn Wines was formed in 1997 by Penny Hart (operations director), David Barnett (winemaker/director), Katrina Barnett (marketing director) and Matthew Barnett (viticulture/cellar director), which may suggest that the operation is rather larger than it in fact is. The business name and label have an unexpectedly complex background, too, involving elements from all the partners. The grapes come from the 11.5-ha Dennistone Vineyard, which is planted to merlot, shiraz, riesling, cabernet sauvignon, chardonnay and lagrein. Exports to Canada, Sweden, Japan and NZ.

ΨΨΨΨΨ **General Store Barossa Shiraz 2005** Full-bodied, with abundant blackberry, licorice and prune fruit framed by balanced and well-integrated oak; the tannins, too, are exactly weighted. Screwcap. 14.5% alc. **Rating** 93 **To** 2020 $30

ΨΨΨΨ **Dennistone Eden Valley Lagrein 2006** Not easy to read the runes of this wine; seems much riper than the alcohol would suggest, and also has more extract than normal. Screwcap. 13.5% alc. **Rating** 88 **To** 2014 $34

Harvey River Bridge Estate   ★★★★☆

Third Street, Harvey, WA 6220 **Region** Geographe
T (08) 9729 2085 **F** (08) 9729 2298 www.harveyfresh.com.au **Open** 7 days 10–4
Winemaker Stuart Pierce **Est.** 2000 **Cases** 45 000
This highly focused business is a division of parent company Harvey Fresh (1994) Ltd,
a producer of fruit juice and dairy products exported to more than 12 countries. It has
12 contract growers throughout the Geographe region, with the wines being made in a
company-owned winery and juice factory. The current releases are decidedly impressive.
Exports to the UK, the US, Canada, Singapore, Japan and Hong Kong.

TTTTT **Joseph River Estate Reserve Geographe Sauvignon Blanc 2008**
Sophisticated winemaking adds a dimension via 10% barrel fermentation in new
French oak without detracting from the gooseberry, grassy varietal fruit and the
clean finish. Screwcap. 12.5% alc. **Rating** 94 **To** 2011 $22

TTTTP **Geographe Sauvignon Blanc Semillon 2008** Fragrant cut grass and
gooseberry, even nectarine; a lively, crisp and long palate, with refreshing finish.
Bargain. Screwcap. 12.3% alc. **Rating** 91 **To** 2011 $15
Joseph River Estate Reserve Geographe Verdelho 2006 Bright straw-
green; a very lively verdelho with an appealing stream of lime citrus through
the long palate; has good balance, and is ageing slowly, with more in front of it.
Screwcap. 13.7% alc. **Rating** 90 **To** 2013 $22

TTTT **Viognier 2008** Well made; early-picked fruit from young vines delivers brightness
to the citrus flavours, but not much varietal character. Screwcap. 12.2% alc.
Rating 87 **To** 2010 $15

Haselgrove Wines   ★★★★☆

150 Main Road, McLaren Vale, SA 5171 **Region** McLaren Vale
T (08) 323 8706 **F** (08) 8323 8049 www.haselgrove.com.au **Open** 7 days 11–4
Winemaker Simon Parker **Est.** 1981 **Cases** 54 000
Between October 2002 and February '08, BankWest took over ownership and management
of Haselgrove Wines in an endeavour to recover the loans it had made to the business. That
achieved, five investors, all with substantial, long-term involvement either in winemaking or
wine marketing, acquired Haselgrove Wines from BankWest in early 2008. The business also
includes McLaren Vale Custom Crush, a contract processing, winemaking and storage facility
adding $1.4 million of annual turnover to the $3 million of Haselgrove Wines. Wines are
released in three ranges: at the top, the Haselgrove Reserve Series (HRS); next the McLaren
Vale series (MVS); and at the bottom the Sovereign series. Exports to Europe and Asia.

TTTTT **HRS Reserve Adelaide Hills Chardonnay 2007** Elegant wine, seamlessly
marrying nectarine and white peach fruit with French oak; caresses the mouth.
Screwcap. 13.5% alc. **Rating** 94 **To** 2013 $24.95

TTTTP **HRS Reserve McLaren Vale Shiraz 2006** Bright colour; intense and lively
juicy cherry fruit on both bouquet and palate; long carry and aftertaste. Well made.
Screwcap. 14% alc. **Rating** 93 **To** 2016 $24.95

TTTT **Vincent's Breeze McLaren Vale Shiraz 2006** Light- to medium-bodied; tangy
style, with more personality and impact than many at this price, although not so
much depth. Screwcap. 14.5% alc. **Rating** 88 **To** 2012 $15.95

Hastwell & Lightfoot   ★★★

Foggos Road, McLaren Vale, SA 5171 (postal) **Region** McLaren Vale
T (08) 8323 8692 **F** (08) 8323 8098 www.hastwellandlightfoot.com.au **Open** By appt
Winemaker James Hastwell, Goe DiFabio (Contract) **Est.** 1990 **Cases** 3800 **Vyds** 15.5 ha
Hastwell & Lightfoot is an offshoot of a rather larger grapegrowing business, with the majority
of the grapes from the vineyard being sold to others. The vineyard was planted in 1988 to

shiraz, cabernet sauvignon, chardonnay, cabernet franc, viognier, tempranillo and barbera. Incidentally, the labels are once seen, never forgotten. Exports to the UK, the US, Canada, Norway, Malaysia and Singapore.

TTTT **McLaren Vale Shiraz 2006** Fresh colour; lighter-bodied than most McLaren Vale shiraz, quite perfumed and open, although American oak is obvious; finishes with fine tannins that give overall balance. Screwcap. 14% alc. **Rating** 89 **To** 2015 $22

Hat Rock Vineyard ★★★★☆
2330 Portarlington Road, Bellarine, Vic 3221 (postal) **Region** Geelong
T (03) 5259 1386 **F** (03) 9833 1150 **www.**hatrockvineyard.com.au **Open** By appt
Winemaker Contract **Est.** 2000 **Cases** 300 **Vyds** 2 ha
Steven and Vici Funnell began the development of Hat Rock in 2000, planting pinot noir. The vineyard derives its name from a hat-shaped rocky outcrop on the Corio Bay shore, not far from the vineyard, a landmark named by Matthew Flinders when he mapped the southern part of Australia. The wines are available through the website.

TTTTT **Bellarine Peninsula Pinot Noir 2007** A powerful wine with intense, spicy plum and black cherry fruit; fine tannins are a feature of both flavour and structure; has considerable length. Screwcap. 13.5% alc. **Rating** 94 **To** 2015 $28

Hay Shed Hill Wines ★★★★★
Harmans Mill Road, Wilyabrup, WA 6280 **Region** Margaret River
T (08) 9755 6046 **F** (08) 9755 6083 **www.**hayshedhill.com.au **Open** 7 days 10.30–5
Winemaker Michael Kerrigan **Est.** 1987 **Cases** 35 000 **Vyds** 17.45 ha
The changes continue at Hay Shed Hill. Highly regarded former winemaker at Howard Park, Mike Kerrigan acquired the business in late 2006 (with co-ownership by the West Cape Howe syndicate) and is now the full-time winemaker. He had every confidence he could dramatically lift the quality of the wines, which is precisely what he has done. Exports to the US, Singapore and china.

TTTTT **Margaret River Chardonnay 2008** Notwithstanding the same modest alcohol as Pitchfork, has much greater intensity of flavour and also length; while barrel fermented in French oak (11 months' maturation), fruit, rather than oak, drives the wine. Screwcap. 12.5% alc. **Rating** 96 **To** 2018 $25
Block 1 Margaret River Semillon Sauvignon Blanc 2008 A very good example of the strength of Margaret River Semillon/Sauvignon Blanc; beautifully balanced and structured, with citrussy/spicy fruit nuanced by some barrel ferment. Screwcap. 12.8% alc. **Rating** 94 **To** 2016 $28
Block 6 Margaret River Chardonnay 2007 Pale straw-green; a precisely focused and balanced wine that accelerates on the back-palate, finish and aftertaste. The restrained alcohol allows zesty, vibrant fruit in a citrus and melon range to fully express itself. Screwcap. 12.8% alc. **Rating** 94 **To** 2015 $33
Margaret River Cabernet Sauvignon 2007 Classic Margaret River cabernet; abundant blackcurrant fruit and firm tannins give structure and balance; 18 months in French oak. Screwcap. 14.5% alc. **Rating** 94 **To** 2017 $25

TTTTT **Pitchfork Margaret River Shiraz 2007** Aromas of violets and cherry blossom on the bouquet lead into a vibrant, fresh palate with cherry and plum fruit leading the way. Excellent value. Screwcap. 13.3% alc. **Rating** 92 **To** 2017 $17
Pitchfork Margaret River Cabernet Merlot 2007 Flush with predominantly redcurrant/red cherry fruits, which show this blend doesn't have to be painfully earthy or savoury; supple mouthfeel adds to the appeal. Great value. Screwcap. 13.3% alc. **Rating** 92 **To** 2016 $17
Margaret River Chardonnay 2007 Unsurprisingly, shares many things in common with Block 6, especially the fruit-flavour profile enhanced by restrained alcohol and perfectly balanced acidity, presumably natural. Screwcap. 12.8% alc. **Rating** 92 **To** 2014 $24

Margaret River Sauvignon Blanc Semillon 2008 Lively citrus/lemon aromas lead into a crisp, tightly structured palate with good acidity and freshness to the long finish. Screwcap. 12.4% alc. **Rating** 91 **To** 2012 $20
Pitchfork Margaret River Chardonnay 2008 Shows what can be achieved with unoaked chardonnay where the quality of the grapes is not in doubt; here a bright display of white peach and a twist of grapefruit does the job. Value. Screwcap. 12.5% alc. **Rating** 90 **To** 2011 $17

♥♥♥♥ **Margaret River Shiraz Tempranillo 2007** An unusual blend, and an unusual wine, with some juicy red fruits interspersed with firm tannins; not yet coherent in its statement. Screwcap. 14% alc. **Rating** 88 **To** 2015 $20
Pitchfork Semillon Sauvignon Blanc 2008 A generous, easygoing dry white wine, exhibiting good winemaking, but needing more fruit thrust for higher points. Screwcap. 12.2% alc. **Rating** 87 **To** 2011 $16

Head Wines

Lot 1, Stonewell Road, Stonewell, SA 5352 **Region** Barossa Valley
T 0413 114 233 **F** (02) 9211 2382 **www**.headwines.com.au **Open** By appt
Winemaker Alex Head **Est.** 2006 **Cases** 600
Head Wines is the intriguing, but highly focused, venture of Alex Head, who came into the wine industry in 1997 with a degree in biochemistry from Sydney University. Experience in fine wine retail stores, wholesale importers and an auction house was followed by vintage work at wineries he particularly admired: Tyrrell's, Torbreck, Laughing Jack and Cirillo Estate. The labelling and naming of the wines reflects his fascination with the Northern Rhône Valley, and, in particular, Côte-Rôtie. The two facing slopes in Côte-Rôtie are known as Côte Blonde and Côte Brune, sometimes combining grapes from the two slopes as Côte Brune et Blonde. Head's Blonde comes from an east-facing slope in the Stonewell subregion of the Barossa Valley (producing 198 cases in 2007), while the Brunette comes from a very low-yielding vineyard in the Moppa subregion. In each case, open fermentation (with whole bunches included) and basket pressing precedes 15 months in seasoned French hogsheads.

♥♥♥♥♥ **The Brunette Single Vineyard Shiraz 2007** Deeper crimson than The Blonde; medium- to full-bodied, and offers very different fruit, with blackberry and licorice to the fore, but also having a lift to the finish that adds a beam of light to illuminate the wine; 66 cases made. Screwcap. 14% alc. **Rating** 96 **To** 2026 $30
The Blonde Single Vineyard Shiraz 2007 Crimson-red; a fragrant bouquet with a mix of red fruits, spice and oak; the medium-bodied palate has very good length and balance, with ripe tannins and oak; 198 cases made. Screwcap. 14% alc. **Rating** 94 **To** 2018 $25

Heafod Glen Winery

8691 West Swan Road, Henley Brook, WA 6055 **Region** Swan Valley
T (08) 9296 3444 **F** (08) 9296 3555 **www**.heafodglenwine.com.au **Open** Wed–Sun 10–5
Winemaker Liam Clarke **Est.** 1999 **Cases** 2400 **Vyds** 40 ha
A combined vineyard and restaurant business, each sustaining the other. The estate plantings are shiraz, cabernet sauvignon, semillon, chenin blanc, chardonnay, verdelho and viognier. Chesters restaurant, created by Paul Smith (famed for establishing Dear Friends restaurant in Perth), is run by Duncan Head and sister Anna, and is situated in a former stable, which has been restored with all of the tables, cabinet works and feature walls crafted from the original timber. Exports to Japan.

♥♥♥♥ **Swan Valley Shiraz Viognier 2007** Quite bright fruit, with redcurrant and savoury notes of roast meat; vibrant acidity greets the palate and provides a fresh medium-bodied backdrop to the finish. Screwcap. 14% alc. **Rating** 89 **To** 2013 $25

Heartland Wines

229 Greenhill Road, Dulwich, SA 5065 **Region** Langhorne Creek/Limestone Coast Zone
T (08) 8431 4322 **F** (08) 8431 4355 **www**.heartlandwines.com.au **Open** Not
Winemaker Ben Glaetzer **Est.** 2001 **Cases** 80 000
This is a joint venture of five industry veterans: winemakers Ben Glaetzer and Scott Collett,
viticulturist Geoff Hardy, General Manager Vicki Arnold and wine industry management
specialist Grant Tilbrook. It uses grapes grown in the Limestone Coast and Langhorne Creek,
predominantly from vineyards owned by the partners. It currently exports 70% of its make
to 38 international markets, and 30% domestic. The wines are principally contract-made at
Barossa Vintners and represent excellent value for money. Exports to all major markets.

ΨΨΨΨ **Langhorne Creek Viognier & Pinot Gris 2007** Clear-cut viognier varietal
character in a peach/apricot spectrum is cut slightly by fresh pinot gris; an odd
couple who nonetheless get on quite well. Screwcap. 13.5% alc. **Rating** 89
To 2010 $20
Stickleback White 2008 A lively, zesty wine, looking as if there is a fifth
component (sauvignon blanc); very good value; fresh as a daisy. Verdelho/Semillon/
Viognier/Pinot Gris. Screwcap. 12.5% alc. **Rating** 87 **To** 2009 $12
Langhorne Creek Limestone Coast Cabernet Sauvignon 2007 Juicy
berry/cassis fruit aromas and flavours yield to a peremptory challenge by savoury
tannins. Screwcap. 14.5% alc. **Rating** 87 **To** 2015 $18
Langhorne Creek Dolcetto & Lagrein 2007 A smorgasbord of juicy red
fruit aromas and flavours, before a twitch of light tannin on the finish. Screwcap.
14.5% alc. **Rating** 87 **To** 2011 $20

Heathcote II

290 Cornella–Toolleen Road, Toolleen, Vic 3551 **Region** Heathcote
T (03) 5433 6292 **F** (03) 5433 6293 **www**.heathcote2.com **Open** W'ends 10–5
Winemaker Peder Rosdal **Est.** 1995 **Cases** 365 **Vyds** 5.4 ha
This is the venture of Danish-born, French-trained, Flying Winemaker (California, Spain and
Chablis) Peder Rosdal and viticulturist Lionel Flutto. The establishment of the vineyard dates
back to 1995, with new plantings in '04 and '08 of shiraz (with the lion's share of 2.6 ha),
cabernet sauvignon, cabernet franc, merlot and tempranillo. The vines are dry-grown on the
famed red Cambrian soil, and the wines are made onsite using hand-plunging, basket press
and (since 2004) French oak maturation. Exports to the US, Switzerland, Denmark, Germany,
Japan and Singapore.

ΨΨΨΨΩ **Shiraz 2006** Massively powerful in every respect: alcohol, fruit impact and
tannins; significant wine travel along the sides of the cork does not suggest the
wine can safely be cellared for the 20 years required for it to settle down, but there
is no choice between a rock and a hard place. 15.7% alc. **Rating** 90 **To** 2026 $39

ΨΨΨΨ **HD Shiraz 2006** Quite developed colour; abundant flavour, but alcohol and
tannins conspire to overshadow the fruit; time won't come to the rescue. Cork.
15.7% alc. **Rating** 89 **To** 2014 $80

Heathcote Winery

183–185 High Street, Heathcote, Vic 3523 **Region** Heathcote
T (03) 5433 2595 **F** (03) 5433 3081 **www**.heathcotewinery.com.au **Open** 7 days 10–5
Winemaker Rachel Brooker **Est.** 1978 **Cases** 10 000 **Vyds** 17 ha
The Heathcote Winery was one of the first to be established in the region. The wines are
produced predominantly from the estate vineyard (shiraz, viognier, chardonnay and marsanne),
and some from local and other growers under long-term contracts; the tasting room facilities
have been restored and upgraded. Exports to Hong Kong.

ㅇㅇㅇㅇㅇ **Curagee Shiraz 2007** An attractive and concentrated blackberry, spice and floral bouquet; thickly textured with copious amounts of dark fruit and spice; the ample level of tannin is swallowed with ease by the generous level of fruit; will require time to be fully appreciated. Screwcap. 14% alc. **Rating** 95 **To** 2020 $60

ㅇㅇㅇㅇㅇ **Mail Coach Shiraz 2007** A little reduction on opening; red and blue fruits framed by a touch of mint and spice; quite a minerally and chewy palate, with lots of tannin and berry fruit on offer; a dark and quite chewy finish. Screwcap. 14.7% alc. **Rating** 91 **To** 2015 $30
Cravens Place Shiraz 2007 A neatly balanced and constructed wine, with attractive, rounded black cherry and plum fruit, the extract and alcohol well controlled. Screwcap. 14.3% alc. **Rating** 90 **To** 2014 $17.50

ㅇㅇㅇㅇ **Thomas Craven MCV 2008** Ripe, clean and attractive peach and nectarine fruit bouquet; fleshy palate, with good acid and an interesting mineral edge to the finish. Marsanne/Chardonnay/Viognier. Screwcap. 13.5% alc. **Rating** 88 **To** 2011 $16.50

Heathvale
Saw Pit Gully Road, via Keyneton, SA 5353 **Region** Eden Valley
T (08) 8564 8248 **F** (08) 8564 8248 **www**.heathvale.com.au **Open** By appt
Winemaker Trevor March **Est.** 1987 **Cases** 1500 **Vyds** 10 ha
The origins of Heathvale go back to 1865 when William Heath purchased the property, building the home and establishing 8 ha of vineyard. The wine was initially made in the cellar of the house, which still stands on the property (now occupied by owners Trevor and Faye March). The vineyards were re-established in 1987, and consist of shiraz, cabernet sauvignon, chardonnay, riesling and sagrantino with future plantings planned. The 2008 vintage wines were produced onsite in the newly built winery. Exports to the US and China.

ㅇㅇㅇㅇㅇ **William Heath Eden Valley Shiraz 2005** Shows Eden Valley to full advantage, especially in terms of texture and structure; the spicy/peppery notes to the black fruits are totally harmonious, as are the tannins. Screwcap. 14% alc. **Rating** 94 **To** 2020 $50

ㅇㅇㅇㅇㅇ **Eden Valley Riesling 2008** Classic Eden Valley lime juice aromas and flavours, heightened by the moderate alcohol; a clear, fluid finish to the long palate. Screwcap. 12% alc. **Rating** 92 **To** 2015 $18

Hedberg Hill
701 The Escort Way, Orange, NSW 2800 **Region** Orange
T (02) 6365 3428 **F** (02) 6365 3428 **www**.hedberghill.com.au **Open** By appt
Winemaker Simon Gilbert **Est.** 1998 **Cases** 400 **Vyds** 5.6 ha
Peter and Lee Hedberg have established their hilltop vineyard 4 km west of Orange, with 0.8 ha each of cabernet sauvignon, merlot, tempranillo, chardonnay, viognier, sauvignon blanc and riesling. It has great views of Mt Canobolas and the surrounding valleys, and visitors are welcome by appointment. A new cellar door is schedule to open in spring 2009.

ㅇㅇㅇㅇㅇ **Lara's Chardonnay 2007** Nicely put together; nectarine and white peach fruit, with balanced barrel ferment French oak inputs, are collectively supported by citrussy acidity on the finish. Screwcap. 13.5% alc. **Rating** 90 **To** 2013 $17

ㅇㅇㅇㅇ **Oscar's Cabernet Sauvignon 2006** Fragrant red berry/cassis fruit on the bouquet flows through onto the palate, which, while relatively light-bodied, has good length and balance. Screwcap. 13.5% alc. **Rating** 88 **To** 2014 $17

Heggies Vineyard
Heggies Range Road, Eden Valley, SA 5235 **Region** Eden Valley
T (08) 8565 3203 **F** (08) 8565 3380 **www**.heggiesvineyard.com **Open** At Yalumba
Winemaker Peter Gambetta **Est.** 1971 **Cases** 13 000 **Vyds** 62 ha

Heggies was the second of the high-altitude (570 m) vineyards established by S Smith & Son. Plantings on the 120-ha former grazing property began in 1973; the principal varieties are riesling, chardonnay, viognier and merlot. There are then two special plantings: a 1.1-ha reserve chardonnay block, and 27 ha of various clonal trials. Exports to all major markets.

♀♀♀♀♀ **Reserve Eden Valley Chardonnay 2006** A beautiful wine that exhibits real poise and amazing fruit definition; pure, focused, fine and lively with many layers that unfold right across the palate; incredibly well made. Screwcap. 13.5% alc. **Rating** 96 **To** 2018 $39.95
Eden Valley Riesling 2008 Light straw-green; intense, voluminous citrus blossom aromas flow into a vibrant, lively palate with citrus lime fruit offset and lengthened by mineral acidity. Screwcap. 11.5% alc. **Rating** 95 **To** 2018 $19.95
Reserve Eden Valley Riesling 2003 Yellow, shot with green; exemplary balance and structure, with a restrained display of lime, apple and acidity. Time to go. Screwcap. 12.5% alc. **Rating** 94 **To** 2013 $28.95
Eden Valley Viognier 2006 Bright green-gold; a rare combination of varietal character and finesse; barrel fermentation with wild yeast has added a textured dimension, but left the stone fruit flavours intact. Screwcap. 14% alc. **Rating** 94 **To** 2012 $29.95

♀♀♀♀♀ **Reserve Eden Valley Riesling 2004** Bright straw-green; yet another classic five-year-old Heggies Riesling, lime juice, honey and toast all coalescing; needed just a touch more acidity. Screwcap. 12.5% alc. **Rating** 93 **To** 2014 $28.95
Eden Valley Chardonnay 2007 The first impression is the strong mineral core to this wine, which is supported by ample levels of stone fruit, moving through to apricot; full of toast and grilled nuts on the finish. Screwcap. 13.5% alc. **Rating** 91 **To** 2013 $26.95
Eden Valley Botrytis Riesling 2007 The green-gold colour and bouquet are arresting, as is the deliciously ripe lime and tropical fruit, honey already apparent on the palate. That said, it really needs more grip and minerally acidity. Screwcap. 11% alc. **Rating** 91 **To** 2012 $26.95
Eden Valley Merlot 2007 A fragrant, gently spicy bouquet, then a neatly balanced palate with offsetting red berry fruits and a hint of forest and olive; exact varietal expression. Cork. 13.5% alc. **Rating** 90 **To** 2017 $28.95

Heidenreich Estate ★★★

PO Box 99, Tanunda, SA 5352 **Region** Barossa Valley
T (08) 8563 2644 **F** (08) 8563 1554 **www**.heidenreichvineyards.com.au **Open** Not
Winemaker Noel Heidenreich **Est.** 1998 **Cases** 2000
The Heidenreich family arrived in the Barossa in 1857, with successive generations growing grapes ever since. It is now owned and run by Noel and Cheryl Heidenreich who, having changed the vineyard plantings and done much work on the soil, were content to sell the grapes from their 4.5 ha of shiraz, cabernet sauvignon, cabernet franc, viognier and chardonnay until 1998, when they and friends crushed a tonne in total of shiraz, cabernet sauvignon and cabernet franc. Since that time, production has increased to around 2000 cases, most exported to San Diego in the US, and a little sold locally.

♀♀♀♀ **The Old School Principals Barossa Valley Shiraz 2005** Traditional Barossa style, albeit with a persistent touch of sweetness running through the blackberry and plum fruit. Screwcap. 15% alc. **Rating** 88 **To** 2014 $26.50
The Old School Graduates Barossa Valley Cabernet Sauvignon 2005 Alcohol impacts more on cabernet than shiraz, investing this wine with inappropriate sweetness; vanilla oak adds its contribution. Does have abundant flavour. Screwcap. 15% alc. **Rating** 87 **To** 2015 $26.50

Helen's Hill Estate

16 Ingram Road, Lilydale, Vic 3140 **Region** Yarra Valley
T (03) 9739 1573 **F** (03) 9739 0350 **www**.helenshill.com.au **Open** 7 days 10–5
Winemaker Scott McCarthy **Est.** 1984 **Cases** 3000 **Vyds** 53 ha

Helen's Hill Estate is named after the previous owner of the property, Helen Fraser. Venture partners, Andrew and Robyn McIntosh and Lewis, Roma and Allan Nalder, combined childhood farming experience with more recent careers in medicine and finance to establish and manage the day-to-day operations of the 65-ha estate. Most of the vines were planted in the mid-1990s, followed by small plantings of chardonnay and pinot noir in the mid-'80s. Immaculately tended vines produce two ranges of 100% estate-grown wines: the entry-point range is of varietals under the Ingram Road label, while flagship wines are released under the Helen's Hill label. Winemaker Scott McCarthy has an impressive record as a Flying Winemaker before coming home to permanently work in Australia. The 140-seat restaurant deservedly has a high reputation, operating with the winery and cellar door complex opened in 2006. Exports to Hong Kong.

♥♥♥♥♀ **Yarra Valley Chardonnay 2007** Bright colour; ripe pear and a suggestion of fig; quite generous palate, with plenty of toast and a layer of citrus providing focus and length. Screwcap. 13.4% alc. **Rating** 93 **To** 2013 $23.50

Ingram Rd Yarra Valley Pinot Noir 2007 Bright colour; savoury bouquet, showing some sulphide complexity and cherry fruit; quite firm and taut on entry, the palate gives way to cherry fruit and a certain mineral complexity. Screwcap. 13.5% alc. **Rating** 92 **To** 2013 $16

Ingram Rd Yarra Valley Cabernet Merlot 2007 Bright colour; cedar and cassis with some savoury black olive notes; the palate is quite firm and serious, with a plummy core to the fruit. Screwcap. 13.8% alc. **Rating** 90 **To** 2014 $16

♥♥♥♥ **Ingram Rd Yarra Valley Sauvignon Blanc 2008** A pure passionfruit bouquet; tropical fruit, and a slightly sweet fruit palate. Screwcap. 11.5% alc. **Rating** 87 **To** 2011 $15

Helm   ★★★★★

Butt's Road, Murrumbateman, NSW 2582 **Region** Canberra District
T (02) 6227 5953 **F** (02) 6227 0207 **www**.helmwines.com.au **Open** Thurs–Mon 10–5
Winemaker Ken Helm **Est.** 1973 **Cases** 3000 **Vyds** 15 ha
Ken Helm, well known as one of the more stormy petrels of the wine industry, is an energetic promoter of his wines and of the Canberra District generally. His wines have been workmanlike at the least, but recent vintages have lifted the quality bar substantially, receiving conspicuous show success and critical acclaim for the Rieslings. Plantings have steadily increased, with riesling, traminer, chardonnay, pinot noir, cabernet sauvignon, merlot, shiraz and cabernet franc. Exports to the UK, Singapore and Macau.

♥♥♥♥♥ **Classic Dry Riesling 2008** Very pale straw; a crisp, dry and tightly focused style, with a mix of citrus and minerally acidity intertwined on the long palate. Two trophies: Canberra Regional Wine Show '08 and Best Riesling at Sydney Wine Show '09. Screwcap. 12% alc. **Rating** 95 **To** 2016 $28

Premium Riesling 2008 Bright, light green-straw; has greater fruit weight and intensity than Classic Dry with a mix of citrussy aromas and flavours. Perversely, I prefer the Classic Dry. Two trophies: Cool Climate Wine Show '08; top gold in its class at Sydney Wine Show '09. Screwcap. 12% alc. **Rating** 94 **To** 2016 $45

♥♥♥♥ **Premium Canberra District Cabernet Sauvignon 2006** Relatively developed colour; very savoury/earthy wine; 30 months in oak; bottling 12 months earlier might have preserved more of the varietal fruit flavour to provide better balance. Screwcap. 14% alc. **Rating** 89 **To** 2014 $52

Henley Hill Wines   ★★★☆

1 Mount Morton Road, Belgrave South, Vic 3160 (postal) **Region** Yarra Valley
T 0414 563 439 **F** (03) 9764 3675 **www**.henleyhillwines.com.au **Open** Not
Winemaker Rob Dolan, Travis Bush (Contract) **Est.** 2003 **Cases** 7000 **Vyds** 12 ha
The history of Henley Hill dates back to 1849 when Rowland Hill began growing crops in the Yarra Valley; the home was built in the 1860s by David Mitchell, Dame Nellie Melba's

father. The property adjoined Gulf Station, but when that property was sold in the 1930s the home was moved to Henley and re-erected by Clive and Hilda Hill. Clive then purchased an 80-ha property adjoining Gulf Station, completing a full circle for the origins of the Henley name. In 2003 Debbie Hill (Clive's granddaughter), Errol Campbell (Debbie's father-in-law) and Nick and Andrew Peters planted chardonnay, sauvignon blanc, pinot gris and shiraz. Errol, Nick and Andrew are long-time partners in various business ventures in the hospitality industry and property development. Exports to India.

ΨΨΨΨΨ **Yarra Valley Cabernet Sauvignon 2007** Fine red fruits, with a splash of black olive; the palate is fine, but quite firm, and some black olive complexity comes through at the finish. Screwcap. 13.5% alc. **Rating** 90 **To** 2016 $19

ΨΨΨΨ **Yarra Valley Sauvignon Blanc 2008** Very pale colour; hints of tropical fruit, with an interesting mineral edge; quite fine and linear, if just a little shy of the necessary concentration. Screwcap. 12% alc. **Rating** 89 **To** 2012 $17.50

Hennings View Vineyard ★★★☆

2562 Heathcote–Rochester Road, Cobinannin, Vic 3559 **Region** Heathcote
T (03) 5432 9266 **F** (03) 5432 9266 **Open** By appt
Winemaker Sergio Carlei (Contract) **Est.** 1998 **Cases** 500 **Vyds** 14 ha
A vineyard devoted entirely to shiraz has been established on part of a family-owned farm founded by Henning Rathjen in 1858. He first planted vines in the 1860s, and award-winning wines were made at the property throughout his lifetime. The vines were removed in the 1920s in favour of broad acre farming, but in 1998 Finlay and Darryl Rathjen (third- and fourth-generation descendants) replanted vines on the original site, and Henning Rathjen's historic cellar once again houses wine. Most of the grapes are sold, but part made by Sergio Carlei for the Hennings View label.

ΨΨΨΨΨ **Heathcote Shiraz 2006** Deeply coloured; slightly sweet and sour, as ripe black fruit stands alongside a slight herbal quality; the palate is rich and generous, with toasty oak, blue fruit and a touch of ironstone lingering on the finish. Screwcap. 14.9% alc. **Rating** 90 **To** 2016 $28

Henry Holmes Wines ★★★★☆

Gomersal Road, Tanunda, SA 5352 **Region** Barossa Valley
T (08) 8563 2059 **F** (08) 8563 2581 **www**.woodbridgefarm.com **Open** By appt
Winemaker Robin Day **Est.** 1998 **Cases** 2500 **Vyds** 31.2 ha
The Holmes family's background runs from Samuel Henry Holmes (whose parents William Henry and Penelope Jane Holmes are co-owners of the property) to Samuel Henry's great-great-grandparents, whose son (and his great-grandfather) Henry Holmes was born en route to Australia from England. A further distinction is that the property owned by the Holmes family today was first planted by the Henschke family in the 1860s. The label denotes the division of opinion between Bill and Penny (as they are known) on the merits of viticulture on the one hand and White Suffolk sheep on the other; shiraz, cabernet sauvignon, grenache, riesling and tempranillo are on one side of the property, sheep on the other (held at bay by a fence). Exports to the US.

ΨΨΨΨΨ **Barossa Valley Shiraz 2006** Light- to medium-bodied; distinctly elegant and lively; multi-spice and licorice nuances run through blackberry and plum fruit; fine tannins; very good value. Screwcap. 14% alc. **Rating** 94 **To** 2016 $25

🍃 Henry Martin Wines NR

Stonyfell Winery, Stonyfell Road, Stonyfell, SA 5066 **Region** Adelaide Hills
T (08) 8431 8293 **F** (08) 8431 8294 **www**.henrymartinwines.com **Open** By appt
Winemaker Carmine De Ieso **Est.** 1858 **Cases** NFP **Vyds** 1 ha
This is a somewhat unusual venture involving a partnership between Adelaide-based Carmine De Ieso and Kuala Lumpur-based expatriates Kym Mensforth and James Coathup. The Henry Martin name is that of the founder of Stonyfell Winery, in 1858; the De Ieso family have been

running the Drumminor Restaurant and the Stonyfell winery complex for many decades. It is hard to claim an establishment date of 1858, but Carmine De Ieso has been making Sparkling Shiraz for 20 years and maturing barrels of fortified wines. The budget-priced wines include Shiraz, Cabernet Sauvignon, Rose, Unwooded Chardonnay, Sauvignon Blanc, Late Picked Sauvignon Blanc and Sparkling Shiraz plus aged Port and Muscat. The majority of the production is exported to Malaysia and Vietnam, and also to Japan, Poland, Singapore and China.

Henschke ★★★★★

Henschke Road, Keyneton, SA 5353 **Region** Eden Valley
T (08) 8564 8223 **F** (08) 8564 8294 **www**.henschke.com.au **Open** Mon–Fri 9–4.30, Sat 9–12, public hols 10–3
Winemaker Stephen Henschke **Est.** 1868 **Cases** 40 000 **Vyds** 107 ha
Regarded as the best medium-sized red wine producer in Australia, Henschke has gone from strength to strength over the past three decades under the guidance of winemaker Stephen and viticulturist Prue Henschke. The red wines fully capitalise on the very old, low-yielding, high-quality vines and are superbly made with sensitive but positive use of new small oak: Hill of Grace is second only to Penfolds Grange as Australia's red wine icon (since 2005 sold with a screwcap). Exports to all major markets.

🍷🍷🍷🍷🍷 **Hill Of Grace 2005** Has a fragrant and expressive bouquet of plum and blackberry fruit with a strong spicy overlay, oak evident but not aggressive; the velvety, supple palate is laden with perfectly ripened black fruits and soft tannins in gentle support; has the hallmark seductive style of Hill of Grace. Shiraz. Screwcap. 14.5% alc. **Rating** 96 **To** 2025
Mount Edelstone 2006 Deep purple-crimson; the bouquet is intense and full of spicy black fruits accurately foretelling the power and purity of the palate; this is an outstanding Mount Edelstone, indeed, I cannot remember any better than this; it has the focus and structure to guarantee a 30-year future, if this is what you are after. Alas, it will long outlive me. How good will the '06 Hill of Grace be? Shiraz. Screwcap. 14% alc. **Rating** 96 **To** 2036
Julius Eden Valley Riesling 2008 A striking wine; absolutely classic aromas and flavours with a mix of lime zest, leaf and a hint of spice, all tightly interwoven. Screwcap. 12.5% alc. **Rating** 96 **To** 2023 $28
Green's Hill Lenswood Riesling 2008 Clean and crisp, with a strong structural underlay courtesy of minerally/flinty notes alongside zesty/citrussy acidity; has very good length. Screwcap. 12.5% alc. **Rating** 95 **To** 2023 $27
Keyneton Estate Euphonium 2006 Attractive medium- to full-bodied wine, with layers of predominantly black fruits garnished with spices and licorice; exemplary oak and tannin integration. Screwcap. 14.5% alc. **Rating** 95 **To** 2021 $45
Peggy's Hill Eden Valley Riesling 2008 Offers a mix of floral blossom and spice on the bouquet, moving on to a classic lime and lemon juice palate; already revealing some of its wares. Screwcap. 12.5% alc. **Rating** 94 **To** 2018 $20
Cyril Henschke Eden Valley Cabernet Sauvignon 2006 The colour is not as bright as the Mount Edelstone; both bouquet and palate have some cedary/earthy nuances and just a hint of mint; it is the length and persistence of flavour on what is a medium-bodied palate that is remarkable, aided by superfine tannins. Cabernet Sauvignon (87%)/Merlot (13%). Screwcap. 14% alc. **Rating** 94 **To** 2021

🍷🍷🍷🍷 **Coralinga Adelaide Hills Sauvignon Blanc 2008** A clean but unobtrusive bouquet, then a contrasting, lively, zesty palate with lingering citrus and redcurrant fruit; excellent balance and mouthfeel. Screwcap. 13% alc. **Rating** 93 **To** 2011 $26
Eleanor's Cottage Eden Valley Sauvignon Blanc Semillon 2008 Fresh, bright and tightly focused, with lemon zest nuances to the well-balanced palate; stylish wine with good mouthfeel. Screwcap. 12.5% alc. **Rating** 93 **To** 2011 $22.20
Littlehampton Innes Vineyard Adelaide Hills Pinot Gris 2008 Has well above average texture and structure; smooth, supple pear and apple flavours backed by good acidity; impressive length. Screwcap. 14% alc. **Rating** 93 **To** 2012 $34

Giles Lenswood Pinot Noir 2007 Tangy more than savoury entry, then lovely small red berry fruits come through strongly on the fine, lingering finish. Screwcap. 14% alc. **Rating** 93 **To** 2016 $40.70

Johann's Garden 2007 A deliciously fruited wine that waltzes away with its alcohol hidden under its skirts; two-thirds grenache, sourced from the Eden and Barossa Valleys. Screwcap. 15.5% alc. **Rating** 92 **To** 2014 $38

Hentley Farm Wines   ★★★★★

Cnr Jenke Road/Gerald Roberts Road, Seppeltsfield, SA 5355 **Region** Barossa Valley
T (08) 8333 0241 **F** (08) 8333 0246 **www**.hentleyfarm.com.au **Open** 7 days 10–5
Winemaker Andrew Quin **Est.** 1999 **Cases** 10 000 **Vyds** 22.7 ha
Keith and Alison Hentschke purchased the Hentley Farm in 1997, then an old vineyard and mixed farming property. Keith has thoroughly impressive credentials, having studied agricultural science at Roseworthy, and then wine marketing, obtaining an MBA. During the 1990s he had a senior production role with Orlando, before moving on to manage one of Australia's largest vineyard management companies, and from 2002 to '06 he worked with Nepenthe. Just under 15 ha of shiraz, 5 ha of grenache, 2 ha of cabernet sauvignon, 0.8 ha of zinfandel and 0.1 ha of viognier are now in production. The vineyard, situated among rolling hills on the banks of Greenock Creek, has red clay loam soils overlaying shattered limestone, lightly rocked slopes and little top soil. Expert handling of the '07 red wines. Exports to the US and other major markets.

ΨΨΨΨΨ The Beauty Barossa Valley Shiraz 2007 Dense purple; a fragrant bouquet and seductive medium- to full-bodied palate do justice to the name; supple blackberry, dark chocolate and mocha flavours fun through to a harmonious finish; has a small jab of viognier. Cork. 15% alc. **Rating** 94 **To** 2022 $50

The Beast Barossa Valley Shiraz 2007 Dense purple; a full-bodied wine that repels invaders, demanding to be left alone for five years or so; the black fruit, licorice, bitter chocolate, tannin and oak are in appropriate balance and the high-quality cork should allow the wine to reach maturity. 15% alc. **Rating** 94 **To** 2027 $80

ΨΨΨΨΩ Clos Otto Barossa Valley Shiraz 2006 Licorice, blackberry and prune; full-bodied, and very nearly carries the alcohol; surely better if less. Cork. 15.5% alc. **Rating** 91 **To** 2017 $120

Fools Bay Dirty Bliss Barossa Valley Grenache Shiraz 2007 A world away from confection fruit, although the tannin profile is softened by the grenache; lively spicy/earthy, light-bodied fruit flavours are unexpectedly delicious on the finish. Good value. Screwcap. 14% alc. **Rating** 90 **To** 2014 $20

Fools Bay Dusty's Desire Barossa Valley Shiraz 2007 Well balanced and constructed, with black fruits and appropriate tannin and oak support; all-purpose style, with good mouthfeel. Screwcap. 15% alc. **Rating** 90 **To** 2014 $20

ΨΨΨΨ Barossa Valley Rose 2008 Vivid light crimson; a red cherry and raspberry bouquet continues on to the well-balanced palate; fruity, but not sweet. Screwcap. 12.5% alc. **Rating** 89 **To** 2010 $23

Barossa Valley Shiraz 2007 An intense bouquet, with strong fruit and oak, the palate a medium- to full-bodied reprise of the warring components of the bouquet; far from at ease with itself. Screwcap. 15% alc. **Rating** 89 **To** 2017 $35

Fools Bay Beached Barossa Valley Shiraz Cabernet 2008 Deep crimson; attractive, richly fruited wine, ideal for barbecue/informal drinking over the next few years. Screwcap. 14.5% alc. **Rating** 88 **To** 2012 $14

Henty Estate   ★★★★

657 Hensley Park Road, Hamilton, Vic 3300 (postal) **Region** Henty
T (03) 5572 4446 **F** (03) 5572 4446 **www**.henty-estate.com.au **Open** Not
Winemaker Peter Dixon **Est.** 1991 **Cases** 1000 **Vyds** 7 ha

Peter and Glenys Dixon have hastened slowly with Henty Estate. In 1991 they began the planting of 4.5 ha of shiraz, 1 ha each of cabernet sauvignon and chardonnay, and 0.5 ha of riesling. In their words, 'we avoided the temptation to make wine until the vineyard was mature', establishing the winery in 2003. Encouraged by neighbour John Thomson, they have limited the yield to 3–4 tonnes per ha on the VSP-trained, dry-grown vineyard.

ΨΨΨΨΨ **Shiraz 2007** A vibrant bouquet, with green peppercorn and raspberry fruit; medium-bodied and refined wine, with fine tannins and acid on the finish. Screwcap. 14% alc. **Rating** 90 **To** 2014 $24

Herbert Vineyard ★★★

Bishop Road, Mount Gambier, SA 5290 **Region** Mount Gambier
T 0408 849 080 **F** (08) 8724 9512 **www**.herbertvineyard.com.au **Open** By appt
Winemaker David Herbert **Est.** 1996 **Cases** 450
David and Trudy Herbert have planted 2 ha of pinot noir, and a total of 0.4 ha of cabernet sauvignon, merlot and pinot gris. The majority of the pinot noir is sold to Foster's for sparkling wine, and the Herberts have built a two-level (mini) winery overlooking a 1600-sq metre maze planted in 2000, which is reflected in the label logo.

ΨΨΨΨ **Mount Gambier Pinot Noir 2006** Excellent clarity and hue for age; has abundant ripe fruit in a black cherry/damson plum spectrum; a subliminal touch of sweetness tends to shorten the length and finish. Screwcap. 13.1% alc. **Rating** 89 **To** 2012 $22

Heritage Estate ★★★☆

Granite Belt Drive, Cottonvale, Qld 4375 **Region** Granite Belt
T (07) 4685 2197 **F** (07) 4685 2112 **www**.heritagewines.com.au **Open** 7 days 9–5
Mt Tambourine (07) 5545 3144
Winemaker John Handy **Est.** 1992 **Cases** 5000 **Vyds** 8.75 ha
Bryce and Paddy Kassulke operate a very successful winery, showcasing their wines through a cellar door at Mt Tamborine in a converted old church, which has views over the Gold Coast hinterland, and includes a restaurant, barbecue area and art gallery. Estate plantings have been steadily expanded, now comprising chardonnay, shiraz, merlot, verdelho, cabernet sauvignon, durif and albarino, with additional varieties purchased from local growers. Heritage Estate has been a prolific award winner in various Qld wine shows, and regional tastings organised by magazines.

ΨΨΨΨΨ **Reserve Cabernet Sauvignon 2007** Deep purple colour; has good varietal expression on both bouquet and palate, with blackcurrant fruit to the fore, and well-balanced tannins and oak in support. Diam. 14.5% alc. **Rating** 91 **To** 2020

ΨΨΨΨ **Reserve Chardonnay 2007** A light- to medium-bodied wine; 13 months in new French oak was a needlessly expensive exercise, but the wine will build on its citrus and stone fruit flavours in the next few years. Diam. 13.5% alc. **Rating** 89 **To** 2014
Granite Belt Chardonnay Pinot Noir 2002 Bottle fermented, with 55 months on lees; bright straw, it has a crisp, firm palate that has not been over-sweetened after disgorgement; doesn't have quite as much length as expected, but a good wine nonetheless. Diam. 12.5% alc. **Rating** 89 **To** 2010
Semillon Sauvignon Blanc 2008 Vibrant, tangy/lemony fruit on bouquet and palate, the 50% semillon doing most of the talking. An incomprehensible decision to forsake Diam and use a synthetic cork. 12.5% alc. **Rating** 88 **To** 2009
Verdelho 2008 Well made, with a tangy/zesty quality to the fruit, and has good length. Synthetic. 13% alc. **Rating** 87 **To** 2010

Heritage Wines ★★★★★

106a Seppeltsfield Road, Marananga, SA 5355 **Region** Barossa Valley
T (08) 8562 2880 **F** (08) 8562 2692 **www**.heritagewinery.com.au **Open** Mon–Fri 10–5,
w'ends & public hols 11–5
Winemaker Stephen Hoff **Est.** 1984 **Cases** 5500 **Vyds** 8 ha
A little-known winery that deserves a far wider audience, for veteran owner/winemaker
Stephen Hoff is apt to produce some startlingly good wines. At various times the Riesling
(from old Clare Valley vines), Cabernet Sauvignon and Shiraz (now the flag-bearer) have all
excelled. Exports to the UK, the US, Thailand, Hong Kong and Malaysia.

♥♥♥♥♥ **Barossa Shiraz 2006** Good colour; a strong, robust medium- to full-bodied
shiraz right in the mainstream of the Heritage style, with abundant blackberry and
dark chocolate fruit plus vanillin oak. Traditional, but good, and carries its alcohol
without a quiver. Cork. 15% alc. **Rating** 94 **To** 2016 $25
Steve Hoff Cabernet Sauvignon 2006 A deeply coloured, potent and strongly
varietal cabernet; blackcurrant, dark chocolate and earth are all in the mix, the
tannin supple yet strongly supportive. Oh, for a screwcap to double the wine's life.
Cork. 14.4% alc. **Rating** 94 **To** 2016 $26.50

♥♥♥♥ **Barossa Semillon 2008** Generously flavoured; picked before the heat and made
without artifice or oak; as honest as they come. Screwcap. 12.2% alc. **Rating** 88
To 2012 $15

Hesketh Wine Company ★★★★

6 Blairgowrie Road, St Georges, SA 5064 **Region** Various
T 0419 003 144 **F** (08) 8344 9429 **www**.heskethwinecompany.com.au **Open** Not
Winemaker Various **Est.** 2006 **Cases** 4000
The Hesketh Wine Company is a New World version of the French Negociant Eleveur,
commonly known in Australia as a virtual winery, and owned by Jonathon Hesketh, wife
Trish and children. Jonathon spent seven years as the Global Sales & Marketing Manager
of Wirra Wirra, two and a half years as General Manager of Distinguished Vineyards in NZ
working with the Möet Hennessy wine and champagne portfolio, plus the Petaluma group,
and also had significant global responsibility for Mars Corporation over a four-year period. He
also happens to be the son of Robert Hesketh, one of the key players in the development of
many facets of the SA wine industry. The model for Hesketh Wine Company is to find wines
that best express the regions they come from and closely monitor their production, but own
neither vineyards nor a winery.

♥♥♥♥♡ **Beautiful Stranger Kremstal Gruner Veltliner 2007** A very attractive wine,
made by Bert Salomon (no stranger to Australia); in federspiel style, leaving the
mouth fresh; will age beautifully. Screwcap. 12.5% alc. **Rating** 92 **To** 2014 $25
The Protagonist Barossa Valley Shiraz 2005 Retains good colour and fruit
intensity; black cherry, plum and blackberry join with fine, ripe tannins and good
oak handling. Screwcap. 14.5% alc. **Rating** 90 **To** 2015 $25

♥♥♥♥ **Scissor Hands Clare Valley Riesling 2008** Solid citrus aromas lead logically
into a rich, full-flavoured palate; more power than finesse despite moderate alcohol.
Screwcap. 12% alc. **Rating** 89 **To** 2014 $20
Usual Suspects McLaren Vale Shiraz 2006 Fresh, light- to medium-bodied
wine, with spicy/earthy nuances finishing with balanced tannins. Screwcap.
14.5% alc. **Rating** 88 **To** 2013 $20
Thirsty Dog Coonawarra Cabernet Sauvignon 2006 An earthy regional/
varietal bouquet then a penetrating palate with pronounced acidity, possibly
over-corrected. Screwcap. 13.5% alc. **Rating** 87 **To** 2014 $20

Hewitson ★★★★★

The Old Dairy Cold Stores, 66 London Road, Mile End, SA 5031
Region Southeast Australia
T (08) 8443 6466 **F** (08) 8443 6866 **www**.hewitson.com.au **Open** By appt
Winemaker Dean Hewitson **Est.** 1996 **Cases** 22 000 **Vyds** 2.7 ha
Dean Hewitson was a winemaker at Petaluma for 10 years, during which time he managed to do three vintages in France and one in Oregon as well as undertaking his Masters at UC Davis, California. It is hardly surprising that the wines are immaculately made from a technical viewpoint. Dean has managed to source 30-year-old riesling from the Eden Valley and 70-year-old shiraz from McLaren Vale; he also makes a Barossa Valley Mourvedre from vines planted in 1853 at Rowland Flat and a Barossa Valley Shiraz and Grenache from 60-year-old vines at Tanunda. Exports to the UK, the US and other major markets.

ŶŶŶŶŶ **Old Garden Barossa Valley Mourvedre 2007** Bright and clear colour and hue; a fragrant bouquet leads into an extremely finely boned and structured palate, a quiet statement of superiority from 150-year-old vines. Screwcap. 14.5% alc. **Rating** 96 **To** 2027 $70
The Mad Hatter McLaren Vale Shiraz 2006 A single-vineyard wine with 20 months in French oak, which is counter-cultural in its elegant, medium-bodied profile and moderate alcohol; red fruits and touches of mocha and chocolate predominate. Screwcap. 14.5% alc. **Rating** 94 **To** 2016 $70
Private Cellar Barossa Valley Shiraz Mourvedre 2006 Powerful, yet very well balanced, the two varieties reacting synergistically; a mix of plum, black cherry and blackberry, with fine but persistent tannins; has swallowed 20 months in French oak; 20-year cellaring ex the label is conservative. Only available in magnum. Screwcap. 14% alc. **Rating** 94 **To** 2040 $170
Miss Harry Dry Grown & Ancient 2007 Elegant wine that is all about the textures – silk, satin and a hint of velvet – to its supple, medium-bodied palate; the flavours are of cherry and plum, the oak subtle. Grenache/Shiraz/Mourvedre. Screwcap. 14% alc. **Rating** 94 **To** 2017 $22

ŶŶŶŶŶ **Ned & Henry's Barossa Valley Shiraz 2007** Full-blooded wine with blackberry, leather and licorice aromas and flavour, along with a touch of mocha oak; good balance and structure. Screwcap. 14% alc. **Rating** 93 **To** 2017 $25
Baby Bush Barossa Valley Mourvedre 2007 Similar colour and flavour to Old Garden; this wine has bright fruits and savoury spices, but without the authority of its parent, Old Garden. Screwcap. 14.5% alc. **Rating** 92 **To** 2015 $29
LuLu Adelaide Hills Sauvignon Blanc 2008 Pleasant wine; throws off a slightly closed bouquet with a mix of passionfruit, gooseberry and apple on the palate. Screwcap. 12.5% alc. **Rating** 91 **To** 2010 $22

ŶŶŶŶ **Gun Metal Eden Valley Riesling 2008** A positive statement of region and variety, but doesn't sing on the finish and aftertaste. Screwcap. 12.5% alc. **Rating** 89 **To** 2016 $22

Hickinbotham of Dromana ★★★

194 Nepean Highway (near Wallaces Road), Dromana, Vic 3936
Region Mornington Peninsula
T (03) 5981 0355 **F** (03) 5987 0692 **www**.hickinbotham.biz **Open** 7 days 11–5
Winemaker Andrew Hickinbotham **Est.** 1981 **Cases** 4000 **Vyds** 6 ha
After a peripatetic period and a hiatus in winemaking, Hickinbotham established a permanent vineyard and winery base at Dromana. It now makes only Mornington Peninsula wines, drawing in part on estate vineyards (chardonnay, aligote, taminga, pinot noir, shiraz, cabernet sauvignon, merlot, cabernet franc and ruby cabernet), and in part on contract-grown fruit.

ŶŶŶŶ **Cabernet Sauvignon 2004** A mature, cool-grown cabernet, fined down by 26 months barrel maturation; has good length and balance, with cedary/earthy overtones to the medium-bodied palate. Screwcap. 14% alc. **Rating** 89 **To** 2014 $30

Hidden Creek ★★★

Eukey Road, Ballandean, Qld 4382 **Region** Granite Belt
T (07) 4684 1383 **www**.hiddencreek.com.au **Open** Mon & Fri 11–3, w'ends 10–4
Winemaker Jim Barnes **Est.** 1997 **Cases** 1200

A beautifully located vineyard and winery on a 1000 m-high ridge overlooking the Ballandean township and the Severn River Valley. The granite boulder–strewn hills mean that the 70-ha property only provides a little over 2 ha of vineyard, in turn divided into six different blocks. The business is owned by a group of Brisbane wine enthusiasts and Jim Barnes, who also runs a contract winemaking business as well as making the Hidden Creek wines. There are three labels: Hidden Creek, Red Bird and Rooklyn. Rooklyn is made from Granite Belt grapes, which are either of outstanding quality, unusual styles, or are emerging varieties, and have had overwhelming success in wine shows.

🍷🍷🍷🍷 **Granite Belt Tempranillo 2007** Good colour and bright blue and red berry fruits; fine, juicy and supple, without any real complexity. Screwcap. 13.5% alc. **Rating** 87 **To** 2012 $22

Highbank ★★★

Riddoch Highway, Coonawarra, SA 5263 **Region** Coonawarra
T 1800 653 311 **F** (08) 8736 3122 **www**.highbank.com.au **Open** By appt
Winemaker Dennis Vice **Est.** 1986 **Cases** 2000 **Vyds** 44 ha

Mount Gambier lecturer in viticulture Dennis Vice makes small quantities of smooth, melon-accented Chardonnay and rather more of a stylish Coonawarra Cabernet blend; they are sold through local restaurants and the cellar door, with limited Melbourne distribution. The major part of the grape production is sold. Exports to the US, Thailand, Singapore, Hong Kong and China.

🍷🍷🍷🍷 **Coonawarra 2004** Good hue for age; spicy/earthy components run parallel with sombre, savoury black fruits on the medium-bodied palate; the tannins are fine, the finish quite long. Cabernet Sauvignon/Merlot/Cabernet Franc. Cork. 13.5% alc. **Rating** 89 **To** 2014 $52

Higher Plane ★★★★☆

165 Warner Glen Road, Forest Grove, WA 6286 **Region** Margaret River
T (08) 9258 9437 **F** (08) 9755 9100 **www**.higherplanewines.com.au **Open** Not
Winemaker Mark Messenger, Kym Eyres **Est.** 1996 **Cases** 2000 **Vyds** 20.35 ha

In late 2006 Higher Plane was purchased by Roger Hill and family (of Juniper Estate), but kept as a stand-alone brand, with different distributors, etc. The Higher Plane vineyards are planted to all of the 11 key varieties, sauvignon blanc foremost, then chardonnay, semillon and cabernet sauvignon (shiraz, merlot, pinot noir, cabernet franc, malbec, petit verdot and viognier make up the rest of the plantings). Exports to Canada and Denmark.

🍷🍷🍷🍷🍷 **Margaret River Merlot 2007** Very good varietal expression, with an interplay between cassis fruit and savoury olive and spice nuances; the tannins are evident but balanced, the oak likewise. Screwcap. 14.5% alc. **Rating** 94 **To** 2015 $34

🍷🍷🍷🍷½ **South by Southwest Margaret River Cabernet Merlot 2007** An intense and focused bouquet of blackcurrant and redcurrant is faithfully reflected in the palate, which has very good texture and balance. Screwcap. 14% alc. **Rating** 92 **To** 2015 $21

🍷🍷🍷🍷 **South by Southwest Margaret River Sauvignon Blanc Semillon 2008** Crisp and clean, with some tropical fruit notes, but is lacking intensity. Screwcap. 13.5% alc. **Rating** 87 **To** 2011 $21

Hill Smith Estate

Flaxmans Valley Road, Eden Valley, SA 5235 **Region** Eden Valley
T (08) 8561 3200 **F** (08) 8561 3393 **www**.hillsmithestate.com **Open** At Yalumba
Winemaker Kevin Glastonbury **Est.** 1979 **Cases** 5000 **Vyds** 12.5 ha
This property, as it name suggests, is part of the Hill Smith Family Vineyards. It has evolved
into a sauvignon blanc specialist, with no other varieties grown, nor other wines made under
the Hill Smith Estate label.

ΨΨΨΨΨ **Eden Valley Sauvignon Blanc 2008** A lively and precise wine, with crystal
clear fruit offering a mix of citrus and gentle tropical fruit; a clean finish to the
quite long palate. Screwcap. 12% alc. **Rating** 90 **To** 2010 $19.95

Hillbillé

Blackwood Valley Estate, Balingup Road, Nannup, WA 6275 **Region** Blackwood Valley
T (08) 9481 0888 **F** (08) 9486 1899 **www**.hillbille.com **Open** W'ends & hols 10–4
Winemaker Woodlands Wines (Stuart Watson) **Est.** 1998 **Cases** 3000 **Vyds** 20 ha
Gary Bettridge has planted shiraz, cabernet sauvignon, merlot, chardonnay and semillon. The
vineyard is situated in the Blackwood Valley between Balingup and Nannup, which the RAC
describes as 'the most scenic drive in the southwest of WA'. A significant part of the grape
production is sold to other makers, but since 2003 part has been vinified for the Hillbillé label.
Exports to Japan, Singapore. and Hong Kong.

ΨΨΨΨΨ **Sauvignon Blanc Semillon 2008** Highly fragrant and floral citrus blossom
aromas; a lovely palate with a mix of lemon and grassy notes; fresh, zippy finish.
Value. Screwcap. 12.5% alc. **Rating** 90 **To** 2011 $15

ΨΨΨΨ **Merlot 2006** Light colour and body; the variety has not been compromised as
much as other reds from the vintage, retaining small red fruits. Screwcap. 12.5% alc.
Rating 87 **To** 2012 $15

Hillcrest Vineyard

31 Phillip Road, Woori Yallock, Vic 3139 **Region** Yarra Valley
T (03) 5964 6689 **F** (03) 5961 5547 **www**.hillcrestvineyard.com.au **Open** By appt
Winemaker David Bryant, Tanya Bryant, Phillip Jones (Consultant) **Est.** 1971 **Cases** 600
Vyds 16.2 ha
The small, effectively dry-grown vineyard was established by Graeme and Joy Sweet, who
ultimately sold it to David and Tanya Bryant. The pinot noir, chardonnay, merlot and
cabernet sauvignon grown on the property have always been of the highest quality and,
when Coldstream Hills was in its infancy, were particularly important resources for it. The
Bryants have developed the Hillcrest label and, under the guiding hand of Phillip Jones, are
progressively taking control of making these excellent wines. No new tastings; spring frosts
meant no wine was made in 2007, and at the time of going to press the '08 vines wines should
be available shortly after publication of this book.

Hirsch Hill Estate

2088 Melba Highway, Dixons Creek, Vic 3775 **Region** Yarra Valley
T 1300 877 781 **F** (03) 9640 0370 **www**.hirschhill.com **Open** Not
Winemaker Yering Farm (Alan Johns) **Est.** 1998 **Cases** 3500
The Hirsch family has planted a 14.5-ha vineyard to pinot noir (predominantly), cabernet
sauvignon, chardonnay, shiraz, merlot, cabernet franc, sauvignon blanc and viognier. The
vineyard is part of a larger racehorse stud, situated in a mini-valley at the northern end of the
Yarra Valley.

ΨΨΨΨ **Yarra Valley Chardonnay 2008** Fresh, delicate light-bodied style, with citrus
and nectarine fruit and a gentle touch of oak; what is there is well-balanced.
Screwcap. 12.5% alc. **Rating** 88 **To** 2013 $20

Hobbs of Barossa Ranges

Cnr Flaxman's Valley Road/Randalls Road, Angaston, SA 5353 **Region** Barossa Valley
T 0427 177 740 **F** (08) 8565 3268 **www.**hobbsvintners.com.au **Open** By appt
Winemaker Peter Schell, Chris Ringland (Consultant) **Est.** 1998 **Cases** 1100 **Vyds** 6.22 ha
Hobbs of Barossa Ranges is a high-profile, if somewhat challenging, venture of Greg and
Allison Hobbs. The estate vineyards revolve around 1 ha of shiraz planted in 1908, another ha
planted in '88, a further ha planted in '97, and, finally, 1.82 ha planted in 2004. There is also
0.4 ha each of white frontignac (1940s), semillon ('60s) and an inspired 0.6 ha of viognier ('88).
All of the wines made by Peter Schell (at Spinifex) push the envelope. The only conventionally
made wine is the Shiraz Viognier, with a production of 130 cases. Gregor, an Amarone-style
Shiraz in full-blooded table wine mode, and a quartet of dessert wines are produced by cane
cutting followed by further desiccation on racks. The Grenache comes from a Barossa floor
vineyard; the Semillon, Viognier and White Frontignac from estate-grown grapes.

ŶŶŶŶŶ **Gregor Shiraz 2006** Deeply coloured, yet bright; a complex bouquet of black
fruits, licorice, spice and cedary oak, then a very powerful palate enriched by
24 months in French oak. From ancient vines and, against all the odds, carries its
alcohol well. Cork. 16.4% alc. **Rating** 94 **To** 2020 $130
Viognier 2006 Deep gold; less luscious than the Semillon, but does have apricot
and honey varietal nuances and arguably better balance. Screwcap. 9.4% alc.
Rating 94 **To** 2012 $39
Semillon 2006 Bright, gleaming gold; intensely rich, luscious citrus and cumquat
with excellent balancing acidity. Screwcap. 8.5% alc. **Rating** 94 **To** 2012 $39

ŶŶŶŶŶ **White Frontignac 2006** Again, spicy muscat characters come through strongly,
the honeyed viscosity of the mid-palate balanced by the acidity. Screwcap. 8.5% alc.
Rating 93 **To** 2012 $39

ŶŶŶŶ **Shiraz Viognier 2006** Light red-purple; a clean, fresh and vibrant bouquet leads
into a light- to medium-bodied, fresh red berry palate; very pleasant wine, but the
price is a puzzle. Cork. 14.7% alc. **Rating** 88 **To** 2014 $110
Grenache 2007 Has retained some red in its hue; I'm far from convinced this
works with its sweet jujube fruit and acidity; its neither one thing nor half a dozen
others. Screwcap. 10.5% alc. **Rating** 88 **To** 2011 $39

Hoddles Creek Estate

505 Gembrook Road, Hoddles Creek, Vic 3139 **Region** Yarra Valley
T (03) 5967 4692 **F** (03) 5967 4692 **www.**hoddlescreekestate.com.au **Open** By appt
Winemaker Franco D'Anna **Est.** 1997 **Cases** 15 000 **Vyds** 25 ha
In 1997, the D'Anna family decided to establish a vineyard on the property that had been
in the family since 1960. The vineyards (chardonnay, pinot noir, sauvignon blanc, cabernet
sauvignon, pinot gris, merlot and pinot blanc) are hand-pruned and hand-harvested. A
300-tonne, split-level winery was completed in 2003. Son Franco is the viticulturist and
winemaker; he started to work in the family liquor store at 13, graduating to chief wine
buyer by the time he was 21, then completed a Bachelor of Commerce degree at Melbourne
University before studying viticulture at CSU. A vintage at Coldstream Hills, then consulting
help from Peter Dredge of Red Edge and Mario Marson (ex Mount Mary), has put an old
head on young shoulders. Together with his uncle Bruno and one other assistant, he is solely
responsible for the vineyard and winery. Exports to South Africa and Singapore.

ŶŶŶŶŶ **Wickhams Road Gippsland Chardonnay 2008** Yellow peach and nectarine
bouquet, with grilled nuts and spice from the toasty oak; generous and thickly
textured, the lemony acidity cleans up the finish, where lingering toasty notes from
the oak also remain. Fantastic value. Screwcap. 13% alc. **Rating** 94 **To** 2015 $14.99
Yarra Valley Chardonnay 2007 Displays the finesse and skilled winemaking
of Wickhams Road, the difference lying in the greater presence and quality
of the nectarine and stone fruit foundation. Screwcap. 13.2% alc. **Rating** 94
To 2015 $18.95

ŢŢŢŢŢ **Yarra Valley Cabernet Sauvignon 2006** Vibrant colour, and a layered, complex and dark bouquet; very silky on entry, then tightens up with a savoury backbone supported by fine tannin and refreshing acidity. Good value. Screwcap. 13% alc. **Rating** 93 **To** 2016 $18.99

Wickhams Road Yarra Valley Pinot Noir 2008 Vibrant cherry red; clean and precise cherry fruit with a touch of stemmy complexity; light-bodied, fresh and focused, with a splash of velvet to conclude; good value again. Screwcap. 13.5% alc. **Rating** 92 **To** 2012 $14.99

1er Yarra Valley Pinot Blanc 2008 The striking label will attract many, the juicy lemon, apple and stone fruit flavours no letdown; has a long palate and a strong finish. Screwcap. 12.8% alc. **Rating** 92 **To** 2013 $35

Wickhams Road Gippsland Chardonnay 2007 Elegant wine from start to finish; finely balanced stone fruit and a fine veil of oak runs through the long palate; quality at bargain basement. Screwcap. 13% alc. **Rating** 90 **To** 2013 $14.95

Hoeyfield

17 Jetty Road, Birchs Bay, Tas 7162 **Region** Southern Tasmania
T (03) 6267 4149 **F** (03) 6267 4249 **Open** By appt
Winemaker Contract **Est.** 1995 **Cases** 110 **Vyds** 0.5 ha
Richard and Jill Pringle-Jones run a postage stamp–size vineyard of 0.25 ha each of pinot noir and chardonnay, planted on a vine-by-vine basis. When they purchased Hoeyfield in 2004, plantings of chardonnay and pinot noir had spread over '98, '00, and '02; Richard and Jill added more pinot noir (the new Dijon clone 777) in '04 and '05. It is very much a weekend and holiday occupation, Richard's real job being with ABN AMRO Morgans Limited.

ŢŢŢŢŢ **D'Entrecasteaux Channel Pinot Noir 2007** Good colour, bright and clear; a fragrant bouquet and fresh, vibrant red cherry and plum fruit on the palate; excellent length. Screwcap. 13.8% alc. **Rating** 92 **To** 2014 $25

D'Entrecasteaux Channel Chardonnay 2006 Still very youthful, crisp and fresh, headed firmly to Chablis in style; has good length and finish to its mineral and citrus palate. Silver Tas Wine Show '07. Screwcap. 13.9% alc. **Rating** 90 **To** 2013 $20

ŢŢŢŢ **D'Entrecasteaux Channel Chardonnay 2008** Big flavour for an unoaked wine; intense and long, the palate spanning stone fruit and grapefruit. Screwcap. 13.3% alc. **Rating** 89 **To** 2012 $20

Hoffmann's

Ingoldby Road, McLaren Flat, SA 5171 **Region** McLaren Vale
T (08) 8383 0232 **F** (08) 8383 0232 **www**.hoffmannswine.com.au **Open** 7 days 11–5
Winemaker Hamish McGuire (Consultant) **Est.** 1996 **Cases** 2500 **Vyds** 4 ha
Peter and Anthea Hoffmann have been growing grapes (cabernet sauvignon and shiraz) at their property since 1978, and Peter has worked at various wineries in McLaren Vale since '79. Both he and Anthea have undertaken courses at the Regency TAFE Institute in Adelaide, and (in Peter's words) 'in 1996 we decided that we knew a little about winemaking and opened a small cellar door'. Exports to the UK, the US and Germany.

ŢŢŢŢŢ **McLaren Vale Shiraz 2007** Deep colour; quintessential McLaren Vale, black fruits and dark chocolate in more or less equal proportion; good mouthfeel to the medium-bodied palate, American oak working very well. Screwcap. 14.5% alc. **Rating** 92 **To** 2017 $24

McLaren Vale Merlot 2007 A well-made merlot; strongly spicy/savoury notes run through the medium-bodied palate; long palate and excellent finish. Screwcap. 13.5% alc. **Rating** 91 **To** 2014 $22

McLaren Vale Cabernet Sauvignon 2007 Medium- to full-bodied, with abundant blackberry fruit interspersed with splashes of dark chocolate; firm tannins to round off the package. Good outcome for the vintage. Screwcap. 14.5% alc. **Rating** 90 **To** 2020 $24

Hollick

Riddoch Highway, Coonawarra, SA 5263 **Region** Coonawarra
T (08) 8737 2318 **F** (08) 8737 2952 **www.**hollick.com **Open** 7 days 9–5
Winemaker Ian Hollick, Matthew Caldersmith **Est.** 1983 **Cases** 40 000 **Vyds** 80 ha
A family business owned by Ian and Wendy Hollick, and winner of many trophies (including
the most famous of all, the Jimmy Watson), its wines are well crafted and competitively
priced. The lavish cellar door and restaurant complex is one of the focal points for tourism
in Coonawarra. The Hollicks have progressively expanded their vineyard holdings: the first
is the 12-ha Neilson's Block vineyard, one of the original John Riddoch selections, but
used as a dairy farm from 1910 to '75, when the Hollicks planted cabernet sauvignon and
merlot. The second is the 80-plus ha Wilgha Vineyard, purchased in '87 with established
dry-grown cabernet sauvignon and shiraz; total area under vine is 45 ha. The last is the Red
Ridge Vineyard in Wrattonbully, where 24 ha have been planted, including trial plantings of
tempranillo and sangiovese. Exports to most major markets.

ŸŸŸŸŸ **Ravenswood Coonawarra Cabernet Sauvignon 2006** Very good, deep
crimson-purple; high-quality fruit and skilled winemaking act in tandem to
produce an exemplary cabernet; pure varietal characters show why Coonawarra
is so suited to the variety. Diam. 14% alc. **Rating** 95 **To** 2016 $80

ŸŸŸŸŸ **Bond Road Chardonnay 2007** Bright colour; most attractive peach blossom
aromas, then an elegant, lively palate with nectarine and white peach to the fore,
oak purely in support. Screwcap. 14% alc. **Rating** 93 **To** 2014 $24
The Nectar 2008 A lovely example of high but clean botrytis at work, leaving
the riesling varietal flavour unimpaired, and presenting it between perfectly
tensioned acidity on the one hand, luscious sweetness on the other. Screwcap.
10.5% alc. **Rating** 93 **To** 2017 $24
Coonawarra Sauvignon Blanc Semillon 2008 A fragrant, almost flowery,
lemon/citrus bouquet, the palate with lemony acidity underlying the gently
tropical fruit; attractive wine; 90% Sauvignon Blanc. Screwcap. 13% alc. **Rating** 91
To 2011 $22
Wilgha Coonawarra Shiraz 2006 Good, although relatively light, hue; pretty
spicy, raspberry, cherry and plum fruit is framed by French oak and gently savoury
tannins. Diam. 14.5% alc. **Rating** 91 **To** 2016 $55
Wrattonbully Shiraz 2006 Denser colour than Wilgha; the palate, like the colour,
is more powerful and concentrated, firmly in the black fruit spectrum; entirely
different style, not so different quality. Diam. 14.5% alc. **Rating** 90 **To** 2018 $24
Coonawarra Wrattonbully Shiraz Cabernet Sauvignon 2006 Bright, crystal
clear colour; supple red cherry and cassis fruit flavours run through the length of
the palate; good finish and aftertaste. Screwcap. 14% alc. **Rating** 90 **To** 2014 $22
Hollaia Wrattonbully Sangiovese Cabernet Sauvignon 2006 An interesting
50/50 blend, sangiovese sour cherry aromas leading the bouquet, cabernet filling
the palate, then both combining to provide the savoury tannins on the finish.
Screwcap. 13.2% alc. **Rating** 90 **To** 2014 $23

ŸŸŸŸ **Coonawarra Cabernet Sauvignon Merlot 2006** Reflects good growing
conditions in an elegant, medium-bodied palate, with small red and black berry
flavours throughout; does fade slightly on the finish. Screwcap. 14% alc. **Rating** 89
To 2015 $24
Coonawarra Cabernet Sauvignon 2006 Pleasing amalgam of cassis fruit,
mocha, oak and soft, ripe tannins; perhaps a little too much oak for the fruit.
Screwcap. 14% alc. **Rating** 89 **To** 2015 $28

Holm Oak

11 West Bay Road, Rowella, Tas 7270 **Region** Northern Tasmania
T (03) 6394 7577 **F** (03) 6394 7350 **www.**holmoakvineyards.com.au **Open** 7 days 11–5
Sept–June, Wed–Sun 11–4 Jun–Aug
Winemaker Rebecca Wilson **Est.** 1983 **Cases** 3500 **Vyds** 10.4 ha

Holm Oak takes its name from its grove of oak trees, planted around the beginning of the 20th century, and originally intended for the making of tennis racquets. In 2004 Ian and Robyn Wilson purchased the property. The vineyard is planted (in descending order) to pinot noir, cabernet sauvignon, riesling, chardonnay, sauvignon blanc, pinot gris, cabernet sauvignon, with small amounts of cabernet franc, merlot and arneis. In 2006 the Wilson's daughter Rebecca (with extensive winemaking experience both in Australia and California) became winemaker, and partner Tim Duffy (a viticultural agronomist) has taken over management of the vineyard. A winery was completed just in time for the 2007 vintage.

ŶŶŶŶ **Chardonnay 2008** Light-bodied; quite elegant citrus and nectarine, but not quite enough fruit weight for higher points. Screwcap. 13% alc. **Rating** 88 **To** 2012 $20
Pig & d'Pooch Moscato 2008 Cleverly made, ultimate cellar door fodder; from Riverland muscat a petit grains; sweetness balanced by acidity. Crown Seal. 6% alc. **Rating** 87 **To** 2009 $22

Home Hill

38 Nairn Street, Ranelagh, Tas 7109 **Region** Southern Tasmania
T (03) 6264 1200 **F** (03) 6264 1069 **www**.homehillwines.com.au **Open** 7 days 10–5
Winemaker Peter Dunbavan **Est.** 1994 **Cases** 3000
Terry and Rosemary Bennett planted their first 0.5 ha of vines in 1994 on gentle slopes in the beautiful Huon Valley. Between 1994 and '99 the plantings were increased to 3 ha of pinot noir, 1.5 ha chardonnay and 0.5 ha sylvaner. Home Hill has had great success with its exemplary Pinot Noir, winning the pinot noir trophy in the Tri Nations '07 challenge between Australia, NZ and South Africa, but this is by no means the only success.

ŶŶŶŶŶ **Sauvignon Blanc 2008** Fragrant and aromatic; delicious array of citrus, passionfruit and tropical; good length helped by a touch of CO_2. **Rating** 94 **To** 2012

ŶŶŶŶŶ **Kelly's Reserve Chardonnay 2007** Elegant wine with very good line, length and balance; the nectarine fruit is still fresh, the oak well integrated. **Rating** 93 **To** 2014

ŶŶŶŶ **White Label Pinot Noir 2008** Good hue; some spicy aromas to the lively red cherry/plum fruit; fades lightly on the finish. **Rating** 88 **To** 2013

Honey Moon Vineyard

PO Box 544, Echunga SA 5153 **Region** Adelaide Hills
T 0419 862 103 **F** (08) 8388 8384 **www**.honeymoonvineyard.com.au **Open** Not
Winemaker Jane Bromley, Hylton McLean **Est.** 2005 **Cases** 500 **Vyds** 0.8 ha
Jane Bromley and Hylton McLean planted 0.4 ha each of pinot noir (clones 777, 114 and 115) and shiraz (selected from two old vineyards known for their spicy fruit flavours) in 2003. The moon is a striking feature in the landscape, particularly at harvest time when, as a full moon, it appears as a dollop of rich honey in the sky – hence the name. The first vintage was 2005, but Jane has been making wine since '01, with a particular interest in Champagne, while Hylton is a winemaker, wine science researcher and wine educator with over 20 years experience. The Chardonnay is made from purchased grapes.

ŶŶŶŶŶ **Adelaide Hills Pinot Noir 2007** Complex fruit aromas and flavours range through plum, black cherry and warm spices, the texture tightening nicely on the back-palate and finish; the aftertaste lingers for some time, continuing to impress. Screwcap. 13.5% alc. **Rating** 94 **To** 2013 $33
Vintage Port 2007 Great colour, deep purple-crimson; very intense wine, with high-quality shiraz and good spirit in a markedly low baumé; with spicy notes to close. Diam. 18% alc. **Rating** 94 **To** 2017 $30

ŶŶŶŶŶ **Adelaide Hills Shiraz 2007** A very well made juicy, spicy wine; great thrust to the light- to medium-bodied palate with small red and black berry fruits, quality French oak and fine tannins. Screwcap. 13.5% alc. **Rating** 93 **To** 2017 $27

Adelaide Hills Chardonnay 2008 Bright straw-green; elegant, finely structured wine with nectarine and melon fruit cradled in subtle French oak; a classic example of winemaking restraint. Screwcap. 13.5% alc. **Rating** 92 **To** 2014 $22

Honeytree Estate ★★★★

16 Gillards Road, Pokolbin, NSW 2321 **Region** Lower Hunter Valley
T (02) 4998 7693 **www.**honeytreewines.com **Open** Wed–Fri 11–4, w'ends 10–5
Winemaker Monarch Winemaking Services **Est.** 1970 **Cases** 1200 **Vyds** 9.8 ha
The Honeytree Estate vineyard was first planted in 1970 and for a period of time wines were produced. It then disappeared, but the vineyard has since been revived by Dutch-born Henk Strengers and family. The vineyard includes semillon, cabernet sauvignon, shiraz and a little clairette; known in the Hunter Valley as blanquette, it has been in existence there for well over a century. Jancis Robinson comments that the wine 'tends to be very high in alcohol, a little low in acid and to oxidise dangerously fast', but in a sign of the times, the first Honeytree Clairette sold out so quickly (in four weeks) that 2.3 ha of vineyard has been grafted over to clairette. Exports to The Netherlands.

🍷🍷🍷🍷🍷 **Paul Alexander Old Vines Hunter Valley Shiraz 2007** Bright colour; a concentrated black fruit bouquet with oak and a touch of mineral; the palate shows firm tannins, with the fruit balancing the savoury finish with ease. Screwcap. 13.2% alc. **Rating** 93 **To** 2015 $25
Veronica Hunter Valley Semillon 2007 The first signs of development to the toasty bouquet, with lemon fruit and straw aromas; the palate is rich, with cleansing acid on the finish; a forward style, perhaps, but has another three years in front of it. Screwcap. 11.2% alc. **Rating** 90 **To** 2013 $18

Hope Estate ★★★★

2213 Broke Road, Pokolbin, NSW 2320 **Region** Lower Hunter Valley
T (02) 4993 3555 **F** (02) 4993 3556 **www.**hopeestate.com.au **Open** 7 days 10–5
Winemaker James Campkin **Est.** 1996 **Cases** 40 000 **Vyds** 91.05 ha
Hope Estate has, in the manner of a hermit crab, cast off its older, smaller shell, and moved into a resplendent new home. New in the sense for Hope Estate, for it is in fact the former Rothbury Estate winery. The timing was serendipitous; the giant miner Xstrata found a rich coal seam under the Saxonvale winery previously owned by Michael Hope, and made an offer he couldn't refuse. It will be interesting to watch the future development of Hope Estate, made more complex by the acquisition of quality vineyards in WA. Plantings are, in descending order, shiraz, merlot, chardonnay, verdelho and semillon. Exports to the UK, the US and other major markets.

🍷🍷🍷🍷🍷 **The Ripper Shiraz 2007** Bright purple hue; extremely potent and intense, with black fruits, licorice, spice and bitter chocolate all intermingling; sure to develop very well if given time. Screwcap. 14.5% alc. **Rating** 92 **To** 2020 $22
Shiraz Malbec 2006 Some spicy/savoury nuances to the red fruits on the bouquet and light- to medium-bodied palate alike; a fresh and lively cool-grown wine. Screwcap. 13.5% alc. **Rating** 91 **To** 2020 $38
Cabernet Sauvignon 2006 Good colour; savoury cool-grown, medium-bodied wine; cassis and black fruits are interwoven with ripe, fine tannins; good oak balance and integration. Screwcap. 13.5% alc. **Rating** 91 **To** 2016 $38

🍷🍷🍷🍷 **Hunter Valley Chardonnay 2008** Has considerable power and thrust to the complex palate with gently sweet stone fruit and melon balanced by good acidity. Worth cellaring for a few years. Screwcap. 13% alc. **Rating** 89 **To** 2014 $18
Hunter Valley Shiraz 2008 Good hue; regional earthy/leathery nuances on bouquet and palate alike, with a black fruit mainframe; will improve with cellaring. Screwcap. 13% alc. **Rating** 89 **To** 2017 $18
The Cracker Cabernet Merlot 2007 Good colour; an as yet unintegrated blend of sweet cassis fruit, oak and tannins; does have the makings of a good wine. Screwcap. 14% alc. **Rating** 88 **To** 2015 $22

Horlin-Smith Wines/Ardent Estates   NR

170 Commercial Road, Salisbury, SA 5108 **Region** McLaren Vale/Adelaide Hills
T (08) 8258 1385 **F** (08) 8281 2486 **www**.horlin-smith.com.au **Open** Not
Winemaker Anthony Horlin-Smith **Est.** 2002 **Cases** 2500 **Vyds** 1 ha
Ardent Estates, owned by Horlin-Smith Wines, is the venture of Donald and Barbara Horlin-Smith, well known in the SA wine trade for many decades. Sons Robert and Anthony are also involved in the business; Anthony as winemaker, Robert as sales manager. The wines come from two regions: Shiraz and Cabernet Sauvignon from McLaren Vale; and Chardonnay, Sauvignon Blanc, Pinot Noir and Cabernet Franc from the Adelaide Hills. Within that split there are three Reserve wines made in limited quantities: Shiraz, Cabernet Sauvignon and Barrel Fermented Chardonnay. Exports to Canada.

Horvat Estate

2444 Ararat-St Arnaud Rd, Landsborough, Vic 3384 **Region** Pyrenees
T (03) 5356 9208 **F** (03) 5356 9208 **www**.wineisa4letterword.com **Open** 7 days 10–5
Winemaker Andrew Horvat, Gabriel Horvat **Est.** 1995 **Cases** 4000 **Vyds** 4.7 ha
The Horvat family (including Janet, Andrew and Gabriel) began developing their shiraz vineyard in 1995, supplementing production with contract-grown grapes. The wines are made using traditional methods and ideas, deriving in part from the family's Croatian background. Exports to China.

ＹＹＹＹ **Premium Family Reserve Pyrenees Shiraz 2006** Cool red fruit and a savoury dried leather edge; medium-bodied with a briny quality that sits well with the fruit on offer; fine acid and tannin in balance with the fruit. Screwcap. 13.4% alc. **Rating** 89 **To** 2015 $37

Houghton

Dale Road, Middle Swan, WA 6065 **Region** Swan Valley
T (08) 9274 9540 **F** (08) 9274 5372 **www**.houghton-wines.com.au **Open** 7 days 10–5
Winemaker Robert Bowen **Est.** 1836 **Cases** NFP
The 5-star rating was once partially justified by Houghton White Burgundy (now called White Classic), one of Australia's largest selling white wines: it is almost entirely consumed within days of purchase, but is superlative with seven or so years' bottle age. The Jack Mann, Gladstones Shiraz, Houghton Reserve Shiraz, the Margaret River reds, Frankland Riesling and the more recent Wisdom range are all of the highest quality, and simply serve to reinforce the rating. To borrow a saying of the late Jack Mann, 'There are no bad wines here.' Exports to all major markets.

ＹＹＹＹＹ **Wisdom Frankland River Cabernet Sauvignon 2004** Still remarkably youthful and fresh; has an array of red and black fruit aromas and flavours on an elegant palate, oak and tannins seamlessly interwoven. Cork. 14% alc. **Rating** 96 **To** 2014 $28.50
Gladstones Margaret River Cabernet Sauvignon 2003 Good colour; an imposing and powerful wine that nonetheless has first-class balance and great length, the tannins supporting cassis-accented fruit. Eight trophies. Cork. 14% alc. **Rating** 96 **To** 2018 $69
Wisdom Frankland River Riesling 2008 Intriguing flowery blossom aromas; a deceptively delicate opening stanza leads into a palate that gains velocity through to the explosive finish and aftertaste; 38-year-old vines. Screwcap. 12.5% alc. **Rating** 95 **To** 2018 $28.50
Wisdom Pemberton Chardonnay 2008 Deeply fruited with grapefruit and a healthy dose of well-handled toasty oak; rich on entry, there is a generous array of ripe stone fruit on the palate; the fruit tightens up on the finish; time will see this wine come into full flower. Screwcap. 13.8% alc. **Rating** 95 **To** 2015 $32

Wisdom Pemberton Chardonnay 2007 A complete chardonnay; great depth and power, yet there is an elegant restraint to the long and even palate; ample levels of pure grapefruit flavour are framed by grilled nuts and cleansing acidity. Gold WA Wine Show '08, multiple trophies Sydney Wine Show '08. Screwcap. 13.5% alc. **Rating** 95 **To** 2017 $28.50

Wisdom Frankland River Shiraz 2005 Like so many of the best, has very good colour and clarity; rich and complete, oak evident but very well integrated; plum, cherry and blackberry. Gold WA Wine Show '08. Screwcap. 13.9% alc. **Rating** 95 **To** 2020 $32

Crofters Great Southern Cabernet Malbec 2007 Vivid purple hue; lovely fruit concentration and aromatic profile; spiced loganberry and cassis fruit, well-handled oak plays a supporting role; the palate is fleshy and accessible, with a lively line of acidity running through its core; very long, fine and harmonious. Great value. Screwcap. 14% alc. **Rating** 95 **To** 2018 $30

Wisdom Pemberton Sauvignon Blanc 2008 Has a vibrantly crisp, fresh and spotlessly clean bouquet; the precisely focused and long palate provides more of the passionfruit and herbal notes promised by the bouquet. Screwcap. 13% alc. **Rating** 94 **To** 2012 $28.50

Wisdom Pemberton Sauvignon Blanc 2007 Fragrant and pure, and as fresh as a daisy; tropical fruit balanced by more herbaceous components and lively acidity; three deserved gold medals (Adelaide, Brisbane and Melbourne '07). Screwcap. 13% alc. **Rating** 94 **To** 2010 $28.50

Museum Release White Classic 1999 Glowing green-gold; plus ça change; Houghton was doing these back releases 10 years ago with similarly successful outcomes; the combination of crisp freshness and flavour is the reason why this wine has three gold medals to its credit. Cork. 13% alc. **Rating** 94 **To** 2015 $32

Crofters Great Southern Cabernet Malbec 2005 Not deep in colour, but has delicious cassis and mulberry fruit in a supple, medium-bodied frame; golds Mount Barker, Perth and National Wine Shows '07. Drink sooner than later. Cork. 14% alc. **Rating** 94 **To** 2013 $30

Wisdom Pemberton Chardonnay Pinot Noir 2004 Distinctive and unusual aromas described by Houghton as toasty and button mushroom; delicate, precisely focused citrus palate, with great length and balance. Cork. 12.5% alc. **Rating** 94 **To** 2010 $32

Museum Release Sparkling Shiraz 2001 A high-flavoured wine that spent two years in oak, then four years on yeast lees; offers licorice, dark chocolate, spice and black fruits on a long, balanced palate. A bargain. Cork. 14% alc. **Rating** 94 **To** 2015 $32

ΨΨΨΨΨ **Houghton Stripe Cabernet Sauvignon 2007** Bright colour; vibrant cassis fruit, cedar and an attractive floral note; accessible, but also quite tightly wound, with real poise and power for such an inexpensive wine; bargain. Screwcap. 14% alc. **Rating** 93 **To** 2016 $14

Wisdom Pemberton Chardonnay Pinot Noir 2005 A tightly framed wine with a strong minerally streak binding the stone fruit and citrus flavours into a seamless line; bottle fermented. Cork. 12.5% alc. **Rating** 93 **To** 2015 $32

Shiraz 2007 Vibrant colour; quite perfumed and attractive, with red and plum fruit and a touch of spice; very juicy but slightly darker on the palate, with good weight, and generous levels of fruit; fine acid to conclude; terrific value. Cork. **Rating** 92 **To** 2014 $14

The Bandit Shiraz Tempranillo 2007 Strong crimson-purple; rich and complex fruit, but not jammy or dead; black cherry/blackberry/mocha flavours; very good tannins. Screwcap. 14% alc. **Rating** 91 **To** 2012 $19.95

Wisdom Frankland River Shiraz 2004 A savoury style, with red fruits, and notes of fresh herb and spice; a little simple on the finish. Cork. 14% alc. **Rating** 90 **To** 2013 $28.50

Wisdom Frankland River Cabernet Sauvignon 2005 More developed than some; a complex, savoury style; threatening to dry out on the finish. Gold WA Wine Show '08. Screwcap. 13.7% alc. **Rating** 90 **To** 2012 $32

Howard Park   ★★★★★

Miamup Road, Cowaramup, WA 6284 **Region** Margaret River/Denmark
T (08) 9756 5200 **F** (08) 9756 5222 **www.**howardparkwines.com.au **Open** 7 days 10–5
Winemaker Tony Davis, Genevieve Stols **Est.** 1986 **Cases** NFP
In the wake of its acquisition by the Burch family and the construction of a large state-of-
the-art winery at Denmark, a capacious cellar door (incorporating Feng Shui principles) has
opened in the Margaret River, where there are also significant estate plantings. The Margaret
River flagships are the Leston Shiraz and Leston Cabernet Sauvignon, but the Margaret River
vineyards routinely contribute to all the wines in the range, from multi-region MadFish at the
bottom, to the icon Cabernet Sauvignon Merlot at the top. Howard Park also operates a cellar
door at Scotsdale Road, Denmark (7 days 10–4). Exports to all major markets.

ΨΨΨΨΨ **Sauvignon Blanc 2008** A vibrant wine from start to finish, with a mix of herbal,
citrus and mineral aromas and flavours, the excellent mouthfeel aided by the
texture derived from partial barrel ferment; lingering finish. Gold WA Wine Show
'08 Screwcap. 12.5% alc. **Rating** 95 **To** 2010 $25
Scotsdale Great Southern Cabernet Sauvignon 2007 Deep, dark and
inky; a complex black olive bouquet, with a very rich, powerful and heady mix of
cassis, cedar and a little violet thrown in for good measure; the oak merely plays
a supporting role; generous, firm and very long. Screwcap. 14% alc. **Rating** 95
To 2018 $40
Abercrombie Cabernet Sauvignon 2005 A complex offering with an
amalgam of red and black fruits, and plenty of cedar and black olive add to the
picture; the palate is full-bodied, but not heavy, and exhibits plenty of enticing
sweet fruit backed up by seriously fine tannins; very long and quite profound.
Definitely a cerebral cabernet. Screwcap. 14% alc. **Rating** 95 **To** 2025 $95
Chardonnay 2008 Bright straw-green; charged with stone fruit, melon
and citrus flavours; barrel ferment inputs are also very much part of the wine.
Screwcap. 13% alc. **Rating** 94 **To** 2016 $40
Chardonnay 2007 A fine citrus-dominant style, with lemon, nectarine and a
little spice from the oak; quite fine on the palate, with underlying power that
really drives through to the finish; very even and harmonious. Screwcap. 13.5% alc.
Rating 94 **To** 2017 $38
Leston Margaret River Shiraz 2007 Deep colour; alluring blackberry bouquet
filled with Asian spice and a mere suggestion of oak; the palate is fleshy, ample
levels of red fruit provide brightness to the fine-grained and quite slippery tannins;
lovely balance. Screwcap. 14.5% alc. **Rating** 94 **To** 2015 $40
MadFish Gold Turtle Shiraz 2007 Good colour; eloquent bouquet of spice,
pepper, black cherry and plum fruit; the medium-bodied palate provides more of
the same flavours, supported by fine tannins and oak; the touch of viognier has
worked well. Screwcap. 14% alc. **Rating** 94 **To** 2020 $27
Leston Margaret River Cabernet Sauvignon 2007 A strong varietal cassis
bouquet, a slight leafy note adding an attractive element; very lively on the palate,
with a juicy core of fruit and lovely restrained power; textbook style. Screwcap.
14% alc. **Rating** 94 **To** 2016 $40
Leston Margaret River Cabernet Sauvignon 2006 Good colour; aromas of
blackcurrant, leaf and cedar on the bouquet; quality oak continues to underpin
the palate, which has attractive cassis/blackcurrant fruit. Screwcap. 14.5% alc.
Rating 94 **To** 2015 $40

ΨΨΨΨΨ **MadFish Gold Turtle Chardonnay 2008** Light green-straw; crisp and bright,
more significantly fruit-driven than the Howard Park Chardonnay, although there
is a barrel ferment oak contribution. Screwcap. 13.5% alc. **Rating** 93 **To** 2015 $27
**MadFish Premium Red Cabernet Sauvignon Merlot Cabernet Franc
2007** A seductive and appealing delivery of juicy fruit and a little mineral
complexity; plenty of flavour, without too much complexity or winemaking to
cloud the fruit; bright, clean and focused. Value. Screwcap. 14.5% alc. **Rating** 92
To 2014 $19

MadFish Gold Turtle Chardonnay 2007 Plenty of depth and complexity; grapefruit and nectarine on the bouquet; rich on the palate with a light coating of spice from the oak, the finish is even and generous. Screwcap. 13.5% alc. **Rating** 92 **To** 2015 $25

MadFish Premium Red Cabernet Sauvignon Merlot Cabernet Franc 2006 An elegant wine showing clearly defined cabernet aromatics; lovely fine-grained tannins flow through on to a long, fine and slightly savoury finish. Screwcap. 14.5% alc. **Rating** 92 **To** 2013 $19

MadFish Gold Turtle Pinot Noir 2008 Bright, light crimson; has abundant, supple and smooth red fruit flavours that swell on the finish. Mount Barker. Screwcap. 14% alc. **Rating** 90 **To** 2014 $27

Scotsdale Great Southern Shiraz 2007 Blackberry and mocha bouquet with a touch of tar; the palate is quite bright with focused acidity, dark fruits and a slight savoury twist to the finish. Screwcap. 14.5% alc. **Rating** 90 **To** 2014 $40

Howard Vineyard   ★★★★

Lot 1, Bald Hills Road, Nairne, SA 5252 **Region** Adelaide Hills
T (08) 8188 0495 **F** (08) 8388 0623 **www**.howardvineyard.com **Open** Mon–Thurs 11–4, Fri 11–8 & w'ends 11–5
Winemaker Ian Northcott, Mark Swann, Michael Sykes **Est.** 2005 **Cases** 3500 **Vyds** 61 ha
This venture began in the late 1990s with the establishment of two vineyards at different locations in the Adelaide Hills. The Schoenthal Vineyard near Lobethal, at an elevation of 440–500 m, is planted primarily to sauvignon blanc and chardonnay, with smaller amounts of pinot noir and pinot gris. The Howard Vineyard is at a lower elevation, and the slightly warmer site has been planted (in descending order) to sauvignon blanc, chardonnay, semillon, cabernet sauvignon, shiraz, viognier and cabernet franc. The substantial quantities of grapes not required for the Howard Vineyard label are sold to other winemakers.

ΨΨΨΨΨ **Adelaide Hills Cabernet Franc 2005** Lifted and floral bouquet, with a gentle hint of spice; the palate is generous on entry, but tightens gracefully to conclude with an even-handed level of red fruit on the finish. Cork. 14.5% alc. **Rating** 93 **To** 2012 $28

Adelaide Hills Botrytis Semillon 2006 Bright colour; lifted, with fresh pineapple and apricot on the bouquet; the palate shows purity, and just a touch of bitterness providing freshness to the finish. Screwcap. 12.5% alc. **Rating** 90 **To** 2012 $16.50

Howards Lane Vineyard   ★★★

Howards Lane, Welby, Mittagong, NSW 2575 **Region** Southern Highlands
T (02) 4872 1971 **www**.howardslane.com.au **Open** 7 days 10–5
Winemaker Michelle Crockett (Contract) **Est.** 1991 **Cases** 500 **Vyds** 3.15 ha
Tony and Mary Betteridge migrated to Australia in 2002 with the dual objectives of finding an attractive place to live and a worthwhile occupation for their retirement. They say 'The beautiful view we chose came with the vineyard, thus determining our occupation. Within a year we had mastered the tractor, pruned our first vines, chosen a name, logo and label … planted a second vineyard, built a rustic cellar door, and added considerably more knowledge of wine culture to our limited experience of simply enjoying Cape (South African) wines.'

ΨΨΨΨ **Southern Highlands Sauvignon Blanc Chardonnay 2008** Juicy and fresh, with berries and a touch of spice; quite dry, yet with an attractive core of sweet, juicy fruit that shows good persistence; a little grip on the finish works well. Screwcap. 11.2% alc. **Rating** 89 **To** 2011 $20

Hugh Hamilton

McMurtrie Road, McLaren Vale, SA 5171 **Region** McLaren Vale
T (08) 8323 8689 **F** (08) 8323 9488 **www**.hughhamiltonwines.com.au **Open** Mon–Fri
10–5.30, w'ends & public hols 11–5.30
Winemaker Peter Leske **Est.** 1991 **Cases** 30 000 **Vyds** 30 ha
Hugh Hamilton is the fifth generation of the famous Hamilton family, who first planted
vineyards at Glenelg in 1837. A self-confessed black sheep of the family, Hugh embraces
non- mainstream varieties such as sangiovese, tempranillo, petit verdot and viognier, and is
one of only a few growing saperavi. Production comes from estate plantings, which includes
the original Church Block, home to McLaren Vale's oldest chardonnay vines, and a vineyard
in Blewitt Springs of 85-year-old shiraz and 65-year-old cabernet sauvignon. The irreverent
black sheep packaging was the inspiration of daughter Mary (CEO). The cellar door is lined
with the original jarrah from Vat 15 from the historic Hamilton's Ewell winery, the largest
wooden vat ever built in the southern hemisphere. Exports to the UK, the US and other
major markets.

ΨΨΨΨΨ **The Rascal McLaren Vale Shiraz 2006** Deep colour; has abundant black fruits
and dark chocolate; inexplicably, but happily, doesn't show any heat from the high
alcohol, simply a twist of spice. Screwcap. 16% alc. **Rating** 92 **To** 2020 $24.50
The Scoundrel McLaren Vale Tempranillo 2006 An interesting suite of
aromas and flavours that are a sombre backdrop to more vibrant cherry and
plum fruit centre stage; the mouthfeel, too, is good. Cork. 14.5% alc. **Rating** 92
To 2015 $24.50
Jekyll & Hyde McLaren Vale Shiraz Viognier 2007 You might pick the
co-fermented viognier, but never guess it is a high 7% contribution, for the wine
has a burly texture and savoury dark fruits. Described (correctly) as bipolar on the
back label. Cork. 15.5% alc. **Rating** 91 **To** 2022 $45
The Villain McLaren Vale Cabernet Sauvignon 2006 Deep, dense colour; it's
far from clear why it was necessary to burden cabernet with this amount of alcohol,
for there is savoury blackcurrant fruit to burn (so to speak). A potentially great wine
allowed to partly lose its way. Screwcap. 15.5% alc. **Rating** 90 **To** 2020 $24.50

ΨΨΨΨ **The Mongrel 2007** An offspring of two Spaniards (Sangiovese/Tempranillo),
the flavours in a red band spectrum; the tannins are fine, and there is no bitterness.
Screwcap. 14.5% alc. **Rating** 88 **To** 2013 $19.50
The Odd Ball McLaren Vale Saperavi 2006 As befits the variety, dense,
impenetrable colour; despite the very high alcohol, shares a lack of mid-palate
flavour with chambourcin and – sometimes – durif. A Russian variety, the name
means 'dryer', and 5% of this would fix up any colour deficiency. Dyed cork
prevents a longer estimated life span. 16% alc. **Rating** 88 **To** 2016 $39
The Loose Cannon McLaren Vale Viognier 2008 Early picking; a citrussy
component aids the mouthfeel, but not the varietal expression. Nonetheless, better
than some. Screwcap. 14% alc. **Rating** 87 **To** 2010 $19.50

Hugo

Elliott Road, McLaren Flat, SA 5171 **Region** McLaren Vale
T (08) 8383 0098 **F** (08) 8383 0446 **www**.hugowines.com.au **Open** Mon–Fri 9.30–5,
Sat 12–5, Sun 10.30–5
Winemaker John Hugo **Est.** 1982 **Cases** 10 000 **Vyds** 29.9 ha
A winery that came from relative obscurity to prominence in the late 1980s with some lovely
ripe, sweet reds, which, while strongly American oak-influenced, were quite outstanding.
Has picked up the pace again after a dull period in the mid-1990s. There are almost 30 ha
of estate plantings, with part of the grape production sold to others. Exports to the UK, the
US and Canada.

ΨΨΨΨΨ **Reserve McLaren Vale Shiraz 2006** Good colour; fragrant black fruits and
quality oak (with some barrel ferment characters) on the bouquet lead into a very
well-balanced palate; perfectly ripened fruit and good length. Screwcap. 14.5% alc.
Rating 94 **To** 2021 $38

♀♀♀♀♀ **Reserve McLaren Vale Cabernet Sauvignon 2006** Excellent focus, balance and intensity to the strong blackcurrant fruit, French oak in the background of a long finish. Screwcap. 14% alc. **Rating** 93 **To** 2026 $38

♀♀♀♀ **McLaren Vale Cabernet Sauvignon 2006** Medium-bodied wine with varietal expression enhanced by the vintage; good balance. Screwcap. 14% alc. **Rating** 89 **To** 2016 $22.50
McLaren Vale Shiraz 2006 The light-bodied palate is counter-cultural for McLaren Vale, and none the worse for that; fresh spicy fruit, restrained alcohol and vanilla oak define the wine. Screwcap. 14.5% alc. **Rating** 88 **To** 2014 $23

Humbug Reach Vineyard ★★★★

72 Nobelius Drive, Legana, Tas, 7277 **Region** Northern Tasmania
T (03) 6330 2875 **F** (03) 6330 2739 **www**.humbugreach.com.au **Open** Not
Winemaker Paul McShane, Guy Wagner **Est.** 1988 **Cases** 400 **Vyds** 1 ha
The Humbug Reach Vineyard was established in the late 1980s on the banks of the Tamar River with plantings of pinot noir; riesling and chardonnay followed. It has been owned by Paul and Sally McShane since 1999, who proudly tend the 5000 or so vines on the property. After frost decimated the 2007 vintage, Sally and Paul, wanting to become a bit involved in winemaking, brought the process closer to home, with Guy Wagner making the Riesling and Chardonnay, Paul making the Pinot Noir. The 2008 vintage wines will become progressively available throughout '09 and into '10.

♀♀♀♀♀ **Riesling 2008** Clean and gently aromatic; ripe citrus/apple fruit on the bouquet and palate; balance and line good. Screwcap. 11.7% alc. **Rating** 90 **To** 2016 $23
Chardonnay 2008 Oak plays a major role on both bouquet and palate, but there is also good nectarine and citrus fruit on the long palate. Screwcap. 13.9% alc. **Rating** 90 **To** 2013 $32

Hungerford Hill ★★★★☆

1 Broke Road, Pokolbin, NSW 2320 **Region** Lower Hunter Valley
T 1800 187 666 **F** (02) 4998 7375 **www**.hungerfordhill.com.au **Open** 7 days 10–5
Winemaker Phillip John, Andrew Thomas **Est.** 1967 **Cases** 50 000 **Vyds** 5 ha
Hungerford Hill, sold by Southcorp to the Kirby family in 2002, has emerged with its home base at the impressive winery previously known as One Broke Road. The development of the One Broke Road complex proved wildly uneconomic, and the rationalisation process has resulted in Hungerford Hill becoming the sole owner. The quality of the wines has seen production soar from 20 000 cases to 50 000 cases, reversing the pattern under prior Southcorp ownership. As the notes indicate, Hungerford Hill now focuses its attention on Tumbarumba and the Hunter Valley, with some wines coming from the Hilltops region. Exports to all major markets.

♀♀♀♀♀ **Hunter Valley Semillon 2008** Incisive herb, grass and lemon aromas and flavours linger on the very long palate and aftertaste; seafood now, chicken in 10 years. Screwcap. 10% alc. **Rating** 94 **To** 2023 $25

♀♀♀♀♀ **Tumbarumba Chardonnay 2008** Tangy, elegant style with grapefruit and white peach flavours running through to a long finish sustained by good acidity and seamless French oak. Screwcap. 13% alc. **Rating** 93 **To** 2015 $30
Tumbarumba Chardonnay 2007 Lively, fragrant bouquet heralding the seamless fruit and oak of the palate; citrussy acidity underwrites the length. Screwcap. 13% alc. **Rating** 93 **To** 2012 $30
Dalliance Pinot Noir Chardonnay 2004 A very attractive and harmonious wine, with stone fruit and bready/yeasty characters intermingling on the long, rich palate. Cork. 12.5% alc. **Rating** 93 **To** 2012 $30
Tumbarumba Pinot Noir 2007 Has considerable intensity, with a mix of cherry, plum and anise/spice supported by fine, gently savoury tannins. Screwcap. 13% alc. **Rating** 92 **To** 2013 $30

Epic Hunter Valley Shiraz 2006 A bottle of epic proportions sets the scene, I suppose, although the wine is no more than medium-bodied; an elegant regional shiraz, with spicy notes to the predominantly red cherry fruits. Screwcap. 14.5% alc. **Rating** 91 **To** 2016 $75

ΨΨΨΨ **Tumbarumba Sauvignon Blanc 2008** Delicate and fresh, with notes of passionfruit and gooseberry, fermentation in used French oak adding more to texture than flavour; a hint of sweetness somewhere in the mix. Screwcap. 12% alc. **Rating** 89 **To** 2010 $25

FishCage Sauvignon Blanc Semillon 2008 Exceedingly pale; grassy herbal citrus flavours are in a semillon spectrum, although there are background touches of gooseberry. Screwcap. 12.5% alc. **Rating** 88 **To** 2011 $16.50

FishCage Shiraz Viognier 2007 Light- to medium-bodied, with pleasant and lively red fruits on a well-balanced palate; the viognier influence is evident but subtle. Screwcap. 14.5% alc. **Rating** 88 **To** 2013 $16.50

Huntington Estate   ★★★★☆

Cassilis Road, Mudgee, NSW 2850 **Region** Mudgee
T 1800 995 931 **F** (02) 6373 3730 **www.**huntingtonestate.com.au **Open** Mon–Sat 10–5, Sun & public hols 10–4
Winemaker Tim Stevens **Est.** 1969 **Cases** 20 000 **Vyds** 41.38 ha
Bob and Wendy Roberts invested a lifetime in Huntington Estate, joined in more recent years by daughter Susie as winemaker. When the time came to sell, it was to next-door neighbour Tim Stevens of Abercorn. The sale included the 2003–05 vintages, which are being progressively released over '08 and '09. Stevens has deliberately remained faithful to the slightly rustic, traditional ageing style of Huntington, picking up from the '06 vintage. Another element of continuity is the music festival held at the winery each November. Transition issues have been overcome, and Huntington Estate is now headed back towards its pre-eminent position in Mudgee.

ΨΨΨΨΨ **Special Reserve Shiraz 2005** Good colour; attractive black fruit and vanillin oak aromas foreshadow a wine with excellent red and black fruit, flavours as the driver of the palate, tannins and oak in balanced support. Screwcap. 13.4% alc. **Rating** 93 **To** 2020 $31

Block 3 Mudgee Cabernet Sauvignon 2006 Attractive medium-bodied cabernet; a fragrant bouquet promises the gentle blackcurrant fruit, which is duly delivered on the palate; the oak and tannins are where they should be. Screwcap. 13% alc. **Rating** 91 **To** 2015 $45

Block 3 Mudgee Cabernet Sauvignon 2005 Good colour for age; more earth, briar and oak than the '06 give it a thoroughly regional profile; there is plenty of dark, black fruit a the core of a medium- to full-bodied wine. Screwcap. 13.3% alc. **Rating** 90 **To** 2014 $45

ΨΨΨΨ **Mudgee Merlot 2006** Good depth to the colour; a robust, earthy/savoury wine that has convincing varietal expression, even if it is not elegant; will mature well. Screwcap. 12.8% alc. **Rating** 89 **To** 2020 $21

Barrel Fermented Mudgee Chardonnay 2007 A big, bold style, with peachy fruit and plenty of oak; best consumed while it retains freshness. Screwcap. 13.6% alc. **Rating** 87 **To** 2009 $19

Special Reserve Mudgee Cabernet Sauvignon 2005 Shows obvious colour development; savoury/earthy components are threatening to dry out the fruit and there is a distinct lift to the finish, perhaps reflecting some volatile acidity. Screwcap. 13.2% alc. **Rating** 87 **To** 2012 $32

Hurley Vineyard   ★★★★★

101 Balnarring Road, Balnarring, Vic 3926 **Region** Mornington Peninsula
T (03) 5931 3000 **F** (03) 5931 3200 **www.**hurleyvineyard.com.au **Open** By appt
Winemaker Kevin Bell **Est.** 1998 **Cases** 600

It's never as easy as it seems. Although Kevin Bell is now a Victorian Supreme Court judge, and his wife Tricia Byrnes has a busy legal life as a family law specialist in a small Melbourne law firm, they have done most of the hard work in establishing Hurley Vineyard themselves, with family and friends. Most conspicuously, Kevin has completed the Applied Science (Wine Science) degree at CSU, drawing on Nat White for consultancy advice, and occasionally from Phillip Jones of Bass Phillip and Domaine Fourrier in Gevrey Chambertin.

♥♥♥♥♥ **Garamond Mornington Peninsula Pinot Noir 2007** Strong, bright colour; a powerful, layered palate with dark plum fruit and considerable length; good oak balance and integration. Needs a minimum of five years. Diam. 13.9% alc. **Rating** 95 **To** 2017 $54

Homage Mornington Peninsula Pinot Noir 2007 Rich, scented bouquet and a supple palate; fruit more to the red spectrum, the tannins fine, oak in its proper place. Diam. 13.8% alc. **Rating** 94 **To** 2015 $49

♥♥♥♥♡ **Lodestone Mornington Peninsula Pinot Noir 2007** Slightly lighter colour than Homage; more savoury/foresty nuances to the bouquet, the palate responding in kind; long, gently savoury finish. Will be ready first. Diam. 13.8% alc. **Rating** 92 **To** 2013 $44

Hutton Wines

PO Box 1214, Dunsborough, WA 6281 **Region** Margaret River
T 0417 923 126 **F** (08) 9759 1246 **www**.huttonwines.com **Open** Not
Winemaker Dr Bradley Hutton **Est.** 2006 **Cases** 375
This is another venture of the Hutton family of Gralyn fame, with brothers (and sons) Bradley and Michael doing their own thing. Bradley Hutton became winemaker at Gralyn in 2001 following the completion of postgraduate studies in oenology at the University of Adelaide, so this is a busman's holiday. Cabernet sauvignon, shiraz and chardonnay are made from grapes purchased from the family vineyard and other growers in the surrounding area.

♥♥♥♥♥ **Triptych Margaret River Shiraz 2007** Fragrant red and black fruits; an intense but elegant palate, silky and supple, finishing with good acidity and integrated oak. Screwcap. 14.4% alc. **Rating** 94 **To** 2027 $50

♥♥♥♥♡ **Triptych Margaret River Chardonnay 2007** Bright, fresh and lively, with citrus, nectarine and melon fruit supported by a fine skein of French oak; sure to expand with age in bottle. Screwcap. 13.6% alc. **Rating** 93 **To** 2017 $40

Hyde Park Wines

8 Chapel Street, Richmond, Vic 3121 (postal) **Region** Grampians
T (03) 9665 2444 **F** (03) 9665 2455 **www**.hydeparkwines.com.au **Open** Not
Winemaker Best's (Ian McKenzie) **Est.** 1997 **Cases** 800 **Vyds** 101 ha
Hyde Park Wines is owned by David Wells, Michael Ramsden and Michael Tilley, who planted their large vineyard in 1997, close to the Seppelt vineyards at Great Western. Seventy per cent of the plantings are shiraz (the balance cabernet sauvignon and merlot) and only 10 tonnes of the annual production are kept for the Hyde Park brand. A super-premium Shiraz is made each year, and, when the quality is appropriately high, a smaller amount of Cabernet Merlot is made. The wines spend 12 months in French oak before being bottled and held for two years prior to sale.

♥♥♥♥♥ **The Pinnacle Shiraz 2006** Deeply coloured; the bouquet has spicy/peppery nuances to the core of black fruits; the medium-bodied palate has good texture, structure and balance, French oak making a positive contribution. Screwcap. 14.2% alc. **Rating** 94 **To** 2018 $24

The Pinnacle Shiraz 2005 Has a very expressive bouquet, with pepper, spice and cedar intermingling with blackberry and plum fruit on both bouquet and palate; a lovely regional wine. Screwcap. 14.3% alc. **Rating** 94 **To** 2016 $22

ŸŸŸŸ♀ **Cabernet Merlot 2005** No doubting the varietal composition, blackcurrant, olive and earth, picking up energy on the finish and aftertaste. Screwcap. 13.1% alc. **Rating** 91 **To** 2015 $22

Immerse   ★★★

1548 Melba Highway, Yarra Glen, Vic 3775 **Region** Yarra Valley
T (03) 5965 2444 **F** (03) 5965 2441 **www**.immerse.com.au **Open** Thurs–Mon 11–5
Winemaker Contract **Est.** 1989 **Cases** 700 **Vyds** 6.8 ha
Steve and Helen Miles purchased the restaurant, accommodation and function complex previously known as Lovey's. A spa-based health farm has eight rooms, with a full range of services. I have to say that the name chosen both for the facility and for the wines is as far left of centre as it is possible to go. As previously, a portion of the grapes produced is sold to other makers in the Yarra Valley, the vineyards having been rehabilitated. The 2009 bushfires destroyed three accommodation units and a barn, but did not destroy the vineyards.

ŸŸŸŸ **Oscar's Reserve Yarra Valley Shiraz 2006** Toasty oak dominates the fruit on the bouquet; the palate shows lively red fruit, spice, and quite slippery texture; a fine and even conclusion. Diam. 14% alc. **Rating** 89 **To** 2014 $42
Shiraz Viognier 2007 Bright colour; slightly savoury mineral bouquet with a splash of blueberry; clean acid, and crisp fruit lead to a savoury finish. Screwcap. 13.5% alc. **Rating** 89 **To** 2014 $26
Yarra Valley Sauvignon Blanc 2008 Guava and a touch of varietally pungent sweaty character; generous palate, with a little grip on the finish. Screwcap. 12% alc. **Rating** 88 **To** 2012 $22
Unwooded Chardonnay 2008 Clean bouquet of citrus and a touch of pear; quite zesty, but a little one-dimensional on the finish. Screwcap. 13.5% alc. **Rating** 87 **To** 2012 $22

Indigo Wine Company

1221 Beechworth-Wangaratta Road, Everton Upper, Vic 3678 **Region** Beechworth
T (03) 5727 0233 **F** (03) 5727 0580 **Open** By appt
Winemaker Brokenwood **Est.** 1999 **Cases** 1900 **Vyds** 46.15 ha
Indigo Wine Company has a little over 46 ha of vineyards planted to 11 varieties, including the top French and Italian grapes. The business was and is primarily directed to growing grapes for sale to Brokenwood, but since 2004 small parcels of grapes have been vinified for the Indigo label. The somewhat incestuous nature of the whole business sees the Indigo wines being made at Brokenwood by Brokenwood CEO Iain Riggs and senior winemaker PJ Charteris.

ŸŸŸŸ♀ **Beechworth Chardonnay 2006** Ripe peach, melon and spice bouquet; rich mid-palate, with good acidity and vibrant fruit on the finish. Screwcap. 14.5% alc. **Rating** 90 **To** 2012 $27
Beechworth Chardonnay Roussanne 2008 Pale colour; prominent straw and honey on the bouquet as the roussanne seems to be taking charge; interesting savoury and textural palate, with a little grip setting off cool stone fruit on the finish. Screwcap. 13.5% alc. **Rating** 90 **To** 2012 $27

Inghams Skilly Ridge Wines

Gillentown Road, Sevenhill via Clare, SA 5453 **Region** Clare Valley
T 0418 423 998 **F** (08) 8843 4330 **Open** W'ends 10–5, or by appt
Winemaker Clark Ingham, O'Leary Walker **Est.** 1994 **Cases** 2000 **Vyds** 24 ha
Clark Ingham has established shiraz, cabernet sauvignon, merlot, chardonnay, riesling, tempranillo and primitivo. Part of the production is made by contract winemaker David O'Leary (with input from Clark Ingham), the remaining grape production is sold. Exports to the UK, Germany and China.

♈♈♈♈ Clare Valley Riesling 2008 Ripe meyer lemon bouquet, with a touch of spice; clean lime fruit, prominent acidity and a dry, talcy conclusion. Screwcap. 12.5% alc. Rating 87 To 2013 $19

Ingoldby

GPO Box 753, Melbourne, Vic 3001 **Region** McLaren Vale
T 1300 651 650 **F** (08) 8383 0790 **www**.ingoldby.com.au **Open** Not
Winemaker Matt O'Leary **Est.** 1983 **Cases** 170 000
Part of the Foster's group, with the wines now having a sole McLaren Vale source. Over the years, Ingoldby has produced some excellent wines, which can provide great value for money.

♈♈♈♈♈ McLaren Vale Cabernet Sauvignon 2007 Well made, particularly in the context of '07; strong varietal character in a savoury blackcurrant spectrum runs through the length of the palate, which has good tannin and oak support. Screwcap. 14.5% alc. Rating 91 To 2017 $19.99

♈♈♈♈ McLaren Vale Shiraz 2006 A pleasant light- to medium-bodied wine, but a shadow of its former robust self; faintly spicy/savoury nuances to the fruit add a degree of interest and length. Screwcap. 14.5% alc. Rating 87 To 2012 $19.99

Inkwell ★★★★★

PO Box 404, McLaren Vale, SA 5171 **Region** McLaren Vale
T 0430 050 115 **Open** Not
Winemaker Dudley Brown **Est.** 2003 **Cases** 400 **Vyds** 12 ha
Inkwell was born in 2003 when Dudley Brown and wife Karen Wotherspoon returned to Australia from California and bought a somewhat rundown vineyard on the serendipitously named California Road. They inherited 5 ha of neglected shiraz, and planted an additional 7 ha to viognier (2 ha), zinfandel (2 ha) and heritage shiraz clones (3 ha). The five-year restoration of the old vines and establishment of the new reads like the ultimate handbook for aspiring vignerons, particularly those who are prepared to work non-stop. The reward has been rich – almost all the grapes are sold, and the grapes go from a mid-range commercial rating to near the top of the tree. The first toe in the water of winemaking came in 2006 with 140 cases produced, rising to 400 cases in '08. Dudley is adamant the production will be capped at 2000 cases.

♈♈♈♈♈ Rebel Rebel McLaren Vale Shiraz 2006 A deep, dark and inky bouquet, with fruitcake spice, black fruits, and an abundance of sweet fruit; the palate is rich and quite chewy; beneath the ample fruit there is plenty of tannin and good fresh acidity. Very good value. Screwcap. 15% alc. Rating 94 To 2016 $25

Iron Gate Estate

Oakey Creek Road, Pokolbin, NSW 2320 **Region** Lower Hunter Valley
T (02) 4998 6570 **F** (02) 4998 6571 **www**.iron-gate-estate.com.au **Open** 7 days 10–4
Winemaker Roger Lilliott **Est.** 1996 **Cases** 6000 **Vyds** 10.11 ha
Iron Gate Estate would not be out of place in the Napa Valley, which favours bold architectural statements made without regard to cost. No expense has been spared in equipping the winery or on the lavish cellar door facilities. The wines are made from estate plantings of semillon, verdelho, chardonnay, cabernet sauvignon and shiraz, and include such exotic offerings as a sweet shiraz and a chardonnay made in the style of a fino sherry. Exports to the UK.

♈♈♈♈♈ Hunter Valley Rose 2008 Vibrant pale pink; bright red fruits with an underpinning of savoury Merlot cedar and olive; the palate has plenty of sweetness, but the flavour is up to the challenge and the finish is quite dry. Cork. 12.5% alc. Rating 90 To 2011 $23

♈♈♈♈ Hunter Valley Semillon Chardonnay 2008 Attractive peach and spice bouquet; generous mid-palate weight, with reasonable persistence. Cork. 11% alc. Rating 88 To 2011 $24

Hunter Valley Shiraz 2006 Good colour; anise, plum and redcurrant bouquet; quite fleshy with good flavour and persistence. Cork. 13.5% alc. **Rating** 87 **To** 2013 $26.50

Iron Pot Bay Wines

766 Deviot Road, Deviot, Tas 7275 **Region** Northern Tasmania
T (03) 6394 7320 **F** (03) 6394 7346 **www**.ironpotbay.com.au **Open** By appt
Winemaker Dr Andrew Pirie **Est.** 1988 **Cases** 2400 **Vyds** 5 ha
Iron Pot Bay was established by the Cuthbert family and continues in family ownership. The vineyard takes its name from a bay on the Tamar River (now called West Bay) and is strongly maritime-influenced, producing delicate but intensely flavoured unwooded white wines. Over half of the vineyard is planted to chardonnay, the remainder semillon, sauvignon blanc, pinot gris, gewurztraminer and riesling.

Riesling 2006 Lively and bright; good focus and intensity; citrus, apple and lime, although it fades a little on the finish. Screwcap. 12.8% alc. **Rating** 91 **To** 2014 $23
Blanc de Blancs 2005 Very bright, fresh, clean and zesty style, with good length; strong citrus components. Crown. 12% alc. **Rating** 91 **To** 2014 $25

Ironbark Hill Estate ★★★

694 Hermitage Road, Pokolbin, NSW 2321 **Region** Lower Hunter Valley
T (02) 6574 7085 **F** (02) 6574 7089 **www**.ironbarkhill.com.au **Open** 7 days 10–5
Winemaker Trevor Drayton **Est.** 1990 **Cases** 5000
Ironbark Hill Estate is owned by Peter Drayton and accountant Michael Dillon. Peter's father, Max Drayton, and brothers John and Greg, run Drayton's Family Wines. There are 14 ha of estate plantings of semillon, chardonnay, verdelho, shiraz, cabernet sauvignon, merlot and tyrian. Peter Drayton is a commercial/industrial builder, so constructing the cellar door was a busman's holiday. The hope is that the striking building and landscape surrounds will bring more wine tourists to the Hermitage Road end of Pokolbin. The quality of the wines, too, is commendable.

Semillon 2008 Very pale, with a touch of pea pod on the bouquet; zesty lemon sherbet fruit, and enough generosity to be enjoyed in its youth; a drink–early style. Screwcap. 10% alc. **Rating** 89 **To** 2014 $15
Chardonnay 2007 Rich and ripe with a distinct toasty aroma; the palate has plenty of depth and richness. Screwcap. 12.5% alc. **Rating** 88 **To** 2012 $15
Verdelho 2008 Crisp and clean, with lively citrus fruit; vibrant acidity plays a key role to the palate. Screwcap. 13.5% alc. **Rating** 87 **To** 2011 $15

Ironwood Estate

2191 Porongurup Road, Porongurup, WA 6234 **Region** Porongurup
T (08) 9853 1126 **F** (08) 9853 1172 **Open** 7 days 11–5
Winemaker Wignalls Wines (Mick Perkins) **Est.** 1996 **Cases** 2500 **Vyds** 5 ha
Ironwood Estate was established in 1996 under the ownership of Jean and Mary Harmer. An estate vineyard planted to riesling, sauvignon blanc, chardonnay, shiraz, merlot and cabernet sauvignon (in more or less equal amounts) has been established on a northern slope of the Porongurup Range.

Porongurup Merlot 2007 Very aromatic, with ripe cherry/cassis/red fruit flavours driving the impressively long palate. Screwcap. 13.5% alc. **Rating** 91 **To** 2014 $20
Reserve Porongurup Chardonnay 2008 Attractive stone fruit aromas, entwined with some barrel ferment French oak, logically lead into a supple palate with some creamy lees contact notes. Screwcap. 14.5% alc. **Rating** 90 **To** 2014 $20

🍷🍷🍷🍷 **Porongurup Shiraz 2007** Spicy/savoury aromas and savoury tannins are the bookends for the red and black fruits on the mid-palate. Screwcap. 13.6% alc. **Rating** 88 **To** 2020 $20

Irvine ★★★★☆

PO Box 308, Angaston, SA 5353 **Region** Eden Valley
T (08) 8564 1046 www.irvinewines.com.au **Open** At Eden Valley Hotel
Winemaker James Irvine, Joanne Irvine **Est.** 1980 **Cases** 10 000 **Vyds** 9.53 ha
Industry veteran Jim Irvine, who has successfully guided the destiny of so many SA wineries, quietly introduced his own label in 1991. The vineyard from which the wines are sourced was planted in 1983 and now comprises a patchwork quilt of vines. The flagship is the rich Grand Merlot. Exports to the UK and other major markets.

🍷🍷🍷🍷🍷 **James Irvine Eden Valley Grand Merlot 2004** Very typical of the Grand Merlot style, with barrel ferment fusing the French Allier oak into the wine, yet not obscuring the varietal statement of the fruit, and helping the superfine tannins. Cork. 14.5% alc. **Rating** 94 **To** 2014 $100

J&J Wines ★★★★☆

Lot 115 Rivers Lane, McLaren Vale, SA 5172 **Region** McLaren Vale
T (08) 8323 9888 **F** (08) 8323 9309 www.jjwines.com.au **Open** By appt
Winemaker Scott Rawlinson, Chris Thomas **Est.** 1998 **Cases** 1600 **Vyds** 5.5 ha
This single-vineyard business began as a grapegrower in 1995, with 5.5 ha of shiraz. When part of the production was not purchased in 2004, owner Jeff Mason had wine made for private use. Since then volume has grown to the point where it is most definitely a commercial venture. Australian sales are made through The Wine Procurer (thewineprocurer@internode. on.net).

🍷🍷🍷🍷🍷 **Limestone Block McLaren Vale Shiraz 2007** A vibrant young wine; red and blackberry fruit show distinct fruitcake spice aromas; the palate is fresh, lively and full of juicy fruit; should be enjoyed in its youth. Screwcap. 15.6% alc. **Rating** 90 **To** 2014 $19.99

🍷🍷🍷🍷 **Limestone Block McLaren Vale Shiraz 2006** Very ripe chocolate-tinged fruit and nuances of vanilla oak makes a seductive wine for some, especially the McLaren Vale Wine Show '07 judges who gave it the trophy for Best Red Under $20. Cork. 15.6% alc. **Rating** 89 **To** 2012 $19.95

Jacob's Creek ★★★★★

Jacob's Creek Visitor Centre, Barossa Valley Way, Rowland Flat, SA 5352 **Region** Barossa Valley
T (08) 8521 3000 **F** (08) 8521 3003 www.jacobscreek.com **Open** 7 days 10–5
Winemaker Philip Laffer, Bernard Hicken **Est.** 1973 **Cases** NFP
Jacob's Creek is one of the largest selling brands in the world and is almost exclusively responsible for driving the fortunes of this French-owned (Pernod Ricard) company. A colossus in the export game, chiefly to the UK and Europe, but also to the US and Asia. Wine quality across the full spectrum from Jacob's Creek upwards has been exemplary, driven by the production skills of Philip Laffer. The global success of the basic Jacob's Creek range has had the perverse effect of prejudicing many critics and wine writers who fail (so it seems) to objectively look behind the label and taste what is in fact in the glass. Jacob's Creek has four ranges, and all the wines have a connection, direct or indirect, with Johann Gramp, who built his tiny stone winery on the banks of the creek in 1847. The four-tier range consists of Icon (Johann Shiraz Cabernet); then Heritage (Steingarten Riesling, Reeves Point Chardonnay, Centenary Hill Barossa Shiraz and St Hugo Coonawarra Cabernet); then Reserve (all of the major varietals); and finally Traditional (ditto).

🍷🍷🍷🍷🍷 **Steingarten Barossa Riesling 2006** Pale straw-green; spotlessly clean lemon/ lime aromas; a focused and intense palate, still developing around its core of citrus fruit and tight acidity. Screwcap. 12.5% alc. **Rating** 94 **To** 2016 $31.95

Jacaranda Ridge Coonawarra Cabernet Sauvignon 2005 Deeply coloured; powerful black fruits on the bouquet, the mouthfilling full-bodied palate with blackcurrant, blackberry and dark chocolate; good tannin and oak support. Screwcap. **Rating** 94 **To** 2025 $63

🍷🍷🍷🍷🍷 **Reserve Riesling 2008** A lively and fresh wine with citrus blossom aromas mirrored on the palate and enhanced by lively acidity on the finish. A superior wine. Screwcap. 12% alc. **Rating** 93 **To** 2018 $18.50

Centenary Hill Barossa Valley Shiraz 2004 Powerful robust, full-bodied shiraz still to lose some rough edges; black fruits have a crosscut of firm tannins; requires a few more years to fully open up. Cork. 14.5% alc. **Rating** 93 **To** 2015 $41.95

St Hugo Coonawarra Cabernet Sauvignon 2005 A medium-bodied wine; the bouquet through to the finish of the palate has a savoury/spicy cast to the black fruits that drive the flavour; dusty tannins linger on the finish. Screwcap. 14% alc. **Rating** 93 **To** 2020 $47

Three Vines Shiraz Grenache Sangiovese 2008 A wine with excellent length and vibrancy, the sangiovese, while only 20% of the total, provides savoury, almost gritty, texture; a seriously good rose, almost crossing into light-bodied dry red. Subliminal sweetness from 3–4 g per litre. Available December '09. **Rating** 92 **To** 2012 $15

Reeves Point Chardonnay 2005 Bright straw-green; thanks in part to the screwcap, is still remarkably fresh and youthful; crisp apple and stone fruit flavours, the oak suitably restrained. Screwcap. 13.5% alc. **Rating** 91 **To** 2013 $34

Shiraz Cabernet 2006 This is a fine testament to the great quality of the 2006 vintage; if the carping critics of Australian wine in the UK were served this blind they would be looking for somewhere to hide; massively over-delivers in flavour, texture and structure. Screwcap. 14% alc. **Rating** 90 **To** 2012 $10.95

Reserve Sauvignon Blanc 2008 Has very good texture and structure built around a core of minerally acidity; the aromas and flavours extend from grassy notes through to passionfruit. A massive leap up from the varietal. 70% Adelaide Hills. Screwcap. 13.5% alc. **Rating** 90 **To** 2010 $18.50

Cabernet Merlot 2005 Exceptional flavour, texture and structure at this price level, and remarkably fresh; offers exactly the fruit profile expected of the blend ranging through blackcurrant, redcurrant and cassis; one wonders whether this was a lucky bottling lot. Screwcap. 13% alc. **Rating** 90 **To** 2012 $10.95

Reserve Chardonnay Pinot Noir 2005 Bright straw-green; attractive fruity aromas; plenty of citrussy stone fruit flavours, not overmuch bready/yeasty notes, but has good balance and fair length. Cork. 12% alc. **Rating** 90 **To** 2010 $19.99

🍷🍷🍷🍷 **Riesling 2008** Light straw-green; has clear varietal expression, with distinct notes of lime; excellent citrussy acidity and length. Predominantly from the Barossa Valley/Langhorne Creek/Clare Valley. Good value. Screwcap. 12.5% alc. **Rating** 89 **To** 2012 $11.40

Reserve Pinot Grigio 2007 Unusual but attractive citrus blossom and wild flowers, even a touch of lantana, then a long palate. Deserves its price. Screwcap. 12.5% alc. **Rating** 89 **To** 2010 $18.50

Reserve Cabernet Sauvignon 2005 Powerful, medium- to full-bodied wine, seemingly from the Limestone Coast; blackcurrant fruit is supported by uncompromising tannins. For the long haul. Screwcap. 14% alc. **Rating** 89 **To** 2020 $17

Reserve Shiraz 2006 Well-made medium-bodied shiraz, albeit with no distinctive regional fruit characters; has adequate tannins and structure. Screwcap. 14% alc. **Rating** 88 **To** 2012 $17

Reserve Chardonnay Pinot Noir 2006 Bottle fermented, and has both balance and complexity in a relatively ripe mode. Cork. 12% alc. **Rating** 88 **To** 2010 $20

Semillon Sauvignon Blanc 2008 Lively wine with an interesting flavour contrast of lemony semillon against pineapple/tropical sauvignon blanc, albeit in a light framework. Good value. Screwcap. 12.5% alc. **Rating** 87 **To** 2010 $11.40

Grenache Shiraz 2008 Bright and clearly defined raspberry fruit bouquet; juicy on entry with fine tannin to conclude; well put together wine. Value. Screwcap. 14% alc. **Rating** 87 **To** 2013 $11.40

Merlot 2007 The best example in its price range; acceptable varietal fruit via red-currant and black olive flavours. Screwcap. 13.5% alc. **Rating** 87 **To** 2010 $10.95

Jamabro Wines

PO Box 434, Tanunda, SA 5352 **Region** Barossa Valley
T 0437 633 575 **F** (08) 8563 3837 **www.**jamabro.com.au **Open** By appt
Winemaker David Heinze **Est.** 2003 **Cases** 500 **Vyds** 21.4 ha
Sixth-generation grapegrower David Heinze and wife Juli moved into winemaking in 2003, just as many of the major companies reduced their intake of Barossa grapes. With a little over 21 ha of vines planted to eight varieties, they started with a full suite of wines, using estate-grown grapes and carrying out all the winemaking (other than bottling) onsite. Real marketing skill is involved with the labelling (Jamabro is taken from a combination of family names), but it is the back labels that catch the eye. The Semillon takes the name of daughter Madison who, having just had her hair straightened for a school photograph, was doused in semillon when a bung came out unexpectedly, causing lengthy and messy re-straightening (and an aversion to the winery); and Mum's Spade Shiraz celebrates the spade given to Juli by her husband when she turned 21. 'Wherever Mum went, so did her spade…When there was something to dig, out of the car boot came the spade. We lost Mum in 2006. Mum's Spade Shiraz is our tribute to Mum and all the other great Australian farming women, often the quiet achievers.'

The PT Barossa Valley Shiraz 2006 A lifted bouquet, with red and black fruits; quite warm, with a slight savoury edge that leaves the palate very dry; good concentration. Screwcap. 15% alc. **Rating** 88 **To** 2012 $40

James Estate

951 Bylong Valley Way, Baerami via Denman, NSW 2333 **Region** Upper Hunter Valley
T (02) 6547 5168 **F** (02) 6547 5164 **www.**wineforlife.com.au **Open** 7 days 10–4.30
Winemaker Graeme Scott, Deane Rose, Tony Hewitt **Est.** 1997 **Cases** 30 000 **Vyds** 97 ha
James Estate has had an unsettled corporate existence at various times since 1997, but should enter on distinctly calmer waters in the years ahead. Graeme Scott has been installed as senior winemaker, having previously worked with Jim Chatto and Ross Pearson at First Creek, and The Rothbury Estate before that. It is to be expected that the wines from 2008 (in part) and 2009 (in whole) will be distinctly better than those made under previous winery management.

Reserve Chardonnay 2008 Relatively early picking has helped preserve freshness in a well-balanced, fruit-driven style. Screwcap. 13% alc. **Rating** 87 **To** 2013 $18

Rose 2008 Bright, light crimson; red and black cherry fruit flavours are neatly tied up by crisp acidity on the finish. Screwcap. 12% alc. **Rating** 87 **To** 2010 $14

James Haselgrove Wines

PO Box 271, McLaren Vale, SA 5171 **Region** McLaren Vale
T (08) 8383 0886 **F** (08) 8383 0887 **www.**haselgrovevignerons.com **Open** Not
Winemaker James Haselgrove **Est.** 1981 **Cases** 200
While in one sense this is now a virtual winery, Nick Haselgrove is quick to point out that it has access to substantial vineyards and winemaking resources. He and James Haselgrove (who founded this winery) are reluctant to see the business disappear, and intend to continue making and releasing wines under the James Haselgrove label. In terms of both price and style they differ from Blackbilly (see separate entry). Exports to the US and Canada.

Futures McLaren Vale Shiraz 2007 Incredibly concentrated and very ripe, possibly pushing the envelope; prunes and chocolate, and unashamedly big in every respect; off 70-year-old vines. Screwcap. 14.9% alc. **Rating** 92 **To** 2020 $55

Jamieson Estate ★★★☆

PO Box 6598, Silverwater, NSW 2128 **Region** Mudgee
T (02) 9737 8377 **F** (02) 9737 9274 **www**.jamiesonestate.com.au **Open** Not
Winemaker Robert Paul **Est.** 1998 **Cases** 6000 **Vyds** 89.2 ha
Generations of the Jamieson family have been graziers in the region for 150 years, and were able to select 100 ha of the most suitable soil from their property on which to establish their vineyard. Beginning in 1998, they have planted over 32 ha of shiraz, almost 24 ha of cabernet sauvignon and 12 ha of chardonnay, with smaller amounts of semillon, petit verdot, sauvignon blanc, merlot and barbera. Until 2005 all of the grapes were sold to leading wineries in the region, but beginning in '06 small amounts of chardonnay, sauvignon blanc, semillon, shiraz and petit verdot were held back for the Jamieson Estate label.

ΨΨΨΨΨ **Guntawang Shiraz 2007** The fragrant, spicy bouquet is mirrored by the lively, spicy black fruits and licorice of the palate; has cool-grown nuances not often found in Mudgee shiraz. Gold medal Mudgee Wine Show '08. Screwcap. 14.5% alc. **Rating** 93 **To** 2015

ΨΨΨΨ **Guntawang Petit Verdot 2006** This wine also reflects the cool site on which Jamieson Estate is established; that said, this notoriously late-ripening variety has reached phenological ripeness with attractive spicy/savoury flavours. Screwcap. 14% alc. **Rating** 89 **To** 2013

Jamieson Valley Estate ★★★☆

52 Stanhope Street, Malvern, Vic 3144 (postal) **Region** Upper Goulburn
T 0402 210 254 **F** (03) 9322 4699 **www**.jamiesonvalleyestate.com.au **Open** Not
Winemaker Helen's Hill (Scott McCarthy) **Est.** 2003 **Cases** 500 **Vyds** 1.8 ha
Anna and Chris Dunphy began the development of their vineyard in 1990. They elected to focus solely on pinot noir and have planted 1.8 ha of clones 114, 115, MV6 and 777. The vineyard is situated on a north-facing slope near the historic gold mining town of Jamieson and benefits from the hot days and cool nights, which are especially suited to pinot. They say their aim is to make an 'approachable wine at a realistic price. We want Jameaux [their pinot] to be a signature that is a mixture of French sensibility and Australian larrakin-ism'.

ΨΨΨΨΨ **Jameaux Pinot Noir 2006** The hue is still holding on to an interesting wine; a strong savoury/foresty component runs through the palate and finish. Clonally selected vineyard: three Dijon clones and MV6. Screwcap. 13.1% alc. **Rating** 90 **To** 2013 $24.50

Jamiesons Run ★★★☆

Coonawarra Wine Gallery, Riddoch Highway, Penola, SA 5277 **Region** Coonawarra
T (08) 8737 3250 **www**.jamiesonsrun.com.au **Open** 7 days 10–5
Winemaker Andrew Hales **Est.** 1987 **Cases** 135 000
The wheel has turned a full circle for Jamiesons Run. It started out as a single-label, mid-market, high-volume brand developed by Ray King during his time as CEO of Mildara. It grew and grew until Mildara, having many years since been merged with Wolf Blass, decided to rename the Mildara Coonawarra winery as Jamiesons Run, with the Mildara label just one of a number falling under the Jamiesons Run umbrella. Now the Jamiesons Run winery is no more, Foster's has sold it, but retained the brand; the cellar door moved to shared accommodation at the Coonawarra Wine Gallery. Exports to the UK.

ΨΨΨΨΨ **Mildara Coonawarra Cabernet Shiraz 2005** A dense and chewy dark fruited wine; the bouquet is full of cassis, floral notes and plenty of spice; the palate is dark and brooding, with plenty of chewy tannins, and a long and slightly savoury finish. Screwcap. 14.5% alc. **Rating** 93 **To** 2015 $28.99

ΨΨΨΨ **Limestone Coast Shiraz 2008** Good crimson colour; a well-made commercial wine, the palate no more than medium-bodied, the flavours a mix of small red fruits and plum. Screwcap. 14% alc. **Rating** 87 **To** 2011 $16.99

Jamsheed

157 Faraday Street, Carlton, Vic 3053 (postal) **Region** Yarra Valley
T 0409 540 414 **F** (03) 5967 3581 **www**.jamsheed.com.au **Open** Not
Winemaker Gary Mills **Est.** 2003 **Cases** 200
Jamsheed is the venture of Gary Mills, proprietor of Simpatico Wine Services, a boutique
contract winemaking company established at the Hill Paddock Winery in Healesville. The
wines are sourced from a 30-year-old, low-yielding vineyard, and are made using indigenous/
wild yeasts and minimal handling techniques. For the short-term future the business will focus
on old vine sites in the Yarra Valley, but will also include a Grampians and Heathcote Shiraz,
along with a Strathbogie Gewurztraminer. The name, incidentally, is that of a Persian king
recorded in the Annals of Gilgamesh.

ᵀᵀᵀᵀᵀ **Great Western Syrah 2007** A layered wine showing red fruit, Asian spice, hints
of earth and a touch of oak; the redcurrant fruit persists on the palate, and the
texture is velvet-like and truly medium-bodied; a long, supple and harmonious
finish. Diam. 14.5% alc. **Rating** 94 **To** 2016 $37

ᵀᵀᵀᵀᵀ **Yarra Valley Syrah 2007** Deep colour; smoky aromas dominate the bouquet;
lively on the palate, with blueberry and blackberry fruit, fine acidity and fine-
grained tannin persisting on the finish. Diam. 14.5% alc. **Rating** 90 **To** 2015 $37

ᵀᵀᵀᵀ **La Syrah 2008** Some reduction, but attractive black fruit and spice aromas come
through; medium-bodied with sweet black fruit and a touch of wild herb on the
finish. Screwcap. 13.5% alc. **Rating** 89 **To** 2014 $20
Pepe le Pinot Noir 2008 Bright colour; spicy red fruit bouquet; quite a
generous palate, exhibiting game and red fruit, and a little smokiness on the finish.
Screwcap. 13.5% alc. **Rating** 88 **To** 2012 $20

Jane Brook Estate

229 Toodyay Road, Middle Swan, WA 6056 **Region** Swan Valley
T (08) 9274 1432 **F** (08) 9274 1211 **www**.janebrook.com.au **Open** 7 days 10–5
Winemaker Mark Baird **Est.** 1972 **Cases** 25 000 **Vyds** 19 ha
Beverley and David Atkinson have worked tirelessly to build up the Jane Brook Estate wine
business over the past 30-plus years. The most important changes during that time have been
the establishment of a Margaret River vineyard, and sourcing grapes from other southern wine
regions in WA. Exports to Hong Kong and Singapore.

ᵀᵀᵀᵀᵀ **Shovelgate Vineyard Margaret River Cabernet Sauvignon 2007** Good
crimson; fragrant blackcurrant aromas foreshadow a delicious medium-bodied
palate, the fruit lively and fine; superfine tannins on the long finish. Bargain.
Screwcap. 14.3% alc. **Rating** 95 **To** 2017 $25

ᵀᵀᵀᵀᵀ **Shovelgate Vineyard Margaret River Sauvignon Blanc 2008** Excellent
depth; tropical fruit profile without heaviness; good balance, length and mouthfeel.
Screwcap. 13.4% alc. **Rating** 90 **To** 2010 $21

ᵀᵀᵀᵀ **Margaret River Chardonnay 2007** Bright straw-green; a generous wine, with
ripe stone fruit and fig flavours, the influence of oak evident but not marked;
finishes a little short. Screwcap. 13.9% alc. **Rating** 89 **To** 2012 $35
Plain Jane Cabernet Shiraz 2007 Over-delivers on price and expectations; the
Margaret River cabernet component meshes neatly with the Swan Valley shiraz;
has good black fruit concentration and structure; ditto length. Screwcap. 13.8% alc.
Rating 89 **To** 2014 $15
Atkinson Family Reserve Shiraz 2007 Plenty of French oak and skilful
winemaking techniques have produced a shiraz that stands out from most Swan
Valley wines; the catch is the alcohol, which heats the finish. So near, yet so far.
Screwcap. 15.4% alc. **Rating** 88 **To** 2015 $50
Margaret River Merlot 2007 Brightly coloured; a fragrant, juicy light- to
medium-bodied palate with clear varietal expression; the tannins fine, oak subtle.
Screwcap. 14.8% alc. **Rating** 88 **To** 2013 $25

Elizabeth Jane Pinot Noir Chardonnay 2006 Salmon colour; complex spicy/bready, red fruit aromas, the chardonnay more evident on the well-balanced palate; bottle fermented. Margaret River/Pemberton. Cork. 12.6% alc. **Rating** 88 **To** 2010 $27

Back Block Shiraz 2007 Deep crimson-purple; shows many of the positive attributes of the Atkinson Family Reserve, including the alcohol heat. Again, such a pity. Screwcap. 15.4% alc. **Rating** 87 **To** 2014 $25

Jansz Tasmania

1216b Pipers Brook Road, Pipers Brook, Tas 7254 **Region** Northern Tasmania
T (03) 6382 7066 **F** (03) 6382 7088 **www.**jansztas.com **Open** 7 days 10–5
Winemaker Natalie Fryar **Est.** 1985 **Cases** 35 000 **Vyds** 30 ha
Jansz is part of the Hill Smith Family Vineyards, and was one of the early sparkling wine labels in Tasmania, stemming from a short-lived relationship between Heemskerk and Louis Roederer. Its 15 ha of chardonnay, 12 ha of pinot noir and 3 ha of pinot meunier correspond almost exactly to the blend composition of the Jansz wines. It is the only Tasmanian winery entirely devoted to the production of sparkling wine under the Jansz Tasmania brand (although the small amount of Dalrymple Estate wines are also made here), and is of high quality. Exports to all major markets.

ꙮꙮꙮꙮꙮ **Premium Vintage Late Disgorged 2001** Freshly toasted brioche on the bouquet, displaying an attractive level of development; creamy and fine on the palate, with a dry, linear and chalky finish; complex and satisfying. Cork. 12% alc. **Rating** 94 **To** 2012 $49.95

ꙮꙮꙮꙮꙮ **Premium Vintage Rose 2005** A fresh and lively palate, with good fruit line and continuity; excellent balance. Cork. 13% alc. **Rating** 92 **To** 2013 $39.95

Premium Vintage Cuvee Brut 2004 A very clean and focused wine; good length to the stone fruit flavours and good balance. Cork. 12.5% alc. **Rating** 91 **To** 2012 $39.95

Premium Non Vintage Rose NV Pale salmon; the eternal auto-suggestion of strawberries on bouquet and palate, along with notes of citrus and rose petals. Cork. 12.5% alc. **Rating** 90 **To** 2010 $24.95

Premium Non Vintage Cuvee NV Attractive wine; has flavour and complexity to its nutty palate, yet is quite delicate and refreshing. Cork. 12.5% alc. **Rating** 90 **To** 2010 $24.95

Jarrah Ridge Winery

651 Great Northern Highway, Herne Hill, WA 6056 **Region** Perth Hills
T (08) 9296 6337 **F** (08) 9403 0800 **www.**jarrahridge.com.au **Open** 7 days 10–5
Winemaker Rob Marshall (Contract) **Est.** 1998 **Cases** 9000 **Vyds** 20.5 ha
Syd and Julie Pond have established their vineyard with shiraz the most important variety, the remainder chenin blanc, chardonnay, cabernet sauvignon, verdelho, viognier and merlot. Children Michael and Lisa are also involved in the business. Most of the wines have a degree of sweetness, which will doubtless appeal to cellar door and restaurant customers. Exports to Canada and Hong Kong.

ꙮꙮꙮꙮ **Chardonnay 2007** Unexpectedly fresh unoaked chardonnay with light, but attractive, stone fruit flavours, and just a touch of citrussy acidity. Screwcap. 13.8% alc. **Rating** 87 **To** 2011 $15

Verdelho 2008 Well-made wine, with particularly good depth and fruit salad fruit at this modest alcohol; good mouthfeel. Screwcap. 11.4% alc. **Rating** 87 **To** 2012 $15

Viognier 2008 Fresh and lively, with notes of orange and a hint of apricot; does have length. Screwcap. 12.6% alc. **Rating** 87 **To** 2012 $15

Marginata Perth Hills Classic White 2008 Fresh and bright, sauvignon blanc doing the hard yards, one suspects. Screwcap. 12.5% alc. **Rating** 87 **To** 2012 $12

Reserve Perth Hills Shiraz 2006 Ripe shiraz fruit has some confit/jam elements, its 16 months in French and American oak also very evident. A little too confected; 2600 bottles made. Screwcap. 15% alc. **Rating** 87 **To** 2013 $26

Jasper Hill   ★★★★★

Drummonds Lane, Heathcote, Vic 3523 **Region** Heathcote
T (03) 5433 2528 **F** (03) 5433 3143 www.jasperhill.com **Open** By appt
Winemaker Ron Laughton, Emily Laughton **Est.** 1975 **Cases** 3500 **Vyds** 25.4 ha
The red wines of Jasper Hill are highly regarded and much sought after, invariably selling out at the cellar door and through the mailing list within a short time of release. These are wonderful wines in admittedly Leviathan mould, reflecting the very low yields and the care and attention given to them. The oak is not overdone, and the fruit flavours show Heathcote at its best. Exports to the UK, the US and other major markets.

� **Emily's Paddock Heathcote Shiraz Cabernet Franc 2007** Good colour; much more savoury than Georgia's Paddock, and slightly lighter in body – and thus more elegant; savoury tannins, too, are in balance. Cork. 15% alc. **Rating** 94 **To** 2017 $96

TTTTT **Georgia's Paddock Heathcote Shiraz 2007** Inky purple-crimson; aromas of damson plum, licorice, prune and spice; powerful structure, but mid-palate vinosity is overshadowed by tannins on the finish. Cork. 15% alc. **Rating** 93 **To** 2015 $73
Cornella Vineyard Heathcote Grenache 2007 Light, slightly hazy crimson-purple; no more than medium-bodied, with spicy/savoury overtones and good length to the red fruit flavours. Cork. 15% alc. **Rating** 91 **To** 2013 $45

TTTT **Georgia's Paddock Heathcote Riesling 2008** Generous style, with depth and power, but not the fragrance of the very best rieslings; cork stands out in a sea of fresher screwcapped wines. 13% alc. **Rating** 89 **To** 2012 $35

jb Wines   ★★★★

PO Box 530, Tanunda, SA 5352 **Region** Barossa Valley
T (08) 8563 0291 **F** (08) 8379 4359 www.jbwines.com **Open** By appt
Winemaker Joe Barritt, Tim Geddes **Est.** 2005 **Cases** 260 **Vyds** 17.7 ha
The Barritt family has been growing grapes in the Barossa since the 1850s, but this particular venture was established in 2005 by Lenore, Joe and Greg Barritt. It is based on shiraz, cabernet sauvignon and chardonnay (with tiny amounts of zinfandel, pinot blanc and clairette) planted between 1972 and 2003. Greg runs the vineyard operations; Joe, with a bachelor of agricultural science degree from Adelaide University, followed by 10 years of winemaking in Australia, France and the US, is now the winemaker together with Tim Geddes at McLaren Vale, where the wines are made.

TTTT **Barossa Valley Shiraz 2006** Has excellent mouthfeel and overall balance; blackberry, mocha and spice seamlessly interwoven with positive oak and tannins. Harmonious wine. Screwcap. 14% alc. **Rating** 93 **To** 2021 $25
Barossa Valley Cabernet Sauvignon 2006 Strong colour; luscious blackcurrant fruit has an array of sidelights ranging from cassis to mocha to chocolate; the tannins and oak also contribute. Screwcap. 14.5% alc. **Rating** 91 **To** 2020 $25

TTTT **Joseph's Barossa Valley Zinfandel 2007** Unconvincing colour, but has some of the flamboyant sweet, spicy flavours of warm-grown California zinfandel. The price is challenging, however. Cork. 15% alc. **Rating** 88 **To** 2012 $35

Jeanneret Wines   ★★★★☆

Jeanneret Road, Sevenhill, SA 5453 **Region** Clare Valley
T (08) 8843 4308 **F** (08) 8843 4251 www.jeanneretwines.com **Open** Mon–Fri 9–5, w'ends & public hols 10–5
Winemaker Ben Jeanneret, Harry Dickinson **Est.** 1992 **Cases** 12 000 **Vyds** 6 ha

Ben Jeanneret has progressively built the range and quantity of wines made by him at the onsite winery. In addition to the vineyards Jeanneret has contracts with owners of an additional 20 ha spread throughout the Clare Valley. All these vines are hand pruned, hand picked and dry-grown. Exports to the US, Canada and Japan.

ŶŶŶŶŶ **Doozie 2008** Richer, more intense than Big Fine Girl; sugar-dry, but fruit sweet, with luscious lime juice flavours. The Vino-Lok glass button self-ejected at high speed like a champagne cork, targeting and smashing an adjacent Riedel glass full of wine waiting to be tasted. Riesling. 12% alc. **Rating** 94 **To** 2015 $40

ŶŶŶŶŶ **Big Fine Girl Clare Valley Riesling 2008** Bright and lively from start to finish; citrus blossom aromas and a brisk, crisp palate has good length. Screwcap. 12.5% alc. **Rating** 90 **To** 2016 $19
Rank and File Clare Valley Shiraz 2006 Strong colour; the alcohol fills the mouth with associated flavours of plum and blackberry jam, plus chocolate and licorice. There is no shortage of flavour here, and some will love it. Screwcap. 15.5% alc. **Rating** 90 **To** 2016 $23

ŶŶŶŶ **Grace & Favour Clare Valley Grenache Shiraz 2005** The particular mark of Clare Valley grenache imposes itself strongly on this wine; it's an acquired taste that hasn't captured my receptors, but there is no technical fault with the wine. Screwcap. 15.5% alc. **Rating** 88 **To** 2013 $18

Jeir Creek   ★★★☆

122 Bluebell Lane, Murrumbateman, NSW 2582 **Region** Canberra District
T (02) 6227 5999 **F** (02) 6227 5900 **www.**jeircreekwines.com.au **Open** Thurs–Mon & hols 10–5 (w'ends only during Aug)
Winemaker Rob Howell **Est.** 1984 **Cases** 4000 **Vyds** 8 ha
Rob and Kay Howell, owner-founders of Jeir Creek, celebrate their 25 years of involvement in 2009. Rob runs the technically advanced winery, while Kay looks after the cellar door. Predominantly an estate-based business, the plantings comprise riesling, semillon, sauvignon blanc, chardonnay, viognier, pinot noir, merlot and cabernet sauvignon.

ŶŶŶŶ **Canberra District Riesling 2008** Rich citrus and apple aromas plus tropical nuances; has good length, depth and focus; good development potential. Screwcap. 12.5% alc. **Rating** 89 **To** 2015 $20

Jerusalem Hollow   ★★★★

6b Glyde Street, East Fremantle, WA 6158 (postal) **Region** Margaret River
T (08) 9339 6753 **F** (08) 9339 5192 **www.**jerusalemhollowwines.com.au **Open** Not
Winemaker Clive Otto (Contract) **Est.** 2000 **Cases** 500 **Vyds** 4.7 ha
Perth eye surgeon Bill Ward, wife (and former nurse) Louise and family began planting their vineyard in 2000. Bill, a long-term admirer of Champagne, was inspired by an article by Max Allen in the *Weekend Australian Magazine* in which Californian sparkling winemaker Harold Osborne (maker of Pelorus for Cloudy Bay in NZ) expressed the view that Margaret River was a good region for sparkling wine. This remains the main thrust of the business, with a side bet on Cabernet Sauvignon and a small amount of Roussanne Chardonnay to follow in due course. The name, incidentally, is a local one, but it so happens that Bill worked at the St John's eye hospital in Jerusalem as a surgical fellow in the late 1980s to early '90s.

ŶŶŶŶŶ **Methode Traditionnelle Chardonnay 2006** A lively wine, the early-picked chardonnay going through full mlf before tiraging and spending two years on yeast lees; has good length. Cork. 12.5% alc. **Rating** 90 **To** 2013 $23
Methode Traditionnelle Pinot Noir 2006 Full salmon-pink; crisp and tangy, with pronounced acidity to the fresh red berry fruits; good finish and aftertaste; an interesting contrast to the Methode Traditionelle Chardonnay. Cork. 12.5% alc. **Rating** 90 **To** 2014 $24

ɥɥɥɥ **Margaret River Chardonnay 2008** Fine, tight mineral and citrus aromas, the palate likewise; nine months in 30% new French oak has been absorbed by the fruit; needs a little more flesh. Screwcap. 13% alc. **Rating** 88 **To** 2012 $20

Jim Barry Wines ★★★★★

Craig's Hill Road, Clare, SA 5453 **Region** Clare Valley
T (08) 8842 2261 **www**.jimbarry.com **Open** Mon–Fri 9–5, w'ends & public hols 9–4
Winemaker Peter Barry **Est.** 1959 **Cases** 80 000 **Vyds** 250 ha
The patriarch of this highly successful wine business, Jim Barry, died in 2004, but the business continues under the active management of several of his many children. There is a full range of wine styles across most varietals, but with special emphasis on Riesling, Shiraz and Cabernet Sauvignon. The ultra-premium release is The Armagh Shiraz, with the McCrae Wood red wines not far behind. Jim Barry Wines is able to draw upon mature Clare Valley vineyards, plus a small holding in Coonawarra. Exports to all major markets.

ɥɥɥɥɥ **The Armagh Shiraz 2006** Inky crimson-purple; laden with voluptuous, but not jammy or dead, fruit in a blackberry, licorice and prune range; the tannins are remarkably soft for a full-bodied wine, oak unobtrusive. Cork. 15.5% alc. **Rating** 96 **To** 2030 $220
The Florita Clare Valley Riesling 2008 Haunting herb and blossom aromas lead into a penetrating, long and precisely structured palate; guaranteed for a long life. Screwcap. 11.5% alc. **Rating** 95 **To** 2023 $39.50
The McRae Wood Shiraz 2006 A very different flavour register to The Armagh; notes of red fruit and mint accompany black fruits; the medium- to full-bodied palate is very supple and smooth. Cork. 15.5% alc. **Rating** 95 **To** 2025 $55
The PB Cabernet Sauvignon 2005 Intense and focused blackcurrant fruit cradled in quality oak; the palate is no more than medium-bodied, but is very long, sustained by fine tannins. Poor quality cork. 15% alc. **Rating** 95 **To** 2025 $90
Watervale Riesling 2008 High-quality riesling at its price, with abundant citrus and herb fruit on the mid-palate, the long finish driven by lemon juice acidity. Screwcap. 11.5% alc. **Rating** 94 **To** 2020 $15

ɥɥɥɥɥ **The Lodge Hill Riesling 2008** A fragrant bouquet of citrus blossom and zest; then a tightly structured, dry palate leading through to a balanced finish. Screwcap. 11.5% alc. **Rating** 93 **To** 2018 $19.50
First Eleven Coonawarra Cabernet Sauvignon 2006 Savoury/spicy nuances swirl around the cassis and blackcurrant fruit on the medium- to full-bodied palate, which has good length. Deserves a better cork. 14.5% alc. **Rating** 93 **To** 2026 $60
Silly Mid On Sauvignon Blanc Semillon 2008 Driven past silly mid on to the boundary by the Adelaide Hills sauvignon blanc component, which is bright and breezy; has hit on a good length, too. Screwcap. 13% alc. **Rating** 91 **To** 2011 $20

ɥɥɥɥ **The Benbournie Cabernet Sauvignon 2004** The most savoury/herbal of the top-end releases, perhaps reflecting the vintage; I'm not convinced the wine comes off, the tannins likely to outlive the fruit. Cork. 14.5% alc. **Rating** 89 **To** 2014 $90

Jimbour Wines ★★★

86 Jimbour Station Road, Jimbour, Qld 4406 **Region** Queensland Zone
T (07) 3236 2100 **F** (07) 3236 0110 **www**.jimbour.com.au **Open** 7 days 10–4.30
Winemaker Peter Scudamore-Smith MW (Consultant) **Est.** 2000 **Cases** 10 000
Vyds 19.3 ha
Jimbour Station was one of the first properties opened in the Darling Downs and the heritage-listed homestead was built in 1876. The property, owned by the Russell family since 1923, has diversified by establishing a vineyard (shiraz, chardonnay, verdelho, cabernet sauvignon, viognier and merlot) and opening a cellar door on the property in a renovated water tower built in 1870. Increasing production is an indication of its role as one of Qld's major wine producers. Exports to Japan, Taiwan, Hong Kong and China.

ΨΨΨΨ   **Ludwig Leichhardt Reserve Shiraz 2007** Quite a porty bouquet of stewed blackberry; the palate is livelier, with plenty of ripe raspberry fruit and a touch of spice on the finish. Screwcap. 14.5% alc. **Rating** 89 **To** 2014 $27.99
Ludwig Leichhardt Reserve Merlot 2006 Dull colour; spiced plum bouquet, with soft fleshy fruit; just a little short, but good flavour. Screwcap. 13% alc. **Rating** 87 **To** 2012 $27.99

Jindalee Estate ★★★

265 Ballan Road, Moorabool, North Geelong, Vic 3221 **Region** Geelong
T (03) 5276 1280 **F** (03) 5276 1537 **www**.jindaleewines.com.au **Open** 7 days 10–5
Winemaker Chris Sargeant **Est.** 1997 **Cases** 700 000
Jindalee is part of the Littore Group, which currently has 1200 ha of premium wine grapes in production and under development in the Riverland. Corporate offices are now at the former Idyll Vineyard, acquired by Jindalee in 1997. Here 16 ha of estate vineyards have been retrellised and upgraded, and produce the Fettlers Rest range. The Jindalee Estate Chardonnay can offer spectacular value. Exports to all major markets.

ΨΨΨΨ   **Littore Family Wines Moscato 2008** Fresh and vibrant, with good acidity and spritz to its fine green apple fruit, and a cleansing chalky acidity on the finish; well made and good value. Screwcap. 5.5% alc. **Rating** 89 **To** 2009 $10.99

Jingalla ★★★☆

49 Bolganup Dam Road, Porongurup, WA 6324 **Region** Porongurup
T (08) 9853 1103 **F** (08) 9853 1023 **www**.jingallawines.com.au **Open** 7 days 10.30–5
Winemaker The Vintage Wineworx, Bill Crappsley (Consultant) **Est.** 1979 **Cases** 4000
Vyds 9 ha
Jingalla is a family business, owned and run by Geoff and Nita Clarke and Barry and Shelley Coad, the latter the ever-energetic wine marketer of the business. The hillside vineyards are low-yielding, with the white wines succeeding best, but they also produce some lovely red wines. A partner in The Vintage Wineworx winery, which means it no longer has to rely on contract winemaking. Exports to Taiwan.

ΨΨΨΨΨ   **Vignerons Select Porongurup Riesling 2008** Faintly dusty aromas are followed by a delicate but very lively palate with a mix of fresh cut apple and citrus; excellent acidity to close. Screwcap. 12.5% alc. **Rating** 92 **To** 2018 $25

Jinglers Creek Vineyard ★★★

288 Relbia Road, Relbia, Tas 7258 (postal) **Region** Northern Tasmania
T (03) 6344 3966 **www**.jinglerscreekvineyard.com.au **Open** Thurs–Sun 11–5
Winemaker Tamar Ridge (Michael Fogarty, Andrew Pirie), Bass Fine Wines (Guy Wagner) **Est.** 1998 **Cases** 870 **Vyds** 2 ha
Irving Fong came to grapegrowing later in life, undertaking the viticulture course at Launceston TAFE when he was 67 years old (where he also met his second wife). They have 1.8 ha of pinot noir, and small plantings of pinot gris, sauvignon blanc and chardonnay.

ΨΨΨΨ   **Riesling 2008** Gentle passionfruit/tropical/citrus; good balance, and will have much to offer in the medium term. Screwcap. 11.6% alc. **Rating** 89 **To** 2012 $21

Jinks Creek Winery ★★★★☆

Tonimbuk Road, Tonimbuk, Vic 3815 **Region** Gippsland
T (03) 5629 8502 **www**.jinkscreekwinery.com.au **Open** Sun 12–5 or by appt
Winemaker Andrew Clarke **Est.** 1981 **Cases** 1000 **Vyds** 3.52 ha
Planting of the Jinks Creek vineyard antedated the building of the winery by 11 years, but to this day all of the wines are made from estate-grown grapes. Perched above the vineyard with an uninterrupted view of the Bunyip State Forest and Black Snake Ranges, a refurbished

100-year-old wool shed has been renovated to house a restaurant, art gallery and cellar door. This venue is constructed entirely from recycled materials sourced from Gippsland, including old lining boards, a kauri pine dance floor and a perfectly preserved pressed-tin ceiling. Huge industrial steel windows open onto an outer deck, next to the sculpture garden and contemporary artworks by well-known Australian artists including Esther Erlich, Christopher Lees, Willy Sheather and Mark Knight. Open on Sundays for wood-fired pizza and wine tasting, the venue is available for private functions by arrangement, and a nearby Victorian weatherboard cottage provides secluded accommodation above the vineyard. Exports to the US.

ΨΨΨΨΨ   **Heathcote Shiraz 2006** An extremely attractive crimson-purple wine, offering the depth of flavour expected of Heathcote without the burden of elevated alcohol; supple blackberry, plum and red cherry fruit, seamless French oak and fine tannins. Diam. 14% alc. **Rating** 95 **To** 2021 $32

ΨΨΨΨΨ   **Yarra Valley Shiraz 2006** An appropriately sharp contrast to the Heathcote, with far more spice and pepper components, and a savoury twist to the long finish; good overall balance. Diam. 13.8% alc. **Rating** 93 **To** 2018 $32
Sauvignon Blanc 2008 An aromatic, clean bouquet in a grass/capsicum/citrus range, which comes through without interruption on the palate until a touch of passionfruit also appears. Screwcap. 12.5% alc. **Rating** 90 **To** 2010 $26

ΨΨΨΨ   **Pinot Gris 2008** Clear varietal character on both bouquet and palate, with clear apple and pear fruit on the well-balanced palate; just a trifle simple. Screwcap. 13.8% alc. **Rating** 88 **To** 2010 $26
West Gippsland Pinot Noir 2006 Distinct development; the flavours have a mix of confit fruit and spice flavours; varietal character moderately expressed. Drink up. Diam. 14% alc. **Rating** 88 **To** 2011 $30
Yarra Valley Cabernet Franc 2006 Light-bodied, with an appealing mix of small red fruits and more savoury characters; has length and balance. Diam. 13.5% alc. **Rating** 88 **To** 2013 $25
Sangiovese 2006 Creditable wine; a mix of cherry, sour cherry and sundry spices run through the bouquet and palate; the oak just a little too sweet and assertive. Diam. 14% alc. **Rating** 88 **To** 2013 $30
Rose 2008 Pale salmon; light flavours, but with a nice savoury edge and some acidity. Screwcap. 13% alc. **Rating** 87 **To** 2009 $25

John Duval Wines   ★★★★★

PO Box 622, Tanunda, SA 5352 **Region** Barossa Valley
T (08) 8563 2591 **F** (08) 8563 0372 **www.**johnduvalwines.com **Open** Not
Winemaker John Duval **Est.** 2003 **Cases** 6900
John Duval is an internationally recognised winemaker, having been the custodian of Penfolds Grange for almost 30 years as part of his role as chief red winemaker at Penfolds. He remains involved with Penfolds as a consultant, but these days is concentrating on establishing his own brand, and providing consultancy services to other clients in various parts of the world. On the principle 'if not broken, don't fix', he is basing his business on shiraz and shiraz blends from old-vine vineyards in the Barossa Valley. The brand name Plexus, incidentally, denotes a network in an animal body that combines elements into a coherent structure. Exports to the UK, the US and other major markets.

ΨΨΨΨΨ   **Eligo Barossa Valley Shiraz 2006** Dense but bright colour; has perfectly pitched blackberry, plum fruit and French oak on both the bouquet and medium- to full-bodied palate, with a very long finish. Cork in deference to the export market. 15% alc. **Rating** 95 **To** 2016 $105
Entity Barossa Valley Shiraz 2007 A fragrant bouquet and high-toned palate, quality oak an essential part of the wine; an almost European restraint in its make-up. Screwcap. 14.5% alc. **Rating** 94 **To** 2017 $48

🍷🍷🍷🍷 **Plexus Barossa Valley Shiraz Grenache Mourvedre 2007** Bright, but light, colour; a fragrant bouquet of red fruits is replicated on the light- to medium-bodied palate, backed by gossamer fine, savoury tannins. Screwcap. 14.5% alc. **Rating** 93 **To** 2015 $39

John Gehrig Wines ★★★★

Oxley-Milawa Road, Oxley, Vic 3678 **Region** King Valley
T (03) 5727 3395 **F** (03) 5727 3699 **www**.johngehrigwines.com.au **Open** 7 days 9–5
Winemaker Ross Gehrig **Est.** 1976 **Cases** 5600 **Vyds** 6 ha

Parents John and Elizabeth Gehrig have effectively passed on the management (and the winemaking) to son Ross, and now look after cellar door and marauding ducks and geese. The estate vineyard is a patchwork quilt of riesling, chenin blanc, chardonnay, pinot noir, cabernet sauvignon, merlot, malbec, shiraz, cabernet franc, petit verdot, tempranillo, muscat gordo blanco, durif and gamay, allowing – indeed demanding – Ross to make wines in a wide variety of styles, continuing to enjoy particular success with Riesling and Chenin Blanc.

🍷🍷🍷🍷 **King Valley Riesling 2008** Ripe lemon, cumquat and a touch of spice; good weight and texture, soft and supple on entry, and with good acidity on the finish. Screwcap. 13% alc. **Rating** 92 **To** 2014 $20

Cremant de Chenin Blanc 2004 Fresh cut green apple bouquet, with a touch of lanolin on the palate; a fresh and well-made example of the variety. Crown Seal. 12% alc. **Rating** 90 **To** 2012 $35

🍷🍷🍷🍷 **King Valley Chenin Blanc 2008** Bright colour; ripe apple bouquet with a little spice; off-dry with moderate intensity, good focus, and fresh acid to clean up the sugar. Screwcap. 13% alc. **Rating** 89 **To** 2013 $20

Cremant de Gamay 2006 Sweet and inoffensive; blueberry fruit with sweet black plums. Crown Seal. 13.5% alc. **Rating** 87 **To** 2011 $40

King Valley Tawny Port NV Deep colour; prune and Christmas cake, with some grilled nut complexity on the finish; a dark tawny style, but good flavour. Screwcap. 18% alc. **Rating** 87 **To** 2012 $30

John Kosovich Wines ★★★★★

Cnr Memorial Avenue/Great Northern Highway, Baskerville, WA 6056 **Region** Swan Valley
T (08) 9296 4356 **www**.johnkosovichwines.com.au **Open** 7 days 10–5.30
Winemaker Anthony Kosovich **Est.** 1922 **Cases** 4000 **Vyds** 12 ha

The name change from Westfield to John Kosovich Wines did not signify any change in either philosophy or direction for this much-admired producer of a surprisingly elegant and complex Chardonnay. The other wines are more variable, but from time to time there have been attractive Verdelho and excellent Cabernet Sauvignon. Since 1998, wines partly or wholly from the family's planting at Pemberton have been made, the Swan Valley/Pemberton blends released under the Bronze Wing label.

🍷🍷🍷🍷🍷 **Reserve Pemberton Cabernet Malbec 2007** Deep crimson-purple; impressive wine; great depth and intensity to the black fruit flavours, yet no hint of over-extraction, the tannins firm, but perfectly balanced; 20% Malbec. Diam. 13.5% alc. **Rating** 95 **To** 2020 $38

Rare Muscat NV Has the olive rim that shows its age; exceedingly rich and complex, with Christmas pudding, burnt toffee and caramel; extremely viscous, very different to Northeast Victoria, but of similar quality. Diam. 19% alc. **Rating** 95 **To** 2010 $75

Pemberton Chardonnay 2008 A very well-made and elegant wine, bringing the best out of Pemberton; while French oak is part of the picture, the primary focus is on the nectarine and grapefruit that drives the long palate. Screwcap. 13.5% alc. **Rating** 94 **To** 2015 $28

🍷🍷🍷🍷 **Verdelho 2008** Unusually fresh and lively, aided by a touch of spritz; citrussy overtones to typical fruit salad and honey flavours; good length. **Rating** 92 **To** 2010 $18

John's Blend

18 Neil Avenue, Nuriootpa, SA 5355 (postal) **Region** Langhorne Creek
T (08) 8562 1820 **F** (08) 8562 4050 **www**.johnsblend.com.au **Open** Not
Winemaker John Glaetzer **Est.** 1974 **Cases** 2500 **Vyds** 23 ha
John Glaetzer was Wolf Blass' right-hand man almost from the word go, the power behind
the throne of the three Jimmy Watson trophies awarded to Wolf Blass Wines in 1974, '75 and
'76, and a small matter of 11 Montgomery trophies for the Best Red Wine at the Adelaide
Wine Show. This has always been a personal venture on the side, as it were, by John and wife
Margarete Glaetzer, officially sanctioned of course, but really needing little marketing effort.
Exports to the UK, the US and other major markets.

ŶŶŶŶŶ **Margarete's Shiraz 2006** As ever, brilliantly made, the rich and supple
Langhorne Creek shiraz cradled in barrel-fermented American (75%) and French
(25%) oak, which provide both flavour and texture; an ultimate statement of his
style. Cork. 14% alc. **Rating** 94 **To** 2016 $35

ŶŶŶŶŸ **Individual Selection Langhorne Creek Cabernet Sauvignon 2005** While
the varietal fruit is clear enough, the wine doesn't have the mid-palate vinosity of
the Shiraz, yet does have length. Cork. 14.5% alc. **Rating** 90 **To** 2015 $35

Johnston Oakbank

18 Oakwood Road, Oakbank, SA 5243 **Region** Adelaide Hills
T (08) 8388 4263 **www**.johnston-oakbank.com.au **Open** Mon–Fri 8–5
Winemaker David O'Leary (Contract), Geoff Johnston **Est.** 1843 **Cases** 8000 **Vyds** 49 ha
The origins of this business owned by the Johnston Group date back to 1839, making it the
oldest family-owned business in SA. The vineyard at Oakbank is substantial, with chardonnay,
pinot noir, sauvignon blanc, shiraz, merlot and cabernet sauvignon.

ŶŶŶŶŸ **Adelaide Hills Shiraz 2005** There is a good showing of vibrant red and black
fruits; savoury at the core, with good tannin and refreshing acid; a very good cork
has certainly helped this wine mature with grace. 14% alc. **Rating** 92 **To** 2015 $20
Adelaide Hills Merlot 2007 Great colour; intense blueberry and plum bouquet
with a generous amount of new oak; the palate is fleshy and well balanced by
ample tannin and focused acidity; quite oaky, but should come together well with
time. Screwcap. 14% alc. **Rating** 92 **To** 2014 $20
Adelaide Hills Pinot Noir 2007 Bright colour; very oaky bouquet, with a
strong element of sweet red fruit and plenty of spice; the palate is fleshy, warm,
generous and exhibits cleansing acidity on the finish; certainly a bigger style.
Screwcap. 13.8% alc. **Rating** 91 **To** 2013 $20

ŶŶŶŶ **Adelaide Hills Sauvignon Blanc 2008** Very pale; cut grass and green nettle
dominate the bouquet; the balancing sweetness provides good texture, with a very
high acid finish. Screwcap. 12.5% alc. **Rating** 87 **To** 2012 $17.95
Adelaide Hills Cabernet Sauvignon 2005 A cassis-driven bouquet with a
slight herbal edge to the fruit; medium-bodied with plenty of sweet fruit on offer.
Screwcap. 14% alc. **Rating** 87 **To** 2014 $20

Jones Road ★★★★

2 Godings Road, Moorooduc, Vic 3933 **Region** Mornington Peninsula
T (03) 5977 7795 **F** (03) 5977 9695 **www**.jonesroad.com.au **Open** Fri–Mon 11–5
Winemaker Sticks (Travis Bush) **Est.** 1998 **Cases** 8000 **Vyds** 26.5 ha
It's a long story, but after establishing a very large and very successful herb-producing business
in the UK, Rob Frewer and family migrated to Australia in 1997. By a circuitous route
they ended up with a property on the Mornington Peninsula, promptly planting pinot
noir and chardonnay, then pinot gris, sauvignon blanc and merlot, and have since leased
another vineyard at Mt Eliza, and purchased Ermes Estate in 2007. Production has increased
significantly in the wake of these purchases. Exports to the UK, Canada, Norway, Sweden,
Singapore and Japan.

ΤΤΤΤ♀ **The Nepean Mornington Peninsula Chardonnay 2007** Light straw-green; has very attractive, bright nectarine and grapefruit flavours that do not depend on obvious oak for their length. Screwcap. 13.5% alc. **Rating** 91 **To** 2013 $42
Mornington Peninsula Chardonnay 2007 While restrained, has good focus, balance and length to the citrus-infused fruit, oak merely a support. Screwcap. 13.5% alc. **Rating** 90 **To** 2014 $22

ΤΤΤΤ **JR Jones Mornington Peninsula Pinot Noir 2008** Good clarity and hue; the bouquet is closed, and the palate distinctly firm early in its life, with hard-edged red fruit flavours; needs to loosen up. Screwcap. 13% alc. **Rating** 87 **To** 2014 $18

Jones Winery & Vineyard   ★★★★☆

Jones Road, Rutherglen, Vic 3685 **Region** Rutherglen
T (02) 6032 8496 **F** (02) 6032 8495 **www**.joneswinery.com **Open** Mon, Tues, Fri 11–4, w'ends & public hols 10–5
Winemaker Mandy Jones **Est.** 1860 **Cases** 2000 **Vyds** 9.19 ha
Jones Winery & Vineyard was established in 1860 and stands testament to a rich winemaking tradition. Since 1927, the winery has been owned and operated by the Jones family. Two blocks of old vines have been preserved (including 1.69 ha of shiraz), supported by further blocks progressively planted between '75 and 2008. Today, Jones Winery & Vineyard is jointly operated by winemaker Mandy Jones, who brings 14 years of experience working at Chateau Carsin in Bordeaux, France, and her brother Arthur Jones. Together they produce a small range of boutique wines. Exports to Finland.

ΤΤΤΤΤ **The Winemaker Rutherglen Durif 2006** Rich and robust, with layers of predominantly black fruits and well-balanced tannins giving good structure and length; impressive wine, developing at a leisurely pace. ProCork. 16% alc. **Rating** 94 **To** 2016 $28

ΤΤΤΤ♀ **LJ 2006** A generous, warm and rich offering of blackberry and plum fruit, with savoury/spicy nuances, perhaps partly stemming from the touch of grenache in the dominant shiraz. ProCork. 14.8% alc. **Rating** 90 **To** 2020 $55

ΤΤΤΤ **Rutherglen Shiraz 2006** A powerful bouquet of ripe fruit leads into a burly full-bodied palate with licorice, plum and prune flavours; not over-extracted, however. ProCork. 14.8% alc. **Rating** 89 **To** 2018 $28
The Winemaker Roussanne Marsanne 2008 Full-bodied white, its character coming from the fruit and its attendant phenolics; food style. Screwcap. 13.5% alc. **Rating** 87 **To** 2010 $25
Classic Rutherglen Muscat NV Very luscious and sweet; really needs more barrel-age. Vino-Lok. 18.5% alc. **Rating** 87 **To** 2009 $30

Josef Chromy Wines   ★★★★★

370 Relbia Road, Relbia, Tas 7258 **Region** Northern Tasmania
T (03) 6335 8700 **F** (03) 6335 8777 **www**.josefchromy.com.au **Open** 7 days 10–5
Winemaker Jeremy Dineen **Est.** 2004 **Cases** 5500
Joe Chromy just refuses to lie down and admit the wine industry in Tasmania is akin to a financial black hole. After escaping from Czechoslovakia in 1950, establishing Blue Ribbon Meats, using the proceeds of sale to buy Rochecombe and Heemskerk Vineyards, then selling those and establishing Tamar Ridge before it, too, was sold, Joe is at it again; this time he's invested $40 million in a wine-based but multi-faceted business. If this were not remarkable enough, Joe is in his late 70s, and spent much of 2006 recovering from a major stroke. Foundation of the new business was the purchase of the large Old Stornoway Vineyard at a receivership sale in 2003; in all, there are 60 ha of 10-year- old vines, the lion's share to pinot noir and chardonnay. He has retained Jeremy Dineen (for many years winemaker at Hood/ Wellington) as winemaker, the winery completed prior to the '07 vintage. Chromy's grandson Dean Cocker is guiding the development of a restaurant, function and equestrian centre, the latter on a scale sufficient to accommodate the Magic Millions yearling sales.

ϔϔϔϔ **Riesling 2008** Intense and penetrating citrus aromas and flavours; the palate has great length, accelerating on the finish, the acidity playing a major part without upsetting the balance of the wine. Screwcap. 12.7% alc. **Rating** 95 **To** 2023 $24
ZDAR Chardonnay 2006 A fine bouquet of white nectarine and framed by gentle spice; textural on the palate from lees stirring, toasty oak, and quite nutty on the long, fine and focused finish; ultimately generous with restraint. Screwcap. 14% alc. **Rating** 94 **To** 2014 $48

ϔϔϔϔ **Chardonnay 2007** A savoury bouquet showing lemon, grilled nuts and attractive charcuterie aromas; the palate is all about texture, soft and fleshy on entry, then tightening with precision and poise; finally a generous amount of lingering fruit on the finish. Screwcap. 13% alc. **Rating** 93 **To** 2014 $28

ϔϔϔϔ **Gewurztraminer 2008** Has some floral/rose petal characters to distinguish it from riesling, the mouthfeel also subtly different, but I'm not convinced. Screwcap. 13.7% alc. **Rating** 89 **To** 2013 $25
Pinot Noir 2007 Relatively light-bodied; clear pinot varietal expression but verging on simple. Screwcap. 13.9% alc. **Rating** 88 **To** 2012 $28

Journeys End Vineyards ★★★☆

248 Flinders Street, Adelaide, SA 5000 (postal) **Region** Southeast Australia
T 0431 709 305 **www.**journeysendvineyards.com.au **Open** Not
Winemaker Ben Riggs (Contract). **Est.** 2001 **Cases** 10 000
A particularly interesting business in the virtual winery category, which, while focused on McLaren Vale shiraz, also has contracts for other varieties in the Adelaide Hills and Langhorne Creek. The shiraz comes in four levels and, for good measure, uses five different clones to amplify the complexity that comes from having grapegrowers in many different parts of McLaren Vale. Exports to the UK, the US and other major markets.

ϔϔϔϔ **Embarkment McLaren Vale Shiraz 2006** Slightly brighter hue than Arrival; literally screams its region so strong are the chocolate flavours, but calms down on the back-palate thanks to savoury, balanced tannins. Screwcap. 14.5% alc. **Rating** 91 **To** 2016 $22.50

ϔϔϔϔ **Arrival McLaren Vale Shiraz 2006** Generous wine, arguably to a fault, the black fruit and dark chocolate fruit having a persistent substrate of vanillin sweetness; a question of style, I suppose; stained cork may have contributed. 14.5% alc. **Rating** 89 **To** 2014 $45
Three Brothers Reunited Shiraz 2007 Bright colour; has distinct spicy/earthy notes, utterly unexpected from a Southeast Australia provenance; the alcohol seems higher than disclosed, but that is a small quibble for a wine at this price. Value. Screwcap. 14.5% alc. **Rating** 87 **To** 2013 $11
The Bobby Dazzler Shiraz 2007 Label cringe (directed at the US market) to one side, the wine has plenty of black fruit flavours and fair length, helped by savoury tannins. Screwcap. 14.5% alc. **Rating** 87 **To** 2015 $16.50

Juniper Estate ★★★★☆

Harmans Road South, Cowaramup, WA 6284 **Region** Margaret River
T (08) 9755 9000 **F** (08) 9755 9100 **www.**juniperestate.com.au **Open** 7 days 10–5
Winemaker Mark Messenger, Kym Eyres **Est.** 1973 **Cases** 16 000 **Vyds** 15.27 ha
When Roger Hill and his wife purchased the Wrights vineyard in 1998, the 10-ha vineyard was already 25 years old, but in need of retrellising and a certain amount of nursing to bring it back to health. All of that has happened, along with the planting of additional shiraz and cabernet sauvignon. The Juniper Crossing wines use a mix of estate-grown and purchased grapes from other Margaret River vineyards. The Juniper Estate releases are made only from the estate plantings. Exports to the UK, the US, Canada, Denmark, Hong Kong and Singapore.

ΨΨΨΨΨ Juniper Crossing Margaret River Semillon Sauvignon Blanc 2008
A complex style, with a mineral element playing support to very pure varietal
fruit; ample on the palate, there is terrific depth to the flavour; linear acidity
sustains an even, harmonious finish. Screwcap. 13% alc. **Rating** 94 **To** 2012 $21.99

ΨΨΨΨΨ Juniper Crossing Margaret River Chardonnay 2007 A fine, clearly defined
wine with nectarine fruit and some compelling toasty complexity from the well-
handled oak; the palate is quite fine, focused and long; real depth and power to the
finish. Screwcap. 13.5% alc. **Rating** 93 **To** 2015 $23
Juniper Crossing Margaret River Tempranillo 2007 Good colour; dark
cherry bouquet, with bramble and spice; juicy blue fruits on the palate, and a very
attractive savoury twist to the finish; firm and tannic, but in balance with the fruit.
Screwcap. 14% alc. **Rating** 92 **To** 2013 $21
Juniper Crossing Margaret River Merlot 2007 Vibrant and focused, with
cedar, redcurrant and a splash of oak; medium-bodied, with a fleshy mid-palate,
the tannins are fine and persistent. Screwcap. 14% alc. **Rating** 90 **To** 2014 $20

ΨΨΨΨ Margaret River Semillon 2007 Barrel ferment inputs tend to overshadow the
varietal fruit, but do invest the wine with complexity; deserves a year or two to
flex its fruit muscles. Screwcap. 13% alc. **Rating** 89 **To** 2013 $28
Juniper Crossing Margaret River Shiraz 2006 Focused red berry fruit, with
cinnamon spice and a medium-bodied palate; fresh acid and slightly savoury tannin
on the finish. Screwcap. 14% alc. **Rating** 89 **To** 2014 $20
Juniper Crossing Margaret River Rose 2008 Pale pink; a dry style, light red
fruits and good texture; finishes quite dry, with a savoury, slightly bitter twist for
interest. Screwcap. 13.5% alc. **Rating** 88 **To** 2012 $18.99
Juniper Crossing Margaret River Cabernet Sauvignon Merlot 2006
Good colour; quite bright fruit aromas, likewise entry into the mouth, finishing
with more savoury notes. Screwcap. 13.5% alc. **Rating** 88 **To** 2012 $21.50

Juul Wines   NR

820 Rosemount Road, Denman, NSW 2328 **Region** Upper Hunter Valley
T (02) 6547 1044 **F** (02) 6547 1280 **www**.roseglenestate.com **Open** By appt
Winemaker Inwine (Barry Koorij) **Est.** NFP **Cases** 12 000 **Vyds** 40 ha
Juul Wines is a partnership between Stephen Bottomley, Ingrid Suijkerbuijk and Karen
Williams, and is part of a larger property offering thoroughbred agistment, lucerne hay and
holiday cottage accommodation. The 40-ha vineyard is substantial, with chardonnay and
verdelho accounting for just under 30 ha, the remainder sauvignon blanc, shiraz and cabernet
sauvignon. The wines were borne of a series of five devastating hail storms in the Upper
Hunter, the first in October 2004. The storms not only gave rise to some evocatively-named
wines, but also an enforced decision to look to Mount Barker, Western Australia and Orange
for the 2005 Shiraz. The substantial production is sold through the usual domestic channels,
together with exports to China and – wait for it – Lord Howe Island.

K1 by Geoff Hardy   ★★★★★

Tynan Road, Kuitpo, SA 5172 **Region** Adelaide Hills
T (08) 8388 3700 **F** (08) 8388 3564 **www**.k1.com.au **Open** W'ends & public hols 11–5
Winemaker Geoff Hardy, Ben Riggs **Est.** 1980 **Cases** 8000 **Vyds** 30 ha
The ultra-cool Kuitpo vineyard in the Adelaide Hills was planted by Geoff Hardy in 1987 after
searching for an ideal location in the hills for premium wine production. As this was the first
significant vineyard planted in the region it became known as the K1 vineyard. All fruit for
Geoff Hardy's K1 brand is sourced from this vineyard, perched on the south-western ridge of
the Adelaide Hills above McLaren Vale. Exports to the UK, the US and other major markets.

ΨΨΨΨΨ Tzimmukin 2006 A powerful, medium-bodied, wine, convincingly matching
blackcurrant and blackberry fruit flavours against each other; the texture is good,
as is the length; the tannins, too, have been precisely judged. Cabernet Sauvignon/
Shiraz. ProCork. 15% alc. **Rating** 95 **To** 2026 $75

Adelaide Hills Shiraz 2007 The very dark hue signals a wine with attractively savoury/earthy/spicy nuances through both bouquet and palate; it has particularly good structure, and persistence to the ripe tannins of the finish. Screwcap. 14.5% alc. **Rating** 94 **To** 2020 $35

Adelaide Hills Cabernet Sauvignon 2007 Deep crimson-purple; a strongly varietal wine on both bouquet and palate; intense blackcurrant fruit receives perfect oak and tannin support, in turn giving rise to excellent balance and length. Screwcap. 14.5% alc. **Rating** 94 **To** 2022 $35

ΨΨΨΨΨ Adelaide Hills Merlot 2006 Great colour; while intense, the palate is no more than medium-bodied, as befits merlot; the varietal expression, too, is spot on, the cassis fruit with black olive and spice undertones. Screwcap. 14% alc. **Rating** 92 **To** 2016 $35

Adelaide Hills Pinot Noir 2007 Bright, clear colour; lively, spicy red fruits course through a precisely structured palate; good line and length. Screwcap. 13.5% alc. **Rating** 91 **To** 2014 $35

ΨΨΨΨ Adelaide Hills Chardonnay 2007 The relatively quiet bouquet leads into an elegant, understated palate that will continue to develop at a leisurely pace; length is its major strength. Screwcap. 13.5% alc. **Rating** 89 **To** 2012 $35

Silver Label Semillon Viognier 2008 I'm not sure about the blend rationale, unless it be that opposites attract; if so, it more or less worked, although most of the attraction is that of the semillon. Screwcap. 13.5% alc. **Rating** 88 **To** 2012 $18

Silver Label Cabernet Tempranillo 2006 A spicy bouquet leads into a medium-bodied palate, with a tangy finish undoubtedly due to the tempranillo; a near miss. Screwcap. 14% alc. **Rating** 87 **To** 2012 $18

Kabminye Wines

Krondorf Road, Tanunda, SA 5352 **Region** Barossa Valley
T (08) 8563 0889 **F** (08) 8563 3828 **www**.kabminye.com **Open** 7 days 11–5
Winemaker Rick Glastonbury **Est.** 2001 **Cases** 3500 **Vyds** 1.5 ha
Richard and Ingrid Glastonbury's cellar door is on land settled in the 1880s by Ingrid's ancestor Johann Christian Henschke. Kabminye is an Aboriginal word meaning 'morning star', and was given to the hamlet of Krondorf as a result of the anti-German sentiment during the Second World War (since changed back to the original Krondorf). The cellar door and café opened in 2003; SA Tourism has since used the building as a sustainable tourism case study. The vineyard is planted to durif, shiraz, mourvedre, carignan, cinsaut, black muscat and black frontignac. Exports to the UK, Malaysia, Hong Kong and China.

ΨΨΨΨΨ Barossa Valley Carignan 2006 Bright, clear crimson-red; fragrant red fruit aromas and flavours, amazingly so given the wine spent 30 months in French oak, bolstered by fine, tight tannins. Screwcap. 14.5% alc. **Rating** 94 **To** 2016 $37.50

ΨΨΨΨΨ Kahl Barossa Valley Shiraz 2006 Full-flavoured, but not overripe; blackberry, plum and dark chocolate coalesce into a fluid medium-bodied palate, the tannins fine, the oak subtle. Screwcap. 15% alc. **Rating** 93 **To** 2020 $32.50

Ilona Barossa Valley Rose 2008 Offers a powerful palate built around Cabernet Sauvignon (55%), plus equal parts Grenache/Dolcetto; buckets of red fruits without sweetness or phenolics. Screwcap. 13.5% alc. **Rating** 91 **To** 2010 $18.50

Barossa Valley Grenache Carignan 2006 Light but bright crimson; the bouquet and palate are also very fresh, with crisp red berry fruits impressive, and unexpected from Barossa Valley Grenache (85%) at this age. Screwcap. 15% alc. **Rating** 90 **To** 2014 $27.50

ΨΨΨΨ Irma Adeline 2006 In typical Barossa style; notwithstanding the very good vintage; no more than medium-bodied, and some confection characters appear; however, notes of warm spice and integrated oak come to the rescue. Shiraz/Mataro/Grenache. Screwcap. 15% alc. **Rating** 89 **To** 2016 $25

Schliebs Block 2006 Bright, clear colour; aromatic, juicy red berry fruits with spice and herb components in the background. Mataro/Carignan/Cinsaut/Black Frontignan. Screwcap. 14.5% alc. **Rating** 89 **To** 2014 $27.50

Kaesler Wines

Barossa Valley Way, Nuriootpa, SA 5355 **Region** Barossa Valley
T (08) 8562 4488 **www.**kaesler.com.au **Open** Mon–Sat 10–5, Sun & public hols 11.30–4
Winemaker Reid Bosward, Stephen Dew **Est.** 1990 **Cases** 22 000 **Vyds** 50 ha
The Kaesler name originated in 1845, when the first members of the family settled in the Barossa Valley. The vineyards date back to 1893, but the Kaesler ownership ended in 1968. After several changes, the present (much-expanded) Kaesler Wines was acquired by a Swiss banking family in conjunction with former Flying Winemaker Reid Bosward and wife Bindy. Bosward's experience shows through in the wines, which now come from estate vineyards, 40 ha adjacent to the winery, and 10 ha in the Marananga area. The latter includes shiraz planted in 1899, with both blocks seeing plantings in the 1930s, '60s, then each decade through to the present. Exports to all major markets.

Stonehorse Barossa Valley Shiraz 2006 Inevitably mouthfilling, but has attractive plum, prune and licorice flavours on the mid-palate, which manage to carry the alcohol very well; scrappy cork. 15.5% alc. **Rating** 93 **To** 2016 $25

 # Kahlon Estate Wines   **NR**

Lot 4 Airport Road, Renmark, SA 5341 **Region** Riverland
T (08) 8586 5744 **www.**kahlonestatewine.com.au **Open** Mon–Fri 8–5, w'ends 9–4
Winemaker Peter McKee **Est.** 2004 **Cases** 22 000 **Vyds** 160 ha
The roots of Kahlon Estate go back to 1990, when founder/owner Mohinder Kahlon began the development of what ultimately became a 160-ha vineyard. Initially simply a grapegrower, the business first diversified into volume wines sold in bulk, and ultimately (in 2004) to cleanskin bottled wines selling for $33 per 12-bottle case, and varietal wines under the Long Tail brand (Chardonnay, Sauvignon Blanc, Shiraz, Petit Verdot and Cabernet Sauvignon) at $50 per case. Export markets include the UK, the US, France, Germany and China.

Kalari Wines

120 Carro Park Road, Cowra, NSW 2794 **Region** Cowra
T (02) 6342 1465 **www.**kalariwines.com.au **Open** Fri–Mon & public hols 10–5
Winemaker Madrez Wine Services (Chris Derrez) **Est.** 1995 **Cases** NA **Vyds** 10.5 ha
The name Kalari was that given by the Wiradjuri people for the nearby Lachlan River before white settlement. The family-owned vineyard saw chardonnay, verdelho and shiraz planted in 1995, followed by cabernet sauvignon, merlot and semillon in '97. Unusually, Kalari produces four different styles of wine from verdelho: a light, dry wine; a semi-sweet table wine; Fortelho, the first fortified wine from the region; and, most recently, a dessert wine (Semillon/Verdelho).

Cowra Shiraz 2008 Dense crimson-purple; a rich, full-bodied palate, with blackberry, plum and prune flavours, remarkable for Cowra; a nice touch of French oak adds to the appeal. Screwcap. 13.5% alc. **Rating** 90 **To** 2018 $20

Cowra Verdelho 2008 Varietal fruit salad is there, but also a commendable touch of distinctly minerally acidity to lift it out of the ruck. Screwcap. 13.4% alc. **Rating** 88 **To** 2011 $17
Cowra Chardonnay 2008 So pale, it is almost white; has good structure and surprising thrust, although the fruit is not particularly expressive; an airbrush of oak is well judged. Screwcap. 14.1% alc. **Rating** 87 **To** 2011 $17

Kalgan River Wines

PO Box 5559, Albany, WA 6332 **Region** Albany
T (08) 9841 4413 **F** (08) 9841 6471 **www**.kalganriverwines.com.au **Open** Not
Winemaker Mike Garland **Est.** 2000 **Cases** 2000 **Vyds** 20 ha
John and Dianne Ciprian have brought different backgrounds to their Kalgan River property.
John has grapegrowing in two generations of ancestral blood in his veins. However, it was
his success as a jeweller that provided the wherewithal for Kalgan River; Dianne started
as a mathematics teacher, and then became a jewellery valuer, both occupations requiring
intellectual rigour. Thanks to what they describe as 'hard yakka', they have established shiraz,
cabernet sauvignon, riesling, chardonnay and viognier.

♀♀♀♀♀ **Great Southern Riesling 2008** Ripe citrus fruit aromas and a touch of spice;
quite fine on the finish with some mineral complexity to add depth. Screwcap.
13.6% alc. **Rating** 90 **To** 2015 $22.95

♀♀♀♀ **Ciprian Great Southern Shiraz 2007** Good colour; the bouquet has an
abundance of red fruits; the palate is very firm and quite dry, but the fruit weight
suggests it will soften with time. Screwcap. 14.3% alc. **Rating** 89 **To** 2016 $44.95
Great Southern Shiraz Viognier 2007 Another brooding dark wine;
full-bodied, dense and quite chewy, with a veritable mountain of tannin to
wade through before getting to the fruit; balance is the question, but its fruit
concentration cannot be denied. Screwcap. 14.7% alc. **Rating** 88 **To** 2017 $34.95

Kalleske

6 Murray Street, Greenock, SA 5360 **Region** Barossa Valley
T (08) 8563 4000 **F** (08) 8563 4001 **www**.kalleske.com **Open** By appt
Winemaker Troy Kalleske **Est.** 1999 **Cases** 7000 **Vyds** 30.2 ha
The Kalleske family has been growing and selling grapes on a mixed farming property at
Greenock for over 100 years. Sixth-generation Troy Kalleske with brother Tony established
the Kalleske winery and created the Kalleske label in 1999. The vineyard is planted to shiraz,
grenache, mataro, chenin blanc, durif, viognier, zinfandel, petit verdot, semillon and tempranillo;
the vines vary in age with the oldest dating back to 1875, and an overall average age of about
50 years. The vineyard is low-yielding, all grapes are grown organically, and the onsite winery
is certified organic; handled the 2007 vintage well. Exports to all major markets.

♀♀♀♀♀ **Johann Georg Old Vine Barossa Valley Shiraz 2006** One of those
rare wines when very high alcohol does not compromise the palate; a mix of
blackberry, dark chocolate and licorice in a savoury spectrum; very good length;
vines planted 1875. Cork. 15.5% alc. **Rating** 96 **To** 2020 $100

♀♀♀♀ **Greenock Barossa Valley Shiraz 2007** An unabashed full-bodied wine, with
fruit, tannins and oak in abundance; really does need time to slim down, which it
will do. Cork. 15% alc. **Rating** 93 **To** 2022 $38
Moppa Barossa Valley Shiraz 2007 Has more light and shade to its aromas
and flavours than the Greenock; medium-bodied rather than full-bodied;
complexity possibly due to a dash of viognier and petit verdot; pleasing splashes of
spice and savoury black fruits. Screwcap. 14.5% alc. **Rating** 93 **To** 2017 $29
Pirathon by Kalleske Barossa Valley Shiraz 2007 The flavour to dollar
ratio is, to say the least, impressive; oceans of plum, prune and blackberry fruits,
and well-controlled extract; good wine from the difficult '07. Cork. 15% alc.
Rating 92 **To** 2017 $23
Pirathon by Kalleske Barossa Valley Shiraz 2006 Deep colour; blackberry,
dark chocolate and blackberry aromas; a richly textured, full-bodied palate, but
with soft, evenly distributed tannins and showing no excessive alcohol or extract
characters; very impressive wine at its price point. Cork. 15% alc. **Rating** 92
To 2016 $23.50

Old Vine Barossa Valley Grenache 2006 From a single vineyard planted in 1935, it is ultra-typical Barossa style, with slight confection overtones to the spicy flavours of the medium-bodied palate; the alcohol is evident. Cork. 15.5% alc. **Rating** 90 **To** 2014 $45
JMK Barossa Valley Shiraz VP (375 ml) 2006 Well put together; spicy fruit with clean spirit, and an admirably dry finish taking it towards Portuguese vintage port. Cork. 19% alc. **Rating** 90 **To** 2015 $24

ȲȲȲ **Clarry's Grenache Shiraz 2007** Some early colour development; plush but very ripe fruit flavours in a cosmetic spectrum ex the grenache. Screwcap. 14.5% alc. **Rating** 89 **To** 2012 $19
Florentine Barossa Valley Chenin Blanc 2008 Very pleasant fruit salad flavours, with a touch of marzipan rumbling somewhere around in the background. Could surprise with a few years bottle age. Screwcap. 12.5% alc. **Rating** 87 **To** 2012 $19

Kangarilla Road Vineyard ★★★★

Kangarilla Road, McLaren Vale, SA 5171 **Region** McLaren Vale
T (08) 8383 0533 **www.**kangarillaroad.com.au **Open** Mon–Fri 9–5, w'ends 11–5
Winemaker Kevin O'Brien **Est.** 1997 **Cases** 40 000 **Vyds** 14 ha
Kangarilla Road was formerly known as Stevens Cambrai. Long-time industry identity Kevin O'Brien and wife Helen purchased the property in 1997, soon establishing the strikingly labelled Kangarilla Road brand. The estate plantings include shiraz, zinfandel, viognier, chardonnay and albarino, intake supplemented by purchases from other vineyards in the region. Exports to the UK, the US and other major markets.

ȲȲȲȲȲ **McLaren Vale Shiraz 2007** Deep purple-crimson; a seriously impressive wine, with blackberry and bitter chocolate fruit underpinned by quality oak, and lingering, ripe tannins. Bargain. Screwcap. 14% alc. **Rating** 93 **To** 2020 $20
McLaren Vale Cabernet Sauvignon 2007 Savoury, brooding black fruits leave no doubt about variety or region, but the elegant, fine tannins on the finish are an unexpected pleasure. Screwcap. 14% alc. **Rating** 92 **To** 2017 $20
The Devil's Whiskers McLaren Vale Shiraz 2006 While only medium-bodied, this is a very potent wine, with an animated palate demanding attention for its display of savoury black fruits. Screwcap. 15% alc. **Rating** 91 **To** 2016 $30
McLaren Vale Viognier 2007 A ripe bouquet of apricot kernel and a touch of spice; full and rich on entry, with a slight phenolic twist to the finish, which keeps the palate fresh; long and even. Screwcap. 14% alc. **Rating** 90 **To** 2012 $21

ȲȲȲȲ **Fleurieu Primitivo 2006** Loaded with sweet red fruit and a light confectionery character; fruitcake spice comes through on the palate, and the finish is warm and generous. Zinfandel. Screwcap. 16% alc. **Rating** 89 **To** 2012 $21
McLaren Vale Chardonnay 2008 Pale colour; a pleasant array of spice and stone fruit aromas; generous and rich on the palate, with quite a toasty full-flavoured finish. Screwcap. 13.5% alc. **Rating** 88 **To** 2014 $16
2 Up Shiraz 2007 A robust, verging on rustic, wine with strong black fruits and a stash of dark chocolate. Screwcap. 14.5% alc. **Rating** 87 **To** 2014 $15

Kara Kara Vineyard ★★★

99 Edelsten Road, St Arnaud, Vic 3478 **Region** Pyrenees
T (03) 5496 3294 **F** (03) 5496 3294 **www.**karakarawines.com.au **Open** Mon–Fri 10.30–6, w'ends 9–6
Winemaker Steve Zsigmond, Hanging Rock Winery **Est.** 1977 **Cases** 1500 **Vyds** 9 ha
Hungarian-born Steve Zsigmond comes from a long line of vignerons and sees Kara Kara as the eventual retirement occupation for himself and wife Marlene. He is a graduate of the Adelaide University (Roseworthy) wine marketing course, and worked for Yalumba and Negociants as a sales manager in Adelaide and Perth. He looks after sales and marketing from the Melbourne premises of Kara Kara, and the wine is made at Hanging Rock, with consistent results.

🍷🍷🍷🍷 **Pyrenees Cabernet Sauvignon 2006** Light- to medium-bodied in a distinctly savoury mode, but with good length and balance, and enough cassis notes to get it over the line. Screwcap. 13.8% alc. **Rating** 88 **To** 2014 **$25**

Karanto Vineyards ★★★

Box 12, Langhorne Creek, SA 5255 **Region** Langhorne Creek
T (08) 8537 3106 **F** (08) 8537 3106 **www**.karanto.com.au **Open** Not
Winemaker Briony Hoare **Est.** 2002 **Cases** 800 **Vyds** 43.5 ha

The Karanto property was purchased by PR Dodd in 1910 who established a mixed horticultural venture. In 1979 it came into the ownership of Dodd's granddaughter Zonda and husband Dennis Elliott, who progressively changed the 44-ha property into a single-purpose viticultural enterprise. Until 2002 all the grapes were sold to major wine companies, but in that year the Elliotts made their first Shiraz; both it and the '03 won significant accolades. The Shiraz continues, but the Elliotts have since established 0.5 ha each of aglianico, greco di tufo, primitivo, fiano and pinot grigio, the first vines made over the 2007 to '09 vintages. The wines are made by former Australian Young Winemaker of the Year, Briony Hoare.

🍷🍷🍷🍷 **Langhorne Creek Fiano 2008** Has more upfront flavour than the Coriole Fiano, thanks in part to much higher alcohol; honey, spice and dried fruit flavours. Screwcap. 14.6% alc. **Rating** 89 **To** 2010 **$20**

Langhorne Creek Pinot Grigio 2007 Has enough flavour and mouthfeel to satisfy; quite evident pear and citrus; has length. Screwcap. 13.7% alc. **Rating** 88 **To** 2009 **$17**

Langhorne Creek Aglianico 2007 Bright colour; light, fresh raspberry and strawberry fruit with none of the residual sweetness sometimes encountered in the variety. Cork. 13.4% alc. **Rating** 88 **To** 2010 **$24**

7A Langhorne Creek Shiraz 2004 Has developed well; juicy/spicy overtones to its berry fruits, along with a dash of chocolate; the alcohol does show up on the finish, however. Diam. 15.3% alc. **Rating** 87 **To** 2011 **$20**

Karra Yerta Wines ★★★★

Lot 534 Flaxman's Valley Road, Wilton, SA 5353 **Region** Eden Valley
T 0438 870 178 **www**.karrayertawines.com.au **Open** By appt
Winemaker James Linke, Peter Gajewski, Peter Schell **Est.** 2006 **Cases** 300 **Vyds** 1.92 ha

The name Karra Yerta is derived from the local Aboriginal language, 'karra' the name for the majestic red gum trees, and 'yerta' meaning country or ground. The landscape has changed little (other than the patches of vineyard) since the ancestors of James and Marie Linke arrived (separately) in SA in 1847. Both James and Marie were born in Angaston, but moved to the Flaxmans Valley in 1985, and in '87 purchased one of the old stone cottages in the region. Much time has been spent in reviving the largely abandoned vineyard, which provides most of their grapes; plantings now include semillon, riesling, shiraz and frontignac. While most of the grapes were sold, they indulged in home winemaking for many years, but have now moved into commercial winemaking on a micro scale. Exports to the UK.

🍷🍷🍷🍷½ **Limited Release Eden Valley Riesling 2008** A taut lemon and mineral bouquet; tightly wound palate, with good focus and persistence; strong mineral notes on the finish; 85 cases made. Screwcap. 12.5% alc. **Rating** 92 **To** 2015 **$20**

KarriBindi ★★★★★

RMB 111, Scott Road, Karridale, WA 6288 (postal) **Region** Margaret River
T (08) 9758 5570 **F** (08) 9758 5570 **www**.karribindi.com.au **Open** Not
Winemaker Naturaliste Vintners (Bruce Dukes) **Est.** 1997 **Cases** NFP **Vyds** 32 ha

KarriBindi has been established by Kevin, Yvonne and Kris Wealand. The name is partly derived from Karridale and the surrounding Karri forests, and from Bindi, the home town of one of the members of the Wealand family. In Nyoongar, 'karri' means strong, special, spiritual, tall tree and Bindi means butterfly, hence the label's picture of a butterfly soaring through

Karri trees. The Wealands have established 15 ha of sauvignon blanc, 6.25 ha chardonnay, 4 ha cabernet sauvignon, 3 ha semillon and 2 ha each shiraz and merlot. The major part of the grape production is sold under contract to Vasse Felix and Leeuwin Estate, with limited amounts released under the KarriBindi label. The core range includes Sauvignon Blanc, Semillon Sauvignon Blanc (a prolific medal-winner, including top gold in its class at the WA Wine Show '08), Shiraz and Chardonnay Pinot.

ŸŸŸŸŸ **Semillon Sauvignon Blanc 2008** Pure and intense aromas give way to a bright incisive palate with a mix of grass and a hint of tropical fruit; lingering acidity; comes up and up the more you taste it. Gold WA Wine Show '08. Screwcap. 12.5% alc. **Rating** 95 **To** 2012 $15

ŸŸŸŸ **Margaret River Sauvignon Blanc 2008** Highly perfumed green nettle bouquet; strong varietal intensity, with juicy mid-palate fruit; fresh pea pod flavour on the finish. Screwcap. 12.6% alc. **Rating** 89 **To** 2011 $20
Margaret River Shiraz 2006 Spicy pepper and light red berry fruit; elegant on the palate, with a distinct savoury edge and prominent refreshing acidity; somewhat European in style. Screwcap. 13.5% alc. **Rating** 89 **To** 2014 $20

Kassebaum Wines   ★★★

Nitschke Road, Marananga, SA 5355 **Region** Barossa Valley
T (08) 8562 2731 **F** (08) 8562 4751 **www**.carobcottage.com.au **Open** By appt
Winemaker Mark Jamieson (Contract) **Est.** 2003 **Cases** 400 **Vyds** 6.9 ha
David and Dianne Kassebaum are third-generation grapegrowers. David has been involved in the wine industry for 20 years, working first with Penfolds in bottling, microbiology and maturation laboratories, and most recently in the Vinpac International laboratory. They have shiraz on two separate vineyards, most of the production being sold, yields vary from 1 to 1.5 tonnes per acre. The small amount of shiraz retained for the Kassebaum Magdalena label is matured in new French and American oak for 12 months.

ŸŸŸŸ **Magdalena Barossa Valley Shiraz 2007** Good colour; aromas of stewed prune and chocolate lead into a ripe, full-flavoured palate; all arms and legs at this point. Screwcap. 14.5% alc. **Rating** 88 **To** 2015 $25

Kate Hill Wines   ★★★★★

PO Box 3052, West Hobart, Tas 7005 **Region** Southern Tasmania
T (03) 6223 5641 **F** (03) 9598 2718 **www**.katehillwines.com.au **Open** Not
Winemaker Kate Hill **Est.** 2008 **Cases** 900
When Kate Hill (and husband Charles) came to Tasmania, Kate had worked as a winemaker in Australia and overseas for 10 years. They arrived in 2006, Kate to grow her winemaking consultancy business and to gradually establish her own label. In 2008 she made a Riesling and Pinot Noir; the wines are made from a number of vineyards across southern Tasmania, the aim being to produce approachable, delicate wines. She achieved precisely that with the gold medal-winning '08 Riesling entered in the Tasmanian Wines Show '09.

ŸŸŸŸŸ **Riesling 2008** Delicate but lingering passionfruit and lime; very good balance, line and length; marked contrast to the more aggressive acidity of young Tasmanian rieslings. Gold medal Tas Wine Show '09. Screwcap. 12% alc. **Rating** 95 **To** 2016 $21.50

Katnook Estate   ★★★★★

Riddoch Highway, Coonawarra, SA 5263 **Region** Coonawarra
T (08) 8737 2394 **www**.katnookestate.com.au **Open** Mon–Sat 10–5, Sun 11–4
Winemaker Wayne Stehbens **Est.** 1979 **Cases** 110 000 **Vyds** 387 ha
One of the largest contract grapegrowers and suppliers in Coonawarra, selling more than half its grape production to others. The historic stone wool shed in which the second vintage in Coonawarra (1896) was made, and which has served Katnook since 1980, has been restored.

Well over half the total estate plantings are cabernet sauvignon and shiraz, other varieties of importance being chardonnay, merlot, sauvignon blanc and pinot noir. The Odyssey Cabernet Sauvignon and Prodigy Shiraz are the icon duo at the top of a multi-tiered production. Freixenet, the Spanish Cava producer, now owns 100% of the business. Exports to all major markets.

ŢŢŢŢŢ **Odyssey Coonawarra Cabernet Sauvignon 2005** An intense wine with tremendous depth of flavour despite modest alcohol; blackcurrant and blackberry fruit resonates through the palate, which has absorbed its lengthy stay in French oak; the tannins, too, are balanced. Screwcap. 14% alc. **Rating** 96 **To** 2025 $98
Prodigy Coonawarra Shiraz 2006 Dense colour; the rich bouquet of black fruits and quality oak is replicated on the palate,which is stylish and intense, extract and alcohol perfectly balanced. Screwcap. 14.5% alc. **Rating** 95 **To** 2026 $98
Odyssey Coonawarra Cabernet Sauvignon 2004 In absolutely classic Odyssey style; three years in new and one-year-old French and American barriques; silky smooth black fruits, cedary oak and tannins all coalesce; the screwcap will underwrite its long future. 14% alc. **Rating** 95 **To** 2024 $95
Coonawarra Chardonnay 2005 Bright green-gold; a very complex bouquet, with some Burgundian characters; grapefruit to the fore on the long and intense palate, which has very good structure and length; 22 months in French oak. Screwcap. 13.5% alc. **Rating** 94 **To** 2013 $28
Coonawarra Cabernet Sauvignon 2005 Medium red-purple; a wine strongly shaped by over two years in predominantly French barriques that have imparted a cedary/spicy overlay to the perfectly ripened blackcurrant fruit; good line and length. Screwcap. 14% alc. **Rating** 94 **To** 2020 $40

ŢŢŢŢŢ **Coonawarra Shiraz 2006** Gently spiced black fruit aromas; a supple, smooth medium-bodied palate, cedary overtones to the predominantly black fruits, with a few red touches; fine tannins. Screwcap. 14% alc. **Rating** 93 **To** 2020 $40
Coonawarra Sauvignon Blanc 2008 Pale straw-green; the bouquet is crisp and fresh, the palate has good intensity and purity to the predominantly herbaceous and gooseberry flavours that run all the way through to the finish. Screwcap. 13.5% alc. **Rating** 92 **To** 2012 $27
Prodigy Coonawarra Shiraz 2005 A dense, dark and powerful wine, full of red fruits and a slight edge of fresh herbs; good length and intensity of fruit. Screwcap. 14% alc. **Rating** 91 **To** 2020 $95
Founder's Block Coonawarra Cabernet Sauvignon 2007 Attractive medium-bodied wine with a harmonious blend of blackcurrant and cassis on the bouquet and palate, the latter with considerable length. Well priced. Screwcap. 13.5% alc. **Rating** 90 **To** 2017 $19
Founder's Block Coonawarra Sparkling Shiraz 2005 A distinctly light-bodied sparkling shiraz, perhaps deliberately, taking it part of the way back to rose, and reducing the assault on the senses some of these wines have; good balance and not excessively sweet. Cork. 13.5% alc. **Rating** 90 **To** 2012 $19

ŢŢŢŢ **Founder's Block Coonawarra Merlot 2006** Katnook has laboured hard with its merlot, and the briary/black olive nuances of this wine are clearly varietal, as is the fine texture. Good value. Screwcap. 13.5% alc. **Rating** 89 **To** 2014 $19
Founder's Block Coonawarra Chardonnay 2006 Neatly balanced and assembled, with stone fruit, citrus and melon augmented by gentle oak; has good length. Screwcap. 13.5% alc. **Rating** 89 **To** 2014 $20
Coonawarra Merlot 2006 Strongly savoury, but equally strongly varietal; earth and black olive frame the blackcurrant and redcurrant fruit; good length. Screwcap. 13.5% alc. **Rating** 89 **To** 2015 $40
Founder's Block Coonawarra Sauvignon Blanc 2008 Has riper, more tropical flavours than the Estate version, although the herb and gooseberry characters do not disappear. Screwcap. 13.5% alc. **Rating** 88 **To** 2010 $19

Founder's Block Coonawarra Shiraz 2006 Bright and clear colour; light- to medium-bodied, with a mix of blackberry, spice and earth aromas and flavours. Screwcap. 13.5% alc. **Rating** 88 **To** 2014 $19

Founder's Block Coonawarra Cabernet Sauvignon 2006 Vanilla oak makes a significant contribution to the otherwise savoury/earthy black fruit flavours and herbal finish. Screwcap. 13.5% alc. **Rating** 88 **To** 2012 $19

Coonawarra Riesling 2008 Pleasant, well-made wine that has fair varietal expression, but lacks thrust and drive. Screwcap. 12% alc. **Rating** 87 **To** 2014 $20

Founder's Block Coonawarra Merlot 2005 Uncompromising varietal expression in a savoury/herbal/earthy black-olive spectrum, red fruits well and truly hidden. Screwcap. 13.5% alc. **Rating** 87 **To** 2011 $19

 # Katoa Wines

PO Box 10, Heathcote, Vic 3523 **Region** Heathcote
T 0401 088 214 **F** (03) 5433 2483 **Open** Not
Winemaker Michael Katoa **Est.** 2005 **Cases** 200

Michael Katoa was introduced to wine at a young age at the behest of his mother, with tastings of up and coming producers in NZ's rapidly developing wine industry. A move to Australia led to work in bars and restaurants, then as a wine retailer. Next came experience working in vineyards and wineries around the Mornington Peninsula, and thereafter Heathcote, with overlapping studies in wine science and viticulture at CSU. He and wife Natasha intend to make Heathcote their permanent home, and ultimately establish a vineyard and winemaking facility of their own. In the meantime, they are purchasing small amounts of shiraz and viognier from local growers, with sangiovese (Natasha has Italian heritage) also in the mix.

▽▽▽▽▽ **Heathcote Shiraz 2006** Strong colour; a richly robed bouquet and palate, with black fruits, licorice and spice, and a low tannin profile. Screwcap. 14.5% alc. **Rating** 92 **To** 2021 $28

Kay Brothers Amery Vineyards

Kay Road, McLaren Vale, SA 5171 **Region** McLaren Vale
T (08) 8323 8211 **F** (08) 8323 9199 **www**.kaybrothersamerywines.com
Open Mon–Fri 9–5, w'ends & public hols 12–5
Winemaker Colin Kay **Est.** 1890 **Cases** 14 000 **Vyds** 19.6 ha

A traditional winery with a rich history and just under 20 ha of priceless old vines; while the white wines have been variable, the red wines and fortified wines can be very good. Of particular interest is Block 6 Shiraz, made from 100-year-old vines; both vines and wines are going from strength to strength. Exports to the UK, the US and other major markets.

▽▽▽▽▽ **Block 6 Shiraz 2006** A dark, brooding wine of rather large proportions, but put together with aplomb; at the core there is an abundance of sweet fruit, and the structure is dense, tannic and chewy and requires a little time to soften; should reward patience well. Screwcap. 15% alc. **Rating** 93 **To** 2020 $65

Hillside McLaren Vale Shiraz 2006 Has lifted red and black fruits with a strong savoury edge; the oak is there, playing a supporting role; the finish is quite firm, but the fruit follows through well. Screwcap. 15.5% alc. **Rating** 90 **To** 2016 $45

▽▽▽▽ **McLaren Vale Viognier 2008** Varietal aromas of apricot kernel and stone fruits are offered on the bouquet; quite rich on entry, but tightens up with a slight amaro bitterness on the finish. Screwcap. 12.5% alc. **Rating** 89 **To** 2012 $25

Keith Tulloch Wine

Hunter Ridge Winery, Hermitage Road, Pokolbin, NSW 2320 **Region** Lower Hunter Valley
T (02) 4998 7500 **www**.keithtullochwine.com.au **Open** Wed–Sun 10–5, or by appt
Winemaker Keith Tulloch **Est.** 1997 **Cases** 11 500 **Vyds** 7.4 ha

Keith Tulloch is, of course, a member of the Tulloch family, who has played such a lead role in the Hunter Valley for over a century. Formerly a winemaker at Lindemans and then Rothbury

Estate, he has developed his own label since 1997. There is the same almost obsessive attention to detail, the same almost ascetic intellectual approach, the same refusal to accept anything but the best as that of Jeffrey Grosset. Exports to the UK, the US, Canada, Sweden, Hong Kong and Singapore.

ŶŶŶŶŶ **Hunter Valley Semillon 2007** The inherent complexity of the wine is starting to express itself; notes of toast, honey and spice joining the lemony fruit of the bouquet and palate. Screwcap. 11% alc. **Rating** 95 **To** 2017 $26
Museum Release Hunter Valley Semillon 2003 Vibrant hue; expressive, classic bouquet with toast, lemon curd and a touch of straw; the palate is generous and quite fine, with focus and finesse on the generous finish. Screwcap. 11.5% alc. **Rating** 95 **To** 2015 $45

ŶŶŶŶŶ **Hunter Valley Semillon 2008** Vibrant colour; green nettle, lemon and straw bouquet; lemon and green apple palate; tightly wound and needs time to gain generosity and weight; will richly repay cellaring as the '07 and '03 prove. Screwcap. 11.5% alc. **Rating** 93 **To** 2015 $26
The Kester Hunter Valley Shiraz 2006 Bright colour; a touch of leather combines with the red fruit and spicy bouquet; quite firm, with an earthy complexity and quite a firm finish. Screwcap. 15% alc. **Rating** 92 **To** 2015 $50
Museum Release Kester Hunter Valley Shiraz 2000 Fully developed with lots of leather, mulled fruit and a little spice; still some sweetness on the palate, with good acid and fine tannin to finish. Cork. **Rating** 92 **To** 2013

ŶŶŶŶ **Hunter Valley Chardonnay 2008** Plenty of toasty oak on the bouquet; quite fresh, with nectarine and cinnamon spice on the finish. Screwcap. 12.5% alc. **Rating** 89 **To** 2012 $26
Hunter Valley Botrytis Semillon 2007 A somewhat oaky bouquet, with moderate complexity and richness; clean and fresh on the finish. Screwcap. 12% alc. **Rating** 88 **To** 2012 $35

Kellybrook   ★★★★

Fulford Road, Wonga Park, Vic 3115 **Region** Yarra Valley
T (03) 9722 1304 **F** (03) 9722 2092 **www**.kellybrookwinery.com.au **Open** Mon 11–5, Tues–Sat 10–5, Sun 11–5
Winemaker Philip Kelly, Darren Kelly **Est.** 1960 **Cases** 2800 **Vyds** 8.5 ha
The vineyard is at Wonga Park, one of the gateways to the Yarra Valley, and has a picnic area and a full-scale restaurant. A very competent producer of both cider and apple brandy (in Calvados style) as well as table wine. When it received its winery licence in 1960, it became the first winery in the Yarra Valley to open its doors in the 20th century, a distinction often ignored or forgotten (by this author as well as others). Exports to the UK and Denmark.

ŶŶŶŶŶ **Yarra Valley Chardonnay 2007** Good example of Yarra chardonnay, with nectarine, melon and spicy French oak seamlessly welded; has good mouthfeel and particularly good length. Screwcap. 14% alc. **Rating** 92 **To** 2013
Yarra Valley Cabernet Merlot 2006 Good colour; clearly defined cassis fruit, with a touch of cedar; elegantly structured with ample fine tannin and fleshy fruit; lively acidity on the finish. Screwcap. 13.5% alc. **Rating** 90 **To** 2015 $27

ŶŶŶŶ **Enfield Yarra Valley Sauvignon Blanc 2008** Pale colour; subdued mineral aroma with a suggestion of fennel; the palate is linear and dry, with a textural, slightly savoury component that is quite appealing. Screwcap. 12.5% alc. **Rating** 89 **To** 2012 $22
Yarra Valley Cabernet Merlot 2007 Good colour; cassis and plum with a little black olive complexity; medium-bodied, fine and fleshy, with moderate, fine-grained tannin. Screwcap. 13.5% alc. **Rating** 89 **To** 2014 $27
Pinot Noir Chardonnay 2004 Pale colour; quite noticeable toasty complexity dominates the bouquet; the palate follows suit and exhibits a slightly creamy mouthfeel, with fairly good length. Diam. 12.5% alc. **Rating** 88 **To** 2013 $30

Kelman Vineyard

2 Oakey Creek Road, Pokolbin, NSW 2320 **Region** Lower Hunter Valley
T (02) 4991 5456 **F** (02) 4991 7555 **www.**kelmanwines.com.au **Open** 7 days 9–5
Winemaker Tower Estate **Est.** 1999 **Cases** 2000 **Vyds** 9 ha
Kelman Vineyards is a California-type development on the outskirts of Cessnock. A 40-ha property has been subdivided into 80 residential development lots, with vines wending between the lots, which are under common ownership. Part of the chardonnay has already been grafted across to shiraz before coming into full production, and the vineyard has the potential to produce 8000 cases a year. In the meantime, each owner receives 12 cases of wine a year.

🍷🍷🍷🍷🍷 **Hunter Valley Shiraz 2007** Proclaims its origin from the first whiff through to the finish; skilled winemaking produces a light- to medium-bodied wine with a silky mouthfeel and long palate. Screwcap. 13% alc. **Rating** 92 **To** 2017 $25
Pond Block Chardonnay 2007 Fresh and lively, unusually so for the Hunter Valley; tangy overtones to the white peach fruit, and French oak lengthens the palate nicely. Screwcap. 14% alc. **Rating** 90 **To** 2014 $23

Kelvedon

PO Box 126, Swansea, Tas 7190 **Region** East Coast Tasmania
T (03) 6257 8283 **F** (03) 6257 8179 **Open** Not
Winemaker Winemaking Tasmania (Julian Alcorso) **Est.** 1998 **Cases** 450 **Vyds** 7 ha
Jack and Gill Cotton began the development of Kelvedon by planting 1 ha of pinot noir in 1998. The plantings were extended in 2000–01 by an additional 5 ha, half to pinot noir and half to chardonnay; the production from this is under contract to CWA. One ha of sauvignon blanc has also been established to provide a second wine under the Kelvedon label; the Pinot Noir can be of excellent quality.

🍷🍷🍷🍷🍷 **Pinot Noir 2007** Fragrant and lively red fruits; good length, balance and focus; mixed red and black fruits with touches of spice. Gold medal Tas Wine Show '09. Screwcap. 13.1% alc. **Rating** 94 **To** 2014 $28

🍇 Kennedy ★★★★☆

Maple Park, 224 Wallenjoe Road, Corop, Vic 3559 (postal) **Region** Heathcote
T (03) 5484 8293 **F** (03) 5484 8148 **www.**kennedyvintners.com.au **Open** Not
Winemaker Sandro Mosele (Contract) **Est.** 2002 **Cases** 1000 **Vyds** 29.2 ha
Having been farmers in the Colbinabbin area of Heathcote for 27 years, John and Patricia Kennedy were on the spot when a prime piece of red Cambrian soil on the east-facing slope of Mt Camel Range became available for purchase. They planted 20 ha of shiraz in 2002. As they gained knowledge of the intricate differences within the site, and worked with contract winemaker Sandro Mosele, further plantings of shiraz, tempranillo and mourvedre followed in '07. The Shiraz is made in small open fermenters, using indigenous yeasts and gentle pigeage before being taken to French oak (20% new) for 12 months maturation prior to bottling.

🍷🍷🍷🍷🍷 **Heathcote Shiraz 2005** A positively elegant wine; bright shiraz fruit are allied with spicy peppery elements; the tannins polished and fine, the oak appropriate; excellent length. Diam. 13.5% alc. **Rating** 94 **To** 2015 $29.95

🍷🍷🍷🍷🍷 **Heathcote Shiraz 2006** Finding the right date for harvest in Heathcote isn't as easy as one might expect; the wine has considerable thrust to its spicy/peppery black fruits, but thins out fractionally on the finish. Nonetheless an impressive addition to Heathcote. Diam. 13.5% alc. **Rating** 90 **To** 2016 $29.95

🍇 Kennedy & Wilson

15/4 North Gateway, Coldstream, Vic 3770 (postal) **Region** Port Phillip Zone
T (03) 9017 4746 **www.**kennedyandwilson.com.au **Open** Not
Winemaker Peter Wilson, James Wilson **Est.** 2005 **Cases** 1000

Kennedy & Wilson is a partnership between brothers James and Peter Wilson, and Juliana Kennedy. James, previously a chemical engineer, completed his master of oenology degree at Adelaide University in 2006, and is currently completing a PhD. Peter worked under Bailey Carrodus at Yarra Yering from 1986 to '96, and established Kennedy & Wilson chocolates in '96 before joining Stuart Wines as chief winemaker in 2003. Juliana, ex-CEO of a smartcard/sim card company and the business mind behind the chocolate venture, now describes herself as 'manager of the worldwide Kennedy & Wilson conglomerate'. A sense of humour in this business is an essential ingredient. The grapes come from the Quarry Ridge Vineyard in Kilmore at an elevation of 400 m on the southern side of the Great Dividing Range. The chardonnay and one of the pinot noir blocks are 20 years old, the balance of the vineyard was planted in 1998. The climate is very cool indeed, the hand-picked fruit ripens between April and May.

ΨΨΨΨΨ **Quarry Ridge Vineyard Chardonnay 2007** Fragrant nectarine and grapefruit aromas lead into a vibrant, elegant, fruit-driven palate; long, cleansing finish. Screwcap. 14% alc. **Rating** 94 **To** 2016 $20
Quarry Ridge Vineyard Cabernet Sauvignon Merlot 2007 Clear crimson-red; while there are earthy/black olive nuances running through the length of the wine, blackcurrant fruit is there to carry these influences; an elegant wine with all the components in balance. Screwcap. 14% alc. **Rating** 94 **To** 2020 $20

ΨΨΨΨΨ **Quarry Ridge Vineyard Shiraz 2006** Bright colour; fragrant and fresh red berry and spice fruit aromas joined by a touch of licorice on the light- to medium-bodied palate, which has both balance and length. Cork. 13.5% alc. **Rating** 91 **To** 2016 $20
Quarry Ridge Vineyard Pinot Noir 2007 An extremely powerful wine with a density to the fruit only partially due to the alcohol; will undoubtedly benefit from maturation. Screwcap. 14% alc. **Rating** 90 **To** 2014 $20

ΨΨΨΨ **Quarry Ridge Vineyard Semillon 2007** Unusual semillon; it has many sauvignon blanc characteristics to its full herbal, asparagus overtones. Screwcap. 11.5% alc. **Rating** 87 **To** 2013 $20

Kersbrook Hill ★★★★★

Lot 102 Bagshaw Road, Kersbrook, SA 5231 **Region** Adelaide Hills
T 0419 570 005 **www.**kersbrookhill.com.au **Open** By appt
Winemaker Ben Jeanneret **Est.** 1998 **Cases** 1500 **Vyds** 4 ha
Paul Clark purchased what is now the Kersbrook Hill property, then grazing land, in 1997, planting 0.4 ha of shiraz on a reality check basis. Encouraged by the results, he increased the plantings to 3 ha of shiraz and 1 ha of riesling two years later. Mark Whisson is consultant viticulturist (Whisson has been growing grapes in the Adelaide Hills for 20 years) and Ben Jeanneret was chosen as winemaker because of his experience with riesling. Exports to the US, China and NZ.

ΨΨΨΨΨ **Adelaide Hills Riesling 2001** Ripe Meyer lemon and spring florals bouquet; a very precise palate, with lively acidity and good texture; very long, bright and pure. Screwcap. 12% alc. **Rating** 95 **To** 2016 $28
Don's Acre Adelaide Hills Shiraz 2006 Good colour; a scented, spicy bouquet leads into an intense and sustained palate with vibrant, shiny black fruits and spice, the tannins in balance; wine-travel along the entire length of two sides of the cork is ominous. 14.6% alc. **Rating** 94 **To** 2016 $120

ΨΨΨΨΨ **Adelaide Hills Shiraz 2007** Deep colour; full-bodied shiraz, with licorice, blackberry and pepper/spice throughout; good length supported by robust tannins. Needs much time. Screwcap. **Rating** 90 **To** 2022 $29

Kies Family Wines ★★★★☆

Barossa Valley Way, Lyndoch, SA 5381 **Region** Barossa Valley
T (08) 8524 4110 **F** (08) 8524 4544 **www**.kieswines.com.au **Open** 7 days 9.30–4
Winemaker Wine Wise Consultancy **Est.** 1969 **Cases** 5000 **Vyds** 26.3 ha
The Kies family has been resident in the Barossa Valley since 1857; the present generation
of winemakers is the fifth, their children the sixth. Until 1969 the family sold almost all
their grapes, but in that year they launched their own brand, Karrawirra. The coexistence of
Killawarra forced a name change in 1983 to Redgum Vineyard; this business was subsequently
sold. Later still, Kies Family Wines opened for business, drawing upon vineyards (up to
100 years old) that had remained in the family throughout the changes, offering a wide range
of wines through the 1880 cellar door. Exports to the UK, Singapore, Hong Kong, China
and Japan.

🍷🍷🍷🍷🍷 **Chaff Mill Barossa Valley Cabernet Sauvignon 2006** Incredible colour;
deeply fruited and full of pure cassis and a great deal of black olive; the palate is
full-bodied and full-blooded; the abundant levels of fruit absorb the tannins with
ease. Cork. 14% alc. **Rating** 94 **To** 2015 $25

🍷🍷🍷🍷 **Monkey Nut Tree Barossa Valley Merlot 2006** Good colour; dark and
savoury with black olive framing the cedar and cassis fruit; prominent acidity,
and quite firm tannin, lead to a savoury and quite dry finish. Cork. 14.5% alc.
Rating 89 **To** 2013 $25
SSB 2008 A regional, varietal blend that works well, the sauvignon blanc
doubtless Limestone Coast; soft tropical fruit and a hint of citrus on an easy-
drinking style. Screwcap. 12.5% alc. **Rating** 88 **To** 2012 $18
Hill Block Barossa Valley Riesling 2008 A mix of citrus and tropical/
pineapple on bouquet and palate; big on flavour, short on finesse, but honest.
Screwcap. 12% alc. **Rating** 87 **To** 2012 $15
Barossa Valley White Muscat NV Made from muscat gordo blanco; clearly
spent time in oak, and has a pleasantly dry biscuity palate. Cork. 18.5% alc.
Rating 87 **To** 2010 $20

Kilikanoon ★★★★★

Penna Lane, Penwortham, SA 5453 **Region** Clare Valley
T (08) 8843 4206 **F** (08) 8843 4246 **www**.kilikanoon.com.au **Open** Thurs–Sun &
public hols 11–5, or by appt
Winemaker Kevin Mitchell **Est.** 1997 **Cases** 40 000 **Vyds** 330 ha
Kilikanoon has over 300 ha of vineyards, predominantly in the Clare Valley but spreading to
all regions around Adelaide and the Barossa Valley. It had the once-in-a-lifetime experience of
winning five of the six trophies awarded at the Clare Valley Wine Show '02, spanning Riesling,
Shiraz and Cabernet, and including Best Wine of Show. In August 2007 it purchased the
iconic Seppeltsfield in the Barossa Valley (see separate entry). Exports to all major markets.

🍷🍷🍷🍷🍷 **Attunga 1865 Clare Valley Shiraz 2006** Powerful, concentrated and complex;
essency black fruit, licorice, tar and a splash of sage; the palate is dense and thickly
textured, with a firm tannin profile, balanced by the abundant fruit; a very long,
pure and fresh finish. Cork. 15% alc. **Rating** 96 **To** 2030 $250
Mort's Reserve Watervale Riesling 2008 A beautiful Riesling; citrus blossom
aromas, then a pure palate, the lime and lemon fruit shimmering all the way
through to the lingering finish. Screwcap. 12.5% alc. **Rating** 95 **To** 2020 $35
R Barossa Valley Shiraz 2006 Dense and powerful bouquet with a real tour
de force of black fruit; essency fruit on the palate, with toasty oak playing a
supporting role; attractive mocha, chocolate finish. Cork. 15% alc. **Rating** 95
To 2025 $120
Parable McLaren Vale Shiraz 2006 Mocha and fruitcake bouquet; quite toasty
on the palate, with chewy/tarry fruit and a seriously firm and dry finish; certainly
large in scale. Screwcap. 15% alc. **Rating** 94 **To** 2025 $40

ꝨꝨꝨꝨꝨ **Killerman's Run Shiraz 2007** Vibrant hue; blackberry, ironstone and tar on the bouquet, with shades of lighter red fruit; thickly textured, amply supported by lively acidity and plentiful tannin; fruitful long and harmonious. Great value. Screwcap. 14.5% alc. **Rating** 93 **To** 2016 $20

Mort's Block Watervale Riesling 2008 Pale straw-green; the clean bouquet leads into a highly focused palate with a core of lime citrus fruit and almost juicy acidity on the finish. Screwcap. 12.5% alc. **Rating** 93 **To** 2017 $22

Barrel Fermented Clare Valley Semillon 2008 It is remarkable that barrel ferment followed by five months' maturation in French oak should leave the semillon fresh and crisp; a win-win outcome, for there is complexity as well. Screwcap. 12.5% alc. **Rating** 93 **To** 2016 $20

Green's Vineyard Barossa Valley Shiraz 2006 Oak-dominant bouquet, with dark chocolate and blackberry essence fruit; the palate reflects the bouquet, and the finish is long, tarry and quite chewy; massively proportioned. Cork. 15% alc. **Rating** 93 **To** 2020 $79

Testament Barossa Valley Shiraz 2006 Quite a dark and savoury personality, with ironstone, tar and licorice on the bouquet; the palate is also dense and rich, showing off the depth of fruit synonymous with the region. Screwcap. 15% alc. **Rating** 93 **To** 2025 $40

The Duke Clare Valley Grenache 2006 Brighter colour and more definition than Prodigal; savoury sage and raspberry fruit bouquet, has a very attractive core of spice; good palate weight, with generous sweet fruit that belies the tannin underneath. Cork. 15% alc. **Rating** 93 **To** 2016 $69

Killerman's Run Shiraz Grenache 2007 Vibrant colour; energetic black and raspberry fruit bouquet; lively palate, with a touch sage and spice; fine, juicy and quite harmonious on the finish. Screwcap. 14.5% alc. **Rating** 92 **To** 2015 $20

Oracle Clare Valley Shiraz 2006 A little reduction, but very good concentration of fruit; dark plum, spice, blackberry and tar; the palate is multilayered and has a dark fruit core; chewy and long, with ironstone on the finish. Cork. 15% alc. **Rating** 92 **To** 2015 $79

Covenant Clare Valley Shiraz 2006 Bright colour; the oak sits apart from the fruit at this point, but there is polished blueberry and spice on the bouquet; ample levels of sweet fruit, the finish is dry and very firm. Screwcap. 15% alc. **Rating** 92 **To** 2020 $40

The Medley 2006 Bright colour; complex; lifted red fruit intermingles with dark, savoury and earthy notes and a hint of mint; fleshy on entry, the palate tightens up and delivers a slightly tarry and chewy finish. Grenache/Shiraz/Mourvedre. Screwcap. 15% alc. **Rating** 91 **To** 2016 $25

Second Fiddle Clare Valley Rose 2008 Vivid crimson; fresh, full-flavoured wine with a mix of Turkish delight, spice and red berry fruits from its base of grenache; good length, dry finish. Screwcap. 13.5% alc. **Rating** 90 **To** 2016 $20

Blocks Road Clare Valley Cabernet Sauvignon 2006 Pure cassis and cedar bouquet; clean, fresh, vibrant and varietal, with a soft and gentle finish that disguises the underlying power well. Screwcap. 14.5% alc. **Rating** 90 **To** 2014 $33

Killara Estate   ★★★★☆

773 Warburton Highway, Seville East, Vic 3139 **Region** Yarra Valley
T (03) 5961 5877 **F** (03) 5961 5629 **www**.killaraestate.com.au **Open** Tues–Sun 11–5
Winemaker David Bicknell, Rob Dolan **Est.** 1997 **Cases** 7000 **Vyds** 92.13 ha
The Palazzo family, one of the largest vineyard holders in the Yarra Valley, have two distinct vineyards at different locations: Killara and Sunnyside, respectively. The varieties overlap with two exceptions: 1.19 ha sangiovese on Sunnyside, and 1.11 ha viognier on Killara. The shared varieties are cabernet sauvignon, chardonnay, merlot, pinot gris, shiraz, pinot noir and sauvignon blanc; pinot noir (almost 33 ha) and chardonnay (over 19 ha) are the most substantial. The largest part of production is sold to producers both within and without the Yarra Valley, but Killara Estate retains sufficient to produce the Killara Estate range (made by David Bicknell) and the Racers & Rascals range (made by Rob Dolan). Exports to the UK.

ＹＹＹＹ **Yarra Valley Chardonnay 2007** Interesting wine; has greater intensity than its alcohol might suggest; nectarine and grapefruit course through the lively and long palate, oak a bit player. Screwcap. 12.5% alc. **Rating** 94 **To** 2013 $20

ＹＹＹＹＹ **Yarra Valley Pinot Noir 2007** Good hue and depth; spice, cherry and a touch of plum; good focus and length, with silky tannins on the finish. Even better value than Racers & Rascals. Screwcap. 12.5% alc. **Rating** 91 **To** 2012 $20

ＹＹＹＹ **Racers & Rascals Yarra Valley Pinot Noir 2007** Unpretentious pinot, hardly surprising at the price; does have authentic varietal expression, and kicks on to the finish. Value. Screwcap. 12.5% alc. **Rating** 89 **To** 2011 $15
Yarra Valley Shiraz 2007 Clear, bright colour; cheerful spicy overtones to a light- to medium-bodied mix of blackberry and cherry fruit; gentle tannins and minimal oak. Screwcap. 13.5% alc. **Rating** 89 **To** 2014 $20

Killerby   ★★★★☆

Caves Road, Wilyabrup, WA 6280 **Region** Margaret River
T 1800 655 722 **F** 1800 679 578 **www**.killerby.com.au **Open** Not
Winemaker Kim Horton **Est.** 1973 **Cases** 9000 **Vyds** 13 ha
In June 2008, the winery established by the late Dr Barry Killerby 35 years ago, was purchased by the Ferngrove wine group. Wines made from the estate plantings (shiraz, chardonnay, sauvignon blanc, semillon and cabernet sauvignon) will be made at Ferngrove, but sold through a new cellar door to be opened at a different address by early 2010. Exports to the US and Denmark.

ＹＹＹＹＹ **Semillon 2008** Has very good intensity and length to the grassy/lemony fruit; barrel fermentation and five months' maturation in new French oak of part of the wine adds both to texture and flavour, producing a maximum result. Screwcap. 12.5% alc. **Rating** 94 **To** 2018 $20

ＹＹＹＹＹ **Sauvignon Blanc 2008** Here, the partial barrel fermentation and three months' maturation in new French oak is more obvious than in the Semillon, but is not in any way distracting as it adds complexity to a naturally high fruit-flavoured wine. Screwcap. 12.5% alc. **Rating** 93 **To** 2011 $20

ＹＹＹＹ **Cabernet Sauvignon 2007** A very austere, savoury wine, but it does have enough blackcurrant and mulberry fruit to give hope that the tannins will loosen their grip over the years ahead. Screwcap. 13.5% alc. **Rating** 89 **To** 2017 $25
Cabernet Merlot 2006 Quite a savoury bouquet, cedar and olive framing vibrant cassis fruit; a cool example, with crisp acidity, and chewy, yet fine, tannins. Screwcap. 14% alc. **Rating** 87 **To** 2012 $20
Cabernet Sauvignon 2005 Strong varietal expression, with cassis and a touch of cedar; clean and well defined. Screwcap. 14% alc. **Rating** 87 **To** 2012 $25

Killibinbin   ★★★★

1 Main Street, Lobethal, SA 5241 **Region** McLaren Vale
T (08) 8339 8664 **www**.killibinbin.com.au **Open** Fri–Sun & public hols 11–5
Winemaker Wayne Anderson **Est.** 1998 **Cases** 4000
Business partners Liz Blanks and Wayne Anderson embarked on their venture (having 'no money, no winemaker, no vineyard and no winery') with the inaugural 1997 Langhorne Creek Shiraz. Robert Parker promptly gave it 92 points, which meant that all of the production went to the US. A challenging set of new label designs straight from the early 1940s have gained (and will gain) much attention. The business has been further strengthened by moving into its own winery prior to the 2008 vintage. Exports to the UK, the US, Canada and Denmark.

ＹＹＹＹＹ **Sandtrap McLaren Vale Shiraz 2006** Fairly and squarely in the middle of McLaren Vale style; blackberry, plum and lashings of dark chocolate, spice and vanilla inputs; good control of extract. Screwcap. 14.5% alc. **Rating** 91 **To** 2020 $15

Adelaide Hills Sauvignon Blanc 2008 The Dali-esque label draws attention to the fact the wine was fermented in new Vosges oak, with only 60 cases made – and well done, giving the wine obvious texture and flavour. Screwcap. 12.5% alc. Rating 90 To 2013 $30

ΥΥΥΥ **Langhorne Creek Cabernet Sauvignon 2006** Dense colour; rich blackcurrant and dark chocolate aromas lead into a powerful palate; tannin and oak are in balance, alcohol nipping at the heels of the wine; 300 cases made. Screwcap. 15% alc. Rating 89 To 2016 $23
Scaredy Cat Adelaide Hills Cabernet Malbec 2005 Where in the Adelaide Hills this wine might come from is not easy to see, for it has the ripeness of a Clare Valley blend of the two varieties. It has an abundance of black fruit flavours and of tannins; 300 cases made. Screwcap. 15% alc. Rating 89 To 2015 $28
Langhorne Creek Blend 2006 Minimal filtration shows through in the slightly hazy colour; jumps around with dark chocolate, black and red fruits and a twang of acidity. Shiraz (52%)/Cabernet Sauvignon (48%). Screwcap. 14.5% alc. Rating 87 To 2015 $18

Kimbarra Wines

422 Barkly Street, Ararat, Vic 3377 **Region** Grampians
T (03) 5352 2238 **www**.kimbarrawines.com.au **Open** Mon–Fri 9–4.30, or by appt
Winemaker Peter Leeke, Ian MacKenzie **Est.** 1990 **Cases** 900 **Vyds** 12 ha
Jim, Peter and David Leeke have established riesling, shiraz and cabernet sauvignon, varieties that have proved best suited to the Grampians region. The particularly well-made, estate-grown wines deserve a wider audience.

ΥΥΥΥΥ **Great Western Cabernet Sauvignon 2006** Well-articulated blackcurrant and earth varietal fruit gives focus and purity; the tannins and oak sit well in a medium-bodied palate. Screwcap. 13% alc. Rating 90 To 2016 $29

ΥΥΥΥ **Great Western Riesling 2008** Light straw-green; a flowery bouquet leads into a palate with a solid mix of tropical and citrus fruits, then a firm, slightly phenolic, finish. Screwcap. 12.9% alc. Rating 89 To 2015 $25
Great Western Late Picked Riesling 2008 Lacks conviction, although the flavours are bright; one less degree of alcohol and 20 g more sugar would make all the difference. Screwcap. 12.4% alc. Rating 87 To 2012 $17

King River Estate   **NR**

3556 Wangaratta-Whitfield Road, Wangaratta, Vic 3678 **Region** King Valley
T (03) 5729 3689 **F** (03) 5729 3688 **www**.kingriverestate.com.au **Open** 7 days 10–5
Winemaker Trevor Knaggs **Est.** 1996 **Cases** 6000 **Vyds** 16 ha
Trevor Knaggs, with the assistance of his father Collin, began the establishment of King River Estate in 1990, making the first wines in '96. The initial plantings were 3.3 ha each of chardonnay and cabernet sauvignon, followed by 8 ha of merlot and 3 ha of shiraz. More recent plantings have extended the varietal range to include verdelho, viognier, barbera and sangiovese. Exports to China.

Kingsdale Wines

745 Crookwell Road, Goulburn, NSW 2580 **Region** Southern New South Wales Zone
T (02) 4822 4880 **www**.kingsdale.com.au **Open** W'ends & public hols 10–5
Winemaker Howard Spark **Est.** 2001 **Cases** 1000 **Vyds** 2.5 ha
Howard and Elly Spark established their vineyard (shiraz, sauvignon blanc, chardonnay, merlot and semillon) south of the burgeoning Southern Highlands region, falling in the Southern NSW Zone. It sits at 700 m above sea level on deep red soils with iron rich sediments (doubtless causing the colour) and limestone. The limestone-clad cellar door overlooks Lake Sooley, 7 mins drive from Goulburn.

ŶŶŶŶ   **Goulburn Rose 2008** Bright fuschia-crimson; has a degree of authority to add interest and length to the cherry fruit. Shiraz. Screwcap. 14% alc. **Rating** 88 **To** 2009 $20
Chardonnay 2008 Unoaked style, which is quite lively, with white peach fruit and crisp acidity. Screwcap. 13.5% alc. **Rating** 87 **To** 2011 $20
Semillon Chardonnay Sauvignon Blanc 2008 Fresh, clean and crisp, with grassy/citrussy flavours to the fore; deserved its bronze medals at the Kiama Wine Show and the Australian Small Winemakers Show. Screwcap. 13% alc. **Rating** 87 **To** 2010 $20

Kingston Estate Wines   ★★★★

Sturt Highway, Kingston-on-Murray, SA 5331 **Region** South Australia
T (08) 8243 3700 **F** (08) 8243 3777 **www.**kingstonestatewines.com **Open** By appt
Winemaker Bill Moularadellis, Brett Duffin, Helen Foggo, Donna Hartwig **Est.** 1979
Cases 300 000 **Vyds** 200 ha
Kingston Estate, under the direction of Bill Moularadellis, has its production roots in the Riverland region, but has long-term purchase contracts with growers in the Clare Valley, Adelaide Hills, Coonawarra, Langhorne Creek and Mount Benson. It has also spread its net to take in a wide range of varietals, mainstream and exotic, under a number of different brands at various price points. Exports the UK, the US and other major markets.

ŶŶŶŶŶ   **Cabernet Sauvignon 2008** Outstanding value; has very good colour, and abundant blackcurrant and cassis fruit on a soft, well-balanced, medium-bodied palate; drink now or later (or both). The good side of a grape surplus. Limestone Coast/Clare Valley. Screwcap. 14.5% alc. **Rating** 93 **To** 2015 $12.99
Echelon Shiraz 2007 Toasty oak and struck match on the bouquet, followed by an abundance of ripe dark fruit; full-bodied with lots of sweet fruit and toasty oak. Screwcap. 14.5% alc. **Rating** 90 **To** 2017 $21.99

ŶŶŶŶ   **Petit Verdot 2008** A full-bodied, fruit-rich wine in a blackberry/blackcurrant spectrum; it only lacks structural complexity, some of which will come with time. Screwcap. 14.5% alc. **Rating** 89 **To** 2014 $12.99
Echelon Petit Verdot 2007 Bright colour; lifted blueberry and violet bouquet; focused black fruit with a fleshy sweet-fruited finish, and a slight briny character adding complexity. Screwcap. 14% alc. **Rating** 89 **To** 2012 $21.99
Shiraz 2007 Sweet red fruit, and a subtle edge of spice; juicy, generous with good flavour; good value. Screwcap. 14.5% alc. **Rating** 87 **To** 2012 $12
Adelaide Hills Limestone Coast Sauvignon Blanc 2008 Clean, lively and correct; tropical fruit with good acidity; good finish. Screwcap. 12.5% alc. **Rating** 87 **To** 2010 $12
Merlot 2008 Light, bright colour; lively, fresh cassis-accented fruits, and a well-balanced finish. Simple but enjoyable. Cork. 14% alc. **Rating** 87 **To** 2013 $12.99

Kinloch Wines   ★★★

'Kainui', 221 Wairere Road, Booroolite, Vic 3723 **Region** Upper Goulburn
T (03) 5777 3447 **F** (03) 5777 3449 **www.**kinlochwines.com.au **Open** 7 days 10–4
Winemaker Al Fencaros (Contract) **Est.** 1996 **Cases** 2000 **Vyds** 4 ha
In 1996 Susan and Malcolm Kinloch began the development of their vineyard, at an altitude of 400 m on the northern slopes of the Great Dividing Range, 15 mins from Mansfield. The vineyard is planted to chardonnay, pinot noir, pinot meunier (primarily used for sparkling wines), sauvignon blanc, riesling and tempranillo, supplemented by purchases of other varieties from local growers. The grapes are hand-picked and contract-made in the Yarra Valley.

ŶŶŶŶ   **Mansfield Unwooded Chardonnay 2008** Hints of green apple and lemon fruit aromas; good concentration and poise, and lively acidity on the finish. Screwcap. 12% alc. **Rating** 89 **To** 2010 $18

Kirrihill Wines

Wendouree Road, Clare, SA 5453 **Region** Clare Valley
T (08) 8842 4087 **F** (08) 8842 4089 **www.**kirrihillwines.com.au **Open** 7 days 12–5
Winemaker Donna Stephens, Marnie Roberts **Est.** 1998 **Cases** 30 000
A large development, with an 8000-tonne, $12 million winery making and marketing its own
range of wines, also acting as a contract maker for several producers. Focused on Clare Valley
and the Adelaide Hills, grapes are sourced from specially selected parcels of Kirribilly's 1300 ha
of managed vineyards as well as the Edwards and Stanway families' properties in these regions.
The quality of the wines is thus no surprise. The Companions range comprises blends of
both regions, while the Single Vineyard Series aims to elicit a sense of place from the chosen
vineyards. Exports to all major markets.

ꟼꟼꟼꟼꟼ **Single Vineyard Series Bothar Umair Clare Valley Cabernet Sauvignon
2006** Has clearly defined varietal aroma and flavour, right in the middle of the
blackcurrant and cassis track; good tannins, length and balance; excellent future.
Screwcap. 14% alc. **Rating** 93 **To** 2020 $19.95
Single Vineyard Series Birchmores Langhorne Creek Shiraz 2006 An
attractive wine; the softly ripe fruit of Langhorne Creek is supported by vanilla
oak ex 18 months in new American barrels. Ready sooner than later. Value.
Screwcap. 14.5% alc. **Rating** 91 **To** 2014 $19.95
Single Vineyard Series Tulach Mor Clare Valley Shiraz 2006 Fragrant fruit,
more in the red spectrum than black, and medium- rather than full-bodied; fine
tannins run through the finish. Screwcap. 14.5% alc. **Rating** 91 **To** 2016 $19.95
Single Vineyard Series Baile An Gharrai Clare Valley Shiraz 2006
Medium- to full-bodied, sonorous black fruits supported by ripe but fine tannins
and well-judged French oak. Screwcap. 13.5% alc. **Rating** 90 **To** 2016 $19.95

ꟼꟼꟼꟼ **Single Vineyard Series Cuaisin Na Sleine Watervale Riesling 2008**
Offers a mix of citrus and tropical fruits with weight and depth in an early-
developing style. Will anyone be game enough to ask for it? Screwcap. 13% alc.
Rating 89 **To** 2013 $19.95
Lizards of Oz Shiraz 2008 Ripe and juicy blueberry fruit with a touch of spice;
clean, varietal and well made, with good acidity and fresh fruit on the finish. Value.
Screwcap. 13.5% alc. **Rating** 88 **To** 2014 $9.95
Single Vineyard Series Serendipity Adelaide Hills Chardonnay 2008
Pale colour; slightly sweet and sour bouquet, with some pear and lemon on
the bouquet; prominent acidity and chalky texture come through on the finish.
Screwcap. 12.5% alc. **Rating** 88 **To** 2013 $19.95
Single Vineyard Series Serendipity Adelaide Hills Pinot Grigio 2008
Has vibrancy and length, sustained by good acidity and minerality backing up the
pear and citrus fruit. Screwcap. 14% alc. **Rating** 88 **To** 2010 $19.95
Companions Clare Valley Shiraz 2007 Redcurrant and spiced mulberry
fruit on the bouquet; fleshy and forward, with good concentration and a touch of
candied orange peel on the palate. Screwcap. 14.9% alc. **Rating** 88 **To** 2013 $14.95
Companions Clare Valley Adelaide Hills Semillon Sauvignon Blanc 2008
A well-established blend; the combination of flavour and structure works well
enough. Screwcap. 13.5% alc. **Rating** 87 **To** 2011 $14.95
Lizards of Oz Chardonnay 2008 Vibrant green hue; peach and straw bouquet;
ripe fruit on the palate, with a little toast on the finish. Screwcap. 13.5% alc.
Rating 87 **To** 2012 $9.95
Companions Clare Valley Adelaide Hills Riesling Pinot Gris 2008 Just
when you think the combination has subtracted rather than added, the length of
the juicy, faintly sweet palate comes to the aid of the wine. Screwcap. 13.5% alc.
Rating 87 **To** 2010 $14.95

🌸 Kiss & Tell Wines ★★★

15 Chaston Street, Wagga Wagga, NSW 2650 (postal) **Region** Tumbarumba
T (02) 6925 5550 **F** (02) 6925 5550 **www**.kissandtellwines.com.au **Open** Not
Winemaker Keiran Spencer **Est.** 2008 **Cases** 300
Kiss & Tell is the virtual winery operation of Keiran Spencer and partner Renae Joyce. Through
Keiran's association with Bidgeebong Wines he and Renae were offered the opportunity to
purchase small quantities of grapes from Tumbarumba (chardonnay) and Gundagai (shiraz).
They say their plan 'is to produce classy wines at an affordable price and have some fun doing
it'. Mostly sold through word of mouth and a small number of select outlets.

� **First Kiss Chardonnay 2008** Nicely balanced ripe stone fruit aromas and
flavours on the mid-palate; does falter on the finish. Screwcap. 14% alc. **Rating** 87
To 2011 $20
First Kiss Gundagai Shiraz 2006 Overflows with ripe and sweet blackberry
and plum fruit, plus a generous amount of oak; the fruit line fades in the face of
fiery tannins on the finish. Screwcap. 14% alc. **Rating** 87 **To** 2013 $20

Kladis Estate ★★★★

Princes Highway, Wandandian, NSW 2540 **Region** Shoalhaven Coast
T (02) 4443 5606 **F** (02) 4443 6485 **www**.kladisestatewines.com.au **Open** 7 days 10–5
Winemaker Steve Dodd **Est.** 1996 **Cases** 10 000
Jim and Niki Kladis have developed 11 ha of shiraz, cabernet sauvignon, grenache, verdelho,
merlot and muscadelle at their Shoalhaven property, and 4 ha of gewurztraminer and cabernet
sauvignon in the Hunter Valley. Additional grapes are also sourced from the Adelaide Hills. The
inspiration has been the medium-bodied red wines Jim grew up with on the Greek island
of Zante. The winery recently had a $1.5 million upgrade to include a conference centre,
restaurant and cellar door. Exports to China, Japan, Fiji and Vanuatu.

♟♟♟♟♟ **Wandanian Cabernet Merlot 2005** Outstanding crimson hue for age; well
made, with clear blackcurrant and cassis fruit on the lusciously fruity palate
supported by gentle tannins. Screwcap. 14% alc. **Rating** 90 **To** 2014 $23
Dion Hunter Valley Cabernet Sauvignon 2006 Good colour; medium-
bodied wine with good length and balance, cabernet expressing itself with black
fruits and a savoury/earthy twist from its Hunter Valley roots. Silver medal from
Vienna '08. Cork. 13.5% alc. **Rating** 90 **To** 2016 $54

♟♟♟♟ **Bandaloop Sauvignon Blanc 2008** Yet another very correct wine from
Kladis, and yet another silver medal from Vienna; sourced from the Yarra Valley, it
has gentle tropical fruit framed by citrussy acidity. Screwcap. 12% alc. **Rating** 89
To 2011 $23
Wandanian Merlot 2005 Has the touch of silk that good merlot should have
somewhere in its make-up; the redcurrant flavours clearly varietal, low extract and
oak handling protecting the fruit. Screwcap. 13% alc. **Rating** 89 **To** 2012 $23
Angelique NV Golden brown; quite complex and rich, with butterscotch and
cumquat flavours, plus balancing acidity; yet another silver medal at Vienna, and
deserved. Botrytis semillon. Cork. 9% alc. **Rating** 89 **To** 2010 $24
Wandanian Shiraz 2005 There is a slight nip to the finish of this wine, but it
has been well made and has the expected flavour and structure of shiraz from
the NSW South Coast. Commendable quality. Screwcap. 14.5% alc. **Rating** 88
To 2012 $23

Knappstein ★★★★★

2 Pioneer Avenue, Clare, SA 5453 **Region** Clare Valley
T (08) 8841 2100 **F** (08) 8841 2101 **www**.knappstein.com.au **Open** Mon–Fri 9–5,
Sat 11–5, Sun & public hols 11–4
Winemaker Julian Langworthy **Est.** 1969 **Cases** 35 000

Knappstein's full name is Knappstein Enterprise Winery & Brewery, reflecting its history before being acquired by Petaluma, and since then part of Lion Nathan's stable. The 115 ha of mature estate vineyards in prime locations supply grapes both for the Knappstein brand and for wider Petaluma use. Despite making seriously good wines, Knappstein can't seem to regularly get across the line to greatness. Exports to all major markets.

ŸŸŸŸŸ **Hand Picked Clare Valley Riesling 2008** Gently perfumed blossom and spice leads into a tightly focused palate; lime and lemon juice flavours run through the long finish; delicious wine. Screwcap. 12.5% alc. **Rating** 94 **To** 2018 $22
Ackland Vineyard Watervale Riesling 2008 Attractive apple blossom and citrus aromas; the palate is intense and very long, with cleansing acidity on the finish. Screwcap. 12.5% alc. **Rating** 94 **To** 2016 $30
Enterprise Vineyard Clare Valley Cabernet Sauvignon 2006 Deeply coloured; a densely fruited, full-bodied cabernet showing luscious black fruits set against firm but balanced tannins and quality French oak. Cork permitting, a long life ahead. 14.5% alc. **Rating** 94 **To** 2021 $40

ŸŸŸŸŸ **Clare Valley Shiraz 2006** Good hue; typical of the Clare Valley, with solid structure underpinning the black fruits; good oak and tannin balance augments the spicy/mocha notes also present. Screwcap. 14.5% alc. **Rating** 91 **To** 2016 $22
Clare Valley Cabernet Merlot 2006 Strong crimson; has quite luscious berry fruit in a mix of red and black flavours framed by savoury tannins on the finish; medium- to full-bodied, with good varietal character. Screwcap. 14.5% alc. **Rating** 91 **To** 2018 $22

ŸŸŸŸ **Three Clare Valley Gewurztraminer Riesling Pinot Gris 2008** As ever, an idiosyncratic blend, the core of riesling being pulled in opposite directions by the other two varieties. A vineyard-driven blend, one suspects. Screwcap. 13.5% alc. **Rating** 88 **To** 2013 $22

 Knee Deep Wines ★★★★

Lot 61 Johnson Road, Wilyabrup, WA 6280 **Region** Margaret River
T (08) 9755 6776 **F** (08) 9755 6779 **www.**kneedeepwines.com.au **Open** 7 days 10–5
Winemaker Bruce Dukes, Bob Cartwright (Consultant) **Est.** 2000 **Cases** 8800
Perth surgeon and veteran yachtsman Phil Childs has found time to acquire a 34-ha farming property in Wilyabrup, and plant a little over 20 ha of chardonnay (3.16 ha), sauvignon blanc (4.1 ha), semillon (1.48 ha), chenin blanc (4.15 ha), cabernet sauvignon (6.34 ha) and shiraz (1.23 ha). The name, Knee Deep Wines, was inspired by absolute commitment to making premium wine (and its concomitant cost) and by a tongue-in-cheek acknowledgement of the grape glut building more or less in tune with the venture. A casual observer noting the 15.3 m racing yacht won the Sydney to Hobart handicap race in 1999 a month after it was launched (then named Yendys), its purchase in 2008 by Phil Childs, and its new name Knee Deep, might think there is also an aquatic angle to the name as the yacht lines up for this year's Sydney–Hobart race. It is as well that Childs has consultant winemaker Bob Cartwright (28 vintages as winemaker at Leeuwin Estate) and consultant viticulturist Greg Nikulinsky (seven years at Ferngrove) to oversee the vineyard management.

ŸŸŸŸŸ **Margaret River Shiraz 2007** Good purple hue, although not entirely bright; generous blackberry, plum and black cherry fruit, with some spicy notes; soft, fine, ripe tannins. Screwcap. 14.2% alc. **Rating** 91 **To** 2015 $24
Margaret River Chardonnay 2006 Bright green-yellow; has more precision and focus than the '07, with grapefruit, nectarine and apple flavours on a crisp and bright palate. Screwcap. 14% alc. **Rating** 90 **To** 2014 $30

ŸŸŸŸ **Margaret River Chardonnay 2007** A complex, pleasantly funky, bouquet leads into a palate that is intense and clean, but slightly congested on the finish. Screwcap. 14.3% alc. **Rating** 89 **To** 2012 $30
Reserve Margaret River Shiraz 2006 Unequivocally cool-grown style, with spicy/peppery notes to the red berry fruits; needs more flesh. Screwcap. 13.5% alc. **Rating** 88 **To** 2012 $33

Knots Wines

A8 Shurans Lane, Heathcote, Vic 3552 **Region** Heathcote
T (03) 5441 5429 **www**.thebridgevineyard.com.au **Open** Select w'ends, or by appt
Winemaker Lindsay Ross **Est.** 1997 **Cases** 1000
This venture of former Balgownie winemaker Lindsay Ross and wife Noeline is part of
a broader business known as Winedrops, which acts as a wine production and distribution
network for the Bendigo wine industry. The Knots wines are sourced from long-established
Heathcote and Bendigo vineyards, providing 0.5 ha each of semillon and chardonnay, and 4
ha each of shiraz and cabernets. The viticultural accent is on low-cropping vineyards with
concentrated flavours, the winemaking emphasis on flavour, finesse and varietal expression.

♥♥♥♥♀ **Top Knot Sangiovese 2006** A single barrel, the capsule made from Kevlar or
more; sommeliers beware. Is strongly, almost painfully, varietal, with rapier-like
cherry fruit and closing acidity. Diam. 14% alc. **Rating** 93 **To** 2016 $80

♥♥♥♥ **Sheepshank Bendigo Shiraz 2005** Deep colour; dense, powerful, black-fruited
shiraz, with aggressive tannins needing to soften before the fruit starts to fade.
Diam. 14% alc. **Rating** 88 **To** 2020 $30
Lark's Head Cabernet Merlot Cabernet Franc 2005 Well and truly varietal;
strong herbaceous elements tied to the tannins on the finish; certainly has length,
however. Cork. 14.5% alc. **Rating** 87 **To** 2014 $30

Knotting Hill Estate Vineyard

247 Carter Road, Wilyabrup WA 6280 **Region** Margaret River
T (08) 9755 3377 **F** (08) 9755 7744 **www**.knottinghill.com.au **Open** 7 days 11–4
Winemaker Flying Fish Cove (Elizabeth Reed) **Est.** 1997 **Cases** 3000 **Vyds** 37.5 ha
The Gould family has been farming in WA since 1907, and still owns the land and grant taken
up on their arrival from Scotland. In 1997 two generations of the family decided to diversify,
and acquired Knotting Hill, their Wilyabrup property in the Margaret River. In 2002 they
leased the wheat farm, and have devoted all their time to Knotting Hill. In 1998, using their
extensive farming background, they propagated 56 000 cuttings by hand in an onsite nursery,
supervised plantings, created a 5.5-ha dam, and built the 45 m bridge entry to the local
limestone cellar door, which opened in '05. The spectacular vineyard setting is established on
a natural amphitheatre, with the lake at the bottom.

♥♥♥♥♥ **Margaret River Cabernet Merlot 2007** A truly excellent example of a blend
that Margaret River has made its own; has great intensity, balance and length
to its blackcurrant and cassis fruit supported by fine-grained, persistent tannins.
Screwcap. 13.6% alc. **Rating** 94 **To** 2017 $28

♥♥♥♥♀ **Margaret River Shiraz 2007** Bright crimson-purple hue; strongly spicy/
savoury/peppery overtones to the core of red fruits and long palate. Screwcap.
13% alc. **Rating** 90 **To** 2015 $28

♥♥♥♥ **Margaret River Verdelho 2008** Striking, pungent pear and baked apple aromas
that back off on the palate; interesting wine. Screwcap. 12.5% alc. **Rating** 89
To 2011 $20
Margaret River Semillon Sauvignon Blanc 2008 The two-thirds semillon
component is very much the foundation of the wine; it needs a year or two
to open up and express itself, which it will do. Screwcap. 13.6% alc. **Rating** 88
To 2014 $20

Kominos Wines

27145 New England Highway, Severnlea, Qld 4352 **Region** Granite Belt
T (07) 4683 4311 **F** (07) 4683 4291 **www**.kominoswines.com **Open** 7 days 9–5
Winemaker Tony Comino **Est.** 1976 **Cases** 6000 **Vyds** 12 ha

Tony Comino, a dedicated viticulturist and winemaker, and wife Mary took over ownership of the winery from his parents on its 21st vintage. Comino is proud of the estate-grown, -made and -bottled heritage of the winery and content to keep a relatively low profile, although the proud show record of the wines might suggest otherwise. In addition to the estate plantings, Comino manages an additional 7 ha. The varieties planted are sauvignon blanc, chenin blanc, semillon, chardonnay, shiraz, merlot, cabernet franc and cabernet sauvignon. Another Qld producer to make seriously good wines, capable of holding their own against all-comers from the south (as Queenslanders refer to anyone not born in the state). Exports to the US, Taiwan, Korea, China and Singapore.

ΨΨΨΨ♀ **Estate Shiraz 2008** Vibrant colour; ripe and spicy with blackberry and pronounced pepper on the bouquet; quite sweet fruited on entry, the spicyness returns with a little firmness, providing focus on the finish. Diam. 14% alc. **Rating** 92 **To** 2015 $20
Reserve Shiraz 2008 Moving into blackberry jam territory with a little oak-derived spice; very dense on the palate, and a little more extract and bitterness on the finish; well constructed and just pushing a little harder than the Estate; a matter of personal taste. Diam. 14% alc. **Rating** 92 **To** 2015 $25

Koonaburra Vineyard   NR
44 Summerhill Road, Bywong, NSW 2621 **Region** Canberra District
T (02) 6236 9019 **F** (02) 6236 9029 **Open** Thurs–Mon 10–5
Winemaker Canberra Winemakers **Est.** 1998 **Cases** 330 **Vyds** 3.2 ha
Nicolaas (Nico) and wife Shawn Duynhoven left Sydney and purchased their block of land 'because we wanted to grow something'. Nico built the house and cellar door/café, and they initially planted 280 hazelnut trees, followed by a little merlot and (progressively) 1 ha each of riesling, sauvignon blanc and pinot noir. They achieved all this while holding down full-time jobs, Nico in home building and Shawn in nursing. By producing a dry Riesling, Riesling Ice Wine, Merlot, Sparkling Merlot and Rose, they have managed to expand the range of their wine portfolio notwithstanding its small estate-grown basis.

Koonara
44 Main Street, Penola, Sa 5277 **Region** Coonawarra
T (08) 8737 3222 **F** (08) 8737 3220 **www**.koonara.com **Open** 7 days 10–6
Winemaker Peter Douglas, Dru Reschke **Est.** 1988 **Cases** 5000 **Vyds** 8 ha
Koonara is a sister, or, more appropriately, a brother company to Reschke Wines. The latter is run by Burke Reschke, Koonara by his brother Dru. Both are sons of Trevor Reschke, who planted the first vines on the Koonara property in 1988. The initial planting was of cabernet sauvignon, followed by shiraz in 1993 and additional cabernet sauvignon in '98. Peter Douglas, formerly Wynns' chief winemaker before moving overseas for some years, has returned to the district and is consultant winemaker. The Bay of Apostles range was released in 2008, with four of the five wines under the label sourced from Vic. A Bay of Apostles cellar door has been opened in the main street of Apollo Bay on the Great Ocean Road. Exports to Malaysia, Singapore and China.

ΨΨΨΨΨ **Ambriel's Gift Coonawarra Cabernet Sauvignon 2006** Bright colour; toasty oak and cassis combine seamlessly to offer a lively and balanced varietal cabernet; red fruits come to the fore on the palate, with a lithe and fresh conclusion. Screwcap. 13.5% alc. **Rating** 94 **To** 2016 $30

ΨΨΨΨ♀ **Bay of Apostles Mount Gambier Sauvignon Blanc 2008** Lively fresh herb, grass and mineral aromas, with nuances of apple and gooseberry joining in on the palate, which has excellent line and length. Screwcap. 12.1% alc. **Rating** 92 **To** 2011 $20
Angel's Footsteps Sauvignon Blanc 2008 While reticent on the bouquet, explodes into life on the bright, zesty palate, with flavours of citrus and gooseberry; a Wrattonbully/Mount Gambier blend that works very well. Screwcap. 12.4% alc. **Rating** 92 **To** 2011 $20

Bay of Apostles Coonawarra Cabernet Sauvignon 2005 Has clear-cut varietal character, with a mix of blackcurrant and mulberry fruit; good tannins; structure will sustain the wine well. Screwcap. 14% alc. **Rating** 90 **To** 2016 $20

ŶŶŶŶ   **Bay of Apostles Geelong Mount Gambier Pinot Noir 2008** Bright colour; varietal cherry and plum bouquet; straightforward and correct, with a bit of grip and toasty oak on the finish. Screwcap. 13.4% alc. **Rating** 89 **To** 2012 $21
Bay of Apostles Shiraz 2006 Fragrant, spicy cool-climate fruit on the bouquet and palate alike; supple red fruits and fine tannins. Screwcap. 14.5% alc. **Rating** 89 **To** 2016 $20
The Temptress Coonawarra Cabernet Sauvignon 2005 Good management of oak and tannins give the wine pleasing mouthfeel; a mix of red and black fruits run through the light- to medium-bodied palate. Screwcap. 13.9% alc. **Rating** 89 **To** 2013 $19
Ambriel's Gift Museum Release Coonawarra Cabernet Sauvignon 2002 Has retained good hue; the savoury/earthy/foresty characters of the cool vintage are intensifying; the wine has reached the point where it should be drunk. The medal display on the label is illegal, as it doesn't specify the year or class of the award. Screwcap. 13.5% alc. **Rating** 88 **To** 2011 $30
Sofiel's Gift Riesling 2007 Has no shortage of flavour in a ripe, tropical spectrum; the finish is a little soft, lacking conviction. Adelaide Hills. Screwcap. 12.2% alc. **Rating** 87 **To** 2012 $17

Koonowla Wines   ·   ★★★★

PO Box 45, Auburn, SA 5451 **Region** Clare Valley
T (08) 8849 2080 **F** (08) 8849 2293 **www**.koonowla.com **Open** Not
Winemaker O'Leary Walker Wines **Est.** 1997 **Cases** 50000 **Vyds** 100 ha
It's not often that a light as large as this can be hidden under a bushel. Koonowla is a historic Clare Valley property; situated just east of Auburn, it was first planted with vines in the 1890s, and by the early 1900s was producing 60 000 litres of wine annually. A disastrous fire in 1926 destroyed the winery and wine stocks, and the property was converted to grain and wool production. Replanting of vines began in 1985, and accelerated after Andrew and Booie Michael purchased the property in '91; there are now 40 ha of cabernet sauvignon, 36 ha riesling, 20 ha of shiraz, and 2 ha each of merlot and semillon. In an all too familiar story, the grapes were sold until falling prices forced a change in strategy; now part of the grapes are vinified by the infinitely experienced David O'Leary and Nick Walker, with the remainder sold. Most of the wines are exported (to the UK, the US, Scandinavia, Malaysia and NZ).

ŶŶŶŶŶ   **Clare Valley Riesling 2008** Strong green-straw colour; the bouquet is stacked with ripe spice and citrus aromas, and the depth and power of the palate comes as no surprise. Great early-drinking style. Screwcap. 12% alc. **Rating** 91 **To** 2013 $20
Clare Valley Shiraz 2006 Loaded with sweet dark fruit and a light seasoning of oak; the palate is quite unctuous and the acidity provides good focus on the finish. Screwcap. 14.5% alc. **Rating** 90 **To** 2014 $22

Kooyong   ★★★★★

PO Box 153, Red Hill South, Vic 3937 **Region** Mornington Peninsula
T (03) 5989 7355 **F** (03) 5989 7677 **www**.kooyong.com **Open** At Port Phillip Estate
Winemaker Sandro Mosele **Est.** 1996 **Cases** 5000 **Vyds** 47.7 ha
Kooyong, owned by Giorgio and Dianne Gjergja, released its first wines in 2001. The vineyard is planted to pinot noir, chardonnay and, more recently, pinot gris. Winemaker Sandro Mosele is a graduate of CSU, and has a deservedly high reputation. He also provides contract winemaking services for others. The Kooyong wines are made at Port Phillip Estate, also owned by the Gjergias. Exports to the UK, the US and other major markets.

ΨΨΨΨΨ Single Vineyard Selection Faultline Chardonnay 2007 A powerful and complex bouquet dominated by mineral complexity and offset with pure lemon aromas; there is real nervosity and tension to the palate, with acid providing a taut backbone to the layered, complex and intriguing fruit components; the final element is the incredible length and the manner in which the wine continues to open up long after it is gone. Cork. 13% alc. **Rating** 96 **To** 2016 $52
Single Vineyard Selection Ferrous Pinot Noir 2007 Dense colour; plush plummy fruit surrounds a core of mineral, with dark cherries adding brightness; the palate is velvet-like on entry, and offers dark, gamey, roast meat characters, which draws out a to a gently spicy and quite tannic conclusion; super concentration, but not in the least heavy. Cork. 13.5% alc. **Rating** 96 **To** 2016 $60
Single Vineyard Selection Meres Pinot Noir 2007 A leaner framework is offered here, with almost sour cherry fruit coming to the fore; the palate draws on the high level of acid and tight red fruits to offer a slightly more savoury, garden herb and game finish; a wine with a slightly more European persuasion. Cork. 13% alc. **Rating** 95 **To** 2015 $60
Single Vineyard Selection Haven Pinot Noir 2007 A more typical Mornington bouquet; generous ripe cherry fruits, gentle and attractive touches of violets and spice; the palate is rich and warm, with slinky tannin, a touch of stem and ample fruit opening gracefully on the finish. Cork. 13% alc. **Rating** 95 **To** 2014 $60
Single Vineyard Selection Farrago Chardonnay 2007 A generous bouquet exhibiting savoury grilled nuts, minerals and grapefruit; the palate is packed with flavour and offers an array of texture and personality; a long, generous and slightly savoury finish. Cork. 13% alc. **Rating** 94 **To** 2016 $52
Massale Mornington Peninsula Pinot Noir 2007 Vivid crimson-purple; very pure varietal fruit expression throughout with black cherry, damson plum and fruit spices; long palate and finish. Will develop with aplomb through to 2012 and beyond. Diam. 13% alc. **Rating** 94 **To** 2015 $30
Estate Mornington Peninsula Pinot Noir 2007 Cherry and plum fruit with a serving of Asian spices and complex ironstone nuances; the palate, fleshy on entry, tightens up with fine-grained tannins and vibrant acidity; a core of pure red fruit takes time to open on the palate. Cork. 13% alc. **Rating** 94 **To** 2015 $42

ΨΨΨΨΨ Clonale Mornington Peninsula Chardonnay 2008 Pale green hue; tightly wound citrus fruit, with an attractive mineral complexity; the palate is very fine and focused and drives seamlessly from start to finish; offers crisp acidity and plenty of texture on the long and even finish. Cork. 13% alc. **Rating** 93 **To** 2012 $25
Estate Mornington Peninsula Chardonnay 2007 Restrained grilled nuts, nectarines and a hint of spice from the oak; the palate is fine and poised, with lively, tangy acidity drawing the wine out to a long and even conclusion. Cork. 13% alc. **Rating** 93 **To** 2014 $36

Kopparossa Wines   ★★★★

PO Box 26, Coonawarra, SA 5263 **Region** Coonawarra
T (08) 8736 3268 **F** (08) 8736 3363 **Open** By appt
Winemaker Gavin Hogg, Mike Press **Est.** 1996 **Cases** 5000 **Vyds** 22 ha
Of the many complicated stories, this is one of the most complicated of all. It was founded by Gavin Hogg and Mike Press in 1996, based on an 80-ha vineyard in the Wrattonbully region, and the Kopparossa label was born in '00. The vineyard was sold in 2002, and Mike retired to pursue separate interests in his Adelaide Hills family vineyard. Various wine releases and events occurred until 2005 when a joint venture between Stentiford Pty Ltd (Kopparossa's parent company) and Estate Licensing Pty Ltd (Olivia Newton John's wine-naming rights company) was entered into. Says Gavin's newsletter, 'Put simply, Stentiford produces and packages wine for the Olivia Label, which is then marketed and sold by Estate Licensing'. Reading on, we are told there are also Kopparossa wines and the possibility of a premium platinum release in the future under the Olivia banner. Please don't ask me to explain this any further. Exports to the UK, the US, Canada and Hong Kong.

ỌỌỌỌỌ **Coonawarra Cabernet Merlot 2006** A generous wine, with layers of black and red fruits ranging from plum, cherry to blackcurrant fruits; ripe tannins and subtle oak. Screwcap. 14% alc. **Rating** 92 **To** 2018 $25

Coonawarra Merlot 2006 Distinctly savoury/earthy aromas carry through onto the palate, which has convincing blackcurrant and plum fruit to match the savoury notes. Screwcap. 14% alc. **Rating** 91 **To** 2015 $25

Wrattonbully Sauvignon Blanc 2007 Unusual wine; tropical fruit on the bouquet and fore-palate followed by intense, lip-smacking citrussy acidity on the back-palate and finish. Screwcap. 12% alc. **Rating** 90 **To** 2010 $20

Coonawarra Shiraz Viognier 2004 Attractive spicy and lively medium-bodied wine; viognier added as wine and not co-fermented; has good mouthfeel, and fine, spicy tannins. Screwcap. 14% alc. **Rating** 90 **To** 2014 $25

Olivia's Personal Reserve Shiraz Viognier 2004 Very similar to the standard wine, the fruit a little brighter, the palate slightly less supple and spicy; same points outcome. Screwcap. 13.5% alc. **Rating** 90 **To** 2014 $24.90

ỌỌỌỌ **Estate Coonawarra Shiraz 2002** A mature wine from a very cool vintage; light- to medium-bodied with spicy notes throughout and gently savoury tannins; ready now or over the next few years. Screwcap. 14% alc. **Rating** 89 **To** 2012 $25

Coonawarra Unwooded Chardonnay 2008 Pale straw-green; has ample stone fruit, grapefruit and melon to provide character and interest; good example of unwooded chardonnay. Screwcap. 13.5% alc. **Rating** 87 **To** 2011 $15

 # Kosciusko Wines

Jingellic Road, Tumbarumba, NSW 2653 **Region** Tumbarumba
T (02) 6948 3843 **F** (02) 6948 3988 **www**.kosciuskowines.com.au **Open** By appt
Winemaker Chris Thomas **Est.** 2005 **Cases** 4000
Adelaide Hills residents Chris and Anne Thomas' love for Flinders Ranges Shiraz, Clare and Eden Valley Rieslings, and SA Cabernet Sauvignon encouraged Chris, a semi-retired engineer, to complete postgraduate oenology studies at Adelaide University, graduating in 2002. Vintages in cooler parts of California and the 2004 vintage in Tumbarumba led to a decision to move from the Adelaide Hills to Tumbarumba in '05. Until Chris' arrival there was no winery or professional winemaker in the region, an earlier sparkling wine facility ceasing to operate many years ago. Five local grapegrowers banded together to own and operate a grape-processing facility where Chris makes the Kosciusko wines, and is a contract maker for others, including the owners of the facility.

ỌỌỌỌỌ **Pinot Noir Chardonnay 2005** Persistent mousse; has stone fruit and some creamy notes on entry into the mouth, tightening up impressively on the long finish. Gold medal and trophy winner at the Canberra Regional Wine Show with Brian Croser as chief judge. Crown. 11.5% alc. **Rating** 92 **To** 2010 $30

ỌỌỌỌ **Riesling 2008** Delicate and crisp, with apple and lemon blossom aromas; the palate has green, grassy notes, which will soften with time. Screwcap. 12% alc. **Rating** 89 **To** 2015 $25

Tumbarumba Chardonnay 2006 Vibrant colour; the citrus bouquet has a touch of spice; nice weight and definition, with a bit of grip on the finish. Screwcap. 12.6% alc. **Rating** 88 **To** 2014 $22

Krinklewood Biodynamic Vineyard

712 Wollombi Road, Broke, NSW 2330 **Region** Lower Hunter Valley
T (02) 6579 1322 **www**.krinklewood.com **Open** W'ends & public hols 10–5
Winemaker Liz Jackson, Rod Windrim **Est.** 1981 **Cases** 6000 **Vyds** 19.9 ha
A boutique, family-owned biodynamic vineyard, Krinklewood produces 100% estate-grown wines reflecting the terroir of the Broke-Fordwich area of the Hunter Valley. The cellar door is set among Provençal-style gardens that overlook the vineyard, with the Wollombi Brook and Brokenback range providing a spectacular backdrop. Exports to Canada, Denmark and Japan.

ŢŢŢŢŢ Lucia Dessert Wine 2008 Bright green–gold; made from botrytised chardonnay, with flavours of peach and cumquat balanced by zesty acidity; excellent length and balance. Screwcap. 11.5% alc. Rating 93 To 2012 $30
Semillon 2008 Attractive, mainstream young semillon, with gently ripe fruit; largely lime/lemon, but with a touch of stone fruit on the palate. Screwcap. 10% alc. Rating 90 To 2016 $22

ŢŢŢŢ Chardonnay 2007 Bright green–straw; complex and lively palate; grapefruit and stone fruit balanced by acidity, presumably adjusted. Well made. Screwcap. 13.2% alc. Rating 89 To 2014 $24
Wild White 2008 Fresh, zesty and lively, benefiting from early picking; attractive palate with good fruit flavours. Screwcap. 12% alc. Rating 89 To 2011 $15

KT & The Falcon ★★★★★

Mintaro Road, Leasingham, SA 5452 5415 **Region** Clare Valley
T 0419 855 500 **F** (08) 8843 0040 **www.**ktandthefalcon.com.au **Open** By appt
Winemaker Kerri Thompson **Est.** 2006 **Cases** 700 **Vyds** 7 ha
KT is winemaker Kerri Thompson and the Falcon is viticulturist Stephen Farrugia. Kerri graduated with a degree in oenology from Roseworthy Agricultural College in 1993, and thereafter made wine in McLaren Vale, Tuscany, Beaujolais and the Clare Valley, becoming well known as the Leasingham winemaker in the Clare. Steve managed vineyards in McLaren Vale and the Clare Valley before establishing the estate vineyard Falcon. Despite Kerri's former role within a very large winemaking organisation, the two have unhesitatingly moved into biodynamic management of their own vineyard (planted chiefly to riesling, but with some shiraz) and one of the vineyards they manage (moving to biodynamic farming in 2003). Kerri resigned from Hardys/Leasingham in 2006 after seven years at the helm, and made the first official KT & The Falcon wines the following year. She makes these wines at Crabtree, where she is winemaker. Exports to the UK.

ŢŢŢŢŢ Peglidis Vineyard Watervale Riesling 2008 A pure lime juice bouquet has a mineral overlay; the palate shows some CO_2, and there is real nerve and drive to the fruit and structure; steely on the finish, with generous fruit-weight providing richness and pleasure to conclude. Screwcap. 12% alc. Rating 95 To 2015 $35
Melva Watervale Riesling 2008 Gently aromatic, with a green apple and perfume talc. bouquet; the off-dry palate shows well-balanced sweetness and the intensity of fruit leaves the finish quite dry; a good example of a little sweetness adding an extra dimension to the variety. Screwcap. 12.5% alc. Rating 94 To 2016 $28

ŢŢŢŢŢ Churinga Vineyard Clare Valley Shiraz 2007 Bright colour; pure blueberry fruit with attractive spicy notes and a touch of choc-mint; quite precise and focused on the palate, with squeaky acidity, and plenty of tannin; firm and full on the finish. Screwcap. 13.5% alc. Rating 93 To 2016 $40

Kurabana ★★★★

580 Hendy Main Road, Mt Moriac, Vic 3240 **Region** Geelong
T 0438 661 273 **F** (03) 5266 1116 **www.**kurabana.com **Open** Not
Winemaker Ray Nadeson, Lee Evans **Est.** 1987 **Cases** 7000 **Vyds** 18 ha
The development of the quite extensive Kurabana Vineyard, west of Geelong in the foothills of Mt Moriac, began in 1987. Pinot noir (7.8 ha) is the largest portion, followed by (in descending order) shiraz, chardonnay, sauvignon blanc, pinot gris and viognier. While some of the grapes are sold, there are also limited purchases from the Geelong area.

ŢŢŢŢŢ Geelong Pinot Noir 2004 As often, the natural cork imparts a distinct woody fingerprint on the bouquet; that said, a thoroughly pleasing pinot that has developed with grace; excellent line, length and finish. Cork. 13.5% alc. Rating 93 To 2012 $19.95

Mt Moriac Estate Chardonnay 2006 Still amazingly youthful and fresh, so much so you wonder whether it will ever fully develop; however, the gentle stone fruit and citrus palate is well balanced, the oak subtle, so perhaps it won't matter. Screwcap. 13% alc. **Rating** 90 **To** 2013 $25.95

Mt Moriac Estate Pinot Noir 2005 Has matured well in bottle, with a pleasing array of spicy/briary notes woven through the black plum and berry fruits; has good texture and mouthfeel. Screwcap. 13.5% alc. **Rating** 90 **To** 2012 $25.95

ŢŢŢŢ **Blanc de Noirs 2005** Pale straw; pleasant style; you would think there was some chardonnay present; flavourful and well balanced. Cork. 13% alc. **Rating** 89 **To** 2010 $29.95

Mt Moriac Estate Pinot Noir 2007 Strong colour; very ripe black plum fruit aromas and flavours; quite intense, but not particularly refined; will likely improve in bottle. Screwcap. 13.5% alc. **Rating** 88 **To** 2012 $16.95

Kurrajong Downs

Casino Road, Tenterfield, NSW 2372 **Region** New England
T (02) 6736 4590 **www**.kurrajongdownswines.com **Open** Thurs–Mon 9–4
Winemaker Ravens Croft Wines, Symphony Hill **Est.** 2000 **Cases** 2000 **Vyds** 5 ha
Jonus Rhodes arrived at Tenterfield in 1858, lured by the gold he mined for the next 40 years, until his death in 1898. He was evidently successful, for the family now runs a 2800-ha cattle grazing property on which Lynton and Sue Rhodes began the development of their vineyard at an altitude of 850 m in 1996. Plantings include shiraz, cabernet sauvignon, merlot, pinot noir, chardonnay and pinot noir.

ŢŢŢŢŢ **Louisa Mary Tenterfield Semillon 2008** Attractive herb, grass and citrus/lemon aromas, the palate even more delicious than the bouquet, with delicate, but persistent, lemon/lime fruit. Very well made. Screwcap. 11% alc. **Rating** 93 **To** 2015 $17

ŢŢŢŢ **Timbarra Gold Tenterfield Chardonnay 2008** Light-bodied, but lively and fresh early-picked style; the mix of grapefruit and stone fruit flavours supported, rather than threatened, by a subtle touch of oak. Screwcap. 12% alc. **Rating** 88 **To** 2012 $18

Kurtz Family Vineyards

PO Box 460, Nuriootpa, SA 5355 **Region** Barossa Valley
T 0418 810 982 **F** (08) 8564 3217 **www**.kurtzfamilyvineyards.com.au **Open** By appt
Winemaker Steve Kurtz **Est.** 1996 **Cases** 4000 **Vyds** 18.4 ha
The Kurtz family has a little over 18 ha of vineyard at Light Pass, with 10 ha of shiraz, the remainder planted to chardonnay, cabernet sauvignon, semillon, sauvignon blanc, petit verdot, grenache, mataro and malbec. Steve Kurtz has followed in the footsteps of his great-grandfather Ben Kurtz, who first grew grapes at Light Pass in the 1930s. After a career working first at Saltram and then Foster's until 2006, Steve gained invaluable experience from Nigel Dolan, Caroline Dunn and John Glaetzer among others. Exports to the US, India, Macau, Hong Kong and China.

ŢŢŢŢŢ **Lunar Block Individual Vineyard Barossa Valley Shiraz 2004** Has many similarities to the '05, but with better colour and slightly more depth and length to the blackberry and spice fruit; perfect tannins and oak balance. Less than 60 dozen bottles made. Cork. 14.5% alc. **Rating** 95 **To** 2016 $41

Lunar Block Individual Vineyard Barossa Valley Shiraz 2005 A most attractive medium-bodied wine, with a spirited display of warm spices on a bed of red and black fruits, the tannins ripe and oak subtle; excellent length. Cork. 14% alc. **Rating** 94 **To** 2015 $41

ŢŢŢŢŢ **Boundary Row Barossa Valley Shiraz 2006** A generous bouquet offers spice, black fruits and vanilla; the medium- to full-bodied palate no less generous, with a deep and seamless line of blackberry and spice fruit, oak providing the chorus line. Screwcap. 14.5% alc. **Rating** 93 **To** 2021 $22

Boundary Row Barossa Valley Grenache Shiraz Mataro 2006 Bold red-purple colour that (correctly) suggests a wine with above-average depth and intensity to its plum, blackberry and black cherry fruit, balanced by gently savoury notes; barely shows 24 months in oak. Cork. 15% alc. **Rating** 93 **To** 2016 $18

ŸŸŸŸ   Seven Sleepers Siebenschlafer 2006 A six-way blend (Shiraz/Grenache/Petit Verdot/Cabernet Sauvignon/Malbec) that has a multiplicity of fruit flavours, none dominant, all different. If nothing else, shows it can be done. Screwcap. 14.5% alc. **Rating** 87 **To** 2013 $15

Kyneton Ridge Estate

90 Blackhill School Road, Kyneton, Vic 3444 **Region** Macedon Ranges
T (03) 5422 7377 **www.**kynetonridge.com.au **Open** W'ends & public hols 10–5, or by appt
Winemaker John Boucher **Est.** 1997 **Cases** 500
Kyneton Ridge Estate has been established by a family team of winemakers, with winemaking roots going back four generations in the case of John and Ann Boucher. Together with Pauline Russell they found what they believe is a perfect pinot noir site near Kyneton, and planted 2.5 ha of pinot noir in 1997; 1.5 ha of chardonnay and 0.5 ha of shiraz were added in '02.

ŸŸŸŸ   Macedon Ranges Pinot Noir 2007 Deep colour; strong foresty/briary overtones to the bouquet foretell a savoury black fruit palate; unusual wine, which could surprise with a year or two in bottle. Screwcap. 13.2% alc. **Rating** 89 **To** 2012 $42
Fortunate Land Macedon Ranges Wooded Chardonnay 2006 Light and fresh, seemingly even lower alcohol than it in fact has; grapefruit, melon and citrus notes with brisk acidity, the barrel ferment oak restrained. Screwcap. 12.5% alc. **Rating** 88 **To** 2012 $25

La Curio

11 Sextant Avenue, Seaford, SA 5169 (postal) **Region** McLaren Vale
T (08) 8327 1442 **F** (08) 8327 1442 **www.**lacuriowines.com **Open** Not
Winemaker Adam Hooper **Est.** 2003 **Cases** 1000
La Curio has been established by Adam Hooper, who purchases small parcels of grapes from vineyards in McLaren Vale with an average age of 40 years, the oldest 80 years. The wines are made at Redheads Studio, a boutique winery in McLaren Vale that caters for a number of small producers. The manacles depicted on the striking label are those of Harry Houdini, and the brand proposition is very cleverly worked through. Winemaking techniques, too, are avant-garde, and highly successful. Exports to the UK, the US and Canada.

ŸŸŸŸŸ   Reserve McLaren Vale Shiraz 2007 While full-bodied, manages to retain life and thrust to the palate; the flavours range through blackberry, cherry, plum and chocolate, with the support of spicy oak. Ratty cork. 15% alc. **Rating** 91 **To** 2017 $28

ŸŸŸŸ   The Nubile McLaren Vale Grenache Shiraz 2007 The 30% blackberry and plum component of the shiraz helps smooth the tannins and adds weight to the mid-palate, providing significantly better balance than the Reserve Grenache. Cork. 15% alc. **Rating** 89 **To** 2017 $19

La Linea

36 Shipsters Road, Kensington Park, SA 5068 (postal) **Region** Adelaide Hills
T (08) 8431 3556 **www.**lalinea.com.au **Open** Not
Winemaker Peter Leske **Est.** 2007 **Cases** 1000
Partners Peter Leske and Jason Quin bring vast experience to this venture. After a number of years with the Australian Wine Research Institute, interacting with many wine businesses, large and small, Peter Leske became chief winemaker at Nepenthe for the better part of a decade. Jason Quin spent years at T'Gallant, one of the pioneers of pinot gris. Working exclusively with tempranillo to produce a serious Rose from a cooler part of the Adelaide Hills, and a dry

red (tempranillo) from a separately owned vineyard in the warmer and drier northern end of the Hills, marks the start of the business. La Linea, Spanish for 'the line', reflects the partners' aim to hold the line in style and quality.

🍷🍷🍷🍷🍷 **Vertigo 25GR Adelaide Hills Riesling 2008** Seductive style, the appreciable sweetness of 25 grammes of residual sugar communicated by the name. Great with Asian food or as an aperitif. Screwcap. 11% alc. **Rating** 90 **To** 2013 **$24**

🍷🍷🍷🍷 **Tempranillo 2007** A mix of juicy berry and more savoury notes; work-in-progress with more depth needed. Screwcap. 13% alc. **Rating** 87 **To** 2011 **$27**

La Pleiade ★★★★★

c/- Jasper Hill, Drummonds Lane, Heathcote, Vic 3523 **Region** Heathcote
T (03) 5433 2528 **F** (03) 5433 3143 **Open** By appt
Winemaker Ron Laughton, Michel Chapoutier **Est.** 1998 **Cases** 600 **Vyds** 9 ha
This is the joint venture of Michel and Corinne Chapoutier and Ron and Elva Laughton. In spring 1998 a vineyard using Australian and imported French shiraz clones was planted. The vineyard is run biodynamically, and the winemaking is deliberately designed to place maximum emphasis on the fruit quality. Exports to the UK, the US and other major markets.

Laanecoorie ★★★★

4834 Bendigo/Maryborough Road, Betley, Vic 3472 **Region** Bendigo
T (03) 5468 7260 **F** (03) 5468 7388 **www**.laanecoorievineyard.com **Open** W'ends & public hols 11–5, Mon–Fri by appt
Winemaker Graeme Jukes, John Ellis (Contract) **Est.** 1982 **Cases** 1000
John and Rosa McQuilten's vineyard (shiraz, cabernet franc, merlot and cabernet sauvignon) produces grapes of high quality, and competent contract winemaking does the rest. Like many Vic vineyards, the 2007 vintage was destroyed; the rating has been rolled over pending the arrival of the '08 wines.

Lady Bay Vineyard ★★★

Cnr Vine & Willis Drive, Lady Bay, SA 5204 **Region** Southern Fleurieu
T 0413 185 771 **F** (08) 8445 1561 **www**.ladybay.com.au **Open** Not
Winemaker Mike Brown **Est.** 1996 **Cases** 1000 **Vyds** 8.64 ha
Lady Bay has cabernet sauvignon (3.64 ha), shiraz (3 ha), tempranillo (1.2 ha), viognier (0.4 ha) and tempranillo (0.3 ha) a mere 500 m from the waters of the Gulf of St Vincent. On the inland side it is protected by the Great Gorge, part of the southern Mount Lofty Ranges. Cool days and warm nights provide good ripening conditions, even for varieties such as cabernet sauvignon.

🍷🍷🍷🍷 **Shiraz Cabernet Sauvignon 2006** Very oaky bouquet, with rich ripe black fruit and focused acidity on the solid finish. Screwcap. 14% alc. **Rating** 88 **To** 2016 **$55**

Lake Barrington Estate ★★★☆

1133-1136 West Kentish Road, West Kentish, Tas 7306 **Region** Northern Tasmania
T (03) 6491 1249 **F** (03) 9662 9553 **www**.lbv.com.au **Open** Wed–Sun 10–5 (Nov–Apr)
Winemaker Steve Lubiana (Sparkling), White Rock, Julian Alcorso (Table) **Est.** 1986 **Cases** 500 **Vyds** 1 ha
Charles and Jill Macek purchased the vineyard from founder Maree Tayler in 2005. Charles is a distinguished company director (Telstra, Wesfarmers). Lake Barrington's primary focus is on high-quality sparkling wine, which has won many trophies and gold medals over the years at the Tasmanian Wine Show, with lesser quantities of high-quality chardonnay and pinot noir. There are picnic facilities at the vineyard and, needless to say, the scenery is very beautiful.

🍷🍷🍷🍷🍷 **Alexandra 2000** Complex, rich, ripe style, with multiple layers of flavour on the long palate. Cork. 13% alc. **Rating** 90 **To** 2012 **$40**

Lake Breeze Wines

Step Road, Langhorne Creek, SA 5255 **Region** Langhorne Creek
T (08) 8537 3017 **F** (08) 8537 3267 www.lakebreeze.com.au **Open** 7 days 10–5
Winemaker Greg Follett **Est.** 1987 **Cases** 15 000 **Vyds** 90 ha
The Folletts have been farmers at Langhorne Creek since 1880, and grapegrowers since the
1930s. Since 1987, increasing amounts of their grapes have been made into wine. The quality
of the releases has been exemplary, with the red wines particularly appealing. Lake Breeze also
owns and makes the False Cape wines from Kangaroo Island. Exports to the UK, the US and
other major markets.

Arthur's Reserve Cabernet Sauvignon Petit Verdot 2005 Impenetrable
colour; a very concentrated bouquet and full-bodied palate; dark fruit and
persistent tannins provide a serious framework, with the alcohol noticeable on
the finish; made for those who like their wines to be big. ProCork. 14.5% alc.
Rating 92 **To** 2016 $32
Bullant Langhorne Creek Cabernet Merlot 2006 Good fruit definition of
cassis, supported by savoury black olives and a little mint; quite deep on the palate,
with fine-grained tannins across the finish; very good for the price. Screwcap.
13.9% alc. **Rating** 91 **To** 2014 $15
Bernoota Langhorne Creek Shiraz Cabernet 2006 Bright and clearly
defined cabernet fruit supported by blackberry shiraz and just a hint of mint; quite
long and savoury. Screwcap. 14.5% alc. **Rating** 91 **To** 2016 $21
Bullant Langhorne Creek Shiraz 2007 Bright colour; plum and mulberry
fruit with a splash of spice and mint; warm and rich on the palate, with ample
levels of dark fruit. Value. Screwcap. 14.5% alc. **Rating** 90 **To** 2014 $14
Bullant Langhorne Creek Shiraz 2006 Clear and bright crimson; fragrant
fruit aromas replicated on the black cherry and raspberry flavours of the light-
to medium-bodied palate; in typical regional fashion, has a pleasingly supple
mouthfeel. Screwcap. 14.5% alc. **Rating** 90 **To** 2015

False Cape Unknown Sailor Cabernet Merlot 2006 Cassis dominant
bouquet, with a strong presence of cedar; medium-bodied; accentuated acidity
and red fruit on the finish. Screwcap. 14% alc. **Rating** 89 **To** 2012 $18
Langhorne Creek Cabernet Sauvignon 2006 Light, fragrant berry aromas; a
typically soft and generous medium-bodied palate, with red and blackcurrant fruit,
tailing off slightly on the finish. Screwcap. 14.5% alc. **Rating** 89 **To** 2013 $23
Langhorne Creek Grenache 2007 Good colour; pure raspberry fruit with
a touch of dried herb; the palate is juicy, with a little savoury, slightly bitter yet
refreshing twist to the finish. Screwcap. 14.8% alc. **Rating** 88 **To** 2012 $18
Langhorne Creek Moscato 2008 Fresh green apple bouquet; lightly sweet
and quite harmonious and juicy on the finish; good and grapey. Crown Seal.
7% alc. **Rating** 88 **To** 2011 $17

Lake Cooper Estate

1608 Midland Highway, Corop, Vic 316 **Region** Heathcote
T (03) 9387 7657 www.lakecooperestate.com.au **Open** W'ends & public hols 11–5
Winemaker Peter Kelliher, Donald Risstrom **Est.** 1998 **Cases** 650 **Vyds** 29.8 ha
Lake Cooper Estate is another substantial venture in the burgeoning Heathcote region, set
on the side of Mt Camel Range with panoramic views of Lake Cooper, Greens Lake and the
Corop township. Planting began in 1998 with 12 ha of shiraz, subsequently extended to 18 ha
of shiraz and 9.5 ha of cabernet sauvignon. Small amounts of merlot, chardonnay, sauvignon
blanc and verdelho have since been planted.

Heathcote Shiraz 2007 A full-bodied wine that might have been better if it
was medium-bodied, the extract and tannins evident from the first sip; at the price,
worth a minor gamble on improvement for five years or so. Screwcap. 14.5% alc.
Rating 88 **To** 2014 $20

Heathcote Verdelho 2008 Ample fruit salad on the fore-palate yields to brisk, citrussy acidity on the finish; give it a year or two, and it might surprise. Screwcap. 13% alc. **Rating** 87 **To** 2012 $15

Heathcote Cabernet Sauvignon 2007 Better hue than other Lake Cooper reds; light- to medium-bodied, with stemmy/savoury/earthy notes to the main blackcurrant fruit stream; developing quickly, drink soon. Screwcap. 14.5% alc. **Rating** 87 **To** 2011 $20

Lake George Winery   ★★★★

Old Federal Highway, Lake George, NSW 2581 **Region** Canberra District
T (02) 9948 4676 **F** (02) 9949 2873 www.lakegeorgewinery.com.au **Open** 7 days 10–5
Winemaker Alex McKay, Nick O'Leary **Est.** 1971 **Cases** 4000 **Vyds** 20 ha
Lake George Winery was sold by founder Dr Edgar Riek some years ago. The plantings of 37-year-old chardonnay, pinot noir, cabernet sauvignon, semillon and merlot have been joined by shiraz and tempranillo, and yet more plantings of pinot gris, viognier, pinot noir and malbec. In March 2008 Lake George acquired the Madew vineyard, providing yet more grape resources. The winemaking techniques include basket pressing and small batch barrel maturation under the expert eyes of consultant winemakers Alex McKay and Nick O'Leary.

ȲȲȲȲȲ Semillon Sauvignon Blanc 2008 The clean bouquet gives little hint of the intense and delicious palate, with the taughtness of the semillon providing great tension to the passionfruit and ripe melon of the sauvignon blanc. Screwcap. 11.5% alc. **Rating** 93 **To** 2012 $18

Shiraz 2007 The fragrant bouquet has black (licorice) and red (cherry and spice) components; a theme carried on by the silky, medium-bodied palate, with its long and pleasing finish. Screwcap. 13.5% alc. **Rating** 92 **To** 2020 $29

ȲȲȲȲ Pinot Noir 2005 The wine is dominated on the bouquet and palate by savoury forest floor and briar; as the primary fruit continues to fade, it will become more so. Drink asap. Screwcap. 14% alc. **Rating** 87 **To** 2010 $60

Lake's Folly   ★★★★★

Broke Road, Pokolbin, NSW 2320 **Region** Lower Hunter Valley
T (02) 4998 7507 www.lakesfolly.com.au **Open** 7 days 10–4 while wine available
Winemaker Rodney Kempe **Est.** 1963 **Cases** 4000 **Vyds** 12.2 ha
The first of the weekend wineries to produce wines for commercial sale, long revered for its Cabernet Sauvignon and nowadays its Chardonnay. Very properly, terroir and climate produce a distinct regional influence and thereby a distinctive wine style. The winery continues to enjoy an incredibly loyal clientele, with much of each year's wine selling out quickly by mail order. Lake's Folly no longer has any connection with the Lake family, having been acquired some years ago by Perth businessman Peter Fogarty. Peter's family company previously established the Millbrook Winery in the Perth Hills, so is no stranger to the joys and agonies of running a small winery.

ȲȲȲȲȲ Lake's Folly Hunter Valley Chardonnay 2008 Very light straw-green; highly fragrant, with elements of citrus and peach blossom; a fine, intense palate reflecting the modest alcohol, verging on cool-climate grapefruit, best of all not swamped by oak. Will be long lived. Screwcap. 12.7% alc. **Rating** 95 **To** 2018 $60

Lake's Folly Hunter Valley Chardonnay 2007 Pale straw-green; melon, fig and stone fruit aromas, oak evident but integrated, lead into a powerful and complex palate, offering the fruit of the bouquet tied up neatly by grainy acidity; has excellent length, and carries its alcohol with aplomb. Radically different style to the '08, reflecting the vintage variation. Cork. 14% alc. **Rating** 95 **To** 2015

Lake's Folly Hunter Valley Cabernets 2007 Bright, light crimson-purple; a multi-faceted bouquet, fruit, oak and earth influences all intermingling; the palate has bright and lively red fruits in a medium-bodied frame; scores for its great balance, line and length. Give it five years' peace, then enjoy for the next 15. Cabernet Sauvignon/Merlot/Petit Verdot. Cork. 13% alc. **Rating** 94 **To** 2027

Lakeview Estate

NR

585 Goodhope Road, Yass, NSW 2582 **Region** Canberra District
T (02) 6227 1253 **F** (02) 6227 1253 **Open** By appt
Winemaker Kyeema Wines (Andrew McEwan) **Est.** 1996 **Cases** 275 **Vyds** 2.5 ha
Lakeview Estate is the venture of John and Jillian Doyle, who began the development of the vineyard at a site 650 m above sea level, 10 km south of Yass. It overlooks the Brindabella Ranges and the Murrumbidgee arm of the Burrinjuck Dam, fully justifying the overused 'spectacular views' tag. The elevation and slope of the vineyard provides perfect air drainage to the Murrumbidgee River, resulting in a frost-free environment, often a problem in this part of the world. The Doyles have planted merlot, shiraz, cabernet sauvignon and semillon, and elect to sell part of the grape production.

Lambert Vineyards

810 Norton Road, Wamboin, NSW 2620 **Region** Canberra District
T (02) 6238 3866 **www**.lambertvineyards.com.au **Open** Thurs–Sun 10–5, or by appt
Winemaker Steve Lambert, Ruth Lambert **Est.** 1998 **Cases** 6000 **Vyds** 9.5 ha
Ruth and Steve Lambert have established riesling (2.5 ha), pinot noir (2 ha), pinot gris and merlot (1.5 ha each), chardonnay (1 ha), cabernet sauvignon and shiraz (0.5 ha each). Steve makes the many wines onsite, and does so with skill and sensitivity. Definitely a winery to watch.

Reserve Canberra District Shiraz 2006 Strong colour; while having many similarities to the varietal, especially in the distinctive flavour register, has more intensity and depth; like the varietal, has absorbed 22 months in French oak. Screwcap. 14.7% alc. **Rating** 92 **To** 2016 $30
Canberra District Riesling 2008 Offers lime and tropical fruit aromas and flavours; the palate is well balanced and long. Screwcap. 12.5% alc. **Rating** 90 **To** 2016 $20
Canberra District Pinot Gris 2007 Alsace style, boldly made; 50% barrel ferment, and very ripe fruit. May not be to everyone's liking, but has masses of flavour and character. Screwcap. 15% alc. **Rating** 90 **To** 2012 $22
Canberra District Merlot 2007 Good colour; at the briary/savoury/olivaceous end of the merlot spectrum, but is strongly varietal, and has plenty of stuffing. Screwcap. 14.7% alc. **Rating** 90 **To** 2015 $25

Canberra District Shiraz 2006 A distinctly savoury style, with unusual tangy, juicy, almost citrussy, elements in the fruit, and a savoury, but low tannin, finish. Screwcap. 14.8% alc. **Rating** 88 **To** 2014 $25
Canberra District Chardonnay 2006 Bold barrel ferment wine with ripe peachy fruit, and just enough acidity to keep the show on the road. Screwcap. 14.5% alc. **Rating** 87 **To** 2012 $22

Lamont's Winery

85 Bisdee Road, Millendon, WA 6056 **Region** Swan Valley
T (08) 9296 4485 **www**.lamonts.com.au **Open** W'ends & public hols 10–5
Winemaker Digby Leddin **Est.** 1978 **Cases** 10 000 **Vyds** 2 ha
Corin Lamont is the daughter of the late Jack Mann, and oversees the making of wines in a style that would have pleased her father. Lamont's also boasts a superb restaurant run by granddaughter Kate Lamont. The wines are going from strength to strength, utilising both estate-grown and contract-grown (from southern regions) grapes. There are two cellar doors, the second (open 7 days) is in the Margaret River at Gunyulgup Valley Drive, Yallingup.

Frankland River Riesling 2008 Flavoursome but the rich palate is slightly broad; nonetheless, awarded a gold medal at the WA Wine Show '08. Screwcap. 12.5% alc. **Rating** 90 **To** 2011 $25

Semillon 2007 A rich bouquet of lemon and fresh toasted bread; while fresh, the palate is thickly textured, and displays evident toast from oak, and added complexity from lees stirring; an interesting textural example of semillon from WA. Screwcap. 12.9% alc. **Rating** 90 **To** 2013 $30

White Monster Chardonnay 2007 Monster by name… Very toasty bouquet, with nectarine and strong element of spice; the palate is dense and textured, with the acidity coming through and cleaning it up well. Screwcap. 14.3% alc. **Rating** 90 **To** 2013 $45

♀♀♀♀ **Chardonnay 2007** A rich and toasty style, with dried fig and melon supported by toasty oak; clean, toasty and with good length. Screwcap. 13.9% alc. **Rating** 89 **To** 2013 $28

Black Monster Malbec 2007 A dense dark and chewy wine, loaded with sweet blue and black fruits and high levels of acid; monster by name, but not so monstrous to drink. Screwcap. 16.1% alc. **Rating** 89 **To** 2012 $55

 # Landhaus Estate

PO Box 2135, Bethany SA 5352 **Region** Barossa Valley
T (08) 8353 8442 **F** (08) 8353 0542 **Open** Not
Winemaker Kane Jaunutis **Est.** 2002 **Cases** 2500

The Jaunutis family (John, Barbara and son Kane) purchased Landhaus Estate in November 2002, and the following month bought 'The Landhaus' cottage and 1-ha vineyard at Bethany. Bethany is the oldest German-established town in the Barossa (1842) and the cottage was one of the first to be built. Kane has worked vintages for Mitolo and Trevor Jones as well as managing East End Cellars, one of Australia's leading fine wine retailers, while John brings decades of owner/management experience and Barbara 20 years in sales and marketing. They decided not to produce any wine in 2003, instead rehabilitating the Bethany vineyard, and establishing contacts with growers of old vines in Greenock, Ebenezer and Stockwell. The strategy worked to perfection, the 2004 and '05 wines selling out quickly.

♀♀♀♀♀ **Reserve Barossa Valley Shiraz 2006** Dense but developed colour; rich black fruits with a strong dash of dark chocolate and mocha borrowed from McLaren Vale's repertoire; delicious mouthfeel due to superfine silky tannins and well-judged oak; great now or later. Screwcap. 14.5% alc. **Rating** 94 **To** 2020 $45

Barossa Valley Shiraz Mourvedre 2006 A delicious blend of equal amounts of shiraz and mourvedre from 70–100-year-old vines; has remarkably fresh fruit with a garnish of spice and sweet leather, the tannins fine and silky. Screwcap. 14.5% alc. **Rating** 94 **To** 2020 $35

Barossa Valley Shiraz Cabernet Sauvignon 2006 The savoury/herbal notes of Cabernet Sauvignon (40%) give the wine an entirely different cast to the Shiraz Mourvedre, but nonetheless synergistically blend with the Shiraz on a long and quite intense palate. Screwcap. 14.5% alc. **Rating** 94 **To** 2020 $35

♀♀♀♀♀ **Barossa Valley Mourvedre Grenache Shiraz 2006** Skilled winemaking invests the wine with above average aromaticity and preservation of fruit flavour, juicy components bonded by gentle but persistent tannins; 70-year-old vines. Screwcap. 14.5% alc. **Rating** 91 **To** 2015 $30

The Saint Shiraz 2006 Like the Reserve, from vines more than 60 years old, from four subregions; a very lively and quite tangy wine, with seamless fruit, oak and tannins. Shiraz. Screwcap. 14.5% alc. **Rating** 90 **To** 2013 $25

The Sinner 2006 Slightly cosmetic fruit on the fore-palate from 40% Grenache is more than balanced by the stronger fruit and tannins from Mourvedre (40%) and Shiraz (20%), which control the back-palate and finish; unoaked; 60–85-year-old vines. Screwcap. 14.5% alc. **Rating** 90 **To** 2015 $25

Landscape Wines

383 Prossers Road, Richmond, Tas 7025 **Region** Southern Tasmania
T (03) 6260 4216 **F** (03) 6260 4016 **Open** By appt
Winemaker Contract **Est.** 1998 **Cases** 120

Knowles and Elizabeth Kerry run the Wondoomarook mixed farming and irrigation property in the heart of the Coal River Valley. In 1998–99 they decided to undertake a small scale diversification, planting 0.5 ha each of riesling and pinot noir. The labels, depicting Antarctic scenes by Jenni Mitchell, hark back to the Kerrys' original occupation in Antarctic scientific research.

ŶŶŶŶŶ Pinot Noir 2007 Bright colour; has aromatic red fruits on the bouquet, and attractive red and black fruits plus spices on the palate, which has energy and drive. Rating 93 To 2014

Lane's End Vineyard ★★★★
885 Mount William Road, Lancefield, Vic 3435 **Region** Macedon Ranges
T (03) 5429 1760 **F** (03) 5429 1760 **www**.lanesend.com.au **Open** By appt
Winemaker Howard Matthews **Est.** 1985 **Cases** 400 **Vyds** 2 ha
Pharmacist Howard Matthews and family purchased the former Woodend Winery in 2000, with 1.8 ha of chardonnay and pinot noir (and a small amount of cabernet franc) dating back to the mid-1980s. Subsequently, the cabernet franc has been grafted over to pinot noir (with a mix of four clones), and the chardonnay now totals 1 ha. After working with next-door neighbour Ken Murchison of Portree Wines for two years gaining winemaking experience, Howard made the first wines in 2003. The 2005 Chardonnay, still available, continues to win trophies at the Macedon Ranges wine show.

ŶŶŶŶŶ Macedon Ranges Chardonnay 2005 An elegant, light- to medium-bodied wine; has good balance of fruit, barrel ferment and mlf influences to the gentle nectarine fruit, giving background creamy/nutty notes; an exercise in restraint. Gold medal Cool Climate Show '06. Screwcap. 13.7% alc. Rating 93 To 2012

Langanook Wines
109 McKittericks Road, Sutton Grange, Vic 3448 **Region** Bendigo
T (03) 5474 8250 **F** (03) 5474 8250 **www**.langanookwines.com.au **Open** W'ends & public hols 11–5, or by appt
Winemaker Matt Hunter **Est.** 1985 **Cases** 1500 **Vyds** 2 ha
When Matt Hunter was looking for a lifestyle change he left his position as Dean, Faculty of Business, Swinburne University and searched for land around the cool, granite soil, apple-growing district of Harcourt. He planted vines in 1985 and kept the vineyard small enough so that he could personally control both the vineyard and winemaking (with help from the wine science course at CSU). Smoke taint meant no wines were made in 2007, but the wines from '05 and '06 are still available at the time of going to press. Exports to Canada.

Langmeil Winery
Cnr Para Road/Langmeil Road, Tanunda, SA 5352 **Region** Barossa Valley
T (08) 8563 2595 **www**.langmeilwinery.com.au **Open** 7 days 10.30–4.30
Winemaker Paul Lindner **Est.** 1996 **Cases** 35 000 **Vyds** 25 ha
Vines were first planted at Langmeil (which possesses the oldest block in Australia) in the 1840s, and the first winery on the site, known as Paradale Wines, opened in 1932. In '96, cousins Carl and Richard Lindner with brother-in-law Chris Bitter formed a partnership to acquire and refurbish the winery and its 5-ha vineyard (planted to shiraz, and including 2 ha planted in 1843). Another vineyard was acquired in 1998, which included cabernet sauvignon and grenache. Exports to all major markets.

ŶŶŶŶŶ The 1843 Freedom Barossa Valley Shiraz 2006 Vibrant colour; surprisingly elegant offering considering the bouquet, plenty of red fruits framing the darker more serious elements; the palate is not in the same vein, with lots of oak, fruit and tannin piled in to create a wine of immense proportions, yet offering subtle complexity. Cork. 15.5% alc. Rating 94 To 2020 $100

Fifth Wave Barossa Grenache 2006 Deep colour; fine and fragrant raspberry and plum fruit has a lot of personality, spice and depth, a surprising amount for a pure grenache; long and juicy. Cork. 15.5% alc. **Rating** 94 **To** 2016 $30

ŸŸŸŸŸ **Jackaman's Barossa Cabernet Sauvignon 2006** Big, rich and ripe, with dark mocha fruit and an underlying cedar and cassis note to point to the variety; the palate exhibits a healthy dose of fruit, but the tannins are ample yet fine. Screwcap. 14.5% alc. **Rating** 93 **To** 2020 $50

The Blacksmith Barossa Cabernet Sauvignon 2006 Rich, generous, luscious cassis, blackcurrant, dark chocolate and cedar all interwoven; ripe tannins on a balanced finish. Cork. 15% alc. **Rating** 93 **To** 2016 $24.95

Barossa Valley Sparkling Shiraz Cuvee NV Good wine; bottle-fermented and a minimum of 10 months on lees; has abundant flavour with no hint of phenolics, so the finish is long, fresh and not the least sweet. One of the best outside Seppelt, Rockford and Primo Estate. Will continue to develop. Disgorged August '08. Cork. 13.5% alc. **Rating** 92 **To** 2015 $35

GWH Barossa Valley Viognier 2008 Good varietal apricot and spice aromas; very rich mid-palate, with balancing acidity for freshness. Screwcap. 14% alc. **Rating** 91 **To** 2010 $19.95

Bella Rouge 2008 Abundant redcurrant and cassis fruit; not overweight or extracted; nice food style. Screwcap. 14% alc. **Rating** 91 **To** 2010 $19.95

Orphan Bank Barossa Valley Shiraz 2006 Crimson-red; unusual oriental spice overtones to the fruit, perhaps a reflection of very ripe grapes; a lingering illusion of sweetness on the finish. Screwcap. 15.5% alc. **Rating** 90 **To** 2016 $49.95

ŸŸŸŸ **Eden Valley Riesling 2008** Abundant soft citrus and tropical aromas flow through onto the easy palate; short-term cellaring. Screwcap. 12.5% alc. **Rating** 88 **To** 2013 $19.50

GCV Barossa Chardonnay 2008 Multiple winemaking inputs (partial barrel ferment, partial mlf) haven't overwhelmed the freshness of the wine, but it is a drink now proposition. Screwcap. 13.5% alc. **Rating** 88 **To** 2010 $15

Valley Floor Barossa Valley Shiraz 2007 Fractionally hazy colour; rich, heady fruit on the bouquet and palate in traditional Barossa style, perhaps partly shaped by the vintage. Cork. 14.5% alc. **Rating** 88 **To** 2014 $24.95

Hangin' Snakes Barossa Valley Shiraz Viognier 2007 Lifted input from the viognier tends to emphasise the ripe confit fruit flavours, when it might have been better to mute them. Screwcap. 14.5% alc. **Rating** 88 **To** 2013 $19.95

Lark Hill   ★★★★☆

521 Bungendore Road, Bungendore, NSW 2621 **Region** Canberra District
T (02) 6238 1393 **F** (02) 6238 1393 **www**.larkhillwine.com.au **Open** Wed–Mon 10–5
Winemaker Dr David Carpenter, Sue Carpenter, Chris Carpenter **Est.** 1978 **Cases** 3000
Vyds 6.5 ha

The Lark Hill vineyard is situated at an altitude of 860 m, level with the observation deck on Black Mountain Tower, and offers splendid views of the Lake George escarpment. The Carpenters have made wines of real quality, style and elegance from the start, but have defied all the odds (and conventional thinking) with the quality of their Pinot Noirs in favourable vintages. Significant changes have come in the wake of son Christopher gaining three degrees, including a double in wine science and viticulture through CSU: the progression towards biodynamic certification of the vineyard and the opening of a restaurant in 2007. They have also planted 1 ha of gruner veltliner; it is hard to understand why there have been so few plantings of this high-quality variety calling Austria its home. Exports to the UK.

ŸŸŸŸŸ **Canberra District Riesling 2008** Restrained green apple and citrus bouquet; light as a feather, but with understated power and finesse; long, fine and harmonious. Screwcap. 12% alc. **Rating** 94 **To** 2015 $25

♀♀♀♀♀ **Museum Release Methode Champenoise Canberra District Pinot Noir Chardonnay 1998** Deep gold, but bright; a very fresh example showing grilled nuts and attractive brioche complexity, and a touch of citrus in the background; the palate is lively and fresh, the acidity chalky and fine. Crown Seal. 12.5% alc. **Rating** 92 **To** 2014 $50
Canberra District Auslese Riesling 2008 Clean, green apple fruit with a lovely balance of sugar and acid; exhibits finesse and grace, and is quite persistent on the finish. Screwcap. 10.5% alc. **Rating** 90 **To** 2014 $20

♀♀♀♀ **Canberra District Pinot Noir 2008** Good concentration with plenty of dark plummy fruit and a strong element of spice; quite firm on the palate, it pushes the varietal envelope to the limit. Screwcap. 13.8% alc. **Rating** 87 **To** 2013 $35
Canberra District Cabernet Sauvignon 2001 Showing some freshness for age; cool cedar characters, with a firm and quite dry, but even palate. Screwcap. 13.8% alc. **Rating** 87 **To** 2012 $50

Larry Cherubino Wines   ★★★★★

PO Box 570, West Perth, WA 6872 **Region** Western Australia
T 0417 848 399 **www.**larrycherubino.com **Open** Not
Winemaker Larry Cherubino **Est.** 2005 **Cases** 2000
Larry Cherubino has had a particularly distinguished winemaking career, first at Hardys Tintara, then Houghton, and thereafter as consultant/Flying Winemaker in Australia, NZ, South Africa, the US and Italy. In 2005 he started Larry Cherubino Wines and has developed three ranges: at the top is Cherubino (Riesling, Sauvignon Blanc, Shiraz and Cabernet Sauvignon); next The Yard, five single-vineyard wines from WA; and at the bottom another five wines under the Ad Hoc label, all single-region wines. As expected, the quality is exemplary. Exports to the UK, the US and Canada.

♀♀♀♀♀ **The Yard Whispering Hill Riesling 2008** Floral lime blossom aromas lead into a superb palate, which has exceptional thrust and length, lime and passionfruit gaining intensity through to the finish and aftertaste. Screwcap. 12.1% alc.
Rating 96 **To** 2020 $25
The Yard Acacia Vineyard Riesling 2008 Fragrant and lissom, with passionfruit and lime interwoven on a delicate but beautifully balanced and long palate. Screwcap. 12.2% alc. **Rating** 95 **To** 2017 $25
Mount Barker Riesling 2008 A spotlessly clean, gently floral bouquet leads into a perfectly balanced and tuned palate, with lime/lemon fruit, mineral notes and acidity all in harmonious balance. Screwcap. 11.2% alc. **Rating** 94 **To** 2018 $35
Ad Hoc Wallflower Riesling 2008 Light, bright green-straw; very appealing passionfruit characters dominate the bouquet and palate; clean, long, balanced finish. Screwcap. 12.4% alc. **Rating** 94 **To** 2016 $16.90
Pemberton Sauvignon Blanc 2008 A sauvignon blanc with as much to do with texture, structure, length and balance as with aroma and flavour; has some affinity with white Bordeaux, and will age. Screwcap. 12.4% alc. **Rating** 94 **To** 2012 $35

♀♀♀♀♀ **The Yard Kalgan River Riesling 2008** A bright, clean bouquet and a firm, yet elegant and poised palate, mineral and citrus notes interwoven; very good length. Screwcap. 12.5% alc. **Rating** 93 **To** 2016 $25
Ad Hoc Straw Man Sauvignon Blanc Semillon 2008 Highly fragrant passionfruit and grass on the bouquet are mirrored on the zippy/zesty palate and reverberate on the aftertaste. Screwcap. 12.5% alc. **Rating** 93 **To** 2011 $16.90
Shiraz 2007 Bright colour; highly fragrant with dark chocolate, raspberry and a touch of spice on display; the oak comes through on the palate, with juicy black fruits and ample gravelly tannins on the finish. Frankland River. Screwcap. 14.5% alc. **Rating** 93 **To** 2016 $65

Cabernet Sauvignon 2007 A concentrated, essency blackcurrant bouquet, with a fairly prominent leafy tone to the fruit; the slightly green theme continues on the palate, but the fruit evolves into cedary complexity; a very young wine that certainly has an interesting future ahead. Margaret River. Cork. 13.8% alc. **Rating** 93 **To** 2018 $75

Ad Hoc Hen & Chicken Chardonnay 2007 Nutty aromas frame the bright grapefruit character; good depth and weight, with a little spice and toast from the oak coming through at the finish. Screwcap. 13% alc. **Rating** 92 **To** 2012 $16.90

The Yard Shiraz 2007 Bright colour; good fruit definition; in a savoury, dry and firm style, there is a tarry/chewy element that screams out for food to accompany. Frankland River. Screwcap. 14.2% alc. **Rating** 91 **To** 2015 $35

The Yard Pedestal Vineyard Semillon Sauvignon Blanc 2008 An elegant bouquet of straw and citrus fruit; the palate has tropical fruit coming to the fore backed by crisp acidity; good texture on the finish. Screwcap. 13% alc. **Rating** 90 **To** 2013 $28

The Yard Margaret River Chardonnay 2008 Fresh and focused, showing ripe grapefruit and spiced nectarine; lively palate, with good fruit and a toasty, crème brûleé finish. Screwcap. 13% alc. **Rating** 90 **To** 2012 $28

The Yard Cabernet Sauvignon 2007 Truly ripe and essency cassis bouquet; the cassis flows through on the palate, and the quite drying and firm tannin takes some time to overcome the weight of the fruit; very dry and very tannic, time will be a good thing for this wine. Frankland River. Screwcap. 13.7% alc. **Rating** 90 **To** 2017 $35

Laughing Jack   ★★★★★

Cnr Parbs Road/Boundry Road, Greenock, SA 5360 **Region** Barossa Valley
T 0427 396 928 **F** (08) 8562 3878 **www.**laughingjackwines.com **Open** By appt
Winemaker Mick Schroeter, Shawn Kalleske **Est.** 1999 **Cases** 2500 **Vyds** 35 ha
The Kalleske family has many branches in the Barossa Valley. Laughing Jack is owned by Shawn, Nathan and Helen, Ian and Carol Kalleske, and Mick and Linda Schroeter. They have just under 35 ha of vines, the lion's share to shiraz (22 ha), with lesser amounts of semillon, chardonnay, riesling and grenache. Vine age varies considerably, with old dry-grown shiraz the jewel in the crown. A small part of the shiraz production is taken for the Laughing Jack Shiraz. As any Australian knows, the kookaburra is also called the laughing jackass, and there is a resident flock of kookaburras in the stands of blue and red gum eucalypts surrounding the vineyards. Exports to the UK and Switzerland.

♟♟♟♟♟ **Jack's Barossa Valley Shiraz 2006** Dark and deep notes to the savoury/tarry core of the fruit; displays good texture on the rich mid-palate and liveliness to the finish; a big, plush over the top example for those who like a little more of everything. Screwcap. 14.5% alc. **Rating** 95 **To** 2016 $20

Barossa Valley Shiraz 2006 Good colour; red fruits and a slight brambly complexity to complement; the palate is generous, with a liveliness that belies the apparent weight and richness of the wine. Screwcap. 15% alc. **Rating** 94 **To** 2014 $38

Laurance of Margaret River   ★★★★

3518 Caves Road, Wilyabrup, WA 6280 **Region** Margaret River
T (08) 9321 8015 **F** (08) 9321 8211 **www.**laurancewines.com **Open** 7 days 10–5
Winemaker Naturaliste Vintners (Bruce Dukes) **Est.** 2001 **Cases** 5000
Dianne Laurance is the driving force of this family business, with husband Peter and son Brendon (and wife Kerrianne) also involved. Brendon is vineyard manager, living on the property with his family. The 40-ha property had 22 ha planted when it was purchased, and since its acquisition it has been turned into a showplace, with a rose garden to put that of Voyager Estate to shame. While the wine is made offsite, a wine storage facility has been built. But it is the bowling pin–shaped bottles that will gain the most attention – and doubtless subsequently used as lamp stands. The way-out packaging does tend to obscure the quality of

the wines in the eyes of intolerant geriatrics such as myself. Exports to Singapore, Hong Kong, Malaysia, Thailand and Japan.

🍷🍷🍷🍷🍷 **Red 2005** Quite a European personality, with a strong sense of cedar, tannin and restrained fruit character; the palate is seriously firm (which belies the flowery and feminine bottle) and the finish, is long, slightly chalky and quite fine. Cabernet Sauvignon/Merlot. Cork. 13.5% alc. **Rating** 92 **To** 2015 $30
Chardonnay 2007 Highly perfumed, with orange zest and grapefruit on the bouquet; a toasty palate, with lively acidity on the finish. Cork. 14% alc. **Rating** 90 **To** 2013 $45

🍷🍷🍷🍷 **Rose 2008** A spicy style, with some fresh herb complexity; quite dry with good depth and richness to the mid-palate and finish. Cork. 13% alc. **Rating** 88 **To** 2012 $25

Laurel Bank

130 Black Snake Lane, Granton, Tas 7030 **Region** Southern Tasmania
T (03) 6263 5977 **F** (03) 6263 3117 **www**.laurelbankwines.com.au **Open** By appt
Winemaker Winemaking Tasmania (Julian Alcorso) **Est.** 1987 **Cases** 900 **Vyds** 3.3 ha
Laurel (hence Laurel Bank) and Kerry Carland began planting their vineyard in 1986 to sauvignon blanc, riesling, pinot noir, cabernet sauvignon and merlot. They delayed the first release of their wines for some years and (by virtue of the number of entries they were able to make) won the trophy for Most Successful Exhibitor at the Hobart Wine Show '95. Things have settled down since; wine quality is solid and reliable.

🍷🍷🍷🍷🍷 **Pinot Noir 2005** Good hue; fragrant red cherry and plum fruit; lively, spicy and tangy palate; lots of structure. Has improved vastly over the last two years. Top gold medal Tas Wine Show '09, and received my Chairman's Trophy in '08. Screwcap. 13.6% alc. **Rating** 96 **To** 2010 $30
Pinot Noir 2007 A complex array of aromas and flavours; spicy notes with moderately sweet plum fruit; good line/balance to a good bigger style example. Gold medal Tas Wine Show '09. Screwcap. 13.6% alc. **Rating** 94 **To** 2016 $30

🍷🍷🍷🍷 **Sauvignon Blanc 2008** Fractionally varnishy/grassy aromas, but has good palate weight and varietal fruit. Screwcap. 12.5% alc. **Rating** 89 **To** 2010 $22
Cabernet Sauvignon Merlot 2007 Vibrant red-purple; vivid red fruits with just a touch of mint and leaf on the cusp of ripeness; tasted in the right food context could be a winner. Screwcap. 13.3% alc. **Rating** 87 **To** 2014 $26

Lavina Estate Wines

263 Main Road, McLaren Vale, SA 5171 **Region** McLaren Vale
T (08) 8323 9646 **www**.lavinawines.com.au **Open** Mon–Fri 10–5, w'ends 11–5
Winemaker Matt Rechner **Est.** 2004 **Cases** 500
Lavina Estate Wines is the venture of Sam and Victoria Daw, born out of a company restructure in 2004 when it moved to McLaren Vale, the core business then and now being the production of private labels and exporting bulk wine through its associated company, World Wine Export Enterprises. (This business handles over 500 000 litres per annum.) Almost as an incidental sideline, a small number of wines were made under the Lavina Select Series and Gold Series labels, the former far superior. On the other side of the business, World Wine Export Enterprises has exported wines to 14 markets, with a strong emphasis on Asia.

🍷🍷🍷🍷🍷 **Select Series McLaren Vale Cabernet Shiraz 2006** Strong colour; a rich generous full-bodied McLaren Vale style, brimming with black fruits, strands of dark chocolate and licorice, and ripe tannins. Far superior to others in stable. Cork. 15% alc. **Rating** 94 **To** 2016 $25

🍷🍷🍷🍷 **Select Series McLaren Vale Shiraz 2006** Full-bodied, solid wine with ultra-ripe black fruits and a dash of chocolate; trails away slightly on the finish despite the alcohol. Cork. 15% alc. **Rating** 89 **To** 2015 $25

Gold Series Barossa Valley Cabernet Merlot 2007 Lifted perfume of cassis, violet and a splash of oak; medium-bodied with a juicy core of black and red fruit, and fleshy on the finish. Screwcap. 14.5% alc. **Rating** 89 **To** 2014

Gold Series Barossa Valley Cabernet Shiraz 2007 Redcurrant bouquet with a touch of spice; clean and juicy on the palate, with fine tannin structure to conclude. Screwcap. 14.5% alc. **Rating** 87 **To** 2013

Lazy Ballerina ★★★★

Woodgate Hill Road, Kuitpo, SA 5172 **Region** McLaren Vale
T (08) 8556 7085 **www**.lazyballerina.com **Open** Fri–Sun & public hols 11–5
Winemaker James Hook **Est.** 2004 **Cases** 800

James Hook, a leading viticulturist, and father Paul have set up a small – perhaps very small is a better description – winery in a converted McLaren Vale garage. The equipment extends to shovels, buckets, open fermenters and a small basket press, and enough French and American oak barrels to allow 20 months' maturation. The grapes come from micro-selections from a number of vineyards in McLaren Vale, chosen with great skill. Exports to the UK and Canada.

♟♟♟♟♟ **Single Vineyard McLaren Vale Shiraz 2007** Slightly lighter colour; admits more light and shade to the texture and flavour of the palate, and is the rapier compared to the bludgeon of the varietal. Cork. 15% alc. **Rating** 92 **To** 2017 $30

McLaren Vale Shiraz 2007 Dense colour; predictably opulent and succulent, with layer-upon-layer of black fruits and some dark chocolate; carries its alcohol quite well. Cork. 15.5% alc. **Rating** 92 **To** 2022 $25

McLaren Vale Shiraz Viognier 2007 Stacked with flavour, the small amount of viognier less relevant than the low-yielding shiraz vines; needs time to smooth out its wrinkles, but will reward patience. ProCork. 14.5% alc. **Rating** 90 **To** 2020 $20

Leabrook Estate ★★★★☆

Cnr Greenhill Road/Reserve Road, Balhannah, SA 5242 **Region** Adelaide Hills
T (08) 8398 0421 **www**.leabrookestate.com **Open** W'ends & public hols 11–5, or by appt
Winemaker Colin Best **Est.** 1998 **Cases** 5000 **Vyds** 2.75 ha

With a background as an engineer and having dabbled in home winemaking for 30 years, Colin (and Chris) Best took the plunge and moved into commercial winemaking in 1998. His wines are found in a who's who of restaurants, and in some of the best independent wine retailers on the east coast. Best says, 'I consider that my success is primarily due to the quality of my grapes (2.25 ha of pinot noir, 0.5 ha of chardonnay), since they have been planted on a 1.2 x 1.2 m spacing and very low yields.' The business has continued to grow, with contract-grown grapes coming from here, there and everywhere. In 2008 the Bests took over the former Spur Creek winery, with a consequent move of cellar door. Exports to the UK, Ireland and Singapore.

♟♟♟♟♟ **Adelaide Hills Chardonnay 2006** Deep colour; rich, ripe peach bouquet, with plenty of skilled winemaking on show; quite toasty, rich and textured palate; a very long and even finish. Screwcap. 13.5% alc. **Rating** 94 **To** 2013 $30

♟♟♟♟♟ **Adelaide Hills Sauvignon Blanc 2008** A restrained bouquet, with ripe tropical fruit, offset by an engaging mineral core; the palate is generous and quite full, with a long sweet-fruited finish. Screwcap. 13% alc. **Rating** 92 **To** 2011 $22

Adelaide Hills Gewurztraminer 2008 Ripe and exotic bouquet with apple, lime and a touch of fresh lychees; lively palate, with good texture and surprisingly racy acidity for the variety. Screwcap. 12.8% alc. **Rating** 90 **To** 2012 $26

♟♟♟♟ **Adelaide Hills Merlot 2006** Spiced red fruit and plum bouquet; black olive palate, with assertive tannin and fresh acidity. Screwcap. 14% alc. **Rating** 89 **To** 2013 $28

George 2006 Deep colour; very ripe fruit, pushing into prune from cassis; full-bodied and full-blooded with dark, ironstone character, and plenty of tannin; a little disjointed. Predominantly Cabernet Sauvignon. Screwcap. 14.5% alc. **Rating** 88 **To** 2016 $42

Adelaide Hills Late Harvest Pinot Gris 2008 Salmon pink; moderate sweetness with good flavour provides a fresh style; best served with fresh fruit. Screwcap. 11.5% alc. **Rating** 87 **To** 2011 $24

Leasingham ★★★★★

Reynell Road, Reynella, SA 5161 **Region** Clare Valley
T (08) 8842 2555 **F** (08) 8842 3293 **www.**leasingham-wines.com.au **Open** Not
Winemaker Simon Osicka **Est.** 1893 **Cases** NFP
Successive big company ownerships and various peregrinations in labelling and branding have not (so far) resulted in any permanent loss of identity or quality. With a core of high-quality, aged vineyards to draw on, Leasingham is in fact going from strength to strength under Constellation's direction. The stentorian red wines take no prisoners, compacting densely rich fruit and layer upon layer of oak into every long-lived bottle; the Bin 7 Riesling often excels. In 2008 CWA put the winery and vineyards on the market, but it is believed the vineyards are highly regarded by senior executives (and winemakers); it would not surprise if it took a long time for the sale to eventuate, nor would it surprise that continued support is given to it in the meantime. Exports to all major markets.

ΨΨΨΨΨ **Bin 7 Clare Valley Riesling 2008** Restrained lime aromas with bath talc. perfume; a tight and linear palate with a very steely backbone, and a dry and taut finish; excellent line and length. Two trophies National Wine Show '08. Screwcap. 12.2% alc. **Rating** 96 **To** 2015 $23
Individual Vineyard Release Provis Shiraz 2007 Very deep colour; ripe redcurrant and blackberry fruit coexist with a myriad spices and plenty of well-handled toasty oak; the palate shows light and shade with great definition of fruit, then raw power and abundant, slippery tannins come to the fore; long, vibrant, juicy and completely engaging. Cork. **Rating** 96 **To** 2025 $120
Bin 8 KS Riesling 2008 Elegant, intense, direct throwback to the Vickery spatlese wines of the early 1970s; very and sweet pure lime juice offset by perfectly balanced acidity; great length and certain to age over 20 years. Screwcap. 10% alc. **Rating** 95 **To** 2028 $23
Single Vineyard Release Schobers Shiraz 2006 A remarkably elegant wine given its provenance; the aromas and flavours are very distinct, the tannins positively silky; more velvet glove than iron fist. Shares its elegance with the cabernet from the same vineyard. **Rating** 95 **To** 2016 $120
Bin 61 Clare Valley Shiraz 2006 Extremely concentrated black fruits and licorice on the palate, supported by positive but very well-balanced tannins; power without alcohol, a blessed relief. Screwcap. 13.5% alc. **Rating** 94 **To** 2021 $26

ΨΨΨΨΨ **Magnus Clare Valley Riesling 2008** Some attractive talc and apple blossom aromas followed by a very crisp and delicate palate, which gains intensity on the finish. Very well priced. Screwcap. 12.5% alc. **Rating** 91 **To** 2016 $16.50
Classic Clare Sparkling Shiraz 2002 Classic Australian sparkling red; mulled blackberry and a touch of leather; well-balanced sugar complements the quality of the fruit; a serious sparkling red. Cork. 14.2% alc. **Rating** 91 **To** 2014 $57

ΨΨΨΨ **Bin 56 Cabernet Sauvignon Malbec 2007** Clean and varietal, travelling along a single plane; the palate is fresh, with good acidity and reasonable flavour; a little simple. Screwcap. 13.3% alc. **Rating** 88 **To** 2014 $26

Leconfield ★★★★

Riddoch Highway, Coonawarra, SA 5263 **Region** Coonawarra
T (08) 8737 2326 **F** (08) 8737 2285 **www.**leconfieldwines.com **Open** Mon–Fri 9–5, w'ends & public hols 10–4.30
Winemaker Paul Gordon, Tim Bailey (Assistant) **Est.** 1974 **Cases** 25 000 **Vyds** 41.1 ha
Sydney Hamilton purchased the unplanted property that was to become Leconfield in 1974, having worked in the family wine business for over 30 years until his retirement in the mid-'50s. When he acquired the property and set about planting it, he was 76, and reluctantly

bowed to family pressure to sell Leconfield to nephew Richard in '81. Richard progressively increased the vineyards to their present level, over 75% to cabernet sauvignon, long the winery's speciality. Exports to the UK, the US and other major markets.

ŶŶŶŶŶ **Old Vines Coonawarra Riesling 2008** Although not the oldest riesling vines in the region (1974 plantings), this is the most powerful, possibly caught by the '08 vintage as it doesn't have the elegance it normally shows, but does exhibit juicy apple and lime fruit. Screwcap. 12.5% alc. **Rating** 93 **To** 2018 $24.95
Coonawarra Cabernet Sauvignon 2006 Medium red-purple; cedary/briary/earthy nuances to the fruit on the bouquet, which carry on to the tangy black fruits of the palate; good length. Screwcap. 14% alc. **Rating** 93 **To** 2016 $30.95

ŶŶŶŶ **McLaren Vale Shiraz 2007** A powerful, quite extractive wine, in a role reversal (normally McLaren Vale looks to Coonawarra); obvious tannins on the blackberry fruit need to soften. Screwcap. 14.5% alc. **Rating** 89 **To** 2020 $24.95

Leeuwin Estate   ★★★★★

Stevens Road, Margaret River, WA 6285 **Region** Margaret River
T (08) 9759 0000 **F** (08) 9759 0001 **www.**leeuwinestate.com.au **Open** 7 days 10–5
Winemaker Paul Atwood **Est.** 1974 **Cases** 60 000 **Vyds** 121 ha
This outstanding winery and vineyard is owned by the Horgan family, with parents Denis and Tricia at the helm, son Justin as general manager. The Art Series Chardonnay is, in my opinion, Australia's finest example, based on the wines of the last 27 vintages. The decision to move to screwcap in 2004 brought a large smile to the faces of those who understand just how superbly the wine ages, unless sabotaged by sporadic oxidation (caused by cork). The large estate plantings, coupled with strategic purchases of grapes from other growers, provide the base for high-quality Art Series Cabernet Sauvignon and Shiraz; a hugely successful, quick-selling Art Series Riesling and Sauvignon Blanc; and lesser priced wines such as Prelude Chardonnay and Siblings Sauvignon Blanc Semillon. Exports to all major markets.

ŶŶŶŶŶ **Art Series Margaret River Chardonnay 2006** Bright and youthful colour; a complex array of nectarine, grapefruit and spice, particularly cinnamon on the bouquet; the palate exhibits understated power, with grilled nuts supporting the very generous, yet refined, level of stone fruit and oak; the finish is staggeringly long, fine and complex. Screwcap. 14.5% alc. **Rating** 97 **To** 2011 $96
Art Series Margaret River Cabernet Sauvignon 2004 An incredibly fresh and vibrant bouquet of red fruit, intermingled with cassis, oak and a little fresh herb edge; the palate is very fleshy on entry, and tightens up on the long, ample and lively finish; good fruit sweetness, and the structure suggests a long and healthy life ahead. Screwcap. 14.5% alc. **Rating** 95 **To** 2020 $59.95
Art Series Margaret River Sauvignon Blanc 2008 Vibrantly pure, fresh and crisp; a wine built upon the purity and energy of the palate, causing plenty of lip smacking after tasting. One-third fermented in older French oak barriques and aged on lees for three months; 7% Semillon. Screwcap. 12.5% alc. **Rating** 94 **To** 2012 $31
Siblings Margaret River Sauvignon Blanc Semillon 2008 Fragrant, pure and bright aromas in the tropical/passionfruit spectrum flow through to the elegant and long palate. 39% barrel-fermented and matured for two months. Screwcap. 12.5% alc. **Rating** 94 **To** 2010 $24
Prelude Vineyards Margaret River Chardonnay 2007 A not-so-junior brother to the Art Series; while the vineyard block sources are different, this is a seriously elegant wine, marrying intensity and finesse on a notably long palate. Screwcap. 14% alc. **Rating** 94 **To** 2015 $33
Art Series Margaret River Shiraz 2007 A fragrant and vibrant wine, with pronounced cool-climate characteristics; spicy/savoury nuances encircle the core of red cherry and plum fruit; very good handling of tannin and oak. Open-fermented, 20% whole bunches. Screwcap. 14% alc. **Rating** 94 **To** 2015 $37

♥♥♥♥♡ **Art Series Margaret River Shiraz 2006** Highly perfumed cherry fruit and spice bouquet; medium-bodied with gravelly tannin and accentuated acidity; cool and savoury on the finish. Screwcap. 13.5% alc. **Rating** 92 **To** 2015 $37.25
Prelude Vineyards Margaret River Cabernet Merlot 2004 The bouquet offers red and black fruits, also exhibiting an alluring floral element; quite firm on entry, the tannins are fully ripe and very fine; the finish has good fruit to offset the savoury intensity. Screwcap. 13.5% alc. **Rating** 92 **To** 2015 $29.80

♥♥♥♥ **Art Series Margaret River Riesling 2007** Still exceptionally pale at 18 months of age; crisp acidity defines the ultra-fine palate; a Peter Pan style that may never grow up; match with oysters. Screwcap. 12.5% alc. **Rating** 89 **To** 2015 $23
Siblings Margaret River Shiraz 2005 Good hue, although light; crisp, light-to medium-bodied palate that is lively but not deep; lunch/picnic style. Screwcap. 13% alc. **Rating** 89 **To** 2011 $24
Siblings Margaret River Shiraz 2006 A clean cherry and loganberry fruit bouquet; a little spice, and quite dry and firm on the finish. Screwcap. 13.5% alc. **Rating** 87 **To** 2013 $24

Lengs & Cooter   ★★★★☆

24 Lindsay Terrace, Belair, SA 5042 **Region** Adelaide Zone
T (08) 8278 3998 **F** (08) 8278 3998 **www.**lengscooter.com.au **Open** Not
Winemaker Colin Cooter, Contract **Est.** 1993 **Cases** 5000
Karel Lengs and Colin Cooter began making wine as a hobby in the early 1980s. Each had (and has) a full-time occupation outside the wine industry, so it was all strictly for fun. One thing has led to another, and although they still possess neither vineyards nor what might truly be described as a winery, the wines have graduated to big-boy status, winning gold medals at national wine shows and receiving critical acclaim from writers across Australia. Exports to the UK, Canada, Singapore and Malaysia.

Lenton Brae Wines   ★★★★★

Wilyabrup Valley, Margaret River, WA 6285 **Region** Margaret River
T (08) 9755 6255 **F** (08) 9755 6268 **www.**lentonbrae.com **Open** 7 days 10–6
Winemaker Edward Tomlinson **Est.** 1983 **Cases** NFP
Former architect and town planner Bruce Tomlinson built a strikingly beautiful winery (now heritage listed by the Shire of Busselton), which is now in the hands of winemaker son Edward, who consistently makes elegant wines in classic Margaret River style. Exports to the UK, Canada, Singapore and Vietnam.

♥♥♥♥♥ **Margaret River Semillon Sauvignon Blanc 2008** A pungent, aromatic bouquet with grassy/herbal semillon to the fore; an attack carried forward on the long and precisely focused palate, with gentle tropical fruits buttressed by lemony acidity. Gold WA Wine Show '08. Screwcap. 13% alc. **Rating** 95 **To** 2010 $23
Wilyabrup Chardonnay 2007 An elegant wine with the usual skilled but subtle use of oak to underpin the finely structured nectarine and grapefruit flavours of the fruit, which now contains 30% Bernard Dijon clones. Screwcap. 13.5% alc. **Rating** 95 **To** 2016 $46
Wilyabrup Cabernet Sauvignon 2007 An elegant wine with delicious blackcurrant and cassis fruit framed by high-quality French oak and fine, savoury tannins; includes 12% merlot; 18 months French oak. Screwcap. 13.5% alc. **Rating** 94 **To** 2022 $60

♥♥♥♥♡ **Margaret River Shiraz 2007** Bright hue; fresh, fragrant, spicy red berry aromas flow through to a lively medium-bodied palate; good length. Screwcap. 13.5% alc. **Rating** 92 **To** 2017 $30
Wilyabrup Cabernet Sauvignon 2005 Somewhat traditional, austere style, particularly given the '05 vintage in Margaret River; however, does have considerable length to the overall savoury flavours of the palate. Screwcap. 14% alc. **Rating** 90 **To** 2015 $45

YYYY **Margaret River Cabernet Merlot 2007** Hints of gum leaf, mint and earth on the bouquet; opens with blackcurrant fruit, then quite dry tannins close in on the finish. Needs to sort itself out. Screwcap. 13.5% alc. **Rating** 87 **To** 2014 $22

Leo Buring ★★★★★

GPO Box 753, Melbourne, Vic 3001 **Region** Barossa Valley
T 1300 651 650 www.leoburing.com.au **Open** Not
Winemaker Peter Munro **Est.** 1931 **Cases** 15 000
Australia's foremost producer of Rieslings over a 35-year period, with a rich legacy left by former winemaker John Vickery. After veering away from its core business with other varietal wines, it has now been refocused as a specialist Riesling producer. The top of the range is the Leonay Eden Valley Riesling under a changing DW bin no. (DWK for 2007, DWL for 2008, etc), supported by Clare Valley Riesling and Eden Valley Riesling at significantly lower prices, and expanding its wings to Tasmania and WA.

YYYYY **Leonay Riesling 2008** DWL18. Low alcohol in a dry style works to perfection; a super-elegant wine that seems to have borrowed the pure lime juice characters of great Eden Valley rieslings, and framed these in a delicate web of spring-fresh acidity. Watervale. Screwcap. 11% alc. **Rating** 96 **To** 2025 $39.99
Eden Valley Riesling 2008 A more fragrant and expressive bouquet than the Clare Valley sister wine, the lime-accented palate logically following on; fine, crisp and long, great now or way down the track thanks to perfect acidity. Screwcap. 12% alc. **Rating** 94 **To** 2020 $21.99
Leopold Tamar Valley Riesling 2008 DWL20. A fragrant/spicy/minerally bouquet leads into an intense and precise palate with flavours of lime and apple; usual excellent acidity and length. Screwcap. 11.5% alc. **Rating** 94 **To** 2017 $39.99

YYYYY **Clare Valley Riesling 2008** A bracing and clean bouquet leads into a classic Clare palate with citrus and mineral components in exact balance; will repay extended cellaring. Screwcap. **Rating** 93 **To** 2018 $21.99

Lerida Estate ★★★★☆

The Vineyards, Old Federal Highway, Lake George, NSW 2581 **Region** Canberra District
T (02) 6295 6640 **F** (02) 6295 6676 www.leridaestate.com **Open** 7 days 10–5
Winemaker Malcolm Burdett **Est.** 1999 **Cases** 5000 **Vyds** 19.42 ha
Lerida Estate owes a great deal to the inspiration of Dr Edgar Riek, planted as it is immediately to the south of the Lake George vineyard. The initial plantings of 7.4 ha were dominated by pinot noir; here, too, Edgar Riek was the inspiration. The vineyard has now more than doubled, with 9.58 ha of pinot noir, and smaller quantities of pinot gris, chardonnay, shiraz, merlot, cabernet franc and viognier. The Glenn Murcutt–designed winery, barrel room, cellar door and café complex has spectacular views over Lake George.

YYYYY **Lake George Shiraz Viognier 2007** Lifted perfume of blue and red berries, cinnamon and a touch of game; the palate is lively and quite silky, very fine-grained tannin on offer; quite sumptuous and lively, a bell-like clarity on the finish. Screwcap. 14.9% alc. **Rating** 95 **To** 2017 $49.50

YYYYY **Lake George Chardonnay 2007** Vibrant colour; cool and restrained bouquet, with white nectarine and a gentle note of spice from the oak; mouthfilling texture, with fresh acidity; complex and fine on the finish. Screwcap. 13.5% alc. **Rating** 93 **To** 2013 $22
Lake George Pinot Gris 2008 Has that bit extra most pinot gris lack; bright apple, citrus and pear fruit flavours with structure from one-third fermented in old oak. Screwcap. 13.2% alc. **Rating** 91 **To** 2010 $28
Lake George Unwooded Chardonnay 2008 Vibrant colour; citrus and mineral bouquet; quite pure, fresh and fine, with good drive and definition. Screwcap. 13.5% alc. **Rating** 90 **To** 2013 $18

ƤƤƤƤ   **Lake George Pinot Noir 2007** Bright colour; black cherry, plum and a touch of ironstone; firm and dry, with the cherry fruit providing definition to the palate; quite a savoury and muscular wine. Screwcap. 14.4% alc. **Rating** 89 **To** 2012 $35
Lake George Botrytis Pinot Gris 2008 Quite sweet with dried apricot and a touch of spice; good line on the finish. Screwcap. 11.8% alc. **Rating** 88 **To** 2012 $24.50

Lethbridge Wines   ★★★★★
74 Burrows Road, Lethbridge, Vic 3222 **Region** Geelong
T (03) 5281 7279 **F** (03) 5281 7221 **www.**lethbridgewines.com **Open** Thurs–Sun & public hols 10.30–5, or by appt
Winemaker Ray Nadeson, Maree Collis **Est.** 1996 **Cases** 2500
Lethbridge was founded by scientists Ray Nadeson, Maree Collis and Adrian Thomas. In Ray Nadeson's words, 'Our belief is that the best wines express the unique character of special places.' As well as understanding the importance of terroir, the partners have built a unique straw-bale winery, designed for its ability to recreate the controlled environment of cellars and caves in Europe. Winemaking is no less ecological: hand-picking, indigenous yeast fermentations, small open fermenters, pigeage (foot-stamping) and minimal handling of the wines throughout the maturation process are all part and parcel of the highly successful Lethbridge approach. Nadeson also has a special touch with Chardonnay, and has a successful contract winemaking limb to the business.

ƤƤƤƤƤ   **Dr Nadeson Portland Riesling 2008** Herb and lime aromas lead into a vibrant and thrusting palate, fruit acidity and deliberate residual sugar playing their part. From the Barrett vineyard in Henty. Dr Loosen tribute. Screwcap. 11% alc. **Rating** 95 **To** 2018 $30
Mietta Geelong Pinot Noir 2006 Strong colour; the potency of the bouquet is remarkable, the ripe fruit of the palate belying the modest alcohol and balanced by acidity running through the long palate and peacock's tail finish. Diam. 13.5% alc. **Rating** 94 **To** 2016 $55
Indra Geelong Shiraz 2006 Bright hue; combines generous black and red fruits with a distinct brush of spice and good acidity, the oak and tannins in the back seat. Screwcap. 14.5% alc. **Rating** 94 **To** 2020 $55

Leura Park Estate   ★★★★☆
1400 Portarlington Road, Curlewis, Vic 3222 **Region** Geelong
T (03) 5253 3180 **F** (03) 5244 3457 **www.**leuraparkestate.com.au **Open** W'ends & public hols 10.30–5, 7 days Jan, or by appt
Winemaker Stephen Webber, Ray Nadeson **Est.** 1995 **Cases** 1800 **Vyds** 15.7 ha
Leura Park Estate's 15-ha vineyard, planted to chardonnay, pinot noir, pinot gris, sauvignon blanc and shiraz was established in 1995. New owners David and Lyndsay Sharp are committed to maintaining minimal interference in the vineyard, and have expanded the estate-grown wine range (Sauvignon Blanc, Pinot Gris, Chardonnay, Pinot Noir and Shiraz) to include Vintage Grand Cuvee (Pinot Noir Chardonnay).

ƤƤƤƤƤ   **Shiraz 2007** Bright colour; fragrant red fruit and spice aromas introduce a super-elegant, medium-bodied palate, the spicy fruit flavours supported by a light veneer of French oak and fine, supple tannins. Gold medal Geelong Wine Show '08. Screwcap. 13.5% alc. **Rating** 94 **To** 2017 $24.95

ƤƤƤƤƤ   **25 d'Gris Bellarine Peninsula Pinot Gris 2008** Scores well for its texture, balance and considerable length, with notes of green apple and nashi pear; sophisticated winemaking. Screwcap. 12.6% alc. **Rating** 91 **To** 2011 $30
Bellarine Peninsula Sauvignon Blanc 2008 A clean and crisp bouquet with herbal/grassy overtones, the palate following in the same track, a hint of barrel (old oak) in the background. Screwcap. 12.6% alc. **Rating** 90 **To** 2011 $21.50

 # Lewood Estate ★★★

80 Shotton Road, Mt Eliza, Vic 3930 **Region** Mornington Peninsula
T (03) 5975 6912 **F** (03) 5975 6912 **Open** By appt
Winemaker Gavin Perry **Est.** 1996 **Cases** 450 **Vyds** 2 ha
Robert and Dale Lee were inspired to plant shiraz on their property after attending a wine dinner at which Port Phillip Estate Cabernet Sauvignon and Shiraz were served. To the Lees, the Shiraz stood out as quite special, and they were able to obtain 350 cuttings from Port Phillip Estate, which were planted in September 1996. Experimental Shirazs made from these vines in 1999 and 2000 both won medals in the amateur winemaking classes at the Victorian Wines Show, which encouraged the Lees to expand the vineyard by taking further cuttings from the Port Phillip-sourced shiraz. Well down the track, 25 of the original cuttings were found to be merlot, and, quite accidentally, the 1.5 ha of shiraz is accompanied by 0.5 ha of merlot. They thus have two varietal releases, and a Rose for good measure.

♟♟♟♟ **Mornington Peninsula Shiraz 2004** Quite bright in colour, the bouquet is spicy and still lively; falls away a little on the finish. Cork. 13.6% alc. **Rating** 87 To 2012 $16

Liebich Wein ★★★☆

Steingarten Road, Rowland Flat, SA 5352 **Region** Barossa Valley
T (08) 8524 4543 **F** (08) 8524 4543 **www**.liebichwein.com.au **Open** Wed–Mon 11–5
Winemaker Ron Liebich **Est.** 1992 **Cases** 2500
Liebich Wein is Barossa Deutsch for 'Love I wine'. The Liebich family have been grapegrowers and winemakers at Rowland Flat since 1919, with CW 'Darkie' Liebich one of the great local characters. His nephew Ron began making wine in 1969, but it was not until '92 that he and wife Janet began selling wine under the Liebich Wein label. The business has grown surely but steadily, with a new warehouse commissioned in 2008 vastly improving storage and handling capacity. Exports to the UK, Mexico, Germany, Switzerland, Malaysia and Singapore.

♟♟♟♟♟ **Ron's Selection Old Vine Shiraz 2005** A massive, full-bodied wine, loaded with prune, plum and blackberry jam fruit, licorice and dark chocolate also in attendance; the alcohol needs no comment; the wine has integrity within the context of the style. Screwcap. 15.8% alc. **Rating** 90 To 2020 $30

Lienert of Mecklenburg ★★★★

Box 5, Lienert Road, She Oak Log, SA 5371 **Region** Barossa Valley
T (08) 8524 9062 **F** (08) 8524 9208 **Open** Not
Winemaker Charles Cimicky (Contract) **Est.** 2001 **Cases** 530 **Vyds** 21.5 ha
The shiraz vineyard owned by John and Cheryl Lienert is planted on land purchased by John's great-grandfather Conrad Lienert in 1880. The Mecklenburg area within the Barossa Valley was given that name in 1854 by émigrés from the Grand Duchy of Mecklenburg. John obtained a diploma of agricultural administration from Marcus Oldham College, Geelong, in 2000 and has overseen the establishment and ongoing management of the vineyard.

♟♟♟♟♟ **Reserve Sauvignon Blanc 2005** Densely coloured; dark fruitcake and a little mocha on the mid-palate; heavy, rich fruit on the finish. Cork. 14.5% alc. **Rating** 90 To 2020 $40

Light's View/Pure Vision Organic Wines ★★★

PO Box 258, Virginia, SA 5120 **Region** Adelaide Plains
T 0412 800 875 **F** (08) 8380 9501 **www**.purevisionwines.com.au **Open** Not
Winemaker David Norman, Jim Irvine, Ken Carypidis **Est.** 2001 **Cases** 25 000
The Carypidis family runs two brands: Pure Vision has 15 ha of certified organically grown grapes, and there's a much larger Light's View (www.lightsviewwines.com.au) planting of 54 ha of conventionally grown grapes. If you are to grow grapes under a certified organic regime,

it makes the task much easier if the region is warm to hot and dry, conditions unsuitable for botrytis and downy mildew. You are still left with weed growth (no herbicides are allowed) and powdery mildew (sulphur sprays are permitted) but the overall task is a much easier one. The Adelaide Plains, where Pure Vision's vineyard is situated, is such a region, and owner Ken Carypidis has been clever enough to secure the services of Jim Irvine as co-winemaker. Light's View wines are exported to the US, Canada, China and Papua New Guinea, and the Pure Vision wines to the US.

ΨΨΨΨ **Light's View The Virginian Adelaide Plains Rose 2008** Light fuschia; has an attractive core of sweet cherry/strawberry fruit, with a hint of sweetness on the finish. Screwcap. **Rating** 87 **To** 2009 $10

Lillian ★★★★

Box 174, Pemberton, WA 6260 **Region** Pemberton
T (08) 9776 0193 **F** (08) 9776 0193 **Open** Not
Winemaker John Brocksopp **Est.** 1993 **Cases** 400 **Vyds** 3.2 ha
Long-serving (and continuing consultant) viticulturist to Leeuwin Estate, John Brocksopp established 2.7 ha of the Rhône trio of marsanne, roussanne and viognier, and shiraz. The varietal mix may seem à la mode, but it in fact comes from John's early experience working for Seppelt at Barooga in NSW, and his formative years in the Barossa Valley. Exports to the UK and Japan.

ΨΨΨΨΨ **Lefroy Brook Pemberton Chardonnay 2007** John Brocksopp's long familiarity with great chardonnay shows through in this wine; an elegant display of varietal fruit in a nectarine/white peach spectrum, the oak subtle, lees contact likewise. Screwcap. 14% alc. **Rating** 93 **To** 2014 $28
Pemberton Viognier 2007 Delicate, but absolutely correct, apricot and peach aromas that flow through onto the elegant palate, which is devoid of unwanted phenolics. Screwcap. 14.5% alc. **Rating** 90 **To** 2012 $26
Pemberton Marsanne Roussanne 2007 What the Viognier delivers today, this wine will deliver in three or four years' time as it builds both weight and flavours; it has the requisite balance and length to do so. Screwcap. 14% alc. **Rating** 90 **To** 2016 $21

ΨΨΨΨ **Lefroy Brook Pemberton Pinot Noir 2007** A light style with dominant savoury/foresty characters; has good length, but at this juncture not enough pinot fruit flavours for higher points. Screwcap. 14% alc. **Rating** 89 **To** 2012 $30

Lillico Wines

297 Copelands Road, Warragul, Vic 3820 **Region** Gippsland
T (03) 5623 4231 **F** (03) 5623 4231 **www.**lillicowines.com.au **Open** Thurs–Sun & public hols 10–6, or by appt
Winemaker Marie Young, Mal Stewart **Est.** 1998 **Cases** 700 **Vyds** 3 ha
Cattle farmer Robert and senior nurse Marie Young impulsively planted 1.7 ha of cabernet sauvignon on their property in 1998; two years later they added 1.3 ha of pinot noir. In the meantime Marie has completed a diploma of horticulture, specialising in viticulture, at Dookie College. The first commercial vintage of cabernet was sold and, encouraged by the quality of the wine made from their grapes, Marie and Rob decided to produce some of their own wine. Marie promptly enrolled in the diploma of wine technology course and now makes the wines. The vineyard is run on a no-pesticide and non-residual chemical regime, and the vines are not irrigated.

ΨΨΨΨ **Gippsland Cabernet Rose 2008** Pale salmon; a dry style, with some varietal cabernet leafy notes; the palate is dry and lively, with fresh acidity and focus to conclude. Screwcap. 12.5% alc. **Rating** 88 **To** 2011 $17

Lillydale Estate   ★★★★

45 Davross Court, Seville, Vic 3139 **Region** Yarra Valley
T (03) 5964 2016 **F** (03) 5964 3009 **www**.mcwilliams.com.au **Open** 7 days 11–5
Winemaker Russell Docy **Est.** 1975 **Cases** NFP **Vyds** 13.4 ha
Lillydale Estate was acquired by McWilliam's in 1994. The major part of the production
comes from the two estate vineyards, Morning Light and Sunnyside, planted in 1976. The
names have been given by McWilliam's: the former is that of the ship that brought Samuel
McWilliam from Ireland to Melbourne in 1857, and Sunnyside is the name of the first winery
and vineyard he established at Corowa in NSW in 1877. The estate production is bolstered by
contract-grown fruit from other growers in the Valley.

 Yarra Valley Pinot Noir 2007 Crimson-red; attractive wine, with supple
plummy fruit on the relatively light-bodied but well-balanced palate; good length.
Screwcap. 13.5% alc. **Rating** 90 **To** 2012 $26

Lillypilly Estate   ★★★

Lillypilly Road, Leeton, NSW 2705 **Region** Riverina
T (02) 6953 4069 **www**.lillypilly.com **Open** Mon–Sat 10–5.30, Sun by appt
Winemaker Robert Fiumara **Est.** 1982 **Cases** 15 000
Botrytised white wines are by far the best from Lillypilly, with the Noble Muscat of
Alexandria unique to the winery; these wines have both style and intensity of flavour and can
age well. However, table wine quality is always steady. Exports to the UK, the US, Canada,
Korea and China.

 Noble Blend 2008 Golden yellow; super-unctuous crystallised fruit characters;
almost honey-like consistency; needs more acidity. Will develop rapidly. Screwcap.
11% alc. **Rating** 89 **To** 2010 $23.50
Domenic Blend Fiumara 7 NV Aged colour; a very rich and sweet liqueur style
of tawny; an absolute knockout at cellar door. Screwcap. 19.5% alc. **Rating** 88
To 2010 $22.50
Tramillon® 2008 An aromatic, grapey blend of Traminer/Semillon, made its own
by Lillypilly almost 30 years ago; serve fully chilled. Screwcap. 12% alc. **Rating** 87
To 2010 $13.50

Limbic   ★★★★☆

295 Morrison Road, Pakenham Upper, Vic 3810 **Region** Port Phillip Zone
T (03) 5942 7723 **F** (03) 5942 7723 **www**.limbicwines.com.au **Open** By appt
Winemaker Michael Pullar **Est.** 1997 **Cases** 600 **Vyds** 7 ha
Jennifer and Michael Pullar have established a vineyard on the hills between Yarra Valley and
Gippsland, overlooking the Mornington Peninsula and Westernport Bay (thus entitled only
to the Port Phillip Zone GI). They have planted pinot noir, chardonnay and sauvignon blanc,
increasingly using organic and thereafter biodynamic practices. 'Limbic' is the word for a
network of neural pathways in the brain that link smell, taste and emotion.

 Sauvignon Blanc 2008 Light straw-green; very fragrant aromas of passionfruit
and tropical fruit salad lead into a lively, fresh, vibrant palate reflecting these aromas;
a bright finish. Screwcap. 13% alc. **Rating** 94 **To** 2010 $22

Chardonnay 2007 Well made, the fruit and oak balanced and seamlessly
integrated; the flavours are of ripe stone fruit, the only question is some lift on the
finish. Diam. 13% alc. **Rating** 90 **To** 2014 $33
Pinot Noir 2006 Very light colour, but has retained good hue; similarly light-
bodied, but has delicious strawberry/cherry fruit running through the mid-palate;
now at or near its peak drinking span. Diam. 13.5% alc. **Rating** 90 **To** 2011 $33

Linda Domas Wines

PO Box 1988, McLaren Flat, SA 5171 **Region** McLaren Vale
T (08) 8383 0069 **F** (08) 8383 0069 **www**.ldwines.com.au **Open** Not
Winemaker Linda Domas **Est.** 2003 **Cases** 5000
Linda Domas and her eponymous wine business started to take shape during years of working
in various parts of Italy, and trips home during the southern hemisphere vintage. Some of the
flying winemaking continues, but the Australian component has become more important. As
well as the Linda Domas brand, contract winemaking is part of the business; the winemaking
is done in leased space at Daringa Cellars. Exports to the UK, the US, Chile, Singapore and
China.

ŸŸŸŸŸ **Boycat Southern Fleurieu Sauvignon Blanc 2008** Interesting wine, which
leaves it to the palate to reveal all; delicate, but intense, flavours of gooseberry,
apple, citrus and a touch of passionfruit; crisp, clean finish. Screwcap. 12% alc.
Rating 93 **To** 2011 $22
Vis a Vis Southern Fleurieu Viognier 2008 Interesting wine, with some of
the structure of viognier from Northern Rhône; the flavours of honeysuckle and
citrus are flanked by touches of peach and apricot, but all sotto voce. Screwcap.
12.5% alc. **Rating** 90 **To** 2011 $22
Shot Bull Southern Fleurieu Rose 2008 Vivid, light crimson; has good red
and black cherry fruit, and some texture and structure; balanced acidity on the
finish. Shiraz. Screwcap. 12.5% alc. **Rating** 90 **To** 2010 $18
Shot Bull Southern Fleurieu Shiraz 2006 A spicy/juicy/tangy medium-
bodied wine, with good length and balance, and attesting to its cool-grown
origins; needs a little more fruit depth to its mid-palate for top points. Screwcap.
13.5% alc. **Rating** 90 **To** 2014 $25
Alchemy McLaren Vale Shiraz Grenache 2007 It seems McLaren Vale
achieves maximum results from this blend with relative ease; here the confection
characters of the grenache fit neatly in the plum and blackberry fruit contrast of
the shiraz to make a coherent whole. Screwcap. 14.5% alc. **Rating** 90 **To** 2014 $20

Lindemans (Coonawarra/Padthaway) ★★★★☆

Coonawarra Wine Gallery, Riddoch Highway, Coonawarra, SA 5263 **Region** Coonawarra
T (08) 8737 3250 **F** (08) 8737 3231 **www**.lindemans.com **Open** 7 days 10–5
Winemaker Brett Sharpe **Est.** 1908 **Cases** 7 million
Lindemans' Limestone Coast vineyards are of increasing significance because of the move
toward regional identity in the all-important export markets, which has led to the emergence
of a range of regional/varietal labels. After a quiet period, the wines are on the march again.
Exports to the UK, the US, Canada and NZ.

ŸŸŸŸŸ **Limestone Ridge 2005** Vivid colour; a great example of this Aussie blend done
well; fine, focused and firm from the cabernet, with a plushness of dark fruits
on the mid-palate provided by the shiraz; very long and very fine on the finish.
Screwcap. 13% alc. **Rating** 96 **To** 2018 $54.99

ŸŸŸŸŸ **Reserve Coonawarra Cabernet Sauvignon 2005** Fresh and vibrant, with
strong varietal cabernet fruit framed by quite toasty oak character; surprisingly
long and firm, this wine offers terrific value for money. Screwcap. 13.5% alc.
Rating 91 **To** 2011 $9.99

ŸŸŸŸ **Reserve Padthaway Shiraz 2006** Light colour; pleasant, light-bodied
commercial style, with shiraz fruit to the fore, and oak invisible. Screwcap.
13.5% alc. **Rating** 87 **To** 2011 $9.99
Reserve Limestone Coast Merlot 2007 Has above-average red fruit flavour
and structure for this price point, lifting it out of the ruck of banality. Screwcap.
13.5% alc. **Rating** 87 **To** 2012 $13.99

Lindemans (Hunter Valley)   ★★★★☆

McDonalds Road, Pokolbin, NSW 2320 **Region** Lower Hunter Valley
T (02) 4998 7684 **F** (02) 4998 7324 **www**.lindemans.com.au **Open** 7 days 10–5
Winemaker Matthew Johnson **Est.** 1843 **Cases** 7 million
One way or another, I have intersected with the Hunter Valley in general and Lindemans in
particular for over 50 years. The wines are no longer made in the Lower Hunter, and the once
mighty Semillon is a mere shadow of its former self. However, the refurbished historic Ben
Ean winery (while no longer making wine) is a must-see for the wine tourist. Exports to the
UK, the US and other major markets.

♀♀♀♀♀ Limited Release Hunter Valley Shiraz 2007 Bin 0703. Vivid colour; dark
fruit abounds with leather and a little wild herb coming to the fore; the red fruits
appear on the palate, framed by a distinctly savoury and quite attractive fine-
tannined finish. Screwcap. 14.5% alc. **Rating** 94 **To** 2016 $25.99

♀♀♀♀♀ Limited Release Hunter Valley Semillon 2008 Bin 0855. Attractive young
wine, made from vines up to 80 years old; the palate has good intensity and focus,
with abundant grass, citrus and lanolin on the mid-palate; one of the best of recent
vintages. Screwcap. 10.5% alc. **Rating** 93 **To** 2017 $20.99

Lindemans (Karadoc)   ★★★☆

Edey Road, Karadoc, Vic 3496 **Region** Murray Darling
T (03) 5051 3285 **F** (03) 5051 3390 **www**.lindemans.com **Open** 7 days 10–4.30
Winemaker Wayne Falkenberg, Hayden Donohue **Est.** 1974 **Cases** 7 million
Now the production centre for all the Lindemans and Leo Buring wines, with the exception
of special lines made in Coonawarra. The very large winery allows all-important economies
of scale, and is the major processing centre for Foster's beverage wine sector (casks, flagons and
low-priced bottles). Exports to all major markets.

♀♀♀♀♀ Bin 95 Sauvignon Blanc 2008 Bright, pale green-straw; clean bouquet; a
very attractive mix of tropical passionfruit and citrus flavours, with a fresh finish;
remarkable value. Screwcap. 10.5% alc. **Rating** 90 **To** 2010 $8.99

♀♀♀♀ Bin 65 Chardonnay 2008 Melon and peach bouquet with a toasty oak overlay;
the palate is generous, albeit with a slightly clipped finish. Screwcap. 13% alc.
Rating 87 **To** 2012 $10.99
Early Harvest Crisp Dry White 2008 A good version of the crisp and dry
low-alcohol style, as opposed to the more usual sweet wines. Screwcap. 8.5% alc.
Rating 87 **To** 2010 $13.99
Bin 40 Merlot 2007 Exceptional value at this price; has lots of juicy flavour, but
is slightly sweet. Screwcap. 13.5% alc. **Rating** 87 **To** 2010 $6.99

Lindenton Wines   ★★★

102 High Street, Heathcote, Vic 3523 **Region** Heathcote
T (03) 5433 3246 **F** (03) 5433 3246 **Open** 7 days 10–4 by appt
Winemaker Adrian Munari, Greg Dedman (Contract) **Est.** 2003 **Cases** 1000 **Vyds** 4 ha
Jim Harrison's Lindenton Wines is a semi-retirement occupation. His business plan is based
on the purchase of grapes from smaller growers in the region who do not have access to
winemaking facilities or outlets for their fruit. From the word go there has been an extensive
range of wines available, running through Verdelho, Chardonnay, Viognier, Marsanne, Merlot,
Shiraz, Shiraz Viognier and top-of-the-tree Melange. Jim's longer range plan is to make the
wines himself.

♀♀♀♀ Limited Release Heathcote Gewurztraminer 2008 Clean and crisp dry
white, with a suggestion of floral aromatics; a tight palate for the variety, with some
grip on the finish. Screwcap. 11.4% alc. **Rating** 89 **To** 2012 $18

Limited Release Heathcote Viognier 2008 Pale colour; varietal spiced apricot bouquet; good texture and clean fruit on the palate, with a lively core of sweet fruit; a touch of residual sugar doesn't hinder the fruit. Screwcap. 14.4% alc. **Rating** 89 **To** 2012 $21

Lindsays ★★★

Cowra Road, Young, NSW 2594 **Region** Hilltops
T (02) 6382 2972 **F** (02) 6382 2972 **www.**lindsayswine.com.au **Open** 7 days 9–5
Winemaker Jill Lindsay **Est.** 1986 **Cases** 4000 **Vyds** 7.25 ha
A subtle name change and radical label redesign coincide with the release of a series of well-made wines, perseverance paying appropriate dividends. The estate vineyards (cabernet sauvignon, shiraz, riesling, sauvignon blanc, merlot, touriga, semillon, chardonnay, pinot meunier and gewurztraminer) have always been dry-grown, with low yields the consequence.

 Reserve Wodonga Hill Cabernet Sauvignon 2003 Now on a plateau of maturity, this medium-bodied wine still retains sweet fruit components among its savoury/foresty tannins. Diam. 13.1% alc. **Rating** 87 **To** 2013 $25
Auslese Gewurztraminer 2008 A difficult proposition to attempt, but has been well made; while more Kabinett than Auslese, is well balanced and there is some varietal character. Diam. 11.5% alc. **Rating** 87 **To** 2012 $18

Linfield Road Wines ★★★☆

65 Victoria Terrace, Williamstown, SA 5351 **Region** Barossa Valley
T (08) 8524 6140 **F** (08) 8524 6427 **www.**linfieldroadwines.com **Open** 7 days 10–4
Winemaker David Norman **Est.** 2002 **Cases** 2500 **Vyds** 19 ha
The Wilson family has been growing grapes at their estate vineyard for over 100 years; Steve and Deb Wilson are fourth-generation vignerons. The vineyard is in one of the coolest parts of the Barossa Valley, in an elevated position near the Adelaide Hills boundary. The estate vineyard is planted to riesling (5.2 ha), cabernet sauvignon (3.1 ha), semillon, shiraz, merlot and grenache (2.4 ha each), and chardonnay (1.1 ha). In 2002 the Wilsons decided to vinify part of the production. Within 12 months of the first release, the wines had accumulated three trophies and five gold medals. A much anticipated ambition to open a cellar door finally came to pass in mid-2008. Exports to the US, Canada, Hong Kong and China.

 The Stubborn Patriarch Shiraz 2006 Good colour and depth to the fruit; fruitcake aromas dominate, with some lively blackberry fruit to complement; warm and chocolatey on the finish. Screwcap. 15% alc. **Rating** 90 **To** 2014 $25

The Black Hammer Cabernet Sauvignon 2006 Colour a little dull; cedar and cassis are evident on the bouquet, with a touch of leathery development; the palate offers plenty of sweet fruit, and finishes quite taut. Screwcap. 15.3% alc. **Rating** 88 **To** 2012 $22
Barossa Riesling 2008 Clean fruited, with lemon zest and a touch of mineral; shows a little width on the palate, but the flavour is fine. Screwcap. 13.5% alc. **Rating** 87 **To** 2012 $18

Little Brampton Wines ★★★★☆

PO Box 61, Clare, SA 5453 **Region** Clare Valley
T (08) 8843 4201 **www.**littlebramptonwines.com.au **Open** By appt
Winemaker Contract **Est.** 2001 **Cases** 800 **Vyds** 10 ha
Little Brampton Wines is a boutique, family-owned business operated by Alan and Pamela Schwarz. They purchased their 24-ha property in the heart of the Clare Valley in the early 1990s (Alan had graduated from Roseworthy in 1981). The property has produced grapes since the 1860s, but the vineyard had been removed during the Vine Pull Scheme of the 1980s. The Schwarzes have replanted 10 ha to riesling, shiraz and cabernet sauvignon on northwest slopes at 520 m; a small proportion of the production is vinified for the Little Brampton label. Exports to the UK.

ΨΨΨΨΨ Clare Valley Riesling 2008 Light straw-green; a wine with tremendous thrust and vitality to the intense lime juice, lime zest/sherbet palate and finish. Now or whenever. Screwcap. 12.6% alc. **Rating** 95 **To** 2018 $19

Little Bridge ★★★

PO Box 499, Bungendore, NSW 2621 **Region** Canberra District
T (02) 6226 6620 **F** (02) 6226 6842 **www**.littlebridgewines.com.au **Open** Not
Winemaker Canberra Winemakers, Mallaluka Winemakers **Est.** 1996 **Cases** 1000 **Vyds** 4 ha
Little Bridge is a partnership between long-term friends John Leyshon, Rowland Clark, John Jeffrey and Steve Dowton. Two ha of chardonnay, pinot noir, riesling and merlot were planted on Rowland Clark's property at Butmaroo, near Bungendore, at an altitude of 860 m. In 2004 a further 2 ha of shiraz, cabernet sauvignon, sangiovese, grenache and gamay were planted on John Leyshon's property near Yass (560 m). Canberra Winemakers makes the white wines, and the reds are made at Mallaluka.

ΨΨΨΨ Canberra District Riesling 2008 The bouquet is clean but reticent, the palate likewise, saved at the death by a touch of citrussy acidity. Screwcap. 12.5% alc. **Rating** 87 **To** 2011 $20

Lloyd Brothers

34 Warners Road, McLaren Vale, SA 5171 **Region** McLaren Vale
T (08) 8323 8792 **F** (08) 8323 8833 **www**.lloydbrothers.com.au **Open** 7 days 10–5
Winemaker Sam Temme **Est.** 2002 **Cases** 3000 **Vyds** 19 ha
The business is owned by David Lloyd (nephew of Mark Lloyd, and son of the late Guy Lloyd of Lloyd Aviation). It has 14 ha of shiraz, and shares a property with a planting of old olive trees, which produces high-quality table olives and extra-virgin olive oil sold through The Olive Grove at McLaren Vale. Lloyd Brothers sells a significant part of its grape production (*inter alia* to d'Arenberg) and sells the entire crop in years where the standard is not considered high enough to warrant an estate release. Brother Matthew also has an Adelaide Hills vineyard planted to 5 ha of chardonnay, verdelho and pinot noir; the Adelaide Hills cellar door is at 94 Main St, Hahndorf.

ΨΨΨΨΨ White Chalk McLaren Vale Shiraz 2005 A massively proportioned wine, with lavish levels of oak, black fruit, mocha and bitter chocolate; a little reduction on the palate, but the weight and generosity of the wine is unmistakable; if you like your wine on a grand scale then this could be for you. Screwcap. 15% alc. **Rating** 94 **To** 2020 $45

Loan Wines

PO Box 106, Tanunda, SA 5352 **Region** Barossa Valley
T (08) 8563 2612 **F** (08) 8563 2978 **www**.loanwines.com.au **Open** Not
Winemaker Richard Loan, Chris Ringland (Consultant) **Est.** 2001 **Cases** 1200 **Vyds** 8.2 ha
Loan Wines is located along Tanunda Creek in one of the first settled areas in the Barossa Valley, the original cottage and cellars, built in 1842, now used to age the Loan wines. Richard and Jessica Loan have 3.5 ha of shiraz, 3.2 ha of alicante bouchet and 1.5 ha of semillon, all in a Certified Organic vineyard. The dry-grown vines were mainly planted in 1992 and '93, with the Front Block of shiraz planted in '96. Exports to the US, Canada and Denmark.

ΨΨΨΨΨ Barossa Valley Shiraz 2005 Holding hue well; a distinctly savoury/earthy style that works well in conjunction with ripe tannins; all building on a core of black fruits. High-quality cork. 17% alc. **Rating** 90 **To** 2015 $38
Barossa Valley Shiraz 2004 Good hue and clarity; spending 30 months in new American oak barrels took too much of the fruit out of the wine; a pity, for there are some really good memories of what was there. Cork. 14.3% alc. **Rating** 90 **To** 2014 $30.80

🍷🍷🍷🍷 **Raven's Barossa Valley Rose 2006** Rich crimson; very surprisingly dry, notwithstanding its low alcohol; good all-purpose food style, particularly for the designated driver. Screwcap. 10.5% alc. **Rating** 88 **To** 2010 $16.50
Barossa Valley Semillon 2005 Developed, bright straw-green; substantial wine, eight months' maturation in old French barriques adding as much to texture as to flavour; does shorten on the finish. Screwcap. 13.3% alc. **Rating** 87 **To** 2010 $18.70

Lobethal Road Wines ★★★★★

Lot 1, Lobethal Road, Mount Torrens, SA 5244 **Region** Adelaide Hills
T (08) 8389 4595 **www**.lobethalroad.com **Open** Thurs–Sun & public hols 11–5
Winemaker Michael Sykes (Contract) **Est.** 1998 **Cases** 1500 **Vyds** 5 ha
Dave Neyle and Inga Lidums bring diverse but very relevant experience to the Lobethal Road vineyard, which has 2 ha of chardonnay, 1.5 ha of shiraz, 0.9 ha of sauvignon blanc and 0.6 ha of riesling. Dave has been in vineyard development and management in SA and Tasmania since 1990, and is currently managing 60 ha in the Adelaide Hills. Inga brings 25 years' experience in marketing and graphic design both in Australia and overseas, with a focus on the wine and food industries. The property is managed with minimal chemical input, and the use of solar power in the pursuit of an environmentally sustainable product and lifestyle.

🍷🍷🍷🍷🍷 **Bacchant Adelaide Hills Chardonnay 2007** Very interesting wine; lovely bouquet; the palate has far more textural play than the low alcohol would suggest, and excellent balance between nectarine and white peach fruit and oak; unusual twin top cork on one-piece body. 13.1% alc. **Rating** 95 **To** 2016 $42
Adelaide Hills Shiraz 2006 Fragrant spicy/peppery overtones to the vibrant, cool-grown black cherry fruit supported by fine, but persistent tannins and good oak. Screwcap. 14% alc. **Rating** 94 **To** 2021 $20

🍷🍷🍷🍷🍷 **Adelaide Hills Sauvignon Blanc 2008** A fragrant and expressive bouquet; attractive passionfruit, gooseberry and spice is followed by a delicate, crisp palate with good acidity to close. Screwcap. 12.5% alc. **Rating** 92 **To** 2010 $20

# Lofty Valley Wines ★★★

PO Box 55, Summertown, SA 5141 **Region** Adelaide Hills
T (08) 8390 0053 **F** (08) 8239 2329 **www**.loftyvalleywines.com.au **Open** Not
Winemaker Simon Greenleaf **Est.** 2004 **Cases** 200 **Vyds** 3 ha
Medical practitioner Brian Gilbert began collecting wine when he was 19, flirting with the idea of becoming a winemaker before being headed firmly in the direction of medicine by his parents. Thirty or so years later he purchased a blackberry and gorse-infested 12-ha property in the Adelaide Hills, eventually obtaining permission to establish a vineyard. Two ha of chardonnay were planted in 2004, and 1 ha of pinot noir in '07, both on steep slopes. A single barrel of (over-oaked) Chardonnay was made in 2007 from the first crop of a little over one-third of a tonne, the '08 Chardonnay bypassing oak altogether.

🍷🍷🍷🍷 **Adelaide Hills Unwooded Chardonnay 2008** A fresh and lively light-bodied wine, the flavours a crossover between sauvignon blanc and chardonnay; at this price, lack of length is barely an issue. Screwcap. 13.5% alc. **Rating** 87 **To** 2010 $10

Logan Wines ★★★★☆

Castelreagh Highway, Apple Tree Flat, Mudgee, NSW 2850 **Region** Mudgee
T (02) 6373 1333 **F** (02) 6373 1390 **www**.loganwines.com.au **Open** 7 days 10–5
Winemaker Peter Logan, Andrew Ling **Est.** 1997 **Cases** 42 000
Logan is a family-owned and operated business with emphasis on cool-climate wines from Orange and Mudgee. The business is run by husband and wife team Peter (winemaker) and Hannah (sales and marketing). Wines are released from three ranges: Logan (from Orange), Weemala and Apple Tree Flat. Exports to the UK, the US and other major markets.

ΨΨΨΨΨ **Orange Sauvignon Blanc 2008** Strong green nettle bouquet, with a splash of passionfruit; generous palate weight, and fresh, clean acidity on the long finish. Trophies at the Murrumbateman Cool Climate Show '08, Orange Wine Show '08 and Sydney Wine Show '09. Screwcap. 14% alc. **Rating** 94 **To** 2011 $22

ΨΨΨΨΩ **Orange Chardonnay 2007** An aromatic, almost flowery bouquet, with aromas of nectarine, grapefruit and a hint of spice, which flow through into the long, finely balanced palate. Screwcap. 13.5% alc. **Rating** 92 **To** 2014 $20
Orange Pinot Noir 2007 Demonstrates that Orange can produce good pinot when conditions are right and the grapes (as here) treated with respect; a light but correct mix of plum, cherry and forest floor; perhaps a little hard on the finish. Screwcap. 14% alc. **Rating** 90 **To** 2012 $35

ΨΨΨΨ **Hannah Orange Rose 2008** A lively fragrant wine, with red fruits and a hint of dried herb; ample on the palate, and fine and even on the finish. Screwcap. 13.5% alc. **Rating** 89 **To** 2012 $22
Weemala Central Ranges Shiraz Viognier 2007 A fragrant, light- to medium-bodied wine with spicy cherry and plum on both bouquet and palate, the tannins fine and soft, oak restrained. Delicious now; no need to wait. Screwcap. 13.5% alc. **Rating** 89 **To** 2010 $17
Vintage M Orange Cuvee 2007 An 'undeclared' rose made from Chardonnay/ Pinot Noir/Pinot Meunier, given 18 months on lees. Bright pale pink, the wine is bone-dry on the mid-palate and firm finish. Oysters recommended. Cork. 12.5% alc. **Rating** 88 **To** 2010 $35
Weemala Orange Riesling 2008 Clean, crisp and minerally, with a light twist of lime/citrus; pleasant seafood style. Screwcap. 11% alc. **Rating** 87 **To** 2010 $16.95
Weemala Orange Pinot Noir 2008 Light savoury/stemmy style that does have pinot varietal expression and belies its alcohol. Screwcap. 14.5% alc. **Rating** 87 **To** 2011 $17
Weemala Central Ranges Merlot 2007 Strongly varietal; the question is how much black olive and earth is too much, however varietal it may be. That said, the wine has good length and structure; this is not a wannabe cabernet. Screwcap. 14.5% alc. **Rating** 87 **To** 2014 $17

Long Gully Estate   ★★★★☆

Long Gully Road, Healesville, Vic 3777 **Region** Yarra Valley
T (03) 9510 5798 **F** (03) 9510 9859 **www.**longgullyestate.com **Open** 7 days 11–5
Winemaker Luke Houlihan **Est.** 1982 **Cases** 12 000
Owned by Reiner and Irma Klapp, this is one of the larger Yarra Valley producers to have successfully established a number of export markets, doubtless due to its core of mature vineyards, which have grown from 2.2 ha to nearly 30 ha, underlining its commercial success. Long-term winemaker Peter Florance retired in 2004, and was replaced by the very experienced and well-regarded Yarra winemaker Luke Houlihan. Exports to the UK, Switzerland and Singapore.

ΨΨΨΨΨ **Yarra Valley Chardonnay 2007** A very well made wine, playing to the strengths of Yarra chardonnay, the oak subtle, the palate elegant, precisely focused, and very long. Screwcap. 13.7% alc. **Rating** 95 **To** 2017 $25

ΨΨΨΨΩ **Yarra Valley Sauvignon Blanc 2008** Clean and bright aromas; fleeting touches of passionfruit lead into a palate with very good thrust, flavour and length before faltering slightly on the finish. Screwcap. 13% alc. **Rating** 91 **To** 2011 $25
Yarra Valley Pinot Noir 2007 Bright, clear colour; the alcohol while modest, is strongly structured, the pinot flavours good given the challenging vintage. Screwcap. 13.2% alc. **Rating** 90 **To** 2012 $26

Longview Creek Vineyard ★★★

150 Palmer Road, Sunbury, Vic 3429 **Region** Sunbury
T (03) 9740 2448 **F** (03) 9740 2495 **www**.longviewcreek.com.au **Open** W'ends 11–5,
or by appt
Winemaker Roland Kaval (Contract) **Est.** 1988 **Cases** 700 **Vyds** 2 ha
Bill and Karen Ashby purchased the Longview Creek Vineyard from founders Dr Ron and
Joan Parker in 2003. It is situated on the brink of the spectacular Longview Gorge, the bulk of
the plantings of chardonnay (0.8 ha), pinot noir (0.6 ha) and chenin blanc (0.4 ha) were made
between 1988 and '90. Thereafter a little cabernet franc and riesling were planted. Simon
Glover oversees viticulture, and Roland Kaval the winemaking. Spring frosts in October 2006
spelt the end of the '07 vintage, with the next new releases to follow in November '08.

ΨΨΨΨ **Riesling 2008** Tightly wound, slate and mineral characters to the fore, and
running through the dry, austere palate; will repay cellaring. Screwcap. 11.1% alc.
Rating 89 **To** 2018 $18

Longview Vineyard

Pound Road, Macclesfield, SA 5153 **Region** Adelaide Hills
T (08) 8388 9694 **F** (08) 8388 9693 **www**.longviewvineyard.com.au **Open** 7 days 11–5
Winemaker Ben Glaetzer (Contract) **Est.** 1995 **Cases** 17 000 **Vyds** 70 ha
Longview Vineyard came to be through the success of Two Dogs, the lemon-flavoured
alcoholic drink created by Duncan MacGillivray and sold in 1995 to the Pernod Ricard
Group (also the owners of Orlando). Shiraz and cabernet sauvignon have been planted
(accounting for a little over half the total), plus significant amounts of chardonnay and merlot,
and smaller plantings of viognier, semillon, riesling, sauvignon blanc, zinfandel, nebbiolo,
pinot gris and albarino. A significant part of the production is sold, but $1.2 million has been
invested in a cellar door and function area, barrel rooms and an administration centre for
the group's activities. All the buildings have a spectacular view over the Coorong and Lake
Alexandrina. In 2008 the Saturno family of Adelaide, with brothers Peter and Mark leading
the way, acquired Longview. Exports to the UK, the US, Canada and Hong Kong.

ΨΨΨΨΨ **Yakka Adelaide Hills Shiraz 2007** Incredibly vibrant colour; truly cool-
grown black fruits and spice, notably cinnamon and clove; the palate is generous
and layered with terrific acidity framing the luscious fruit on offer and silky fine
tannins sustain a very long finish. Screwcap. 14.5% alc. **Rating** 95 **To** 2016 $28.99

ΨΨΨΨΨ **The Boat Shed Adelaide Hills Nebbiolo Rose 2008** Salmon hue; a strongly
savoury bouquet with tar to the fore and framing red fruits; quite sweet at first, the
nebbiolo tannin kicks in, and the generosity of sugar and fruit is appreciated; very
interesting and best quite cold. Screwcap. 13.8% alc. **Rating** 90 **To** 2013 $19.99

Loom Wine ★★★★

90 Chalk Hill Road, McLaren Vale, SA 5171 **Region** McLaren Vale
T (08) 8323 8623 **F** (08) 8323 8694 **www**.loomwine.com **Open** 7 days 10–5
Winemaker Steve Grimley **Est.** 2005 **Cases** 250 000
Steve Grimley runs a substantial offsite winemaking business, which includes the Loom Wine
and Willundry Road brands of Shiraz, and contract winemaking services for others. All of the
grapes used are contract-grown. The large production reflects contract-made wines for various
private label customers. The wines made under the Loom banner are a tiny part, usually less
than 500 cases in each lot. Exports to the UK, the US and other major markets.

ΨΨΨΨΨ **Single Vineyard Blewitt Springs Shiraz 2007** Oaky bouquet, with chocolate
and blackberry fruit beneath; prominent acidity draws out the red fruit, and the
finish is chewy and ripe; a big wine, not for the faint of heart. Screwcap. 14% alc.
Rating 92 **To** 2016 $22

t=1 shiraz 2007 Good colour; a supple, medium-bodied wine has polished texture to the middle of the medium-bodied palate, before fine tannins make their appearance on the finish. Single Vineyard Blewitt Springs. ProCork. 14% alc. **Rating** 92 **To** 2017 $32

Long Yarn Clare Valley Riesling 2008 A ripe bouquet, exhibiting quince and lemon; a touch of sweetness provides a good foil for quite weighty fruit; dry on the finish, with a little grip. Screwcap. 12.5% alc. **Rating** 91 **To** 2014 $12

Individual Vineyard Wrattonbully Shiraz 2007 Very ripe fruit character, of loganberry and a little fruitcake; ample palate, with a core of red fruit and a warm finish. Screwcap. 14% alc. **Rating** 90 **To** 2015 $15

♀♀♀♀ **Long Yarn McLaren Vale Shiraz 2008** Strong colour; has abundant blackberry flavour with an unexpected touch of spice and some slight volatile lift; excellent value. Screwcap. 14% alc. **Rating** 89 **To** 2016 $14

Lost Lake ★★★★

Lot 3 Vasse Highway, Pemberton, WA 6260 **Region** Pemberton
T (08) 9776 1251 **F** (08) 9776 1919 **www.**lostlake.com.au **Open** 7 days 10–4
Winemaker Mark Aitken **Est.** 1990 **Cases** 3000 **Vyds** 7 ha
Previously known as Eastbrook Estate, its origins go back to 1990, to the acquisition of an 80-ha farming property, which was subdivided into three portions: 16 ha, now known as Picardy, were acquired by Dr Bill Pannell, 18 ha became the base for Lost Lake, and the remainder was sold. The initial plantings in 1990 were of pinot noir and chardonnay, followed by shiraz, sauvignon blanc, merlot and cabernet sauvignon. A jarrah and cedar winery with a crush capacity of 150 tonnes was built in 1995, together with a large restaurant. Steve and Karen Masters acquired the property in 2006 and moved from Perth to live full-time at the property.

♀♀♀♀♀ **Barrel Select Chardonnay 2007** Some colour development; quite intense peach flavours, oak also contributing, but not excessively. Flavoursome, if old-fashioned, mouthful. **Rating** 90 **To** 2013 $35

Barrel Selection Single Vineyard Pemberton Cabernet Sauvignon 2007 Despite its modest alcohol, is a medium- to full-bodied wine with a cascade of red berry fruits offset by nicely balanced tannins; shortens just a little on the finish. Screwcap. 13% alc. **Rating** 90 **To** 2016 $35

♀♀♀♀ **Classic Red 2007** Bright and clear colour; light- to medium-bodied, but well balanced, with a nice crosscut of silky tannins on the red and black fruits. Shiraz/Cabernet Sauvignon/Merlot. **Rating** 89 **To** 2013 $18

Barrel Selection Single Vineyard Pemberton Pinot Noir 2007 Positive varietal character on the bouquet and palate entry with plum and spice, but a short finish. Shows promise. Screwcap. 13.6% alc. **Rating** 88 **To** 2012 $35

Single Vineyard Pemberton Shiraz 2007 Bright colour; a fresh bouquet and light- to medium-bodied palate, with spicy/peppery red fruits. Ready to drink. Screwcap. 13.6% alc. **Rating** 87 **To** 2013 $25

Lost Valley Winery ★★★☆

PO Box 4123, Wishart, Vic 3189 **Region** Upper Goulburn
T (03) 9592 3531 **F** (03) 9551 9560 **www.**lostvalleywinery.com **Open** By appt
Winemaker Alex White (Contract) **Est.** 1995 **Cases** 5000 **Vyds** 12 ha
Dr Robert Ippaso established the Lost Valley vineyard at an elevation of 450 m on the slopes of Mt Tallarook, planting merlot, shiraz, cortese, sauvignon blanc and riesling. This cortese is the only planting in Australia. It pays homage to Dr Ippaso's birthplace: Savoie, in the Franco-Italian Alps, where cortese flourishes. Exports to the US, Canada, Hong Kong, Singapore and Indonesia.

♀♀♀♀♀ **Mountain Country Central Victoria Cortese 2008** Distinct lemon blossom scent on the bouquet, and a vibrant palate to follow suit. Here is a rare variety worth pursuing and buying. Screwcap. 11.5% alc. **Rating** 92 **To** 2013 $29.95

ＹＹＹＹ **Mountain Country Central Victoria Sauvignon Blanc 2008** A minerally/
grassy style, with good length and balance, the structure to evolve in the short
term. Screwcap. 12% alc. **Rating** 87 **To** 2011 $27

Lou Miranda Estate

Barossa Valley Way, Rowland Flat, SA 5352 **Region** Barossa Valley
T (08) 8524 4537 www.loumirandaestate.com.au **Open** Mon–Fri 10–4, w'ends 11–4
Winemaker Lou Miranda **Est.** 2005 **Cases** 15 000 **Vyds** 23.29 ha
Lou Miranda's daughters Lisa and Victoria are the driving force behind the estate, albeit with
continuing hands-on involvement from Lou. The jewels in the crown of the estate plantings
are 1 ha of shiraz and 0.5 ha of mourvedre planted in 1898, plus 1.5 ha of shiraz planted in
1907. The remaining vines have been planted gradually since '95, the varietal choice widened
by cabernet sauvignon, merlot, chardonnay and pinot grigio. The cellar door works on the
principle that there should be a wine for every conceivable taste. Exports to the UK and other
major markets.

Lowe Family Wines ★★★★

Tinja Lane, Mudgee, NSW 2850 **Region** Mudgee
T (02) 6372 0800 **F** (02) 6372 0811 www.lowewine.com.au **Open** 7 days 10–5
Winemaker David Lowe, Jane Wilson **Est.** 1987 **Cases** 6000 **Vyds** 10 ha
Business partners David Lowe and Jane Wilson have consolidated their operations in Mudgee,
moving back from the Hunter Valley. They have started a new business, Mudgee Growers,
at the historic Fairview winery. The main business is here, and they have spread their wings,
successfully introducing less well-known varieties, and looking to other regions more suited
for both mainstream styles (e.g. Orange for pinot gris and sauvignon blanc) and alternative
varieties (e.g. Orange roussanne). Since 2006, all wines are classified as organic. Exports to
the UK.

ＹＹＹＹＹ **Tinja Mudgee Riesling 2008** Enlivened by a touch of spritz and crisp, natural
acidity from early picking/low alcohol; a nice touch of lemon on the finish.
Screwcap. 11.8% alc. **Rating** 90 **To** 2017 $20
Tinja Orange Sauvignon Blanc 2008 An unusual, but intense, bouquet of grass
and lantana (precisely described on the back label) that flows through into the
palate, which is well balanced. Screwcap. 13.5% alc. **Rating** 90 **To** 2010 $20
Mudgee Sangiovese Blend 2005 Has retained a bright, light red hue;
the blend of Sangiovese/Merlot has logic, the red fruits and savoury herbal
counterpoints of each variety in tune with the other. Cork. 13% alc. **Rating** 90
To 2014 $28

ＹＹＹＹ **Reserve Mudgee Shiraz 2006** Brighter colour and a clear step up from the
varietal; more concentration and complexity, with licorice evident, supporting the
juicy dark fruits. Cork. 13.5% alc. **Rating** 89 **To** 2014 $45
Reserve Merlot 2006 Slightly better focus than the varietal; more red berry
fruits and some savoury black olive notes; plump on the medium-bodied finish.
Cork. 14% alc. **Rating** 89 **To** 2011 $45
Climate Change Red NV Clever name for a wine from two radically opposed
vintages: a tough '07 merlot and a light, peppery '08 shiraz; still ends up a little
tight and green. Screwcap. 13% alc. **Rating** 88 **To** 2012 $25
Reserve Zinfandel 2006 Ripe and almost syrupy, the fruit shows the riper
spectrum of zinfandel personality; very succulent and very varietal. Cork.
14.8% alc. **Rating** 88 **To** 2011 $45
Tinja Central Ranges Pinot Noir 2007 Very well handled in the winery;
savoury/stemmy/spicy nuances offsetting dry red fruit characters – problems in
the vineyard climate. Screwcap. 14% alc. **Rating** 87 **To** 2013 $25
Mudgee Merlot 2006 Sweet and ripe with good fruit concentration; nice
texture and palate weight; a little simple, but with good flavour. Cork. 13.5% alc.
Rating 87 **To** 2010 $28

Lucas Estate ★★★★

329 Donges Road, Severnlea, Qld 4352 **Region** Granite Belt
T (07) 4683 6365 **F** (07) 4683 6356 **www.**lucasestate.com.au **Open** 7 days 10–5
Winemaker Louise Samuel **Est.** 1999 **Cases** 1500 **Vyds** 2.7 ha
Louise Samuel and her late husband Colin Sellers purchased Lucas Estate in 2003. The wines are made from the estate vineyard (at an altitude of 825 m), which is planted to chardonnay, cabernet sauvignon, muscat hamburg, merlot, verdelho and shiraz, and also from purchased grapes. A new winery was completed in time for the 2008 vintage, with a pneumatic press for the white wines, leaving the basket press for reds. Later that year Colin Sellers succumbed to cancer; after it had been diagnosed 18 months earlier, he and Louise agreed that Lucas Estate should continue, and that is what she is doing.

ŸŸŸŸŸ **The McKinlay Estate Cabernet Sauvignon 2006** Packs a considerable punch; strong blackcurrant and cassis supported by slightly powdery tannins; success at Qld wine shows explains the price. Diam. 13.5% alc. **Rating** 90 **To** 2016 $45

ŸŸŸŸ **Classic Dry Rose 2008** Pale fuschia; has persistence to its cherry-accented fruit, and a largely dry finish. Well made. Screwcap. 13.5% alc. **Rating** 88 **To** 2009 $22
The Joyce Mary Verdelho 2008 Good varietal character and fruit weight, with well-balanced acidity giving length. Screwcap. 14% alc. **Rating** 87 **To** 2010 $25

Luke Lambert Wines ★★★★

PO Box 403, Yarra Glen, Vic 3775 (postal) **Region** Yarra Valley
T 0448 349 323 **www.**lukelambertwines.com.au **Open** By appt
Winemaker Luke Lambert **Est.** 2003 **Cases** 500 **Vyds** 3 ha
Luke Lambert graduated from CSU's wine science course in 2002, aged 23, cramming in winemaking experience at Mount Pleasant, Coldstream Hills, Mount Prior, Poet's Corner, Palliser Estate in Martinborough, and Badia di Morrona in Chianti. With this background he has established a virtual winery, purchasing grapes from quality-conscious growers in the Yarra Valley and Heathcote. After several trial vintages, the first wines were released from the 2005 vintage. He has now settled in the Yarra Valley, leasing slightly less than 1 ha of Heathcote nebbiolo, and similar amounts of Yarra Valley shiraz and Yarra Valley nebbiolo (newly grafted). The wines are wild yeast-fermented and bottled without fining or filtration.

ŸŸŸŸŸ **Yarra Valley Syrah 2007** Has cranberry, raspberry and some very attractive bramble notes on the bouquet; a medium-bodied palate with some blue fruits, supported by crunchy acidity and very fine-grained tannin structure; long and harmoniously savoury, proves you can get good flavour at low alcohol. Diam. 12.6% alc. **Rating** 95 **To** 2020 $36

Lunar Wines ★★★★

RSD 108 Seppeltsfield Road, Marananga, SA 5355 (postal) **Region** Barossa Valley
T 0427 186 295 **www.**lunarwines.com.au **Open** Not
Winemaker Corey Chaplin **Est.** 2004 **Cases** 600
Corey Chaplin had served 3.5 years as an apprentice chef, but at the last moment decided winemaking rather than cheffing was where he wanted to go. He got a foot in the door picking grapes for Rolf Binder, doing a little home winemaking on the side; this was sufficient for him to get a cellar hand job at Rockford Wines the following vintage, and he remained at Rockford for the next four years working in most areas of the business. After spending all day at Rockford he would ride his bike to Paul Lindner's Langmeil Wines, working on the red wines until the early hours of the morning, gaining a reputation as a lunatic. In 2004 he took the last step, selling his house and putting all the money into starting Lunar, sourcing grapes from Marananga, Greenock, Dorrien, Ebenezer and Seppeltsfield. If this weren't enough, he alternated hemispheres, working in Spain for the 2006 and '07 vintages. It has to be said the high-alcohol style works much better with shiraz than it does with cabernet sauvignon from the Barossa Valley.

Barossa Valley Shiraz 2006 Good colour; the bouquet has some dried fruit characters, but there is plenty of stuffing and sweet fruit on the palate, the French and American oak well integrated. Cork. 15.4% alc. **Rating** 90 **To** 2016 $25
Barossa Valley Shiraz 2005 A very seriously concentrated wine, with dark mocha fruit and blackberry conserve on offer; the palate is rich and sweetly voluptuous; a polarising style. Cork. 15.9% alc. **Rating** 90 **To** 2015 $35
Barossa Valley Shiraz 2004 Another very sweet ultra-ripe wine, but with this vintage there is a subtle difference in the fruit; there appears to be more brightness and the finish is more cohesive. Cork. 14.5% alc. **Rating** 90 **To** 2015

Mabrook Estate ★★★

258 Inlet Road, Bulga, NSW 2330 **Region** Lower Hunter Valley
T (02) 9971 9994 **F** (02) 9971 9924 **www.**mabrookestate.com **Open** W'ends 10–4
Winemaker Larissa Kalt, Michael McManus **Est.** 1996 **Cases** 500 **Vyds** 7 ha
The Swiss-born Kalt family began the establishment of Mabrook Estate in 1996, planting 3 ha each of semillon and shiraz, and 1 ha of verdelho. Parents Mona and Tony have used organic growing methods from the word go, but the vineyard is not certified. Daughter Larissa, having obtained an Honours degree in Medical Science at the University of Sydney, decided to pursue winemaking by working as a 'lab rat' and cellar hand at a local winery, and visited Switzerland and Italy to observe small-scale family winemaking in those countries. The red wines are all very light in structure and extract, which may be intentional. Exports to Switzerland.

Wombat Creek Paddock Hunter Valley Verdelho 2008 A quite deep and luscious palate, replete with tropical fruit salad flavours; all one can ask for. Screwcap. 13.2% alc. **Rating** 87 **To** 2012 $18

McAdams Lane ★★★★

90 McAdams Lane, Bellarine, Vic 3223 (postal) **Region** Geelong
T 1300 651 485 **F** (03) 9602 3388 **www.**mcadamslane.com.au **Open** Not
Winemaker Anthony Brain **Est.** 2003 **Cases** 1000 **Vyds** 4.6 ha
Retired quantity surveyor Peter Slattery bought the 48-ha property in 2001, intending to plant the vineyard, make wine and develop a restaurant. He has achieved all of this (with help from others, of course), planting shiraz (0.5 ha), pinot noir (1.8 ha), pinot gris (1 ha), picolit (0.6 ha), chardonnay (0.4 ha) and zinfandel (0.3 ha). Picolit is the most interesting, a highly regarded grape in northern Italy where it makes small quantities of high-quality sweet wine. It has proved to be very temperamental here, as in Italy, with very unreliable fruitset. The restaurant has been built and will open in the latter part of 2009.

 Terindah Estate Bellarine Peninsula Chardonnay 2007 Tangy/nutty/barrel ferment characters match well with the underlying citrus and stone fruit flavours; good length. Screwcap. 13% alc. **Rating** 90 **To** 2013 $25

Macaw Creek Wines ★★★★

Macaw Creek Road, Riverton, SA 5412 **Region** Mount Lofty Ranges Zone
T (08) 8847 2237 **F** (08) 8847 2237 **www.**macawcreekwines.com.au **Open** By appt
Winemaker Rodney Hooper **Est.** 1992 **Cases** 5000 **Vyds** 10 ha
The property on which Macaw Creek Wines is established has been owned by the Hooper family since the 1850s, but development of the estate vineyards did not begin until 1995. The Macaw Creek brand was established in 1992 with wines made from grapes from other regions, including the Preservative-Free Yoolang Cabernet Shiraz. Rodney Hooper is a highly qualified and skilled winemaker with experience in many parts of Australia and in Germany, France and the US. Exports to the UK, the US, Canada and China.

 Preservative Free Shiraz 2008 Very dense, deep colour; similarly deep, densely structured palate with blackberry, dark chocolate and continuous ripe tannins. With its screwcap, could live for years. 14% alc. **Rating** 90 **To** 2014 $17

Preservative Free Shiraz 2005 Thanks to the screwcap, is showing no sign of oxidation; dark chocolate characters are evident on both the bouquet and palate, as well as blackberry and some spice. 14.5% alc. **Rating** 90 **To** 2011 $17

Reserve Shiraz Cabernet 2005 Full-bodied; a powerful mix of blackberry, black cherry and blackcurrant fruit, with streaks of earth and dark chocolate. Cork. 14.5% alc. **Rating** 90 **To** 2015 $25

ŶŶŶŶ **Mt Lofty Ranges Riesling 2008** A substantial wine, with ample, grainy, minerally acidity supporting quite ripe, citrus-accented fruit. Screwcap. 12% alc. **Rating** 89 **To** 2014 $15

Reserve Shiraz Cabernet 2004 Medium-bodied, with a wraparound of vanilla oak encircling the black fruits and soft tannins; ageing nicely and has good balance. Cork. 14.5% alc. **Rating** 89 **To** 2013 $24

Shiraz 2004 Medium- to full-bodied wine, with that streak of dark chocolate that is characteristic of Macaw Creek, allied with generous blackberry fruit and a fractionally sweet finish. Twin top. 14.5% alc. **Rating** 88 **To** 2014 $14

🍇 Macedon Ridge Wines ★★★★

c/- Level 5, 288 Lorimer Street, Port Melbourne, Vic 3207 (postal) **Region** Macedon Ranges
T (03) 9646 6666 **F** (03) 9646 8383 www.macedonridge.com.au **Open** Not
Winemaker Austin's Wines **Est.** 1984 **Cases** 500 **Vyds** 3 ha
The Macedon Ridge vineyard was established in 1984 on the northern slopes of Mt Macedon. Right from the outset the aim was to produce sparkling wines, and, with this in mind, 2 ha of chardonnay and 1 ha of pinot noir were established. Owners Geoff and Leesa Mackay are responsible for the meticulous management of the vines.

ŶŶŶŶŶ **Blanc de Blanc Brut 2004** Bright straw-green; base wine 100% mlf, then minimum 20 months on lees; a finely structured, elegant, dry style with good length and a crisp, clean finish. Cork. 12% alc. **Rating** 91 **To** 2012 $44

macforbes ★★★★★

770 Healesville-Koo Wee Rup Road, Healesville. Vic 3777 **Region** Yarra Valley
T (03) 9818 8099 **F** (03) 9818 8299 www.macforbes.com **Open** By appt
Winemaker Mac Forbes, Tony Fikkers **Est.** 2004 **Cases** 2000
Mac Forbes cut his vinous teeth at Mount Mary, where he was winemaker for several years before heading overseas in 2002. He spent two years in London working for Southcorp in a marketing liaison role, then travelled to Portugal and Austria to gain further winemaking experience. He returned to the Yarra Valley prior to the 2005 vintage, purchasing grapes for the two-tier portfolio: first, the Victorian range (employing unusual varieties or unusual winemaking techniques); and, second, the Yarra Valley range of multiple terroir-based offerings of Chardonnay and Pinot Noir. The business has grown steadily, with Tony Fikkers joining the winemaking team, and Dylan Grigg as viticulturist guiding the contract grapegrowers upon whom macforbes relies. Exports to the UK, the US, Dubai and Japan.

ŶŶŶŶŶ **RS37 Strathbogie Ranges Riesling 2008** Single vineyard; delicious wine with superb balance of residual sugar and acidity, the varietal expression crystal clear. Screwcap. 9.5% alc. **Rating** 95 **To** 2018 $28

RS9 Strathbogie Ranges Riesling 2008 Sophisticated winemaking, the 9 g/l residual sugar neatly offset by a touch of CO_2 and excellent acidity; takes the Strathbogie Ranges towards the Mosel Valley. Screwcap. 12.5% alc. **Rating** 94 **To** 2015 $28

Gruyere Pinot Noir 2007 Light, bright crimson-purple; despite low alcohol, has more depth to the red and black fruit flavours than the Coldstream; very good length. Screwcap. 12% alc. **Rating** 94 **To** 2015 $38

Woori Yallock Pinot Noir 2007 Good colour; a fragrant bouquet and a silky palate with a mix of plum, cherry and savoury, fine tannins; impressive length and aftertaste. Screwcap. 12.5% alc. **Rating** 94 **To** 2015 $48

♥♥♥♥♡ **Coldstream Pinot Noir 2007** Light red, showing the first signs of development; light-bodied, but with length and focus, the gentle red berry fruit given emphasis and length by the spicy tannins and good acidity. Screwcap. 13% alc. **Rating** 93 To 2014 $38
Yarra Valley Pinot Noir 2007 Light-bodied, fine and delicate; Mac Forbes' time at Mount Mary evident in the elegant, understated style of these wines; the finish has considerable length and thrust. Screwcap. 12% alc. **Rating** 91 To 2013 $28
Hugh Cabernet Sauvignon 2006 An elegant, light-bodied cabernet, doubtless deliberately made in this style, but really needs a touch more flesh. Screwcap. 12.5% alc. **Rating** 90 To 2014 $42

♥♥♥♥ **Yarra Valley Chardonnay 2007** Seems softer and riper than its alcohol would suggest, with creamy melon fruit and subtle oak; does have good balance. Screwcap. 12% alc. **Rating** 89 To 2013 $28

McGlashan's Wallington Estate ★★★★

225 Swan Bay Road, Wallington, Vic 3221 **Region** Geelong
T (03) 5250 5760 **F** (03) 5250 5760 **www**.mcglashans.com.au **Open** W'ends & public hols 11–5, 7 days in Jan
Winemaker Robin Brockett (Contract) **Est.** 1996 **Cases** 1500 **Vyds** 10 ha
Russell and Jan McGlashan began the establishment of their vineyard in 1996. Chardonnay and pinot noir make up the bulk of the plantings, the remainder shiraz and pinot gris; the wines are made by Robin Brockett, with his usual skill and attention to detail. Local restaurants around Geelong and the Bellarine Peninsula take much of the wine, although a newly opened cellar door offering food and music will see an increase in direct sales.

♥♥♥♥♡ **Bellarine Peninsula Pinot Noir 2007** Well-made pinot; harmonious texture, structure and flavour; the red cherry and plum fruit is neatly trimmed by light foresty/savoury tannins. Screwcap. 14% alc. **Rating** 92 To 2014 $26
Bellarine Peninsula Chardonnay 2007 Starting to develop colour; a complex wine with ripe peachy fruit, creamy/nutty nuances and a balanced finish. Screwcap. 13.5% alc. **Rating** 90 To 2013 $24

McGuigan Wines ★★★★★

Cnr Broke Road/McDonald Road, Pokolbin, NSW 2321 **Region** Lower Hunter Valley
T (02) 4998 7400 **F** (02) 4998 7401 **www**.mcguiganwines.com.au **Open** 7 days 9.30–5
Winemaker Peter Hall **Est.** 1992 **Cases** 1.4 million
A public-listed company – the ultimate logical expression of Brian McGuigan's marketing drive and vision, which is on a par with that of Wolf Blass in his heyday. The overall size of the company has been measurably increased by the acquisition of Simeon Wines; Yaldara and Miranda, now also part of the business, made wine industry headlines in 2006 when it terminated a large number of grape purchase contracts, a decision likely to cost it dearly in the 2008 and '09 vintages. In 2007 McGuigan Simeon acquired Nepenthe Vineyards, a move that surprised many. In 2008 the group was renamed Australian Vintage Limited, a slightly curious moniker. Exports to all major markets, particularly active in export markets, notably the US and more recently China.

♥♥♥♥♥ **Genus 4 Eden Valley Riesling 2008** A beautifully crafted wine; a floral bouquet and a lime juice palate, reflecting region and variety at its best; a very sustained, lip-smacking finish. Screwcap. 12% alc. **Rating** 94 To 2023 $18.99
Earth's Portrait Eden Valley Riesling 2005 Glowing, almost incandescent, yellow-green; dry mineral, citrus and straw aromas and flavours, which are particularly well balanced. Winner of five trophies at the Adelaide Wine Show '08, including Best Wine of Show. Screwcap. 11.5% alc. **Rating** 94 To 2013 $18.99
The Shortlist Adelaide Hills Chardonnay 2008 Lively, bright and crisp, nectarine and grapefruit flavours having absorbed new French oak impact; very good length. Screwcap. 13.5% alc. **Rating** 94 To 2015 $26

Handmade Langhorne Creek Shiraz 2007 Strong purple-crimson; a rich and luscious wine with perfectly ripened fruit offering plum and blackberry on the supple palate; tannin and oak have been precisely judged. Cork. 14% alc. Rating 94 To 2020 $45

ŸŸŸŸŸ **Genus 4 Eden Valley Riesling 2007** A complex wine, with an array of lime, toast and spice aromas and flavours; good length and focus. Screwcap. 12% alc. Rating 93 To 2017 $18.99

Earth's Portrait Eden Valley Riesling 2004 Bright green-gold; has good continuity of line and flavour, the lime juice and toast flavours running smoothly through to the finish. Screwcap. 11% alc. Rating 92 To 2012 $18.99

Personal Reserve Hunter Valley Chardonnay 2007 Ripe peach, fresh fig and straw bouquet; lively palate with some citrus fruit and toasty oak; rich and harmonious. Diam. 13% alc. Rating 92 To 2013 $30

The Shortlist Barossa Valley Shiraz 2007 While the alcohol is said to be (only) 14%, has an abundance of blackberry, plum, licorice and dark chocolate fruit on the medium- to full-bodied palate, the tannins ripe and soft. Very good outcome for the vintage. Screwcap. 14% alc. Rating 91 To 2017 $26

Genus 4 Old Vine Hunter Valley Chardonnay 2008 Picking and winemaking decisions have delivered a maximum result for the Hunter Valley; has citrus overtones to the stone fruit core; the oak is well integrated. Screwcap. 12.5% alc. Rating 90 To 2013 $19

Handmade Langhorne Creek Shiraz 2006 Bright and lively, bordering edgy, red berry fruits; may settle down into a positive, fruit-driven style in a year or two. Given the benefit of the doubt. Cork. 14.5% alc. Rating 90 To 2016 $45

The Shortlist GSM 2007 Light, but bright, hue; a distinctly savoury/spicy edge runs through the wine, but there is enough substance to carry the wine on for some years. Screwcap. 14.5% alc. Rating 90 To 2015 $26

The Shortlist Coonawarra Cabernet Sauvignon 2007 An uncompromisingly robust wine, with blackcurrant, black olive and earthy tannins intermingling; needs time. Screwcap. 14% alc. Rating 90 To 2020 $26

ŸŸŸŸ **Genus 4 Old Vine Hunter Valley Shiraz 2007** Light, bright crimson; has a gentle mix of red and black fruits on a light- to medium-bodied palate; good balance. Screwcap. 13% alc. Rating 88 To 2013 $19

Limestone Coast Rose 2008 Well made and neatly balanced; supple red cherry/strawberry fruit; dry finish. Screwcap. 13.5% alc. Rating 87 To 2010 $16

Brian McGuigan's Personal Reserve Tawny Port NV Ageing evident on rim (more than 15 years), but is as much muscat in style as anything else. Diam. 18% alc. Rating 87 To 2010 $25

McGuigan Wines (Barossa Valley)   ★★★

Chateau Yaldara, Hermann Thumm Drive, Lyndoch, SA 5351 **Region** Barossa Valley **T** (08) 8524 0200 **F** (08) 8524 0240 **www.**yaldara.com.au **Open** 7 days 10–5 **Winemaker** James Evers **Est.** 1947 **Cases** 5000

At the end of 1999, Yaldara became part of the publicly listed Simeon Wines, the intention being that it (Yaldara) should become the quality flagship of the group. Despite much expenditure and the short-lived stay of at least one well-known winemaker, the plan failed to deliver the expected benefits. In 2002 McGuigan Wines made a reverse takeover for Simeon, and the various McGuigan brands will (presumably) fill the role intended for Yaldara. Exports to all major markets.

ŸŸŸŸ **Yaldara the Farms Barossa Valley Shiraz 2006** Stacked to the rafters with ripe black fruit flavours that overwhelm the finish and aftertaste; picked too late? Cork. 15% alc. Rating 88 To 2016 $70

Yaldara Limited Edition Tawny Port NV Traditional luscious and sweet Australian tawny style. Cork. 18.5% alc. Rating 88 To 2010 $25

McHenry Hohnen Vintners ★★★★★

PO Box 1480, Margaret River, WA 6285 **Region** Margaret River
T (08) 9757 7600 **F** (08) 9757 7999 **www**.mchv.com.au **Open** Not
Winemaker David Hohnen, Freya Hohnen, Ryan Walsh **Est.** 2004 **Cases** 8000 **Vyds** 120 ha
McHenry Hohnen is owned by the McHenry and Hohnen families, sourcing grapes from
four vineyards owned by various members of the families. In all, 120 ha of vines have been
established on the McHenry, Calgardup Brook, Rocky Road and McLeod Creek properties.
A significant part of the grape production is sold to others (including Cape Mentelle) but
McHenry Hohnen have 18 varieties to choose from in fashioning their wines. The family
members with direct executive responsibilities are leading Perth retailer Murray McHenry,
Cape Mentelle founder and former long-term winemaker David Hohnen, and Freya Hohnen,
who shares the winemaking duties with father David. In 2007 David Hohnen received the
inaugural Len Evans Award for Leadership. Exports to the UK, Japan, Singapore, Hong Kong
and NZ.

ŢŢŢŢŢ **Rocky Road Vineyard Margaret River Chardonnay 2007** Very different style
to Calgardup Brook; maximum focus on the delicious white peach and grapefruit
in classic Margaret River style; an intense and long palate and finish. Screwcap.
14% alc. **Rating** 96 **To** 2017 $34.99
Calgardup Brook Vineyard Margaret River Chardonnay 2008 Light straw-
green; an extremely bright, fresh and lively wine, the fruit and oak seamlessly
interwoven on the long and focused palate; is almost painfully youthful, but the
future is undoubted. Screwcap. 13.5% alc. **Rating** 95 **To** 2020 $36
Rocky Road Vineyard Margaret River Chardonnay 2008 Light straw-green;
while it shares many of the characters of Calgardup Brook, the fruit is a little more
evident, the acidity a little softer, and will likely develop a little quicker. Screwcap.
13.5% alc. **Rating** 95 **To** 2018 $36
Calgardup Brook Vineyard Margaret River Chardonnay 2007 A notably
elegant and fine wine notwithstanding the level of French oak; gains velocity and
thrust as it moves to the back-palate and finish; has good texture and structure.
Screwcap. 13.5% alc. **Rating** 95 **To** 2013 $37

ŢŢŢŢŢ **3 Amigos White 2007** Deep colour; a nutty, complex bouquet, with ripe
grapefruit and straw coming to the fore; thickly textured with a savoury
undertone that delivers a different drinking experience from the norm. Marsanne/
Chardonnay/Roussanne. Screwcap. 13.5% alc. **Rating** 90 **To** 2012 $22

ŢŢŢŢ **Rocky Road Margaret River Zinfandel 2007** Stewed plum aromas lead into
a gently juicy raspberry/plum compote palate, which has good length. Screwcap.
14.5% alc. **Rating** 89 **To** 2013 $37

McIvor Estate ★★★★

80 Tooborac-Baynton Road, Tooborac, Vic 3522 **Region** Heathcote
T (03) 5433 5266 **F** (03) 5433 5358 **www**.mcivorestate.com.au **Open** W'ends & public
hols 10–5, or by appt
Winemaker Various contract **Est.** 1997 **Cases** 2000
McIvor Estate is situated at the base of the Tooborac Hills, at the southern end of the
Heathcote wine region, 5 km southwest of Tooborac. Gary and Cynthia Harbor have planted
5.3 ha of marsanne, roussanne, shiraz, cabernet sauvignon, merlot, nebbiolo and sangiovese.

ŢŢŢŢŢ **Shiraz 2006** Bright colour; loaded with black fruit, mineral backbone and a little
tar; dark, chewy and quite rugged, with a long, savoury and quite tarry finish; a big
wine needing time. Screwcap. 14.5% alc. **Rating** 93 **To** 2020 $30
Cabernet Merlot 2006 Generous cassis and black olive bouquet; the palate is
firm, but lively with ample fine-grained tannins and fine blueberry fruit on the
finish. Screwcap. 14.5% alc. **Rating** 91 **To** 2015 $25

McKellar Ridge Wines

Point of View Vineyard, 2 Euroka Avenue, Murrumbateman, NSW 2582
Region Canberra District
T (02) 6258 1556 **www**.mckellarridgewines.com.au **Open** Sun 12–5, or by appt Sept–Jun
Winemaker Dr Brian Johnston **Est.** 2000 **Cases** 600 **Vyds** 6 ha
Dr Brian Johnston and his wife Janet are the partners in McKellar Ridge Wines. Brian has been undertaking a postgraduate diploma in science at CSU, focusing on wine science and wine production techniques. The wines come from low-yielding, mature vines and have had significant show success. They are made using a combination of traditional and new winemaking techniques, the emphasis being on fruit-driven styles.

🍷🍷🍷🍷 **Basket Press Canberra District Shiraz Viognier 2007** A lively and vibrant palate throws off the trace of reduction on the bouquet, with zesty red fruits lifted by the viognier; good length. Screwcap. 14.5% alc. **Rating** 89 **To** 2015 $24
Canberra District Chardonnay 2008 Citrus and nectarine fruit with crisp acidity and the barest hint of oak; simple but well balanced. Screwcap. 13% alc. **Rating** 87 **To** 2012 $22

McLaren Ridge Estate

Whitings Road, McLaren Vale, SA 5171 **Region** McLaren Vale
T (08) 8383 0504 **F** (08) 8383 0504 **www**.mclarenridge.com **Open** 7 days 11–5
Winemaker Brian Light **Est.** 1997 **Cases** 5000 **Vyds** 6 ha
Peter and Heather Oliver have 5 ha of shiraz and 1 ha of grenache, planted over 50 years ago on the ridge that now gives their estate its name. The cellar door opened in 2007, and luxury vineyard accommodation is available. Exports to the UK and Canada.

🍷🍷🍷🍷 **Shiraz 2006** Has retained good hue, and also regional typicity; gently sweet, juicy fruit has the telltale touch of chocolate; medium-bodied, and made without artifice. ProCork. 14.5% alc. **Rating** 89 **To** 2015 $20
Shiraz Cabernet Franc Merlot 2006 The uncommon blend comes together remarkably well, the region stamping a dark chocolate overlay to the array of black and red fruits; good control of extract. Cork. 14.5% alc. **Rating** 89 **To** 2014 $20
SSB 2008 Well made, offering attractive tropical fruit flavours balanced by a clean, crisp and juicy finish. Screwcap. 13% alc. **Rating** 88 **To** 2010 $20

McLaren Vale III Associates ★★★★☆

130 Main Road, McLaren Vale, SA 5171 **Region** McLaren Vale
T 1800 501 513 **www**.associates.com.au **Open** Mon–Fri 9–5, tasting by appt
Winemaker Brian Light **Est.** 1999 **Cases** 12 000 **Vyds** 34 ha
The three associates in question all have a decade or more of wine industry experience; Mary Greer is managing partner, Reginald Wymond chairing partner, and Christopher Fox partner. The partnership has two vineyards, one owned by Mary and John Greer, the other by Reg and Sue Wymond. An impressive portfolio of affordable quality wines has been the outcome, precisely as the partners wished. Exports to the US, Canada, Germany and Singapore.

🍷🍷🍷🍷🍷 **Giant Squid Ink 2006** Less dense colour than the '07 Squid Ink Reserve, perhaps simply due to age; has an elegant, medium-bodied supple palate with entrancing mouthfeel from the silky web of red and black fruits, the tannins fine. The price is another issue. Shiraz. Cork. 14.5% alc. **Rating** 95 **To** 2016 $150

🍷🍷🍷🍷🍷 **Three Score & 10 Grenache 2006** Some brick hues developing; complex bottle-developed flavours on top of the varietal character; spicy plum notes are pleasantly sweetened by the alcohol. Screwcap. 15% alc. **Rating** 90 **To** 2014 $27.90
Premiado Tempranillo 2008 Good colour; has an abundance of small red and black berry juicy fruits flavours; no oak obvious; enjoy now or in five years. Screwcap. 14% alc. **Rating** 90 **To** 2013 $30

Squid Ink Reserve Shiraz 2007 Dense purple-crimson; well named, for this is dense and powerful, with lots of extract underlining the savoury bitter chocolate notes; a little too robust. Cork. 14.5% alc. **Rating** 89 **To** 2017 $45
Memento Cabernet Sauvignon 2007 Good colour; quite fragrant, with a mix of redcurrant and more leafy characters; has good length, then a tart finish. Screwcap. 14.5% alc. **Rating** 87 **To** 2013 $27.90

McLean's Farm

barr-Eden Vineyard, Menglers Hill Road, Tanunda, SA 5352 **Region** Barossa Valley
T (08) 8564 3340 **www.**mcleansfarm.com **Open** W'ends 10–5, or by appt
Winemaker Bob McLean **Est.** 2001 **Cases** 2500
At various times known as the Jolly Green Giant and Sir Lunchalot, Bob McLean has gone perilously close to being a marketing legend in his own lifetime, moving from Orlando to Petaluma and then St Hallett. The farm shed on the home property houses the winery which handles the estate-grown red grapes, which amount to 30 tonnes (or less) a year. Production has been 'downsized' in the wake of the decision to only use estate-grown grapes. Exports to the UK and US.

Eden Valley Riesling 2008 Pleasant wine; gentle mineral/talc. flavours with regional lime/citrus; a light finish that is fractionally short; may improve. Screwcap. 12.5% alc. **Rating** 88 **To** 2015 $25
Eden Valley Riesling 2007 Notable depth to the colour; showing a touch of kerosene and lemon sherbet on the bouquet; rich on entry, the finish is quite tight and lemony. Screwcap. 11.5% alc. **Rating** 88 **To** 2014 $25

McLeish Estate

462 De Beyers Road, Pokolbin, NSW 2320 **Region** Lower Hunter Valley
T (02) 4998 7754 **F** (02) 4998 7754 **www.**mcleishhunterwines.com.au **Open** 7 days 10–5, or by appt
Winemaker Andrew Thomas (Contract) **Est.** 1985 **Cases** 6000 **Vyds** 14 ha
Bob and Maryanne McLeish began planting their vineyard in 1985, and now have semillon, chardonnay, verdelho, shiraz, merlot and cabernet sauvignon. They have also opened their cellar door, having accumulated a number of gold medals for their wines, thanks in no small measure to the winemaking skills of Andrew Thomas. Exports to the UK and the US.

Hunter Valley Cabernet Sauvignon Merlot 2007 Good red-purple colour; has entirely unexpected, deliciously bright and juicy red berry fruit flavours running through to a long finish; oak positive but not aggressive; major surprise. Screwcap. 14.2% alc. **Rating** 94 **To** 2015 $22

Hunter Valley Semillon 2008 Very correct focus and balance; crisp and minerally acidity rounds off a tangy/lemony palate. Screwcap. 9.8% alc. **Rating** 93 **To** 2018 $18
Reserve Hunter Valley Shiraz 2007 An oaky bouquet, with red fruits and a touch of leather; fresh and lively, the palate is dominated by oak at this point, but the concentration indicates that patience will be rewarded. Cork. 14% alc. **Rating** 91 **To** 2018 $35
Hunter Valley Cabernet Sauvignon Merlot 2008 Bright colour; a mostly red fruit bouquet with a varietal cedar and black olive note; medium-bodied and bright on the palate; ripe tannins and a slightly juicy finish. Screwcap. 13.5% alc. **Rating** 90 **To** 2014 $22
Hunter Valley Cabernet Sauvignon 2008 Vibrant and bright, showing the house style to perfection; juicy red fruit aromas; vibrant acidity, clear definition, and a generous level of fruit to finish. Screwcap. 13.5% alc. **Rating** 90 **To** 2014 $22

Hunter Valley Semillon Sauvignon Blanc 2008 A fractionally sweaty bouquet does not impinge on the generous flavours of the palate, largely driven by the 30% sauvignon blanc component. Screwcap. 12.1% alc. **Rating** 89 **To** 2011 $16

Hunter Valley Chardonnay 2008 Ripe peach and fresh fig bouquet, with some complementary vibrant lemon; fresh and focused, with good line. Screwcap. 13% alc. **Rating** 89 **To** 2013 $20

Hunter Valley Merlot 2008 A crunchy cranberry and dark cherry bouquet; crisp and defined palate, with a little savoury note to conclude. Screwcap. 13.5% alc. **Rating** 88 **To** 2014 $22

McPherson Wines   ★★★★☆

PO Box 767, Hawthorn, Vic 3122 **Region** Nagambie Lakes
T (03) 9832 1700 **F** (03) 9832 1750 **www**.mcphersonwines.com **Open** Not
Winemaker Andrew McPherson, Geoff Thompson **Est.** 1993 **Cases** 400 000 **Vyds** 250 ha
McPherson Wines is not well known in Australia but is, by any standards, a substantial business. Its wines are largely produced for the export market, with some sales in Australia. Made at various locations from the estate vineyards and supplemented with contract-grown grapes, they represent very good value. For the record, McPherson Wines is a joint venture between Andrew McPherson and Alister Purbrick (Tahbilk), both of whom have had a lifetime of experience in the industry. Exports to all major markets.

ΨΨΨΨΨ **Chapter Three Shiraz Viognier 2006** Good hue; spicy black fruit aromas flow into a palate with great drive and energy to its mix of black fruits and strongly savoury notes, in turn fuelling the great length of the palate. Screwcap. 14.5% alc. **Rating** 94 **To** 2021 $29.99

ΨΨΨΨΨ **Basilisk Shiraz Mourvedre 2007** Good colour; the bouquet and palate offer a convincing array of blackberry, plum, dark chocolate and spice, the tannins fine, the oak subtle. Screwcap. 14.5% alc. **Rating** 92 **To** 2017 $17.99

Basilisk Marsanne Viognier 2007 The musk and apricot of the viognier are more obvious than the marsanne, but it provides the freshness and structure to a successful blend. Value. Screwcap. 12.5% alc. **Rating** 90 **To** 2013 $17.99

Basilisk Sauvignon Blanc 2008 A firmly structured wine, with a core of mineral surrounded by tropical fruit flavours; good length and balance helped by citrussy acidity. Screwcap. 12.5% alc. **Rating** 90 **To** 2010 $17.99

ΨΨΨΨ **Shiraz 2008** Good colour; as honest as they come, with abundant plum and blackberry fruit; fractionally coarse finish, but no complaint at this price. Screwcap. 14.5% alc. **Rating** 87 **To** 2011 $10.99

Cabernet Sauvignon 2008 Has clearly expressed varietal character on a well-structured, medium-bodied palate; comprehensively over-delivers at its price point. Value. Screwcap. 14% alc. **Rating** 87 **To** 2011 $10.99

Macquariedale Estate   ★★★

170 Sweetwater Road, Rothbury, NSW 2335 **Region** Lower Hunter Valley
T (02) 6574 7012 **www**.macquariedale.com.au **Open** Fri–Mon, school & public hols 10–5
Winemaker Ross McDonald **Est.** 1993 **Cases** 4000 **Vyds** 13 ha
Macquariedale is an acorn to oak story, beginning with a small hobby vineyard in Branxton many years ago, and now extending to three certified organic (in conversion) vineyards around the Lower Hunter with semillon, chardonnay, pinot noir, shiraz, merlot, mataro and cabernet sauvignon. This has led to Ross McDonald (and family) leaving a busy Sydney life to be full-time grapegrower and winemaker. Exports to Canada, Japan and China.

ΨΨΨΨ **Thomas Reserve Hunter Valley Shiraz 2007** Fresh, light- to medium-bodied wine, with predominantly red fruits; has good length and freshness; while the front label displays 'certified organic', the back label reveals certified biodynamic status. Low-sulphur levels used in the wine and no fining agents, thus suitable for vegans. Diam. 13% alc. **Rating** 89 **To** 2013 $40

Hunter Valley Cabernet Sauvignon 2007 A convincing example of Hunter Valley cabernet sauvignon, with sustained blackcurrant and cassis fruit, the oak and tannins balanced for the long haul. Diam. 13.5% alc. **Rating** 89 **To** 2020 $25

Hunter Valley Chardonnay 2008 Organic/biodynamic/low SO₂ wine, which is developing quickly, already with plenty of peachy flavour; good acidity may hold the wine together, but better to be safe than sorry. Screwcap. 13% alc. **Rating** 88 **To** 2010 $20

McWilliam's   ★★★★★

Jack McWilliam Road, Hanwood, NSW 2680 **Region** Riverina
T (02) 6963 0001 **www.**mountpleasantwines.com.au **Open** Mon–Sat 9–5
Winemaker Jim Brayne, Corey Ryan **Est.** 1916 **Cases** NFP **Vyds** 445 ha
The best wines to emanate from the Hanwood winery are from other regions, notably the Barwang Vineyard at Hilltops (see separate entry), Coonawarra (Brand's Laira), Yarra Valley, Tumbarumba and Eden Valley. As McWilliam's viticultural resources have expanded, they have been able to produce regional blends from across Australia of startlingly good value. The 2006 sale of McWilliam's Yenda winery to Casella has led to a major upgrade in both the size and equipment at the Hanwood winery, now the nerve centre of the business. Exports to all major markets via a major distribution joint venture with Gallo.

ŦŦŦŦŦ **1877 Cabernet Sauvignon Shiraz 2005** Super-concentrated, with a complex array of black fruits, spice and herb; the rich palate has great line and focus, the abundant tannins effortlessly swallowed by the fruit; a great example of power and finesse. Screwcap. 14.5% alc. **Rating** 96 **To** 2025 $95
Limited Release Riverina Botrytis Semillon 2007 Deeply botrytised with apricot and a touch of spicy marmalade; the palate is luscious and rich, with toffee and a dried fruit finish; lovely balance. Screwcap. 12% alc. **Rating** 95 **To** 2014 $29.95

ŦŦŦŦŸ **Hanwood Estate Sauvignon Blanc 2008** Reflects the diverse regional fruit resources of McWilliam's; has impressive intensity to the amalgam of gooseberry, passionfruit and citrus flavours; above average length. Screwcap. 11.5% alc. **Rating** 91 **To** 2010 $12.99
Catching Thieves Margaret River Cabernet Merlot 2007 Very good colour and clarity; a supple, medium-bodied palate is primarily driven by blackcurrant and cassis fruit, but there is an appropriate background of tannins and a touch of oak. Value plus. Screwcap. 14% alc. **Rating** 90 **To** 2015 $16.99

ŦŦŦŦ **Catching Thieves Margaret River Semillon Sauvignon Blanc 2008** Driven primarily by the semillon; clean, crisp grassy notes, and crisp, minerally acidity on the finish, tropical nuances in the background. Screwcap. 13% alc. **Rating** 89 **To** 2012 $16.99
Hanwood Estate Semillon Sauvignon Blanc 2008 Bright, lively, juicy grassy/lemony wine, built around the structure of the semillon. Screwcap. 11% alc. **Rating** 88 **To** 2010 $12.99
Inheritance Shiraz Cabernet 2008 This traditional blend works well with a range of cherry, plum and black fruits in a light- to medium-bodied, but well-structured and balanced palate. Value. Screwcap. 13.5% alc. **Rating** 87 **To** 2011 $7.50
Inheritance Cabernet Merlot 2007 Unusually clearly expressed varietal characters at such a low price point; equally meritorious is the structure. Outstanding value. Screwcap. 13.5% alc. **Rating** 87 **To** 2011 $7.50

McWilliam's Mount Pleasant   ★★★★★

Marrowbone Road, Pokolbin, NSW 2320 **Region** Lower Hunter Valley
T (02) 4998 7505 **www.**mountpleasantwines.com.au **Open** 7 days 10–5
Winemaker Phillip Ryan, Andrew Leembruggen **Est.** 1921 **Cases** NFP **Vyds** 119 ha
McWilliam's Elizabeth and the glorious Lovedale Semillon are generally commercially available with four to five years of bottle age, they are undervalued treasures with a consistently superb show record. The individual vineyard wines, together with the Maurice O'Shea memorial wines, add to the lustre of this proud name. Exports to many countries, the most important being the UK and Canada.

ᵀᵀᵀᵀᵀ Maurice O'Shea Shiraz 2006 Dark and understated bouquet; flashes of oak, blackberry, redcurrant, spice and a touch of leather; the palate reveals a powerful array of flavours, not the least of which is the rich core of black fruit, complemented by tarry tannins; the finish is very long and the structure impeccable; this should age gracefully for decades. Screwcap. 14.5% alc. **Rating** 96 To 2026 $65

Maurice O'Shea Shiraz 2005 A rich and complex wine, both in terms of texture and flavour; the predominantly black fruits have regional background nuances of earth, with an obvious but appropriate French oak infusion from completion of fermentation in barrel. Predominantly from the 125-year-old vines of the Old Hill Vineyard. Screwcap. 15% alc. **Rating** 95 To 2030 $65

Lovedale Limited Release Hunter Valley Semillon 2004 Quite deep colour; restrained toast, lemon and straw bouquet; generous on entry, the fruit tightens up and shows a fine line at the core; toasty and a very long finish. Screwcap. 11.8% alc. **Rating** 94 To 2016 $65

Lovedale Limited Release Hunter Valley Semillon 2003 Bright colour; a rich and toasty bouquet with straw and lemon; pristine and pure, it is quite ready to enjoy now; providing the cork is good, the wine will hold together well for some time to come. **Rating** 94 To 2016 $65

Original Vineyard OP&OH Hunter Valley Shiraz 2005 Delicately perfumed with red fruit, leather, spice and a touch of sage; plenty of oak, but the fruit sits with it well; medium-bodied, and very fine on the finish. Screwcap. 15% alc. **Rating** 94 To 2025 $39.99

Original Vineyard OP&OH Hunter Valley Shiraz 2004 Despite the similarity of vineyard influences (Old Paddock was planted in 1921, adjacent to Old Hill) this is very different to the O'Shea, more savoury and in some ways with greater energy, the oak more subtle. Cork. 14.5% alc. **Rating** 94 To 2024 $39.99

Original Vineyard Rosehill Hunter Valley Shiraz 2004 The vineyard was purchased in 1945, and has produced some great wines over the years, notably the '59. Despite its alcohol, it is medium-bodied, with a display of black and red fruits cradled in the French and American oak in which the wine finished its fermentation, the tannins fine and ripe. Cork. 15% alc. **Rating** 94 To 2024 $33.99

ᵀᵀᵀᵀᵀ Original Vineyard Rosehill Hunter Valley Shiraz 2005 Concentrated redcurrant and spicy oak bouquet; medium-bodied and quite even on the palate, with a slight toasty finish; exhibits a true sense of place. Screwcap. 15% alc. **Rating** 93 To 2020 $33.99

Elizabeth Semillon 2004 Cellar Release. Bright green-gold; despite the colour development, is youthful, with lemon tart flavours set against a background of acidity and a touch of CO_2. Screwcap. 10.5% alc. **Rating** 92 To 2013 $17.99

Florence Semillon Sauvignon Blanc 2008 Very crisp and lively, the palate with considerable thrust and assertive lemony acidity. Despite Florence (a name used by Maurice O'Shea in the 1950s), there is no claim of regional origin. Hunter Semillon (87%) and WA Sauvignon Blanc most likely. Screwcap. 10.5% alc. **Rating** 90 To 2012 $16.99

Philip Hunter Valley Shiraz 2006 Bright colour; quite firm fruit in a blackberry/red and black cherry spectrum does the talking, tannins and oak are bystanders. Early release pays dividends; best for many years. Screwcap. 14% alc. **Rating** 90 To 2014 $17.99

Mad Dog Wines   ★★★★☆

PO Box 166, Tanunda, SA 5352 **Region** Barossa Valley
T (08) 8563 2758 **F** (08) 8563 2027 **Open** Not
Winemaker Jeremy Holmes, Matthew Munzberg **Est.** 1999 **Cases** 400 **Vyds** 45 ha
Geoff (aka Mad Dog) Munzberg, a third-generation grapegrower, has joined with Jeremy and Heidi Holmes, Aaron and Kirsty Brasher and son Matthew to create Mad Dog Wines. The principal wine, Shiraz, comes from vines with an average age of 35 years; most of the grapes

are sold, with the best kept for the Mad Dog label. The purchase of a neighbouring vineyard in 2006 has led to the inclusion of some 100-year-old vine fruit, and the range will be slightly extended with small amounts of Moscato and Sangiovese. Exports to the UK.

Maddens Rise ★★★★

19 Maddens Lane, Coldstream, Vic 3770 (postal) **Region** Yarra Valley
T (03) 8608 2560 **F** (03) 8608 1115 **Open** Not
Winemaker Luke Lambert **Est.** 1996 **Cases** 2500 **Vyds** 25.4 ha
Justin Fahey has established a vineyard planted to chardonnay, viognier, pinot noir, pinot meunier, shiraz, merlot and cabernet sauvignon. Planting began in 1996, although the first wines were not released until 2004. The vines are grown using organic/biological farming practices that focus on soil and vine health, low yields and hand picking to optimise the quality. Part of the grape production is sold to other Yarra Valley wineries.

ΨΨΨΨΨ **Reserve Yarra Valley Chardonnay 2008** A very slight difference in alcohol; the Reserve, however, is nothing if not consistent, although here the fruit is purer and tighter, the oak subservient. Screwcap. 12.6% alc. **Rating** 90 **To** 2013 $37.50
Reserve Yarra Valley Shiraz 2008 Light but bright colour; spicy/stemmy notes on the bouquet are replayed on the lively, red fruit-centred palate; light- to medium-bodied, and the oak is restrained. Screwcap. 12.6% alc. **Rating** 90 **To** 2016 $45
Reserve Yarra Valley Cabernet Sauvignon 2008 Crimson; has clear varietal character in an elegant, light- to medium-bodied style; the decision to bottle early is justified; the decision to make the lower-alcohol wine the Reserve is interesting; the price is challenging. Screwcap. 12.7% alc. **Rating** 90 **To** 2015 $45

ΨΨΨΨ **Yarra Valley Shiraz 2008** A slightly fuller-bodied, darker-hued wine than the Reserve, but without the same finesse. Interesting contrast. Screwcap. 12.9% alc. **Rating** 89 **To** 2016 $24
Yarra Valley Cabernet Sauvignon 2008 Fresh and elegant cassis and black-berry fruit, the oak subtle and integrated; like the Reserve, is light- to medium-bodied, with similarly fine tannins. Screwcap. 13.1% alc. **Rating** 89 **To** 2014 $24
Yarra Valley Chardonnay 2008 Seems riper than the alcohol would suggest, the fruit sweeter and the oak not entirely sympathetic; wild yeast, unfiltered chardonnay is a bold throw of the dice. Screwcap. 12.7% alc. **Rating** 87 **To** 2012 $24

Maglieri of McLaren Vale ★★★

GPO Box 753, Melbourne, Vic 3001 **Region** McLaren Vale
T 1300 651 650 **Open** Not
Winemaker Alex MacKenzie **Est.** 1972 **Cases** 10 000
One of the better-kept secrets among the wine cognoscenti, but not among the many customers who drink thousands of cases of white and red Lambrusco every year; an example of niche marketing at its profitable best. It was a formula that proved irresistible to Beringer Blass, which acquired Maglieri in 1999. Its dry red wines are generously proportioned and full of character, the Shiraz particularly so.

ΨΨΨΨ **Shiraz 2008** Deep crimson-purple; densely flavoured blackberry, plum and dark chocolate fruit; solid tannin and oak foundation. Poor cork (wine-stained) threatens its future. 14.5% alc. **Rating** 89 **To** 2014 $20.99
Cabernet Sauvignon 2006 Good colour; the ripe cassis and plum-accented fruit a little congested on the finish. Cork. 15% alc. **Rating** 87 **To** 2014 $21.99

Magpie Estate ★★★★☆

PO Box 126, Tanunda, SA 5352 **Region** Barossa Valley
T (08) 8562 3300 **F** (08) 8562 1177 **Open** Not
Winemaker Rolf Binder, Noel Young **Est.** 1993 **Cases** 5000

This is a partnership between Rolf Binder and Cambridge (England) wine merchant Noel Young. It came about in 1993 when there was limited demand for or understanding of Southern Rhône–style blends based on shiraz, grenache and mourvedre. Initially a small, export-only brand, the quality of the wines was such that it has grown over the years, although the intention is to limit production. The majority of the wines are reasonably priced, the super-premiums more expensive. Exports to the UK, the US, Canada, Austria, Finland, Belgium and the Bahamas.

Magpie Springs

RSD 1790 Meadows Road, Hope Forest, SA 5172 **Region** Adelaide Hills
T (08) 8556 7351 **www**.magpiesprings.com.au **Open** Fri–Sun & public hols 10–5
Winemaker James Hastwell, Reg Wilkinson **Est.** 1991 **Cases** 1000 **Vyds** 16.2 ha
Stuart Brown and Rosemary (Roe) Gartelmann purchased the property on which Magpie Springs is now established in 1983, for growing flowers commercially and grazing cattle. Chardonnay was planted experimentally, and were among the earliest vines in the area. In 1991 the commencement of the vineyard proper led to the planting of a little over 16 ha of semillon, chardonnay, sauvignon blanc, pinot noir, merlot, shiraz and riesling. Roe paints professionally from the Magpie Springs studio, and many classes and workshops have been held over the years. Her studio can be visited during cellar door hours.

ŶŶŶŶŶ **Lenore Adelaide Hills Chardonnay 2006** Light, bright straw-green; bright nectarine, white peach and grapefruit flavours are the major players, barrel ferment and oak maturation far less obvious. Very good wine at an even better price. Screwcap. 13.2% alc. **Rating** 93 **To** 2014 $22
Adelaide Hills Merlot 2006 Medium-bodied, a good varietal expression; red and black fruit flavours with a savoury flourish; how much better would it have been if 14 or 14.5% alc/vol. Screwcap. 15% alc. **Rating** 90 **To** 2014 $18

ŶŶŶŶ **Adelaide Hills Riesling 2007** The clean bouquet is yet to develop, but there is plenty of ripe citrus fruit on the palate, and sufficient acidity for the future. Screwcap. 12.5% alc. **Rating** 89 **To** 2016 $18
Adelaide Hills Sauvignon Blanc 2008 Crisp and fresh, with good structure and length, but still to open up and display its wares in full. Screwcap. 13.5% alc. **Rating** 88 **To** 2010 $18
Adelaide Hills Pinot Noir 2005 Still has good colour and an abundance of ripe fruit in a plum spectrum ranging from fresh to confit. Screwcap. 14% alc. **Rating** 88 **To** 2013 $22

Main Ridge Estate

80 William Road, Red Hill, Vic 3937 **Region** Mornington Peninsula
T (03) 5989 2686 **www**.mre.com.au **Open** Mon–Fri 12–4, w'ends 12–5
Winemaker Nat White **Est.** 1975 **Cases** 1200 **Vyds** 2.8 ha
Nat White gives meticulous attention to every aspect of his viticulture, doing annual battle with one of the coolest sites on the Peninsula. The same attention to detail extends to the winery and the winemaking. Despite such minuscule production, exports to Singapore.

ŶŶŶŶŶ **Mornington Peninsula Chardonnay 2007** Glowing yellow-green; richly textured wine, with barrel ferment and malolactic components central to the style; some honeyed nutty elements adding to the flavour and mouthfeel. Screwcap. 13.5% alc. **Rating** 94 **To** 2014 $52
Half Acre Mornington Peninsula Pinot Noir 2006 Bright hue; typical elegant, finely polished wine; red cherry fruit offset by some savoury notes on the finish and aftertaste. Screwcap. 13.5% alc. **Rating** 94 **To** 2012 $69

Majella

Lynn Road, Coonawarra, SA 5263 **Region** Coonawarra
T (08) 8736 3055 **F** (08) 8736 3057 **www**.majellawines.com.au **Open** 7 days 10–4.30
Winemaker Bruce Gregory **Est.** 1969 **Cases** 15 000 **Vyds** 60 ha

Majella is one of the foremost grapegrowers in Coonawarra, with important vineyards, principally shiraz and cabernet sauvignon, and with a little riesling and merlot. The Malleea is one of Coonawarra's greatest wines, The Musician one of Australia's most outstanding red wines selling for less than $20. Exports to the UK, the US and other major markets.

ΨΨΨΨΨ **The Malleea 2005** Bright colour, very good hue; a delicious wine, has thrust and vitality to the range of red and black fruits on both bouquet and palate, the two varieties weld seamlessly together, and with the oak. High-quality cork. 15% alc. **Rating** 96 **To** 2020 $66

ΨΨΨΨΨ **Coonawarra Shiraz 2006** Bright colour, good hue; fresh, focused cassis blackcurrant fruit and clear-cut acidity; lingering but fine tannins. Screwcap. 14.5% alc. **Rating** 93 **To** 2020 $28
Coonawarra Cabernet Sauvignon 2006 Bright deep colour; classic medium-bodied cabernet; at once juicy yet firm, with tannins guiding the long finish; earth yet to appear, but it will. Screwcap. 14.5% alc. **Rating** 93 **To** 2021 $28
The Musician Coonawarra Cabernet Shiraz 2007 Majella has come up with yet another stylish Musician punching above its price weight; blackberry, plum and blackcurrant do all the flavour singing, while tannins handle the percussion. Screwcap. 14.5% alc. **Rating** 92 **To** 2015 $17

ΨΨΨΨ **Melody Coonawarra Rose 2008** Strongly herbal/leafy nuances; plenty of character in an offbeat style. Screwcap. 13% alc. **Rating** 88 **To** 2010 $16

 # Malone Wines   ★★★★☆

PMB 47, Naracoorte, SA 5271 **Region** Wrattonbully
T (08) 8764 6075 **F** (08) 8764 6060 **www.**malonewines.com.au **Open** Not
Winemaker Paulett **Est.** 2005 **Cases** 500 **Vyds** 23 ha
The third and fourth generations of the Malone family continue to farm the Talinga property, owned by the family since 1930. The planting of vines in '98 was a minor diversification from the core businesses of producing prime lamb, hay and pasture seed. The decision was taken to focus on shiraz and cabernet sauvignon, with most of the grapes being sold, and limited amounts made under the Malone label. The results have been impressive, to say the least.

ΨΨΨΨΨ **Wrattonbully Shiraz 2006** Impressive hue; an intense bouquet of plum and black fruits leads into a supple, medium-bodied palate with those fruits girdled by dark chocolate and quality.oak. Trophy Limestone Coast Wine Show '08. Screwcap. 14.5% alc. **Rating** 95 **To** 2020 $25

ΨΨΨΨΨ **Wrattonbully Cabernet Sauvignon 2006** Rich blackcurrant fruit, with touches of licorice and bitter chocolate, has good tannin support, likewise oak; good mouthfeel and overall balance. Screwcap. 14.5% alc. **Rating** 92 **To** 2021 $25

 # Mandala   ★★★★

1568 Melba Highway, Dixons Creek, Vic 3775 **Region** Yarra Valley
T (03) 5965 2016 **F** (03) 5965 2589 **www.**mandalawines.com.au **Open** 7 days 10–5
Winemaker Scott McCarthy (Contract) **Est.** 2007 **Cases** 5000 **Vyds** 27.4 ha
Mandala was officially opened in July 2008 by owner Charles Smedley. The estate vineyard has vines up to 20 years old, but the spectacular restaurant and cellar door complex is entirely new. The restaurant has deservedly achieved considerable praise under chef Mauro Callegari, whose stellar career began in Buenos Aires before moving between Melbourne and London, in each case working at acclaimed restaurants. The vineyards are primarily at the home base, Dixons Creek, with chardonnay (10.1 ha); sauvignon blanc, cabernet sauvignon and pinot noir (a little over 4 ha each); shiraz (1.7 ha) and merlot (0.4 ha); and a separate 2.5-ha vineyard of pinot noir at Yarra Junction with an impressive clonal mix.

ΨΨΨΨΨ **Prophet Yarra Valley Pinot Noir 2006** Light- to medium-bodied, but has plenty of varietal aromas and flavours in a red cherry and plum spectrum; better still is the persistence and length. Screwcap. 13.5% alc. **Rating** 92 **To** 2013 $45

Yarra Valley Chardonnay 2007 Has surprising weight and richness to its melon and stone fruit flavours, balanced by a touch of citrussy acidity. Drink sooner rather than later. Screwcap. 13% alc. **Rating** 90 **To** 2012 $25

ỢỢỢỢ   **Yarra Valley Sauvignon Blanc 2008** Restrained, gently grassy aromas on a clean bouquet; the palate has satisfying weight and flavour. Screwcap. 12.8% alc. **Rating** 89 **To** 2011 $18

Yarra Valley Pinot Noir 2007 Good crimson-purple hue; early picking has protected some varietal fruit expression, and the acidity is good; the flip side is diminished texture and mouthfeel. Screwcap. 13% alc. **Rating** 89 **To** 2013 $25

Yarra Valley Cabernet Merlot 2006 Good hue; light- to medium-bodied, with attractive cassis berry fruit; balanced tannins and oak. Screwcap. 14% alc. **Rating** 89 **To** 2014 $18

Yarra Valley Chardonnay 2006 Gentle melon and stone fruit, with a touch of oak; well balanced, but lacks intensity. Screwcap. 13% alc. **Rating** 87 **To** 2010 $22

Yarra Valley Pinot Noir 2006 Fresh, light colour; light-bodied plum, spice and forest notes; some acidity. Screwcap. 13% alc. **Rating** 87 **To** 2009 $22

Mandalay Estate ★★★

Mandalay Road, Donnybrook, WA 6239 **Region** Geographe
T (08) 9732 2006 **F** (08) 9732 2006 **www**.mandalayroad.com.au **Open** 7 days 10–5
Winemaker Fermoy Estate (Liz Dawson) **Est.** 1997 **Cases** 1000 **Vyds** 4 ha
Tony and Bernice O'Connell left careers in science and education to establish plantings of shiraz, chardonnay, zinfandel and cabernet sauvignon on their property in 1997. What started off as a fun venture has quickly turned into serious grapegrowing and winemaking. A hands-on approach with low yields has brought out the best characteristics of the grape varieties and the region. Exports to the US.

ỢỢỢỢ   **Mandalay Road Zinfandel 2007** A spicy/zesty wine with pleasant and persistent fruit, but not a great deal of structure. Young vines, perhaps. Screwcap. 15.2% alc. **Rating** 88 **To** 2011 $25

🌿 Marchand & Burch ★★★★★

C/- PO Box 1518, West Perth, WA 6872 **Region** Great Southern
T (08) 9336 9600 **F** (08) 9336 9622 **www**.marchandburchwines.com.au **Open** Not
Winemaker Pascal Marchand, Jeff Burch **Est.** 2006 **Cases** 1100
This is the first stage of a joint venture between Canadian-born and Burgundian-trained Pascal Marchand and the Burch family, who owns Howard Park. The first releases are of Chardonnay and Pinot Noir sourced from the Porongurup and Mount Barker subregions of the Great Southern and Shiraz from Frankland River/Margaret River. The Chardonnay, in particular, is outstanding. In late 2009, two Burgundies from '07 will be released: Gevrey Chambertin ($100) and Chambertin Clos de Beze ($465). Both will be screwcapped. Exports to the UK and the US.

ỢỢỢỢỢ   **Great Southern Chardonnay 2007** A thoroughly impressive wine; outstanding texture and mouthfeel invite comparison with Grand Cru White Burgundy; the length, too, is excellent, with seamless fruit and oak. Screwcap. 13.5% alc. **Rating** 97 **To** 2013 $65

Great Southern Chardonnay 2008 Grapefruit and stone fruit aromas give some clue of what is to come, but the wine literally explodes on the palate with the urgency of its thrust and energy; oak, nectarine, grapefruit and touches of cashew all coalesce on the finish. Screwcap. 13.5% alc. **Rating** 96 **To** 2018 $65

ỢỢỢỢỢ   **Mount Barrow Mount Barker Pinot Noir 2008** Excellent clarity and line, similar to the Gibraltar Rock; has more energy and thrust, with a pleasingly tangy edge to the small red fruits of the palate and finish. Screwcap. 13.5% alc. **Rating** 93 **To** 2016 $70

Margaret River Frankland River Shiraz 2007 Offers a panoply of aromas and flavours with spice, pepper, fine tannins and oak the main drivers; high-quality wine, but the winemaker inputs have partially marked the fruit. Screwcap. 14% alc. **Rating** 93 **To** 2017 $70

Gibraltar Rock Porongurup Pinot Noir 2008 A distinct step up from the '07 Great Southern Pinot; floral red fruits on the bouquet flow into the palate, which has sweet fruit until the savoury finish provides flavour balance. Screwcap. 13% alc. **Rating** 92 **To** 2015 $70

Great Southern Pinot Noir 2007 Deep crimson-purple; a complex wine, with strong oak influence on top of ripe dark fruits; not as exciting as the Chardonnay. Screwcap. 14.5% alc. **Rating** 91 **To** 2013 $70

Marcus Hill Vineyard   ★★★

560 Banks Road, Marcus Hill, Vic 3222 (postal) **Region** Geelong
T (03) 5222 5764 **www.**marcushillvineyard.com.au **Open** Not
Winemaker Darren Burke, Justyn Baker (Contract) **Est.** 2000 **Cases** NFP **Vyds** 3.58 ha
In 2000, Richard and Margot Harrison, together with 'gang pressed friends', planted 2 ha of pinot noir overlooking Port Lonsdale, Queenscliffe and Ocean Grove, a few kilometres from Bass Strait and Port Phillip Bay. Since then chardonnay, shiraz and pinot noir have been added. The vineyard is run with minimal sprays, and the aim is to produce elegant wines that truly express the maritime site.

♟♟♟♟ **Bellarine Peninsula Chardonnay 2007** Developed yellow–gold; a broad, rich, peachy style with barrel ferment influences adding to the overall impact. Screwcap. 12.5% alc. **Rating** 87 **To** 2011 $25

Mardia Wines   ★★★

Light Pass Road, Tanunda, SA 5352 **Region** Barossa Valley
T (08) 8563 1520 **F** (08) 8563 1697 **Open** Not
Winemaker Marco Litterini **Est.** 1987 **Cases** 250
A change of name (from Barossa Ridge Wine Estate) and of philosophy, now focusing on old vineyards in the Gomersal area of the Barossa Valley to produce Shiraz Cabernet under the Litterini label. Increasing retail distribution in Australia; exports to Switzerland, Germany, Malaysia and Thailand.

♟♟♟♟ **Litterini Barossa Valley Shiraz Cabernet 2007** A very savoury/earthy wine, with notes of chocolate and earth; not in the same league as the excellent '06, but that's vintage variation at work. Screwcap. 14.3% alc. **Rating** 89 **To** 2016 $29.95

Margan Family   ★★★★★

1238 Milbrodale Road, Broke, NSW 2330 **Region** Lower Hunter Valley
T (02) 6579 1317 **F** (02) 6579 1267 **www.**margan.com.au **Open** 7 days 10–5
Winemaker Andrew Margan **Est.** 1997 **Cases** 30 000 **Vyds** 100 ha
Andrew Margan, following in his father's footsteps, entered the wine industry over 20 years ago, and has covered a great deal of territory since, working as a Flying Winemaker in Europe, then for Tyrrell's. Andrew and wife Lisa now have over 80 ha of fully mature vines at their Ceres Hill property at Broke, and lease the nearby Vere Vineyard. Wine quality is consistently good. The rammed earth cellar door and restaurant are highly recommended. Exports to the UK, the US and other major markets.

♟♟♟♟♟ **Limited Release Shiraz Mourvedre 2007** Great colour; the only such blend in the Hunter Valley I am aware of, slightly surprising given the suitability of the climate; a lovely wine, the two components seamlessly woven in synergistic support. Screwcap. 14% alc. **Rating** 95 **To** 2022 $30

Hunter Valley Semillon 2008 Pale colour; pure lemon sherbet aroma; the palate is tightly knit with vibrant acidity and fruit, and just enough generosity for early drinking; the structure is there to reward patient cellaring. Screwcap. 11.5% alc. **Rating** 94 **To** 2020 $18

Limited Release Shiraz 2007 Deep purple-red; great example of the depth of flavour that the Hunter Valley can achieve with restrained alcohol; plum, blackberry and mocha flavours to a plushly textured palate; excellent oak and tannin balance. Screwcap. 13.5% alc. **Rating** 94 **To** 2022 $50

Limited Release Cabernet Sauvignon 2007 Elegant medium-bodied wine, with some slightly earthy regional overtones; blackcurrant fruit has juicy components alongside fine, savoury tannins. Very good wine for the region. Screwcap. 13.5% alc. **Rating** 94 **To** 2020 $30

ŸŸŸŸŸ **Limited Release Semillon 2007** Still at the dawn of its adult life, but showing the first hint of development; the bouquet is quiet, but the palate has great drive and length, with mouthfilling lemon, herb and minerally flavours. Screwcap. 11% alc. **Rating** 93 **To** 2020 $30

Hunter Valley Shiraz 2006 Bright red-purple; focused blackberry fruit is surrounded by well-handled French oak and persistent but fine tannins. Very good value; 40-year-old vines. Screwcap. 14.5% alc. **Rating** 92 **To** 2016 $20

Limited Release Barbera 2007 Strong crimson colour; fragrant and lively, offering plum, cherry and herbal flavours on the medium-bodied, well-balanced palate. A Margan speciality. Screwcap. 14% alc. **Rating** 91 **To** 2014 $30

Hunter Valley Barbera 2006 Well made and balanced, with tangy red fruits dusted with spice and a splash of oak; the variety doesn't trumpet its identity, but it's a good wine. Screwcap. 14% alc. **Rating** 90 **To** 2015 $25

ŸŸŸŸ **Hunter Valley Verdelho 2008** A generous smoky style, with an exuberant personality; dried straw comes through on the palate, with a zesty citrus finish. Screwcap. 13.5% alc. **Rating** 88 **To** 2012 $18

Hunter Valley Merlot 2006 A well-made, medium-bodied wine with all the requisite structure and balance, lacking only positive varietal character, not the fault of the winemaker. Screwcap. 13.5% alc. **Rating** 88 **To** 2014 $20

Marius Wines   ★★★★★

PO Box 545, Willunga, SA 5172 **Region** McLaren Vale
T 0402 344 340 **F** (08) 8556 4839 **www**.mariuswines.com.au **Open** By appt
Winemaker Roger Pike, James Hastwell **Est.** 1994 **Cases** 1000 **Vyds** 1.8 ha

Roger Pike says he has loved wine for over 30 years; that for 15 years he has had the desire to add a little bit to the world of wine; and that over a decade ago he decided to do something about it, ripping the front paddock and planting shiraz in 1994. He sold the grapes from the 1997–99 vintages, but when the '98 vintage became a single-vineyard wine (made by the purchaser of the grapes), selling in the US at $40, the temptation to make his own wine became irresistible. Exports to the US and Denmark.

ŸŸŸŸŸ **Symphony Single Vineyard McLaren Vale Shiraz 2007** Dense purple-crimson; has more concentration and depth than Simpatico, but is not overblown or extractive; comes from a small portion of the vineyard shared with Simpatico. Screwcap. 14.2% alc. **Rating** 94 **To** 2022 $35

Simpatico Single Vineyard McLaren Vale Shiraz 2006 A powerful, full-bodied wine that abounds with black fruits, licorice and bitter chocolate; while initially confronting, the appeal grows on retasting. Screwcap. 14.5% alc. **Rating** 94 **To** 2021 $25

ŸŸŸŸŸ **Simpatico Single Vineyard McLaren Vale Shiraz 2007** The bouquet immediately shows dark chocolate notes typical of the region and which join with the savoury blackberry fruit of the palate; good handling of French oak. Screwcap. 14% alc. **Rating** 92 **To** 2017 $25

Symposium McLaren Vale Shiraz Mourvedre 2007 A 50/50 blend, the mourvedre making its presence felt in no uncertain way with strong, tarry black fruits to the fore; the tannins are, however, controlled. Screwcap. 14.5% alc. **Rating** 91 **To** 2022 $30

Marlargo Wines

PO Box 371, Glenside, SA 5065 **Region** Various
T 0438 987 255 **F** (08) 8379 0596 **www**.marlargowines.com **Open** Not
Winemaker Various contract **Est.** 2003 **Cases** 10 000
This is the ultimate virtual winery, with virtual homes in Yarra Glen, McLaren Vale, Adelaide
Hills and the Clare Valley. Each of the garishly labelled wines is contract-made by a different
winemaker at a different winery, and the range is being extended further. The partners in the
venture are Simon Austerberry, a sixth-generation farmer in the Pyrenees, and Mark Gibbs, a
financial adviser from Melbourne. I'm far from convinced by the labels and purple prose (the
Latina Cabernet said 'be seduced...sultry, seductive, sensual' and assured us the wine is matured
in 'charismatic oak'). Both prices and production volume aspirations have been significantly –
and sensibly – reduced. Exports to the US, Canada and Singapore.

🍷🍷🍷🍷🍷 **Clare Valley Riesling 2008** Has an attractive range of citrus and tropical
fruit notes, gaining thrust and energy on the back-palate and finish. Well made.
Screwcap. 12% alc. **Rating** 91 **To** 2016 $20

🍷🍷🍷🍷 **Riverina Petit Verdot 2007** Petit verdot has an extraordinary ability to thrive in
irrigated vineyards without losing its power and spicy black fruits; only the tannins
are tamed, a good thing. Screwcap. 14.5% alc. **Rating** 88 **To** 2013 $25

Marsh Estate

Deasy's Road, Pokolbin, NSW 2321 **Region** Lower Hunter Valley
T (02) 4998 7587 **www**.marshestate.com.au **Open** Mon–Fri 10–4.30, w'ends 10–5
Winemaker Andrew Marsh **Est.** 1971 **Cases** 6000 **Vyds** 32 ha
Through sheer consistency, value for money and unrelenting hard work, the Marsh family has
built up a sufficiently loyal cellar door and mailing list clientele to allow all the production
to be sold direct. Wine style is always direct, with oak playing a minimal role, and prolonged
cellaring paying handsome dividends.

🍷🍷🍷🍷🍷 **Sinclair Hunter Valley Shiraz 2007** Bright colour; red, blue and black fruits
coexist, with oak providing spice; a big wine, with lively acidity, and great depth of
flavour; tannic, but fine-grained and long. Cork. 13.5% alc. **Rating** 94 **To** 2020 $55

🍷🍷🍷🍷🍷 **Vat S Hunter Valley Shiraz 2007** Dark mocha and fruitcake bouquet; plum
and blackberry coulis on the palate, with oak and tannin coming to the fore on
the conclusion; a little disjointed at this point in time. Cork. 13% alc. **Rating** 91
To 2018 $28.50
Holly's Block Hunter Valley Semillon 2008 A ripe style, straw and a touch of
nettle; lively palate, with prominent acidity, and plenty of lemon fruit on the finish.
Screwcap. 10.5% alc. **Rating** 90 **To** 2015 $27.50
Vat R Hunter Valley Shiraz 2007 Vibrant hue; blackberry and ironstone
bouquet, spice in the background; warm and ripe, with chewy tannin and slightly
prominent acidity on the finish. Diam. 13.5% alc. **Rating** 90 **To** 2016 $32.50

🍷🍷🍷🍷 **Hunter Valley Semillon 2008** Tight and taut lemon fruit bouquet; delivers the
same on the palate, with taut fruit and acidity on the finish. Screwcap. 10.5% alc.
Rating 87 **To** 2014 $21

Mason Wines

27850 New England Highway, Glen Aplin, Qld 4381 **Region** Granite Belt
T (07) 4684 1341 **www**.masonwines.com.au **Open** 7 days 11–4
Winemaker Jim Barnes **Est.** 1998 **Cases** 4000 **Vyds** 28.2 ha
Robert and Kim Mason set strict criteria when searching for land suited to viticulture: a long
history of commercial stone fruit production with well-drained, deep soil. The first property
was purchased in 1997, the vines planted thereafter. A second property was purchased in
2000, and a cellar door was constructed. They have planted cabernet sauvignon, chardonnay,
shiraz, merlot, verdelho, viognier, semillon, sauvignon blanc and petit verdot. Yet another
Queenslander on the ascent. Exports to Japan.

ᵀᵀᵀᵀᵀ **Granite Belt Semillon Sauvignon Blanc 2008** Has well above–average length and intensity to the quite luscious citrus, gooseberry and tropical fruit. Value from the Granite Belt. Screwcap. 13% alc. **Rating** 90 **To** 2012 $18

Granite Belt Cabernet Sauvignon 2007 Excellent blackcurrant fruit on the bouquet and palate, with notes of chocolate and cedar, in turn supported by ripe tannins. Estate-grown. Screwcap. 13.8% alc. **Rating** 90 **To** 2015 $18

ᵀᵀᵀᵀ **Granite Belt Shiraz 2007** Strong colour; generous blackberry and plum fruit; however, the texture of the wine does not flow easily; needed finishing. Screwcap. 14.5% alc. **Rating** 87 **To** 2013 $20

Massena Vineyards   ★★★★★

PO Box 54, Tanunda, SA 5352 **Region** Barossa Valley
T (08) 8564 3037 **F** (08) 8564 3038 **www.**massena.com.au **Open** By appt
Winemaker Dan Standish, Jaysen Collins **Est.** 2000 **Cases** 5000 **Vyds** 4 ha
Massena Vineyards draws upon 1 ha each of mataro (mourvedre), saperavi, primitivo (petite syrah) and tannat at Nuriootpa, also purchasing grapes from other growers. It is an export-oriented business although the wines can be purchased by mail order, which, given both the quality and innovative nature of the wines, seems more than ordinarily worthwhile. Exports to the UK, the US and other major markets.

ᵀᵀᵀᵀᵀ **The Surly Muse Barossa Valley Viognier 2008** A deft and poised bouquet, exhibiting attractive peach kernel and spice aromas; the palate is ample but not in the least bit heavy with focused fruit, and lively acidity; the conclusion is seamlessly balanced and fine. Now! Screwcap. 13.5% alc. **Rating** 95 **To** 2012 $17.50

The Howling Dog Barossa Valley Durif 2006 Bright colour; serious wine with the structure expected of this variety; rich plum/blackberry fruit and ripe tannins; good balance and length. Cork. 14.5% alc. **Rating** 94 **To** 2014 $35

ᵀᵀᵀᵀ **The Moonlight Run 2006** Very concentrated, but the fruit a little dead; very ripe, and quite sweet right across the palate, with the same confectionery character coming to the fore. Cork. 14.5% alc. **Rating** 88 **To** 2014 $25

Matilda's Estate   ★★★★

18 Hamilton Road, Denmark, WA 6333 **Region** Denmark
T (08) 9848 2622 **F** (08) 9848 2633 **www.**matildasestate.com **Open** 7 days 11–5
Winemaker Coby Ladwig, Brenden Smith **Est.** 1990 **Cases** 5000 **Vyds** 10 ha
In 2003 the founders of Matilda's Meadow (as it was then known), Don Turnbull and Pamela Meldrum, sold the business to former citizen of the world Steve Hall. It is a thriving business based on the estate plantings of chardonnay, semillon, sauvignon blanc, pinot noir, cabernet sauvignon, cabernet franc and merlot. Exports to Malaysia, Singapore and Hong Kong.

ᵀᵀᵀᵀᵀ **Chardonnay 2008** Brilliant straw-green; a stylish wine with a tightly focused varietal display of nectarine and grapefruit; oak held in restraint. Screwcap. 13.5% alc. **Rating** 92 **To** 2016 $35

Shiraz 2007 Fragrant spicy cool-grown style, light- to medium-bodied, but has both intensity and length to its mix of red and black fruit flavours. Screwcap. 13.5% alc. **Rating** 91 **To** 2016 $25

Cabernet Merlot Franc 2007 Light, but vivid crimson-purple; bright red fruits and snow pea notes attesting to cool growing conditions; silky tannins adorn the finish. Screwcap. 13% alc. **Rating** 91 **To** 2017 $25

Sauvignon Blanc 2008 Gentle but clean and clear-cut tropical fruit flavours run through a well-balanced and long palate. Screwcap. 12% alc. **Rating** 90 **To** 2011 $25

Pinot Noir 2007 A juicy, tangy wine with faint nuances of citrus and mint behind its primary red cherry and plum fruit; has good mouthfeel and length. Screwcap. 13.5% alc. **Rating** 90 **To** 2013 $35

ΨΨΨΨ **Classic White 2008** Bright, light green-straw; unusual blend (Chardonnay/ Semillon) in cool climates, but works well in a breezy, citrussy style; minerally acidity finishes the palate well. Screwcap. 12.5% alc. **Rating** 89 **To** 2012 $18

Maverick Wines

Lot 141 Light Pass Road, Vine Vale, Moorooroo, SA 5352 **Region** Barossa Valley
T (08) 8563 3551 **F** (08) 8563 3554 www.maverickwines.com.au **Open** By appt
Winemaker Christopher Taylor, Ronald Brown **Est.** 2004 **Cases** 8000 **Vyds** 37.6 ha
A new and ambitious venture of Ronald Brown, Jeremy Vogler, Adrian Bell and Christopher Taylor. Taking advantage of (likely short-lived) excess grape production in Australia, the partners have acquired four vineyards in key areas of the Eden Valley and Barossa Valley. With vines ranging in age from 40 to over 100 years. The wines are made in small batches in tanks of half a tonne to 3-tonne capacity, and are then matured in French oak. For a relatively new kid on the block – and a strong emphasis on export to countries ranging from Japan to the UK, the US and Russia – Maverick has already achieved celebrity listings in top restaurants and fine wine retailers such as Tetsuya's and Ultimo Wine Centre in Sydney, a dazzling array of hotels and restaurants in Tokyo, and the Hilton Hotel in Osaka.

ΨΨΨΨΨ **Trial Hill Eden Valley Shiraz 2006** A classy, medium-bodied wine, with an appealing mix of spicy and juicy fruit notes, and equally pleasing fine savoury tannins, smoky oak also contributing. Cork. 14.7% alc. **Rating** 96 **To** 2016 $60
Trial Hill Eden Valley Riesling 2008 Loaded to the gills with saturated lime juice aromas and flavours, yet not heavy thanks to sherbet acidity and a touch of CO_2. Now or much later. Screwcap. 12.5% alc. **Rating** 95 **To** 2016 $25

ΨΨΨΨΨ **Twins Barossa Shiraz 2007** Not an easy vintage, but this blend of three estate vineyards (one in the Eden Valley) shows that high alcohol was not the answer; an attractive array of juicy plum and blackberry fruit, with fine tannins. Screwcap. 14% alc. **Rating** 93 **To** 2017 $25
Twins Barossa Grenache Shiraz Mourvedre 2007 Very attractive, with fragrant red fruits and spices on both bouquet and palate; notwithstanding the alcohol, has freshness and good acidity. Screwcap. 15% alc. **Rating** 93 **To** 2014 $25
Greenock Rise Barossa Valley Grenache Shiraz Mourvedre 2007 Light, bright crimson; scented jujube confectionery grenache very much in the vanguard of both bouquet and palate, the mourvedre and shiraz providing structure. Cork. 15% alc. **Rating** 92 **To** 2015
Twins Barossa Cabernet Sauvignon Merlot Cabernet Franc 2007 A fragrant, light- to medium-bodied wine that demonstrates all things are possible; it has good varietal character, is not alcoholic, or tannic. Screwcap. 14% alc. **Rating** 90 **To** 2014 $25
Twins Eden Valley Chardonnay 2007 A clearly cut and polished wine, with precise stone fruit and citrus flavours, oak in the background of a long finish and aftertaste. Screwcap. 13.5% alc. **Rating** 90 **To** 2013

ΨΨΨΨ **Greenock Rise Barossa Valley Shiraz 2006** Potentially good varietal fruit from 50-year-old vines has to fight against a powdery mix of tannins and oak, and comes off second best. Cork. 15% alc. **Rating** 89 **To** 2014
Trial Hill Eden Valley Chardonnay 2007 Quite an exotic wine, and very toasty; the fruit exhibits a strong apricot aroma, which follows through on the palate; rich, but a little heavy. Cork. 13.5% alc. **Rating** 88 **To** 2010 $35

Maxwell Wines

Olivers Road, McLaren Vale, SA 5171 **Region** McLaren Vale
T (08) 8323 8200 **F** (08) 8323 8900 www.maxwellwines.com.au **Open** 7 days 10–5
Winemaker Mark Maxwell, Maria de Una **Est.** 1979 **Cases** 15 000
Maxwell Wines has come a long way since opening in 1979 using an amazing array of Heath Robinson equipment in cramped surroundings. A state-of-the-art and much larger winery was built in 1997. The brand has produced some excellent wines in recent years; it is also sourcing grapes from Kangaroo Island. Exports to all major markets.

ΨΨΨΨ **Ellen Street McLaren Vale Shiraz 2006** Very attractive; luscious blackberry, plum and chocolate fruit on the fleshy medium-bodied palate, with soft tannins and good oak. Screwcap. 15% alc. **Rating** 95 **To** 2026 $32.95

Minotaur Reserve McLaren Vale Shiraz 2006 Massively proportioned with dark chocolate, blackberry and a touch of tar and leather; the palate is thick, powerful and brooding, a slight bitter twist highlights the very attractive core of fruit that runs through to the finish. Cork. 15% alc. **Rating** 95 **To** 2025 $75

Lime Cave McLaren Vale Cabernet 2006 Expresses both variety and region on bouquet and palate, cassis and blackcurrant fruit framed by dark chocolate, the tannins fine and soft. Screwcap. 14.9% alc. **Rating** 94 **To** 2018 $32.95

ΨΨΨΨΨ **Four Roads McLaren Vale Shiraz Grenache Viognier 2006** Quite perfumed red and slightly spicy; raspberry with a hint of apricot from the viognier provide a juicy fine wine, underpinned by a steely backbone of dark shiraz fruit; very good value. Screwcap. 14.5% alc. **Rating** 91 **To** 2015 $19.95

ΨΨΨΨ **Silver Hammer McLaren Vale Shiraz 2006** A powerful full-bodied palate; abundant black fruits, and even more abundant tannins needing to soften their grip. Screwcap. 14.5% alc. **Rating** 88 **To** 2015 $19.95

Little Demon McLaren Vale Cabernet Merlot 2006 Solid, ripe, medium- to full-bodied wine speaking more loudly about its region of origin than its varietal origin; has no shortage of flavour. Screwcap. 14.5% alc. **Rating** 88 **To** 2013 $16.95

Mayer
★★★★☆

66 Miller Road, Healesville, Vic 3777 **Region** Yarra Valley
T (03) 5967 3779 **www**.timomayer.com.au **Open** By appt
Winemaker Timo Mayer **Est.** 1999 **Cases** 600

Timo Mayer, also winemaker at Gembrook Hill Vineyard, teamed with partner Rhonda Ferguson to establish Mayer Vineyard on the slopes of Mt Toolebewoong, 8 km south of Healesville. The steepness of those slopes is presumably 'celebrated' in the name given to the wines (Bloody Hill). There is just under 2.5 ha of vineyard, the lion's share to pinot noir, and smaller amounts of shiraz and chardonnay – all high-density plantings. Mayer's winemaking credo is minimal interference and handling, and no filtration.

ΨΨΨΨΨ **Close Planted Yarra Valley Pinot Noir 2007** Charry oak is prominent on the bouquet, with some whole berry complexity providing interest beside the dark plum and cherry fruit; initially quite firm and strict, the bright plum fruit opens on the back of the palate with sweet-fruited generosity. Diam. 13.2% alc. **Rating** 93 **To** 2014 $50

Big Betty Yarra Valley Shiraz 2007 Reductive on opening, showing tar and pitch on the bouquet; the palate tells the real story with blue and red fruits intermingling to provide a spicy medium-bodied platform from which to launch; savoury and engaging on the finish. Diam. 13.8% alc. **Rating** 93 **To** 2017 $35

Bloody Hill Yarra Valley Chardonnay 2007 Fresh-fruited with melon and a splash of lemon and spice; the palate is lively with focused acidity; distinctly savoury; a mineral edge to the finish. Diam. 13.2% alc. **Rating** 90 **To** 2014 $30

Bloody Hill Yarra Valley Pinot Noir 2007 A little reduced, with a distinct charry edge to the fruit; bright cranberry fruit on the palate, and a spicy stem character coming through on the finish. Diam. 13.2% alc. **Rating** 90 **To** 2012 $27

Mayfield Vineyard
★★★★★

Icely Road, Orange, NSW 2800 **Region** Orange
T (02) 6365 9292 **www**.mayfieldvineyard.com **Open** W'ends 10–5, or by appt
Winemaker Jon Reynolds (Contract) **Est.** 1998 **Cases** 7000 **Vyds** 37 ha

The property – including the house in which owners Richard and Kathy Thomas now live, and its surrounding arboretum – has a rich history as a leading Suffolk sheep stud, founded upon the vast fortune accumulated by the Crawford family via its biscuit business in the UK. The Thomases planted the vineyard in 1998, with merlot (15.3 ha) leading the way, followed (in descending order) by cabernet sauvignon, sauvignon blanc, chardonnay, pinot noir, riesling and sangiovese. The wines are marketed under the Mayfield Vineyard and Icely Road brands. Exports to the UK.

ՈՈՈՈՈ **Single Vineyard Orange Riesling 2008** Distinct citrus blossom aromas; a delicate, yet precise and intense, palate, with a mix of lime and mineral flavours, finishing with zest. Screwcap. 12.5% alc. **Rating** 94 **To** 2016 $28
Icely Road Orange Chardonnay 2007 A fragrant bouquet leads into a remarkably focused and intense palate, with stone fruit, grapefruit and cashew flavours running through to a long finish. Screwcap. 13.5% alc. **Rating** 94 **To** 2015 $21.50

ՈՈՈՈՑ **Icely Road Orange Sauvignon Blanc 2008** A crisp and clean bouquet; the palate has good drive and concentration, yet further proof of the quality of Orange sauvignon blanc, with an appealing touch of passionfruit lifting the flavour, and more grassy notes giving structure. Screwcap. 13.5% alc. **Rating** 92 **To** 2010 $21.50
Icely Road Orange Sangiovese 2007 Bright hue; an eminently enjoyable cherry/sour cherry-driven wine, without any uncomfortable savoury tannins. Screwcap. 14.5% alc. **Rating** 90 **To** 2012 $25

ՈՈՈՈ **Icely Road Orange Riesling 2008** Very pale; a slightly reductive bouquet and palate partially obscures the citrus and herb fruit. Screwcap. 12.5% alc. **Rating** 87 **To** 2014 $21.50
Icely Road Orange Cabernet Merlot 2006 Light colour; a pleasant, well-balanced, light- to medium-bodied wine with red fruits and gossamer tannins; ready to drink right now. Screwcap. 14% alc. **Rating** 87 **To** 2011 $21.50
Single Vineyard Orange Cabernet Sauvignon 2006 A pleasant wine, with red fruits, but lacking depth in the colour and flavour; perhaps over-cropped. Screwcap. 14.5% alc. **Rating** 87 **To** 2012 $28

Maygars Hill Winery ★★★★

53 Longwood-Mansfield Road, Longwood, Vic 3665 **Region** Strathbogie Ranges
T 0402 136 448 **F** (03) 5798 5457 **www.**strathbogieboutiquewines.com **Open** By appt
Winemaker Plunkett Fowles **Est.** 1997 **Cases** 950 **Vyds** 3.2 ha
Jenny Houghton purchased this 8-ha property in 1994, planting shiraz (1.9 ha) and cabernet sauvignon (1.3 ha), and establishing a stylish B&B cottage. The name comes from Lieutenant Colonel Maygar, who fought with outstanding bravery in the Boer War in South Africa in 1901, and was awarded the Victoria Cross. In World War I he rose to command the 8th Light Horse Regiment, winning yet further medals for bravery. He died on 1 November 1917. Exports to Fiji.

ՈՈՈՈՑ **Cabernet Sauvignon 2007** Bright and clean, with redcurrant and a splash of dried herb; sweet-fruited palate with fine structure and a fresh finish. Screwcap. 14% alc. **Rating** 90 **To** 2012 $20

ՈՈՈՈ **Shiraz 2007** Bright colour; smoky bouquet, with redcurrant fruit beneath; the palate is fleshy, but dries out a little at the end. Screwcap. 14.5% alc. **Rating** 87 **To** 2014 $22

Meadowbank Estate ★★★★☆

699 Richmond Road, Cambridge, Tas 7170 **Region** Southern Tasmania
T (03) 6248 4484 **F** (03) 6248 4485 **www.**meadowbankwines.com.au **Open** 7 days 10–5
Winemaker Contract **Est.** 1974 **Cases** 6000
An important part of the Ellis family business on what was once a large grazing property on the banks of the Derwent. Increased plantings are under contract to Hardys, and a splendid winery has been built to handle the increased production. The winery complex has expansive entertainment and function facilities, plus a large restaurant, and presents an arts and music program. Exports to Germany, Sweden, the Netherlands and Hong Kong.

ΨΨΨΨΨ **FGR Riesling 2008** A quiet bouquet, then a delicious palate with near-explosive energy; lime juice sweetness balanced by acidity and CO_2. Screwcap. 8.2% alc. **Rating** 94 **To** 2015 $31

ΨΨΨΨΨ **Salvation Devil's Own Brut NV** Pale rose; elegant and crisp, showing strong pinot component; bracing acidity demands a food background. Diam. 12% alc. **Rating** 90 **To** 2013 $29

ΨΨΨΨ **Unwooded Chardonnay 2006** Has abundant flavour and length; stone fruit and citrus on a long palate. Screwcap. 13.5% alc. **Rating** 88 **To** 2011 $29

Medhurst
★★★★

24–26 Medhurst Road, Gruyere, Vic 3770 **Region** Yarra Valley
T (03) 5964 9022 **F** (03) 5964 9033 **www**.medhurstwines.com.au **Open** Fri–Mon 10–5
Winemaker Dominique Portet **Est.** 2000 **Cases** 2500 **Vyds** 14 ha
The wheel has come full circle for Ross and Robyn Wilson. In the course of a very distinguished corporate career, Ross was CEO of Southcorp during the time it brought the Penfolds, Lindemans and Wynns businesses under the Southcorp banner. For her part, Robyn spent her childhood in the Yarra Valley, her parents living less than a kilometre away as the crow flies from Medhurst. Immaculately sited and tended vineyard blocks, most on steep, north-facing slopes, promise much for the future. The vineyard is planted to sauvignon blanc, chardonnay, pinot noir, cabernet sauvignon and shiraz, all run on a low-yield basis. Red Shed is the newly introduced second label, taking its name from the recently opened café.

ΨΨΨΨΨ **Yarra Valley Chardonnay 2008** An interesting and convincing example of early picking, which has resulted in elegance and freshness, but not stripped the palate of flavour or length. Will develop well. Screwcap. 12% alc. **Rating** 92 **To** 2016 $22.50
Yarra Valley Pinot Noir 2006 Despite a stained cork, retains a bright red hue; has plenty of red cherry and plum fruit, with a touch of forest on the finish giving complexity. 13.5% alc. **Rating** 91 **To** 2012 $30

ΨΨΨΨ **Yarra Valley Rose 2008** An unusually savoury style, some spicy notes before an emphatic, dry finish. Screwcap. 14% alc. **Rating** 89 **To** 2009 $18.50
Yarra Valley Shiraz 2006 An elegant, but distinctly savoury wine, the spicy blackberry fruit supported by prominent tannins; needs more time. Cork. 14% alc. **Rating** 89 **To** 2014 $25
Yarra Valley Cabernet Sauvignon 2005 Leaf, spice, cedar and berry fruit aromas coalesce on a well-balanced palate, which has good length and balance. Cork. 14% alc. **Rating** 89 **To** 2013 $25
Yarra Valley Sauvignon Blanc 2008 Has aromas of grass and capsicum, the palate in a similar spectrum, adding a touch of asparagus; food style, perhaps. Screwcap. 14% alc. **Rating** 88 **To** 2010 $20

Meerea Park
★★★★★

188 Palmers Lane, Pokolbin, NSW 2320 **Region** Lower Hunter Valley
T (02) 4998 7474 **www**.meereapark.com.au **Open** At The Boutique Wine Centre, Pokolbin
Winemaker Rhys Eather **Est.** 1991 **Cases** 10 000
All the wines are produced from grapes purchased from growers primarily in the Pokolbin area, but also from the Upper Hunter, and as far afield as Young. It is the brainchild of Rhys Eather, a great-grandson of Alexander Munro, a leading vigneron in the mid-19th century; he makes the wine at the former Little's Winery at Palmers Lane in Pokolbin, which was purchased in 2007 and is now named Meerea Park. Exports to the UK, the US, and other major markets.

ΨΨΨΨΨ **Alexander Munro Individual Vineyard Hunter Valley Shiraz 2006** Good crimson hue; distinguished Hunter style, certain to age gracefully, the black fruits supported by perfect tannins. Screwcap. 14.5% alc. **Rating** 95 **To** 2030 $70
Epoch Semillon 2008 Right in the mainstream of young Hunter Valley semillon, its future assured; grass, herb and lemon zest flavours are supported and balanced by crisp acidity. Screwcap. 10% alc. **Rating** 94 **To** 2016 $20

Alexander Munro Individual Vineyard Hunter Valley Semillon 2004
Bright straw-green; complex toasty/smoky aromas, then a hyper-intense palate
with driving acidity coating the lemon fruit at its core. Screwcap. 10.5% alc.
Rating 94 **To** 2015 $35
Terracotta Hunter Valley Shiraz 2006 Bright colour; the inclusion of 5%
co-fermented viognier works well, taking the wine outside the usual context of
Hunter shiraz into lifted red fruit territory; finishes with fine tannins. Screwcap.
14% alc. **Rating** 94 **To** 2020 $55

ρρρρ♀ **Hell Hole Hunter Valley Semillon 2008** Typical young semillon, the bouquet
locked up, but the wine springs to life on the palate, with grainy, zesty lemon-
accented fruit. The future is assured. Screwcap. 10.5% alc. **Rating** 93 **To** 2018 $25
Terracotta Semillon 2004 Bright straw-green; strikingly similar aromas to the
Alexander Munro, the palate less intense but better balanced, perhaps. A pair of
striking wines. Screwcap. 10.5% alc. **Rating** 93 **To** 2014 $30
Hell Hole Hunter Valley Shiraz 2006 Deep, but bright colour; voluminous
shiraz fruit aromas and flavours are supported by positive tannins; long range
proposition and will reward. Screwcap. 13.5% alc. **Rating** 93 **To** 2026 $55
XYZ Hunter Valley Shiraz 2007 Good hue and depth of colour; fresh, bright
fruit profile, the flavours in a cherry/raspberry range. Experimental wine; 110 cases
made. Screwcap. 13.5% alc. **Rating** 92 **To** 2016 $40
Alexander Munro Individual Vineyard Hunter Valley Chardonnay 2008
Pleasant wine, with ripe stone fruit and melon flavours, bolstered by enough
acidity to provide balance and length. Screwcap. 13% alc. **Rating** 90 **To** 2012 $30

ρρρρ **The Aunts Shiraz 2006** Light, bright colour; dark cherry and plum fruit is
neatly supported by a light web of ripe tannins and vanilla oak. Will develop well.
Screwcap. 13.5% alc. **Rating** 89 **To** 2016 $26
Shiraz Viognier 2007 The 5% viognier component was co-fermented with
the shiraz, but I remain to be convinced that Hunter Valley shiraz (in common
with other warm areas) is enhanced by viognier. A pleasant wine, but no more.
Screwcap. 14% alc. **Rating** 89 **To** 2014 $20
Verdelho 2008 Light fruit salad aromas and flavours, possibly early picked to
thwart vintage rain; fresh finish Screwcap. 12.5% alc. **Rating** 87 **To** 2011 $15
Viognier 2007 A touch of French oak adds to the texture, but also shapes aspects
of the flavour, clearly adding interest to the wine. Screwcap. 14% alc. **Rating** 87
To 2011 $23

 # Melross Estate   **NR**
50 Brooke Street, Moonambel, Vic 3478 **Region** Pyrenees
T (03) 5467 2203 **www**.melrossestate.com **Open** W'ends & public hols 10–4, or by appt
Winemaker Graeme Jukes **Est.** 2002 **Cases** 5000 **Vyds** 10 ha
Ross and Helen Camfield planted their vineyard in 2002; the plantings were of shiraz
(4.5 ha), with cuttings taken from the Old Block at Best's, sangiovese (2 ha) and pinot gris
(3.5 ha). Further plantings of merlot and tempranillo will follow at the end of 2009. The vines
are grafted onto drought-resistant rootstocks, and the soil is grey-brown loamy sand with
small granules of quartz stone on top of a red clay base. Until 2007 the wines were made
by Dominique Portet, the Pinot Gris in a deliberate 'French' style. Eighty per cent of the
production is exported to China.

Mermerus Vineyard
60 Soho Road, Drysdale, Vic 3222 **Region** Geelong
T (03) 5253 2718 **F** (03) 5251 1555 **www**.mermerus.com.au **Open** Sun 11–4
Winemaker Paul Champion **Est.** 2000 **Cases** 600 **Vyds** 2.5 ha
Paul Champion has established pinot noir, chardonnay and riesling at Mermerus since 1996.
The wines are made from the small but very neat winery on the property, with small batch
handling and wild yeast fermentation playing a major part in the winemaking, oak taking a
back seat. He also acts as contract winemaker for small growers in the region.

ŢŢŢŢ   **Chardonnay 2007** Rich and ripe, with fresh fig, peach and a little nectarine; toasty, a touch of butterscotch on the palate; good acidity and focus on the finish Screwcap. 13.7% alc. **Rating** 88 **To** 2012 $20
Dry White 2008 Fresh and zesty with straw complementing the lemon fruit; vibrant and lively finish. Screwcap. 13% alc. **Rating** 87 **To** 2011 $16.50
Pinot Noir 2007 Vibrant colour; ripe cherry fruit bouquet; quite firm and showing lots of extract and tannin on the palate; the varietal fruit is dominated by the structure at this point in time. Screwcap. 14% alc. **Rating** 87 **To** 2012 $22

Merops Wines   ★★★

5992 Caves Road, Margaret River, WA 6825 **Region** Margaret River
T (08) 9757 9195 **F** (08) 9757 3193 **www.**meropswines.com.au **Open** By appt
Winemaker Flying Fish Cove **Est.** 2000 **Cases** 3000 **Vyds** 5.3 ha
Jim and Yvonne Ross have been involved in horticulture for over 25 years, in production, retail nurseries and viticulture. They established a nursery and irrigation business in the Margaret River township in 1985 before establishing a rootstock nursery. In 2000 they removed the nursery and planted cabernet sauvignon, cabernet franc, merlot and shiraz on the laterite gravel over clay soils. They use the practices developed by Professor William Albrecht in the US 50 years ago, providing mineral balance and thus eliminating the need for insecticides and toxic sprays. Organic pre-certification was completed in 2007, which resulted in the '08 vintage being certified organic. Over the years the wines have won numerous bronze medals at Australian wine shows, Ornatus having particular success at the International Wine & Spirit Competition (London), with Best in Class silver medals. Exports to the US and Singapore.

Merricks Estate

Thompsons Lane, Merricks, Vic 3916 **Region** Mornington Peninsula
T (03) 5989 8416 **F** (03) 9613 4242 **www.**merricksestate.com.au **Open** 1st w'end of month, each w'end in Jan & public hol w'ends 12–5
Winemaker Paul Evans **Est.** 1977 **Cases** 750
Melbourne solicitor George Kefford, with wife Jacquie, runs Merricks Estate as a weekend and holiday enterprise. Right from the outset it has produced distinctive, spicy, cool-climate Shiraz, which has accumulated an impressive array of show trophies and gold medals. For some inexplicable reason, no Shiraz was tasted for this edition.

ŢŢŢŢŢ   **Close Planted Mornington Peninsula Pinot Noir 2007** Bright colour; highly fragrant; has a vibrant palate replete with red and black fruits, and a strikingly long finish; lovely pinot. Diam. 13.5% alc. **Rating** 96 **To** 2017 $57
Close Planted Mornington Peninsula Pinot Noir 2006 Light colour showing some development; spicy/savoury fragrance flows through to the palate, which is seriously long and very fine. Cork. 13.5% alc. **Rating** 95 **To** 2016 $57
Mornington Peninsula Pinot Noir 2007 Slightly deeper colour than Close Planted; an altogether bigger wine, with luscious plum and black cherry; good line and length. Diam. 13.5% alc. **Rating** 94 **To** 2016 $46

🍇 Michael Hall Wines

10 George Street, Tanunda, SA 5352 (postal) **Region** Mount Lofty Ranges Zone
T 0419 126 290 **F** (08) 8562 2172 **www.**michaelhallwines.com **Open** Not
Winemaker Michael Hall **Est.** 2008 **Cases** 300
For reasons no longer relevant (however interesting) Michael Hall was once a jewellery valuer for Sotheby's in Switzerland. He came to Australia in 2001 to pursue winemaking, a lifelong interest, and undertook the wine science degree at CSU, graduating as dux in 2005. His vintage work in Australia and France is a veritable who's who: in Australia with Cullen, Giaconda, Henschke, Shaw & Smith, Coldstream Hills and Veritas; in France with Domaine Leflaive, Meo-Camuzet, Vieux Telegraphe and Trevallon. He now works for Rocland Estate in Nuriootpa, but has the right to make his own wines in the Rocland winery. They are as impressive as his CV suggests they should be.

🍷🍷🍷🍷🍷 Piccadilly Valley Chardonnay 2007 Super-concentrated and rich; peach, nectarine and fig fruit framed by strong barrel ferment French oak; obvious lees and mlf influences. Striking wine in all respects. Diam. 14% alc. **Rating** 94 **To** 2014 $45

Sang de Pigeon Barossa Shiraz Saignee 2008 Has considerable grip and texture without bitterness; a rose built from the ground up with intensity, balance, length and a dry finish. Screwcap. 14.1% alc. **Rating** 94 **To** 2010 $25

Flaxman's Valley Eden Valley Syrah 2007 Medium red-purple; a spicy/savoury bouquet and palate, almost as if there was a touch of grenache (there isn't); very sophisticated winemaking gives the wine great drive on the back-palate and finish. Diam. 14.8% alc. **Rating** 94 **To** 2020 $45

Michael Unwin Wines   ★★★★

2 Racecourse Road, on the Western Highway, Beaufort, Vic 3373 **Region** Western Victoria Zone
T (03) 5349 2021 **F** (03) 5349 2032 **www**.michaelunwinwines.com.au **Open** Mon–Fri 8.30–5, w'ends 11–4.30
Winemaker Michael Unwin **Est.** 2000 **Cases** 2000
Michael Unwin, a veteran of 27 vintages, learned the art of winemaking around the world with some of the most influential and forward thinking winemakers of our time. The winery location was chosen because it is the geographical centre of the best viticultural areas in Western Victoria. The grapes are grown in up to six mature vineyards, all with different site climates. In all, approximately 2 ha of shiraz and 1 ha each of cabernet sauvignon, sangiovese, barbera, durif, riesling and chardonnay are grown or contracted.

🍷🍷🍷🍷🍷 Acrobat Umbrella Man Riesling 2008 A generous wine with tropical overtones to the fruit, but without becoming soft or blowsy; good length and aftertaste. Screwcap. 12% alc. **Rating** 90 **To** 2014 $20

Acrobat Umbrella Man Merlot 2006 Clear-cut merlot aromas and flavours, spice, olive, cassis and blackcurrant all interwoven on the medium-bodied palate, which has good length and texture. Screwcap. 13.5% alc. **Rating** 90 **To** 2014 $26

🍷🍷🍷🍷 Acrobat Umbrella Man Chardonnay 2007 Bright green-gold; a curious wine, in some ways quite developed, in some respects rich, but not in others. Difficult to read. Screwcap. 13% alc. **Rating** 88 **To** 2013 $26

Acrobat Umbrella Man Cabernet Sauvignon 2006 Some spicy/herbal nuances to the bouquet and repeat on the light- to medium-bodied palate; some regional mint also evident. Screwcap. 13% alc. **Rating** 87 **To** 2014 $26

Michelini Wines

Great Alpine Road, Myrtleford, Vic 3737 **Region** Alpine Valleys
T (03) 5751 1990 **F** (03) 5751 1410 **www**.micheliniwines.com.au **Open** 7 days 10–5
Winemaker Greg O'Keefe **Est.** 1982 **Cases** 10 000 **Vyds** 34 ha
The Michelini family is among the best known grapegrowers in the Buckland Valley of Northeast Victoria. Having migrated from Italy in 1949, the Michelinis originally grew tobacco, diversifying into vineyards in 1982. The vineyard, on terra rossa soil, is at an altitude of 300 m, mostly with frontage to the Buckland River. The winery can handle 1000 tonnes of fruit, which eliminates the problem of moving grapes out of a declared phylloxera area. Exports to NZ.

🍷🍷🍷🍷 Pinot Grigio 2008 Pale in colour; lemon, straw and a touch of pear aromas; a little savoury on the palate, with the straw lending a distinctly Italian feel to the wine. Screwcap. 13.5% alc. **Rating** 89 **To** 2012 $17.50

Middlesex 31

PO Box 367, Manjimup, WA 6258 **Region** Manjimup
T (08) 9771 2499 **F** (08) 9771 2499 **Open** Not
Winemaker Brenden Smith, Dave Cleary, Mark Aitken **Est.** 1990 **Cases** 1000 **Vyds** 6.5 ha

Dr John Rosser (a local GP who runs the Manjimup Medical Centre) and Rosemary Davies have planted 6.5 ha of vines, predominantly to shiraz, chardonnay and verdelho, but with a little patch of pinot noir.

Chardonnay 2007 Attractive, harmonious and supple with ripe, generous, peachy fruit. Screwcap. 14.2% alc. **Rating** 93 **To** 2011 $18

Mihi Creek Vineyard ★★★

1292 Enmore Road, Mihi via Uralla, NSW 2358 (postal) **Region** New England
T (02) 6778 2166 www.home.bluepin.net.au/mihicreek **Open** Not
Winemaker Merilba Estate (Shaun Cassidy) **Est.** 2003 **Cases** NFP **Vyds** 1.8 ha
Andrew and Belinda Close purchased 180 ha of what was part of a large sheep and cattle property called Mihi Station in 2001. The property is situated at an elevation of 1000 m, planted with trial amounts of sauvignon blanc, viognier, pinot noir, cabernet sauvignon and merlot on a 1.8-ha vineyard in 2003. Sauvignon Blanc has performed best, and small amounts were made (and sold) from the 2006 and '07 vintages. Says Andrew Close, 'At the moment, the Sauvignon Blanc seems to be going really well. The viognier, merlot and cabernet sauvignon are a real struggle and the pinot noir over time I think will improve…if it doesn't kill me in the meantime.'

New England Sauvignon Blanc 2006 Well made; a fresh and lively palate, with lemongrass, herb and gooseberry flavours; clean finish. Screwcap. 12% alc. **Rating** 88 **To** 2009 $15

Mike Press Wines ★★★★☆

PO Box 224, Lobethal, SA 5241 **Region** Adelaide Hills
T (08) 8389 5546 **F** (08) 8389 5548 www.mikepresswines.com.au **Open** Not
Winemaker Mike Press **Est.** 1998 **Cases** 10 000 **Vyds** 23.2 ha
Mike and Judy Press established their Kenton Valley Vineyards in 1998, when they purchased 34 ha of land in the Adelaide Hills at an elevation of 500 m. Over the next two years they planted mainstream, cool-climate varieties (merlot, shiraz, cabernet sauvignon, sauvignon blanc, chardonnay and pinot noir), intending to sell the grapes to other wine producers. Even an illustrious 42-year career in the wine industry did not prepare Mike for the downturn in grape prices that followed, and that led to the development of the Mike Press wine label. They produce Sauvignon Blanc, Chardonnay, Pinot Noir, Merlot, Shiraz, Cabernet Merlot and Cabernet Sauvignon, which, despite accumulating gold medals and trophies, are sold at low prices.

MP1 Adelaide Hills Cabernet Sauvignon 2007 Strong crimson-purple; potent, rich and powerful blackcurrant fruit powers the luscious palate; the tannins are fine, the oak in a back-seat role. Screwcap. 14% alc. **Rating** 94 **To** 2020 $25

Adelaide Hills Merlot 2006 Attractive mix of small red berry fruits and more savoury notes entirely appropriate for merlot. Screwcap. 13.8% alc. **Rating** 90 **To** 2014 $12.99
Adelaide Hills Shiraz 2007 Strong crimson; black and red fruit aromas with plenty of mid-palate richness, yet retaining a fresh and lively finish; good acidity, little or no oak evident. Bargain. Screwcap. 14% alc. **Rating** 90 **To** 2012 $10.99

Adelaide Hills Cabernet Sauvignon 2007 Bright hue; some minty fruit notes and lots of oak before evening out on the quite long finish. Screwcap. 14.5% alc. **Rating** 88 **To** 2012 $11.60

Miles from Nowhere ★★★☆

PO Box 8129, Subiaco East, WA 6008 **Region** Margaret River
T (08) 9212 9100 **F** (08) 9212 9199 www.milesfromnowhere.com.au **Open** Not
Winemaker Brian Fletcher **Est.** 2007 **Cases** 6000 **Vyds** 20 ha

Miles from Nowhere is the born again business of Franklin (Frank) and Heather Tate; Frank was CEO of Evans & Tate for many years, and Brian Fletcher was his chief winemaker. The demise of Evans & Tate has been well chronicled, but has not prevented the Tates (and Brian) from doing what they know best. The plantings of petit verdot, chardonnay, shiraz, sauvignon blanc, semillon, viognier, cabernet sauvignon and merlot are scattered across the Margaret River region, miles from nowhere.

ΨΨΨΨΨ **Margaret River Sauvignon Blanc Semillon 2008** A complex bouquet of grass, asparagus and citrus leads into a palate full of flavour and zest, with some tropical fruit components; acidity keeps the wine in good balance. Screwcap. 12.5% alc. **Rating** 91 **To** 2012 $17

ΨΨΨΨ **Margaret River Cabernet Merlot 2007** There is some lift to the aromas of berry, leaf and mint, characters that flow though the light- to medium-bodied palate; good length. Screwcap. 14% alc. **Rating** 89 **To** 2014 $17

Milhinch Wines

PO Box 655, Greenock, SA 5360 **Region** Barossa Valley
T (08) 8563 4003 **F** (08) 8563 4003 www.seizetheday.net.au **Open** At Barossa Small Winemakers, Chateau Tanunda
Winemaker Contract **Est.** 2003 **Cases** 1200 **Vyds** 4 ha
Peter Milhinch and Sharyn Rogers have established 2 ha each of shiraz and cabernet sauvignon near the Greenock Creek, which (sometimes) flows through their Seppeltsfield property. At the foot of their vineyard is Seppeltsfield Vineyard Cottage, a restored German settlers cottage offering luxury accommodation for one couple. The Cottage has won three successive SA Tourism Awards, two National Tourism Awards and was inducted into the SA Tourism Hall of Fame in 2007. The Cottage project and Peter and Sharyn's wine production began in 2003 when Peter was recovering from cancer. They gained inspiration and hope from legendary American cyclist Lance Armstrong's own cancer journey, so much so that the Seize the Day phrase on their wine labels has been borrowed from Lance's book, *It's Not About the Bike*. Exports to Singapore.

ΨΨΨΨΨ **Seize the Day Single Vineyard Barossa Valley Cabernet Sauvignon 2006** Serious cabernet with complex aromas of violets, cedar, cassis and a touch of black olive; wonderfully pure on the palate, with great depth to the full-bodied fruit. Screwcap. 14.5% alc. **Rating** 94 **To** 2018 $38

ΨΨΨΨΨ **Seize the Day Single Vineyard Barossa Valley Shiraz 2006** Deep colour; slightly savoury notes, with red fruits and hints of mocha; good weight with bright acidity, and good persistence of dark fruits on the finish. Screwcap. 14.9% alc. **Rating** 91 **To** 2018 $38

Millamolong Estate

Millamolong Road, Mandurama, NSW 2792 **Region** Orange
T 0429 635 191 **F** (02) 6367 4088 www.millamolong.com **Open** 7 days 9–4
Winemaker Madrez Wine Services, Lowe Family Wines **Est.** 2000 **Cases** 1000
This is a book about wine, not polo, but it so happens that Millamolong Estate has been the centrepiece of Australian polo for over 80 years. For an even longer period, generations of James Ashton (differentiated by their middle name) have been at the forefront of a dynasty to make *Rawhide* or *McLeod's Daughters* seem tame. In the context of this, 28 ha of chardonnay, riesling, cabernet, shiraz and merlot may seem incidental, but it happens to add to the luxury accommodation at the main homestead, which caters for up to 18 guests.

ΨΨΨΨΨ **26 Ponies Orange Chardonnay 2007** Bright straw-green; fragrant white peach and nectarine fruit drives the bouquet and palate; attractive mouthfeel with balanced oak and acidity. Screwcap. 13% alc. **Rating** 93 **To** 2015 $20

ΨΨΨΨ **56 Miles Orange Shiraz 2007** A fragrant, spicy array of red and black fruits on the bouquet, and long, vibrant light- to medium-bodied palate. Not profound, but has plenty of charm. Screwcap. 13.9% alc. **Rating** 89 **To** 2013 $20

24 Goals Orange Riesling 2007 Tight structure and texture around a core of bitter lemon flavour; good acidity. Screwcap. 11.5% alc. **Rating** 88 **To** 2014 $20

Millbrook Winery ★★★★★

Old Chestnut Lane, Jarrahdale, WA 6124 **Region** Perth Hills
T (08) 9525 5796 **F** (08) 9525 5672 **www**.millbrookwinery.com.au **Open** 7 days 10–5
Winemaker Damian Hutton, Josh Uren **Est.** 1996 **Cases** 20 000 **Vyds** 7.8 ha
The strikingly situated Millbrook Winery is owned by the highly successful Perth-based entrepreneur Peter Fogarty and wife Lee. They also own Lake's Folly in the Hunter Valley and Deep Woods Estate in Margaret River, and have made a major commitment to the quality end of Australian wine. Millbrook draws on vineyards in the Perth Hills, planted to sauvignon blanc, semillon, chardonnay, viognier, cabernet sauvignon, merlot, shiraz and petit verdot. The wines (Millbrook and Barking Owl) are of consistently high quality. Exports to Ireland, Belgium, Germany, Denmark, Poland, Russia, Malaysia, Hong Kong, China and Japan.

♥♥♥♥♥ **LR Viognier 2008** At the top end of the complexity scale, yet with no oily or coarse phenolic characters; barrel fermentation in older oak has added to texture, complementing the apricot and stone fruit flavours. Screwcap. 14.5% alc. **Rating** 94 **To** 2011 $40
Estate Viognier 2008 A fragrant bouquet leads into an interesting palate with apricot and a twitch of ginger, oak not part of a quite complex and satisfying palate. Value. Screwcap. 14% alc. **Rating** 94 **To** 2012 $35

♥♥♥♥♡ **Barking Owl Shiraz Viognier 2007** Good colour courtesy of viognier; a terrific wine at the price, at once showing lifted fruit contributed by the viognier along with spicy/savoury flavours on the medium-bodied palate, which has great energy and drive. Screwcap. 14% alc. **Rating** 93 **To** 2017 $17.95

♥♥♥♥ **Viognier 2008** The third-ranked release of three viogniers, but nonetheless well above average, with clear-cut varietal fruit characters on both bouquet and palate, and no hint of over-extraction. Value. Screwcap. 14.5% alc. **Rating** 89 **To** 2011 $22
Sauvignon Blanc 2008 Unusual aromas of custard apple, lychee and feijoa; rich tropical fruit on the full-flavoured palate. Screwcap. 12% alc. **Rating** 89 **To** 2010 $19.95
Barking Owl Semillon Sauvignon Blanc 2008 Clean and quite varietal, with a dominating green nettle note; fine and juicy, if just a little one-dimensional. Screwcap. 12% alc. **Rating** 87 **To** 2012 $16.95
Barking Owl Rose 2008 Squashed berry fruit flavours; not sweet but not brilliant. Cabernet Sauvignon. Screwcap. 12.5% alc. **Rating** 87 **To** 2010 $18.20
Barking Owl Cabernet Sauvignon Merlot 2007 Rather austere in the context of the very good vintage; thins out somewhat on the finish, although has length. Screwcap. 14.5% alc. **Rating** 87 **To** 2012 $17.95

Miller's Dixons Creek Estate ★★★★☆

1620 Melba Highway, Dixons Creek, Vic 3775 **Region** Yarra Valley
T (03) 5965 2553 **F** (03) 5965 2320 **www**.graememillerwines.com.au **Open** 7 days 10–5
Winemaker Graeme Miller **Est.** 2004 **Cases** 6000 **Vyds** 30.4 ha
Graeme Miller is a Yarra Valley legend in his own lifetime, having established Chateau Yarrinya (now De Bortoli) in 1971, and as a virtual unknown winning the Jimmy Watson Trophy in '78 with the '77 Chateau Yarrinya Cabernet Sauvignon. He sold Chateau Yarrinya in 1986 and, together with wife Bernadette, established a vineyard that has steadily grown to over 30 ha with chardonnay, pinot gris, cabernet sauvignon, shiraz, pinot noir, sauvignon blanc, petit verdot and merlot. A significant part of the production is sold, but the opening of the winery in 2004, and a cellar door thereafter, has seen production increase.

♥♥♥♥♥ **Yarra Valley Chardonnay 2008** Pale colour and bright; nectarine and pear flesh bouquet; grilled nuts and a touch of spice with a core of slatey minerality; very poised, pure and persistent on the finish. Screwcap. 13.5% alc. **Rating** 94 **To** 2014 $28

ÏÏÏÏÏ Yarra Valley Sauvignon Blanc 2008 Pale colour; ripe exotic fruit bouquet, with an attractive talc. overlay; the palate is fresh and fine, with good texture and an even finish. Screwcap. 13.5% alc. **Rating** 90 **To** 2012 $16

Yarra Valley Cuvee Extra Brut 2006 Pale colour; vibrant, focused and full of citrus fruit, a touch of toasty complexity; the palate is poised and precise, with zest and verve and a clean chalky acid finish. Diam. 12.5% alc. **Rating** 90 **To** 2012 $35

Milton Vineyard

14635 Tasman Highway, Cranbrook, Tas 7190 **Region** East Coast Tasmania
T (03) 6257 8298 **F** (03) 6257 8297 **www**.miltonvineyard.com.au **Open** 7 days 10–5
Winemaker Winemaking Tasmania (Julian Alcorso) **Est.** 1992 **Cases** 2840 **Vyds** 6.3 ha
Michael and Kerry Dunbabin have one of the most historic properties in Tasmania, dating back to 1826. The property is 1800 ha, meaning the vineyard (2.7 ha of pinot noir, 1.4 ha of riesling, 1.2 ha of pinot gris and 1 ha of gewurztraminer) has plenty of room for expansion. Michael says, 'I've planted some of the newer pinot clones in 2001, but have yet to plant what I reckon will prove to be some of the best vineyard sites on the property.' Initially the grapes were sold to Hardys, but since 2005 much of the production has been retained for the Milton Vineyard label. Exports to Japan.

ÏÏÏÏÏ Freycinet Coast Riesling 2008 Relatively closed bouquet, but the palate has intense fruit and good line and length; sure to blossom with age. Screwcap. 12.1% alc. **Rating** 93 **To** 2018 $23

ÏÏÏÏ Iced Riesling 2007 Ice wine style; nicely balanced and made; will mooch on, even if a little simple. Screwcap. 9% alc. **Rating** 89 **To** 2013 $23

Minko Wines

13 High Street, Willunga, SA 5172 **Region** Southern Fleurieu
T (08) 8556 4987 **F** (08) 8556 2688 **www**.minkowines.com **Open** Wed–Mon 11–5
Winemaker Hawkers Gate, Mark Day (Consultant) **Est.** 1997 **Cases** 2000 **Vyds** 10.5 ha
Mike Boerema (veterinarian) and Margo Kellet (ceramic artist) established the Minko vineyard on their cattle property at Mt Compass. The vineyard is planted to pinot noir, merlot, cabernet sauvignon, chardonnay and pinot gris, and managed using sustainable eco-agriculture; 60 ha of the 160-ha property is heritage listed. Exports to the UK.

ÏÏÏÏÏ Southern Fleurieu Pinot Noir 2006 Has retained excellent hue; a generous mouthfilling mix of spicy plum fruit, round and soft in the mouth, but not jammy; does shorten fractionally on the finish. Screwcap. 14% alc. **Rating** 91 **To** 2013 $25

ÏÏÏÏ Southern Fleurieu Pinot Grigio 2008 Is genuinely placed in the grigio side of the divide, with considerable texture, and a display of pear and apricot fruit flavours. Screwcap. 13.5% alc. **Rating** 89 **To** 2010 $20

Minnow Creek

5 Hillside Road, Blackwood, SA 5051 (postal) **Region** McLaren Vale
T 0404 288 108 **F** (08) 8278 8248 **www**.minnowcreekwines.com.au **Open** Not
Winemaker Tony Walker **Est.** 2005 **Cases** 1500
Former Fox Creek winemaker Tony Walker has set up Minnow Creek in partnership with William Neubauer, the grapes grown by Don Lopresti at vineyards just west of Willunga. The name of the venture reflects the intention of the partners to keep the business focused on quality rather than quantity, and to self-distribute much of the wine through the large number of highly regarded Adelaide restaurants. Exports to the US, Canada and Germany.

ÏÏÏÏ McLaren Vale Shiraz 2006 Medium-bodied, with a gently sweet mix of red and black fruits plus a dusting of chocolate; slightly hot finish. Screwcap. 14.5% alc. **Rating** 88 **To** 2014 $25

Minot Vineyard

Lot 4 Harrington Road, Margaret River, WA 6285 **Region** Margaret River
T (08) 9757 3579 **F** (08) 9757 2361 **www**.minotwines.com.au **Open** By appt 10–5
Winemaker Fraser Gallop Estate **Est.** 1986 **Cases** 3000 **Vyds** 4.2 ha
Minot, which takes its name from a small chateau in the Loire Valley, is the husband and
wife venture of the Miles family. It produces just two wines from the plantings of semillon,
sauvignon blanc and cabernet sauvignon. Exports to the UK and Singapore.

ΨΨΨΨΨ **Margaret River Sauvignon Blanc Semillon 2008** Has very considerable
depth and textural richness, without heaviness; deliciously ripe gooseberry/tropical
fruit, with a long finish. 12.2% alc. **Rating** 93 **To** 2011 $15

Mintaro Wines ★★★

Leasingham Road, Mintaro, SA 5415 **Region** Clare Valley
T (08) 8843 9150 **F** (08) 8843 9050 **www**.mintarowines.com.au **Open** 7 days 10–4.30
Winemaker Peter Houldsworth **Est.** 1984 **Cases** 4000 **Vyds** 10 ha
Has produced some very good Riesling over the years, developing well in bottle. The red
wines, too, have improved significantly. The labelling is nothing if not interesting, from the
depiction of a fish drinking like a fish, not to mention the statuesque belles femmes. Exports
to Singapore.

ΨΨΨΨ **Clare Valley Late Picked Riesling 2008** Bright colour; lemon and talc.
bouquet; good flavour, lightly sweet, and with quite a dry finish. Screwcap.
13.5% alc. **Rating** 87 **To** 2012 $16

Miramar

Henry Lawson Drive, Mudgee, NSW 2850 **Region** Mudgee
T (02) 6373 3874 **F** (02) 6373 3854 **www**.miramarwines.com.au **Open** 7 days 9–5
Winemaker Ian MacRae **Est.** 1977 **Cases** 6000 **Vyds** 41.42 ha
Industry veteran Ian MacRae has demonstrated his skill with every type of wine over the
decades, ranging from Rose to Chardonnay to full-bodied reds. All have shone under the
Miramar label at one time or another; in 2005 there was a marked swing to white wines, with
which Ian has always had a special empathy. The majority of the production from the estate
vineyard is sold to others, the best being retained for Miramar's own use.

ΨΨΨΨΨ **Mudgee Sauvignon Blanc 2008** This is a considerable achievement, for it has
flowery passionfruit nuances on the bouquet; the palate is lively and quick on its
feet, leaving a clean embrace. Screwcap. 11.5% alc. **Rating** 91 **To** 2010 $15

ΨΨΨΨ **Mudgee Semillon 2006** Excellent pale green-straw; starting to open up, with
the first hints of honey and lightly browned toast starting to appear; has good
balance and length. Screwcap. 11.9% alc. **Rating** 89 **To** 2015 $15
Eurunderee Rose 2008 Very pale crimson-pink; Ian MacRae is an old hand,
giving this dry style a nice touch of spritz; ideal for summer alfresco drinking.
Screwcap. 12.5% alc. **Rating** 88 **To** 2010 $15

Mistletoe Wines

771 Hermitage Road, Pokolbin, NSW 2320 **Region** Lower Hunter Valley
T (02) 4998 7770 **F** (02) 4998 7792 **www**.mistletoewines.com **Open** 7 days 10–6
Winemaker Nick Paterson **Est.** 1989 **Cases** 7000 **Vyds** 5.5 ha
Mistletoe Wines, owned by Ken and Gwen Sloan, can trace its history back to 1909, when
a vineyard was planted on what was then called Mistletoe Farm. The Mistletoe Farm brand
made a brief appearance in the late 1970s. The wines are made onsite by Nick Paterson, who
has had significant experience in the Hunter Valley. The quality, and the consistency of these
wines is irreproachable, as is their price.

🍷🍷🍷🍷🍷 **Home Vineyard Hunter Valley Semillon 2008** Bright colour; straw and tart lemon on bouquet and palate; a touch of nettle comes through on the finish; tight and taut, with line and length, showing true potential to age. Screwcap. 9.5% alc. **Rating** 94 **To** 2018 $18

Mitchell ★★★★★

Hughes Park Road, Sevenhill via Clare, SA 5453 **Region** Clare Valley
T (08) 8843 4258 **F** (08) 8843 4340 **www.**mitchellwines.com **Open** 7 days 10–4
Winemaker Andrew Mitchell **Est.** 1975 **Cases** 30 000 **Vyds** 69 ha
One of the stalwarts of the Clare Valley, producing long-lived Rieslings and Cabernet Sauvignons in classic regional style. The range now includes very creditable Semillon, Grenache and Shiraz. A lovely old stone apple shed provides the cellar door and upper section of the compact winery. Exports to the UK, the US, Canada, Singapore, Hong Kong and NZ.

🍷🍷🍷🍷🍷 **McNicol Clare Valley Riesling 2007** Ripe lemon fruit with mineral and talc. on the bouquet; the palate is generous, but there is restraint in the personality, as the flavour takes time to build and unwind across the palate; a textural and intriguing finish. Screwcap. 13.5% alc. **Rating** 95 **To** 2015 $32
Peppertree Vineyard Shiraz 2006 Bright crimson-purple; full-bodied wine, with strong blackberry fruit and robust tannins; needs time, but should come through well. Screwcap. 15% alc. **Rating** 94 **To** 2021 $25

🍷🍷🍷🍷🍷 **Watervale Riesling 2008** Vibrant colour; delicate florals are offset by pure lime and talc. aromas; tight and textural, with a distinctly mineral core enhancing the lime fruit and focused acidity. Screwcap. 13% alc. **Rating** 93 **To** 2015 $22
Clare Valley Semillon 2007 A rich bouquet; straw and savoury spice notes from the oak; vibrant and lively, with citrus fruit aplenty and a very harmonious finish, if a little oaky at this point; a very interesting journey ahead. Screwcap. 13.5% alc. **Rating** 93 **To** 2016 $22
McNicol Clare Valley Shiraz 2001 A little development, but still very fresh; red fruit and a touch of mint, framed by an undercurrent of leather; the palate is soft and approachable, showing the value of time in bottle before release; very fine and even finish. Screwcap. 14.5% alc. **Rating** 93 **To** 2014 $40
Sevenhill Vineyard Clare Valley Cabernet Sauvignon 2005 Bright redcurrant and cedar bouquet; medium-bodied with prominent, cleansing acidity and tightly wound fruit; dry and savoury finish. Screwcap. 13.5% alc. **Rating** 90 **To** 2014 $27

 # Mitchell Harris Wines ★★★★☆

515 Havelock Street, Soldiers Hill, Vic 3350 (postal) **Region** Pyrenees
T 0438 301 471 **www.**mitchellharris.com.au **Open** Not
Winemaker John Harris **Est.** 2008 **Cases** 550
Mitchell Harris Wines is a partnership between Alicia and Craig Mitchell, and Shannyn and John Harris, the latter winemaker for this little producer and for the somewhat larger Mount Avoca winery. John began his career at Mount Avoca, then spent eight years as winemaker at Domaine Chandon in the Yarra Valley, cramming in northern hemisphere vintages in California and Oregon. The Mitchells grew up in the Ballarat area, and have an affinity for the Macedon and Pyrenees Ranges districts. While the total make is not large, a lot of thought has gone into the creation of each of the wines.

🍷🍷🍷🍷🍷 **Pyrenees Cabernet Sauvignon 2006** Pure cassis and blackcurrant aromas are precisely reflected on the palate, which has very good balance, texture and structure; everything in its place. Screwcap. 13.5% alc. **Rating** 94 **To** 2018 $21.95

🍷🍷🍷🍷🍷 **Pyrenees Sauvignon Blanc 2008** Very successful use of partial wild yeast barrel fermentation in older oak to balance the fresh grassy components, and allow the riper fruit to express itself on the finish and aftertaste. Screwcap. 11.5% alc. **Rating** 92 **To** 2011 $21.95

Pyrenees Shiraz 2007 Bright crimson-purple; a fragrant bouquet, then a medium-bodied palate offering black cherry and blackberry fruit, sustained by savoury tannins. Screwcap. 14% alc. **Rating** 92 **To** 2017 $33.95

Mitchelton ★★★★★

Mitchellstown via Nagambie, Vic 3608 **Region** Nagambie Lakes
T (03) 5736 2222 **F** (03) 5736 2266 **www**.mitchelton.com.au **Open** 7 days 10–5
Winemaker Ben Haines **Est.** 1969 **Cases** 220 000
Acquired by Petaluma in 1994 (both now part of Lion Nathan), having already put the runs on the board in no uncertain fashion with gifted winemaker Don Lewis (who retired in '04). His successor, Ben Haines, won the Wine Society Winemaker of the Year Award '08 (from a pool of Australian and NZ winemaking talent). Mitchelton, which celebrates its 40th birthday in 2009, boasts an array of wines across a broad spectrum of style and price, each carefully aimed at a market niche. Exports to all major markets.

ҮҮҮҮ **Print Shiraz 2004** As ever, a full-bodied wine with strong varietal focus and expression through its black fruits and subliminal spice; has very good length and texture; seriously stained cork a worry. 14.5% alc. **Rating** 94 **To** 2014 $51
Crescent Mourvedre Shiraz Grenache 2004 Red fruits and a hint of mint jump out of the glass; the palate is really lively, juicy and poised, especially given its age; almost velvety in texture, with a little dried herb edge to the finish. Screwcap. 14.5% alc. **Rating** 94 **To** 2014 $26

ҮҮҮҮҮ **Shiraz 2007** Bright colour; blueberry, damson plum and plenty of spice; the palate is dense with dark fruit coming to the fore, complemented by spicy oak and good tannins; bright-fruited, long, firm and dry. Great value. Screwcap. 14.5% alc. **Rating** 93 **To** 2016 $20
Parish Shiraz Viognier 2006 Highly perfumed red fruits and a touch of florals and spicy oak; much darker on the palate with the shiraz taking over from the more aromatic quality of the viognier; more tannic than expected, the wine is assertive, firm and needing time to integrate. Screwcap. 14.5% alc. **Rating** 93 **To** 2018 $30
Airstrip Roussanne Marsanne Viognier 2005 Glowing yellow-green; honeysuckle, honey and toast aromas, apricot nuances joining on the palate; crisp mineral/talc. acidity on the finish. Screwcap. 14% alc. **Rating** 92 **To** 2011 $26
Blackwood Park Riesling 2008 Tightly focused fruit with nectarine and lime coming to the fore; lean, crisp and quite fine on the finish, with an underlying generosity that gives the wine real presence on the finish. Screwcap. 13% alc. **Rating** 92 **To** 2016 $18
Preece Shiraz 2007 Good colour; red and blue fruit with a touch of bay leaf; medium-bodied and quite fleshy, with some savoury/spicy notes for complexity; good flavour. Screwcap. 14.5% alc. **Rating** 90 **To** 2014 $15

ҮҮҮҮ **Shiraz 2006** A clean, quite fragrant bouquet; strong blackberry and spice fruit, the structure building quickly with persistent tannins on the mid-palate through to the finish. Screwcap. 14.5% alc. **Rating** 89 **To** 2016 $21
Blackwood Park Botrytis Riesling 2008 Nice level of botrytis, but not particularly sweet; burnt marmalade and ripe lime flavours remain on the palate. Screwcap. 12.5% alc. **Rating** 89 **To** 2012 $17
Airstrip Roussanne Marsanne Viognier 2007 Very deep colour; ginger and honeysuckle bouquet; the palate is quite fresh despite the colour, drawing out the dried fig, peach and toast. Screwcap. 13.5% alc. **Rating** 88 **To** 2012 $26
Preece Cabernet Sauvignon 2007 Sweet cassis fruit; good flavour and weight, with juicy red and black fruit on the palate. Screwcap. 14% alc. **Rating** 88 **To** 2012 $15
Blackwood Park Riesling 2007 Significant colour development at 12 months; ripe tropical fruit aromas and flavours, with pineapple overtones; slightly broad finish. Screwcap. 13.5% alc. **Rating** 87 **To** 2009 $18

Clarke's Block Riesling 30 GR 2008 Clean green apple bouquet, with good acidity, and a slightly chalky refreshing finish; lacks a little drive. Screwcap. 11.5% alc. **Rating** 87 **To** 2011 $26

Mitolo Wines ★★★★★

PO Box 520, Virginia, SA 5120 **Region** McLaren Vale
T (08) 8282 9012 **F** (08) 8282 9062 **www.**mitolowines.com.au **Open** Not
Winemaker Ben Glaetzer **Est.** 1999 **Cases** 20 000
Frank Mitolo began making wine in 1995 as a hobby, and soon progressed to undertaking formal studies in winemaking. His interest grew year by year, and in 2000 he took the plunge into the commercial end of the business, retaining Ben Glaetzer to make the wines. Since that time, a remarkably good series of wines have been released. Imitation being the sincerest form of flattery, part of the complicated story behind each label name is pure Torbreck, but Mitolo then adds a Latin proverb or saying to the name. The '07 vintage has left its mark. Exports to all major markets.

♟♟♟♟♟ **Savitar McLaren Vale Shiraz 2007** Dense, deep purple-crimson; full-bodied, with rich and luscious plum, blackberry and dark chocolate is supported by good oak and appropriate tannins. Screwcap. 15% alc. **Rating** 94 **To** 2020 $80

♟♟♟♟♀ **Jester McLaren Vale Sangiovese Rose 2008** Bright fuschia pink; attractive red fruits dance the song to a beat of dry, spicy minerality. Good food style. Screwcap. 13% alc. **Rating** 91 **To** 2009 $22
Jester McLaren Vale Shiraz 2007 Loaded with sweet red and black fruits, fruitcake spice and a lively juicy personality; the palate is fleshy, full and quite chewy on the finish. Screwcap. 14.5% alc. **Rating** 90 **To** 2016 $28
G.A.M. McLaren Vale Shiraz 2007 Strong colour; dusty/bitter chocolate aromas lead into a powerful wine that really needs more fruit on the mid-palate. Screwcap. 15% alc. **Rating** 90 **To** 2017 $55
Jester McLaren Vale Cabernet Sauvignon 2007 Light but bright and clear colour; a mix of blackcurrant, savoury black olive and bitter chocolate aromas and flavours; restrained oak. Screwcap. 14.5% alc. **Rating** 90 **To** 2014 $28

♟♟♟♟ **Reiver Barossa Valley Shiraz 2007** A wine that, in common with many from the vintage, has impact, but not enough fruit or finesse. Screwcap. 15% alc. **Rating** 89 **To** 2014 $55

Molly Morgan Vineyard ★★★

496 Talga Road, Rothbury, NSW 2320 **Region** Lower Hunter Valley
T (02) 4930 7695 **F** (02) 4006 3004 **www.**mollymorgan.com **Open** Fri 1–5; w'ends 10–5 (summer), w'ends 10–4.30 (winter) or by appt
Winemaker Simon Miles **Est.** 1963 **Cases** 1100 **Vyds** 12.44 ha
Molly Morgan has been acquired by Andrew and Hady Simon, who established the Camperdown Cellars Group in 1971, which became the largest retailer in Australia, before moving on to other pursuits. They were joined by Grant Breen, their former general manager at Camperdown Cellars. The property includes unirrigated semillon vines over 40 years old (used for the Old Vines Semillon), 1.97 ha of chardonnay, 3.68 ha shiraz and a few riesling vines. Exports to Japan and China.

♟♟♟♟ **Hunter Valley Semillon 2008** Vibrant hue; slightly closed lemon and straw bouquet; correct flavour, but lacks a little concentration and drive. Screwcap. 11.4% alc. **Rating** 87 **To** 2014 $20

 Molly's Cradle **NR**

356 Tuckers Lane, North Rothbury, NSW 2335 **Region** Lower Hunter Valley
T (02) 9979 1471 **F** (02) 9979 1472 **www.**mollyscradle.com.au **Open** By appt
Winemaker Gary Reed **Est.** 2002 **Cases** 10 000 **Vyds** 9 ha

Steve Skidmore and Deidre Broad created the Molly's Cradle brand concept in 1997, moving to reality with the first planting of estate vines in 2000, the first vintage following in '02. They have 2 ha each of verdelho, chardonnay, merlot and shiraz, plus 1 ha of petit verdot, but also look to other regions to supplement the estate-grown grapes. Thus, for the time being, shiraz comes from Wrattonbully, merlot from Mudgee and sauvignon blanc (for blending with Hunter semillon) from Orange. A significant part of the business is the luxury Cradle Lodge, built as a '5-star adult retreat comfortably accommodating up to three couples'. A new cellar door is in the final stages of construction, expected to open in early 2010. Exports to Indonesia and Malaysia.

Mollydooker Wines

8/938 South Road, Edwardstown, SA 5039 (postal) **Region** South Australia
T (08) 8179 6500 **F** (08) 8179 6555 **www**.mollydookerwines.com.au **Open** By appt
Winemaker Sarah Marquis, Sparky Marquis **Est.** 2005 **Cases** 70 000 **Vyds** 157 ha
As Sarah and Sparky Marquis wound their way through Fox Creek, Henry's Drive, Parsons Flat, Marquis Philips and Shirvington, they left a vivid trail of high-flavoured, medal-winning wines in their wake. After 10 years they took the final step, launching Mollydooker Wines, with Robert Parker their number one ticket holder. Everything about their wines and their business is larger than life, with a 70 000-case winery established in McLaren Vale in the twinkling of an eye, and a core of estate plantings of shiraz (106 ha), cabernet sauvignon (27 ha), merlot (15 ha) and verdelho (8 ha); they also buy grapes from other regions. All this in the fast lane. Oh, and incidentally, 'mollydooker' is Australian slang for left-handed, an attribute shared by Sarah, Sparky and Robert Parker. The primary market for the wines will be the US, and that market should add five points to each of my scores. The 2007 acquisition of Classic McLaren Wines gives them a real base, and underwrites the future of the business. Exports to the US, the UK and other major markets.

Momentum Wines

Canal Rocks Road, Yallingup, WA 6282 **Region** Margaret River
T (08) 9755 2028 **F** (08) 9755 2101 **www**.momentum.com **Open** W'ends & hols 10–5
Winemaker Egidijus Rusilas, Sharna Kowalczuk, Siobhan Lynch **Est.** 1978 **Cases** 2500
Vyds 4 ha
The vineyard, planted to semillon, sauvignon blanc, riesling and cabernet sauvignon, was established by David Hunt in 1978. Originally called Sienna Estate, it has now passed into the ownership of the Rusilas family, which has significantly enhanced its legacy. Exports to Lithuania.

ŸŸŸŸŸ **Momentum of Passion Margaret River Semillon Sauvignon Blanc 2008** Pale colour; a delicate bouquet of nettle, tropical fruit and straw; the palate is taut and fine, with chalky acidity and attractive texture. Value. Screwcap. 13.4% alc. **Rating** 92 **To** 2011 $14.90

ŸŸŸŸ **Momentum of Love Margaret River Cabernet Sauvignon 2007** A slightly leafy cassis fruit bouquet; a medium-bodied palate, with a quite vibrant acid and tannin profile on the finish. Screwcap. 13.5% alc. **Rating** 89 **To** 2014 $19.90

Monahan Estate

319 Wilderness Road, Rothbury, NSW 2320 **Region** Lower Hunter Valley
T (02) 4930 9070 **F** (02) 4930 7679 **www**.monahanestate.com.au **Open** Wed–Sun 10–5
Winemaker Tower Estate, McLean Winemaking **Est.** 1997 **Cases** 1500 **Vyds** 7.1 ha
Monahan Estate is bordered by Black Creek in the Lovedale district, an area noted for its high-quality semillon; the old bridge adjoining the property is displayed on the wine label. As the website discloses in some detail, Monahan Estate offers wine with lower than normal levels of sulphur dioxide, the wines winning a number of medals.

ŸŸŸŸ **Hunter Valley Semillon 2008** Clean, fresh wine with a mix of grassy and citrussy aromas and flavours, but not as piercing or as long as the best. Screwcap. 10.5% alc. **Rating** 88 **To** 2014 $17

Mongrel Creek Vineyard ★★★

109 Hayes Road, Yallingup Siding, WA 6281 **Region** Margaret River
T 0417 991 065 **F** (08) 9755 5708 **Open** W'ends, school & public hols 10–5
Winemaker Tony Davis, Genevieve Stols **Est.** 1996 **Cases** 1250 **Vyds** 2.8 ha

Larry and Shirley Schoppe both have other occupations, Larry as vineyard supervisor at Howard Park's Leston Vineyard, Shirley as a full-time nurse. Thus the vineyard, planted to shiraz, semillon and sauvignon blanc in 1996, is still a weekend and holiday business. Given the viticultural and winemaking expertise of those involved, it is hardly surprising that the wines have been consistent show medal winners.

🍷🍷🍷🍷 **Le Mongrel Champers NV** Quite toasty notes on the bouquet; the palate is zesty and full of lemon fruit; good texture and flavour on the finish. Cork. 12.3% alc. **Rating** 87 **To** 2012 **$20**

Le Mongrel Champers Rouge NV Raspberry and blackberry fruit, with a touch of spice; quite dry and evenly poised on the finish. Cork. 13.2% alc. **Rating** 87 **To** 2012 **$2**

Monichino Wines ★★★☆

70 Berrys Road, Katunga, Vic 3640 **Region** Goulburn Valley
T (03) 5864 6452 **www**.monichino.com.au **Open** Mon–Sat 9–5, Sun 10–5
Winemaker Carlo Monichino, Terry Monichino **Est.** 1962 **Cases** 18 000 **Vyds** 22 ha

This winery was an early pacesetter for the region, with clean, fresh wines in which the fruit character was (and is) carefully preserved; it also showed a deft touch with its Botrytis Semillon. It has moved with the times, introducing an interesting range of varietal wines while preserving its traditional base. Plantings include chardonnay (6 ha), sauvignon blanc and shiraz (3 ha each), merlot (2 ha) and 1 ha each of riesling, pinot gris, semillon, white frontignan, orange muscat and brown muscat.

🍷🍷🍷🍷½ **Vintage Port 2004** The large number of gold and silver medals attests to the quality of the wine; it is spicy, and the spirit is of high quality, but the sweetness is higher than that of the very best wines of the future. Cork. 18% alc. **Rating** 90 **To** 2014 **$30**

🍷🍷🍷🍷 **Sauvignon Blanc 2008** Light straw-green; has a well balanced juxtaposition of citrus and sweeter stone fruit and pineapple components; slightly sweet finish will add to popular appeal. Screwcap. 13% alc. **Rating** 87 **To** 2010 **$16**

Cabernet Sauvignon 2007 Good colour; well made, with soft berry fruit and some warm oak notes appear on the smooth, light- to medium-bodied palate. Screwcap. 14.9% alc. **Rating** 87 **To** 2013 **$17**

Montalto Vineyards ★★★★★

33 Shoreham Road, Red Hill South, Vic 3937 **Region** Mornington Peninsula
T (03) 5989 8412 **F** (03) 5989 8417 **www**.montalto.com.au **Open** 7 days 11–5
Winemaker Robin Brockett **Est.** 1998 **Cases** 5000 **Vyds** 11.1 ha

John Mitchell and family established Montalto Vineyards in 1998, but the core of the vineyard goes back to '86. There are 5.6 ha of pinot noir, 3 ha of chardonnay, 1 ha of pinot gris, and 0.5 ha each of semillon, riesling and pinot meunier. Intensive vineyard work opens up the canopy, with yields ranging between 1.5 and 2.5 tonnes per acre. Wines are released under two labels, the flagship Montalto and Pennon, the latter a lower-priced, second label. All offer good value.

🍷🍷🍷🍷🍷 **Mornington Peninsula Pinot Noir 2007** A generous pinot, with red berry fruits, and a soft velvet-like palate; good fruit definition, with a gentle splash of spice and a truly expansive array of flavours on the finish. Screwcap. 13.2% alc. **Rating** 94 **To** 2014 **$42**

Pennon Hill Shiraz 2007 Deep colour; has more weight and structure than most cool-climate shirazs, with powerful red and black fruits surrounded by spicy tannins and a touch of oak. Screwcap. 14% alc. **Rating** 94 **To** 2022 **$28**

ΨΨΨΨΨ **Mornington Peninsula Chardonnay 2007** A complex wine showing, creamy oak, nectarine and a touch of nutty complexity; the palate is rich, with fine acidity, and a creamy texture on the finish. Screwcap. 13.1% alc. **Rating** 91 **To** 2012 $36
Pennon Hill Rose 2008 Slight salmon tinge to the pink; good structure and texture; crisp, dry finish built around appropriate acidity. Pinot Noir/Pinot Meunier. Screwcap. 13.5% alc. **Rating** 90 **To** 2010 $21
Pennon Hill Mornington Peninsula Pinot Noir 2007 A substantial wine with strong plummy fruit and fine savoury tannins; moderate length, and will build with a few more years. Screwcap. 14% alc. **Rating** 90 **To** 2015 $28

ΨΨΨΨ **Pennon Hill Pinot Grigio 2008** Razor sharp varietal pear aromas and a bracing palate and finish. Serve ice cold with shellfish on a hot summer's day. Screwcap. 13.5% alc. **Rating** 88 **To** 2010 $24
Mornington Peninsula Riesling 2007 A pleasant riesling, with gentle citrus and tropical fruits, but lacks the energy and thrust needed for higher points. Screwcap. 12.5% alc. **Rating** 87 **To** 2014 $23

Montgomery's Hill ★★★★

South Coast Highway, Upper Kalgan, Albany, WA 6330 **Region** Albany
T (08) 9844 3715 **F** (08) 9844 3819 **www**.montgomeryshill.com.au **Open** 7 days 11–5
Winemaker The Vintage Wineworx, Bill Crappsley (Consultant) **Est.** 1996 **Cases** 6000
Montgomery's Hill is 16 km northeast of Albany on a north-facing slope on the banks of the Kalgan River. Previously used as an apple orchard; it is a diversification for the third generation of the Montgomery family. Chardonnay, cabernet sauvignon, cabernet franc, sauvignon blanc, shiraz and merlot were planted in 1996–97. The wines are made with a gentle touch.

ΨΨΨΨΨ **Albany Shiraz 2007** Deeply coloured, with blackberry, mulberry and a touch of spice; dense on the palate with chewy, ripe tannins and a long, full-bodied and full-blooded finish. Screwcap. 14.4% alc. **Rating** 92 **To** 2016 $20

Moombaki Wines ★★★☆

341 Parker Road, Kentdale via Denmark, WA 6333 **Region** Denmark
T (08) 9840 8006 **F** (08) 9840 8006 **www**.moombaki.com **Open** 7 days 11–5
Winemaker Harewood Estate (James Kellie) **Est.** 1997 **Cases** 1200 **Vyds** 2 ha
David Britten and Melissa Boughey (with three young sons in tow) established vines on a north-facing gravel hillside, with picturesque Kent River frontage. Not content with establishing the vineyard, they put in significant mixed tree plantings to increase wildlife habitats. It is against this background that they chose Moombaki as their vineyard name: a local Aboriginal word meaning 'where the river meets the sky'. Exports to the UK, Switzerland, Malaysia and Singapore.

ΨΨΨΨΨ **Shiraz 2007** Deep fruited with cranberry, blackberry and some dried herb notes; the palate has a savoury, tar-like character that complements the dark fruit well; chewy tannins and full on the finish. Screwcap. 14% alc. **Rating** 92 **To** 2015 $29

ΨΨΨΨ **Chardonnay 2007** Clearly expressed melon and stone fruit on bouquet and palate; some slightly rough characters do break the line of the palate, but should settle down. Screwcap. 13.5% alc. **Rating** 89 **To** 2012 $28

Moondah Brook ★★★★☆

Dale Road, Middle Swan, WA 6056 **Region** Swan Valley
T (08) 9274 9540 **F** (08) 9274 5172 **www**.moondahbrook.com.au **Open** At Houghton
Winemaker Courtney Treacher **Est.** 1968 **Cases** NFP
Part of the Constellation wine group, Moondah Brook has its own special character, as it draws part of its fruit from the large Gingin vineyard, 70 km north of the Swan Valley, and part from the Margaret River and Great Southern. From time to time it has excelled even its own reputation for reliability with some quite lovely wines, in particular honeyed, aged

Chenin Blanc, generous Shiraz and finely structured Cabernet Sauvignon. Exports to the UK and other major markets.

ITTTT Verdelho 2008 Fragrant; fine, tight, some citrus notes on top of fruit salad; elegance and length, to a wine of exceptional varietal expression. Gold WA Wine Show '08. Screwcap. 13.5% alc. **Rating** 94 **To** 2012 $18

ITTTI Shiraz 2007 The spicy/peppery complexity of the bouquet and palate doubtless reflects the various regional components of the wine; the structure, too, is very good; masterly blending in the winery, and will develop further. Value. Screwcap. 14% alc. **Rating** 90 **To** 2017 $18
Cabernet Sauvignon 2007 Bright colour; the bouquet has lifted blue and black fruit, violet and a little cedar; poised and precise with fresh acidity, fine tannin and a very bright finish. Screwcap. 13.7% alc. **Rating** 90 **To** 2014 $18

ITTT Cabernet Rose 2008 As expected, a thoroughly professional rose from the first producer of cabernet rose in Australia decades ago; sleek red fruits on a long, balanced palate. Screwcap. 12.5% alc. **Rating** 89 **To** 2010 $18

Moondarra

45 Grange Road, Sandringham, Vic 3191 (postal) **Region** Gippsland
T (03) 9598 3049 **F** (03) 9598 0677 **Open** Not
Winemaker Neil Prentice **Est.** 1991 **Cases** 3200 **Vyds** 12 ha
In 1991 Neil Prentice and family established their Moondarra Vineyard in Gippsland, eventually focusing on the 2 ha of low-yielding pinot noir. Subsequently, they began planting their Holly's Garden vineyard at Whitlands in the King Valley, where they have 6 ha of pinot gris and 4 ha of pinot noir. It is from this vineyard that all but 200 cases of their wines come, sold under the Holly's Garden label. Exports to the US, Singapore, Hong Kong, Philippines, Korea and Japan.

ITTT Holly's Garden Pinot Gris 2008 A late harvest, sweet palate; theoretically must have been picked at over 15° baumé; not sure what the style is, other than Alsace Vendage Tardive attempt. Screwcap. 15% alc. **Rating** 88 **To** 2011 $26.50
Holly's Garden Luddite Pinot Noir 2006 Deep colour; a dark, massively extracted style, the tannins biting from the moment the wine enters the mouth – they will soften with time, but there isn't enough varietal fruit to outlast the tannins. Cork. 13.5% alc. **Rating** 87 **To** 2015 $40

Moorebank Vineyard

Palmers Lane, Pokolbin, NSW 2320 **Region** Lower Hunter Valley
T (02) 4998 7610 **www.**moorebankvineyard.com.au **Open** 7 days 10–5
Winemaker Gary Reed **Est.** 1977 **Cases** NA
Ian Burgess and Debra Moore own a mature 6-ha vineyard planted to chardonnay, semillon, gewurztraminer and merlot, with a small cellar door operation offering immaculately packaged wines in avant-garde style. Exports to the UK, Canada, China and Japan.

ITTTI Charlton Hunter Valley Chardonnay 2006 Has an attractive, zesty quality to its white peach and citrus fruit, French oak present but kept in its place. The thin and long 500 ml bottle would drive those with fixed-rack cellars insane, and won't be purchased for that reason. Screwcap. 13% alc. **Rating** 90 **To** 2012 $28.50
Hunter Valley Merlot 2006 Succeeds where the shiraz fails; has the olivaceous, savoury nuances that are an important part of merlot's varietal expression; touches of earth and leather are regional; all these characters could overwhelm the cassis fruit, but don't. Screwcap. 14% alc. **Rating** 90 **To** 2013 $29.50

ITTT Summar Hunter Valley Semillon 2006 Very light and crisp, with stony/minerally flavours and a bone-dry finish; odd packaging from start to finish, including 'BEC medals in 1996, '97 and '98' a throwback to 19th century European labelling; 500 ml. Screwcap. 10.5% alc. **Rating** 88 **To** 2012 $26.50

Moores Hill Estate

3343 West Tamar Highway, Sidmouth, Tas 7270 **Region** Northern Tasmania
T (03) 6394 7649 **F** (03) 6394 7647 **www**.mooreshill.com.au **Open** 7 days 10–5
Winemaker Winemaking Tasmania (Julian Allpart) **Est.** 1997 **Cases** 2500 **Vyds** 4.5 ha
Rod and Karen Thorpe established Moores Hill Estate in 1997 on the gentle slopes of the
West Tamar Valley. The vineyard has riesling, chardonnay, pinot noir, merlot and cabernet
sauvignon. The vineyard represents a full circle for the Thorpes, who bought the farm 30 years
ago and ripped out a small vineyard. The Wine Centre (built in 2002 mainly from timber
found on the property) overlooks the vineyard.

ŢŢŢŢŢ **Riesling 2008** Sweet, lime-accented fruit, which does have conviction and line to
its long palate; time to go. Screwcap. 11.6% alc. **Rating** 90 **To** 2017 $30

ŢŢŢŢ **Chardonnay 2007** Bright green-straw; firm, quite minerally wine; oak well
integrated; just a touch green perhaps. Screwcap. 13.5% alc. **Rating** 87 **To** 2014 $22

Moorilla Estate

655 Main Road, Berriedale, Tas 7011 **Region** Southern Tasmania
T (03) 6277 9900 **F** (03) 6249 4093 **www**.moorilla.com.au **Open** 7 days 10–5
Winemaker Conor van der Reest **Est.** 1958 **Cases** 9400 **Vyds** 14.3 ha
Moorilla Estate is an icon in the Tasmanian wine industry, and is thriving. However, in
the future it will not be known so much for its wines as for the largest and most highly
accredited (in terms of air quality, temperature and humidity, etc) museum in the southern
hemisphere. It will stage exhibitions of priceless paintings not hitherto shown in Australia
once the facility is complete and open for business in 2010. The three-year construction
process, estimated by observers (though not confirmed or denied by Moorilla Estate) to cost
upwards of $100 million, will be integrated with one of the best winery restaurants, if not the
best, in Tasmania, and also with the original Alcorso House, designed by Sir Roy Grounds. A
microbrewery, fastidiously equipped and surgically clean, also operates onsite to make superb
beer under the Moo Brew label. Almost incidental will be the construction of a new, purpose-
built winery. Exports to the US, Denmark and Hong Kong.

ŢŢŢŢŢ **Muse Chardonnay 2007** Very good green-straw; a complex wine; with lots of
oak, and lots of ripe fruit; rather less finesse. Screwcap. 13.7% alc. **Rating** 90 $45
Muse Pinot Gris 2008 Pale straw; lively and fresh; light fruit but has good
acidity and freshness. Screwcap. 13.5% alc. **Rating** 90 **To** 2010 $35
Praxis Pinot Noir 2008 Has a quite silky, sappy texture; attractive red fruits and
spices; very good thrust and length. Screwcap. 14.6% alc. **Rating** 90 **To** 2014 $25

ŢŢŢŢ **Praxis Shiraz Rose 2008** A firm, dry style; a crisp, linear palate with red berry
fruits, finishing with brisk acidity. Screwcap. 12.7% alc. **Rating** 88 **To** 2010 $25

Moorooduc Estate

501 Derril Road, Moorooduc, Vic 3936 **Region** Mornington Peninsula
T (03) 5971 8506 **www**.moorooducestate.com.au **Open** W'ends 11–5, 7 days in Jan
Winemaker Dr Richard McIntyre **Est.** 1983 **Cases** 2300 **Vyds** 6.5 ha
Richard McIntyre has taken Moorooduc Estate to new heights, having completely mastered
the difficult art of gaining maximum results from wild yeast fermentations. While the
Chardonnays remain the jewels in the crown, the Pinot Noirs are also very impressive. The
viticulturist is Hugh Robinson, who tends the vines with same attention to detail he bestows
on his own vineyard. An additional attraction is the restaurant, with Richard McIntyre's wife,
Jill, producing unfailingly exquisite food. Exports to Hong Kong and Singapore.

ŢŢŢŢŢ **The Moorooduc Chardonnay 2007** By some measure, the most complex
wine of the three '07 Moorooduc chardonnays, with strong structure surrounding
the fruit; its strength lies in its depth as much as its length. Screwcap. 13.5% alc.
Rating 96 **To** 2019 $55

McIntyre Vineyard Pinot Noir 2007 Excellent colour; fragrant cherry and plum, then a supple and long palate, full of all the right fruit flavours, expanding on the spicy, lingering finish. Screwcap. 14% alc. Rating 96 To 2015 $35
McIntyre Vineyard Chardonnay 2007 A super-fragrant bouquet is followed by a finely drawn, elegant palate, everything in the right place and of the right shape and size; terrific finish. Screwcap. 13.5% alc. Rating 95 To 2017 $35
Robinson Vineyard Chardonnay 2007 Tighter and sharper in profile than McIntyre Vineyard, with more tangy citrussy fruit; as with McIntyre, the oak influence is subtle. Screwcap. 13.5% alc. Rating 94 To 2015 $35
Pinot Gris 2007 It is remarkable how good winemaking – very good – can uncover what lies hidden in most pinot gris; the wine has great texture and mouthfeel, and abundant pear and stone fruit flavour. Screwcap. 14% alc. Rating 94 To 2011 $30
The Moorooduc Pinot Noir 2007 Similar deep colour to McIntyre Vineyard; an extremely powerful wine, with layers of fruit and substantial, but balanced, tannins; may well cruise past McIntyre when ready, but not now. Screwcap. 14% alc. Rating 94 To 2017 $55
Shiraz 2006 Classic fragrant and lively cool-grown shiraz, with red and black fruits and spices seamlessly interwoven, tannins and oak bystanders. Screwcap. 14% alc. Rating 94 To 2018 $30

Moorooroo Park Vineyards ★★★

Nitschke Road, Tanunda, SA 5352 Region Barossa Valley
T (08) 8563 1123 F (08) 8563 0727 www.jacobscreekretreat.com.au Open 7 days 10–5
Winemaker Stephen Black, Wyndham House Est. 2000 Cases NFP Vyds 1.2 ha
Moorooroo Park Vineyards is owned by Wyndham and Patricia House, who have had many years experience in the catering business. It is part of a larger venture known as the Jacobs Creek Retreat, established in 1996 for accommodation, with ongoing restoration of the historic buildings set among lavish French-inspired gardens. It has nothing to do with the Pernod Ricard Jacob's Creek; place names cannot be trademarked, hence the ability to use the Jacobs Creek name. They have a little over 1 ha of shiraz planted to clone 1654, and also purchase grapes from other growers. Exports to the US.

ᵠᵠᵠᵠ Lotties Barossa Valley Shiraz 2004 A distinctly savoury/spicy bouquet and fore-palate are smartly replaced by a decidedly warm alcohol afterglow on the palate; a wine in parts. Screwcap. 15% alc. Rating 89 To 2014 $35
Late Harvest Semillon 2004 The golden colour suggests this wine is at its peak and should be consumed asap while the crisp acidity holds the palate together. Cork. 12% alc. Rating 88 To 2010 $17.50
Samuel Nitschke Barossa Valley Cabernets 2005 Very late harvesting has resulted in a semi-Amarone style; whether this suits Cabernet Sauvignon (85%)/ Cabernet Franc (15%) is debatable. Screwcap. 15% alc. Rating 87 To 2015 $35
Silentium Barossa Valley Sparkling Shiraz 2005 Light- to medium-bodied; spice and licorice with complexity to the fruit; low alcohol helps keep phenolics under control. Cork. 12.5% alc. Rating 87 To 2012 $30

Moppa Wilton Vineyards ★★★

Cnr Stonewell Road/Seppeltsfield Road, Marananga, SA 5355 Region Barossa Valley
T 0408 821 657 F (08) 8562 3878 Open By appt
Winemaker Shawn Kalleske Est. 2004 Cases 250 Vyds 42 ha
Shawn Kalleske (who has his fingers in a number of Barossa pies) has joined forces with Joel Mattschoss to begin the development of Moppa Wilton Vineyards. Joel has 30 ha of vineyards and Shawn 12 ha, the lion's share in each case shiraz, but also with significant quantities of grenache. Only a small amount of the grapes from the two vineyards are retained for the Moppa Wilton label, by far the largest portion being sold to other Barossa wineries. The name Maczos for the Shiraz goes back five generations to the Maczos family being forced to

leave Hungary and settle in Germany in the early 1600s, changing their name to the more German-friendly Mattschoss.

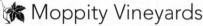 Moppity Vineyards ★★★★

Moppity Road, Young, NSW 2594 (postal) **Region** Hilltops
T (02) 6382 6222 **F** (02) 6382 6222 **www**.moppity.com.au **Open** Not
Winemaker Martin Cooper **Est.** 1973 **Cases** 1000 **Vyds** 73 ha
Jason Brown (and wife Alecia) have a background in retailing fine wines; Jason says he was indoctrinated into the world of fine wine at the age of eight, and hasn't lost the taste for it. He is president of the Hilltops Wine Growers Association, not surprising, given the size of the vineyard: shiraz (23 ha), cabernet sauvignon (21 ha), chardonnay (13 ha), riesling and merlot (6 ha each), nebbiolo (2 ha), and semillon and viognier (1 ha each). Jason's ambition is to produce world-class wine, and he has made a convincing start. Exports to the UK.

ΨΨΨΨΨ **Reserve Hilltops Shiraz 2007** Deep purple colour; blue and black fruits are complemented by a gently spicy personality; a touch of mint comes through on the palate, and the fruit is dark and generous; quite firm, but with a succulent nature to the finish. Screwcap. 14.5% alc. **Rating** 93 **To** 2014 $48.95
Reserve Hilltops Shiraz 2006 Attractive aromatic bouquet of spicy cherry and plum fruit, the palate with similar flavours in a medium-bodied spectrum, not impacted by the alcohol. Screwcap. 15% alc. **Rating** 92 **To** 2020 $48.95

ΨΨΨΨ **Hilltops Shiraz 2006** Vibrant colour; quite spicy on the bouquet with red fruit to match; fine, juicy and even on the palate. Screwcap. 13.8% alc. **Rating** 89 **To** 2013 $19.95
Tumbarumba Chardonnay 2008 Early picking allied with its cool-grown origin gives the wine Chablis-like elegance, but needs a bit more authority to the fruit; will develop in the short term. Screwcap. 12.5% alc. **Rating** 88 **To** 2013 $19.95

Morambro Creek Wines ★★★☆

PMB 98, Naracoorte, SA 5271 (postal) **Region** Padthaway
T (08) 8765 6043 **F** (08) 8765 6011 **www**.morambrocreek.com.au **Open** Not
Winemaker Ben Riggs **Est.** 1994 **Cases** 30 000 **Vyds** 170.5 ha
The Bryson family has been involved in agriculture for more than a century, moving to Padthaway in 1955 as farmers and graziers. Since the 1990s, they have progressively established large plantings of shiraz (88.5 ha), cabernet sauvignon (47.5 ha) and chardonnay (34.5 ha), lifting production from 6000 cases, and establishing export markets, including the UK and the US. The wines have been consistent winners of bronze and silver medals.

ΨΨΨΨ **Padthaway Shiraz 2006** A positive bouquet of blackberry and plum fruit plus obvious oak promises more than the palate delivers, the line breaking up on the finish. Screwcap. 14.9% alc. **Rating** 88 **To** 2013 $22.95
Mt Monster Shiraz 2007 Red berry bouquet with a touch of spice; medium-bodied with good acidity, and a firm finish. Good value. Screwcap. 14.5% alc. **Rating** 87 **To** 2013 $12.99
Jip Jip Rocks Chardonnay 2008 Deeply coloured; nectarine fruit, with vibrant acidity; fresh, with a fair bit of weight on the finish. Screwcap. 13.5% alc. **Rating** 87 **To** 2012 $16.99
Padthaway Cabernet Sauvignon 2007 Clearly delineated briary/savoury/ earthy black fruits, with a firm, dry finish. Screwcap. 15.7% alc. **Rating** 87 **To** 2014 $22.95

Morgan Simpson ★★★☆

PO Box 39, Kensington Park, SA 5068 **Region** McLaren Vale
T 0417 843 118 **F** (08) 8364 3645 **www**.morgansimpson.com.au **Open** Not
Winemaker Richard Simpson **Est.** 1998 **Cases** 1200 **Vyds** 27.1 ha

Morgan Simpson was founded by South Australian businessman George Morgan (since retired) and winemaker Richard Simpson, who is a graduate of CSU. The grapes are sourced from the Clos Robert Vineyard (where the wine is made) planted to shiraz (10 ha), cabernet sauvignon (7 ha), chardonnay (3.5 ha), mourvedre and sauvignon blanc (2.5 ha each) and pinot noir (1.6 ha), established by Robert Allen Simpson in 1972. Most of the grapes are sold, the remainder used to provide the reasonably priced, drinkable wines for which Morgan Simpson has become well known.

ŸŸŸŸ   **Two Clowns McLaren Vale Chardonnay 2006** Deep colour; very ripe, a smoky element to the fruit; very rich and generous. Screwcap. **Rating** 88 **To** 2012 $15

Morning Sun Vineyard ★★★★

337 Main Creek Road, Main Ridge, Vic 3928 **Region** Mornington Peninsula
T (03) 5989 6571 **www**.morningsunvineyard.com.au **Open** Thurs–Sun 10–5
Winemaker Owen Goodwin **Est.** 1995 **Cases** 1500 **Vyds** 5.5 ha
When Mario Toniolo retired, aged 70, and purchased a property on the hills of Main Ridge, he had ideas for a yabby farm and a few cattle on what was an abandoned apple orchard. His Italian blood got the better of him, and he now has 5 ha of pinot noir, pinot grigio and chardonnay, and a 1.8-ha olive grove. In 2005 he employed Owen Goodwin as viticultural manager; Owen had worked at Yarra Yarra while studying wine science at CSU, and thereafter worked vintages overseas. His first vintage at Morning Sun in 2006 resulted in gold medals for both the Chardonnay and Pinot Noir and a silver medal for the Pinot Grigio (never easy to gain).

ŸŸŸŸŸ   **Trial Series Claudia Block O Mornington Peninsula Gewurztraminer 2008** Green apple, spice and lychee bouquet; quite sweet, with plenty of exotic fruit, vibrant acidity, and a clean and focused finish; not typical, but certainly enjoyable. Screwcap. 10.5% alc. **Rating** 90 **To** 2012 $29

Morningside Vineyard ★★★☆

711 Middle Tea Tree Road, Tea Tree, Tas 7017 **Region** Southern Tasmania
T (03) 6268 1748 **F** (03) 6268 1748 **www**.morningsidevineyard.com.au **Open** By appt
Winemaker Peter Bosworth **Est.** 1980 **Cases** 600 **Vyds** 3 ha
The name Morningside was given to the old property on which the vineyard stands because it gets the morning sun first; the property on the other side of the valley was known as Eveningside. Consistent with the observation of the early settlers, the Morningside grapes achieve full maturity with good colour and varietal flavour. Production will increase as the vineyard matures, and as recent additions of clonally selected pinot noir (including 8104, 115 and 777) come into bearing. The Bosworth family, headed by Peter and wife Brenda, do all the vineyard and winery work, with conspicuous attention to detail.

ŸŸŸŸ   **Pinot Noir 2007** Pleasant light- to medium-bodied red fruits; a little simple, but has varietal character. Diam. 13.5% alc. **Rating** 87 **To** 2012 $34

Morris ★★★★★

Mia Mia Road, Rutherglen, Vic 3685 **Region** Rutherglen
T (02) 6026 7303 **www**.morriswines.com **Open** Mon–Sat 9–5, Sun 10–5
Winemaker David Morris **Est.** 1859 **Cases** 100 000
One of the greatest of the fortified winemakers, ranking with Chambers Rosewood. Just to confuse matters a little, Morris has decided to move away from the 4-tier classification structure used by other Rutherglen winemakers (other than Chambers, that is) and simply have two levels: varietal and Old Premium. The oldest components of the Old Premium are entered in a handful of shows, but the trophies and stratospheric gold medal points they receive are not claimed for the Old Premium wines. The art of these wines lies in the blending of very old and much younger material. They have no equivalent in any other part of the world.

ŢŢŢŢŢ Old Premium Liqueur Tokay NV Mahogany, with an olive rim; aromas of
Christmas cake and tea; incredibly viscous and rich, with layer upon layer of
flavours ranging through ginger snap, burnt butterscotch, and every imaginable
spice, the length and depth of the palate is as extraordinary as is that of the
aftertaste. Released in tiny quantities each year that maintain the extreme average
age of each release. **Rating** 97 **To** 2010
Old Premium Tawny Port NV Medium depth to the colour, true tawny and
not liqueur; a vibrant palate, with rich and luscious fruit, then extreme rancio
provides perfect balance, the acidity neither biting nor volatile. Great texture. Cork.
18% alc. **Rating** 96 **To** 2010 $51.50
Rutherglen Durif 2005 In traditional, and very good indeed, Morris style;
Christmas cake, chocolate, plum, prune and blackberry, the tannins and oak both
subtle. Bargain. Cork. 15% alc. **Rating** 94 **To** 2015 $21
Liqueur Muscat NV More touches of red-brown than the Liqueur Tokay,
precisely as it should be; fragrant raisin varietal fruit luring you into the second
glass; perfect balance. Screwcap. 18% alc. **Rating** 94 **To** 2010 $19.60

ŢŢŢŢŢ Blue Imperial Cinsaut 2007 Tangy/spicy, almost leafy overtones to the red
berry fruits; has a lively, fresh finish. Impressive example of cinsaut. Screwcap.
13.7% alc. **Rating** 91 **To** 2016 $19

ŢŢŢŢ Rutherglen Shiraz 2006 Has really attractive mouthfeel; medium-bodied, but
quite rich, with black fruits, mocha, dark chocolate and tannins all intermingling;
over-delivers at its price. Screwcap. 14.5% alc. **Rating** 89 **To** 2014 $15
Cabernet Sauvignon 2005 Generous, well-made wine with broad appeal; is
smooth and well balanced, black fruits offset by correct tannins. Good value; high-
quality cork. 14% alc. **Rating** 89 **To** 2015 $15
Sparkling Shiraz Durif NV A little tar frames the dark fruits, with a slight Amaro
bitterness; the sugar is in balance and finishes with a dry, complex and interesting
finish. Cork. 13.5% alc. **Rating** 87 **To** 2012 $18.50

Morrisons Riverview Winery   ★★★

Lot 2, Merool Lane, Moama, NSW 2731 **Region** Perricoota
T (03) 5480 0126 **F** (03) 5480 7144 **www**.morrisons.net.au **Open** Tues–Sun 10–5
Winemaker John Ellis **Est.** 1996 **Cases** 3000 **Vyds** 10 ha
Alistair and Leslie Morrison purchased this historic piece of land in 1995. Plantings began in
1996 with shiraz and cabernet sauvignon, followed in '97 by sauvignon blanc, and frontignac
in '98. Its restaurant has received an award for Restaurant of the Year for southern NSW.

ŢŢŢŢ Reserve Shiraz 2005 Notes of spice and dried gum leaf (the latter, perhaps an
autosuggestion of the label) on the bouquet and medium-bodied palate, which
has a twist of acidity to close. Impressive for the region. Screwcap. 14.5% alc.
Rating 88 **To** 2013 $31

Mortimers of Orange   ★★★

'Chestnut Garth', 786 Burrendong Way, Orange, NSW 2800 **Region** Orange
T (02) 6365 8689 **F** (02) 6365 8689 **www**.mortimerswines.com.au **Open** W'ends 11–5
Winemaker Simon Gilbert **Est.** 1996 **Cases** 3600 **Vyds** 6 ha
Peter and Julie Mortimer began the establishment of their vineyard (named after a quiet
street in the Humberside village of Burton Pidsea in the UK) in 1996. The vineyard includes
chardonnay, sauvignon blanc, shiraz, cabernet sauvignon, merlot and pinot noir. Exports to
the UK.

ŢŢŢŢ Chestnut Garth Sauvignon Blanc 2008 Cut grass, on a slightly herbaceous
bouquet; hints of tropical fruit on the palate, which has good texture and weight.
Screwcap. 12.2% alc. **Rating** 88 **To** 2011 $23
BFL Brothers for Life Pinot Noir 2005 Quite lively and bright; cherry and
plum with just a touch of spice; good texture and weight, with a touch of mint
coming to the fore on the finish. Screwcap. 14% alc. **Rating** 88 **To** 2012 $28

Moss Brothers

★★★★☆

3857 Caves Road, Wilyabrup, WA 6280 **Region** Margaret River
T (08) 9755 6270 **F** (08) 9755 6298 **www**.mossbrothers.com.au **Open** 7 days 10–5
Winemaker Navneet Singh, David Moss (Consultant) **Est.** 1984 **Cases** 20 000 **Vyds** 9.6 ha
Established by long-term viticulturist Jeff Moss and his family, notably sons Peter and David
and Roseworthy graduate daughter Jane, and Michelle as general manager of the operation.
A 400-tonne winery constructed in 1992 draws upon both estate-grown and purchased
grapes. It processes 200 tonnes a year for the Moss Brothers label, and also provides contract
winemaking services. The vineyard is planted to semillon, sauvignon blanc, chardonnay,
cabernet sauvignon, cabernet franc, grenache, merlot and petit verdot, and is supplemented by
several long-term grape contract purchase agreements. Exports to Canada, Germany, Hong
Kong, Singapore and China.

♟♟♟♟♟ **Wilyabrup Cabernet Sauvignon Merlot 2007** Typical Margaret River
cabernet merlot blend, the two varieties working synergistically in a medium- to
full-bodied frame, cassis and blackcurrant seamlessly woven through fine tannins
and good oak. Cork. 14.5% alc. **Rating** 94 **To** 2017 $35

♟♟♟♟♟ **Single Vineyard Margaret River Chardonnay 2007** Bright light green;
harmonious wine, with fruit and oak seamlessly married; grapefruit and stone fruit
flavours run through the long palate. Screwcap. 13.5% alc. **Rating** 93 **To** 2015 $35

♟♟♟♟ **Margaret River Semillon 2008** Has abundant flavours of herb, grass and citrus,
almost moving into sauvignon blanc territory; the line falters slightly on the finish.
Screwcap. 13% alc. **Rating** 89 **To** 2014 $25
Margaret River Sauvignon Blanc 2008 Pleasant tropical passionfruit aromas,
with gooseberry joining in on the palate; no frills style. Screwcap. 13% alc.
Rating 89 **To** 2010 $25
Big Barrel Margaret River Grenache 2007 Bright, fresh raspberry, cherry and
plum fruit is given texture by spicy notes; good varietal example. Interesting wine.
Screwcap. 14% alc. **Rating** 89 **To** 2015 $24
Wilyabrup Cabernet Sauvignon Merlot 2005 Pleasing medium-bodied wine,
with cassis and blackcurrant fruit, which has retained freshness; does back off a
little on the finish. Cork. 14.5% alc. **Rating** 88 **To** 2013
Jane Moss Margaret River Semillon Sauvignon Blanc 2008 Well-balanced
wine with a mix of citrus, grass and gooseberry fruit on both bouquet and palate.
Screwcap. 13% alc. **Rating** 87 **To** 2010 $22

Moss Wood

★★★★★

Metricup Road, Wilyabrup, WA 6284 **Region** Margaret River
T (08) 9755 6266 **F** (08) 9755 6303 **www**.mosswood.com.au **Open** By appt
Winemaker Keith Mugford, Josh Bahen, Amanda Shepherdson **Est.** 1969 **Cases** 15 000
Widely regarded as one of the best wineries in the region, capable of producing glorious
Semillon in both oaked and unoaked forms, unctuous Chardonnay and elegant, gently
herbaceous, superfine Cabernet Sauvignon, which lives for many years. In 2000 Moss
Wood acquired the Ribbon Vale Estate; the Ribbon Vale wines are now treated as vineyard-
designated within the Moss Wood umbrella. Exports to all major markets.

♟♟♟♟♟ **Margaret River Cabernet Sauvignon 2005** A classic, pure, autocratic portrayal
of cabernet, opening with a degree of reticence but revealing more and more
along the length of the palate, gaining in velocity near the finish and into the
aftertaste. Screwcap. 14% alc. **Rating** 95 **To** 2025 $85.50
Ribbon Vale Vineyard Margaret River Merlot 2007 Light crimson-red;
the bouquet is a fragrant mix of cassis, snow pea and olive, the elegant light- to
medium-bodied palate reflecting those characters; has great purity and varietal
focus, length and balance flawless. Screwcap. 13.5% alc. **Rating** 94 **To** 2015

ŢŢŢŢŢ **Ribbon Vale Vineyard Margaret River Cabernet Sauvignon Merlot**
2007 Stylistically similar to the Merlot, but medium-bodied rather than light- to medium-bodied, and with blackcurrant to the fore, the tannins providing more structure. Nonetheless, retains the elegance and effortless length of the Merlot. Screwcap. 14% alc. **Rating** 93 **To** 2017
Margaret River Semillon 2008 Pungent pea pod aromas, intermingling with zesty lemon fruit; the palate is dry and vibrant, with good mid-palate texture and line on the finish. Screwcap. 14% alc. **Rating** 92 **To** 2012 $38
Amy's 2007 The bouquet exhibits strong cassis and underlying spice and cedar from the oak; the palate is generous on entry, but the strictness of the varieties comes through finish with firmness and a look to the future. Cabernet Sauvignon/ Petit Verdot/Malbec. Screwcap. 14% alc. **Rating** 92 **To** 2016 $37
Ribbon Vale Vineyard Margaret River Semillon Sauvignon Blanc 2008 Some complexity, straw and restrained cut grass characters; textured and generous, with a fine, even and layered finish. Screwcap. 13.5% alc. **Rating** 91 **To** 2012 $29

Motton Terraces

119 Purtons Road, North Motton, Tas 7315 **Region** Northern Tasmania
T (03) 6425 2317 **www**.cradlecoastwines.info/ **Open** Tues–Sun 10–5
Winemaker Flemming Aaberg **Est.** 1990 **Cases** 140 **Vyds** 1 ha
Another of the micro-vineyards, which seem to be a Tasmanian speciality; Flemming and Jenny Aaberg planted slightly less than 0.5 ha of chardonnay and riesling in 1990, and have now increased that to 1 ha with more riesling and some tempranillo. The exercise in miniature is emphasised by the permanent canopy netting to ward off possums and birds.

ŢŢŢŢ   **Chardonnay 2008** Pleasant wine, gently peachy fruit, achieving good balance through fresh acidity. Unoaked. Diam. 12.8% alc. **Rating** 87 **To** 2011 $15

Mount Alexander Winery

410 Harcourt Road, Sutton Grange, Vic 3448 **Region** Bendigo
T (03) 5474 2567 **www**.mawine.com.au **Open** W'ends & public hols 11–5, or by appt
Winemaker Bill Blamires **Est.** 2001 **Cases** 1000 **Vyds** 7 ha
Bill and Sandra Blamires acquired their property after a two-year search of the southern Bendigo area for what they considered to be an ideal location. They have firmly planted their faith in shiraz (6 ha), with merlot, cabernet sauvignon, chardonnay, merlot and viognier contributing another hectare. The winery was previously called Blamires Butterfly Crossing (because of the butterfly population on Axe Creek, which runs through the property) but has been changed due to confusion with Angove's Butterfly Ridge.

ŢŢŢŢ   **Shiraz 2007** A medium- to full-bodied Shiraz with ripe blackberry fruit; has potential. Screwcap. 14.9% alc. **Rating** 87 **To** 2013 $16.50

Mount Ashby Estate

RMB 403 Nowra Road, Moss Vale, NSW 2577 **Region** Southern Highlands
T (02) 4869 3736 **www**.mountashby.com.au **Open** Fri–Sun & public hols 10–5
Winemaker High Range Vintners **Est.** 1999 **Cases** 600
Chris Harvey and wife Sally Beresford purchased the Mirrabooka property in 1999, part of one of the earliest dairy farms established in the Southern Highlands in the 19th century. They run one of the few remaining Holstein cattle studs in the region, but also planted 1 ha each of merlot and pinot gris. The cellar door is a replica of the original dairy, but also includes the relocated barrel produce store (circa 1918) used to restore provincial antique furniture for sale in Sally's antique shops (and the cellar door, of course).

ŢŢŢŢŢ **Galante Southern Highlands Pinot Gris 2007** Mention of sugar would be appropriate on the label, but there is no doubt the essence of the grape variety has been captured; exotic candied orange and pear fruit linger, with clean acidity and appealing concentration. Screwcap. 12% alc. **Rating** 92 **To** 2016 $27

Southern Highlands Pinot Gris 2007 A quite exotic style, with pure pear aromas and flavours; the essence of the wine lies in the texture and just a hint of bitterness that ultimately adds interest to this pinot gris, made in an Alsatian style. Screwcap. 13% alc. **Rating** 91 **To** 2015 $25

Mount Avoca ★★★★

Moates Lane, Avoca, Vic 3467 **Region** Pyrenees
T (03) 5465 3282 **F** (03) 5465 3544 **www.**mountavoca.com **Open** 7 days 10–5
Winemaker John Harris, Matthew Barry **Est.** 1970 **Cases** 12 000 **Vyds** 24.4 ha
A winery that has long been one of the stalwarts of the Pyrenees region, and is steadily growing. There has been a significant refinement in the style and flavour of the red wines over the past few years. I suspect a lot of worthwhile work has gone into barrel selection and maintenance. Reverted to family ownership in 2003 after a short period as part of the ill-fated Barrington Estates group. Exports to China.

ΨΨΨΨΩ Pyrenees Shiraz 2006 Good hue; red and black cherry fruits are at the centre of a palate with good texture and structure, the tannins spot on. Excellent value. ProCork. 14% alc. **Rating** 92 **To** 2010 $20
Pyrenees Merlot 2006 Strong, bright colour; has abundant cassis fruit; impressive Australian version of merlot, even if headed to cabernet in flavour terms. Well priced. Cork. 13.5% alc. **Rating** 91 **To** 2015 $20
Pyrenees Chardonnay 2006 Well made, with nectarine and melon fruit framed by just the right amount of barrel ferment oak; good overall balance. Screwcap. 13.5% alc. **Rating** 90 **To** 2012 $20

ΨΨΨΨ Trioss Red 2005 Has well above-average flavour and structure for a wine at this price, black fruits providing an impressive backbone. Shiraz/Cabernet Sauvignon. Screwcap. 13% alc. **Rating** 89 **To** 2012 $12
Pyrenees Cabernet Sauvignon 2007 A clean and juicy red fruit bouquet; the palate has a generous, yet somewhat one-dimensional, dollop of varietal fruit. Screwcap. 14.5% alc. **Rating** 89 **To** 2014 $20
Pyrenees Cabernet Sauvignon 2006 A pretty wine, but doesn't have quite the same depth as the other '06 reds of Mount Avoca; gentle cassis/berry fruits are smooth and supple. ProCork. 14% alc. **Rating** 89 **To** 2014 $20
Pyrenees Semillon Sauvignon Blanc 2008 Has more mouthfeel and flavour than the Sauvignon Blanc; ripe citrus flavours run through to the finish. Screwcap. 11.5% alc. **Rating** 88 **To** 2010 $15
Pyrenees Merlot 2007 Bright colour; lifted plum and floral bouquet; medium-bodied with fleshy fruit and tight acidity on the finish; clean and vibrant with a bit of stuffing. Screwcap. 13.5% alc. **Rating** 88 **To** 2015 $20
Pyrenees Sauvignon Blanc 2008 Light, bright green-straw; well made, but not enough fruit from the vineyard. Screwcap. 11.5% alc. **Rating** 87 **To** 2010 $17

Mt Bera Vineyards ★★★★☆

PO Box 372, Gumeracha, SA 5233 **Region** Adelaide Hills
T (08) 8389 2433 **F** (08) 8389 2418 **www.**mtberavineyards.com.au **Open** Not
Winemaker Jeanneret Wines **Est.** 1997 **Cases** 600 **Vyds** 12 ha
In 2008 Greg and Katrina Horner (plus four kids and a growing collection of animals) purchased Mt Bera from Louise Warner. Both Greg and Katrina grew up on farms, and the 75-ha property, with its homestead built in the 1880s, was irresistible. The property is located in a sanctuary overlooking the Torrens Valley, looking out to Adelaide, 45 mins drive away. For the time being, at least, most of the production is sold to Penfolds, but the intention is to increase the range and quantity of wines available. Exports to the UK.

Mt Billy   ★★★★

18 Victoria Street, Victor Harbor, SA 5211 (postal) **Region** Southern Fleurieu
T 0416 227 100 **F** (08) 8552 8333 **www**.mtbillywines.com.au **Open** Not
Winemaker Dan Standish, Peter Schell **Est.** 2000 **Cases** 2000 **Vyds** 2.4 ha

Having been an avid wine collector and consumer since 1973, John Edwards (a dentist)
and wife Pauline purchased a 3.75-ha property on the hills behind Victor Harbor, planting
chardonnay and pinot meunier. There have been various viticultural peregrinations since that
time, culminating in the grafting over of half the original plantings; 0.5 ha of chardonnay
and 0.6 ha of pinot meunier remain for sparkling wine, the remainder of the vineyard now
planted to 0.7 ha of clonally selected shiraz, plus small amounts of viognier, mourvedre, petite
syrah, malbec and sangiovese, all of which are destined for a vineyard blend. In the meantime,
grapes are purchased from the Barossa and Clare Valleys. Exports to the US, Canada, Maldives,
Japan and China.

 Circe Southern Fleurieu Shiraz 2007 Bright colour; fruitcake, plum and
touch of undergrowth; the palate is loaded with sweet black fruit, and there is real
definition to the red fruit on the palate; a rich, ripe and warm style. Screwcap.
14.7% alc. **Rating** 90 **To** 2015 $28.95

Mount Buninyong Winery   ★★★

210 Platts Road, Scotsburn, Vic 3352 **Region** Ballarat
T (03) 5341 8360 **www**.mountbuninyongwinery.com.au **Open** 7 days 11–6
Winemaker Peter Armstrong, Sandra Armstrong, Robert Taylor **Est.** 1993 **Cases** NA
Vyds 4 ha

Mount Buninyong Winery is the venture of Peter and Jan Armstrong, assisted by son and
daughter-in-law Malcolm and Sandra Armstrong. It is situated just south of Ballarat, near
Scotsburn, and is planted to riesling, chardonnay, pinot noir and cabernet sauvignon. A range
of table, fortified, sparkling and organic wines are made.

 Cabernet Sauvignon 1998 Family Reserve. As the wine has aged, the herbal/
leafy/minty components have become more obvious; the gold medal it won at the
Victorian Wines Show when six months old is yesterday's story. Cork. 12.9% alc.
Rating 87 **To** 2012 $49

Mount Burrumboot Estate   ★★★★☆

3332 Heathcote-Rochester Road, Colbinabbin, Vic 3559 **Region** Heathcote
T (03) 5432 9238 **www**.burrumboot.com **Open** W'ends & public hols 11–5, or by appt
Winemaker Cathy Branson **Est.** 1999 **Cases** 1500 **Vyds** 16.5 ha

To quote: 'Mount Burrumboot Estate was born in 1999, when Andrew and Cathy Branson
planted vines on the Home Block of the Branson family farm, Donore, on the slopes of
Mt Burrumboot, on the Mt Camel Range, above Colbinabbin. Originally the vineyard was
just another diversification of an already diverse farming enterprise. However, the wine bug
soon bit Andrew and Cathy, and so a winery was established. The first wine was contract-
made in 2001 by contract – however, 2002 vintage saw the first wine made by Cathy in the
machinery shed, surrounded by headers and tractors. Very primitive, and the appearance of
the new 50-tonne winery in 2002 was greeted with great enthusiasm!' And then you taste
the wines. Amazing. The original plantings of a little over 11 ha of shiraz and merlot have
since been expanded to take in lesser amounts of petit verdot, sangiovese, tempranillo, gamay,
marsanne and viognier. There is no intention to expand the business further.

Heathcote Shiraz 2006 Attractive medium-bodied wine, with particularly
good mouthfeel and balance, not always the case in Heathcote; supple plum and
blackberry fruit, with touches of spice and licorice; good oak handling. Diam.
14% alc. **Rating** 94 **To** 2021 $30

Heathcote Sangiovese 2006 The wine has the fine structure of sangiovese
from Tuscany, and great continuity and line; the mix of sour cherry, cherry and
spice is also very good indeed. Diam. 13.2% alc. **Rating** 93 **To** 2016 $25

Heathcote Marsanne Viognier 2008 Once again, manages to squeeze that little bit extra, investing the wine with character and overall flavour; should develop nicely. Screwcap. 13.5% alc. **Rating** 90 **To** 2014 $25

Heathcote Merlot 2006 Toward the upper end of Australian Merlot, although not at the top; the flavours are of redcurrant with a dressing of herb and olive, the tannins fine, mouthfeel balanced. Diam. 14% alc. **Rating** 90 **To** 2013 $28

ŢŢŢŢ **Mad Uncle Jack's Heathcote Petit Verdot 2006** Usual deep colour and flavour; will need to age for a decade to achieve the grace the other Mount Burrumboot wines have when young. Diam. 14% alc. **Rating** 89 **To** 2026 $28

Heathcote Tempranillo 2006 Has good depth and complexity, with distinct savoury components not always present in Australian tempranillo; spicy red and black fruits are the main message. Diam. 14% alc. **Rating** 89 **To** 2014 $25

Heathcote Gamay 2006 Interesting wine; retains good colour, but the bramble and forest characters are out-muscling the fresh fruit expected of the style; plenty of potential, especially when 6–12 months old. Screwcap. 13.5% alc. **Rating** 87 **To** 2009 $30

Mount Camel Ridge Estate ★★★★

473 Heathcote-Rochester Road, Heathcote, Vic 3523 **Region** Heathcote
T (03) 5433 2343 **www.**mountcamelridgeestate.com **Open** By appt
Winemaker Ian Langford, Gwenda Langford **Est.** 1999 **Cases** 350 **Vyds** 17 ha
Ian and Gwenda Langford commenced planting their vineyard in 1999, the majority to shiraz (8.5 ha), cabernet sauvignon (3.4 ha) and merlot (3.4 ha), with a little over 0.5 ha each of petit verdot, viognier and mourvedre. The land has been developed using organic principles, using composted chicken manure every three years, the application of seaweed fertiliser and mulching of the prunings. The vineyard is dry-grown, and no copper, lime or sulphur fungicide has been used. The Langfords say, 'As a result, worms have reappeared, and there is now an extensive frog population, ladybirds and other invertebrates and a range of beautiful spiders.' Scientists from University of Melbourne, La Trobe University and the University of California, Davis, have commenced a survey in the vineyard to establish the connection between the health of the vines and the resident invertebrate population. The red wines are made in open half-tonne vats, basket-pressed and matured in French oak. Exports to the US.

ŢŢŢŢŢ **Heathcote Shiraz 2007** Extremely savoury/spicy aromas and flavours, the palate lacking the desired depth; perhaps the prolonged drought prevented full maturation of the grapes; 100% wild fermentation. Diam. 13.2% alc. **Rating** 90 **To** 2015 $45

Heathcote Cabernet Sauvignon 2007 The wine does not show green fruit characters, although does have earthy black olive overtones to its black fruits; heavily wine-stained Diam suggest some mischance at bottling or storage. Diam. 12.5% alc. **Rating** 90 **To** 2016 $45

Mount Charlie Winery ★★★☆

228 Mount Charlie Road, Riddells Creek, Vic 3431 **Region** Macedon Ranges
T (03) 5428 6946 **F** (03) 5428 6946 **www.**mountcharlie.com.au **Open** Most w'ends & Wed 10–3
Winemaker Trefor Morgan **Est.** 1991 **Cases** 600 **Vyds** 3 ha
Mount Charlie's wines are sold principally by mail order and through selected restaurants. A futures program encourages mailing-list sales with a discount of over 25% on the release price. Owner/winemaker Trefor Morgan is perhaps better known as Professor of Physiology at Melbourne University. He also acts as a contract maker for others in the region.

ŢŢŢŢŢ **Tempranillo 2007** The cool-climate enhances the almost citrussy finish, but theoretically should prove well suited to the variety, bringing out delicious morello cherry flavours. May prove to be a real winner. Screwcap. 14.2% alc. **Rating** 90 **To** 2014 $22

ŸŸŸŸ   **Malbec 2007** Light-bodied; sweet plummy fruit of the variety, but not its lusciousness when fully ripe. Tempranillo is a much better bet than this late-ripening variety. Screwcap. 13.1% alc. **Rating** 87 **To** 2011 $22

Mount Eyre Vineyards   ★★★★

173 Gillards Road, Pokolbin, NSW 2321 **Region** Lower Hunter Valley
T 0438 683 973 **F** (02) 6842 4513 **www**.mounteyre.com **Open** Tues–Sun 11–5
Winemaker Stephen Hagan, Aniello Iannuzzi, Rhys Eather **Est.** 1970 **Cases** 5000
Vyds 33 ha
This is the venture of two families whose involvement in wine extends in an unbroken line back several centuries. The Tsironis family in the Peleponese, Greece, and the Iannuzzi family in Vallo della Lucania, Italy. Their vineyards are at Broke (the largest) and a smaller vineyard at Pokolbin. The three principal varieties planted are chardonnay, shiraz and semillon, with small amounts of merlot, viognier and chambourcin. Exports to Mexico, Thailand, Maldives, Malaysia, China and Hong Kong.

ŸŸŸŸŸ   **Hunter Valley Semillon 2008** Delicious young semillon, with unusually good balance making for enjoyable drinking now, as well as in the long term, the latter guaranteed by the screwcap. Screwcap. 10% alc. **Rating** 94 **To** 2018 $13.95

ŸŸŸŸ   **Hunter Valley Semillon Chardonnay 2008** Fresh and lively, the contribution of stone fruit from the chardonnay driving the flavour, the semillon the structure. Good value. Screwcap. 11.5% alc. **Rating** 89 **To** 2012 $13.95
Three Ponds Hunter Valley Shiraz 2007 Good hue; a fragrant bouquet leads into a light- to medium-bodied palate with a mix of red and black fruits; pleasant wine. Screwcap. 13.5% alc. **Rating** 88 **To** 2015 $29.95

Mount Gisborne Wines   ★★★★

83 Waterson Road, Gisborne, Vic 3437 **Region** Macedon Ranges
T (03) 5428 2834 **www**.mountgisbornewines.com.au **Open** Wed–Sun 10–6
Winemaker David Ell, Stuart Anderson **Est.** 1986 **Cases** 1200 **Vyds** 2.9 ha
David and Mary Ell planted pinot noir and chardonnay between 1986 and '90. The first wines were made in '91, signalling a partnership with the veteran Stuart Anderson, who is now theoretically in retirement. Exports to Canada, Singapore and Malaysia.

ŸŸŸŸŸ   **Montague Macedon Ranges Rose 2008** Brilliant light crimson; the strawberry aromas are pure pinot noir joined on the palate by spicy notes and crisp acidity. Impressive example. Screwcap. 14% alc. **Rating** 92 **To** 2010 $19
Florina Macedon Ranges Sauvignon Blanc 2008 Bright, light-green-straw; a vivacious blend of grass, citrus and tropical fruit; clear varietal fruit expression, above the norm for the region; excellent value. Screwcap. 14% alc. **Rating** 91 **To** 2010 $19

ŸŸŸŸ   **Macedon Ranges Chardonnay 2007** Reflects cool climate, with light melon, stone fruit and cashew aromas and flavours; has a long, minerally, finish. Diam. 13% alc. **Rating** 89 **To** 2014 $28
Macedon Ranges Pinot Noir 2007 Excellent depth of colour; a very savoury/ briary/earthy wine; picking the right time to most enjoy it won't be easy, depending on the tug-of-war between extract and fruit. Diam. 14% alc. **Rating** 89 **To** 2013 $32

Mount Horrocks   ★★★★★

The Old Railway Station, Curling Street, Auburn, SA 5451 **Region** Clare Valley
T (08) 8849 2243 **www**.mounthorrocks.com **Open** W'ends & public hols 10–5
Winemaker Stephanie Toole **Est.** 1982 **Cases** 4500 **Vyds** 11.1 ha
Mount Horrocks has well and truly established its own identity in recent years, aided by positive marketing and, equally importantly, wine quality, which has resulted in both show

success and critical acclaim. Stephanie Toole has worked long and hard to achieve this, and I strongly advise you (or anyone else) not to get in her way. Exports to the UK, the US and other major markets.

ȲȲȲȲȲ **Clare Valley Cabernet Sauvignon 2006** As expected, a far purer and more elegant expression of cabernet than any others from the region (except for Grosset Gaia); juicy blackcurrant and cassis fruit is cradled in the finest of tannins and quality French oak. Screwcap. 14% alc. **Rating** 95 **To** 2021 $35

Clare Valley Semillon 2008 In a 100% barrel ferment style unique to the Clare Valley; Mitchell and Tim Adams other notable makers; the strength of the lemony citrus fruit absorbs the impact of the oak; complex food style; good length and balance. Screwcap. 13.5% alc. **Rating** 94 **To** 2015 $27

Watervale Shiraz 2007 Bright crimson; a super-fragrant bouquet of red berry fruits changes direction on the spicy/savoury palate with fine tannins providing framework for the red berry fruits at the heart of the wine. Screwcap. 14% alc. **Rating** 94 **To** 2017 $35

Watervale Shiraz 2006 Bright hue; shows the '06 vintage to full advantage, with vibrant fruits ranging through red and black berries; overall, has great freshness and elegance. Screwcap. 14% alc. **Rating** 94 **To** 2016 $35

ȲȲȲȲȲ **Cordon Cut 2008** Glowing yellow-green; stacked to the rafters with preserved lime and lime juice flavours, the acidity perfectly balanced. Needs age to build complexity. Riesling. Screwcap. 11% alc. **Rating** 93 **To** 2014 $35

Watervale Riesling 2008 Light bright green-gold; complex aromas of lime and subliminal toast, the palate still locked up and inwards looking; requires patience. Screwcap. 12.5% alc. **Rating** 91 **To** 2016 $29.95

Clare Valley Semillon 2007 The 100% barrel fermentation impact is certainly there, but it is well integrated with and does not subjugate the lemon, honey and toast fruit. A specific style. Screwcap. 13.5% alc. **Rating** 91 **To** 2014 $27

Mt Jagged Wines   ★★★★

Main Victor Harbor Road, Mt Jagged, SA 5211 **Region** Southern Fleurieu
T (08) 8554 9520 **F** (08) 8554 9520 **www.**mtjaggedwines.com.au **Open** 7 days 11–5
Winemaker Duane Coates **Est.** 1989 **Cases** 10 000 **Vyds** 27.5 ha
Mt Jagged's vineyard was established in 1989 by the White family, with close-planted semillon, chardonnay, merlot, cabernet sauvignon and shiraz. The vineyard sits at 350 m above sea level on a diversity of soils ranging from ironstone/clay for the red varieties to sandy loam/clay for the whites. The cool-climate vineyard (altitude and proximity to the ocean) produces fresh, crisp, zingy white wines and medium-bodied savoury reds of complexity and depth. The vineyard has good rainfall and natural spring water in abundance, and is currently in the process of conversion to organic/biodynamic viticulture principles. Exports to the UK, the US, Canada and China.

ȲȲȲȲȲ **Single Vineyard Southern Fleurieu Shiraz 2006** A lively, juicy and delicious medium-bodied wine, clearly benefiting from 2% co-fermented viognier; silky mouthfeel and gossamer-fine tannins, French oak barely perceptible. Good value. Screwcap. 14% alc. **Rating** 92 **To** 2014 $22

Bullock Road Fleurieu Semillon Sauvignon Blanc 2008 A fragrant bouquet, with voluminous herb and cut grass aromas, the equally flavoursome palate moving into citrus, guava and apple territory. Value plus. Screwcap. 12.5% alc. **Rating** 91 **To** 2011 $15

Southern Fleurieu Sauvignon Blanc Semillon 2008 Crisp and clearly defined fruit; straw and a touch of gooseberry; quite fleshy on entry, but fine and poised on the finish. Value. Screwcap. 13% alc. **Rating** 90 **To** 2012 $18

Single Vineyard Reserve Southern Fleurieu Chardonnay 2007 Clean and fine, with stone fruits and a light touch of toasty oak; cinnamon spice on the palate marries well with generous texture and weight on the finish. Screwcap. 13% alc. **Rating** 90 **To** 2015 $25

Single Vineyard Southern Fleurieu Merlot Cabernet Sauvignon 2005
A well-made blend of Merlot (60%)/Cabernet Sauvignon (40%); has very attractive silky mouthfeel to the cedary palate with its red and black fruit interplay, the tannins fine. Screwcap. 14% alc. **Rating** 90 **To** 2014 $22

ŦŦŦŦ **Bullock Road Fleurieu Shiraz Cabernet Merlot 2006** A lively, savoury/spicy light- to medium-bodied palate, with fine tannins to close. Screwcap. 14.5% alc. **Rating** 87 **To** 2013 $15

Mount Langi Ghiran Vineyards ★★★★★

Warrak Road, Buangor, Vic 3375 **Region** Grampians
T (03) 5354 3207 **www.**langi.com.au **Open** Mon–Fri 9–5, w'ends 10–5
Winemaker Dan Buckle, Kate Petering **Est.** 1969 **Cases** 60 000
A maker of outstanding cool-climate peppery Shiraz, crammed with flavour and vinosity, and very good Cabernet Sauvignon. The Shiraz points the way for cool-climate examples of the variety. The business was acquired by the Rathbone family group in 2002, and hence the marketing has been integrated with the Yering Station, Parker Coonawarra and Xanadu Estate wines, a synergistic mix with no overlap. Exports to all major markets.

ŦŦŦŦŦ **Langi Shiraz 2007** Near-identical deep crimson colour to all six shiraz releases; has the multi-layered flavours promised by the bouquet, and more texture from the fine, ripe tannins, which run through the medium- to full-bodied palate and lingering aftertaste. Screwcap. 14.5% alc. **Rating** 96 **To** 2022 $75
Cliff Edge Riesling 2008 Very crisp, lively and fresh; a wine that reinforces the right of the Grampians to be regarded as a top-class region for riesling, the green apple, citrus and pear flavours delicate yet intense. Screwcap. 12% alc. **Rating** 94 **To** 2018 $25
Cliff Edge Pinot Gris 2008 Exceptionally vibrant and zesty, with energy and drive seldom encountered in the variety; has crunchy nashi pear fruit and citrussy/tangy acidity. Screwcap. 13% alc. **Rating** 94 **To** 2012 $25
Moyston Hills Vineyard Shiraz 2007 A vibrant wine in colour, aroma and flavour, with spicy black pepper fruits on the light- to medium-bodied palate, and a penetrating, zesty finish to the notably long palate. Screwcap. 14.5% alc. **Rating** 94 **To** 2017 $27
Billi Billi Shiraz 2007 Excellent hue and clarity; has a compelling mix of spice and licorice overtones to the medium-bodied, supple palate, all components in balance. Screwcap. 14.5% alc. **Rating** 94 **To** 2017 $15

ŦŦŦŦ̵ **Cliff Edge Shiraz 2007** Good colour; is more fragrant and lively, with strong spice notes to the plum and blackberry of the palate; has more zest and life perhaps, but not necessarily better than Billi Billi. Screwcap. 14.5% alc. **Rating** 93 **To** 2020 $27
Nowhere Creek Vineyard Shiraz 2007 Like Moyston Hills, the fruit is dominantly used in Cliff Edge, but a few barrels selected to be bottled separately; a fuller, richer wine than the others in the line-up, but carries its alcohol with nonchalance. Screwcap. 15% alc. **Rating** 93 **To** 2020 $27
Cliff Edge Sparkling Shiraz NV Deep colour; serious bottle-fermented style with some lees age; is neither oaky nor sweet, thanks to minimal phenolics; good length and finish. Cellaring will be rewarded. Crown Seal. 14.5% alc. **Rating** 92 **To** 2014 $35
Nut Tree Hill Sangiovese 2006 A fragrant, lively and fresh bouquet is precisely reflected by the palate, with a mix of red and sour cherries backed by notes of cedar and spice. Screwcap. 13.5% alc. **Rating** 91 **To** 2014 $27
The Gap Vineyard Shiraz 2007 Yet another building block for Cliff Edge; a strong/savoury spicy herbal edge to both bouquet and palate; while its worth in the blend is obvious, it is less convincing on its own. Screwcap. 14% alc. **Rating** 90 **To** 2017 $27

♀♀♀♀　Billi Billi Pinot Grigio 2008 A faint touch of straw ex the grape is no issue; a junior brother to Cliff Edge, pleasant but little more. Screwcap. 12% alc. **Rating** 87 **To** 2010 $15

Mt Lofty Ranges Vineyard ★★★★

Harris Road, Lenswood, SA 5240 **Region** Adelaide Hills
T (08) 8389 8339 **F** (08) 8389 8349 **Open** W'ends 11–5, or by appt Aug–May
Winemaker Adelaide Hills Fine Wine Centre, Simon Greenleaf, Peter Leske
(Consultants) **Est.** 1992 **Cases** 600 **Vyds** 4.6 ha
Owners Alan Herath and Jan Reed developed and operate the vineyard (pinot noir, sauvignon blanc, chardonnay and riesling), cellar door, and self-distribute the wines in SA. Skilled contract winemaking has brought rewards and recognition to the brand.

♀♀♀♀♀　Five Vines Riesling 2008 Finely structured wine, with citrus and green apple aromas and flavours; the palate is bone dry, with well-balanced acidity lengthening the finish. Great value. Screwcap. 12.5% alc. **Rating** 92 **To** 2017 $16
Old Pump Shed Lenswood Pinot Noir 2007 Light crimson-purple; has more intensity than the colour suggests, both bouquet and palate with a fine amalgam of cherry, plum and spice; good acidity draws out the finish. Excellent value, for early consumption. Screwcap. 14% alc. **Rating** 92 **To** 2012 $20
Sauvignon Blanc 2008 An evocative bouquet of citrus, herb and grass, then a delicate, lively palate, balanced acidity giving it freshness and length. Well priced. Screwcap. 12.5% alc. **Rating** 90 **To** 2010 $16

♀♀♀♀　Lenswood Chardonnay 2007 An unusually but commendably elegant wine, with stone fruit and ripe apple flavours set against subtle oak. Good value. Screwcap. 14% alc. **Rating** 89 **To** 2013 $16

Mount Majura Vineyard

RMB 314 Majura Road, Majura, ACT 2609 (postal) **Region** Canberra District
T (02) 6262 3070 **www**.mountmajura.com.au **Open** Thurs–Mon 10–5
Winemaker Dr Frank van de Loo **Est.** 1988 **Cases** 3000 **Vyds** 9.31 ha
The first vines were planted in 1988 by Dinny Killen on a site on her family property that had been especially recommended by Dr Edgar Riek; its attractions were red soil of volcanic origin over limestone, with reasonably steep east and northeast slopes providing an element of frost protection. The tiny vineyard established in '88 has been significantly expanded since it was purchased in '99. The pre-existing blocks of pinot noir, chardonnay and merlot have all been increased, and have been joined by pinot gris, shiraz, tempranillo, riesling, graciano, cabernet franc and touriga.

♀♀♀♀♀　Canberra Chardonnay 2007 Bright citrus fruit dominates the bouquet, with an underlying mineral complexity; concentrated fruit, with vibrant acidity, and just a touch of amaro bitterness, which provides a savoury interest to the finish. Screwcap. 12.6% alc. **Rating** 94 **To** 2015 $20

♀♀♀♀♀　Canberra District Shiraz 2007 Dark and savoury fruit bouquet, with a lift of fragrant floral character; spicy, medium-bodied and showing plenty of fine-grained tannins on the long and silky finish. Screwcap. 14.1% alc. **Rating** 93 **To** 2016 $25
Canberra District Riesling 2008 Tight, and quite surprisingly concentrated; the palate is generous yet fine and linear, with richness and poise that extends right through to the finish. Screwcap. 12.2% alc. **Rating** 90 **To** 2015 $18

♀♀♀♀　Canberra District Pinot Gris 2008 Pear and candied orange fruit bouquet; some green character on the palate, but this provides lively acidity and crisp texture on the finish. Screwcap. 12.3% alc. **Rating** 89 **To** 2014 $20
Canberra District Graciano 2007 Bright colour, with cranberry and a little spice; prominent acidity, and clean fruit provides an interesting, slightly savoury and tannic finish. Screwcap. 12.3% alc. **Rating** 88 **To** 2012 $20

Mount Mary

Coldstream West Road, Lilydale, Vic 3140 **Region** Yarra Valley
T (03) 9739 1761 **F** (03) 9739 0137 **www**.mountmary.com.au **Open** Not
Winemaker Rob Hall **Est.** 1971 **Cases** 3500 **Vyds** 13.6 ha
Superbly refined, elegant and intense Cabernets and usually outstanding and long-lived Pinot
Noirs fully justify Mount Mary's exalted reputation. The Triolet blend is very good; more
recent vintages of Chardonnay are even better. Founder and long-term winemaker, the late
Dr John Middleton, was one of the great, and truly original, figures in the Australian wine
industry. He liked nothing more than to tilt at windmills, and would do so with passion.
His annual newsletter grew longer as each year passed, although the paper size did not. The
only change necessary was a reduction in font size, and ultimately very strong light or a
magnifying glass (or both) to fully appreciate the barbed wit and incisive mind of this great
character. The determination of the family to continue the business is simply wonderful, even
if the 2007 vintage was severely reduced by frost. Limited quantities of the wines are sold
through the wholesale/retail distribution system in Victoria, New South Wales, Queensland
and South Australia.

Mount Moliagul

Clay Gully Lane, Moliagul, Vic 3472 **Region** Bendigo
T (03) 9809 2113 **www**.mountmoliagulwines.com.au **Open** By appt 0427 221 641
Winemaker Terry Flora **Est.** 1991 **Cases** 400
Terry and Bozenka Flora began their tiny vineyard in 1991, gradually planting 0.5 ha each
of shiraz and cabernet sauvignon, and 0.2 ha of chardonnay. Terry Flora has completed two
winemaking courses, one with Winery Supplies and the other at Dookie College, and has
learnt his craft very well. Unfortunately the 2006 vintage was destroyed by drought, and at
the time of going to press the '07 had not been bottled. The rating is that of the last wines
tasted ('05).

Mt Pilot Estate

208 Shannons Road, Byawatha, Vic 3678 **Region** North East Victoria Zone
T (03) 5726 5434 **F** (03) 5726 5434 **www**.mtpilotestatewines.com.au **Open** By appt
Winemaker Mandy Jones **Est.** 1996 **Cases** 800 **Vyds** 12 ha
Lachlan and Penny Campbell have planted to shiraz (5 ha), cabernet sauvignon (3 ha), and
durif and viognier (2 ha each). The vineyard is situated on thin granite soils at an altitude
of 250 m near Eldorado, 20 km from Wangaratta, and 35 km from Beechworth. The 2006
Shiraz won a silver medal at the Rutherglen Wine Show '08, placed in the top 20 out of 200
wines.

ɥɥɥɥɥ **Shiraz 2006** Good colour; the concentrated black fruits reflect the very low yield,
and largely carry the new oak maturation. Silver medal Rutherglen Wine Show
'08. Cork. 14.3% alc. **Rating** 90 **To** 2015 $25

ɥɥɥɥ **Cabernet Sauvignon 2006** Very ripe, almost essency cassis fruit character on
the bouquet; the palate is soft, rich, and full of sweet cassis fruit. Cork. 14.5% alc.
Rating 88 **To** 2014 $25

Mount Stapylton Vineyard ★★★

1212 Northern Grampians Road, Laharum, Vic 3401 (postal) **Region** Grampians
T (03) 9824 6680 **www**.mtsv.com.au **Open** Not
Winemaker Don McRae **Est.** 2002 **Cases** 100 **Vyds** 1 ha
Mount Stapylton Vineyard forms part of the historic Goonwinnow Homestead farming
property on the northwest side of the Grampians in front of Mt Stapylton. Owners Howard
and Samantha Staehr began the development of the shiraz vineyard (two-thirds Great Western
Old Block clone and one-third clone 1654) in 2002, and the vines have already produced
four highly acclaimed vintages; expansion of the vineyard will follow over the next few
years. Winemaker Don McRae is a busy man: he has been involved to a minor degree in the

Vic wine industry since undertaking a vine propagation and vineyard establishment course at Wangaratta TAFE in 1987, following this with a wine science degree at CSU in Wagga, finishing in 2000, while also involved in hospital work and studies.

 **Grampians Shiraz 2007** A potent wine with a confronting bouquet and palate; masses of black fruits, but some hard-to-define nuances and edges that may or may not settle down. Twin top. 14% alc. **Rating** 88 **To** 2015 $40

Mt Terrible

289 Licola Road, Jamieson, Vic 3723 **Region** Central Victoria Zone
T (03) 5777 0703 **www**.mtterrible-pinot.com **Open** By appt
Winemaker Delatite (Jane Donat) **Est.** 2001 **Cases** 400 **Vyds** 2 ha
John Eason and wife Janene Ridley began the long, slow (and at times very painful) business of establishing their vineyard in 1992, just north of Mt Terrible – hence the choice of name. The original plantings were trials, DIY home winemaking likewise, aided by an extensive library of how-to books. In 2001 they found the courage to plant 2 ha of pinot noir (MV6, 115, 114 and 777 clones) on a gently sloping, north-facing river terrace adjacent to the Jamieson River. The DIY trials persuaded John Eason to have the first commercial vintage in 2006 contract-made by Jane Donat, then Delatite winemaker. Construction has begun on an underground fireproof wine cellar, a cellar door to be built above. The Central Victoria Zone is shown as the region, as the vineyard is 5 km outside the boundary of the Upper Goulburn region.

 Jamieson Pinot Noir 2006 Excellent retention of red-purple hue; new generation French clones and MV6, plus sophisticated winemaking have produced a very pure, highly focused, razor sharp Pinot Noir, with a long palate and varietal definition. Screwcap. 14% alc. **Rating** 95 **To** 2014 $38.50

Mt Toolleen ★★★★

Level 12, North Tower, 459 Collins Street, Melbourne, Vic 3000 (postal)
Region Barossa Valley/Heathcote
T (03) 9885 1367 **F** (03) 9885 1367 **www**.mttoolleen.com.au **Open** Not
Winemaker Mark Jamieson (Contract) **Est.** 2000 **Cases** 1500 **Vyds** 17.5 ha
Mt Toolleen is owned by a group of Melbourne investors by a somewhat complicated joint venture scheme that gives Mt Toolleen access to 100 ha of shiraz grown in Barossa Valley, and ownership of a 17.5-ha vineyard in Heathcote. Exports to Canada, China, Taiwan, United Arab Emirates and Hong Kong.

 Kavel Barossa Valley Shiraz 2005 Bright colour; well-defined dark fruit, with a firm and tarry palate; quite tannic, but the fruit handles the structure well. Screwcap. 14.9% alc. **Rating** 90 **To** 2018

Mount Torrens Vineyards ★★★★★

PO Box 1679, Mt Torrens, SA 5244 **Region** Adelaide Hills
T 0418 822 509 **www**.solstice.com.au **Open** Not
Winemaker Torbreck (David Powell) **Est.** 1996 **Cases** 1000
Mount Torrens Vineyards has 2.5 ha of shiraz and viognier, and the distinguished team of Mark Whisson as viticulturist and David Powell as contract winemaker. The excellent wines are available by mail order and selected retailers, but are chiefly exported to the UK, the US and other major markets. The marketing is handled by owner and founder, David Thompson.

Solstice Adelaide Hills Shiraz 2006 Great hue and clarity; a spotlessly clean, gently spicy/peppery bouquet leads into a zesty/spicy palate with energy and thrust to its array of black fruits; excellent line and length. Screwcap. 14.2% alc. **Rating** 95 **To** 2018 $38
Solstice Adelaide Hills Shiraz Viognier 2005 Very good colour; has much more energy and intensity than the '06, with spicy black fruits and licorice lifting on the long finish and aftertaste. Screwcap. 14.3% alc. **Rating** 94 **To** 2020 $35

ϘϘϘϘϘ Solstice Adelaide Hills Shiraz 2005 Retains good hue; fragrant spice pepper, plum and black cherry fruit on the bouquet and palate; good mouthfeel and balance. Screwcap. 14.4% alc. **Rating** 93 **To** 2020 $38

Solstice Adelaide Hills Viognier 2006 Has substantially more going for it than most; there is strong varietal character in a stone fruit spectrum and palate richness; the twitch of heat on the finish has no ready explanation. Screwcap. 13.7% alc. **Rating** 90 **To** 2012 $29

Solstice Adelaide Hills Shiraz Viognier 2006 Neither the colour nor the flavours shows the normal intensity or lift of viognier; very different to both the '04 and '05 vintages; seems that the 10% addition was simply too high. Screwcap. 14.2% alc. **Rating** 90 **To** 2013 $35

ϘϘϘϘ Solstice Late Harvest Viognier 2008 Is an impressive example if you think Late Harvest Viognier is the way to go; I'm afraid I don't. Screwcap. **Rating** 87 **To** 2010 $32

Mount Trio Vineyard

2534 Porongurup Road, Mount Barker WA 6324 **Region** Porongurup
T (08) 9853 1136 **F** (08) 9853 1120 **www.**mounttriowines.com.au **Open** By appt
Winemaker Gavin Berry **Est.** 1989 **Cases** 7000 **Vyds** 8 ha
Mount Trio was established by Gavin Berry and Gill Graham shortly after they moved to the Mount Barker area in late 1988. They have slowly built up the business, increasing estate plantings from 2.5 ha to 8 ha of shiraz, riesling, pinot noir and sauvignon blanc. Exports to the UK, Denmark, Japan and Singapore.

ϘϘϘϘϘ Sauvignon Blanc 2008 Fragrant passionfruit-accented aromas; intense but quite juicy tropical fruits on the mid-palate, then citrus and mineral acidity to close. Screwcap. 12% alc. **Rating** 94 **To** 2011 $16

ϘϘϘϘϘ Gravel Pit Great Southern Riesling 2008 Restrained lemon fruit bouquet, with a serious mineral edge; this follows through on the palate, with a dry, high acid finish; time is needed. Screwcap. 11% alc. **Rating** 90 **To** 2016 $19.50

Great Southern Cabernet Merlot 2007 Dark varietal fruit, with black olive, cassis and a hint of plummy sweetness at the core; juicy, fine and surprisingly long on the finish. Very good value. Screwcap. 14% alc. **Rating** 90 **To** 2016 $16

ϘϘϘϘ Gravel Pit Great Southern Pinot Noir 2007 A firm wine, still to open up and soften sufficiently to let the varietal fruit express itself; two to three years may surprise. Screwcap. 13.5% alc. **Rating** 89 **To** 2013 $20

Gravel Pit Great Southern Riesling 2008 A mineral style of riesling that is very linear and very dry; lacks a little generosity, but will build. Screwcap. 11.5% alc. **Rating** 87 **To** 2020 $19.95

Gravel Pit Great Southern Shiraz 2007 Gravelly sums up the wine, as the dark fruit on offer is diminished by firm and gravelly tannins on the finish. Screwcap. 14% alc. **Rating** 87 **To** 2014 $19.50

Tempranillo 2007 Needs to put on more flesh and muscle, although the raspberry fruit flavours are pleasant enough. Screwcap. 13.5% alc. **Rating** 87 **To** 2012 $16

Mount View Estate

Mount View Road, Mount View, NSW 2325 **Region** Lower Hunter Valley
T (02) 4990 3307 **F** (02) 4991 1289 **www.**mtviewestate.com.au **Open** Mon–Sat 10–5, Sun 10–4
Winemaker Janelle Zerk **Est.** 1971 **Cases** 4000 **Vyds** 16 ha
John and Polly Burgess became the owners of Mount View Estate (8 ha) in 2000, and in '04 purchased the adjoining Limestone Creek Vineyard (8 ha); planted in 1982, it fits seamlessly into the Mount View Estate production.

♥♥♥♥♥ **Flagship Museum Release Shiraz 2003** A beautifully crafted wine with incredibly concentrated dark fruits, spice and an alluring overlay of violets; the palate is dense and chewy, but has an elegance and finesse that belies the obvious power; long and harmonious. Cork. 14.5% alc. **Rating** 95 **To** 2018 $55
Flagship Shiraz 2007 Densely concentrated black fruit core with a restrained spice character; quite fleshy with very fine tannin structure, the brightness of the fruit on the finish is very appealing. Screwcap. 14.5% alc. **Rating** 94 **To** 2016 $55

♥♥♥♥♀ **Reserve Museum Release Hunter Valley Semillon 2002** Has abundant developed toast and honey aromas; the palate also shows lots of toasty fruit, but the acid is quite tight and lemony, and the finish is long. Cork. 10% alc. **Rating** 93 **To** 2014 $28
Reserve Hunter Valley Pinot Noir 2007 Bright colour; a vibrant cherry fruit bouquet with a touch of spicy complexity; the palate is soft and supple, with fine tannin and vibrant acidity on the finish; a well-balanced wine. Screwcap. 14.5% alc. **Rating** 93 **To** 2013 $24
Reserve Hunter Valley Semillon 2008 Clean and focused with lemon and a touch of straw on the bouquet; the palate is zesty and linear, with hint of pea pod; quite generous and ready for early drinking. Screwcap. 11% alc. **Rating** 90 **To** 2014 $24
Limestone Creek Vineyard Chardonnay 2006 Quite restrained, with a fine and focused lemon fruit bouquet; the palate is zesty, has good acidity and finishes with grilled nuts. Screwcap. 14% alc. **Rating** 90 **To** 2012 $25
Limestone Creek Vineyard Verdelho 2008 An interesting and quite exotic bouquet of pear and ripe apple; there is generosity of fruit on the palate, and the vibrant acidity cleans up and prolongs the flavour with aplomb. Screwcap. 13% alc. **Rating** 90 **To** 2012 $21

♥♥♥♥ **Reserve Hunter Valley Chardonnay 2006** Vibrant colour; hints of nectarine and peach on the bouquet, with quite a distinct mineral edge; fresh and focused acidity, draws out some fig flavours on the finish; good balance. Screwcap. 14% alc. **Rating** 89 **To** 2013 $25
Willow Flat Chardonnay Semillon 2008 Clearly defined nectarine and green apple fruit on the bouquet; fresh acidity, and a slightly chalky element conclude the dry and zesty palate. Screwcap. 12% alc. **Rating** 89 **To** 2012 $17
Hunter Valley Late Harvest Semillon 2008 Pale colour; CO_2 on opening; medium sweet, with green nettle bouquet, dried straw and good acid; very clean and precise on the finish. Screwcap. 10% alc. **Rating** 88 **To** 2014 $20
Hunter Valley Sauvignon Blanc 2008 Pale colour; subdued bouquet, with a mere suggestion of tropical fruit; vibrant and quite juicy with a guava-like finish to the palate; a user-friendly style. Screwcap. 12.5% alc. **Rating** 87 **To** 2011 $20

Mount William Winery ★★★★☆

Mount William Road, Tantaraboo, Vic 3764 **Region** Macedon Ranges
T (03) 5429 1595 **F** (03) 5429 1998 **www.**mtwilliamwinery.com.au **Open** 7 days 11–5
Winemaker David Cowburn (Contract), Murray Cousins **Est.** 1987 **Cases** 3000 **Vyds** 7.5 ha
Adrienne and Murray Cousins purchased a 220-ha grazing property in 1985; the sheep and Angus cattle remain the principal part of the general farming program, but between 1987 and '99 they established pinot noir, chardonnay, cabernet franc, semillon and merlot. The quality of the wines has been consistently good, and are sold through a stone cellar door, and at a number of fine wine retailers around Melbourne.

♥♥♥♥♀ **Macedon 2001** Pale green–straw; exceptionally fine and crisp given five years on lees; citrus peel flavours and a long, dry finish; will flourish for several years on cork. Cork. 12% alc. **Rating** 92 **To** 2013 $35
Pinot Noir 2005 Light colour is deceptive; the wine is very intense and long, with predominantly spicy/foresty notes wrapped around red fruits. Short-term cellaring while the fruit holds. Screwcap. 13.5% alc. **Rating** 90 **To** 2012 $28

Mountadam   ★★★★☆

High Eden Road, Eden Valley, SA 5235 **Region** Eden Valley
T (08) 8564 1900 **F** (08) 8564 1999 **www**.mountadam.com.au **Open** By appt
Winemaker Con Moshos **Est.** 1972 **Cases** 35 000 **Vyds** 80 ha
Founded by the late David Wynn for the benefit of winemaker-son Adam, Mountadam was
(somewhat surprisingly) purchased by Cape Mentelle (doubtless under the direction of Möet
Hennessy Wine Estates) in 2000. Rather less surprising has been its sale in '05 to Adelaide
businessman David Brown, who has extensive interests in the Padthaway region. The arrival
of Con Moshos (long-serving senior winemaker at Petaluma) has already made a significant
impact in lifting the quality of the wines. One should hope so, because Con Moshos eats
(well, almost), drinks and sleeps Mountadam. Exports to the UK, France, Switzerland, Poland
and Hong Kong.

ⵑⵑⵑⵑⵑ **Eden Valley Pinot Gris 2008** Pale blush-pink; very attractive pinot gris with
a near-Alsace richness, yet without phenolics; long and spicy pear nuances, two
months in used French oak adding texture. Screwcap. 14.7% alc. **Rating** 94
To 2011 $25

ⵑⵑⵑⵑⵑ **High Eden Estate Chardonnay 2007** Bright straw-green; harmonious
bouquet and palate, with stone fruit, melon and oak well balanced and integrated; a
fractionally hard finish detracts a little. Screwcap. 13.5% alc. **Rating** 91 To 2014 $35
Eden Valley Riesling 2008 Flinty/spicy nuances to the bouquet lead into a
precise, as yet austere, palate; pleads for time in bottle, but will open up slowly.
Screwcap. 13.2% alc. **Rating** 90 To 2017 $25
Barossa Shiraz 2007 A light- to medium-bodied wine with strongly spicy/
savoury overtones to the fruit; doesn't show much impact from the Barossa Valley
component. An uncompromising and quite deliberate style. Screwcap. 14.2% alc.
Rating 90 To 2014 $18
Patriarch High Eden Shiraz 2006 Surprisingly light colour, although the hue is
good; a savoury, light- to medium-bodied wine, with spicy nuances to the savoury
fruit and minimal tannins. Just a little too restrained. Cork. 14% alc. **Rating** 90
To 2014 $35
Eden Valley Shiraz Viognier 2007 Good hue, but not the depth or intensity
of colour often achieved; the 8% co-fermented viognier has added considerably to
the fragrance of the red fruits on both the bouquet and light- to medium-bodied
palate. Screwcap. 14.5% alc. **Rating** 90 To 2014 $25

ⵑⵑⵑⵑ **The Red 2006** Clear and bright colour; like the Shiraz, is a bright, light-bodied
wine, with zesty fruit but needing more depth and structure. Merlot/Cabernet
Sauvignon/Shiraz/Cabernet Franc. Cork. 14% alc. **Rating** 89 To 2013 $35
Eden Valley Riesling 2007 Very much in the austere style established by Con
Moshos; flint, green apple and spice components, but not a lot of flesh on the
bones. Screwcap. 12.8% alc. **Rating** 88 To 2016 $25

Mr Riggs Wine Company   ★★★★★

Main Road, McLaren Vale, SA 5171 **Region** McLaren Vale
T (08) 8556 4460 **F** (08) 8556 4462 **www**.mrriggs.com.au **Open** 7 days 10–5
Winemaker Ben Riggs **Est.** 2001 **Cases** 20 000 **Vyds** 6.28 ha
After 24 years' winemaking experience, Ben Riggs is now well established under his own
banner. Ben sources the best fruit from individual vineyards in McLaren Vale, Clare Valley,
Adelaide Hills, Langhorne Creek, Coonawarra, and from his own Piebald Gully vineyard
(shiraz and viognier). Each wine is intended to express the essence of not only the vineyard,
but also the region's terroir. The vision of the Mr Riggs brand is unpretentious and personal,
'to make the wines I love to drink'. Exports to the UK, the US and other major markets.

ⵑⵑⵑⵑⵑ Yacca Paddock Adelaide Hills Tempranillo 2007 Clear, bright colour; has a
strong dark cherry and licorice cast to the aromas and fore-palate before a savoury,
well-balanced finish. Screwcap. 14.5% alc. **Rating** 95 To 2015 $25

Watervale Riesling 2008 A fragrant and fine bouquet foretells a similarly immaculately poised and balanced palate offering a pas de deux of citrus and acidity. Screwcap. 12% alc. **Rating** 94 **To** 2018 $22

Adelaide Viognier 2008 Complex winemaking inputs are obvious on the bouquet, and to a lesser degree on the rich palate; wild yeast, oak and partial mlf all build layers, yet don't make the wine phenolic. Points added for the degree of difficulty. Screwcap. 13.5% alc. **Rating** 94 **To** 2012 $25

McLaren Vale Shiraz 2007 Good colour; a complex, but strongly regional style; with the near-obligatory dark chocolate surrounding the plum and blackberry fruit; is medium- to full-bodied, with excellent balance and mouthfeel. A pity the US market still insists on cork. 15% alc. **Rating** 94 **To** 2022 $50

ΨΨΨΨΨ **Piebald Shiraz Viognier 2007** Lovely concentration, the shiraz getting a small floral lift from the viognier component; very good texture. Screwcap. 14.5% alc. **Rating** 93 **To** 2017 $27

Adelaide Hills Riesling VOR-GS 2008 The clean and correct bouquet does not point to the very rich and sweet mouthfeel of tropical fruit that follows. Screwcap. 11.5% alc. **Rating** 92 **To** 2013 $22

ΨΨΨΨ **The Gaffer McLaren Vale Shiraz 2007** Has some curious smoky/spicy aromas, most likely from whatever oak medium has been used; the texture is gently chewy, the balance very good. Screwcap. 15% alc. **Rating** 89 **To** 2017 $22

Coonawarra Cabernet 2007 While the wine falls short of the hyperbole on the back label, it does show good regional cabernet; the underlying hint of earth is sure to develop in the years ahead, joining the black fruits which dominate today. Screwcap. 14.5% alc. **Rating** 89 **To** 2015 $25

Sticky End McLaren Vale Viognier 2008 Desiccated on racks; lively acidity gives the wine appeal, although it is not especially sweet. Screwcap. 11.5% alc. **Rating** 89 **To** 2012 $22

Mulyan ★★★

North Logan Road, Cowra, NSW 2794 **Region** Cowra
T (02) 6342 1336 **F** (02) 6341 1015 **Open** W'ends & public hols 10–5, or by appt
Winemaker Contract **Est.** 1994 **Cases** 2000
Mulyan is a 1350-ha grazing property purchased by the Fagan family in 1886 from Dr William Redfern, a leading 19th-century figure in Australian history. The current-generation owners, Peter and Jenni Fagan, began planting in 1994, and intend the vineyard area to be 100 ha in all. Presently there are 29 ha of shiraz, 14.5 ha of chardonnay, and 4.6 ha each of merlot and viognier. The label features a statue of the Roman god Mercury, which has stood in the homestead garden since being brought back from Italy in 1912 by Peter Fagan's grandmother. Exports to the UK and China.

ΨΨΨΨ **Cowra Viognier 2007** An abundant apricot, pear and peach assemblage with just enough acidity to balance the high alcohol. Ready now. Screwcap. 15.1% alc. **Rating** 87 **To** 2009 $20

Cowra Shiraz 2007 Strongly oaky bouquet, with smoky black fruits and some leathery complexity; strong tannins need to soften. Screwcap. 14.2% alc. **Rating** 87 **To** 2014 $20

Munari Wines ★★★★

Ladys Creek Vienyard, 1129 Northern Highway, Heathcote, Vic 3523 **Region** Heathcote
T (03) 5433 3366 **F** (03) 5433 3905 **www**.munariwines.com **Open** Tues–Sun 11–5
Winemaker Adrian Munari, Deborah Munari **Est.** 1993 **Cases** 2500 **Vyds** 6.9 ha
Established on one of the original Heathcote farming properties, Ladys Creek Vineyard is situated on the narrow Cambrian strip 11 km north of the town. Adrian Munari has harnessed traditional winemaking practices with New World innovation to produce complex, fruit-driven wines that marry concentration and elegance. They are produced form estate plantings of shiraz, cabernet sauvignon, cabernet franc, malbec and merlot. Exports to France and Taiwan.

ŢŢŢŢŢ The Beauregard Heathcote Shiraz 2006 A dense and brooding wine; dark fruit abounds, with tar and earth on the bouquet; the palate is thick and chewy, but has a lively core of fruit; the finish is long, generous and even. Screwcap. 15% alc. **Rating** 92 **To** 2015 $30

Ladys Pass Heathcote Shiraz 2006 Dense and dark, showing a blackberry bouquet with a touch of mint; the palate is quite thick on entry, and a little forward; warm, rich and slightly spicy on the finish. Cork. 14.5% alc. **Rating** 90 **To** 2014 $45

ŢŢŢŢ Heathcote Cabernet Sauvignon 2006 Strong cassis aromas; quite a rich and warm palate, with ample sweet fruit from start to finish. Cork. 14% alc. **Rating** 87 **To** 2013 $35

Murchison Wines   ★★★☆

105 Old Weir Road, Murchison, Vic 3610 **Region** Goulburn Valley
T (03) 5826 2294 **F** (03) 5826 2510 **www**.murchisonwines.com.au **Open** W'ends & most public hols 10–5, or by appt
Winemaker Guido Vazzoler **Est.** 1975 **Cases** 4000 **Vyds** 8.1 ha
Sandra (ex kindergarten teacher turned cheesemaker) and Guido Vazzoler (ex Brown Brothers) acquired the long-established Longleat Estate vineyard in 2003 (renaming it Murchison Wines), after living on the property (as tenants) for some years. The mature vineyard comprises 3.2 ha of shiraz, 2.3 ha of cabernet sauvignon, 0.8 ha each of semillon, sauvignon blanc and chardonnay, and 0.2 ha petit verdot. Exports to Hong Kong.

ŢŢŢŢŢ Longleat Estate Semillon 2008 Attractive lemon/lemongrass aromas, the palate following suit, flavourful despite the low alcohol; drink now or later. Top value. Screwcap. 11.5% alc. **Rating** 90 **To** 2014 $15

ŢŢŢŢ Longleat Estate Chardonnay 2008 Very light-bodied, but fragrant, the delicate stone fruit flavours not imperilled by the touch of oak. Screwcap. 13% alc. **Rating** 87 **To** 2012 $15

Murdoch Hill   ★★★★☆

Mappinga Road, Woodside, SA 5244 **Region** Adelaide Hills
T (08) 8389 7081 **F** (08) 8389 7991 **www**.murdochhill.com.au **Open** By appt
Winemaker Brian Light (Contract), Michael Downer **Est.** 1998 **Cases** 2550 **Vyds** 20.5 ha
A little over 20 ha of vines were established on the undulating, gum-studded countryside of Charlie and Julie Downer's 60-year-old Erinka property, 4 km east of Oakbank. In descending order of importance, the varieties planted are sauvignon blanc, shiraz, cabernet sauvignon and chardonnay. Son Michael, with a Bachelor of Oenology degree from Adelaide University, is assistant winemaker. Exports to the UK and Canada.

Murdock   ★★★★★

Riddoch Highway, Coonawarra, SA 5263 **Region** Coonawarra
T (08) 8737 3700 **F** (08) 8737 2107 **www**.murdockwines.com **Open** By appt
Winemaker Balnaves (Pete Bissell) **Est.** 1998 **Cases** 4500 **Vyds** 24.7 ha
The Murdock family has established 10.4 ha of cabernet sauvignon, 2 ha of shiraz, 1 ha of merlot, 0.8 ha of riesling and 0.5 ha of chardonnay in Coonawarra, and produces small quantities of an outstanding Cabernet Sauvignon, contract-made by Pete Bissell. A second vineyard has been added in the Barossa Valley, with 5.8 ha of shiraz and 2.1 ha each of semillon and cabernet sauvignon. The labels, incidentally, are ultra-minimalist; there's no flood of propaganda here. The Barossa Valley cellar door is now open 7 days 10–5 (Magnolia Road, Vine Vale). Exports to Canada and Singapore.

ŢŢŢŢŢ Coonawarra Cabernet Sauvignon 2004 Great colour; super-intense blackcurrant and earthy Coonawarra cabernet fruit on the bouquet and medium-bodied palate; tannins and extract are perfectly balanced; would have a much longer life under screwcap. Cork. 14.5% alc. **Rating** 96 **To** 2020 $45

Coonawarra Riesling 2008 Clean, fresh, tight wine with excellent focus and structure to the apple and citrus flavours; will blossom with age in bottle. Screwcap. 13.3% alc. **Rating** 94 **To** 2018 $19

Murray Street Vineyard ★★★★

Lot 723, Murray Street, Greenock, SA 5360 **Region** Barossa Valley
T (08) 8562 8373 **F** (08) 8562 8414 **Open** 7 days 10–4.30
Winemaker Andrew Seppelt **Est.** 2001 **Cases** 10 000
Andrew Seppelt has moved with a degree of caution in setting up Murray Street Vineyard, possibly because of inherited wisdom and the business acumen of partner Bill Jahnke, a successful investment banker with Wells Fargo. Andrew is a direct descendant of Benno and Sophia Seppelt, who built Seppeltsfield and set the family company bearing their name on its path to fame. The partnership has 46 ha of vineyards, one block at Gomersal, the other at Greenock, with the lion's share going to shiraz, followed by grenache, mourvedre, viognier, marsanne, semillon and zinfandel. Most of the grapes are sold, with a small (but hopefully increasing) amount retained for the Murray Street Vineyard brand. The Benno (Shiraz Mataro) is the icon tribute on the masculine side; the Sophia (Shiraz) the feminine icon. Unusually good point of sale/propaganda material. No red wines submitted for this edition. Exports to the UK, the US, Canada and Denmark.

ŸŸŸŸŸ Eden Valley Riesling 2008 Quite fragrant aromas in a citrus spectrum, the palate retreating into stony/minerally notes and a dry finish. Screwcap. 12.5% alc. **Rating** 90 **To** 2013 $20
Barossa Valley Rose 2008 A dry and crisp mix of herbs and spices take this wine well into Provençale style; ideal for summer salads. Screwcap. 12.3% alc. **Rating** 90 **To** 2009 $20

ŸŸŸŸ Barossa Valley Semillon 2008 A bright and lively wine, happily unadorned by oak; has good length and thrust to its lemony fruit. Screwcap. 12% alc. **Rating** 89 **To** 2013 $20
Barossa Valley Viognier Marsanne 2008 Rich and ripe, spiced apricot bouquet; thickly textured, with a lightly bitter twist to the finish. Screwcap. 14.5% alc. **Rating** 87 **To** 2011 $25

Murrindindi Vineyards ★★★★

30 Cummins Lane, Murrindindi, Vic 3717 **Region** Upper Goulburn
T (03) 5797 8448 **F** (03) 5797 8448 **www**.murrindindivineyards.com **Open** Not
Winemaker Hugh Cuthbertson **Est.** 1979 **Cases** 3000 **Vyds** 15 ha
Situated in an unequivocally cool climate, which means that special care has to be taken with the viticulture to produce ripe fruit flavours. In more recent vintages, Murrindindi has by and large succeeded in so doing.

ŸŸŸŸŸ Family Reserve Yea Valley Chardonnay 2008 A lively, crisp and vibrant wine, driven by nectarine and grapefruit aromas and flavours, oak precisely positioned. Will age gracefully. Screwcap. 13.5% alc. **Rating** 93 **To** 2016 $28
Family Reserve Yea Valley Shiraz 2006 Bright, spicy/savoury and fragrant overtones on the bouquet and to the black fruits of the medium-bodied palate; silky tannins on the fine finish. Screwcap. 14% alc. **Rating** 93 **To** 2016 $25
Don't Tell Dad Cabernet Sauvignon 2004 Has held colour remarkably well since first tasted Oct '05; a very powerful, almost inky, cabernet with black fruits and tannins still in in an Indian arm wrestle, but the fruit will win. Screwcap. 14% alc. **Rating** 93 **To** 2019 $18.80
Don't Tell Dad Yea Valley Riesling 2008 Has good overall intensity and varietal character; ripe citrus notes on the bouquet intensify on the well-balanced palate. Screwcap. 13% alc. **Rating** 90 **To** 2015 $18.80

Myola Vineyard

137 Griffins Road, Coghills Creek, Vic 3364 (postal) **Region** Ballarat
T (03) 5343 4368 **F** (03) 5343 4369 **Open** Not
Winemaker Eastern Peake (Norman Latta) **Est.** 1996 **Cases** 50 **Vyds** 2.5 ha
Cheryl Hines and Anthony Fergusson purchased Conihfer Park in 2003. It is part agistment farm and part vineyard, with 1.5 ha of pinot noir and 1 ha of chardonnay planted in 1996. The vines were in full bearing, and the grapes were sold to other wineries in the region. One tonne of pinot was retained and vinified for Myola Vineyard in 2005, followed by another small make in '07. The partners hope to eventually make some pinot each year, with chardonnay part of the mix. Finally, they have made a sparkling wine for their daughter's wedding, and intend to follow this up with limited releases in the years to come.

ΨΨΨΨΥ **Pinot Noir 2007** Good clarity and hue; clearly delineated cool-climate pinot fruit characters, tangy and brisk; good length. Screwcap. 13% alc. **Rating** 90 To 2013 $30

Myrtaceae

53 Main Creek Road, Main Ridge, Vic 3928 **Region** Mornington Peninsula
T (03) 5989 2045 **Open** 1st w'end of month, public hols & Jan w'ends 12–5
Winemaker Julie Trueman **Est.** 1985 **Cases** 300 **Vyds** 1 ha
Owners John Trueman (viticulturist) and wife Julie (winemaker) began the planting of Myrtaceae in 1985, intending to make a Bordeaux-style red blend. It became evident that these late-ripening varieties were not well suited to the site, so the vineyard was converted to 0.5 ha each of pinot noir and chardonnay in 1998. Part of the property is devoted to the Land for Wildlife Scheme; the integrated Australian garden is a particular feature.

ΨΨΨΨΥ **Mornington Peninsula Chardonnay 2007** Straw-green; in the suave, slightly creamy, traditional style of Mornington Peninsula chardonnay, all the stone fruit, oak and fermentation characters seamlessly folded together. Screwcap. 13.5% alc. **Rating** 90 To 2013 $30

Naked Range Wines

125 Rifle Range Road, Smiths Gully, Vic 3760 **Region** Yarra Valley
T (03) 9710 1575 **F** (03) 9710 1655 **www**.nakedrangewines.com **Open** By appt
Winemaker Simon Wightwick (Contract) **Est.** 1996 **Cases** 2500 **Vyds** 5.8 ha
Mike Jansz has established his vineyard on a steep and rocky site, one-third sauvignon blanc, a small patch of pinot noir and the remainder cabernet sauvignon (predominant), merlot and chardonnay. The wines are made at Punt Road and marketed under the striking Naked Range label, with a second label, Duet, using grapes from other Victorian regions and exported to Asia.

ΨΨΨΨΥ **Sauvignon Blanc 2008** Very well made, the partial barrel ferment in no way diminishing the passionfruit-accented aroma and flavour of what is a light-bodied wine. Screwcap. 12.7% alc. **Rating** 90 To 2011 $18

ΨΨΨΨ **Yarra Valley Pinot Noir 2006** Has plenty of presence with forceful sappy/minty edges to the palate; a little more flesh on its bones needed. Screwcap. 13.5% alc. **Rating** 89 To 2012 $22

Nardone Baker Wines

PO Box 386, McLaren Vale, SA 5171 **Region** McLaren Vale
T (08) 8445 8100 **F** (08) 8445 8200 **www**.nardonebaker.com **Open** Not
Winemaker Brian Light (Contract) **Est.** 1999 **Cases** 23 000
Italian-born Joe Nardone and English-born John Baker were brought together by the marriage of Joe's daughter and John's son. Both were already in the wine industry, John studying at Roseworthy Agricultural College and establishing a vineyard. The second generation of Frank Nardone and Patrick Baker, the latter having also studied at Roseworthy,

now run what is a significant virtual winery, sourcing grapes from all over SA, with contract winemaking by Brian Light at Boar's Rock. There are five ranges, headed by The Wara Manta Reserve, followed by the Nardone Baker, Blaxland's Legacy, Treeview Selection and Wara Manta (non-reserve). Exports to various markets including the UK and the US.

♀♀♀♀♀ The Wara Manta Reserve McLaren Vale Shiraz 2006 There can be no complaints about the quality of this wine, with similar fruit to the varietal, the main difference being the American oak in which it spent 18 months. The price relativity is a conundrum beyond my comprehension. Cork. 14.5% alc. **Rating** 91 **To** 2016 $78

♀♀♀♀ Shiraz 2006 All in all, a very smart wine at this price; no frills, the great vintage and blackberry fruit selection doing the work; good tannin support. Cork. 14.5% alc. **Rating** 89 **To** 2014 $13.95

Narkoojee

170 Francis Road, Glengarry, Vic 3854 **Region** Gippsland
T (03) 5192 4257 **F** (03) 5192 4238 **www**.narkoojee.com **Open** 7 days 10.30–4.30
Winemaker Harry Friend, Axel Friend **Est.** 1981 **Cases** 3000
Narkoojee Vineyard (originally a dairy farm owned by the Friend family) is within easy reach of the old gold mining town of Walhalla and looks out over the Strzelecki Ranges. The wines are produced from a little over 10 ha of estate vineyards, with chardonnay accounting for half the total. Former lecturer in civil engineering and extremely successful amateur winemaker Harry Friend changed horses in 1994 to take joint control, with Axel Friend, of the family vineyard and winery, and hasn't missed a beat since; their skills show through with all the wines, none more so than the Chardonnay. Exports to Canada, Ireland, Maldives, Japan, Hong Kong and Singapore.

♀♀♀♀♀ Gippsland Cabernet Sauvignon 2006 Perfectly ripened fruit invests the wine with freshness and offering vibrant cassis-accented varietal fruit; has grace and length. Diam. **Rating** 94 **To** 2016 $28

♀♀♀♀♀ Isaac Gippsland Shiraz 2007 Crimson-red; has intense cherry, plum and blackberry fruit with spice and pepper notes in the background; medium-bodied, but has considerable drive and length. Diam. 14.5% alc. **Rating** 93 **To** 2022 $28
The Athelstan Gippsland Merlot 2006 Very deep colour; quite serious red fruits and black olives; vibrant acidity, and plentiful fine-grained tannins; quite long, savoury and well structured. Cork. 13.5% alc. **Rating** 92 **To** 2016 $28
Lily Grace Gippsland Chardonnay 2008 Deep, but bright, colour; ripe stone fruit on entry moves more into nutty/creamy flavours and textures on the mid-palate; generous style. Diam. 13.5% alc. **Rating** 90 **To** 2012 $20

♀♀♀♀ Yorkie's Gully Gippsland Rose 2008 Crisp, tangy wine aged for some months in old barriques; savoury notes on the palate and energetic finish. Bargain. Screwcap. 14% alc. **Rating** 88 **To** 2010 $12
Gippsland Pinot Noir 2007 Very deep colour; concentrated, deep plum fruit; impressive in every respect except for the lack of finesse and blossoming on the back-palate expected of pinot noir. Diam. 14% alc. **Rating** 88 **To** 2015 $24

Nazaaray

266 Meakins Road, Flinders, Vic 3929 **Region** Mornington Peninsula
T (03) 5989 0126 **www**.nazaaray.com.au **Open** 1st weekend of each month, or by appt
Winemaker Paramdeep Ghumman **Est.** 1996 **Cases** 900
Paramdeep Ghumman is, as far as I am aware, the only Indian-born winery proprietor in Australia. He and his wife migrated from India over 20 years ago, and purchased the Nazaaray vineyard property in 1991. An initial trial planting of 400 vines in 1996 was gradually expanded to the present level of 1.6 ha of pinot noir, 0.4 ha of pinot gris and 0.15 ha of chardonnay. Notwithstanding the micro size of the estate, all the wines are made and bottled onsite. Exports to Singapore.

♱♱♱♱ **Mornington Peninsula Sauvignon Blanc 2008** A varietal bouquet of green nettle and passionfruit; fresh palate, with slightly raspy acidity and persistent gunsmoke flavour. Screwcap. 12.5% alc. **Rating** 88 **To** 2012 $25

Mornington Peninsula Pinot Gris 2008 Ripe pear aromas and flavours provide presence, but the line of the palate is not clear enough for higher points. Screwcap. 14.5% alc. **Rating** 87 **To** 2009 $25

Neagles Rock Vineyards ★★★★☆

Lot 1 & 2 Main North Road, Clare, SA 5453 **Region** Clare Valley
T (08) 8843 4020 **www**.neaglesrock.com **Open** Mon–Sat 10–5, Sun 11–4
Winemaker Steve Wiblin, Ang Meaney (Consultant) **Est.** 1997 **Cases** 11 000 **Vyds** 16.1 ha
Owner-partners Jane Willson and Steve Wiblin have taken the plunge in a major way, simultaneously raising a young family, resuscitating two old vineyards, and – for good measure – stripping a dilapidated house to the barest of bones and turning it into a first-rate, airy restaurant-cum-cellar door. They bring decades of experience, gained at all levels of the wine industry, to Neagles Rock, and built upon this by the 2003 acquisition of the outstanding and mature vineyards of Duncan Estate, adding another level of quality to their wines. Listed for sale in April 2009 by specialist wine industry brokers and advisers Gaetjens Langley. Exports to the UK, the US and other major markets.

♱♱♱♱♱ **Clare Valley Cabernet Sauvignon 2006** Clear, deep red-purple; attractive, lively blackcurrant and redcurrant fruits with an echo of mint; fine, supple mouthfeel. Screwcap. 14.5% alc. **Rating** 93 **To** 2016 $25

Clare Valley Riesling 2008 Spotlessly clean; fresh lime and lemon fruit against a gentle background of minerally acidity; ready to drink sooner than later. Screwcap. 12% alc. **Rating** 92 **To** 2016 $19

Clare Valley Semillon Sauvignon Blanc 2008 Cleverly made; a touch of barrel-fermented semillon in new French oak results in a complex, but not heavy, wine with gentle tropical fruits giving way to the crisp and lively green apple flavours of the semillon on the finish. Screwcap. 13.5% alc. **Rating** 91 **To** 2012 $19

Mr Duncan Clare Valley Cabernet Shiraz 2007 Replete with blackberry, blackcurrant, chocolate, spice and a dash of vanilla oak, all balanced by soft, ripe tannins; nothing to dislike, everything to like, including the price. Screwcap. 14.5% alc. **Rating** 91 **To** 2016 $20

Clare Valley Sangiovese 2006 A complex but quite supple array of cherry, strawberry, cedar and spice flavours on the long palate. Screwcap. 14.5% alc. **Rating** 91 **To** 2014 $25

Clare Valley Shiraz 2006 Some colour development; abundant flavour, with strong mocha and vanilla flavours tending to somewhat submerge the fruit, but the texture and structure are good. Screwcap. 14.5% alc. **Rating** 90 **To** 2016 $25

Misery Clare Valley Grenache Shiraz 2007 Typical light colour; vibrant and fresh aromas and flavours in a raspberry and cherry spectrum; avoids cosmetic notes. Screwcap. 14.5% alc. **Rating** 90 **To** 2012 $20

♱♱♱♱ **Clare Valley Sangiovese 2007** Nebbiolo may be harder, but sangiovese is no bed of roses, sweet or not; the pretty red cherry fruits are encircled by dusty tannins. Screwcap. 13.5% alc. **Rating** 87 **To** 2009 $25

Neil Hahn Wines ★★★★

PO Box 64, Stockwell, SA 5355 **Region** Barossa Valley
T (08) 8562 3002 **F** (08) 8562 1111 **www**.hahnbarossa.com **Open** Not
Winemaker Mark Jamieson **Est.** 1885 **Cases** 3500 **Vyds** 45.52 ha
Neil Hahn Wines has a very long history. On 25 January 1839 Johann Christian Hahn and wife Maria Elizabeth left their home in Silesia to travel to SA on the sailing ship Catharina. They were among the earliest white settlers to arrive, and in 1846 Johann purchased 32 ha of land in the Barossa Valley. In 1885 son Johann Christian II bought land of his own, situated

on Light Pass Road. Mixed farming and viticulture were common and now, after being in the Hahn family for five generations, the property is totally planted to vines under the care and ownership of Neil and Sandy Hahn. There are 19.6 ha at this vineyard, and a further 30 ha in the Ebenezer Vineyard. The wines, contract-made by Mark Jamieson, overflow with luscious red and black fruit flavours and copious amounts of American oak.

ŶŶŶŶŶ **Yanyarrie Riesling 2005** Starting to show the benefits of bottle development, lime and lemon juice flavours emerging, balanced by minerally acidity and (perhaps) the faintest touch of residual sweetness. Exceptional value. Screwcap. 12% alc. **Rating** 92 **To** 2013 $13.95

Yanyarrie Riesling 2008 Highly fragrant mix of lemon, lime and apple blossom aromas, then a crisp and penetrating palate; a dry finish; but with a question mark about some volatility. Screwcap. 12.5% alc. **Rating** 91 **To** 2015 $13.95

Catharina Shiraz 2006 Holding deep crimson hue; a heroic wine, jam-packed with ripe shiraz fruit and integrated vanillin American oak. Screwcap. 15% alc. **Rating** 91 **To** 2020 $28.95

Catharina Shiraz 2004 Holding red-purple hue very well; has blackberry, prune, licorice and dark chocolate flavours in abundance, but seems much higher than 15% alcohol. Screwcap. 15% alc. **Rating** 91 **To** 2014 $28.95

Catharina Shiraz 2005 Strong crimson-red; an effusive bouquet of lush, ripe fruits, followed by a high octane, fruit-driven palate. What you see is what you get, but is nonetheless a polarising style. Screwcap. 15% alc. **Rating** 90 **To** 2020 $28.95

ŶŶŶŶ **Yanyarrie Riesling 2007** Pale straw-green; a tightly wound, minerally wine, promising more for the future than it delivers today; the balance and acidity are good. Screwcap. 12% alc. **Rating** 89 **To** 2014 $13.95

Yanyarrie Shiraz 2006 There is no doubting the generosity of the flavour, nor the warmth to the mouthfeel. Top barbecue red. Screwcap. 15% alc. **Rating** 87 **To** 2013 $17.95

Nepenthe ★★★★

Jones Road, Balhannah, SA 5242 **Region** Adelaide Hills
T (08) 8398 8888 **F** (08) 8388 1100 **www**.nepenthe.com.au **Open** 7 days 10–4
Winemaker Andre Bondar **Est.** 1994 **Cases** 70 000 **Vyds** 108.64 ha
The Tweddell family has 100 ha of close-planted vineyards in the Adelaide Hills, with an exotic array of varieties. In late 1996 it obtained the second licence to build a winery in the Adelaide Hills (Petaluma was the only prior successful applicant, back in '78). Nepenthe quickly established its reputation as a producer of high-quality wines. Founder Ed Tweddell died unexpectedly in 2006; in March '07 son James announced that McGuigan Simeon had purchased the winery, causing many industry observers to scratch their heads. In '09 the Adelaide Hills winery was closed, and winemaking operations transferred to Australian Vintage (aka McGuigan Simeon's principal SA winery). Exports to the UK, the US and other major markets.

ŶŶŶŶŶ **Ithaca Adelaide Hills Chardonnay 2006** Bright colour; quite restrained, but showing a powerful mix of stone fruit, oak and mineral complexity; thickly textured on entry, the palate delivers a lively and crisp acid finish. Screwcap. 13.5% alc. **Rating** 93 **To** 2014 $38

The Rogue Adelaide Hills Cabernet Shiraz Merlot 2006 Bright colour; a savoury bouquet of wild herb, blackberry and plum; medium-bodied with good texture, and really vibrant fruit at the core; clean, spicy, complex and quite long. Screwcap. 14.5% alc. **Rating** 92 **To** 2015 $24

Adelaide Hills Sauvignon Blanc 2008 A positive bouquet, with passionfruit, gooseberry, and a touch of citrus, characters that flow through to the well-balanced palate. Screwcap. 13.5% alc. **Rating** 90 **To** 2010 $22.99

ŶŶŶŶ **The Rogue Adelaide Hills Cabernet Shiraz Merlot 2005** Bright, fresh light- to medium-bodied mix of blackcurrant, blackberry, mint, leaf and cedar. Screwcap. 14% alc. **Rating** 89 **To** 2012 $21

Tempranillo 2008 Good colour; prominent choc-mint bouquet, bright and focused cherry and plum fruit; a little spice comes forward on the palate, and the texture is generous and focused. Screwcap. 13.5% alc. **Rating** 89 **To** 2013 $25

Charleston Adelaide Hills Pinot Noir 2007 Bright cherry and plum fruit with a touch of mint; a spicy palate, and also quite firm and long; a big expression of the variety. Screwcap. 13.5% alc. **Rating** 88 **To** 2013 $24

Adelaide Hills Zinfandel 2006 A good example of the sweet zinfandel varietal character, with a dry, sour cherry finish. Screwcap. 14.5% alc. **Rating** 88 **To** 2012 $35

Neqtar Wines

Campbell Avenue, Irymple, Vic 3498 **Region** Murray Darling
T (03) 5024 5704 **F** (03) 5024 6605 **www**.neqtarwines.com.au **Open** Mon–Sat 10–4.30
Winemaker Robert Pezzaniti, Gary Compton, Peter Lyons **Est.** 1998 **Cases** 400 000
This is yet another Australian–UK joint venture in similar vein to Willunga 100 Wines. The UK end is distributor HwCg, while the Australian components include the former Evans & Tate–owned Salisbury Winery at Irymple, and Roberts Estate at Merbein. A $2 million upgrade of the Salisbury Winery was completed prior to the 2007 vintage. The wines come in three price levels: at the bottom is the Roberts Estate brand, the Commissioner's Block next and, at the top, Calder Grove. Exports to the UK and Asia.

Salisbury White Label Cabernet Shiraz 2008 Bright colour; spicy red and black fruit bouquet; clean and fresh, with focused acid and moderate length on the finish. Good value. Screwcap. 14.6% alc. **Rating** 88 **To** 2012 $9.95

Salisbury White Label Semillon Chardonnay 2008 Clean and crisp, with nectarine, straw and a touch of lemon; a vibrant palate with a fresh finish. Screwcap. 13.1% alc. **Rating** 88 **To** 2011 $9.95

Salisbury Premium Semillon Sauvignon Blanc 2008 Pale colour; clean, crisp with a touch of tropical and green fruit character; fresh, lively and dry on the finish. Screwcap. 12.6% alc. **Rating** 87 **To** 2012 $11.95

Calder Grove Chardonnay 2008 Clear, clean, juicy stone fruit flavours; good balance and length; reflects chardonnay surplus. Screwcap. 13.9% alc. **Rating** 87 **To** 2011 $15.95

Commissioner's Block Shiraz 2006 Simple bright red and black fruit flavours without obvious oak embellishment, but lifted by a touch of viognier. Well priced. Screwcap. 14% alc. **Rating** 87 **To** 2010 $11.95

New Era Vineyards

PO Box 391, Woodside SA 5244 **Region** Adelaide Hills
T (08) 8389 7715 **F** (08) 8389 7715 **www**.neweravineyards.com.au **Open** Not
Winemaker Robert Baxter, Reg Wilkinson **Est.** 1988 **Cases** 600 **Vyds** 12.5 ha
The New Era vineyard is situated over a gold reef that was mined for 60 years until all recoverable gold had been extracted (mining ceased in 1940). The vineyard was originally planted to chardonnay, shiraz, cabernet sauvignon, merlot and sauvignon, mostly contracted to Foster's. Recently 2 ha of cabernet sauvignon and 1.1 ha of merlot have been grafted over to sauvignon blanc. The small amount of wines made has been the subject of favourable reviews, and it's not hard to see why.

Basket Pressed Adelaide Hills Shiraz 2003 The colour is still remarkably deep; potent black fruits, licorice, spice and pepper are evident from the word go; a wine of great power and intensity and sold at a price bordering on silly. Cork. 13.5% alc. **Rating** 94 **To** 2023 $16

Adelaide Hills Merlot 2003 A fragrant bouquet of cassis, leaf and olive lead into a quite vibrant medium-bodied palate with an abundance of varietal fruit, finishing with fine-grained tannins. Cork. 13.5% alc. **Rating** 93 **To** 2013 $16

♈♈♈♈   Adelaide Hills Cabernet Sauvignon 2003 Very powerful and intense, but is just a little too earthy/savoury; needs more sweet fruit. Cork. 13.5% alc. **Rating** 89 **To** 2014 $16

Newtons Ridge   ★★★☆

1170 Cooriemungle Road, Timboon, Vic 3268 **Region** Geelong
T (03) 5598 7394 **www.**newtonsridge.com.au **Open** 7 days 11–5 Nov–Apr, or by appt
Winemaker David Newton **Est.** 1998 **Cases** 1500 **Vyds** 4 ha
David and Dot Newton say that after milking cows for 18 years, they decided to investigate the possibility of planting a northeast-facing block of land that they also owned. Their self-diagnosed mid-life crisis also stemmed from a lifelong interest in wine. They planted 2 ha of chardonnay and pinot noir in 1998, and another 2 ha of pinot gris, pinot noir and sauvignon blanc the following year. Having done a short winemaking course at Melbourne University (Dookie campus), the Newtons completed a small winery in 2003. Originally called Heytesbury Ridge, the winery had a speedy name change to Newtons Ridge after a large legal stick was waved in their direction.

♈♈♈♈♈   Shiraz 2007 Its cool-grown origins are clear-cut; spice, pepper, tar and a touch of licorice, but there are also some attractive black fruit notes, and good length. Screwcap. 14% alc. **Rating** 90 **To** 2015 $20

 # Nick O'Leary Wines   ★★★★

129 Donnelly Road, Bungendore, NSW 2621 **Region** Canberra District
T (02) 6161 8739 **F** (02) 6166 0572 **www.**nickolearywines.com.au **Open** By appt
Winemaker Nick O'Leary **Est.** 2007 **Cases** 750 **Vyds** 0.5 ha
At the ripe old age of 28 years, Nick O'Leary had been involved in the wine industry for over a decade, working variously in retail, wholesale, viticulture and winemaking. Two years earlier he had laid the foundation for Nick O'Leary Wines, purchasing shiraz from local vignerons (commencing in 2006) and riesling following in '08. His wines have had extraordinary success in the Winewise Small Vignerons Show, which is a very exacting competition. The 2006 Shiraz and '08 Riesling both won gold medals, the Riesling topping its class. Similar success was achieved at the Canberra District Wine Show '08.

♈♈♈♈♈   Riesling 2008 Bright, pale green-straw; a spotlessly clean and lively mix of citrus, green apple and a touch of spice; good balance and length, and a promising future already. Screwcap. 12.5% alc. **Rating** 93 **To** 2018 $24

♈♈♈♈   Shiraz 2007 Relatively light colour; light- to medium-bodied, with savoury/spicy aromas and flavours to the fore; needed more fruit. Screwcap. 13.5% alc. **Rating** 88 **To** 2015 $27

 # Nine Fingers   ★★★

PO Box 212, Lobethal, SA 5241 **Region** Adelaide Hills
T (08) 8389 6049 **Open** By appt at The Adelaide Hills Wine Cellar, Lobethal
Winemaker Contract **Est.** 1999 **Cases** 200 **Vyds** 1 ha
Simon and Penny Cox established their sauvignon blanc vineyard after encouragement from local winemaker Robb Cootes of Leland Estate. The small vineyard has meant that they do all the viticultural work, and meticulously tend the vines. They obviously have a sense of humour, which may not be shared by their youngest daughter Olivia. In 2002 two-year-old Olivia's efforts to point out bunches that needed to be thinned resulted in Penny's secateurs cutting off the end of Olivia's finger. A race to hospital and successful microsurgery resulted in the full restoration of the finger; strangely, Olivia has shown little interest in viticulture ever since, but will be reminded of the incident by the name of the business and the design of the label.

♈♈♈♈   Adelaide Hills Sauvignon Blanc 2008 A lean steely style; strong mineral character on the bouquet, but needs more fruit on the palate for higher points. Screwcap. 13% alc. **Rating** 87 **To** 2011 $18.99

919 Wines

NR

Section 919, Hodges Road, Berri, SA 5343 **Region** Riverland
T (08) 8582 4436 **www**.919wines.com.au **Open** Thurs–Mon 10–5
Winemaker Eric Semmler, Jenny Semmler **Est.** 2002 **Cases** 5000 **Vyds** 2.9 ha
Eric and Jenny Semmler have been involved in the wine industry since 1986, and have a special
interest in fortified wines. Eric previously made fortified wines for Hardys at Berri Estates, and
worked at Brown Brothers. Jenny has worked for Strathbogie Vineyards, Pennyweight Wines,
St Huberts and Constellation. They have planted micro-quantities of varieties specifically for
fortified wines: palomino, durif, tempranillo, muscat a petits grains, tinta cao, shiraz, tokay and
touriga nacional. Notwithstanding their Riverland GI, they use minimal water application
and deliberately reduce the crop levels, practising organic and biodynamic techniques where
possible. Grapes are purchased from other growers if the need arises; the grapes are hand-
picked, fermented in open fermenters and basket-pressed before the juice is fortified.

Nintingbool

56 Wongerer Lane, Smythes Creek, Vic 3351 (postal) **Region** Ballarat
T (03) 5342 4393 **F** (03) 5342 4393 **www**.nintingbool.com **Open** Not
Winemaker Peter Bothe **Est.** 1998 **Cases** 200 **Vyds** 2 ha
Peter and Jill Bothe purchased the Nintingbool property in 1982 and built the home in
which they now live in '84, using old bluestone dating back to the goldrush period. They
established an extensive Australian native garden and home orchard, but in 1998 diversified
with the planting of pinot noir, a further planting the following year lifted the total to 2 ha; a
small amount of the property remains to be planted with pinot gris. This is one of the coolest
mainland regions, and demands absolute attention to detail (and a warm growing season)
for success. In 2002 and '03 the grapes were sold to Ian Watson, the wine made and released
under the Tomboy Hill label but with the Nintingbool Vineyard shown on the label (the '02
was quite a beautiful wine). In '04 they decided to make the wines themselves, the opening
vintage producing a tiny 44 cases.

ŸŸŸŸŸ **Ballarat Pinot Noir 2007** Light, bright crimson; a light-bodied, tangy/savoury/
foresty pinot, with a subtle core of red fruits and ultra-fine tannins; will never be
generous, but that is Ballarat. Screwcap. 13.7% alc. **Rating** 91 **To** 2013 $37

Nocton Park

373 Colebrook Road, Richmond, Tas 7025 **Region** Southern Tasmania
T (03) 6260 2088 **F** (03) 6260 2880 **www**.noctonpark.com.au **Open** By appt
Winemaker Winemaking Tasmania (Julian Alcorso) **Est.** 1998 **Cases** 7000 **Vyds** 31.6 ha
Nocton Park is part of a corporate group, which aims to become a significant supplier of
Tasmanian wine. It employs a full-time viticulturist under whose direction and skill Nocton
Park continues to lift the quality of grapes it delivers to its chosen winemakers who produce
wines destined for both domestic and export markets. The connection with Domaine A
remains fundamental, because it was Peter Althaus of Domaine A who, in 1995, showed
Nocton Park executive Chris Ellis a 100-ha site that he (Althaus) described as the best
vineyard land in the Coal River Valley. Today that site has plantings of pinot noir, chardonnay,
merlot and sauvignon blanc. Exports to China.

ŸŸŸŸŸ **Chardonnay 2007** Good straw-green; obvious oak on the bouquet, but
intense stone fruit/grapefruit flavours take control on the palate. Cork. 13.5% alc.
Rating 90 **To** 2014 $25

ŸŸŸŸ **Pinot Noir 2007** Powerful, concentrated ripe black fruits; finishes with some
savoury notes typical of the vintage. Cork. 13.5% alc. **Rating** 89 **To** 2014 $25
Pinot Noir Rose 2008 Vivid light fuschia; abundant fruit flavour, but needed
a touch more acidity to give energy and length. Screwcap. 12.7% alc. **Rating** 88
To 2010 $20

Nolan Vineyard

217 Badger Creek Road, Badger Creek, Vic 3777 **Region** Yarra Valley
T (03) 5962 3435 **Open** Fri–Mon & public hols 10–5
Winemaker Paul Evans (Contract) **Est.** 2000 **Cases** 100 **Vyds** 1.8 ha
John and Myrtle Nolan have established low-yielding, non-irrigated pinot noir using clones
114, 115 and MV6. Myrtle had worked in Yarra Valley vineyards for 10 years across all sectors
of the Valley, and (one assumes it is Myrtle who says) 'John is a faithful supporter of the
vineyard endeavours and is highly valued at picking time because of his large and extended
family.' The vineyard, incidentally, is very close to the Healesville Sanctuary.

ΨΨΨΨ   **Yarra Valley Pinot Noir 2006** Bricking colour; undergrowth, spice and a touch
of plum; certainly developed, but with some richness to the finish. Diam. 14% alc.
Rating 87 **To** 2011 $22.50

Norfolk Rise Vineyard

Limestone Coast Road, Mount Benson, SA 5265 **Region** Mount Benson
T (08) 8768 5080 **F** (08) 8768 5083 **www**.norfolkrise.com.au **Open** Mon–Fri 9–5
Winemaker René Bezemer **Est.** 2000 **Cases** 85 000 **Vyds** 130.3 ha
This is by far the largest and most important development in the Mount Benson region. It
is ultimately owned by a privately held Belgian company, G & C Kreglinger, established in
1797. In early 2002 it acquired Pipers Brook Vineyard; it will maintain the separate brands
of the two ventures. The Mount Benson development commenced in 2000, with a large
vineyard and a 2000-tonne winery, primarily aimed at the export market. Exports to the UK,
the US and other major markets.

ΨΨΨΨΨ   **Mount Benson Cabernet Sauvignon 2006** Good colour; has the weight and
conviction lacking in other Norfolk Rise wines; strong blackcurrant varietal fruit
supported by balanced tannins and a long finish. Screwcap. 14.5% alc. **Rating** 92
To 2016 $16

ΨΨΨΨ   **Mount Benson Merlot 2006** Light colour and body, but in an almost
Burgundian fashion; has surprising flavour and movement on the palate and finish.
At its best now. Screwcap. 14% alc. **Rating** 88 **To** 2010 $16
Mount Benson Pinot Grigio 2008 Crisp and lively, with good length to pear
and apple flavours; clean finish. Screwcap. 12.5% alc. **Rating** 87 **To** 2009 $17

Normanby Wines

Rose-Lea Vineyard, 178 Dunns Avenue, Harrisville, Qld 4307 **Region** Queensland Zone
T (07) 5467 1214 **F** (07) 5467 1021 **www**.normanbywines.com.au **Open** 7 days 10–5
Winemaker Golden Grove Estate (Ray Costanzo) **Est.** 1999 **Cases** 700 **Vyds** 2.84 ha
Normanby Wines, about 50 km due south of Ipswich, fills in more of the Qld viticultural
jigsaw puzzle. The vineyard has just under 3 ha planted to verdelho, shiraz, merlot, viognier,
chambourcin, durif and grenache.

ΨΨΨΨΨ   **Chauvel Shiraz 2007** Clear crimson-red; very well-made wine, with a fragrant
bouquet and delicious mix of red and black fruits on the medium-bodied, supple
palate. Another strike for Qld. Screwcap. 14.6% alc. **Rating** 93 **To** 2017 $25

Norton Estate ★★★☆

758 Plush Hannans Road, Lower Norton, Vic 3401 **Region** Western Victoria Zone
T (03) 5384 8235 **F** (03) 5384 8235 **www**.nortonestate.com.au **Open** Wed–Sun 10–5
Winemaker Best's Wines **Est.** 1997 **Cases** 1250 **Vyds** 4.32 ha
In 1996 the Spence family purchased a run-down farm at Lower Norton and, rather than
farming the traditional wool, meat and wheat, trusted their instincts and planted vines on
the elevated frost-free buckshot rises. The surprising vigour of the initial planting of shiraz
prompted further plantings of shiraz, cabernet sauvignon and sauvignon blanc. The vineyard
is halfway between the Grampians and Mt Arapiles, 6 km northwest of the Grampians GI

and will have to be content with the Western Victoria Zone, but the wines show regional Grampians character and style. A traditional Wimmera ripple iron barn has been converted into a cellar door.

ŸŸŸŸŸ **Shiraz 2005** Remarkable colour retention; an elegant and lively medium-bodied palate with black and red fruits in equal proportions, the tannins fine, oak restrained. Screwcap. 13.5% alc. **Rating** 90 **To** 2015 $22

ŸŸŸŸ **Sauvignon Blanc 2008** Has considerable presence thanks to the abundance of tropical fruits that roll across the palate; generous and ready to drink. Screwcap. 13% alc. **Rating** 89 **To** 2010 $17.50
Arapiles Run Shiraz 2007 Good red-purple; powerful wine, with ripe red and black fruits, and tannins needing to smooth out the rough edges. Screwcap. 13.5% alc. **Rating** 89 **To** 2017 $35
Shiraz 2006 Excellent bright colour; has a somewhat loose structure, fruit at one end, tannins and acidity at the other; this should come together over the next few years. Screwcap. 14% alc. **Rating** 89 **To** 2016 $22

Norton Summit Vineyards   ★★★★

59 Nicholls Road, Norton Summit, SA 5136 **Region** Adelaide Hills
T (08) 8390 1986 **F** (08) 8390 1986 **www.**nsv.net.au **Open** By appt
Winemaker Kenn Fisher **Est.** 1998 **Cases** 500 **Vyds** 2.5 ha
Dr Kenn Fisher and partner Meredyth Taylor planted the 1.5 ha of pinot noir and 0.5 ha of chardonnay in 1998. The vineyard has five blocks, each with its own mesoclimate, orientation and soil type. To add further complexity, four clones have been utilised. With additional vine age, the use of new French oak has been increased to 30%. Kenn makes the wines using traditional Burgundian methods of open fermenters and a basket press.

ŸŸŸŸŸ **Reserve Adelaide Hills Pinot Noir 2007** More depth to the colour than the Estate; very much in the savoury/foresty end of the spectrum, although extract and oak kept in restraint. Screwcap. 13.5% alc. **Rating** 91 **To** 2013 $35
Estate Adelaide Hills Pinot Noir 2006 Brighter hue than the Reserve, although showing development; a mix of sappy/minty notes and black cherry fruit; fine tannins, subtle oak. Screwcap. 13.5% alc. **Rating** 90 **To** 2012 $27.50

ŸŸŸŸ **Adelaide Hills Chardonnay 2006** Bright green-straw; a fresh and precise palate, with juicy stone fruits and a squeeze of grapefruit; subtle oak. Screwcap. 13.5% alc. **Rating** 89 **To** 2012 $25
Adelaide Hills Chardonnay 2007 A light-bodied mix of stone fruits, apple and a touch of citrus, the softening effect of mlf and barrel ferment a little too evident. Screwcap. 13.5% alc. **Rating** 88 **To** 2012 $27.50

Nova Vita Wines   ★★★★★

GPO Box 1352, Adelaide, SA 5001 **Region** Adelaide Hills
T (08) 8356 0454 **F** (08) 8356 1472 **www.**novavitawines.com.au **Open** Not
Winemaker Peter Leske, Mark Kozned **Est.** 2005 **Cases** 16 000 **Vyds** 46 ha
Mark and Jo Kozned spent months of painstaking research before locating the property on which they have now established their vineyard. Situated 4 km outside of Gumeracha, it has gentle slopes, plenty of water and, importantly, moderately fertile soils. Here the 30-ha Woodlands Ridge Vineyard is planted (in descending order of size) to chardonnay, sauvignon blanc, pinot gris and shiraz. They have subsequently established the Tunnel Hill Vineyard near Forreston, with 16 ha planted to pinot noir, shiraz, cabernet sauvignon, sauvignon blanc, semillon, verdelho, merlot and sangiovese. The name Nova Vita reflects the beginning of the Kozneds' new life, the firebird on the label coming from the Kozneds' Russian ancestry. It is a Russian myth that only a happy or lucky person may see the bird or hear its song. The increased vineyard resources have led to the Mad Russian range, exclusive to Cellarmasters in Australia, but also exported. Exports to the US, Singapore and Hong Kong.

🍷🍷🍷🍷🍷 **Single Vineyard Chardonnay 2007** A delicious and very well made Adelaide Hills chardonnay, with perfectly ripened nectarine, melon and grapefruit flavours balanced by quality French oak running through the long palate and aftertaste. Screwcap. 13% alc. **Rating** 95 **To** 2016 $30

Firebird Adelaide Hills Sauvignon Blanc 2008 A powerful bouquet running through herb, gooseberry and passionfruit promises much, and the palate doesn't disappoint, delivering all those flavours on a long palate and finish. Screwcap. 11.5% alc. **Rating** 94 **To** 2011 $22

Mad Russian Adelaide Hills Sauvignon Blanc 2008 A very interesting contrast, picked later and fermented bone dry, the accent on citrussy/grassy/herbal flavours, the finish fine but long. Screwcap. 13% alc. **Rating** 94 **To** 2011 $22.99

Mad Russian Adelaide Hills Chardonnay 2008 A similar, fascinating contrast as with the Sauvignon Blancs; this is a less flamboyant wine, with stone fruit, crisp apple and citrus flavours on the long, even palate, oak again controlled. Both are exemplary, but very different styles. Screwcap. 13.5% alc. **Rating** 94 **To** 2015 $22.99

Firebird Adelaide Hills Chardonnay 2008 Brilliant straw-green; has an opulent array of stone fruit, fig and citrus aromas and flavours, which drive both bouquet and palate, a touch of barrel ferment lurking in the background. Screwcap. 13.8% alc. **Rating** 94 **To** 2014 $22

🍷🍷🍷🍷½ **Firebird Adelaide Hills Pinot Gris 2008** Straw colour, quite acceptable, likely ex skin contact; complex and full-bodied, in genuine gris (Alsace) style; has good texture, and does not rely on sweetness. Nonetheless, strange it is more expensive than the Chardonnay. Screwcap. 14% alc. **Rating** 93 **To** 2012 $25

Firebird Adelaide Hills Shiraz 2007 Strong colour; a complex bouquet of spiced black fruits leads into an intense medium- to full-bodied palate, with some foresty nuances along with spice and pepper; lingering finish. Screwcap. 14.5% alc. **Rating** 93 **To** 2020 $25

Mad Russian Adelaide Hills Pinot Grigio 2008 Certainly more to grigio style, but not all the way, for it retains positive pear fruit; has good acidity. Screwcap. 13.5% alc. **Rating** 91 **To** 2011 $22.99

Mad Russian Adelaide Hills Shiraz 2006 Fragrant spicy red fruits on the bouquet are replicated on the medium-bodied palate, but without any extra characters; that said, does have length and balance. Screwcap. 14% alc. **Rating** 90 **To** 2020 $26.99

🍷🍷🍷🍷 **Mad Russian Adelaide Hills Pinot Noir 2008** Strong colour, and a bouquet and palate to match; black cherry and plum, with a strong foresty backdrop; will improve. Cork. 14.5% alc. **Rating** 89 **To** 2013 $26.99

Nugan Estate ★★★★★

60 Banna Avenue, Griffith, NSW 2680 **Region** Riverina
T (02) 6962 1822 **F** (02) 6962 6392 **www**.nuganestate.com.au **Open** Mon–Fri 9–5
Winemaker Darren Owers **Est.** 1999 **Cases** 400 000

Nugan Estate arrived on the scene like a whirlwind. It is an offshoot of the Nugan Group headed by Michelle Nugan, inter alia the recipient of an Export Hero Award in 2000. In the mid-1990s the company began developing vineyards, and is now a veritable giant with 310 ha at Darlington Point, 52 ha at Hanwood and 120 ha at Hillston (all in NSW), 100 ha in the King Valley and 10 ha in McLaren Vale. In addition, it has contracts in place to buy 1000 tonnes of grapes per year from Coonawarra. It sells part of the production as grapes, part as bulk wine and part under the Cookoothama and Nugan Estate labels. Both brands are having considerable success in wine shows, large and small. Exports to the UK, the US and other major markets.

🍷🍷🍷🍷🍷 **Alcira Vineyard Coonawarra Cabernet Sauvignon 2005** Thirty months in new and used French oak has not overwhelmed the juicy redcurrant, mulberry and blackcurrant fruit; good texture, balance and length. Screwcap. 14% alc. **Rating** 94 **To** 2015 $22.95

Alfredo Frasca's Lane Vineyard King Valley Sangiovese Merlot 2006
A major surprise, the two varieties working symbiotically and synergistically in
a spray of cherry and raspberry fruit aromas and flavours; fine tannins. Screwcap.
14% alc. **Rating** 94 **To** 2016 $22.95

ŸŸŸŸŸ **Frasca's Lane Vineyard King Valley Sauvignon Blanc 2008** Has a lifted,
aromatic bouquet, the promise fulfilled by the palate with its intense mix of
tropical and more grassy flavours, which are, however, seamless. Screwcap. 13% alc.
Rating 93 **To** 2010 $19.95
Parish Vineyard McLaren Vale Shiraz 2006 Bright colour; generous, plush,
blackberry, plum and chocolate flavours on the medium-bodied palate; ripe
tannins, good oak. Screwcap. 14.5% alc. **Rating** 93 **To** 2018 $22.95
Cookoothama Darlington Point Cabernet Merlot 2006 Good colour; a
dark savoury bouquet complemented by well-handled oak; bright, juicy, complexed
by a chewy finish. Great value. Screwcap. 14% alc. **Rating** 92 **To** 2013 $14.95
Manuka Grove Vineyard Durif 2007 Has the usual deep colour and powerful
black fruits on bouquet and palate; savoury, albeit fine, tannins are a distinct plus.
Screwcap. 14.5% alc. **Rating** 90 **To** 2017 $22.95

ŸŸŸŸ **Manuka Grove Vineyard Durif 2006** Good colour; red and black plum, and
blackberry fruit on a medium-bodied palate; good tannins. Screwcap. 14.5% alc.
Rating 89 **To** 2012 $22.95
Cookoothama King Valley Riesling 2008 Generously proportioned and
flavoured; tropical fruits with balanced acidity to close; no need to wait. Screwcap.
12.5% alc. **Rating** 87 **To** 2011 $14.95
Talinga Park Semillon Sauvignon Blanc 2008 Hard to deny at this price, the
King Valley sauvignon blanc component lifting the Riverina semillon; inevitably,
just a little light-on, but given a leg up courtesy of its price. Screwcap. 12% alc.
Rating 87 **To** 2010 $9.95
King Valley Pinot Grigio 2008 Whether the grigio label (rather than gris) is
appropriate is arguably beside the point; has plenty of pear and apple flavour, but
does shorten on the finish. Screwcap. 13.5% alc. **Rating** 87 **To** 2009 $19.95

Nuggetty Vineyard ★★★☆

280 Maldon-Shelbourne Road, Nuggetty, Vic 3463 **Region** Bendigo
T (03) 5475 1347 **F** (03) 5475 1647 **www.**nuggettyvineyard.com.au **Open** W'ends &
public hols (10–5 winter, 10–6 summer), or by appt
Winemaker Greg Dedman **Est.** 1993 **Cases** 2000 **Vyds** 6 ha
This family-owned business is managed by Greg Dedman and daughter Meisha; Greg has a
formidable array of degrees: biology, then aquatic biology, then CSU oenology, and finally
business administration from Deakin University. If this were not enough, he has 25 vintages
under his belt, spreading from Jaboulet in the Rhône Valley to Seppelt Great Western,
Lindemans Karadoc and Best's before joining Blue Pyrenees in 1997. Apart from Nuggetty
Vineyard, his principal present occupation is that of senior winemaker at Bendigo Institute of
TAFE. Exports to the UK and China.

ŸŸŸŸŸ **Bendigo Cabernet Sauvignon 2006** Bright colour; red fruit, sage and a little
thyme on the bouquet; medium-bodied, with fine tannin and focused fruit on the
finish. Screwcap. 13.5% alc. **Rating** 90 **To** 2014 $20

ŸŸŸŸ **Barrel Fermented Semillon 2008** Quite restrained flavour and weight, but
good overall flavour and weight. Screwcap. 12.5% alc. **Rating** 87 **To** 2012 $15

Nursery Ridge Estate

8514 Calder Highway, Red Cliffs, Vic 3496 **Region** Murray Darling
T (03) 5024 3311 **F** (03) 5024 3114 **Open** Thurs–Sun, school & public hols 10–4.30
Winemaker Bob Shields **Est.** 1999 **Cases** 2000 **Vyds** 60.8 ha

The estate takes its name from the fact that the first vineyard was situated on the site of the original vine nursery at Red Cliffs. The holdings have since been expanded to plantings on three additional vineyards: Wilga Road, Cottrell's Hill Road and Calder. It is a family-owned and operated affair, with shiraz, cabernet sauvignon, chardonnay, petit verdot, pinot noir, ruby cabernet and viognier. The well-priced wines are usually well made, with greater richness and depth of fruit flavour than most other wines from the region.

ΨΨΨΨ **Coorong Petit Verdot 2008** Bright colour; lifted violet perfume and lots of cassis; fresh and lively, without a great deal of complexity. Screwcap. 14% alc. **Rating** 88 **To** 2012 $18

O'Donohoe's Find ★★★

PO Box 460, Berri, SA 5343 **Region** Riverland
T 0414 765 813 **F** (08) 8583 2228 **www**.tomsdrop.com.au **Open** By appt
Winemaker Michael O'Donohoe **Est.** 2002 **Cases** 600 **Vyds** 2.8 ha
Michael O'Donohoe pays tribute to his Irish grandfather, Thomas O'Donohoe, and six great-uncles, who arrived from Ireland in 1881 to search for gold, ending up distilling salty bore water into fresh water. A century later Michael O'Donohoe runs a small vineyard in the Riverland that was certified organic in 1990, receives very little water and crops at around 2 tonnes per acre. A further 4 ha of vines and native trees were planted in 2008. The wines (released under the Tom's Drop label) are made using a tiny crusher, a small hand-operated basket press, and open fermenters. Exports to the UK, the US and Singapore.

ΨΨΨΨ **Tom's Drop Mourvedre Shiraz 2007** Leather, licorice and spice components drive both the bouquet and medium-bodied palate, which has good structure, mouthfeel and length. Screwcap. 13.5% alc. **Rating** 89 **To** 2015 $30
Tom's Drop Shiraz 2007 Relatively pale colour; light- to medium-bodied; savoury spicy fruit has surprising length and persistence, the finish and aftertaste clean. Screwcap. 13.8% alc. **Rating** 87 **To** 2013 $25

O'Leary Walker Wines

Main Road, Leasingham, SA 5452 (PO Box 49, Watervale, SA 5452) **Region** Clare Valley
T (08) 8843 0022 **www**.olearywalkerwines.com **Open** Mon–Fri 10–7, w'ends by appt
Winemaker David O'Leary, Nick Walker **Est.** 2001 **Cases** 18 000 **Vyds** 35 ha
David O'Leary and Nick Walker together had more than 30 years' experience as winemakers working for some of the biggest Australian wine groups when they took the plunge in 2001, and backed themselves to establish their own winery and brand. Initially the principal focus was on the Clare Valley, with 10 ha of riesling, shiraz, cabernet sauvignon and semillon the main plantings; thereafter attention swung to the Adelaide Hills, where they now have 25 ha of chardonnay, cabernet sauvignon, pinot noir, shiraz, sauvignon blanc and merlot. Exports to the UK, Ireland and Singapore.

ΨΨΨΨΨ **Polish Hill River Riesling 2008** Apple, lime and slate aromas; a beautifully structured and focused palate, the flavour flowing on evenly from the bouquet; thoroughly impressive line and length. Screwcap. 12% alc. **Rating** 95 **To** 2016 $20
Clare Valley McLaren Vale Shiraz 2006 Crimson-purple; sumptuously rich and velvety fruit on the medium- to full-bodied palate is supported by good oak and ripe tannins. Screwcap. 14.5% alc. **Rating** 95 **To** 2021 $22.50
Clare Valley Cabernet Sauvignon 2006 Rich, juicy blackcurrant fruit aromas and flavours are perfectly supported by ripe tannins on the medium-bodied palate; quality oak adds to the picture. Screwcap. 14.5% alc. **Rating** 95 **To** 2021 $22.50

ΨΨΨΨΨ **Adelaide Hills Sauvignon Blanc 2008** Elegant and crisp, with clearly defined varietal fruit on bouquet and palate, ranging through grassy to passionfruit notes; good length and finish. Screwcap. 12.5% alc. **Rating** 93 **To** 2010 $18.50
Watervale Riesling 2008 Lime blossom bouquet and palate; very fresh and lively, with a minerally backbone; lacks the complexity of the Polish Hill. Screwcap. 12% alc. **Rating** 91 **To** 2013 $18.50

Blue Cutting Road Clare Valley Cabernet Merlot 2006 A bright and clearly defined red berry, cedar and coffee bouquet; the palate shows generous levels of ripe fruit, with cleansing acidity and slightly savoury tannins. Great value. Screwcap. 14.5% alc. **Rating** 90 **To** 2014 $15

Blue Cutting Road Clare Valley Adelaide Hills Semillon Sauvignon Blanc 2008 Developed, although bright, colour; a clean, relatively restrained bouquet leads into a palate full of energy and thrust with grassy fruit and brassy acidity; an ideal match for fish and chips. Screwcap. 11.5% alc. **Rating** 90 **To** 2010 $15

ŸŸŸŸ **Hurtle Adelaide Hills Pinot Noir Chardonnay 2004** Quite a limey bouquet; good flavour and quite dry and chalky on the palate; pulls up a little short. Cork. 12% alc. **Rating** 87 **To** 2013 $28

Oakdene Vineyards   ★★★★

255 Grubb Road, Wallington, Vic 3221 **Region** Geelong
T (03) 5256 3886 **F** (03) 5256 3881 **www**.oakdene.com.au **Open** 7 days noon–11 pm
Winemaker Ray Nadeson, Robin Brockett **Est.** 2001 **Cases** 1500 **Vyds** 10.4 ha
Bernard and Elizabeth Hooley purchased Oakdene in 2001. Bernard focused on planting the vineyard (shiraz, pinot gris, sauvignon blanc, pinot noir, merlot, cabernet franc and cabernet sauvignon), while Elizabeth worked to restore the 1920s homestead. In 2004 they opened the Oakdene restaurant, through which much of the wine is sold. Ray Nadeson makes Chardonnay, Pinot Noir and Shiraz; Robin Brockett makes the Sauvignon Blanc.

ŸŸŸŸŸ **Elizabeth Chardonnay 2007** Attractive, relatively subtle, barrel ferment aromas augment the grapefruit, apple and honeydew melon fruit, with some creamy cashew notes along the way. Screwcap. 13.5% alc. **Rating** 91 **To** 2013 $28

Jessica Sauvignon Blanc 2008 Delicate aromas of passionfruit and gooseberry with a counterpoint of grass/herb lead into a lively palate, fresh acidity giving both balance and length. Screwcap. 12.5% alc. **Rating** 90 **To** 2010 $28

ŸŸŸŸ **Pinot Noir 2007** Complex aromas of spice, briar and charcuterie/smoked meat; the light palate has good intensity, plum and cherry surrounded by spicy/briary notes. Screwcap. 13% alc. **Rating** 89 **To** 2012 $28

Oakover Wines

14 Yukich Close, Middle Swan, WA 6056 **Region** Swan Valley
T (08) 9374 8000 **F** (08) 9250 7544 **www**.oakoverwines.com.au **Open** 7 days 11–4
Winemaker Rob Marshall, Craig Newton **Est.** 1990 **Cases** 60 000 **Vyds** 100 ha
Oakover Wines is a family-operated winery located in the Swan Valley. Formerly part of Houghton, in 1990 it came under the Yukich family's control as Oakover Estate. Prominent Perth funds manager Graeme Yukich and his family have been involved in the region since Nicholas Yukich purchased his first block of land in 1929. In 2002 Oakover Estate became Oakover Wines and Rob Marshall joined the team as chief winemaker and general manager, overseeing the construction of a new winery and managing the extensive vineyard operations on the property. Today, Oakover is the third-largest winery in the Swan Valley. Oakover's White Label brand is currently sold in over 500 independent liquor outlets in WA and Vic, with expansion into NSW and Qld planned. Exports to China, Indonesia, Malaysia and Singapore.

ŸŸŸŸŸ **White Label Classic White 2008** Chardonnay, verdelho and chenin blanc come together in time-honoured fashion; crisp and lively now, developing into a fuller bodied wine (without heaviness) in a few years. Gold medal Swan Valley Wine Show '08 and trophy for Best Value Table Wine. Screwcap. 11.8% alc. **Rating** 90 **To** 2012 $10

ŸŸŸŸ **White Label Swan Valley Chenin Blanc 2008** Quite fresh and lively; gentle fruit salad flavours, which will gain presence over the next three–five years. Gold medal Swan Valley Wine Show '08. Screwcap. 11% alc. **Rating** 89 **To** 2013 $12.99

White Label Margaret River Cabernet Merlot 2007 Not a great Margaret River cabernet merlot, but a good wine at a very good price, with authentic varietal character and good balance. Screwcap. 14.4% alc. **Rating** 88 **To** 2014 $12.99

Oakridge ★★★★★

864 Maroondah Highway, Coldstream, Vic 3770 **Region** Yarra Valley
T (03) 9738 9900 **F** (03) 9739 1923 **www.**oakridgewines.com.au **Open** 7 days 10–5
Winemaker David Bicknell **Est.** 1978 **Cases** 15 000 **Vyds** 8.9 ha
The long, dark shadow of Evans & Tate's ownership is now totally dispelled. Life is never easy, but winemaker (and now CEO) David Bicknell has proved his worth time and again as an extremely talented winemaker. At the top of the brand tier is 864, all Yarra Valley vineyard selections, and only released in the best years (Chardonnay, Shiraz, Cabernet Sauvignon, Riesling); next is the Oakridge core label (the Chardonnay, Pinot Noir and Sauvignon Blanc come from the cooler Upper Yarra Valley; the Shiraz, Cabernet Sauvignon and Viognier from the Lower Yarra); and the Over the Shoulder range, drawn from all of the sources available to Oakridge (Sauvignon Blanc, Pinot Grigio, Pinot Noir, Shiraz Viognier, Cabernet Sauvignon). Exports to Hong Kong and NZ.

ΤΤΤΤΤ **864 Yarra Valley Chardonnay 2008** Pale colour, vibrant hue; a tightly wound bouquet offering pear, lemon, gunflint and a delicate toasty overtone from the oak; a pure palate, with intense citrus fruit driving it, and a complex array of flavours lying in wait to open and enchant over time; a great future. Screwcap. 13% alc. **Rating** 96 **To** 2018 $60
864 Yarra Valley Cabernet Sauvignon 2005 Bright colour; vivid cabernet characters on both bouquet and palate; incisively fresh blackcurrant fruit on a notably long and persistent palate built on ripe tannin structure. Screwcap. 14% alc. **Rating** 96 **To** 2025 $60
Yarra Valley Chardonnay 2008 A distinctly cool opening with nectarine and a touch of citrus on the bouquet; fleshy and slightly creamy on the palate, the line returns for a fine, even and elegant finish; good now, it will improve substantially over the next 12 months. Screwcap. 12.5% alc. **Rating** 94 **To** 2016 $32

ΤΤΤΤΤ **Yarra Valley Pinot Noir 2008** A distinctly softer and fleshier wine than Over the Shoulder, with spiced cherry and plum on the bouquet; fleshy and vibrant on the palate; the oak plays a supporting role, with a dry, but fruit-filled, finish. Screwcap. 13.5% alc. **Rating** 93 **To** 2014 $32
Over the Shoulder Yarra Valley Shiraz Viognier 2007 Vibrant crimson-purple colour accurately foretells the fresh, vibrant red fruit flavours; fine tannins on the finish give the wine the structure sometimes lacking. Delicious drink-now style. Screwcap. 13.5% alc. **Rating** 93 **To** 2017 $19
Over the Shoulder Yarra Valley Pinot Grigio 2008 Pale colour and restrained pear bouquet; a little straw comes through on the palate, with pronounced acidity and fresh citrus fruit to conclude. Screwcap. 12.5% alc. **Rating** 91 **To** 2012 $19.50
Limited Release Yarra Valley Fume Blanc 2008 A strong mineral character, with a struck gunflint, green mango and ripe lemon bouquet; lively on the palate; restrained on the finish, and should age well. Screwcap. 11.5% alc. **Rating** 90 **To** 2014 $32
Over the Shoulder Yarra Valley Chardonnay 2008 Ripe pear and nectarine bouquet, showing a touch of spice from the oak; generous for its age, good texture and weight; an honest wine. Screwcap. 12.5% alc. **Rating** 90 **To** 2014 $19.50
864 Yarra Valley Pinot Noir 2008 Bright colour; very oaky bouquet with the fruit well and truly taking a back seat to the winemaking; some bright cherry fruit at the core, the palate is very firm and again oak dominant; time will tell if the fruit will be able to eat the oak. Screwcap. 13.5% alc. **Rating** 90 **To** 2014 $60
Over the Shoulder Yarra Valley Shiraz Viognier 2008 Bright colour; highly perfumed blueberry bouquet, with an attractive array of spices; medium-bodied and quite fleshy, with supple tannin and generous fruit to finish. Screwcap. 13.5% alc. **Rating** 90 **To** 2014 $19.50

Limited Release Yarra Valley Blanc de Blancs 2005 Green apple and lanolin bouquet; tight and taut, with prominent citrus and green apple fruit providing almost startling freshness and acidity on the palate. Diam. 12% alc. **Rating** 90 **To** 2014 $38

ŶŶŶŶ **Over the Shoulder Yarra Valley Pinot Noir 2008** A bit of savoury reduction on the bouquet; slightly tarry and quite chewy on the palate; a muscular young wine, with cherry the dominant fruit on display. Well priced. Screwcap. 13.5% alc. **Rating** 89 **To** 2013 $19.50

Oakvale

1596 Broke Road, Pokolbin, NSW 2320 **Region** Lower Hunter Valley
T (02) 4998 7088 **F** (02) 4998 7077 **www.**oakvalewines.com.au **Open** 7 days 10–5
Winemaker Steve Hagan **Est.** 1893 **Cases** 15 000 **Vyds** 20.62 ha
Richard and Mary Owens purchased the historic winery and vineyard in 1999. For three-quarters of a century it was in the ownership of the founding Elliot family, whose original slab hut homestead is now a museum. One of the 'must see' destinations in the Hunter. Exports to the US, Mexico and Japan.

ŶŶŶŶŶ **Reserve Elliot's Well Semillon 2008** Restrained, tight and a little angular, with lemon and a touch of straw in the background; tightly wound and classic in structure, the finish is very long and quite fine. Screwcap. 11% alc. **Rating** 94 **To** 2016 $25

ŶŶŶŶŶ **Gold Rock Shiraz 2007** Vivid purple; plum and spice aromas are supported by some earthy complexity and a touch of oak; the palate is fresh and lively, the tannins fine and plentiful. Screwcap. 13.9% alc. **Rating** 92 **To** 2016 $25
Reserve Peach Tree Chardonnay 2008 Melon and fig with a gentle touch of creamy oak; quite rich on the palate, with a zesty, citrus and focused finish. Screwcap. 13% alc. **Rating** 90 **To** 2013 $27
Reserve Peppercorn Shiraz 2007 A slight blackberry pastille bouquet framed by spicy oak; good concentration, with depth and richness to the sweet mid-palate; long and fruitful on the finish. Screwcap. 13.9% alc. **Rating** 90 **To** 2015 $35

ŶŶŶŶ **Reserve Block 37 Verdelho 2008** Restrained nectarine and lime bouquet; quite sweet on the palate, but the balancing acidity provides a long and interesting finish. Screwcap. 12.5% alc. **Rating** 88 **To** 2012 $22.50
Gold Rock Semillon 2008 Ripe lemon fruit with a touch of tropical; a juicy and generous palate, forward and ready for drinking. Screwcap. 11.5% alc. **Rating** 87 **To** 2012 $20

Oakway Estate

575 Farley Road, Donnybrook, WA 6239 **Region** Geographe
T (08) 9731 7141 **F** (08) 9731 7190 **www.**oakwayestate.com.au **Open** By appt
Winemaker Sharna Kowalczuk **Est.** 1998 **Cases** 1500 **Vyds** 2 ha
Ria and Wayne Hammond run a vineyard, beef cattle and sustainable blue gum plantation in undulating country on the Capel River in the southwest of WA. The grapes are grown on light gravel and loam soils that provide good drainage, situated high above the river, giving even sun exposure to the fruit and minimising the effects of frost. Varieties include shiraz, merlot, cabernet sauvignon and chardonnay, and have won a number of medals at wine shows.

ŶŶŶŶŶ **Sauvignon Blanc Semillon 2008** Vibrant hue; focused vibrant fruit, with good mid-palate weight and juicy tropical fruit on the palate; the finish shows poised acid, and vibrant texture. Screwcap. 12.3% alc. **Rating** 92 **To** 2012 $20
Unwooded Chardonnay 2008 A fine and fleshy wine, with lemon and grapefruit on the bouquet and palate; fine and full of fresh lemon fruit on the finish. Good value. Screwcap. 12.5% alc. **Rating** 90 **To** 2012 $16

♈♈♈♈   **Blue Gum Ridge Cabernet Merlot 2007** Light- to medium-bodied; fresh, vibrant, zesty; very good line and balance, although not concentrated. **Rating** 88 **To** 2012 $22

Observatory Hill Vineyard ★★★★☆

107 Centauri Drive, Mt Rumney, Tas 7170 **Region** Southern Tasmania
T (03) 6248 5380 **Open** By appt
Winemaker Frogmore Creek **Est.** 1991 **Cases** 600
Glenn and Chris Richardson's Observatory Hill Vineyard has been developing since 1991 when Glenn and his late father-in-law Jim Ramsey planted the first of the 8500 vines that now make up the estate. Together with the adjoining property owned by Chris' brother Wayne and his wife Stephanie, the vineyard now covers 3 ha, with new plantings having been made each year. The name 'Observatory Hill' comes from the state's oldest observatory, which is perched on the hill above the vineyard.

♈♈♈♈♈   **Pinot Noir 2006** Medium- to full-bodied; very good bouquet, fruit and oak are seamless, with supple mouthfeel; still a slight query on tannins, which were very obvious when first tasted in Jan '07, though no longer. Gold medal Tas Wine Show '09. Screwcap. 13.8% alc. **Rating** 94 **To** 2011 $32

♈♈♈♈♀   **Cabernet Sauvignon 2007** Great crimson-purple; pure varietal fruit, cassis and earth; positive oak, ripe tannins. Screwcap. 12.4% alc. **Rating** 93 **To** 2017 $29

♈♈♈♈   **Riesling 2008** Lemon/citrus flavours; firm palate; with apple and citrus entwined with Tasmanian acidity. Screwcap. 12.6% alc. **Rating** 88 **To** 2015 $22

Occam's Razor ★★★☆

c/- Jasper Hill, Drummonds Lane, Heathcote, Vic 3523 **Region** Heathcote
T (03) 5433 2528 **F** (03) 5433 3143 **Open** By appt
Winemaker Emily Laughton **Est.** 2001 **Cases** 300 **Vyds** 2.5 ha
Emily Laughton has decided to follow in her parents' footsteps after first seeing the world and having a range of casual jobs. Having grown up at Jasper Hill, winemaking was far from strange, but she decided to find her own way, buying the grapes from a small vineyard owned by Jasper Hill employee Andrew Conforti and his wife Melissa. She then made the wine 'with guidance and inspiration from my father'. The name comes from William of Ockham (1285–1349), also spelt Occam, a theologian and philosopher responsible for many sayings, including that appearing on the back label of the wine: 'what can be done with fewer is done in vain with more'. Exports to the UK, the US, Canada and NZ.

♈♈♈♈   **Heathcote Shiraz 2007** A powerful wine with extravagant tannins, which may never soften enough before the fruit is gone. Earlier picking might have helped. Cork. 15% alc. **Rating** 88 **To** 2020 $42

Oceans Estate ★★★

Courtney Road, Karridale, WA 6288 (postal) **Region** Margaret River
T (08) 9758 2240 **F** (08) 9758 2240 **www.**oceansestate.com.au **Open** Not
Winemaker Frank Kittler **Est.** 1999 **Cases** 5000 **Vyds** 22 ha
Oceans Estate was purchased by the Tomasi family (headed by Frank Tomasi) in 1995, and, between '99 and 2007, chardonnay, sauvignon blanc, pinot noir, merlot and cabernet sauvignon were planted. The cool climate has proved a problem for the cabernet sauvignon, which is likely to be grafted to semillon. Likewise, the pinot noir is to be grafted to cabernet franc in late 2009. Since 2006 the wines have been made at the onsite winery, adequate to handle the 180 to 220 tonnes of grapes that will come once the vineyards are in full bearing.

♈♈♈♈   **Margaret River Cabernet Merlot 2005** Holding colour well; much greater depth and texture than the '06, with black and red fruits supported by balanced tannins. Screwcap. 13.7% alc. **Rating** 88 **To** 2014 $15

Margaret River Sauvignon Blanc 2007 The screwcap has kept the wine clean and fresh; has good acidity to support the grassy flavours and the dry finish. 12.5% alc. **Rating** 87 **To** 2010 $15

Margaret River Cabernet Sauvignon 2005 Has a savoury/earthy cast to its blackcurrant fruit, which is not unattractive; firm tannins lengthen the finish. Screwcap. 13.6% alc. **Rating** 87 **To** 2011 $17

Oddfellows Wines   ★★★★

PO Box 88, Langhorne Creek, SA 5255 **Region** Langhorne Creek
T (08) 8537 3326 **F** (08) 8537 3319 **www.**oddfellowswines.com.au **Open** Not
Winemaker David Knight **Est.** 1997 **Cases** 2000 **Vyds** 40 ha
Oddfellows is the name taken by a group of five individuals who decided to put their expertise, energy and investments into making premium wine. Langhorne Creek vignerons David and Cathy Knight were two of the original members, and in 2007 took over ownership and running of the venture. David worked with Greg Follett from Lake Breeze to produce the wines, gradually taking over more responsibility, and is now both winemaker and viticulturist for the estate's vineyard. This vineyard also produces the Winners Tank label (in conjunction with Reid Bosward of Kaesler Wines in the Barossa); the first two vintages were made for export only (Canada), with limited domestic distribution of the '06 vintage. Exports to the UK, Canada, Singapore, Indonesia, Hong Kong and China.

ŶŶŶŶŶ **Langhorne Creek Shiraz 2006** Good colour; a fragrant bouquet leads into a lively palate, with complex spice, pepper and licorice overtones to the core of juicy fruits; long finish. Cork. 14.9% alc. **Rating** 94 **To** 2016 $25

ŶŶŶŶ **Langhorne Creek Cabernet Sauvignon 2006** Typical generous, fleshy Langhorne Creek style, with a mix of blackcurrant, dark chocolate and vanilla flavours, finishing with soft tannins. Cork. 14.6% alc. **Rating** 89 **To** 2016 $25

Old Kent River   ★★★★★

1114 Turpin Road, Rocky Gully, WA 6397 **Region** Frankland River
T (08) 9855 1589 **www.**oldkentriver.com.au **Open** At Kent River, Denmark
Winemaker Alkoomi (Contract), Michael Staniford **Est.** 1985 **Cases** 3000
Mark and Debbie Noack have earned much respect from their neighbours and from the other producers to whom they sell more than half the production from the 16.5-ha vineyard on their sheep property. The quality of their wines has gone from strength to strength, Mark having worked particularly hard with his Pinot Noir. Exports to the UK, the US, Hong Kong, Malaysia and Singapore.

ŶŶŶŶŶ **Frankland River Pinot Noir 2002** Good colour for its age; has developed impressively in bottle, with considerable complexity; there is great balance between the plummy pinot fruit and the fine, savoury tannins; also has excellent length. Drink by its 10th birthday. Cork. 11.5% alc. **Rating** 95 **To** 2012 $30

Frankland River Pinot Noir 2007 Spicy cherry and plum fruit; excellent texture and mouthfeel to mid-palate (but doesn't quite accelerate on finish). Gold WA Wine Show '08. Screwcap. 13.5% alc. **Rating** 94 **To** 2012 $27

Frankland River Shiraz 2007 Most attractive cool-grown shiraz; spicy overtones to the red fruit aromas and flavours, the medium-bodied palate silky and supple, oak well integrated. Screwcap. 13.5% alc. **Rating** 94 **To** 2017 $30

ŶŶŶŶŶ **Frankland River Chardonnay 2008** Bright straw-green; fragrant nectarine on the bouquet is joined by grapefruit on the palate, and complexed by barrel ferment in old French oak; has considerable length. Screwcap. 13% alc. **Rating** 93 **To** 2015 $30

Frankland River Sauvignon Blanc 2008 Crisp snow pea and citrus aromas and flavours; the palate has good length and vibrant natural acidity. Screwcap. 11.5% alc. **Rating** 92 **To** 2011 $20

Frankland River Pinot Noir 2005 Has retained hue well; a focused and precise pinot, with a mix of bright red fruits and spicy/foresty components; good line and length. Cork. 13% alc. **Rating** 90 **To** 2012 $26

Diamondtina 2006 Pale straw-bronze; bottle-fermented pinot noir; well balanced and long, with a mix of spice and strawberry flavours; will develop further on cork. 12.5% alc. **Rating** 90 **To** 2012 $30

Old Plains   ★★★

6 Winser Avenue, Seaton, SA 5023 (postal) **Region** Adelaide Plains
T 0407 605 601 **F** (08) 8355 3603 **www**.oldplains.com **Open** Not
Winemaker Domenic Torzi, Tim Freeland **Est.** 2003 **Cases** 2000 **Vyds** 11 ha
Old Plains is a partnership between Tim Freeland and Domenic Torzi who have located and acquired small parcels of old vine shiraz (8 ha), grenache (2 ha) and cabernet sauvignon (1 ha) in the Adelaide Plains region. A large portion of the consistently high-quality wines, sold under the Old Plains and Longhop labels, are exported to the US, Denmark, Hong Kong. Singapore and China.

♥♥♥♥ **Longhop Old Vine La Quattro 2008** Early picking beat the heat, and provides a lively and fresh wine with a range of citrus flavours. Chenin Blanc/Riesling/Semillon/Sauvignon Blanc. Screwcap. 11% alc. **Rating** 87 **To** 2009 $15

Olivers Taranga Vineyards   ★★★★★

Seaview Road, McLaren Vale, SA 5171 **Region** McLaren Vale
T (08) 8323 8498 **F** (08) 8323 7498 **www**.oliverstaranga.com **Open** 7 days 10–4
Winemaker Corrina Wright **Est.** 1841 **Cases** 10 000 **Vyds** 96.99 ha
William and Elizabeth Oliver arrived from Scotland in 1839 to settle at McLaren Vale. Six generations later, members of the family are still living on the Whitehill and Taranga farms. The Taranga property has 16 grape varieties planted (the lion's share to shiraz and cabernet sauvignon, with lesser quantities of chardonnay, chenin blanc, durif, fiano, grenache, mataro, merlot, petit verdot, sagrantino, sauvignon blanc, semillon, tempranillo, viognier and white frontignac); grapes from the property have been sold, but since 1994 a portion has been made under the Olivers Taranga label. Since 2000 the wine has been made by Corrina Wright (the Oliver family's first winemaker and a sixth-generation family member). Exports to the US, Canada, Belgium, Singapore, Thailand and Hong Kong.

♥♥♥♥♥ **HJ Reserve McLaren Vale Shiraz 2005** A perfect example of less is more, a vibrant wine that caresses the mouth with its silky, gently spicy, black fruits perfectly balanced by tannins. Cork. 14.5% alc. **Rating** 95 **To** 2020 $48

Corrina's McLaren Vale Shiraz Cabernet Sauvignon 2006 Co-fermentation is logical, although seldom used; this wine may cause a rethink, as the cabernet exercises excellent control; harmonious yet firm, there is no sign of heat or dead fruit, and the tannins are perfect. Screwcap. 15% alc. **Rating** 94 **To** 2021 $30

♥♥♥♥♀ **McLaren Vale Shiraz 2006** Dense, deep colour; big, bold full-bodied wine that fills every corner of the mouth with black fruits, bitter chocolate, tannins and oak. Tatty cork may imperil its slow march to maturity. 15% alc. **Rating** 92 **To** 2020 $30

McLaren Vale Viognier 2008 Well made, has a varietal apricot kernel bouquet with some attractive spice elements; soft acid with rich texture; to be enjoyed in its youth. Screwcap. 13% alc. **Rating** 91 **To** 2012 $24

♥♥♥♥ **Cadenzia McLaren Vale Grenache 2007** Small Batch 2666. Deceptively light in colour and body as a pinot, for it has clearly defined varietal flavour and a persistent finish. Screwcap. 14.5% alc. **Rating** 89 **To** 2013 $30

Olsen   ★★★

RMB 252 Osmington Road, Osmington, WA 6285 **Region** Margaret River
T (08) 9757 4536 **www**.olsen.com.au **Open** At Margaret River Regional Wine Centre
Winemaker Jarrad Olsen **Est.** 1986 **Cases** 4000 **Vyds** 13.5 ha

Steve and Ann Marie Olsen have planted cabernet sauvignon, sauvignon blanc, chardonnay, semillon and verdelho, which they tend with the help of their four children. It was the desire to raise their children in a healthy country environment that prompted the move to establish the vineyard, coupled with a long-standing dream to make their own wine. Not to be confused with Olsen Wines in Melbourne. Exports to Canada.

ΨΨΨΨ **Margaret River Classic Red 2004** Offers a generous mouthful and works much better than Classic White; warm blackberry/spicy fruit and soft tannins to close. Drink whenever. Screwcap. 13.5% alc. **Rating** 87 **To** 2012 $15.95

Olsen Wines Victoria

131 Koornang Road, Carnegie, Vic 3163 **Region** Port Phillip Zone
T (03) 9569 2188 **www**.vin888.com **Open** Mon–Thurs 10.30–8, Fri–Sat 10.30–9
Winemaker Glenn Olsen **Est.** 1991 **Cases** 55 000
Glenn Olsen, a science and engineering graduate of the University of Melbourne, has been involved in the wine industry since 1975, initially importing wines and spirits from Europe, then moving into retailing. In 1991, he started Olsen Wines, claiming to be Melbourne's first inner suburban winery. Several others may dispute this claim, but that is perhaps neither here nor there. Most of the wines come either from grapes grown on the Murray River in Northeast Victoria, or from the Yarra Valley. Exports to the US, Canada, Japan, China and Hong Kong.

ΨΨΨΨΨ **Personal Reserve Yarra Valley Cabernet Sauvignon 2006** Excellent crimson colour; pure varietal aromas herald the perfectly ripened blackcurrant and cassis of the palate, there supported by good tannins and oak. Yet another in a line-up of very good cabernets from Olsen. Screwcap. 14.5% alc. **Rating** 94 **To** 2016 $38

ΨΨΨΨΨ **Yarra Valley Cabernet Sauvignon 2005** Good depth and hue; has an abundance of black fruits and licorice supported by good oak; the tannins are still softening, with more to go. Screwcap. 13.9% alc. **Rating** 91 **To** 2017 $23.99

ΨΨΨΨ **Preservative Free Yarra Valley Cabernet Sauvignon 2007** Dense colour; very ripe cassis and blackcurrant fruit on the bouquet and palate, the texture very soft and plush. A very good option for those allergic to SO_2. Screwcap. 14.7% alc. **Rating** 89 **To** 2012 $23.99
Premium Sparkling Shiraz 2005 Better than many sparkling red wines, and surmounts its alcohol to provide a pleasantly dry spicy/savoury wine with good balance. Cork. 14.9% alc. **Rating** 89 **To** 2012 $18.99
Shiraz 2005 The relatively light colour heralds a light- to medium-bodied wine, with sweet red fruits offset by a dusting of pepper and spice. Screwcap. 14.9% alc. **Rating** 88 **To** 2015 $18.99

Olssens of Watervale

Sollys Hill Road, Watervale, SA 5452 **Region** Clare Valley
T (08) 8843 0065 **F** (08) 8843 0065 **Open** Thurs–Sun & public hols 11–5, or by appt
Winemaker Kevin Olssen, Julian Midwinter **Est.** 1994 **Cases** 4000 **Vyds** 32 ha
Kevin and Helen Olssen first visited the Clare Valley in 1986. Within two weeks they and their family decided to sell their Adelaide home and purchased a property in a small, isolated valley 3 km north of the township of Watervale. As a result of the acquisition of the Bass Hill Vineyard, estate plantings have risen to 32 ha, including unusual varieties such as carmenere and primitivo di Gioia. The Bass Hill project is a joint venture between parents Kevin and Helen and children David and Jane Olssen. Exports to the US, Sweden and Hong Kong.

ΨΨΨΨΨ **The Olssen Six 2006** Good colour; highly intense and focused wine, the power coming not from the tannins or extract so much as the array of mainly black, with some red, fruits; there is remarkable elegance amid this precocious display of power. Cabernet Sauvignon/Malbec/Cabernet Franc/Carmenere/Petit Verdot. Screwcap. 14.5% alc. **Rating** 96 **To** 2031 $65

Clare Valley Riesling 2008 A fresh and lively bouquet, then seamless citrus and mineral flavours running through the length of the well-balanced palate. Screwcap. 12.5% alc. **Rating** 94 **To** 2018 $20

Clare Valley Shiraz Mataro 2006 Good colour; has a rich and complex bouquet and palate, the blackberry and licorice fruits seamlessly married with French oak (20 months) and ripe tannins; very good balance and length. Screwcap. 14.5% alc. **Rating** 94 **To** 2021 $25

ŸŸŸŸŸ **Second Six 2006** Has the power and much of the black fruit flavours of The Six, but more obvious extract and tannins; that said, has a greater reservoir of fruit, and given time might emerge in front of it. Cabernet Franc/Merlot/Petit Verdot/Malbec/Cabernet Sauvignon/Carmenere. Screwcap. 14.5% alc. **Rating** 93 **To** 2021 $28

Second Six 2005 Some of the synergistic fragrance has started to appear on the bouquet, but the wine is still unready, needing another year or two for the fruit, oak and tannins to fully coalesce. Cabernet Franc/Merlot/Petit Verdot/Malbec/Cabernet Sauvignon/Carmenere. Screwcap. 15% alc. **Rating** 91 **To** 2015 $28

Bass Hill Vineyard Mataro 2006 Savoury/spicy and vibrant, with no overripe or cosmetic characters; good structure, the tannins not excessive. Attractive small single vineyard example. Screwcap. 14% alc. **Rating** 90 **To** 2015 $30

Onannon ★★★★☆

PO Box 190, Flinders, Vic 3929 **Region** Port Phillip Zone
T 0448 900 229 **Open** Not
Winemaker Sam Middleton, Kaspar Hermann, Will Byron **Est.** 2008 **Cases** 80
Onannon is the venture of Sam Middleton, Kaspar Hermann and Will Byron, who donated the last two or three letters of their surnames to come up with Onannon. They share many things in common, not the least working vintages at Coldstream Hills, Will Byron for six years, Sam Middleton for two (before ultimately returning to the family's winery, Mount Mary) and Kaspar Hermann for one. Strictly speaking, I should disqualify myself from making any comment about them or their wine, but you would have to go a long way to find three more open-hearted and utterly committed winemakers; the world is their oyster, their ambitions unlimited.

ŸŸŸŸŸ **Gippsland Pinot Noir 2008** Bright hue, even though neither fined nor filtered; full-flavoured pinot, with abundant plum and spice; superfine tannins expand and lengthen the finish. Diam. 13.7% alc. **Rating** 93 **To** 2014 $27

145°02′23″E 37°11′16″S ★★★★

27 Hilltop Road, Clareville, NSW 2107 (postal) **Region** Central Victorian Zone
T 0414 246 564 **Open** Not
Winemaker Steve Fitzmaurice **Est.** 2008 **Cases** 500 **Vyds** 2.02 ha
Steve Fitzmaurice was a professional yachtsman who, aged 40, had a 'typical mid-life crisis and uprooted the family from Sydney and headed to Wagga (CSU) to study oenology'. An academic experience that didn't find altogether rewarding. A complicated turn of events lead him to Adrian Munari's vineyard and winery in Heathcote, where he became involved in the making of the Sugarloaf Creek Shiraz from 2001, notwithstanding that Sugarloaf Creek is in fact in the Goulburn Valley, not Heathcote. He continued to learn pruning in the vineyard, and winemaking in the winery, which lead to his securing a three-year-plus-three-year option lease of Sugarloaf Creek, and making his 2008 Broadford Shiraz. The tasting note that follows was made before I read the life story and winemaking aims, and it would seem he has succeeded in making a wine precisely as he wished. That is a happy ending; however, one of these days he will get tired of restaurants and retailers throwing up their hands at the yachting-inspired name, which is the exact GPS position of the vineyard.

ŸŸŸŸŸ **Broadford Shiraz 2008** Strong colour; luscious, but not overripe or jammy, fruit in a blackberry and plum spectrum, with notes of pepper, spice and licorice; good oak integration. Screwcap. 14.5% alc. **Rating** 90 **To** 2018 $29

 Optimiste

PO Box 4214, Castlecrag, NSW 2068 **Region** Mudgee
T (02) 9967 3294 **F** (02) 9967 3295 **www.**optimiste.com.au **Open** Not
Winemaker Michael Slater, Barry Kooij **Est.** 1998 **Cases** 2000 **Vyds** 11 ha
Steven and Sharlene Dadd had been growing grapes for over a decade before realising a long
held dream to launch their own wines under the Optimiste label. The name is inspired by
their son's struggle with deafness and a quote by Helen Keller: 'Optimism is the faith that leads
to achievement. Nothing can be done without hope and confidence.' The first vines planted
were cabernet sauvignon, petit verdot and merlot, with more recent plantings of viognier,
semillon, tempranillo and pinot gris (chardonnay is purchased). A cellar door is planned to
open in late 2009.

♀♀♀♀♀ **Mudgee Shiraz 2006** Good colour; attractive medium-bodied palate, with good
varietal expression from blackberry, dark chocolate and ripe tannins, some vanilla
oak in balance. Screwcap. 14.5% alc. **Rating** 90 **To** 2015 $18

♀♀♀♀ **Mudgee Cabernet Sauvignon 2005** Light but bright hue; fresh, clean and
well-made, with pleasant cassis fruit and good length; not over-extracted nor over-
oaked. Screwcap. 14% alc. **Rating** 89 **To** 2014 $18
Marquis Mudgee Cabernet Sauvignon Merlot Petit Verdot 2006
Light but bright hue; fresh, clean and well-made, with pleasant cassis fruit and
good length; not over-extracted nor over-oaked. Screwcap. 14.5% alc. **Rating** 89
To 2014 $20
Mudgee Petit Verdot 2006 Like all the Optimiste wines, remarkable for its
purity and clarity of colour, aroma and flavour; an elegant version of the normally
robust petit verdot. Screwcap. 14.5% alc. **Rating** 89 **To** 2013 $18
Mudgee Chardonnay 2007 Light, but ripe, stone fruit on the bouquet and
palate has an even lighter touch of oak; sensitive winemaking has paid dividends.
Screwcap. 13.5% alc. **Rating** 88 **To** 2013 $18

Oranje Tractor

198 Link Road, Albany, WA 6330 **Region** Albany
T (08) 9842 5175 **F** (08) 9842 5175 **www.**oranjetractor.com **Open** Fri–Sun & hols 11–5
Winemaker Rob Diletti, Mike Garland (Contract) **Est.** 1998 **Cases** 1000 **Vyds** 3 ha
The name celebrates the 1964 vintage, orange-coloured, Fiat tractor, acquired when Murray
Gomm and Pamela Lincoln began the establishment of the vineyard. Murray was born next
door, but moved to Perth to work in physical education and health promotion. Here he met
nutritionist Pamela, who completed the wine science degree at CSU in 2000, before being
awarded a Churchill Fellowship to study organic grape and wine production in the US and
Europe. When the partners established their vineyard, they went down the organic path.

♀♀♀♀♀ **Albany Riesling 2004** One stage further advanced than the '05, and all the better
for it, with delicious sweet lime juice flavours balanced by acidity. The four years
since first tasted has transformed it. Screwcap. 12.6% alc. **Rating** 95 **To** 2014 $18.50
Albany Riesling 2005 Has continued to develop in bottle very well over
the past two years, and will continue to do so. Screwcap. 12.5% alc. **Rating** 94
To 2015 $19.50
Albany Riesling 2003 Bright green-yellow; intense spicy/lemony aromas; great
length and vibrancy. Gold WA Wine Show '08. Screwcap. 12% alc. **Rating** 94
To 2013 $29

♀♀♀♀♀ **Albany Sauvignon Blanc 2008** The bouquet is clean although as yet unevolved,
but the palate has thrust and vibrancy, tropical fruit offset by crisp, crunchy acidity.
Screwcap. 13% alc. **Rating** 92 **To** 2011 $22.50

♀♀♀♀ **Reverse Riesling 2008** Attractive Mosel style with an appreciable touch of
sweetness; needs a little more intensity, or perhaps acidity, for higher points.
Screwcap. 11% alc. **Rating** 89 **To** 2014 $17.50

Piston Broke Pinot Noir NV Has appreciable varietal fruit in a very savoury/ foresty mode, and the colour is still good. Quite an achievement for a blend of '04, '05 and '06 vintages. Cork. 12.6% alc. **Rating** 89 **To** 2012 $29

Organic Vignerons Australia

Section 395 Derrick Road, Loxton North, SA 5333 **Region** South Australia
T (03) 9646 6666 **F** (03) 9646 8383 **www**.ova.com.au **Open** Not
Winemaker David Bruer **Est.** 2002 **Cases** 6000
Organic Vignerons Australia is a very interesting winemaking business. It consists of the owners of five certified organic SA properties: Claire and Kevin Hansen at Padthaway, Bruce and Sue Armstrong at Waikerie, Brett and Melissa Munchenberg at Loxton, Terry Markou at Adelaide Plains and David and Barbara Bruer at Langhorne Creek. The wines are made by David Bruer at Temple Bruer, which is itself a certified organic producer. The company went into liquidation, but by early 2008 had commenced trading again.

ŢŢŢŢŢ **Shiraz Cabernet Sauvignon 2005** Bright, lively succulent red fruits set in a medium-bodied frame; sufficient tannins to give structure and longevity. Screwcap. 14.5% alc. **Rating** 90 **To** 2014 $18

ŢŢŢŢ **Shiraz Cabernet Sauvignon 2008** Bright colour; vibrant and juicy redcurrant fruit, with a touch of fruitcake spice; juicy, clean and quite polished on the finish. Screwcap. 14% alc. **Rating** 89 **To** 2013 $17
Semillon Chardonnay 2007 Has plenty of warm-grown buttery/nutty/peachy fruit balanced by acidity on the finish. Screwcap. 13.5% alc. **Rating** 87 **To** 2010

Orlando

Jacob's Creek Visitor Centre, Barossa Valley Way, Rowland Flat, SA 5352
Region Barossa Valley
T (08) 8521 3000 **F** (08) 8521 3003 **www**.orlandowines.com **Open** 7 days 10–5
Winemaker Philip Laffer, Bernard Hicken **Est.** 1847 **Cases** NFP
Orlando is the parent who has been divorced by its child, Jacob's Creek (see separate entry). Orlando is 160 years old, Jacob's Creek little more than 34 years. For what are doubtless sound marketing reasons, Orlando aided and abetted the divorce, but the average consumer is unlikely to understand the logic, and – if truth be known – care about it even less.

ŢŢŢŢŢ **Lawson's Padthaway Shiraz 2004** Speaks clearly of Padthaway, with its mix of red berry fruit, a touch of chocolate and savoury, but balanced, tannins; oak well integrated. Cork. 14% alc. **Rating** 94 **To** 2020 $63

ŢŢŢŢŢ **Gramp's Shiraz 2005** Great colour; plenty of sweet primary black fruit and sweet oak; the palate is lively and well constructed, intense black fruits lingering on the finish. Ever reliable value. Cork. 14.5% alc. **Rating** 90 **To** 2014 $19.99
Gramp's Shiraz 2006 Densely coloured; a dark fruitcake wine with extravagant levels of ripe fruit; warm, thick and ample on the palate, with chewy tannin and a distinct mocha flavour to the finish. Screwcap. 14.5% alc. **Rating** 90 **To** 2015 $20

Otway Estate ★★★

20 Hoveys Road, Barongarook, Vic 3249 **Region** Geelong
T (03) 5233 8400 **www**.otwayestate.com.au **Open** Mon–Fri 11–4.30, w'ends 10–5
Winemaker Matthew di Sciascio **Est.** 1983 **Cases** 1800 **Vyds** 6.4 ha
The history of Otway Estate dates back to 1983 when the first vines were planted by Stuart and Eileen Walker. The current group of six family and friends have expanded the scope of the business: the vineyard is planted primarily to chardonnay (3 ha) and pinot noir (1 ha) with small patches of riesling, semillon, sauvignon blanc and gewurztraminer. Current winemaker Matthew di Sciascio (who also makes the Bellbrae/Longboard wines) believes the climate is much cooler than the norm for Geelong, closer to parts of Tasmania. Thus the future direction will focus on sparkling wines, Chardonnay, Pinot Noir and aromatic white wines.

ŸŸŸŸ   **Semillon Sauvignon Blanc 2008** Pale colour; lemon fruit with a touch of straw; clean, crisp and fresh. Screwcap. 12% alc. **Rating** 87 **To** 2011 $19

Outlook Hill ★★★★
97 School Lane, Tarrawarra, Vic 3777 **Region** Yarra Valley
T (03) 5962 2890 **F** (03) 5962 2890 **www**.outlookhill.com.au **Open** Fri–Sun 11–4.45
Winemaker Al Fencaros, Peter Snow **Est.** 2000 **Cases** 2000 **Vyds** 5.4 ha
After several years overseas, former Melbourne professionals Peter and Lydia Snow returned in 1997 planning to open a wine tourism business in the Hunter Valley. However, they had second thoughts, and in 2000 moved to the Yarra Valley, where they have now established three tourist B&B cottages, a vineyard, a terrace restaurant and adjacent cellar door outlet, backed by a constant temperature wine storage cool room. Exports to Denmark and Japan.

 # Oxford Landing ★★★☆
Pipeline Road, Nuriootpa, SA 5355 **Region** Riverland
T (08) 8561 3200 **F** (08) 8561 3393 **www**.oxfordlanding.com.au **Open** By appt
Winemaker Matthew Pick **Est.** 1958 **Cases** NA **Vyds** 250 ha
Oxford Landing is, so the website tells us 'A real place, a real vineyard. A place distinguished by clear blue skies, rich red soil and an abundance of golden sunshine.' In the 50+ years since the vineyard was planted, the brand has grown to reach all corners of the world. Success has been due to over-delivery against expectations at its price points, and has largely escaped the scorn of the UK wine press. In 2008 a five-year experiment began to determine whether a block of vines could survive and produce an annual crop with only 10% of the normal irrigation. This apart, there is now 1 ha of native vegetation for every ha of vineyard. Exports to the UK, the US and NZ.

ŸŸŸŸŸ   **Cabernet Rose 2008** Vivid pink; this is precisely how a cabernet rose should taste; savoury, leafy, almost minerally, flavours on a crisp and energetic palate, not a hint of sugar to spoil the party. Screwcap. 12% alc. **Rating** 90 **To** 2010 $8.95

ŸŸŸŸ   **Sauvignon Blanc 2008** A clean but slightly subdued bouquet does not prepare you for the slashing palate, with grass and gooseberry and zingy acidity. Screwcap. 11% alc. **Rating** 89 **To** 2010 $8.95
Shiraz 2007 Clean, fresh and juicy; red and blue fruits, with good persistence of flavour. Screwcap. 13.5% alc. **Rating** 87 **To** 2012 $8.95

 # Padthaway Block 1 NR
121 Greenhill Road, Unley, SA 5061 (postal) **Region** Padthaway
T (08) 8357 0655 **F** (08) 8373 5075 **www**.pb1.net.au **Open** Not
Winemaker O'Leary Walker Wines **Est.** 2006 **Cases** 10 000 **Vyds** 30 ha
This is a somewhat challenging name for a wine business that, while having a 30-ha planting of cabernet sauvignon in Padthaway, has been a virtual winery between 2002 and '06, with two Cabernet Shiraz blends made in '02 (Southern Roo and Scrub Paddock) and two Shirazs in '04 (Lizard Flat and 1 Mile Dam). Some of the information suggests these were made by a number of winemakers in the district (Padthaway) and the Barossa Valley, although the O'Leary Walker winery is in fact situated in the Clare Valley. It would seem that a significant part of the production is exported (China and Singapore).

Padthaway Estate ★★★☆
Riddoch Highway, Padthaway, SA 5271 **Region** Padthaway
T (08) 8734 3148 **F** (08) 8734 3188 **www**.padthawayestate.com **Open** 7 days 10–4
Winemaker Ulrich Grey-Smith **Est.** 1980 **Cases** 6000
For many years, until the opening of Stonehaven, this was the only functioning winery in Padthaway, in a large and gracious old stone wool shed set in the superb grounds of the estate; the homestead is in the Relais et Chateaux mould, offering luxurious accommodation and fine food. Sparkling wines are the speciality. Padthaway Estate also acts as a tasting centre for other Padthaway-region wines.

ﾏﾏﾏﾏ♀ **Eliza Late Tirage Pinot Noir Chardonnay 2002** Quite deep colour, there is a nice toasty complexity that is supported by delicate creamy fruit on the bouquet and palate; good flavour. Cork. 12.5% alc. **Rating** 90 **To** 2013 $50

ﾏﾏﾏﾏ **Eliza Pinot Noir Chardonnay 2005** A quite toasty bouquet, with strong nutty complexity; some nice citrus fruit character on the palate, with freshness coming through on the finish. Cork. 12.5% alc. **Rating** 88 **To** 2012 $25

Palandri Wines

Cnr Boundary Road/Bussell Highway, Cowaramup, WA 6284 **Region** Margaret River
T (08) 9756 5656 **F** (08) 9755 5722 **www**.palandri.com.au **Open** 7 days 10–5
Winemaker Ben Roodhouse **Est.** 1999 **Cases** 160 000 **Vyds** 355.51 ha
When Palandri went into voluntary administration in February 2008, some industry observers simply asked why had it taken so long to happen. There were eerie echoes of the collapse of Adelaide Steamship's byzantine corporate structure, as five Palandri group companies followed the sixth (Palandri Finance Pty Ltd), which had gone into administration a little under two weeks earlier. In June '08, 3 Oceans Wine Company Pty Ltd acquired the Margaret River winery, the 30-year-old Margaret River vineyard and 347 ha of Frankland River vineyards. In October '08 it also acquired the Palandri and Baldivis Estate brands. Exports to the UK and other major markets.

ﾏﾏﾏﾏ♀ **The Estates Sauvignon Blanc Semillon 2008** Pale colour; aromas of tropical fruit and straw; a clean and vibrant palate, with a generous and juicy finish. Screwcap. 11.5% alc. **Rating** 90 **To** 2012 $19.95
Vita Novus Margaret River Cabernet Sauvignon 2007 Bright colour; essency cassis bouquet, with a gentle seasoning of oak; full-bodied with ample tannin and dark fruit at the core; fruity finish. Cork. 14.5% alc. **Rating** 90 **To** 2014 $24.95

ﾏﾏﾏﾏ **Vita Novus Margaret River Great Southern Shiraz 2007** Quite an oaky bouquet, with redcurrant and sage; gravelly and dry on the palate, the red fruits come to the fore and draw out to a lightly spicy; red fruit to finish. Cork. 14.5% alc. **Rating** 89 **To** 2014 $24.95
The Estates Merlot 2007 Deep colour and dark fruited; pure plum, spice and a little touch of black olive; medium-bodied with firm structure, and a drying, savoury finish. Screwcap. 14% alc. **Rating** 89 **To** 2013 $19.95
The Estates Cabernet Merlot 2005 Polished cedar, cassis and red fruit bouquet; medium-bodied, with fine-grained tannin and vibrant acidity. Screwcap. 14% alc. **Rating** 88 **To** 2012 $19.95
Baldivis Estate Shiraz 2006 The Western Australian appellation suggests various regions have contributed to give the wine some ripe red fruit flavours. Good value. Screwcap. 14% alc. **Rating** 87 **To** 2012 $13.95

Palmer Wines

1271 Caves Road, Dunsborough, WA 6281 **Region** Margaret River
T (08) 9756 7388 **F** (08) 9756 7399 **www**.palmerwines.com.au **Open** 7 days 10–5
Winemaker Mark Warren **Est.** 1977 **Cases** 6000 **Vyds** 51.4 ha
Stephen and Helen Palmer began the planting of their vineyard in 1977; with encouragement and direction from Dr Michael Peterkin of Pierro, the plantings have been increased over the years, and are now headed by chardonnay, sauvignon blanc, shiraz, cabernet sauvignon, merlot, semillon, malbec and cabernet franc. Exports to Indonesia (Bali).

ﾏﾏﾏﾏﾏ **Reserve Shiraz 2007** Crimson-purple; black fruit and licorice aromas on the bouquet are amplified on the palate by touches of spice to a remarkably juicy and intense palate. Screwcap. 15% alc. **Rating** 95 **To** 2027
Margaret River Shiraz 2007 While the lowest rung of the Palmer ladder, it has excellent colour, and is laden with rich blackberry and plum fruit supported by good tannins. Screwcap. 15% alc. **Rating** 94 **To** 2022

ŸŸŸŸŸ **Margaret River Merlot 2007** Good colour; a fragrant bouquet of small red berry fruits is replayed on the palate, given some complexity by very fine tannins. Screwcap. 14.5% alc. **Rating** 91 **To** 2014

Margaret River Sauvignon Blanc 2008 Exudes varietal characters on the bouquet, with the downside of a trace of reduction. Firmly in the tropical/passionfruit camp, the palate balanced and not sweet. Screwcap. 12.5% alc. **Rating** 90 **To** 2010

Margaret River Chardonnay 2007 An unusually crisp and delicate wine by Margaret River standards; has considerable length, the oak well integrated. Screwcap. 14% alc. **Rating** 90 **To** 2013

ŸŸŸŸ **Cabernet Sauvignon 2007** Has clear varietal character, expressed by the blackcurrant fruit, but not the length or intensity of other reds of the vintage. Screwcap. 15.5% alc. **Rating** 88 **To** 2015

Margaret River Semillon Sauvignon Blanc 2008 Pleasant and well balanced, but needs more energy and thrust to the gently tropical fruits. Screwcap. 13% alc. **Rating** 87 **To** 2010

 Pangallo Estate ★★★

PO Box 1578, Dee Why, NSW 2099 **Region** Lower Hunter Valley
T (02) 9984 1288 **F** (02) 9971 0455 **www**.pangalloestate.com.au **Open** Not
Winemaker Contract **Est.** 2003 **Cases** NFP **Vyds** 10 ha
Mick and Lyn Pangallo have a mixed vineyard and olive grove, the Italian connection evident in many ways, seemingly with their planting of zibbibo. This is in fact the Italian synonym for muscat of alexandria.

ŸŸŸŸ **Hunter Valley Shiraz Rose 2008** Bright colour, plenty of sugar and flavour, but could do with a touch more acidity. Screwcap. 12.5% alc. **Rating** 87 **To** 2011 $14

Pankhurst ★★★☆

'Old Woodgrove', Woodgrove Road, Hall, NSW 2618 **Region** Canberra District
T (02) 6230 2592 **www**.pankhurstwines.com.au **Open** W'ends, public hols, or by appt
Winemaker Lark Hill, Brindabella Hills **Est.** 1986 **Cases** 2000 **Vyds** 5 ha
Agricultural scientist and consultant Allan Pankhurst and wife Christine (with a degree in pharmaceutical science) have established a split-canopy vineyard. The first wines produced showed considerable promise. Pankhurst has had success with Pinot Noir and Chardonnay. Exports to China.

Paper Eagle/Ekhidna ★★★★

151 Main Road, McLaren Vale, SA 5171 **Region** McLaren Vale
T (08) 8323 8496 **F** (08) 8323 8490 **www**.papereagle.com.au **Open** 7 days 11–5
Winemaker Matthew Rechner **Est.** 2001 **Cases** 3500
Matt Rechner entered the wine industry in 1988, spending most of the intervening years at Tatachilla Winery in McLaren Vale, starting as laboratory technician and finishing as operations manager. Frustrated by the constraints of large winery practice, he decided to strike out on his own in 2001 via the virtual winery option. His long experience has meant he is able to buy grapes from high-quality producers. A restructuring of the former McLaren Wines has resulted in two brands, Paper Eagle and Ekhidna (the old spelling of echidna). Exports to the US, NZ and India.

ŸŸŸŸŸ **Paper Eagle Rarefied Air McLaren Vale Shiraz 2007** A massive wine, with lots of dark fruit, mocha and fruitcake on the bouquet; the palate is incredibly tannic and the acid sits apart from the fruit, but there is certainly more of everything; the wine needs time, and is structured for those who just want more. Screwcap. 14.5% alc. **Rating** 92 **To** 2020 $80

ΨΨΨΨ   **Ekhidna McLaren Vale Shiraz 2007** Rich blackberry bouquet with a touch of spice; warm-fruited and juicy on the finish. Screwcap. 14.5% alc. **Rating** 88 **To** 2014 $17.50

Ekhidna McLaren Vale Shiraz Rose 2008 Bright colour; red fruit and a touch of spice on the palate, with a dry slightly tart finish. Screwcap. 12.5% alc. **Rating** 87 **To** 2011 $15

Paracombe Wines   ★★★★☆

Main Road, Paracombe, SA 5132 **Region** Adelaide Hills
T (08) 8380 5058 **F** (08) 8380 5488 **www**.paracombewines.com **Open** By appt
Winemaker Paul Drogemuller **Est.** 1983 **Cases** 7700 **Vyds** 17.7 ha
Paul and Kathy Drogemuller established Paracombe following the devastating Ash Wednesday bushfires in 1983. It has become a successful business, producing a range of wines that are never less than good, often very good. The wines are made onsite in the 250-tonne winery with every part of the production process through to distribution handled from the winery. Exports to Canada, Sweden, Switzerland, Singapore, Taiwan, Hong Kong, Malaysia and India.

ΨΨΨΨΨ   **Somerville Adelaide Hills Shiraz 2005** Incredibly deep colour; very ripe and pushing the boundary a little, as the aromas step into the liqueur end of the spectrum; the palate is dense and thickly textured, and the alcohol has a noticeable presence; massively proportioned this wine is not for everyone, but there is plenty to ruminate over. Cork. 17% alc. **Rating** 93 **To** 2016 $69

Holland Creek Adelaide Hills Riesling 2008 Elements of spice and candied fruit frame the bouquet; the palate shows a zesty lemon personality, with a talcy texture and zesty citrus finish. Screwcap. 13.5% alc. **Rating** 92 **To** 2014 $19

Adelaide Hills Shiraz 2005 Vibrant colour; youthful and fine, with plenty of blue fruit and spice on offer; juicy on entry, but pulls up, leaving a fragrant, spicy and slightly mineral note to the finish. Screwcap. 16% alc. **Rating** 92 **To** 2016 $21

Adelaide Hills Shiraz Viognier 2006 A spicy, medium-bodied bouquet, with an attractive overlay of perfume; the palate is juicy on entry, and offers a slight silky quality to the finish. Screwcap. 16% alc. **Rating** 92 **To** 2014 $21

Adelaide Hills Cabernet Sauvignon 2005 Shows a nice level of cassis and savoury bramble complexity; the palate is quite fine and the tannins plentiful; a well-balanced finish. Screwcap. 15.5% alc. **Rating** 90 **To** 2014 $21

ΨΨΨΨ   **Adelaide Hills Pinot Gris 2008** A balanced bouquet of pear and a hint of mineral complexity; thickly textured, with fresh acid on the finish to clean it up. Screwcap. 13.5% alc. **Rating** 89 **To** 2012 $19

Adelaide Hills Cabernet Franc 2006 Plenty of perfume, with tight red berry fruit, a little spice and a savoury, slightly earthy, high acid finish. Screwcap. 14.5% alc. **Rating** 87 **To** 2012 $27

Paradigm Hill   ★★★★★

26 Merricks Road, Merricks, Vic 3916 **Region** Mornington Peninsula
T (03) 5989 9000 **F** (03) 5989 8555 **www**.paradigmhill.com.au **Open** 1st w'end of month, public hols or by appt
Winemaker Dr George Mihaly **Est.** 1999 **Cases** 1200 **Vyds** 4.2 ha
Dr George Mihaly (with a background in medical research, biotech and pharmaceutical industries) and wife Ruth (a former chef and caterer) have realised a 30-year dream of establishing their own vineyard and winery, abandoning their previous careers to do so. George had all the necessary scientific qualifications, and built on those by making the 2001 Merricks Creek wines, moving to home base at Paradigm Hill in '02, all along receiving guidance and advice from Nat White of Main Ridge Estate. The vineyard, under Ruth's control with advice from Shane Strange, is planted to 2.1 ha of pinot noir, 0.9 ha of shiraz, 0.8 ha of riesling and 0.4 ha of pinot gris. Exports to Singapore, Indonesia, Malaysia and China.

ΨΨΨΨΨ   **Les Cinq Mornington Peninsula Pinot Noir 2007** Finer and more savoury than L'Ami Sage, red fruits as well as black; long, elegant palate. Two utterly different styles, both very good. Screwcap. 13.8% alc. **Rating** 95 **To** 2014 $58

L'Ami Sage Mornington Peninsula Pinot Noir 2007 Clear, deep purple-red; a fragrant bouquet leads into a very intense and vibrant palate, the fruit flavours in the black cherry and plum spectrum. Screwcap. 13.8% alc. **Rating** 95 **To** 2015 $48

Mornington Peninsula Pinot Gris 2008 The most complex (and expensive) pinot gris on the market; 100% barrel ferment, with 50% new French oak followed by five months' maturation; notwithstanding, the varietal fruit still shines through, the finish rich but bone dry. Screwcap. 14% alc. **Rating** 94 **To** 2012 $40

Col's Block Mornington Peninsula Shiraz 2007 Vivid crimson-purple; a fragrant, perfumed bouquet of black cherry and spice is faithfully repeated on the fine, but intense, palate, with perfectly judged oak and tannin support. Screwcap. 13.6% alc. **Rating** 94 **To** 2020 $40

♀♀♀♀ **Transition Mornington Peninsula Pinot Noir Rose 2008** Very pale crimson; well balanced although bone dry; attractive strawberry and spice flavours. Screwcap. 13.6% alc. **Rating** 89 **To** 2010 $30

Mornington Peninsula Riesling 2008 Very aromatic; picking on three days over a week has added to the flavour, but the palate lacks thrust and intensity; may develop, for the acidity is good. Screwcap. 12.8% alc. **Rating** 88 **To** 2013 $26

Paradise IV   ★★★★

45 Dog Rocks Road, Batesford, Vic 3221 (postal) **Region** Geelong
T (03) 5276 1536 **F** (03) 5276 1665 **Open** Not
Winemaker Graham Bonney, Doug Neal **Est.** 1988 **Cases** 1000
The former Moorabool Estate has been renamed Paradise IV for the very good reason that it is the site of the original Paradise IV Vineyard planted in 1848 by Swiss vigneron Jean-Henri Dardel. It is owned by Ruth and Graham Bonney in partnership with former school teacher and wine lover Douglas Neal, who has the agency for various French barrel makers in Australia and South Africa. Neal is also a self-trained winemaker, and his role in the partnership is to make and sell the wines, with Graham and Ruth responsible for the vineyard. In practice, the functions overlap to a degree, as one would expect with a relatively small business. The winery has an underground barrel room, and the winemaking turns around wild yeast fermentation, natural mlf, gravity movement of the wine and so forth. The vineyard is planted to equal quantities of chardonnay, shiraz and cabernet sauvignon.

♀♀♀♀♀ **Dardel Shiraz 2006** Good red-purple; succulent black fruits, licorice and spice on entry, finishing with pleasantly earthy tannins; will develop very well. Diam. 13.8% alc. **Rating** 93 **To** 2026 $37

Batesford Geelong Shiraz Cabernet 2006 Medium-bodied; smooth, supple briary/leafy components ex cabernet add to complexity. Diam. 13.8% alc. **Rating** 90 **To** 2016 $29

Paramoor Wines

439 Three Chain Road, Carlsruhe via Woodend, Vic 3442 **Region** Macedon Ranges
T (03) 5427 1057 **F** (03) 5427 3927 **www**.paramoor.com.au **Open** 7 days 10–5
Winemaker William Fraser **Est.** 2003 **Cases** 900 **Vyds** 1.6 ha
Paramoor Wines is the retirement venture of Will Fraser, formerly Managing Director of Kodak Australasia. To be strictly correct, he is Dr Will Fraser, armed with a PhD in chemistry from Adelaide University. Much later he added a Diploma of wine technology from the University of Melbourne, Dookie Campus, to his qualifications. Paramoor's winery is set on 17 ha of beautiful country not far from Hanging Rock, originally a working Clydesdale horse farm, with a magnificent heritage-style barn now used for cellar door sales and functions. Will has planted 0.8 ha each of pinot noir and pinot gris, and supplements the product range by purchasing varieties more suited to warmer climates than the chilly hills of the Macedon Ranges.

♀♀♀♀♀ **Riesling 2008** A glorious modern riesling, with lime and apple aromas leading into a seductive palate, which is fruit-sweet in a citrus, apple and tropical range; just an echo of sweetness on the finish. Screwcap. 12% alc. **Rating** 95 **To** 2018 $18

ỲỲỲỲ♀ **Kathleen Shiraz 2006** Opaque crimson-purple; the anticipated extract is present, but the wine is in balance, and the alcohol does not show through. Limitless patience will be repaid. Diam. 15% alc. **Rating** 93 **To** 2026 $24

The Fraser Cabernet Sauvignon Merlot 2005 A complex medium-bodied wine that is developing well, the blackcurrant and cassis fruit neatly folded into chocolatey nuances and cedary French oak. Diam. 14% alc. **Rating** 93 **To** 2015 $22

Paringa Estate   ★★★★★

44 Paringa Road, Red Hill South, Vic 3937 **Region** Mornington Peninsula
T (03) 5989 2669 **F** (03) 5931 0135 **www**.paringaestate.com.au **Open** 7 days 11–5
Winemaker Lindsay McCall **Est.** 1985 **Cases** 16 000 **Vyds** 21.85 ha
Schoolteacher-turned-winemaker Lindsay McCall has shown an absolutely exceptional gift for winemaking across a range of styles, but with immensely complex Pinot Noir and Shiraz leading the way. The wines have an unmatched level of success in the wine shows and competitions Paringa Estate is able to enter, the limitation being the relatively small production of the top wines in the portfolio. His skills are no less evident in contract winemaking for others. Winery of the Year 2007 Wine Companion. Exports to the UK, Denmark, South Korea, Singapore, Taiwan and Hong Kong.

ỲỲỲỲỲ **Reserve Special Barrel Selection Pinot Noir 2007** Very bright colour; monolithic in proportion with more of everything, handled with great control; dark plum, bright cherry, allspice, game and charry oak intermingle for a heady mix of aromas; the palate relays this conviction with real depth and power on entry, and lightness returns as the flavours cascade from start to finish; needs much time, but will richly reward patience. Screwcap. 14.5% alc. **Rating** 96 **To** 2016 $90

Estate Pinot Noir 2007 As ever, deeply coloured; an altogether serious pinot with magisterial depth to both the dark plum flavour and structure, and commensurate length. Born to stay. Screwcap. 14.5% alc. **Rating** 96 **To** 2015 $60

Estate Shiraz 2007 Vibrant colour; a heady mixture of elegance and ripe, luscious black fruit; plum, blackberry, pepper and fresh sage engage on the bouquet; medium-bodied with racy acidity and really silky tannin; the not inconsiderable oak is a mere afterthought in the wake of the expansive fruit on offer. Screwcap. 14.5% alc. **Rating** 96 **To** 2020 $50

Peninsula Pinot Noir 2008 Bright and focused red cherry fruit with a very attractive spice component; lovely purity on the palate, with drive, nerve and a bit of grip from the vibrant fruit on offer; a shining example of the fruit showing its personality without winemaking clouding the offering. Screwcap. 14% alc. **Rating** 95 **To** 2014 $27

ỲỲỲỲ♀ **Estate Chardonnay 2007** A prominently savoury bouquet of grilled nuts, lemon and mineral; the palate is grippy and textural, with a high level of toast on the melon-fruit finish. Screwcap. 14.5% alc. **Rating** 91 **To** 2013 $35

ỲỲỲỲ **Estate Pinot Gris 2008** Pale colour; the bouquet has pear fruit and a little spice; cleansing acidity on the palate, with good texture; savoury and demanding food. Screwcap. 14.5% alc. **Rating** 89 **To** 2012 $25

Peninsula Chardonnay 2007 Elegant lemon fruit with a touch of mineral; the palate is tightly wound with pronounced fresh acidity and citrus fruit on the finish. Screwcap. 14.5% alc. **Rating** 88 **To** 2012 $22

Parish Hill Wines   ★★★

Parish Hill Road, Uraidla, SA 5142 **Region** Adelaide Hills
T (08) 8390 3927 **F** (08) 8390 0394 **www**.parishhill.com.au **Open** By appt
Winemaker Andrew Cottell **Est.** 1998 **Cases** 600 **Vyds** 1.6 ha
Andrew Cottell and Joy Carlisle have a tiny vineyard on a steep, sunny, exposed slope adjacent to their house, and a micro-winery (which has approval for a total crush of 15 tonnes), but they take the venture very seriously. Andrew studied wine science and viticulture at CSU, where he was introduced to the Italian varieties; this led to the planting of arneis, nebbiolo,

vermentino, negro amaro and dolcetto. An attempt to use an organic spray program in 2002 failed, and while adopting integrated pest management, soft environmental practices and beneficial insects, they have moved to conventional vineyard management.

ŶŶŶŶ   **Pinot Grigio 2008** Deeply coloured with plenty of pink; exotic and very ripe fruit bouquet; good weight and texture, but a little soft on the finish. Screwcap. 12.5% alc. **Rating** 87 **To** 2012 $25

Parker Coonawarra Estate   ★★★★★

Riddoch Highway, Coonawarra, SA 5263 **Region** Coonawarra
T (08) 8737 3525 **www**.parkercoonawarraestate.com.au **Open** 7 days 10–4
Winemaker Peter Bissell (Contract) **Est.** 1985 **Cases** 7000
Parker Coonawarra Estate is at the southern end of Coonawarra, on rich terra rossa soil over limestone. Cabernet sauvignon is the predominant variety (17.45 ha), with minor plantings of merlot and petit verdot. Acquired by the Rathbone family in 2004. Exports to all major markets.

ŶŶŶŶŶ   **Terra Rossa First Growth 2006** There can be no doubt this is by far the best Parker cabernet merlot, or that it is a very good wine by any standards; multiple layers of flavour, texture and structure, cassis and blackcurrant interweaving with new French oak and ripe tannins. Screwcap. 15% alc. **Rating** 96 **To** 2030 $110
Terra Rossa Cabernet Sauvignon 2006 Deeply coloured; an extremely powerful, dense wine with blackcurrant and blackberry fruit obscuring the French oak and, to a degree, the tannins. One for the grandchildren. Screwcap. 15% alc. **Rating** 96 **To** 2035 $39.50
Favourite Son Chardonnay 2007 Bright and lively; citrus/grapefruit intermingles with stone fruit on the long palate, where French oak is seen rather than heard; has excellent length. Screwcap. 13.5% alc. **Rating** 94 **To** 2015 $23
Terra Rossa Merlot 2006 An extremely elegant, finely structured wine, with great mouthfeel and continuity of line; no one flavour stands out among the multiplicity of spicy/earthy/red fruit/cedary French oak components. Screwcap. 14% alc. **Rating** 94 **To** 2020 $39.50

ŶŶŶŶŶ   **Favourite Son Shiraz 2006** More elegant and spicy than one might expect at this alcohol level, but all the better for that; its array of spice, pepper, cedar and earth flavours are in total harmony. Screwcap. 14.5% alc. **Rating** 92 **To** 2016 $23
Favourite Son Cabernet Merlot 2006 Attractive berry, spice, olive and earth aromas; the palate has good texture from fine tannins and quality French oak. Screwcap. 14.5% alc. **Rating** 91 **To** 2016 $23
Favourite Son Cabernet Merlot 2005 A slightly fuller and richer wine than the '06, the slightly riper fruit with more obvious tannins; preference turns on style, not quality. Screwcap. 15% alc. **Rating** 91 **To** 2015 $23

Parri Estate   ★★★★

Sneyd Road, Mount Compass, SA 5210 **Region** Southern Fleurieu/McLaren Vale
T (08) 8554 9660 **F** (08) 8554 9694 **www**.parriestate.com.au **Open** 7 days 11–4
Winemaker Linda Domas **Est.** 1998 **Cases** 10 000 **Vyds** 32 ha
Alice, Peter and John Phillips have established a business with a clear marketing plan and an obvious commitment to quality. The vineyard is planted to chardonnay, viognier, sauvignon blanc, semillon, pinot noir, cabernet sauvignon and shiraz, using modern trellis and irrigation systems. In 2004 a second property on Ingoldby Road, McLaren Vale was acquired, with a second cellar door (open 7 days 11–5) and shiraz, grenache and cabernet sauvignon plantings up to 60 years old. Exports to the UK, the US and other major markets.

ŶŶŶŶŶ   **Phillips Family Selection Limited Release McLaren Vale Cabernet Shiraz 2007** Attractive medium-bodied wine, strongly spicy, but not green; the tannins are fine, the oak (French and American) balanced and integrated; the finish is long and persistent; 400 cases made. Cork. 13% alc. **Rating** 93 **To** 2017 $40

Southern Fleurieu Pinot Noir 2007 Shows to advantage, even in a warm vintage. Authentic and attractive varietal expression, with savoury/spicy elements to the cherry fruit; good length and balance. A new region emerging? Screwcap. 12% alc. **Rating** 91 **To** 2014 $22

ŸŸŸŸ **Southern Fleurieu Viognier Chardonnay 2008** An interesting outcome; chardonnay does most of the talking and adds freshness, but the viognier sneaks in to put its apricot stamp on the back-palate. Screwcap. 13.5% alc. **Rating** 88 **To** 2011 $19

Passing Clouds ★★★★

RMB 440 Kurting Road, Kingower, Vic 3517 **Region** Bendigo
T (03) 5438 8257 **www.**passingclouds.com.au **Open** W'ends 12–5, Mon–Fri by appt
Winemaker Graeme Leith, Cameron Leith **Est.** 1974 **Cases** 3000 **Vyds** 22 ha
In 1974, Graeme Leith and Sue Mackinnon planted the first vines at Passing Clouds, 60 km northwest of Bendigo. Graeme is one of the great personalities of the wine industry, with a superb sense of humour, and makes lovely regional reds with cassis, berry and mint fruit. Sheltered by hills of ironbark forest, the valley offers an ideal growing climate for premium red wine. The vineyard is planted to shiraz (9 ha), cabernet sauvignon (5 ha), chardonnay and pinot noir (4 ha each). With the passing of years (and clouds), Graeme is gradually handing over winemaking responsibilities to son Cameron. Wines from the Three Wise Men joint venture are also available (see separate entry). Exports to the UK and the US.

ŸŸŸŸŸ **Graeme's Blend Shiraz Cabernet 2005** Clean, fragrant red and black fruits; supple and smooth texture to the medium-bodied palate offering blackberry, plum and blackcurrant; soft supporting tannins and oak. Diam. 13.4% alc. **Rating** 93 **To** 2018 $30
Pinot Noir 2007 Good colour; considerable body and depth of flavour at this low alcohol; savoury black fruits, which are positively ripe. Screwcap. 12.6% alc. **Rating** 91 **To** 2014 $25
The Angel Cabernet Sauvignon 2005 A fragrant mix of blackcurrant and mint fruit aromas; a medium-bodied palate, with silky texture and good length, pleasantly savoury tannins making a contribution. Diam. **Rating** 91 **To** 2015 $30

ŸŸŸŸ **Musk Chardonnay 2006** Still bright straw-green; from a vineyard near Daylesford at 720 m; light mineral and apple flavours backed by firm acidity. A Peter Pan style. Screwcap. 11.5% alc. **Rating** 88 **To** 2014 $23

Patina ★★★★

109 Summerhill Lane, Orange, NSW 2800 **Region** Orange
T (02) 6362 8336 **www.**patinawines.com.au **Open** W'ends 11–5, or by appt
Winemaker Gerald Naef **Est.** 1999 **Cases** 2500 **Vyds** 3 ha
Gerald Naef's home in Woodbridge in the Central Valley of California was surrounded by the vast vineyard and winery operations of Gallo and Robert Mondavi. It would be hard to imagine a more different environment than that provided by Orange. Gerald and wife Angie left California in 1981, initially establishing an irrigation farm in the northwest of NSW; 20 years later they moved to Orange, and by 2006 Gerald was a final-year student of wine science at CSU. He set up a micro-winery at the Orange Cool Stores, and his first wine was a 2003 Chardonnay, made from vines planted by him in '99. At its first show entry it won the trophy for Best White Wine of Show at the Orange Wine Show '06, of which I was Chairman. Dream starts seldom come better than this.

ŸŸŸŸŸ **Orange Sauvignon Blanc 2007** A lively and precise wine on both the clean bouquet and palate, with a mix of passionfruit, apple and tropical fruit; still pale in colour, and very fresh. Screwcap. 12.5% alc. **Rating** 90 **To** 2010 $27
Orange Cabernet Sauvignon 2004 Bottle age has softened the fruit, but, if anything, enhanced the length of the palate, with cedary oak complementing the rounded black fruits; fine tannins to close. Cork. 14% alc. **Rating** 90 **To** 2014 $27

Patrick T Wines

Cnr Ravenswood Lane/Riddoch Highway, Coonawarra, SA 5263 **Region** Coonawarra
T (08) 8737 3687 **F** (08) 8737 3689 **www**.patricktwines.com **Open** 7 days 10–5
Winemaker Pat Tocaciu **Est.** 1996 **Cases** 6600 **Vyds** 50.5 ha
Patrick Tocaciu is a district veteran, setting up Patrick T Winemaking Services after prior
careers at Heathfield Ridge Winery and Hollick Wines. He and his partners have over
40 ha of vines at Wrattonbully, and another 8 ha of cabernet sauvignon in Coonawarra. The
Wrattonbully plantings cover all the major varieties, while the Coonawarra plantings give rise
to the Home Block Cabernet Sauvignon. Also carries out contract winemaking for others.
Exports to Chile, Korea and NZ.

ΨΨΨΨΨ **Museum Release Home Block Coonawarra Cabernet Sauvignon 2002**
An elegant wine that has prospered mightily in bottle (and from the cool vintage).
The fruit flavours are still wonderfully fresh, the structure impeccable, the length
remarkable. Worth every cent of its price. Cork. 14% alc. **Rating** 96 **To** 2017 $80

ΨΨΨΨΨ **Estate Grown Wrattonbully Riesling 2008** The bouquet ranges through
apple blossom and mineral; the delicate palate has a light touch of sweetness neatly
balanced by acidity. Seductive style. Screwcap. 11% alc. **Rating** 92 **To** 2015 $21
Estate Grown Mount Gambier Pinot Noir 2007 Excellent hue; further proof
that Mount Gambier is far more suited to Pinot Noir than any other Limestone
Coast region; a mix of supple red cherry and plum fruit with a balanced finish.
Biodynamically grown. Screwcap. 13% alc. **Rating** 91 **To** 2012 $21
Mother of Pearl Limestone Coast Shiraz 2006 Attractive light- to medium-
bodied wine with a flamboyant display of juicy red fruits framed by spice, black
pepper and good acidity. Screwcap. 14% alc. **Rating** 90 **To** 2014 $18
Reserve Selection Coonawarra Sparkling Shiraz NV Carefully made; the
base wine spent two years in French oak before fermentation in bottle, then two
years on yeast lees prior to disgorgement. Has plenty of flavour, and the dosage has
been precisely calibrated. Cork. 14% alc. **Rating** 90 **To** 2015 $50

ΨΨΨΨ **Mother of Pearl Limestone Coast Chardonnay 2008** Has gently ripe,
clear-cut varietal character in a stone fruit spectrum, with depth to the mouthfeel;
no oak to be seen. Screwcap. 13.5% alc. **Rating** 87 **To** 2012 $18
Estate Grown Wrattonbully Shiraz 2005 Light- to medium-bodied; spicy,
earthy, slightly leafy nuances to the predominantly red fruits. Screwcap. 14% alc.
Rating 87 **To** 2014 $25
Reserve Release Margaret River Cabernet Sauvignon 2004 Relatively
light-bodied, but with clear varietal character in a cedary/earthy mode; ready now.
Screwcap. 13.5% alc. **Rating** 87 **To** 2010 $18

Paul Bettio Wines

34 Simpsons Lane, Moyhu, Vic 3732 **Region** King Valley
T (03) 5727 9308 **F** (03) 5727 9344 **www**.paulbettiowines.com.au **Open** 7 days 10–5
Winemaker Damien Star **Est.** 1995 **Cases** 10 000 **Vyds** 27 ha
Paul and Helen Bettio have been growing grapes in the King Valley since 1988. The plantings
include cabernet sauvignon, merlot, sauvignon blanc, pinot grigio, barbera and chardonnay
(the latter three grown by Paul's father Joe).

ΨΨΨΨΨ **King Valley Barbera 2005** Good colour; blueberry fruit with a touch of spice;
good acidity and clean low-tannin finish; has a touch of the varietal bramble
character on the finish; very fresh for its age. Screwcap. 12.8% alc. **Rating** 90
To 2012 $18

ΨΨΨΨ **King Valley Cabernet Sauvignon 2008** Good colour; quite European
bouquet; high-toned, with a relatively high-acid palate. Screwcap. 14% alc.
Rating 87 **To** 2012 $15

Paul Conti Wines

529 Wanneroo Road, Woodvale, WA 6026 **Region** Greater Perth Zone
T (08) 9409 9160 **F** (08) 9309 1634 **www**.paulcontiwines.com.au **Open** Mon–Sat 10–5,
Sun by appt
Winemaker Paul Conti, Jason Conti **Est.** 1948 **Cases** 6000 **Vyds** 21.5 ha
Third-generation winemaker Jason Conti has assumed control of winemaking, although
father Paul (who succeeded his father in 1968) remains interested and involved in the business.
Over the years Paul Conti challenged and redefined industry perceptions and standards; the
challenge for Jason Conti was to achieve the same degree of success in a relentlessly and
increasingly competitive market environment, and he is doing just that. Plantings at the
Carabooda Vineyard have been expanded with 1 ha of tempranillo, petit verdot and viognier,
and pinot noir is purchased from Manjimup. In a further extension, a property has been
acquired at Cowaramup in Margaret River, with 1 ha each of petit verdot and viognier
planted at this stage. Exports to the UK, Malaysia and Japan.

ᵀ ᵀ ᵀ ᵀ ᵀ **The Tuarts Cabernet Sauvignon 2007** Strong crimson-purple; the medium-
bodied palate is flooded with blackcurrant and redcurrant fruit, French oak playing
a sure-footed support role. Screwcap. 14% alc. **Rating** 92 **To** 2016 $20
Medici Ridge Pinot Noir 2008 Clear light crimson; good varietal expression
with quite strongly spiced plum fruit; tannins spot-on, length good. Value.
Screwcap. 14% alc. **Rating** 90 **To** 2013 $20
Mariginiup Shiraz 2006 Well-made, with ripe, but not overripe, fruit; pleasing
spicy components to a medium-bodied wine of good length and balance. Cork.
15% alc. **Rating** 90 **To** 2014 $28

ᵀ ᵀ ᵀ ᵀ **Roccella Grenache Shiraz 2007** A convincing blend, the bouquet and
medium-bodied palate ranging through red and black fruits, spice and notes of
vanilla. Good value. Screwcap. 14.5% alc. **Rating** 89 **To** 2013 $16
Mariginiup Shiraz 2007 Generous medium- to full-bodied palate, offering
blackberry and plum fruit, ripe tannins and vanilla oak. Screwcap. 14.5% alc.
Rating 89 **To** 2015 $28
The Tuarts Chenin Blanc 2008 Strong varietal fruit salad in a tropical mode;
will become even richer in the years ahead. Screwcap. 13.5% alc. **Rating** 88
To 2012 $16
Medici Ridge Pinot Noir 2007 Good colour and plenty of depth; at the
ripe end of the spectrum, perhaps bordering on some dry red characters. Cork.
14.5% alc. **Rating** 87 **To** 2011 $23.99

Paul Osicka

Majors Creek Vineyard at Graytown, Vic 3608 **Region** Heathcote
T (03) 5794 9235 **F** (03) 5794 9288 **Open** By appt
Winemaker Paul Osicka **Est.** 1955 **Cases** NFP **Vyds** 14 ha
The Osicka family arrived in Australia from Czechoslovakia in the early 1950s. Vignerons
in their own country, they settled at Graytown, and commenced planting vines in 1955.
Their vineyard was the first new venture in Central and Southern Victoria for over half a
century. It keeps a low profile, but produces consistently good shiraz from the 10 ha of estate
plantings (the remainder cabernet sauvignon, merlot and riesling). Exports to Canada, Ireland
and Hong Kong.

ᵀ ᵀ ᵀ ᵀ ᵀ **Majors Creek Vineyard Heathcote Shiraz 2006** A complex but balanced
wine, with blackberry, dark chocolate and licorice seamlessly integrated with
evident new oak and ripe tannins. Diam. 15% alc. **Rating** 94 **To** 2021 $35

Paulett

Polish Hill Road, Polish Hill River, SA 5453 **Region** Clare Valley
T (08) 8843 4328 **F** (08) 8843 4202 **www**.paulettwines.com.au **Open** 7 days 10–5
Winemaker Neil Paulett **Est.** 1983 **Cases** 13 000 **Vyds** 26 ha

The Paulett story is a saga of Australian perseverance, commencing with the 1982 purchase of a property with 1 ha of vines and a house, promptly destroyed by the terrible Ash Wednesday bushfires of the following year. Son Matthew has joined Neil and Alison Paulett as a partner in the business, responsible for viticulture on a much-expanded property holding of 147 ha. The winery and cellar door have wonderful views over the Polish Hill River region, the memories of the bushfires long gone. Exports to the UK, NZ and China.

ŸŸŸŸŸ **Antonina Polish Hill River Riesling 2007** Has outstanding texture, structure and balance; the intense lime/citrus flavours driving through the palate from the start to the long finish and aftertaste; the acidity guarantees a long and prosperous life. Value. Screwcap. 12% alc. **Rating** 96 **To** 2022 $40

Andreas 2005 Very good colour reveals an intense, highly focused wine with great texture and structure to the seamless spicy black fruits, oak and tannins. Shiraz. Screwcap. 14.5% alc. **Rating** 95 **To** 2025 $45

ŸŸŸŸŸ **Polish Hill River Shiraz 2005** Developing slowly but surely; a mix of red and black fruits with spice and pepper complexity to the medium-bodied palate. Screwcap. 14.5% alc. **Rating** 92 **To** 2015 $22

Polish Hill River Riesling 2008 Focused and flinty with lime juice bouquet; good texture and fresh acid; but will build. Screwcap. 12.5% alc. **Rating** 90 **To** 2018 $20

Polish Hill River Aged Release Riesling 2003 Plenty of toasty aromatics, leading toward kerosene; better palate, with plenty of sweet fruit, showing a strong lemon zest character; long and toasty on the finish. Screwcap. 12% alc. **Rating** 90 **To** 2014 $30

ŸŸŸŸ **Polish Hill River Cabernet Merlot 2005** Distinct nuances of mint and briar to the black fruits; this blend is often a challenge in the Clare Valley. Screwcap. 14.5% alc. **Rating** 88 **To** 2012 $22

Paxton ★★★★★

Wheaton Road, McLaren Vale, SA 5171 **Region** McLaren Vale
T (08) 8323 9131 **F** (08) 8323 8903 **www**.paxtonvineyards.com **Open** 7 days 10–5
Winemaker Michael Paxton **Est.** 1979 **Cases** 18 000 **Vyds** 74.5 ha

David Paxton is one of Australia's best known viticulturists and consultants. He founded Paxton Vineyards in McLaren Vale with his family in 1979, and has since been involved in various capacities in the establishment and management of vineyards in several leading regions across the country. Former Flying Winemaker, son Michael (with 14 years' experience in Spain, South America, France and Australia) is responsible for making the wines. There are five vineyards in the family holdings: the Thomas Block (28 ha), the Jones Block (22 ha), Quandong Farm (19 ha), Landcross Farm (2 ha) and Maslin Vineyard (3.5 ha). By 2006 all of the five vineyards were managed using full biodynamic principles. Paxton has become the first member of 1% For the Planet (www.onepercentfortheplanet.org). An underground barrel store has been completed and a cellar door opened in the original shearing shed. Exports to the UK, the US, Canada, Denmark, Sweden, Germany and Taiwan.

ŸŸŸŸŸ **Elizabeth Jean 100 Year McLaren Vale Shiraz 2006** An elegant wine from start to finish, in no way reflecting any alcohol heat or dead fruit characters; supple black fruits have a touch of spice, the tannins are fine but persistent, the oak entirely persistent. Screwcap. 15% alc. **Rating** 95 **To** 2021 $85

Jones Block McLaren Vale Shiraz 2005 A very impressive wine for a vintage considered (however unfairly) inferior to '04 and '06; the super-elegant, supple and harmonious blend of black fruits, oak and tannin push all the right buttons. Screwcap. 14.5% alc. **Rating** 95 **To** 2020 $39

ŸŸŸŸŸ **Quandong Farm McLaren Vale Shiraz 2007** Ripe dark fruits, with mocha and fruitcake coming to the fore on the bouquet; sweet and supple on the palate, the wine offers a hint of dried herb relief from the abundance of sweet black and, surprisingly evident, red fruits. Screwcap. 13% alc. **Rating** 93 **To** 2015 $30

McLaren Vale Shiraz Rose 2008 Brilliant crimson; delicious style for broad appeal; residual sugar balanced by crisp acidity; raspberry and cherry fruit flavours. Screwcap. 12% alc. **Rating** 91 **To** 2010 **$**19.99

AAA McLaren Vale Shiraz Grenache 2007 Light but fresh crimson colour announces an even fresher and brighter wine on the palate, with juicy raspberry notes ex the grenache (33%) adding life to the quality shiraz (67%). Screwcap. 14% alc. **Rating** 90 **To** 2013 **$**23

Temprano McLaren Vale Tempranillo 2007 Bright crimson-purple; piercing red fruits with the twist of lemon rind that is typical of Australian tempranillo; bright finish. May repay cellaring even though the extract is not high. Screwcap. 13% alc. **Rating** 90 **To** 2016 **$**23

Payne's Rise ★★★☆

10 Paynes Road, Seville, Vic 3139 **Region** Yarra Valley
T 0408 618 346 **F** (03) 5961 9383 **www**.paynesrise.com.au **Open** By appt
Winemaker Jeff Wright, Keith Salter, Franco D'Anna (Contract) **Est.** 1998 **Cases** 500 **Vyds** 4 ha

Tim and Narelle Cullen have progressively established 1 ha each of cabernet sauvignon, shiraz, chardonnay and sauvignon blanc since 1998, supplemented by grapes purchased from local growers. They carry out all the vineyard work; Tim is also a viticulturist for a local agribusiness, and Narelle is responsible for sales and marketing. The contract-made wines have won several awards at the Victorian Wine Show.

🍷🍷🍷🍷🍷 **Yarra Valley Cabernet Sauvignon 2006** Crimson-red; well made, with attractive blackcurrant varietal fruit supported by fine tannins and balanced oak; has good line and a fresh finish. Diam. 13.5% alc. **Rating** 90 **To** 2016 **$**22

🍷🍷🍷🍷 **Yarra Valley Sauvignon Blanc 2008** Has considerable intensity to its citrussy/grassy/stone fruit flavours, perhaps with a touch of sweetness. Screwcap. 12.5% alc. **Rating** 88 **To** 2010 **$**18

Pearson Vineyards ★★★

Main North Road, Penwortham, SA 5453 **Region** Clare Valley
T (08) 8843 4234 **F** (08) 8843 4141 **Open** As per roadside sign
Winemaker Jim Pearson **Est.** 1993 **Cases** 500 **Vyds** 2.3 ha

Jim Pearson makes the Pearson Vineyard wines at Mintaro Cellars. The estate vineyards (cabernet franc, riesling, cabernet sauvignon, shiraz and semillon) surround the beautiful little stone house, which acts as a cellar door – and which appears on the cover of my book *The Wines, The History, The Vignerons of the Clare Valley*. Exports to the US.

🍷🍷🍷🍷 **Clare Valley Riesling 2008** Lime and mineral bouquet; good acidity and even fruit on the palate; good length. Screwcap. 12.5% alc. **Rating** 87 **To** 2012 **$**19

Peel Estate ★★★☆

290 Fletcher Road, Karnup, WA 6171 **Region** Peel
T (08) 9524 1221 **F** (08) 9524 1625 **www**.peelwine.com.au **Open** 7 days 10–5
Winemaker Will Nairn, Mark Morton **Est.** 1974 **Cases** 5000 **Vyds** 16 ha

The icon wine is the Shiraz, a wine of considerable finesse and with a remarkably consistent track record. Every year Will Nairn holds a Great Shiraz Tasting for 6-year-old Australian Shirazs, and pits Peel Estate (in a blind tasting attended by 100 or so people) against Australia's best. It is never disgraced. The wood-matured Chenin Blanc is another winery speciality, although not achieving the excellence of the Shiraz. Exports to the UK, the US and Japan.

🍷🍷🍷🍷🍷 **Wood Matured Chenin Blanc 2004** In time-honoured style, ripe fruit salad and honey fruit flavours given an extra dimension courtesy of the oak; ageing nicely. Screwcap. 14% alc. **Rating** 90 **To** 2012 **$**22

ŶŶŶŶ   **Chardonnay 2006** Soft, peachy fruit is supported by a subtle infusion of oak; medium-bodied and ready soon. Screwcap. 14% alc. **Rating** 88 **To** 2012 $22
Cabernet Sauvignon 2003 Juicy red berry fruit is the foundation, oak and tannins in the back seat; does have overall balance. Diam. 13.5% alc. **Rating** 88 **To** 2013 $30

Pelican's Landing Maritime Wines   ★★★

PO Box 1143, Stirling, SA 5152 **Region** Southern Fleurieu
T 0411 552 077 **F** (08) 8370 1052 **www.**plmwines.com **Open** Not
Winemaker Helen Marzola **Est.** 2001 **Cases** 2000 **Vyds** 7 ha
Helen Marzola is the owner and winemaker of Pelican's Landing, the second vineyard to be established on Hindmarsh Island. The 32-ha property was previously a cattle farm; it now has cabernet sauvignon, chardonnay and viognier in production, the first vintage in 2004.

ŶŶŶŶ   **Mr Percival Cabernet Sauvignon 2007** A noticeable tang of the sea; slightly briny with red fruit in support; very firm and savoury. Screwcap. 14% alc.
Rating 87 **To** 2013 $15

Pembroke

191 Richmond Road, Cambridge, Tas 7170 **Region** Southern Tasmania
T (03) 6278 3808 **F** (03) 6234 5481 **www.**pembrokewines.com **Open** By appt
Winemaker Contract **Est.** 1980 **Cases** 200 **Vyds** 1.3 ha
The Pembroke vineyard was established in 1980 by the McKay and Hawker families and is still owned by them. It is predominantly planted to pinot noir and chardonnay, with tiny quantities of riesling and sauvignon blanc.

ŶŶŶŶŶ   **Pinot Noir 2006** Bright colour; quite jubey/raspberry fruit bouquet with a bit of spice and a slight waxy note; fleshy on the palate, with the toasty oak playing a role; firm on the finish. Gold medal Tas Wine Show '08. Screwcap. 13.3% alc.
Rating 94 **To** 2013 $39.95

ŶŶŶŶŶ   **Pinot Noir 2007** Bright colour; raspberry and spiced plum bouquet, with a touch of mint; the palate is lively and fresh, with good fruit concentration; the mint plays a leading role at this point in time. Screwcap. 13.8% alc. **Rating** 90 **To** 2014 $27.95

Penfolds

Tanunda Road, Nuriootpa, SA 5355 **Region** Barossa Valley
T (08) 8568 9389 **F** (08) 8568 9489 **www.**penfolds.com.au **Open** Mon–Fri 10–5, w'ends & public hols 11–5
Winemaker Peter Gago **Est.** 1844 **Cases** 1.4 million
Senior among the numerous wine companies or stand-alone brands of Foster's, and undoubtedly one of the top wine companies in the world in terms of quality, product range and exports. The consistency of the quality of the red wines and their value for money has long been recognised worldwide; the white wines, headed by the ultra-premium Yattarna Chardonnay, are now on a par with the red wines. Exports to the UK, the US and other major markets.

ŶŶŶŶŶ   **Grange 2004** Saturated purple-crimson colour; has an amazing depth to the bouquet, oak and black fruits already seamlessly woven; the longer you spend inhaling the aromas, the more you learn about the wine within, in much the same way as a Grand Cru red burgundy. The palate delivers all that the bouquet promises, and then some; it has absolutely perfect proportions to the river of flavours running through blackberry, Satsuma plum, licorice and spice; the tannins are quite active, but totally balanced and ripe. Cork. 14.3% alc. **Rating** 98 **To** 2054

Yattarna Chardonnay 2006 A brilliantly intense and focused wine, with nectarine, grapefruit and white peach flavours driving the extremely long, immaculately balanced palate. Like all great chardonnays, has eaten the oak in which it was barrel-fermented and matured. Screwcap. **Rating** 96 **To** 2016 $129.99

RWT Barossa Valley Shiraz 2006 Great colour; oozes blackberry and licorice from the bouquet, and then improbably gains greater impact on the dense, plush palate; just when you think that is it, the freakishly vibrant and juicy finish and aftertaste take over. Screwcap. 14.5% alc. **Rating** 96 **To** 2036 $169.99

Bin 707 Cabernet Sauvignon 2006 An effortlessly luxuriant and pure wine, with juicy blackcurrant and cassis fruit supported by positive, but fine and ripe tannins; only Penfolds can use 100% American oak to such good effect. Great 707. Screwcap. **Rating** 96 **To** 2036 $184.99

Bin 389 Cabernet Shiraz 2006 Great colour, and as befits the vintage, is an intense and complex wine of great breed; it has many layers of blackberry, blackcurrant, licorice, earth and chocolate, the powerful tannins in balance, the oak likewise. Screwcap. 14.5% alc. **Rating** 96 **To** 2036 $59.99

Bin 51 Eden Valley Riesling 2008 Potent bouquet promising the intense lime juice and apple flavours that emerge on the long palate; has some minerally notes on the finish and aftertaste. A seriously good riesling. Screwcap. 11.5% alc. **Rating** 95 **To** 2018 $31.95

Reserve Bin Chardonnay 2007 Bin 07A. Shows the continuing evolution of the Penfolds white wines as they become steadily finer and more elegant; fruit to the fore, with seamless oak behind. This is a great example of that evolution, marrying intensity with delicacy. Screwcap. **Rating** 95 **To** 2017 $89.99

Cellar Reserve Barossa Valley Cabernet Sauvignon 2006 Is not far short of the material used in Special Bins or 707, possible only in years such as '06; lovely, expressive, cassis fruit with seamless tannins and oak; lingering finish. Screwcap. **Rating** 95 **To** 2026 $250

Bin 407 Cabernet Sauvignon 2005 Very typical Penfolds style, with strong structure built around a base of black fruits, tannin and oak seamlessly interwoven on the medium- to full-bodied palate and long finish. Screwcap. 14.5% alc. **Rating** 95 **To** 2025 $44.99

Bin 707 Cabernet Sauvignon 2005 Clear red-purple; the fragrant bouquet proclaims its class from the first whiff; the web of blackcurrant, cassis and mulberry fruit is complexed further by American oak, a match that only Penfolds can carry off. Cork. 14.5% alc. **Rating** 95 **To** 2020 $174.99

Bin 311 Tumbarumba Chardonnay 2008 Vibrantly crisp and piercing, proclaiming its cool-grown origins, with nectarine and grapefruit the driver, French oak the second tier. Screwcap. 13% alc. **Rating** 94 **To** 2015 $42.99

Kalimna Bin 28 Shiraz 2006 In the heartland of Penfolds' red wine style; blackberry fruit, ripe tannins and vanilla oak; needs time, but everything is in balance. Screwcap. 14.5% alc. **Rating** 94 **To** 2026 $33.99

St Henri 2005 A substantial wine in all respects, with more richness and mouthfeel than many of the 1980s and '90s; the array of black fruits with a twist of cassis is perfectly balanced, as is the oak and tannin support. Screwcap. **Rating** 94 **To** 2025 $94.99

Koonunga Hill Seventy Six Shiraz Cabernet 2007 Crimson-purple; a rich, amply proportioned wine with layers of blackberry, blackcurrant and plum fruit cradled in subtle oak and persistent, but fine, tannins. On-premise release. Trophy Sydney Wine Show '08 for Best Dry Red in the commercial classes. Screwcap. 14.5% alc. **Rating** 94 **To** 2020 $35

Bin 407 Cabernet Sauvignon 2006 Has classic cabernet character, with a distinctly austere framework surrounding the blackcurrant and earth fruit; the tannins are in balance and not dry, the oak likewise in balance. An appallingly heavily wine-stained cork. 14.5% alc. **Rating** 94 **To** 2021 $49.99

Cellar Reserve Barossa Valley Sangiovese 2007 Deeper hue than any other Australian sangiovese; a powerful, textured palate with ripe black cherry fruit running through to the long finish. Should age superbly. Cork. 14.5% alc. Rating 94 To 2020 $51.99

Cellar Reserve Barossa Valley Sangiovese 2006 Has got its act together, with both structure and length to the sour cherry fruit; fine tannins. Cork. 14.5% alc. Rating 94 To 2012 $51.99

ⓉⓉⓉⓉⓎ Thomas Hyland Adelaide Riesling 2008 Bright straw-green; has a highly aromatic, almost pungent, bouquet of citrus and tropical fruit, the emphatic palate following suit. Screwcap. 12% alc. Rating 93 To 2016 $20.99

Bin 128 Coonawarra Shiraz 2007 Strong colour; has considerable richness and depth to bouquet and palate alike; plummy black fruits are supported by positive oak and emphatic tannins; long-lived style sure to improve. Screwcap. 14.5% alc. Rating 93 To 2027 $33.99

Bin 311 Tumbarumba Chardonnay 2007 Clean and precise, with nectarine and white peach fruit coming to the fore; has excellent balance and length thanks to minerally acidity. Screwcap. 12.5% alc. Rating 92 To 2013 $42.99

Koonunga Hill Seventy Six Shiraz Cabernet 2006 Packed with sweet fruit reminiscent of Christmas cake and blackberries; quite juicy on the palate, with a hint of cassis on the finish. Screwcap. 14.5% alc. Rating 92 To 2020 $35

Bin 138 Barossa Valley Grenache Shiraz Mourvedre 2006 Well balanced, with no confection and a vast array of red and dark fruits; a little spice comes through on the quite tannic finish. Screwcap. 14.5% alc. Rating 92 To 2021 $33.99

Bin 138 Barossa Valley Grenache Shiraz Mourvedre 2007 Bright clear colour; a harmonious blend of spicy red and black fruits, licorice, chocolate and vanilla oak; the fine tannins provide a neat framework for the wine. Screwcap. 14.5% alc. Rating 91 To 2018 $33.99

Cellar Reserve Woodbury Vineyard Eden Valley Gewurztraminer 2008 As always, one of the best traminers going, perfectly balanced and appealing, but with less varietal expression than it achieves in the best vintages. Screwcap. 13.5% alc. Rating 90 To 2016 $34.99

Koonunga Hill Semillon Sauvignon Blanc 2008 Spotlessly clean, with gentle tropical nuances on the bouquet; the palate is fresh and lively, featuring grass, lemon and pineapple flavours. Screwcap. 12% alc. Rating 90 To 2011 $11.99

Koonunga Hill Shiraz Cabernet 2007 Bright and fresh; black and red fruits in very good balance, and supported by gentle tannins, oak second fiddle. Very different to the Seventy Six. Screwcap. 13.5% alc. Rating 90 To 2015 $15.99

Koonunga Hill Shiraz Cabernet 2006 Savoury/spicy nuances to the bouquet give way to blackberry fruit on the medium-bodied palate; supported by fine tannins and an echo of oak. Screwcap. 13.5% alc. Rating 90 To 2014 $11.99

Thomas Hyland Cabernet Sauvignon 2007 Correct colour; a quite fragrant bouquet leads into an elegant, medium-bodied palate with clearly defined cabernet fruit and good tannin structure. Coonawarra must be a contributor to this wine. Screwcap. 14% alc. Rating 90 To 2020 $20.99

Bluestone 10 Aged Tawny NV Pale brick; has good rancio characters on bouquet and palate; likewise good length. Cork. Rating 90 To 2010 $23.99

Penfolds Magill Estate ★★★★★

78 Penfold Road, Magill, SA 5072 **Region** Adelaide Zone
T (08) 8301 5400 **F** (08) 8301 5544 **www.**penfolds.com **Open** 7 days 10.30–4.30
Winemaker Peter Gago **Est.** 1844 **Cases** 3000 **Vyds** 5.2 ha
This is the birthplace of Penfolds, established by Dr Christopher Rawson Penfold in 1844, his house still part of the immaculately maintained property. It includes 5.2 ha of precious shiraz used to make Magill Estate; the original and subsequent winery buildings, most still in operation or in museum condition; and the much-acclaimed Magill Restaurant, with panoramic views of the city, a great wine list and fine dining. All this is a 20-min drive from Adelaide's CBD. Exports to the UK, the US and other major markets.

ΨΨΨΨΨ Shiraz 2006 A fragrant and gently spicy bouquet; a gloriously structured and flavoured wine, with a cascade of supple, rich black fruits, tannins and oak in a perfectly judged support role. Surely the best Magill Estate made to date. Why, oh why, a cork – simply to give the recorking clinic work? **Rating** 97 **To** 2030 $99.99

Penley Estate   ★★★★☆

McLeans Road, Coonawarra, SA 5263 **Region** Coonawarra
T (08) 8736 3211 **F** (08) 8736 3124 **www.**penley.com.au **Open** 7 days 10–4
Winemaker Kym Tolley, Greg Foster **Est.** 1988 **Cases** 40 000 **Vyds** 111 ha
Owner winemaker Kym Tolley describes himself as a fifth-generation winemaker, the family tree involving both the Penfolds and the Tolleys. He worked 17 years in the industry before establishing Penley Estate and has made every post a winner since, producing a succession of rich, complex, full-bodied red wines and stylish Chardonnays. These are made from precious estate plantings. Exports to all major markets.

ΨΨΨΨΨ Chertsey 2006 Bright colour; the promise of the fragrant red and black fruits on the bouquet comes to fruition in the mouth, juicy cassis fruit running through the long palate; high-quality cork. Cabernet Sauvignon/Merlot/Cabernet Franc. 15% alc. **Rating** 94 **To** 2020 $50.50

ΨΨΨΨ̊ Special Select Coonawarra Shiraz 2006 Good red-purple; a complex medium-bodied wine with spice, earth, blackberry and plum fruit plus vanilla oak and fine tannins. Cork. 15% alc. **Rating** 93 **To** 2016 $50.50
Over the Moon 2008 Bright red; while it abounds with red cherry fruit, has a balanced finish thanks to firm acidity; good length. Likely a shiraz base. Value plus. Screwcap. 14.5% alc. **Rating** 91 **To** 2009 $15
Phoenix Coonawarra Cabernet Sauvignon 2007 A fragrant bouquet of spicy red and dark fruits; a medium-bodied palate with bright cassis-accented fruit; good tannins and length. Value. Screwcap. 15% alc. **Rating** 91 **To** 2017 $19.99

ΨΨΨΨ Reserve Coonawarra Cabernet Sauvignon 2006 Has a complex bouquet, with cedary/earthy aromas at one end, and strong tannins on the finish; a heavily wine-stained cork doesn't inspire confidence. 15% alc. **Rating** 89 **To** 2015 $50.50
Cabernet Shiraz 2007 Cassis and blackberry, with focus and poise; good concentration and weight on the palate, with an even, if slightly forward, finish. Screwcap. 15% alc. **Rating** 89 **To** 2012 $19.99
Hyland Coonawarra Shiraz 2007 Pleasant light- to medium-bodied wine with ripe fruit on the mid-palate and a touch of spice/earth; heats up a little on the finish. Screwcap. 15% alc. **Rating** 88 **To** 2014 $19.99
Gryphon Coonawarra Merlot 2007 Despite the alcohol, is at the savoury/herbal end of the spectrum, redeemed in part by the red and black fruits of the mid-palate Screwcap. 15% alc. **Rating** 87 **To** 2012 $19.99

Penmara

Suite 42, 5-13 Larkin Street, Camperdown, NSW 2050 (postal)
Region Upper Hunter Valley/Orange
T (02) 9517 4429 **F** (02) 9517 4439 **www.**penmarawines.com.au **Open** Not
Winemaker Hunter Wine Services (John Horden) **Est.** 2000 **Cases** 25 000 **Vyds** 120 ha
Penmara was formed with the banner 'Five Families: One Vision', pooling most of their grapes, with a central processing facility, and marketing focused exclusively on exports. The six sites are Lilyvale Vineyards in New England; Tangaratta Vineyards at Tamworth; Birnam Wood, Rothbury Ridge and Martindale Vineyards in the Hunter Valley; and Highland Heritage at Orange. In all, these vineyards give Penmara access to 120 ha of shiraz, chardonnay, cabernet sauvignon, semillon, verdelho and merlot, mainly from the Hunter Valley and Orange. Exports to the US and other major markets.

ŢŢŢŢŢ **Reserve Orange Sauvignon Blanc 2008** A strong green nettle character complements the gooseberry fruit bouquet; the palate shows pronounced acidity, but delivers an even finish, full of varietal character. Screwcap. 11% alc. **Rating** 90 **To** 2012 $21.99

ŢŢŢŢ **Marawarpina Clare Valley Orange Shiraz 2005** A hitherto unique regional blend, the cool-climate component from Orange dominating both bouquet and palate, with spicy/leafy/menthol notes. I'm not convinced about this one. Screwcap. 14% alc. **Rating** 89 **To** 2015 $34.95
Five Families Riesling 2008 Clean, fine and focused lemon and orange zest aromas; quite generous on the palate, with good flavour, and a dry chalky finish. Screwcap. 12% alc. **Rating** 88 **To** 2013 $15.99

Penna Lane Wines   ★★★★☆

Lot 51, Penna Lane, Penwortham via Clare, SA 5453 **Region** Clare Valley
T (08) 8843 4364 **F** (08) 8843 4349 **www**.pennalanewines.com.au **Open** Thurs–Sun & public hols 11–5, or by appt
Winemaker Ray Klavins, Paulett Wines **Est.** 1998 **Cases** 3000 **Vyds** 4.5 ha
A seachange brought Ray Klavins and Stephen Stafford-Brookes together. Ray ran a landscaping business in Adelaide and Stephen was a sales rep in the UK. Both decided to get into wine production and, with enormous support from their wives, began studying oenology and viticulture at Roseworthy College in 1991. Ray and wife Lynette purchased their 14-ha property in the Skilly Hills in '93; it was covered with rubbish, Salvation Jane, a derelict dairy and tumbledown piggery. They spent all their spare time clearing up the property, living in a tent and the old shearing shed, and planted the first vines in '94. In '98 the Klavins and Stafford-Brookes families formed a partnership to produce and sell wine under the Penna Lane label. Exports to Hong Kong and Korea.

ŢŢŢŢŢ **The Willsmore Shiraz 2006** Deep colour; gorgeously rich Clare shiraz; masses of blackberry, licorice and spice on a supple but full-bodied palate; has absorbed 20 months in new French oak. Screwcap. 14.5% alc. **Rating** 96 **To** 2026 $48

ŢŢŢŢŢ **Clare Valley Shiraz 2006** Inky, opaque purple-red; lush prune, licorice and blackberry fruit drives a medium- to full-bodied wine that might have been better still had it been picked earlier. Screwcap. 15% alc. **Rating** 92 **To** 2021 $25
Clare Valley Cabernet Sauvignon 2006 Deeply coloured; black fruits, licorice and a touch of tar; the tannins are firm and marginally dry; will evolve well. Screwcap. 14% alc. **Rating** 90 **To** 2018 $25

ŢŢŢŢ **Clare Valley Riesling 2008** A clean, firmly structured wine, with the requisite balance to age well in bottle. Screwcap. 12.9% alc. **Rating** 88 **To** 2014 $21
Clare Valley Sauvignon Blanc Semillon 2008 Has plenty of power, depth and length, albeit without the lifted aromatics of WA wines in this category; may develop well, however. Screwcap. 12% alc. **Rating** 88 **To** 2012 $19

Penny's Hill   ★★★★☆

Main Road, McLaren Vale, SA 5171 **Region** McLaren Vale
T (08) 8556 4460 **F** (08) 8556 4462 **www**.pennyshill.com.au **Open** 7 days 10–5
Winemaker Ben Riggs **Est.** 1988 **Cases** 9000
Penny's Hill is owned by Adelaide advertising agency businessman Tony Parkinson and wife Susie. The vineyard is 43.5 ha and, unusually for McLaren Vale, is close-planted with a thin vertical trellis/thin vertical canopy, the work of consultant viticulturist David Paxton. The innovative red dot packaging was the inspiration of Tony Parkinson, recalling the red dot 'sold' sign on pictures and giving rise to the Red Dot Art Gallery at Penny's Hill. The restaurant was named as Australia's Best Restaurant in a Winery for 2007/08. Exports to all major markets, particularly via the Woop Woop joint venture between Ben Riggs and Penny's Hill.

🍷🍷🍷🍷🍷 **Specialized McLaren Vale Shiraz Cabernet Merlot 2007** The savoury blackcurrant characters of the cabernet and merlot blend synergistically with shiraz, and it is these two that define the cedary, blackcurrant characters of the wine; has a long, fine finish. Good value. Screwcap. 14.5% alc. **Rating** 94 **To** 2017 $22

🍷🍷🍷🍷 **McLaren Vale Cabernet Sauvignon 2007** A deeply coloured, luscious offering of black fruits backed by a touch of savoury spice and a lick of chocolate; the tannins are fine and the oak well integrated. Screwcap. 14.5% alc. **Rating** 92 **To** 2017 $24

McLaren Vale Shiraz 2007 Classic McLaren Vale, even more, a Ben Riggs style, aimed at giving maximum enjoyment and maximum flavour in a softly textured frame. Drink now or in 10 years. Screwcap. 14.5% alc. **Rating** 90 **To** 2020 $27

🍷🍷🍷🍷 **McLaren Vale Merlot 2007** Has a mix of cassis, blackcurrant and savoury/olive characters, which come together well on the back-palate and finish, the alcohol not intruding. Screwcap. 15% alc. **Rating** 89 **To** 2015 $22

McLaren Vale Chardonnay 2008 Cleverly made by keeping the winemaker's thumb prints at a low level, with only 20% barrel ferment in older French oak; this has preserved as much as possible of the fruit profile, and also given good mouthfeel. Screwcap. 13.5% alc. **Rating** 88 **To** 2011 $22

Footprint McLaren Vale Shiraz 2006 Lots of sweet fruit and a slight dried herb character to the bouquet; layers of sweet fruit on the palate, but the wine appears a little forward for its age. Cork. 14.5% alc. **Rating** 88 **To** 2015 $50

Woop Woop Shiraz 2007 Clean, fresh and full of red fruits; medium-bodied with good persistence, but a little simple on the finish. Screwcap. 15% alc. **Rating** 87 **To** 2016 $13

The Black Chook Shiraz Viognier 2007 No-holds-barred aromas, flavours and alcohol; needs a big black chook cooked in this wine for company. Screwcap. 15% alc. **Rating** 87 **To** 2012 $18

Peos Estate ★★★☆

Graphite Road, Manjimup, WA 6258 **Region** Manjimup
T (08) 9772 1378 **F** (08) 9772 1372 **www**.peosestate.com.au **Open** 7 days 10–4
Winemaker Forest Hill Vineyard **Est.** 1996 **Cases** 5000 **Vyds** 36.8 ha

The Peos family has farmed the West Manjimup district for over 50 years, the third generation of four brothers commencing the development of the vineyard in 1996; there is a little over 36 ha of vines, with shiraz (12 ha), merlot (6.8 ha), chardonnay (7 ha), cabernet sauvignon (4 ha), sauvignon blanc (3 ha), and pinot noir and verdelho (2 ha each). Exports to Canada, Denmark and Singapore.

🍷🍷🍷🍷 **Manjimup Cabernet Sauvignon 2007** Deeply coloured; a very ripe bouquet, pushing the limit but not overstepping the mark; the palate is dense and very tannic, and will show marked improvement with some time in the bottle; just a little heat on the finish. Screwcap. 14.5% alc. **Rating** 90 **To** 2015 $21

🍷🍷🍷🍷 **Manjimup Sauvignon Blanc 2008** A slightly savoury style, with fresh cut hay and citrus fruit on the bouquet; the palate shows richness on entry, and cleans up with vibrant acid on the finish. Screwcap. 12.5% alc. **Rating** 87 **To** 2012 $16

Pepper Tree Wines ★★★★★

Halls Road, Pokolbin, NSW 2321 **Region** Lower Hunter Valley
T (02) 4998 7539 **www**.peppertreewines.com.au **Open** Mon–Fri 9–5, w'ends 9.30–5
Winemaker Jim Chatto **Est.** 1993 **Cases** 50 000 **Vyds** 179 ha

The Pepper Tree winery is part of a complex that also contains The Convent guest house and Roberts Restaurant. In 2002 it was acquired by a company controlled by Dr John Davis, who owns 50% of Briar Ridge. The appointment of Jim Chatto as chief winemaker in March 2007 brings the expertise of the best young wine judge on the Australian wine show circuit, with winemaking talents to match, and should bring further improvement (vintage conditions accepted). It sources the majority of its Hunter Valley fruit from its Tallavera Grove vineyard at Mt View, but also has premium vineyards at Orange, Coonawarra and Wrattonbully, which provide its Grand Reserve and Reserve (single region) wines. Exports to the US, Canada, Singapore, China and NZ.

ŸŸŸŸŸ **The Gravels Single Vineyard Reserve Wrattonbully Shiraz Viognier 2007** Deep purple-crimson; a highly aromatic bouquet leads into a wine bursting with vibrantly spicy fruit that accelerates on the finish; 3% co-fermented viognier works to perfection; even the tannins are sweet, if that were possible. Terrific value. Screwcap. 14.5% alc. **Rating** 96 **To** 2025 $31

Venus Block Single Vineyard Reserve Orange Chardonnay 2008 Pale straw-green; a fragrant bouquet with some blossom aromas, then a mouth-wateringly intense palate, with nectarine, apple and citrus rind, the barrel ferment oak completely absorbed by the fruit. Great value. Screwcap. 14.5% alc. **Rating** 95 **To** 2016 $26

Coquun Single Vineyard Reserve Hunter Valley Shiraz 2007 Very good purple hue and depth; a mouthfilling wine with intense plum, blackberry and spice fruit; excellent texture and structure guarantee a long life. Made from vines planted in the 1960s. Screwcap. 14.5% alc. **Rating** 95 **To** 2030 $31

Elderslee Road Single Vineyard Reserve Wrattonbully Cabernet Sauvignon 2006 Dense purple-crimson; an altogether different wine to its junior brother; classic cabernet fruit flavour in a blackcurrant, earth and black olive spectrum, balanced by firm, but perfectly weighted, tannins, the oak largely absorbed. Screwcap. 14.2% alc. **Rating** 95 **To** 2030 $31

Limited Release Hunter Valley Semillon 2008 Tangy, crisp and fresh; vibrantly juicy lemon and lemongrass flavours run through a very long palate, those flavours persisting well into the aftertaste. Great now or any time to 10+ years. Screwcap. 11% alc. **Rating** 94 **To** 2020 $26

Grand Reserve Hunter Valley Semillon 2005 Overlooked when first tasted at six months old, and even when four years of age; still bright, crisp and youthful, with intense lemony fruit and lingering acidity, which comes through an unbroken stream, and is in balance. Demands another four years. Screwcap. 10.5% alc. **Rating** 94 **To** 2018 $39

Semillon Sauvignon Blanc 2008 Pale straw-green; a spotlessly clean burst of passionfruit and gooseberry on the bouquet with an undertow of grassy/lemony fruit, which defines the thrust and intensity of the palate. Screwcap. 11.5% alc. **Rating** 94 **To** 2012 $19

Elderslee Road Single Vineyard Reserve Wrattonbully Cabernet Sauvignon 2007 Pure dark fruit bouquet of cassis, violet and black olive; quite firm, the fruit is poised, polished and pristine, with a long even and harmonious palate; the oak is a mere seasoning component. Screwcap. 14.8% alc. **Rating** 94 **To** 2018

ŸŸŸŸ̆ **Calcare Single Vineyard Reserve Coonawarra Cabernet Sauvignon 2007** Good colour; cassis, cedar and a touch of mint, shows a classic Coonawarra personality; quite dark and dense, with generous texture, and fresh acidity to draw out the finish. Screwcap. 14.8% alc. **Rating** 93 **To** 2015

Strandlines Single Vineyard Grand Reserve Wrattonbully Cabernet Shiraz 2006 The bouquet offers an array of black fruits with undertones of spice and cedar; on the palate the wine has a degree of austerity, needing to loosen its grip somewhat, although this is not a tannin issue. Screwcap. 14.5% alc. **Rating** 93 **To** 2026 $65

Strandlines Single Vineyard Grand Reserve Wrattonbully Cabernet Shiraz 2007 A dark and chewy wine, with strong leather notes to frame the pure cassis and blackberry fruit; very tannic, but the fruit concentration is there to see it through; needs a little patient cellaring. Screwcap. 14.9% alc. **Rating** 92 **To** 2020

14 Shores Single Vineyard Reserve Wrattonbully Merlot 2006 Bright colour; fragrant red fruit aromas lead into a fresh and lively medium-bodied wine, with cassis and raspberry fruits sustained by fine savoury tannins. Screwcap. 14.5% alc. **Rating** 90 **To** 2015 $31

ŶŶŶŶ   **Coonawarra Wrattonbully Cabernet Sauvignon 2006** Good colour; a
fragrant bouquet and a light- to medium-bodied palate with cassis and black
fruits, the tannin and oak support well balanced. Screwcap. 14.5% alc. **Rating** 89
To 2014 $19

Peregrine Ridge

19 Carlyle Street, Moonee Ponds, Vic 3039 (postal) **Region** Heathcote
T 0411 741 772 **F** (03) 9326 2885 **www**.peregrineridge.com.au **Open** Not
Winemaker Graeme Quigley, Sue Kerrison **Est.** 2001 **Cases** 900 **Vyds** 5.5 ha
Graeme Quigley and Sue Kerrison were wine lovers and consumers before they came to
growing and making their own wine. Having purchased a property high on the Mt Camel
Range (the name comes from the peregrine falcons that co-habit the vineyard and the
ridgeline that forms the western boundary of the property), they progressively planted their
vineyard solely to shiraz. Irrigation is used sparingly, with the yields restricted to 2.5 to
3.5 tonnes per ha; the grapes are hand-picked into small baskets, transported direct to small
open fermenters and made in small batches.

ŶŶŶŶŶ **Winemaker's Reserve Heathcote Shiraz 2006** Bright colour; quite dark and
savoury aromas with leather, spice and chocolate framing red and blue fruit; the
palate is very fresh, and belies the slightly forward nature of the bouquet; bright
acid, and fine, almost slippery, tannins on the finish. Cork. 15.2% alc. **Rating** 94
To 2016 $60

ŶŶŶŶŶ **American Oak Blend Heathcote Shiraz 2006** Bright colour; biscuity oak and
bright blueberry fruit jump out on the bouquet; the palate is fleshy and fragrant,
with good concentration and flavour; juicy and forward, certainly approachable as
a young wine. Screwcap. 15.1% alc. **Rating** 90 **To** 2015 $35

ŶŶŶŶ   **Winemaker's Reserve Heathcote Sparkling Shiraz 2005** Bright colour;
blackberry and spicy oak bouquet; good flavour and weight, with nice precision
on the charry finish. Diam. 13.9% alc. **Rating** 88 **To** 2014 $55

Pertaringa

Cnr Hunt Road/Rifle Range Road, McLaren Vale, SA 5171 **Region** McLaren Vale
T (08) 8323 8125 **F** (08) 8323 7766 **www**.pertaringa.com.au **Open** Mon–Fri 10–5,
w'ends & public hols 11–5
Winemaker Ben Riggs **Est.** 1980 **Cases** 23 000 **Vyds** 26 ha
Pertaringa has been owned and operated for three decades by viticulturists Geoff Hardy
and Ian Leask, with Ben Riggs complementing the creative team as consultant winemaker.
The vineyard in the foothills of McLaren Vale was first established in 1969. In 2006, Ian's son
Richard Leask took over the day-to-day management of the vineyard and since then there
has been a 'back to the future' approach with the introduction of biodynamics and biological
farming techniques, as well as 15 ha of shiraz being carefully regenerated to its original early
'70s shape. Although not always grammatically correct, the Two Gentlemen farmers will
continue to pour their experience into Pertaringa. Exports to all major markets.

ŶŶŶŶŶ **Undercover McLaren Vale Shiraz 2007** Bright colour; a dark and dense,
almost mysterious array of aromas, with mulled blackberry and slightly tarry
elements coming to the fore; the palate is lively and has a vibrant, essency core
of fruit, handling the quite firm structure with ease; long, savoury and well put
together. Screwcap. 14.5% alc. **Rating** 95 **To** 2018 $22

ŶŶŶŶŶ **Rifle & Hunt Cabernet Sauvignon 2007** Waves of blackcurrant and dark
chocolate come through on the bouquet, gaining further strength on the full-
bodied palate; will be a very long-lived wine. ProCork. 14.5% alc. **Rating** 93
To 2022 $35
Bonfire Block Adelaide Semillon 2008 A 'brief interlude' in new French oak
has made as much impact on texture as flavour; a concentrated wine with good
balance and length. Screwcap. 13.5% alc. **Rating** 90 **To** 2014 $18

Scarecrow Adelaide Sauvignon Blanc 2008 Minerally grass and capsicum characters are the drivers of the palate, which has freshness and length. Screwcap. 12.5% alc. **Rating** 90 **To** 2010 $18

Over The Top McLaren Vale Shiraz 2007 Medium- to full-bodied, and strongly regional, black fruits interwoven with dark chocolate and a twist of licorice; has good length and carries the alcohol well. ProCork. 15% alc. **Rating** 90 **To** 2020 $39

Stage Left Adelaide Merlot 2007 A robust wine, with rich and velvety cassis/blackcurrant fruit supported by appropriate tannins and oak. Will repay cellaring. Screwcap. 14.5% alc. **Rating** 90 **To** 2013 $20

Understudy McLaren Vale Cabernet Petit Verdot 2007 Strong crimson-purple; a quite firm, but still medium-bodied, palate features fresh blackcurrant and blackberry fruit supported by balanced tannins. Screwcap. 15% alc. **Rating** 90 **To** 2017 $20

ᵞᵞᵞᵞ **Two Gentlemens McLaren Vale Grenache 2007** More in the Barossa style than McLaren Vale; light in colour and body, with sweet confection fruit flavours (not residual sugar). Screwcap. 15% alc. **Rating** 88 **To** 2012 $26

Petaluma   ★★★★★

Spring Gully Road, Piccadilly, SA 5151 **Region** Adelaide Hills
T (08) 8339 9300 **www**.petaluma.com.au **Open** At Bridgewater Mill, Bridgewater
Winemaker Andrew Hardy **Est.** 1976 **Cases** 50 000 **Vyds** 186 ha
The Lion Nathan group comprises Petaluma, Knappstein, Mitchelton, Stonier and Smithbrook. The Petaluma range has been expanded beyond the core group of Croser Sparkling, Clare Valley Riesling, Piccadilly Chardonnay and Coonawarra (Cabernet Sauvignon/Merlot). Newer arrivals of note include Adelaide Hills Viognier and Adelaide Hills Shiraz. Bridgewater Mill is the second label, which consistently provides wines most makers would love to have as their top label. The South Australian plantings in the Clare Valley, Coonawarra and Adelaide Hills provides a more than sufficient source of estate-grown grapes and wines. Exports to all major markets.

ᵞᵞᵞᵞᵞ **Piccadilly Valley Chardonnay 2007** Precise and polished bouquet of grapefruit, nectarine and grilled nuts; the palate is silky and fine with tightly wound fruit, and very fine acidity; gloriously long and harmonious. Screwcap. 14% alc. **Rating** 96 **To** 2016 $45

Croser Piccadilly Valley Pinot Noir Chardonnay 1998 Still as fresh and as tight as a daisy; perfect balance despite zero dosage when disgorged in Feb '08 after nine years on yeast lees. Bargain. Cork. 12.5% alc. **Rating** 96 **To** 2013 $49.95

Tiers Piccadilly Valley Chardonnay 2004 Just when you think this is a nice, neatly balanced, bottle-developed chardonnay, the wine accelerates on the back-palate and reverberates on the finish and aftertaste, lifting it into the top echelon. Cork. 13.5% alc. **Rating** 95 **To** 2012 $120

Tiers Piccadilly Valley Chardonnay 2006 Deep colour, vibrant green hue; a worked bouquet, with grilled nuts, grapefruit, ripe pear and plenty of spice from new oak; the palate is surprisingly fine and restrained, with weight and complexity building toward the back of the palate; the stamp of winemaking lies heavily on the wine at this point in time. Screwcap. 13% alc. **Rating** 94 **To** 2014 $115

Adelaide Hills Shiraz 2006 Elegant but positive cool-grown shiraz; black fruits shot through with spice, the palate long, the tannins fine. Screwcap. 13.5% alc. **Rating** 94 **To** 2021 $48

Croser Piccadilly Valley Pinot Noir Chardonnay 2005 As always, supremely elegant and understated, but has a little more mid-palate fruit than some prior vintages, the lees contribution subtle; very good length, of course. Cork. 13% alc. **Rating** 94 **To** 2010 $35

ΨΨΨΨΨ **Tiers Piccadilly Valley Chardonnay 2005** Complex and toasty, almost mealy on the bouquet, with ripe peach and straw evident; the palate is thickly textured, but not heavy, with lingering toasty notes playing a key role in the wine; very savoury on the finish. Cork. 13.5% alc. **Rating** 93 **To** 2013 $115

Adelaide Hills Shiraz 2007 Vibrant colour; dark and brooding with lots of spicy oak framing the fruit; the palate is earthy and rich, with a savoury roast meat component; the wine needs time for all parts to integrate. Screwcap. 14% alc. **Rating** 93 **To** 2016 $49

Coonawarra Merlot 2005 New oak, black olive and a little cassis; the palate is plump and generous, with a tightly wound core of fruit providing the backbone for longevity. Cork. 14.5% alc. **Rating** 93 **To** 2016 $55

Coonawarra 2006 Pencilly oak sits atop the cassis fruit; good drive and energy to a firm and strict palate only revealing its personality slowly; needs time, but will reward patience. Cabernet Sauvignon/Merlot. Screwcap. 14% alc. **Rating** 93 **To** 2018 $65

Hanlin Hill Clare Valley Riesling 2008 As with all the top screwcapped rieslings, not a breath of reduction; a wine still tightly wrapped up, but the perfect balance and length give a gold-plated guarantee the wine will grow exponentially in bottle over decades to come. 12.5% alc. **Rating** 91 **To** 2028 $25

Project Company Adelaide Hills Riesling 2008 Lifted and ripe, with stone fruit and pear offset by grapefruit; the palate is generous, very dry and shows a touch of spice and just a little grip on the finish. Screwcap. 13% alc. **Rating** 91 **To** 2014 $30

Bridgewater Mill Adelaide Hills Chardonnay 2007 Good flavour and fruit definition, with a strong spicy oak influence dominating the palate; a little grip and savoury complexity comes through on the finish. Screwcap. 13.5% alc. **Rating** 90 **To** 2012 $24

ΨΨΨΨ **Bridgewater Mill Adelaide Hills Sauvignon Blanc 2008** High-flavoured wine, its feet firmly planted at the tropical end of the spectrum, making for easy, early drinking. Screwcap. 13% alc. **Rating** 89 **To** 2010 $22

Bridgewater Mill Adelaide Hills Rose 2008 Bright colour; cherry and raspberry bouquet; focused acidity provides a fresh and vibrant palate, with a pleasant helping of spice on the finish. Screwcap. 12% alc. **Rating** 89 **To** 2012 $22

Peter Douglas Wines   ★★★★☆

c/- 288 Lorimer Street, Port Melbourne, Vic 3207 (postal) **Region** Coonawarra
T (03) 9646 6666 **F** (03) 9646 8383 **www.**peterdouglaswines.com.au **Open** Not
Winemaker Peter Douglas **Est.** 2007 **Cases** 1500
Peter Douglas made a name for himself while working as a senior winemaker with Wynns Coonawarra Estate in the 1980s. For various reasons, he and his medical practitioner wife headed overseas, briefly in the US, and thereafter Sicily. The wheel has now turned full circle with the Douglases once again living in Coonawarra, Peter both making wine under his own label, and running an extensive winemaking consultancy business. He makes two Cabernets: Chime Hoop, matured in American oak, and designed for early drinking; and Bulge Hoop, matured in French oak, with greater depth and richness, and a longer life.

ΨΨΨΨΨ **Bulge Hoop Coonawarra Cabernet Sauvignon 2006** A lifted bouquet, with blueberry, cassis and a touch of earth; initially the palate verges on the tart, but the fruit offers generosity, and ultimately a satisfying level of complexity. Screwcap. 14.4% alc. **Rating** 93 **To** 2012 $45

Chime Hoop Coonawarra Cabernet Sauvignon 2006 Pure-fruited bouquet with a bright and polished blackcurrant and red fruit personality; fine, vibrant and very fresh on the finish. Screwcap. 14.2% alc. **Rating** 92 **To** 2015 $30

Peter Lehmann

Para Road, Tanunda, SA 5352 **Region** Barossa Valley
T (08) 8563 2100 **F** (08) 8563 3402 **www**.peterlehmannwines.com **Open** Mon–Fri
9.30–5, w'ends & public hols 10.30–4.30
Winemaker Andrew Wigan, Ian Hongell, Kerry Morrison, Phil Lehmann **Est.** 1979
Cases 750 000

Under the benevolent ownership of the Swiss/Californian Hess Group, Peter Lehmann has
continued to flourish, making wines from all the major varieties at multiple price points, the
common link being over-delivery against expectations. Its record with its Reserve Eden Valley
Riesling (usually released when five years old) is second to none, and it has refined its semillons
to the point where it can take on the Hunter Valley at its own game with five-year-old releases,
exemplified by the recent Reserve releases. At the base level, the Semillon is the largest seller
in that category in the country. Yet it is as a red winemaker that Peter Lehmann is best known
in both domestic and export markets, with some outstanding wines leading the charge. Grapes
are purchased from 180 growers in the Barossa and Eden Valleys, and the quality of the wines
has seen production soar. Exports to all major markets.

PPPPP **Wigan Eden Valley Riesling 2003** Gleaming green-gold; stacked to the rafters
with luscious lime juice aromas and flavours, augmented by touches of honey on
the mid-palate; tremendous length. Screwcap. 11% alc. **Rating** 96 **To** 2018 $40
Margaret Barossa Semillon 2004 Bright gold, with a green hue; the bouquet
is layered with straw, lemon, mineral and a touch of marzipan; fresh and lively
with a long road to travel, the texture is refreshing, and the drive on the back of
the palate truly harmonious; long, toasty and fresh all rolled into one complete
package. Remarkable. Screwcap. 11.4% alc. **Rating** 96 **To** 2016 $30
The 1885 Shiraz 2006 Has the fragrance, elegance and exceptional length that
120-year-old vines often produce; the flavours on the medium-bodied palate range
through black cherry, blackberry and licorice; tannins and French oak are perfectly
balanced. Screwcap. 14.5% alc. **Rating** 96 **To** 2026 $50
Stonewell Shiraz 2004 Bright colour; dark and tarry on the surface, the
bouquet reveals a vibrant, pure and poised core of black fruit interlaced with
well-handled oak; the palate is dense and chewy, but shows a deft hand of balance
between the elements of fruit, tannin, acid and the slight savoury complexity; very
long and quite tannic, time will treat this wine with kindness. Cork. 14.3% alc.
Rating 96 **To** 2025 $90
Mentor 2004 Very good hue; classic cabernet on both bouquet and palate, oak
seamlessly integrated by finishing fermentation in French hogsheads, the cork a
tribute to the flat-earth American market; very good structure and great length.
14% alc. **Rating** 96 **To** 2020 $40
Eden Valley Riesling 2008 Bright straw-green; a fragrant and aromatic lime-
accented bouquet; excellent mouthfeel and length; very harmonious, the fruit
running through to the finish and aftertaste; great future, although seductive now.
Screwcap. 11% alc. **Rating** 95 **To** 2016 $19.50
Wigan Eden Valley Riesling 2004 Glowing green-yellow; a fragrant and
vibrant bouquet with lime blossom and a hint of toast, then an elegant, but intense,
palate, finishing crisp and clear. Screwcap. 12.5% alc. **Rating** 95 **To** 2020 $40
Margaret Barossa Semillon 2003 A vinous pheromone for those who know
the implications; the bouquet has already developed complex toasty/quasi-oaky
notes, moving decisively to honey on the palate. The winemaking team has got
this style nailed. Screwcap. 11.5% alc. **Rating** 95 **To** 2018 $30
Eight Songs Shiraz 2005 Pure fruitcake and chocolate bouquet; loaded with
blackberry on the palate, there are ample levels of dark fruit, tar, licorice and a
touch of spice; rich on entry, the acidity provides freshness and contrast. Screwcap.
14.5% alc. **Rating** 95 **To** 2025 $40
Black Queen Sparkling Shiraz 2001 Seppelt, Rockford, Primo Estate and
Peter Lehmann are the top makers of mature sparkling shiraz; has great, supple
mouthfeel, the flavours of high-quality spicy shiraz; the dosage is perfect; seven
years on lees, disgorged July '08. Cork. 14% alc. **Rating** 95 **To** 2014 $40

ττττ? **Ruediger Cabernet Sauvignon 2006** Fragrant blackcurrant fruit on the bouquet leads into an elegant, vibrant and juicy medium-bodied palate; fine ripe tannins and cedary oak to the finish. Screwcap. 14.5% alc. **Rating** 93 **To** 2016 $28

Barossa Semillon 2006 Bright green-tinged colour; has flourished with two years bottle age, touches of honey and toast starting to appear on the foundation of citrus fruit; has further to go. Screwcap. 12% alc. **Rating** 92 **To** 2013 $13.50

Futures Shiraz 2006 Rich, generous blackberry and plum fruit is framed by integrated but positive French oak, the tannins in balance. Cork. 14.5% alc. **Rating** 92 **To** 2020 $30

Mudflat Shiraz 2005 Very well-constructed, medium-bodied wine, with red and black fruits couched in the well-integrated oak, finishing with fine tannins. Screwcap. 14% alc. **Rating** 92 **To** 2017 $25

Eight Songs Shiraz 2004 Bright colour; dark savoury fruit of mocha, blackberry and some mulberry is supported amply by well-handled toasty oak; the palate is also dark and thickly textured; a complex, well-constructed wine. Cork. 14.5% alc. **Rating** 92 **To** 2018 $40

Botrytis Semillon 2008 A very pure bouquet with candied pear and strong varietal expression; sweet on the palate, with cleansing acidity balancing it convincingly. Screwcap. 10% alc. **Rating** 91 **To** 2013 $30

Barossa Rose 2008 Concentrated red fruit flavours, yet not heavy; has length and vibrancy; dry finish. Screwcap. 12.5% alc. **Rating** 90 **To** 2010 $16.50

Barossa Cabernet Sauvignon 2006 Rich and ripe, great depth and fruit weight; a little bit of heat comes through on the finish, and a lick of oak, but the fruit handles these elements with aplomb. Screwcap. 14% alc. **Rating** 90 **To** 2015 $19.50

Mentor 2005 Fine and expressive bouquet; cassis and cedar, with a distinctly medium-bodied personality. Cabernet Sauvignon. Screwcap. 14.1% alc. **Rating** 90 **To** 2014 $40

The King AD 2018 1997 Three gold medals when young; the wine is spicy, but too sweet for most aficionados of its Portuguese equivalent. Vintage Port. Cork. 19.5% alc. **Rating** 90 **To** 2015 $25

Pettavel   ★★★★

65 Pettavel Road, Waurn Ponds, Vic 3216 **Region** Geelong
T (03) 5266 1120 **F** (03) 5266 1140 **www**.pettavel.com **Open** 7 days 10–5.30
Winemaker Peter Flewellyn **Est.** 2000 **Cases** 13 000 **Vyds** 65 ha
Pettavel is a major landmark in the Geelong region. Mike and wife Sandi Fitzpatrick sold their large Murray Darling winery and vineyards and moved to Geelong, and in 1990 began developing vineyards at Sutherlands Creek. They have been joined by daughter Robyn (who manages the overseas business) and son Reece (who co-ordinates the viticultural resources). A striking winery/restaurant complex was opened in 2002. Exports to the UK, the US and other major markets.

ττττ? **Evening Star Late Harvest Riesling 2008** Consistently does well with this style; intense lime juice with neatly balanced acidity. Screwcap. 9.5% alc. **Rating** 91 **To** 2013 $18

Evening Star Geelong Sauvignon Blanc 2008 Generously flavoured, with an array of gooseberry, lychee and passionfruit elements, tightened and freshened by minerally acidity on the finish. Screwcap. 13% alc. **Rating** 90 **To** 2010 $18

ττττ **Evening Star Geelong Pinot Noir 2007** Fresh purple-red; aromatic plum and cherry fruit on the bouquet, the palate has contrasting sous bois notes and fractionally green tannins. Screwcap. 13% alc. **Rating** 89 **To** 2012 $18

Evening Star Geelong Shiraz 2007 Mint, spice and leaf nuances on the bouquet replay on the palate, although juicy black and red fruits do most of the talking. Screwcap. 14.5% alc. **Rating** 89 **To** 2015 $18

Platina Geelong Chardonnay 2006 Ripe and rich peachy fruit has been fleshed out further by mlf and lees contact into a full-blown style. Screwcap. 13.5% alc. **Rating** 88 **To** 2012 $27

Platina Geelong Pinot Noir 2006 Deep colour; a massive wine, with an avalanche of red and black fruits achieved at the expense of extractive tannins; many years in bottle might help. Screwcap. 13.5% alc. **Rating** 88 **To** 2015 $27
Evening Star Geelong Cabernet Sauvignon Merlot 2007 Fragrant and spicy; has the Pettavel mark of bright fruits opposed by somewhat dry tannins; remedial action would have been a major help. Screwcap. 13.5% alc. **Rating** 88 **To** 2017 $18

Pewsey Vale ★★★★★

Browns Road, Eden Valley, SA 5353 (postal) **Region** Eden Valley
T (08) 8561 3200 **F** (08) 8561 3393 **www**.pewseyvale.com **Open** At Yalumba
Winemaker Louisa Rose **Est.** 1847 **Cases** 20 000 **Vyds** 48 ha
Pewsey Vale was a famous vineyard established in 1847 by Joseph Gilbert, and it was appropriate that when S Smith & Son began the renaissance of the Adelaide Hills plantings in 1961, it should do so by purchasing Pewsey Vale and establishing 40 ha of riesling and 4 ha each of gewurztraminer and pinot gris. The Riesling has also finally benefited from being the first wine to be bottled with a Stelvin screwcap in 1977. While public reaction forced the abandonment of the initiative for almost 20 years, Pewsey Vale never lost faith in the technical advantages of the closure. A quick taste (or better, a share of a bottle) of five- to seven-year-old Contours Riesling will tell you why. Exports to all major markets.

♟♟♟♟♟ Prima Eden Valley Riesling 2008 Incredibly fragrant and expressive aromas of lime blossom, apple blossom and fruit spice (and more) is of 100-point quality; inevitably, the palate, while excellent, does not have quite the same vibrancy and intensity. That said, a must-buy. Screwcap. 9.5% alc. **Rating** 95 **To** 2018 $24.95
Eden Valley Riesling 2008 Strong colour; a powerful, complex bouquet leads into a palate bursting with lime juice fruit; has thrust and length. Screwcap. 12.5% alc. **Rating** 94 **To** 2018 $17.95
Museum Release The Contours Eden Valley Riesling 2003 Bright green-yellow; a flowery bouquet leads into a crisp, lime and lemon palate, which gains thrust on the long finish and aftertaste, sustained by perfect acidity. Screwcap. 12.5% alc. **Rating** 94 **To** 2018 $27.95
Individual Vineyard Selection Eden Valley Gewurztraminer 2008 Achieves the rare feat (in Australia) of combining good varietal expression and elegance; spicy rose water and a touch of lychee run through to the finish. Screwcap. 12% alc. **Rating** 94 **To** 2016 $24.95

♟♟♟♟ Individual Vineyard Selection Eden Valley Pinot Gris 2008 Elegant and understated wine, with good texture and balance, but needs more fruit at this price. Screwcap. 13.5% alc. **Rating** 87 **To** 2010 $24.95

Pfeiffer Wines

167 Distillery Road, Wahgunyah, Vic 3687 **Region** Rutherglen
T (02) 6033 2805 **F** (02) 6033 3158 **www**.pfeifferwines.com.au **Open** Mon–Sat 9–5, Sun 10–5
Winemaker Chris Pfeiffer, Jen Pfeiffer **Est.** 1984 **Cases** 20 000 **Vyds** 28 ha
Family-owned and run, Pfeiffer wines occupies one of the historic wineries (built 1880) that abound in Northeast Victoria, and which is worth a visit on this score alone. The fortified wines are good, and the table wines have improved considerably over recent vintages, drawing upon estate plantings. In 2009 Pfeiffer celebrated its 25th vintage in fine style. Exports to the UK, the US and other major markets (under the Carlyle and Three Chimneys labels).

♟♟♟♟♟ Rare Rutherglen Tokay NV Deep dark mahogany-olive rim; here the step up is as much to do with intensity as complexity; the flavours penetrate every corner of the mouth; burnt toffee and Christmas cake. Screwcap. 17.5% alc. **Rating** 97 **To** 2010 $110

Rare Rutherglen Muscat NV Not the most concentrated example, but beautifully balanced and poised; the old material is held in check by winemaking that maintains precision, and it is not until you taste the wine that its full force is revealed; wonderfully long and complex, this once again shows why these wines are national treasures. Screwcap. 17.5% alc. **Rating** 96 **To** 2010 $110

Grand Rutherglen Tokay NV The colour has moved towards light mahogany; a serious step up in intensity and complexity, yet retains excellent balance and length. Screwcap. 17.5% alc. **Rating** 95 **To** 2010 $70

Grand Rutherglen Muscat NV Deep colour, with toffee, raisins, grilled nuts and lip-smacking floral fruit; the palate is rich yet lithe, also focused with a seamless and effortless grace; there is great freshness to the beautiful old material held within. Screwcap. 17.5% alc. **Rating** 95 **To** 2010 $70

Old Distillery Rutherglen Tawny NV The colour is a little deeper than the Grand, the bouquet is more complex and the palate distinctly richer and more viscous in texture; however, it is the varietal character of tokay still doing the work. Screwcap. 17.5% alc. **Rating** 94 **To** 2010 $29

�♀ Old Distillery Classic Rutherglen Muscat NV Attractive flamboyant muscat bouquet, with fruitcake and a hint of toffee on offer; the palate is luscious for this level and shows a fine balance between sweetness and freshness on the finish. Screwcap. 18% alc. **Rating** 92 **To** 2010 $29

Frontignac 2008 Intense spicy/grapey aromas and flavours are entirely correct; the residual sweetness no issue for the style, particularly given the twist of lemony acidity on the finish. Value. Screwcap. 11% alc. **Rating** 90 **To** 2010 $12.90

Shiraz 2006 A very ripe and very dark fruit bouquet, with a little cinnamon spice and blackberry confiture; sweet-fruited and ripe with a leathery aspect to the palate; certainly warm, but still quite bright. Screwcap. 14% alc. **Rating** 90 **To** 2015 $21

Cabernet Sauvignon 2006 Deep bright colour; ripe blood plum bouquet with a suggestion of cassis; the palate shows life and liveliness with good tannin and acid balance; quite generous on the finish. Screwcap. 14% alc. **Rating** 90 **To** 2014 $21

Old Distillery Pale Dry Flor Fino NV Lightly nutty rancio bouquet, with a fresh, vibrant and nicely focused finish; serve chilled; do not cellar. Cork. 18% alc. **Rating** 90 **To** 2010 $29

Christopher's VP 2005 Good colour and concentration; fresh dark berries on the bouquet and an attractive splash of spice; juicy and forward, this should be enjoyed in the full flush of youth. Screwcap. 18% alc. **Rating** 90 **To** 2012 $24.50

Rutherglen Tokay NV Bright golden-brown; has absolutely classic varietal character with cold tea and butterscotch characters; good spirit. Screwcap. 17.5% alc. **Rating** 90 **To** 2010 $19.90

� Old Distillery Classic Rutherglen Tawny NV Fresh oak, vibrant red fruit, pleasant rancio complexity, all working well with the fruit on offer; clean and forward; good value early drinking tawny. Screwcap. 19% alc. **Rating** 89 **To** 2010 $19.90

The Carson Gewurztraminer 2008 Tight and crisp, the varietal character subdued, but nonetheless apparent; good winemaking achieves a better than average wine. Screwcap. 13% alc. **Rating** 89 **To** 2012 $16.50

Riesling 2008 Pale colour; lime and mineral bouquet; tight and dry palate, with chalky acidity to finish. Screwcap. 12.5% alc. **Rating** 88 **To** 2013 $17

Riesling 2007 Discrete style, but is well made and balanced; pleasant citrus notes on the light-bodied palate. Screwcap. 12.5% alc. **Rating** 88 **To** 2012 $17

Chardonnay 2007 Quite restrained for its origins; nectarine and a little spice; nice texture and weight, with a soft and generous finish. Screwcap. 14% alc. **Rating** 88 **To** 2012 $17

Rutherglen Muscat NV Strong varietal characters of raisins; sweet and luscious, although not especially complex. Screwcap. 18% alc. **Rating** 88 **To** 2010 $16.90

Marsanne 2008 Clean and fresh, with a suggestion of honeysuckle and lemon; a fresh entry, with a slight nutty finish and good acidity; clean and well made. Screwcap. 13.5% alc. **Rating** 87 **To** 2013 **$17**

Pfitzner ★★★★☆

PO Box 1098, North Adelaide, SA 5006 **Region** Adelaide Hills
T (08) 8332 4194 **Open** Not
Winemaker Petaluma **Est.** 1996 **Cases** 1000 **Vyds** 5.55 ha
The subtitle to the Pfitzner name is Eric's Vineyard. The late Eric Pfitzner purchased and aggregated a number of small, subdivided farmlets to protect the beauty of the Piccadilly Valley from ugly rural development. His three sons inherited the vision, with the vineyard planted principally to chardonnay and pinot noir, plus small amounts of sauvignon blanc and merlot. Half the total property has been planted, the remainder preserving the natural eucalypt forest. Roughly half the production is sold in the UK, no surprise given the bargain basement prices asked for these lovely wines.

🍷🍷🍷🍷🍷 **Eric's Vineyard Piccadilly Valley Chardonnay 2007** Has a highly aromatic bouquet of both nectarine fruit and oak, then a fruit-driven, long and fine palate, with bright acidity. Lovely wine. Screwcap. 13.8% alc. **Rating** 94 **To** 2017 **$28**

Phaedrus Estate ★★★★☆

220 Mornington-Tyabb Road, Moorooduc, Vic 3933 **Region** Mornington Peninsula
T (03) 5978 8134 **www**.phaedrus.com.au **Open** W'ends & public hols 11–5
Winemaker Ewan Campbell, Maitena Zantvoort **Est.** 1997 **Cases** 3000 **Vyds** 2.5 ha
Since Maitena Zantvoort and Ewan Campbell established Phaedrus Estate, they have gained a reputation for producing premium cool-climate wines. Their winemaking philosophy brings art and science together to produce wines showing regional and varietal character with minimal winemaking interference. Exports to Hong Kong.

🍷🍷🍷🍷🍷 **Mornington Peninsula Shiraz 2007** Deep, dense crimson-purple; an aromatic bouquet leads into a vibrant palate, with licorice, spice, damson plum and black cherry fruit, the fine tannins giving excellent mouthfeel and length. Screwcap. 13.9% alc. **Rating** 95 **To** 2020 **$22**

🍷🍷🍷🍷½ **Mornington Peninsula Pinot Noir 2008** Good colour; a full-flavoured Pinot; a mix of plum, cherry and spicy fruit running through a long, balanced palate. Screwcap. 13.9% alc. **Rating** 90 **To** 2015 **$22**

🍷🍷🍷🍷 **Mornington Peninsula Chardonnay 2008** A complex wine; peachy fruit is at the top end of the ripeness scale, even though the alcohol is moderate, and shows numerous winemaking inputs. Screwcap. 13.9% alc. **Rating** 89 **To** 2014 **$20**
Reserve Mornington Peninsula Pinot Noir 2006 Very powerful and complex, with strong briary/foresty/savoury accents throughout, but not quite enough fruit to provide sufficient balance. Screwcap. 13.9% alc. **Rating** 89 **To** 2013 **$45**
Mornington Peninsula Pinot Gris 2008 Definitely in the Alsatian gris style, mouthfilling and rich, fruit sweetness running through to the finish. Screwcap. 14.3% alc. **Rating** 88 **To** 2011 **$20**

PHI ★★★★★

Lusatia Park Vineyard, Owens Road, Woori Yallock, Vic 3139 **Region** Yarra Valley
T (03) 5964 6070 **www**.phiwines.com **Open** By appt
Winemaker Steve Webber **Est.** 1985 **Cases** NFP
This is a joint venture between two very influential wine families: De Bortoli and Shelmerdine. The key executives are Stephen Shelmerdine and Steve Webber (and their respective wives). It has a sole viticultural base: the Lusatia Park vineyard of the Shelmerdine family. Unusually, however, it is of specific rows of vines, not even blocks, although the rows are continuous. They are pruned and managed quite differently to the rest of the block, with the deliberate

aim of strictly controlled yields. While the joint venture was entered into in 2005, De Bortoli has been buying grapes from the vineyard since '02, and has had the opportunity to test the limits of the grapes. The outcome has been wines of the highest quality, and a joint venture that will last for many years. The name, incidentally, is derived from the 21st letter of the ancient Greek alphabet, symbolising perfect balance and harmony. It's courageous pricing for a new kid on the block, but reflects the confidence the families have in the wines. Exports to the UK.

ΨΨΨΨΨ **Lusatia Park Vineyard Yarra Valley Chardonnay 2007** A complex and restrained wine, exhibiting, pear, mineral and a hint of citrus character on the bouquet; the palate is tightly wound with refined texture, and a delicate use of oak that merely acts as seasoning; long, fine and worthy of serious consideration for ageing. Screwcap. 12% alc. **Rating** 96 **To** 2018 $48
Lusatia Park Vineyard Yarra Valley Sauvignon 2008 Has the incisive palate that is the mark of this wine, relying on texture, structure and length rather than primary fruit; echoes of top-quality Sancerre. Screwcap. 12% alc. **Rating** 94 **To** 2012 $42
Lusatia Park Vineyard Yarra Valley Pinot Noir 2007 Fresh red fruits, elements of spice and even a hint of fresh cut herbs; the palate is incredibly fine, supple, focused and long, with savoury, almost gamey, complexity showing through on the fan-like finish. Screwcap. 12.5% alc. **Rating** 94 **To** 2014 $65

Philip Lobley Wines ★★★★☆

1084 Eucalyptus Road, Glenburn, Vic 3717 (postal) **Region** Upper Goulburn
T (03) 5797 8433 **F** (03) 5797 8433 **Open** Not
Winemaker Philip Lobley **Est.** 2008 **Cases** 400 **Vyds** 3.4 ha
The micro, patchwork quilt vineyard was first planted by Philip Lobley in 1995 with pinot noir, merlot and cabernet sauvignon. In 2008 nebbiolo, semillon, sauvignon blanc and muscato giallo (or gold muskateller, thought to be a version of muscat a petits grains) were added. These are high-density plantings and, with shoot and crop thinning, yield is kept to 600–800 grammes per vine. The red wines are wild yeast-fermented and neither filtered nor fined; the Yarra Valley Sauvignon Blanc (purchased) is whole bunch-pressed and wild yeast-fermented.

ΨΨΨΨΨ **Merlot 2007** A lively and very correct varietal expression on both bouquet and palate, the latter with remarkable intensity and precision; the spicy, savoury red fruits on the finish lead to the need for another glass; four barrels made. Screwcap. 13% alc. **Rating** 94 **To** 2013 $25

ΨΨΨΨΨ **Reserve Pinot Noir 2007** Light colour; slight minty edges to the otherwise savoury/foresty fruit aromas and flavours; does have good mouthfeel and length, and is varietal. Screwcap. 12.8% alc. **Rating** 91 **To** 2014 $40

Philip Shaw Wines ★★★★☆

Koomooloo Vineyard, Caldwell Lane, Orange, NSW 2800 **Region** Orange
T (02) 6365 2334 **www**.philipshaw.com.au **Open** W'ends 12–5, or by appt
Winemaker Philip Shaw **Est.** 1989 **Cases** 10 000 **Vyds** 45 ha
Philip Shaw, former chief winemaker of Rosemount Estate and then Southcorp, first became interested in the Orange region in 1985. In 1988 he purchased the Koomooloo Vineyard and began extensive plantings, the varieties including merlot (10 ha), chardonnay (8 ha), pinot noir (6 ha), shiraz (7 ha), sauvignon blanc (5 ha), cabernet franc (4 ha), cabernet sauvignon (3 ha) and viognier (2 ha). Exports to the UK, the US and other major markets.

ΨΨΨΨΨ **No 5 Orange Cabernet Sauvignon 2006** Skilled winemaking brings out the best qualities of the fruit, which has classic varietal character framed by fine tannins and harmonious cedary oak. Screwcap. 13.5% alc. **Rating** 94 **To** 2021 $75

ΨΨΨΨΨ **No. 19 Orange Sauvignon Blanc 2008** Attractive tropical/gooseberry aromas and flavours, the palate light on its feet, and with a crisp and lively finish. Screwcap. 13% alc. **Rating** 92 **To** 2011 $23

Phillip Island Vineyard ★★★★★

44 Berrys Beach Road, Phillip Island, Vic 3922 **Region** Gippsland
T (03) 5956 8465 **F** (03) 5956 8465 **www**.phillipislandwines.com.au **Open** 7 days 12–5
Winemaker David Lance, James Lance **Est.** 1993 **Cases** 3000 **Vyds** 1.7 ha
The first harvest from the Phillip Island Vineyard was marked in 1997, and the vineyard (sauvignon blanc, chardonnay, merlot, cabernet sauvignon and pinot noir) is totally enclosed in the permanent silon net, which acts both as a windbreak and protection against birds. The quality of the wines across the board make it clear that this is definitely not a tourist-trap cellar door; it is a serious producer of quality wine. Exports to Indonesia.

ΨΨΨΨΨ **Chardonnay 2007** A high-quality, immaculately balanced and harmonious wine; nectarine fruit is seamlessly married to quality French oak, the palate as supple as it is long, thanks to citrussy acidity. Screwcap. 14% alc. **Rating** 96 **To** 2017 $28
Pinot Noir 2007 Vivid crimson; as the colour suggests, there is spicy plum fruit on bouquet and palate alike, the wine perfectly balanced and with excellent line and length. Screwcap. 13.5% alc. **Rating** 95 **To** 2015 $50
Chardonnay 2008 Bright straw-green; an intensely fruited wine, nectarine and grapefruit flavours perfectly integrated with French oak; shows no heat from the alcohol. Screwcap. 14.5% alc. **Rating** 94 **To** 2015 $28
Cabernet Merlot 2007 Crimson-purple; a generous palate in terms of both structure and flavour, the luscious black and red fruits perfectly balanced by fine, ripe tannins and controlled oak. Screwcap. 13.5% alc. **Rating** 94 **To** 2017 $28

ΨΨΨΨΨ **Rose 2008** Pale crimson; a highly aromatic bouquet of red fruits reflecting its merlot base, the finish has a savoury flourish, the aftertaste dry. Screwcap. 13.5% alc. **Rating** 91 **To** 2009 $19
Cabernet Sauvignon 2006 Has that little, but vital, bit of extra ripeness; still has the restrained Phillip Island Vineyard style, and the balance between cassis/blackcurrant fruit and olive nuances on the finish is good. Screwcap. 14% alc. **Rating** 91 **To** 2016 $28
The Nobbies Pinot Noir 2006 A delicate, light-bodied wine that is moving rapidly toward its best-by date, although it is seductively drinkable right now, with its fusion of red fruits and spices. Screwcap. 13% alc. **Rating** 90 **To** 2010 $24

ΨΨΨΨ **Merlot 2006** Good hue; a light- to medium-bodied wine with strong herb and olive flavours on the finish that tend to obscure the red fruits of the mid-palate. Screwcap. 13% alc. **Rating** 88 **To** 2014 $28
Berrys Beach Cabernet Sauvignon 2006 Excellent bright crimson hue; the fragrant bouquet has an early-warning touch of green, which is confirmed on the bright, but slightly bitter, palate. Screwcap. 13.5% alc. **Rating** 88 **To** 2013 $24

Phillips Brook Estate

118 Redmond-Hay River Road, Redmond, WA 6332 **Region** Albany
T (08) 9845 3124 **www**.phillipsbrook.com.au **Open** Wed–Sun 11–4
Winemaker Harewood Estate (James Kellie) **Est.** 1975 **Cases** 1800 **Vyds** 12 ha
Bronwen and David Newbury first became viticulturists near the thoroughly unlikely town of Bourke, in western NSW, but in 2001 they moved back to the Great Southern region. The name comes from the adjoining Phillips Brook Nature Reserve and the permanent creek on their property. Riesling and cabernet sauvignon (4 ha) had been planted in 1975, but thoroughly neglected. The Newburys have rehabilitated the old plantings, and have added chardonnay, merlot, cabernet franc and sauvignon blanc.

ΨΨΨΨΨ **Albany Riesling 2008** Exceedingly pale; has delicious passionfruit nuances to the citrus base of the bouquet and palate, inviting immediate consumption, but will live much longer. Screwcap. 12% alc. **Rating** 94 **To** 2017 $18

ΨΨΨΨΨ **Albany Chardonnay 2007** A very complex, funky Burgundian bouquet, the palate likewise, although the oak is a little intrusive. Excellent value. Screwcap. 14% alc. **Rating** 91 **To** 2015 $20

ΨΨΨΨ **Albany Sauvignon Blanc 2008** Crisp, fresh and zesty, ironically without the passionfruit of the Riesling; nonetheless, the gooseberry and lychee flavours of the light-bodied palate hang together well. Screwcap. 12.5% alc. **Rating** 89 **To** 2010 $18

Albany Merlot 2007 Bright, light crimson; a fragrant red fruit and spice bouquet is followed by a very light and savoury palate, which really needs more vinosity; best drunk fresh. Screwcap. 14% alc. **Rating** 87 **To** 2010 $18

Pialligo Estate

18 Kallaroo Road, Pialligo, ACT 2609 **Region** Canberra District
T (02) 6247 6060 **F** (02) 6262 6074 **www.**pialligoestate.com.au **Open** 7 days 10–5
Winemaker Andrew McEwin, Frank Van de Loo (Contract) **Est.** 1999 **Cases** 1500
Vyds 4 ha
Sally Milner and John Nutt planted their vineyard (1 ha of riesling and 0.6 ha each of pinot gris, merlot, shiraz and cabernet sauvignon) in 1999. The newly extended and renovated cellar door and café has views of Mt Ainslie, Mt Pleasant, Duntroon, the Telstra Tower, Parliament House and the Brindabella Ranges beyond. The property, which has a 1-km frontage to the Molonglo River, is only a 5-min drive from the centre of Canberra.

ΨΨΨΨΨ **Canberra Pinot Grigio 2008** Fragrant pear and apple aromas, then a punchy palate with more attitude than most pinot gris. Commendable and commended (though fully priced). Screwcap. 12.7% alc. **Rating** 90 **To** 2010 $25

ΨΨΨΨ **Canberra Riesling 2008** A clean, but as yet subdued, bouquet followed by a firm palate with good balance and length. Best still to come. Screwcap. 11.2% alc. **Rating** 89 **To** 2015 $20

Canberra Sangiovese 2007 Strongly flavoured wine, which is totally impressive until the very end of the palate, where there is a touch of bitterness; nonetheless can't be denied. Screwcap. 13.4% alc. **Rating** 88 **To** 2014 $25

Canberra Cabernet Sauvignon 2006 Earthy, dusty, cedar nuances to both bouquet and palate circumscribe the red and black berry fruits, but not unpleasantly so. Screwcap. 13.8% alc. **Rating** 87 **To** 2013 $20

Piano Gully

Piano Gully Road, Manjimup, WA 6258 **Region** Manjimup
T (08) 9316 0336 **F** (08) 9316 0336 **www.**pianogully.com.au **Open** By appt
Winemaker Naturaliste Vintners **Est.** 1987 **Cases** 3500 **Vyds** 6 ha
The Piano Gully vineyard, established in 1987 on rich Karri loam, 10 km south of Manjimup, includes chardonnay, sauvignon blanc, cabernet sauvignon, viognier, shiraz and merlot. The name of the road (and the winery) commemorates the shipping of a piano from England by one of the first settlers in the region. The horse and cart carrying the piano on the last leg of the long journey were within sight of their destination when the piano fell from the cart and was destroyed.

ΨΨΨΨΨ **Shiraz 2007** Dense purple-crimson; a fragrant bouquet redolent with spicy blackberry fruit, the elegant medium-bodied palate picking up those flavours through to the long finish. Diam. 13.5% alc. **Rating** 93 **To** 2020 $27

Sauvignon Blanc 2008 Lively and fresh, with a pleasant mix of herbaceous and citrus aromas and flavours; good length and persistence. Screwcap. 12% alc. **Rating** 90 **To** 2012 $18

Unwooded Chardonnay 2008 Has abundant varietal fruit aromas of nectarine and peach, backed by pleasant acidity. A much better than average example of the style. Great value. Screwcap. 13.5% alc. **Rating** 90 **To** 2012 $16

Chardonnay 2007 Gathers momentum and weight as it moves through to the back-palate, where nuances of tropical fruit/passionfruit emerge, the oak well balanced. Screwcap. 13.5% alc. **Rating** 90 **To** 2012 $30

Viognier 2007 A complex bouquet and palate, apricot and peach astride a saddle of French oak; the finish is fruity, the aftertaste dry. Screwcap. 13% alc. **Rating** 90 **To** 2011 $27

Picardy ★★★★

Cnr Vasse Highway/Eastbrook Road, Pemberton, WA 6260 **Region** Pemberton
T (08) 9776 0036 **F** (08) 9776 0245 **www**.picardy.com.au **Open** By appt
Winemaker Bill Pannell, Dan Pannell **Est.** 1993 **Cases** 6000 **Vyds** 10 ha
Picardy is owned by Dr Bill Pannell, wife Sandra, son Daniel and daughter Jodie; Bill and
Sandra founded Moss Wood winery in Margaret River in 1969. Picardy initially reflected Bill's
view that the Pemberton area was one of the best regions in Australia for Pinot Noir and
Chardonnay, but it is now clear Pemberton has as much Rhône and Bordeaux as Burgundy
in its veins. The Pannell Family wines are a separate venture to Picardy. Exports to the UK,
the US and other major markets.

♀♀♀♀♀ **Pemberton Chardonnay 2007** Deep colour; heavy toasty oak dominates the
bouquet; the weight and depth of the citrussy fruit is undoubted, but the level
of oak makes it hard to define at this point in time. Cork. 13% alc. **Rating** 90
To 2013 $35

♀♀♀♀ **Pannell Family Tete de Cuvee Pinot Noir 2006** Light colour, with some
development; light cherry fruit, with strong sappy/savoury/leafy overtones; seems
to lack full phenological ripeness. Cork. 13% alc. **Rating** 89 To 2012 $50

Pier 10 ★★★★

10 Shoreham Road, Shoreham, Vic 3916 **Region** Mornington Peninsula
T (03) 5989 8848 **www**.pier10.com.au **Open** Wed–Sun 11–5, 7 days Dec–Mar
Winemaker Kevin McCarthy (Contract) **Est.** 1996 **Cases** NA **Vyds** 3.2 ha
Eric Baker and Sue McKenzie began the development of Pier 10 with the aim of creating
first a lifestyle, then perhaps a retirement business. Both helped set up the vineyard while
continuing to work in Melbourne before handing over viticultural management to Mark
Danaher. Chardonnay, pinot gris and pinot noir are planted.

♀♀♀♀♀ **Family Reserve Mornington Peninsula Chardonnay 2004** Lively, fresh
and focused with nectarine, peach and just a hint of fresh fig; the well-handled
oak provides a spicy framework on the palate, and there is an attractive savoury
complexity to the finish. Impressive. Screwcap. 14% alc. **Rating** 92 To 2015 $28
Mornington Peninsula Pinot Noir 2006 Brighter and more focused than
the '05; cherry, and a little plum, enriched by spice and a touch of game; evenly
textured and supple through to the finish. Cork. 13.8% alc. **Rating** 91 To 2012 $28
Alexander Lightly Oaked Mornington Peninsula Chardonnay 2003
Melon, fresh fig and a light touch of spice; good depth to the palate, with quite a
fresh and lively finish. Screwcap. 13.6% alc. **Rating** 90 To 2011 $25

♀♀♀♀ **Heathcote Shiraz 2006** Blue and black berry fruit, with a hint of mint on the
bouquet; medium-bodied with some mineral complexity running through the
core. Cork. 13.8% alc. **Rating** 89 To 2014 $45

Pierro ★★★★★

Caves Road, Wilyabrup via Cowaramup, WA 6284 **Region** Margaret River
T (08) 9755 6220 **F** (08) 9755 6308 **www**.pierro.com.au **Open** 7 days 10–5
Winemaker Dr Michael Peterkin **Est.** 1979 **Cases** 10 000 **Vyds** 8.65 ha
Dr Michael Peterkin is another of the legion of Margaret River medical practitioners; for
good measure, he married into the Cullen family. Pierro is renowned for its stylish white
wines, which often exhibit tremendous complexity; the Chardonnay can be monumental in
its weight and texture. That said, its red wines from good vintages can be every bit as good.
Exports to the UK, the US, Japan and Indonesia.

♀♀♀♀♀ **Margaret River Chardonnay 2007** Bright straw-green; the very complex
bouquet has distinct Burgundian overtones, as does the incisive and long palate,
with its lingering finish and aftertaste. First-class winemaking, first-class grapes.
Screwcap. 14% alc. **Rating** 96 To 2022 $69.90

Reserve Margaret River Cabernet Sauvignon Merlot 2005 Retains good hue; has excellent balance and structure to the array of cassis and blackcurrant fruit, finishing with fine tannins. Cork. 14% alc. **Rating** 94 **To** 2015 $62.90

ŢŢŢŢŢ **Cabernet Sauvignon Merlot 2004** Obvious colour development; a medium-bodied palate, with gently sweet red and blackberry fruits offset by cedary oak and savoury tannins; elegant finish. Cork. 13% alc. **Rating** 93 **To** 2015 $69
Margaret River Semillon Sauvignon Blanc LTC 2008 Bright green-straw; a time-honoured regional blend, along with the touch of chardonnay to add intrigue and a degree of muscle; mouthfilling and flavoursome. Screwcap. 13.5% alc. **Rating** 92 **To** 2013 $26.90

Pike & Joyce ★★★★☆

PO Box 54, Sevenhill, SA 5453 **Region** Adelaide Hills
T (08) 8843 4370 **F** (08) 8843 4353 www.pikeandjoyce.com.au **Open** Not
Winemaker Neil Pike, John Trotter **Est.** 1998 **Cases** 45000
This is a partnership between the Pike family (of Clare Valley fame) and the Joyce family, related to Andrew Pike's wife, Cathy. The Joyce family have been orchardists at Lenswood for over 100 years, but also have extensive operations in the Riverland. Together with Andrew they have established 1 ha of vines; the lion's share to pinot noir, sauvignon blanc and chardonnay, followed by merlot, pinot gris and semillon. The wines are made at Pikes Clare Valley winery. Exports to the UK, the US, Canada, Singapore and Japan.

ŢŢŢŢŢ **Adelaide Hills Chardonnay 2007** Bright straw-green; a very well made wine from the first whiff through to the finish and aftertaste; has classic cool-grown nectarine white peach and grapefruit flavours, supported by quality French oak. Screwcap. 13.5% alc. **Rating** 95 **To** 2015 $35

ŢŢŢŢŢ **Adelaide Hills Pinot Noir 2007** Lightly coloured; a spicy/savoury bouquet, then a spiced black cherry palate; its deceptive length becomes apparent on retasting. Screwcap. 13.5% alc. **Rating** 91 **To** 2013 $35
Adelaide Hills Sauvignon Blanc 2008 Vibrant tropical fruit aromas with a touch of mineral complexity; fresh, generous and quite fine on the finish. Screwcap. 13% alc. **Rating** 90 **To** 2012 $22.95

ŢŢŢŢ **Adelaide Hills Pinot Gris 2008** A clean and juicy wine; not particularly complex or concentrated, but it exhibits the right amount of fruit and slippery texture for an easy-drinking style. Screwcap. 13% alc. **Rating** 88 **To** 2011 $22.95

Pikes ★★★★★

Polish Hill River Road, Sevenhill, SA 5453 **Region** Clare Valley
T (08) 8843 4370 **F** (08) 8843 4353 www.pikeswines.com.au **Open** 7 days 10–4
Winemaker Neil Pike, John Trotter **Est.** 1984 **Cases** 35 000 **Vyds** 65 ha
Owned by the Pike brothers: Andrew was for many years the senior viticulturist with Southcorp, Neil was a winemaker at Mitchell. Pikes now has its own winery, with Neil presiding. In most vintages its white wines, led by Riesling, are the most impressive. Planting of the vineyards has been an ongoing affair, with a panoply of varietals, new and traditional, reflected in the 2007 plantings of an additional 4.3 ha of riesling (26 ha in total), 3.5 ha of shiraz and a first-up planting of 1.24 ha of albarino. Exports to the UK, the US and other major markets.

ŢŢŢŢŢ **The EWP Reserve Clare Valley Shiraz 2006** Dense purple; an even more evocative bouquet than that of Eastside, full of promise for what is to come, and which the palate duly delivers; how much the 2% viognier contributes is irrelevant, the wine has glorious length and concentration to its treasure trove of black fruits. A bargain at the price. Screwcap. 14.5% alc. **Rating** 97 **To** 2036 $65
Eastside Clare Valley Shiraz 2006 Deep purple; a voluminous bouquet of black fruits, spice and licorice; a medium- to full-bodied and rich palate, flooded with black fruit and spice flavours; great tannin and oak support. Screwcap. 14.5% alc. **Rating** 95 **To** 2021 $26

The Merle Reserve Clare Valley Riesling 2008 A pure expression of Clare, with fresh lime juice and talc. aromas framing an abundance of zesty, fine fruit on the long, dry and even palate. Screwcap. 12% alc. **Rating** 94 **To** 2020 $38

ŶŶŶŶŶ Traditionale Clare Valley Riesling 2008 Pale straw with green hues; floral lime fruit bouquet; linear and fine, with a racy, yet still juicy, finish to the palate. Screwcap. 12% alc. **Rating** 91 **To** 2016 $23

ŶŶŶŶ Luccio Clare Valley Pinot Grigio Semillon Sauvignon Blanc 2008 Against all the odds, this blend works; the wine does not lose its grigio identity, mainly because of its drying lemony acidity on the finish. Screwcap. 12% alc. **Rating** 89 **To** 2010 $17

Pindarie   ★★★★

PO Box 341, Tanunda, SA 5352 **Region** Barossa Valley
T (08) 8524 9019 **F** (08) 8524 9090 **www**.pindarie.com.au **Open** Not
Winemaker Mark Jamieson **Est.** 2005 **Cases** 2500 **Vyds** 28.5 ha
Owners Tony Brooks and Wendy Allan met at Roseworthy College in 1985, but had very different family backgrounds. Tony was the sixth generation of farmers in SA and WA, and was studying agriculture; NZ-born Wendy was studying viticulture. On graduation Tony worked overseas managing sheep feedlots in Saudi Arabia, Turkey and Jordan, while Wendy worked for the next 12 years with Penfolds, commencing as a grower liaison officer and working her way up to become a senior viticulturist. She also found time to study viticulture in California, Israel, Italy, Germany, France, Portugal, Spain and Chile, working vintages and assessing vineyards for wine projects. In 2001 she completed a graduate diploma in wine business. Today they are renovating the original bluestone homestead and outbuildings, while managing the vineyards, mixed farm enterprises, a wine business and raising three children. Small wonder they have retained Mark Jamieson as executive winemaker. Exports to the US.

ŶŶŶŶŶ Reserve Black Hinge Barossa Valley Shiraz 2006 Deep purple-crimson; powerful, full-bodied wine with the full complement of black fruit flavours on the luscious and intense palate, ripe tannins and oak framing the fruit nicely. Cork. 14.5% alc. **Rating** 93 **To** 2016 $55
Bar Rossa Tempranillo Sangiovese Shiraz 2008 Good colour; interesting Mediterranean blend, with spicy overtones to the ripe black fruits at its core, spicy/savoury tannins to round it off. Screwcap. 14.5% alc. **Rating** 90 **To** 2014 $22

ŶŶŶŶ Barossa Valley Shiraz 2007 A powerful, beefy wine, with built-in tannins running through the length of the palate; flavours in the blackberry, dark chocolate and Christmas cake spectrum. Screwcap. 14.5% alc. **Rating** 89 **To** 2015 $23

Pipers Brook Vineyard   ★★★★★

1216 Pipers Brook Road, Pipers Brook, Tas 7254 **Region** Northern Tasmania
T (03) 6382 7527 **F** (03) 6382 7226 **www**.pipersbrook.com **Open** 7 days 10–5
Winemaker René Bezemer **Est.** 1974 **Cases** 100 000 **Vyds** 185 ha
The Pipers Brook Tasmanian empire has 185 ha of vineyard supporting the Pipers Brook and Ninth Island labels, with the major focus, of course, being on Pipers Brook. Fastidious viticulture and winemaking, immaculate packaging and enterprising marketing create a potent and effective blend. Pipers Brook operates two cellar door outlets, one at headquarters, the other at Strathlyn. In 2001 it became yet another company to fall prey to a takeover, in this instance by Belgian-owned sheepskin business Kreglinger, which has also established a large winery and vineyard at Mount Benson in SA. Exports to all major markets.

ŶŶŶŶŶ Kreglinger Vintage Brut Rose 2003 Salmon pink – a Tibetan sunset, says the back label; very fine wine with very clear strawberry notes ex the 100% pinot noir base; has great balance and very good length; bell-clear finish and aftertaste. Cork. 12.5% alc. **Rating** 95 **To** 2013 $50

Estate Chardonnay 2007 Vibrant, fresh and crisp, with the spine of natural acidity that is so much the mark of Tasmanian white wines; there are crushed citrus leaf nuances, and a stony/minerally acidity, which add to the overall impact. Screwcap. 13.5% alc. **Rating** 94 **To** 2017 $34

Ninth Island Pinot Grigio 2008 Faint blush tint; unusually scented rose petal, spice and tropical aromas lead into a very long palate, with a mineral and citrus backbone; very good balance. Tasmania is clearly suited to the variety. Screwcap. 13.5% alc. **Rating** 94 **To** 2010 $21.50

Ninth Island Pinot Noir 2007 Bright colour; fragrant and pure pinot, presented without adornment, simply because it doesn't need it. Small wonder it is one of the best value pinots on the market today. Screwcap. 13.5% alc. **Rating** 94 **To** 2012 $23.50

ŶŶŶŶŶ Ninth Island Sauvignon Blanc 2008 Very well made; an ideal combination of tropical and grassy/minerally components giving immediate pleasure. Screwcap. 13.5% alc. **Rating** 93 **To** 2010 $21.50

Ninth Island Pinot Noir 2008 Good colour hue and depth; fragrant and vibrant, with abundant red fruits and a touch of forest floor/sap to add interest. Screwcap. 13.5% alc. **Rating** 93 **To** 2014 $27.50

Estate Riesling 2008 A very refined and understated wine, driven by the framework of minerally acidity that frames the delicate citrus fruit. Development guaranteed. Screwcap. 13% alc. **Rating** 92 **To** 2018 $27.50

Ninth Island Riesling 2007 Fresh, vibrant and focused with a mineral streak through the citrus/lemon fruit; good length and balance. Screwcap. 13% alc. **Rating** 92 **To** 2015 $21.50

Estate Chardonnay 2005 Developing slowly but surely, sustained by typical Tasmanian acidity; grapefruit and stone fruit flavours dominate through to the long finish. Screwcap. 13.5% alc. **Rating** 92 **To** 2015 $34

The Summit Single Site Chardonnay 2004 Bright green-gold; the contribution of the cork is obvious in sea of screwcapped wines; an austere palate has both intensity and length to the grapefruit flavours; bold acidity to close. 13.5% alc. **Rating** 92 **To** 2012 $53.95

Estate Pinot Gris 2008 Bracing and crisp, but not without texture, thanks to some oak inputs; crisp granny smith apple and green pear flavours, finishing with bright acidity. Screwcap. 13.5% alc. **Rating** 92 **To** 2012 $27.50

Kreglinger Vintage Brut 2002 Attractive and delicate wine, but without the vibrancy and length of the Rose; that said, does have good stone fruit and bready notes ex yeast autolysis; will live on. Cork. 12.5% alc. **Rating** 92 **To** 2013 $50

Ninth Island Chardonnay Pinot Noir Pinot Meunier NV Fine, persistent mousse; elegant, intense wine built around green apple and citrus fruit, plus touches of creamy/toasty notes; very good finish and aftertaste. Cork. 12.5% alc. **Rating** 92 **To** 2013 $26.95

Estate Gewurztraminer 2008 Very pale colour; extremely delicate spice and rose petal nuances; nicely balanced and pure, with sustaining acidity. Screwcap. 13.5% alc. **Rating** 90 **To** 2013 $27.50

ŶŶŶŶ Estate Pinot Noir 2007 Perfect colour and clarity; a challenging wine due to the persistent, savoury, drying tannins surrounding a red fruit core; hopefully will come into balance with time. Screwcap. 13.5% alc. **Rating** 89 **To** 2015 $41.50

Pirie Estate ★★★★★

17 High Street, Launceston, Tas 7250 (postal) **Region** Northern Tasmania
T (03) 6334 7772 **F** (03) 6334 7773 **www.**pirietasmania.com.au **Open** Not
Winemaker Andrew Pirie **Est.** 2004 **Cases** 8000
Pirie Estate is the eponymous brand of Andrew Pirie. He manages 30 ha of vineyards in the Tamar Valley region (riesling, sauvignon blanc, gewurztraminer, chardonnay, pinot gris and pinot noir), but only part of the production is vinified for sale under the various Pirie labels.

Moreover, his main responsibility is that of his role as CEO of Tamar Ridge, where he is in overall charge of winemaking. Wines are released under the Pirie (varietal and Reserve) and South labels.

ŸŸŸŸŸ **South Chardonnay 2007** Pale, bright straw-green; a complex wine with strong winemaker thumbprints shaping the texture and flavours that embroider, rather than obscure, the core of stone fruit flavours, adding creamy/nutty nuances. Screwcap. 13.5% alc. **Rating** 94 **To** 2016 $23

Non Vintage NV Pale colour; focused and fresh lemon fruit and spring blossom bouquet; generous and creamy mouthfeel, with linear acidity and well-handled dosage; very good focus. Diam. 12.5% alc. **Rating** 94 **To** 2014 $32

Clark's Botrytis Riesling 2007 Super rich, super intense, super viscous; at least the equivalent of Beerenauslese; needs to be served fully chilled. 375 ml. Screwcap. 9% alc. **Rating** 94 **To** 2012 $30

ŸŸŸŸŸ **Pinot Noir 2007** Bright, clear colour and hue; firm, finely focused and structured plum and black cherry are dominant on a long palate and finish. Will develop. Screwcap. 13.5% alc. **Rating** 93 **To** 2015 $37.20

South Pinot Gris 2008 A faint touch of pink-bronze to the colour heralds a racy wine with bright fruit and crisp acidity, as much grigio as gris, if those words are in fact worth anything in the broader market. Screwcap. 13% alc. **Rating** 91 **To** 2012 $23

South Pinot Noir 2007 Light, bright colour; fresh red fruits and a hint of stem and forest; good length and balance; plenty of oak. Screwcap. 13.5% alc. **Rating** 91 **To** 2013 $23.60

Gewurztraminer 2007 Delicate floral aromas and even more delicate flavours define the wine by what it isn't (riesling); scores for its balance and length. Screwcap. 13.5% alc. **Rating** 90 **To** 2015 $29

ŸŸŸŸ **South Pinot Noir 2008** Fresh red cherry and strawberry fruit; very attractive wine for immediate consumption. Screwcap. 13.7% alc. **Rating** 89 **To** 2010 $23.70

South Sauvignon Blanc 2008 Clean, fresh and lively citrus and mineral character on the bouquet; the palate is fine and quite crisp, if lacking a little concentration. Screwcap. 13.5% alc. **Rating** 87 **To** 2012 $23

Piromit Wines   ★★★★

113 Hanwood Avenue, Hanwood, NSW 2680 **Region** Riverina
T (02) 6963 0200 **F** (02) 6963 0277 **www.**piromitwines.com.au **Open** Mon–Fri 10–4
Winemaker Sam Mittiga **Est.** 1998 **Cases** 50 000
I simply cannot resist quoting directly from the background information kindly supplied to me. 'Piromit Wines is a relatively new boutique winery situated in Hanwood, NSW. The 1000-tonne capacity winery was built for the 1999 vintage on a 14-acre site which was until recently used as a drive-in. Previous to this, wines were made on our 100-acre vineyard. The winery site is being developed into an innovative tourist attraction complete with an Italian restaurant and landscaped formal gardens.' It is safe to say this extends the concept of a boutique winery into new territory, but then it is a big country. Exports to Canada, Sweden and Italy.

ŸŸŸŸŸ **Pinot Grigio 2008** Very crisp and crunchy; if ever there was an Australian pinot grigio this is it; having won a gold medal at the National Wine Show '08 (and one at the Riverina Wine Show '08), disclosing it also won a bronze medal at the Dubbo Wine Show is a strange marketing decision. Screwcap. 13% alc. **Rating** 93 **To** 2010 $12.50

ŸŸŸŸ **Botrytis Semillon 2006** Butterscotch and honey, with some cumquat; good balance, but drink soon. Screwcap. 11.5% alc. **Rating** 87 **To** 2010 $16

Pirramimma

Johnston Road, McLaren Vale, SA 5171 **Region** McLaren Vale
T (08) 8323 8205 **F** (08) 8323 9224 **www**.pirramimma.com.au **Open** Mon–Fri 9–5,
Sat 11–5, Sun, public hols 11.30–4
Winemaker Geoff Johnston **Est.** 1892 **Cases** 50 000 **Vyds** 192 ha
A long-established, family-owned company with outstanding vineyard resources. It is using
those resources to full effect, with a series of intense old-vine varietals including Semillon,
Sauvignon Blanc, Chardonnay, Shiraz, Grenache, Cabernet Sauvignon and Petit Verdot, all
fashioned without over-embellishment. There are two quality tiers, both offering excellent
value, the packaging significantly upgraded recently. Exports to the UK, the US and other
major markets.

ΨΨΨΨΨ **McLaren Vale Cabernet Sauvignon 2006** A totally convincing mix of
elegance and intensity in a medium-bodied wine with great length and perfect
balance; gently savoury overtones to the black fruits add to both flavour and
texture. Reversing the use of cork and screwcap with Stock's Hill would have
been a smart move. Cork. 14% alc. **Rating** 95 **To** 2016 $26.50

ΨΨΨΨΨ **McLaren Vale Petit Verdot 2005** Good colour still with red nuances;
blackberry, blackcurrant, bitter chocolate, with a sweet fruit core. Cork. 14% alc.
Rating 92 **To** 2015 $26.50
Stock's Hill McLaren Vale Shiraz 2005 A supremely honest, no frills example
of McLaren Vale Shiraz, with supple mouthfeel and very good length; the twist
of spice on the finish is the legacy of restrained alcohol. Great value. Screwcap.
14% alc. **Rating** 90 **To** 2014 $15
Stock's Hill McLaren Vale Cabernet Merlot 2005 Complexity starting to
develop, with a mix of blackcurrant, cedar, mocha and a wisp of dark chocolate;
tannins are evident but ripe. Screwcap. 14% alc. **Rating** 90 **To** 2013 $15
Stock's Hill McLaren Vale Cabernet Sauvignon 2006 Cabernet sauvignon
doesn't come any better at this price, the blackcurrant fruit making light of the
American oak in which it was matured; the tannins are spot on. Screwcap. 14% alc.
Rating 90 **To** 2014 $15

ΨΨΨΨ **12 Year Old McLaren Vale Liqueur Tawny NV** Lively, spicy/tawny with
clear rancio character lengthening and partially drying the finish. Bargain. Cork.
18.5% alc. **Rating** 89 **To** 2010 $15
Pirra McLaren Vale Grenache Shiraz 2006 Has a basket of unusual aromas
and flavours, which may or may not reflect early picking; chocolate, vanilla,
Turkish delight and spice all jostle for attention. Screwcap. 11.5% alc. **Rating** 88
To 2012 $15
Stock's Hill McLaren Vale Cabernet Merlot 2006 A sturdy wine, with a
strong regional face to its blend of black fruits and dark chocolate; enough tannin
structure to sustain it for the next five years or so. Screwcap. 14% alc. **Rating** 88
To 2013 $15
McLaren Vale Sauvignon Blanc 2008 Very unusual wine, presumably very
early picked, although the alcohol may have been reduced by reverse osmosis;
either way, is crisp but somewhat thin. Screwcap. 9.5% alc. **Rating** 87 **To** 2009 $15

Pizzini

175 King Valley Road, Whitfield, Vic 3768 **Region** King Valley
T (03) 5729 8278 **F** (03) 5729 8495 **www**.pizzini.com.au **Open** 7 days 10–5
Winemaker Alfred Pizzini, Joel Pizzini **Est.** 1980 **Cases** 20 000 **Vyds** 50.2 ha
Fred and Katrina Pizzini have been grapegrowers in the King Valley for over 25 years, with
more than 50 ha of vineyard. Originally much of the grape production was sold, but today
80% is retained for the Pizzini brand, and the focus is on winemaking, which has been
particularly successful. Their wines rank high among the many King Valley producers. It is
not surprising that their wines should span both Italian and traditional varieties, and I can
personally vouch for their Italian cooking skills. Exports to Japan.

ŶŶŶŶŶ **King Valley Merlot Sangiovese 2004** A very complex wine, the bouquet with startlingly spicy, cherry and cedar aromas, the palate revolving around the sangiovese tannins; the high-quality cork will pay its way as the wine ages further. Available only at cellar door. 14.2% alc. **Rating** 92 **To** 2015 $29

King Valley Nebbiolo 2003 Light colour, but still predominantly red; ultra savoury/cedary/spicy flavours run through a palate with very considerable length, but less depth; good outcome for such a difficult variety. Cork. 14.5% alc. **Rating** 91 **To** 2013 $56

King Valley Shiraz 2005 Good hue retention; spicy overtones to the volumes of red fruits on the bouquet and the thrusting palate; has all the length one could wish for. Screwcap. 14% alc. **Rating** 91 **To** 2015 $24

King Valley Arneis 2008 A wine made with a true Italian leaning; savoury anise, grapefruit, pear and straw flavours and aromas are complemented by tangy mouth-watering acidity. Screwcap. 12.9% alc. **Rating** 90 **To** 2012 $20

King Valley Merlot 2005 Has good bottle-developed character, spicy notes coming through on the bouquet and the medium-bodied palate, which has varietal cassis and snow pea flavours. Screwcap. 13.8% alc. **Rating** 90 **To** 2012 $18

Il Barone 2004 An interesting, if unconventional, blend, with sweet fruit offset by strong savoury complexity; the tannins are intense and plentiful, as the fruit takes a back seat to the structure, in the truest of Italian traditions. Cabernet Sauvignon/Shiraz/Sangiovese/Nebbiolo. Screwcap. 14.3% alc. **Rating** 90 **To** 2014 $43

ŶŶŶŶ **King Valley Sangiovese Shiraz 2008** The character of the medium-bodied wine is largely driven by the cherry/sour cherry and savoury tannins of the sangiovese, tempered by the shiraz. Screwcap. 13.8% alc. **Rating** 89 **To** 2015 $17.50

King Valley Pinot Grigio 2008 Lemon fruit and straw, bright acidity, and food-friendly texture on the finish. Screwcap. 12.2% alc. **Rating** 87 **To** 2012 $18.50

King Valley Verduzzo 2008 Has some depth to the colour, possibly from the small portion of barrel ferment in new French oak barriques; the flavours wander, the wine is more about texture and its bone-dry finish. Screwcap. 14.2% alc. **Rating** 87 **To** 2011 $21

King Valley Sangiovese 2006 Holding hue well; has a clean and fresh bouquet, and there are fleeting glimpses of red fruits before Tarzan's Grip tannins take hold of the palate; insists on rich Italian meat and pasta dishes. Screwcap. 14% alc. **Rating** 87 **To** 2016 $28

Coronamento King Valley Nebbiolo 2003 Light tawny-red; nebbiolo strikes again with its sour cherry fruit enmeshed in drying tannins. Varietal expression is decidedly expensive, it seems. Cork. 13.8% alc. **Rating** 87 **To** 2012 $135

Plan B   ★★★★

PO Box 139, Cowaramup, WA 6284 **Region** Margaret River
T 0413 759 030 **F** (08) 9755 6267 **www.**planbwines.com **Open** At Arlewood Estate
Winemaker Bill Crappsley **Est.** 2005 **Cases** 10 000 **Vyds** 18 ha
This is a joint venture between Bill Crappsley, a 43-year veteran winemaker/consultant; Martin Miles, who has a wine distribution business in the southwestern part of the state; Gary Gosatti, of Arlewood Estate; and Terry Chellappah, wine consultant and now also in partnership with Gary. The shiraz is sourced from Bill's Calgardup Vineyard, the remaining wines from Arlewood and all are single-vineyard releases. Exports to the UK, Canada, Sweden, Norway, Singapore, Hong Kong and China.

ŶŶŶŶŶ **Frankland River Shiraz 2007** Strong crimson-purple; a dense and powerful wine, with strong licorice and spicy black fruits finishing with ripe tannins and oak. Will live for decades. Screwcap. 15% alc. **Rating** 93 **To** 2027 $18.99

Frankland River Chardonnay 2007 Charged with masses of nectarine, melon and grapefruit on the medium-bodied palate, oak irrelevant (if, indeed, present). Screwcap. 14.5% alc. **Rating** 90 **To** 2013 $18.99

Plantagenet ★★★★★

Albany Highway, Mount Barker, WA 6324 **Region** Mount Barker
T (08) 9851 3131 **F** (08) 9851 1839 **www**.plantagenetwines.com **Open** 7 days 9–5
Winemaker John Durham, Andries Mostert **Est.** 1974 **Cases** 90 000 **Vyds** 127 ha
The senior winery in the Mount Barker region, making superb wines across the full spectrum of variety and style: highly aromatic Riesling, tangy citrus-tinged Chardonnay, glorious Rhône-style Shiraz and ultra-stylish Cabernet Sauvignon. Exports to all major markets.

ⵧⵧⵧⵧⵧ **Mount Barker Cabernet Sauvignon 2005** Light but bright hue; pure and fragrant cabernet varietal aromas lead logically into a long, fruit-driven palate with a silky texture and admirable balance. Screwcap. 13.5% alc. **Rating** 95 **To** 2020 $35
Great Southern Riesling 2008 A little reductive on opening; incredibly tight lemon fruit, and a super-strong core of minerality; there is also a touch of exotic fruit on the palate, but the line and length suggest great longevity. Screwcap. 11.5% alc. **Rating** 94 **To** 2025 $23
Great Southern Shiraz 2007 A ripe and savoury bouquet with redcurrant and blackberry, framed by mineral complexity and a little roast meat; the palate is quite chewy in texture, but has a litheness to the fruit that draws out the very long, and quite juicy conclusion. Screwcap. 14.5% alc. **Rating** 94 **To** 2020 $40
Mount Barker Cabernet Sauvignon 2007 Strong crimson-purple; classic Great Southern cabernet; while it has fully ripe and lush blackcurrant fruit, there is also a savoury/spicy cool-climate twist to the finish; has good length and balance. Screwcap. 14.5% alc. **Rating** 94 **To** 2022 $35
Ringbark Riesling 2008 Bright straw-green; very clean and pure riesling; abundant lime juice flavours on the long finish, which is at once intense and balanced. Screwcap. 11% alc. **Rating** 94 **To** 2014 $25

ⵧⵧⵧⵧⵧ **Omrah Cabernet Merlot 2006** Very good varietal expression of the two varieties ranging through red and black berry fruits; exceptional for the vintage, especially the tannin structure. Screwcap. 14% alc. **Rating** 90 **To** 2015 $18
Hazard Hill Semillon Sauvignon Blanc 2008 Aromas of fresh cut grass, with a touch of citrus are offered on the bouquet; clean, varietal fruit with real persistence to the very fresh, clean finish. Screwcap. 13% alc. **Rating** 90 **To** 2012 $12
Great Southern Chardonnay 2007 Loaded with sweet nectarine fruit and a slight pine element; toasty and rich with a strong mineral component coming to the fore. Screwcap. 13.5% alc. **Rating** 90 **To** 2013 $25

ⵧⵧⵧⵧ **Omrah Sauvignon Blanc 2008** Straw-green; the palate opens quietly, but progressively builds tropical fruit flavours through to the emphatic finish. Screwcap. 13.5% alc. **Rating** 89 **To** 2010 $18
Hazard Hill Shiraz 2006 Red fruits and spice, showing clove, pepper and a fine touch of oak; the palate is medium-bodied and the tannins a little chewy, providing a savoury edge to the finish. Screwcap. 14.5% alc. **Rating** 89 **To** 2014 $12
Omrah Unoaked Chardonnay 2008 One of the pioneers of unoaked chardonnay; aromatic, verging tropical, with a brisk citrus finish. Screwcap. 13.5% alc. **Rating** 87 **To** 2010 $18
Omrah Shiraz 2006 Lively, supple, light- to medium-bodied wine, with a mix of black and red fruits; good balance. Screwcap. 14% alc. **Rating** 87 **To** 2013 $18

Plum Hill Vineyard

45 Coldstream West Road, Chirnside Park, Vic 3116 **Region** Yarra Valley
T (03) 9735 0985 **F** (03) 9735 4109 **Open** By appt
Winemaker Contract **Est.** 1998 **Cases** 2000 **Vyds** 7.2 ha
Ian and June Delbridge had been breeding cattle on their 36-ha property since the early 1970s before deciding to establish a vineyard in '98 on the advice of the late Dr John Middleton. They have planted pinot noir, merlot, shiraz and cabernet sauvignon in the distinguished neighbourhood of Mount Mary, Bianchet and Yarra Edge. Grapes from the first two vintages were sold, but in 2003 the decision was taken to make wine under the Plum Hill Vineyard

label. The '06 wines will be on release for some time; the '07 and '09 vintages were affected by smoke (as was the case throughout the Yarra Valley) and the grapes from '08 were sold.

ŸŸŸŸŸ **Yarra Valley Merlot 2006** Quite expressive merlot fruit on both the bouquet and light- to medium-bodied palate; spicy/savoury notes, but not quite enough small berry fruit on the mid-palate. Screwcap. 13.4% alc. **Rating** 90 **To** 2013 $20

ŸŸŸŸ **Yarra Valley Shiraz 2006** Medium-bodied; an elegant fusion of black cherry fruit and soft oak, fine tannins; needs a little more conviction. Screwcap. 14.1% alc. **Rating** 89 **To** 2012 $20

Plunkett Fowles

Cnr Hume Freeway/Lambing Gully Road, Avenel, Vic 3664 **Region** Strathbogie Ranges
T (03) 5796 2150 **F** (03) 5796 2147 **www**.plunkettfowles.com.au **Open** 7 days 9–5
Winemaker Sam Plunkett, Victor Nash, Lindsay Brown, Michael Clayden **Est.** 1968
Cases 30 000 **Vyds** 193.64 ha

Plunkett Fowles is the new face for two families committed to building a prominent international wine business. The co-managers, Sam Plunkett and Matt Fowles, are in their late 30s and late 20s, with both winemaking and business skills. The two families have had a long association with this dry, cool, granitic region, which has given them a deep understanding of their extensive vineyards (chardonnay, shiraz, cabernet sauvignon, sauvignon blanc, pinot noir, merlot, riesling, semillon, viognier, gewurztraminer, verdelho, albarino, tempranillo and lagrein). They are committed to a strategy of selling wine that exceeds the expectations for any given price point. Exports to the UK, the US and other major markets.

ŸŸŸŸŸ **The Rule Reserve Strathbogie Ranges Shiraz 2006** Good colour; a polished, spicy red berry fruit bouquet exhibiting a nice seasoning of well-handled oak; medium-bodied with attractive velvet texture and an abundance of red fruits; the oak is noticeable, but merely extends the finish. Screwcap. 14.5% alc. **Rating** 94 **To** 2015 $39.95
Plunkett Reserve Strathbogie Ranges Cabernet Sauvignon 2004
Well-made wine, with ripe cassis and black fruits on bouquet and medium-bodied palate; fine tannins and vanillin oak. Screwcap. 14.5% alc. **Rating** 94 **To** 2019 $39.95

ŸŸŸŸ **Stone Dwellers Strathbogie Ranges Riesling 2008** Has good varietal expression and focus, citrus-dominant, but with hints of apple and stone fruit; good acidity and a dry finish. Screwcap. 13% alc. **Rating** 89 **To** 2016 $21.95
Stone Dwellers Strathbogie Ranges Gewurztraminer 2008 Has clear-cut rose petal and spice varietal aromas that come through on the palate; good example of this difficult variety. Screwcap. 14.5% alc. **Rating** 89 **To** 2013 $21.95
Stone Dwellers Strathbogie Ranges Sauvignon Blanc 2008 Has more flavour and varietal character than the other sauvignon blancs from Plunkett Fowles; a pleasing mix of passionfruit and gooseberry offset by cleansing acidity. Screwcap. 13.5% alc. **Rating** 89 **To** 2011 $21.95
Stone Dwellers Strathbogie Ranges Pinot Noir 2008 Well-made, capturing all the varietal character available; spicy/briary notes are authentic; clever use of higher than normal acidity to balance the alcohol; surprise packet. Screwcap. 15% alc. **Rating** 89 **To** 2011 $24.95
Blackwood Ridge Sauvignon Blanc 2008 Firmly structured wine, with solid gooseberry fruit, but doesn't have the thrust and vitality of the best examples. Screwcap. 13% alc. **Rating** 88 **To** 2010 $16.95
Stone Dwellers Strathbogie Ranges Shiraz 2006 Seek and ye shall find, in this case the explanation for the particular scent of the bouquet is a dash of viognier (though still unusual); the palate is very savoury and earthy; the wine abounds with questions. Screwcap. 14.5% alc. **Rating** 88 **To** 2014 $24.95
490 m Cabernet Merlot 2005 Gentle spicy/savoury aromas and flavours; the medium-bodied palate is well-balanced, the tannins fine, the oak subtle. Screwcap. 14.5% alc. **Rating** 87 **To** 2012 $14.95

Poacher's Ridge Vineyard ★★★★★

1630 Spencer Road, Narrikup, WA 6326 **Region** Mount Barker
T (08) 9857 6066 **F** (08) 9857 6077 **www**.prv.com.au **Open** Fri–Sun 10–4 or by appt
Winemaker Robert Diletti (Contract) **Est.** 2000 **Cases** 1400 **Vyds** 7 ha
Alex and Janet Taylor purchased the Poacher's Ridge property in 1999; before then it had
been used for cattle grazing. The vineyard includes shiraz, cabernet sauvignon, merlot, riesling,
marsanne and viognier. The first small crop came in 2003, a larger one in '04, together making
an auspicious debut. However, winning the Tri Nations merlot class against the might of
Australia, NZ and South Africa in 2007 with its '05 Louis' Block Great Southern Merlot was
a dream come true.

ŸŸŸŸŸ **Louis' Block Great Southern Riesling 2007** Fine, tight, classic style; crisp
and dry; very pure, lingering acidity; fresh waxy finish. Gold WA Wine Show '08.
Screwcap. 12.5% alc. **Rating** 94 **To** 2015 $18.99
Louis' Block Great Southern Merlot 2007 Bright crimson; has remarkable
intensity, focus and length, with exemplary varietal fruit, redcurrant/cassis and just
a hint of black olive. Screwcap. 14.9% alc. **Rating** 94 **To** 2017 $23.99
Louis' Block Great Southern Cabernet Sauvignon 2007 Crimson-purple;
fragrant cassis and blackcurrant aromas, a medium-bodied and very pure varietal
palate, with good balance and length. Screwcap. 14% alc. **Rating** 94 **To** 2020 $19.99

ŸŸŸŸŸ **Sophie's Yard Great Southern Shiraz 2007** Bright crimson; notes of spice
and herb on the bouquet merge into the red fruits of the medium-bodied palate,
and fine tannins. Screwcap. 14.5% alc. **Rating** 91 **To** 2016 $25.99
Louis' Block Great Southern Riesling 2008 Classic riesling, very tight and
minerally; slightly tweaky acidity needs to settle down, which, on the evidence of
the '07, will happen. Screwcap. 11.7% alc. **Rating** 90 **To** 2014 $18.99

ŸŸŸŸ **Louis' Block Great Southern Marsanne 2008** Typical of the faintly chalky,
dusty aroma of marsanne from the Rhône Valley; touches of honeysuckle on
the palate, which has overall delicacy. Cellaring will pay off. Screwcap. 12.9% alc.
Rating 89 **To** 2014 $16.99

Point Leo Road Vineyard ★★★★

214 Point Leo Road, Red Hill South, Vic 3937 **Region** Mornington Peninsula
T 0406 610 815 **F** (03) 9882 0327 **www**.pointleoroad.com.au **Open** By appt
Winemaker Phillip Kittle, Andrew Thomson, David Cowburn **Est.** 1996 **Cases** 1100
Vyds 5.7 ha
John Law and family planted 1.9 ha of pinot noir and 1.5 ha of chardonnay in 1996 as contract
growers for several leading Mornington Peninsula wineries. Plantings have been progressively
expanded with small amounts of pinot gris, lagrein, sauvignon blanc and gewurztraminer. Part
of the grapes are now contract-made, and they have two labels: Point Leo Road for premium
wines, and Point Break the second label.

ŸŸŸŸŸ **Mornington Peninsula Chardonnay 2006** A harmonious wine with perfectly
ripened stone fruit and melon chardonnay matched by well-weighted French oak.
Screwcap. 13.5% alc. **Rating** 92 **To** 2014 $27
Salmon Mornington Peninsula Blanc de Noir 2005 Very delicate and fresh,
notwithstanding 30 months on lees prior to disgorgement; has flavours of small red
berries and strawberries. Diam. 12.5% alc. **Rating** 91 **To** 2012 $35
The Tom Thumb Mornington Peninsula Pinot Noir 2005 Retains good
hue; an unusually durable pinot, ripe plummy fruit is reinforced with foresty/
savoury, but balanced, tannins. Screwcap. 13.5% alc. **Rating** 90 **To** 2012 $45

Polin & Polin Wines ★★★

Mistletoe Lane, Pokolbin, NSW 2230 **Region** Hunter Valley
T 0422 511 348 **F** (02) 9969 9665 **www**.polinwines.com.au **Open** Not
Winemaker Peter Orr, Patrick Auld **Est.** 1997 **Cases** 2000 **Vyds** 10 ha

The first of the two vineyards of the business was established by Lexie and Michael Polin (and family) in 1997 near Denman, in the Upper Hunter. An additional 4 ha was acquired in Pokolbin in 2003, and all of the wines have been produced from single-vineyard sites. The name was chosen to honour forebears Peter and Thomas Polin, who migrated from Ireland in 1860, operating a general store in Coonamble. Limb of Addy has a distinctly Irish twist to it, but is in fact a hill immediately to the east of the vineyard. Subsequent wine names directly or indirectly reflect movement to Australia by 19th-century migrants.

ŸŸŸŸ **Convicts and Catholics Hunter Valley Shiraz 2005** Light in colour and body, but with a stealthy insistence and length to the bright red fruits of the palate. Screwcap. 13% alc. **Rating** 89 **To** 2015 $19.99
Ships of the Line Hunter Valley Verdelho 2007 Very rich, full-bodied style, with ripe tropical fruit flavours. Screwcap. 14% alc. **Rating** 87 **To** 2010 $17.99

Politini Wines

65 Upper King River Road, Cheshunt, Vic 3678 **Region** King Valley
T (03) 5729 8277 **F** (03) 5729 8373 **www.**politiniwines.com.au **Open** 7 days 11–5
Winemaker Luis Simian **Est.** 1989 **Cases** 6000 **Vyds** 20.68 ha
The Politini family have been grapegrowers in the King Valley supplying major local wineries since 1989, selling to Brown Brothers, Miranda and the Victorian Alps Winery. In 2000 they decided to move into winemaking, and have steadily increased their wine production to its present level. They have also planted pinot gris, sangiovese, nero d'Avola and graciano to accompany the previously planted cabernet sauvignon, shiraz, merlot and sauvignon blanc. Luis Simian is a winemaker with a significant track record of success in many places, including Chile. Exports to Hong Kong and China.

ŸŸŸŸŸ **King Valley Cabernet Sauvignon 2005** Strong colour; a cedary/earthy/ oaky bouquet; the palate has blackcurrant fruit framed by those characters; still remarkably fresh. Very stained cork. 13.5% alc. **Rating** 90 **To** 2015 $18

ŸŸŸŸ **King Valley Merlot 2005** Bright colour; a surprise packet, with deep, dark fruit on both bouquet and palate, the latter with black olive notes on a substantial finish. Value. Cork. 13.5% alc. **Rating** 89 **To** 2012 $16
King Valley Pinot Grigio 2008 Fragrant apple, citrus and pear blossom aromas; a lively, tangy palate with no reliance on residual sugar. Screwcap. 13.5% alc. **Rating** 89 **To** 2010 $17.50
King Valley Vermentino 2008 A quite fragrant and flowery bouquet, then a fresh palate built around citrussy acidity. Further evidence that this is a worthwhile variety. Screwcap. 13.1% alc. **Rating** 89 **To** 2012 $19.50
King Valley Sangiovese Rose 2008 Distinctive aromas of spice and cherry are repeated on the long and persistent palate, finishing with good acidity. Value. Screwcap. 13.5% alc. **Rating** 88 **To** 2010 $14
King Valley Cabernet Sauvignon 2002 Distinct cedary/earthy overtones to the black fruits of the palate; fully mature. Cork. 13.5% alc. **Rating** 87 **To** 2011 $18

Polleters

80 Polleters Road, Moonambel, Vic 3478 **Region** Pyrenees
T (03) 9569 5030 **www.**polleters.com **Open** W'ends 10–5
Winemaker Mark Summerfield **Est.** 1994 **Cases** 1500 **Vyds** 8.5 ha
Pauline and Peter Bicknell purchased the 60-ha property on which their vineyard now stands in 1993, at which time it was part of a larger grazing property. The first vines were planted in '94, and include shiraz, cabernet sauvignon, cabernet franc and merlot. In the first few years the grapes were sold, but since 2001 part of the production has been used to produce the impressively rich and powerful wines. The grapes are hand-picked, fermented in open vats with hand-plunging, and matured for 18 months in American oak.

ΨΨΨΨ **Moonambel Shiraz 2006** Medium- to full-bodied, with all the velvety richness Central Victorian regions can produce, yet not overripe or extractive; has layers of plum and blackberry fruit neatly wrapped up in a fine sheath of oak and tannins. Screwcap. 14.5% alc. **Rating** 94 **To** 2021 $25

ΨΨΨΨΨ **Moonambel Merlot 2006** Has abundant red berry fruit on the bouquet and medium-bodied palate, where some savoury/plummy notes add to the depth of the flavour; more regional than varietal, perhaps. Screwcap. 14.5% alc. **Rating** 92 **To** 2016 $25
Morgan's 2006 Good colour; mocha overtones add to the inherent sweetness of the fruit, chocolate also part of the mix; good balance. Cabernet Sauvignon/ Cabernet Franc/Merlot/Shiraz. Screwcap. 14.1% alc. **Rating** 91 **To** 2016 $25

ΨΨΨΨ **Moonambel Cabernet Franc 2005** Interesting medium-bodied wine; distinct tobacco/coffee aromas and flavours, plus cedary tannins in an overall savoury mode. Screwcap. 14.5% alc. **Rating** 89 **To** 2013 $25

Pondalowie Vineyards ★★★★★

6 Main Street, Bridgewater-on-Loddon, Vic 3516 **Region** Bendigo
T (03) 5437 3332 **F** (03) 5437 3332 www.pondalowie.com.au **Open** By appt
Winemaker Dominic Morris, Krystina Morris **Est.** 1997 **Cases** 2500 **Vyds** 10 ha
Dominic and Krystina Morris both have strong winemaking backgrounds gained from working in Australia, Portugal and France. Dominic has worked alternate vintages in Australia and Portugal since 1995, and Krystina has also worked at St Hallett and at Boar's Rock. They have established 5.5 ha of shiraz, 2 ha each of tempranillo and cabernet sauvignon, and a little viognier and malbec. Incidentally, the illustration on the Pondalowie label is not a piece of barbed wire, but a very abstract representation of the winery kelpie dog. Exports to the UK, Singapore, Macau, Hong Kong and Japan.

ΨΨΨΨ **Special Release Shiraz 2006** As deep as the varietal, but with more crimson; abounds with luscious, but complex, spice and pepper black fruits, licorice and plum; the palate has multiple layers. Screwcap. 14.5% alc. **Rating** 95 **To** 2026 $50
Special Release Tempranillo 2006 Deep, dense colour; without question, the most serious and complex tempranillo from Australia, equalling the plush intensity of the best examples from Spain. By extension, should live for decades. Screwcap. 13.5% alc. **Rating** 95 **To** 2026 $50

ΨΨΨΨΨ **Shiraz 2006** Deep colour; seems to have gained weight and substance since first tasted Feb '08, the fruit gaining another dimension, the savoury finish more bite. Screwcap. 14.5% alc. **Rating** 92 **To** 2020 $25
Vineyard Blend Shiraz Cabernet Tempranillo 2006 Deep colour; a rich and dense wine, packed with black fruits of all shapes and sizes, and just a tweak of spicy red fruit on the finish. Top value. Screwcap. 14.5% alc. **Rating** 91 **To** 2015 $20

Poole's Rock/Cockfighter's Ghost ★★★★

DeBeyers Road, Pokolbin, NSW 2321 **Region** Lower Hunter Valley
T (02) 4998 7356 **F** (02) 4998 6866 www.poolesrock.com.au **Open** 7 days 9.30–5
Winemaker Patrick Auld, Usher Tinkler **Est.** 1988 **Cases** NFP
Sydney merchant banker David Clarke has had a long involvement with the wine industry. The 18-ha Poole's Rock vineyard, planted purely to chardonnay, is his personal venture; it was initially bolstered by the acquisition of the larger, adjoining Simon Whitlam Vineyard. However, the purchase of the 74-ha Glen Elgin Estate, upon which the 2500-tonne former Tulloch winery is situated, takes Poole's Rock (and its associated brands, Cockfighter's Ghost and Firestick) into another dimension. Exports to all major markets.

ΨΨΨΨΨ **Cockfighter's Ghost Premium Reserve Coonawarra Cabernet Sauvignon 2004** Elegant medium-bodied wine, with savoury/earthy regional overtones to the blackcurrant fruit; has good length, and accelerates on the tangy finish. Screwcap. 13.8% alc. **Rating** 93 **To** 2015 $39.99

♥♥♥♥ **Cockfighter's Ghost Orange Pinot Noir Chardonnay 2006** Salmon-pink; delicate, dry, savoury aperitif style; hefty price. Cork. 12.5% alc. **Rating** 89 To 2012 $39.99
Cockfighter's Ghost Pinot Gris 2008 A brisk, citrussy wine with nuances of apple and pear; not especially distinctive. Screwcap. 13.5% alc. **Rating** 87 To 2010 $24.99

Pooley Wines

Cooinda Vale Vineyard, Barton Vale Road, Campania, Tas 7026 **Region** Southern Tasmania
T (03) 6260 2895 **F** (03) 6260 2895 **www**.pooleywines.com.au **Open** 7 days 10–5
Winemaker Matt Pooley **Est.** 1985 **Cases** 2600 **Vyds** 10.2 ha

Three generations of the Pooley family have been involved in the development of Pooley Wines, although the winery was previously known as Cooinda Vale. Plantings have now reached over 10 ha in a region that is warmer and drier than most people realise. In 2003 the family planted 1.2 ha of pinot noir and 1.3 ha of pinot grigio at Belmont Vineyard, 1431 Richmond Road, Richmond, a heritage property with an 1830s Georgian home and a second cellar door in the old sandstone barn and stables.

♥♥♥♥♥ **Coal River Pinot Noir 2007** Good hue; a complex offering of savoury/spicy/foresty/stemmy aromas and flavours, along with ripe red fruits; good length and mouthfeel. Screwcap. **Rating** 94 To 2014 $30
Butchers Hill Pinot Noir 2007 Plenty of substance and flavour with a complex and harmonious mix of small berry fruits and spicy/savoury notes; the oak level may worry some tasters. Screwcap. **Rating** 94 To 2015 $35

♥♥♥♥♡ **Coal River Riesling 2008** Nicely balanced, well-made wine; ripe but not flabby; pushes through a long palate; good balance. Screwcap. **Rating** 93 To 2015 $25
Coal River Pinot Noir 2006 Holding vibrant colour; zesty plum and black cherry fruit with a touch of green acidity, but hard done by when tasted Jan '08. Screwcap. **Rating** 90 To 2013 $30

Poonawatta Estate

PO Box 340, Angaston, SA 5353 **Region** Eden Valley
T (08) 8565 3248 **F** (08) 8565 3248 **www**.poonawatta.com **Open** Not
Winemaker Reid Bosward, Jo Irvine, Andrew Holt **Est.** 1880 **Cases** 800 **Vyds** 3.6 ha

The Poonawatta Estate story is complex, stemming from 1.8 ha of shiraz planted in 1880. When Andrew Holt's parents purchased the Poonawatta property, the vineyard had suffered decades of neglect, and a slow process of restoration began. While that was underway, the strongest canes available from the winter pruning of the 1880s block were slowly and progressively dug into the stony soil of the site. It took seven years to establish the matching 1.8 ha, and the yield is even lower than that of the 1880s block. In 2004 Andrew and wife Michelle were greeted with the same high yields that were obtained right across South Eastern Australia, and this led to declassification of part of the production, giving rise to a second label, Monties Block, which sits underneath The Cuttings (from the 'new' vines) and, at the top, The 1880. In 2005 a Riesling was introduced, produced from a single vineyard of 2 ha hand-planted by the Holt family in the 1970s. Exports to the US, France and Denmark.

♥♥♥♥♥ **The 1880 Eden Valley Shiraz 2007** Great colour; a wine of exceptional complexity both in flavour and structure, with a raft of spicy/savoury notes coursing through the fine black fruits; dismisses its alcohol with a flick of its hand. Cork. 15% alc. **Rating** 96 To 2027 $80
The Centenarian Single Barrel Reserve Eden Valley Shiraz 2005 Retains excellent hue; an extremely powerful wine, with intense focus to its black fruits, which have revelled in 22 months' maturation in new French oak; still in its infancy, and deserves another 10, if not 20, years' maturation; 300 bottles made. Cork. 14.5% alc. **Rating** 96 To 2030 $160
The Eden Riesling 2008 Powerful and intense, yet in no way heavy or phenolic; grainy/minerally notes add texture to the lime and apple fruit; has an energetic finish. Screwcap. 12% alc. **Rating** 94 To 2020 $25

Monties Block Eden Valley Shiraz 2007 Very well crafted; satin smooth blackberry, plum and licorice running along an intense but supple palate, with particularly good balance and length. Screwcap. 14% alc. **Rating** 94 **To** 2020 $29

ŶŶŶŶ **Golden Eden Ratafia Riesling 2006** Interesting wine, but doesn't really work because the spirit is too fierce. Screwcap. 18% alc. **Rating** 87 **To** 2011 $20

Port Phillip Estate ★★★★★

261 Red Hill Road, Red Hill, Vic 3937 **Region** Mornington Peninsula
T (03) 5989 2708 **F** (03) 5989 3017 **www**.portphillip.net **Open** 7 days 11–5
Winemaker Sandro Mosele **Est.** 1987 **Cases** 4000 **Vyds** 9.37 ha
Port Phillip Estate has been owned by Giorgio and Dianne Gjergja since 2000. The ability of the site (enhanced, it is true, by the skills of Sandro Mosele) to produce outstanding Syrah, Pinot Noir, Chardonnay, and very good Sauvignon Blanc, is something special. Whence climate change? Quite possibly the estate may have answers for decades to come. A futuristic, multimillion-dollar restaurant, cellar door and winery complex will be completed by 2010. Exports to the UK, Canada and Singapore.

ŶŶŶŶŶ **Mornington Peninsula Chardonnay 2007** In typical powerful and focused mode, the vineyard speaking as loudly as the maker; flavours of nectarine, white peach and grapefruit are all to be found, French oak acting as a projector of those flavours onto the palate screen. Diam. 13% alc. **Rating** 95 **To** 2015 $27
Mornington Peninsula Pinot Noir 2007 Bright crimson; has exceptional focus, intensity and clarity of line, the predominantly red fruit flavours swelling on the finish in peacock's tail fashion. Diam. 13.5% alc. **Rating** 95 **To** 2016 $37
Mornington Peninsula Sauvignon Blanc 2008 A wine with considerable depth of flavour; and likewise texture and complexity partially due to a barrel ferment component; the bouquet and palate alike are, however, ultimately built on perfectly ripened fruit. Screwcap. 13.5% alc. **Rating** 94 **To** 2012 $24
Quartier Mornington Peninsula Arneis 2007 The most expressive Arneis yet tasted, with notes of mandarin, ginger and grapefruit on the long and intense palate. Screwcap. 13.5% alc. **Rating** 94 **To** 2013 $25
Rimage Tete de Cuvee Mornington Peninsula Syrah 2007 Excellent crimson colour; an explosively fragrant bouquet with scented/perfumed red fruits; the spicy/savoury palate heads off in a direction of its own. Possibly picked a little too soon? Diam. 13.5% alc. **Rating** 94 **To** 2020 $42
Mornington Peninsula Shiraz 2006 Bright crimson; a sparkling fresh bouquet and palate with an abundance of red fruits, spice and pepper; while only medium-bodied, has great length and intensity. Diam. 13.5% alc. **Rating** 94 **To** 2020 $30

ŶŶŶŶŶ **Morillon Tete De Cuvee Mornington Peninsula Pinot Noir 2007** Bright, light crimson; a firm, quite severe style, with tangy/savoury fruit and a long finish. Will evolve. Diam. 13.5% alc. **Rating** 92 **To** 2017 $42
Salasso 2008 A fragrant bouquet, and a lissom palate, finishing spicy and dry. High-quality example of shiraz rose. Screwcap. 13.5% alc. **Rating** 90 **To** 2011 $21

Portsea Estate ★★★★

PO Box 3148, Bellevue Hill, NSW 2023 **Region** Mornington Peninsula
T (02) 9328 6359 **F** (02) 9326 1984 **www**.portseaestate.com **Open** Not
Winemaker Paringa Estate (Lindsay McCall) **Est.** 2000 **Cases** 700
Warwick Ross and sister (and silent partner) Caron Wilson-Hawley may be relative newcomers to the Mornington Peninsula (the first vintage was 2004), but they have had exceptional success with their Pinot Noir, the '05 winning top gold medal at the Ballarat Wine Show '07, and the '06 taking Champion Wine of the Show of the National Cool Climate Wine Show '07 (against all varietal comers). The vines are planted on calcareous sand and limestone (the chardonnay is in fact on the site of a 19th-century limestone quarry) only 700 m from the ocean. Warwick has been a very successful film producer and says 'I'm not sure if that makes me a filmmaker with a passion for wine, or a vigneron with a passion for film. Either way, I'm very happy with the collision of the two.'

YYYY Mornington Peninsula Pinot Noir 2007 Very rich and ripe with plenty of dark fruit on offer; the palate is full of sweet, dark fruit with a touch of spice and plenty of richness on the finish. Cork. 13.8% alc. **Rating** 89 **To** 2012 $32

Possums Vineyard

31 Thornber Street, Unley Park, SA 5061 (postal) **Region** McLaren Vale
T (08) 8272 3406 **F** (08) 8272 3406 **www.**possumswines.com.au **Open** Not
Winemaker Pieter Breugem **Est.** 2000 **Cases** 10 000 **Vyds** 60 ha
Possums Vineyard is owned by Dr John Possingham and Carol Summers. They have two vineyards in McLaren Vale, one at Blewitt Springs, the other at Willunga, covering shiraz (23.5 ha), cabernet sauvignon (17 ha), chardonnay (9 ha), viognier (2 ha), pinot gris (1.2 h), sauvignon blanc (1 ha) and malbec (0.7 ha). In 2007 they completed construction of a 500-tonne winery at Blewitt Springs and sell both bottled and bulk wine. Pieter Breugem, the winemaker, has come from South Africa via the US and Constellation Wines. Exports to the UK, Denmark, Germany and Hong Kong.

YYYYY McLaren Vale Shiraz 2006 Retains very good hue; while it has a harmonious and complex array of aromas and flavours, is at the elegant end of the McLaren Vale spectrum, and is all the better for that; has deceptive length. Screwcap. 14.5% alc. **Rating** 94 **To** 2019 $19.99

YYYYY McLaren Vale Shiraz 2007 A luscious, but not jammy, palate, with superfine tannins underpinning the blackberry fruit, dark chocolate and well-handled oak the finishing touches. Value. Screwcap. 14.5% alc. **Rating** 93 **To** 2022 $19.99
McLaren Vale Cabernet Sauvignon 2006 In contradistinction to the '07, the variety speaks louder than the region; most attractive blackcurrant and cassis fruit is supported by ripe tannins on the medium-bodied palate. Great value. Screwcap. 14.2% alc. **Rating** 93 **To** 2021 $19.99
Two in the Pouch McLaren Vale Shiraz Cabernet Sauvignon 2008 Good crimson; well-balanced and integrated fruit and oak; luscious flavours, with some confit fruit elements on the way through to the finish. Ludicrous price. Screwcap. 14.5% alc. **Rating** 90 **To** 2017 $6.50

YYYY Two in the Pouch McLaren Vale Chardonnay Viognier 2008 A highly aromatic bouquet, with the viognier definitely adding apricot nuances to the stone fruit of the chardonnay; fractionally hot on the finish. Incredible price. Screwcap. 13.5% alc. **Rating** 89 **To** 2012 $6.50
McLaren Vale Cabernet Sauvignon 2007 More regional than varietal, thanks to that strong dark chocolate component that runs right through the palate. Screwcap. 14.4% alc. **Rating** 89 **To** 2017 $19.99
Blewitt Springs Viognier 2008 Strangely, seems less effusive than it does in the chardonnay blend, although it does have some varietal character achieved without the downside of phenolics. Screwcap. 13.8% alc. **Rating** 88 **To** 2011 $12.50
Willunga Shiraz 2007 Not up to the quality of the 2006, hardly surprising; a mix of dark chocolate, herb, leaf and black fruits, and a slightly edgy finish. Screwcap. 14.5% alc. **Rating** 88 **To** 2012 $15.99

Postcode Wines

PO Box 769, Cessnock, NSW 2325 **Region** Various
T (02) 4998 7474 **F** (02) 4998 7974 **www.**postcodewines.com.au **Open** At The Boutique Wine Centre, Pokolbin
Winemaker Rhys Eather **Est.** 2004 **Cases** 1000
This is a new and separate venture for Rhys and Garth Eather (of Meerea Park) taking as its raison d'etre wines that clearly show their postcode by exhibiting true regional character. The initial releases were two Shirazs from the Hunter Valley [2320] with a Cabernet Sauvignon from Hilltops [2587], and with several white wines in the future mix.

ŸŸŸŸ **Pokolbin 2320 Reserve Shiraz 2005** Strongly earthy regional style, as befits the brand; positive short-term development. Screwcap. 14% alc. **Rating** 87 **To** 2013 $25

Hilltops 2587 Cabernet Sauvignon 2005 Mature, savoury/earthy overtones to light- to medium-bodied cabernet varietal fruit; easy-drinking style. Screwcap. 14% alc. **Rating** 87 **To** 2012 $20

Poverty Hill Wines ★★★★☆

PO Box 76, Springton, SA 5235 **Region** Eden Valley
T (08) 8568 2220 **www.**povertyhillwines.com.au **Open** Fri–Mon 10–5
Winemaker John Eckert **Est.** 2002 **Cases** 6000
I'm not sure whether there is a slight note of irony in the name, but Poverty Hill Wines brings together men who have had a long connection with the Eden Valley. Robert Buck owns a small vineyard on the ancient volcanic soils east of Springton, producing both Shiraz and Cabernet Sauvignon. Next is Stuart Woodman, who owns the vineyard with the riesling that produced glorious wines in the early 1990s, and also has high-quality, mature-vine cabernet sauvignon. Finally, there is John Eckert, who once worked at Saltram. He not only works as winemaker at Poverty Hill, but manages Rob Buck's vineyard and his own small block of young riesling in the highlands of Springton. Exports to the US, Hong Kong and NZ.

ŸŸŸŸŸ **Eden Valley Shiraz 2006** Good colour; a dense, tarry bouquet, with ample levels of dark fruit; the palate is rich and generous, and the structure cuts through with a chewy, savoury and bright acid finish; long and well balanced. Screwcap. 15% alc. **Rating** 94 **To** 2016 $30

Prancing Horse Estate ★★★★★

39 Paringa Road, Red Hill South, Vic 3937 **Region** Mornington Peninsula
T (03) 5989 2602 **F** (03) 9827 1231 **www.**prancinghorseestate.com **Open** By appt
Winemaker Sergio Carlei, Pascal Marchand **Est.** 1990 **Cases** 800 **Vyds** 4.5 ha
Anthony and Catherine Hancy acquired the Lavender Bay Vineyard in early 2002, renaming it the Prancing Horse Estate, and embarking on increasing the estate vineyards, with 2 ha each of chardonnay and pinot noir, and 0.5 ha of pinot gris. The vineyard moved to organic farming in '03, progressing to biodynamic in '07. They appointed Sergio Carlei as winemaker, and the following year became joint owners with Sergio in Carlei Wines. An additional property, 150 m west of the existing vineyard, has been purchased, and 2 ha of vines will be planted in the spring of '09. Exports to the UK, the US and Sweden.

ŸŸŸŸŸ **Mornington Peninsula Chardonnay 2007** Has barely moved since it was bottled; still very tight and compressed, with citrus and stone fruit components, oak and minerally acidity all locked in a tight embrace. Screwcap. 13% alc. **Rating** 94 **To** 2020 $50

Macedon Ranges Pinot Gris 2008 This truly is a gris style, with a strong nod to Alsace; cool-grown fruit and partial barrel ferment has given the wine unusually good texture and flavour in a pear/citrus spectrum. Screwcap. 12% alc. **Rating** 94 **To** 2012 $40

Mornington Peninsula Pinot Noir 2007 Deep colour; despite moderate alcohol, is from the big end of town, with great power and depth to the layered black fruits. Will be very long lived and improve further. Screwcap. 13% alc. **Rating** 94 **To** 2020 $60

Pressing Matters ★★★★★

PO Box 2119, Lower Sandy Bay Road, Tas 7005 **Region** Southern Tasmania
T 0439 022 988 **Open** Not
Winemaker Winemaking Tasmania (Julian Alcorso) **Est.** 2002 **Cases** NFP **Vyds** 6.7 ha
Greg Melick simultaneously wears more hats than most people manage in a lifetime. He is a top-level barrister (Senior Counsel), a Major General (thus the highest ranking officer in the

Australian Army Reserve) and has presided over a number of headline special commissions and enquiries into subjects as diverse as cricket match fixing allegations against Mark Waugh and others, to the Beaconsfield mine collapse. Yet, if asked, he would probably nominate wine as his major focus in life. Having built up an exceptional cellar of the great wines of Europe, he has turned his attention to grapegrowing and winemaking, planting riesling (2.9 ha) at his vineyard on Middle Tea Tree Road in the Coal River Valley. It is a perfect north-facing slope, and the early wines promise much for the future, the Mosel-style Rieslings jumping out of the box. Equally promising are the multiple blocks of pinot noir (2.9 ha) with an exceptional mix of Dijon and Australian clones.

ΨΨΨΨΨ **R139 Riesling 2008** Intense lime juice at Beerenauslese baumé; seduction on a stick; great balancing acidity. Trophy and gold medal Tas Wine Show '09. Screwcap. 9.2% alc. **Rating** 95 **To** 2014 $26
RO Riesling 2007 Fragrant and delicate, but quite piercing and surprisingly long; great potential. Gold medal Tas Wine Show '09. Screwcap. 9.4% alc. **Rating** 94 **To** 2016 $29
R69 Riesling 2008 A vibrant and intense wine, the substantial residual sugar (69 g per l) balanced by perfectly judged acidity. Gold medal Tas Wine Show '09. Screwcap. 9.1% alc. **Rating** 94 **To** 2014 $29

ΨΨΨΨ **RO Riesling 2008** A clean bouquet; ripe citrus flavours to a generous, early developing style. Screwcap. 9.2% alc. **Rating** 88 **To** 2014 $29

Preston Peak

31 Preston Peak Lane, Toowoomba, Qld 4352 **Region** Darling Downs
T (07) 4630 9499 **F** (07) 4630 9499 **www**.prestonpeak.com **Open** Wed–Sun 10–5
Winemaker Mark Ravenscroft, Mike Hayes, Peter Scudamore-Smith MW, Peter Stark (Contract) **Est.** 1994 **Cases** 5000
Dentist owners Ashley Smith and Kym Thumpkin have a substantial wine and tourism business. The large, modern cellar door accommodate functions of up to 150 people, and is used for weddings and other events. It is situated less than 10 mins drive from the Toowoomba city centre, with views of Table Top Mountain, the Lockyer Valley and the Darling Downs.

ΨΨΨΨΨ **Single Vineyard Reserve Shiraz 2006** Particularly well made; excellent mouthfeel, balance and length, the focus on the display of blackberry and plum fruit running through to the long finish. Screwcap. 14% alc. **Rating** 94 **To** 2020 $32

ΨΨΨΨΨ **Single Vineyard Reserve Verdelho 2007** A high-toned bouquet, with the small percentage of barrel ferment quite obvious, but less so on the vibrant palate, where fruit salad and lemon juice share the bill. Screwcap. 14.5% alc. **Rating** 90 **To** 2011 $32
Single Vineyard Reserve Cabernet Sauvignon 2005 Retains excellent hue; not particularly intense, but is well made and balanced; cassis fruit framed by an appropriate amount of oak and fine tannins. Screwcap. 14.7% alc. **Rating** 90 **To** 2013 $32

ΨΨΨΨ **Single Vineyard Syrah Viognier Mourvedre 2006** The 15% viognier (and 4% mourvedre) co-fermented was counterproductive; simply too much viognier gives a rather strange aroma and flavour to the wine, the mourvedre not restoring structure. Screwcap. 13.5% alc. **Rating** 88 **To** 2012 $32

Preveli Wines

Bessell Road, Rosa Brook, Margaret River, WA 6285 **Region** Margaret River
T (08) 9757 2374 **F** (08) 9757 2790 **www**.preveliwines.com.au **Open** At Prevelly General Store, 7 days 10–8
Winemaker Vasse River Wines (David Johnson) **Est.** 1998 **Cases** 5000 **Vyds** 7.5 ha
Andrew and Greg Home have turned a small business into a larger one, with 7.5 ha of vineyards at Rosabrook (supplemented by contracts with local growers), and winemaking

spread among a number of contract makers. The wines are of consistently impressive quality. The Prevelly General Store (owned by the Homes) is the main local outlet.

ŢŢŢŢŢ **Margaret River Chardonnay 2007** Elegant, very well-balanced and structured wine; stone fruit and melon; good oak; nothing out of place. Gold WA Wine Show '08. Screwcap. 13.5% alc. **Rating** 94 **To** 2013 $23.95

ŢŢŢŢŢ **Margaret River Pinot Noir 2007** Relatively light-bodied, and very much in a foresty/savoury/spicy spectrum, but has good length, and is not over-extracted. Screwcap. 14% alc. **Rating** 90 **To** 2012 $24.95

ŢŢŢŢ **Margaret River Semillon Sauvignon Blanc 2008** Bright straw-green; has crisp citrus fruit extending into grapefruit territory; lively acidity on the finish prolongs the length. Screwcap. 13% alc. **Rating** 89 **To** 2011 $18.95

Prime Premium Wines   NR

Lot 2, Rivers Lane, McLaren Vale, SA 5171 **Region** McLaren Vale
T (08) 8323 8297 **www**.primepremiumwine.com.au **Open** By appt
Winemaker Longwood Wines (Phil Christiansen) **Est.** 2002 **Cases** 200 **Vyds** 4.1 ha
This is the business of Warwick, Jenny and Robert Prime, who acquired a block on the fringe of McLaren Vale township first farmed by the Aldersey family in the mid-19th century. The philosophy in choosing the block worked on the principle that the early settlers had first choice of the best land. The Prime family believes they made the right decision, the production from the 3.4 ha of cabernet sauvignon, 0.5 ha of shiraz and 0.2 ha of grenache is contracted to Mollydooker Wines and finding its way to an enthusiastic market in the US. A very small amount of grapes are held back for the Prime Premium Wines label, and the quantity made will not exceed 300 to 400 cases per year.

Primo Estate   ★★★★★

McMurtie Road, McLaren Vale, SA 5171 **Region** McLaren Vale
T (08) 8323 6800 **F** (08) 8323 6888 **www**.primoestate.com.au **Open** 7 days 11–4
Winemaker Joseph Grilli, Daniel Zuzdo **Est.** 1979 **Cases** 30 000 **Vyds** 34 ha
One time Roseworthy dux Joe Grilli has always produced innovative and excellent wines. The biennial release of the Joseph Sparkling Red (in its tall Italian glass bottle) is eagerly awaited, the wine immediately selling out. Also unusual and highly regarded are the vintage-dated extra virgin olive oils. However, the core lies with the La Biondina, the Il Briccone Shiraz Sangiovese and the Joseph Cabernet Merlot. The business has expanded to take in both McLaren Vale and Clarendon, with plantings of colombard, shiraz, cabernet sauvignon, riesling, merlot, sauvignon blanc, chardonnay, pinot gris, nebbiolo and merlot. Exports to all major markets.

ŢŢŢŢŢ **Joseph Moda McLaren Vale Cabernet Sauvignon Merlot 2006** Strong colour; ripe but vibrant blackcurrant, mulberry and spice aromas and flavours; a medium-bodied palate that easily carries the alcohol, and has very good texture and structure. Cork. 15% alc. **Rating** 95 **To** 2014 $65
Joseph Sparkling Red NV Obvious age in colour; very complex leather/spice/tar/licorice aromas; mouthfilling flavours; quite unique; some oak inevitably part of the picture; perfect dosage. Cork. 13.5% alc. **Rating** 95 **To** 2010 $65
Joseph La Magia Botrytis Riesling Traminer 2008 A super-elegant wine, retaining dominant riesling varietal character; the balance between sweetness and acidity cannot be faulted. Continues a long tradition. (The 15% traminer is from Coonawarra.) Screwcap. 11% alc. **Rating** 94 **To** 2010 $25

ŢŢŢŢŢ **Joseph McLaren Vale Nebbiolo 2006** Light red, some brown; achieves as much as can be expected for this perverse variety, its rose petal aromas lulling you into a false sense of security before the savoury tannin attack of the palate. Cork. 14% alc. **Rating** 92 **To** 2013 $75

Joseph Pinot Grigio d'Elena 2008 A warm allspice and ripe pear bouquet leads into a mid-palate with similar characters, moving into a minerally finish. Screwcap. 14% alc. **Rating** 91 **To** 2010 $25

La Biondina Colombard Sauvignon Blanc 2008 Delicious, upfront wine busting with aroma and flavour; juicy tropical fruits and perfect acidity; never better than right now. Screwcap. 12% alc. **Rating** 90 **To** 2008 $15

Shale Stone McLaren Vale Shiraz 2006 Deep colour; mocha and blackberry fruit bouquet with spicy oak aplenty; a little hot on the palate, the weight is undeniable; loaded with sweet fruit and a light chocolate edge. Twin top. 14.5% alc. **Rating** 90 **To** 2016 $32

Zamberlan McLaren Vale Cabernet Sauvignon Sangiovese 2006 Cassis and a distinct bramble/undergrowth note to the bouquet; very warm on the palate, with lots of juicy black fruit cleaned up by the pronounced acidity. Screwcap. 14.5% alc. **Rating** 90 **To** 2014 $28

▼▼▼▼ **Il Briccone McLaren Vale Shiraz Sangiovese 2007** Pronounced cherry and blue fruit bouquet; quite a challenging high acid palate, but the fruit works well; definitely an Italian influence shows through in this wine. Screwcap. 14% alc. **Rating** 89 **To** 2014 $22

Merlesco McLaren Vale Merlot 2008 Ripe and plummy bouquet, with blue fruits and a little spice; the palate is fleshy, with a little leafy edge to the fruit. 13.5% alc. Screwcap. **Rating** 88 **To** 2012 $15

Prince Albert   ★★★★☆

100 Lemins Road, Waurn Ponds, Vic 3216 **Region** Geelong
T (03) 5241 8091 **F** (03) 5241 8091 **Open** By appt
Winemaker Bruce Hyett, Fiona Purnell **Est.** 1975 **Cases** 400 **Vyds** 2 ha
In 2007 Dr David Yates, with a background based on a degree in chemistry, purchased the pinot noir–only Prince Albert vineyard from founder Bruce Hyett. David's plans are to spend 6–12 months running the vineyard and winery exactly as it has been, with advice from Bruce on winemaking and Steve Jones in the vineyard. So far as the latter is concerned, Yates is firmly committed to retaining the certified organic status for Prince Albert, and at this juncture sees no reason to change the style of the wine, which he has always loved. Exports to the UK.

▼▼▼▼▼ **Geelong Pinot Noir 2007** Strong colour; has the depth and texture that truly reflects an exceptional site; layers of dark berry fruits and supporting tannins. The best for many years. Screwcap. 14% alc. **Rating** 93 **To** 2015 $30

Prince Hill Wines   ★★★

1220 Sydney Road, Mudgee, NSW 2850 **Region** Mudgee
T (02) 6373 1245 **www.**princehillwines.com **Open** Mon–Sat 9–5, Sun 10–4
Winemaker Michelle Heagney **Est.** 1993 **Cases** 35 000 **Vyds** 25.5 ha
Prince Hill Wines has become the new name and identity for Simon Gilbert Wines. It is now associated with the Watson Wine Group, which has the difficult task of returning the business to profit. One might have thought the large, well-designed winery was well placed to take grapes from the various regions along the western side of the Great Dividing Range of NSW, but observers have questioned whether this can become a reality. In the meantime, the estate plantings of shiraz, merlot, petit verdot, cabernet sauvignon, zinfandel and sangiovese, all in reasonably significant amounts, provide the estate-grown wines. Exports to the UK, the US, Canada, Sweden, Dubai, China and NZ.

▼▼▼▼ **Card Collection Chardonnay 2007** Crisp pear and melon fruit bouquet; clean and precise, with generous levels of fruit. Screwcap. 13.5% alc. **Rating** 88 **To** 2012 $19.95

Prince of Orange

'Cimbria', The Escort Way, Borenore, NSW 2800 **Region** Orange
T (02) 6365 2396 **F** (02) 6365 2396 **www**.princeoforangewines.com.au **Open** Sat &
long w'ends 10–5, or by appt
Winemaker Monarch Winemaking Services **Est.** 1996 **Cases** 3000
Harald and Coral Brodersen purchased the 40-ha Cimbria property in 1990, and planted
3 ha of sauvignon blanc and 2 ha of cabernet sauvignon in '96, followed by more recent and
smaller plantings of merlot, viognier, shiraz and semillon. The name and label design were
inspired by the link between Thomas Livingstone Mitchell, Surveyor-General of NSW, who
served in the British Army during the Peninsular Wars against Napoleon alongside Willem,
Prince of Orange, who was aide-de-camp to the Duke of Wellington. It was Mitchell who
named the town Orange in honour of his friend, who had by then been crowned King
Willem II of The Netherlands.

ŶŶŶŶ   **Sauvignon Blanc 2008** Some complexity and tropical fruit on the bouquet;
zesty and fresh, with vibrant citrus fruit cleaning up the finish. Screwcap. 11.7% alc.
Rating 89 **To** 2012 $18
Rose 2008 Aromatic red fruits on the bouquet, with a touch of spice; quite dry
and focused on the palate. Screwcap. 13.3% alc. **Rating** 87 **To** 2011 $18

Principia

139 Main Creek Road, Red Hill, Vic 3937 (postal) **Region** Mornington Peninsula
T (03) 5931 0010 **www**.principiawines.com.au **Open** Not
Winemaker Darrin Gaffy **Est.** 1995 **Cases** 450 **Vyds** 3.5 ha
Darren and Rebecca Gaffy spent their honeymoon in SA, and awakened their love of wine. In
due course they gravitated to Burgundy, and began the search in Australia for a suitable cool-
climate site to grow pinot noir and chardonnay. In 1995 they began to develop their vineyard,
planting pinot noir and chardonnay. Darren continues to work full-time as a toolmaker (and
in the vineyard on weekends and holidays); while Rebecca's career as a nurse took second
place to the Bachelor of Applied Science (Wine Science) course at CSU, graduating in 2002.
Along the way she worked at Red Hill Estate, Bass Phillip, Virgin Hills and Tuck's Ridge, and
as winemaker at Massoni Homes. A cellar door is planned.

ŶŶŶŶŶ   **Mornington Peninsula Pinot Noir 2007** Showing some development, the
bouquet with ripe cherry, plum, spice and a slight herbal note; elegantly structured
with a mere suggestion of oak, the texture is the key with good persistence, and a
velvet-like quality to conclude. Diam. 13.6% alc. **Rating** 94 **To** 2013 $36

Printhie Wines

489 Yuranigh Road, Molong, NSW 2866 **Region** Orange
T (02) 6366 8422 **F** (02) 6366 9328 **www**.printhiewines.com.au **Open** Mon–Sat 10–4
Winemaker Drew Tuckwell **Est.** 1996 **Cases** 25 000 **Vyds** 33 ha
Jim and Ruth Swift have planted shiraz, cabernet sauvignon, merlot, pinot gris and viognier,
and built the largest winery in the region, with sons Dave and Ed now assuming much of
the business responsibility. Winemaking passed from Robert Black to Drew Tuckwell in late
2007, having achieved exceptional results for the multiple trophy-winning red wines from
'06. Notwithstanding its estate vineyards, Printhie also purchases grapes from growers in the
Orange region. The wines are modestly priced, and will gain further weight as the vines age.
Printhie can fairly claim to be the premier winery in the Orange region. Exports to the US
and Denmark.

ŶŶŶŶŶ   **Orange Chardonnay 2008** Fragrant and elegant, its cool-climate characters
nailed to the masthead; white peach and nectarine fruit is supported by subtle
French oak; good line and length. Screwcap. 13% alc. **Rating** 94 **To** 2016 $17
Orange Shiraz 2008 Deep crimson; an exceptionally rich, but not overripe,
wine with an array of blackberry, plum and spice aromas and flavours; excellent
control of oak and tannins. Screwcap. 14.5% alc. **Rating** 94 **To** 2023 $17

ŢŢŢŢ♀ **Mount Canobolas Collection Orange Chardonnay 2008** Cool, white nectarine bouquet; tight lemon fruit palate, with a touch of mineral complexity; good line and length. Screwcap. 13.5% alc. **Rating** 91 **To** 2013 $32
Orange Sauvignon Blanc 2008 A potent but distinctly sweaty/reduced bouquet, a pity given the intensity and impact of the tangy palate; points a matter of personal taste. Screwcap. 12.5% alc. **Rating** 90 **To** 2011 $17
Orange Pinot Gris 2008 Has well above-average depth to its flavour and texture; gently honeyed fruit has been augmented by a touch of barrel ferment and lees contact. Sophisticated winemaking. Screwcap. 13.5% alc. **Rating** 90 **To** 2010 $17
Mount Canobolas Collection Orange Shiraz Viognier 2008 Bright blueberry bouquet with a touch of violet and spice; medium-bodied with citrus acidity, and fine tannin to conclude; evenly balanced. Screwcap. 14% alc. **Rating** 90 **To** 2014 $32
Orange Cabernet Sauvignon 2008 A high-flavoured wine, with cassis, raspberry and blackcurrant aromas and flavours; while correct, it needs to loosen up and soften with time in bottle. Screwcap. 14% alc. **Rating** 90 **To** 2016 $17

ŢŢŢŢ **Orange Riesling 2008** Talc. and orange blossom bouquet, with a splash of spice; quite textural on the palate, with good acidity on the finish. Screwcap. 12.5% alc. **Rating** 89 **To** 2015 $24
Mount Canobolas Collection Orange Shiraz Cabernet 2008 Pronounced orange citrus bouquet with cranberry fruit in support; light- to medium-bodied with a touch of sage. Screwcap. 14.5% alc. **Rating** 89 **To** 2013 $26
Orange Shiraz Cabernet 2007 Bright colour; effusive aromas of cassis and blackcurrant promise more than the light-bodied palate delivers, although the flavours are attractive enough. Screwcap. 13.5% alc. **Rating** 89 **To** 2013 $17
Orange Merlot 2008 Has fragrant cassis/red fruit aromas, the light- to medium-bodied palate following down the same track, with just a touch of savoury/black olive fruit on the finish. Screwcap. 14% alc. **Rating** 89 **To** 2014 $17
Orange Merlot 2007 Light- to medium-bodied; clear-cut varietal character, with notes of black olive through to mint; problems lie with the clone(s) of merlot used in Australia. Screwcap. 13.5% alc. **Rating** 88 **To** 2012 $17

Provenance Wines   ★★★★☆

870 Steiglitz Road, Sutherlands Creek, Vic 3331 **Region** Geelong
T (03) 5281 2230 **F** (03) 5281 2205 **www**.provenancewines.com.au **Open** By appt
Winemaker Scott Ireland, Kirilly Gordon, Sam Vogel **Est.** 1995 **Cases** 2000
Scott Ireland and partner Jen Lilburn established Provenance Wines in 1997 as a natural extension of Scott's years of winemaking experience, both here and abroad. Located in the Moorabool Valley, the winery team of Scott, Kirilly Gordon and Sam Vogel focus on the classics in a cool-climate sense – Pinot Gris, Chardonnay, Pinot Noir in particular, as well as Shiraz. Fruit is sourced both locally within the Geelong region and further afield (when the fruit warrants selection). They are also major players in contract making for the Geelong region. Exports to the UK.

ŢŢŢŢŢ **Geelong Pinot Noir 2007** Bright, light crimson; elegant pinot, with delicious red fruit aromas, the palate fine and precise, the texture and balance perfect; outstanding length and aftertaste. Screwcap. 13.5% alc. **Rating** 96 **To** 2015 $29

ŢŢŢŢ♀ **Pinot Gris 2008** Strong bruised pear and apple aromas feed through into the palate, which has good length and acidity; gris or grigio? Screwcap. 13.5% alc. **Rating** 90 **To** 2011 $27

Providence Vineyards   ★★★★☆

236 Lalla Road, Lalla, Tas 7267 **Region** Northern Tasmania
T (03) 6395 1290 **F** (03) 6395 2088 **www**.providence.com.au **Open** 7 days 10–5
Winemaker Frogmore Creek (Alain Rousseau), Bass Fine Wines (Guy Wagner) **Est.** 1956
Cases 750 **Vyds** 2.6 ha

Providence incorporates the pioneer vineyard of Frenchman Jean Miguet, now owned by the Bryce family, who purchased it in 1980. The original 1.3-ha vineyard has been doubled, and unsuitable grenache and cabernet (from the original plantings) have been grafted over to chardonnay, pinot noir and riesling. Miguet called the vineyard 'La Provence', reminding him of the part of France he came from, but after 40 years the French authorities forced a name change. The cellar door offers 70 different Tasmanian wines.

ŸŸŸŸŸ **Black Reserve Pinot Noir 2008** Good colour; a dark-fruited, spicy bouquet leads into an intense and long palate, with distinct savoury/foresty nuances to the fruit core. Screwcap. 13.5% alc. **Rating** 94 **To** 2015 $38

ŸŸŸŸŸ **Monet Riesling 2008** Has the intensity that Tasmania seems to effortlessly achieve, leaving the mouth fresh and thirsting for more, the acidity masked by the luscious fruit and perhaps a gram or two of residual sugar. Screwcap. 12.2% alc. **Rating** 93 **To** 2018 $19
Cecile Pinot Rose 2008 Seriously good pinot rose, dry and spicy; strawberry/cherry fruit and a long palate. Screwcap. 13% alc. **Rating** 91 **To** 2010 $19.50

Puddleduck Vineyard

992 Richmond Road, Richmond, Tas 7025 **Region** Southern Tasmania
T (03) 6260 2301 **www**.puddleduckvineyard.com.au **Open** 7 days 10–5
Winemaker Frogmore Creek **Est.** 1997 **Cases** 1500 **Vyds** 3.5 ha
After working the majority of their adult lives at vineyards in southern Tasmania, Darren and Jackie Brown bought land in 1996 with the dream of one day having their own label and cellar door. The dream is now reality, with the vineyard planted to pinot noir, riesling, chardonnay and sauvignon blanc, and the next step is a small cheesery making cheese from their small goat herd to complement the wines, which are sold exclusively through the cellar door.

ŸŸŸŸ **Rose 2008** Bright colour; lively, tangy and citrussy characters give the wine thrust and drive; dry finish. Screwcap. 11.8% alc. **Rating** 89 **To** 2010 $26
Pinot Noir 2007 Has an abundance of ripe, dark fruits on bouquet and palate; very different style to the '06; flavour rather than finesse. Screwcap. 13.5% alc. **Rating** 89 **To** 2013 $32
Cabernet Sauvignon 2007 A firm wine, with blackcurrant fruit, but persistent tannins threaten its future. Screwcap. 13.5% alc. **Rating** 88 **To** 2016 $38

Punch

2130 Kinglake Road, St Andrews, Vic 3761 (postal) **Region** Yarra Valley
T (03) 9710 1155 **F** (03) 9710 1369 **www**.punched.com.au **Open** Not
Winemaker James Lance **Est.** 2004 **Cases** 315 **Vyds** 3.45 ha
In the wake of Graeme Rathbone taking over the brand (but not the real estate) of Diamond Valley, the Lances' son James and his wife Claire leased the vineyard and winery from David and Catherine Lance, including the 0.25-ha block of close-planted pinot noir. In all, Punch has 2.25 ha of pinot noir (including the close planted), 0.8 ha of chardonnay and 0.4 ha of cabernet sauvignon.

ŸŸŸŸŸ **Lance's Vineyard Close Planted Yarra Valley Pinot Noir 2006** A veritable cornucopia of aromas; damson plum, dark cherry, game, earth, Asian spices and a lick of oak; the palate truly opens like a peacock's tail, with red fruit on entry, followed by silky texture, some mineral components and again a touch of game and forest floor, all balanced by nerve and drive from the citrussy acidity. Screwcap. 13.5% alc. **Rating** 96 **To** 2015 $80
Lance's Vineyard Yarra Valley Chardonnay 2007 Vibrant green hue; quite a savoury bouquet, with some leesy complexity, white pear and a touch of peach; the palate is rich on entry, with good texture and very fine acidity to draw out the toasty finish. Screwcap. 13.5% alc. **Rating** 95 **To** 2015 $40

Lance's Vineyard Yarra Valley Pinot Noir 2007 Bright colour; highly aromatic bouquet, with an array of red and dark fruits and some spice; super fresh acidity and a vibrant core of fruit are supported handsomely by a firm and slightly savoury finish; will reward cellaring. Screwcap. 13% alc. **Rating** 94 **To** 2016 $40

♀♀♀♀♀ **Lance's Vineyard Yarra Valley Pinot Noir 2006** Quite a pungent bouquet, with roast meat, dried herbs and ripe plum; pronounced acidity gives the wine drive, and the style is full throttle and quite challenging; not classic varietal, but certainly classic Lance. Screwcap. 12.5% alc. **Rating** 93 **To** 2014 $40

Punt Road

10 St Huberts Road, Coldstream, Vic 3770 **Region** Yarra Valley
T (03) 9739 0666 **F** (03) 9739 0633 **www**.puntroadwines.com.au **Open** 7 days 10–5
Winemaker Kate Goodman **Est.** 2000 **Cases** 15 000 **Vyds** 75 ha
Commencing in 2007, Punt Road began to change the focus of its business, a move triggered by the Napoleone family acquiring full ownership of the winery. The annual crush has decreased by two-thirds to 1200 tonnes, and the amount of contract winemaking significantly curtailed. The emphasis is now on wines produced from vines owned by the Napoleone family; this has resulted in the introduction of the Airlie Bank range, a sub-$20 Yarra Valley range made in a fruit-driven, lightly-oaked style. While these plans will stay in place for the foreseeable future, the '07 vintage was frost-ravaged, and '09 significantly affected by smoke taint. Exports to the UK, the US and other major markets.

♀♀♀♀♀ **Botrytis Semillon 2007** Glowing gold; a complex bouquet, with notes of cumquat, cinnamon and nutmeg; with the advent of the new, low-alcohol style for botrytis semillon; has delicacy. Screwcap. 10% alc. **Rating** 94 **To** 2014 $32

♀♀♀♀♀ **Airlie Bank Yarra Valley Shiraz Viognier 2007** Impressive at the price; highly aromatic and fragrant, the co-fermented viognier pitched at just the right level; a come-hither style. Screwcap. 13.5% alc. **Rating** 91 **To** 2012 $19
Airlie Bank Yarra Valley Sauvignon Blanc 2008 Interesting style, the touch of barrel fermentation adding complexity to both the bouquet and palate of a wine in a grassy, citrussy style; fresh and cleansing. Screwcap. 12.5% alc. **Rating** 90 **To** 2012 $19
Airlie Bank Yarra Valley Chardonnay 2007 Lively and fresh nectarine and melon fruit, with the length of palate typical of good Yarra wine, the oak influence perceptible but minimal. Screwcap. 13% alc. **Rating** 90 **To** 2014 $19
Yarra Valley Cabernet Sauvignon 2006 As usual with Punt Road, a well-made, medium-bodied wine with all the components in balance; good length and finish to the cool-grown cabernet fruit flavours. Screwcap. 14% alc. **Rating** 90 **To** 2016 $25

♀♀♀♀ **Yarra Valley Chardonnay 2007** Melon, stone fruit and citrus fruit is given complexity by subtle barrel ferment, which introduces some nutty/creamy notes. Screwcap. 13.5% alc. **Rating** 89 **To** 2014 $23
Yarra Valley Pinot Gris 2008 Clearly defined varietal character with pear, musk and honeysuckle all present, pear dominant; achieves flavour without obvious sweetness. Screwcap. 13.5% alc. **Rating** 89 **To** 2010 $23
Yarra Valley Shiraz 2006 Supple, smooth, light- to medium-bodied shiraz; carefully calibrated oak and tannin inputs to the spicy medium-bodied palate with its plum and black cherry fruit. Screwcap. 14% alc. **Rating** 89 **To** 2015 $25
Airlie Bank Yarra Valley Pinot Noir 2007 Light, but bright, hue; savoury/foresty notes to the light plum fruit; not much depth. Screwcap. 13% alc. **Rating** 87 **To** 2011 $19
Airlie Bank Yarra Valley Cabernet Sauvignon Merlot 2006 Quite fragrant, and proclaims the cool climate from start to finish; a savoury/foresty/olivaceous style. Screwcap. 14% alc. **Rating** 87 **To** 2012 $19

Pycnantha Hill Estate ★★★★

Benbournie Road, Clare, SA 5453 (postal) **Region** Clare Valley
T (08) 8842 2137 **F** (08) 8842 2137 **www**.pycnanthahill.com.au **Open** Not
Winemaker Jim Howarth **Est.** 1997 **Cases** 800 **Vyds** 2.4 ha
The Howarth family progressively established the vineyard from 1987, and made its first
commercial vintage in '97. *Acacia pycnantha* is the botanical name for the golden wattle that
grows wild over the hills of the Howarth farm, and they say it was 'a natural choice to name
our vineyards Pycnantha Hill'. I am not too sure that marketing gurus would agree, but there
we go.

♟♟♟♟♟ **Clare Valley Shiraz 2006** A medium- to full-bodied wine; an abundance of
black fruits and dark chocolate, supported by generous, but not excessive, tannins
and oak; a reflection of the good vintage. Screwcap. **Rating** 90 **To** 2016 $18

Pyramid Hill Wines ★★★★

194 Martindale Road, Denman, NSW 2328 **Region** Upper Hunter Valley
T (02) 6547 2755 **F** (02) 6547 2735 **www**.pyramidhillwines.com **Open** By appt
Winemaker First Creek Winemaking Services **Est.** 2002 **Cases** 5000 **Vyds** 72 ha
Pyramid Hill is a partnership between the Adler and Hilder families. Richard Hilder is a
veteran viticulturist who oversaw the establishment of many of the Rosemount vineyards.
Nicholas Adler and Caroline Sherwood made their mark in the international film industry
before moving to Pyramid Hill in 1997. The vineyard (chardonnay, semillon, shiraz, verdelho
and merlot) has a computer-controlled irrigation system connected to a network of radio-
linked weather and soil moisture sensors that constantly relay data detailing the amount of
available moisture at different soil depths to a central computer, thus avoiding excess irrigation
and preventing stress. Most of the grapes are sold, but part has been vinified, with cautious
expansion planned. Exports to the UK, Canada, Japan and Singapore.

Pyren Vineyard ★★★☆

22 Errard Street North, Ballarat, Vic 3350 (postal) **Region** Pyrenees
T (03) 5467 2352 **F** (03) 5021 0804 **www**.pyrenvineyard.com **Open** By appt
Winemaker Mount Avoca Winery, Pyrenees Ridge **Est.** 1999 **Cases** 4500 **Vyds** 34 ha
Martin and Kevyn Joy have planted 25 ha of shiraz, 3 ha each of cabernet sauvignon and
viognier, 1 ha of durif and 2 ha comprising cabernet franc, malbec and petit verdot on the
slopes of the Warrenmang Valley near Moonambel. Yield is restricted to between 1.5 and
2.5 tonnes per acre.

♟♟♟♟♟ **Block E Pyrenees Shiraz 2007** Medium- to full-bodied, with blackberry, plum
and spice on the lively, almost juicy, mid-palate, before the tannins on the finish
introduce a more savoury note. Screwcap. 14.2% alc. **Rating** 91 **To** 2017 $27

♟♟♟♟ **Broken Quartz Pyrenees Shiraz 2007** Dark hue; a powerful, ripe wine with
black fruits, dark chocolate and earthy notes in a very different style to Block E.
Screwcap. 14% alc. **Rating** 89 **To** 2017 $17
Broken Quartz Pyrenees Cabernet Sauvignon 2007 Bright colour; light-
to medium-bodied cabernet, with cassis-accented fruit to the fore, some spicy oak
and fine tannins on the finish. Screwcap. 13.7% alc. **Rating** 89 **To** 2014 $17

Pyrenees Ridge Winery ★★★★☆

532 Caralulup Road, Lamplough via Avoca, Vic 3467 **Region** Pyrenees
T (03) 5465 3320 **www**.pyreneesridge.com.au **Open** Thurs–Mon & public hols 10–5
Winemaker Graeme Jukes **Est.** 1998 **Cases** 4000 **Vyds** 15.3 ha
Notwithstanding the quite extensive winemaking experience (and formal training) of Graeme
Jukes, this started life as small-scale winemaking in the raw version of the French garagiste
approach. Graeme and his wife Sally-Ann now have 10 ha of shiraz, 3 ha cabernet sauvignon,
with lesser amounts of chardonnay, merlot and a hatful of viognier. There are plans to plant

a further 3–4 ha of shiraz. After a fire in Sept 2007 destroyed the winery and cellar door, the facility has been rebuilt, bigger and better than before. Exports to Canada, Germany, Singapore, Hong Kong, China and Japan.

ỢỢỢỢỢ **Reserve Shiraz 2007** Good colour; blueberry and plenty of spice, with an underpinning of savoury ironstone; the tannins are firm and dry, and there is plenty of rich, ripe and dense dark fruit to soak them up. Time will reward. Cork. 14.5% alc. **Rating** 94 **To** 2016 $50

ỢỢỢỢỢ **Shiraz 2007** Vibrant purple colour; intense purple and black fruit bouquet and quite a bit of oak; sweet-fruited and vibrant on entry, the finish is oaky and distinctly tannic; will need some time to reach its full potential. Cork. 14.2% alc. **Rating** 92 **To** 2016 $28

Quarisa Wines ★★★★

743 Slopes Road, Tharbogang, NSW 2680 (postal) **Region** Various
T (02) 6963 6222 **F** (02) 6963 6473 **www**.quarisa.com.au **Open** Not
Winemaker John Quarisa **Est.** 2005 **Cases** 20 000
Quarisa Wines was established by John and Josephine Quarisa (plus their three young children). John has had a distinguished career as a winemaker spanning 22 years, working for some of Australia's largest wineries including McWilliam's, Casella and Nugan Estate. He was also chiefly responsible for winning the Jimmy Watson Trophy in 2004 (Melbourne) and the Stodart Trophy (Adelaide). In a busman's holiday venture, they have set up a small family business using grapes from various parts of Australia and made in leased space. After a slightly uncertain start, the current releases offer exemplary value for money, and it is no surprise that leading national distributor, Domaine Wine Shippers, has taken on the brand. Exports to the UK, Canada, Sweden, Indonesia, Israel, China and NZ.

ỢỢỢỢỢ **Treasures McLaren Vale Shiraz Viognier 2007** The viognier, whether co-fermented or not, makes a major difference to the varietal shiraz; this is much more juicy and vibrant, with red fruits lining up alongside the black fruit nuances. Very good value. Screwcap. 14.5% alc. **Rating** 91 **To** 2015 $14.99
Treasures Barossa Valley Shiraz 2006 Well made, fully reflecting the excellent vintage and over-delivering on price; blackberry fruit is supported by fine tannins on the medium-bodied palate, oak in restraint. Value. Screwcap. 14.5% alc. **Rating** 90 **To** 2015 $14.99

ỢỢỢỢ **Johnny Q Adelaide Hills Semillon Sauvignon Blanc 2008** May be on the delicate side, but it cleverly captures the essence of the Adelaide Hills flavours of these varieties, and is a bargain for those who enjoy a touch of passionfruit with a drizzle of lemon juice. Screwcap. 13.5% alc. **Rating** 89 **To** 2011 $11.99
Johnny Q Shiraz 2008 Good colour; has considerable fruit density, with plum and blackberry supported by positive, ripe and balanced tannins. Very good value. Screwcap. 14.5% alc. **Rating** 89 **To** 2013 $11.99
Treasures Langhorne Creek Shiraz 2006 Good hue; savoury/briary/chocolatey aromas are reminiscent of McLaren Vale, and the palate provides more of the same. Screwcap. 14.5% alc. **Rating** 89 **To** 2014 $14.99

Quattro Mano ★★★★★

PO Box 189, Hahndorf, SA 5245 **Region** Barossa Valley
T 0439 677 001 **F** (08) 8388 1736 **www**.quattromano.com.au **Open** Not
Winemaker Anthony Carapetis, Christopher Taylor, Philippe Morin **Est.** 2006 **Cases** 600
Vyds 1 ha
Anthony Carapetis, Philippe Morin and Chris Taylor have a collective experience of over 50 years working in various facets of the wine industry, Morin as a leading sommelier for 25 years, and presently as Director of French Oak Cooperage, Carapetis and Taylor as long-serving winemakers. The dream of Quattro Mano began in the mid-1990s, but only became a reality in '06. Their intention is to develop a small range of wines including Tempranillo and

Mourvedre, as well as a limited number of other, less common, red and white grape varieties sourced from whatever regions provide the best opportunities. They have made an impressive debut with their first Tempranillo from Lyndoch in the southern Barossa.

🍷🍷🍷🍷🍷 **La Reto Barossa Valley Tempranillo 2006** Strong colour; has more density and structure than most Australian tempranillos, and will undoubtedly repay prolonged cellaring; the flavours are of spiced fruits, ranging from blackcurrant to plum. Diam. 14.5% alc. **Rating** 94 **To** 2020 **$28**

Quealy ★★★★☆

Merricks General Store, 3458-3460 Frankston-Flinders Road, Merricks, Vic 3916
Region Mornington Peninsula
T (03) 5989 8088 **www**.quealy.com.au **Open** 7 days 9–5
Winemaker Kathleen Quealy **Est.** 1982 **Cases** 5000 **Vyds** 8 ha
Kathleen Quealy and husband Kevin McCarthy lost no time after their ties with T'Gallant (purchased from them by Foster's in 2003) were finally severed. As they were fully entitled to do, they already had their ducks set up in a row, and in short order acquired Balnarring Estate winery (being significantly upgraded) and leased Earl's Ridge Vineyard near Flinders. In a move reminiscent of Janice McDonald at Stella Bella/Suckfizzle in the Margaret River, they launched their business with Pobblebonk (a white blend) and Rageous (a red blend), plus a Pinot Noir and a Pinot Gris with a passing nod to convention. The estate plantings are 2 ha each of pinot noir, tocai friulano and pinot gris, and 1 ha each of chardonnay and muscat giallo. Kathleen (with five children) is a human dynamo; this is a business sure to succeed.

🍷🍷🍷🍷🍷 **Earls Ridge Vineyard Pinot Noir 2007** Great colour; a precise evocation of pinot, with pure cherry and plum fruit without the distraction of obvious oak; outstanding balance and line. Screwcap. 14% alc. **Rating** 94 **To** 2013 **$35**

🍷🍷🍷🍷🍷 **Seventeen Rows Pinot Noir 2007** Extraordinary crimson-purple Jan '08; the palate reflects the depth of the colour, with awesome power and intensity to its black cherry and stewed plum fruit; needs years to relax; from a block planted in 1982. Screwcap. 13.7% alc. **Rating** 93 **To** 2020 **$50**
Senza Nome 2008 A fragrant, perfumed wine, with a savoury quality that relies on texture more than all-out fruit power; light-bodied with great acidity and focus on the finish. Screwcap. 11.3% alc. **Rating** 92 **To** 2014 **$20**
Rageous 2007 Bright, light crimson; a fresh, lively, crisp red that avoids any green/herbal notes; seems to be designed for early, light-hearted consumption, the price not so much. Sangiovese/Shiraz/Pinot Noir. Screwcap. 13.5% alc. **Rating** 91 **To** 2012 **$35**
Pobblebonk 2008 A crisp, crunchy structure is filled out by ripe apple, pear and stone fruit flavours; has good length and persistence. Screwcap. 12.5% alc. **Rating** 91 **To** 2012 **$25**
Independence Earls Ridge Vineyard Pinot Gris 2008 A typically full-flavoured wine from the long-term mistress of the variety, ranging from apple to pear to citrus to spice. Screwcap. 13.5% alc. **Rating** 90 **To** 2010 **$28**

Radford Wines ★★★★★

RSD 355, Eden Valley, SA 5235 (postal) **Region** Eden Valley
T (08) 8565 3256 **F** (08) 8565 3244 **www**.radfordwines.com **Open** Not
Winemaker Gill Radford, Ben Radford **Est.** 2003 **Cases** 900 **Vyds** 4 ha
I first met Ben Radford when he was working as a head winemaker at the Longridge/ Winecorp group in Stellenbosch, South Africa. A bevy of international journalists grilled Ben, a French winemaker and a South African about the wines they were producing for the group. The others refused to admit there were any shortcomings in the wines they had made (there were), while Ben took the opposite tack, criticising his own wines even though they were clearly the best. He and wife Gill are now the proud owners of a vineyard in the Eden Valley, with 1.2 ha of riesling planted in 1930, another 1.1 ha planted in '70, and 1.7 ha of shiraz planted in 2000. Following Ben's appointment as winemaker at Rockford in '07,

executive winemaking responsibilities are now Gill's. Exports to the UK, the US, Denmark and South Africa.

ΨΨΨΨΨ Eden Valley Riesling 2008 The floral aromas have a background of stony nuances; the palate is disciplined and taut, with lemony acidity on the long finish; complex making including nine months on lees, small portion barrel ferment. Cries out for time. Screwcap. 12.5% alc. **Rating** 94 **To** 2018 $23
Eden Valley Riesling 2007 A precise reflection of Eden Valley terroir on both bouquet and palate, with lime juice, mineral and apple notes all interwoven on a long, balanced palate. Screwcap. 11.5% alc. **Rating** 94 **To** 2020 $22

ΨΨΨΨΨ Eden Valley Shiraz 2006 Bright colour; touch of reduction, with a savoury dark array of fruit; medium-bodied, dry and with a mineral quality to the palate; a firm and long finish. Screwcap. 14.5% alc. **Rating** 93 **To** 2018 $38

Ralph Fowler Wines   ★★★☆

Limestone Coast Road, Mount Benson, SA 5275 **Region** Mount Benson
T (08) 8768 5000 **F** (08) 8768 5008 **www.**ralphfowlerwines.com.au **Open** 7 days 10–4
Winemaker Ralph Fowler **Est.** 1999 **Cases** 5000 **Vyds** 5.94 ha
Established in 1999 by the Fowler family, headed by well-known winemaker Ralph Fowler, with wife Deborah and children Sarah (Squires) and James all involved in the venture. Ralph began his winemaking career at Tyrrell's, rising to the position of chief winemaker before heading off to various wineries. In 2005 he passed on the operation of the business to Sarah. Exports to Canada, The Netherlands, China, Malaysia and Singapore.

ΨΨΨΨΨ Riesling 2007 Pale colour; a slatey bouquet with lemon and a touch of lime; poised and precise on entry, just falls away a touch; savoury and certainly complex flavour profile. Screwcap. 12.5% alc. **Rating** 92 **To** 2014 $15

ΨΨΨΨ Viognier 2007 Deep colour; a bit of struck match complexity, with straw and spiced apricot on the palate; rich and long. Screwcap. 13.5% alc. **Rating** 89 **To** 2012 $20
Shiraz Viognier 2006 A strong Rhône-like savoury bouquet; briny with black and red fruit and a touch of dried herb; the palate is softer than expected, with cleansing acid and good focus. Screwcap. 14% alc. **Rating** 89 **To** 2013 $20

Ramsay's Vin Rose   ★★★

30 St Helier Road, The Gurdies, Vic 3984 **Region** Gippsland
T (03) 5997 6531 **F** (03) 5997 6158 **www.**vinrosewinery.com **Open** 7 days 11–5
Winemaker Dianne Ramsay **Est.** 1995 **Cases** 500 **Vyds** 2 ha
The slightly curious name (which looks decidedly strange in conjunction with Riesling and Cabernet Sauvignon) stems from the original intention of Alan and Dianne Ramsay to grow roses on a commercial scale on their property. Frank Cutler, at Western Port Winery, persuaded them to plant wine grapes instead; the plantings comprise pinot noir, chardonnay, cabernet sauvignon, merlot and riesling. They opened their micro-winery in 1999, and have four self-contained units set around their 800-bush rose garden.

ΨΨΨΨ Merlot 2006 Good colour; a potent wine that does, however, display good varietal characteristics on a long, savoury palate and should improve over the short term. Cork. 14% alc. **Rating** 88 **To** 2013 $20
Pinot Noir 2007 A lighter touch in the winery would have been better; the wine has formidable power and extract, and only just enough varietal fruit to get it across the line. Cork. 14% alc. **Rating** 87 **To** 2012 $20

Random Valley Organic Wines   ★★★★☆

410 Brockman Highway, Karridale, WA 6288 **Region** Margaret River
T (08) 9758 6707 **F** (08) 9758 6743 **www.**randomvalley.com **Open** 7 days 10–5
Winemaker Naturaliste Vintners (Bruce Dukes) **Est.** 1995 **Cases** 1000 **Vyds** 7 ha

The Little family has established sauvignon blanc, semillon, cabernet sauvignon (2 ha each) and shiraz (1 ha), with a certified organic grapegrowing program. No chemical-based fertilisers, pesticides or herbicides are used in the vineyard, building humus and biological activity in the soil. Given that the vineyard produces 50 tonnes per year, it is evident that the approach has worked well. The cellar door (opened Dec 2007) has a unique air-conditioning system provided by 13 750 recycled wine bottles filled with water, producing a cooling effect in summer, and a warming effect in winter.

ՔՔՔՔՔ **Margaret River Shiraz 2007** Bright colour; cranberry fruit and a touch of dried leaf on the bouquet; gravelly tannins dominate the palate, with a lively core of red fruit and spice on offer as well; vibrant and focused on the finish. ProCork. 14% alc. **Rating** 94 **To** 2014 $25

ՔՔՔՔՔ **Cabernet Sauvignon 2007** Brilliantly clear colour; a robust, earthy style, black fruits supported by persistent tannins. Cork. 13.6% alc. **Rating** 90 **To** 2014 $22

Ravens Croft Wines   ★★★

274 Spring Creek Road, Stanthorpe, Qld 4380 **Region** Granite Belt
T (07) 4683 3252 **www.**ravenscroftwines.com.au **Open** Fri–Sun 10–4.30, or by appt
Winemaker Mark Ravenscroft **Est.** 2002 **Cases** 700 **Vyds** 1.4 ha
Mark Ravenscroft was born in South Africa, and studied oenology there. He moved to Australia in the early 1990s, and in '94 became an Australian citizen. His wines come from estate plantings of verdelho (1 ha) and pinotage (0.4 ha), supplemented by contract-grown grapes from other vineyards in the region. A new winery has recently been completed. Exports to Japan.

Ravensworth   ★★★★

312 Patemans Lane, Murrumbateman, ACT 2582 **Region** Canberra District
T (02) 6226 8368 **F** (02) 6226 8378 **www.**ravensworthwines.com.au **Open** Not
Winemaker Bryan Martin **Est.** 2000 **Cases** 1600 **Vyds** 7.5 ha
Winemaker, vineyard manager and partner Bryan Martin (with dual wine science and wine growing degrees from CSU) has a background of wine retail, food and beverage in the hospitality industry, and teaches part-time in that field. He is also assistant winemaker to Tim Kirk at Clonakilla, after seven years at Jeir Creek. Judging at wine shows is another string to his bow. Ravensworth has two vineyards: Rosehill planted in 1998 to cabernet sauvignon, merlot and sauvignon blanc; and Martin Block planted 2000–01 to shiraz, viognier, marsanne and sangiovese.

ՔՔՔՔՔ **Hunter Valley Shiraz 2007** Unusually deep and intense colour; a rich, flamboyant style but one that will age for decades thanks to the depth of the blackberry fruit and balanced tannins. Screwcap. 14% alc. **Rating** 93 **To** 2027 $22
Murrumbateman Sangiovese 2008 Good colour; sour cherry and a touch of bramble/undergrowth on the bouquet; cool, fresh and focused with lively tannin and acid providing a savoury finish; a good example of the variety. Screwcap. 12% alc. **Rating** 92 **To** 2012 $20
Murrumbateman Marsanne 2007 Has admirable focus and intensity, with aromas and flavours of honeysuckle and lemon zest; texture is partly chalky, partly minerally. Will age beautifully. Screwcap. 13.5% alc. **Rating** 92 **To** 2017 $22
Murrumbateman Sangiovese 2007 A thoroughly enjoyable rendition of sangiovese; delicious red cherry dominant, halfway between sour and maraschino cherry, and no earthy/green olive notes to disrupt the aftertaste. Screwcap. 13.5% alc. **Rating** 90 **To** 2011 $20
Murrumbateman Viognier 2007 Amazing, glowing yellow-green colour more typical of a 10-year-old wine than a 1-year-old; has plenty of spicy apricot varietal character and, if skin contact produced the colour, the expected phenolics don't appear on the finish. Screwcap. 14.5% alc. **Rating** 90 **To** 2010 $25

♏♏♏♏ **Murrumbateman Marsanne 2008** Deep colour; exotic and very ripe with spicy tropical fruit on display; the palate has a slight bitterness, but the level of extract is an interesting counterbalance. Screwcap. 13% alc. **Rating** 88 **To** 2012 $20

Murrumbateman Shiraz Viognier 2007 Bright red-purple typical of the blend; the wine enters the mouth with bright fruit, but leaves a tide mark of drying tannins that needed fining. Screwcap. 13.5% alc. **Rating** 88 **To** 2014 $27

Murrumbateman Riesling 2008 Firm style from start to finish; strong, grainy/mineral structure; not particularly welcoming yet. Screwcap. 12% alc. **Rating** 87 **To** 2014 $18

Murrumbateman Viognier 2008 Quite subtle with ripe stone fruit and apricot at the edges; fairly neutral palate, with reasonable texture and length. Screwcap. 13% alc. **Rating** 87 **To** 2011 $20

Red Hill Estate

53 Shoreham Road, Red Hill South, Vic 3937 **Region** Mornington Peninsula
T (03) 5989 2838 **F** (03) 5931 0143 **www**.redhillestate.com.au **Open** 7 days 11–5
Winemaker Michael Kyberd, Luke Curry **Est.** 1989 **Cases** 40 000 **Vyds** 74 ha
Red Hill Estate was established by Sir Peter Derham and family, and has three vineyard sites: Range Road, Red Hill Estate (the home vineyard), and The Briars. Taken together, the vineyards make Red Hill Estate one of the larger producers of Mornington Peninsula wines. The tasting room and ever-busy restaurant have a superb view across the vineyard to Westernport Bay and Phillip Island. In 2007 it (surprisingly) merged with Arrowfield Estate in the Hunter Valley; one can only assume marketing synergies are expected to drive the new InWine Group Australia. Exports to the UK, the US and other major markets.

♏♏♏♏♏ **Reserve Pinot Noir 2006** Cool, fine and polished red fruit bouquet, with Asian allspice and attractive toasty oak notes; the palate is very fine and quite silky with a long and complex, cool and expansive finish. Screwcap. **Rating** 94 **To** 2014

Mornington Peninsula Shiraz 2007 A red fruit bouquet loaded with attractive spice and undergrowth aromas; medium-bodied, fleshy and exhibiting fine-grained tannins and a long and developing finish. Screwcap. 14.5% alc. **Rating** 94 **To** 2016

Briars Mornington Peninsula Cabernet Sauvignon 2006 Dusty cigar-box perfume, with sweet blackcurrant fruit beneath; the palate is dark and complex, and the structure fine yet firm; a long, balanced finish. Screwcap. 13.8% alc. **Rating** 94 **To** 2020

♏♏♏♏♍ **Mornington Peninsula Chardonnay 2007** A complex and leesy bouquet, with creamy stone fruit aromas; the palate is quite nutty and shows some grapefruit and focused acidity on the finish; fresh, understated and quite long. Screwcap. 13.5% alc. **Rating** 93 **To** 2014

Mornington Peninsula Pinot Noir 2007 Bright colour; cherry fruit with a touch of mint and a lot of spice; red fruits continue on the palate, with a restrained and elegant level of spice, and a generous core of cool red fruits. Screwcap. 13.5% alc. **Rating** 93 **To** 2014 $22

Reserve Mornington Peninsula Chardonnay 2006 Quite deep colour; restrained peach and nectarine bouquet; rich, but with precision on the finish. Screwcap. **Rating** 92 **To** 2014

Cellar Door Release Mornington Peninsula Sauvignon Blanc 2008 Restrained and fine, with citrus and some gun flint; creamy texture, with vibrant acidity and lingering tropical fruit on the finish. Screwcap. 12.7% alc. **Rating** 90 **To** 2011

Mornington Peninsula Blanc de Blancs 2006 Pale colour; chalky lemon fruit with a touch of green apple; quite good texture, with focused acidity, and a refreshing finish; very clean. Diam. 13.7% alc. **Rating** 90 **To** 2012 $35

ΨΨΨΨ   **Mornington Peninsula Blanc de Noirs 2006** Restrained red fruit bouquet; clean and well-defined, with a very dry and slightly savoury finish. Diam. 13.4% alc. **Rating** 87 **To** 2012 $35

Redbank Victoria ★★★★☆

Whitfield Road, King Valley, Vic 3678 **Region** King Valley
T (03) 5729 3604 **F** (08) 8561 3411 **www**.redbankwines.com **Open** Fri–Mon 11–11
Winemaker Kevin Glastonbury **Est.** 2005 **Cases** 75 000
The Redbank brand was for decades the umbrella for Neill and Sally Robb's Sally's Paddock. In 2005 Hill Smith Family Vineyards acquired the Redbank brand from the Robbs, leaving them with the Redbank Winery and Sally's Paddock. Hill Smith Family Vineyards is most unhappy with the continued designation of the Robb's winery as Redbank, while the Robbs say it is simply the name of the winery as shown in district maps, district signposts and at the gate, and is in no sense a brand. Redbank Victoria purchases grapes from the King Valley, Whitlands, Beechworth and the Ovens Valley (among other vineyards sources). Exports to all major markets.

ΨΨΨΨΨ   **The Anvil Shiraz 2006** Good colour and wonderful fruit purity; blackberry and ironstone, framed by good oak; the palate is fleshy and fine, and has terrific structure on the finish. Beechworth. Cork. 14.5% alc. **Rating** 94 **To** 2016 $24.95

ΨΨΨΨ♀   **Sunday Morning King Valley Pinot Gris 2008** Has the fruit others lack, with a fine display of pear, apple and musk, then a cleansing finish. Screwcap. 13.5% alc. **Rating** 90 **To** 2011 $24.95

ΨΨΨΨ   **Emily Moscato NV** Very cunningly made from King Valley pinot gris and 'muscat rouge' (presumably red frontignac); very fruity, yet zesty and well balanced; possibly goes over the top for many of its consumers. Crown Seal. 8.5% alc. **Rating** 89 **To** 2009 $17

Redden Bridge Wines ★★★

PMB 147, Naracoorte, SA 5271 (postal) **Region** Wrattonbully
T (08) 8764 7494 **F** (08) 8764 7501 **www**.reddenbridge.com **Open** Not
Winemaker Robin Moody (Contract) **Est.** 2002 **Cases** 800
This is the venture of Greg and Emma Koch, Greg with a quarter-century of viticultural experience, first in Coonawarra (17 years) and thereafter turning his attention to Wrattonbully, buying land there in 1995 and setting up Terra Rossa Viticultural Management to assist growers across the Limestone Coast. Greg and Emma now have 24 ha of cabernet sauvignon and 22 ha of shiraz, and in 2002 obtained the services of the immensely experienced Robin Moody to oversee the making of the Redden Bridge wines at Cape Jaffa Estate.

ΨΨΨΨ   **The Crossing Wrattonbully Cabernet Sauvignon 2005** Prominent oak on the bouquet, with red fruit in support; there is a little development, but the flavour is good and the definition of fruit and black olive on the finish combine with ease. Screwcap. 13.8% alc. **Rating** 89 **To** 2014 $24

Redesdale Estate Wines

Redesdale Hotel, 2640 Kyneton-Heathcote Road, Redesdale, Vic 3444 **Region** Heathcote
T (03) 5425 3236 **www**.redesdale.com **Open** Tues–Wed 2–8, Thurs–Sun 11–late
Winemaker Tobias Ansted (Contract) **Est.** 1982 **Cases** 800 **Vyds** 4 ha
Planting of the Redesdale Estate vines began in 1982 on the northeast slopes of a 25-ha grazing property, fronting the Campaspe River on one side. The rocky quartz and granite soil meant the vines had to struggle, and when Peter Williams and wife Suzanne Arnall-Williams purchased the property in 1988 the vineyard was in a state of disrepair. They have rejuvenated the vineyard, planted an olive grove, and, more recently, erected a two-storey cottage surrounded by a garden, which is part of the Victorian Open Garden Scheme (and cross-linked to a villa in Tuscany).

ϔϔϔϔϔ Heathcote Shiraz 2006 Bright colour; a strong minerally character envelopes dark fruits, sage and a touch of blueberry; medium-bodied with vibrant acidity, well-defined dark fruit and a little bay leaf on the palate; long, fine and supple on the finish. Screwcap. 14.3% alc. **Rating** 94 **To** 2020 $40

Redgate ★★★★★

Boodjidup Road, Margaret River, WA 6285 **Region** Margaret River
T (08) 9757 6488 **F** (08) 9757 6308 **www.**redgatewines.com.au **Open** 7 days 10–5
Winemaker Simon Keall **Est.** 1977 **Cases** 7500 **Vyds** 22.83 ha
Founder and owner of Redgate, Bill Ullinger, chose the name not simply because of the nearby eponymous beach, but also because – so it is said – a local farmer (with a prominent red gate at his property) had run an illegal spirit-still 100 or so years ago, and its patrons would come to the property and ask whether there was any 'red gate' available. True or not, Ullinger, one of the early movers in the Margaret River, now has over 22 ha of mature estate plantings (the majority to sauvignon blanc, semillon, cabernet sauvignon, cabernet franc, shiraz and chardonnay). Exports to the US, Switzerland, Denmark, Japan and Singapore.

ϔϔϔϔϔ Shiraz 2007 Restrained savoury bouquet with sage and thyme framing the red fruit; medium-bodied with ample flesh, and fine drying tannins; even, harmonious and surprisingly long; a real sleeper with potential. Screwcap. 14.5% alc. **Rating** 94 **To** 2016 $30
Bin 588 2007 Vibrant colour; redcurrant and a touch of cedar on the bouquet leads into approachable and fleshy sweet fruit on the palate; well-handled oak; a little savoury complexity lingers on the finish. Screwcap. 13.5% alc. **Rating** 94 **To** 2014 $22.50

ϔϔϔϔϙ Margaret River Cabernet Sauvignon 2007 Elegant; cool red fruit and a light seasoning of oak; the palate is fine and quite linear, with gentle, yet plush tannin and an even line from start to finish. Screwcap. 13.5% alc. **Rating** 90 **To** 2014 $35

ϔϔϔϔ OFS Margaret River Semillon 2008 A pronounced green nettle bouquet follows onto the palate, with some generosity, although a little too green. Screwcap. 13% alc. **Rating** 87 **To** 2011 $25
Margaret River Sauvignon Blanc Semillon 2008 Strong nettle bouquet, very assertive; quite crisp, but a little simple. Screwcap. 12.5% alc. **Rating** 87 **To** 2011 $21

Redheads Studios ★★★

Cnr Foggo Road/Kangarilla Road, McLaren Vale, SA 5171 **Region** McLaren Vale
T (08) 8323 7799 **F** (08) 8323 0080 **www.**redheadswine.com.au **Open** By appt
Winemaker Adam Hooper, Peter Kennedy **Est.** 2003 **Cases** 80 000
The Redheads Studio winery has always been, and will continue to be, constantly evolving, and a sometimes secret wine business, venture of young or youngish winemakers. It has its roots in the Flying Winemaker days of the late 1980s and '90s, when Australia's best and brightest would travel to Europe for the northern hemisphere vintage, only to return home to continue their employment with mega wineries, unable to apply any of the ideas they picked up in Europe. Eventually, some money was scraped up to buy a former curry house restaurant called Redheads, and the founders saw no reason to change the name. It is now a place where small producers can come and go making their own wines behind closed doors in the dead of night, returning to work the following morning to their unsuspecting employer somewhat the worse for wear. It was inevitable that Redheads would start developing its own labels, and this it has done, the names of the wines giving further curry flavour to the venture. Exports to the UK, the US, Canada, Denmark and Singapore.

ϔϔϔϔ Laithwaite The Back Shed McLaren Vale Shiraz Grenache 2006 Deep, dark and full of mocha and chocolate; the palate is full-bodied, of moderate length and plenty of weight on the finish. Cork. 15% alc. **Rating** 89 **To** 2014 $20

Yard Dog White 2008 Lively bouquet of lemon and a touch of spice; clean and crisp on the finish. Chardonnay/Traminer/Sauvignon Blanc/Viognier/Semillon. Screwcap. 13.5% alc. **Rating** 87 **To** 2011 $12.50

Redman ★★★

Main Road, Coonawarra, SA 5263 **Region** Coonawarra
T (08) 8736 3331 **www**.redman.com.au **Open** Mon–Fri 9–5, w'ends 10–4
Winemaker Bruce Redman, Malcolm Redman, Daniel Redman **Est.** 1966 **Cases** NFP
Vyds 32 ha
In March 2008 the Redman family celebrated 100 years of winemaking in Coonawarra. The 2008 vintage also marked the arrival of Daniel as the fourth-generation Redman winemaker. Daniel gained winemaking experience in Central Victoria, the Barossa Valley and the US before taking up his new position. It was felicitous timing, for the 2004 Cabernet Sauvignon and '04 Cabernet Merlot were each awarded a gold medal from the national wine show circuit in '07, the first such accolades for a considerable time.

Reilly's Wines ★★★

Cnr Hill Street/Burra Street, Mintaro, SA 5415 **Region** Clare Valley
T (08) 8843 9013 **F** (08) 8843 9275 **www**.reillyswines.com.au **Open** 7 days 10–4
Winemaker Justin Ardill **Est.** 1994 **Cases** 25 000 **Vyds** 125 ha
Cardiologist Justin and Julie Ardill are no longer newcomers in the Clare Valley, with 10 or so vintages under their belt. An unusual sideline of Reilly's is the production of extra virgin olive oil, made from wild olives found in the Mintaro district of the Clare Valley. Justin also does some contract making for others. Reilly's has a second cellar door in Adelaide, which also holds wine classes. Exports to the US, Canada, Ireland, Malaysia, China and Singapore.

 Clare Valley Coonawarra Semillon Sauvignon Blanc 2008 The foray to Coonawarra for sauvignon blanc pays dividends; grassy/herbal notes offset by sweet passionfruit/tropical nuances. Screwcap. 12.5% alc. **Rating** 89 **To** 2011 $18
Barking Mad Clare Valley Rose 2008 A well-made blend of Cabernet Sauvignon/Sangiovese; is fruity, albeit dry, with some sweet cherry notes. Screwcap. 13.5% alc. **Rating** 88 **To** 2010 $15
Dry Land Clare Valley Shiraz 2004 A slightly reduced wine on both bouquet and palate should benefit from vigorous decanting, for there are bright fruit flavours underneath. Screwcap. 14.7% alc. **Rating** 88 **To** 2015 $27

Renards Folly ★★★

PO Box 499, McLaren Vale, SA 5171 **Region** McLaren Vale
T (08) 8556 2404 **F** (08) 8556 2404 **Open** Not
Winemaker Tony Walker **Est.** 2005 **Cases** 1000
The dancing foxes on the label, one with a red tail, give a subliminal hint that this is a virtual winery, owned by Linda Kemp (who looks after the marketing and sales) and Mark Dimberline, who has spent 16 years in the wine industry. Aided by friend and winemaker Tony Walker, they source grapes from McLaren Vale, and allow the Vale to express itself without too much elaboration, the alcohol nicely controlled. Exports to the US, Canada, Germany an Singapore.

 McLaren Vale Sauvignon Blanc Semillon 2008 Has unexpectedly voluminous tropical fruit without blowsiness, the restraint of the semillon helping. Drink and enjoy now. Screwcap. 13% alc. **Rating** 89 **To** 2010 $15.95
McLaren Vale Sangiovese Cabernet 2007 Has authentic sangiovese fruit in a sour cherry/savoury cherry spectrum, the cabernet not particularly obvious in a light- to medium-bodied wine. Screwcap. 14% alc. **Rating** 87 **To** 2012 $16.95

Reschke Wines

Level 1, 183 Melbourne Street, North Adelaide, SA 5006 (postal) **Region** Coonawarra
T (08) 8239 0500 **F** (08) 8239 0522 **www**.reschke.com.au **Open** Not
Winemaker Peter Douglas (Contract) **Est.** 1998 **Cases** 10 000 **Vyds** 143.86 ha
It's not often that the first release from a new winery is priced at $100 per bottle, but that
was precisely what Reschke Wines achieved with its 1998 Cabernet Sauvignon. The family
has been a landholder in Coonawarra for 100 years, with a large holding that is partly terra
rossa, part woodland. Cabernet sauvignon (with 108 ha) takes the lion's share of the plantings,
with merlot, shiraz and petit verdot making up the balance. Exports to the UK, the US and
other major markets.

♥♥♥♥♥ **Empyrean Cabernet Sauvignon 2004** A wine full of impressive dark fruit
and toasty well-handled oak; deep, dark and generous, there is ample fruit to
complement the winemaking involved; warm and fleshy, and unashamedly full-
bodied. Cork. 14.5% alc. **Rating** 94 **To** 2020 $120

♥♥♥♥♀ **Bos Cabernet Sauvignon 2004** Vibrant colour; fresh and focused cassis with
a touch of mint bouquet; good texture and weight, ample fine-grained tannins
to match the abundant fruit. Cork. 14.5% alc. **Rating** 93 **To** 2015 $38

🍇 Resolution Vineyard   **NR**

4 Glen Street, South Hobart, Tas 7004 (postal) **Region** Southern Tasmania
T (03) 6224 9497 **www**.theresolutionvineyard.com **Open** Not
Winemaker Frogmore Creek **Est.** 2003 **Cases** 145 **Vyds** 0.8 ha
Owners Charles and Alison Hewitt live in England and entrust the care of the property and
vineyard to Alison's father Peter Brown, with support from former Parks & Wildlife ranger
Val Dell, who also has a small vineyard. A love of red burgundy and fishing was sufficient for
Charles to establish the vineyard planted to three clones of pinot noir in Tasmania, the place
where Alison had spent most of her formative years. The vineyard is on a north-facing slope
overlooking the D'Entrecasteaux Channel. The 2-tonne crush in 2008 does not provide
enough information to make a call on the quality to be expected in the years ahead.

Richard Hamilton

Cnr Main Road/Johnston Road, McLaren Vale, SA 5171 **Region** McLaren Vale
T (08) 8323 8830 **F** (08) 8323 8881 **www**.leconfieldwines.com **Open** Mon–Fri 10–5,
w'ends & public hols 11–5
Winemaker Paul Gordon, Tim Bailey **Est.** 1972 **Cases** 25 000 **Vyds** 74 ha
Richard Hamilton has outstanding estate vineyards, some of great age, all fully mature. The
arrival (in 2001) of former Rouge Homme winemaker Paul Gordon has allowed the full
potential of those vineyards to be expressed. His move to lower alcohol white wines (without
sacrificing flavour) is to be commended, as is the limit of 14.5% alc. on the old vineyard red
wines. Exports to the UK, the US and other major markets.

♥♥♥♥♥ **Hamilton Centurion Old Vine Shiraz 2006** A bright wine with intermingling
red and black fruits; very supple and fine, with a flowing and very even palate;
beautifully balanced, fine and long. Screwcap. 14.5% alc. **Rating** 95 **To** 2020 $59.95
Burton's Vineyard Old Bush Vine McLaren Vale Grenache Shiraz 2005
Savoury/spicy aromas, more toward black than red; while only medium-bodied,
has the spine and focus that often eludes the Barossa; dark plums with just a hint
of raspberry. Stained cork is ominous. 14.5% alc. **Rating** 94 **To** 2015 $39.95

♥♥♥♥♀ **Gumprs' McLaren Vale Shiraz 2007** A new label design for an old vineyard
name tricking subeditors into inserting the missing 'e'; a very substantial, full-
bodied wine, but with more focus than the Leconfield brother of this wine. Good
value. Screwcap. 14.5% alc. **Rating** 90 **To** 2016 $17.95

♥♥♥♥ Almond Grove McLaren Vale Chardonnay 2008 There is a subtle infusion of oak immediately obvious on the bouquet, but not so much on the tangy palate, which flourishes with citrussy acidity. Well priced. Screwcap. 13.5% alc. **Rating** 89 To 2012 $14.95

McLaren Vale Sauvignon Blanc Semillon 2008 Well put together, the desired synergy achieved in a crisp, light and fresh wine with some contrasting passionfruit and grassy notes. Screwcap. 13% alc. **Rating** 89 **To** 2010 $14.95

Slate Quarry McLaren Vale Riesling 2008 A solid wine, typical of McLaren Vale, with ripe aromas and flavours bordering on tropical; well-priced, early-consumption style. Screwcap. 12.5% alc. **Rating** 88 **To** 2012 $14.95

Richfield Estate

Bonshaw Road, Tenterfield, NSW 2372 **Region** New England
T (02) 6737 5488 **F** (02) 6737 5598 **www.**richfieldvineyard.com.au **Open** By appt 10–4
Winemaker John Cassegrain **Est.** 1997 **Cases** 6000 **Vyds** 30 ha
Singapore resident Bernard Forey is the Chairman and majority shareholder of Richfield Estate. The 500-ha property, at an altitude of 720 m, was selected after an intensive survey by soil specialists. Shiraz, cabernet sauvignon, verdelho, merlot, semillon and chardonnay are planted. Winemaker John Cassegrain is a shareholder in the venture, and much of the wine is exported to Canada, Malaysia and Thailand.

♥♥♥♥ New England Chardonnay 2007 Early-picked style that shows some green leaf notes and distinct citrus, veering towards sauvignon blanc territory; is fresh, however. Screwcap. 13% alc. **Rating** 87 **To** 2012 $16.95

Tenterfield Shiraz 2006 Bright but quite light colour; continues the style with early-picked characters leaving the wine with nuances of green olive and leaf. Screwcap. **Rating** 87 **To** 2011 $16.95

Richmond Grove

Para Road, Tanunda, SA 5352 **Region** Barossa Valley
T (08) 8563 7303 **www.**richmondgrovewines.com **Open** 7 days 10.30–4.30
Winemaker Steve Clarkson, John Vickery (Consultant) **Est.** 1983 **Cases** 150 000
Richmond Grove, owned by Orlando Wyndham, draws its grapes from diverse sources. The Richmond Grove Barossa Valley and Watervale Rieslings made by the team directed by consultant winemaker John Vickery represent excellent value for money (for Riesling) year in, year out. Exports to the UK.

♥♥♥♥♥ Limited Release Watervale Riesling 2008 A relatively quiet opening on the bouquet and fore-palate, but takes off on the brilliant and vibrant finish; full of zesty, tangy fruit entwined with acidity. Screwcap. 11.5% alc. **Rating** 94 **To** 2020 $22

♥♥♥♥♡ Limited Release Barossa Vineyards Shiraz 2006 A delicious medium-bodied Shiraz, reinforcing what a great vintage '06 was in the Barossa Valley; a range of red and black fruits that are intense but not the least heavy or jammy; a wine which will age with extreme grace. Screwcap. 14.5% alc. **Rating** 93 **To** 2021 $21.99

Limited Release Adelaide Hills Chardonnay 2008 Fully reflects its Adelaide Hills birthplace via stone fruit and citrus aromas and flavours; the oak, too, has been well handled. Value. Screwcap. 14% alc. **Rating** 91 **To** 2014 $22

Limited Release Adelaide Hills Chardonnay 2007 Clean, crisp and clearly defined stone fruit aromas; good weight and texture, with a fine, even and bright-fruited finish. Screwcap. 13.5% alc. **Rating** 91 **To** 2014 $23.99

Limited Release Adelaide Hills Pinot Noir 2007 Gently fragrant and pure red cherry/strawberry fruit, then a focused, silky palate, even if a fraction light; impressive first-up Pinot for the brand. Screwcap. 13% alc. **Rating** 91 To 2012 $23.99

Limited Release Mount Lofty Ranges Sangiovese 2007 No-holds-barred savoury/briary overtones to the intense cherry fruit flavours. Screwcap. 13% alc. **Rating** 90 **To** 2012 $21.99

Rickety Gate

1949 Scotsdale Road, Denmark, WA 6333 **Region** Great Southern
T (08) 9840 9504 **www**.ricketygate.com.au **Open** Fri–Mon & hols 11–4
Winemaker John Wade **Est.** 2000 **Cases** 3500 **Vyds** 3 ha
The Rickety Gate vineyard is situated on north-facing slopes of the Bennet Ranges, in an area specifically identified by Dr John Gladstones as highly suited to cool-climate viticulture. The property was purchased by Russell and Linda Hubbard at the end of 1999, and 1.8 ha of merlot, 0.8 ha of riesling and 0.5 ha of chardonnay and pinot noir were planted in 2000. John Wade contract-makes the wines at the small onsite winery.

ŸŸŸŸŸ **Chardonnay 2007** Has good focus and intensity to its mix of white peach, grapefruit and barrel ferment oak inputs, all adding to the line and length of the wine. Screwcap. 13.6% alc. **Rating** 91 **To** 2014 $25

ŸŸŸŸ **Denmark Riesling 2008** Green nettle, lemon and a light stony character; tight and lemony palate, with good acidity and interesting texture. Screwcap. 12.2% alc. **Rating** 87 **To** 2013 $22.50

RidgeView Wines

273 Sweetwater Road, Rothbury, NSW 2335 **Region** Lower Hunter Valley
T 0419 475 221 **F** (02) 9534 5468 **www**.ridgeview.com.au **Open** Fri–Sun 10–5
Winemaker Cameron Webster, Darren Scott, Gary MacLean **Est.** 2000 **Cases** 2500
Vyds 9 ha
Darren and Tracey Scott (plus their four children and extended family) have transformed a 40-ha timbered farm into a vineyard together with self-contained accommodation and cellar door. The lion's share of the plantings are 4.5 ha of shiraz, with cabernet sauvignon, chambourcin, merlot, pinot gris, viognier and traminer making up a somewhat eclectic selection of varieties. Exports to Japan.

ŸŸŸŸŸ **Generations Reserve Hunter Valley Semillon 2008** Pungent green nettle bouquet; dry, lean, focused and plenty of lemon on the palate; all the pieces are there, now for a little time. Screwcap. 10.5% alc. **Rating** 90 **To** 2018 $22

ŸŸŸŸ **Hunter Valley Semillon 2008** Varietal lemon and straw bouquet; clean and precise; could use a little more concentration. Screwcap. 10.5% alc. **Rating** 88 **To** 2013 $18
Hunter Valley Merlot 2006 Bright colour; cherry bouquet and a touch of spice and earth; juicy and bright on the finish. Screwcap. 13.5% alc. **Rating** 88 **To** 2012 $22
Hunter Valley Cabernet Sauvignon 2007 Cassis, redcurrant and leather bouquet; soft, fleshy and forward with good concentration of fruit; a little one-dimensional. Screwcap. 14.5% alc. **Rating** 87 **To** 2014 $22

Riposte

PO Box 256, Lobethal, SA 5241 **Region** Adelaide Hills
T (08) 8389 8149 **F** (08) 8389 8178 **www**.timknappstein.com.au **Open** Not
Winemaker Tim Knappstein **Est.** 2006 **Cases** 7000
It's never too late to teach an old dog new tricks when the old dog in question is Tim Knappstein. With 40 years of winemaking and more than 500 wine show awards under his belt, Tim has started yet another new wine life with Riposte, a subtle response to the various vicissitudes he has suffered in recent years. While having no continuing financial interest in Lenswood Vineyards, established many years ago, Tim is able to source grapes from this vineyard, and also makes selections from other prime sites in surrounding areas. Exports to the UK.

ŸŸŸŸŸ **The Foil Adelaide Hills Sauvignon Blanc 2008** Spotlessly clean aromas, then a palate with a sunburst of tropical fruits with splashes of passionfruit and gooseberry; good acidity on the long finish. Screwcap. 13% alc. **Rating** 94 **To** 2010 $19

ŢŢŢŢ♀ **The Stiletto Adelaide Hills Pinot Gris 2008** Grainy/minerally notes add to the interest, citrus, nashi pear and spiced apple likewise. A pinot gris with character. Screwcap. 13% alc. **Rating** 91 **To** 2010 $25
The Sabre Adelaide Hills Pinot Noir 2007 Abundant red and black cherry fruit on the bouquet, which flows through into the quite fruit-sweet palate; enjoyable wine, ready now. Screwcap. 14.5% alc. **Rating** 90 **To** 2012 $28

ŢŢŢŢ **The Rapier Adelaide Hills Traminer 2008** Expertly made, but really needs more development in bottle to start showing its varietal wares. The suspicion is that the clone or clones of gewurztraminer in this country are not good. Screwcap. 13% alc. **Rating** 89 **To** 2014 $19

Rivendell ★★★☆

Wildwood Road, Yallingup, WA 6282 **Region** Margaret River
T (08) 9755 2090 **www**.rivendellwines.com.au **Open** Thurs–Mon 10–4
Winemaker James Pennington **Est.** 1987 **Cases** 3000 **Vyds** 1.5 ha
Rivendell was established in 1987 by a local family and became recognised for its gardens, restaurant and wines. The property was purchased by private investors in 2004, who have renovated the restaurant (with locally renowned chef Peter Clatworthy) and cellar door. The new owners have employed James Pennington to oversee the improvements to the winery and its production, based in part upon estate plantings of cabernet sauvignon, semillon and sauvignon blanc. Exports to Singapore.

ŢŢŢŢ♀ **Margaret River Shiraz 2006** Good colour; has an intense palate, verging on full-bodied, an exceptional achievement in the rain-drenched vintage, the fruit flavour fully ripe, likewise the tannins. Screwcap. 13.5% alc. **Rating** 92 **To** 2016 $18

ŢŢŢŢ **Margaret River Semillon Sauvignon Blanc 2008** A light-bodied and fresh wine, with delicate grassy and tropical nuances; clean finish. Screwcap. 12.5% alc. **Rating** 87 **To** 2010 $17

Robert Channon Wines ★★★★

32 Bradley Lane, Stanthorpe, Qld 4380 **Region** Granite Belt
T (07) 4683 3260 **F** (07) 4683 3109 **www**.robertchannonwines.com **Open** Mon–Fri 11–4, w'ends & public hols 10–5
Winemaker Mark Ravenscroft **Est.** 1998 **Cases** 3000 **Vyds** 8 ha
Peggy and Robert Channon have established verdelho, chardonnay, pinot gris, shiraz, cabernet sauvignon and pinot noir under permanent bird protection netting. The initial cost of installing permanent netting is high, but in the long term it is well worth it: it excludes birds and protects the grapes against hail damage. Also, there is no pressure to pick the grapes before they are fully ripe. The winery has established a particular reputation for its Verdelho.

ŢŢŢŢ♀ **Reserve Chardonnay 2007** Complex, pleasantly funky, barrel ferment aromas; light-bodied stone fruit flavours assert themselves on the palate and finish. Screwcap. 13.5% alc. **Rating** 91 **To** 2013 $35
Verdelho 2008 One of the secrets of Robert Channon Verdelho is its crisp, citrussy acidity which bolsters the more usual tropical fruit salad flavours leading to above-average length. Screwcap. 12.5% alc. **Rating** 91 **To** 2013 $24.50
Shiraz 2007 Bright crimson; well-made medium-bodied wine with nicely balanced and integrated fruit, oak and tannins, in a plum and blackberry spectrum. Screwcap. 14% alc. **Rating** 90 **To** 2017 $20
Cabernet Sauvignon 2007 Shows good varietal character throughout in a medium-bodied frame, cassis, blackcurrant and fine tannins intermingling. Screwcap. 14% alc. **Rating** 90 **To** 2015 $20

ŢŢŢŢ **Pinot Gris 2008** Crisp, clean and bright fruit, with citrus elements complementing pear and apple; good dry finish. Screwcap. 12% alc. **Rating** 89 **To** 2010 $22.50

Robert Johnson Vineyards ★★★☆

Old Woollen Mill, Lobethal, SA 5241 **Region** Eden Valley
T (08) 8359 2600 **www**.robertjohnsonvineyards.com.au **Open** Fri–Sun 11–4
Winemaker Robert Johnson **Est.** 1997 **Cases** 3000 **Vyds** 3.86 ha
The home base for Robert Johnson is a 12-ha vineyard and olive grove purchased in 1996,
with 0.4 ha of merlot and 5 ha of dilapidated olive trees. The olive grove has been rehabilitated,
and 2.1 ha of shiraz, 1.2 ha of merlot and a small patch of viognier have been established.
Wines made from the estate-grown grapes are released under the Robert Johnson label; these
are supplemented by Alan & Veitch wines purchased from the Sam Virgara vineyard in the
Adelaide Hills, and named after Robert Johnson's parents. Exports to the UK and the US.

ΨΨΨΨΥ **Eden Valley Shiraz 2006** A lively medium-bodied wine, with spicy/peppery
nuances surrounding the blackberry and licorice fruit, in turn supported by fine
tannins. Screwcap. 14.5% alc. **Rating** 90 **To** 2016 $32

ΨΨΨΨ **Alan & Veitch Adelaide Hills Sauvignon Blanc 2008** Has an array of herb,
grass, apple and mineral flavours, with moderate intensity and length. Screwcap.
12.5% alc. **Rating** 88 **To** 2010 $22
Alan & Veitch Woodside Merlot 2005 Savoury/earthy/oaky aromas and
flavours; a soft entry to the palate, but does tighten up on the finish. Screwcap.
14.5% alc. **Rating** 88 **To** 2014 $26

Robert Oatley Vineyards ★★★★☆

Craigmoor Road, Mudgee, NSW 2850 **Region** Mudgee
T (02) 6372 2208 **www**.robertoatley.com.au **Open** 7 days 10–4
Winemaker James Manners **Est.** 2006 **Cases** NFP **Vyds** 461.83 ha
Robert Oatley Vineyards is the latest venture of the Oatley family, previously best known
as the owners of Rosemount Estate until it was sold to Southcorp. The founder of both
businesses is chairman Bob Oatley; the new venture is run by son Sandy, with considerable
hitting power added by deputy executive chairman Chris Hancock. Wild Oats, as anyone with
the remotest interest in yachting and the Sydney–Hobart Yacht Race will know, has been the
name of Bob Oatley's racing yachts. The family has long owned vineyards in Mudgee, but
the new business has been rapidly expanded by the acquisition of the Montrose winery, the
Craigmoor cellar door and restaurant, and vineyards spread across the Mudgee region. The
family recently completed a $10 million upgrade of the Montrose winery. The quality of the
current releases is much improved, an interesting sidelight being some of the oldest plantings
of barbera (10.06 ha) and sangiovese (17.17 ha) in Australia. Exports to the US.

ΨΨΨΨΨ **Montrose Stony Creek Mudgee Chardonnay 2007** Bright green-yellow; a
particularly elegant style for the region, and very well made; nectarine and melon
fruit lead the way, oak following behind; good length and finish. Screwcap. 13% alc.
Rating 94 **To** 2015 $23.95

ΨΨΨΨΥ **Montrose Mudgee Rose of Barbera 2007** Salmon-pink; interesting spice and
herb aromas that carry on as a background to rose petal fruit on a bone-dry palate.
Serious rose style at a serious price. Screwcap. 13% alc. **Rating** 92 **To** 2010 $23.95
Montrose Pietra Mudgee Sangiovese 2006 Clearly defined and presented
varietal fruit with cherry and sour cherry the mainspring; minimal tannins. Perfect
for antipasto. Screwcap. 14% alc. **Rating** 92 **To** 2013 $25.95
Wild Oats Pinot Grigio 2008 An unusually fragrant bouquet of apple, pear
and talc aromas; the palate has substance and thrust and is pleasantly dry. Quite an
achievement. Screwcap. 13.5% alc. **Rating** 90 **To** 2010 $18.99
Sauvignon Blanc 2008 Cool, fine and focused pea pod bouquet; the palate is
lively and certainly varietal, with a touch of tropical generosity to offset the crisp
herbaceous edge. Screwcap. **Rating** 90 **To** 2012 $24.99
Shiraz 2007 Good colour; a lifted bouquet of plum, blackberry and a hint
of apricot; the palate is sweet and supple and has a dark element of tar to
complement the chewy finish. Screwcap. **Rating** 90 **To** 2014 $24.99

Montrose Black Mudgee Shiraz 2006 Bright crimson-purple; an attractive array of red and black fruits on the medium-bodied palate; controlled oak and tannins; good length. Screwcap. 14% alc. **Rating** 90 **To** 2018 $28.95

Montrose Omaggio Mudgee Barbera 2006 Excellent hue; spicy/savoury black fruits, with prominent acidity on the long finish; definitely needs food. Screwcap. 14% alc. **Rating** 90 **To** 2014 $25.95

ΥΥΥΥ **Wild Oats Sauvignon Blanc Semillon 2008** A fragrant and tangy bouquet of crushed citrus leaves, and a zesty palate with herbal/grassy acidity. Screwcap. 12.2% alc. **Rating** 89 **To** 2011 $18.99

Montrose Black Mudgee Shiraz 2007 Good colour; quite dense and dark with a touch of spice; warm on the palate, with a light savoury edge to the firm and ample finish. Screwcap. 14.5% alc. **Rating** 89 **To** 2013 $28.99

Chardonnay 2007 Developed colour; has an abundance of yellow peach fruit in an overall retro style, although that (apparently) was not intended; drink now, not later. Screwcap. 13.5% alc. **Rating** 88 **To** 2010 $24.95

Shiraz Viognier 2006 A blend of Langhorne Creek/Mudgee/Barossa Valley, with an added (not co-fermented?) touch of viognier; fresh, but light-bodied, and presumably designed for early consumption. Screwcap. 14% alc. **Rating** 88 **To** 2011 $24.95

Cabernet Merlot 2007 Vibrant colour; essency redcurrant fruit and a touch of oak on the bouquet; the acidity is quite pronounced and lends a high-toned quality to the palate, and the fruit is vibrant. Screwcap. **Rating** 88 **To** 2014 $24.99

Wild Oats Rose 2008 Fragrant wine; light red fruit flavours poised between sweetness and acidity. Screwcap. 13.5% alc. **Rating** 87 **To** 2009 $18.99

Wild Oats Cabernet Merlot 2007 Quite clean essency cassis fruit bouquet; follows through on the palate, with juicy fruit and reasonable structure. Screwcap. 14.5% alc. **Rating** 87 **To** 2012 $18.99

Robyn Drayton Wines ★★★★

Cnr McDonalds Road/Pokolbin Mountain Road, Pokolbin, NSW 2321 **Region** Lower Hunter Valley
T (02) 4998 7523 **F** (02) 4998 7523 www.robyndraytonwines.com.au **Open** 7 days 10–5
Winemaker Robyn Drayton, Andrew Spanazi **Est.** 1989 **Cases** 5000 **Vyds** 17 ha
In 1994 Robyn Drayton inherited the business started by her parents following their death in a plane crash. Together with her sons, Justin, Liam and Taylor, she has grown the business exponentially. The cellar door has been expanded twice, a new café and function centre opened, and an additional 6 ha of vines planted. Robyn is a fifth-generation Drayton, and continues the proud tradition of 154 years of Drayton winemaking in the Hunter Valley.

ΥΥΥΥΥ **Reginald Reserve Hunter Valley Semillon 2007** A delicious young semillon, with an abundance of lemon, lemongrass and a little white peach flavours; has very good texture, balance and length. Top-flight drinking over the next five–seven years. Screwcap. 12.5% alc. **Rating** 94 **To** 2009 $30

ΥΥΥΥ **Liam Reserve Hunter Valley Verdelho 2007** Has good varietal flavour enlivened by a splash of lemony acidity. Screwcap. 13.9% alc. **Rating** 87 **To** 2010 $25

RockBare

PO Box 395, Stirling, SA 5152 **Region** McLaren Vale
T (08) 8124 9042 **F** (08) 8370 8840 www.rockbare.com.au **Open** Not
Winemaker Tim Burvill, Marty O'Flaherty **Est.** 2000 **Cases** 20 000 **Vyds** 47 ha
A native of WA, Tim Burvill moved to SA in 1993 to do the winemaking course at the Adelaide University Roseworthy campus. Having completed an Honours degree in oenology, he was recruited by Southcorp, and quickly found himself in a senior winemaking position responsible for super-premium whites including Penfolds Yattarna. He makes the RockBare wines under lend-lease arrangements with other wineries. Exports to all major markets.

ŸŸŸŸŸ **Barossa Babe Shiraz 2004** Retains good hue, mainly crimson; has excellent intensity and length, the sheer depth of the black fruits carrying the alcohol. Cork. 15% alc. **Rating** 94 **To** 2019 $45

ŸŸŸŸŸ **Mojo Shiraz 2006** A positive bouquet foretells a palate with rich blackberry wrapped in dark chocolate, and which carries its alcohol with relative ease, oak in sotto voce support. Great value. Screwcap. 15% alc. **Rating** 93 **To** 2017 $17
Mojo Sauvignon Blanc 2008 Sourced from the Adelaide Hills, showing its origins with its structure and length, the latter aided by perfectly balanced acidity. Screwcap. 13% alc. **Rating** 90 **To** 2011 $17

ŸŸŸŸ **McLaren Vale Chardonnay 2008** Interesting wine with 3% semillon from the Adelaide Hills; a certain degree of underlying austerity is outside the norm for McLaren Vale, but no bad thing. Screwcap. 13.5% alc. **Rating** 89 **To** 2013 $20
McLaren Vale Shiraz 2007 Has an earthy/savoury edge to the fruit, along with regional dark chocolate nuances, but is a little deficient in mid-palate vinosity, perhaps the vintage. Screwcap. 14.5% alc. **Rating** 89 **To** 2017 $24
McLaren Vale Grenache Shiraz Mourvedre 2006 A potent, heady mix of Grenache/Shiraz/Mourvedre; demands food to quell the fire. Screwcap. 15.5% alc. **Rating** 89 **To** 2016 $22

Rockfield Estate ★★★★☆

Rosa Glen Road, Margaret River, WA 6285 **Region** Margaret River
T (08) 9757 5006 **www**.rockfield.com.au **Open** 7 days 11–5 or by appt
Winemaker Andrew Gaman Jr **Est.** 1997 **Cases** 7000 **Vyds** 11 ha
Rockfield Estate Vineyard is very much a family affair. Dr Andrew Gaman wears the hats of chief executive officer, assistant winemaker and co-marketing manager; wife Anne is a director; son Alex is the viticulturist; Andrew Gaman Jr is winemaker; and Anna Walter (née Gaman) helps with the marketing. Chapman Brook meanders through the property, the vines run from its banks up to the wooded slopes above the valley floor. Exports to the UK.

ŸŸŸŸŸ **Reserve Margaret River Chardonnay 2007** An intense, yet restrained, wine that achieves complexity on both bouquet and palate; has very good length to the grapefruit and white peach fruit. Screwcap. 13.5% alc. **Rating** 94 **To** 2017 $42

ŸŸŸŸŸ **Reserve Margaret River Shiraz 2006** Excellent colour for the vintage, bold and strong; the spicy/gamey bouquet is likewise impressive, the palate with abundant fruit supported by good tannins. Screwcap. 14% alc. **Rating** 92 **To** 2020 $45
Reserve Margaret River Merlot 2007 An intense evocation of merlot in Margaret River style, cassis, blackberry and cherry fruit embraced by fine, ripe tannins and quality French oak. Screwcap. 14% alc. **Rating** 92 **To** 2017 $45
Margaret River Semillon Sauvignon Blanc 2008 A quality example of the blend, led by the grassy/citrussy fruit of the semillon, the structure enhanced by a touch of barrel ferment. Good value. Screwcap. 12.5% alc. **Rating** 91 **To** 2013 $19
Semillon 2008 Plenty of flesh and accompanying structure due to oak inputs; good balance and length. Screwcap. 13% alc. **Rating** 90 **To** 2013 $22

ŸŸŸŸ **Sauvignon Blanc 2008** Stacked full of flavour, but is distinctly sweaty; love it or leave it. Screwcap. 13% alc. **Rating** 89 **To** 2011 $22
Reserve Extra Brut Margaret River Grande Cuvee Blanc de Blancs 2004 Bright green-gold; while there is complex stone fruit on the palate, and the wine spent time both in barrel and on lees, it is surprisingly short. Cork. 12.8% alc. **Rating** 87 **To** 2011 $42

Rockford ★★★★★

Krondorf Road, Tanunda, SA 5352 **Region** Barossa Valley
T (08) 8563 2720 **F** (08) 8563 3787 **www**.rockfordwines.com.au **Open** 7 days 11–5
Winemaker Robert O'Callaghan, Ben Radford **Est.** 1984 **Cases** NFP

Rockford can only be described as an icon, no matter how overused that word may be. It has a devoted band of customers who buy most of the wine through the cellar door or mail order (Rocky O'Callaghan's entrancing annual newsletter is like no other.) Some wine is sold through restaurants, and there are two retailers in Sydney, and one each in Melbourne, Brisbane and Perth. Whether they will have the Basket Press Shiraz available is another matter; it is as scarce as Henschke Hill of Grace (and less expensive). Exports to the UK, Canada, Switzerland, Korea, Singapore and NZ.

ΨΨΨΨΨ **Basket Press Barossa Valley Shiraz 2006** The brown glass, high-shouldered proprietary bottle gives the right message: this is a classic, gently understated Barossa Shiraz that will sail on for decades if the dubiously short cork permits. Drinking it sooner would not be a capital offence. 14.5% alc. **Rating** 95 **To** 2026 $51
Black Shiraz NV Disgorged August '08; the flavours, while intense, are positively elegant, a rare phenomenon indeed; the wine is beautifully balanced. Cork. 13.5% alc. **Rating** 95 **To** 2018 $56
Rifle Range Barossa Valley Cabernet Sauvignon 2006 In archetypal elegant, unfussed Rockford style, with a core of cassis/blackcurrant fruit complexed by savoury nuances that are wholly varietal; oak is a junior partner. Cork. 14.5% alc. **Rating** 94 **To** 2016 $35

ΨΨΨΨΨ **Handpicked Eden Valley Riesling 2006** Bright colour; has developed very well to this point; ripe citrus/lime fruit on a serene, flowing palate; now or over the next five years. Cork. 12% alc. **Rating** 92 **To** 2014 $19
Moppa Springs Barossa Valley Grenache Mataro Shiraz 2004 Has the expected range of spice and Christmas cake aromas; the palate is medium-bodied, and red fruits come to the fore before spice notes reassert themselves on the finish. Cork. 14.5% alc. **Rating** 92 **To** 2014 $23.50
Rod & Spur 2005 A mainstream mix of blackberry and blackcurrant fruit, the tannins balanced and ripe, the oak largely incidental. Will develop nicely. Cabernet Sauvignon/Shiraz. Cork. 14.5% alc. **Rating** 92 **To** 2015 $29.50

ΨΨΨΨ **Local Growers Barossa Valley Semillon 2005** Bright yellow tinged with green; the cork, while not musty, introduces a touch of woody (oaky) notes to the wine, interwoven between the toasty lemon butter flavours. 11.5% alc. **Rating** 89 **To** 2012 $18
Alicante Bouchet 2008 Bright, pale fuschia; very well made, with sweet, juicy small red fruits balanced and lengthened by crisp acidity. Rose. Screwcap. 9.5% alc. **Rating** 89 **To** 2010 $17
Barossa Valley White Frontignac 2008 Grapey, crisp and fresh, with just enough alcohol to give texture; bone dry finish. Screwcap. 10.8% alc. **Rating** 87 **To** 2010 $15.50

Rocky Passes Estate ★★★★

1590 Highlands Road, Seymour, Vic 3660 **Region** Upper Goulburn
T (03) 5796 9366 **F** (03) 5796 9366 **www.**rockypassesestate.com.au **Open** W'ends 10–5
Winemaker Vitto Oles **Est.** 2000 **Cases** 800 **Vyds** 2 ha
Vitto Oles and Candida Westney run this tiny, cool-climate vineyard situated at the southern end of the Strathbogie Ranges, which in fact falls in the Upper Goulburn region. They have planted 1.6 ha of shiraz and 0.4 ha of viognier, growing the vines with minimal irrigation and preferring organic and biodynamic soil treatments. Vitto is also a fine furniture designer and maker, with a studio at Rocky Passes.

ΨΨΨΨΨ **Upper Goulburn Syrah 2006** Impressive first-up effort; a silky texture to the medium-bodied palate, where juicy red and blackberry fruits slide through to the finish and aftertaste. Diam. 14% alc. **Rating** 92 **To** 2016 $20

ΨΨΨΨ **Sugarloaf Syrah 2007** Light- to medium-bodied palate; some elements of sweet and sour, moving from confit flavours on the mid-palate to a savoury finish. Diam. 13% alc. **Rating** 87 **To** 2012 $18

Rocland Estate

PO Box 679, Nuriootpa, SA 5355 **Region** Barossa Valley
T (08) 8562 2142 **F** (08) 8562 2182 **www**.roclandestate.com **Open** By appt
Winemaker Peter Gajewski **Est.** 2000 **Cases** 4000 **Vyds** 6 ha
Rocland Wines is primarily a bulk winemaking facility for contract work, but Frank Rocca does have 6 ha of shiraz to make the Rocland wines, largely destined for export markets (the US, Singapore, China and NZ), but with retail distribution in Adelaide.

ΩΩΩΩΩ **Lot 147 Barossa Valley Shiraz 2007** Crimson-red; has ripe and generous black fruit aromas replayed on the very even, supple palate; the tannins are balanced, as is the oak. Screwcap. 14.5% alc. **Rating** 93 **To** 2020 $28
Marsanne Viognier Roussanne 2008 Is well balanced, and has its whole life in front of it; will develop considerable character over the next five years. Screwcap. 14.5% alc. **Rating** 90 **To** 2015 $20
Shiraz 2007 More earthy than Lot 147, the mouthfeel less smooth; however, it does have plenty of fruit stuffing. Screwcap. 14.5% alc. **Rating** 90 **To** 2015 $22

ΩΩΩΩ **Duck's & Goose Barossa Shiraz 2005** Pleasant medium-bodied wine, which spent 30 months in used French and American oak, softening the blackberry fruit without overwhelming it with oak; soft tannins on the finish. Screwcap. 14.5% alc. **Rating** 89 **To** 2013 $17

Roennfeldt Wines

13 Augusta Street, Maylands, SA 5069 (postal) **Region** Barossa Valley
T 0411 180 960 **F** (08) 8363 9431 **Open** Not
Winemaker David Heinze **Est.** 2005 **Cases** 600 **Vyds** 18.2 ha
The Roennfeldt family emigrated from Germany in 1849 and has been growing grapes in the Barossa Valley for five generations. The vineyards, currently owned by Brett and Ruth Roennfeldt, are mainly 10–18 years old, with small sections of 50-year-old shiraz, mourvedre and grenache; 60% of the plantings are shiraz. The vineyard produces around 120 tonnes of grapes a year, almost all of which are sold to leading Barossa wineries. In 2005 five tonnes of seven- and 12-year-old shiraz were vinified to make the first release under the Roennfeldt label, marketed as 2005 Genesis Barossa Shiraz. No wine was made in the excellent 2006 vintage because the Roennfeldts were waiting to see how the '05 would be received. When it was placed sixth out of the 416 entries in the Visy Great Australian Shiraz Challenge '07 they had their answer, and production promptly resumed. The wine will always be a single-vineyard, estate-grown shiraz.

ΩΩΩΩ **Genesis Shiraz 2005** Dark and tarry on the bouquet; blackberry pastille palate, with lots of sweet fruit on the finish. Screwcap. 15% alc. **Rating** 89 **To** 2013 $25
Genesis Shiraz 2007 Colour a little dull; confected bouquet, loaded with sweet, almost jammy fruit; more life on the palate, with red fruit and fruitcake on offer. Screwcap. 13.5% alc. **Rating** 87 **To** 2014 $30

Rohrlach Family Wines

PO Box 864, Nuriootpa, SA 5355 **Region** Barossa Valley
T (08) 8562 4121 **F** (08) 8562 4202 **www**.rohrlachfamilywines.com.au **Open** Not
Winemaker Peter Schell (Contract) **Est.** 2000 **Cases** 1000 **Vyds** 160.6 ha
Brothers Kevin, Graham and Wayne Rohrlach, with wives Lyn, Lynette and Kaylene, are third-generation owners of prime vineyard land, the first plantings made back in 1930 by their paternal grandfather. Until 2000 the grapes were sold to two leading Barossa wineries, but (in a common story) in that year some of the grapes were retained to make the first vintage of what became Rohrlach Family Wines. In '03 the family received the ultimate local accolade when the Barons of the Barossa gave them the title of 'Vignerons of the Year'.

Rokewood Junction ★★★☆

123 Georges Road, Cambrian Hill, Vic 3352 (postal) **Region** Ballarat
T (03) 5342 0307 **Open** Not
Winemaker Graham Jacobsson **Est.** 1995 **Cases** 200 **Vyds** 2.5 ha
Western District farmer Graham Jacobsson planted pinot noir on a steep north-facing slope
in 1995. There are vertical slabs of shaley rock both under and on the surface, and the roots of
the vines penetrate the fissures. With no top soil and a very windy, exposed site, the vineyard
is basically devoid of diseases, and minimal vineyard intervention is needed. For a period of
time, Jacobsson sold his grapes to Tomboy Hill, but since 2005 has made wine under his own
label. Plantings include 1 ha each of shiraz and pinot noir, and 0.5 ha of viognier.

ΨΨΨΨΨ **Pinot Noir 2006** Light-bodied, but brightly coloured, and with a light, but
positive, core of small red fruits; and a fresh finish. Screwcap. 13.5% alc. **Rating** 90
To 2012 $25

ΨΨΨΨ **Pinot Noir 2007** An ultra-fine and very savoury/stemmy/foresty wine with
good texture and length, but not enough sweet fruit for higher points. Screwcap.
13.7% alc. **Rating** 89 **To** 2013 $25

Romney Park Wines ★★★★★

Lot 100, Johnson Road, Balhannah, SA 5242 **Region** Adelaide Hills
T (08) 8398 0698 **F** (08) 8398 0698 **Open** By appt
Winemaker Rod Short, Rachel Short **Est.** 1997 **Cases** 500 **Vyds** 3 ha
Rod and Rachel Short began the planting of chardonnay, shiraz and pinot noir in 1997.
The first vintage was in 2002, made from 100% estate-grown grapes. Yields are limited to
3.7–5 tonnes per hectare for the red wines, and 2–3 tonnes for the chardonnay. The vineyard
is managed organically, with guinea fowl cleaning up the insects. Most of the grapes are sold;
the limited production is sold by mail order. The property, incidentally, was previously known
as Balhannah Estate.

ΨΨΨΨΨ **Reserve Adelaide Hills Chardonnay 2006** Has very good balance and
structure; cashew, nectarine, melon, citrus, quality oak and wild yeast components
all coalesce in a very stylish wine. Diam. 13.5% alc. **Rating** 94 **To** 2014 $32
Barossa Shiraz 2006 Vibrant red-purple; an aromatic and scented bouquet leads
into luscious and mouthfilling blackberry and plum fruit; good oak and tannin
management to a high-quality wine. Diam. 14.5% alc. **Rating** 94 **To** 2021 $58
Adelaide Hills Shiraz 2006 Bright colour; red fruits dominate the bouquet
with a gentle lick of oak and spice; quite firm and focused, with silky tannin and
vibrant acidity. Diam. 14.5% alc. **Rating** 94 **To** 2016 $36

ΨΨΨΨΨ **Pinot Noir 2007** Bright colour; concentrated perfume of dark cherries and
a touch of mint; quite firm and tannic, with dark fruit being tightly wound at
this point; a big wine needing some time to soften. Diam. 14% alc. **Rating** 93
To 2014 $39
Adelaide Hills Shiraz 2007 Good colour; lifted black and red fruit bouquet
with a dose of cinnamon spice; medium-bodied and with silky texture, finishing
with tarry red fruit and focused acidity. Diam. 14.5% alc. **Rating** 93 **To** 2016 $36

Rookery Wines ★★★☆

PO Box 132, Kingscote, Kangaroo Island, SA 5223 **Region** Kangaroo Island
T (08) 8553 9099 **F** (08) 8553 9201 **www.**rookerywines.com.au **Open** By appt
Winemaker Garry Lovering **Est.** 1999 **Cases** 1000 **Vyds** 8.3 ha
Garry and Gael Lovering have established 2.8 ha of cabernet sauvignon and 1.8 ha of shiraz,
with smaller plantings of sauvignon blanc, tempranillo, saperavi, sangiovese, chardonnay,
merlot, petit verdot, riesling and primitivo. Kangaroo Island is one of SA's best-kept secrets,
a place of genuine magic with its aquatic life, amazing coastline sculpture, wild flowers and
prolific native fauna.

ρρρρ Kangaroo Island Sangiovese 2006 Light colour and relatively light-bodied, but at this price no one should complain because the flavours are authentic; the tannins are fine and light. Screwcap. 14.5% alc. **Rating** 89 **To** 2014 $17

Kangaroo Island Petit Verdot 2006 A massive, full-bodied Petit Verdot; inwards looking, and with years to go, although the black fruits are ripe and the balance is intrinsically good. Simply needs patience. Screwcap. 14.5% alc. **Rating** 89 **To** 2020 $17

Kangaroo Island Riesling 2008 Has an appealing mix of lime and tropical fruits, and plenty of mid-palate fruit. Screwcap. 12.5% alc. **Rating** 89 **To** 2013 $19.50

Kangaroo Island Shiraz 2006 Attractive notes of spice and licorice on the bouquet also find their way into the medium-bodied palate to define its character; just a little light on. Screwcap. 14.8% alc. **Rating** 88 **To** 2014 $18

Kangaroo Island Unwooded Chardonnay 2008 Aromatic stone fruit and grapefruit characters on the bouquet, repeated on the palate, which is generous, if inevitably simple. Screwcap. 13.5% alc. **Rating** 87 **To** 2010 $18

Rosby ★★★☆

122 Strikes Lane, Mudgee, NSW 2850 **Region** Mudgee
T (02) 6373 3856 **F** (02) 6373 3109 **www.**rosby.com.au **Open** By appt
Winemaker Tim Stevens **Est.** 1997 **Cases** 800 **Vyds** 6 ha
Gerald and Kaye Norton-Knight have 4 ha of shiraz and 2 ha of cabernet sauvignon established on what is truly a unique site in Mudgee. Many new vignerons like to think that their vineyard has special qualities, but in this instance the belief is well based. It is situated in a small valley, with unusual red basalt over a quartz gravel structure, encouraging deep root growth, and making the use of water far less critical than normal. Tim Stevens of Abercorn and Huntington Estate has purchased much of the production, and has no hesitation in saying it is of the highest quality (it formed an important part of his multi-trophy winning A Reserve range).

ρρρρρ Mudgee Cabernet Sauvignon 2006 Strong red-purple; medium- to full-bodied, with blackcurrant and black cherry fruit supported by persistent, but balanced, tannins; good length. Trophy Best Cabernet of Show, Mudgee Wine Show. Screwcap. 13.6% alc. **Rating** 92 **To** 2016 $18.30

ρρρρ Mudgee Shiraz 2006 Medium-bodied, with gently ripe plummy fruit; overtones of mocha and chocolate, finishing with ripe tannins. Silver Mudgee Wine Show '08. Screwcap. 13.8% alc. **Rating** 88 **To** 2012 $20

Rose Hill Estate Wines

1400 Oxley Flats Road, Milawa, Vic 3678 **Region** King Valley
T (03) 5727 3930 **www.**rosehillestatewines.com.au **Open** Fri–Mon 10–6
Winemaker Jo Hale **Est.** 1996 **Cases** 400
The Rose Hill vineyard, winery and house are all the work of Milawa cabinetmaker Stan Stafford (and friends). The house, using 150-year-old bricks from a former chapel at Everton, came first, almost 30 years ago. Then came the vineyard, with merlot planted in 1987, and durif planted in 2002 to fill in the gaps where the merlot had died. It's a strange mix of bedfellows, but it's easy to tell which is which. In '04, after many sleepless nights weighing up the pros and cons, Jo Hale and Kevin de Henin purchased the estate from Stan. They knew what they were doing: Jo had helped Stan in both vineyard and winery in the last few years while studying wine science at CSU, and working for Brown Brothers, Gapsted Wines and Sam Miranda; Kevin had also worked at many regional vineyards and wineries.

ρρρρ King Valley Merlot 2006 Good colour; offers a mix of tarry/savoury notes alongside red and blackcurrant fruit in a medium-bodied frame. Screwcap. 14.7% alc. **Rating** 88 **To** 2013 $18

Rosemount Estate (Hunter Valley)

McDonalds Road, Pokolbin, NSW 2320 **Region** Upper Hunter Valley
T (02) 4998 6670 **F** (02) 4998 6680 **www.**rosemountestates.com **Open** 7 days 10–5
Winemaker Matthew Koch **Est.** 1969 **Cases** 3 million
Under the energetic and highly successful ownership of the founding Oatley family,
Rosemount Estate was one of the brightest stars in the Australian wine sky. It merged with
Southcorp in 2001, and what seemed to be a powerful and synergistic merger turned out to
be little short of a disaster. It is now part of Foster's, and ongoing efforts are being made to
re-establish the brand value the business once had. The bleak economic outlook for the world,
and continuing wine surpluses in Australia, seem likely to make the process slow. Exports to
all major markets.

ŶŶŶŶ **Show Reserve Chardonnay 2007** A toasty bouquet of ripe peach and straw;
rich and full on the palate, with a lingering toast, straw and melon finish. Screwcap.
13.5% alc. **Rating** 89 **To** 2013 $19.99
Diamond Label Shiraz 2007 While medium-bodied, has plenty of complexity
and texture to the blackberry fruits; balanced tannins and good length. Screwcap.
13.5% alc. **Rating** 89 **To** 2013 $15.99
Diamond Label Merlot 2007 While only light- to medium-bodied, does have
the combination of a red fruit entry to the mouth and a slightly savoury twist to
the finish expected of the variety. Screwcap. 13.5% alc. **Rating** 87 **To** 2011 $15.99

Rosemount Estate (McLaren Vale)

Chaffeys Road, McLaren Vale, SA 5171 **Region** McLaren Vale
T (08) 8323 8250 **F** (08) 8323 9308 **www.**rosemountestate.com.au **Open** Mon–Sat 10–5,
Sun & public hols 11–4
Winemaker Charles Whish **Est.** 1888 **Cases** 3 million
The specialist red wine arm of Rosemount Estate, responsible for its prestigious Balmoral
Syrah, Show Reserve Shiraz and GSM, as well as most of the other McLaren Vale–based
Rosemount brands. These wines come in large measure from 325 ha of estate plantings.
Exports to all major markets.

ŶŶŶŶŶ **Show Reserve GSM 2005** Retains very good hue; a vibrant and juicy mix of
blackberry, raspberry and dark chocolate, balanced by firm but ripe tannins; best
for some years. Screwcap. 14.5% alc. **Rating** 94 **To** 2015 $20.95

ŶŶŶŶŶ **Show Reserve Traditional 2006** A full-bodied wine, replete with blackcurrant,
blackberry, licorice and dark chocolate fruit, the tannins firm but in balance, oak
in the back seat. Will develop very well. Cabernet Sauvignon/Merlot/Petit Verdot.
Screwcap. 14.5% alc. **Rating** 93 **To** 2026 $19.99
Show Reserve Shiraz 2005 Good hue; a complex wine both in terms of
fruit flavours and structure; excellent savoury offsets to the blackberry and dark
chocolate fruit, fine tannins running through the length of the palate. Screwcap.
14.5% alc. **Rating** 92 **To** 2015 $20.95
Balmoral Syrah 2004 Brick hue; a dark and tarry bouquet with a touch
of leather, mocha and dried plums; the palate is very firm, quite savoury and
developed; dense and chewy on the finish. Screwcap. 14.5% alc. **Rating** 92
To 2014 $67.99
Show Reserve Coonawarra Cabernet Sauvignon 2006 Clear regional and
varietal character, with all the marks of perfectly ripened cabernet; the tannins
do need to soften, so leave alone for some years. Screwcap. 14.5% alc. **Rating** 92
To 2021 $20.95
Show Reserve GSM 2006 Bright colour; raspberry, spice and a touch of
bramble; focused sweet fruit is played off with a savoury core; dark and chewy,
there is plenty of interest on the finish. Grenache/Shiraz/Mourvedre. Screwcap.
14.5% alc. **Rating** 90 **To** 2015 $19.99

Rosenthal Wines   ★★★☆

PO Box 1458, South Perth, WA 6951 **Region** Blackwood Valley
T 0407 773 966 **F** (08) 9368 6445 **www.**rosenthalwines.com.au **Open** Not
Winemaker The Vintage Wineworx (Greg Jones) **Est.** 2001 **Cases** 1000 **Vyds** 4 ha
Perth medical specialist Dr John Rosenthal heads Rosenthal Wines, which is a small part
of the much larger 180-ha Springfield Park cattle stud situated between Bridgetown and
Manjimup. He acquired the property from Gerald and Marjorie Richings, who in 1997 had
planted a small vineyard as a minor diversification. The Rosenthals extended the vineyard,
which is equally divided between shiraz and cabernet sauvignon. All of the wines have had
significant show success, chiefly in WA-based shows. No wine was made in 2007; the '08 red
wines are to be released early in '10.

♀♀♀♀♀ **Cabernet Shiraz 2005** Scented, with some smoky bacon oak; a complex
palate, with tannins still needing time to fully soften, but should do so. Gold WA
Wine Show '08, and trophies in regional wine shows in '08. Screwcap. 13% alc.
Rating 93 **To** 2015 $30

♀♀♀♀ **Shiraz Cabernet 2006** Good hue; a light- to medium-bodied wine with fresh
blackberry and cherry fruits; does not require cellaring; minimal tannin and oak
inputs. Screwcap. 13% alc. **Rating** 88 **To** 2012 $20

Rosenvale Wines   ★★★★☆

Lot 385 Railway Terrace, Nuriootpa, SA 5355 **Region** Barossa Valley
T 0407 390 788 **F** (08) 8565 7206 **www.**rosenvale.com.au **Open** By appt
Winemaker James Rosenzweig, Mark Jamieson **Est.** 2000 **Cases** 4000 **Vyds** 80 ha
The Rosenzweig family vineyards, some old and some new, are planted to riesling, semillon,
chardonnay, pinot noir, grenache, shiraz and cabernet sauvignon. Most of the grapes are sold
to other producers, but since 2000 select parcels have been retained and vinified for release
under the Rosenvale label. Exports to the UK, the US and other major markets.

♀♀♀♀♀ **Estate Barossa Valley Cabernet Sauvignon 2006** At the full end of the
spectrum, but equally shows what a good vintage '06 was for cabernet in the
Barossa Valley; cassis and blackcurrant are complemented by French oak, the
tannins well-balanced and ripe. Cork. 14.5% alc. **Rating** 93 **To** 2016 $24
Reserve Barossa Valley Shiraz 2006 Dense colour; a potent medium-
to full-bodied wine offering layers of blackberry, licorice, tar and plum with
well-integrated oak, the tannins ripe. Diam. 14.5% alc. **Rating** 93 **To** 2020 $40
Barossa Valley Shiraz Cabernet 2005 Very much in the powerful, concentrated style of Rosenvale; layers of blackcurrant and blackberry fruit; good structure
and balance to a long-lived wine. Diam. 14.5% alc. **Rating** 90 **To** 2015 $28

♀♀♀♀ **Estate Barossa Valley Shiraz 2006** Medium-bodied, with opulent blackberry
and plum fruit; oak invests the wine with a touch of vanilla; good balance. Diam.
Rating 89 **To** 2015 $24
Estate Barossa Valley Semillon 2008 Powerful wine from vines almost
70 years old; unoaked, but otherwise in traditional Barossa style, trenchantly
mouthfilling. Screwcap. 13.5% alc. **Rating** 88 **To** 2012 $24

Rosily Vineyard   ★★★★☆

Yelveton Road, Wilyabrup, WA 6284 **Region** Margaret River
T (08) 9755 6336 **F** (08) 9221 3309 **www.**rosily.com.au **Open** W'ends 10–5 during hols
Winemaker Mike Lemmes, Dan Pannell (Consultant) **Est.** 1994 **Cases** 6500 **Vyds** 11.77 ha
The partnership of Mike and Barb Scott and Ken and Dot Allan acquired the Rosily
Vineyard site in 1994. Under the direction of consultant Dan Pannell (of *the* Pannell family),
the vineyard was planted over the next three years to sauvignon blanc, semillon, chardonnay,
cabernet sauvignon, merlot, shiraz, grenache and cabernet franc. The first crops were sold to
other makers in the region, but in 1999 Rosily built a winery with 120-tonne capacity, and is
now moving to fully utilise that capacity. Exports to the UK, Hong Kong and Singapore.

ΥΥΥΥΥ Shiraz 2005 Vibrant colour; wonderful penetrating, pure and long; a lovely cool-climate style, with length and a harmonious finish. Gold WA Wine Show '08. Screwcap. 14.4% alc. **Rating** 95 **To** 2015 $22

ΥΥΥΥΥ **Margaret River Sauvignon Blanc 2008** Grassy capsicum aromas, with more depth/ripeness on the palate; has length. Screwcap. 13.4% alc. **Rating** 93 **To** 2015 $18

The Cartographer 2005 A good varietal Bordeaux blend, with elements of sweet black fruit, cassis and just a little hint of oak; medium-bodied, fine and well balanced. Screwcap. 14% alc. **Rating** 92 **To** 2015 $23

Margaret River Chardonnay 2007 Generously proportioned, with an abundance of stone fruit flavours and a drizzle of grapefruit; has two of the Dijon clones so successful in eastern states. Screwcap. 13.5% alc. **Rating** 91 **To** 2014 $23

🍇 Roslyn Estate ★★★★

409 White Kangaroo Road, Campania, Tas 7026 **Region** Southern Tasmania
T (03) 6260 4077 **F** (03) 6260 4072 **www**.roslynestate.com.au **Open** By appt
Winemaker Hood Wines **Est.** 2001 **Cases** 11 000 **Vyds** 45 ha
The 408-ha Roslyn Estate is part of a much larger property dating back to 1821, which has had only three owners in the intervening time. In 2000, when the property was divided, the homestead and surrounding land was purchased by the Allen family. In 2001 the planting of vines began on various parts of the property, selected by soil type and a north-facing aspect; in all, there are 27 different blocks at different altitudes, the lion's share given to just under 18 ha of pinot noir and a little over 11 ha of chardonnay. Other varieties planted are sauvignon blanc, riesling, merlot, cabernet sauvignon, cabernet franc and petit verdot. The 2006 Unwooded Chardonnay won silver medals in '07 and '08 at the Tasmanian Wines Show, the '07 Sauvignon Blanc won a gold medal in '08. Exports to the Maldives.

ΥΥΥΥΥ Sauvignon Blanc 2007 Strong herb and nettle aromas, but with very good fruit-weight underneath; a long, crisp, lingering dry finish; gold medal Tas Wine Show '07. **Rating** 94 **To** 2010

ΥΥΥΥ Pinot Noir 2006 Good varietal character, with red cherry and plum, plus a touch of spice; well put together. **Rating** 89 **To** 2010

Cabernet Merlot 2006 Quite complex and layered; cedar frames a little splash of cassis on the palate, followed by a dry, firm finish. **Rating** 87 **To** 2013

Ross Estate Wines ★★★★

Barossa Valley Way, Lyndoch, SA 5351 **Region** Barossa Valley
T (08) 8524 4033 **F** (08) 8524 4533 **www**.rossestate.com.au **Open** 7 days 10–4
Winemaker Neville Falkenberg, Alex Peel **Est.** 1999 **Cases** 20 000 **Vyds** 43 ha
Darius and Pauline Ross laid the foundation for Ross Estate Wines when they purchased a vineyard that included two blocks of 75- and 90-year-old grenache. Also included were blocks of 30-year-old riesling and semillon, and 13-year-old merlot; plantings of chardonnay, sauvignon blanc, cabernet sauvignon, cabernet franc, shiraz and tempranillo have followed. Neville Falkenberg has moved to Ross Estate from Chain of Ponds to take the place of Rod Chapman, who has retired. Exports to the UK, the US and other major markets.

ΥΥΥΥΥ Altona Reserve Shiraz 2006 Quite a rich and forward wine, full of mocha and blackberry; good concentration, but ready to go, and should be enjoyed in the shorter term. Cork. 15% alc. **Rating** 91 **To** 2013 $45

Lynedoch Cabernet Sauvignon Cabernet Franc Merlot 2006 Sweet fruited bouquet and palate; juicy and generous, with a bit of warmth and some tarry character on the finish. Screwcap. 14.5% alc. **Rating** 90 **To** 2014 $25

ΥΥΥΥ Single Vineyard Shiraz 2006 Concentrated and powerful wine; the alcohol is a little prominent, and the fruit quite sweet, supple and forward. Screwcap. 14.5% alc. **Rating** 89 **To** 2014 $26

Single Vineyard Old Vine Barossa Valley Grenache 2007 Candied raspberry fruit bouquet with a touch of spice; good weight with a touch of undergrowth coming through on the palate. Screwcap. 14.5% alc. **Rating** 88 To 2015 $20

Ross Hill Vineyard

62 Griffin Road, Orange, NSW 2800 **Region** Orange
T (02) 6360 0175 **www**.rosshillwines.com.au **Open** Sat 11–5 or by appt
Winemaker David Lowe (Contract) **Est.** 1994 **Cases** 3000 **Vyds** 12 ha
Peter and Terri Robson began planting vines in 1994. Chardonnay, merlot, sauvignon blanc, cabernet franc, shiraz and pinot noir have been established on north-facing, gentle slopes at an elevation of 800 m. No insecticides are used in the vineyard, the grapes are hand-picked and the vines are hand-pruned. Ross Hill also has an olive grove with Italian and Spanish varieties. Exports to the UK.

ȚȚȚȚ **Orange Rose 2008** Cherry fruit, with a touch of herb and spice; the palate is quite dry, and shows plenty of red fruit on the finish; evenly balanced. Screwcap. 13.1% alc. **Rating** 88 To 2011 $21
Mack's Block Orange Shiraz 2007 Bright colour; restrained plum bouquet, also exhibiting a little leather and spice; medium-bodied, refreshing acidity cleaning up the finish. Screwcap. 14% alc. **Rating** 88 To 2014 $25
Maya Orange Chardonnay 2006 Peach, fig and straw bouquet; rich palate, with a noticeable, slightly oxidative grilled nut finish. Screwcap. 13.5% alc. **Rating** 87 To 2011 $21
Jessica Orange Merlot 2007 Plum and cherry on the bouquet; a little spice and cedar frames the cool fruit well. Screwcap. 14% alc. **Rating** 87 To 2012 $21

Roundstone Winery & Vineyard ★★★★

54 Willow Bend Drive, Yarra Glen, Vic 3775 **Region** Yarra Valley
T (03) 9730 1181 **F** (03) 9730 1151 **www**.roundstonewine.com.au **Open** Wed–Sun & public hols 10–5, or by appt
Winemaker John Derwin **Est.** 1998 **Cases** 5000 **Vyds** 8 ha
John and Lynne Derwin lost everything in the Black Saturday bushfires on 7 February 2009: their house, the winery, the restaurant, all bottled wine on the premises, and the trellising and irrigation system in the scorched and blackened vines. Poignantly, their distributor John Davey, his wife, and two children died in the Kinglake fire. The only thing spared was bulk-bottled stock stored elsewhere, which will be gradually sold until the Derwins are able to fully come to grips with the financial consequences of the fire. They do not wish to walk away from 10 years of effort building the brand, but what they will rebuild, and when the process will begin, is as yet uncertain.

ȚȚȚȚȚ **Yarra Valley Sauvignon Blanc 2008** Very pale colour; tight, crisp and clear aromas and flavours run through a notably long palate; seafood and summer style. Screwcap. 12.9% alc. **Rating** 90 To 2011 $25
Yarra Valley Gamay 2008 Bright crimson-red; a fresh, fruit-forward style that does full justice to its varietal origin; ready to drink right now. Screwcap. 13.5% alc. **Rating** 90 To 2009 $22

ȚȚȚȚ **Yarra Valley Rose 2008** Pale salmon; distinct overtones of Tavel rose, barrel-fermented with wild yeast; gently spicy and bone dry; good tapas style. Screwcap. 13.6% alc. **Rating** 88 To 2010 $22

Rowans Lane Wines

40 Farnham Road, Dennington, Vic 3280 **Region** Henty
T (03) 5565 1586 **F** (03) 5565 1586 **www**.rowanslanewines.com.au **Open** W'ends & public hols 10.30–5, or by appt
Winemaker Ted Rafferty **Est.** 2003 **Cases** 500

Ted and Judy Rafferty expanded their lifetime interest in wine by establishing an experimental 0.8-ha vineyard at their Rowans Lane property in 1999, making their first Pinot Noir in 2003. This encouraged them to expand their plantings to 3.6 ha at a second site at Dennington, on the banks of the Merri River. To supplement their own production, they have purchased grapes from other leading Henty grapegrowers, each with an impressive track record.

TTTTT Shiraz 2007 Bright red and blue fruit bouquet, full of spice and a touch of gamey complexity; medium-bodied with velvety texture and bright and focused fruit on the finish; there is an appealing European quality to the texture of this wine. Cork. 13.4% alc. **Rating** 92 **To** 2015 $25

Rowanston on the Track ★★★★☆

2710 Burke & Wills Track, Glenhope, Vic 3444 **Region** Macedon Ranges
T (03) 5425 5492 **www**.rowanston.com **Open** Thurs–Sun 9–5, or by appt
Winemaker John Frederiksen **Est.** 2003 **Cases** 2500 **Vyds** 9.3 ha
John (a social worker) and Marilyn (a former teacher turned viticulturist) Frederiksen are no strangers to grapegrowing and winemaking in the Macedon Ranges. They founded Metcalfe Valley Vineyard in 1995, planting 5.6 ha of shiraz, going on to win gold medals at local wine shows. They sold the vineyard in early 2003, moving to their new property in the same year, which now has 9.3 ha of vines. In descending order of size the plantings are of shiraz, merlot, riesling, and sauvignon blanc. The heavy red soils and basal ridges hold moisture, which allows watering requirements to be kept to a minimum. Exports to the US.

TTTTT Riesling 2008 Brilliant straw-green; has very good focus and intensity to the mix of lime juice fruit and almost spicy minerality; has all the ingredients for a long life. Top value. Screwcap. 12.5% alc. **Rating** 93 **To** 2018 $17

Rumbalara

137 Fletcher Road, Fletcher, Qld 4381 **Region** Granite Belt
T (07) 4684 1206 **F** (07) 4684 1299 **www**.rumbalarawines.com.au **Open** 7 days 10–5
Winemaker Mike Cragg **Est.** 1974 **Cases** 4000 **Vyds** 3.25 ha
Established by Bob and Una Gray, who produced some of the Granite Belt's finest honeyed Semillon and silky, red berry Cabernet Sauvignon, it was purchased by Kime and Bobbi Cragg in 2002. The winery incorporates a spacious restaurant, and there are also barbecue and picnic facilities. A most impressive line-up (the first tastings for some years) for this edition.

TTTTT Shiraz 2007 Well made, with positive varietal character; blackberry and some unexpected spice; has excellent length and mouthfeel, and over-delivers on price. Screwcap. 14% alc. **Rating** 91 **To** 2016 $22
Shiraz Merlot Cabernet Sauvignon 2008 A burst of fresh red berry, cassis and raspberry fruits, unencumbered by oak or obvious tannins. Brilliant drink-now style; brilliant price. Screwcap. 13% alc. **Rating** 90 **To** 2010 $13
Merlot 2005 Has a little more structural complexity than the '06, and the fruit flavours are every bit as vibrant; enhances the impact of the of the suite of wines from Rumbalara. Diam. 13.3% alc. **Rating** 90 **To** 2016 $25
Cabernet Sauvignon 2007 A well-made medium-bodied Cabernet that pushes all the right buttons, with blackcurrant and mulberry fruit; soft, but adequate, tannins and integrated oak. Screwcap. 14% alc. **Rating** 90 **To** 2015 $22
Cabernet Sauvignon 2005 Good depth and hue to the colour; much the most powerful of the Rumbalara reds, and needs more time than the others; however, the blackcurrant fruit holds its own with the tannins, and the wine is balanced. Diam. 13.8% alc. **Rating** 90 **To** 2017 $25

TTTT Merlot 2007 Yet another well-made wine from Granite Belt grapes, with good colour and distinct spicy notes to the red cherry/berry fruits of the palate; good length. Screwcap. 13% alc. **Rating** 89 **To** 2014 $20
Verdelho 2008 Crisp, clean and fresh; well made; serve chilled with seafood. Screwcap. 13.9% alc. **Rating** 87 **To** 2009 $18

Shiraz 2005 Full of plum and chocolate flavour, but doesn't have the finesse of the '06; the tannins have distracting rough edges. Screwcap. 13.6% alc. **Rating** 87 To 2013 $25

🍇 Rupert's Ridge Estate Vineyard ★★★★

843 Metcalfe-Redesdale Road, Redesdale, Vic 3444 (postal) **Region** Heathcote
T (03) 5425 3297 **F** (03) 5425 3297 **www.**rupertsridge.com **Open** Not
Winemaker Cobaw Ridge (Alan Cooper) **Est.** 2003 **Cases** 140 **Vyds** 4 ha
Christina (Chris) Gillies and husband John Williams were grandparents before they embarked on a search for what became Rupert's Ridge in 2003. Armed with the bravery of ignorance, a book on how to plant a vineyard, and Alan Cooper of Cobaw Ridge to give advice in moments of crisis, they began planting 2.5 ha of shiraz and viognier. There was no such thing as delegation; they planted the vines themselves, and came to know each one by name. Bloodied but unbowed, the following year they planted another 2 ha, mainly shiraz but with 0.25 ha each of vermentino and sagrantino. The first crop (6 tonnes) came in '06, and over the next two years they retained 1 tonne (producing 70 cases) selling the remainder of the grapes. The intention was to double the production in '09, but the terrible bushfires are more likely than not to have put paid to that. Chris and John were overseas, but last ditch defence by family friends, Redesdale locals and local winemakers largely saved the vineyard (though not the crop), but the house burnt down. A bit of adversity is not going to deter Chris and John from turning the galvanised iron former pig shed (which did survive the fire) into a cellar door, and once the house is rebuilt, it will be business as usual. The name, incidentally, is that of their great dane mastiff who provides a 24-hour security service, and escaped the fire.

🍷🍷🍷🍷🍷 **Shiraz 2006** Deeply coloured; rich black fruit and licorice aromas lead into a full-bodied palate supported by firm, gently savoury tannins; will be long lived. Diam. 13.5% alc. **Rating** 93 **To** 2021 $25
Shiraz 2007 Blackberry, blackcurrant and licorice aromas are replicated on the medium-bodied palate, with savoury tannins asserting themselves on the finish. Patience will reward. Diam. 14% alc. **Rating** 90 **To** 2015 $25

Russell Wines ★★★★★

45 Murray Street, Angaston, SA 5353 **Region** Barossa Valley
T (08) 8564 2511 **F** (08) 8564 2533 **www.**russellwines.com.au **Open** By appt
Winemaker Shawn Kalleske (Contract) **Est.** 2001 **Cases** 3500 **Vyds** 32.5 ha
John Russell (and wife Rosalind) came to the Barossa in 1990 to create the Barossa Music Festival. The winemaking bug soon bit, and in '94 they planted vines at Krondorf (expanded over the years) and on three vineyards at St Vincent, Augusta and Greenock Farm, which in turn give rise to the three labels. The cellar door is situated in the old Angaston Court House, where wine, food, music and art exhibitions are all on offer. Shawn Kalleske not only makes the wine, but oversees both his and Russell Wines' vineyards; part of the grape production from the latter is sold to other Barossa wineries. Exports to Switzerland.

🍷🍷🍷🍷🍷 **St Vincent Barossa Valley Shiraz 2006** Strong crimson-red; complex, but immaculately balanced and structured, with black fruits, quality oak and ripe tannins seamlessly welded; high-quality cork. 14.5% alc. **Rating** 95 **To** 2026 $40
Greenock Farm The Fenceline 2004 Deep crimson-purple due to the co-fermentation of at least some of the potpourri of varieties (Grenache/Shiraz/Mourvedre/Semillon/Riesling/Red Frontignan/White Frontignan/Tokay). The flavours are harmonious, the texture supple, and the alcohol not pervasive. Surely Australia's most unusual wine. Cork. 15% alc. **Rating** 94 **To** 2025 $100

🍷🍷🍷🍷🍷 **Augusta Barossa Valley Shiraz 2006** A dark and tarry bouquet, with fruitcake and essence of blackberry; the palate is rich and dense, with chewy tannins and plenty of oak for the fruit to use in support. Cork. 14.5% alc. **Rating** 93 To 2020 $25

Augusta Chardonnay 2006 Impressive chardonnay given its region and age; while full-flavoured in every department, it still has good focus, structure and freshness. Ready now. Screwcap. 13.5% alc. **Rating** 90 **To** 2012 $15

St Vincent Barossa Valley Chardonnay 2006 More complex and weightier than the Augusta, but not necessarily better; shares the family style, and has good length. Screwcap. 13.5% alc. **Rating** 90 **To** 2012 $20

The Victor Greenock Farm Barossa Valley Shiraz 2006 Dense colour; has the power and impact on the palate promised by the colour and alcohol, but some attractive shiraz flavours of licorice and confit plum do escape; the balance is surprisingly good. Cork. 15.5% alc. **Rating** 90 **To** 2016 $85

ΨΨΨΨ **St Vincent Barossa Valley Cabernet 2006** Deep colour; the bouquet has warm and sweet cassis fruit; essency fruit palate; a little one-dimensional. Cork. 14.5% alc. **Rating** 87 **To** 2013 $30

Rusticana ★★★★

Lake Plains Road, Langhorne Creek, SA 5255 **Region** Langhorne Creek
T (08) 8537 3086 **F** (08) 8537 3220 **www**.rusticanawines.com.au **Open** 7 days 10–5
Winemaker John Glaetzer (Consultant) **Est.** 1998 **Cases** 1000 **Vyds** 10 ha
Brian and Anne Meakins are also owners of Newman's Horseradish, which has been on the SA market for over 80 years. Increasing demand for the horseradish forced a move from Tea Tree Gully to Langhorne Creek in 1985. It wasn't until 1997 that they succumbed to the urging of neighbours and planted 4.5 ha each of shiraz and cabernet sauvignon, adding 0.5 ha each of durif and zinfandel several years later.

ΨΨΨΨΨ **Langhorne Creek Durif 2007** Deeply coloured; vibrant spiced blackberry bouquet, with good concentration and lively structure on the palate; a well-handled example of this sometimes over-the-top variety, carrying the 16.2% alcohol with ease. Screwcap. 16.2% alc. **Rating** 90 **To** 2014 $30

Rutherglen Estates ★★★★

Cnr Great Northern Road/Murray Valley Highway, Rutherglen, Vic 3685 **Region** Rutherglen
T (02) 6032 7999 **F** (02) 6032 7998 **www**.rutherglenestates.com.au **Open** At Tuileries Building, Rutherglen 7 days 10–6
Winemaker Nicole Esdaile, Marc Scalzo **Est.** 2000 **Cases** 50 000
Rutherglen Estates is an offshoot of a far larger contract crush-and-make business, with a winery capacity of 4000 tonnes (roughly equivalent to 280 000 cases). Rutherglen is in a declared phylloxera region, which means all the grapes grown within that region have to be vinified within it, itself a guarantee of business for ventures such as Rutherglen Estates. It also means that some of the best available material can be allocated for the brand, with an interesting mix of varieties. Smart, upgraded, packaging is yet another part of the marketing mix. Exports to the UK, the US and other major markets.

ΨΨΨΨΨ **Renaissance Viognier Roussanne Marsanne 2007** The bouquet shows plenty of ripe fruit and powerful apricot, spice and a touch of honeysuckle; the palate is vibrant and appealing, with many layers opening over the duration. Screwcap. 14% alc. **Rating** 91 **To** 2014 $30.95

Renaissance Zinfandel 2007 A nicely balanced combination of bright red fruits and a touch of blackberry; there is a little varietal sweetness to the fruit, and an elegant aspect that delivers a complex example while maintaining balance. Screwcap. 14% alc. **Rating** 90 **To** 2014 $34.95

ΨΨΨΨ **Marsanne Viognier 2007** A clean, albeit neutral bouquet, leads into a palate with good weight and texture; the fruit profile of melon and a touch of citrus, helped by well-balanced acidity, but without any defining character. Screwcap. 13.5% alc. **Rating** 89 **To** 2010 $15.95

Shiraz Viognier 2007 Has the typical bright colour and lifted fruit flavours achieved by co-fermentation with a small percentage of viognier; cherry and plum flavours, the tannins soft. Screwcap. 14.5% alc. **Rating** 89 **To** 2014 $20.95

Durif 2007 Inky purple; unashamedly full-bodied, with prune and blackberry conserve surrounded by firm, dusty tannins, which in fact save the wine from itself. Screwcap. 14.5% alc. **Rating** 89 **To** 2017 $21.95

Viognier 2008 A rich, well-made wine, with some barrel ferment adding complexity to the honeyed tropical fruit flavours; does show its alcohol on the finish. Screwcap. 14.5% alc. **Rating** 88 **To** 2012 $19.95

Sparkling Shiraz Durif 2007 Vibrant colour and juicy young blue fruit bouquet; quite sweet, but the balance offers a fun sparkling red. Cork. 14.5% alc. **Rating** 88 **To** 2012 $26.95

Rymill Coonawarra   ★★★★

Riddoch Highway, Coonawarra, SA 5263 **Region** Coonawarra
T (08) 8736 5001 **F** (08) 8736 5040 **www**.rymill.com.au **Open** 7 days 10–5
Winemaker Sandrine Gimon **Est.** 1974 **Cases** 35 000 **Vyds** 150 ha

The Rymills are descendants of John Riddoch and have long owned some of the finest Coonawarra soil, upon which they have grown grapes since 1970. The promotion of Champagne-trained Sandrine Gimon to chief winemaker (after three years as winemaker at Rymill) is interesting. Sandrine is a European version of a Flying Winemaker, having managed a winery in Bordeaux, and made wine in Champagne, Languedoc, Romania and WA. Given the size of the vineyards, and the onsite winery, Rymill has never quite lived up to the high expectations it engenders. Exports to all major markets.

ΨΨΨΨΨ **12 Years on Lees Chardonnay Pinot Noir 1994** Pale straw-green; incredibly fine and fresh, presumably sustained in part by the high acidity and low pH of the base wine; citrus and berry fruit, with a long, clean finish; 110 cases made. Diam. 12% alc. **Rating** 93 **To** 2015 $50

ΨΨΨΨ **Rose 2008** Bright, pale pink; subtle red fruit bouquet, with good weight and fine acidity; a quite dry finish. Screwcap. 13% alc. **Rating** 88 **To** 2011 $18

Sauvignon Blanc 2008 Pleasant wine, moving from a herbaceous bouquet to soft, tropical fruit salad flavours on the palate. Screwcap. 12% alc. **Rating** 87 **To** 2009 $17.95

S Kidman Wines   ★★★★

Riddoch Highway, Coonawarra, SA 5263 **Region** Coonawarra
T (08) 8736 5071 **www**.kidmanwines.com.au **Open** 7 days 10–5
Winemaker John Innes (Contract) **Est.** 1984 **Cases** 8000

One of the district pioneers, with a 16-ha estate vineyard, which is now fully mature. Limited retail distribution in Melbourne and Adelaide; exports through Australian Prestige Wines.

ΨΨΨΨΨ **Coonawarra Cabernet Sauvignon 2005** Good colour; sweet cassis fruit bouquet, with a touch of tar and leather; the firm palate is long, savoury and quite poised on the finish. ProCork. 14% alc. **Rating** 92 **To** 2016 $20

Sabella Vineyards   NR

Lot 51 McMurtrie Road, McLaren Vale, SA 5171 **Region** McLaren Vale
T 0416 361 369 **F** (08) 8323 8270 **www**.sabella.com.au **Open** Not
Winemaker Michael Petrucci **Est.** 1999 **Cases** 2000

Giuseppe (Joe) Petrucci was born in the Molise region of Italy, where his family were farmers. His father migrated to Australia in 1960, the rest of the family following him in '66. In 1976 Joe and wife Rosa (and children) moved to McLaren Vale where they purchased their first vineyard in McMurtrie Road; since then their vineyards have increased from 10 ha to 44 ha, their grapes sold to various wineries. In 1999 they decided to keep some grapes back for release under the Sabella label; Sabella derives from a pseudonym given to the Petrucci name six generations ago. A cellar door is planned for 2009.

2004 Sabella Vineyards Reserve McLaren Vale Shiraz Truth stranger than fiction; a plastic collar inserted in the neck of the bottle prevents the exit of the block of oak put in each bottle in lieu of conventional oak maturation. NR for obvious reasons. Screwcap. 15% alc **Rating** NR **To** 2009 $20

Saddlers Creek ★★★★

Marrowbone Road, Pokolbin, NSW 2320 **Region** Lower Hunter Valley
T (02) 4991 1770 **F** (02) 4991 2482 **www**.saddlerscreek.com **Open** 7 days 10–5
Winemaker John Johnstone **Est.** 1989 **Cases** 6000 **Vyds** 10 ha
Made an impressive entrance to the district with full-flavoured and rich wines, and has continued on in much the same vein, with good wines across the spectrum. Estate plantings include shiraz (5 ha), cabernet sauvignon (3 ha) and merlot (2 ha). Exports to Sweden and the Pacific region.

♀♀♀♀♀ **Bluegrass Langhorne Creek Cabernet 2006** Very fine fruit of cassis and cedar, with an overlay of mint to be expected; the palate has lovely sweet fruit followed by a very long, fine-grained tannin finish. Screwcap. 15% alc. **Rating** 93 **To** 2016 $26
Classic Hunter Semillon 2007 Clean, fine, fresh and focused, with lemon and a touch of straw; the palate is crisp, long and even. Screwcap. 11% alc. **Rating** 90 **To** 2016 $23
Reserve Chardonnay 2007 Rich and ripe, full of dried figs and toasty oak and a touch of lemon butter; full on the palate, but with fine balancing acidity that provides length. Screwcap. 14% alc. **Rating** 90 **To** 2014 $28
Single Vineyard Hunter Shiraz 2003 Medium-bodied; has developed to fully express earthy/leathery regional characters, yet retains a core of savoury/dusty fruit on a long finish. Cork. 14.5% alc. **Rating** 90 **To** 2013 $45
Botrytis Supreme NV Bright gold; butterscotch, lemon tart, mandarin and cumquat; fine acidity. Screwcap. 12.7% alc. **Rating** 90 **To** 2012 $36

♀♀♀♀ **Classic Hunter Semillon 2008** Very tightly wound, with lemon sherbet fruit, and a touch of green nettle; the palate is fresh, tight, linear and needs time in the classic Hunter style. Screwcap. 11% alc. **Rating** 89 **To** 2020 $23

St Aidan ★★★

754 Ferguson Road, Dardanup, WA 6236 **Region** Geographe
T (08) 9728 3007 **www**.saintaidan.com **Open** W'ends & public hols 10–5, or by appt
Winemaker Mark Messenger (Contract) **Est.** 1996 **Cases** 1500
Phil and Mary Smith purchased their property at Dardanup in 1991, a 20-min drive from the Bunbury hospitals where Phil works. They first ventured into Red Globe table grapes, planting 1 ha in 1994–05, followed by 1 ha of mandarins and oranges. With this experience, and with Mary completing a TAFE viticulture course, they extended their horizons by planting 1 ha each of cabernet sauvignon and chardonnay in 1997, half a hectare of muscat in 2001, and semillon and sauvignon blanc thereafter.

♀♀♀♀ **Chardonnay 2006** Very developed colour; very complex, strong wild yeast/barrel ferment characters. **Rating** 89 **To** 2010 $15
Geographe Cabernet Merlot 2007 Smooth and supple, ripe blackcurrant/cassis fruit making the first impression, before gentle tannins come through to support the finish. Cork. **Rating** 89 **To** 2013

St Hallett ★★★★★

St Hallett Road, Tanunda, SA 5352 **Region** Barossa Valley
T (08) 8563 7000 **F** (08) 8563 7001 **www**.sthallett.com.au **Open** 7 days 10–5
Winemaker Stuart Blackwell, Toby Barlow **Est.** 1944 **Cases** 100 000
Nothing succeeds like success. St Hallett merged with Tatachilla to form Banksia Wines, which was then acquired by NZ's thirsty Lion Nathan. St Hallett understandably continues

to ride the Shiraz fashion wave, with Old Block the ultra-premium leader of the band (using grapes from Lyndoch and the Eden Valley) supported by Blackwell (taking its grapes from Greenock, Ebenezer and Seppeltsfield). It has also had conspicuous success with its Eden Valley Rieslings, and its big-volume Poacher's range. Exports to all major markets.

ΨΨΨΨΨ **Old Block Barossa Shiraz 2006** Red-purple; a fragrant bouquet leads into a particularly well-balanced medium-bodied palate with lush, but not jammy, blackberry and raspberry fruit, ripe tannins and balanced oak. A welcome return to top form. Screwcap. 14.5% alc. **Rating** 95 **To** 2021 $75
Sub-Region Release Eden Valley Shiraz 2006 Very good, bright, colour; has all the elegance and intensity that the Eden Valley can provide; great structure and mouthfeel to the long palate, replete with black cherry, blackberry and spice fruits. Screwcap. 14.3% alc. **Rating** 95 **To** 2025 $35
Blackwell Barossa Shiraz 2007 Strong crimson-purple; rich and concentrated, but with no dead or confit fruit flavours; excellent texture and structure. Screwcap. 14.5% alc. **Rating** 94 **To** 2020 $34.95

ΨΨΨΨΨ **Eden Valley Riesling 2008** Very elegant, almost delicate, style with fragrant blossom aromas and a long, pleasingly dry finish. For the classicists. Screwcap. 11% alc. **Rating** 92 **To** 2020 $21

ΨΨΨΨ **Faith Barossa Shiraz 2007** Bright crimson; some spicy/savoury elements among the main drivers of red and black fruits; good tannins. Screwcap. 14.5% alc. **Rating** 89 **To** 2015 $21
Barossa Cabernet Sauvignon 2006 Deep magenta; good concentration of dark berry fruit, with a sweet-fruited juicy cassis palate, and moderate levels of tannin. Screwcap. 13% alc. **Rating** 88 **To** 2013 $22.99
Poacher's Blend Barossa Semillon Sauvignon Blanc 2008 Cleverly made, with very pleasant fruit salad flavours and a balanced finish. Screwcap. 11.5% alc. **Rating** 87 **To** 2009 $14
Frivola 2008 Notwithstanding pink colour, made from gewurztraminer and not too sweet; not too sure where it fits, other than as a pleasant aperitif. Crown Seal. 8.8% alc. **Rating** 87 **To** 2009 $18

St Huberts

★★★★☆

Cnr Maroondah Highway/St Huberts Road, Coldstream, Vic 3770 **Region** Yarra Valley
T (03) 9739 1118 **www**.sthuberts.com.au **Open** Mon–Fri 9–5, w'ends 10.30–5.30
Winemaker Greg Jarratt **Est.** 1966 **Cases** 10 000
A once famous winery (in the context of the Yarra Valley) that is now part of Foster's. The wines are now made at Coldstream Hills, and on an upwards trajectory. (I have no part in their making.)

ΨΨΨΨΨ **Yarra Valley Chardonnay 2007** Bright straw-green; a highly fragrant bouquet and a palate bursting with lively nectarine and citrus fruit, oak barely registering; has the hallmark thrust and length of fine Yarra chardonnay. Screwcap. 13% alc. **Rating** 95 **To** 2013 $26.95

ΨΨΨΨΨ **Yarra Valley Cabernet Merlot 2006** Bright, fresh purple hues still retained; fragrant cassis/redcurrant aromas, then a light-footed, fresh palate with cassis fruit to the fore, finishing with fine tannins, the oak subtle. Screwcap. 13.5% alc. **Rating** 92 **To** 2011 $30.99
Hubert the Stag Yarra Valley Pinot Noir 2008 Good colour; quite a toasty bouquet with redcurrant, cherry and a touch of spice; quite firm on the palate, with plenty of sweet red fruit on the finish. Screwcap. 13.5% alc. **Rating** 91 **To** 2012 $33.90
Yarra Valley Pinot Noir 2007 An uninhibited successor to the trophy-winning '06 makes a bold statement, but perhaps without the same depth of mid-palate plum fruit; has good balance. Screwcap. 13.5% alc. **Rating** 91 **To** 2013 $26.95

St Michael's Vineyard ★★★★☆

503 Pook Road, Toolleen, Vic 3521 **Region** Heathcote
T (03) 5433 2580 **F** (03) 5433 2612 **Open** By appt
Winemaker Mick Cann **Est.** 1994 **Cases** 300 **Vyds** 4.5 ha
Owner/winemaker Mick Cann has established vines on the famous deep red Cambrian clay loam on the east face of the Mt Camel Range. Planting began in 1994–95, with a further extension in 2000. Shiraz (3 ha), merlot (1 ha) and petit verdot (0.3 ha) are the main varieties, with a smattering of cabernet sauvignon and semillon. Part of the grape production is sold to David Anderson of Wild Duck Creek, the remainder made by Mick, using open fermentation, hand plunging of skins and a basket press, a low-technology but highly effective way of making high-quality red wine. The period poster-style labels do the wines scant justice.

🍷🍷🍷🍷🍷 **Limited Release Heathcote Shiraz 2006** Dense colour; immensely concentrated, reflecting the extremely low yields of half a tonne to the acre, but not showing the alcohol in the flavours of black fruits, anise and fine, savoury tannins; only three hogsheads (French and Russian) made. Screwcap. 16% alc. **Rating** 94 **To** 2021 $25

🍷🍷🍷🍷 **Heathcote Vintage Fortified Shiraz 2008** Spicy black fruits are set against a relatively low baumé background; should age well for those with patience; 375 ml. Screwcap. 18.5% alc. **Rating** 89 **To** 2018 $12.50

St Regis ★★★★

35 Princes Highway, Waurn Ponds, Vic 3216 **Region** Geelong
T (03) 5241 8406 **F** (03) 5241 8946 **www**.stregis.com.au **Open** 7 days 11–5
Winemaker Peter Nicol **Est.** 1997 **Cases** 600 **Vyds** 5 ha
St Regis is a family-run boutique winery focusing on estate-grown Shiraz, Chardonnay and Pinot Noir. Each year the harvest is hand-picked by members of the family and friends, with Peter Nicol (assisted by wife Viv) the executive, onsite winemaker. While Peter has a technical background in horticulture, he is a self-taught winemaker, and has taught himself well, also making wines for others.

🍷🍷🍷🍷🍷 **The Reg Geelong Shiraz 2007** Dense purple-crimson; potent black fruits, licorice and spice drive the bouquet and the medium- to full-bodied palate, the tannins in strong support. Needs time. Screwcap. 14% alc. **Rating** 91 **To** 2016 $25

Salena Estate ★★★☆

Bookpurnong Road, Loxton, SA 5333 **Region** Riverland
T (08) 8584 1333 **F** (08) 8584 1388 **www**.salenaestate.com.au **Open** Mon–Fri 8.30–4.30
Winemaker Melanie Kargas **Est.** 1998 **Cases** 300 000 **Vyds** 207 ha
This business encapsulates the once hectic rate of growth across the entire Australian wine industry. Its 1998 crush was 300 tonnes, and by '01 it was processing around 7000 tonnes. It is the venture of Bob and Sylvia Franchitto, the estate being named after their daughter Salena. The future is uncertain in the wake of the near collapse of the Murray Darling river system. Exports to the US, the UK and other major markets.

🍷🍷🍷🍷🍷 **Bookpurnong Hill Block 267 2005** Good colour retention; attractive medium-bodied palate, with savoury/spicy components seldom seen in the Riverland; the core of blackcurrant fruit is long and fine, as are the tannins. Cabernet Sauvignon/Petit Verdot/Shiraz. Cork. 14% alc. **Rating** 92 **To** 2015 $29

🍷🍷🍷🍷 **Sangiovese 2006** Good colour; sour cherry fruit with a touch of sage; varietally lean fruit, with good acidity, and assertive tannin; a good example of the variety in Australia. Screwcap. 12.5% alc. **Rating** 89 **To** 2011 $12

Lyrup Crossing Shiraz Cabernet 2007 Dark colour; bright fruit, with cassis and a touch of spice; medium-bodied and fresh finish. Screwcap. 13.5% alc. **Rating** 87 **To** 2012 $7

Amore Fortified Chardonnay NV Technically well done, but the fortifying spirit is a little raw; gold medal in a wine competition in Vienna in '08. Screwcap. 16% alc. **Rating** 87 **To** 2010 $15

Salitage ★★★★★

Vasse Highway, Pemberton, WA 6260 **Region** Pemberton
T (08) 9776 1771 **F** (08) 9776 1772 **www.**salitage.com.au **Open** 7 days 10–4
Winemaker Patrick Coutts **Est.** 1989 **Cases** 17 000 **Vyds** 22.7 ha
Salitage is the showpiece of Pemberton. If it had failed to live up to expectations, it is a fair bet the same fate would have befallen the whole of the Pemberton region. The quality and style of Salitage did once vary, presumably in response to vintage conditions and yields, but it has found its way, with a succession of attractive wines. Exports to the UK, the US and other major markets.

♟♟♟♟♟ **Pemberton Pinot Noir 2007** A stylish pinot from a good vintage, showing Pemberton on its best behaviour; fragrant and spicy, with a delicate mid-palate, then a peacock's tail finish. Screwcap. 13% alc. **Rating** 94 **To** 2012 $40
Pemberton 2005 Bright colour; elegant, light-bodied style with Bordeaux overtones; it is deceptive, for the sweet red berry fruits are not immediately obvious but shows up on retasting; the tannins are gossamer fine, the finish long. Cabernet Sauvignon/Merlot/Petit Verdot/Cabernet Franc. Screwcap. 13% alc. **Rating** 94 **To** 2015 $33

♟♟♟♟♟ **Pemberton Sauvignon Blanc 2008** A wine with above average depth to the ripe/tropical fruit flavours, offset and cleansed by minerally acidity on the dry finish. Screwcap. 13% alc. **Rating** 91 **To** 2011 $22
Pemberton Chardonnay 2007 A rich and complex array of ripe stone fruit aromas and flavours, tightened nicely by citrussy acidity and integrated French oak. Screwcap. 13.5% alc. **Rating** 90 **To** 2013 $35

♟♟♟♟ **Treehouse Chardonnay Verdelho 2008** A fragrant bouquet of tropical fruit is followed by a generous palate with stone fruit also contributing to the appeal. Screwcap. 14% alc. **Rating** 89 **To** 2012 $17
Treehouse Pemberton Chardonnay 2008 Fresh, lively and flavoursome, with stone fruit running from white peach to tropical; no oak evident. Screwcap. 13.5% alc. **Rating** 87 **To** 2011 $17
Treehouse Pemberton Pinot Noir 2007 A light-bodied, savoury palate made for early consumption with brasserie food. Screwcap. 13% alc. **Rating** 87 **To** 2010 $20

Sally's Paddock ★★★★☆

Redbank Winery, 1 Sally's Lane, Redbank, Vic 3478 **Region** Pyrenees
T (03) 5467 7255 **www.**sallyspaddock.com.au **Open** Mon–Sat 9–5, Sun 10–5
Winemaker Neill Robb **Est.** 1973 **Cases** 2500 **Vyds** 18.5 ha
The Redbank brand and stocks (Long Paddock, etc) were acquired by the Hill Smith Family Vineyards (aka Yalumba) several years ago. The winery and surrounding vineyard that produces Sally's Paddock were retained by Neill and Sally Robb, and continue to produce (and sell) this single-vineyard, multi-varietal red wine and the Sally's Hill range. There is some disagreement on the use of the Redbank Winery name (see Redbank Victoria entry), but there is no dispute about Sally's Paddock. Exports to the US, Germany, Czech Republic and Asia.

♟♟♟♟♟ **Sally's Paddock 2006** Attractive, clean, medium-bodied wine; red and black fruits are supported by a web of fine, savoury tannins and balanced oak; not effusive, but shows its pedigree. Diam. 13.5% alc. **Rating** 93 **To** 2020 $59.20
Sally's Hill Shiraz 2006 Attractive medium-bodied Shiraz with a strong spicy/savoury component on both bouquet and palate, but not at the expense of the plum and red berry fruits. Diam. 14.5% alc. **Rating** 92 **To** 2016 $21.90

Salmon Run ★★★★

C/- 288 Lorimer Street, Port Melbourne, Vic 3207 (postal) **Region** Margaret River
T (03) 9646 6666 **F** (03) 9646 8383 **www.**salmonrunwines.com.au **Open** Not
Winemaker Flying Fish Cove (Damon Eastaugh) **Est.** 2008 **Cases** 3000
This virtual winery is anchored to the Margaret River region. It takes its name from the large
schools of salmon that migrate from the Great Australian Bight, west along the coast around
Cape Leeuwin, then north towards Rottnest Island on their spawning run. Local fishermen
take full advantage of the abundance of fish for a few brief weeks, and the Salmon Run wines
are (with a certain amount of poetic licence) made to enjoy with salmon.

♀♀♀♀♀ **Margaret River Sauvignon Blanc Semillon 2008** Pale colour; an expressive
bouquet of nettle and tropical fruit; fleshy and full with a vibrant cleansing acid
finish. Screwcap. 13% alc. **Rating** 92 **To** 2011 $21
Margaret River Chardonnay 2008 Quite a fresh bouquet of lemon and a
touch of spice; accentuated acidity with real drive and nerve; a tight grapefruit
core of fruit on the finish. Screwcap. 12.5% alc. **Rating** 92 **To** 2014 $21

Salomon Estate ★★★★☆

PO Box 829, McLaren Vale, SA 5171 **Region** Southern Fleurieu
T 0417 808 243 **F** (08) 8323 8668 **www.**salomonwines.com **Open** Not
Winemaker Bert Salomon, Simon White, Boar's Rock **Est.** 1997 **Cases** 7000
Bert Salomon is an Austrian winemaker with a long-established family winery in the Kremstal
region, not far from Vienna. He became acquainted with Australia during his time with import
company Schlumberger in Vienna; he was the first to import Australian wines (Penfolds) into
Austria in the mid-1980s, and later became head of the Austrian Wine Bureau. He was so
taken by Adelaide that he moved his family there for the first few months each year, sending
his young children to school and setting in place an Australian red winemaking venture. He
retired from the Bureau and is a full-time travelling winemaker, running the family winery
in the northern hemisphere vintage, and overseeing the making of the Salomon Estate wines
at Boar's Rock in the first half of the year. The circle closes as Mike Farmilo, former Penfolds
chief red winemaker, now makes Salomon Estate wines at Boar's Rock. Exports to the UK,
the US, and other major markets.

♀♀♀♀♀ **Fleurieu Peninsula Syrah Viognier 2006** Dark chocolate and red berry fruit
bouquet; quite earthy on attack, but the core of fruit is sweet and ample; sweet-
fruited and silky on the finish. Vino-Lok. 14% alc. **Rating** 94 **To** 2016 $30

♀♀♀♀♀ **Finniss River Shiraz 2006** Essency black pastille fruit, with an element of earthy
spice; the palate is fine and lithe, with well-integrated oak and tannin; juicy, long
and fine. Cork. 14.5% alc. **Rating** 92 **To** 2016 $40
Norwood Shiraz Cabernet 2007 Deep colour; very oaky bouquet, with cassis
fruit and black olive sitting behind; dense and oaky on the palate, there are florals
to be enjoyed with red and black fruits; a good decanting will be necessary. Cork.
14.5% alc. **Rating** 90 **To** 2016 $26
Finniss River Cabernet Merlot 2006 Cassis and redcurrant fruit, framed by
elegant oak-handling; medium- to full-bodied, with depth and weight of fruit
driving the palate; savoury and chewy on the finish. Cork. 14% alc. **Rating** 90
To 2016 $38

Saltram ★★★★★

Nuriootpa Road, Angaston, SA 5355 **Region** Barossa Valley
T (08) 8561 0211 **F** (08) 8561 0232 **www.**saltramwines.com.au **Open** Mon–Fri 9–5,
w'ends & public hols 10–5
Winemaker Shavaugn Wells **Est.** 1859 **Cases** 150 000
There is no doubt that Saltram has taken giant strides toward regaining the reputation it held
30 or so years ago. Under Nigel Dolan's stewardship, grape sourcing has come back to the
Barossa Valley for the flagship wines, a fact of which he is rightly proud. The red wines, in

particular, have enjoyed great show success over the past few years, with No. 1 Shiraz, Mamre Brook and Metala leading the charge. Nigel Dolan retired in late 2007, taking with him the best wishes of all in the industry who knew him. Exports to the UK, the US and other major markets.

ＰＰＰＰＰ **Barossa Shiraz Cabernet 2006** A well-crafted wine showing the strength of the union; blackberry generosity meets strict cassis and cedar on the palate; fleshy, firm and surprisingly long, the oak works seamlessly with the fruit. Screwcap. 14.5% alc. **Rating** 94 **To** 2015 $19.99

Pepperjack Stylus 2008 Bright colour; fresh raspberry, cherry and Asian spice; a forward, juicy and accessible wine, with great purity of fruit and fine acid structure; unencumbered by artefact. Grenache/Shiraz/Merlot. Screwcap. 12% alc. **Rating** 94 **To** 2012 $24.99

ＰＰＰＰＰ **Mamre Brook Barossa Shiraz 2006** Deep colour; in the powerful, full-bodied style expected of Mamre Brook, oozing with black fruits, tar, licorice and prune flavours that partially obscure the alcohol; the most surprising aspect is the tatty, pockmarked, wine-stained cork for a wine with an otherwise minimum 20-year cellaring future. 15.5% alc. **Rating** 93 **To** 2020 $29.99

Mamre Brook Barossa Cabernet Sauvignon 2006 Powerful, incisive, full-bodied cabernet; tarry black fruits, licorice and dark chocolate are interwoven through obvious oak, the tannins also very evident. Needs longer than the cork may give it. 15% alc. **Rating** 93 **To** 2020 $29.99

Pepperjack Barossa Cabernet Sauvignon 2007 A generously proportioned and wholly satisfying cabernet in which all of the fruit, oak and tannin components are in harmony; the soft, blackcurrant and plum fruit are supported by ripe tannins. Screwcap. 14% alc. **Rating** 92 **To** 2022 $23.99

Mamre Brook Eden Valley Riesling 2008 A fine, floral bouquet leads into a still-delicate and crisp palate; has balance and length, its best years in front of it. Screwcap. 11.5% alc. **Rating** 91 **To** 2016 $22.99

Metala Langhorne Creek Shiraz Cabernet 2006 Good colour; bright fruit with blackberry and spice, a touch of mint and a little cassis; fine and persistent, with clean fruit and vibrant acidity on the finish. Screwcap. 14.5% alc. **Rating** 91 **To** 2014 $21.99

Pepperjack Barossa Shiraz Viognier 2007 A rich and luscious wine, with waves of black fruits and licorice, the texture full and round; avoids over-extraction, and will cellar well. Screwcap. 14.5% alc. **Rating** 90 **To** 2017 $23.99

ＰＰＰＰ **Pepperjack Barossa Shiraz 2007** Solid, full-bodied wine with plenty of ripe fruit flavour, but not much finesse. Screwcap. 15% alc. **Rating** 87 **To** 2015 $23.99

Metala Original Plantings Langhorne Creek Shiraz 2005 A robust wine, with plenty of earthy/berry flavour, and somewhat rough tannins. Disappointing to say the least. Poor wine-stained cork. 15% alc. **Rating** 87 **To** 2013 $56.99

Sam Miranda of King Valley   ★★★☆

1019 Snow Road, Oxley, Vic 3678 **Region** King Valley
T (03) 5727 3888 **F** (03) 5727 3853 **www**.sammiranda.com.au **Open** 7 days 10–5
Winemaker Sam Miranda **Est.** 2004 **Cases** 15 000 **Vyds** 15 ha
Sam Miranda, grandson of Francesco Miranda, joined the family business in 1991, striking out on his own in '04 after Miranda Wines was purchased by McGuigan Simeon. The High Plains Vineyard is in the Upper King Valley at an altitude of 450 m; estate plantings are supplemented by some purchased grapes. In 2005 Sam purchased the Symphonia Wines business, and intends to keep its identity intact and separate from the Sam Miranda brand. Rewarded with gold medals for its 2006 Saperavi and '06 Las Triadas Tempranillo. Exports to China.

ＰＰＰＰＰ **High Plains Glenrowan Shiraz 2008** Well-constructed, pleasingly restrained, medium-bodied wine, with plum and blackberry fruit sustained by fine, ripe tannins and French oak; deliberate and successful choice of Glenrowan for the variety. Screwcap. 14% alc. **Rating** 90 **To** 2014 $17

ΨΨΨΨ **High Plains Cabernet Sauvignon 2008** Appealing, fresh light- to medium-bodied palate, with juicy cassis berry fruit, subtle oak (40% matured in French oak) and gently ripe tannins. Ready now or whenever. Screwcap. 14% alc. **Rating** 89 **To** 2013 $17
High Plains Merlot 2008 In mainstream King Valley style, with cassis/blackcurrant fruit offset by varietal savoury/olive/spice notes on the finish. Screwcap. 14% alc. **Rating** 88 **To** 2012 $17
High Plains Sauvignon Blanc 2008 Slightly muted varietal character, but with enough tropical notes on the palate to get it over the line. Screwcap. 12.5% alc. **Rating** 87 **To** 2009 $16

Samuel's Gorge   ★★★★☆

Lot 10 Chaffeys Road, McLaren, SA 5171 **Region** McLaren Vale
T (08) 8323 8651 **F** (08) 8323 8673 **www.**gorge.com.au **Open** First w'end of spring until sold out, or by appt
Winemaker Justin McNamee **Est.** 2003 **Cases** 1250 **Vyds** 10 ha
After a wandering winemaking career in various parts of the world, Justin McNamee became a winemaker at Tatachilla in 1996, where he remained until 2003, leaving to found Samuel's Gorge. He has established his winery in a barn built in 1853, part of a historic property known as the old Seaview Homestead. The property was owned by Sir Samuel Way, variously Chief Justice of the South Australian Supreme Court and Lieutenant Governor of the State. The grapes come from small contract growers spread across the ever-changing (unofficial) subregions of McLaren Vale, and are basket-pressed and fermented in old open slate fermenters lined with beeswax – with impressive results. Exports to the UK, the US and Canada.

ΨΨΨΨΨ **McLaren Vale Shiraz 2006** Very deep colour; dense, powerful and chock full of Christmas cake and black fruits; a massive wine, but lively, vibrant and very long on the finish. Cork. 14.5% alc. **Rating** 94 **To** 2020 $40

ΨΨΨΨΩ **McLaren Vale Grenache 2006** Rich and ripe with an abundance of sweet red fruits, and a slight garrigue note at the edge; long and sweet, with a toasty finish. Cork. 14.5% alc. **Rating** 91 **To** 2014 $40
McLaren Vale Tempranillo 2007 Tangy cherry/plum fruit with a squeeze of sweet lemon juice; fine tannins and good length. Cork. 13.5% alc. **Rating** 90 **To** 2015 $40

Sandalford   ★★★★★

3210 West Swan Road, Caversham, WA 6055 **Region** Margaret River
T (08) 9374 9374 **F** (08) 9274 2154 **www.**sandalford.com **Open** 7 days 10–5
Winemaker Paul Boulden, Hope Metcalf **Est.** 1840 **Cases** 100 000 **Vyds** 92 ha
Some years ago the upgrading of the winery and the appointment of Paul Boulden as chief winemaker resulted in far greater consistency in quality, and the proper utilisation of the excellent vineyard resources of the vineyard planted in 1970. Things have continued on an even keel since, with the entry level Element range (from various parts of WA), Protege (from Margaret River) at the mid-level, and Single Vineyard Estate (Margaret River) at the top level. Exports to all major markets.

ΨΨΨΨΨ **Estate Reserve Margaret River Chardonnay 2006** A notably complex wine, with rich cashew/creamy overtones to the fig/melon/white peach fruit; barrel ferment and 12 months lees contact have worked well, with very good mouthfeel. Typical Margaret River. Screwcap. 13.5% alc. **Rating** 94 **To** 2015 $23.95
Estate Reserve Cabernet Sauvignon 2005 Nicely ripened fruit gives supple mouthfeel and very good overall balance; tannins on finish evident. Gold WA Wine Show '08. Screwcap. 14.6% alc. **Rating** 94 **To** 2015 $35

ΨΨΨΨΩ **Margaret River Shiraz 2008** Crimson-red; a high-quality Shiraz, with bright spicy notes to its plum and blackberry fruit, sustained by fine, but positive, tannins and integrated oak. Value. Screwcap. 14.5% alc. **Rating** 93 **To** 2016 $18.99

Margaret River Rose 2008 Vivid crimson-purple; very appealing raspberry and cherry fruit runs through the long, well-balanced palate; barest hint of sweetness on the finish. Screwcap. 13% alc. **Rating** 93 **To** 2011 $18.95

Margaret River Classic Dry White 2008 Tropical fruit balanced by a slight herbaceous edge; very good texture, and fine and long on the finish. Screwcap. 12% alc. **Rating** 92 **To** 2010 $18.95

Estate Reserve Sauvignon Blanc Semillon 2008 Deliciously vibrant, lively and fresh; lemon/citrus/mineral notes interwoven on bouquet and palate, then a bright, fresh finish with a farewell of passionfruit. Screwcap. 13% alc. **Rating** 91 **To** 2011 $20.95

Margaret River Unoaked Chardonnay 2008 A floral bouquet, with stone fruit and citrus on the delicate but focused palate; very good example of unwooded chardonnay. Screwcap. 14% alc. **Rating** 91 **To** 2012 $18.95

Estate Reserve Margaret River Shiraz 2005 Very good colour and clarity; distinct chocolate and mocha notes ex oak; good mouthfeel. Screwcap. 14.5% alc. **Rating** 91 **To** 2015 $33.95

Margaret River Sauvignon Blanc Semillon 2008 Well made; seamless integration and balance between the grassy/minerally components and citrus/tropical flavours. Screwcap. 13% alc. **Rating** 90 **To** 2010 $22.95

Margaret River Verdelho 2008 Bright green-straw; has considerable character – and varietal character – on both bouquet and palate, with tangy citrus elements in the vibrant multi-fruit flavours. Screwcap. 13.5% alc. **Rating** 90 **To** 2011 $22.95

Estate Reserve Margaret River Verdelho 2008 Has good varietal expression to both bouquet and palate, in a gentle tropical spectrum, with pineapple and banana rather than passionfruit. Screwcap. 13.5% alc. **Rating** 90 **To** 2011 $20.95

♥♥♥♥ **Margaret River Cabernet Merlot 2008** Good colour and overall flavour; a combination of blackcurrant, spice and black olive fruit, the tannin structure good. Screwcap. 14% alc. **Rating** 89 **To** 2014 $18.99

Margaret River Cabernet Merlot 2007 Vibrant colour with clearly defined cassis fruit coming to the fore; clean, fleshy and fine, with a savoury twist to the finish. Screwcap. 14% alc. **Rating** 88 **To** 2012 $18.95

Margaret River Shiraz 2006 Light colour; pleasant light-bodied palate with spicy red fruits, although not much depth or structure. Screwcap. 14% alc. **Rating** 87 **To** 2012 $18.95

Sandhurst Ridge   ★★★★

156 Forest Drive, Marong, Vic 3515 **Region** Bendigo
T (03) 5435 2534 **F** (03) 5435 2548 **www**.sandhurstridge.com.au **Open** 7 days 11–5
Winemaker Paul Greblo, George Greblo **Est.** 1990 **Cases** 3000 **Vyds** 7.1 ha
The Greblo brothers (Paul and George), with combined experience in business, agriculture, science, and construction and development, began the establishment of Sandhurst Ridge in 1990, planting the first 2 ha of shiraz and cabernet sauvignon. Plantings have increased to over 7 ha, principally cabernet and shiraz, but also a little merlot and nebbiolo. As the business has grown, the Greblos have supplemented their crush with grapes grown in the region. Exports to Canada, Norway, Taiwan, Hong Kong and China.

♥♥♥♥♥ **Bendigo Shiraz 2007** Good colour; bright red and blue fruit bouquet has a touch of bay leaf; medium-bodied with a soft and quite velvet-like core of fruit; understated, fine and very attractive. Cork. 14.5% alc. **Rating** 94 **To** 2015 $28

♥♥♥♥♀ **Fringe Bendigo Shiraz Cabernet 2007** Good colour; red fruit and noticeable spice on the bouquet; a strong sense of wild herb follows on the palate, with ample sweet fruit. Screwcap. 14.5% alc. **Rating** 90 **To** 2013 $22

Sanguine Estate   ★★★★☆

77 Shurans Lane, Heathcote, Vic 3523 **Region** Heathcote
T (03) 9646 6661 **F** (03) 9646 1746 **www**.sanguinewines.com.au **Open** By appt
Winemaker Mark Hunter, Ben Riggs (Consultant) **Est.** 1997 **Cases** 7500 **Vyds** 22.25 ha

The Hunter family – parents Linda and Tony at the head, their children Mark and Jodi, with their respective partners Melissa and Brett – began establishing the vineyard in 1997. It has grown to 20.23 ha of shiraz, and 2.02 ha of chardonnay, viognier, merlot, tempranillo, petit verdot, cabernet sauvignon and cabernet franc. Low-yielding vines and the magic of the Heathcote region have produced Shiraz of exceptional intensity, which has received rave reviews in the US, and led to the 'sold out' sign being posted almost immediately upon release. With the ever-expanding vineyard, Mark has become full-time vigneron, and Jodi Marsh part-time marketer and business developer. Exports to the UK, the US, Canada, Singapore and Hong Kong.

ΨΨΨΨΨ **D'Orsa Heathcote Shiraz 2006** Deep crimson-purple; the bouquet promises opulent black fruits with a dash of oak and spice, and so it is, but on a quality level above expectations; incredibly rich and supple, but not jammy; generous oak and ripe tannins finish the taste. The cork is of high quality, as it should be. 14.8% alc. **Rating** 96 **To** 2031 $59.95

ΨΨΨΨΨ **Progeny Heathcote Shiraz 2006** A very respectable little brother of D'Orsa, with lashings of ripe fruits, the alcohol on the upside, and introducing a touch of confit; however, its generosity cannot be denied. Screwcap. 15% alc. **Rating** 90 **To** 2016 $19.95

Saracen Estates   ★★★★★

3517 Caves Road, Wilyabrup, WA 6280 **Region** Margaret River
T (08) 9755 6000 **F** (08) 9755 6011 **www**.saracenestates.com.au **Open** 7 days 10–6
Winemaker Bob Cartwright (Consultant) **Est.** 1998 **Cases** 7000 **Vyds** 16.96 ha
Luke and Maree Saraceni have almost 17 ha of vines on their 80-ha property, with a striking restaurant and cellar door opened in 2007. This was followed by a visitor facility in 2008 incorporating a craft brewery, a beer garden, and restaurant. Exports to the UK, Singapore, Malaysia, Hong Kong, India and Denmark.

ΨΨΨΨΨ **Reserve Margaret River Cabernet Sauvignon 2007** Deep crimson-purple; a full-bodied cabernet with outstanding varietal character and structure, which has devoured the 100% new French oak in which it spent 21 months; great mouthfeel and balance. Screwcap. 13.3% alc. **Rating** 96 **To** 2030 $60
Margaret River Sauvignon Blanc Semillon 2008 Quite a rich and ripe style, with tropical fruit in abundance, offset by a touch of nettle; the palate is thickly textured on entry, but moves to a lighter conclusion; an interesting style. Screwcap. 13.1% alc. **Rating** 94 **To** 2013 $22

ΨΨΨΨΨ **Margaret River Sauvignon Blanc 2008** Accentuated pea pod and green nettle bouquet; fresh and clean, with good concentration; suitable for those who enjoy the greener end of the spectrum. Screwcap. 12.8% alc. **Rating** 90 **To** 2012 $24

ΨΨΨΨ **Reserve Margaret River Cabernet Sauvignon 2006** A considerable achievement to produce this much fruit in '06, but the alcohol and the lack of structure tell the tale. Nice enough wine, but overpriced. Screwcap. 12.8% alc. **Rating** 89 **To** 2014 $60

Sarsfield Estate   ★★★★☆

345 Duncan Road, Sarsfield, Vic 3875 **Region** Gippsland
T (03) 5156 8962 **F** (03) 5156 8970 **www**.sarsfieldestate.com.au **Open** By appt
Winemaker Dr Suzanne Rutschmann **Est.** 1995 **Cases** 1200 **Vyds** 2 ha
Owned by Suzanne Rutschmann, who has a PhD in Chemistry, a Diploma in Horticulture and a BSc (Wine Science) from CSU, and Swiss-born Peter Albrecht, a civil and structural engineer who has also undertaken various courses in agriculture and viticulture. For a part-time occupation, these are exceptionally impressive credentials. Their vineyard (pinot noir, cabernet, shiraz and merlot) was planted between 1991 and '98. Sarsfield Pinot Noir has enjoyed conspicuous success in both domestic and international wine shows over the past few years. No insecticides are used in the vineyard, the winery runs on solar and wind energy,

and relies entirely on rain water. No Pinot Noir was made in 2007 owing to smoke taint; the rating is that of last year. The previously released 2006 Pinot Noir won a gold medal at the Mondial du Pinot Noir competition, held in Switzerland and attracting 1100 wines from 19 countries, judged by 53 international wine judges, who thus had 40 wines for each panel to taste. Exports to Ireland.

 ## Sautjan Vineyards

PO Box 1317, Kyneton, Vic 3444 **Region** Macedon Ranges
T 0400 582 747 **F** (03) 5024 7401 **www**.s17.com.au **Open** Not
Winemaker John Ellis (Contract), Damien Pitt **Est.** 2006 **Cases** 500 **Vyds** 3.2 ha
Owner and founder Damien Pitt was looking for a cool-climate site, and he certainly found one. The vineyard, situated on a north-facing slope of Mt Jim Jim at an elevation of 650 m, has close-planted chardonnay, viognier and pinot gris. Until they come into bearing, grapes are being purchased from various Victorian cool-climate vineyards.

ΨΨΨΨ **Macedon Ranges Chardonnay 2007** Typical flinty/bony style of the region (excepting Curly Flat and Bindi); not complex, but has good poise and length, particularly given the modest alcohol; French oak is very restrained. Screwcap. 12.5% alc. **Rating** 88 **To** 2014 $20
Kilmore Ranges Shiraz 2007 A bracing, light- to medium-bodied wine, which reflects its markedly cool climate with red cherry and raspberry fruits; the finish is savoury, possibly slightly smoke-tainted. Screwcap. 13% alc. **Rating** 88 **To** 2016 $20
Strathbogie & King Valley Sauvignon Blanc 2008 Very minerally style, with length and persistence of green apple flavour its strength. Strathbogie Ranges (70%), King Valley (30%). Screwcap. 12.5% alc. **Rating** 87 **To** 2011 $16

SC Pannell

14 Davenport Terrace, Wayville, SA 5034 (postal) **Region** McLaren Vale
T (08) 8299 9256 **F** (08) 8299 9274 **www**.scpannell.com.au **Open** Not
Winemaker Stephen Pannell **Est.** 2004 **Cases** 4500
The only surprising piece of background is that it took (an admittedly still reasonably youthful) Stephen Pannell (and wife Fiona) so long to cut the painter from Constellation/ Hardys and establish their own winemaking and consulting business. Steve radiates intensity, and extended experience backed by equally long experimentation and thought has resulted in wines of the highest quality right from the first vintage. At present the focus of their virtual winery (they own neither vineyards nor winery) is grenache and shiraz grown in McLaren Vale. This is a label well on its way to icon status.

ΨΨΨΨΨ **McLaren Vale Shiraz Grenache 2007** Bright crimson; an exercise in restrained elegance; spicy/savoury elements to the fore, and a long, perfectly balanced palate, co-fermentation and French oak wrapping up the parcel to perfection. Screwcap. 14% alc. **Rating** 94 **To** 2020 $55

ΨΨΨΨΨ **Adelaide Hills Nebbiolo 2007** True nebbiolo brick colour; restrained with red fruit and a touch of sage; the palate is strict, firm and high acid; complex and intriguing, and a good example of the variety. Better your money than mine. Screwcap. 14% alc. **Rating** 90 **To** 2015 $65
Adelaide Hills Nebbiolo 2006 Hand-harvested; five clones; open-fermented for 18 days; old oak puncheons for 28 months. It's a long and hard road, and those tannins are still there waiting to stitch your mouth together. Points are largely meaningless. Screwcap. 14% alc. **Rating** 90 **To** 2020 $65

ΨΨΨΨ **Pronto Tinto 2007** Doubtless a deliberate choice of light-bodied material to fashion a savoury but ready-to-drink style for consumption with tapas. Garnacha/ Monastrell/Syrah/Touriga. Screwcap. 14% alc. **Rating** 89 **To** 2011 $25
Adelaide Hills Pronto Bianco 2008 A Bill Clinton blend, simply because it can be done; juicy and fresh, a wine for summer and the beach. Sauvignon Blanc/ Riesling/Pinot Gris. Screwcap. 13.5% alc. **Rating** 87 **To** 2009 $25

Scaffidi Wines

Talunga Cellars, Adelaide-Mannum Road, Gumeracha, SA 5233 **Region** Adelaide Zone
T (08) 8389 1222 **www**.talunga.com.au **Open** Wed–Sun & public hols 10.30–5
Winemaker Vince Scaffidi **Est.** 1994 **Cases** 4000 **Vyds** 95.91 ha
Owners Vince and Tina Scaffidi have sold their interest in the 80-ha Gumeracha Vineyards,
but have retained 2.8 ha of sauvignon blanc and chardonnay at their Gumeracha house
property. They also have a little over 93 ha on their One Tree Hill Vineyard, planted to shiraz,
cabernet sauvignon, merlot, sangiovese, nebbiolo, petit verdot, tempranillo and chardonnay, the
majority of the grape production being sold. The cellar door and restaurant is named Talunga
Cellars. The wines are exceptionally well-priced

ΨΨΨΨ **Adelaide Hills Unwooded Chardonnay 2008** Pale colour; nectarine and a
touch of spice; soft and fleshy with a bit of grip on the finish. Screwcap. 13.5% alc.
Rating 87 **To** 2012 $15.50
One Tree Hill Shiraz 2008 Bright purple hue; young and vibrant blackberry
fruit with a little spice; sweet and a little one-dimensional, but with good flavour.
Screwcap. 15% alc. **Rating** 87 **To** 2012 $10.50

Scalawag Wines

PO Box 743, West Perth, WA 6872 **Region** Great Southern
T (08) 9322 5144 **F** (08) 9322 5740 **www**.scalawag.com.au **Open** Not
Winemaker Harewood Estate, Garlands **Est.** 1998 **Cases** 8000 **Vyds** 73 ha
Peter Hodge, Laurence Huck, Kevin Tangney and Alf Baker are the owners of Scalawag Wines,
and have made a substantial investment in the large estate vineyard, planted to shiraz (24.5 ha),
cabernet sauvignon (18.8 ha), chardonnay (12 ha), merlot (7.3 ha), sauvignon blanc (6.1 ha)
and riesling (4.2 ha). The planting material came from the Forest Hill Vineyard, the oldest in
the Mount Barker region. The Scalawag property has well-known vineyards on three sides, the
Hay River and Yamballup Creek forming the southern boundary of the vineyard. Emphasis
in the vineyard is on organic products, and minimum chemical use. The prices of the wines
are mouth-watering.

ΨΨΨΨ **Mount Barker Classic White 2007** A very rich mouthful of tropical fruits with
some minor citrus nuances, a worthy companion to the Scalawag Shiraz, and great
value. Screwcap. 14.5% alc. **Rating** 88 **To** 2010 $12
Mount Barker Shiraz 2007 A remarkably good expression of Mount Barker
at this price, with spicy black fruits and some tannin support; the alcohol is not a
problem. Top value. Screwcap. 15% alc. **Rating** 88 **To** 2013 $12

Scarborough Wine Co

179 Gillards Road, Pokolbin, NSW 2320 **Region** Lower Hunter Valley
T (02) 4998 7563 **F** (02) 4998 7786 **www**.scarboroughwine.com.au **Open** 7 days 9–5
Winemaker Ian Scarborough, Jerome Scarborough **Est.** 1985 **Cases** 20 000 **Vyds** 14 ha
Ian Scarborough honed his white winemaking skills during his years as a consultant, and has
brought all those skills to his own label. He makes three different styles of Chardonnay: the
Blue Label is a light, elegant, Chablis style for the export marke; a richer barrel-fermented
wine (Yellow Label) is primarily directed to the Australian market; the third is the White
Label, a cellar door–only wine made in the best vintages. However, the real excitement for the
future lies with the portion of the old Lindemans Sunshine Vineyard, which he has purchased
(after it lay fallow for 30 years) and planted with semillon and (quixotically) pinot noir. The
first vintage from the legendary Sunshine Vineyard was made in 2004. Exports to the UK
and the US.

ΨΨΨΨΨ **White Label Hunter Valley Chardonnay 2007** Bright straw-green; similar to
the Blue Label, the more intense, the oak more than balanced by that fruit. A top-
quality Hunter Valley chardonnay. Screwcap. 13% alc. **Rating** 94 **To** 2015 $30

🍷🍷🍷🍷🍷 **Blue Label Chardonnay 2007** Very well made; a finely structured wine, with crisp melon and stone fruit flavours embraced by a subtle web of French oak. Value. Screwcap. 13% alc. **Rating** 90 **To** 2013 $19

Late Harvest Semillon 2008 In the new interpretation of the style; modest alcohol, and not lusciously sweet, simply fruitily sweet with balancing acidity. Screwcap. 10% alc. **Rating** 90 **To** 2014 $20

🍷🍷🍷🍷 **White Label Hunter Valley Semillon 2008** Very fresh, but still to build the flavour presently latent in the glass; some CO_2 spritz will help sustain the ageing process. Screwcap. 10% alc. **Rating** 88 **To** 2016 $25

Scarpantoni Estate ★★★★★

Scarpantoni Drive, McLaren Flat, SA 5171 **Region** McLaren Vale
T (08) 8383 0186 **F** (08) 8383 0490 **www**.scarpantoniwines.com **Open** Mon–Fri 9–5, w'ends & public hols 11–5
Winemaker Michael Scarpantoni, Filippo Scarpantoni **Est.** 1979 **Cases** 30 000 **Vyds** 40 ha
With 20 ha of shiraz, 11 ha of cabernet sauvignon, 3 ha each of chardonnay and sauvignon blanc, 1 ha each of merlot and gamay, and 0.5 ha of petit verdot, Scarpantoni has come a long way since Domenico Scarpantoni purchased his first property in 1958. He was working for Thomas Hardy at its Tintara winery and subsequently became vineyard manager for Seaview Wines. In 1979 his sons Michael and Filippo built the winery, which has now been extended to enable all the grapes from the estate plantings to be used to make wine under the Scarpantoni label. A second label, Oxenberry Farm, has been introduced using contract-grown grapes, with the rationale of matching site, variety and style. Exports to the UK and other major markets.

🍷🍷🍷🍷🍷 **Block 3 McLaren Vale Shiraz 2006** Shouts its regional origin from the rooftops; a rich coating of dark chocolate wraps around the plum and blackberry fruit, so much so you don't worry about the alcohol. Screwcap. 15.5% alc. **Rating** 94 **To** 2021 $30

Brothers Block McLaren Vale Cabernet Sauvignon 2006 A somewhat controversial winner of the Jimmy Watson Trophy '07; certainly in the flamboyantly generous mould of very ripe McLaren Vale cabernet sauvignon. What is most remarkable is the decision to hold the price to $30. Points in deference to the trophy. Screwcap. 15.5% alc. **Rating** 94 **To** 2021 $30

Black Tempest NV Complex flavours of black fruits and spices have built in bottle; the wine is far lighter, drier and more elegant than most sparkling reds; is a wine to be drunk, not just sipped. Cork. 13.5% alc. **Rating** 94 **To** 2013 $28

🍷🍷🍷🍷🍷 **Oxenberry The Star of Greece Shiraz 2007** Medium- to full-bodied in traditional McLaren Vale style; rich, complex, and warm, with dark fruits and chocolate, moving to a peremptory finish that brooks no argument. Screwcap. 15% alc. **Rating** 90 **To** 2022 $35

Oxenberry Blackfellows Well 2007 Fragrant red fruit aromas ex grenache, which also contribute lively spicy red fruit components to the palate alongside the darker flavours of the shiraz. Screwcap. 14.5% alc. **Rating** 90 **To** 2015 $30

🍷🍷🍷🍷 **Oxenberry The Sermon Tree 2008** Faint pink-grey blush perfectly acceptable in true grigio style, flinty and precise, with touches of nashi pear and good balance. Pinot Grigio. Screwcap. 13% alc. **Rating** 89 **To** 2010 $22

Oxenberry Jack of all Trades 2008 Bright, light crimson; while the blend is unconventional, bordering on implausible, it is fresh and flavoursome, with good balance and length, finishing spicy and dry; a good light-bodied dry red. Tempranillo/Chardonnay. Screwcap. 12% alc. **Rating** 89 **To** 2010 $22

School Block McLaren Vale Shiraz Cabernet Merlot 2006 Strongly, almost stridently, regional, with a thick coating of dark chocolate in magnum ice-cream style; also generous amounts of very ripe fruit; barbecue rump steak style. Screwcap. 14.8% alc. **Rating** 88 **To** 2014 $15

Ceres Rose 2008 Fresh, crisp and tangy gamay; blindfold, you'd guess it is a white wine. Screwcap. 12% alc. **Rating** 87 **To** 2009 $14

Schild Estate Wines

Cnr Barossa Valley Way/Lyndoch Valley Road, Lyndoch, SA 5351 **Region** Barossa Valley
T (08) 8524 5560 **F** (08) 8524 4333 **www**.schildestate.com.au **Open** 7 days 10–5
Winemaker Wine Wise (Jo Irvine) **Est.** 1998 **Cases** 30 000 **Vyds** 159.5 ha
Ed Schild is a Barossa Valley grapegrower who first planted a small vineyard at Rowland Flat
in 1952, steadily increasing his vineyard holdings over the next 50 years to their present level.
Currently 12% of the production from these vineyards (now managed by son Michael Schild)
is used to produce Schild Estate Wines, and the plan is to increase this percentage. The flagship
wine is made from 150-year-old shiraz vines on the Moorooroo Block. The cellar door is in
the old ANZ Bank at Lyndoch, and provides the sort of ambience that can only be found in
the Barossa Valley. Exports to the UK, the US and other major markets.

ΨΨΨΨΨ **Barossa Cabernet Sauvignon 2005** Nicely made wine, the French oak
balanced and integrated with gentle blackcurrant fruit; silky tannins provide
good mouthfeel. Two international gold medals. Screwcap. 14.5% alc. **Rating** 92
To 2018 $20

ΨΨΨΨ **Old Bush Vine Barossa Grenache Mataro Shiraz 2008** Light- to medium-
bodied, but a good example of Barossa Valley blend of these varieties; juicy
berry flavours are not drowned by the alcohol. Screwcap. 15% alc. **Rating** 89
To 2013 $16
Ben Schild Reserve Barossa Shiraz 2006 The combined effect of American
(and Hungarian) oak and ripe fruit gives the wine an overall confection gloss
bordering on sweetness. A style to polarise opinion. Screwcap. 15% alc. **Rating** 88
To 2015 $35
Moorooroo Shiraz 2005 Very rich and concentrated shiraz fruit, but the oak is
very strong; time will cure part of the problem, and the style may appeal to some.
Cork. 15% alc. **Rating** 88 To 2020 $85
Old Bush Vine Barossa Grenache Mataro Shiraz 2007 Light colour and
body for a wine from (average age) 70-year-old vineyards, and dominated by the
55% grenache component; very pleasant, but not as distinguished as it should be.
Screwcap. 15% alc. **Rating** 88 To 2013 $16
Barossa Sparkling Shiraz 2006 Full-flavoured young wine; the relatively high
dosage needed to balance the phenolic background. Time in bottle will greatly
assist. Cork. 13% alc. **Rating** 87 To 2014 $25
Barossa Frontignac 2008 Well made; attractive grapey varietal fruit flavour, a
touch of spritz, and a nice, dry finish. Screwcap. 12% alc. **Rating** 87 To 2010 $14

Schubert Estate

Roennfeldt Road, Marananga, SA 5355 **Region** Barossa Valley
T (08) 8562 3375 **F** (08) 8562 4338 **www**.schubertestate.com.au **Open** Not
Winemaker Steve Schubert **Est.** 2000 **Cases** 600 **Vyds** 14 ha
Steve and Cecilia Schubert are primarily grapegrowers, with 13 ha of shiraz and 1 ha of
viognier. They purchased the 25-ha property in 1986, when it was in such a derelict state
that there was no point trying to save the old vines. Both were working in other areas, so
it was some years before they began replanting, at a little under 2 ha per year. Almost all
the production is sold to Torbreck. In 2000 they decided to keep enough grapes to make a
barrique of wine for their own (and friends') consumption. They were sufficiently encouraged
by the outcome to venture into the dizzy heights of two hogsheads a year (since increased to
four or so). The wine is made with wild yeast, open fermentation, basket pressing and bottling
without filtration. Found the 2007 vintage difficult – as did most. Exports to the UK, the US,
Canada, Germany and Holland.

ΨΨΨΨΨ **The Gosling Barossa Valley Shiraz 2007** Bright colour; quite sweet and pure
blackberry fruit on display, with the fruit taking the front seat to the winemaking;
juicy, fresh, vibrant and focused. Screwcap. 14.5% alc. **Rating** 91 To 2015 $24.50

ＴＴＴＴ   **Goose-yard Block Barossa Valley Shiraz 2007** Dull colour; a little stewed and heavy; the concentration is unmistakable, but the fruit shows some shrivel and lacks life on the finish; a victim of the vintage. Cork. 14.5% alc. **Rating** 87 **To** 2014 $65

Schutz Barossa

Stonewell Road, Marananga, SA 5355 **Region** Barossa Valley
T 0409 547 478 **F** (08) 8563 3472 **www.**schutzbarossa.com **Open** By appt
Winemaker Troy Kalleske **Est.** 1997 **Cases** 800 **Vyds** 25 ha
Tammy Schutz (nee Pfeiffer) may be a sixth-generation grapegrower, but she was only 19 when in 1997 she purchased the 27-ha property now known as Schutz Barossa. At that time there were 2.4 ha of shiraz plantings, the remainder was grazing land with a beautiful view towards the Seppeltsfield palm avenue. The existing shiraz had been sourced from 80-year-old vines grown in the Moppa district, and Tammy has since established another 5.3 ha of shiraz and 2 ha of cabernet sauvignon. She carries out much of the work on the vineyards herself, using sustainable vineyard practices wherever possible. The Stonewell area, in which the vineyard is situated, is well known for its high-quality shiraz fruit. The winemaking is done by her good friend and cousin Troy Kalleske. Exports to France, Denmark, The Netherlands, Ireland, Israel and Asia.

ＴＴＴＴＴ   **Red Nectar Barossa Valley Shiraz 2006** Deep colour; luscious blackberry and plum fruit, with soft but persistent tannins; no sign of alcohol heat; 320 cases made. Screwcap. 15% alc. **Rating** 92 **To** 2021 $28

ＴＴＴＴ   **Red Nectar Barossa Valley Cabernet Sauvignon 2006** Good colour, strong and bright; has abundant flavour, but the varietal fruit line is blurred by the alcohol; a pity. Screwcap. 15% alc. **Rating** 89 **To** 2015 $28

Schwarz Wine Company

PO Box 182, Tanunda, SA 5352 **Region** Barossa Valley
T 0417 881 923 **F** (08) 8562 3534 **www.**schwarzwineco.com.au **Open** By appt
Winemaker Jason Schwarz **Est.** 2001 **Cases** 1300
The economical name is appropriate for a business that started with 1 tonne of grapes making two hogsheads of wine in 2001. The shiraz was purchased from Jason Schwarz's parents' vineyard in Bethany, the vines planted 60 years ago; the following year half a tonne of grenache was added, once again purchased from the parents. Production remained static until 2005 when the grape sale agreements to another (larger) winery were terminated, freeing up 1.8 ha of shiraz and 0.8 ha of grenache. From this point on things moved more quickly: in 2006 Jason, while working with Peter of Spinifex, formed a partnership (Biscay Road Vintners) with Peter Schell giving each total control over production. Using grapes purchased from other growers, Jason hopes to eventually increase production to 3000–4000 cases. Exports to the UK, the US, Canada, The Netherlands, Denmark, Singapore and Hong Kong.

ＴＴＴＴＴ   **Nitschke Block Barossa Valley Shiraz 2007** Deep colour; a rich, full-bodied densely textured shiraz with blackberry, satsuma plum, licorice and mocha flavours and aromas supported by ripe tannins. Screwcap. 15% alc. **Rating** 92 **To** 2020 $32
The Dust Kicker Barossa Valley Shiraz Mataro 2007 Strong, bright colour; the inclusion of 18% mataro (mourvedre) works well, adding complexity to both the texture and flavour; black fruits have slashes of bitter chocolate and earth; the finish is lively and clear. Screwcap. 14.5% alc. **Rating** 92 **To** 2015 $25
Thiele Road Barossa Valley Grenache 2007 Typically light hue, and typically light-bodied, but has more definition to the spicy red fruits, and less outright confection flavour. Nowhere near McLaren Vale in style, but better than many Barossa counterparts. Screwcap. 15% alc. **Rating** 91 **To** 2013 $26

ＴＴＴＴ   **The Dust Kicker Hunt & Gather 2007** Driven by the dominant grenache and shiraz components; has quite good flavour, but lacks structure. Grenache/Shiraz/Mataro/Cabernet Sauvignon. Screwcap. 14% alc. **Rating** 87 **To** 2013 $20

Scion Vineyard & Winery ★★★☆

74 Slaughterhouse Road, Rutherglen, Vic 3685 **Region** Rutherglen
T (02) 6032 8844 **www**.scionvineyard.com **Open** W'ends & public hols 10–5
Winemaker Jan Milhinch **Est.** 2002 **Cases** 1200
Former audiologist Jan Milhinch is a great-great-granddaughter of GF Morris, founder of the most famous Rutherglen wine family. She was in her 50s and at the height of her professional career when she decided to take what she describes as a 'vine change', moving from Melbourne to establish a little over 3 ha of durif, grenache, orange muscat, brown muscat and viognier on a quartz-laden red clay slope, planted in 2002, but with a viticultural history stretching back to 1890.

ŸŸŸŸ **Rutherglen Durif 2004** Remarkably deep purple; the flavours are fresh, although not intense; a wine full of interesting philosophical approaches, not the least is the aim of producing a low-alcohol Durif. Cork. 12.6% alc. **Rating** 89 **To** 2013 $36
The Melba Special Release Rutherglen Muscat NV Still predominantly russet red, but has good varietal expression with raisin toast, spice and toffee notes, the spirit less evident. Screwcap. 19% alc. **Rating** 89 **To** 2009 $58
Fleur 2008 Great green-straw colour; delicately fruity, with good mouthfeel for a low alcohol wine; lacks thrust for higher points. Orange Muscat. Screwcap. 10.5% alc. **Rating** 87 **To** 2010 $19
Sweet Rutherglen Durif 2008 Effectively a vintage port style; while not over-sweet, the spirit is somewhat fiery, and tends to take over the finish. Should benefit from a few years in bottle. Cork. 18% alc. **Rating** 87 **To** 2013 $29

Scorpiiion ★★★★☆

32 Waverley Ridge Road, Crafers, SA 5152 (postal) **Region** Various
T 0409 551 110 **F** (08) 8353 1562 **www**.scorpiiionwines.com.au **Open** Not
Winemaker Spinifex (Peter Schell) **Est.** 2002 **Cases** 1200
Scorpiiion Wines was the concept of Mark Herbertt who decided to buy a small quantity of McLaren Vale and Barossa grapes in 2002 and have the wine made for himself, friends and family. In 2004 Paddy Phillips and Michael Szwarcbord – like Mark Herbertt, they share the Scorpio birth sign – joined the partnership. It is a virtual winery, with the grapes purchased, and the wines contract-made by the brilliant Peter Schell. They say 'We share a number of likes and dislikes in relation to Australian red wines – apart from that, we don't really agree on anything ... We aim for a fruit-driven style with elegant oak, rather than a big, oak-driven style.' Oh, and they are united in their insistence on using screwcaps rather than corks. As a postscript, the poor 2007 vintage, low in yield and quality, means only one wine (Grenache Shiraz Mataro) is likely to be released.

ŸŸŸŸŸ **Barossa Valley Shiraz 2006** Bright crimson; a most appealing medium-bodied wine with a freshness and life to its red and black fruit flavours not common in the Barossa Valley; a balanced finish to the long palate; all the marks of great winemaking. Screwcap. 14.9% alc. **Rating** 94 **To** 2021 $21

Scorpo Wines ★★★★★

23 Old Bittern-Dromana Road, Merricks North, Vic 3926 **Region** Mornington Peninsula
T (03) 5989 7697 **F** (03) 5989 7697 **www**.scorpowines.com.au **Open** By appt
Winemaker Paul Scorpo, Sandro Mosele (Contract) **Est.** 1997 **Cases** 3500 **Vyds** 9.21 ha
Paul Scorpo has a 27-year background as a horticulturist/landscape architect, working on major projects ranging from private gardens to golf courses in Australia, Europe and Asia. His family has a love of food, wine and gardens, all of which led to them buying a derelict apple and cherry orchard on gentle rolling hills between Port Phillip and Westernport bays. Part of a ridge system that climbs up to Red Hill, it offers north and northeast-facing slopes on red-brown, clay loam soils. They have established pinot gris (4.74 ha), pinot noir (2.8 ha), chardonnay (1.06 ha) and shiraz (1.05 ha). Exports to Canada and Singapore.

ŶŶŶŶŶ **Mornington Peninsula Pinot Noir 2007** A sheer powerhouse of pinot; dark and brooding plum, redcurrant and layers of spice are offered on the bouquet; the palate is rich, but not in the least heavy, as the mineral ironstone and dark fruit is lifted by a core of vibrant cherry fruit; long, deep and satisfying, the journey is worth the effort. Diam. 13.5% alc. **Rating** 96 **To** 2015 $40
Noirien Mornington Peninsula Pinot Noir 2008 Vibrant cherry fruit jumps out of the glass, supported by an attractive spice component; the palate is juicy, generous, fine and thoroughly delicious, and volumes about sheer pleasure; best in the full flush of youth. Diam. 14% alc. **Rating** 95 **To** 2012 $30
Mornington Peninsula Pinot Gris 2008 Pale colour; exuberant personality of spiced pear and candied lemon; the palate is layered and fresh, exhibiting a core of ripe pear fruit, offset by an assertive mineral aspect; a true representation of the Gris style, yearning for an interesting food match. Diam. 14% alc. **Rating** 94 **To** 2012 $34

ŶŶŶŶŶ **Aubaine Mornington Peninsula Chardonnay 2008** Pale colour; a nectarine and stony/mineral bouquet; the emphasis is on the textural, with vibrant acidity providing a counterpoint to the depth of mid-palate fruit; long and savoury finish. Diam. 13.5% alc. **Rating** 93 **To** 2014 $30
Mornington Peninsula Shiraz 2007 Bright colour, purple hue; cranberry, bramble and a touch of spice; slightly tart acid profile, but it serves to accentuate the cool nature of the wine; long, polished and poised, this is one to polarise opinion. Diam. 13.5% alc. **Rating** 93 **To** 2015 $40
Mornington Peninsula Chardonnay 2007 Nectarine and spiced fruit bouquet; quite deep and concentrated, and again showing an added element of texture and grip, with a cleansing touch of citrus to conclude; certainly richer and a little less lively than Aubaine. Diam. 13.5% alc. **Rating** 92 **To** 2012 $38

Scotchmans Hill   ★★★★★

190 Scotchmans Road, Drysdale, Vic 3222 **Region** Geelong
T (03) 5251 3176 **www**.scotchmanshill.com.au **Open** 7 days 10.30–5.30
Winemaker Robin Brockett, Marcus Holt **Est.** 1982 **Cases** 70 000
Situated on the Bellarine Peninsula, southeast of Geelong, with a well-equipped winery and first-class vineyards. It is a consistent performer with its Pinot Noir and has a strong following in Melbourne and Sydney for its astutely priced, competently made wines. The second label, Swan Bay, has been joined at the other end of the spectrum with top-end individual vineyard wines. Exports to the UK and other major markets.

ŶŶŶŶŶ **Geelong Sauvignon Blanc 2008** Distinguished sauvignon blanc; abundant gooseberry, passionfruit and tropical fruit on the bouquet, and the well-balanced palate, which has both line and length. Screwcap. 13% alc. **Rating** 94 **To** 2011 $25
Geelong Chardonnay 2007 Light straw-green; as expected, very well made, the nectarine fruit framed by precisely weighted French oak; natural acidity retained by the inhibition of mlf, but texture gained from lees stirring, giving supple mouthfeel. Screwcap. 13.5% alc. **Rating** 94 **To** 2013 $29.50
Cornelius Pinot Gris 2007 A complex and intense wine; barrel ferment, six months in oak and lees stirring offset the piercing palate driven by a very low pH; a wine built to live. Screwcap. 14.5% alc. **Rating** 94 **To** 2013 $36
Cornelius Syrah 2006 Delicious wine; sophisticated winery handling, with 25% whole bunches in 3-tonne fermenters, 16 months in one-third new French oak all adding to the appeal; very good balance and mouthfeel. Screwcap. 15% alc. **Rating** 94 **To** 2021 $45

ŶŶŶŶŶ **Cornelius Sauvignon 2007** Very pale notwithstanding barrel ferment and six months' maturation in French oak; an intense palate has soaked up the oak, with a penetrating and long finish. Screwcap. 14% alc. **Rating** 93 **To** 2014 $36

Sutton Vineyard Bellarine Peninsula Chardonnay 2005 Deep golden yellow; there is more of everything here; super-ripe peach bouquet, lots of very toasty oak and grilled nuts and spice result; the palate is densely packed full of fruit, and the finish cleans up with reasonable acidity, and a bit of grip; the price stretches things a little. Screwcap. 13.3% alc. **Rating** 91 **To** 2013 $75

Geelong Pinot Noir 2007 Medium-bodied, carefully crafted in a year requiring just that; offers plum and spice aromas and flavours on a palate with adequate balance and length. Screwcap. 14% alc. **Rating** 90 **To** 2012 $34.50

ŶŶŶŶ   **Swan Bay Chardonnay 2007** A fragrant and supple chardonnay from Mornington Peninsula/Geelong; mouthfilling stone fruit flavours drive what is at best a lightly oaked, perhaps unoaked, wine. Screwcap. 13.5% alc. **Rating** 89 **To** 2012 $19

Swan Bay Pinot Grigio 2008 Clear-cut varietal expression in a pear and quince spectrum; has good length and doesn't rely on residual sugar. Screwcap. 13.5% alc. **Rating** 89 **To** 2011 $19

Norfolk Vineyard Bellarine Peninsula Pinot Noir 2005 Browning colour; quite developed and completely savoury with a roast meat and game bouquet; firm and minerally on the palate, there is a core of dark fruit to provide lift and light; oaky on the finish. Screwcap. 13.4% alc. **Rating** 89 **To** 2012 $75

The Hill Chardonnay 2008 Seemingly unoaked, but has sufficient fruit to stand on its own, with a mix of ripe melon and stone fruit flavours. King Valley (60%)/ Geelong (40%). Great price. Screwcap. 13.5% alc. **Rating** 87 **To** 2010 $12.50

Seabrook Wines ★★★★★

Lot 350 Light Pass Road, Tanunda, SA 5352 **Region** Barossa Valley
T 0427 224 353 **F** (08) 8563 1210 **Open** By appt
Winemaker Hamish Seabrook **Est.** 2004 **Cases** 600 **Vyds** 2 ha
Hamish Seabrook is the youngest generation of a proud Melbourne wine family once involved in wholesale and retail distribution, and as leading show judges of their respective generations. Hamish, too, is a wine show judge, but was the first to venture into winemaking, working with Best's and Brown Brothers in Vic before moving to SA with wife Joanne. Here they have a small planting of shiraz (recently joined by viognier) but also continue to source small amounts of shiraz from the Barossa and Pyrenees. In February 2008 Hamish set up his own winery located on the family property in Vine Vale, having previously made the wines at Dorrien Estate and elsewhere. Exports to the UK.

ŶŶŶŶŶ   **Barossa Valley Shiraz 2006** Good hue; a scented bouquet; notes of licorice and spice lead into an elegant, medium-bodied palate with excellent texture and structure; black fruits; savoury tannins and quality oak all meld on the finish. Screwcap. 14.5% alc. **Rating** 94 **To** 2021 $35

Seaforth Estate ★★★★★

520 Arthurs Seat Road, Red Hill, Vic 3937 **Region** Mornington Peninsula
T (03) 5989 2362 **F** (03) 5989 2506 **www**.seaforthwines.com.au **Open** First w'end each month 11–5, or by appt
Winemaker Contract (Phillip Kittle) **Est.** 1994 **Cases** 1800 **Vyds** 4.1 ha
Seaforth Estate is a family-owned and operated business. Andrew and Venetia Adamson continue to undertake much of the management of their vineyard on red volcanic soil at the top of Red Hill. At 300 m above sea level, Seaforth Estate is one of the highest vineyards on the Mornington Peninsula, sited on a north-facing slope overlooking Port Phillip Bay to the distant Melbourne skyline. Wines marketed under the Seaforth Estate label are 100% estate-grown and the Pinot Noir, Chardonnay and Pinot Gris have consistently performed well.

ŶŶŶŶŶ   **Mornington Peninsula Chardonnay 2006** An aromatic, tangerine-accented bouquet leads into an intense and long palate, with grapefruit joining the fray; well-balanced and integrated oak. Screwcap. 13.8% alc. **Rating** 94 **To** 2013 $26

Mornington Peninsula Chardonnay 2005 Has developed slowly over the two and a half years since first tasted, fulfilling its early promised; very good length and balance to the nectarine fruit and subtle oak. Screwcap. 13.8% alc. **Rating** 94 **To** 2012 $26

Secret Garden Wines   ★★★★

251 Henry Lawson Drive, Mudgee, NSW 2850 **Region** Mudgee
T (02) 6373 3874 **F** (02) 6373 3854 **Open** Fri–Sun & public hols 9–5
Winemaker Ian MacRae **Est.** 2000 **Cases** NA
Secret Garden Wines is owned by Ian and Carol MacRae, and is a sister operation to their main business, Miramar Wines. Estate plantings consist of 10 ha of shiraz and around 2 ha each of cabernet sauvignon and chardonnay. The wines are made at Miramar, the cellar door is at Secret Garden. The property is only 5 km from Mudgee and fronts Craigmoor Road, giving it a prime position in the so-called 'golden triangle'.

ＹＹＹＹＹ **Eljamar Mudgee Chardonnay 2005** A still youthful wine, which swept all before it at the Mudgee Wine Show '07; gentle honeydew melon and stone fruit favours with subtle oak. Certainly well made. Screwcap. 13.9% alc. **Rating** 92 **To** 2013 $25

Sedona Estate

182 Shannons Road, Murrindindi, Vic 3717 **Region** Upper Goulburn
T (03) 9730 2883 **www.**sedonaestate.com.au **Open** W'ends & public hols 11–5, or by appt
Winemaker Paul Evans **Est.** 1998 **Cases** 2000 **Vyds** 4 ha
The Sedona Estate vineyard was chosen by Paul and Sonja Evans after a long search for what they considered to be the perfect site. Situated on north-facing and gently undulating slopes, with gravelly black soils, it is planted (in descending order) to shiraz, cabernet sauvignon, merlot and sangiovese. Paul (former Oakridge winemaker) also contract-makes wines for a number of other small Yarra Valley producers.

ＹＹＹＹＹ **Yea Valley Cabernet Sauvignon 2006** Excellent colour, deep and bright; a powerful, intense wine, which explains the success of the Cabernet Merlot, and the less successful Merlot; abundant blackcurrant fruit runs through to the finish. Diam. 13.5% alc. **Rating** 94 **To** 2021 $25

ＹＹＹＹＹ **Yea Valley Cabernet Merlot 2005** The bright hue is partly explained by the December '08 bottling; the flavours are similarly fresh, with blackcurrant, plum and cedar fruit backed by well-balanced tannins. Screwcap. 13.5% alc. **Rating** 91 **To** 2015 $18
Sauvignon Blanc 2008 Well-made wine, with good mouthfeel and length to its array of grass, gooseberry and kiwi fruit flavours. Screwcap. 12% alc. **Rating** 90 **To** 2010 $21

Seplin Estate Wines

36 Chifley Road, Wee Waa, NSW 2388 **Region** Western Plains Zone
T (02) 6795 3636 **F** (02) 6795 3636 **www.**seplinestatewines.com.au **Open** 7 days 10–10
Winemaker James Estate (Peter Orr) **Est.** 1998 **Cases** 6000 **Vyds** 9.8 ha
Seplin Estate was established by the late Seppi Widauer and wife Lindy. It was the culmination of a long-held ambition to have their own wines and their own cellar door. When Seppi died suddenly in March 2004, his wife and children (Jamie and Simon) decided to continue the project, opening the cellar door and function centre in April '06. It is situated in a 70-year-old building overlooking the nearby lagoon and gum trees. Most of the wine comes from 5.2 ha of shiraz and 4.6 ha of chardonnay, supplemented by some purchases of cabernet sauvignon.

ＹＹＹＹ **Kangaloon Chardonnay 2007** Has abundant peachy flavour on the medium-bodied palate; much more successful than the red wines. However, drink asap. Screwcap. 13% alc. **Rating** 87 **To** 2009 $20

Seppelt ★★★★★

Moyston Road, Great Western, Vic 3377 **Region** Grampians
T (03) 5361 2239 **F** (03) 5361 2328 www.seppeltwines.com.au **Open** 7 days 10–5
Winemaker Joanna Marsh **Est.** 1908 **Cases** 150 000

Australia's best known producer of sparkling wine, always immaculate in its given price range but also producing excellent Great Western–sourced table wines, especially long-lived Shiraz and Australia's best Sparkling Shirazs. The glitzy labels of the past have rightly been consigned to the rubbish bin, and the product range has been significantly rationalised and improved. Following the sale of Seppeltsfield to Kilikanoon, this is the sole operating arm of Seppelt under Foster's ownership. Exports to the UK, the US and other major markets.

ΨΨΨΨΨ **St Peters Grampians Shiraz 2006** Very deep colour; an epic, multi-faceted, engaging and complex wine; a vast array of red to black fruit aromas, intermingle with a dark heart of minerals and tar; lovely ripe, chewy tannins perfectly frame the abundant fruit. Screwcap. 13.5% alc. **Rating** 96 **To** 2026 $59.99

Drumborg Vineyard Chardonnay 2007 Still pale straw-green; sensitive, skilled use of barrel ferment has enhanced the purity of the nectarine, apple and citrus fruit; minerally acidity is the anchor on the finish. Screwcap. 13% alc. **Rating** 95 **To** 2017 $44.99

Chalambar Bendigo Grampians Shiraz 2007 A full-bodied wine crammed with spicy black fruits, licorice and lingering tannins running through the length of the palate; good oak, and a dyed-in-the-wool stayer. Screwcap. 14% alc. **Rating** 95 **To** 2030 $26.99

Benno Seppelt Bendigo Shiraz 2006 Lively dark fruits leap out of the glass; the tannin management is wonderful, as the palate is quite velvety, long and has a very attractive savoury twist to the finish. Screwcap. 14% alc. **Rating** 95 **To** 2020 $54.99

Jaluka Drumborg Vineyard Chardonnay 2008 Bright straw-green; very tight and very youthful; grapefruit leads the way, followed by white peach and apple; the wine has devoured the French oak in which it was barrel-fermented. Will be very long lived. Screwcap. 12.5% alc. **Rating** 94 **To** 2020 $26.99

Drumborg Vineyard Pinot Gris 2008 From the very cool Henty region in the far southwest of Vic. Floral apple blossom aromas; as always, very pure and focused, with a long and bright fruit palate, balanced acidity. Screwcap. 13.5% alc. **Rating** 94 **To** 2010 $26.99

Benno Seppelt Bendigo Shiraz 2007 Deep purple; the bouquet has plum, licorice and spice, the full-bodied palate with wonderful texture and structure anchored by lacy tannins that run through its length and aftertaste. Screwcap. 14% alc. **Rating** 94 **To** 2022 $54.99

St Peters Grampians Shiraz 2007 Aromatic red and black fruit nuances on the bouquet lead into a gently spicy medium-bodied palate, which has true elegance and harmony. Screwcap. 13.5% alc. **Rating** 94 **To** 2020 $59.99

Mt Ida Vineyard Shiraz 2006 Vivid purple hue; a very dark wine with tar, earth and spicy oak complementing an abundance of dark fruits with a hint of blueberry; quite tannic, but in balance for the abundant fruit; very long. Screwcap. 13.5% alc. **Rating** 94 **To** 2026 $54.99

ΨΨΨΨΩ **Heathcote Shiraz 2006** The innate power of the wine expresses itself in the length of the palate and finish rather than the more usual depth of flavour, which will appeal to those looking for elegance and subtlety. Great price. Screwcap. 14.5% alc. **Rating** 92 **To** 2016 $18.95

Silverband Grampians Shiraz 2006 Squeaky clean; lifted violet aromas intermingle with red and dark berry fruits; impeccably structured, the fruit subordinate to the tannin and acid at this point. Screwcap. 14% alc. **Rating** 92 **To** 2012 $35

Original Sparkling Shiraz 2005 Strong colour and mousse; complex spicy black fruit aromas are precisely reflected on the palate, which is neither oaky nor, praise be, sweet. Cork. 13% alc. **Rating** 92 **To** 2010 $20.99

Drumborg Riesling 2008 Absolutely locked up, with little fruit aroma or flavour escaping the net, just crisp acidity on a long finish. The track record of this wine guarantees it will flower with time, but how brilliantly is hard to tell. Screwcap. 12% alc. **Rating** 91 **To** 2020 $31.99

Aerin's Vineyard Single Vineyard Heathcote Shiraz 2008 Vibrant colour; a clean and bright blue and black fruit bouquet with a minerally edge; medium-bodied and quite firm, the fruit takes a back seat to the minerality and savoury nature of the wine; quite tarry on the finish. Screwcap. 14% alc. **Rating** 91 **To** 2015 $17.99

Silverband Grampians Sparkling Shiraz NV Elegant spicy red fruits are immediately enjoyable, but do expose some sweetness on the finish, which some will greatly enjoy. Crown Seal. 13% alc. **Rating** 90 **To** 2010 $35

Moyston Grampians Bendigo Cabernet Sauvignon 2007 Is very much in the traditional style of Moyston, savoury black olive notes appearing alongside cassis and blackcurrant fruit right from the outset. Screwcap. 13.5% alc. **Rating** 90 **To** 2017 $26.99

Salinger 2005 Bright straw-green; good mousse; abundant fruity flavour and good acidity; has balance and length. Fall from grace. Cork. 13% alc. **Rating** 90 **To** 2010 $24.99

ŶŶŶŶ   **Grampians Chardonnay 2007** An elegant, juicy palate with persistence and length, the new style chardonnay evident in the alcohol; the fruit profile is slightly diminished, however. Screwcap. 12.5% alc. **Rating** 89 **To** 2012 $18.95

Aerin's Vineyard Heathcote Grenache Shiraz Mourvedre 2008 Vibrant raspberry and blackberry bouquet, with a slight undergrowth complexity; juicy on entry with good definition, but lacks a little generosity on the mid-palate. Screwcap. 13.5% alc. **Rating** 89 **To** 2014 $17.99

Victoria Chardonnay 2005 Fresh for its age, and showing melon and peach fruit aromas; just missing drive and line across the palate. Screwcap. 13.5% alc. **Rating** 88 **To** 2011 $17.99

Aerin's Vineyard Mornington Peninsula Pinot Grigio 2008 Quite deep colour; neutral straw bouquet with a suggestion of lemon; engaging phenolic palate, and a true grigio finish. Screwcap. 12.5% alc. **Rating** 88 **To** 2012 $17.99

Seppeltsfield   ★★★★★

1 Seppeltsfield Road, Seppeltsfield via Nuriootpa, SA 5355 **Region** Barossa Valley
T (08) 8568 6217 **www**.seppelt.com.au **Open** Mon–Fri 10–5, w'ends & public hols 11–5
Winemaker James Godfrey **Est.** 1851 **Cases** 150 000
In August 2007 this historic property and its treasure trove of great fortified wines dating back to 1878 was purchased by the Kilikanoon group. A series of complicated lease-back arrangements and supply agreements were entered into between Kilikanoon and vendor Foster's, further complicated by Foster's keeping the Seppelt brand for table and sparkling wines (mostly produced at Great Western, Vic; see separate entry), but the Seppelt brand for fortified wines vesting in purchaser Kilikanoon. The winery was fully recomissioned for the 2008 vintage, including the gravity flow system designed by Benno Seppelt in 1878.

ŶŶŶŶŶ   **100 Year Old Para Liqueur 1908** The colour is slightly less dense than that of the 1918, yet paints the glass so thoroughly it resists attempts to rinse it. It combines all the expected intensity with an unexpected degree of elegance. (Tasted on its own, elegance would likely be the last thing in your mind, but such is the comparative element of all mega-tastings of great wines.) An extra element of spice and cedar appears moments before the flavours surge across the palate, then emphatic rancio on a finish that knows no end. **Rating** 100 **To** 2010

Rare Rutherglen Tokay NV Full mahogany, olive rim; an intensely fragrant and equally complex bouquet; the flavours are more intense and piercing than those of the Muscat, rancio now a cornerstone, but the wine is not heavier or more luscious, simply marking the difference between tokay and muscat; 375 ml. Cork. 17% alc. **Rating** 97 **To** 2010 $59

Rare Rutherglen Muscat NV Deep mahogany-brown grading to olive on the rim; explosively rich on the palate; raisins, singed toffee, plum pudding, almond and multi-spices race along the vibrant, wonderfully complex palate; rancio and associated acidity keeps the wine lithe and lively; 375 ml. Cork. 17% alc. **Rating** 97 **To** 2010 $59

Rare Tawny DP90 NV Full-on tawny colour; the bouquet immediately proclaims the age and the class of the wine; the palate is electric in its intensity and vibrancy, the rancio penetrating and lingering; the aftertaste goes on and on, and it is here that the glorious breed and quality of the wine is most apparent. Cork. 20.5% alc. **Rating** 96 **To** 2010 $69

Grand Rutherglen Tokay NV Bright mahogany, with a rim of olive; in another tokay category altogether, its piercing complexity coupled with elegance, a vivid line of rancio running through the butterscotch, tea leaf and honey flavours; has great length and balance. Serve chilled; 500 ml. Screwcap. 16.5% alc. **Rating** 96 **To** 2010 $32

Selma Melitta Rare Luscious NV Bright mahogany brown, a blush of olive on the rim; into another realm of richness and sweetness, yet always with the counter-punch of rancio; flavours of slightly burnt toffee and raisined sultanas; the finish has great balance; 500 ml. Screwcap. 18.5% alc. **Rating** 95 **To** 2010 $40

Flora Fino DP117 NV Pale straw-green; a great bouquet, highly aromatic, tangy and fresh; the palate follows precisely in the footsteps of the bouquet, with a mix of nutty/green apple characters on the mid-palate, then a gloriously fresh, dry and breezy finish. This has more character than Manzanilla; 500 ml. Screwcap. 16.1% alc. **Rating** 95 **To** 2010 $22

Para 1987 In a unique heavy base, clear glass bottle with a fascinating variant of screwcap. True tawny colour, the aromas are of hazelnut, mocha, dried fruits and spice, the flavours an intense array infinitely complexed by rancio cut. By far the best commercial liqueur-style tawny on the market. 19.5% alc. **Rating** 95 **To** 2010 $75

Grand Rutherglen Muscat NV Brown-gold; another step up in richness and lusciousness; an unctuous, essency palate with spicy plum pudding and caramel overtaking outright raisin flavours; the finish is sleek and lingering; 10–15 years barrel age. Serve chilled; 500 ml. Screwcap. 17% alc. **Rating** 95 **To** 2010 $32

Glenpara GSM Barossa Clare Valley Grenache Shiraz Mataro 2006 Has good balance, weight (medium-bodied) and structure, but, above all, a synergistic union between the regional and varietal components; has excellent black and red fruit flavours, and good tannins. Screwcap. 15% alc. **Rating** 94 **To** 2021 $25

Clara Blanca Amontillado DP116 NV Yellow bronze/old gold; nutty, dried fruit peel aromas, then a palate that plays hide and seek; one moment with sweet honeyed nuances, the next dry and nutty, with the crosscut of rancio driving the finish; 500 ml. Screwcap. 21.7% alc. **Rating** 94 **To** 2010 $26

Vera Viola Rare Rich Oloroso DP38 NV Light golden brown, with just a hint of olive; here the honeyed flavours are more persistent, accompanied by dried fruit and nut flavours. Has tremendous length; it is not until the aftertaste that the rancio dries out the mouth, demanding another sip to start the process again. Average age of 18 years, but as fresh as a daisy; 500 ml. Screwcap. 21.1% alc. **Rating** 94 **To** 2010 $32

ҮҮҮҮҮ **Vintage Port 2001** An elegant, spicy true vintage port style, much closer to Portuguese than older examples; the blend of shiraz and a little touriga has some impact, but it is really the lower level of sweetness that enlivens the palate, allowing the licorice and black fruits to express themselves. Its balance and length means it can be enjoyed now or on its 15th birthday; 375 ml. **Rating** 93 **To** 2016 $18

Grand Para NV In a squat, heavy base, clear glass bottle; a very substantial step up the quality tree, the dried fruit/Christmas cake flavours perfectly balanced by gentle rancio. This is a wine that leads you on and on. Average age 10 years; 500 ml. Screwcap. 19.1% alc. **Rating** 93 **To** 2010 $32

Glenpara Pump House Barossa Valley Shiraz 2006 Fractionally fresher colour; medium- to full-bodied, and has more rich fruit than Head Office, ranging through blackberry, licorice and bramble, with some earthy notes and a dry, savoury finish. Screwcap. 15% alc. **Rating** 91 **To** 2016 $25

Cellar No. 6 Rutherglen Tokay NV Pale golden brown; tea leaf, honey, shortbread biscuit and malt aromas; a succulent, supple and rich palate, varietal fruit to the fore, rancio yet to develop much impact. Previously released under the DP37 label. Screwcap. 16.5% alc. **Rating** 91 **To** 2010 $20

Cellar No. 8 Rutherglen Muscat NV Tawny gold-amber; the bouquet is redolent of raisins and a hint of rose petal; a quite vigorous palate, with luscious raisin fruit balanced by a neat spear of acidity. Screwcap. 16.5% alc. **Rating** 91 **To** 2010 $20

ŸŸŸŸ   Glenpara Elm Walk Clare Valley Riesling 2008 Quite rich and ripe, with citrus and some tropical fruits; relatively forward style for next few years. Screwcap. 12.5% alc. **Rating** 89 **To** 2012 $19

Glenpara Head Office Barossa Valley Shiraz 2006 Some development in colour; a quite earthy/savoury wine, somewhat at odds with its alcohol, for there is certainly no surfeit of ripe fruit; may appeal for that very reason. Screwcap. 15% alc. **Rating** 89 **To** 2014 $40

Cellar No. 7 Tawny NV No red tints anywhere to be seen; the wine is distinctly rich and quite sweet, with brandysnap and cake nuances; rancio is in the background. Serve chilled is the wise instruction. Screwcap. 18% alc. **Rating** 89 **To** 2010 $20

Ruby Lightly Fortified Grenache Rose NV The instruction on the back label not to binge drink is appropriate; this could get anyone into trouble, regardless of age and experience, so cleverly has it been put together, the spirit doing little more than holding the red, spicy raspberry and cherry fruit together. Screwcap. 16% alc. **Rating** 87 **To** 2010 $20

Serafino Wines   ★★★★☆

McLarens on the Lake, Kangarilla Road, McLaren Vale, SA 5171 **Region** McLaren Vale
T (08) 8323 0157 **F** (08) 8323 0158 **Open** Mon–Fri 10–5, w'ends & public hols 10–4.30
Winemaker Charles Whish **Est.** 2000 **Cases** 20 000 **Vyds** 98 ha
In the wake of the sale of Maglieri Wines to Beringer Blass in 1998, Maglieri founder Steve Maglieri acquired the McLarens on the Lake complex originally established by Andrew Garrett. The accommodation has been upgraded and a larger winery was commissioned in 2002. The operation draws upon 40 ha each of shiraz and cabernet sauvignon, 7 ha of chardonnay, 2 ha each of merlot, semillon, barbera, nebbiolo and sangiovese, and 1 ha of grenache. Part of the grape production is sold. Exports to the UK, the US and other major markets.

ŸŸŸŸŸ   McLaren Vale Cabernet Sauvignon 2007 Strong red-purple; briary/earthy/ chocolate aromas and flavours are wrapped around a core of black fruit, finishing with firm tannins. Screwcap. 14.5% alc. **Rating** 91 **To** 2017 $24

Single Vineyard McLaren Vale Nebbiolo 2007 Bright, light red-purple, good for the variety; while light-bodied, has delicious cherry, strawberry and spice aromas and flavours; good length, and no green abrasive tannins. Screwcap. 12.5% alc. **Rating** 91 **To** 2014 $20

Goose Island McLaren Vale Sangiovese Rose 2008 Has well above average character, with red and sour cherry fruit set against a spicy background; good length and balance. Screwcap. **Rating** 90 **To** 2011 $13

Sharktooth McLaren Vale Shiraz 2007 Full-on McLaren Vale Shiraz, with full-bodied potent black fruits and a strong veneer of dark chocolate; the tannin structure is good. Screwcap. 15% alc. **Rating** 90 **To** 2022 $50

Goose Island McLaren Vale Shiraz 2006 Laden with rich and succulent black fruits and dark chocolate; the finish is mildly surprising, for it has the warmth of a wine with higher alcohol; a curate's egg. Screwcap. 14.5% alc. **Rating** 90 **To** 2016 $13

Sorrento Dry Grown McLaren Vale Grenache 2007 Bright crimson hue; highly aromatic and flowery red fruits on the bouquet, with a more savoury/spicy medium-bodied palate; balanced finish. Screwcap. 14.5% alc. **Rating** 90 To 2013 $15

ŶŶŶŶ **McLaren Vale Shiraz 2007** Good commercial wine; honest blackberry shiraz flavours on a medium-bodied palate, appropriate oak and tannins. Screwcap. 14.5% alc. **Rating** 88 **To** 2015 $24
Goose Island McLaren Vale Cabernet Merlot 2006 Has ripe fruit aromas and flavours in a red/morello cherry and juicy berry spectrum. Screwcap. 14.5% alc. **Rating** 88 **To** 2014 $13
McLaren Vale Grenache Tempranillo Shiraz 2007 A light- to medium-bodied savoury/spicy/juicy assemblage of three varieties with very different characters; designed by a committee. Screwcap. 14.5% alc. **Rating** 87 **To** 2014 $22
McLaren Vale Tempranillo 2007 A very savoury wine from start to finish, with earthy/green nuances, but does have length. Screwcap. 14.5% alc. **Rating** 87 To 2010 $22

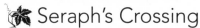

Seraph's Crossing   ★★★

PO Box 5753, Clare, SA 5453 **Region** Clare Valley
T 0412 132 549 **Open** Not
Winemaker Harry Dickinson **Est.** 2006 **Cases** 400 **Vyds** 5 ha
In a moment of enlightened madness, Harry Dickinson gave up his career as a lawyer in a major London law firm to work in the wine business. He helped run the International Wine Challenge for three years, followed by stints with various wine retailers, and some PR work for the German Wine Information Service. He worked his first vintage in Australia at Hardys Tintara winery in 1997 with Stephen Pannell and Larry Cherubino; their work with open fermenters, basket presses and winemaking philosophy made a huge impression. Following a period as a wine retailer in North Adelaide, he returned to winery work in 1999, moving around various wineries in the Clare Valley. During this time he and wife Chan bought a 75-ha property. They restored the 1880s house on the property, and the vineyards have been extended from the original 1 ha to now comprise shiraz, grenache, mourvedre and zinfandel. The shiraz is hand-picked, de-stemmed, fermented with wild yeast, and, at the end of fermentation, is pressed directly to barrel where it remains for 28 months (with no racking) prior to blending and bottling with no fining or filtration. Exports to the UK and the US.

ŶŶŶŶ **Clare Valley Shiraz 2006** Wow. There is no question aromas and flavours are obtained at very high alcohol that are impossible to achieve at lower levels; confit/jam/conserved fruit are just the start. *Chacun à son goût*, I suppose. Screwcap. 16.4% alc. **Rating** 88 **To** 2016 $35

Serrat   ★★★★☆

PO Box 478, Yarra Glen, Vic 3775 **Region** Yarra Valley
T (03) 9730 1439 **F** (03) 9730 1579 **www**.serrat.com.au **Open** Not
Winemaker Tom Carson **Est.** 2001 **Cases** 25
Serrat is the family business of Tom Carson (after a 12-year reign at Yering Station, now running Yabby Lake and Heathcote Estate for the Kirby family) and partner Nadege Suné. They have close-planted (at 8800 vines per ha) 0.8 ha each of pinot noir and chardonnay, 0.42 ha of shiraz, and a sprinkling of viognier. The vineyard was significantly damaged by the Black Saturday bushfires of 7 February 2009. Exports to Singapore.

ŶŶŶŶŶ **Yarra Valley Pinot Noir 2007** Excellent hue; vibrant and lively, with a scented bouquet leading into a pristine cherry/plum palate, oak and gossamer tannins cradling the fruit. Screwcap. 13.5% alc. **Rating** 94 **To** 2013 $30

ŶŶŶŶ♀ **Yarra Valley Grenache Noir 2005** Light, bright red after four years; a quixotic yet successful desire to make a Yarra Valley grenache, in a climate that should be too cool; no confection flavours, instead spices and small red fruits, cherry, strawberry and cassis. Screwcap. 14.5% alc. **Rating** 90 **To** 2013 $30

Setanta Wines ★★★★★

RSD 43 Williamstown Road, Forreston, SA 5233 (postal) **Region** Adelaide Hills
T (08) 8380 5516 **F** (08) 8380 5516 **www**.setantawines.com.au **Open** Not
Winemaker Rod Chapman, Rebecca Wilson **Est.** 1997 **Cases** 5000

Setanta is a family-owned operation involving Sheilagh Sullivan, her husband Tony, and brother Bernard; the latter is the viticulturist, while Tony and Sheilagh manage marketing, administration and so forth. Of Irish parentage (they are first-generation Australians), they chose Setanta, Ireland's most famous mythological hero, as the brand name. The beautiful and striking labels tell the individual stories that give rise to the names of the wines. Unexplained problems occurred with the tastings for this edition, emerging when it was too late to investigate. Further tastings will appear on www.winecompanion.com.au in due course. The winery rating is an interim measure. Exports to Ireland, of course; also to the UK, Dubai, Singapore, Hong Kong and Japan.

🍷🍷🍷🍷½ **Black Sanglain Adelaide Hills Cabernet Sauvignon 2007** Good colour; elements of cassis and a touch of spicy oak; medium-bodied, with good varietal fruit expression and length. Screwcap. 13.5% alc. **Rating** 90 **To** 2013 **$29**

Settlement Wines ★★★☆

Lot 101 Seaview Road, McLaren Vale, SA 5171 **Region** McLaren Vale
T (08) 8323 7344 **F** (08) 8323 7355 **www**.settlementwines.com.au **Open** Mon–Fri 10–5, w'ends & public hols 11–5
Winemaker Vincenzo Berlingieri **Est.** 1992 **Cases** 3500

Vincenzo Berlingieri is a bigger than life graduate of Perugia University, Italy. He arrived in Melbourne with beard flowing and arms waving (his words) in 1964 as a research scientist to work in plant genetics. He subsequently moved to SA, and gained considerable publicity for the winery he then owned, and for his larger than life wines. There is nothing new in the reincarnated Settlement Wines, it still has big table wines, but with specialities in liqueurs and fortified wines.

🍷🍷🍷🍷½ **Black Pedro Ximinex NV** Olive rim attests to its age; very rich and luscious with Christmas pudding/crystallised fruit/brandy snap and malt all coinciding; good rancio, clean spirit. Cork. 18% alc. **Rating** 93 **To** 2010 **$30**

🍷🍷🍷🍷 **McLaren Vale Cabernet Sauvignon 2004** Well balanced and modulated, the blackcurrant fruit offset by some black olive and earthy notes on the finish. Screwcap. 13.5% alc. **Rating** 87 **To** 2012 **$20**

Sevenhill Cellars ★★★★☆

College Road, Sevenhill, SA 5453 **Region** Clare Valley
T (08) 8843 4222 **www**.sevenhill.com.au **Open** Mon–Fri 9–5, w'ends & public hols 10–5
Winemaker Liz Heidenreich, Brother John May, Neville Rowe **Est.** 1851 **Cases** 20 000
Vyds 72.46 ha

One of the historical treasures of Australia; the oft-photographed stone wine cellars are the oldest in the Clare Valley, and winemaking is still carried out under the direction of the Jesuitical Manresa Society. Value for money is excellent, particularly that of the powerful Shiraz and Riesling; all the wines reflect the estate-grown grapes from old vines. Exports to the UK, the US, Indonesia, Korea, Singapore and Japan.

🍷🍷🍷🍷🍷 **Inigo Clare Valley Shiraz 2006** Dense colour; spectacularly rich and dense wine, with multiple layers of blackberry, licorice and dark chocolate flavours supported by ripe tannins; carries alcohol, although those who enjoy full-bodied wines will appreciate it most. Screwcap. 15% alc. **Rating** 94 **To** 2026 **$19**

🍷🍷🍷🍷½ **St Aloysius Riesling 2007** Talc and lime juice bouquet; classic dry palate, minerals interplaying pleasingly with the fruit; zesty on the conclusion. Screwcap. 12.5% alc. **Rating** 93 **To** 2014 **$29**

Inigo Semillon 2008 Deep colour; straw and ripe lemon aromas and flavours to a generous and textured semillon; good finish. Screwcap. 12% alc. **Rating** 91 **To** 2013 $19

Inigo Merlot 2006 Good colour; powerful, intense wine, with savoury tannins evident from the outset; some dark berry and fruitcake notes, but needs time. Screwcap. 14% alc. **Rating** 90 **To** 2014 $19

ŶŶŶŶ **Inigo Clare Valley Riesling 2008** Quite deep colour; a touch of kerosene with lime and mineral notes; quite rich on the palate with a strong quince flavour evident. Screwcap. 12.5% alc. **Rating** 88 **To** 2015 $19

Clare Valley Semillon 2007 Full-throated lemon, honey and a touch of toast on the mid-palate; shortens/slows down on the finish. Screwcap. 11% alc. **Rating** 88 **To** 2011 $19

Inigo Clare Valley Cabernet Sauvignon 2006 Savoury dark fruits, framed by a little mint on the bouquet; good depth to the fruit, with an abundance of dark fruit and earth on the finish. Screwcap. 14.5% alc. **Rating** 88 **To** 2014 $19

Clare Valley Verdelho 2008 Deep colour; a ripe bouquet of nectarine with a touch of rose; the palate is generous and rich, finishing quite dry and full. Screwcap. 13.5% alc. **Rating** 87 **To** 2011 $19

Clare Valley Barbera 2006 A little bit of animal complexity; bramble, blackberry and a touch of spice; fleshy, with high acid and good fruit-weight. Screwcap. 15% alc. **Rating** 87 **To** 2012 $19

Clare Valley Fine Old Tawny NV A light and freshly raisined style of tawny; quite clean with a gentle touch of red fruits and nuts to the finish. Screwcap. 18% alc. **Rating** 87 **To** 2014 $19

Seville Estate   ★★★★★

65 Linwood Road, Seville, Vic 3139 **Region** Yarra Valley
T (03) 5964 2622 **F** (03) 5964 2633 **www.**sevilleestate.com.au **Open** 7 days 10–5
Winemaker Dylan McMahon **Est.** 1970 **Cases** 3500 **Vyds** 8 ha
Dr Peter McMahon and wife Margaret commenced planting Seville Estate in 1972, part of the resurgence of the Yarra Valley. Peter and Margaret retired in 1997, selling to Brokenwood. Graham and Margaret Van Der Meulen acquired the property in '05, bringing it back into family ownership. Graham and Margaret are hands-on in the vineyard and winery, working closely with winemaker Dylan McMahon, who is the grandson of Peter and Margaret. The philosophy is to capture the fruit expression of the vineyard in styles that reflect the cool climate. Exports to Hong Kong and Singapore.

ŶŶŶŶŶ **Old Vine Reserve Vine Yarra Valley Cabernet Sauvignon 2007** A particularly rich and generous cabernet from this southern, red soil side of the valley, coming from the original 1972 plantings; has an abundance of cassis and blackcurrant fruit, ripe tannins and good oak. Screwcap. 14% alc. **Rating** 96 **To** 2037 $50

Reserve Yarra Valley Chardonnay 2006 Like the varietal, bright straw-green; here the more intense and more tightly focused fruit leads the way on the bouquet and palate; supple and smooth white peach and citrus run through to the finish, accompanied by fine French oak. Screwcap. 14% alc. **Rating** 95 **To** 2016 $45

Yarra Valley Chardonnay 2006 Bright straw-green; a complex bouquet with fruit and oak both having their say; attractive stone fruit and melon is lifted by citrussy acidity on the long finish. Screwcap. 14.5% alc. **Rating** 94 **To** 2013 $27

Reserve Yarra Valley Pinot Noir 2007 Light but clear colour; deceptively light-bodied on entry to the mouth, but builds progressively on the back of fine, gently spicy tannins. Screwcap. 14% alc. **Rating** 94 **To** 2015 $55

Old Vine Reserve Yarra Valley Shiraz 2006 Deeper colour than the varietal; while medium-bodied, has considerable depth to the complex flavours of black cherry, blackberry, spice, licorice and pepper supported by lingering tannins. Screwcap. 14.5% alc. **Rating** 94 **To** 2021 $60

ΨΨΨΨΨ **Yarra Valley Pinot Noir 2007** Similar colour to Reserve; a more fruit-forward, juicy style with cherry and strawberry fruit; good balance and length; delicious now. Screwcap. 14% alc. **Rating** 92 **To** 2012 $30
Yarra Valley Shiraz 2006 Spicy/earthy/peppery nuances are immediately obvious in this silky, light- to medium-bodied wine; red berry fruits carry the mid-palate through to the finish. Screwcap. 14.5% alc. **Rating** 92 **To** 2016 $27
The Barber Yarra Valley Rose 2008 Made with estate-grown Shiraz (90%)/ Cabernet Sauvignon (10%); has well above average intensity to the black cherry fruit, and a pleasingly dry finish. Screwcap. 13% alc. **Rating** 91 **To** 2010 $16

ΨΨΨΨ **The Barber Pinot Gris 2008** A blend of Beechworth/Upper Yarra grapes says more about texture (ex lees contact) and complexity (regional blend) than pinot gris varietal fruit – no bad thing. Screwcap. 13.5% alc. **Rating** 89 **To** 2011 $23

Seville Hill   ★★★★

8 Paynes Road, Seville, Vic 3139 **Region** Yarra Valley
T (03) 5964 3284 **F** (03) 5964 2142 **www.**sevillehill.com.au **Open** 7 days 10–6
Winemaker Dominic Bucci, John D'Aloisio **Est.** 1991 **Cases** 3000
John and Josie D'Aloisio have had a long-term involvement in the agricultural industry, which ultimately led to the establishment of the Seville Hill vineyard in 1991. There they have 2.4 ha of cabernet sauvignon and 1.3 ha each of merlot, shiraz and chardonnay. John makes the wines with Dominic Bucci, a long-time Yarra resident and winemaker.

ΨΨΨΨΨ **Yarra Valley Sauvignon Blanc 2008** Opens quietly on the bouquet and fore-palate, but then gathers pace and intensity to the citrus and passionfruit flavours on the finish. Diam. 13% alc. **Rating** 90 **To** 2011 $22
Yarra Valley Merlot 2005 Maturing slowly; demonstrates the capacity of the Yarra Valley to produce quality Merlot; the medium-bodied palate has pleasing tension between the cassis fruit and black olive/leaf components. Diam. 14% alc. **Rating** 90 **To** 2013 $25

ΨΨΨΨ **Yarra Valley Tempranillo 2005** A complex wine, for sure, but without the razor sharp spicy red berry fruits of the best Tempranillos; many parts to the palate, more bass than treble. Cork. 14.8% alc. **Rating** 88 **To** 2012 $45

Shadowfax   ★★★★★

K Road, Werribee, Vic 3030 **Region** Geelong
T (03) 9731 4420 **F** (03) 9731 4421 **www.**shadowfax.com.au **Open** 7 days 11–5
Winemaker Matt Harrop **Est.** 2000 **Cases** 15 000
Shadowfax is part of an awesome development at Werribee Park, a mere 20 mins from Melbourne. The truly striking winery, designed by Wood Marsh Architects, built in 2000, is adjacent to the extraordinary private home built in the 1880s by the Chirnside family and known as The Mansion. It was then the centrepiece of a 40 000-ha pastoral empire, and the appropriately magnificent gardens were part of the reason why the property was acquired by Parks Victoria in the early 1970s. The Mansion is now The Mansion Hotel, with 92 rooms and suites. Exports to the UK, Japan, NZ and Singapore.

ΨΨΨΨΨ **Chardonnay 2007** Very well crafted, subtle complexities bubbling under the surface; a generous mid-palate is tightened and lengthened by delicious lemony acidity, oak lost in the background. Screwcap. 13% alc. **Rating** 94 **To** 2016 $30
Viognier 2008 A singularly well made Viognier, with clear varietal flavour and texture, yet avoids a phenolic finish; barrel fermentation in old French oak barriques; works to perfection. Value. Goulburn Valley/Yarra Valley. Screwcap. 13.5% alc. **Rating** 94 **To** 2011 $25
Shiraz 2007 Perfumed, spicy red/black fruit aromas lead into an intensely flavoured palate with spicy red fruits to the fore, French oak in the background; fine tannins and excellent length. Screwcap. 13.5% alc. **Rating** 94 **To** 2015 $18

ŢŢŢŢŢ **Adelaide Hills Sauvignon Blanc 2008** Filled to the brim with ripe tropical fruit aromas and flavours, with consequently generous mouthfeel. Drink asap. Screwcap. 13% alc. **Rating** 90 **To** 2009 $18

Rose 2008 Made from pinot noir macerated then lightly pressed and fermented in old oak; salmon-pink, it is fresh and lively, with spicy notes and a dry finish. Screwcap. 13% alc. **Rating** 90 **To** 2009 $18

ŢŢŢŢ **Riesling 2008** Dressed in a striking retro brown glass bottle; has plenty of flavour, but the structure is loose, perhaps reflecting the maritime climate. Screwcap. 13% alc. **Rating** 89 **To** 2014 $22

Shantell   ★★★★☆

1974 Melba Highway, Dixons Creek, Vic 3775 **Region** Yarra Valley
T (03) 5965 2155 **F** (03) 5965 2331 **www**.shantellvineyard.com.au **Open** 7 days 10.30–5
Winemaker Shan Shanmugam, Turid Shanmugam **Est.** 1980 **Cases** 1800 **Vyds** 10 ha
The fully mature Shantell vineyards provide the winery with a high-quality fruit source; part is sold to other Yarra Valley makers, the remainder vinified at Shantell. Chardonnay, Semillon and Cabernet Sauvignon are its benchmark wines, sturdily reliable, sometimes outstanding. Exports to the UK and Singapore.

ŢŢŢŢŢ **Yarra Valley Chardonnay 2006** Outstanding straw-green; has developed a totally seductive smoothness to the flow of stone fruit and grapefruit across the mid-palate, then thrusting through on the complex, well-balanced finish. Screwcap. 13% alc. **Rating** 94 **To** 2015 $28

ŢŢŢŢŢ **Yarra Valley Pinot Noir 2005** Light red, showing development; spicy, lively cherry and strawberry fruits on the light-bodied, well-balanced and long palate. Screwcap. 13% alc. **Rating** 90 **To** 2012 $30

Yarra Valley Cabernet Sauvignon 2004 Elegant cool-climate style, with blackcurrant and cassis fruit, fine-grained and modest oak influence; the ProCork membrane appears to have failed. 13% alc. **Rating** 90 **To** 2016 $28

Sharmans   ★★★★☆

Glenbothy, 175 Glenwood Road, Relbia, Tas 7258 **Region** Northern Tasmania
T (03) 6343 0773 **F** (03) 6343 0773 **www**.sharmanswines.com **Open** W'ends 10–5
Winemaker Tamar Ridge (Andrew Pirie), Josef Chromy Wines (Jeremy Dineen), Bass Fine Wines (Guy Wagner) **Est.** 1987 **Cases** 1000 **Vyds** 4.047 ha
Mike Sharman pioneered one of the more interesting wine regions of Tasmania, not far south of Launceston but with a distinctly warmer climate than (say) Pipers Brook. Ideal north-facing slopes are home to the vineyard (planted to pinot choir, chardonnay, riesling, sauvignon blanc, cabernet sauvignon and malbec). This additional warmth gives the red wines greater body than most Tasmanian counterparts.

ŢŢŢŢŢ **Chardonnay 2008** Bright colour; a lively, fine and focused bouquet, with mineral complexity framing the pure lemon fruit; the palate is very fresh, vibrant and focused with fine texture and a very long and very attractive finish; a fine example of the potential of Tasmanian chardonnay. Gold medal Tas Wine Show '09. Screwcap. 13.4% alc. **Rating** 95 **To** 2015 $22

ŢŢŢŢ **Shaman 2005** Delicate style, with some blossom aromas and a comparatively long finish. Sparkling. Cork. 12.5% alc. **Rating** 88 **To** 2012 $25

Sharpe Wines of Orange   ★★★

789 Icely Road, Emu Swamp, Orange, NSW 2800 **Region** Orange
T (02) 6361 9046 **www**.sharpewinesoforange.com.au **Open** W'ends 12–4, or by appt
Winemaker Margot Sharpe **Est.** 1998 **Cases** 1000 **Vyds** 4 ha
When Tony and Margot Sharpe planted their vineyard in 1998, the wheel of fortune turned a sharp 180 degrees. Their ancestors, strict Methodists, established Sharpe Bros cordials in

1868 to provide the working man with an alternative to the demon alcohol at the end of his working day. The vicissitudes of this life of wine are reflected in the names of their wines: Shattered Margot, Battered Sauv, Gentleman's Claret (a nod to the forebears), Lazy Rosy, Redemption Chardonnay and Just Franc (cabernet franc).

ΨΨΨΨ   **Redemption Cabernet Sauvignon 2005** A savoury/earthy cabernet, offering black fruits with a web of fine tannins; good winemaking has given the wine balance and a certain harmony. Diam. 14.2% alc. **Rating** 88 **To** 2015 $18

Shaw & Smith   ★★★★★

Lot 4 Jones Road, Balhannah, SA 5242 **Region** Adelaide Hills
T (08) 8398 0500 **www**.shawandsmith.com **Open** Sat–Mon & public hols 11–4
Winemaker Martin Shaw, Darryl Catlin **Est.** 1989 **Cases** NFP **Vyds** 93 ha
Has progressively moved from a contract grapegrown base to estate production with the development of a vineyard at Balhannah, followed in 2000 by a state-of-the-art, beautifully designed and executed winery, which ended the long period of tenancy at Petaluma. From a single wine (Sauvignon Blanc) operation, it now makes three benchmark wines (Sauvignon Blanc, M3 Chardonnay and Shiraz) and smaller quantities of cellar door specialities (Riesling and Pinot Noir), all of the highest quality. Exports to all major markets.

ΨΨΨΨΨ   **Adelaide Hills Shiraz 2006** Brilliant crimson; voluminous plum, black cherry and spice aromas, replayed on the very intense and focused palate, which has glorious length and line. Screwcap. 14% alc. **Rating** 97 **To** 2020 $40
M3 Vineyard Adelaide Hills Chardonnay 2008 A fragrant bouquet of nectarine, white peach and a hint of citrus rind leads into a vibrant, fresh and very long palate; you know the French oak is there, but it speaks very quietly. Screwcap. 13.5% alc. **Rating** 96 **To** 2018 $38
M3 Vineyard Adelaide Hills Chardonnay 2007 A beautifully crafted wine with great depth and power; incredibly rich, with lashings of fine French oak and stone fruits; the depth and power is offset by lively acidity, and a complex mineral core. Screwcap. 13% alc. **Rating** 96 **To** 2017 $40
Adelaide Hills Shiraz 2007 Deep crimson-purple; a classy bouquet promises spicy black fruits and quality oak, which the medium- to full-bodied palate delivers in spades, with layers of flavour and perfect balance; right up there with the great '06. Screwcap. 14% alc. **Rating** 96 **To** 2027 $38
Adelaide Hills Pinot Noir 2007 Positive red-purple hue; aromatic spice, berry and sous bois fruit on the bouquet translates into a generous palate, with plenty of ripe fruit running through the long finish. Screwcap. 13.5% alc. **Rating** 94 **To** 2015 $45

ΨΨΨΨ￼   **Adelaide Hills Sauvignon Blanc 2008** Its flavour profile builds progressively through to a rich mid- and back-palate, with flavours in the tropical/gooseberry range; good length and balance, yet slightly disappointing. Screwcap. 13% alc. **Rating** 93 **To** 2011 $28

Shaw Vineyard Estate   ★★★★☆

34 Isabel Drive, Murrumbateman, NSW 2582 **Region** Canberra District
T (02) 6227 5827 **www**.shawvineyards.com.au **Open** Wed–Sun & public hols 10–5
Winemaker Bryan Currie, Graeme Shaw **Est.** 1999 **Cases** 10 000 **Vyds** 33 ha
Graeme and Ann Shaw established their vineyard (semillon, riesling, shiraz, merlot and cabernet sauvignon) in 1998 on a 280-ha fine wool–producing property established in the mid-1800s known as Olleyville. It is one of the largest privately owned vineyard holdings in the Canberra area, and one of the few to produce 100% estate-grown wines. The two children are fully employed in the family business, Michael as viticulturist and Tanya as cellar door manager. As well as the restaurant, there is a ceramics gallery of handmade pieces from Deruta in Italy. Exports to France, Belgium, Ukraine, Macau and Singapore.

ŶŶŶŶŶ Premium Murrumbateman Riesling 2008 Lime juice, spice and minerally
acidity are seamlessly woven together on a perfectly balanced and very long palate;
drink any time over the next five to eight years. Screwcap. 12% alc. **Rating** 94
To 2017 $22

ŶŶŶŶŶ Premium Murrumbateman Semillon Sauvignon Blanc 2008 Bright straw-
green; has abundant tropical sweet fruit on the palate, balanced by citrussy acidity
on the finish. Screwcap. 13.5% alc. **Rating** 91 To 2011 $22
Semi Sweet Murrumbateman Riesling 2008 The wine is more minerally than
sweet, with gentle lime flavours balanced by good acidity; has had wine competition
success, but I expected more. Screwcap. 11.2% alc. **Rating** 90 To 2014 $22

Sheep's Back ★★★★★

PO Box 441, South Melbourne, Vic 3205 **Region** Barossa Valley
T (03) 9696 7018 **F** (03) 9686 4015 **Open** Not
Winemaker Dean Hewitson **Est.** 2001 **Cases** 3000 **Vyds** 4 ha
Sheep's Back is a joint venture between Neil Empson (with 30 years' experience as an
exporter to Australia and elsewhere of Italian wines) and Dean Hewitson. They decided to
produce a single estate-grown shiraz after an extensive search found a vineyard of 75-year-old
shiraz. With Dean at the helm of winemaking and with Neil's input on style, the aim is to
produce a wine that is not overwhelmed by alcohol or oak, but that reflects the varietal aspects
of this essency, old vine shiraz. Exports to the US, Canada, Hong Kong and Singapore.

ŶŶŶŶŶ Old Vine Barossa Valley Shiraz 2004 From 75-year-old vines, and spent
22 months in French oak, a distinguished foundation for a distinguished wine;
quite juicy and supple fruit is elegantly framed by French oak and fine-grained
tannins. Cork. 14% alc. **Rating** 95 To 2019 $50

Shelmerdine Vineyards ★★★★★

Merindoc Vineyard, Lancefield Road, Tooborac, Vic 3522 **Region** Heathcote
T (03) 5433 5188 **F** (03) 5433 5118 **www**.shelmerdine.com.au **Open** 7 days 10–5
Winemaker De Bortoli (Yarra Valley) **Est.** 1989 **Cases** 10 000 **Vyds** 120 ha
Stephen Shelmerdine has been a major figure in the wine industry for well over 20 years,
like his family (who founded Mitchelton Winery) before him, and has been honoured for his
many services to the industry. The venture has vineyards spread over three sites: Lusatia Park
in the Yarra Valley, and Merindoc Vineyard and Willoughby Bridge in the Heathcote region.
Substantial quantities of the grapes produced are sold to others; a small amount of high-quality
wine is contract-made. Exports to the UK, Singapore and Hong Kong.

ŶŶŶŶŶ Merindoc Vineyard Heathcote Shiraz 2007 Deep and concentrated, there is
rich blackberry and fruitcake on the bouquet; the palate is dense and long, with
multiple layers of licorice and blackberry fruit balanced by firm tannins. Screwcap.
13.5% alc. **Rating** 95 To 2014 $65
Heathcote Shiraz 2007 Lifted blueberry bouquet with elements of mint, oak
and slightly dusty complexity; the palate is very firm, with an abundance of tannin
and acid; a complex wine that needs time to fully integrate, and especially for the
tannin to soften. Screwcap. 13.5% alc. **Rating** 94 To 2020 $36
Merindoc Vineyard Heathcote Shiraz 2006 A strong minty bouquet, but
the palate offers a different experience: red fruits intermingle with spice and earth;
while medium-bodied, has a firm and fine-grained tannin finish, acidity leaving
the wine fresh and vibrant. Screwcap. 13.5% alc. **Rating** 94 To 2016 $65

ŶŶŶŶŶ Heathcote Cabernet Sauvignon 2007 Pure blueberry bouquet with
sage thrown in for good measure; the palate is forceful and rich, with a strong
tannin and bright acid presence on the long and firm finish. Screwcap. 13% alc.
Rating 93 To 2015 $33

ŶŶŶŶ Yarra Valley Rose 2008 Salmon blush; very dry, and deliberately made in
a European/French style, with old oak barrel fermentation. A particular style.
Screwcap. 13.5% alc. **Rating** 89 To 2011 $20

Shepherd's Hut   ★★★★☆

PO Box 194, Darlington, WA 6070 **Region** Porongurup
T (08) 9299 6700 **F** (08) 9299 6703 **www**.shepherdshutwines.com **Open** Not
Winemaker Rob Diletti **Est.** 1996 **Cases** 2000 **Vyds** 15.5 ha
The shepherd's hut that appears on the wine label was one of four stone huts used in the 1850s
to house shepherds tending large flocks of sheep. When WA pathologist Dr Michael Wishart
(and family) purchased the property in 1996, the hut was in a state of extreme disrepair. It
has since been restored, still featuring the honey-coloured Mount Barker stone. Riesling,
chardonnay, sauvignon blanc, shiraz and cabernet sauvignon have been established; the daily
running of the vineyard is the responsibility of son Philip, who also runs a large farm of mainly
cattle; son William helps with marketing and sales. Most of the grapes are sold to other makers
in the region. Exports to the UK.

ＹＹＹＹＹ **Porongurup Shiraz 2005** Very good colour; a complete and beautifully
composed wine, even if on the full-bodied side of the ledger; blackberry and
licorice; great length. Gold WA Wine Show '08. Screwcap. 15% alc. **Rating** 95
To 2018 $20

ＹＹＹＹＹ **Porongurup Sauvignon Blanc 2008** Spicy herbal aromas; good depth and
mouthfeel in a generous mould. Screwcap. 13% alc. **Rating** 90 To 2011 $19

Shingleback   ★★★★★

Cnr Main Road/Stump Hill Road, McLaren Vale, SA 5171 **Region** McLaren Vale
T (08) 8323 7388 **F** (08) 8323 7336 **www**.shingleback.com.au **Open** 7 days 10–5
Winemaker John Davey, Dan Hills **Est.** 1995 **Cases** 100 000 **Vyds** 90 ha
Shingleback has substantial vineyards in McLaren Vale, all of which is vinified for the
Shingleback labels. Originally a specialist export business, but now the wines are also available
in Australia. Quality has risen greatly, as has total production. Which is the chicken, which
is the egg? It doesn't really matter, is the best answer. It has followed its 2006 Jimmy Watson
Trophy for its '05 D Block Cabernet Sauvignon with continuing success for that wine and
similar wines in both domestic and overseas wine shows. Exports to the UK, the US and
other major markets.

ＹＹＹＹＹ **The Gate McLaren Vale Shiraz 2006** Good colour; a surprisingly reserved
wine, exhibiting red fruit elements, mocha and some gentle spicy character; the
palate is quite velvety in texture, with an ample level of fruit and fresh acidity;
exhibits true harmony, as the sum of all the parts work seamlessly together. Cork.
14.5% alc. **Rating** 95 To 2018 $34.95
D Block Reserve McLaren Vale Shiraz 2006 Generously proportioned, with a
large amount of sweet dark fruit, and fruitcake spice on offer, dark and chewy; the
sweet fruit at the core is the essence of the wine; long and generous on the finish.
Cork. 14.5% alc. **Rating** 94 To 2016 $59.95

ＹＹＹＹＹ **McLaren Vale Shiraz 2006** Essency blackberry fruit, mocha and just a touch
of bramble; really bright fruit at the core, with dense chewy fruit; a rich, ripe and
generous style. Screwcap. 14.5% alc. **Rating** 93 To 2016 $24.95
D Block Reserve McLaren Vale Cabernet Sauvignon 2006 The bouquet
has essency fruit, with a slight mineral/savoury edge that adds complexity; the
flavour is rich and ripe, and extends gracefully along the entire palate. Cork.
14.5% alc. **Rating** 92 To 2016 $59.95
Red Knot McLaren Vale Shiraz 2007 Redcurrant fruit and fruitcake spice are
evident on the bouquet; juicy and quite slippery on the palate; the wine offers
very good value. Screwcap. 14% alc. **Rating** 90 To 2014 $14.95
McLaren Vale Chardonnay 2008 Lively and focused with nectarine and peach
fruit on the bouquet; quite rich on the palate, with the acid offering a zesty, fresh
finish. Screwcap. 13% alc. **Rating** 90 To 2012 $19.95
McLaren Vale Cabernet Sauvignon 2006 Squeaky clean fruit, showing a
touch of cassis and redcurrant; juicy and fine on entry, with attractive sweet fruit
and plenty of fine-grained tannin. Screwcap. 14.5% alc. **Rating** 90 To 2014 $24.95

🍷🍷🍷🍷 **Cellar Door McLaren Vale Shiraz 2007** Ripe and essency blueberry fruit with a touch of vanilla and spice; very juicy on the palate, some dark tarry character providing light and shade. Screwcap. 14% alc. **Rating** 88 **To** 2014 $17.95
Red Knot McLaren Vale Chardonnay 2008 Quite toasty, rich and varietal bouquet, with generous stone fruit; clean and well made. Screwcap. 13% alc. **Rating** 87 **To** 2012 $14.95
Cellar Door McLaren Vale Chardonnay 2008 Quite a peachy bouquet with a gentle dollop of spice; forward and fleshy; best consumed early. Screwcap. 13.5% alc. **Rating** 87 **To** 2011 $17.95
Red Knot McLaren Vale Cabernet Sauvignon 2007 Clean and varietal bouquet; fresh and vibrant fruit on the palate; clean and well made. Screwcap. 14% alc. **Rating** 87 **To** 2012 $14.95

Shottesbrooke

Bagshaws Road, McLaren Flat, SA 5171 **Region** McLaren Vale
T (08) 8383 0002 **F** (08) 8383 0222 **www.**shottesbrooke.com.au **Open** Mon–Fri 10–4.30, w'ends & public hols 11–5
Winemaker Nick Holmes, Hamish Maguire **Est.** 1984 **Cases** 12 000 **Vyds** 24 ha
For many years the full-time business of former Ryecroft winemaker Nick Holmes (now with stepson Hamish Maguire), drawing primarily on estate-grown grapes at his Myoponga vineyard (shiraz, merlot, cabernet sauvignon and chardonnay). He has always stood out for the finesse and elegance of his wines compared with the dam-buster, high-alcohol reds for which McLaren Vale has become famous (or infamous, depending on one's point of view). Now the wheel has started to turn full circle, and finesse and elegance are much more appreciated. Listed for sale in April 2009 by specialist wine industry brokers and advisers Gaetjens Langley. Exports to the UK, the US and other major markets.

🍷🍷🍷🍷🍷 **Eliza McLaren Vale Shiraz 2006** In typical Shottesbrooke fashion, offers an alternative but utterly delicious expression of McLaren Vale fruit, with lively, spicy fruit, daubs of chocolate and licorice running through the long and vibrant palate. Screwcap. 14.5% alc. **Rating** 94 **To** 2018 $38

🍷🍷🍷🍷🍷 **McLaren Vale Cabernet Sauvignon 2007** Deep crimson; pure varietal blackcurrant fruit drives the bouquet and palate; there are some of the dusty tannin of the merlot, but here the volume of fruit sustains them. Good value. Screwcap. 14.5% alc. **Rating** 93 **To** 2020 $19.95
Punch McLaren Vale Cabernet Sauvignon 2006 Has very good varietal definition to both bouquet and palate; black fruit with a dusting of dark chocolate runs through an even palate with excellent line and balance. Screwcap. 14% alc. **Rating** 93 **To** 2016 $38
McLaren Vale Shiraz 2007 In the elegant, medium-bodied frame that is the Shottesbrooke style; black fruits, bitter chocolate and dashes of spice and licorice on the finish – even in this vintage. Screwcap. 14.5% alc. **Rating** 91 **To** 2015 $19.95

🍷🍷🍷🍷 **McLaren Vale Chardonnay 2008** Peach and nectarine fruit, with a touch of straw; brassy fruit on the palate, with plenty of flavour and a long, slightly toasty finish. Screwcap. 13.5% alc. **Rating** 89 **To** 2012 $19.95
McLaren Vale Merlot 2007 Has the red berry/cassis fruit of the maker, but the tannins teeter on the edge; a few years will tell where they will fall, right now, I'm not sure. Screwcap. 13.5% alc. **Rating** 88 **To** 2014 $19.95
Bernesh Bray Fine Old Liqueur Tawny NV Blended from 10 vintages: 1990–99 inclusive; an atypical liqueur tawny, for the spirit is obvious and the wine is not particularly luscious. Cork. 20.5% alc. **Rating** 88 **To** 2010 $30

Sidewood Estate

2 Hunt Road, Hahndorf, SA 5245 (postal) **Region** Adelaide Hills
T (08) 8388 7084 **F** (08) 8388 1752 **www.**sidewoodestate.com.au **Open** Not
Winemaker Shaw & Smith (Darryl Catlin) **Est.** 2000 **Cases** 1500 **Vyds** 49.67 ha

The establishment date of Sidewood Estate in fact marks the year when 32 ha of vineyard were planted by the Lloyd family of Coriole. Owen and Cassandra Inglis purchased the property in 2004, not only because of the vines, but also with an eye on the horse stables and horse training facilities. Owen has owned, ridden and raced horses since his early childhood, and both he and Cassandra were committed wine drinkers, which sealed the deal. They have since planted more sauvignon blanc, pinot gris, chardonnay (Dijon clone) and shiraz. Much care and attention has been given to the vineyard, and in 2008 Owen sold his Hong Kong business (he lived in Hong Kong and China for many years). It is not surprising that the principal export markets are Hong Kong and Singapore.

ⵜⵜⵜⵜⵜ **Adelaide Hills Chardonnay 2008** A highly scented, almost flowery, citrus and stone fruit bouquet, followed by an intense mouth-watering palate, with a long finish. Screwcap. 13.5% alc. **Rating** 93 **To** 2014 $18
Adelaide Hills Sauvignon Blanc 2008 Complex aromas of tropical and asparagus fruit come through strongly on the long, positive flavours of the palate. Screwcap. 12.9% alc. **Rating** 90 **To** 2011 $18

Sieber Road Wines   ★★★☆

Sieber Road, Tanunda, SA 5352 **Region** Barossa Valley
T (08) 8562 8038 **F** (08) 8562 8681 **www**.sieberwines.com **Open** 7 days 11–4
Winemaker Tony Carapetis **Est.** 1999 **Cases** 4000 **Vyds** 18 ha
Richard and Val Sieber are the third generation to run Redlands, the family property, traditionally a cropping/grazing farm. They have diversified into viticulture with shiraz (14 ha) the lion's share, the remainder viognier, grenache and mourvedre. Son Ben Sieber is a viticulturist. Exports to Canada.

ⵜⵜⵜⵜⵜ **Barossa Valley Grenache Shiraz Mourvedre 2007** Good hue and clarity; the flavours are complex, primarily black, and not too much confection from the grenache; balanced tannins a plus. Screwcap. 14.9% alc. **Rating** 90 **To** 2014 $18

ⵜⵜⵜⵜ **Barossa Valley Mataro 2007** Good varietal character, juxtaposing sweet berry fruits with firm, spicy tannins, some Christmas cake squeezed in between. Screwcap. 14% alc. **Rating** 89 **To** 2015 $25
Ernest Barossa Valley Shiraz 2007 A ripe and powerful wine, with black fruits, then a finish dominated by savoury, slightly green tannins. Screwcap. 14.5% alc. **Rating** 87 **To** 2015 $20

Silk Hill   NR

324 Motor Road, Deviot, Tas 7275 **Region** Northern Tasmania
T (03) 6394 7385 **F** (03) 6394 7392 **Open** By appt
Winemaker Gavin Scott **Est.** 1989 **Cases** 500
Pharmacist Gavin Scott has been a weekend and holiday viticulturist for many years, having established the Glengarry Vineyard, which he sold, and then establishing the 1.5-ha Silk Hill (formerly Silkwood Vineyard) in 1989, planted exclusively to pinot noir.

Silkwood Wines   ★★★☆

5204/6249 Channybearup Road, Pemberton, WA 6260 **Region** Pemberton
T (08) 9776 1584 **F** (08) 9776 1540 **www**.silkwoodwines.com.au **Open** Fri–Mon 10–4
Winemaker Blair Meiklejohn **Est.** 1998 **Cases** 8000 **Vyds** 25 ha
Third-generation farmers Pam and John Allen returned from a short break running small businesses in Adelaide and Perth to purchase Silkwood in 1998. Plantings began with 5 ha of shiraz and sauvignon blanc in 1999, followed by a further 5.5 ha of riesling, pinot noir, merlot and cabernet sauvignon in '00. The vineyard is patrolled by a large flock of guinea fowl, eliminating most insect pests and reducing the use of chemicals. Under new ownership (2004), a modern winery was built in time for the '06 vintage, and in '05 purchased Phillips Estate, lifting estate vineyard holdings to 25 ha. A new cellar door now looks over a large lake on the property.

ŸŸŸŸŸ **Pemberton Chardonnay 2007** Lively, fresh chardonnay, with delicious nectarine and grapefruit flavours on a long, even palate. Screwcap. 13.5% alc. **Rating** 92 **To** 2016 $24

ŸŸŸŸ **Pemberton Sauvignon Blanc 2007** There are some attractive tropical nuances to the wine, and just enough emphasis to the finish. Screwcap. 12.5% alc. **Rating** 87 **To** 2010 $22
Pemberton Pinot Noir 2005 Good colour; dark fruits are offset by some briary/foresty/stemmy notes, the two components not entirely cohesive after almost four years. Cork. 14.1% alc. **Rating** 87 **To** 2012 $25

Silverstream Wines

2365 Scotsdale Road, Denmark, WA 6333 **Region** Great Southern
T (08) 9840 9119 **www**.silverstreamwines.com **Open** W'ends & public hols 11–4
Winemaker John Wade (Contract) **Est.** 1999 **Cases** 800 **Vyds** 8.95 ha
Tony and Felicity Ruse have 8.95 ha of chardonnay, merlot and cabernet franc in their vineyard 23 km from Denmark. The wines are contract-made, and after some hesitation, the Ruses decided their very pretty garden and orchard more than justified their recently opened cellar door, a decision supported by the quality on offer at very reasonable prices.

ŸŸŸŸ **Denmark Cabernet Franc Rose 2008** Very pale pink; has unexpected flavour and character on the palate with spicy red cherry and redcurrant nuances; pleasingly dry finish. Screwcap. 13% alc. **Rating** 89 **To** 2010 $19

Silverwood Wines ★★★★☆

66 Bittern-Dromana Road, Balnarring, Vic 3926 **Region** Mornington Peninsula
T 0419 890 317 **F** (03) 8317 6642 **www**.silverwoodwines.com.au **Open** Not
Winemaker Paul Dennis, Phillip Kittle, Andrew Thomson **Est.** 1997 **Cases** 900 **Vyds** 3.2 ha
Paul and Denise Dennis were inspired to establish Silverwood after living in France for a year. They, with members of their family, did much of the establishment work on the vineyard (pinot noir, chardonnay and sauvignon blanc), which is meticulously maintained. All of the grapes are now used for Silverwood (in earlier years some were sold), not surprising given that the 2005 Pinot Noir topped its class at the strictly judged Winewise Small Vignerons Awards '06 in Canberra. Exports to Hong Kong and Singapore.

ŸŸŸŸŸ **Estate Mornington Peninsula Pinot Noir 2007** Bright colour; cherry and a touch of plum with an attractive spice backbone to the fruit; quite velvety on entry, with good fruit definition, and a brightness to the finish that is even, fine and long. Screwcap. 13.4% alc. **Rating** 94 **To** 2014 $31.95

ŸŸŸŸ **Estate Mornington Peninsula Chardonnay 2007** Restrained melon and nectarine bouquet, framed by quite spicy oak; a worked style, good texture and weight, leading to a nutty yet fresh finish. Screwcap. 13.9% alc. **Rating** 89 **To** 2013 $27.95
Estate Mornington Peninsula Pinot Noir 2006 A closed bouquet, but the palate offers some richness and texture; good flavour, but doesn't accelerate on the finish. Screwcap. 13.9% alc. **Rating** 87 **To** 2012 $35.95

Simon Hackett

Budgens Road, McLaren Vale, SA 5171 **Region** McLaren Vale
T (08) 8323 7712 **F** (08) 8323 7713 **Open** Wed–Sun 11–5
Winemaker Simon Hackett **Est.** 1981 **Cases** 15 000
In 1998 Simon Hackett acquired the former Taranga winery in McLaren Vale, which has made his winemaking life a great deal easier. He purchases grapes from long-term contract growers in McLaren Vale and the Barossa Valley, with a total of 40 ha. Exports to the UK, the US and other major markets.

ＴＴＴＴＴ Adelaide Hills Sauvignon Blanc 2008 Has a vibrant and fresh palate, with a lively display of citrus and gooseberry fruit; crisp finish. Value. Screwcap. 13.5% alc. **Rating** 90 **To** 2010 $15

ＴＴＴＴ McLaren Vale Shiraz 2005 A welcome medium-bodied wine that is still strongly regional; spicy black fruits, chocolate and vanilla American oak all contribute. Value. Screwcap. 14% alc. **Rating** 89 **To** 2015 $15
McLaren Vale Cabernet Sauvignon 2006 An equal display of regional and varietal expression in an unobtrusive, medium-bodied framework. Well priced. Screwcap. 14% alc. **Rating** 87 **To** 2014 $15

Sinapius Vineyard   ★★★★☆

111 Archers Road, Hillwod, Tas 7252 (postal) **Region** Northern Tasmania
T 0417 341 764 **Open** Not
Winemaker Vaughn Dell, Linda Morice **Est.** 2005 **Cases** 400 **Vyds** 1.2 ha
When Vaughn Dell and Linda Morice purchased the former Golders Vineyard from Richard Crabtree in 2005, they were only 24. Both were originally from Tasmania, but between '01 and '05 lived in various parts of Australia; Linda completed a university degree in occupational therapy and Vaughn worked at wineries in the Hunter Valley, Yarra Valley (at Wedgetail Estate) and Margaret River (Barwick Estates) before returning to Tasmania to undertake vintage at Tamar Ridge in '05. The vineyard had 1 ha of mature pinot noir and 0.2 ha of mature chardonnay. They have now also leased the Bellingham Vineyard, which has 1.2 ha of riesling and 0.8 ha of chardonnay. Vaughn made the 2007 Pinot Noir and Chardonnay at Holm Oak under the guidance of Rebecca Wilson; a small winery and cellar door are planned but until the winery is completed future wines will be made at nearby Delamere.

ＴＴＴＴＴ Chardonnay 2007 Finely focused; delicate style, but with lots of nervous energy and drive to the stone fruit and grapefruit flavours. Top gold medal Tas Wine Show '09. Screwcap. 14% alc. **Rating** 95 **To** 2017 $32

Sinclair's Gully   ★★★

Lot 3 Colonial Drive, Norton Summit, SA 5136 **Region** Adelaide Hills
T (08) 8390 1995 **www**.sinclairsgully.com **Open** W'ends & public hols 12–4 (Aug–June), Fri 5–9 (Nov–Mar), or by appt
Winemaker Contract **Est.** 1998 **Cases** 600 **Vyds** 1 ha
Sue and Sean Delaney purchased their 10.5 ha property at Norton Summit in 1997. The property had a significant stand of remnant native vegetation, with a State Conservation Rating, and since acquiring the property much energy has been spent in restoring 8 ha of pristine bushland, home to 130 species of native plants and 66 species of native birds, some recorded as threatened or rare. It has been a DIY venture for the Delaneys (supported by family and friends) with Sue hand pruning the 0.4 ha each of chardonnay and sauvignon blanc planted in 1998. The adoption of biodynamic viticulture has coincided with numerous awards for the protection of the natural environment, and most recently, including eco-tourism; they operate the only eco-certified cellar door in the Adelaide Hills.

ＴＴＴＴ Adelaide Hills Chardonnay 2007 A powerful wine from start to finish, seemingly higher in alcohol than it is; ripe stone fruit and vanilla oak fill the palate to overflowing. Screwcap. 13% alc. **Rating** 87 **To** 2012 $28
Adelaide Hills Pinot Noir 2005 Light, developed colour; light spicy/savoury fruit, but already tiring somewhat. Screwcap. 13.5% alc. **Rating** 87 **To** 2010 $28
Adelaide Hills Rubida 2006 Light salmon-orange; basket-pressed and barrel-fermented is a far from usual process for sparkling wine base, but it very nearly works for this citrus-driven wine. Cork. 13% alc. **Rating** 87 **To** 2011 $45

Singlefile Estate

PO Box 487, West Perth, WA 6872 **Region** Denmark
T 1300 885 807 **F** 1300 884 087 **www**.singlefileestate.com **Open** Not
Winemaker Brenden Smith, Coby Ladwig (contract) **Est.** 2007 **Cases** 500 **Vyds** 5 ha
Reading the background to Singlefile Estate, and its marketing and mission statements, might lead one to think that this is a 50 000-case venture, not a 500-case business, based on 2.5 ha of 24-year-old estate chardonnay, and 1.25 ha each of merlot and shiraz (supplemented by purchases of semillon, sauvignon blanc and cabernet sauvignon). Owners Phil and Viv Snowden took a circuitous path to the Denmark subregion, exiting Zimbabwe to join academia in South Africa (with a mining focus) before migrating to Australia in the late 1980s to start an Australian mining consultancy. When they sold the business in 2004 for just under $15 million, it had 200 employees and was one of the leaders in its field in WA. This is downsizing on a grand scale.

ΨΨΨΨΨ **Reserve Chardonnay 2008** Light, fresh, crisp and delicate style, with nectarine and white peach joined by subtle French oak; well made, and not forced. Screwcap. 13.4% alc. **Rating** 92 **To** 2014 $45
Semillon Sauvignon Blanc 2008 Citrus, grass, herbs and mineral notes run through both bouquet and palate, which scores for its lingering finish and aftertaste. Screwcap. 12.6% alc. **Rating** 90 **To** 2012 $24
Chardonnay 2008 Very tangy, citrussy aromas and flavours ranging from grapefruit to green apple; good cool-grown, unoaked style. Screwcap. 12.8% alc. **Rating** 90 **To** 2015 $22

ΨΨΨΨ **Shiraz 2007** Bright hue; a light- to medium-bodied palate, with strong spicy peppery components alongside red berry fruits; pleasant, early maturing wine. Screwcap. 13.6% alc. **Rating** 89 **To** 2014 $33

Sir Paz Estate

384 George Street, Fitzroy, Vic 3065 (postal) **Region** Yarra Valley
T (03) 9417 3121 **F** (03) 9417 3981 **www**.sirpaz.com **Open** Not
Winemaker Gary Mills, John Zapris **Est.** 1997 **Cases** 5500 **Vyds** 15.5 ha
The Zapris family established Sir Paz Estate in 1997, planting just under 6 ha of shiraz; the first release of '01 scored an emphatic gold medal at the Victorian Wines Show '03 as the highest scored entry. The success led to the planting of an additional 3.5 ha ha of merlot, and 3 ha each of chardonnay and sauvignon blanc. It is not hard to see the anagrammatic derivation of of the name. Exports to the UK, Germany, Sri Lanka, Dubai and China.

ΨΨΨΨ **Parker Road Bin 8 2007** Lifted and bright bouquet, with red fruit and tar on offer; the palate is medium-bodied with high levels of acidity, cranberry fruit and a gravelly tannin finish. Shiraz/Merlot. Diam. 14% alc. **Rating** 89 **To** 2014 $26
Yarra Valley Shiraz 2007 Black fruit and leather on the bouquet; very firm palate, with just enough fruit to balance; a very savoury wine. Diam. 14% alc. **Rating** 88 **To** 2014 $33

Sirromet Wines

850-938 Mount Cotton Road, Mount Cotton, Qld 4165 **Region** Queensland Coastal
T (07) 3206 2999 **F** (07) 3206 0900 **www**.sirromet.com **Open** 7 days 10–5
Winemaker Adam Chapman, Velten Tiemann **Est.** 1998 **Cases** 100 000
This was an unambiguously ambitious venture, which has succeeded in its aim of creating Qld's premier winery. The founding Morris family retained a leading architect to design the striking state-of-the-art winery; the state's foremost viticultural consultant to plant the four major vineyards (in the Granite Belt), which total over 100 ha; and the most skilled winemaker practising in Qld, Adam Chapman, to make the wine. It has a 200-seat restaurant, a wine club offering all sorts of benefits to its members, and is firmly aimed at the domestic and international tourist market, taking advantage of its situation, halfway between Brisbane and the Gold Coast. Exports to the Netherlands, Malaysia, Taiwan, Singapore, Japan and China.

ŸŸŸŸŸ **Seven Scenes Granite Belt Cabernet Sauvignon 2007** Opens quite softly, but picks up speed and intensity on the mid- to back-palate with quite luscious blackcurrant fruit; good tannin and oak management. Screwcap. 13.5% alc. **Rating** 90 **To** 2017 $25

Seven Scenes Granite Belt Chardonnay 2007 Well made, the balance between fruit and oak spot-on; quite tight and crisp, but not green; stone fruit and melon flavours run through the long palate. Screwcap. 12.8% alc. **Rating** 90 **To** 2014 $25

Seven Scenes Granite Belt Shiraz Viognier 2007 Savoury/spicy/tangy aromas and flavours coalesce around a core of black fruits on the medium-bodied palate; very well made. Screwcap. 13.9% alc. **Rating** 90 **To** 2017 $25

ŸŸŸŸ **820 Above Pinot Gris 2008** Clean and ripe candied pear fruit bouquet; fresh and fine on the finish. Screwcap. 12.4% alc. **Rating** 89 **To** 2010 $15

Seven Scenes Granite Belt Viognier 2007 A clever decision to pick early is reflected in the clarity and freshness of the wine, which also has good acidity, and enough varietal expression to satisfy. Screwcap. 12.7% alc. **Rating** 89 **To** 2012 $25

First Step Reduced Carbon Footprint Cabernet Merlot 2005 An altogether strange feeling when you pick up the plastic bottle – is it empty? No, it's full. Also it has the positive statement 'best before 30 June 2010'. The wine itself is not as remarkable as the package. Screwcap. 14.1% alc. **Rating** 87 **To** 2010 $12

Sittella Wines ★★★★☆

100 Barrett Street, Herne Hill, WA 6056 **Region** Swan Valley
T (08) 9296 2600 **www.**sittella.com.au **Open** Tues–Sun & public hols 11–5
Winemaker Matthew Bowness **Est.** 1998 **Cases** 7000 **Vyds** 15 ha
Perth couple Simon and Maaike Berns acquired a 7-ha block (with 5 ha of vines) at Herne Hill, making the first wine in 1998 and opening a most attractive cellar door facility later in the year. They also own the 10-ha Wildberry Springs Estate vineyard in the Margaret River region. Consistent and significant wine show success has brought well-deserved recognition for the wines.

ŸŸŸŸŸ **Berns Reserve Cabernet Sauvignon 2007** Fragrant cassis aromas; more elegance than power; neatly balanced, and has excellent length. Gold WA Wine Show '08. Screwcap. 14.5% alc. **Rating** 94 **To** 2015 $32

ŸŸŸŸŸ **Pinot Noir Chardonnay 2006** Good mousse; fresh, bright lemon, citrussy; good balance and length. Cork. 12% alc. **Rating** 91 **To** 2011 $34

Unwooded Chardonnay 2008 Elegant cool-climate style with citrussy/tangy fruit; good balance and a seductive finish. Screwcap. 13.4% alc. **Rating** 90 **To** 2012 $16.50

ŸŸŸŸ **Silk 2008** The four-varietal blend works very well at the luscious end of the spectrum; the abundant flavours neatly tied together by crisp acidity on the finish. Verdelho/Chardonnay/Chenin Blanc/Semillon. Screwcap. 13.1% alc. **Rating** 89 **To** 2012 $16.50

Shiraz 2007 Luscious, ripe, confit plum and blackberry fruit, if nothing else, expressive of the region. Screwcap. 14.5% alc. **Rating** 89 **To** 2014 $21

Muscat of Alexandria 2008 Has an appropriate level of grapey sweetness that runs through to the back-palate, acidity drying it fractionally on the finish. Screwcap. 12% alc. **Rating** 89 **To** 2010 $18

Six Gates ★★★★

14 Sitters Memorial Drive, Burnside, SA 5066 (postal) **Region** Barossa Valley
T 0412 469 285 **F** (08) 8332 0124 **www.**6gates.com.au **Open** Not
Winemaker Contract **Est.** 1998 **Cases** 1200
The name Six Gates originates from the six entries to the ancient city of Shiraz, and it is thus appropriate that this organically managed vineyard should be predominantly planted to

that variety (12.8 ha; 4 ha of cabernet sauvignon make up the balance). While there is a long history of viticulture on the property, the present plantings were established in 1998 on highly suitable soil, with 25 cm of loam on 60 cm of red clay over well-decayed limestone, thus providing both good drainage and water holding capacity. Every one of the 18 000 vines is pruned by the vineyard manager, Bruce Wutke, who has spent a long time as a grapegrower.

ȚȚȚȚȚ **The Majnun Barossa Valley Shiraz 2006** Has a pronounced, lifted bouquet, with plenty of sweet fruit and fruitcake aromas on offer; the palate is quite juicy, and the tannins ample, with a little black olive savoury edge to the finish. Screwcap. 15.8% alc. **Rating** 90 **To** 2016 $23

Skillogalee ★★★★★

Trevarrick Road, Sevenhill via Clare, SA 5453 **Region** Clare Valley
T (08) 8843 4311 **F** (08) 8843 4343 **www.**skillogalee.com.au **Open** 7 days 10–5
Winemaker Dave Palmer, Daniel Palmer **Est.** 1970 **Cases** 16 000 **Vyds** 50.3 ha
David and Diana Palmer purchased the small hillside stone winery from the George family at the end of the 1980s and have fully capitalised on the exceptional fruit quality of the Skillogalee vineyards. All the wines are generous and full-flavoured, particularly the reds. In 2002 the Palmers purchased next-door neighbour Waninga Vineyards, with 30 ha of 30-year-old vines, allowing an increase in production without any change in quality or style. Exports to the UK, Canada, Switzerland, Hong Kong, Malaysia, Singapore and NZ.

ȚȚȚȚȚ **Trevarrick Clare Valley Riesling 2008** Delicate fragrant lime blossom aromas; vibrantly crisp and fresh, with pure lime and lemon riesling fruit; a minerally and fresh finish. God medal Clare Valley Wine Show '08. Screwcap. 11.5% alc. **Rating** 95 **To** 2020 $40
Trevarrick Single Contour Clare Valley Cabernet Sauvignon 2004 Remarkably deep crimson colour for a five-year-old cabernet; a massively robust full-bodied wine, still nowhere near ready for consumption, its opulent cassis and blackcurrant fruit and French oak being overshadowed by relentless tannins. It will, however, become a great wine with another 10 years in bottle, as the components are in balance. Screwcap. 14.5% alc. **Rating** 95 **To** 2034 $60

ȚȚȚȚȚ **Single Vineyard Clare Valley Riesling 2008** A complex bouquet with citrus and a touch of tropical fruit; the palate is at once flavoursome yet light on its feet; good balance, line and length. Screwcap. 13% alc. **Rating** 93 **To** 2018 $20
Harvest Gold 2005 Has good balance, sweet citrussy riesling fruit offset by crisp acidity; most impressive is its leisurely development. Gold medal Clare Valley Wine Show '08. Screwcap. 11.5% alc. **Rating** 92 **To** 2013 $22
Clare Valley Gewurztraminer 2008 Usually produces the best gewurztraminers in the Barossa Zone, and this is no exception. Has the weight and texture of Alsace, and ripe lychee fruit. Screwcap. 13.5% alc. **Rating** 90 **To** 2014 $22.50
Lees Stirred Clare Valley Chardonnay 2006 A very interesting wine, which has some early-picked zest as well as some alcohol heat on the finish; all in all, has far more going for it than most Clare chardonnays, and is developing slowly. Screwcap. 14.5% alc. **Rating** 90 **To** 2014 $21.50
Cabernet Malbec Rose 2008 Distinctive fuschia-pink; an aromatic red fruit bouquet leads into a lively palate, with good intensity and acidity; 15% malbec. Well above average. Screwcap. 13.5% alc. **Rating** 90 **To** 2010 $18.50

ȚȚȚȚ **The Cabernets 2005** A mix of minty, leafy flavours on the one hand, and medium-bodied black and red fruits on the other; there is a slight sharpness to the wine, which it may never lose. Cabernet Sauvignon/Cabernet Franc/Malbec. Screwcap. 14.5% alc. **Rating** 87 **To** 2013 $25.50

Smallfry Wines ★★★★★

13 Murray Street, Angaston, SA 5353 **Region** Barossa Valley
T (08) 8564 2182 **www.**smallfrywines.com.au **Open** By appt tel 0412 153 243
Winemaker Wayne Ahrens, Colin Forbes, Tim Smith **Est.** 2005 **Cases** 1500 **Vyds** 27 ha

The engagingly-named Smallfry Wines is the venture of Wayne Ahrens and partner Suzi Hilder. Wayne comes from a fifth-generation Barossa family, Suzi is the daughter of well-known Upper Hunter viticulturist Richard Hilder and wife Del, partners in Pyramid Hill Wines. Both have degrees from CSU, and both have extensive experience – Suzi as a senior viticulturist for Foster's, and Wayne's track record includes seven vintages as a cellar hand at Orlando Wyndham and other smaller Barossa wineries. They have a 10.7-ha vineyard in the Eden Valley (led by cabernet sauvignon and riesling), and a long-established 16.3-ha vineyard in the Vine Vale subregion of the Barossa Valley has no less than 16 varieties, led by shiraz, grenache, semillon, mourvedre, cabernet sauvignon and riesling. Most of the grapes are sold to other Barossa wineries, enough retained from each vineyard to meet Smallfry Wines' needs.

ŶŶŶŶŶ **Barossa Semillon 2008** Sophisticated winemaking on a micro scale (175 dozen) runs from the start (early picking) through fermentation (25% new French oak) to the refined, crisp palate and finish. Tour de force. Screwcap. 11.5% alc. **Rating** 94 To 2015 $15
Eden Valley Cabernet Grenache Rose 2008 Relatively deep crimson; has abundant flavour from 10% carbonic maceration and 24 hours cold-soak skin contact for the cabernet, then wild yeast fermentation. A red wine drinker's rose made from the ground up. Screwcap. 12.5% alc. **Rating** 94 To 2010 $18

ŶŶŶŶŶ **Eden Valley Red Blend 2007** Deep purple-crimson; a seriously concentrated wine, with considerable depth to its black fruits and tannins; needs much time; 80 dozen made. Screwcap. 14.5% alc. **Rating** 92 To 2022 $28
Barossa Grenache 2007 Light colour; attractive spicy overtones to the varietal confection fruit flavours; it is amazing how the wine carries its alcohol; 50 dozen made. Screwcap. 16% alc. **Rating** 91 To 2013 $28
Eden Valley Riesling 2008 A delicate, crisp mineral-accented wine, with great purity and length. As yet reticent, but will bloom given time in bottle. Screwcap. 12% alc. **Rating** 90 To 2018 $18

Smidge Wines   ★★★★☆

62 Austral Terrace, Malvern, SA 5061 (postal) **Region** Southeast Australia
T (08) 8272 0369 **F** (08) 8272 8491 **www**.smidgewines.com **Open** Not
Winemaker Matt Wenk **Est.** 2004 **Cases** 1000

Matt Wenk and Trish Callaghan have many things in common: joint ownership of Smidge Wines, marriage, and their real day jobs. Matt has a distinguished record as a Flying Winemaker and, in Australia, working with Tim Knappstein and then Peter Leske at Nepenthe Wines. These days he is the winemaker for Two Hands Wines (and Sandow's End). Trish holds a senior position in one of the world's largest IT services companies, and was a finalist in the Australian Young Business Woman of the Year '03. The elegantly labelled wines are Le Grenouille (The Frog) Adelaide Hills Merlot, from a small vineyard in Verdun, and The Tardy Langhorne Creek Zinfandel, which (and I quote) 'is named The Tardy in honour of Matt's reputation for timekeeping (or lack thereof)'. Exports to the UK and the US.

ŶŶŶŶŶ **S Smitch Barossa Valley Shiraz 2006** Slightly deeper colour – crimson-purple – than the Adamo; an intense, complex and multi-layered full-bodied wine, ranging through licorice, plum, prune, blackberry and vanilla, fruit, oak and tannins in a seamless stream, largely keeping the alcohol at bay. Cork. 15.5% alc. **Rating** 94 To 2026 $65

ŶŶŶŶŶ **Adamo Barossa Valley Shiraz 2006** Crimson-red; an eloquent bouquet of black fruits, dark chocolate and quality oak flows into an equally expressive medium-bodied palate; a pity, however, the bottles and closures weren't reversed, giving the S Smitch the benefit of a screwcap. Screwcap. 15.5% alc. **Rating** 93 To 2021 $26
The Cellar-pod Adelaide Hills Viognier 2007 Early picking has given the wine great vitality and freshness, but diminished its varietal expression. I'll take the rock (early picking) over the hard place (varietal impact) any day. Screwcap. 12.5% alc. **Rating** 90 To 2011 $26

Houdini Adelaide Hills Sauvignon Blanc 2008 Clean, crisp, tight and restrained in a mineral/grass/citrus/apple spectrum; fades a little on the finish. Screwcap. 13.5% alc. **Rating** 87 **To** 2010 $16

Houdini Red 2006 A marriage of convenience of Shiraz/Zinfandel/Merlot that begot a pleasant, light- to medium-bodied red-fruited wine. Screwcap. 14.5% alc. **Rating** 87 **To** 2012 $16

Smith & Hooper ★★★★☆

Caves Edward Road, Naracoorte, SA 5271 **Region** Wrattonbully
T (08) 8762 0622 **F** (08) 8762 0514 **www**.smithandhooper.com **Open** By appt
Winemaker Peter Gambetta **Est.** 1994 **Cases** 13 000 **Vyds** 82 ha
On one view of the matter, this is simply one of many brands within various of the Hills Smith family financial/corporate structures. However, it is estate-based, with cabernet sauvignon (21 ha) and merlot (13 ha) planted on the Hooper Vineyard in 1994, and cabernet sauvignon (15 ha) and merlot (9 ha) planted on the Smith Vineyard in '98. Spread across both vineyards are 15 ha of shiraz and 9 ha of trial varieties. Exports to all major markets.

Reserve Wrattonbully Merlot 2006 Brightly fruited and clearly defined, with mouth-watering acidity providing a counterpoint to the vibrant red fruits; dry and pleasingly savoury on the finish. Cork. 13% alc. **Rating** 95 **To** 2016 $39.95

Wrattonbully Cabernet Sauvignon Merlot 2006 Clearly defined cabernet fruit; fleshy and generous; a light touch of oak and a core of bright fruit linger on the long, fine-tannin finish. Cork. 14% alc. **Rating** 93 **To** 2016 $17.95

Wrattonbully Merlot 2006 Holding crimson hue well; a mix of sweet red berry fruit and fine, but savoury tannins. Cork. 13.5% alc. **Rating** 89 **To** 2012 $17.95

Wrattonbully Cabernet Sauvignon Merlot 2007 A medium-bodied wine, with the accent on red and black fruits rather than oak or tannins (though both are certainly there). Good balance. Cork. 14% alc. **Rating** 89 **To** 2015 $17.95

Smithbrook ★★★★

Smithbrook Road, Pemberton, WA 6260 **Region** Pemberton
T (08) 9772 3557 **www**.smithbrook.com.au **Open** Mon–Fri 9–4, w'ends by appt
Winemaker Ashley Lewkowski **Est.** 1988 **Cases** 8000
Smithbrook is a major player in the Pemberton region, with over 60 ha of vines in production. Owned by Petaluma/Lion Nathan, but continues its role as a contract grower for other companies, as well as supplying Petaluma's needs and making relatively small amounts of wine under its own label. Perhaps the most significant change has been the removal of Pinot Noir from the current range of products, and the introduction of Merlot. The Far Flung second label offers great value. Exports to the UK, Canada and Japan.

The Yilgarn Pemberton Sauvignon Blanc Semillon 2008 Oaky on the bouquet, with tropical fruit and a mere suggestion of nettle; the palate offers more, with a rich middle and an elongated, textural finish; will rapidly improve as the oak integrates with the fruit. Screwcap. 12.5% alc. **Rating** 91 **To** 2013 $28

Smiths Vineyard

27 Croom Lane, Beechworth, Vic 3747 **Region** Beechworth
T 0412 475 328 **www**.smithsvineyard.com.au **Open** W'ends & public hols 10–5, or by appt
Winemaker Will Flamsteed **Est.** 1978 **Cases** 1000 **Vyds** 3.3 ha
Pete and Di Smith established the first vineyard in Beechworth in 1978, with the encouragement of John Brown Jr of Brown Brothers. In 2003 the winery and vineyard was taken over by their daughter Sarah and husband Will Flamsteed. At 550 m, the vineyard is predominantly chardonnay (1.8 ha), with some cabernet sauvignon (1 ha) and merlot (0.5 ha), which make the estate wines. Will and Sarah made their first Beechworth Shiraz in 2006. The Heathcote Shiraz was a response to the smoke taint and frost damage in 2007.

ŸŸŸŸŸ **Heathcote Shiraz 2007** Good colour; vibrant blueberry fruit bouquet with touches of mint and spice; quite warm and ripe on the palate, with a soft and gentle conclusion. Screwcap. 14.4% alc. **Rating** 90 **To** 2013 $25

Somerled ★★★★

7 Heath Road, Crafers, SA 5152 (postal) **Region** McLaren Vale
T (08) 8339 2617 **F** (08) 8339 2617 **www.**somerled.com.au **Open** Not
Winemaker Rob Moody **Est.** 2001 **Cases** 1500
This is the venture of Robin and Heather Moody, and daughters Emma and Lucinda. The quietly spoken Robin (with a degree in oenology) joined Penfolds in 1969, and remained with Penfolds/Southcorp until 2001. This is a classic negociant business in the strict sense of that term: it produces only full-bodied McLaren Vale Shiraz, selected by Robin from parcels of young wine, during or soon after fermentation. The wines are blended and matured at Boar's Rock Winery at McLaren Vale. The name comes from the bay gelding that Robin's grandfather raced to victory in the amateur steeplechase at the Oakbank Picnic Races in 1908, and which took its name from the Scottish king who defeated the Vikings in 1156. So there you are. Exports to Hong Kong.

ŸŸŸŸŸ **McLaren Vale Shiraz 2004** Heady levels of sweet dark fruit, dark chocolate and sweet oak; the palate is dense and unctuous, delivering copious amounts of sweet fruit; a big ripe style, handled well. Cork. 14.8% alc. **Rating** 93 **To** 2015 $20

Somerset Hill Wines ★★★★

540 McLeod Road, Denmark, WA 6333 **Region** Denmark
T (08) 9840 9388 **F** (08) 9840 9394 **www.**somersethillwines.com.au **Open** 7 days 11–5 summer, 11–4 winter
Winemaker Graham Upson (red), Harewood Estate (white) **Est.** 1995 **Cases** 2000
Vyds 10.28 ha
Graham Upson commenced planting pinot noir, chardonnay, semillon, merlot, pinot meunier and sauvignon blanc in 1995, on one of the coolest and latest-ripening sites in WA. The limestone cellar door area has sweeping views out over the ocean and to the Stirling Ranges, selling everything from Belgian chocolates to farm-grown mushrooms (and, of course, wine). Exports to the UK, Denmark, Russia, Poland and Canada.

ŸŸŸŸŸ **Semillon 2008** A clean but unusual bouquet with some hints of passionfruit, the palate with very intense fruit ranging across a citrus spectrum on its way to a long, lingering finish. Screwcap. 12.5% alc. **Rating** 93 **To** 2015
Sauvignon Blanc 2008 An aromatic bouquet of herb and gooseberry shifts gears radically on the palate with generous and soft tropical fruit; does tighten up on the finish. Screwcap. 12.5% alc. **Rating** 90 **To** 2011

Songlines Estates ★★★★

PO Box 221, Cessnock, NSW 2325 **Region** Lower Hunter Valley
T (02) 4932 0054 **F** (02) 4998 7058 **www.**songlinesestates.com **Open** By appt
Winemaker David Fatches, John Duval **Est.** 2002 **Cases** 7000 **Vyds** 29 ha
This is another of the multinational, multi-talented boutique wine operations springing up like mushrooms after autumn rain. The English end is represented by Martin Krajewski (who also owns Chateau de Sours in Bordeaux) and in Australia by David Fatches and John Duval as winemakers. While the red wines are made from McLaren Vale grapes, Songlines is from 110-year-old vines, the wines are in fact made in the Lower Hunter Valley winery, which takes advantage of 3 ha each of chardonnay and semillon to produce estate-based varietal releases of these wines. Songlines heads the three-tiered range of wines, followed by Bylines and then Leylines. Exports to the UK, Canada, France and Hong Kong.

ŢŢŢŢŢ **Bylines McLaren Vale Shiraz 2007** Powerful full-bodied shiraz with regional character running through the length of the palate, where black fruits, dark chocolate, oak and tannins coalesce. Screwcap. 14.5% alc. **Rating** 93 **To** 2022 $49
Bylines Hunter Valley Semillon 2008 Well made, and has plenty of flavour in a complex spectrum, swelling on the finish with almost tropical fruits, but is fully priced. Screwcap. 10.5% alc. **Rating** 91 **To** 2018 $35
Songlines McLaren Vale Shiraz 2006 Deeply coloured and deeply complex; dark, brooding and quite chewy with a sweetness of fruit to the core that is supported by ample fine-grained tannins and fruitcake spice; almost old-fashioned in style, there is a charm about the wine that is compelling. Cork. 14.5% alc. **Rating** 90 **To** 2015 $120

ŢŢŢŢ **Songlines McLaren Vale Shiraz 2007** Good hue of medium depth; medium-bodied wine, primarily shaped by 20 months in new French oak, both in terms of flavour and texture; despite old vine estate-grown origin, the fruit has not yet reasserted itself. Cork. 14.5% alc. **Rating** 89 **To** 2017 $120
Bylines Hunter Valley Chardonnay 2008 Light, bright colour; light, clean and fresh palate, with some barrel ferment and stone fruit flavours, but neither complex nor long. Screwcap. 13.5% alc. **Rating** 88 **To** 2013 $38
Bylines Hunter Valley Chardonnay 2007 Strong sulphide complexity dominates the bouquet, and the palate is a little hard and unyielding; a complex style; the price tag is daunting. Screwcap. 13% alc. **Rating** 87 **To** 2015 $55
Leylines McLaren Vale Shiraz 2007 A wine in two parts; medium-bodied and savoury on entry before rugged tannins cut in on the back-palate and finish. Time may, or may not, resolve the conflict. Screwcap. 14.5% alc. **Rating** 87 **To** 2015 $25

Sons of Eden   ★★★★★

PO Box 261, Angaston, SA 5353 **Region** Barossa Valley
T (08) 8564 2363 **F** (08) 8564 3823 **www**.sonsofeden.com **Open** Not
Winemaker Corey Ryan **Est.** 2000 **Cases** 5000 **Vyds** 52 ha
Sons of Eden is the venture of winemaker Corey Ryan and viticulturist Simon Cowham, who both learnt and refined their skills in the vineyards and cellars of Eden Valley. Corey is a trained oenologist with 22 vintages under his belt, having cut his teeth as a winemaker at Henschke. Thereafter he worked for Rouge Homme and Penfolds in Coonawarra, backed up with winemaking stints in the Rhône Valley, and in 2002 took the opportunity to work in NZ, heading up the winemaking team for Villa Maria Estates (remaining a consultant to Villa Maria). In 2007 he won the Institute of Masters of Wine scholarship, awarded to the student with the highest marks across the theory and practical sections of wine assessment. Simon has a similarly international career covering such diverse organisations as Oddbins, UK and the Winemakers' Federation of Australia. Switching from the business side to grapegrowing when he qualified as a viticulturist, he worked for Yalumba as technical manager of the Heggies and Pewsey Vale vineyards. With this background, it comes as no surprise to find the estate-grown wines are of outstanding quality. Exports to the US.

ŢŢŢŢŢ **Freya Eden Valley Riesling 2008** Has quite remarkable intensity to its flavour, with citrus, apple and even stone fruit wrapped around a core of stony acidity. Built to last. Screwcap. 11.5% alc. **Rating** 94 **To** 2020 $22
Remus Old Vine Eden Valley Shiraz 2005 Strong colour; a rich bouquet of dark berries, then a velvety palate with a mix of black fruits, spice and licorice running through to a long finish. Cork. 15% alc. **Rating** 94 **To** 2020 $49
Kennedy Barossa Valley Grenache Shiraz Mourvedre 2006 Good colour; a prime example of the synergy of the blend, shiraz the glue that holds the other parts together; a cascade of red and black fruits with fine-grained tannins. Great price. Screwcap. 15% alc. **Rating** 94 **To** 2016 $22

ŢŢŢŢŢ **Zephyrus Barossa Valley Shiraz Viognier 2005** Good colour; a quiescent bouquet is followed by a palate that has thrust and energy building progressively through to the vibrant finish. Screwcap. 15% alc. **Rating** 93 **To** 2018 $32

Freya Eden Valley Riesling 2006 Is developing very slowly but equally surely; lemon zest/peel notes on the back-palate lead into a clean, bracing finish and aftertaste. Screwcap. 12.5% alc. **Rating** 92 **To** 2016 $22

Romulus Old Vine Barossa Valley Shiraz 2005 Like Remus, good colour; curiously, the alcohol is less than Remus, the palate is distinctly riper and sweeter, with mocha and chocolate notes. Cork. 14.5% alc. **Rating** 90 **To** 2015 $49

Sorby Adams Wines ★★★

Lot 18, Gawler Park Road, Angaston, SA 5353 **Region** Eden Valley
T (08) 8564 2741 **F** (08) 8564 2437 **www**.sorbyadamswines.com **Open** 7 days 10–5
Winemaker Simon Adams **Est.** 2004 **Cases** 15 000 **Vyds** 12 ha
Simon Adams and wife Helen purchased a 3.2-ha vineyard in 1996, which had been planted by Pastor Franz Julius Lehmann (none other than Peter Lehmann's father) in 1932. Peter Lehmann always referred to it as 'Dad's Block'. They have added 0.25 ha of viognier, which, as one might expect, is used in a shiraz viognier blend. Most recent plantings are of shiraz (2.5 ha), riesling (1.7 ha), cabernet sauvignon (0.7 ha) and traminer (1.5 ha). Nonetheless, the top wines, The Family Shiraz and The Thing Shiraz, need no assistance from viognier. Only six barrels of The Thing are made each year, using the best grapes from Dad's Block. The name Sorby Adams has overtones of a chameleon: it comes from a female ancestor of long-serving Yalumba winemaker Simon Adams, whose full name is Simon David Sorby Adams. Exports to the US, Canada, Germany, Hong Kong and China.

ŸŸŸŸ **Jellicoe Estate Grown Eden Valley Cabernet Sauvignon 2007** Minty notes dominate the bouquet, but there is ample black fruit and toasty oak to add relief; has quite tight and focused flavours. Screwcap. 14% alc. **Rating** 88 **To** 2014 $22

Sorrenberg ★★★★★

Alma Road, Beechworth, Vic 3747 **Region** Beechworth
T (03) 5728 2278 **F** (03) 5728 2278 **www**.sorrenberg.com **Open** By appt
Winemaker Barry Morey, Jan Morey **Est.** 1986 **Cases** 1200 **Vyds** 3.5 ha
Barry and Jan Morey keep a low profile, but the wines from their vineyard at Beechworth have a cult following not far removed from that of Giaconda; chardonnay, sauvignon blanc, semillon, cabernet sauvignon and gamay are the principal varieties planted on the north-facing, granitic slopes. Gamay and Chardonnay are the winery specialities.

ŸŸŸŸŸ **Sauvignon Blanc Semillon 2008** Creamy oak aroma dominates the bouquet with an underpinning of tropical fruit; the palate is focused and lively, with a long and harmonious joining of fruit and oak; a complex example of this classic blend. Cork. 13.6% alc. **Rating** 94 **To** 2013 $32

Cabernet Sauvignon Cabernet Franc Merlot 2006 Elegantly framed red fruits, and a touch of bramble and spice; medium-bodied with an attractive violet character showing through on the palate; very fine tannin structure on the finish. Cork. 13.5% alc. **Rating** 94 **To** 2016 $45

Soul Growers

PO Box 805, Tanunda, SA 5352 (postal) **Region** Barossa Valley
T 0417 851 317 **Open** By appt
Winemaker James Lindner, Paul Lindner, David Cruickshank **Est.** 1998 **Cases** 600
James Lindner is a fifth-generation Barossan, working in every area of the wine industry since he left school. In 1998 he acquired a small property on the hills of Seppeltsfield, planting 1.6 ha of shiraz, 0.8 ha of grenache, 0.3 ha of mourvedre, and a little cabernet sauvignon and black muscat. The first three varieties are separately open-fermented and given two years barrel age before the wine is blended and bottled (without filtration or fining). Exports to Canada and Singapore.

ΨΨΨΨ♀ **Barossa Valley Shiraz 2006** No fining, no filtration policy shows in the lack of absolute clarity in colour; a luscious mouthfeel of sweet black fruits, alcohol partly involved. Cork. 15% alc. **Rating** 90 **To** 2016 $49.99
Barossa Valley Shiraz Grenache Mourvedre 2006 Quite developed colour; typical Barossa Valley blend; light- to medium-bodied, with some spicy/earthy/cedary characters to both the fruit and the tannins; good length. Cork. 14.5% alc. **Rating** 90 **To** 2013 $24.99

ΨΨΨΨ **Barossa Valley Shiraz Cabernet 2006** Juicy, vibrant and clean; a little volatile acidity lifts the red fruits; reasonable length. Cork. 14.5% alc. **Rating** 87 **To** 2014 $29.95

Souter's Vineyard

390 Happy Valley Road, Rosewhite, Vic 3737 **Region** Alpine Valleys
T (03) 5752 1077 **www.**happyvalley75.com.au/soutersvineyard/ **Open** Fri–Sun 10–4,
7 days in Jan
Winemaker Eleana Anderson **Est.** 1983 **Cases** 250 **Vyds** 2.13 ha
Melbourne professional couple Kay and Allan Souter acquired the former Rosewhite Vineyard in late 2003. The vineyard, one of the oldest in the Alpine Valleys region, had been run down significantly owing to the age and ill health of the former owners, and the Souters have invested much time and effort in rehabilitating, retrellising and regrafting the vineyard to more suitable varieties.

ΨΨΨΨ **Alpine Valleys Cabernet Sauvignon 2006** Good hue; lively cassis/red fruits on both bouquet and the medium-bodied palate; fine, savoury tannins lengthen the finish. Screwcap. 14.8% alc. **Rating** 88 **To** 2014 $25
Alpine Valleys Cabernet Sauvignon 2005 An austere style, but with clear varietal definition at the savoury/leafy/minty end of the spectrum, and enough fruit to satisfy. Cork. 14% alc. **Rating** 88 **To** 2014 $22.50
Alpine Valleys Shiraz 2006 Ripe berry aromas flow through onto the light- to medium-bodied palate, with touches of licorice and spice joining the blackberry fruit; good balance. Screwcap. 14.8% alc. **Rating** 87 **To** 2014 $25
Alpine Valleys Shiraz 2005 While the colour is relatively light, retains good hue; has a light- to medium-bodied array of red fruit flavours and spices, the tannins minimal. Cork. 14% alc. **Rating** 87 **To** 2012 $25

Southern Highland Wines

Oldbury Road, Sutton Forest, NSW 2577 **Region** Southern Highlands
T (02) 4868 2300 **www.**southernhighlandwines.com **Open** 7 days 10–5
Winemaker Eddy Rossi, Ben McDonald **Est.** 2003 **Cases** 6000 **Vyds** 20 ha
The venture is owned by its five directors, who together have 50 years of experience in the wine industry and in commerce. John Gilbertson ran Ericsson in NZ and then in China between 1983 and '00. Darren Corradi and Eddy Rossi, in charge of viticulture and winemaking, respectively, both had lengthy careers in various Griffith wineries, also the training ground for production director Frank Colloridi. NZ-born Simon Gilbertson graduated from Lincoln University with a degree in agriculture, and after 13 years in corporate life, purchased three vineyards in Hawke's Bay, NZ; he is de facto general manager and sales director. Exports to the US and China.

ΨΨΨΨ♀ **Oldbury Reserve Chardonnay 2005** Glowing straw-green; holding together well, with classic nectarine, peach and grapefruit supported by subtle oak; good overall balance. Screwcap. 13.2% alc. **Rating** 92 **To** 2013 $38
Cool Climate Riesling 2008 A focused lime and lemon bouquet, with an underpinning of minerality; a quite generous and lively palate of citrus and stone fruit; very clean finish, with quite linear acidity. Screwcap. 11.5% alc. **Rating** 91 **To** 2014 $20

ҮҮҮҮ **Cool Climate Shiraz 2006** Clear crimson; well made, unforced and elegant; strong spicy/savoury components leave no doubt about the climate; needs a little more flesh, but it's a very promising start. Screwcap. 13.5% alc. **Rating** 89 **To** 2014 $20

Cool Climate Cabernet Sauvignon 2006 Totally ambiguous labelling; the flavours and light-bodied weight of the wine suggest it could come from the Southern Highlands, with notes of cassis, mint and leaf, and minimal tannins. Screwcap. 13% alc. **Rating** 88 **To** 2015 $20

Cool Climate Pinot Noir 2006 Retains red hues; has clear varietal character, but the oak (French and American) does not flatter the wine; succeeds in spite of that oak. Screwcap. 13% alc. **Rating** 87 **To** 2012 $20

Altitude 676 Shiraz Cabernet 2006 A surprise packet, with riper fruit flavours than either the alcohol or the altitude would suggest; oak sweetness largely obscures the trace of green mint on the finish. Screwcap. 13% alc. **Rating** 87 **To** 2012 $15

SpearGully Wines

455 Lusatia Park Road, Hoddles Creek, Vic 3139 **Region** Yarra Valley
T 0417 331 599 **F** (03) 5967 4496 **Open** Not
Winemaker Tony Jordan **Est.** 1999 **Cases** 500 **Vyds** 2.6 ha

SpearGully is the venture of Dr Anthony (Tony) and Michele Jordan, both prominent figures in the Australian wine industry, albeit in different fields. Tony has had a distinguished career, first as a lecturer and consultant, then as CEO of Domaine Chandon, broken for several years as the senior technical director for the worldwide operations of Möet Hennessy, before returning to Domaine Chandon and the Yarra Valley. Wife Michele has spent many years in public relations, marketing and sales, based variously in the UK and Australia. They have established chardonnay, sauvignon blanc and pinot noir on the hillsides surrounding their home in the Upper Yarra Valley, and the wines have both domestic and international distribution (the UK and Japan), though in small quantities.

ҮҮҮҮҰ **Shiraz 2006** Bright colour; blackberry and sage bouquet; medium-bodied with good focus and a tidy freshness to the fruit; surprisingly long. Screwcap. **Rating** 92 **To** 2015 $28

Yarra Valley Chardonnay 2007 Ripe peach, straw and a little spice; the palate is quite full on entry, with nutty complexity being framed by nectarine fruit; then a long finish. Screwcap. 13% alc. **Rating** 90 **To** 2014 $28

Shiraz 2004 Still quite fresh; good acidity and plenty of red berry fruit; tar and a touch of licorice, with ample chewy tannin on the palate. Yarra Valley/Heathcote/McLaren Vale. Cork. 13.5% alc. **Rating** 90 **To** 2014 $28

Spinifex

PO Box 511, Nuriootpa, SA 5355 **Region** Barossa Valley
T (08) 8564 2059 **F** (08) 8564 2079 **www.**spinifexwines.com.au **Open** Not
Winemaker Peter Schell **Est.** 2001 **Cases** 3500

Peter Schell and Magali Gely are a husband and wife team from NZ who came to Australia in the early 1990s to study oenology and marketing, respectively, at Roseworthy College. Together they have spent four vintages making wine in France, mainly in the south where Magali's family were vignerons for generations near Montpellier. The focus at Spinifex is the red varieties that dominate in the south of France: mataro (more correctly mourvedre), grenache, shiraz and cinsaut. The wine is made in open fermenters, basket-pressed, partial wild (indigenous) fermentations, and relatively long post-ferment maceration. This is at once a very old approach, but nowadays à la mode. The wines are made at Spinifex's winery in Vine Vale, where Peter also makes wines for a number of clients to whom he consults. So far as I am concerned Spinifex out-Torbrecks Torbreck. Exports to the UK, the US, Canada, Belgium, Taiwan and Singapore.

ŸŸŸŸŸ **Barossa Shiraz Viognier 2007** Inviting vibrant colour; quite a polished and poised bouquet of allspice redcurrant and blackberry fruit; at the core of the wine there is a mineral complexity that is thoroughly engaging, and the hedonistic level of sweet fruit marries seamlessly with it and the toasty oak; beautifully constructed, on a large scale, the balancing acidity provides brightness to the finish. Diam. 14.5% alc. **Rating** 96 **To** 2020 $48

Esprit 2007 Good colour; clearly defined raspberry fruit is backed seamlessly by spicy shiraz, and meaty mataro; the palate is lively, and exhibits pronounced perfume; tightly focused and very inviting on the juicy finish. Shiraz/Grenache/Mataro/Carignan/Cinsaut. Diam. 14.5% alc. **Rating** 94 **To** 2015 $28

ŸŸŸŸŸ **Taureau 2007** Quite a savoury bouquet with sour cherry, briar and a touch of spice; loaded with sweet red fruit on entry, there is an attractive savoury mineral note that provides focus and energy to the finish. Tempranillo/Carignan/Cabernet Sauvignon/Graciano. Screwcap. 14.3% alc. **Rating** 93 **To** 2015 $24

Lola 2008 An unusual blend that delivers a distinctly European styled wine; straw, pear and a touch of citrus come through on the bouquet and the palate; nutty and full on the finish, texture is the key. Semillon/Marsanne/Ugni Blanc/Vermentino/Viognier. Screwcap. 13.5% alc. **Rating** 91 **To** 2012 $19

Papillon 2008 Certainly a fun-time wine; bright and juicy with appealing spice and a strong sense of red and blue fruit; lively, almost squeaky, acidity provides a juicy and lifted finish to the wine. Grenache/Cinsaut/Mataro/Shiraz. Screwcap. 13.8% alc. **Rating** 91 **To** 2014 $22.50

Spook Hill Wines   NR
PO Box 335, Cadell, SA 5321 **Region** Riverland
T 0428 403 235 **F** (08) 8540 3126 **www**.spookhillwines.com **Open** Not
Winemaker Jock Gordon **Est.** 1999 **Cases** 600 **Vyds** 8 ha
Owner and winemaker Jock Gordon Jr's family have been grapegrowers for three generations, but in 1999 Jock Gordon took the plunge into commercial winemaking after a successful career as an amateur winemaker. He has 8 ha of shiraz, and purchases grenache and mourvedre from local growers. The Spook Hill vineyard is situated in the Cadell Valley, a former oxbow of the Murray River now bypassed by the current river channel; silt soil deposited in the ancient river valley is especially suited to viticulture. All of the wines are open-fermented, basket-pressed and matured in the onsite winery.

Spring Vale Vineyards   ★★★★
130 Spring Vale Road, Cranbrook, Tas 7190 **Region** East Coast Tasmania
T (03) 6257 8208 **F** (03) 6257 8598 **www**.springvalewines.com **Open** 7 days 10–4
Winemaker Kristen Cush, David Cush **Est.** 1986 **Cases** 10 000 **Vyds** 12.1 ha
Rodney Lyne has progressively established pinot noir (6.5 ha), chardonnay (2 ha), gewurztraminer (1.6 ha), pinot gris and sauvignon blanc (1 ha each). In 2007 Spring Vale purchased the Melrose Vineyard from Bishops Rock (not the Bishops Rock brand or stock), planted to pinot noir (3 ha), sauvignon blanc, riesling (1 ha each) and chardonnay (0.5 ha). Exports to the US, Canada and Taiwan.

ŸŸŸŸ **Gewurztraminer 2008** Offers gentle touches of lychee; has fair length and acidity, and undoubted varietal character. Screwcap. 13.2% alc. **Rating** 88 **To** 2012 $28

Chardonnay 2008 Offers tropical fruit aromas and flavours; soft and mouthfilling, offset by balanced acidity. Screwcap. 12.8% alc. **Rating** 88 **To** 2012 $22

Melrose Pinot Noir Pinot Meunier 2008 An elegant, light-bodied wine, part of its character deriving from the pinot meunier, giving it some leafy/savoury characters. Screwcap. 13.2% alc. **Rating** 88 **To** 2011 $22

Springs Hill Vineyard

Schuller Road, Blewitt Springs, SA 5171 **Region** Fleurieu Zone
T (08) 8383 7001 **F** (08) 8383 7001 **www**.springshill.com.au **Open** By appt
Winemaker Anthony Whaite, Gary Whaite **Est.** 1998 **Cases** 1000 **Vyds** 17 ha
Anthony and Gary Whaite began the planting of their vineyard in 1975 with cabernet sauvignon and shiraz and have slowly expanded it over the following years with merlot, mourvedre and grenache. The vines are dry-grown, and the whole operation from vine to wine is carried out by the pair. They use traditional small batch winemaking techniques of open fermenters which are hand-plunged, basket-pressed, etc.

ŤŤŤŤŤ **Blewitt Springs Shiraz 2007** Dense colour; rich, luscious and concentrated; blackberry and plum run through the medium-bodied palate, oak and tannins playing a well-judged support role. Particularly good outcome for the vintage. Screwcap. 14.5% alc. **Rating** 94 **To** 2017 $35
Blewitt Springs Mourvedre 2007 Dense purple-crimson; a very complex bouquet, with notes of spice, tobacco and cedar alongside black fruits; a generous and welcoming style of mourvedre which should age very well. Screwcap. 14.5% alc. **Rating** 94 **To** 2022 $35

ŤŤŤŤŤ **Blewitt Springs Merlot 2007** In the full-blown style of McLaren Vale merlot pioneered by Tatachilla with great show success, but less admired these days. Vivid crimson, it has luscious, soft fruit and even, soft tannins. Screwcap. 14.5% alc. **Rating** 90 **To** 2015 $35

ŤŤŤŤ **Blewitt Springs Cabernet Sauvignon 2007** Good colour and fragrance; a mix of earthy and sweet cassis fruit, the two components needing to agree to an armistice; needs a year or two. Screwcap. 14.5% alc. **Rating** 89 **To** 2015 $35

Staindl Wines

63 Shoreham Road, Red Hill South, Vic 3937 (postal) **Region** Mornington Peninsula
T (03) 9813 1111 **www**.staindlwines.com **Open** By appt
Winemaker Phillip Jones (Contract) **Est.** 1982 **Cases** 600 **Vyds** 3.1 ha
As often happens, the establishment date for a wine producer can mean many things. In this instance it harks back to the planting of the vineyard by the Ayton family, and the establishment of what was thereafter called St Neots. Juliet and Paul Staindl acquired the property in 2002, and, with the guidance of Phillip Jones, have extended the plantings to 2.6 ha of pinot noir, 0.3 ha of chardonnay and 0.2 ha of riesling. The vineyard is run on a low chemical regime, heading towards biodynamic viticulture. Paul says, 'It's all good fun and lots of learning.' I would add it's also more than slightly demanding.

ŤŤŤŤŤ **Mornington Peninsula Chardonnay 2006** Bright pale green-straw; classic Mornington Peninsula style, with stone fruit, melon and cashew running through a supple and long palate, oak merely an interested bystander; great length and harmony. Screwcap. 13.7% alc. **Rating** 94 **To** 2014 $35

ŤŤŤŤŤ **Mornington Peninsula Riesling 2007** Apple, herb and citrus aromas lead into a bright palate with considerable thrust, finishing with crisp acidity. Screwcap. 12.9% alc. **Rating** 92 **To** 2015 $25
Mornington Peninsula Pinot Noir 2007 Clear red-purple; distinct touches of herb and mint add a tangy facade to the core of plummy fruit behind. Diam. 13.5% alc. **Rating** 90 **To** 2013 $40

ŤŤŤŤ **Mornington Peninsula Chardonnay 2007** Has abundant flavour, but has a jumbled fruit line in the mouth, with citrus/herbal notes alongside riper flavours. Might sort itself out with time. Screwcap. 13.5% alc. **Rating** 87 **To** 2013 $35

Stanley Lambert Wines

Barossa Valley Way, Tanunda, SA 5352 **Region** Barossa Valley
T (08) 8563 3375 **F** (08) 8563 3758 **www**.stanleylambert.com.au **Open** Mon–Fri 10–5,
w'ends & public hols 11–5
Winemaker Lindsay Stanley **Est.** 1994 **Cases** 15 000 **Vyds** 16.2 ha
Former Anglesey winemaker and industry veteran Lindsay Stanley established his own
business in the Barossa Valley when he purchased (and renamed) the former Kroemer Estate in
late 1994. As one would expect, the wines are competently made, although often light-bodied.
The estate plantings have provided virtually all the grapes for the business (shiraz, riesling,
chardonnay, cabernet sauvignon, zinfandel, tempranillo, mourvedre, merlot and viognier).
Exports to the UK, the US and other major markets.

ΨΨΨΨΨ **The Family Tree Barossa Valley Shiraz 2005** A supple, smooth, medium-
bodied palate with gently ripe plum fruit enfolded in a swathe of American oak
which fits well in the style. Diam. 14.5% alc. **Rating** 90 **To** 2016 $65

ΨΨΨΨ **Nordic Frost Barossa Valley Riesling 2008** Hand-picked bunches chilled to
2°C before pressing has achieved the intention of preserving maximum riesling
flavour in a traditional Barossa Valley spectrum. Innovative approach. Diam.
11.5% alc. **Rating** 89 **To** 2015 $18
August Barossa Valley Shiraz 2005 Nicely weighted and structured wine, in
mainstream Barossa style; warm fruit tones are supported by vanillin oak and soft
tannins; good overall balance. Diam. 14% alc. **Rating** 89 **To** 2015 $30
Full Sister Barossa Valley Semillon 2006 Now at its best, fleshed out by skin
contact prior to fermentation; these characters tend to blow out over time. Diam.
13.5% alc. **Rating** 87 **To** 2010 $15
Three's Company Barossa Valley Grenache Shiraz Mourvedre 2006
Good hue and clarity; very typical light to medium-bodied Barossa blend with
a mix of Turkish delight/confection and spiced cake notes. Diam. 13.5% alc.
Rating 87 **To** 2011 $20

Stanton & Killeen Wines

Jacks Road, Murray Valley Highway, Rutherglen, Vic 3685 **Region** Rutherglen
T (02) 6032 9457 **www**.stantonandkilleenwines.com.au **Open** Mon–Sat 9–5, Sun 10–5
Winemaker Michael Oxlee, Brendan Heath **Est.** 1875 **Cases** 20 000 **Vyds** 35.52 ha
The tragic and premature death of Chris Killeen was much mourned by his numerous
admirers, myself included. However, son Simon is already studying wine science, and 18-year-
old daughter Natasha is likely to enrol in a wine marketing course. In the meantime Michael
Oxlee, Chris's assistant for 15 years, continues the winemaking, with assistance from Brendan
Heath, who spent a similar time with Campbells. Exports to the UK and Denmark.

ΨΨΨΨΨ **Rutherglen Durif 2006** Strong colour; a heady bouquet of raisins, licorice and
dark chocolate; the palate carries the alcohol with contemptuous ease; a wine as
full of character as body. Diam. 15% alc. **Rating** 94 **To** 2021 $32
Rutherglen Vintage Fortified 2004 Good colour; in classic Stanton &
Killeen style, less sweet than most of what used to be called vintage port; the
complex varietal base, including port varieties, pays dividends, as does the balanced
sweetness. Cork. 18.5% alc. **Rating** 94 **To** 2024 $29

ΨΨΨΨΨ **Rutherglen Shiraz Durif 2006** Good hue and depth; a luscious palate with
blackberry, plum and prune flavours backed by well-integrated oak and ripe, but
soft, tannins. Diam. 14.5% alc. **Rating** 92 **To** 2016 $20
Rutherglen Tokay NV Classic toffee, caramel and cold tea aromas and flavours,
then a pleasingly fresh, almost dry, finish. Cork. 17.5% alc. **Rating** 91 **To** 2010 $17

Star Lane

RMB 1167 Star Lane, Beechworth, Vic 3747 **Region** Beechworth
T (03) 5728 7268 **Open** By appt
Winemaker Savaterre **Est.** 1996 **Cases** NA
Liz and Brett Barnes have established 4 ha of shiraz and merlot (planted in 1996) with further plantings of riesling and chardonnay planned. When Liz Barnes completes her winemaking course, she will take responsibility for winemaking from Keppell Smith (of Savaterre), but even then, they will continue to sell 70% of their grape production.

ΨΨΨΨΨ **Beechworth Shiraz 2005** Great colour; a very serious wine with red fruits, Asian spices and well-handled oak in abundance; the palate is quite fine, despite the fruit weight, and the freshness for the vintage is commendable. Cork. 14.2% alc. **Rating** 94 **To** 2018 $70

 ## Starvedog Lane

Reynell Road, Reynella, SA 5161 (postal) **Region** Adelaide Hills
T (08) 8392 2222 **F** (08) 8392 2202 **www.**starvedoglane.com.au **Open** Not
Winemaker Glenn Barry **Est.** 1999 **Cases** NFP
Starvedog Lane came into existence as part of a joint venture with John and Helen Edwards of Ravenswood Lane, who had established 28 ha of vineyards in 1993. Part of that production was sold to the joint venture for the Starvedog Lane brand, part reserved for release under the Ravenswood Lane brand, which morphed into The Lane (see seperate entry). Confusing, but the situation is now much simpler, as the Edwards and Hardys (technically, Constellation Wines Australia) have severed all commercial ties. The Starvedog Lane brand is wholly owned by CWA and relies on contract-grown grapes from growers in the Adelaide Hills.

ΨΨΨΨΨ **Adelaide Hills Cabernet Merlot 2006** Good crimson-purple; the bouquet has abundant cool-grown black fruit and spice aromas, which come through positively on the medium-bodied palate, there joined by substantial tannins and oak. Screwcap. 13.5% alc. **Rating** 93 **To** 2016 $25.50
Adelaide Hills Sauvignon Blanc 2008 Exotic guava and grapefruit bouquet; good weight on entry with fresh acid and a touch of mineral on the finish. Screwcap. **Rating** 91 **To** 2012 $26

ΨΨΨΨ **Adelaide Hills Pinot Noir 2008** Bright colour; a little dried leaf, herbal edge to the bouquet, with plummy fruit in support; quite focused and big boned, with a juicy fruited, yet savoury, finish. Screwcap. **Rating** 89 **To** 2013 $28.50
Adelaide Hills Pinot Grigio 2007 This in no way convinces me these wines improve past their second birthday, although it does have some impact. Screwcap. 13.5% alc. **Rating** 87 **To** 2009 $26

Steels Creek Estate ★★★★

1 Sewell Road, Steels Creek, Vic 3775 **Region** Yarra Valley
T (03) 5965 2448 **www.**steelsckestate.com.au **Open** W'ends & public hols 10–6, or by appt
Winemaker Simon Peirce **Est.** 1981 **Cases** 400 **Vyds** 1.7 ha
The Steels Creek vineyard (chardonnay, shiraz, cabernet sauvignon, cabernet franc and colombard), family-operated since 1981, is located in the picturesque Steels Creek Valley with views toward the Kinglake National Park. Red wines are made onsite, white wines with the assistance of consultants. Visitors can view the winemaking operations from the cellar door.

ΨΨΨΨΨ **Yarra Valley Chardonnay 2008** Vibrant colour; pear flesh and spice, especially cinnamon; vibrant and focused fruit on the palate, with taut acidity, and layered texture on the finish. Screwcap. 13.5% alc. **Rating** 92 **To** 2014 $22

Stefani Estate

389 Heathcote-Rochester Road, Heathcote, Vic 3523 **Region** Heathcote
T (03) 9570 8750 **F** (03) 9579 1532 **www.**stefaniestatewines.com.au **Open** By appt
Winemaker Mario Marson **Est.** 2002 **Cases** 2200 **Vyds** 27.6 ha

Stefano Stefani came to Australia in 1985. Business success has allowed Stefano and wife Rina to follow in the footsteps of Stefano's grandfather, who had a vineyard and was an avid wine collector. The first property they acquired was at Long Gully Road in the Yarra Valley, planted with pinot grigio, cabernet sauvignon, chardonnay and pinot noir. The next was in Heathcote, where he acquired a property adjoining that of Mario Marson, built a winery and established 14.4 ha of vineyards, planted to shiraz, cabernet sauvignon, merlot, cabernet franc, malbec and petit verdot. In 2003 a second Yarra Valley property named The View, reflecting its high altitude, was acquired and Dijon clones of chardonnay and pinot noir were planted. In addition, 1.6 ha of sangiovese, mammolo bianco, malvasia, aleatico, trebbiano and crepolino bianco have been established, using scion material from the original Stefani vineyard in Tuscany (released for planting after three years in Australian quarantine). Mario Marson (ex Mount Mary) oversees the operation of all the vineyards and is also the winemaker. He is also able to use the winery to make his own brand wines, completing the business link. Exports to China.

♓♓♓♓♓ **The View Yarra Valley Chardonnay 2006** Has the length and persistence of all top Yarra chardonnay, the flavours within a tight ring of nectarine and grapefruit, the oak balanced and integrated. Diam. 14% alc. **Rating** 94 **To** 2015 $50
Heathcote Vineyard Shiraz 2006 Dense crimson; an archetypal Heathcote shiraz, with layers of black fruits, licorice and a touch of pepper on the bouquet and palate alike; full-bodied, the black fruits having a juicy element balanced by the tannins. Diam. 14.5% alc. **Rating** 94 **To** 2026 $50

Stefano Lubiana ★★★★★

60 Rowbottoms Road, Granton, Tas 7030 **Region** Southern Tasmania
T (03) 6263 7457 **www.slw.com.au Open** Sun–Thurs 11–3 (closed some public hols)
Winemaker Steve Lubiana **Est.** 1990 **Cases** NFP **Vyds** 18 ha
When Stefano (Steve) Lubiana moved from the Riverland to Tasmania, he set up a substantial contract sparkling winemaking facility to help cover the costs of the move and the establishment of his new business. Over the years, he has steadily decreased the amount of contract winemaking, now focusing on his estate-grown wines from beautifully located vineyards sloping down to the Derwent River. Exports to the UK, Sweden, Korea, Singapore and Japan.

♓♓♓♓♓ **Estate Chardonnay 2005** In pure Chablis style, with stony/minerally overtones to the bouquet and palate, tangy/citrussy fruit and bright acidity; long finish. Screwcap. 13.5% alc. **Rating** 95 **To** 2014 $43
Estate Pinot Noir 2006 Positive, deep colour; fragrant plum aromas lead into a generously proportioned palate, which also has excellent balance and fine supporting tannins; the oak is well integrated and balanced. Cork. 13.5% alc. **Rating** 95 **To** 2014 $53
Vintage Brut 2003 Very complex wine, with citrus, bready/brioche notes and spice running through the long palate, which has very low dosage; bottle-fermented. Diam. 12.5% alc. **Rating** 94 **To** 2016 $52

♓♓♓♓♓ **Merlot 2006** Excellent hue and clarity; while medium-bodied at best, has attractive redcurrant fruit and fine, savoury tannins in true merlot style. Diam. 14% alc. **Rating** 92 **To** 2014 $35

♓♓♓♓ **Alfresco 2008** In typical Lubiana fashion; is lemony, long and largely dry, residual sugar neutralised by high acidity. Screwcap. 8.5% alc. **Rating** 89 **To** 2010 $29

Steinborner Family Vineyards ★★★★

91 Siegersdorf Road, Tanunda, SA 5352 **Region** Barossa Valley
T 0414 474 708 **F** (08) 8522 4898 **www.sfvineyards.com.au Open** By appt
Winemaker David Reynolds, Neil Doddridge, Sally Blackwell **Est.** 2003 **Cases** 3000
Vyds 10 ha
This is a partnership between David and Rebecca Reynolds, and Rebecca's parents, Michael and Heather Steinborner. They say 'David, hailing from UK/Irish heritage and with a chance

meeting in Tokyo (with Rebecca), brings some fresh blood to the Steinborner clan. He oversees (or does himself wherever possible) much of both the vineyard and wine production.' The oldest vines include some 80-year-old shiraz, and all the other varieties of semillon, viognier, durif and marsanne are planted on the typical sand-over-clay profile of Vine Vale, one of the noted subregions of the Barossa Valley. Exports to Switzerland, Indonesia, Hong Kong, China and Japan.

Stella Bella Wines ★★★★★

PO Box 536, Margaret River, WA 6285 **Region** Margaret River
T (08) 9757 6377 **F** (08) 9757 6022 **www.**stellabella.com.au **Open** Not
Winemaker Janice McDonald, Stuart Pym **Est.** 1997 **Cases** 50 000 **Vyds** 40 ha
This enormously successful, privately owned winemaking business produces wines of true regional expression with fruit sourced from the central and southern parts of Margaret River. Owns or controls more than 80 ha of vineyards, recently acquired a 3000-tonne (potential) winemaking facility at Karridale, and a cellar door is in the pipeline, just minutes from the township at the original Isca vineyard. It's hard to imagine the wines getting better, but we shall see. Exports of Stella Bella, Suckfizzle and Skuttlebutt labels to the UK, the US, Canada, China, Hong Kong and Singapore.

ΨΨΨΨΨ **Suckfizzle Margaret River Sauvignon Blanc Semillon 2006** A distinguished blend in full White Bordeaux fashion, the fruit and oak seamless, the length and aftertaste impeccable. Screwcap. 13% alc. **Rating** 96 **To** 2012 $45
Sauvignon Blanc 2008 A fragrant, flowery bouquet and a lissom palate, with passionfruit, kiwi fruit and redcurrant flavours; has vibrancy and thrust, with a long, clean finish. Screwcap. 13% alc. **Rating** 94 **To** 2012 $21
Margaret River Shiraz 2007 A highly fragrant and spicy bouquet leads into a medium-bodied palate with a display of red and black fruits, the tannins fine, the oak perfectly weighted. Screwcap. 14% alc. **Rating** 94 **To** 2022 $27
Margaret River Sangiovese Cabernet Sauvignon 2007 A masterly blend of the two varieties that flow seamlessly together in a stream of red fruits, the tannins silky and fine. Totally delicious, and a must on any Italian restaurant wine list worthy of the name. Screwcap. 14% alc. **Rating** 94 **To** 2015 $30

ΨΨΨΨ **Skuttlebutt Sauvignon Semillon 2008** Fresh and breezy, but there is a lot of flavour to be had, redcurrant and passionfruit at opposite ends of the spectrum, bound by appealing citrussy acidity. Screwcap. 12.5% alc. **Rating** 92 **To** 2012 $16
Margaret River Semillon Sauvignon Blanc 2008 A rich wine, the sauvignon blanc speaking louder than the semillon, even though it is the junior partner; an assemblage of tropical fruits drive the palate; best served fully chilled. Screwcap. 13% alc. **Rating** 91 **To** 2012 $21
Margaret River Viognier 2007 Pale straw-green; gently fragrant apricot blossom aromas lead into a palate that has good structure and length, and avoids phenolics. Screwcap. 13.5% alc. **Rating** 91 **To** 2010 $28
Suckfizzle Margaret River Cabernet Sauvignon 2006 A testament to cabernet's resistance to rain (its thick skins) and to the skill of the winemaking team; the colour is good, the cassis-accented fruit is ripe, as are the tannins, and the oak is integrated. Screwcap. 13.5% alc. **Rating** 91 **To** 2016 $50

ΨΨΨΨ **Margaret River Chardonnay 2007** Clean, fleshy and lively; pulls up a little short, and the fruit is a little one dimensional. Screwcap. 13% alc. **Rating** 89 **To** 2013 $28
Skuttlebutt Shiraz Cabernet 2006 Bright, clear purple-red; delicious light-bodied cassis, raspberry and redcurrant fruit in an uncomplicated style. Screwcap. 13.5% alc. **Rating** 89 **To** 2014 $16
Cabernet Sauvignon Merlot 2006 Bright, clear colour; a fragrant bouquet with blackcurrant aromas followed by a more sombre, savoury palate, changing gear once again on the well-defined, elegant finish, oak where it should be. Screwcap. 14% alc. **Rating** 89 **To** 2015 $28

Skuttlebutt Shiraz Merlot Rose 2007 Gently spicy elements to the tangy fruit, with a dry, balanced finish. Screwcap. 13.5% alc. **Rating** 88 **To** 2010 $16

Margaret River Tempranillo 2007 Very good crimson-purple; the most robust, powerful and tannic Tempranillo in Australia; Rioja would give it three years of constant egg white fining; here a barbecue is the only likely antidote. Screwcap. 14% alc. **Rating** 87 **To** 2020 $30

Stephen John Wines   ★★★☆

Sollys Hill Road, Watervale, SA 5452 **Region** Clare Valley
T (08) 8843 0105 **F** (08) 8843 0105 **www**.stephenjohnwines.com **Open** 7 days 11–5
Winemaker Stephen John **Est.** 1994 **Cases** 10 000 **Vyds** 5 ha
The John family is one of the best known in the Barossa Valley, with branches running Australia's best cooperage (AP John & Sons) and providing the former chief winemaker of Lindemans (Philip John) and the former chief winemaker of Quelltaler (Stephen John). Stephen and Rita John have now formed their own family business in the Clare Valley, based on a vineyard overlooking Watervale, and supplemented by grapes from a few local growers. The cellar door is a renovated 80-year-old stable full of rustic charm. Exports to Canada, Malaysia, Thailand, Maldives and Singapore.

🍷🍷🍷🍷🍷 **Dry Grown Clare Valley Shiraz 2007** A no-holds-barred full-bodied wine brimming with blackberry, tar and prune, backed in turn by abundant tannins; needs much patience, but is not alcoholic. Screwcap. 14.5% alc. **Rating** 90 **To** 2027 $25

🍷🍷🍷🍷 **Watervale Riesling 2008** Bright straw-green; a sturdy and powerful wine in the mainstream of traditional Clare Valley style, with citrus and mineral fruit; needs a few years to open up. Screwcap. 12% alc. **Rating** 89 **To** 2015 $25

The Loquat Tree MGS 2007 In the mainstream of Clare Valley style for this blend (Mourvedre/Grenache/Shiraz), with some varietal confection/Turkish delight characters, partially balanced by fine, savoury tannins. Screwcap. 15% alc. **Rating** 89 **To** 2014 $20

Oak Matured Classic Tawny NV In the strongly fruited Australian tawny style; rich and will be better with more time yet in oak. Cork. 18.5% alc. **Rating** 87 **To** 2010 $15

Sticks   ★★★★☆

179 Glenview Road, Yarra Glen, Vic 3775 **Region** Yarra Valley
T (03) 9730 1022 **F** (03) 9730 1131 **www**.sticks.com.au **Open** 7 days 10–5
Winemaker Rob Dolan, Travis Bush **Est.** 2000 **Cases** 60 000
In 2005 the former Yarra Ridge winery, with a 3000-tonne capacity, and 25 ha of vineyards planted mainly in 1983, was acquired by a partnership headed by Rob 'Sticks' Dolan. The estate production is significantly supplemented by contract-grown grapes sourced elsewhere in the Yarra Valley. He makes all the Sticks wines here, and also provides substantial contract-making facilities for wineries throughout the Yarra Valley. The partnership with Mike Fitzpatrick of Squitchy Lane Vineyard will be part of a new unit of Sticks dedicated to producing small volume, high-quality wines. Exports to the UK, the US and other major markets.

🍷🍷🍷🍷🍷 **No. 29 Yarra Valley Chardonnay 2006** Bright colour; now this is a seriously good wine, with delicious nectarine fruit at its heart, and all the length one expects from the best Yarra Valley chardonnays; the oak is at once important and unimportant. Screwcap. 13.5% alc. **Rating** 96 **To** 2016 $30

🍷🍷🍷🍷🍷 **No. 29 Yarra Valley Pinot Noir 2006** A deliberately restrained and light-bodied style; cherry/strawberry/raspberry fruits are sprinkled with spice, and lengthened by fine tannins. Screwcap. 13.5% alc. **Rating** 92 **To** 2014 $40

No. 29 Yarra Valley Cabernet Sauvignon 2006 The best advice I can give is to buy a bottle; if you like it, buy a dozen or so, but leave the wine alone for at least five years; it has everything, but those tannins have to be tamed by time. Screwcap. 14% alc. **Rating** 92 **To** 2031 $35

Yarra Valley Sauvignon Blanc 2008 A wine that creeps up on you, saving the best for last as the finish surges with passionfruit, lemon and gooseberry flavours. Screwcap. 12% alc. **Rating** 90 **To** 2010 $18

ȚȚȚȚ   **Shiraz Viognier 2008** Good colour; a juicy wine showing just what viognier can achieve, with lift and life to the bundle of fruit flavours. Ready to roll right now.; value plus. Screwcap. 14.5% alc. **Rating** 89 **To** 2012 $14.50
Yarra Valley Pinot Noir 2008 Bright colour; a light spicy/savoury style that needs more mid-palate vinosity. Screwcap. 12.5% alc. **Rating** 88 **To** 2012 $22
Cabernet Merlot Petit Verdot 2006 A medium-bodied but distinctly savoury wine, with briar and black olive notes underpinning the blackcurrant fruit; best at a barbecue, but fairly priced. Screwcap. 13.5% alc. **Rating** 87 **To** 2014 $14.50

🍂 Stomp   ★★★

891 Milbrodale Road, Broke, NSW 2330 (postal) **Region** Lower Hunter Valley
T (02) 6579 1400 **F** (02) 6579 1400 **www**.stompwine.com.au **Open** Not
Winemaker Michael McManus **Est.** 2004 **Cases** 450
After a lifetime in the food and beverage industry, Michael and Meredith McManus have finally made a decisive move to full-time occupation in all aspects of winemaking. They have set up Stomp Winemaking, a contract winemaker designed to keep small and larger parcels of grapes separate through the fermentation and maturation process, thus meeting the needs of boutique wine producers in the Hunter Valley. The addition of their own label, Stomp, is a small but important part of their business, the Chardonnay, Verdelho and Shiraz made from purchased grapes.

ȚȚȚȚ   **Hunter Valley Shiraz 2007** A lively medium-bodied wine with sweet, juicy black cherry fruit, yet which is dry, the oak influence minimal, the tannins fine. Screwcap. 13% alc. **Rating** 89 **To** 2014 $17
Hunter Valley Chardonnay 2007 Full flavoured, but needs more length for higher points. Price ok. Screwcap. 13.5% alc. **Rating** 87 **To** 2011 $15

🍂 Stone Bridge Wines   ★★★★☆

Section 113 Gillentown Road, Clare, SA 5453 **Region** Mount Lofty Ranges Zone
T (08) 8843 4143 **F** (08) 8843 4143 **Open** Thurs–Mon 10–4
Winemaker Craig Thomson **Est.** 2005 **Cases** 2000 **Vyds** 0.5 ha
Stone Bridge Wines started out as a hobby but has turned into a commercial enterprise for its owners, Craig and Lisa Thomson. They say that Craig's 16 years as a baker has assisted in the art of winemaking: 'It's all about the mix'. Their small patch of shiraz provides only a small part of the annual crush; riesling, pinot gris, cabernet sauvignon and malbec are purchased from local growers. The cellar door is a rammed earth and iron building with picturesque surrounds.

ȚȚȚȚȚ   **Clare Valley Shiraz 2006** Dense purple; fills the mouth with flavour, yet is in no way extractive; plum, blackberry and dark chocolate ripple along the palate, the tannins ripe. Bargain basement. Screwcap. 14.5% alc. **Rating** 94 **To** 2018 $18

ȚȚȚȚȚ   **Clare Valley Cabernet Malbec 2005** Good colour; very much in the luscious, faintly chocolatey, fruit spectrum typical of Clare cabernet malbec; has good balance and considerable appeal for an already drinkable medium- to full-bodied wine. Value-plus. Screwcap. 14.8% alc. **Rating** 92 **To** 2015 $18
Clare Valley Riesling 2006 A concise and focused style, the bridge to the future built on its lime/citrus fruit, the first hints of toast starting to appear on the long palate. Screwcap. 12% alc. **Rating** 92 **To** 2020 $20
Clare Valley Riesling 2008 Has an abundance of power and varietal expression to its lime juice palate; sure to repay extended cellaring, but can be drunk right now. Screwcap. 12% alc. **Rating** 91 **To** 2018 $18

Stonehaven

Riddoch Highway, Padthaway, SA 5271 **Region** Padthaway
T (08) 8765 6166 **F** (08) 8765 6177 **www**.stonehavenvineyards.com.au **Open** Not
Winemaker Paul Lapsley **Est.** 1998 **Cases** NFP **Vyds** 400 ha
Stonehaven has fallen victim to the CWA move (in 2008) to aggressively reduce its regional winery and vineyard holdings. The scale of operations at the winery was significantly reduced for the 2009 vintage, and it will cease to be operational thereafter until such time as it is sold. CWA continues to take all but a small part of the grape production from the estate vineyards. Exports to the UK, the US, Canada and Europe.

Stepping Stone Shiraz 2006 Good fruit concentration and shows a slight savoury/mineral quality on the palate; fresh and fine on the finish. Screwcap. 14% alc. **Rating** 87 **To** 2014 $16
Stepping Stone Merlot 2007 A savoury bouquet, with red fruit and a slight green herbal edge; the palate is lively, with some juicy fruit persisting on the finish. Screwcap. 13.3% alc. **Rating** 87 **To** 2012 $16

Stoney Rise

Hendersons Lane, Gravelly Beach, Tas 7276 **Region** Northern Tasmania
T (03) 6394 3678 **F** (03) 6394 3684 **www**.stoneyrise.com **Open** Thurs–Mon 11–5
Winemaker Joe Holyman **Est.** 2000 **Cases** 1500
This is the venture of Joe and Lou Holyman. The Holyman family has been involved in vineyards in Tasmania for 20 years, but Joe's career in the wine industry, first as a sales rep, then as a wine buyer, and more recently working in wineries in NZ, Portugal, France, Mount Benson and Coonawarra, gave him an exceptionally broad-based understanding of wine. In 2004 Joe and Lou purchased the former Rotherhythe vineyard, which had been established in '86 but was in a somewhat rundown state when it was purchased, and set about restoring the vineyard to its former glory, with 3 ha of pinot noir and 1 ha of chardonnay. There are two ranges: the Stoney Rise wines focusing on fruit and early drinkability, the Holyman wines with more structure, more new oak and the best grapes, here the focus on length and potential longevity. The 2006 Pinots had spectacular success at the Tas Wine Show '07. Exports to the UK.

Holyman Pinot Noir 2007 Very good purple-crimson; both bouquet and palate have wonderfully pure pinot fruit expression and admirable line and length, albeit with considerable oak assistance. Screwcap. 14% alc. **Rating** 94 **To** 2016 $45

Tamar Valley Pinot Noir 2007 Very good hue and clarity; the fragrant, although oaky, bouquet has red fruits and a faint touch of mint, the very long palate adding black fruit flavours (dark plum) and some spice. Screwcap. 13.5% alc. **Rating** 91 **To** 2015 $29

Stonier Wines

Cnr Thompson's Lane/Frankston-Flinders Road, Merricks, Vic 3916
Region Mornington Peninsula
T (03) 5989 8300 **F** (03) 5989 8709 **www**.stoniers.com.au **Open** 7 days 11–5
Winemaker Michael Symons **Est.** 1978 **Cases** 25 000
One of the most senior wineries on the Mornington Peninsula, now part of the Petaluma group, which is in turn owned by Lion Nathan of NZ. Wine quality is assured, as is the elegant, restrained style of the Chardonnay and Pinot Noir. In 2008 long-serving winemaker Geraldine McFaul left to take up another position, and it remains to be seen whether the style will change. Replacement winemaker Mike Symons has a track record of nearly 20 years with the Petaluma group, both before and after its acquisition by Lion Nathan. Exports to all major markets.

♔♔♔♔♔ **Mornington Peninsula Pinot Noir 2007** Deeper colour than usual for Stonier, the aromas and flavours likewise stronger and deeper, but without any hint of dead/shrivelled fruit; instead there are delicious cherry and plum flavours running through the long, supple palate. Screwcap. 13% alc. **Rating** 96 **To** 2017 $28
Reserve Mornington Peninsula Pinot Noir 2007 Bright, clear colour; fragrant cherry and plum aromas lead into a finely sculpted wine with bell-clear varietal expression and a faultless structure. Screwcap. 13.5% alc. **Rating** 96 **To** 2014 $50
Reserve Mornington Peninsula Chardonnay 2007 Vibrant hue; a very complex array of aromas, from nectarine and pear, flowing through to lightly toasted cashews; the palate shows great intensity, but is balanced by linear acidity and great drive; the finish is very long, even and fresh, and the wine should age gracefully indeed. Screwcap. 13.5% alc. **Rating** 95 **To** 2016 $42
Windmill Vineyard Pinot Noir 2006 Quite intensely stemmy, with cherry and allspice coming to the fore; the structure is quite serious and the fruit takes a backward step in this regard; firmer than the KBS, the wine is complex and offers a fine sweet spot on the mid-palate; to choose between the two is a matter of personal taste. Screwcap. 13.5% alc. **Rating** 95 **To** 2015 $60
KBS Vineyard Pinot Noir 2006 Quite pale colour; a vibrant array of red fruits from cherry through to plum, and complemented by attractive spice and undergrowth complexity; truly exhibiting a peacock's tail of flavour as the palate builds from light red fruits to a veritable cornucopia of complex flavours, not the least of which is Asian allspice; the structure belies the colour and the flavour is very long indeed. Screwcap. 13% alc. **Rating** 95 **To** 2013 $60

♔♔♔♔♕ **Mornington Peninsula Chardonnay 2007** Vibrant nectarine fruit framed by a delicate seasoning of toasty oak; generously textured, with plenty of ripe fruit, and vibrant acidity framing the wine well; always good value. Screwcap. 14% alc. **Rating** 93 **To** 2014 $25
KBS Vineyard Chardonnay 2006 A complex leesy bouquet; lots of buttered toast and grilled nuts; a vibrant palate, with the structure being the cornerstone of the wine; everything in the winemakers arsenal has been thrown at the KBS, and it is a style that will polarise opinion. Screwcap. 13.5% alc. **Rating** 93 **To** 2014 $60
Mornington Peninsula Pinot Noir Chardonnay 2006 Pale, vibrant hue; attractive lemon biscuit bouquet, with a touch of creamy lees complexity; the palate is tight, fine, linear and just a little chalky; very dry on the finish. Cork. 12.5% alc. **Rating** 93 **To** 2014 $28

Stringy Brae of Sevenhill   ★★★★☆

Sawmill Road, Sevenhill, SA 5453 **Region** Clare Valley
T (08) 8843 4313 **F** (08) 8843 4319 **www.**stringybrae.com.au **Open** By appt
Winemaker O'Leary Walker **Est.** 1991 **Cases** 2000 **Vyds** 5 ha
Donald and Sally Willson began planting their vineyard in 1991, having purchased the property in '83. In 2004 daughter Hannah Rantanen took over day-to-day management. Subsequently, the estate vineyard has been trimmed to 5 ha of cabernet sauvignon, and wine production reduced. On the other side of the equation, shiraz and malbec are purchased from Clare Valley growers. Exports to Canada and Denmark.

♔♔♔♔♕ **Clare Valley Cabernet Shiraz Malbec 2005** Very attractive blend of the three red varieties most suited to the Clare Valley; juicy fruit flavours are complexed by notes of spice and dark chocolate; no more than medium-bodied, but has excellent length and balance. Screwcap. 15% alc. **Rating** 93 **To** 2018 $24
Battle Cry Clare Valley Malbec 2005 A convincing example of Malbec, with its slightly jammy varietal blackberry and prune fruit and its backdrop of savoury spices; little or no tannins, hence its blend with cabernet sauvignon. Screwcap. 15% alc. **Rating** 92 **To** 2015 $50
Clare Valley Shiraz 2005 Deep colour; a muscular, full-bodied red, with blackberry, plum, prune and dark chocolate fruit flavours; the tannins and oak contribution is less than expected. Screwcap. 15% alc. **Rating** 91 **To** 2020 $24

Clare Valley Cabernet Sauvignon 2005 A strong wine, fusing black and red fruits, dark chocolate, mint, tannins and oak in a medium- to full-bodied framework. Will be long lived. Screwcap. 15% alc. **Rating** 90 **To** 2025 $24

Stringybark

2060 Chittering Road, Chittering, WA 6084 **Region** Perth Hills
T (08) 9571 8069 **www.**stringybarkwinery.com.au **Open** Wed–Sat 12–late, Sun 9–8
Winemaker Lilac Hill Estate (Steven Murfitt) **Est.** 1985 **Cases** 420 **Vyds** 2 ha
Bruce and Mary Cussen have a vineyard dating back to 1985, but the development of the cellar door and restaurant complex is far more recent. The vineyard consists of chardonnay (1 ha), verdelho and cabernet sauvignon (0.5 ha each). Impressive contract winemaking makes its mark.

ΨΨΨΨ **Chittering Verdelho 2008** Has good varietal character, if in a restrained, slightly minerally/grainy mode, along with more conventional fruit salad. From 25-year-old vines. Screwcap. 13.5% alc. **Rating** 87 **To** 2012 $22.50

Stuart Wines ★★★★★

105 Killara Road, Gruyere, Vic 3770 (postal) **Region** Yarra Valley
T (03) 5964 9312 **F** (03) 5964 9313 **www.**stuartwinesco.com.au **Open** Not
Winemaker Peter Wilson **Est.** 1999 **Cases** 85 000 **Vyds** 127.4 ha
The Indonesian Widjaja family have major palm oil plantations in Java, with downstream refining. Hendra Widjaja was sent to Australia to establish a vineyard and winery, and he initially chose the Yarra Valley for the first vineyard, thereafter establishing a larger one in Heathcote. The Yarra Valley vineyard is 61.9 ha (pinot noir, shiraz, cabernet sauvignon, merlot, chardonnay, sangiovese, pinot gris, mataro, petit verdot and viognier), the Heathcote vineyard 75.5 ha (shiraz, nebbiolo, tempranillo, merlot, viognier and cabernet sauvignon). Since 2004 all the wines have been made at a new winery at Heathcote. While the major part of the production is exported, there are also direct sales in Australia. Wines are released under the Cahillton, White Box and Buddha's Wine labels; 50¢ per bottle of the proceeds of sales of all of the Buddha's Wine are donated to the Buddha's Global Childrens Fund, www. buddhaswine. com.au. Exports to Germany, The Netherlands, Indonesia, China and NZ.

ΨΨΨΨΨ **Cahillton Deja Vu Heathcote Shiraz 2006** A plum/blackberry and spice bouquet leads into a juicy and highly flavoured palate with an array of fruit and oak flavours, the tannins long and balanced. Screwcap. 14.5% alc. **Rating** 94 **To** 2020 $22.50
White Box Heathcote Shiraz 2006 Deep crimson-purple; has intermingling black cherry, plum, licorice and dark chocolate aromas and flavours; the palate is long, the finish well balanced, the oak subtle. Great value. Screwcap. 14.5% alc. **Rating** 94 **To** 2016 $19.50

ΨΨΨΨΨ **Buddha's Wine Yarra Valley Sangiovese 2006** A light-bodied, delicate style that works well; the pure mix of red cherry and sour cherry fruit is not cluttered by tannins, and the finish is long. Screwcap. 14% alc. **Rating** 90 **To** 2013 $19.50

ΨΨΨΨ **White Box Heathcote Tempranillo 2007** While somewhat savoury and tannic, is far better balanced and less extractive than the Buddha's Wine; spicy plum and berry fruits revealed for all to see. Screwcap. 14.5% alc. **Rating** 87 **To** 2012 $19.50

Studley Park Vineyard

5 Garden Terrace, Kew, Vic 3101 (postal) **Region** Port Phillip Zone
T (03) 9254 2777 **F** (03) 9853 4901 **www.**studleypark.com **Open** Not
Winemaker Llew Knight (Contract) **Est.** 1994 **Cases** 250 **Vyds** 0.5 ha
Geoff Pryor's Studley Park Vineyard is one of Melbourne's best-kept secrets. It is on a bend of the Yarra River barely 4 km from the Melbourne CBD, on a 0.5-ha block once planted to vines, but for a century used for market gardening, then replanted with cabernet sauvignon. A

spectacular aerial photograph shows that immediately across the river, and looking directly to the CBD, is the epicentre of Melbourne's light industrial development, while on the northern and eastern boundaries are suburban residential blocks.

ŶŶŶŶ   Cabernet 2005 Very savoury/earthy/briary style, but does have considerable length and persistence. Screwcap. 14% alc. **Rating** 88 **To** 2015 $25

Stumpy Gully

1247 Stumpy Gully Road, Moorooduc, Vic 3933 **Region** Mornington Peninsula
T (03) 5978 8429 **F** (03) 5978 8419 **www**.stumpygully.com.au **Open** W'ends 11–5
Winemaker Wendy Zantvoort, Frank Zantvoort, Michael Zantvoort **Est.** 1988
Cases 9500 **Vyds** 33 ha
Frank and Wendy Zantvoort began planting their first vineyard in 1988; Wendy, having enrolled in the oenology course at CSU, subsequently graduated with B. App.Sc (Oenology). Together with son Michael, the Zantvoorts look after all aspects of grapegrowing and winemaking. In addition to the original vineyard, they have deliberately gone against prevailing thinking with their Moorooduc vineyard, planting it solely to red varieties, predominately cabernet sauvignon, merlot and shiraz. They believe they have one of the warmest sites on the Peninsula, and that ripening will present no problems. In all they now have 10 varieties planted, producing 18 different wines (Peninsula Panorama is their second label). Exports to all major markets.

ŶŶŶŶŶ   Mornington Peninsula Pinot Grigio 2008 Clean and fresh with pear fruit offset by a touch of nutty complexity; generous on the palate, with good acidity on the finish. Screwcap. 14.1% alc. **Rating** 90 **To** 2012 $22
Mornington Peninsula Pinot Noir 2008 Deeply coloured with a strong spicy element and plenty of sweet plummy fruit; the palate is rich, warm and spicy, and shows depth and adequate structure. Screwcap. 14.3% alc. **Rating** 90 **To** 2012 $25

ŶŶŶŶ   Peninsula Panorama Pinot Noir 2008 Vibrant cherry fruit bouquet; sweet-fruited on the palate, with focus and freshness on the finish. Screwcap. 14.6% alc. **Rating** 87 **To** 2011 $15

Sugarloaf Ridge

336 Sugarloaf Road, Carlton River, Tas 7173 **Region** Southern Tasmania
T (03) 6265 7175 **www**.sugarloafridge.com **Open** Fri–Mon 10–5 Oct–May
Winemaker Winemaking Tasmania (Julian Alcorso) **Est.** 1999 **Cases** 300
Dr Simon Stanley and wife Isobel are both microbiologists, but with thoroughly unlikely specialities: he in low-temperature microbiology, taking him to the Antarctic, and she in a worldwide environmental geosciences company. Sugarloaf Ridge is an extended family business, with daughter Kristen and husband Julian Colville partners. Multiple clones of pinot noir, sauvignon blanc, pinot gris, viognier and lagrein have been planted, and 1580 native trees, 210 olive trees and 270 cherry trees have also helped transform the property.

ŶŶŶŶŶ   Chardonnay 2006 Fruit-driven style with appealing stone fruit and melon aromas and flavours. Gold medal Tas Wine Show '09. **Rating** 93 **To** 2012

ŶŶŶŶ   Sauvignon Blanc 2008 A generous wine, with ample fruit salad flavours and good acidity; perhaps slightly sweet. **Rating** 88 **To** 2010

Summerfield

5967 Stawell-Avoca Road, Moonambel, Vic 3478 **Region** Pyrenees
T (03) 5467 2264 **www**.summerfieldstudioapartments.com **Open** 7 days 9–5
Winemaker Mark Summerfield **Est.** 1979 **Cases** 8000 **Vyds** 13.49 ha
A specialist red wine producer, the particular forté of which is Shiraz. The red wines are consistently excellent: luscious and full-bodied and fruit-driven, but with a slice of vanillin oak to top them off. Founder Ian Summerfield has now handed over the winemaking reins to son Mark, who, with consulting advice, produces consistently outstanding and awesomely

concentrated Shiraz and Cabernet Sauvignon, both in varietal and Reserve forms. The red wines are built for the long haul, and richly repay cellaring. Exports to the US, Canada, Hong Kong and China.

🍷🍷🍷🍷🍷 **Reserve Shiraz 2007** Strong colour; powerful, full-bodied wine, with luscious blackberry fruit at its core, yet with a sheath of more savoury characters surrounding that core; as excellent length and balance, but its best years are a long way distant. Screwcap. 14.4% alc. **Rating** 95 **To** 2027 $55
Shiraz 2007 Right in the mainstream of the big, bold Summerfield style, luscious black fruits intermingling with the savoury notes more evident on the Reserve wine. A very long life ahead. Screwcap. 14.4% alc. **Rating** 94 **To** 2022 $35
Cabernet 2007 One of the best varietal Cabernets from Summerfield, if not the best; has distinct elegance to its symbiotic union of cassis, black fruits and more savoury notes. Screwcap. 13.9% alc. **Rating** 94 **To** 2020 $35
Reserve Cabernet 2007 A deeper and more powerful mode than the varietal, and – if nothing else – needing more time to show its best. Other than that, is a cloned big brother. Screwcap. 13.3% alc. **Rating** 94 **To** 2027 $55

🍷🍷🍷🍷🍷 **Merlot 2007** For all its size, has managed to keep varietal character in the frame, wit touches of savoury black olive and spice to blackcurrant fruit, the tannin likewise controlled. Screwcap. 14.7% alc. **Rating** 92 **To** 2020 $35
Tradition 2007 Generously endowed, but not extractive; the luscious fruits are ripe, the alcohol an inevitable partner, but it works. Screwcap. 14.3% alc. **Rating** 91 **To** 2017 $35

Surveyor's Hill Winery ★★★☆

215 Brooklands Road, Wallaroo, NSW 2618 **Region** Canberra District
T (02) 6230 2046 **www.**survhill.com.au **Open** W'ends & public hols, or by appt
Winemaker Brindabella Hills Winery **Est.** 1986 **Cases** 1000 **Vyds** 10 ha
The Surveyor's Hill vineyard is on the slopes of the eponymous hill, at 550 m–680 m above sea level. It is an ancient volcano, producing granite-derived coarse-structured (and hence well-drained) sandy soils of low fertility. This has to be the ultimate patchwork quilt winery, with 1 ha each of chardonnay, shiraz and viognier; 0.5 ha each of roussanne, marsanne, aglianico, nero d'alpha, mourvedre, grenache, muscadelle, moscato giallo, cabernet franc and riesling; and lesser amounts of semillon, sauvignon blanc, touriga nacional and cabernet sauvignon.

Sutherland Estate ★★★

2010 Melba Highway, Dixons Creek, Vic 3775 **Region** Yarra Valley
T 0402 052 287 **www.**sutherlandestate.com.au **Open** Fri–Sun & public hols 10–5
Winemaker Alex White, Phil Kelly (Contract) **Est.** 2000 **Cases** 1200 **Vyds** 4 ha
Catherine Phelan, her parents Ron and Sheila, and her partner Angus Ridley, purchased an established vineyard in Dixons Creek in 2000. Supplementary plantings included gewurztraminer and tempranillo. Catherine has almost completed the CSU wine science degree, while Angus is at Coldstream Hills, and is the winemaker for the new Tollana Mornington Peninsula Pinot Noir. The cellar door, built by Ron, enjoys one of the best views of the Yarra Valley.

🍷🍷🍷🍷 **Yarra Valley Rose 2008** Very pale salmon; spotlessly clean strawberry and cherry fruit, the subliminal touch of sweetness balanced by a twist of acidity on the finish; 100% estate-grown pinot noir. Screwcap. 12.5% alc. **Rating** 89 **To** 2009 $16
Yarra Valley Pinot Noir Chardonnay 2006 Salmon-bronze; has more aroma and flavour than many; an expressive, spicy bouquet leads into a palate with a mix of strawberry and citrus aromas. Diam. 11% alc. **Rating** 88 **To** 2011 $28

Sutherlands Creek Wines ★★★☆

PO Box 1665, Geelong, Vic 3220 **Region** Geelong
T (03) 5281 1811 **F** (03) 5281 1877 **www.**sutherlandscreek.com **Open** By appt
Winemaker Brett Snelson **Est.** 2000 **Cases** 12 500 **Vyds** 42 ha

The five investor-owners of Sutherlands Creek bring a wide range of international business backgrounds to the venture, spanning the UK, Hong Kong, Asia and Australia. The total investment in the venture was $12 million; there are two separate vineyard properties, together planted to pinot noir, viognier, shiraz, zinfandel, sauvignon blanc, pinot gris and semillon. In addition there is a 2.4-ha planting of 42 varietals, rootstocks and clones at the Russells Bridge Vineyard, including varieties such as gamay, nebbiolo, mourvedre and roussanne. A winery has been built, which will be expanded in the years ahead if the need arises.

ΨΨΨΨΨ **Geelong Shiraz 2006** Plum and bramble with a touch of clove; medium-bodied with fresh acidity, and a plush, quite savoury, character on the finish. Cork. 14.5% alc. **Rating** 90 **To** 2014 $26.95

Sutton Grange Winery ★★★★

Carnochans Road, Sutton Grange, Vic 3448 **Region** Bendigo
T (03) 5474 8277 **www**.suttongrangewines.com **Open** Mon–Fri 9–4, w'ends 11–5
Winemaker Gilles Lapalus **Est.** 1998 **Cases** 4000 **Vyds** 12.5 ha
The 400-ha Sutton Grange property is a thoroughbred stud acquired in 1996 by Peter Sidwell, a Melbourne businessman with horse racing and breeding interests. A lunch visit to the property by long-term friends Alec Epis and Stuart Anderson led to the decision to plant syrah, merlot, cabernet sauvignon, viognier and sangiovese, and to the recruitment of French winemaker Gilles Lapalus, who just happens to be the partner of Stuart's daughter. The winery, built from WA limestone, was completed in 2001. Exports to the UK, Canada, Switzerland and Malaysia.

ΨΨΨΨΨ **Fairbank Fiano 2008** Pale colour; pear, almond and attractive subtle spice; incredibly fresh and vibrant, with the high level of acid sitting well with the tightly wound and savoury character; long, crisp and slightly exotic finish. Screwcap. 13.5% alc. **Rating** 92 **To** 2012 $25
Fairbank Viognier 2008 Vibrant hue; understated power, with spiced apricot and a touch of grapefruit on the bouquet; thickly textured with a savoury mineral core to the fruit; a bit of phenolic grip on the finish, providing contrast to the rich varietal expression. Screwcap. 14% alc. **Rating** 92 **To** 2012 $25
Estate Syrah 2006 Good concentration of dark fruit, with a distinct leathery/savoury edge to the bouquet; the palate is quite firm and dry, with plenty of volume and a hint of bay leaf on the finish. Diam. 13.8% alc. **Rating** 92 **To** 2018 $50
Fairbank Syrah 2006 Redcurrant and bay leaf bouquet, with a nice layer of toasty oak; truly medium-bodied with fine-grained tannin and persistent roast meat character on the finish. Screwcap. 13.5% alc. **Rating** 91 **To** 2016 $25

ΨΨΨΨ **Fairbank Cabernet Sauvignon 2005** Bright colour; cassis and black olive and a well-defined, savoury personality; quite fleshy, but also very firm, with an assertive tannin structure at this point in time. Diam. 13.5% alc. **Rating** 89 **To** 2014 $25
Estate Giove 2006 Bright colour; bit of reduction on opening; cherry and plum bouquet; firm, dry and savoury palate with pronounced acidity; a distinctly European feel to the structure. Sangiovese/Cabernet Sauvignon/Merlot. Diam. 13% alc. **Rating** 89 **To** 2012 $50

Swan Valley Wines ★★★

261 Haddrill Road, Baskerville, WA 6065 **Region** Swan Valley
T (08) 9296 1501 **www**.swanvalleywines.com.au **Open** Fri–Sun & public hols 10–5
Winemaker Rachael Robinson **Est.** 1999 **Cases** 6000
Peter and Paula Hoffman, with sons Paul and Thomas, acquired their 6-ha property in 1989. It had a long history of grapegrowing, and the prior owner had registered the name Swan Valley Wines back in 1983. In 1999 the family built a modern winery to handle the grapes from 5.5 ha of chenin blanc, grenache, semillon, malbec, cabernet sauvignon and shiraz. Exports to the UK and Japan.

♀♀♀♀ **Semillon 2008** Fresh, well-made Semillon with herb, citrus and mineral components running through to the distinctly herbal finish. Screwcap. 12.5% alc. **Rating** 87 **To** 2014 $15
Chenin Blanc 2008 Well made, with as much character as is ever likely from young chenin blanc; tropical fruit salad. Screwcap. 13.4% alc. **Rating** 87 **To** 2011 $15

Swinging Bridge

'Belubula', Fish Fossil Drive, Canowindra, NSW 2804 **Region** Central Ranges Zone
T 0409 246 609 **F** (02) 6344 3232 **www**.swingingbridge.com.au **Open** By appt
Winemaker Tom Ward, Chris Derrez (Contract) **Est.** 1995 **Cases** 800 **Vyds** 77 ha
The Ward (Mark and Anne, Tom and Georgie) and Patten (Michael and Helen) families commenced the development of a large vineyard at Canowindra in 1995. There are 45 ha of chardonnay, 18 ha of shiraz, 8 ha of merlot and 6 ha of cabernet sauvignon; most of the grapes are sold, with small amounts of Shiraz and Chardonnay made under the Swinging Bridge label. The outstanding success Swinging Bridge achieved with its 2007 wines was not a bolt from the blue, its '04 Chardonnay also had major show success. It is obvious the very best grapes are used for the brand, the skilled winemaking of Chris Derrez equally obvious.

♀♀♀♀♀ **Canowindra Chardonnay 2007** A complex bouquet with some Burgundian funk; the palate, too, is complex, with strong barrel ferment inputs, which do not threaten the fruit. Remarkable for the region. Trophy Best Single Vineyard Wine Melbourne Wine Show. Screwcap. 14.5% alc. **Rating** 94 **To** 2012 $18.99

♀♀♀♀♀ **Canowindra Shiraz 2007** Convincing colour; medium-bodied, with a soft entry to the red and black fruits on the palate, firming up on the finish, tannins still to soften. Red Wine of the Year, NSW Wine Awards '08. Screwcap. 14.8% alc. **Rating** 92 **To** 2012 $18.99

Swings & Roundabouts

2807 Caves Road, Yallingup, WA 6232 **Region** Margaret River
T (08) 9756 6640 **F** (08) 9756 6736 **www**.swings.com.au **Open** 7 days 10–5
Winemaker Brian Fletcher **Est.** 2004 **Cases** NFP
The Swings & Roundabouts name comes from the expression used to encapsulate the eternal balancing act between the various aspects of grape and wine production. Swings aims to balance the serious side with a touch of fun. There are now four ranges: Kiss Chasey, Life of Riley, Swings & Roundabouts and the top-shelf Laneway. I am not too sure in which order these events occurred, but previous winemaker Mark Lane left Swings & Roundabouts to come east to Balgownie Estate around the same time as he was made Winestate Winemaker of the Year '08.

♀♀♀♀♀ **Creek View Vineyard Margaret River Shiraz Viognier 2004** A radical label design change usually announces the arrival of a new brand manager; whatever, this elegant wine is maturing slowly but impressively, with a lovely array of spice and pepper supporting the black fruits. Screwcap. 14% alc. **Rating** 93 **To** 2015 $29

♀♀♀♀ **Russo Vineyard Margaret River Nebbiolo Sangiovese 2004** Preordained to be tannic, but in fact the tannins are not over the top, and the cherry/sour cherry flavours come through well in an offhand way. Screwcap. 13.5% alc. **Rating** 88 **To** 2012 $29
Margaret River Sauvignon Blanc Semillon 2008 A pleasant wine, with gentle tropical fruits supported by the structure of the semillon. Screwcap. 12.5% alc. **Rating** 87 **To** 2010 $19

Swooping Magpie

860 Commonage Road, Yallingup, WA 6282 **Region** Margaret River
T 0417 921 003 **F** (08) 9756 6227 **www**.swoopingmagpie.com.au **Open** W'ends &
public hols 11–5, or by appt
Winemaker Mark Standish (Contract) **Est.** 1998 **Cases** 2000 **Vyds** 2.5 ha
Neil and Leann Tuffield have established their vineyard in the hills behind the coastal town of
Yallingup. The name, they say, 'was inspired by a family of magpies who consider the property
part of their territory'. One ha each of semillon and cabernet franc and 0.5 ha of verdelho
is supplemented by purchased sauvignon blanc, chenin blanc, shiraz, cabernet sauvignon and
merlot to produce the wines. Exports to the US.

ＰＰＰＰＰ **Margaret River Sauvignon Blanc Semillon 2008** Elegant and fresh, the two
varieties symbiotically joined with grass and herbs softened and lifted by gentle
tropical notes. Screwcap. 12.2% alc. **Rating** 90 **To** 2011 $17

ＰＰＰＰ **Margaret River Shiraz 2005** A light- to medium-bodied wine, which probably
didn't need 24 months in used French and American oak, more like 15 or so; does
have quite vibrant flavours, but not much depth. Screwcap. 14% alc. **Rating** 89
To 2014 $20

Sylvan Springs

RSD 405 Blythmans Road, McLaren Flat, SA 5171 (postal) **Region** McLaren Vale
T (08) 8383 0500 **F** (08) 8383 0499 **www**.sylvansprings.com.au **Open** Not
Winemaker Brian Light (Consultant) **Est.** 1974 **Cases** 4600 **Vyds** 49.47 ha
The Pridmore family has been involved in grapegrowing and winemaking in McLaren Vale for
four generations, spanning over 100 years. The pioneer was Cyril Pridmore, who established
The Wattles Winery in 1896, and purchased Sylvan Park, one of the original homesteads in the
area, in 1901. The original family land in the township of McLaren Vale was sold in '78, but
not before third-generation Digby Pridmore had established vineyards (in '74) near Blewitt
Springs. When he retired in '90, his son David purchased the 50-ha vineyard (planted to 10
different varieties) and, with sister Sally, began assisting with winemaking in '96. Exports to
the UK, the US and Canada.

ＰＰＰＰ **McLaren Vale Shiraz 2007** A medium-bodied wine, with regional black
fruits and dark chocolate, with a savoury, although slightly short, finish. Screwcap.
14.5% alc. **Rating** 87 **To** 2016 $18

Symphonia Wines

1019 Snow Road, Oxley, Vic 3678 **Region** King Valley
T (03) 5727 3888 **F** (03) 5727 3853 **www**.sammiranda.com.au **Open** At Sam Miranda
Winemaker Sam Miranda **Est.** 1998 **Cases** 3000 **Vyds** 15 ha
Peter Read and his family were veterans of the King Valley, commencing the development
of their vineyard in 1981 to supply Brown Brothers. As a result of extensive trips to both
Western and Eastern Europe, Peter embarked on an ambitious project to trial a series of grape
varieties little known in this country. The process of evaluation and experimentation produced
a number of wines of great interest and no less merit. In 2005 Rachel Miranda (wife of Sam
Miranda), with parents Peter and Suzanne Evans, purchased the business, and keeps its identity
intact and separate from the Sam Miranda brand. Exports to China.

ＰＰＰＰＰ **Quintus King Valley Saperavi Tempranillo Tannat Merlot Cabernet
2006** Has an element of Bill Clinton's 'because I can', but the outcome is far
more successful, with a velvety mix of black fruits, licorice, plum, prune and spice.
Screwcap. 14.5% alc. **Rating** 92 **To** 2015 $40
King Valley Riesling 2006 Some unusual spicy ginger nuances to the bouquet,
the palate dry and crisp, with good length, the ginger not reappearing. Screwcap.
12.5% alc. **Rating** 90 **To** 2014 $20

King Valley Petit Manseng 2008 A candidate, in this vintage at least, for the most character; some Japanese pickled vegetable flavours are one stream, the piercing dry finish another. Points for distinctiveness. Screwcap. 13.5% alc. Rating 90 To 2011 $20

ŶŶŶŶ **King Valley Pinot Grigio 2008** A fresh and pleasingly savoury style, with a touch of herb along with apple and pear; bone dry finish. Screwcap. 12.5% alc. Rating 89 To 2011 $20

King Valley Arneis 2008 A vibrant and brisk palate has good length, the flavours oscillating and hard to pin down. Screwcap. 13% alc. Rating 89 To 2011 $20

King Valley Albarino 2008 Offers more flavour impact on the fore-palate than most other alternative white varieties in a zesty lemon and green apple spectrum. Screwcap. 12.5% alc. Rating 89 To 2011 $20

King Valley Tannat 2006 The legendary, fearsome tannins are in fact not fearsome in this wine, rather defining its character and framing the black fruits of the mid-palate. Screwcap. 14.5% alc. Rating 89 To 2014 $24

King Valley Rosata Tempranillo 2008 Pale crimson; fragrant and aromatic, but well and truly off-dry. Screwcap. 12.8% alc. Rating 87 To 2010 $20

Symphony Hill Wines ★★★★☆

2017 Eukey Road, Ballandean, Qld 4382 **Region** Granite Belt
T (07) 4684 1388 **F** (07) 4684 1399 **www.**symphonyhill.com.au **Open** 7 days 10–4
Winemaker Mike Hayes **Est.** 1999 **Cases** 6000 **Vyds** 14 ha
Ewen and Elissa Macpherson purchased what was then an old table grape and orchard property in 1996. In partnership with Ewen's parents, Bob and Jill Macpherson, they developed 4 ha of vineyards, while Ewen completed his Bachelor of Applied Science in viticulture (2003). The vineyard (now much expanded) has been established using state-of-the-art technology; vineyard manager and winemaker Mike Hayes has a degree in viticulture and is a third-generation viticulturist in the Granite Belt region. It is planted to verdelho, viognier, pinot noir, shiraz, cabernet sauvignon, chardonnay, sauvignon blanc and pinot gris. Symphony Hill has firmly established its reputation as one of the Granite Belt's foremost wineries. Exports to Singapore and China.

ŶŶŶŶŶ **Family Reserve Snowvember Release Cabernet Sauvignon 2007** Deep colour; a strongly structured medium- to full-bodied wine with blackcurrant, dark chocolate and hints of cassis supported by firm tannins and quality oak; 65 cases made. Screwcap. 15% alc. Rating 94 To 2027 $65

ŶŶŶŶŶ **Reserve Merlot 2007** Strong colour; an altogether serious merlot, with cassis and blackcurrant fruit on a firm, long, medium- to full-bodied palate. Screwcap. 14% alc. Rating 93 To 2020 $45

Reserve Sauvignon Blanc 2008 Clean, crisp herb, grass and citrus aromas come through strongly on the palate, which has good energy and length. Screwcap. 11.5% alc. Rating 90 To 2010 $25

Shiraz 2007 Light, bright purple; plum and a host of spices spring from the bouquet and equally strongly from the light- to medium-bodied palate; unusual but attractive wine, best enjoyed soon. Screwcap. 14.3% alc. Rating 90 To 2013 $25

Reserve Cabernet Sauvignon 2007 Crimson-red; an elegant wine with bright aromas and flavours of cassis and black fruits neatly girdled by mocha oak, and supported by fine, satiny tannins. Screwcap. 14.8% alc. Rating 90 To 2017 $45

ŶŶŶŶ **Pinot Gris 2008** Clean and fresh, with an array of subtly intermingling fruit aromas and flavours; apple, pear, stone fruit – take your pick. Screwcap. 13.5% alc. Rating 89 To 2011 $30

Wild Child Viognier 2008 Like the Verdelho, has good texture and structure, and does have some varietal apricot flavours along with good balance and mouthfeel. Screwcap. 13.6% alc. Rating 89 To 2011 $45

Reserve Petit Verdot 2007 Typical deep colour; abundant ripe black fruits and equally abundant soft tannins and oak; flavour rather than finesse, usually the case with petit verdot. Screwcap. 15% alc. **Rating** 89 **To** 2014 $45

Reserve Verdelho 2008 Has more structure than some, with tropical fruit offset by minerally acidity. Screwcap. 13.8% alc. **Rating** 87 **To** 2011 $25

Family Reserve Pinot Noir 2007 Very good colour; well made and balanced, but is definitely in dry red territory, varietal expression all but absent. Screwcap. 14.3% alc. **Rating** 87 **To** 2013 $65

Granite Belt Cabernet Sauvignon 2007 Savoury/briary/earthy elements are varietal, but the wine needs more blackcurrant fruit to provide balance; a long way from the '06. Screwcap. 15% alc. **Rating** 87 **To** 2013 $25

Syrahmi   ★★★★☆

PO Box 438, Heathcote, Vic 3523 **Region** Heathcote
T 0407 057 471 **Open** Not
Winemaker Adam Foster **Est.** 2004 **Cases** 750
Adam Foster worked as a chef in Vic and London before moving to the front of house and becoming increasingly interested in wine. He then worked as a cellar hand with a who's who from Australia and France, including Torbreck, Chapoutier, Mitchelton, Domaine Ogier, Heathcote Winery, Jasper Hill and Domaine Pierre Gaillard. He became convinced that the Cambrian soils of Heathcote could produce the best possible Shiraz, and since 2004 has purchased grapes from the region, using the full bag of open ferment techniques with 30% whole bunches, extended cold soak, wild yeast and mlf and hand plunging, then 13 months in French oak. Bottled unfined and unfiltered. Exports to the US.

ŸŸŸŸŸ **La La Shiraz Viognier 2006** Bright colour; highly perfumed and attractive bouquet, showing redcurrant, Asian spices and French oak; the palate is silky, with ample fine-grained tannins; the oak dominates the finish, but should integrate well with time. Screwcap. 14% alc. **Rating** 94 **To** 2015 $90

T'Gallant   ★★★★

1385 Mornington-Flinders Road, Main Ridge, Vic 3928 **Region** Mornington Peninsula
T (03) 5989 6565 **F** (03) 5989 6577 **www**.tgallant.com.au **Open** 7 days 10–5
Winemaker Kevin McCarthy **Est.** 1990 **Cases** 40 000
Husband-and-wife consultant winemakers Kevin McCarthy and Kathleen Quealy carved out such an important niche market for the T'Gallant label that in 2003, after protracted negotiations, it was acquired by Beringer Blass. The acquisition of a 15-ha property, and the planting of 10 ha of pinot gris gives the business a firm geographic base, as well as providing increased resources for its signature wine. La Baracca Trattoria is open 7 days for lunch and for specially booked evening events.

ŸŸŸŸ̦ **Imogen Pinot Gris 2008** Has plenty of flavour and mouthfeel, the flavours correct, as is the structure, but would be better still with a touch more acidity. Screwcap. 14.5% alc. **Rating** 90 **To** 2011 $23.99

Volante 2008 Has considerable thrust and length to the apple and citrus palate; bone dry finish. Obvious food style. Screwcap. 13% alc. **Rating** 90 **To** 2012 $23.99

Cyrano Pinot Noir 2006 Elegant light-bodied style, with a mix of berry fruits and distinct savoury/stemmy/foresty notes on the back-palate and finish. Screwcap. 14% alc. **Rating** 90 **To** 2011 $24.99

ŸŸŸŸ **Volante 2006** Pale straw-green; fresh, bright apple, pear and citrus fruit running through a lively light- to medium-bodied palate finishing with crisp acidity. Screwcap. 14% alc. **Rating** 89 **To** 2012 $21.99

Tribute Mornington Peninsula Pinot Noir 2006 Has abundant flavour in a dark berry spectrum, but is flawed by excess and faintly green tannins. Screwcap. 13.5% alc. **Rating** 89 **To** 2011 $32.99

Grace Pinot Grigio 2008 Has some citrus edges to the more conventional pear and apple flavours; has good length. Screwcap. 12.5% alc. **Rating** 87 **To** 2010 $23.99

Grace Pinot Grigio 2007 Good structure, but the flavours don't sing or excite, simply in the mainstream dry style. Screwcap. 12.5% alc. **Rating** 87 **To** 2009 $21.99
Juliet Moscato 2008 Vibrantly juicy grapey flavours, with a citrus twang to enliven the finish. Screwcap. 6% alc. **Rating** 87 **To** 2009 $19.99

Taemas Wines ★★★

121 Magennis Drive, Murrumbateman, NSW 2582 **Region** Canberra District
T (02) 6227 0346 **F** (02) 6227 0346 **www.**taemaswines.com.au **Open** By appt
Winemaker Dr Brian Johnston **Est.** 1997 **Cases** 300 **Vyds** 4 ha
Taemas is situated 15 km southwest of Murrumbateman and roughly 10 km north of the ACT, in a topographical area of the same name bestowed by Hume and Hovell when they passed through the district in the early 1820s; it is believed to be an old variation of the word Thames. Owners Peter McPherson and Peter Wheeler began planting the vineyard in 1997, and over eight years established 1 ha each of shiraz and cabernet sauvignon, adding 0.6 ha each of merlot, pinot noir (clone MV6) and shiraz in '99 and '00, finishing with 0.1 ha each of viognier and pinot noir (clone 777), the last planted in '05. Interestingly, the 150 vines of viognier were sourced from Yarra Yering, a different clone to that of Yalumba. The 2007 vintage was destroyed by frost; the '08 vintage has produced four barriques each of Pinot Noir, Merlot and Shiraz Viognier, with release due in the second half of '09.

ŸŸŸŸ **Canberra District Shiraz 2006** A cool and savoury style, with pepper and game showing through the red and dark fruits; quite fine and abundant tannins, with vibrant, fresh and cool acidity. Screwcap. 14% alc. **Rating** 88 **To** 2014 $20
Canberra District Pinot Noir 2005 A cool and elegant style; gently spicy, cherry fruit and lively acidity on the finish. Screwcap. 13% alc. **Rating** 87 **To** 2012 $40
Limited Release Canberra District Shiraz Viognier 2006 Quite reductive, with a strong, savoury/leather and earth character; the palate is quite firm and dry, with red fruits coming to the fore on the finish. Screwcap. 14% alc. **Rating** 87 **To** 2014 $37

Tahbilk ★★★★★

Goulburn Valley Highway, Tabilk, Vic 3608 **Region** Nagambie Lakes
T (03) 5794 2555 **www.**tahbilk.com.au **Open** Mon–Sat 9–5, Sun 11–5
Winemaker Alister Purbrick, Neil Larson, Alan George **Est.** 1860 **Cases** 120 000
Vyds 222 ha
A winery steeped in tradition (with National Trust classification), which should be visited at least once by every wine-conscious Australian, and which makes wines – particularly red wines – utterly in keeping with that tradition. The essence of that heritage comes in the form of the tiny quantities of Shiraz made entirely from vines planted in 1860. In 2005 Tahbilk opened its wetlands project, with a series of walks connected (if you wish) by short journeys on a small punt. Exports to all major markets.

ŸŸŸŸŸ **1860 Vines Shiraz 2003** A lovely, bright and vibrant wine, that is multi-faceted with a strong mineral core adding to the wine's overall complexity and appeal. Cork. 13.5% alc. **Rating** 94 **To** 2018 $135
Eric Stevens Purbrick Shiraz 2003 Excellent hue; a powerful wine, built to last, with fruit and tannins jousting for space, neither subduing the other; scores for its considerable length and refreshingly low alcohol. Cork. 13% alc. **Rating** 94 **To** 2018 $70

ŸŸŸŸŸ **Shiraz 2005** Bright red-crimson; a full-flavoured but elegant wine, with an abundance of black cherry and blackberry fruit; best for many years; extract perfectly managed. Screwcap. 14.5% alc. **Rating** 93 **To** 2020 $19.75
Marsanne 2008 A quite backward bouquet with honeysuckle and apple in evidence; tightly wound, yet quite generous on the palate, with a fine line of minerality following through to the conclusion. Screwcap. 12.5% alc. **Rating** 91 **To** 2015 $14.95

Eric Stevens Purbrick Cabernet Sauvignon 2003 A condensed, powerful, introspective array of black fruits on the full-bodied palate is accompanied by persistent tannins, which are a little dry. Cork. 14% alc. **Rating** 91 **To** 2020 $70
Cabernet Sauvignon 2005 Dark berry fruit bouquet with hints of leather and earth; quite generous and deep-fruited on the palate, fine-grained tannins and a very long and even finish. Screwcap. 14.5% alc. **Rating** 90 **To** 2015 $19.75

ŸŸŸŸ **Riesling 2008** Generously flavoured wine, with a mix of citrus and tropical fruits; somewhat soft overall. Screwcap. 12.5% alc. **Rating** 87 **To** 2012 $18

Tait   ★★★☆

Yaldara Drive, Lyndoch, SA 5351 **Region** Barossa Valley
T (08) 8524 5000 **F** (08) 8524 5220 **www**.taitwines.com.au **Open** By appt
Winemaker Bruno Tait **Est.** 1994 **Cases** 11 000 **Vyds** 5 ha
The Tait family has been involved in the wine industry in the Barossa for over 100 years, making not wine but barrels. Their more recent venture into winemaking was immediately successful. Their estate vineyards (3 ha of shiraz and 2 ha of 80-year-old cabernet sauvignon) is supplemented by contract-grown grapes. Winemaker Bruno Tait works with wife Michelle and brother Michael looking after various facets of the business. Exports to the US, Canada, Israel and Singapore.

ŸŸŸŸŸ **Basket Pressed Barossa Valley Shiraz 2006** Deep colour; the wine has everything in equal proportions: colour, fruit, tannins, oak and alcohol; for those who can live with the alcohol, a knockout wine. Screwcap. 16.2% alc. **Rating** 90 **To** 2026 $40

ŸŸŸŸ **Basket Pressed Barossa Valley Shiraz 2005** Full-bodied wine, the alcohol here even more evident than in the '06; there is no doubting its flavour or character, but it's not my style, period fullstop. Screwcap. 16% alc. **Rating** 89 **To** 2020 $40
The Ball Buster 2007 Curiously named, for the alcohol (on numbers) is lower than the other wines; however, in the mouth the wine lets the secret out that it is well named. Screwcap. 15.5% alc. **Rating** 88 **To** 2017 $23

Tallavera Grove Vineyard & Winery   ★★★★

749 Mount View Road, Mount View, NSW 2325 **Region** Lower Hunter Valley
T (02) 4990 7535 **www**.tallaveragrove.com.au **Open** Thurs–Mon 10–5
Winemaker Luke Watson **Est.** 2000 **Cases** 2500 **Vyds** 40 ha
Tallavera Grove is one of the many wine interests of John Davis and family. The family is a 50% owner of Briar Ridge, a 12-ha vineyard in Coonawarra, a 100-ha vineyard at Wrattonbully (Stonefields Vineyard) and a 36-ha vineyard at Orange (Jokers Peak). The 40-ha Hunter Valley vineyards are planted to chardonnay, shiraz, semillon, verdelho, cabernet sauvignon and viognier. The Mount View winery will eventually be equipped to handle 200–300 tonnes of fruit.

ŸŸŸŸŸ **Hunter Valley Shiraz 2007** Strong crimson-purple; an intense, medium-bodied wine with a panoply of black fruits interwoven with leather and oak, Hunter earth in the background. Well made. Screwcap. 14.5% alc. **Rating** 91 **To** 2020 $22
Hunter Valley Verdelho 2008 Well above average richness and intensity to the fruit salad flavours, which swell on the mid- to back-palate; a verdelho with attitude. Screwcap. 13% alc. **Rating** 90 **To** 2012 $18

ŸŸŸŸ **Two in the Bush Hunter Valley Semillon Verdelho 2008** The semillon has the upper hand, with intense citrus and mineral notes, but there is synergy to the blend; the wine will assuredly develop well. Screwcap. 11.5% alc. **Rating** 89 **To** 2013 $16
Jokers Peak Orange Sauvignon Blanc 2008 Hyper-tangy and incisive green apple, citrus and asparagus flavours on a long, lingering finish and aftertaste. Screwcap. 13% alc. **Rating** 88 **To** 2010 $18

Jokers Peak Orange Chardonnay 2008 Has a little more weight and complexity than the Hunter Valley Chardonnay, but a similar structure and focus; short-term development. Screwcap. 13.5% alc. **Rating** 88 **To** 2014 $20
Hunter Valley Chardonnay 2008 Crisp, lively and citrussy, with a suitably restrained touch of oak; has considerable length thanks to acidity, whether natural or adjusted. Screwcap. 13% alc. **Rating** 87 **To** 2013 $20

Tallis Wine   ★★★☆

PO Box 10, Dookie, Vic 3646 **Region** Central Victoria Zone
T (03) 5823 5383 **F** (03) 5828 6532 **www**.talliswine.com.au **Open** Not
Winemaker Richard Tallis, Gary Baldwin (Consultant) **Est.** 2000 **Cases** 2000 **Vyds** 24 ha
Richard and Alice Tallis have 14 ha of shiraz, 5 ha of cabernet sauvignon, 2 ha of viognier and a small planting of sangiovese and merlot. While most of the grapes are sold, they have embarked on winemaking with the aid of Gary Baldwin, and have had considerable success. The philosophy of their winemaking and viticulture is minimal intervention to create a low-input and sustainable system; use of environmentally harmful sprays is minimised. The searing heat in January 2009 resulted in the destruction of 80% of the crop, and the hand-picking and selection of the remainder. It was a scenario repeated in various parts of South Eastern Australia, as far south as the Yarra Valley.

♀♀♀♀♀ **Dookie Hills Shiraz 2005** Spice and sweet leather aromas lead into a medium-bodied palate of red and black fruits supported by spicy tannins and oak. Screwcap. 13% alc. **Rating** 90 **To** 2013 $18

♀♀♀♀ **Dookie Hills Viognier 2007** Solid, ripe varietal expression in a peachy spectrum, nicely offset by acidity. Screwcap. 14% alc. **Rating** 89 **To** 2012 $18
The Silent Showman Shiraz Viognier 2005 Developed colour; has distinct spicy/savoury characters outside the norm for this blend, but has considerable length and persistence. Screwcap. 14% alc. **Rating** 89 **To** 2015 $25

Taltarni   ★★★★☆

339 Taltarni Road, Moonambel, Vic 3478 **Region** Pyrenees
T (03) 5459 7900 **F** (03) 5467 2306 **www**.taltarni.com.au **Open** 7 days 10–5
Winemaker Loïc Le Calvez **Est.** 1972 **Cases** 80 000 **Vyds** 139 ha
Taltarni continues to be a major player in the context of Victoria, but given the age and size of its vineyards, and apart from occasional bursts of activity, it seems unable to maintain its momentum and to consistently realise its full potential. Exports to all major markets.

♀♀♀♀♀ **Reserve Pyrenees Shiraz Cabernet 2004** A concentrated, full-bodied wine with an array of blackberry, mocha, vanilla and Central Victorian mint aromas and flavours; has good tannin support for the long haul, the long but thoroughly wine-stained cork not so. 14% alc. **Rating** 94 **To** 2014 $65

♀♀♀♀♀ **Estate Pyrenees Cabernet Sauvignon 2006** Deep colour; very powerful in every way, blackcurrant fruit and obvious French on bouquet and palate alike; on the back-palate and finish earthy tannins take hold; it is uncertain whether they will soften before the fruit fades; given the benefit of the doubt. Cork. 14% alc. **Rating** 90 **To** 2020 $32

Tamar Ridge   ★★★★★

Auburn Road, Kayena, Tas 7270 **Region** Northern Tasmania
T (03) 6394 1111 **F** (03) 6394 1126 **www**.tamarridge.com.au **Open** 7 days 10–5
Winemaker Andrew Pirie, Tom Ravech, Matt Lowe **Est.** 1994 **Cases** 80 000 **Vyds** 137 ha
Gunns Limited, of pulp mill fame, purchased Tamar Ridge in 2003. With the retention of Dr Richard Smart as viticultural advisor, the largest expansion of Tasmanian plantings is now underway, with several vineyards in the vicinity of the winery. Richard Smart has constructed a micro-vinification winery, with $1.9 million (including a Federal grant of $900 000) as

funding to employ a number of doctor of philosophy students. Their subjects are varied, ranging from clonal trials to canopy trials. A further development at Coombend, on the east coast, is also underway. Dr Andrew Pirie is CEO and chief winemaker, adding further lustre to the brand. Exports to the UK, the US and other major markets.

ΨΨΨΨΨ **Kayena Vineyard Pinot Noir 2007** Clear, bright crimson hue; precisely calibrated fruit on both bouquet and palate, with damson plum and cherry flavours; fine, silky palate with a long finish. Screwcap. 14% alc. **Rating** 95 **To** 2013 $29.70
Research Series 83-1 Viognier 2007 The first viognier from Tasmania, and promises much; the varietal fruit is present, but the palate has the vibrancy and thrust lacking from so many viogniers. This is quite something. Screwcap. 14.5% alc. **Rating** 94 **To** 2012 $28.30
Research Series 81-1 Albarino 2007 Yet another first, and yet another wine full of promise. Like the viognier, bright, light, straw-green in colour, the palate with exceptional velocity to the citrus spice and pear fruit. Screwcap. 13% alc. **Rating** 94 **To** 2013 $28.30

ΨΨΨΨΨ **Kayena Vineyard Riesling 2007** A clean and vibrant bouquet, the palate featuring precise, highly focused citrus fruit and typical Tasmanian acidity. Will develop very well. Screwcap. 12.5% alc. **Rating** 93 **To** 2015 $22.10
Devil's Corner Chardonnay 2008 Pale colour; a focused citrus fruit bouquet with a little mineral complexity; nectarine and lemon combine on the palate, with generous weight and texture; a fresh and focused finish. Screwcap. 13% alc. **Rating** 93 **To** 2013 $18
Limited Release Kayena Reserve Pinot Noir 2006 The bouquet has restrained power, showing red and dark fruits, spice and a touch of forest floor; quite rich on the palate, with darker fruit to the fore and a bit of muscle entering the equation; firm and long. Screwcap. 14% alc. **Rating** 93 **To** 2014 $50
Limited Release Kayena Reserve Botrytis Riesling 2006 Bright pale gold; plenty of botrytis with candied orange and a touch of spiced apricot complexity; the palate is very sweet, has good acidity, and nice drive and line, providing focus and energy for the sugar. Screwcap. 7.5% alc. **Rating** 93 **To** 2014 $39
Devil's Corner Riesling 2008 A lifted, exotic bouquet with lime and tropical fruit; the palate is generous and rich with an abundance of sweet fruit coming through on the finish. Screwcap. 12% alc. **Rating** 91 **To** 2014 $18

ΨΨΨΨ **Devil's Corner Pinot Noir 2008** Bright crimson; clear-cut varietal fruit in a plum spectrum, but with some green leaf/stem notes that detract. Screwcap. 13.5% alc. **Rating** 89 **To** 2012 $18.90
Research Series 74-1 Gewurztraminer 2007 Nicely balanced and textured, but – despite clonal selection and appropriate alcohol – has little or no varietal expression. Curious to say the least. Screwcap. 14% alc. **Rating** 88 **To** 2012 $28.30
Kayena Vineyard Gewurztraminer 2007 Not particularly varietal, but does have weight to the fruit, and good balance; may well develop more varietal character over the next few years. Screwcap. 14% alc. **Rating** 88 **To** 2013 $22
Devil's Corner Sauvignon Blanc 2008 Offers a mix of herbal/grassy characters with more tropical fruit; shortens slightly on the finish. Screwcap. 13.5% alc. **Rating** 88 **To** 2010 $18.90

Tamburlaine ★★★★★

358 McDonalds Road, Pokolbin, NSW 2321 **Region** Lower Hunter Valley
T (02) 4998 7570 **F** (02) 4998 7763 **www**.mywinery.com **Open** 7 days 9.30–5
Winemaker Mark Davidson, Simon McMillan, Patrick Moore **Est.** 1966 **Cases** 80 000
A thriving business that sells over 90% of its wine through the cellar door and by mailing list (with an active tasting club members' cellar program offering wines held and matured at Tamburlaine). The maturing of the estate-owned Orange vineyard has led to a dramatic rise in quality across the range. Both the Hunter Valley and Orange vineyards are now Australian Certified Organic. Exports to the UK, the US, Sweden, Denmark, Japan, China and Nepal.

ŸŸŸŸŸ **Members Reserve Hunter Semillon 2008** Has classic length and structure, which guarantees the long-term future; worth the investment, although the lemony fruit does encourage early drinking. Screwcap. 10.5% alc. **Rating** 94 **To** 2018 $28

ŸŸŸŸ♀ **Reserve Orange Syrah 2007** A classic case of the alcohol figure being misleading; the wine is in the spicy/savoury spectrum, with no dead or confit fruit characters, and considerable length. Screwcap. 15.4% alc. **Rating** 93 **To** 2017 $40
Reserve Orange Merlot 2007 Good colour; a vibrant wine, with tangy red fruit flavours that utterly belie the alcohol; good tannin and oak support adds to the appeal. Screwcap. 15.2% alc. **Rating** 93 **To** 2015 $32
Reserve Hunter Valley Merlot Cabernet 2007 Has excellent fruit definition thanks to the vintage rather than the region; cassis and blackcurrant with ripe tannins and good oak. Screwcap. 12.9% alc. **Rating** 93 **To** 2020 $32
Members Reserve Orange Sauvignon Blanc 2008 Has well above average texture and structure with a harmonious, if slightly unusual, fusion of passionfruit and Granny Smith apple flavours. Screwcap. 12.6% alc. **Rating** 92 **To** 2011 $28
Members Reserve Hunter Verdelho 2008 Has an appealing, tangy bouquet, the citrus hinted at appearing positively on the long palate; will flourish with a couple of years in bottle. Screwcap. 13.6% alc. **Rating** 92 **To** 2013 $28

ŸŸŸŸ **Members Reserve Orange Riesling 2008** Has plenty of varietal presence on both bouquet and palate, with a mix of citrus and tropical flavours; just a fraction heavy, perhaps. Screwcap. 12.3% alc. **Rating** 89 **To** 2014 $28
Reserve Hunter Chardonnay 2008 Despite the moderate alcohol, the fruit flavours are at the tropical end of the spectrum, creamy vanilla notes adding to the impact. Screwcap. 12.8% alc. **Rating** 89 **To** 2013 $28
Reserve Orange Chardonnay 2008 The green–gold colour suggests some skin contact prior to fermentation, and the flavour of the wine likewise, bolstered by quite prominent oak. Screwcap. 12.5% alc. **Rating** 89 **To** 2014 $28
Reserve Hunter Valley Syrah 2007 Bright, but light, hue; savoury/earthy/leathery nuances are regional, but the wine needs more conviction to the back-palate and finish. Screwcap. 14.4% alc. **Rating** 89 **To** 2015 $40
Reserve Orange Cabernet Sauvignon 2007 Slightly minty/leafy/savoury nuances are as persistent as they are unexpected; not easy to guess where this will head. Screwcap. 14.4% alc. **Rating** 87 **To** 2017 $32

Taminick Cellars ★★★★☆

339 Booth Road, Taminick via Glenrowan, Vic 3675 **Region** Glenrowan
T (03) 5766 2282 **www.**taminickcellars.com.au **Open** Mon–Sat 9–5, Sun 10–5
Winemaker James Booth **Est.** 1904 **Cases** 4000 **Vyds** 19.7 ha
Peter Booth is a third-generation member of the Booth family, who have owned this winery since Esca Booth purchased the property in 1904. James Booth, fourth-generation and current winemaker, completed his wine science degree at CSU in 2008. The red wines are massively flavoured and very long lived, notably from the 9 ha of shiraz planted in 1919. Trebbiano and alicante bouchet were also planted in 1919, with much newer arrivals including nero d'Avola. The wines are sold through the cellar door, mail order and a selection of independent retailers in Melbourne and Sydney.

ŸŸŸŸŸ **Generations IV Shiraz 2006** Bright, but relatively light, hue; a deliciously, and surprisingly, light- to medium-bodied fresh wine that could have been grown in a cool climate; in fact from 86-year-old estate vines, open-fermented and matured in used French oak; skilled and sensitive winemaking. Screwcap. 14.1% alc. **Rating** 94 **To** 2021 $20

ŸŸŸŸ♀ **Special Release Cabernet Sauvignon 2006** A luscious and rich cabernet, infinitely better than the standard release; ripe but not jammy, with French oak adding a further flavour dimension. Cork. 14.2% alc. **Rating** 90 **To** 2016 $18

♥♥♥♥   **Premium Shiraz 2006** A richer, riper and much warmer full-bodied wine than Generations, looking back where Generations looks forward, but there is nothing wrong with respecting traditional regional medium- to full-bodied styles. Has all the flavour one could wish for. Cork. 14.5% alc. **Rating** 89 **To** 2016 $18
Merlot 2007 As with the Shiraz, astute winemaking has given the wine elegance, freshness and more varietal character than a region such as this should produce; ready to enjoy right now. Screwcap. 13.5% alc. **Rating** 89 **To** 2013 $15
Liqueur Muscat NV Extremely rich, full-on muscat, with masses of raisin fruit; bargain, but would have been something else if left in barrel for another 10+ years. Screwcap. 18.2% alc. **Rating** 87 **To** 2010 $15

Tanjil Wines   ★★★

1171 Moe Road, Willow Grove, Vic 3825 (postal) **Region** Gippsland
T 0409 773 037 **F** (03) 9773 0378 **www**.tanjilwines.com **Open** Not
Winemaker Robert Hewet, Olga Garot **Est.** 2001 **Cases** 1000 **Vyds** 3 ha
Robert Hewet and Olga Garot have planted pinot noir, pinot grigio and albarino on a north-facing slope at an altitude of 200 m between the Latrobe and Tanjil valleys. The cool climate allows the vines to grow without irrigation, yields are kept low and the wines are made onsite using traditional methods and minimal intervention. The modest prices do not reflect the quality of the wines. Exports to the US.

♥♥♥♥   **Gippsland Pinot Noir 2008** A deep bouquet of red fruits and spice; good concentration, but just a little short. Screwcap. 13.8% alc. **Rating** 87 **To** 2011 $18

Tapanappa   ★★★★★

PO Box 174, Crafers, SA 5152 **Region** South Australia
T 0419 843 751 **F** (08) 8370 8374 **www**.tapanappawines.com.au **Open** Not
Winemaker Brian Croser **Est.** 2002 **Cases** 3250 **Vyds** 16 ha
The Tapanappa partners are Brian Croser (formerly of Petaluma), Jean-Michel Cazes of Chateau Lynch-Bages in Pauillac and Société Jacques Bollinger, the parent company of Champagne Bollinger. The partnership has three vineyard sites in Australia: the 8-ha Whalebone Vineyard at Wrattonbully (planted to cabernet sauvignon, shiraz and merlot 30 years ago), the 4 ha of Tiers Vineyard (chardonnay) at Piccadilly in the Adelaide Hills (the remainder of the Tiers Vineyard chardonnay continues to be sold to Petaluma) and, the most recent, the 4-ha Foggy Hill Vineyard on the southern tip of the Fleurieu Peninsula (pinot noir). Exports to all major markets.

♥♥♥♥♥   **Tiers Vineyard Piccadilly Valley Chardonnay 2007** Bright pale green-straw; as expected, an immaculately proportioned and balanced wine with great drive and impeccable line; all the vineyard and winemaker inputs are seamlessly welded, making flavour descriptors unnecessary. Cork. 13.5% alc. **Rating** 96 **To** 2013 $75
Whalebone Vineyard Wrattonbully Merlot 2005 Perfectly ripened fruit highlights the deficiencies of the majority of Australian Merlots; bright small red berry fruits, a faint nuance of snow pea and fine, persistent, ripe tannins. Cork. 14% alc. **Rating** 95 **To** 2015 $75

Tapestry   ★★★★☆

Olivers Road, McLaren Vale, SA 5171 **Region** McLaren Vale
T (08) 8323 9196 **F** (08) 8323 9746 **www**.tapestrywines.com.au **Open** 7 days 11–5
Winemaker Jon Ketley **Est.** 1971 **Cases** 18 000 **Vyds** 37.5 ha
After a relatively brief period of ownership by Brian Light, the former Merrivale Winery was acquired in 1997 by the Gerard family, previously owners of Chapel Hill. It has 30-year-old vineyards in McLaren Vale and in the distinctly different Bakers Gully location. Less than half the grapes are used for the Tapestry label. Very limited tastings for this edition. Exports to the US, Canada, Singapore, Hong Kong, India, Indonesia and China.

ŶŶŶŶŶ **McLaren Vale Shiraz 2007** A fine and juicy style, black and red fruit working alongside each other with ease; chocolate and fruitcake richness comes through on the palate; really bright and elegant for the region and vintage. Screwcap. 14.5% alc. **Rating** 94 **To** 2015 $25

ŶŶŶŶŶ **Bakers Gully & Vignerons McLaren Vale Shiraz 2007** Deep colour; very ripe bouquet with confit blackberry fruit coming to the fore; rich and sweet-fruited, the palate offers a chocolate and savoury tar finish. Value. Screwcap. 14% alc. **Rating** 90 **To** 2014 $15

ŶŶŶŶ **The Vincent McLaren Vale Shiraz 2006** Some volatility and shrivel here, yet has good concentration, dark pruney fruit and a fair amount of oak; more life on the finish, with chocolate and fruitcake to conclude. Cork. 14.5% alc. **Rating** 89 **To** 2014 $45
Fifteen Barrels Cabernet Sauvignon 2006 Deep colour; a very oaky bouquet, with essency cassis fruit sitting beneath; the palate is worked and the fruit pushing the ripeness envelope; hot on the finish. Cork. 15.5% alc. **Rating** 87 **To** 2014 $45

Tar & Roses/Trust

61 Vickers Lane, Nagambie, Vic 3608 (postal) **Region** Central Victoria Zone
T (03) 5794 1811 **F** (03) 5794 1833 **www**.trustwines.com.au **Open** Not
Winemaker Don Lewis, Narelle King **Est.** 2004 **Cases** 15 000 **Vyds** 5 ha
Tar & Roses is one of the more interesting new arrivals on the Australian winemaking scene, even though the partners, Don Lewis and Narelle King, have been making wine together for many years at Mitchelton and – for the past three years – Priorat, Spain. Don came from a grapegrowing family in Red Cliffs, near Mildura, and in his youth was press-ganged into working in the vineyard. When he left home he swore never to be involved in vineyards again, but in 1973 found himself accepting the position of assistant winemaker to Colin Preece at Mitchelton, where he remained until his retirement 32 years later. Narelle, having qualified as a chartered accountant, set off to discover the world, and while travelling in South America met a young Australian winemaker who had just completed vintage in Argentina, and who lived in France. The lifestyle appealed greatly, so on her return to Australia she obtained her winemaking degree from CSU and was offered work by Mitchelton as a bookkeeper and cellar hand. Together they are making wines that are a mosaic of Australia, Italy and Spain in their inspiration.

ŶŶŶŶŶ **Tar & Roses Heathcote Shiraz 2007** Dense purple-red; a very complex wine, with 7% cabernet sauvignon from the Strathbogie Ranges; has the intense plum, blackberry and licorice of Heathcote, the cabernet adding to the structure and length. Screwcap. 14.5% alc. **Rating** 95 **To** 2020 $18
Tar & Roses Miro 2006 Great colour; fruit and tannins are interwoven like a tapestry, the grenache far firmer than that of either France or Australia; the flavours of black fruits with notes of tar and roses (what else?). Grenache/Shiraz/Cabernet Sauvignon, from Priorat, Spain. Cork. 15% alc. **Rating** 94 **To** 2020 $50

ŶŶŶŶŶ **Tar & Roses Pinot Grigio 2008** A bright, distinct splash of pale pink leads into a wine with unusual but most attractive nuances of strawberries, as well as the more usual pear. Screwcap. 13.5% alc. **Rating** 92 **To** 2011 $18
Tar & Roses Heathcote Tempranillo 2007 Good crimson-purple; fragrant red fruits with a hint of cinnamon, the palate lively and fresh; good balance and length. Screwcap. 13.5% alc. **Rating** 91 **To** 2014 $24
Tar & Roses Heathcote Sangiovese 2007 Classic sour cherry aromas and flavours are a breezy start, the Italianate tannins a formidable finish. As should be the case, demands food. Screwcap. 14% alc. **Rating** 90 **To** 2014 $24

Tarrawarra Estate   ★★★★★

Healesville Road, Yarra Glen, Vic 3775 **Region** Yarra Valley
T (03) 5962 3311 **F** (03) 5962 3887 **www**.tarrawarra.com.au **Open** 7 days 11–5
Winemaker Clare Halloran **Est.** 1983 **Cases** 18 000 **Vyds** 29 ha

Clare Halloran has lightened the Tarrawarra style, investing it with more grace and finesse, but without losing complexity or longevity. The opening of the large art gallery (and its attendant café/restaurant) in early 2004 added another dimension to the tourism tapestry of the Yarra Valley. The gallery is open Wed–Sun and, as the Michelin Guide says, it is definitely worth a detour. The deluxe MDB label made its way (very quietly, because of the tiny production) in '09. The release of the new Reserve range introduced a second tier, followed by the Tarrawarra varietal releases alongside the Tin Cows range, which is not 100% estate grown nor necessarily limited to the Yarra Valley. Exports to the UK, the US and other major markets.

¶¶¶¶¶ **MDB Yarra Valley Pinot Noir 2006** Less than 100 dozen bottles made from two small selections of the oldest vines on the vineyard, and matured in two French puncheons. A spectacular pinot with exceptional drive and, above all, length and persistence of flavour. Screwcap. 13.8% alc. **Rating** 96 **To** 2017 $100
MDB Yarra Valley Chardonnay 2006 An unusually complex and textured wine with elements of top Margaret River chardonnays in its makeup; stone fruit, melon and fig flavours within a gentle swathe of French oak run through the long palate. Screwcap. 13.8% alc. **Rating** 95 **To** 2016 $100
Yarra Valley Chardonnay 2002 Appropriately developed yellow-green; has flourished in bottle since Oct '04, adding texture to the stone fruit/grapefruit flavours, the oak balance exact. Screwcap. 14% alc. **Rating** 95 **To** 2012 $50
Reserve Yarra Valley Pinot Noir 2006 Slightly hazy colour; a very intense palate with great thrust and drive to the savoury-nuanced black cherry and plum fruit running through to the finish and lingering aftertaste. Screwcap. 14% alc. **Rating** 95 **To** 2015 $50
Yarra Valley Chardonnay 2008 Bright green-straw; immaculately structured and balanced, at once complex yet elegant, with melon and white peach fruit, a touch of hazelnut and cream seamlessly woven with French oak. Screwcap. 13.5% alc. **Rating** 94 **To** 2016 $22
Reserve Chardonnay 2006 Bright green-yellow; an elegant wine marries finesse with complexity; has all the hallmark length of Yarra Valley, with a tangy/savoury finish and aftertaste. Screwcap. 13.5% alc. **Rating** 94 **To** 2016 $50
MRV 2008 A flowery, fresh, elegant wine with excellent length and balance; nuances of honeysuckle, apple and talc. on the lingering aftertaste. Marsanne/Roussanne/Viognier. Screwcap. 13% alc. **Rating** 94 **To** 2013 $40

¶¶¶¶¶ **Tin Cows Yarra Valley Heathcote Shiraz 2006** An elegant and bright medium-bodied wine, with lively spicy red fruits supported by fine tannins and subtle oak; an exercise in winemaking restraint paying big dividends. Screwcap. 14.5% alc. **Rating** 93 **To** 2016 $22
Yarra Valley Pinot Noir 2008 Bright, but light, colour; a big brother to the Rose, with marked texture and structure to the plum, spice and briar flavours of the long palate. Priced low in a tough market. Screwcap. 14% alc. **Rating** 92 **To** 2014 $22
Pinot Noir Rose 2008 Serious, bone-dry rose with texture ex barrel ferment as well as cherry/spicy/strawberry fruits; long finish. Screwcap. 12.1% alc. **Rating** 91 **To** 2010 $22
Tin Cows Yarra Valley Sauvignon Blanc 2008 An uncompromisingly crisp and punchy wine, driven by cut grass, herb and mineral inputs; long, dry, finish. Screwcap. 12.5% alc. **Rating** 90 **To** 2012 $22
Tin Cows Pinot Noir 2006 Bright colour; has an overall savoury/foresty cast, which is not a fault, but which takes the wine out of the flavour and texture profile expected at this price point. Screwcap. 13.8% alc. **Rating** 90 **To** 2012 $22

 PPPP **Pinot Noir Rose 2007** Salmon-pink; a powerful rose with more alcohol impact than most; leading artist John Olsen's designed label is way out of the normal Tarrawarra frame. Screwcap. 14.3% alc. **Rating** 89 **To** 2009 $17

Tin Cows Yarra Valley Merlot 2006 An elegant light- to medium-bodied wine; good varietal typicity courtesy of blackcurrant, cassis and black olive flavours supported by silky tannins. Screwcap. 13.9% alc. **Rating** 89 **To** 2014 $22

Tin Cows Yarra Valley Heathcote Shiraz 2005 A medium-bodied wine that has varietal expression, but does not deliver the profundity/density expected of a Yarra/Heathcote blend. Screwcap. 14% alc. **Rating** 87 **To** 2012 $22

Tassell Park Wines

Treeton Road, Cowaramup, WA 6284 **Region** Margaret River
T (08) 9755 5440 **F** (08) 9755 5442 **www.**tassellparkwines.com **Open** 7 days 10.30–5
Winemaker Peter Stanlake (Consultant) **Est.** 2001 **Cases** 4250 **Vyds** 6.8 ha
One of the light brigade of newcomers to the Margaret River region. Ian and Tricia Tassell have sauvignon blanc, shiraz, cabernet sauvignon, chenin blanc, petit verdot, semillon, chardonnay and merlot. Their white wines have proved so successful that some of the red varieties have been grafted over to white varieties, with the emphasis on their trophy-winning Sauvignon Blanc Semillon.

PPPPP **Private Bin Margaret River Shiraz 2007** A wine that fully reflects the excellent vintage Margaret River enjoyed, with vibrant red and black fruit aromas repeated on the medium- to full-bodied palate; here spicy notes join ripe tannins and good oak. Screwcap. 14% alc. **Rating** 93 **To** 2022 $38

Private Bin Margaret River Cabernet Sauvignon 2007 Deeper colour and distinctly riper fruit aromas than the standard cabernet, the palate verging on robust; strong tannins underpin blackcurrant fruit, and demand patience. Screwcap. 13% alc. **Rating** 93 **To** 2020 $38

Margaret River Sauvignon Blanc Semillon 2008 Very delicate and fine, fully reflecting its unusually low (by Margaret River standards) alcohol; flavours of passionfruit, citrus and grass emerge on retasting the wine. Screwcap. 11.8% alc. **Rating** 90 **To** 2013 $22

PPPP **Margaret River Cabernet Sauvignon 2007** An elegant light- to medium-bodied wine picked at the lower end of ripeness, but which is savoury (and a little minty) rather than green. May surprise with its tenacity over the next five years. Screwcap. 12.5% alc. **Rating** 89 **To** 2014 $28

Margaret River Sauvignon Blanc 2008 Light-bodied, a touch of smoke on the bouquet; fine palate. Screwcap. 12.8% alc. **Rating** 88 **To** 2010 $22

Margaret River Cabernet Sauvignon Merlot 2007 Fragrant red berry fruit aromas lead into a light- to medium-bodied palate with cassis/redcurrant fruit and a hint of sweetness. Screwcap. 13.5% alc. **Rating** 88 **To** 2012 $23

Margaret River Chenin Blanc 2008 Quite vibrant flavours of tropical fruits garnished with a drizzle of lemon; modest cellaring potential. Screwcap. 12.8% alc. **Rating** 87 **To** 2011 $18

Tatachilla

151 Main Road, McLaren Vale, SA 5171 **Region** McLaren Vale
T (08) 8323 8656 **F** (08) 8323 9096 **www.**tatachillawines.com.au **Open** Not
Winemaker Fanchon Ferrandi **Est.** 1903 **Cases** 50 000
Tatachilla was reborn in 1995 but has had an at-times tumultuous history going back to 1903. Between 1903 and '61 the winery was owned by Penfolds; it was closed in 1961 and reopened in '65 as the Southern Vales Co-operative. In the late 1980s it was purchased and renamed The Vales but did not flourish; in '93 it was purchased by local grower Vic Zerella and former Kaiser Stuhl chief executive Keith Smith. After extensive renovations, the winery was officially reopened in 1995 and won a number of tourist awards and accolades. It became part of Banksia Wines in 2001, in turn acquired by Lion Nathan in '02. Exports to all major markets.

ŶŶŶŶ Growers Sauvignon Blanc Semillon 2008 Exceptional value for a wine that has an abundance of gently sweet tropical fruit offset by good acidity; good length. Value. Screwcap. 12% alc. **Rating** 89 **To** 2010 $11
McLaren Vale Chardonnay 2008 A fragrant and juicy wine, with a mix of nectarine and grapefruit on the well-balanced palate, oak playing no part. Screwcap. 11.5% alc. **Rating** 88 **To** 2011 $18
McLaren Vale Shiraz 2007 A considerable amount of apparent oak on both bouquet and palate needs to subside to let the quite rich fruit come forward. Screwcap. 14.5% alc. **Rating** 87 **To** 2013 $22.95

Tatler Wines

477 Lovedale Road, Lovedale, NSW 2321 **Region** Lower Hunter Valley
T (02) 4930 9139 **F** (02) 4930 9145 **www.**tatlerwines.com **Open** 7 days 9.30–5.30
Winemaker Daniel Binet **Est.** 1998 **Cases** 6500 **Vyds** 11 ha
Tatler Wines is a family-owned company headed by Sydney hoteliers Theo and Spiro Isak (Isakidis). The name comes from the Tatler Hotel on George Street, Sydney, which was purchased by James (Dimitri) Isak from the late Archie Brown, whose son Tony is general manager of the wine business. Together with wife Deborah, Tony runs the vineyard, cellar door, café and accommodation. The 40-ha property has 11 ha of chardonnay, shiraz and semillon. In 2008 Tatler acquired and renovated the Allanmere winery, where 75% of Tatler wines are now made under the direction of Daniel Binet. Exports to the US.

ŶŶŶŶŶ Museum Release Nigel's Hunter Valley Semillon 2004 Bright, glowing light green; still in its youth, with the clearest possible link to the '08, the flavours just a little more intense and complex. You can't fault the wine, but the price is ambitious. Screwcap. 10.5% alc. **Rating** 95 **To** 2014 $48
Nigel's Hunter Valley Semillon 2008 Pale straw; a very tight and focused wine, with zesty lemon juice flavours, and a long finish. Appealing price. Screwcap. 10% alc. **Rating** 94 **To** 2018 $20

ŶŶŶŶŶ Over the Ditch Hunter Valley Marlborough Semillon Sauvignon Blanc 2008 A bold blend that has worked well for Tatler; a really attractive mix of juicy/ citrussy/grassy flavours from this side of the ditch, and passionfruit and gooseberry from the other side. Screwcap. 10.8% alc. **Rating** 93 **To** 2014 $24
The Sticky Hunter Valley Botrytis Semillon 2008 Deep gold; vibrant orange, lemon and cumquat zest flavours; zingy acidity balancing and lengthening the palate. 375 ml. Screwcap. 10% alc. **Rating** 92 **To** 2013 $22

ŶŶŶŶ The Butlers Selection Semillon Sauvignon Blanc 2008 A Hunter Valley Semillon (65%)/Yarra Valley Sauvignon Blanc (35%) blend that provides plenty of enjoyable flavour, but doesn't have the same punch as Over The Ditch. Screwcap. 10.3% alc. **Rating** 89 **To** 2011 $18

Taylor Ferguson

Level 1, 62 Albert Street, Preston, Vic 3072 (postal) **Region** South Eastern Australia
T (03) 9487 2599 **F** (03) 9487 2588 **www.**alepat.com.au **Open** Not
Winemaker Norman Lever **Est.** 1996 **Cases** NFP
Taylor Ferguson is the much-altered descendant of a business of that name established in Melbourne in 1898. A connecting web joins it with Alexander & Paterson (1892) and the much more recent distribution business of Alepat Taylor. The development of the Taylor Ferguson wine label under the direction of winemaker Norman Lever, using grapes purchased in Coonawarra, Langhorne Creek and the Riverina, is yet another strand. The wines have a strong export focus on Germany, Denmark, China, Nauru and Taiwan.

ŶŶŶŶ Premium Selection Langhorne Creek Shiraz 2006 Bright colour; lots of sweet red fruit aromas with a touch of mint; vibrant and fine, with fleshy fruit and good structure. Screwcap. 14% alc. **Rating** 88 **To** 2014 $15

Premium Selection Langhorne Creek Shiraz Cabernet 2006 A good example of these two varieties working together; plump blackberry fruit, with a hint of mint is complemented by a fine and firm backbone of cassis and cedar; fresh acidity provides very good focus of fruit on the finish. Screwcap. 14% alc. **Rating** 88 **To** 2014 $15

Taylors ★★★★★

Taylors Road, Auburn, SA 5451 **Region** Clare Valley
T (08) 8849 1111 **F** (08) 8849 1199 **www.**taylorswines.com.au **Open** Mon–Fri 9–5, Sat & public hols 10–5, Sun 10–4
Winemaker Adam Eggins, Helen McCarthy **Est.** 1969 **Cases** 580 000
The family-founded and owned Taylors continues to flourish and expand, its vineyards now total over 500 ha, by far the largest holding in Clare Valley. There have also been changes both in terms of the winemaking team and in terms of the wine style and quality, particularly through the outstanding St Andrews range. With each passing vintage, Taylors is managing to do the same for the Clare Valley as Peter Lehmann is doing for the Barossa Valley. Off the pace with this year's submissions; rated on previous years, and (indirectly) on value. Exports (under the Wakefield brand due to trademark reasons) to all major markets.

ΨΨΨΨΨ **St Andrews Clare Valley Riesling 2005** Very pale colour; an amazingly fresh bouquet, exhibiting pure lime juice and floral aromas; the palate delivers precision and length, with rapier-like acidity and a generous dollop of fruit coursing all the way to the finish. Screwcap. 13.5% alc. **Rating** 96 **To** 2025 $37.95
Jaraman Clare Valley Coonawarra Cabernet Sauvignon 2006 This has been very well constructed, the two components clearly contributing, the Clare Valley with its bold dark fruit richness, Coonawarra with its elegance, fragrance and length. A great outcome. Screwcap. 14.5% alc. **Rating** 94 **To** 2020 $29.95
St Andrews Clare Valley Cabernet Sauvignon 2004 Bright colour; finer and more delicate than many Clare cabernets; predominantly black fruits (some cassis notes) are supported by powdery tannins and cedary French oak. Screwcap. 14.5% alc. **Rating** 94 **To** 2019 $62.50
Jaraman Margaret River Adelaide Hills Sauvignon Blanc 2008 The first such regional blend I have tasted, and one that succeeds brilliantly, with a haunting fragrance of fruit blossom and grass on the bouquet and a juicily fresh palate of passionfruit and green apples. Screwcap. 13% alc. **Rating** 94 **To** 2010 $29.95

ΨΨΨΨ♀ **Jaraman Clare Valley McLaren Vale Shiraz 2005** Good colour; attractive medium-bodied wine, with excellent purity and varietal expression to both bouquet and palate; blackberry and plum fruit, with a touch of dark chocolate. Screwcap. 14.5% alc. **Rating** 93 **To** 2018 $29.95
Jaraman Clare Valley Eden Valley Riesling 2008 A lifted bouquet of fresh lime and slate/talc. bouquet; a very dry and precise palate, with a sense of freshly squeezed lime juice, and almost searing acidity; great line, but requires time. Screwcap. 11.8% alc. **Rating** 92 **To** 2018 $29.95
Clare Valley Adelaide Hills Gewurztraminer 2008 Gentle musk aromas are framed by lifted orange peel and ripe lemon characters; the palate is generous and rich, but cleans up nicely with a good dose of acidity on the finish. Screwcap. 13.5% alc. **Rating** 92 **To** 2014 $18.95
Jaraman Clare Valley McLaren Vale Shiraz 2006 A medium-bodied wine that shows the synergy available from this blend; supple and smooth, it ranges through red and black fruits, licorice and dark chocolate, but no one character dominant. Screwcap. 14.5% alc. **Rating** 92 **To** 2016 $29.95
St Andrews Clare Valley Shiraz 2003 Shows some leathery development to a core of red fruits complemented by some savoury complexity; the palate is sweet-fruited, complex and long. Screwcap. 15% alc. **Rating** 92 **To** 2015 $59.95
Jaraman Clare Valley Eden Valley Riesling 2007 Bright brassy colour; interesting wine that relies as much on structure as it does flavour; some floral/blossom notes, but its strength is the pure finish. Screwcap. 13% alc. **Rating** 90 **To** 2014 $24.95

Jaraman Clare Valley Adelaide Hills Chardonnay 2007 Bright straw-green; the Adelaide Hills component gives the wine definition and verve it could never get from the Clare Valley; has attractive grapefruit nuances, and the oak is balanced. Screwcap. 14% alc. **Rating** 90 **To** 2012 $24.95

Jaraman Clare Valley Coonawarra Cabernet Sauvignon 2005 Very good colour; clear blackcurrant and blackberry fruit characters; good tannin structure and length. Screwcap. 14.5% alc. **Rating** 90 **To** 2015 $29.95

ΨΨΨΨ **Clare Valley Shiraz 2007** Good colour; well-made, supremely honest, medium-bodied shiraz with plum and blackberry fruit cradled in vanillin oak. Screwcap. 14.5% alc. **Rating** 89 **To** 2014 $18.95

Eighty Acres Clare Valley Shiraz Viognier 2006 Bright colour; attractive lifted red berry fruits with some spicy notes and vanilla oak; fine tannins. Screwcap. 14.5% alc. **Rating** 89 **To** 2014 $16.95

Adelaide Hills Clare Valley Pinot Gris 2008 Good flavour and depth to the fruit; light mineral edge to the pear and straw aromas; good persistence and cleansing acidity. Screwcap. 13% alc. **Rating** 88 **To** 2012 $19.95

Clare Valley Merlot 2007 This is not a great wine, but it's an attractive light- to medium-bodied merlot driven by small red fruits, and not over-extracted or oaked. Screwcap. 14.5% alc. **Rating** 88 **To** 2013 $18.95

Clare Valley Riesling 2008 A rich example of Clare riesling; ripe, slightly exotic fruit bouquet is followed by a fractionally tart fruit finish. Screwcap. 13% alc. **Rating** 87 **To** 2014 $18.95

Adelaide Hills Sauvignon Blanc 2008 Clean and crisp with tropical fruit aromas and a touch of straw; vibrant and poised on the palate. Screwcap. 13.5% alc. **Rating** 87 **To** 2011 $18.95

St Andrews Clare Valley Chardonnay 2005 A worked style, with oak, lees stirring and winemaking driving the bouquet; the palate is tighter and fresher, but the oak dominates the finish. Screwcap. 14.5% alc. **Rating** 87 **To** 2015 $37.95

Adelaide Hills Pinot Noir 2008 Great colour; has much flavour, but is on the tannic side and should have been picked earlier and fined more enthusiastically. May improve in bottle. Screwcap. 14.5% alc. **Rating** 87 **To** 2012 $18.95

TeAro Estate

Lot 501 Fromm Square Road, Williamstown, SA 5351 **Region** Barossa Valley
T (08) 8524 6860 **F** (08) 8524 6860 **www**.tearoestate.com **Open** By appt
Winemaker Mark Jamieson, Neville Falkenberg **Est.** 2001 **Cases** 2000 **Vyds** 57.5 ha
TeAro Estate is a family owned and operated wine business located in Williamstown in the southern Barossa Valley. In 1919 great-grandfather Charlie Fromm married Minnie Kappler who named their home block TeAro. Today fourth-generation vigneron Ryan Fromm and brother-in-law Todd Rowett work closely with winemakers Neville Falkenberg and Mark Jamieson to capture the fruit characters produced by the slightly cooler climate and varied soils. The vineyards are planted (in descending size) to shiraz, cabernet sauvignon, semillon, chardonnay, pinot noir, riesling, viognier, sauvignon blanc, pinot gris, tempranillo, merlot, mourvedre and grenache. Exports to China and Hong Kong.

ΨΨΨΨΨ **Barossa Valley Cabernet Sauvignon 2006** Good colour; fully reflects the quality of the vintage for Barossa Valley cabernet sauvignon; strong blackcurrant fruit with overtones of dark chocolate and cedar; carries its alcohol well. Screwcap. 15% alc. **Rating** 93 **To** 2020 $25

Barossa Valley Shiraz 2006 Relatively unscathed by its alcohol; medium-bodied and spicy/savoury nuances to its black cherry and plum fruit; unusual style. Screwcap. 15.1% alc. **Rating** 91 **To** 2016 $25

ΨΨΨΨ **Iron Fist Barossa Valley Grenache 2006** If this is not a misnomer, I have never seen one; offers typical raspberry, strawberry, confection/Turkish delight flavours on a light, supple palate. Screwcap. 14.7% alc. **Rating** 88 **To** 2012 $18

Temple Bruer

Milang Road, Strathalbyn, SA 5255 **Region** Langhorne Creek
T (08) 8537 0203 **www.**templebruer.com.au **Open** Mon–Fri 9.30–4.30
Winemaker David Bruer, Vanessa Altmann **Est.** 1980 **Cases** 10 000 **Vyds** 19.2 ha
Temple Bruer was in the vanguard of the organic movement in Australia and was the focal
point for the formation of Organic Vignerons Australia. Part of the production from its estate
vineyards is used for its own label, part sold. Winemaker-owner David Bruer also has a vine
propagation nursery, likewise run on an organic basis. Exports to the US and Japan.

ŸŸŸŸ **Preservative Free Langhorne Creek Cabernet Merlot 2008** A medium- to
full-bodied, rich and dense wine that, despite preservative-free status, needs time in
bottle; the screwcap will not let it down. 13.5% alc. **Rating** 89 **To** 2013 $18.50
Preservative Free Langhorne Creek Verdelho 2007 Strong varietal
fruit evident from start to finish, with good balance. Screwcap essential with
no-preservative wines. 13.5% alc. **Rating** 87 **To** 2009 $18.50

Tempus Two Wines

Broke Road, Pokolbin, NSW 2321 **Region** Lower Hunter Valley
T (02) 4993 3999 **F** (02) 4993 3988 **www.**tempustwo.com.au **Open** 7 days 9–5
Winemaker Scott Comyns **Est.** 1997 **Cases** 100 000
Tempus Two is the name for what was once Hermitage Road Wines. It is a mix of Latin
(Tempus means time) and English; the change was forced on the winery by the EU Wine
Agreement and the prohibition of the use of the word 'hermitage' on Australian wine labels.
It has been a major success story, production growing from 6000 cases in 1997 to over 100
000 cases today. Its cellar door, restaurant complex (including the Oishii Japanese restaurant),
and small convention facilities are situated in a striking building. The design polarises opinion;
I like it. Exports to all major markets.

ŸŸŸŸŸ **Pewter Vine Vale Shiraz 2007** An engaging bouquet of redcurrant, plum,
spices and fresh herbs; the palate is soft and lithe, with a core of red fruits that
provides focus and nerve; the tannins are very silky and are a testament to the
skill of the winemaker. Diam. 13.5% alc. **Rating** 95 **To** 2016 $35
Pewter Coonawarra Cabernet 2007 Deeply coloured; pure cassis bouquet, a
touch of cedar, and some red fruit in support; the palate is silky and focused, with
a compelling level of complexity and interest; medium-bodied with an elegant and
long fine-grained tannin finish. Diam. 14% alc. **Rating** 94 **To** 2016 $35

ŸŸŸŸŸ **Copper Zenith Semillon 2004** A tightly wound, pure lemon bouquet; the
palate is completely unevolved with searingly high acidity set against considerable
fruit richness; its future still hangs in the balance, for it may be a Peter Pan, blessed
(or condemned) by eternal youth. Screwcap. 11% alc. **Rating** 93 **To** 2020 $30
Pewter Pinot Gris 2008 Pale and vibrant hue; ripe pear and candied orange
bouquet with a racy green edge to the fruit; the palate is rich and shows real
personality and verve; cleansing acidity prolongs the finish harmoniously. Diam.
12.5% alc. **Rating** 92 **To** 2012 $30
Copper Wilde Chardonnay 2007 Ripe grapefruit, melon and a touch of
toast on the bouquet; the palate is thickly textured, with lingering toasty notes
dominating the fleshy peach fruit on the finish. Screwcap. 13.5% alc. **Rating** 91
To 2013 $25

Ten Miles East

8 Debneys Road, Norton Summit, SA 5136 **Region** Adelaide Hills
T (08) 8390 1723 **F** (08) 8390 1723 **www.**tenmileseast.com **Open** Sun 11–4
Winemaker John Greenshields, Taiita Champniss, James Champniss **Est.** 2003 **Cases** 1000
Vyds 1.8 ha
Ten Miles East takes its name from the fact that it is that distance and direction from
the Adelaide GPO. It is the venture of industry veteran John Greenshields, and Robin

Smallacombe and Judith Smallacombe and is, to put it mildly, an interesting one. Its home vineyard in the Adelaide Hills is planted principally to riesling and sauvignon blanc, with smaller plantings of arneis, pinot noir, shiraz, carmenere and saperavi, a Joseph's coat if ever there was one. Next, there is a joint venture vineyard on the Yorke Peninsula planted to shiraz (3000 vines) and carmenere (1000 vines). Finally, Ten Miles East purchases 2–4 tonnes of shiraz per year from Wrattonbully (where, many years ago, John founded Koppamurra, now Tapanappa). The winery is in what was the Auldwood Cider Factory built in 1962, and also houses the cellar door that opened in 2009.

ΨΨΨΨ **Adelaide Hills Riesling 2008** Lime and lemon comes through on the palate; juicy and forward; should be enjoyed in the short term. Screwcap. 12.4% alc. **Rating** 88 **To** 2012 $15

Ten Minutes by Tractor   ★★★★★

1333 Mornington-Flinders Road, Main Ridge, Vic 3928 **Region** Mornington Peninsula **T** (03) 5989 6455 **www.**tenminutesbytractor.com.au **Open** 7 days 11–5 **Winemaker** Richard McIntyre, Martin Spedding **Est.** 1999 **Cases** 7200 **Vyds** 17 ha
The energy, drive and vision of Martin Spedding has transformed Ten Minutes by Tractor since he acquired the business in early 2004. He has entered into long-term leases of the three original vineyards, thus having complete management control over grape production courtesy of vineyard manager Alan Murray, who has been involved with those vineyards since 1999. A fourth vineyard has been added on the site of the new cellar door and restaurant; its first vintage was 2008, and it has been managed organically since day one. It is being used to trial various organic viticultural practices, which will ultimately be employed across all of the plantings. Martin is completing a wine science degree at CSU, and has taken over active winemaking alongside Richard McIntyre (the latter as an all-important mentor). The restaurant has one of the best wine lists to be found at any winery. Exports to the UK, Canada, Hong Kong and Singapore.

ΨΨΨΨΨ **10X Mornington Peninsula Pinot Noir 2007** Great colour; a great example of grace and power; fine cherry, plum and a touch of game on the bouquet; the palate builds from start to finish, with fine and precise fruit, framed by complex aromas and flavours that will gather momentum over the next few years; long, luscious and showing velvet-like quality on the finish. Screwcap. 14% alc. **Rating** 96 **To** 2015 $36
Wallis Vineyard Mornington Peninsula Pinot Noir 2007 Distinctly darker hue than Judd or McCutcheon; as the colour suggests, stronger dark fruit flavours run through the palate, which has good balance. Will repay cellaring. Screwcap. 13.5% alc. **Rating** 95 **To** 2016 $70
McCutcheon Vineyard Mornington Peninsula Chardonnay 2007 A very complex wine, with deliberately funky barrel ferment aromas leading into a minerally/savoury palate of considerable depth. Very different to Wallis Vineyard. Screwcap. 12.8% alc. **Rating** 94 **To** 2019 $55
Wallis Vineyard Mornington Peninsula Chardonnay 2007 Finer and purer than McCutcheon Vineyard, the delicate stone fruit and apple aromas and flavours set against gentle barrel ferment inputs; has immaculate balance and length. Screwcap. 12.8% alc. **Rating** 94 **To** 2016 $55
Judd Vineyard Mornington Peninsula Pinot Noir 2007 Has plenty of richness, concentration and length, black cherry flavour building through to the back-palate and finish. Screwcap. 13.5% alc. **Rating** 94 **To** 2014 $70
McCutcheon Vineyard Mornington Peninsula Pinot Noir 2007 Mid-red-purple; fragrant, with some slightly sappy nuances to add interest, a counterpoint to the small red fruits of the mid-palate. Screwcap. 13.5% alc. **Rating** 94 **To** 2014 $70

ΨΨΨΨΩ **10X Mornington Peninsula Chardonnay 2007** Has good intensity and depth; white peach and a touch of cashew are framed by quality French oak. Screwcap. 13.5% alc. **Rating** 92 **To** 2015 $30

X Tractor Mornington Peninsula Chardonnay 2008 A tight structure and texture, with apple and stone fruit flavours running through to a crisp finish; seafood style; will develop. Screwcap. 13.8% alc. **Rating** 90 **To** 2012 $22

10X Mornington Peninsula Pinot Gris 2008 Has some textural complexity befitting the gris label, and also pear and apple fruit; well above average, but expensive. Screwcap. 13.5% alc. **Rating** 90 **To** 2011 $28

X Mornington Peninsula Pinot Noir 2007 Showing a little spice and stem, with the primary fruit taking a back seat to earthy, slightly undergrowth tones; the palate is ample, fine and shows plenty of personality. Screwcap. 13% alc. **Rating** 90 **To** 2013 $23

Terra Felix

PO Box 2029, Wattletree Road, Malvern East, Vic 3134 **Region** Upper Goulburn
T (03) 9807 9778 **F** (03) 9923 6167 **www.**terrafelix.com.au **Open** Not
Winemaker Terry Barnett **Est.** 2001 **Cases** 14 600
Terra Felix was for many years a brand of Tallarook Wines, jointly owned by the Riebl family and by Peter Simon, Stan Olszewski and John Nicholson. In 2005 it was decided to separate the businesses, with Luis Riebl now solely concerned with the production of the Tallarook wines. Peter Simon and Stan Olszewski had run the Stanley Wine Company in Clare over 20 years ago, leaving it in the early 1980s, but always harbouring a desire to be involved in the industry as owners. Grapes continue to be sourced from Tallarook, and supplemented by other local growers. They have worked hard to establish export markets as well as on-premise distribution in Australia, with one-third of the production exported to the US, China and Hong Kong.

Chardonnay 2008 Candied orange fruit bouquet; ripe on entry, lemon fruit takes over on the palate and provides freshness on the finish. Screwcap. 13.9% alc. **Rating** 87 **To** 2012 $14.90

Central Victoria Viognier 2008 A full-flavoured varietal mix of apricot and yellow peach without any oak influence, no bad thing. Screwcap. 14% alc. **Rating** 87 **To** 2010 $16.50

La Vie En Rose 2008 A fragrant style of rose, with plenty of flavour and texture; the hint of sweetness balances the savoury nature of the mourvedre well. Screwcap. 12.9% alc. **Rating** 87 **To** 2012 $16.50

Tertini Wines

Kells Creek Road, Mittagong, NSW 2575 **Region** Southern Highlands
T (02) 4878 5213 **www.**tertiniwines.com.au **Open** Thurs–Mon 10–5, or by appt
Winemaker High Range Vintners **Est.** 2000 **Cases** 3000 **Vyds** 7.9 ha
When Julian Tertini began the development of Tertini Wines in 2000, he followed in the footsteps of Joseph Vogt 145 years earlier. History does not relate the degree of success that Joseph had, but the site he chose then was, as it is now, a good one. Tertini has pinot noir and riesling (1.8 ha each), cabernet sauvignon and chardonnay (1 ha each), arneis (0.9 ha), pinot gris (0.8 ha), merlot (0.4 ha) and lagrein (0.2 ha). Early indications that riesling and arneis would be particularly well suited have been brought to fruition. Exports to Asia.

Tertini & Knight Private Cellar Collection Riesling 2006 An exceptionally intense and vibrant palate, with lime juice flavours obscuring other characters, which you sense more than taste; has begun its leisurely development towards maturity. Screwcap. 11.9% alc. **Rating** 94 **To** 2016 $27

Eighteen 55 Berrima Valley Riesling 2006 Well-made wine; a complex, yet unified, mix of lime, apple and mineral aromas and flavours, finishing with lemony acidity. Screwcap. 11.8% alc. **Rating** 91 **To** 2015 $25

Reserve Southern Highlands Arneis 2008 Very crisp, bright and at once juicy and minerally; the aftertaste is clear and fresh. Perfect for Italian seafood. Screwcap. 12.7% alc. **Rating** 90 **To** 2011 $35

Teusner ★★★★★

29 Jane Place, Tanunda, SA 5352 (postal) **Region** Barossa Valley
T (08) 8252 4147 **www**.teusner.com.au **Open** By appt tel 0409 351 166
Winemaker Kym Teusner, Michael Page **Est.** 2001 **Cases** 15 000
Teusner is a partnership between former Torbreck winemaker Kym Teusner and brother-in-law Michael Page, and is typical of the new wave of winemakers determined to protect very old, low-yielding, dry-grown Barossa vines. Kym Teusner was crowned *Gourmet Traveller* Young Winemaker of the Year in 2007. The winery approach is based on lees ageing, little racking, no fining or filtration, and no new American oak. The reasonably priced wines are made either from 100% shiraz or from Southern Rhône blends. Exports to the UK, the US Canada, The Netherlands and Hong Kong.

ΨΨΨΨΨ **The Astral Series Riebke FG Barossa Valley Shiraz 2006** Deep purple-crimson; an exceptional wine from a great vintage; both bouquet and palate with a wonderful array of black fruits and bitter chocolate supported by quality oak and ripe tannins; no hint of dead fruit or alcohol here. Dreadnought bottle. Cork. 15% alc. **Rating** 96 **To** 2039 $130
Avatar 2006 Good depth and hue; an unambiguously top-end Rhône blend with a delicious mix of black and red fruits, licorice and spice flavours; perfect tannin and oak inputs to a seriously good wine. Quality cork. Grenache/Mataro/Shiraz. 14.5% alc. **Rating** 96 **To** 2026 $32
Albert 2006 Great colour; an abundance of sweet ripe black fruit, with the oak playing a supporting role on the bouquet; the palate reveals a layered, subtle, complex and powerful array of flavours and texture; there is plenty of fine tannin, and all of the elements indicate a long and fruitful existence. Shiraz. Cork. 14.5% alc. **Rating** 95 **To** 2025 $48
The Astral Series Barossa Valley Moppa Mataro 2006 A seriously dark wine, full of licorice, blackberry fruit, earth and ironstone; dense and concentrated, with strong chewy tannins that are completely ripe and in balance with the fruit; exceptionally complex, with many years ahead, which is presumably why it is in a bottle that can withstand an atomic blast. Cork. 14.5% alc. **Rating** 95 **To** 2025 $98
The Riebke Northern Barossa Shiraz 2008 Impressive colour; rich, ripe and pure, with a plummy Christmas cake bouquet; light on its feet despite its apparent ripeness; juicy, vibrant, rich and long, showing the strength of Barossa shiraz without too much oak. Screwcap. 14.5% alc. **Rating** 94 **To** 2015 $20
Joshua 2007 Good colour; a luscious array of raspberry fruit, wild herbs and spice on the bouquet; the palate is warm and rich, but shows clear definition of dark fruit for structure; long and a little savoury on the finish, with a generous splash of red fruit to conclude. Grenache/Mataro/Shiraz. Cork. 14.5% alc. **Rating** 94 **To** 2015

ΨΨΨΨΨ **Woodside Adelaide Hills Sauvignon Blanc 2008** Ripe tropical aromas with passionfruit coming to the fore; a textured palate with a dry, chalky and even finish. Screwcap. 13.5% alc. **Rating** 90 **To** 2012 $18
Barossa Valley Salsa 2008 Vibrant, juicy red fruit with alluring spice and floral aromas; the palate is dry, with a fine savoury wild herb edge to the fruit. Rose. Screwcap. 13.5% alc. **Rating** 90 **To** 2012 $18

The Blok Estate

Riddoch Highway, Coonawarra, SA 5263 **Region** Coonawarra
T (08) 8737 2734 **F** (08) 8737 2994 **www**.blok.com.au **Open** 7 days 10–5
Winemaker Kopparossa Wines (Gavin Hogg) **Est.** 1999 **Cases** 2000 **Vyds** 1 ha
The Trotter family (Luke, Rebecca, Gary and Ann) purchased The Blok Estate in 2005, and have significantly increased production. The cellar door is in a renovated, old stone home surrounded by gardens and 1 ha of cabernet sauvignon.

ΨΨΨΨ♀ **Coonawarra Shiraz 2004** Is maturing confidently, the bouquet a fragrant blend of spicy oak and red fruits, the palate introducing some black fruits together with fine, ripe tannins; has excellent length and a good cork. 14% alc. **Rating** 93 **To** 2015 $24.50

ΨΨΨΨ **Coonawarra Riesling 2008** An appealing blend of citrus and apple blossom aromas flow through onto a very delicate palate; just a little too delicate, indeed. Screwcap. 11.5% alc. **Rating** 89 **To** 2015 $18
Coonawarra Chardonnay 2008 Fragrant stone fruit and melon aromas are joined by citrussy notes on the lively, fruit-driven palate; some development potential. Screwcap. 13.5% alc. **Rating** 89 **To** 2013 $18.50
Coonawarra Cabernet Sauvignon 2005 An elegant, light- to medium-bodied wine with good fruit definition and length; needs a little more depth. Cork. 14% alc. **Rating** 88 **To** 2014 $26

The Carriages Vineyard ★★★

549 Kotta Road, Echuca, Vic 3564 **Region** Goulburn Valley
T (03) 5483 7767 **F** (03) 5483 7767 **www**.thecarriages.com.au **Open** By appt
Winemaker Nuggetty Vineyard (Greg Dedman) **Est.** 1996 **Cases** 1000 **Vyds** 6 ha
David and Lyndall Johnson began the development of The Carriages in 1996, and now have cabernet sauvignon (2.5 ha), merlot (2 ha), chardonnay (1 ha) and semillon (0.5 ha). The name and the innovative packaging stems from four old railway carriages, which the Johnsons have painstakingly rehabilitated, and now live in. Each bottle is identified with a cardboard rail ticket that is strikingly similar to the tickets of bygone years. The ticket manages to show the brand name, the vintage, the variety, the number of standard drinks, the alcohol and the bottle number (which is in fact the ticket number, or vice versa). The ticket is fixed to the label with fine twine, so it can be removed either as a memento or for further orders.

ΨΨΨΨ **Reserve Echuca Cabernet Sauvignon 2005** Bright colour; generous levels of ripe and sweet cassis fruit on the bouquet; quite juicy, with good acid and definition on the palate. Cork. 14.5% alc. **Rating** 89 **To** 2014 $30
Echuca Chardonnay 2008 Toasty straw and peach bouquet; fresh fruited and generous with a distinctly warm-origin personality. Screwcap. 12.5% alc. **Rating** 87 **To** 2012 $16

The Colonial Estate ★★★★★

PO Box 851, Nuriootpa, SA 5355 **Region** Barossa Valley
T (08) 8562 1244 **F** (08) 8562 1288 **www**.maltus.com **Open** Not
Winemaker Jonathan Maltus, Neil Whyte **Est.** 2002 **Cases** 25 000 **Vyds** 39.85 ha
The brand names of The Colonial Estate wines tell part of the story: Exile, Emigre, Exodus, Explorateur, Etranger, Envoy, Expatrie, Evangeliste and Enchanteur. It will come as no surprise, then, to find that this is a French-managed business with an extensive export program to many parts of the world including France and other European countries. Thoroughly European winemaking methods are used, most obviously being two sorting tables, one for the bunches before they pass through the de-stemmer, and another for individual berries after the de-stemming process. The company runs an active membership program for direct sales.

ΨΨΨΨΨ **Emissaire Reserve Eden Valley Riesling 2008** A vibrant, early-picked style; the bouquet of crisp lime and green apple, the palate has tremendous energy, thrust and drive with a rapier edge to the lemony acidity on the long finish. Long-term development. Screwcap. 11.5% alc. **Rating** 95 **To** 2023 $33
Mungo Park Single Vineyard Barossa Valley Shiraz 2006 Full of thrust and vitality, paradoxically turning its alcohol into a virtue; ripples of plum, blackberry and mulberry; balancing acidity is the key. US market, of course. Cork. 15.5% alc. **Rating** 95 **To** 2017 $110
Explorateur Old Vine Barossa Valley Shiraz 2006 Abundant black cherry and blackberry fruit with spicy components; good oak and tannin handling; a nice twist of acidity to freshen the finish. Cork. 14.5% alc. **Rating** 94 **To** 2016 $33

John Speke Single Vineyard Barossa Valley Grenache Shiraz Mourvedre 2006 More spice and distinctly more weight and length than the other wines in this range; seamless fruit and oak handling; the alcohol does not unduly disrupt the line. Cork. 15.5% alc. **Rating** 94 **To** 2020 $75

ⵀⵀⵀⵀⵀ **Richard Lander Single Vineyard Barossa Valley Shiraz 2006** Very powerful full-bodied style with great appeal to some, less to others; low-cropped shiraz and French oak work well until the very finish, when an afterglow of alcohol heats the mouth. Cork. 15.5% alc. **Rating** 93 **To** 2016 $79

Eclaireur Old Vine Barossa Valley Grenache 2006 Has more fruit focus than the Alexander Laing, ranging between the more normal red fruits, and black cherry and licorice. These are very supple wines, with little tannin support. Cork. 14.5% alc. **Rating** 91 **To** 2014 $33

Envoy Barossa Valley Grenache Shiraz Mourvedre 2006 The shiraz component adds some structure to the blend, but the flavours are essentially driven by the grenache. All of these wines have elements of Southern Rhône. Cork. 14.5% alc. **Rating** 91 **To** 2015 $33

Alexander Laing Single Vineyard Old Vine Barossa Valley Grenache 2006 Weak colour typical of much Barossa Valley grenache; the undoubted impact of the palate owes as much to alcohol as anything else; one man's cup of tea... Exceedingly difficult to point. From 100-year-old vines. Cork. 15.5% alc. **Rating** 90 **To** 2014 $75

Etranger Barossa Valley Cabernet Sauvignon 2006 Leafy/earthy aromas follow through into the back-palate, where the accent changes to black olive and herb woven through cassis fruit. Cork. 14.5% alc. **Rating** 90 **To** 2016 $33

The Grapes of Ross ★★★

PO Box 14, Lyndoch, SA 5351 **Region** Barossa Valley
T (08) 8524 4214 **F** (08) 8524 4214 **www**.grapesofross.com.au **Open** Not
Winemaker Ross Virgara **Est.** 2006 **Cases** 2000
Ross Virgara spent much of his life in the broader food and wine industry, finally taking the plunge into commercial winemaking in 2006. The grapes come from a fourth-generation family property in the Lyndoch Valley, and the aim is to make fruit-driven styles of quality wine. His fondness for frontignac led to the first release of Moscato, followed in due course by Rose, Merlot Cabernet and Old Bush Vine Grenache. Exports to China.

ⵀⵀⵀⵀ **Barossa Valley Moscato 2008** The most amazing moscato, smelling and tasting like a cross between Solo and sparkling lime juice. Great thirst quencher for a summer's day. Screwcap. 8.5% alc. **Rating** 87 **To** 2008 $18

Ruby Tuesday Barossa Valley Rose 2008 Vivid fuschia-purple; a Shiraz/Sangiovese base to a red berry fruit style, the amount of sweetness not necessary. Screwcap. 12.5% alc. **Rating** 87 **To** 2008 $18

The Growers ★★★★☆

1071 Wildwood Road, Yallingup, WA 6282 **Region** Margaret River
T (08) 9755 2121 **F** (08) 9755 2286 **www**.thegrowers.com **Open** 7 days 10–5
Winemaker Philip May **Est.** 2002 **Cases** 40 000
The Growers (once AbbeyVale) has had a turbulent history since it was founded in 2002, with legal disputes between various partners making life complicated. In February 2006 all that was put behind it, and it is now a syndicate of 17 growers with vineyards spread across all six regions in South West Australia, and 400 ha planted to all the major varieties. Five shareholders have key vineyards in the Margaret River region, where it is based. The wines are released in four tiers: Peppermint Grove at the $12–15 entry point; The Growers Reward (Margaret River) at $15–25; The Growers Limited Release Reward (single-vineyard, single-varietal Margaret River) at $20–30; and The Growers Palate, with six wines identically vinified across three different styles to showcase single-region vineyard expression at $30. It's an interesting concept, already gaining significant exports into the US and Asia.

ΨΨΨΨ Ϋ **Dedication Series Riesling 2004** Glowing gold-yellow; a complex bouquet, with some kerosene and toasty bottle-developed characters. Screwcap. 13.5% alc. **Rating** 90 **To** 2012 $20

ΨΨΨΨ **Reward Chardonnay 2007** Has gently funky complexity to the bouquet; a medium-bodied palate with good length, but with a slight break in line. Screwcap. 13.5% alc. **Rating** 89 **To** 2010 $20
Reward Cabernet Sauvignon 2007 Light- to medium-bodied; a savoury palate, but with neatly balanced extract. Screwcap. 14% alc. **Rating** 89 **To** 2013 $25
Reward Margaret River Verdelho 2004 Bright straw-green; a well-structured, clean wine with fair varietal character, but how it won a double gold at the Sydney International Wine Competition '07 is not easy to work out. Screwcap. 14% alc. **Rating** 87 **To** 2014 $18

The Islander Estate Vineyards   ★★★★★

PO Box 96, Parndana, SA 5220 **Region** Kangaroo Island
T (08) 8553 9008 **F** (08) 8553 9228 **www**.iev.com.au **Open** By appt
Winemaker Jacques Lurton **Est.** 2000 **Cases** 5000 **Vyds** 11 ha
Established by one of the most famous Flying Winemakers in the world, Bordeaux-born, trained and part-time Australian resident Jacques Lurton. He has established 10 ha of close-planted vineyard; the principal varieties are cabernet franc, shiraz and sangiovese, with lesser amounts of grenache, malbec, semillon and viognier. The wines are made and bottled at the onsite winery, in true estate style. The flagship wine (Yakka Jack) is an esoteric blend of sangiovese and cabernet franc. Exports to the US, Canada, France, Denmark, Holland, United Arab Emirates and Hong Kong.

ΨΨΨΨΨ **Wally White Kangaroo Island Semillon Viognier 2007** Straw, Meyer lemon and some toasty oak on the bouquet; rich on entry, it tightens across the palate, finishing with a slightly savoury/toasty conclusion. Made in a style reflecting Lurton's vinous birth in white Bordeaux amniotic fluid. Screwcap. 14% alc. **Rating** 94 **To** 2014 $44
Majestic Plough Kangaroo Island Malbec 2006 Bright colour; blueberry and violet perfume, with a fairly healthy seasoning of new oak; the palate is dense and quite firm, with plenty of fruit to balance the savoury notes on the finish. Screwcap. 14% alc. **Rating** 94 **To** 2016 $44

The Lake House Denmark   ★★★★☆

106 Turner Road, Denmark, WA 6333 **Region** Denmark
T (08) 9848 2444 **F** (08) 9848 3444 **www**.lakehousedenmark.com.au **Open** 7 days 11–5
Winemaker Harewood Estate (Jamie Kellie) **Est.** 1995 **Cases** 3000 **Vyds** 5.2 ha
When Gary Capelli and partner Leanne Rogers purchased the vineyard (formerly known as Jindi Creek) in 2005, it had vines planted 10 years earlier to no less than six mainstream varieties: chardonnay (2 ha), sauvignon blanc (1 ha) and pinot noir and merlot (0.8 ha each). They have since moved to incorporate biodynamic principles into the vineyard, which also has small plantings of semillon and marsanne.

ΨΨΨΨΨ **Pinot Noir 2007** Bright, clear colour; a fragrant bouquet of red fruits with a touch of spice; silky mouthfeel building to a long finish where spicy tannins add the right amount of texture. Screwcap. 13.5% alc. **Rating** 94 **To** 2014 $40

ΨΨΨΨ Ϋ **Unwooded Chardonnay 2008** Lively, zesty and full of interest, showing yet again the worth of unwooded chardonnay from cool regions; bursting with nectarine and grapefruit, the palate with great balance and length. Screwcap. 13.5% alc. **Rating** 91 **To** 2012 $19
Semillon Sauvignon Blanc 2008 Fragrant grass, grapefruit and gooseberry aromas, with more tropical flavours on the generously fruited palate. Screwcap. 12.5% alc. **Rating** 90 **To** 2011 $24

ŢŢŢŢ   **He Said She Said Classic White 2008** The ultimate fruit salad style, diced very fine, and with cool-climate zest. Screwcap. 13% alc. **Rating** 87 **To** 2010 $16.99
He Said She Said Classic Red 2007 A spicy/savoury wine showing its Cabernet Sauvignon/Merlot base, with green and black olive nuances on the finish. Screwcap. 14% alc. **Rating** 87 **To** 2012 $16.99

The Lane Vineyard   ★★★★★

Ravenswood Lane, Hahndorf, SA 5245 **Region** Adelaide Hills
T (08) 8388 1250 **F** (08) 8388 7233 **www**.thelane.com.au **Open** 7 days 10–4.30
Winemaker Michael Schreurs, Hugh Guthrie **Est.** 1993 **Cases** 30 000 **Vyds** 56.55 ha
After 15 years at The Lane Vineyard, Helen and John Edwards, and their sons Marty and Ben, have taken an important step in realising their long held dream – to grow, make and sell estate-based wines that have a true sense of place. In 2005, at the end of the Starvedog Lane joint venture with BRL Hardy, they commissioned a state-of-the-art 500-tonne winery, bistro and cellar door overlooking the family's vineyards on picturesque Ravenswood Lane. Exports to all the UK, the US, Ireland, Belgium and China.

ŢŢŢŢŢ   **Block 10 Single Vineyard Adelaide Hills Sauvignon Blanc 2008** Clean, crisp and clearly defined, with an extra element of texture, and a suggestion of guava and cut grass; a very lively palate; a quite long and even finish. Screwcap. 13% alc. **Rating** 94 **To** 2011 $25
Block 3 Single Vineyard Adelaide Hills Chardonnay 2008 Vibrant hue; a restrained nectarine and grapefruit bouquet; lightly toasty palate, with zesty lemon acidity and some appealing mineral complexity; long and even finish. Screwcap. 13.5% alc. **Rating** 94 **To** 2014 $30

ŢŢŢŢŢ   **Gathering Single Vineyard Adelaide Hills Sauvignon Blanc Semillon 2008** Quite a complex style; guava, straw and mineral character; real depth to the palate, with texture playing an integral role; weighty on the finish. Screwcap. 13.5% alc. **Rating** 93 **To** 2012 $35
19th Meeting Single Vineyard Adelaide Hills Cabernet Sauvignon 2007 A lifted red fruit bouquet with a touch of violets; the palate is linear and fine with pronounced acidity; a poised and polished cool-grown cabernet. Screwcap. 14% alc. **Rating** 92 **To** 2014 $65
Single Vineyard Adelaide Hills Pinot Grigio 2008 Touch of pink; focused and lively aroma of pear and a touch of spice; while quite ripe, there is a crispness to the finish that is quite appealing. Screwcap. 13.5% alc. **Rating** 90 **To** 2011 $35
Single Vineyard Adelaide Hills Viognier 2007 Apricot with a touch of spice from oak; clean palate, with some anise framing the fruit; generous and rich; quite a long varietal, warm finish. Screwcap. 13.5% alc. **Rating** 90 **To** 2011 $39

ŢŢŢŢ   **Block 2 Single Vineyard Adelaide Hills Pinot Gris 2008** Salmon pink; a very ripe style, with an abundance of candied orange and a little spice; fresh acidity cleans up the finish, leaving a slightly savoury/earthy character. Screwcap. 13% alc. **Rating** 88 **To** 2012 $30
Ravenswood Lane Single Vineyard Adelaide Hills Shiraz 2007 Bright crimson; fragrant mint and cassis; light- to medium-bodied; fresh but a little thin on the mid-palate; will fill out somewhat. Screwcap. 13.5% alc. **Rating** 88 **To** 2010 $39
Block 11 Single Vineyard Adelaide Hills Semillon Sauvignon Blanc 2008 Fresh and crisp with a strong showing from the semillon; a touch of straw on the palate. Screwcap. 13.5% alc. **Rating** 87 **To** 2011 $30

The Little Wine Company   ★★★☆

Small Winemakers Centre, 426 McDonalds Road, Pokolbin, NSW 2320
Region Lower Hunter Valley
T (02) 6579 1111 **www**.thelittlewinecompany.com.au **Open** 7 days 10–5
Winemaker Ian Little, Suzanne Little **Est.** 2000 **Cases** 12 000

Having sold their previous winery, Ian and Suzanne Little moved in stages to their new winery at Broke. The Little Wine Company is part-owner of the 20-ha Lochleven Vineyard in Pokolbin, and contracts three vineyards in the Broke-Fordwich area (where the winery is situated). It also has access to the Talga Vineyard in the Gundaroo Valley near Canberra. Exports to Hong Kong, Taiwan, China and Japan.

🍷🍷🍷🍷🍷 **Shiraz 2006** Good colour; red berry fruit with a touch of earth; medium-bodied, fine and focused with poise on the red berry and high-acid finish. Screwcap. 14.6% alc. **Rating** 90 **To** 2016 $37

The Old Faithful Estate ★★★★☆

c/- PO Box 235 (Kangarilla Road), McLaren Vale, SA 5171 **Region** McLaren Vale
T 0419 383 907 **F** (08) 8323 9747 **Open** By appt
Winemaker Nick Haselgrove, Warren Randall **Est.** 2005 **Cases** 2500

This is a 50/50 joint venture between American John Larchet (with one-half) and a quartet of Nick Haselgrove, Warren Randall, Warren Ward and Andrew Fletcher. Larchet has long had a leading role as a specialist importer of Australian wines into the US, and guarantees the business whatever sales it needs there. The shiraz, grenache and mourvedre come from selected blocks within Tinlins wine resources, with which the quartet has a close association. It's a winning formula.

🍷🍷🍷🍷🍷 **Cafe Block McLaren Vale Shiraz 2007** A concentrated and rich bouquet of blackberry and mocha; the palate is dense and chewy, with a strong element of tar playing an important role; a massive and dark spirited wine. Diam. 14.9% alc. **Rating** 92 **To** 2016 $75

🍷🍷🍷🍷 **Top of the Hill McLaren Vale Shiraz 2007** A high-toned bouquet, showing black fruit confiture and savoury, tarry notes; thickly textured, the finish is a little clipped and tart. Diam. 14.9% alc. **Rating** 87 **To** 2013 $75

The Ritual ★★★

233 Haddrill Road, Baskerville, WA 6056 (postal) **Region** Peel
T 0417 095 820 **F** (08) 9296 0681 **www**.theritual.com.au **Open** Not
Winemaker John Griffiths **Est.** 2005 **Cases** 2000 **Vyds** 20 ha

The Ritual is the product of a partnership between two Perth wine identities. John Griffiths is winemaker, and Bill Healy owns the 40-ha Orondo Farm Vineyard in Dwellingup, where John Griffiths obtains much of the grapes for his own (Faber) and other labels. The modest line-pricing and simplicity of the product range reflect no more than sober experience.

🍷🍷🍷🍷 **Shiraz Viognier 2008** Typically good colour; the viognier definitely adds lift, but also acts to break the continuity of the palate early in the life of the wine; may settle down with time. Screwcap. 14% alc. **Rating** 89 **To** 2014 $19.50

Grenache Mourvedre Shiraz 2008 Light, bright crimson; has a highly fragrant bouquet of spicy/tangy red fruits, the palate identical; attractive light-bodied red; serve slightly chilled on a hot day, and don't delay. Screwcap. 14% alc. **Rating** 89 **To** 2011 $19.50

Viognier 2008 Has positive viognier mouthfeel, and – to a degree – flavour in a peachy spectrum; isn't phenolic. Screwcap. 15% alc. **Rating** 88 **To** 2011 $19.50

Shiraz Viognier 2007 Has very unusual aromas and flavours, with hints of lantana on the bouquet and palate; more conventional spicy notes also evident. Screwcap. 14% alc. **Rating** 87 **To** 2013 $19.50

The Story Wines ★★★★☆

6/5 Arnold Street, Cheltenham, Vic 3192 (postal) **Region** Grampians
T 0411 697 912 **F** (03) 9534 8881 **www**.thestory.com.au **Open** Not
Winemaker Rory Lane **Est.** 2004 **Cases** 800

Over the years I have come across winemakers with degrees in atomic science, innumerable doctors with specialities spanning every human condition, town planners, sculptors and painters, the list going on and on, and Rory Lane adds yet another, a degree in ancient Greek literature. He says that after completing his degree, and 'desperately wanting to delay an entry into the real world, I stumbled across and enrolled in a postgraduate wine technology and marketing course at Monash University, where I soon became hooked on ... the wondrous connection between land, human and liquid.' Vintages in Australia and Oregon germinated the seed, and he zeroed in on the Grampians, where he purchases small parcels of high-quality grapes for his one and only wine, Shiraz, making it in a small factory shell where he has assembled a basket press, a few open fermenters, a mono pump and some decent French oak.

ŢŢŢŢŢ **Grampians Shiraz 2007** An elegant style, with some undergrowth framing the red berry fruit; fresh acidity, and a savoury finish. Screwcap. 14% alc. **Rating** 92 **To** 2014 $22

The Trades   ★★★☆

13/30 Peel Road, O'Connor, WA 6163 (postal) **Region** Various
T (08) 9331 2188 **F** (08) 9331 2199 **Open** Not
Winemaker Geoff Johnston (Contract) **Est.** 2006 **Cases** 1600
Thierry Ruault and Rachel Taylor have run a wholesale wine business in Perth since 1993, representing a group of top-end Australian and imported producers. By definition, the wines they offered to their clientele were well above $20 per bottle, and they decided to fill the gap with a contract-made Shiraz from the Adelaide Hills, and a Sauvignon Blanc from Margaret River, selling at $17.50. This is, without question, a virtual winery.

ŢŢŢŢŢ **Butcher's McLaren Vale Adelaide Hills Shiraz 2005** A well-conceived and executed blend, the spicy notes of the Adelaide Hills a pleasing counterpoint to the chocolatey black fruits of McLaren Vale, and drawing out the lingering finish. Value. Cork. 14% alc. **Rating** 90 **To** 2013 $17.50

The Vintners Ridge Estate   ★★★

Lot 18 Veraison Place, Yallingup, Margaret River, WA 6285 **Region** Margaret River
T (08) 9447 2086 **F** (08) 9448 0018 **www.**vintnersridge.com.au **Open** By appt
Winemaker Vasse River Wines (Sharna Kowalczuk) **Est.** 2001 **Cases** 530 **Vyds** 2.1 ha
When Maree and Robin Adair purchased The Vintners Ridge vineyard in 2006, it had already produced three crops, having been planted in Nov '01 (which is a perfectly permissible establishment date). Small acorns, great oaks. The vineyard (cabernet sauvignon) overlooks the picturesque Geographe Bay.

ŢŢŢŢ **Margaret River Cabernet Sauvignon 2007** Good colour; good concentration of fruit, with clean, vibrant fruit on offer; exists on one dimension, but that is fine. Screwcap. 14.5% alc. **Rating** 87 **To** 2012 $30

The Wanderer   ★★★★☆

2850 Launching Place Road, Gembrook, Vic 3783 **Region** Yarra Valley
T 0415 529 639 **F** (03) 5968 1699 **www.**wandererwines.com **Open** By appt
Winemaker Andrew Marks **Est.** 2005 **Cases** 500
Andrew Marks is the son of Ian and June Marks, owners of Gembrook Hill, and after graduating from Adelaide University with a degree in oenology he joined Southcorp, working for six years at Penfolds (Barossa Valley) and Seppelt (Great Western), as well as undertaking vintages in Coonawarra and France. He has since worked in the Hunter Valley, Great Southern, Sonoma County in the US and Costa Brava in Spain – hence the name of his business.

ŢŢŢŢŢ **Yarra Valley Shiraz 2007** Clear, but deep, purple; spice and pepper nuances to the plum and blackberry fruit are classic cool-grown characters, as are the fine tannins; the palate is long, as is the aftertaste. Screwcap. 13.4% alc. **Rating** 94 **To** 2017 $32

ΨΨΨΨΨ **Yarra Valley Pinot Noir 2007** Light, but bright, colour; a pinot built around savoury tannins and oak, but with enough fruit to carry those characters; distinctive style. Screwcap. 13.4% alc. **Rating** 91 **To** 2014 $32

The Willows Vineyard

Light Pass Road, Light Pass, Barossa Valley, SA 5355 **Region** Barossa Valley
T (08) 8562 1080 **F** (08) 8562 3447 **www**.thewillowsvineyard.com.au **Open** Wed–Mon 10.30–4.30, Tues by appt
Winemaker Peter Scholz, Michael Scholz **Est.** 1989 **Cases** 6500 **Vyds** 42.6 ha
The Scholz family have been grapegrowers for generations and have over 40 ha of vineyards, selling part and retaining the remainder of the crop. Current generation winemakers Peter and Michael Scholz make smooth, well-balanced and flavoursome wines under their own label, all marketed with some bottle age. Exports to the UK, the US, Canada, NZ and Singapore.

ΨΨΨΨΨ **Bonesetter Barossa Shiraz 2006** Mocha, tar, leather and fruitcake on the bouquet; toasty oak comes through on the palate and frames the abundant sweet fruit; a little time will see the fruit come to prominence in this wine. Cork. 14.5% alc. **Rating** 94 **To** 2018 $58

ΨΨΨΨΨ **Single Vineyard Barossa Valley Semillon 2006** Fresh cut hay and lemon bouquet; a generous level of fruit, with a slight toasty note to conclude. Screwcap. 12% alc. **Rating** 90 **To** 2012 $15

ΨΨΨΨ **Barossa Valley Seven 2007** Quite approachable on entry; finishes dry and savoury, with a prominent minty streak framing the red fruit. Grenache/Shiraz. Screwcap. 15% alc. **Rating** 87 **To** 2012 $20
Barossa Valley Cabernet Sauvignon 2006 A strong combination of mint and cassis on the bouquet; medium-bodied, clean and fresh, but pulls up a little quickly. Screwcap. 14.5% alc. **Rating** 87 **To** 2014 $26

🍇 The Wine Doctor

Wine iQ, 104 Buckingham Street, Surry Hills, NSW 2010 **Region** McLaren Vale
T 1300 946 347 **F** (02) 9318 1231 **www**.winedoctor.info **Open** Not
Winemaker Brian Light (Contract) **Est.** 2008 **Cases** 2000
The Wine Doctor is the brand name of Resveratrol Wines Pty Ltd, a joint venture between Dr Phil Norrie, former owner of Pendarves Estate (which has now been sold, though he retains the Pendarves brand name, currently inactive) and Wine iQ, itself owned by PR veteran Adrian Read and his partners. The wines are contract-made in McLaren Vale, which is likely to be the base for the foreseeable future. Their resveratrol content has been boosted to 100 mg/l, compared to the trace elements normally found in white wine, and much lower levels in red wines. Researchers are still divided on the cardiovascular protective effects of resveratrol, although it is true much of the debate concerns the extent of the effect, and the absence of large scale epidemiological trials.

ΨΨΨΨ **McLaren Vale Chardonnay 2008** Contains 100 mg/l resveratrol compared to normal 1–2 mg/l for white wines. Not a great wine, but better tasting than most medicines. Screwcap. 13.5% alc. **Rating** 87 **To** 2010
McLaren Vale Shiraz 2006 Like its white wine sister, a pleasant but unremarkable McLaren Vale red, other than its added resveratrol, 20 times normal levels. Screwcap. 14% alc. **Rating** 87 **To** 2011

Third Child

134 Mt Rumney Road, Mt Rumney, Tas 7170 (postal) **Region** Southern Tasmania
T 0419 132 184 **F** (03) 6223 8042 **Open** Not
Winemaker John Skinner, Rob Drew **Est.** 2000 **Cases** 250 **Vyds** 3 ha
John and Marcia Skinner planted 2.5 ha of pinot noir and 0.5 ha of riesling in 2000. It is very much a hands-on operation, the only concession being the enlistment of Rob Drew (from an adjoining property) to help John Skinner with the winemaking. When the first vintage (2004)

was reaching the stage of being bottled and labelled, the Skinners could not come up with a name and asked their daughter Claire. 'Easy,' she said. 'You've got two kids already; considering the care taken and time spent at the farm, it's your third child.'

ŸŸŸŸ   **Riesling 2008** Early picked and with a touch of sweetness; young vines limit the flavour intensity. Screwcap. 11% alc. **Rating** 87 **To** 2012 $15
        Benjamin Daniel Pinot Noir 2007 Bright, light colour; a fresh wine with minty/leafy overtones; good texture, but not quite ripe enough. Screwcap. 12.5% alc. **Rating** 87 **To** 2011 $25

Thistle Hill

74 McDonalds Road, Mudgee, NSW 2850 **Region** Mudgee
T (02) 6373 3546 **F** (02) 6373 3540 **www.**thistlehill.com.au **Open** Mon–Sat 9.30–4.30, Sun & public hols 9.30–4
Winemaker Lesley Robertson, Philip van Gent **Est.** 1976 **Cases** 3500
The Robertson family owns and operates Thistle Hill. The estate-grown wines are made onsite with the help of Robert Paul, whatever additional assistance is needed is happily provided by the remaining wine community of Mudgee. The vineyard, incidentally, is registered by the National Association for Sustainable Agriculture Australia (NASAA), which means no weedicides, insecticides or synthetic fertilisers – the full organic system. Exports to the UK, the US, Canada and Japan.

ŸŸŸŸŸ   **Mudgee Riesling 2008** Very well made, conjuring up maximum varietal character without any semblance of phenolics; apple and citrus flavours. Screwcap. 13% alc. **Rating** 90 **To** 2014 $20

ŸŸŸŸ   **Mudgee Chardonnay 2008** Well made, with fruit and oak neatly balanced and integrated; light stone fruit is given freshness by crisp acidity. Screwcap. 13% alc. **Rating** 87 **To** 2014 $20

Thomas New England Estate

Delungra, NSW 2403 **Region** New England
T (02) 6724 8508 **F** (02) 6724 8507 **Open** 7 days 10–5
Winemaker John Cassegrain (Contract) **Est.** 1997 **Cases** NA **Vyds** 33 ha
New England Estate is 33 km west of Inverell; Ross Thomas and wife Rae have established chardonnay, cabernet sauvignon, merlot, shiraz and viognier, with further plantings of durif and tannat planned. The cellar door has barbecue and picnic facilities, regional produce, arts and crafts and a children's play area; there is also a museum and accommodation available.

ŸŸŸŸ   **Chardonnay 2008** A ripe nectarine bouquet; clean, fresh and generous on the finish. Screwcap. 13.5% alc. **Rating** 87 **To** 2012 $14

Thomas Wines

c/- The Small Winemakers Centre, McDonalds Road, Pokolbin, NSW 2321
Region Lower Hunter Valley
T (02) 6574 7371 **F** (02) 6574 7371 **www.**thomaswines.com.au **Open** 7 days 10–5
Winemaker Andrew Thomas, Phil Le Messurier **Est.** 1997 **Cases** 4000
Andrew Thomas came to the Hunter Valley from McLaren Vale, to join the winemaking team at Tyrrell's. After 13 years with Tyrrell's, he left to undertake contract work and to continue the development of his own label, a family affair run by himself and his wife, Jo. He makes individual vineyard wines, simply to underline the subtle differences between the various subregions of the Hunter. Plans for the construction of an estate winery have been delayed and pro tem has leased the James Estate winery on Hermitage Road through to Dec 2010; all being well, the '11 vintage will be in his new winery. It hasn't prevented his being voted Winemaker of the Year '08 by his Hunter Valley winemaking peers, nor winning gold medals for each of his '06, '07 and '08 Braemore Semillon at the Sydney Wine Show '09. Exports to Canada and Singapore.

ŶŶŶŶŶ **Kiss Individual Vineyard Hunter Valley Shiraz 2007** The most concentrated and complex of the '07 Thomas red wines, but with no hint of overripe or dead fruit; the palate flows effortlessly within a gossamer envelope of spicy/savoury tannin and oak notes. Screwcap. 14.3% alc. **Rating** 95 **To** 2022 $60
Braemore Individual Vineyard Hunter Valley Semillon 2008 Typical pale colour, with pure lemon sherbet fruit, excellent concentration and a fine, focused and long varietal finish; good now, but will age gracefully. Screwcap. 10.2% alc. **Rating** 94 **To** 2025 $25
Sweetwater Individual Vineyard Hunter Valley Shiraz 2007 Great colour; the juicy medium-bodied palate has great balance and energy thanks to the savoury/earthy tannins that emerge on the finish and lingering aftertaste. Screwcap. 13.8% alc. **Rating** 94 **To** 2022 $35
TBC Individual Vineyard Hunter Valley Shiraz 2007 A rich bouquet of sweet leather and confit plums, then a succulent palate redolent of black, gently savoury fruits, rounded tannins and quality oak; revels in its moderate alcohol and finishes with good acidity. Screwcap. 13.5% alc. **Rating** 94 **To** 2020 $30

ŶŶŶŶŶ **Six Degrees Vineyard Selection Hunter Valley Semillon 2008** Very interesting wine taking a leaf out of the riesling makers book by emulating the structure and flavour of Mosel Kabinett styles; the distinct residual sugar is neatly balanced by lemony acidity. A devilish wine for the options guessing game. Screwcap. 8% alc. **Rating** 90 **To** 2014 $20

Thompson Estate   ★★★★★

Harmans Road South, Wilyabrup, WA 6284 **Region** Margaret River
T (08) 9386 1751 **F** (08) 9386 1708 **www**.thompsonestate.com **Open** Wed–Sun 10–5
Winemaker Various contract **Est.** 1998 **Cases** 4000
Cardiologist Peter Thompson planted the first vines at Thompson Estate in 1994, inspired by his and his family's shareholdings in the Pierro and Fire Gully vineyards, and by visits to many of the world's premium wine regions. A total of 15 ha has been established: cabernet sauvignon, cabernet franc, merlot, chardonnay and pinot noir. The Thompsons have split the winemaking between specialist winemakers: Cabernet Merlot by Mark Messenger of Juniper Estate (previously of Cape Mentelle), Pinot Noir by Flying Fish Cove and Pinot Chardonnay by Harold Osborne of Fraser Woods. Exports to the UK, the US and other major markets.

ŶŶŶŶŶ **Margaret River Chardonnay 2007** Beautifully crafted, with pure grapefruit and nectarine on the bouquet; gently spiced with very polished oak, and lovely grip, weight and depth to the powerful yet fine palate. Screwcap. 14.5% alc. **Rating** 95 **To** 2017 $38
Margaret River Semillon Sauvignon Blanc 2008 A very precise green nettle bouquet, with vibrant citrus and a mere hint of tropical fruit; the palate is taut, with fine line and drive; long and harmonious. Screwcap. 11% alc. **Rating** 94 **To** 2014 $25
Margaret River Cabernet Merlot 2005 Still vibrant colour; red fruit and cassis combine seamlessly with cigar box and black olive; the oak frames the fruit well, and there is a slight leafy varietal firmness on the finish; textbook stuff. Screwcap. 14.5% alc. **Rating** 94 **To** 2018 $28
Margaret River Cabernet Sauvignon 2005 Very good colour; generous but high-quality blackcurrant fruit immediately appears on the fragrant bouquet backed by cedary oak, and continues on the well-balanced and structured palate, which has ample tannin support. Cork. 14.5% alc. **Rating** 94 **To** 2018 $38

ŶŶŶŶ **Margaret River Chardonnay Pinot Noir 2005** Lemon and green apple bouquet; good flavour and intensity, but just a little coarse on the finish. Cork. 12.5% alc. **Rating** 88 **To** 2012 $38

Thorn-Clarke Wines ★★★★★

Milton Park, Gawler Park Road, Angaston, SA 5353 **Region** Barossa Valley
T (08) 8564 3036 **F** (08) 8564 3255 **www**.thornclarkewines.com.au **Open** Mon–Fri 9–5
Winemaker Derek Fitzgerald **Est.** 1987 **Cases** 80 000 **Vyds** 267.88 ha
Established by David and Cheryl Clarke (née Thorn), and son Sam, Thorn-Clarke is one of
the largest family-owned, estate-based businesses in the greater Barossa region. Their winery
is close to the border between the Barossa and Eden valleys, and they are often regarded as
a Barossa Valley winery. In fact three of their four vineyards are in the Eden Valley, the Mt
Crawford Vineyard is at the southern end of the Eden Valley, while the Milton Park and
Sandpiper vineyards are further north in the Eden Valley. The fourth vineyard is at St Kitts in
the northern end of the Barossa Ranges, established when no other vignerons had ventured
onto what was hitherto considered unsuitable soil. In all four vineyards careful soil mapping
has resulted in matching of variety and site, with all of the major varieties represented. The
quality of grapes retained for the Thorne-Clarke label has resulted in a succession of trophy
and gold medal-winning wines at very competitive prices. Exports to all major markets.

♟♟♟♟♟ **Sandpiper Eden Valley Riesling 2008** Clean lime and apple blossom aromas;
very well-delineated lime juice flavours; considerable length. Screwcap. 12.5% alc.
Rating 94 **To** 2016 $16
William Randell Barossa Shiraz 2006 Very dense colour; a super-rich wine
with layers of black fruits glued together by fine, but persistent, tannins and quality
oak; needs to shed some weight, but will undoubtedly do so. Wine-stained cork.
15% alc. **Rating** 94 **To** 2021 $49

♟♟♟♟♀ **Shotfire Barossa Shiraz 2007** Bright crimson-purple; a fragrant bouquet leads
into cherry and plum fruit on the mid-palate; finish still to fully integrate, but will
almost certainly do so. Cork. 14% alc. **Rating** 91 **To** 2015 $22
Sandpiper Barossa Cabernet Sauvignon 2007 Good weight and depth of
dark berry fruit; a little black olive comes through on the very generous finish, with
a bright core of red fruit and oak. Screwcap. 13.5% alc. **Rating** 91 **To** 2015 $16
Shotfire Eden Valley Chardonnay 2007 Big, brassy, rich and ripe; figs and
toasted bread, with plenty of grilled nut flavour coming through on the finish.
Screwcap. 13% alc. **Rating** 90 **To** 2011 $22
Sandpiper Barossa Shiraz 2007 Has abundant, carefree plum and blackberry
fruit on both bouquet and palate, with well-integrated and balanced oak in
support. Screwcap. 13.5% alc. **Rating** 90 **To** 2015 $16
Sandpiper Barossa Merlot 2007 Good hue and depth; a rich, rollicking, juicy
red wine which has immediate appeal, and just enough savoury tannins to express
varietal flavour. Value. Screwcap. 13% alc. **Rating** 90 **To** 2014 $15

♟♟♟♟ **Shotfire Barossa Quartage 2007** Good hue; fresh and vibrant; red fruits and
savoury flavours on the light- to medium-bodied palate; minimal tannins; not
as complex as prior vintages. Cabernet Sauvignon/Petit Verdot/Merlot/Malbec.
Screwcap. 13.5% alc. **Rating** 89 **To** 2014 $20
Sandpiper Eden Valley Pinot Gris 2007 Clean, fresh and well made; pear
and a touch of spice, with pleasant texture and surprising length on the finish.
Screwcap. 12.5% alc. **Rating** 88 **To** 2012 $15

3 Drops ★★★★★

PO Box 1828, Applecross, WA 6953 **Region** Mount Barker
T (08) 9315 4721 **F** (08) 9315 4724 **www**.3drops.com **Open** Not
Winemaker Robert Diletti (Contract) **Est.** 1998 **Cases** 4500 **Vyds** 21.5 ha
The 3 Drops are not the three owners (John Bradbury, Joanne Bradbury and Nicola Wallich),
but wine, olive oil and water, all of which come from the substantial property at Mount Barker.
The plantings are riesling, sauvignon blanc, semillon, chardonnay, cabernet sauvignon, merlot,
shiraz and cabernet franc, like the olive trees, irrigated by a large wetland on the property. The
business expanded significantly in 2007 with the purchase of the 14.7-ha Patterson's Vineyard.
Exports to the UK, Canada and Hong Kong.

ΨΨΨΨΨ Mount Barker Riesling 2008 Lively and pure bouquet of lemon and ripe exotic fruit; linear and fine, lime takes over on the palate with unexpected depth and persistence; finely balanced. Screwcap. 12.5% alc. **Rating** 94 **To** 2015 $22
Mount Barker Riesling 2007 Ultra-correct citrus and mineral; smooth, supple, toasty nuances, then a silky, clean finish. Gold WA Wine Show '08. Screwcap. 13% alc. **Rating** 94 **To** 2015 $22

ΨΨΨΨΨ Mount Barker Chardonnay 2007 Elegantly framed with spicy oak and ripe melon and grapefruit aromas; fresh, focused, and very even throughout the palate; nicely balanced with real poise and finesse. Screwcap. 14% alc. **Rating** 93 **To** 2014 $24
Mount Barker Sauvignon Blanc 2008 A fresh and vibrant wine exhibiting a nice balance of ripe tropical fruits, with a little hint of nettle for complexity and interest; fine and fragrant on the finish. Screwcap. 13% alc. **Rating** 92 **To** 2012 $22
Mount Barker Shiraz 2007 Dense plum and mulberry fruit bouquet; tar and blackberry comes to the fore on the palate, and the oak sits nicely with the fruit; bright and chewy on the finish. Screwcap. 14% alc. **Rating** 92 **To** 2014 $24

ΨΨΨΨ Mount Barker Merlot 2007 Light fresh redcurrant fruit aromas and flavours on entry, then more savoury/olive notes on the back-palate and finish. Varietal but a little edgy. Screwcap. 14% alc. **Rating** 88 **To** 2013 $25

Three Wise Men ★★★

Woongarra Estate, 95 Hayseys Road, Narre Warren East, Vic 3804 **Region** Port Phillip Zone
T (03) 9796 8886 **www**.threewisemen.com.au **Open** Thurs–Sun 9–5, or by appt
Winemaker Graeme Leith **Est.** 1994 **Cases** 800
The Three Wise Men label was conceived to make a top-quality single-vineyard Pinot Noir grown at Woongarra Estate, a well-drained, cool and moist site close to the Yarra Valley. An agreement between the Jones's of Woongarra and Passing Clouds (see separate entries) winemaker Graeme Leith means that the wine is made at Passing Clouds. A variety of winemaking techniques are used, varying according to vintage conditions. Each of the partners takes half of the resulting wine and sells it through their respective cellar doors.

ΨΨΨΨ Sauvignon Blanc 2008 May be a little light-on, but everything that is present is correct; attractive touches of herb, citrus and passionfruit. Great price. Screwcap. 12.5% alc. **Rating** 89 **To** 2010 $12

Three Wishes Vineyard

604 Batman Highway, Hillwood, Tas 7252 **Region** Northern Tasmania
T (03) 6331 2009 **F** (03) 6331 0043 **www**.threewishesvineyard.com.au
Open 7 days 11–5 Boxing Day to Easter, or by appt
Winemaker Bass Fine Wines **Est.** 1998 **Cases** 600
Peter and Natalie Whish-Wilson began the establishment of their vineyard in 1998 while they were working in Hong Kong, delegating the management tasks to parents Rosemary and Tony until 2003. Peter and Natalie took a year's sabbatical to do the first vintage, with their children aged six and four also involved in tending the vines. The seachange became permanent, Peter completing his wine growing degree from CSU in 1996. The original 2.8 ha of pinot noir, chardonnay and riesling are being extended by the planting of a further ha of pinot noir.

ΨΨΨΨ Riesling 2008 Commercial style; flavoursome, but the sweet tropical fruit needed more acidity for balance. Drink soon. Screwcap. 13% alc. **Rating** 87 **To** 2012 $20
Pinot Noir 2007 Supple and lively array of red and black fruits; good length; slightly simple. Screwcap. 13.5% alc. **Rating** 87 **To** 2013 $35

Tidswell Wines ★★★☆

PO Box 94, Kensington Park, SA 5068 **Region** Limestone Coast Zone
T (08) 8363 5800 **F** (08) 8363 1980 **www**.tidswellwines.com.au **Open** Not
Winemaker Ben Tidswell, Wine Wise Consultancy **Est.** 1994 **Cases** 7000 **Vyds** 134 ha
The Tidswell family (now in the shape of Andrea and Ben Tidswell) has two large vineyards
in the Limestone Coast Zone near Bool Lagoon; lion's share is planted to shiraz and cabernet
sauvignon, with smaller plantings of merlot, chardonnay, semillon and sauvignon blanc. Fifty
percent of the vineyards are organically certified, and more will be converted in due course.
Wines are released under the Jennifer, Heathfield Ridge and Caves Road labels. Exports to
Canada, Denmark, Germany, Singapore and Japan.

♀♀♀♀♀ **Heathfield Ridge Cabernet Sauvignon 2005** Generous wine, with pleasing,
ripe blackcurrant and cassis fruit supported by well-integrated French oak; the
tannins are likewise ripe. Screwcap. 14.5% alc. **Rating** 92 **To** 2020 $22.50

Tilbrook ★★★★★

17/1 Adelaide Lobethal Road, Lobethal, SA 5241 **Region** Adelaide Hills
T (08) 8389 5318 **F** (08) 8389 5315 **www**.marketsatheart.com/tilbrookestate
Open Fri–Sun 11–5 & public hols, or by appt
Winemaker James Tilbrook **Est.** 2001 **Cases** 1500 **Vyds** 4.8 ha
James and Annabelle Tilbrook have 4.4 ha of multi-clone chardonnay and pinot noir,
and 0.4 ha of sauvignon blanc at Lenswood. The winery and cellar door are in the old
Onkaparinga Woollen Mills building in Lobethal; this not only provides an atmospheric
home, but also helps meet the very strict environmental requirements of the Adelaide Hills
in dealing with winery waste water. English-born James came to Australia in 1986, aged 22,
but a car accident led to his return to England. Working for Oddbins and passing the WSET
diploma set his future course. He returned to Australia, met wife Annabelle, purchased the
vineyard and began planting the vineyard in 1999. Plantings are continuing for the Tilbrook
label, and for the moment the major part of the plantings (chardonnay and pinot noir) is sold
to Foster's. Exports to the UK.

♀♀♀♀♀ **Lenswood Vineyard Reserve Chardonnay 2006** All the bells and whistles
have paid handsome dividends: hand-picked, whole bunch–pressed, barrel-
fermented in one-third new French oak, two-thirds through mlf, extended lees
contact and two years in barrel have not diminished the vibrancy, freshness and
length of the wine. Cork. 13.5% alc. **Rating** 96 **To** 2020 $30
Adelaide Hills Chardonnay 2006 A subtle fusion of grapefruit and stone fruit,
French oak and acidity in an understated but perfectly balanced wine. Screwcap.
13.5% alc. **Rating** 94 **To** 2013 $20

♀♀♀♀♀ **Adelaide Hills Sauvignon Blanc 2008** Has strong varietal expression via
gooseberry and passionfruit on the bouquet and palate, then a firm finish.
Screwcap. 13.5% alc. **Rating** 91 **To** 2010 $20

Tim Adams ★★★★★

Warenda Road, Clare, SA 5453 **Region** Clare Valley
T (08) 8842 2429 **F** (08) 8842 3550 **www**.timadamswines.com.au **Open** Mon–Fri 10.30–5,
w'ends 11–5
Winemaker Tim Adams **Est.** 1986 **Cases** 50 000 **Vyds** 70 ha
After almost 20 years slowly and carefully building the business, based on the classic Clare
Valley varieties of riesling, semillon, grenache, shiraz and cabernet sauvignon, Tim and Pam
Goldsack decided to increase their production from 35 000 to 50 000 cases. Like their move
to a total reliance on screwcaps, there is nothing unexpected in that. However, the makeup
of the new plantings is anything but usual: they will give Tim Adams more than 10 ha of
tempranillo and pinot gris, and about 3.5 ha of viognier, in each case with a very clear idea
about the style of wine to be produced. Exports to all major markets.

♡♡♡♡♡ Reserve Clare Valley Riesling 2007 Intensely wound citrus/grapefruit aromas; excellent mouthfeel, with slippery acidity supporting mouth-watering citrus and apple flavours. Screwcap. 11% alc. **Rating** 95 **To** 2018 $35

Clare Valley Riesling 2008 An excellent bouquet offers a range of blossom and spice aromas, and leads into a refined and precise palate, citrus fruit and acidity perfectly balanced. Cellar special. Screwcap. 11.5% alc. **Rating** 94 **To** 2020 $22

Clare Valley Semillon 2007 Twelve hours skin contact and barrel fermentation in new French oak then five months' oak maturation has been very well handled; the wine is still fresh and in no way phenolic, simply complex. Not my style, but impressive and very good value. Trophy Best International Semillon International Wine Challenge '08. Screwcap. 13% alc. **Rating** 94 **To** 2015 $22

♡♡♡♡♀ Clare Valley Riesling 2007 Classic regional evocation without any distortion from heat or drought; almost slippery citrus fruit flavour; good line, likewise finish. Screwcap. 12% alc. **Rating** 93 **To** 2012 $22

The Aberfeldy 2006 Bright and quite polished red fruits, with earth and a little supporting mint; the palate exhibits pronounced acidity, but the fruit is ample enough; quite fine and long on the even finish. Shiraz. Screwcap. 14.5% alc. **Rating** 91 **To** 2018 $59

Reserve Clare Valley Tempranillo 2006 An attractive array of red fruits with an equally emphatic input of new French oak; languorous tannins add to the pleasure factor. Screwcap. 13% alc. **Rating** 90 **To** 2010 $29

♡♡♡♡ Clare Valley Shiraz 2006 Good hue and depth; a curious earthy component to both bouquet and palate gives the wine a certain austerity, but also complexity. Difficult to point. Screwcap. 14.5% alc. **Rating** 89 **To** 2015 $26

The Fergus 2006 An eclectic blend of Grenache/Cabernet Sauvignon/Shiraz/ Malbec/Cabernet Franc comes together in a light- to medium-bodied palate made for easy drinking. Screwcap. 14.5% alc. **Rating** 88 **To** 2011 $19

Tim Gramp ★★★★☆

Mintaro /Leasingham Road, Watervale, SA 5452 **Region** Clare Valley
T (08) 8344 4079 **www**.timgrampwines.com.au **Open** W'ends & hols 11–4
Winemaker Tim Gramp **Est.** 1990 **Cases** 6000 **Vyds** 16 ha
Tim Gramp has quietly built up a very successful business and by keeping overheads to a minimum provides good wines at modest prices. Over the years the estate vineyards (shiraz, riesling, cabernet sauvignon and grenache) have been expanded significantly. Exports to the UK, Taiwan, Malaysia and NZ.

♡♡♡♡♡ Gilbert Valley Reserve Mount Lofty Ranges Shiraz Cabernet 2005 A lovely wine, which speaks its mind from the first whiff of cedar, spice and black fruits, then through the perfectly balanced and textured palate, the flavours tracking the bouquet. The 10% cabernet adds to the length, as do the superfine tannins; 230 dozen made. Cork. 14.5% alc. **Rating** 96 **To** 2020 $58

♡♡♡♡♀ Watervale Riesling 2008 A tight, linear and very dry style; floral aromas mixed with freshly squeezed lime juice and a hint of mineral in the background; dry and focused. Screwcap. 12.5% alc. **Rating** 91 **To** 2016 $19.80

Tim McNeil Wines ★★★★

PO Box 1088, Clare, SA 5453 **Region** Clare Valley
T (08) 8843 4348 **F** (08) 8843 4272 **www**.timmcneilwines.com.au **Open** Not
Winemaker Tim McNeil **Est.** 2004 **Cases** 600 **Vyds** 3 ha
When Tim and Cass McNeil established Tim McNeil Wines, Tim had long since given up his teaching career, graduating with a degree in oenology from Adelaide University in 1999. During his university years he worked at Yalumba, then moved with Cass to the Clare Valley in 2001, spending four years as a winemaker at Jim Barry Wines before moving to Kilikanoon in '05, where he currently works as a winemaker alongside Kevin Mitchell. The McNeils'

16-ha property at Watervale includes mature, dry-grown riesling, and they intend to plant shiraz, currently purchasing that variety from the Barossa Valley. A cellar door facility is under construction and will open by the end of 2009.

ɣɣɣɣɣ **Clare Valley Riesling 2008** Bright, light straw-green; a vibrant, zesty and crisp palate, flowery lime fruit at one edge, minerally notes at the other; good length and thrust. Very good value. Screwcap. 12.5% alc. **Rating** 93 **To** 2018 $19.99

ɣɣɣɣ **Barossa Shiraz 2006** Well-balanced and structured medium- full-bodied wine, with slightly spicy fruit, oak and fine tannins all coalescing. Screwcap. 15% alc. **Rating** 89 **To** 2016 $24.99

Tim Smith Wines   ★★★★

PO Box 446, Tanunda, SA 5352 **Region** Barossa Valley
T (08) 8563 0939 **F** (08) 8563 0939 **Open** Not
Winemaker Tim Smith **Est.** 2001 **Cases** 1000
Tim Smith aspires (and succeeds) to make wines in the mould of the great producers of Côte Rôtie and Chateauneuf du Pape, but using a New World approach. It is a business in its early stages, with only four wines: a Shiraz, Botrytis Semillon, Viognier and Grenache/Shiraz/Mourvedre. Exports to the UK and the US.

ɣɣɣɣɣ **Barossa Mataro Grenache Shiraz 2006** Good colour; very powerful and intense, belying its region and alcohol; the black and red fruits with unusual intensity and length. Screwcap. 14.5% alc. **Rating** 93 **To** 2016 $27
Barossa Shiraz 2006 Impressively deep, dark and just a little spicy, with a dried herb edge; mouth-coating texture, with a slight mocha element fighting through to the fruit on the finish. Screwcap. 14.5% alc. **Rating** 92 **To** 2016 $32
tsw Shiraz 2005 Colour still very strong and dense; a full-bodied wine, with layers of black fruit and supple tannins; some alcohol-derived sweetness the only issue. Cork. 15.5% alc. **Rating** 92 **To** 2015 $60

ɣɣɣɣ **Adelaide Hills Viognier 2008** Faint bronze tint; elegant wine with supple mouthfeel and gently sweet fruit (not sugar) but lacks varietal punch. Screwcap. 14% alc. **Rating** 89 **To** 2011 $28

Tin Soldier Wine   ★★★★★

60 Arabella Street, Longueville, NSW 2066 (postal) **Region** Lower Hunter Valley
T 0437 121 302 **F** (02) 8088 1066 **www.tinsoldierwine.com.au** **Open** Not
Winemaker First Creek (Liz Jackson), Daniel Binet **Est.** 2008 **Cases** 4000 **Vyds** 11.2 ha
When I tasted this range of wines, I had never heard of the name and knew nothing about the origin of the wines. However, skilled winemaking was apparent in every wine, and it also seemed improbable that they could have been made from young vines. And, indeed, I subsequently learnt that the vineyard goes back as far as 1970, with some intervening plantings, although none in recent years. It was previously owned by the Gartelmann Estate, and was used in the production of their wine up to and including 2006. When Russell and Katrina Leslie purchased the vineyard, they found a toy tin soldier among the vines; it not only provided the name, but the striking label design and packaging. While Tin Soldier has had significant show success, the tasting notes make it clear I was, and am, particularly impressed by the range of wines.

ɣɣɣɣɣ **Hunter Valley Semillon 2008** Fragrant grass and herb aromas lead into a vibrant, lemon-charged palate, with abundant flavour and length sustained by bright acidity. Screwcap. 9.7% alc. **Rating** 95 **To** 2016 $25
Reserve Hunter Valley Semillon 2007 Has the focus, intensity and precision absent from the varietal, with sweet lemon/citrus fruit and a long, crisp finish. Why only $2 difference? Screwcap. 10.2% alc. **Rating** 94 **To** 2016 $27

Hunter Valley Chardonnay 2007 Completes a remarkable run of wines from Tin Soldier, all flawlessly made; nectarine and citrus flavours have the poise and balance of cool-grown chardonnay; the oak is perfectly balanced. Screwcap. 13.2% alc. **Rating** 94 **To** 2015 $16

♀♀♀♀♀ Hunter Valley Merlot 2007 Brilliant clarity and hue; comes together remarkably well; the Hunter Valley is not supposed to make merlot this good, with delicious cassis fruit and equally good texture and structure. Screwcap. 12% alc. **Rating** 93 **To** 2016 $25
Hunter Valley Shiraz 2007 Light, bright crimson; a refreshing and elegant wine; the palate is no more than medium-bodied, but has length and balance to its red fruit flavours. Screwcap. 13% alc. **Rating** 92 **To** 2017 $32
Hunter Valley Semillon Sauvignon Blanc 2008 Interestingly, has stuck with the Hunter Valley for its sauvignon blanc, most going to Orange, Tumbarumba or Margaret River; as expected the focus is on semillon, although the sauvignon blanc pokes its head up momentarily on the mid-palate; all works well enough. Screwcap. 10.7% alc. **Rating** 91 **To** 2014 $25
Hunter Valley Semillon 2007 Bright straw-green; some hints of development with hints of honey and straw; good length, but needed a touch more acidity. Screwcap. 10.3% alc. **Rating** 90 **To** 2014 $25

♀♀♀♀ Hunter Valley Chardonnay 2008 Fresh, crisp fruit-driven style, with good focus and length, subtle oak adding a dimension to the structure. Like all the Tin Soldiers, very well drilled. Screwcap. 12.8% alc. **Rating** 89 **To** 2013 $25

Tinderbox Vineyard   ★★★★
Tinderbox, Tas 7054 **Region** Southern Tasmania
T (03) 6229 2994 **Open** By appt
Winemaker Contract **Est.** 1994 **Cases** 96 **Vyds** 2 ha
Liz McGown may have retired from specialist nursing (some years ago), but is busier than ever, having taken on the running of the 400-ha Tinderbox fat lamb and fine merino wool property after a lease (which had run for 22 years) terminated. Liz describes Tinderbox as a vineyard between the sun and the sea, and looking out over the vineyard towards Bruny Island in the distance, it is not hard to see why. The attractive label was designed by Barry Tucker, who was so charmed by Liz's request that he waived his usual (substantial) fee.

♀♀♀♀♀ Pinot Noir 2007 Good colour; a delicate but vigorous palate with red cherry fruit framed by some spicy/foresty notes; has achieved the ripeness missing in some. Screwcap. 13.6% alc. **Rating** 91 **To** 2014 $30

Tinklers Vineyard   ★★★★
Pokolbin Mountains Road, Pokolbin, NSW 2320 **Region** Lower Hunter Valley
T (02) 4998 7435 **F** (02) 4998 7469 **www**.tinklers.com.au **Open** 7 days 10–5
Winemaker Usher John Tinkler **Est.** 1997 **Cases** 1500 **Vyds** 41 ha
Three generations of the Tinkler family have been involved with the property since 1942. Originally a beef and dairy farm, vines have been both pulled out and replanted at various stages, and part of the adjoining 80-year-old Ben Ean Vineyard acquired. Plantings include semillon (14 ha), shiraz (11.5 ha), chardonnay (6.5 ha) and smaller plantings of merlot, muscat and viognier. In 2008 a new winery, adjoining the cellar door, was completed; all Tinklers wines are now vinified here, distinguished by a gold strip at the bottom of the label. The majority of the grape production continues to be sold to McWilliam's.

♀♀♀♀♀ School Block Hunter Valley Semillon 2007 Well made and balanced, with juicy, sweet citrus flavours on the mid-palate followed by a dry, minerally finish. Screwcap. 11.3% alc. **Rating** 91 **To** 2017 $18
U & I Reserve Shiraz 2006 Attractive medium-bodied wine, with clear regional character, although black cherry and blackberry are more potent than the earthy/leathery nuances. Screwcap. 14% alc. **Rating** 91 **To** 2016 $32

Hunter Valley Shiraz Viognier 2007 Bright crimson-purple reflecting 5% co-fermented viognier, the lifted spice and musk aromas likewise; the juicy medium-bodied palate will give maximum pleasure over the next five to seven years. Screwcap. 14% alc. **Rating** 91 **To** 2016 $25

Tintara   ★★★★★

202 Main Road, McLaren Vale, SA 5171 **Region** McLaren Vale
T (08) 8329 4124 **F** (08) 8392 2202 **www.**tintara.com.au **Open** 7 days 10–4.30
Winemaker Paul Carpenter **Est.** 1863 **Cases** NFP
Tintara was the third of the three substantial winery and vineyard enterprises in the early days of McLaren Vale. It was established by Dr Alexander Kelly, who purchased 280 ha of land in 1861 and planted the first vines in 1863. It grew rapidly – indeed, too rapidly, because it ran into financial difficulties and was acquired by Thomas Hardy in 1876. He in turn recovered his purchase price by wine sales over the following year. It has been a proud label for almost 150 years, but gained additional vigour with the 2008 release of the Single Vineyard wines, which in the years prior to their release collected a swag of trophies and accolades.

🍷🍷🍷🍷🍷 **Single Vineyard Upper Tintara Shiraz 2004** The most complete wine of the three Tintara Single Vineyard Shirazs; has grace with power thanks to glistening, fine tannins; total harmony. From the vineyard owned by Bob Hardy. Three trophies, and three gold medals. **Rating** 96 **To** 2024 $80
Single Vineyard McLaren Flat Shiraz 2004 Has abundant red and black fruits with strands of dark chocolate and spice running through the palate; quality oak and fine tannins frame a beautiful wine, the red fruits echoing on the finish and aftertaste; 60-year-old vines; 4 gold medals. **Rating** 95 **To** 2024 $80
McLaren Vale Grenache 2007 Clear crimson-red; fills the bouquet and palate with an array of spicy/savoury red fruits; has intensity and great balance. One of the very best examples. Cork. 14% alc. **Rating** 95 **To** 2022 $52
Single Vineyard Blewitt Springs Shiraz 2004 An altogether aristocratic wine, filled to the brim with dark fruits supported by persistent, faintly dusty, tannins on a long, lingering finish. One trophy, eight gold medals. **Rating** 95 **To** 2024 $80
McLaren Vale Shiraz 2006 Dense crimson; a wine that manages to retain elegance even though it is full of plum, blackberry and dark chocolate fruit; the texture is silky, the oak integrated, the tannins fine. Cork. 14% alc. **Rating** 94 **To** 2021 $27
McLaren Vale Cabernet Sauvignon 2006 Deeply coloured; a powerful wine, speaking more or less equally of its region and variety; lush blackcurrant fruit at one end, dark chocolate in the middle, and savoury/earthy tannins at the other end. Curious use of cork for a long-lived wine; for US consumption? 13.5% alc. **Rating** 94 **To** 2020 $27

🍷🍷🍷🍷🍷 **Reserve Shiraz 2002** A brooding powerhouse, full of fruit, oak and, given its absolute weight and power, is incredibly precise; however the oak still dominates, which poses the question whether the fruit can come through. Cork. 14% alc. **Rating** 91 **To** 2027 $50
McLaren Vale Sangiovese 2007 Light red; clear varietal expression on bouquet and palate alike, offering spicy red fruits with inbuilt, but very fine, tannins; this is sangiovese without the pain. Cork. 14% alc. **Rating** 91 **To** 2013 $25

🍷🍷🍷🍷 **McLaren Vale Tempranillo 2006** Aromas of spice, leather, dark chocolate and cherry accompany the wine through to the palate, with its spicy finish. Cork. 14% alc. **Rating** 89 **To** 2013 $25

Tintilla Wines   ★★★★

725 Hermitage Road, Pokolbin, NSW 2320 **Region** Lower Hunter Valley
T (02) 6574 7093 **F** (02) 9767 6894 **www.**tintilla.com.au **Open** 7 days 10.30–6
Winemaker James Lusby **Est.** 1993 **Cases** 3500 **Vyds** 7.5 ha

The Lusby family has established shiraz, sauvignon blanc, merlot, semillon, sangiovese and cabernet sauvignon on a northeast-facing slope with red clay and limestone soil. Tintilla was the first winery to plant sangiovese in the Hunter Valley (1995). They have also planted an olive grove producing four different types of olives, which are cured and sold from the estate.

ŸŸŸŸŸ **Angus Hunter Semillon 2008** Classic Hunter semillon, showing the intensity of flavour and extreme palate length that can be achieved at this (typical) low alcohol; will get better with age. Screwcap. 10.5% alc. **Rating** 93 **To** 2018 $24
Pebbles Brief Hunter Valley Chardonnay 2008 Attractive stone fruit and melon aromas, the French oak neatly balanced; on the palate, moves into a more citrussy spectrum, with pronounced acidity on the finish. Screwcap. 13% alc. **Rating** 90 **To** 2014 $25
Rosato di Jupiter Hunter Valley Sangiovese 2008 An early-picked, feather-light, dry rose with sour cherry fruit flavours that work very well in a gently savoury mode. Screwcap. 11.5% alc. **Rating** 90 **To** 2010 $20
Reserve Hunter Valley Shiraz 2007 Distinctive regional sweet leather and earth notes to the bouquet; the medium-bodied palate has a well-balanced mix of blackberry and plum fruit, then soft tannins to close. Screwcap. 13% alc. **Rating** 90 **To** 2017 $28
Patriarch Hunter Valley Shiraz 2005 A bright wine with a savoury personality; red fruits on entry give way to darker, more earthy tones, and the tannin and fruit weight come through on the finish. Screwcap. 13.5% alc. **Rating** 90 **To** 2016 $60

ŸŸŸŸ **James Hunter Valley Cabernet Merlot 2007** There is no shortage of sweet fruits in a cassis and blackcurrant range; just a little soft. Screwcap. 13% alc. **Rating** 89 **To** 2015 $26
Catherine de 'M Hunter Valley Sangiovese Merlot 2007 A light- to medium-bodied, but intense wine, the cherry/sweet cherry of the sangiovese melding into the red fruits of the merlot, each having a savoury twist in its tail. Screwcap. 13% alc. **Rating** 89 **To** 2015 $26
James Hunter Valley Cabernet Merlot 2006 Attractive light- to medium-bodied blend of cassis red fruits and a savoury twist in the tail. Screwcap. 13% alc. **Rating** 88 **To** 2014 $26

Tisdall Wines   ★★★

19-29 Cornelia Creek Road, Echuca, Vic 3564 **Region** Goulburn Valley
T (03) 5482 1911 **F** (03) 5482 2516 **Open** 7 days 9.30–5 at Murray Esplande Cellars
Winemaker Robin Querre, John Mackley **Est.** 1971 **Cases** 28 000 **Vyds** 40.77 ha
Tisdall Wines is not so much a new winery, as a reborn one. The vineyard, with most of the mainstream varieties, has been in continuous production since 1971. It is planted to chardonnay, merlot, sauvignon blanc, cabernet sauvignon, riesling, semillon and shiraz. Under the ownership of the Ballande Groupe, which acquired the business in 1999, the focus has been international markets, with exports to the China, India, Belgium and NZ.

ŸŸŸŸ **Sauvignon Blanc 2008** Has good structure and texture, the flavours subtle but ranging from mineral to grapefruit and stone fruit. Screwcap. 13% alc. **Rating** 88 **To** 2010 $14.99

Tobin Wines

34 Ricca Road, Ballandean, Qld 4382 **Region** Granite Belt
T (07) 4684 1235 **F** (07) 4684 1235 **www**.tobinwines.com.au **Open** 7 days 10–5
Winemaker Adrian Tobin, David Gianini **Est.** 1964 **Cases** 1000 **Vyds** 7.5 ha
In the early 1960s the Ricca family planted table grapes, followed by shiraz and semillon in 1964–66, which are said to be the oldest vinifera vines in the Granite Belt region. The Tobin family (headed by Adrian and Frances) purchased the vineyard in 2000 and have increased plantings, which now consist of shiraz, cabernet sauvignon, merlot, tempranillo, semillon, verdelho, chardonnay and sauvignon blanc, with some remaining rows of table grapes. The emphasis has changed towards quality bottled wines, with some success.

ŸŸŸŸ **Isabella Semillon 2008** Typical young semillon; crisp and minerally, with a long finish, myriad future flavours waiting in the wings. Pleads for time to grow up. Screwcap. 11% alc. **Rating** 88 **To** 2018 $28
Lily Chardonnay 2008 Early-picked style on the verge of sauvignon blanc/ semillon territory, but does score for its fresh and lively fruit and good length. Screwcap. 12.2% alc. **Rating** 87 **To** 2011 $28
Jacob Tempranillo 2008 Is distinctively varietal in the Australian context, with that citrussy twist on the finish contrasting with the raspberry and cherry flavours. Screwcap. 13% alc. **Rating** 87 **To** 2010 $28

Tokar Estate

6 Maddens Lane, Coldstream, Vic 3770 **Region** Yarra Valley
T (03) 5964 9585 **F** (03) 5964 9587 **www.tokarestate.com.au Open** 7 days 10–5
Winemaker Paul Evans **Est.** 1996 **Cases** 5000
Leon Tokar established 12.4 ha of now mature pinot noir, shiraz, cabernet sauvignon and tempranillo at Tokar Estate, one of many vineyards on Maddens Lane. All the wines are from the estate, badged Single Vineyard (which they are), and have performed well in regional shows, with early success for the Tempranillo.

ŸŸŸŸŸ **Yarra Valley Tempra Rosa 2008** Pale pink; fine array of red fruit and a gentle touch of spice; the palate is vibrant and quite dry, with a slight chalky minerality to the finish. Tempranillo. Screwcap. 12% alc. **Rating** 90 **To** 2011 $19

ŸŸŸŸ **The Reserve Syrah 2006** Toasty oak and roast meat/savoury bouquet; quite firm and savoury on the palate, with an earthy tone to frame the red fruit finish. Screwcap. 14.5% alc. **Rating** 89 **To** 2016 $48
Estate Pinot Noir 2006 Very savoury/stemmy/earthy varietal expression; does have length, albeit without changing the beat of the drum. Screwcap. 13.8% alc. **Rating** 88 **To** 2012 $26

Tollana

GPO Box 753, Melbourne, Vic 3001 **Region** Southeast Australia
T 1300 651 650 **Open** Not
Winemaker Angus Ridley **Est.** 1888 **Cases** 10 000
Tollana survived a near-death experience during the turbulent days of the Rosemount management of Southcorp; where it will ultimately fit in the Foster's scheme of things remains to be seen, but in the meantime, Tollana is back in business.

ŸŸŸŸŸ **Robinson Family Bin TR474 Pinot Noir 2008** Bright, light hue; an extremely fragrant bouquet with an infusion of spicy red fruits and some oak; outstanding palate with great drive and thrust to the vibrant black cherry and plum fruit finishing with spicy tannins. Made at Coldstream Hills from Mornington Peninsula grapes. **Rating** 95 **To** 2014

Tomboy Hill

204 Sim Street, Ballarat, Vic 3350 (postal) **Region** Ballarat
T (03) 5331 3785 **Open** Not
Winemaker Scott Ireland (Contract) **Est.** 1984 **Cases** 1400 **Vyds** 4.2 ha
Former schoolteacher Ian Watson seems to be following the same path as Lindsay McCall of Paringa Estate (also a former schoolteacher) in extracting greater quality and style than any other winemaker in his region, in this case Ballarat. Since 1984 Watson has slowly and patiently built up a patchwork quilt of small plantings of chardonnay and pinot noir. In the better years, the single-vineyard wines of Chardonnay and/or Pinot Noir are released; Rebellion Chardonnay and Pinot Noir are multi-vineyard blends, but all 100% Ballarat. I have a particular fondness for the style, not necessarily shared by others. Exports to the UK and Canada.

¶¶¶¶¶ **Smythes Creek Ballarat Goldfields Pinot Noir 2007** Brilliantly clear colour; the bouquet tells you this has the fully ripened fruit the Rebellion lacks; a totally delicious wine, with red cherry and raspberry fruit on a long, super-silky palate. Screwcap. 13.3% alc. **Rating** 95 **To** 2013 $50
Rebellion Ballarat Goldfields Chardonnay 2007 Bright straw-green; a totally delicious chardonnay offering nectarine and grapefruit harmoniously balanced by integrated quality French oak. Screwcap. 13.5% alc. **Rating** 94 **To** 2017 $30
The Tomboy Ballarat Goldfields Chardonnay 2007 Remarkably, has even more intensity and length than the Rebellion, and the fruit seems a little riper; at the end of the day, there is little to choose between the wines; both are of very high quality. Screwcap. 13.2% alc. **Rating** 94 **To** 2018 $45
The Tomboy Ballarat Goldfields Pinot Noir 2007 Is positioned between Rebellion and Smythes Creek, having the red fruits of the latter, and some of the savoury structure giving it more complexity, and possibly longevity. Screwcap. 13.2% alc. **Rating** 94 **To** 2015 $70

¶¶¶¶ **Rebellion Ballarat Goldfields Pinot Noir 2007** Bright purple hue; a spotlessly clean bouquet is followed by a very savoury/briary/stemmy palate that needs more ripe fruit components; does have serious length. Screwcap. 12.7% alc. **Rating** 89 **To** 2013 $35

Tomich Hill Wines   ★★★★

87 King William Road, Unley, SA 5061 (postal) **Region** Adelaide Hills
T (08) 8272 9388 **F** (08) 8373 7229 **www**.tomichhill.com.au **Open** Not
Winemaker John Tomich, Peter Leske (Contract) **Est.** 2002 **Cases** 4600
There is an element of irony in this family venture. Patriarch John Tomich was born on a vineyard near Mildura, where he learnt first-hand the skills and knowledge required for premium grapegrowing. He went on to become a well-known Adelaide ear, nose and throat specialist. Taking the wheel full circle, he completed postgraduate studies in winemaking at the University of Adelaide in 2002, and is now venturing on to the Master of Wine revision course from the Institute of Masters of Wine. His son Randal is a cutting from the old vine (metaphorically speaking), having invented new equipment and techniques for tending the family's 80-ha vineyard in the Adelaide Hills near Woodside, resulting in a 60% saving in time and fuel costs. Most of the grapes are sold, but the amount of wine made under the Tomich Hill brand is far from a hobby. Exports to Malaysia and Hong Kong.

¶¶¶¶¶ **Adelaide Hills Sauvignon Blanc 2008** A fragrant, fine wine, with bell-clear fruit in a passionfruit and citrus spectrum; the palate is fresh, the acidity perfect. Screwcap. 12.8% alc. **Rating** 94 **To** 2010 $19

¶¶¶¶ **Adelaide Hills Pinot Noir 2007** Very light bodied and delicate, but the varietal red fruit flavours are pure and unforced. Drink asap. Screwcap. 14% alc. **Rating** 88 **To** 2010 $26.50
Adelaide Hills Riesling 2008 Plenty of ripe citrus flavours, almost into stone fruit, but the finish is unconvincing. Screwcap. 12% alc. **Rating** 87 **To** 2012 $16
Adelaide Hills GSR 2008 Enigmatic labelling; sweet lime juice and tropical fruits intermingle; hard to pick a fight with it. Screwcap. 13% alc. **Rating** 87 **To** 2010 $17

Toms Cap Vineyard   ★★★

322 Lays Road, Carrajung Lower, Vic 3844 **Region** Gippsland
T (03) 5194 2215 **F** (03) 5194 2369 **www**.tomscap.com.au **Open** 7 days 10–5
Winemaker Owen Schmidt (Contract) **Est.** 1994 **Cases** 600
Graham Morris began the development of the vineyard in 1992 on a 40-ha property surrounded by the forests of the Strzelecki Ranges, the Ninety Mile Beach at Woodside, and the Tarra Bulga National Park, one of the four major areas of cool temperature rainforest in Vic. The vineyard has 2.4 ha of cabernet sauvignon, chardonnay, sauvignon blanc and riesling. In 2007 a 100-seat restaurant was opened offering a variety of local and overseas foods.

ŸŸŸŸ   **Cabernet Sauvignon 2006** Redcurrant and cedar fruit with a suggestion of
floral aromas; quite fine tannin and vibrant acidity; fine and even on the finish.
Screwcap. 12.5% alc. **Rating** 88 **To** 2013 $24
Mesana Late Picked Sauvignon Blanc 2008 Bright green–gold; barely off-
dry, but has enough flavour and length to satisfy and will develop a little more over
the next two years or so. Screwcap. 10.4% alc. **Rating** 87 **To** 2011 $20

Toolangi Vineyards   ★★★★★

PO Box 9431, South Yarra, Vic 3141 **Region** Yarra Valley
T (03) 9827 9977 **F** (03) 9827 6626 **www.**toolangi.com **Open** Not
Winemaker Various contract **Est.** 1995 **Cases** 12 000 **Vyds** 13 ha
Garry and Julie Hounsell acquired their property in the Dixons Creek subregion of the
Yarra Valley, adjoining the Toolangi State Forest, in 1995. The primary accent is on pinot
noir and chardonnay, accounting for all but 2.8 ha, which is predominantly shiraz and a little
viognier. Winemaking is by Yering Station, Giaconda and Shadowfax, as impressive a trio of
winemakers as one could wish for.

ŸŸŸŸŸ   **Estate Yarra Valley Chardonnay 2007** Vibrant hue; a restrained bouquet with
pear, nectarine and gentle spice from the well-handled oak; fine and tightly wound
with rapier-like acidity, and a pure fruit palate; very long and extremely fine and
poised. Screwcap. 12.5% alc. **Rating** 95 **To** 2015 $50
Reserve Yarra Valley Shiraz 2006 Perfumed and bright, with Asian spice and
red fruit at the core; the palate is lithe and quite lean, but builds to an apex of
flavour that is defined by a subtle bramble undercurrent; very long and quite silky
on the finish. Screwcap. 14% alc. **Rating** 95 **To** 2018 $65
Reserve Yarra Valley Chardonnay 2007 Ripe and highly expressive bouquet
with lots of toasty oak, grilled nuts and nectarine; the wine has pure power at all
levels, and needs time to integrate all of its parts, and will go a long way. Screwcap.
14.2% alc. **Rating** 94 **To** 2015 $75

ŸŸŸŸŸ   **Yarra Valley Shiraz 2006** A little reduction on opening; quite a firm and rugged
savoury wine, with roast meat and raspberry fruit at the heart; grainy tannins and
slightly unintegrated oak define the wine at this point in time; time will see it
soften. Screwcap. 14% alc. **Rating** 90 **To** 2015 $25

ŸŸŸŸ   **Yarra Valley Chardonnay 2007** Fresh and lean, with nectarine and a touch
of spice; quite fleshy and fine on the finish. Screwcap. 12.5% alc. **Rating** 89
To 2012 $25

Toolleen Vineyard   **NR**

Level 12, North Tower, 454 Collins Street, Melbourne, Vic 3000 (postal) **Region** Heathcote
T (03) 9831 7000 **F** (03) 9831 7099 **Open** Not
Winemaker Mark Jamieson **Est.** 1996 **Cases** 1500 **Vyds** 17.5 ha
Owned by Mr KC Huang and family, Toolleen's 17.5 ha of shiraz, cabernet sauvignon,
merlot, cabernet franc and durif are planted on the western slope of Mt Camel, 18 km north
of Heathcote. The lower Cambrian red soils are now well recognised for their suitability for
making full-bodied and strongly structured red wines. Most of the wine (80%) is exported to
Canada, United Arab Emirates, Taiwan, Hong Kong and China.

Toorak Winery

Vineyard 279 Toorak Road, Leeton, NSW 2705 **Region** Riverina
T (02) 6953 2333 **www.**toorakwines.com.au **Open** Mon–Fri 10–5, Sat by appt
Winemaker Robert Bruno **Est.** 1965 **Cases** 200 000 **Vyds** 150 ha
A traditional, long-established Riverina producer with a strong Italian-based clientele around
Australia. Production has been increasing significantly, utilising 150 ha of estate plantings and
grapes purchased from other growers, both in the Riverina and elsewhere. Wines are released
under the Willandra Estate, Toorak Estate, Casuarina Creek and Amesbury Estate labels. While,

in absolute terms, the quality is not great, the low-priced wines in fact over-deliver in many instances. Exports to the US, India, Singapore and China.

♀♀♀♀ **Willandra Estate Premium Tumbarumba Chardonnay 2008** Clearly shows its cool-climate birthplace, with grapefruit aromas and flavours leading this fruit-driven wine; oak incidental. Worth a year or two in the cellar. Screwcap. 13.5% alc. **Rating** 88 **To** 2013 $16

Willandra Estate Premium King Valley Sauvignon Blanc 2008 Not particularly aromatic, but has an incisive cut grass palate and a fresh, minerally finish. Screwcap. 13% alc. **Rating** 87 **To** 2010 $16

Casuarina Creek Unwooded Chardonnay 2008 A considerable achievement to make an unwooded Riverina Chardonnay with such life and juicy varietal fruit; a little simple, but that is a small issue. Screwcap. 14% alc. **Rating** 87 **To** 2009 $12

Willandra Estate Premium Langhorne Creek Shiraz 2006 A convincing example of Langhorne Creek's ability to grow relatively cheap grapes, yet retain soft, almost silky, red fruit flavours; easy light- to medium-bodied, early-drinking style. Screwcap. 14.5% alc. **Rating** 87 **To** 2011 $16

Topper's Mountain Vineyard

5 km Guyra Road, Tingha, NSW 2369 **Region** New England
T (02) 6723 3506 **F** (02) 6723 3222 **www.**toppers.com.au **Open** By appt
Winemaker John Cassegrain (Contract), Symphony Hill **Est.** 2000 **Cases** 4000 **Vyds** 9.6 ha
Yet another New England venture, owned by the Kirkby and Birch families, with Mark Kirkby having the primary management responsibilities. Planting began in the spring of 2000, with the ultimate fruit salad trial of 15 rows each of innumerable varieties and clones. The total area planted was made up of 28 separate plantings, many of these with only 200 vines in a block. As varieties proved unsuited, they were grafted to those that hold the most promise. Thus far, gewurztraminer and sauvignon blanc hold most promise among the white wines, the Mediterranean reds doing better than their French cousins.

♀♀♀♀ **Thunderbolt's Combo Dry Red 2007** The 75% field blend of Petit Verdot and Tannat (both very tannic varieties) has been tempered by 25% Tempranillo; fresh and juicy, great for a summer's day. Screwcap. 13.5% alc. **Rating** 89 **To** 2011 $16

New England Tempranillo 2007 Clean, fresh and well made, with zesty raspberry and cherry fruit plus a squeeze of lemon. Screwcap. 13.5% alc. **Rating** 88 **To** 2014 $20

Torbreck Vintners

Roennfeldt Road, Marananga, SA 5352 **Region** Barossa Valley
T (08) 8562 4155 **F** (08) 8562 4195 **www.**torbreck.com **Open** 7 days 10–6
Winemaker David Powell **Est.** 1994 **Cases** 50 000 **Vyds** 70.95 ha
Of all the Barossa Valley wineries to grab the headlines in the US, with demand pulling prices up to undreamt levels, Torbreck stands supreme. David Powell has not let success go to his head, or subvert the individuality and sheer quality of his wines, all created around very old, dry-grown, bush-pruned vineyards. The top trio are led by The RunRig (Shiraz/Viognier); then The Factor (Shiraz) and The Descendant (Shiraz/Viognier); next The Struie (Shiraz) and The Steading (Grenache/Mataro/Shiraz). Notwithstanding the depth and richness of the wines, they have a remarkable degree of finesse. In 2008 the ownership was restructured, Californian vintner Peter Kight (of Quivira Vineyards) acquired the shares held by the investors who had been introduced earlier in the decade. Exports to all major markets.

♀♀♀♀♀ **The Factor 2006** Shows exceptional generosity from start to finish, yet retains finesse; the predominantly red fruits positively dance on the back-palate and finish, uninhibited by the fine-grained tannins; stained cork a worry. Shiraz. 14.5% alc. **Rating** 96 **To** 2017 $125

RunRig 2006 A very fragrant bouquet attests to the influence of viognier, which also may be part of the reason why the palate does not show the high alcohol, and is simply supple and velvety, even showing a hint of spice. Shiraz/viognier. Cork. 15.5% alc. **Rating** 96 **To** 2021 $225

ŸŸŸŸ♀ **Descendant 2007** Deep colour; an ultra-powerful wine, crammed with flavour, but which hasn't entirely escaped the hot vintage effect. Will settle down, methinks. Shiraz/Viognier. Cork. 15% alc. **Rating** 93 **To** 2022 $125

Barossa Valley Viognier Marsanne Roussanne 2008 The wine relies mainly on texture and structure, for the varieties quite properly merge without a break in the line; honeysuckle, apple and pear are all in the picture. What will be most interesting is the wine in five years' time. Cork. 14% alc. **Rating** 92 **To** 2013 $37.50

Descendant 2006 Bright colour; thoroughly unusual Shiraz/Viognier, mainly due to the texture and mouthfeel tightly bound within a web of all-embracing furry tannins. Cork. 14.5% alc. **Rating** 90 **To** 2021 $125

The Steading 2006 Very light colour; typical Barossa Valley Rhône blend dominated by grenache (60%) with soft, gently ripe fruit and minimal tannins. Grenache/Mataro/Shiraz. Cork. 14.5% alc. **Rating** 90 **To** 2014 $40

ŸŸŸŸ **Woodcutter's Barossa Valley Shiraz 2007** Pleasing medium-bodied wine, with sweet berry fruit married with sweet oak; however, no residual sugar sweetness. Screwcap. 14% alc. **Rating** 89 **To** 2012 $21

Cuvee Juveniles 2008 Bright crimson; full of lively sweet berry fruits and soft tannin in support; for drinking, not analysis. Grenache/Shiraz/Mataro. Screwcap. 14.5% alc. **Rating** 89 **To** 2012 $25

Woodcutter's Barossa Valley Semillon 2008 Plenty of flavour, but needs more zest and vibrancy to grab attention. Screwcap. 14% alc. **Rating** 87 **To** 2011 $17.50

Torzi Matthews Vintners   ★★★★☆

Cnr Eden Valley Road/Sugarloaf Hill Road, Mount McKenzie, SA 5353 **Region** Eden Valley
T (08) 8565 3393 **F** (08) 8565 3393 **www.torzimatthews.com.au Open** By appt
Winemaker Domenic Torzi **Est.** 1996 **Cases** 2500 **Vyds** 13 ha
Domenic Torzi and Tracy Matthews, former Adelaide Plains residents, searched for a number of years before finding a 6-ha block at Mt McKenzie in the Eden Valley. The block they chose is in a hollow and the soil is meagre, and they were in no way deterred by the knowledge that it would be frost-prone. The result is predictably low yields, concentrated further by drying the grapes on racks and reducing the weight by around 30% (the appassimento method is used in Italy to produce Amarone-style wines). Four wines are made: Riesling and Shiraz under both the Frost Dodger and Schist Rock labels, the Shiraz wild yeast fermented and neither fined nor filtered. Newer plantings of sangiovese and negroamaro, and an extension of the original plantings of shiraz and riesling, is likely to see the wine range increase in the future. Exports to the UK, the US, Denmark and Singapore.

ŸŸŸŸŸ **Frost Dodger Eden Valley Shiraz 2006** Leather, licorice and spice aromas carry through onto the medium-bodied palate, which has very good length and silky tannins; strong regional character. Screwcap. 14.5% alc. **Rating** 94 **To** 2020 $30

ŸŸŸŸ♀ **Schist Rock Eden Valley Riesling 2008** Spice and apple blossom aromas; very attractive flavour and mouthfeel, with apple, lime juice and tropical fruit; shortens fractionally. Screwcap. 12% alc. **Rating** 92 **To** 2011 $15

ŸŸŸŸ **Schist Rock Eden Valley Shiraz 2007** Light, slightly hazy colour; spice and herb overtones to the bouquet and palate; picks up somewhat on the finish with well-judged tannins. Screwcap. 14% alc. **Rating** 88 **To** 2012 $17

Tower Estate   ★★★★★

Cnr Broke Road/Hall Road, Pokolbin, NSW 2320 **Region** Lower Hunter Valley
T (02) 4998 7989 **F** (02) 4998 7919 **www.towerestatewines.com.au Open** 7 days 10–5
Winemaker Scott Stephens **Est.** 1999 **Cases** 10 000 **Vyds** 4.9 ha
Tower Estate was founded by the late Len Evans, with the award-winning 5-star Tower Lodge accommodation and convention centre a part of the development. It is anticipated there will be little day-to-day change in either part of the business. Tower Estate will continue to draw

upon varieties and regions that have a particular synergy, the aim being to make the best possible wines in the top sector of the wine market. Exports to the UK, Hong Kong, Japan and Canada.

ŸŸŸŸŸ **Hunter Valley Shiraz 2006** Bright, youthful hue; a rich bouquet with black fruits, polished leather and a hint of earth around the corner; the palate, too, is rich, and backed by savoury/earthy tannins. Good-quality cork may sustain the wine. 13.5% alc. **Rating** 95 **To** 2026 $42

Barossa Shiraz 2006 As it is intended to be, in classic (and best) Barossa Valley style; the fragrant bouquet of black and red fruits leads into a precise, lively evocation of young shiraz; the spicy nuances lead you to another sip, another glass, and another bottle... Cork. 14.5% alc. **Rating** 95 **To** 2016 $42

Hunter Valley Chardonnay 2006 Surprisingly, has more freshness and vigour than the Adelaide Hills version, which would doubtless please the late Len Evans; some attractive nectarine and even a touch of grapefruit invigorate the wine. Cork. 13.5% alc. **Rating** 94 **To** 2013 $35

Barossa Shiraz 2005 Shares many things in common with the '06; a perfect union of generous black fruits, quality oak and fine, ripe tannins; the line, length, finish and aftertaste cannot be faulted. Cork. 14.5% alc. **Rating** 94 **To** 2025 $42

Coonawarra Cabernet Sauvignon 2005 Retains good hue; a very powerful and concentrated wine, with lush blackcurrant fruit framed by quite powerful, although ripe, tannins. Needs a minimum of 10 years, which the perfect cork should provide. 14.5% alc. **Rating** 94 **To** 2025 $42

ŸŸŸŸŸ **Tasmania Pinot Noir 2007** Brilliantly clear hue; a high-quality pinot, with a fragrant red berry bouquet, then a racy, incisive palate that is 99% ripe, and has great length. Perfect cork, perfectly inserted. 13% alc. **Rating** 93 **To** 2015 $58

Hunter Valley Semillon 2008 A trifle closed on the bouquet; a generously flavoured palate for a young semillon, but does have the zesty, minerally acidity needed for the future. Screwcap. 11% alc. **Rating** 91 **To** 2015 $26

Hunter Valley Sparkling Shiraz 2003 Superior example, with the base wine matured before tiraging, then two years on lees prior to disgorgement. A fraction sweeter than it needed to be, but better than most. Cork. 14% alc. **Rating** 91 **To** 2013 $42

ŸŸŸŸ **Adelaide Hills Sauvignon Blanc 2008** Offers gentle tropical fruit aromas and flavours, but lacks incisiveness. Screwcap. 14% alc. **Rating** 89 **To** 2010 $32

Adelaide Hills Chardonnay 2006 Soft stone fruit and melon, with subtle oak and the influence of the cork (as natural wood) all adding to the parcel. Needs more acidity/vibrancy. 13.5% alc. **Rating** 89 **To** 2012 $35

Towerhill Estate ★★★

Albany Highway, Mount Barker, WA 6324 **Region** Mount Barker
T (08) 9851 1488 **F** (08) 9851 2982 **Open** Fri–Sun 10–5 (7 days during school hols)
Winemaker Harewood Estate (James Kellie) **Est.** 1993 **Cases** NA
The Williams family, headed by Alan and Diane, began the establishment of Towerhill Estate in 1993, planting 6.5 ha of chardonnay, cabernet sauvignon, riesling and merlot. Initially the grapes were sold to other producers, but since 1999 limited quantities have been made for Towerhill.

ŸŸŸŸ **Riesling 2008** Delicate and fine lime, leaf and mineral aromas repeated on the palate, which, while delicate, has good length. **Rating** 89 **To** 2014

 Trahna Rutherglen Wines ★★★

404 Buckinghams Road, Norong, Vic 3682 **Region** Rutherglen
T (02) 6033 2016 **F** (02) 6033 0285 **Open** At Victoria Hotel, Rutherglen
Winemaker Cofield (David White) **Est.** 2002 **Cases** NFP **Vyds** 10 ha

Roger King began a career in the retail wine business in 1972, but it was not until '99 that he (and wife Dale) realised a long-held ambition to start their own winery. In that year they purchased a property near Rutherglen called Trahna, which had been the site of a substantial winery and vineyard until the wool boom arrived in 1952, and sheep devoured the vines. All the fermentation vats and wine equipment were destroyed or removed but the huge three-gabled shed built with tree trunks and corrugated iron remained standing. Notwithstanding (or perhaps because of) Roger's experience in the wine industry, they have no intention to re-equip the winery, preferring to have the wine made by David White at Cofield. The 8.9 ha of vines on the property are equally divided between viognier, petit verdot, tempranillo and durif; Trahna also has access to a small block of much older shiraz situated 3 km away.

♀♀♀♀ **SVP Shiraz Petit Verdot 2006** Not, as one might expect, dense and heavy, but light- to medium-bodied, with red berry fruits and a vanilla topping. Screwcap. 14.2% alc. **Rating** 87 **To** 2010 $13.95
Petit Verdot 2005 A moderately firm structure to dark fruit flavours; then a surprisingly fine finish with good length. Screwcap. 13.3% alc. **Rating** 87 **To** 2010 $12.95

Train Trak   ★★★★

957 Healesville-Yarra Glen Road, Yarra Glen, Vic 3775 **Region** Yarra Valley
T (03) 9730 1314 **F** (03) 9427 1510 **www**.traintrak.com.au **Open** Wed–Sun
Winemaker Contract **Est.** 1995 **Cases** 6000 **Vyds** 16 ha
The unusual name comes from the Yarra Glen to Healesville railway, which was built in 1889 and abandoned in 1980 – part of it passes by the Train Trak vineyard. The vineyard is planted (in descending order) to pinot noir, cabernet sauvignon, chardonnay and shiraz. The restaurant makes exceptional pizzas in a wood-fired oven. Train Trak has had a hard time of it in recent years, the 2007 crop destroyed by frost, the '09 by fire and smoke taint. Exports to Canada, Pacific Islands, China and Japan.

♀♀♀♀♀ **Sojourn Yarra Valley Chardonnay 2008** A thoroughly modern style; a showpiece for the length of flavour of Yarra Valley chardonnay and for its bright citrus and stone fruit flavours; as good an unoaked style as you are likely to find. Screwcap. 12.5% alc. **Rating** 91 **To** 2012 $18

Trentham Estate   ★★★★☆

Sturt Highway, Trentham Cliffs, NSW 2738 **Region** Murray Darling
T (03) 5024 8888 **F** (03) 5024 8800 **www**.trenthamestate.com.au **Open** 7 days 9.30–5
Winemaker Anthony Murphy, Shane Kerr **Est.** 1988 **Cases** 60 000 **Vyds** 48.57 ha
Remarkably consistent tasting notes across all wine styles from all vintages attest to the expertise of ex-Mildara winemaker Tony Murphy, a well-known and highly regarded producer, with estate vineyards on the Murray Darling. With an eye to the future, but also to broaden the range of the wines on offer, Trentham Estate is selectively buying grapes from other regions with a track record for the chosen varieties. The value for money is unfailingly excellent. Exports to the UK and other major markets.

♀♀♀♀♀ **Heathcote Shiraz 2006** Bright colour; altogether unexpected finesse and elegance, notwithstanding the trademark of Heathcote; lots of spice and pepper accompany the red cherry and plum fruit; tannins and oak in balance. Screwcap. 14.5% alc. **Rating** 94 **To** 2016 $30

♀♀♀♀♀ **La Famiglia Sangiovese Rose 2008** Bright salmon-pink; while light on its feet, has above-average complexity to its spicy/cherry/plummy fruit; dry, crisp finish. Great value. Screwcap. 13.5% alc. **Rating** 91 **To** 2010 $14
Pinot Noir 2007 Bright colour; very pure and precise varietal fruit on both bouquet and palate; light-bodied but with enticing cherry and strawberry fruit flavours; incidental oak and tannins. Screwcap. 13.5% alc. **Rating** 91 **To** 2012 $14

Shiraz 2006 Although the vintage was a very good one, to produce this silk purse from the Riverland is a considerable achievement – but then Tony Murphy has done it so often before. The medium-bodied palate has faultless balance and good length. Screwcap. 14% alc. **Rating** 90 **To** 2012 $14

Estate Merlot 2006 Fresh, lively, small red berry fruits in a light- to medium-bodied frame; keeps its balance and thrust through to the finish. Punches above its weight. Screwcap. 13.5% alc. **Rating** 90 **To** 2012 $16

ŢŢŢŢ **Estate Chardonnay 2007** As ever, very well made, investing the wine with finesse without sacrificing flavour; classic melon/stone fruit and subtle oak. Screwcap. 13% alc. **Rating** 89 **To** 2012 $16

La Famiglia Vermentino 2008 Has even more to it than the Albarino, with lively lemon fruit adding to the flavour and mouthfeel. Gold medal Qld Wine Show '08. Screwcap. 11.5% alc. **Rating** 89 **To** 2012 $16

Mount Macedon Pinot Noir Chardonnay NV Neatly balanced citrus and stone fruit; dosage also spot-on; lacks a little intensity. Cork. 12% alc. **Rating** 89 **To** 2012 $35

Noble Taminga 2005 Golden yellow; luscious apricot, honey, vanilla and toffee flavours are well balanced by acidity, but the wine is not particularly complex. Screwcap. 11% alc. **Rating** 89 **To** 2011 $16

Estate Chardonnay 2008 As ever, very well made, with peachy/stone fruit flavours enhanced by a touch of barrel ferment French oak. Screwcap. 13.5% alc. **Rating** 88 **To** 2011 $16

Estate Albarino 2008 A variety worth persevering with; stone fruit and citrus acidity make a good pair in this context. Screwcap. 12% alc. **Rating** 88 **To** 2012 $16

Sauvignon Blanc 2008 Crisp and firm, but needs more varietal fruit expression for higher points; does have good balance and length. Screwcap. 12.5% alc. **Rating** 87 **To** 2009 $14

Two Thirds Semillon Sauvignon Blanc 2008 The two-thirds refers not to the blend, but to the alcohol level; reverse osmosis used, not stopping the ferment (which would produce a very sweet wine); pleasantly crisp. Screwcap. 8.5% alc. **Rating** 87 **To** 2009 $14

Trevelen Farm   ★★★★

506 Weir Road, Cranbrook, WA 6321 **Region** Great Southern
T (08) 9826 1052 **F** (08) 9826 1209 **www.**trevelenfarmwines.com.au
Open Fri–Mon 10.30–4.30, or by appt
Winemaker Harewood Estate (James Kellie) **Est.** 1993 **Cases** 2300 **Vyds** 6.5 ha
In 2008 John and Katie Sprigg decided to pass ownership of their 1300-ha wool, meat and grain-producing farm to son Ben and wife Louise. However, they have kept control of the 6.5 ha of sauvignon blanc, riesling, chardonnay, cabernet sauvignon and merlot planted in 1993. Henceforth, each wine will be made as a 100% varietal, and if demand requires, they will increase production by purchasing grapes from growers in the Frankland River region. Riesling will remain the centrepiece of the range. Exports to Denmark, Japan, Malaysia and Hong Kong.

ŢŢŢŢŢ **Riesling 2008** Restrained lime and stone fruit bouquet; fresh and focused, with a little grip on the finish; dry, tight and linear. Screwcap. 12.5% alc. **Rating** 91 **To** 2014 $25

Sauvignon Blanc 2008 Pale colour; clean and crisp, with tropical fruit and a little spice; fine, juicy and focused on the finish. Screwcap. 12.5% alc. **Rating** 90 **To** 2011 $16

ŢŢŢŢ **Aged Release Riesling 2002** Very toasty, and a prominent kerosene bouquet; fresher on the palate, with vibrant lime juice and slate character. Screwcap. 11.5% alc. **Rating** 88 **To** 2013 $30

Trevor Jones/Kellermeister ★★★★★

Barossa Valley Highway, Lyndoch, SA 5351 **Region** Barossa Valley
T (08) 8524 4303 **F** (08) 8524 4880 **www**.kellermeister.com.au **Open** 7 days 9–6
Winemaker Trevor Jones, Matthew Reynolds **Est.** 1976 **Cases** 35 000 **Vyds** 2 ha
Trevor Jones is an industry veteran, with vast experience in handling fruit from the Barossa
Valley, Eden Valley and the Adelaide Hills. His business operates on two levels: Kellermeister
was founded in 1976 with the emphasis on low-cost traditional Barossa wine styles. In '96
he expanded the scope by introducing the ultra-premium Trevor Jones range, with a strong
export focus. Exports to the US, Switzerland, Denmark, Macau, Singapore and Japan.

ŸŸŸŸŸ **Trevor Jones Wild Witch Reserve Barossa Valley Shiraz 2006** Excellent
crimson-purple hue; an extravagantly heavy bottle holds a vibrantly fragrant
wine exuding spicy black fruits on the bouquet, following through on the long,
intense and silky medium- to full-bodied palate, with immaculate oak and tannins;
tremendous length. Cork. 14.7% alc. **Rating** 97 **To** 2026 $60

Trevor Jones Wicked Witch Reserve Dry Grown Barossa Cabernet 2006
Another behemoth bottle houses a very good old vine cabernet, which has easily
absorbed its 28-month sojourn in new French oak; has wholly remarkable intensity
and length, with admirable varietal character. The Barossa Valley only occasionally
produces cabernet of this quality. Cork. 14.5% alc. **Rating** 96 **To** 2026 $60

TJ Hand Selected Barossa Shiraz 2003 Made from 90-year-old vines in
the Eden Valley and 125-year-old vines from Ebenezer in the Barossa Valley, both
yielding less than one tonne per acre. Ultra spicy and savoury, with notes of bitter
chocolate and licorice among a persistent filigree of tannins running through
the length of the palate. Amazing achievement for a poor vintage. Cork. 15% alc.
Rating 95 **To** 2015 $100

Trevor Jones Boots Eden Valley Riesling 2008 A floral array of spice, apple
and citrus aromas; impressive palate; intense fruit running through to a long,
lingering finish. Screwcap. 12.5% alc. **Rating** 94 **To** 2017 $17.50

Trevor Jones Dry Grown Barossa Shiraz 2006 A medium- to full-bodied
wine with lusciously ripe, but not overripe, fragrant and sumptuous blackberry,
plum and licorice fruit supported by fine tannins and quality oak. Screwcap.
14.5% alc. **Rating** 94 **To** 2020 $40

ŸŸŸŸ **Trevor Jones The Elusive Chardonnay 2007** Given the vintage (and perhaps
region) a more than creditable wine, with stone fruit girdled by just the right
amount of oak; good mouthfeel, and ready now. Screwcap. 13.8% alc. **Rating** 89
To 2011 $24

Trevor Jones Virgin Chardonnay 2007 Strong nectarine and melon aromas
with an element of spice; a textural wine with plenty of depth, and just a little grip
on the clean finish. Screwcap. 13.5% alc. **Rating** 88 **To** 2011 $18

Kellermeister Barossa Valley Albarino 2008 Quite a fragrant wine, with a
zesty lemon fruit bouquet, and quite noticeable acidity on the oxidative nutty and
quite textural finish. Screwcap. 12.8% alc. **Rating** 87 **To** 2012 $24

🍃 Troll Creek Wines

Lot 362 Bethany Road, Bethany, SA 5352 **Region** Barossa Valley
T (08) 8563 2961 **F** (08) 8563 2961 **www**.trollcreek.com **Open** By appt
Winemaker Christian Canute **Est.** 1998 **Cases** 350 **Vyds** 35 ha
Sixth-generation grapegrower James Hage, and wife Jo, first put their toe in winemaking water
in 1998, enlisting cousin Christian Canute to make a single barrel for home consumption.
The quality of the wine encouraged them to modestly expand production, using the best
rows of old vine shiraz and cabernet from the Home Block, which has been owned by the
Hage family since the early 1900s. The name comes from an old redgum slab bridge spanning
a tiny creek among the vines, under which a legendary troll lives to the delight and fear of
successive generations of Hage children. Exports to Denmark and Singapore.

ŸŸŸŸŸ **Barossa Valley Cabernet Sauvignon 2006** An elegant, medium-bodied, juicy Cabernet, which has excellent texture, structure and length; can be enjoyed at any time over the next 10 years. Cork. 14% alc. **Rating** 93 **To** 2020 $65

ŸŸŸŸ **Barossa Valley Shiraz 2005** Generously flavoured and rich, but 7.93 g/l acidity breaks the line and balance. Cork. 14.5% alc. **Rating** 88 **To** 2013 $65
Shiraz Cabernet Sauvignon 2006 Advanced colour; the fruit flavours are sweeter and riper than the alcohol would suggest, but there is some acidity to tighten up the finish. Screwcap. 14.5% alc. **Rating** 87 **To** 2012 $30
Barossa Valley Cabernet Sauvignon 2005 Medium-bodied, with strong foresty/briary overtones; the vineyard yields only 2 tonnes per ha, one might have expected more weight; however, does pick up on the aftertaste. Cork. 14.5% alc. **Rating** 87 **To** 2015 $55

Truffle Hill Wines   ★★★★★

PO Box 1538, Osborne Park, WA 6916 **Region** Pemberton
T (08) 9777 2474 **F** (08) 9204 1013 **www.**wineandtruffle.com.au **Open** 7 days 10–4.30
Winemaker Mark Aitken **Est.** 1997 **Cases** 10 000 **Vyds** 11 ha
Owned by a group of investors from various parts of Australia who share the common vision of producing fine wines and black truffles. The winemaking side is under the care of Mark Aitken, who, having graduated as dux of his class in applied science at Curtin University in 2000, joined Chestnut Grove as assistant winemaker in 2002. The truffle side of the business is run by former CSIRO scientist Dr Nicholas Malajcsuk. He oversaw the planting of 13 000 truffle-inoculated hazelnut and oak trees on the property, which have now produced truffles, some of prodigious size. Exports to Japan.

ŸŸŸŸŸ **Reserve Series Pemberton Chardonnay 2007** A complex and fine bouquet of grapefruit and nectarine, seasoned well with spicy oak; a creamy texture, with ripe stone fruit and well-handled leesy complexity; fresh, fine and focused. Screwcap. 14.5% alc. **Rating** 94 **To** 2014 $26
Reserve Series Pemberton Shiraz 2007 Good colour; has an extra level of richness and complexity; blue and red fruits, with some cinnamon and clove; the palate is fine, with a slippery texture to the fruit; fresh and clean on the finish. Screwcap. 13.9% alc. **Rating** 94 **To** 2015 $35

ŸŸŸŸ **Pemberton Merlot 2007** Dark fruited, with elements of cassis, earth and olive; quite tannic and savoury on the finish. Screwcap. 14.5% alc. **Rating** 89 **To** 2013 $20
Reserve Series Pemberton Riesling 2007 A touch of kerosene development; quite ripe, with quince and lemon fruit; generous palate weight, with some grip and phenolic complexity. Screwcap. 13% alc. **Rating** 88 **To** 2014 $24
Pemberton Shiraz 2007 Bright colour; a lifted blueberry mulberry bouquet; medium-bodied spicy and quite juicy on the finish. Screwcap. 13.8% alc. **Rating** 88 **To** 2013 $20
Pemberton Shiraz Cabernet Merlot 2007 Clean and fresh, with redcurrant and cassis; juicy, fine and well-balanced on the finish. Screwcap. 13.5% alc. **Rating** 88 **To** 2012 $17
Pemberton Sauvignon Blanc Semillon 2008 Clean and crisp with a tropical fruit bouquet and palate; a zesty finish. Screwcap. 12.8% alc. **Rating** 87 **To** 2011 $17

Tuck's Ridge   ★★★★★

37 Shoreham Road, Red Hill South, Vic 3937 **Region** Mornington Peninsula
T (03) 5989 8660 **F** (03) 5989 8579 **www.**tucksridge.com.au **Open** 7 days 11–5
Winemaker Peninsula Winemakers **Est.** 1985 **Cases** 4000 **Vyds** 3.9 ha
Tuck's Ridge has changed focus significantly since selling its large Red Hill vineyard. Estate plantings are now an eclectic mix of chardonnay (2 ha), pinot noir (1.2 ha) and albarino (0.7 ha), and contract grape purchases have been reduced. Quality, not quantity, is the key. Exports to the US, Germany, the Netherlands and Hong Kong.

ŦŦŦŦŦ **Buckle Vineyard Chardonnay 2007** Brilliant straw-green; intensely focused wine, abounding with power and energy; has the layered complexity of great White Burgundy, and will live for many years to come thanks to the screwcap. 13.6% alc. **Rating** 97 **To** 2020 $70
Buckle Vineyard Pinot Noir 2007 Deeply coloured, and has a remarkably intense bouquet and palate, the wine surging in the mouth to the pulsating finish built on great pinot fruit and superfine tannins. Screwcap. 13.7% alc. **Rating** 97 **To** 2020 $80
Turramurra Vineyard Chardonnay 2007 Tight, fine and elegantly structured grapefruit and white peach flavours framed by quality oak; has very considerable length and purity. Screwcap. 13.7% alc. **Rating** 96 **To** 2020 $60
Mornington Peninsula Pinot Noir 2007 Vibrant, light crimson-purple; a powerful yet elegant wine, full of spicy plum fruit, supported by savoury tannins; long finish. Screwcap. 13.6% alc. **Rating** 94 **To** 2015 $39

ŦŦŦŦŸ **Mornington Peninsula Chardonnay 2007** Light straw-green; quality chardonnay, unfairly put in the shade by the Buckle and Turramurra Vineyard wines; all the inputs are in balance, the melon and stone fruit driving the wine with the aid of citrussy acidity. Screwcap. 13.7% alc. **Rating** 93 **To** 2014 $29

ŦŦŦŦ **Grosso 2007** Good colour, of course; fairly and squarely raises the question whether Mornington Peninsula can ripen Cabernet Sauvignon/Shiraz/Merlot/Petit Verdot/Cabernet Franc, or whether it should try. This is like a cold shower at boarding school. Screwcap. 13.3% alc. **Rating** 89 **To** 2020 $39

Tulloch   ★★★★★

'Glen Elgin' 638 De Beyers Road, Pokolbin, NSW 2321 **Region** Lower Hunter Valley **T** (02) 4998 7580 **F** (02) 4998 7226 **www.**tulloch.com.au **Open** 7 days 10–5
Winemaker Jay Tulloch, Monarch Winemaking Services, Jim Chatto **Est.** 1895 **Cases** 40 000
The revival of the near-death Tulloch brand continues apace. Angove's, the national distributor of the brand, has invested in the business, the first time the Angove family has taken a strategic holding in any business other than its own. Inglewood Vineyard (aka Two Rivers) also has a shareholding in the venture, and is the primary source of grapes for the white wines. A lavish cellar door and function facility has opened, and Jay Tulloch is in overall control, with his own label, JYT Wines, also available at the cellar door. The return of the classic Dry Red and Private Bin Dry Red labels (only slightly rejigged) brings back memories of the great wines of the 1950s and '60s, and is a sign of the continuing resurgence of this brand. Exports to Belgium, Canada, Philippines, Singapore, Hong Kong, Malaysia, Japan and China.

ŦŦŦŦŦ **Hector of Glen Elgin Limited Release Shiraz 2005** A concentrated, very long and unusually powerful wine, produced from a block with vines over 100 years old. Begs to be cellared for at least a decade, and will go on for another 40 years (at least) thereafter. Screwcap. 14% alc. **Rating** 96 **To** 2045 $50
Private Bin Pokolbin Dry Red Shiraz 2007 An historic label, first appearing in the 1950s; classic medium-bodied Hunter, with red and black fruits highlighted by balanced acidity and fine tannins; some of the vines well over 100 years old. Screwcap. 14% alc. **Rating** 94 **To** 2027 $40

ŦŦŦŦŸ **Limited Release Julia Semillon 2007** Quite generous levels of lemon sherbet and a hint of straw; crisp, clean and focused with a taut, yet rich, finish. Screwcap. 11% alc. **Rating** 92 **To** 2018 $28
Vineyard Selection Hunter Valley Semillon 2008 A lively, crisp wine made from an Upper Hunter vineyard; mineral, grass and herbs lurk in the background, a touch of lemon in the foreground. Plenty to come. Screwcap. 10% alc. **Rating** 91 **To** 2017 $20
Hunter Valley Semillon 2008 Dominated by crisp snow pea green aromas, the palate is lively, fresh and surprisingly long and fine. Screwcap. 10% alc. **Rating** 90 **To** 2015 $16

Semillon Sauvignon Blanc 2008 Attractive wine at the price; the main contribution of the WA sauvignon blanc is to fill out the palate, but it also adds to the overall flavour, without diminishing the precision and focus of the wine. Screwcap. 10.5% alc. **Rating** 90 **To** 2011 $16

Cellar Door Release Hunter Valley Petit Verdot 2007 Impressive colour for such modest alcohol; petit verdot is a chameleon, a late-ripening Bordeaux variety that actually enjoys much warmer climates; this has good black fruit flavours and a bright, almost crisp, finish. Screwcap. 12% alc. **Rating** 90 **To** 2014 $22

ȲȲȲȲ **Cellar Door Release Hunter Valley Marsanne 2008** A worthy example of the variety snatched from the jaws of the rain ravaged vintage, with a honeysuckle opening and lemon/citrus/mineral acidity to close. Screwcap. 11.5% alc. **Rating** 89 **To** 2013 $20

Creme de Vin NV A complex wine, but very expensive at this price. It is a fortified verdelho, based on a small solera established in 1973; nice toffee and crystallised fruit characters. 375 ml. Screwcap. 18.5% alc. **Rating** 89 **To** 2010 $40

EM Limited Release Chardonnay 2007 Quite toasty, with melon and fig, mingling with straw; rich on the palate, with a real twang of acidity running across the finish; a little disjointed as yet. Screwcap. 13.5% alc. **Rating** 88 **To** 2013 $28

Hunter Valley Verdelho 2008 Clean, crisp and full of lemon and nectarine fruit; juicy and vibrant, and best consumed early. Screwcap. 13% alc. **Rating** 88 **To** 2012 $16

Cellar Door Release Hunter Valley Shiraz Cabernet 2006 Light red; a lively, light- to medium-bodied wine with snappy, fresh fruit and minimal tannins; slightly curious price. Screwcap. 13% alc. **Rating** 87 **To** 2012 $25

Turkey Flat   ★★★★★

Bethany Road, Tanunda, SA 5352 **Region** Barossa Valley
T (08) 8563 2851 **F** (08) 8563 3610 **www.turkeyflat.com.au Open** 7 days 11–5
Winemaker Julie Campbell **Est.** 1990 **Cases** 25 000 **Vyds** 44.9 ha
The establishment date of Turkey Flat is given as 1990 but it might equally well have been 1870 (or thereabouts), when the Schulz family purchased the Turkey Flat vineyard, or 1847, when the vineyard was first planted to the very old shiraz that still grows there today alongside 8 ha of equally old grenache. Plantings have since expanded significantly, now comprising shiraz (24 ha), grenache (10.5 ha), cabernet sauvignon (6.7 ha), mataro (2.2 ha), viognier (1 ha) and dolcetto (0.5 ha). Exports to the UK, the US and other major markets.

ȲȲȲȲȲ **Barossa Valley Shiraz 2007** Bright colour; pure Barossa fruit, with blackberry, redcurrant and fruitcake on the bouquet; the abundant sweet fruit is offset by a savoury/tarry complexity that drives the palate to its ultimately long and tannin-textured finish. Screwcap. 14.5% alc. **Rating** 95 **To** 2020 $47

Barossa Valley Rose 2008 Bright fuschia; as elegant as always, made by a team that has developed great expertise with the style; offers an array of gently sweet red fruits on the mid-palate, then a balanced dry finish. Screwcap. 13% alc. **Rating** 94 **To** 2010 $23

ȲȲȲȲȲ **Butchers Block Barossa Valley Marsanne Viognier Roussanne 2008** A big-boned dry white, with apricot, honeysuckle and straw on offer; the palate is rich, but exhibits a liveliness and texture that offers harmony on the finish. Screwcap. 14% alc. **Rating** 91 **To** 2012 $25

Butchers Block Shiraz Grenache Mourvedre 2007 A ripe, raspberry and fruitcake spice bouquet, also showing a slight briny complexity; stricter on the palate, with a generous core of sweet red fruit on the mid-palate; finishes dry and firm. Screwcap. 14.5% alc. **Rating** 91 **To** 2014 $27.50

ȲȲȲȲ **Barossa Valley Mourvedre 2007** A dark and savoury bouquet, full of spice and sage; the palate is tannic and shows lots of sweet dark fruit, but the savoury component dominates alongside the tannins. Screwcap. 14.5% alc. **Rating** 89 **To** 2014 $35

Turner's Crossing Vineyard ★★★★☆

PO Box 103, Epsom, Vic 3551 **Region** Bendigo
T (03) 5448 8464 **www.**turnerscrossing.com **Open** W'ends tel (03) 5944 4599
Winemaker Sergio Carlei **Est.** 2002 **Cases** 8000 **Vyds** 41 ha
The name of this outstanding vineyard comes from local farmers crossing the Loddon River in the mid- to late-1800s on their way to the nearest town. The vineyard was planted in 1999 by former corporate executive and lecturer in the business school at La Trobe University, Paul Jenkins. However, Jenkins' experience as a self-taught viticulturist dates back to 1985, when he established his first vineyard at Prospect Hill, planting all the vines himself. The grapes from both vineyards have gone to a who's who of winemakers in Central Victoria, but an increasing amount is being made under the Turner's Crossing label, not surprising given the exceptional quality of the wines. Phil Bennett and winemaker Sergio Carlei have joined Paul Jenkins as co-owners of the vineyard, with Sergio putting his money where his winemaking mouth is. Exports to the UK, the US, Canada, China and Taiwan.

 Bendigo Shiraz Viognier 2007 Incredibly ripe redcurrant and blackberry bouquet, with a suggestion of bay leaf; very warm on entry, there is a generous quality to the fruit; the tannins sit apart at this stage, but given the dimensions of the wine, time will be of great assistance. Diam. **Rating** 94 **To** 2018 $25

 The Cut Shiraz 2006 Very concentrated dark fruit with a prominent bay leaf quality; thickly textured and very tannic, the heat is a touch troublesome on the palate; massively proportioned, time will be the key. Diam. **Rating** 90 **To** 2016 $85

Twelve Acres ★★★

Nagambie-Rushworth Road, Bailieston, Vic 3608 **Region** Goulburn Valley
T (03) 5794 2020 **F** (03) 5794 2020 **Open** Thurs–Mon 10.30–5.30
Winemaker Peter Prygodicz, Jana Prygodicz **Est.** 1994 **Cases** 300
The property name comes from the fact that the original subdivision created a tiny 12-acre block in the midst of 1000-acre properties, giving rise to the local nickname of 'Bastard Block', less suited for a winery brand. When purchased in 1987, it was completely overgrown, and Peter and Jana Prygodicz have done all the work themselves, doing it the tough way without any mains power, relying on a generator and solar panels. This is their house, winery and cellar door block; the grapes for the wines come from local grapegrowers.

♀♀♀♀ **Grenache 2002** A remarkable testament to the very cool vintage, for Swan Hill grenache should normally be drunk asap; spicy and savoury flavours are offset by a flash of heat (ex alcohol) on the finish. Zork. 16% alc. **Rating** 87 **To** 2010 $16

24 Karat Wines ★★★★☆

PO Box 165, Mosman Park, WA 6912 **Region** Margaret River
T (08) 9383 4242 **F** (08) 9383 4502 **www.**24karat.com.au **Open** Not
Winemaker Claudia Lloyd, Bruce Dukes (Contract) **Est.** 1998 **Cases** 1000 **Vyds** 46.3 ha
In 1979 Dr Graham Lloyd, a qualified metallurgist with particular expertise in gold mining, established his now world-leading metallurgical services company Ammtec. By 1997 he was ready for a new challenge, and as he and his family had a long association with the Augusta area, the idea of a vineyard was natural. He found an 82-ha property in Karridale, and acquired it in 1997. He then did what many fail to do: in 1998 he signed a 15-year contract with Brookland Valley for sale of the grapes, but included the right to retain 10% for his own label. The 46-ha vineyard has the major varieties of the region, importantly including 8.7 ha of six clones (including the outstanding French Dijon clones) of chardonnay all planted in individual blocks. It is managed with biodynamic principles, and the driving force is to procure quality-based bonus grape payments from Brookland Valley. Graham and Penny's younger daughter Claudia is a winemaker with both Australian and overseas experience, and the expectation is that she will have a long-term involvement with the business.

♟♟♟♟ **Chardonnay 2007** A particularly elegant wine, 100% barrel-fermented in French oak, which has absorbed that oak in the intense grapefruit and nectarine flavours of the long palate and fresh finish. Screwcap. 13.4% alc. **Rating** 94 **To** 2015 $37

♟♟♟♟ **Cabernet Sauvignon 2007** A fragrant cassis bouquet, then a medium- to full-bodied palate with more cassis plus blackcurrant backed by fine, savoury tannins; good focus and length. Screwcap. 13.5% alc. **Rating** 92 **To** 2017 $36
Sauvignon Blanc 2008 A fresh, spotlessly clean bouquet with no hint of sweatiness; the gentle tropical gooseberry/citrus fruit of the palate is enlivened by a touch of CO_2, which will help the wine retain its freshness for a year or two. Screwcap. 12.5% alc. **Rating** 90 **To** 2011 $25

Two Dorks Estate   NR
PO Box 19204, Southbank, Vic 3006 **Region** Heathcote
T 0409 134 332 **Open** Not
Winemaker Mark Bladon **Est.** 2001 **Cases** 44 **Vyds** 2 ha
Owners Mark Bladon and Nektaria Achimastos (described by Mark as 'Vineyard Goddess') have an exceptionally keen sense of humour. Having chosen a site in the southern end of Heathcote off the Cambrian soil ('In truth the land in the area is not the best' Mark admits) they planted 2 ha of dry-grown vines in 2001. The ensuing seven years of drought meant that development of the vines has been painstakingly slow, and simultaneously demanding much TLC and that sense of humour. The vineyard is predominantly shiraz, with a patch of viognier and 0.5 ha of cabernet sauvignon and merlot. Says Mark, 'The merlot doesn't like the area and the conditions much, I fear; although while it's growing I don't have the heart to dig it up.' That said, replanting will be with shiraz. The first tiny crop ('barely sufficient to bother, really') came in 2008, and was not put in oak. Mark thinks that Heathcote wines can often be too extracted and overoaked, and while future vintages will be matured in new and used French oak, the aim will be for a medium-bodied wine with restrained alcohol.

Two Hands Wines   ★★★★★
Neldner Road, Marananga, SA 5355 **Region** Barossa Valley
T (08) 8562 4566 **F** (08) 8562 4744 **www**.twohandswines.com **Open** 7 days 10–5
Winemaker Matthew Wenk **Est.** 2000 **Cases** 30 000 **Vyds** 15 ha
The 'hands' in question are those of SA businessmen Michael Twelftree and Richard Mintz, Michael in particular having extensive experience in marketing Australian wine in the US (for other producers). On the principle that if big is good, bigger is better, and biggest is best, the style of the wines has been aimed fairly and squarely at the palate of Robert Parker Jr and *Wine Spectator's* Harvey Steiman. Grapes are sourced from the Barossa Valley (where the business has 15 ha of shiraz), McLaren Vale, Clare Valley, Langhorne Creek and Padthaway. The retention of cork closures, the emphasis on sweet fruit, and the soft tannin structure, all signify the precise marketing strategy of what is a very successful business. Exports to the UK, the US and other major markets.

♟♟♟♟ **Max's Garden Heathcote Shiraz 2007** Rich, dense and dark, with a cool overlay to the fruit; there is an element of cranberry complementing the tar, earth, spice and well-handled oak that delivers not only on the bouquet, but also on the palate; bright and clean on the finish. Cork. 14.9% alc. **Rating** 95 **To** 2017 $60
Gnarly Dudes Barossa Valley Shiraz 2007 Bright colour; an accessible and fine bouquet of redcurrant, mocha and blackberry; the palate is lively, fresh, focused and very long and even; much brighter on the palate than expected. Screwcap. 14.8% alc. **Rating** 94 **To** 2014 $27
Barney's Block Single Vineyard McLaren Vale Shiraz 2007 Impenetrable colour; thick, dark, dense, chewy and massive in every respect; there is a little lack of freshness in the wine; inky fruit, with prune-like intensity; thick and tannic, with bitter chocolate providing some relief from the overwhelming intensity on the palate. If you like them big, then this is for you. Cork. 15.4% alc. **Rating** 94 **To** 2020 $100

Lily's Garden McLaren Vale Shiraz 2007 Unflinchingly in the biggest is best camp; deeply coloured, with luscious, mouthfilling black fruits and dark chocolate; demands that you share the bottle with three others and order a thick rump steak. Not my style, but well made. Cork. 15.7% alc. **Rating** 94 **To** 2022 $60

Ares Barossa Valley McLaren Vale Shiraz 2006 Dense crimson; there is no point in grumbling about the alcohol, for the wine takes no prisoners. Recalls Robert Parker's glowing description of a Barossa red as unfortified vintage port to which he gave 99 or so points. In that context, this is as good as they come. Cork. 16% alc. **Rating** 94 **To** 2030 $165

Aphrodite Barossa Valley Cabernet Sauvignon 2006 Dense colour; an exuberant, voluptuous cabernet, which clearly says 'take me on my terms or not at all'; somehow or other, avoids the dead, jammy flavours normally associated with cabernet at this alcohol level. Cork. 15.5% alc. **Rating** 94 **To** 2030 $165

ΨΨΨΨΨ **Bella's Garden Barossa Valley Shiraz 2007** Pure Barossa mocha, blackberry and fruitcake, blended with a generous serve of toasty oak; thick and unctuous on entry, the quite gravelly tannin refocuses the wine, to conclude with more toast and ample levels of sweet fruit. Cork. 15.5% alc. **Rating** 93 **To** 2015 $60

Bad Impersonator Single Vineyard Barossa Valley Shiraz 2007 Distinctly savoury personality, showing black fruit and a briny, slightly pruney character; medium-bodied and quite drying, the finish displays more earth, iron and roast meat than fruit. Screwcap. 14.8% alc. **Rating** 92 **To** 2014 $45

Zippy's Block Single Vineyard Barossa Valley Shiraz 2007 More life here, with some red fruit providing lift to the concentrated fruitcake and chocolate beneath; the oak and fruit work in tandem and provide a rich, but not overwhelming, level of interest on the finish; chewy with some nerve to conclude. Cork. 14.7% alc. **Rating** 92 **To** 2020 $100

The Wolf Clare Valley Riesling 2008 Focused lime fruit and talc bouquet; precise on the palate, but in a delicate framework; pronounced lime character on the finish. Screwcap. 13.5% alc. **Rating** 91 **To** 2014 $25

Angels Share McLaren Vale Shiraz 2007 Bright colour; loaded with sweet fruit and attractive spice from the oak-handling; rich and juicy, the wine provides a generous level of sweet fruit. Screwcap. 15.5% alc. **Rating** 90 **To** 2013 $27

Brave Faces Barossa Valley Shiraz Grenache Mataro 2007 Bright colour; ripe raspberry, blackberry and thyme bouquet; medium-bodied palate, with ample sweet fruit, complemented by savoury wild herb complexity; quite zesty acidity on the finish. Screwcap. 15% alc. **Rating** 90 **To** 2013 $27

Fly by Nighters Vintage Port 2007 Deep and concentrated with liqueur kirsch and a hint of violets; quite spicy and complex; the style is forward, but should show some ability to age. Cork. 19.2% alc. **Rating** 90 **To** 2020 $25

ΨΨΨΨ **Sophie's Garden Padthaway Shiraz 2007** Quite dark fruited, with a distinctly earthy character; the fruit is concentrated, but there is a question over the freshness; very dry and tarry on the finish. Cork. 16.4% alc. **Rating** 88 **To** 2013 $60

Coach House Block Single Vineyard Barossa Valley Shiraz 2007 Lots of colour and a very heavy bottle do not a great wine make; there is a distinct lack of freshness, as the wine is pruney, hot and really heavy; the palate is disjointed with tannin sitting apart from the fruit, and with lead in its legs; hard work. Cork. 15.8% alc. **Rating** 87 **To** 2020 $100

For Love or Money Barossa Valley Cane Cut Semillon 2007 Incredibly sweet and concentrated; candied orange and lemon fruit; could do with a little more zest. Cork. 12.5% alc. **Rating** 87 **To** 2012 $50

 # 2 Mates

62 Sunnyside Road, Glen Osmond, SA 5064 **Region** McLaren Vale
T 0418 821 273 **F** (08) 8338 0087 **www.2mates.com.au** **Open** Not
Winemaker Matt Rechner **Est.** 2006 **Cases** 450

The two mates are Mark Venable and David Minear, who say, 'Over a big drink in a small bar in Italy a few years back, we talked about making "our perfect Australian Shiraz". When we got back, we decided to have a go.' The wine (2005) was duly made, and went on to win a silver medal at the *Decanter Magazine* World Wine Awards in London, along with some exalted company. In my opinion, they went one – perhaps many – better with the '06.

ŶŶŶŶŶ **Shiraz 2006** Excellent crimson colour, and the wine does not disappoint; while medium-bodied, has great energy and intensity to the blackberry, plum and licorice fruit; very good tannin and oak management. Striking packaging. Screwcap. 14.8% alc. **Rating** 94 **To** 2021 $29.90

Two Way Range   ★★★★☆

PO Box 7, Tanunda, SA 5352 **Region** Barossa Valley
T (08) 8563 3210 **F** (08) 8563 0304 **www.**twowayrange.com **Open** Not
Winemaker Iain Seabrook, Jules Campbell **Est.** 2001 **Cases** 400 **Vyds** 30 ha
Two Way Range is owned by Seabrook & Clancy Wine Co, and is a joint venture between the Seabrook and Clancy families. Ian and Wendy Seabrook are part of the celebrated Melbourne Seabrook wine family, while Paul and Fran Clancy are retired wine industry book publishers who have run an historic vineyard on the upper reaches of Jacob's Creek at Krondorf for nearly 20 years. The vineyard has a gilt-edged list of purchasers including Rockford, John Duval, Spinifex, Charlie Melton and Massena Wines. The exceptionally high quality of the grapes is thought to be due to the very young soils (200 000 years) originating high on Kaiser Stuhl hill, the cold gully winds from the adjacent Eden Valley. Ian and Paul are both Vietnam veterans, and 'two way range' was an expression of black humour when Australians went out on patrol: akin to a rifle range where the targets shoot back. The wine is matured in a mix of new and used French oak for 18 months. Exports to Canada, Dubai, Singapore, Hong Kong and China.

ŶŶŶŶŶ **Barossa Valley Shiraz 2006** An elegant example of Barossa Shiraz, with blackberry fruit framed by spice and wild herbs; the acidity is truly vibrant, and the ample tannins frame the fruit well; quite supple on the finish. Cork. 14.5% alc. **Rating** 94 **To** 2016 $39

ŶŶŶŶŶ **Barossa Valley Shiraz 2004** Fresh and vibrant, with a touch of leather developing alongside the ample blackberry fruit; the palate is dense and chewy, but also showing attractive finesse and poise; a long, juicy and savoury finish; holds the high alcohol with aplomb. Cork. 15.5% alc. **Rating** 93 **To** 2014 $38
Barossa Valley Shiraz 2002 True to style, ageing gracefully and showing some tarry development; the palate is vibrant and dense, and while very ripe, there is a litheness to the palate that is really attractive. Cork. 15.6% alc. **Rating** 93 **To** 2013 $38

Tyrone Estate   ★★★☆

PO Box 2187, Berri, SA 5343 **Region** Riverland
T (08)b8584 1120 **F** (08) 8584 1388 **www.**tyroneestate.com.au **Open** Not
Winemaker Melanie Kargas **Est.** 2008 **Cases** 20 000
While this is the venture of Bob and Sylvia Franchitto, it has been set up for the benefit of their son Tyrone. When Bob began his various horticultural and farming activities, he applied a holistic view, preferring the use of selected cover crops and mulching instead of chemicals for weed control and soil conditioning. Care for the environment also extends to the winemaking process: the winery is fully undercover, eliminating storm water run off and allowing the collection of rain water for further use. The water used in winery wash-down procedures is processed before being recycled for supplementary irrigation of the vineyards. All the marc and grape skins are taken offsite and distilled to recover alcohol and tartaric acid before being combined with other ingredients for organic fertilisers. This is a sister winery to that of Salena Estate. Exports to Singapore, Taiwan, Korea and China.

ϺϺϺϺϘ **Home Block Barossa Valley Shiraz 2005** Fresh blackberry with mocha and a touch of spice; really vibrant palate, with good focus and an element of savoury tar and mineral to add complexity. Screwcap. 13.5% alc. **Rating** 92 **To** 2015 $17.99

ϺϺϺϺ **Three Generations Semillon Sauvignon Blanc 2008** An appealing wine, with juicy flavours ranging through grass and citrus to more tropical characters. Well made. Screwcap. 12% alc. **Rating** 88 **To** 2010 $11.99

Three Generations Shiraz 2008 Good colour; slightly more complex version of the varietal, aided by a light veneer of oak; fair balance and length to the red fruits of the palate. Screwcap. 13.5% alc. **Rating** 87 **To** 2012 $11.99

Three Generations Merlot 2007 Generous sweet small berry fruit in a medium-bodied frame; avoids dead fruit; good outcome. Screwcap. 13.5% alc. **Rating** 87 **To** 2011 $11.99

Reserve Cabernet Sauvignon 2007 Good colour; has more than adequate varietal flavour and structure, with nice savoury offsets to the cassis/blackcurrant fruit. Surprise packet. Cork. 13.5% alc. **Rating** 87 **To** 2014 $19.99

Home Block Cabernet Sauvignon 2006 Good concentration; pure cassis fruit and a little black olive; medium-bodied with juicy fruit on the finish. Screwcap. 13.5% alc. **Rating** 87 **To** 2012 $13.99

Tyrrell's   ★★★★★

Broke Road, Pokolbin, NSW 2321 **Region** Lower Hunter Valley
T (02) 4993 7000 **F** (02) 4998 7723 **www**.tyrrells.com.au **Open** 7 days 8.30–5
Winemaker Andrew Spinaze, Mark Richardson **Est.** 1858 **Cases** 500 000 **Vyds** 226 ha
One of the most successful family wineries, a humble operation for the first 110 years of its life which has grown out of all recognition over the past 40 years. In 2003 it cleared the decks by selling its Long Flat range of wines for an eight-figure sum, allowing it to focus on its premium, super-premium and ultra-premium wines: Vat 1 Semillon is one of the most dominant wines in the Australian show system, and Vat 47 Chardonnay is one of the pacesetters for this variety. It has an awesome portfolio of single-vineyard Semillons released when five–six years old. Exports to all major markets.

ϺϺϺϺϺ **Vat 1 Hunter Semillon 2005** Bright straw-green, it has a strikingly perfumed bouquet of grass, herbs and wild flowers, the palate charged with lemon juice and lemon zest flavours, crisp acid driving the long palate and lingering finish. Screwcap. 11.3% alc. **Rating** 96 **To** 2025 $55

Single Vineyard Stevens Hunter Semillon 2005 Pale colour, vibrant hue; tightly wound and completely pristine and unevolved, with lemon sherbet and the merest suggestion of straw; the palate is coiled and ungiving, but the potential is palpable, as the flavour lingers with attractive texture for a very long time. Screwcap. 11.4% alc. **Rating** 96 **To** 2025 $30

Vat 1 Hunter Semillon 2002 Still pale and bright; small wonder it has such a spectacular show record (9 golds stretching from 2002 to '07); it has the feminine delicacy of all great Hunter semillons, yet has layer-upon-layer of flavour, in a seamless mix of lemon, honey and acidity, toasty notes yet to come. Pray all corks are as good as this one. 10% alc. **Rating** 96 **To** 2017 $49

Vat 47 Hunter Chardonnay 2007 Surprisingly austere, with citrus fruit gambolling alongside tightly focused oak; the palate shows finesse and a great deal of power, with a crescendo-like build to the finish; the wine is completely unevolved and should age with grace. Screwcap. 14.3% alc. **Rating** 96 **To** 2018 $50

Single Vineyard Old Patch 1867 Hunter Shiraz 2007 Vibrant colour; bright red and blue fruit bouquet, lots of spice and a seriously engaging mineral core; medium-bodied with silky tannins and vibrant acidity; the focus, poise and length are admirable. Screwcap. 13.5% alc. **Rating** 96 **To** 2020 $100

Belford Reserve Semillon 2004 Vibrant green hue; pea pod and straw bouquet with a touch of lemon; the palate shows some generosity, and is approachable now, while still remaining tightly wound; beautifully precise on the finish. Screwcap. 11.2% alc. **Rating** 95 **To** 2020 $30

Museum Release Vat 1 Hunter Semillon 2003 A mere suggestion of toasty development, with lemon butter and straw; generous on entry, the texture provides a bit of grip, drawing the palate out harmoniously; one of the most age-worthy from the vintage. Screwcap. 10.9% alc. **Rating** 95 **To** 2020 $50

Winemaker's Selection 4 Acres Hunter Valley Shiraz 2007 Bright purple hue; blueberry, violets and ironstone bouquet; thickly textured with a vibrant core of blue and red fruit, underpinned by seamlessly integrated oak; fine tannin and slightly plummy fruit persist on the finish. Screwcap. 13.5% alc. **Rating** 95 **To** 2020 $100

Vat 9 Hunter Shiraz 2007 Very noticeable new oak influence on the bouquet, with an abundance of bright red fruit, spice and a touch of sage and mint; the palate shows leather and tannin, with savoury nuances prolonging the red fruit on the finish. Screwcap. 13.5% alc. **Rating** 95 **To** 2025 $65

Vat 8 Shiraz 2006 Brightly coloured; ripe, almost sweet black fruit bouquet; plummy and full of spice on entry, the complexity builds up, and more savoury and dark fruit comes through with a complexing element of dried herb and leather; medium-bodied, long and richly fruited on the finish. Screwcap. 13.3% alc. **Rating** 95 **To** 2020 $50

Belford Single Vineyard Hunter Chardonnay 2006 A complex Chardonnay, with unquestioned varietal expression courtesy of stone fruit, fig and melon; integrated French oak and good acidity round off a high-quality wine. Dry-grown vines planted 1991. Screwcap. 13% alc. **Rating** 94 **To** 2013 $38.99

Single Vineyard Stevens Hunter Shiraz 2006 Oak dominant bouquet of mocha and coffee with redcurrant, blackberry and a touch of spice; light to medium-bodied with the fragrance really coming forward on the palate; fine and elegant on the finish. Screwcap. 13.5% alc. **Rating** 94 **To** 2015 $35

Brokenback Hunter Valley Shiraz 2006 Bright colour; red and blue fruit bouquet with a subtle underpinning of leather and earth; the palate is beautifully bright and focused, the slippery tannins providing length to the ample levels of fruit; very seductive spice on the finish. Screwcap. 13% alc. **Rating** 94 **To** 2018 $30

Winemaker's Selection 4 Acres Hunter Valley Shiraz 2004 Bright cherry fruit; a supple and elegant structure, with an attractive and silky, almost light-bodied, palate, which has deceptive length. From vines well over 100 years old. Cork. 12.6% alc. **Rating** 94 **To** 2015 $100

ㅜㅜㅜㅜㅜ **Moon Mountain Hunter Valley Chardonnay 2008** Elegant and restrained bouquet of ripe lemon and minerals; the palate is zesty, thanks to the lack of mlf, and the weight of the fruit builds profoundly; taut and minerally on the finish. Screwcap. 12.5% alc. **Rating** 93 **To** 2015 $25

Belford Single Vineyard Hunter Chardonnay 2007 Bright colour; a toasty straw bouquet, with a hint of peach; thickly textured and warm on entry, the palate provides light and shade with vibrant acidity, and is a lively expression of Hunter Chardonnay. Screwcap. 15.1% alc. **Rating** 92 **To** 2014 $35

Old Winery Hunter Valley Semillon 2008 Outstanding structure and mouthfeel for a wine at its price; Tyrrell's experience shining through; attractive lemony fruit, balanced acidity. Screwcap. 10.5% alc. **Rating** 91 **To** 2014 $12

Old Winery Verdelho 2008 Nicely poised fruit, with lime and straw notes; quite fleshy on entry, and then cleans up with lime fruit on the long finish. Screwcap. 12.5% alc. **Rating** 90 **To** 2010 $12

Old Winery Shiraz 2006 Fragrant red and black fruit aromas are picked up on the lively light- to medium-bodied palate, joined by spice/savoury nuances on the finish. Top value; ready to roll. Screwcap. 14% alc. **Rating** 90 **To** 2012 $12

Rufus Stone McLaren Vale Shiraz 2006 Potent aromas, with a faint suggestion of reduction on the bouquet; blackberry and licorice and bitter chocolate drive the intense palate, oak incidental. Screwcap. 14.5% alc. **Rating** 90 **To** 2016 $24.95

Ulithorne ★★★★

The Middleton Mill, 29 Mill Terrace, Middleton, SA 5213 **Region** McLaren Vale
T 0419 040 670 **F** (08) 8554 2433 **www**.ulithorne.com.au **Open** By appt
Winemaker Rose Kentish, Brian Light, Natasha Mooney (Contract) **Est.** 1971 **Cases** 2000
Sam Harrison and partner Rose Kentish have sold the Ulithorne vineyard (but with the right
to select and buy part of the production each vintage) and have purchased the Middleton
Mill on the south coast of the Fleurieu Peninsula. It is now their home, and Sam has resumed
full-time painting while Rose is running a wine bar in the Middelton Mill with Ulithorne
and other local wines, beers and platters of regional food on offer. In 2008 Rose was made
McLaren Vale's Bushing Queen, the title going to the maker of the best wine at the McLaren
Vale Wine Show. Exports to the UK, the US and other major markets.

� **Frux Frugis McLaren Vale Shiraz 2006** Some colour development; rich soft
     black fruits with some caramel elements; even palate-feel and flow, with some fruit
     sweetness ex alcohol. Screwcap. **Rating** 91 **To** 2016 $45

Umamu Estate ★★★★

PO Box 1269, Margaret River, WA 6285 **Region** Margaret River
T (08) 9757 5058 **F** (08) 9757 5058 **www**.umamuestate.com **Open** Not
Winemaker Bruce Dukes (Contract) **Est.** 2005 **Cases** 7500 **Vyds** 20.8 ha
Chief executive Charmaine Saw explains 'my life has been a journey towards Umamu. An
upbringing in both eastern and western cultures, graduating in natural science, training as a
chef, combined with a passion for the arts, and experience as a management consultant have
all contributed to my building the business creatively yet professionally.' The palindrome
Umamu, says Saw, is inspired by balance and contentment. In practical terms this means an
organic approach to viticulture and a deep respect for the terroir. In 2004 Charmaine Saw
purchased the property and its plantings, dating back to '78, of cabernet sauvignon (6.9 ha),
shiraz (4.1 ha), chardonnay (3.5 ha), merlot (2 ha), semillon and sauvignon blanc (1.5 ha each)
and cabernet franc (0.7 ha); the maiden vintage under the Umamu label following in '05.
Exports to the UK, Hong Kong, Malaysia and Singapore.

♥♥♥♥♀ **Margaret River Chardonnay 2007** A very oaky bouquet, with grapefruit and
     straw on offer; the palate is fresh and lively with good acidity and drive; the oak
     dominates, and hopefully time will see it integrate with the generous level of fruit.
     Screwcap. 13.5% alc. **Rating** 91 **To** 2014 $50
     Margaret River Cabernet Merlot 2006 Bright colour; focused red and
     blackcurrant fruit, with cedar and some leafy tones; bright and quite juicy, with
     charry oak coming through on the finish. Great achievement in the wet vintage.
     Screwcap. 13% alc. **Rating** 90 **To** 2015 $28

♥♥♥♥ **Margaret River Shiraz 2006** A light and spicy bouquet due to the vintage; red
     fruits and a little green pepper on display; the palate is quite light, with fine tannin
     and good flavour. Screwcap. 13% alc. **Rating** 88 **To** 2014 $28

 # Uplands ★★★★☆

174 Richmond Road, Cambridge, Tas 7170 **Region** Southern Tasmania
T (03) 6248 5460 **Open** By appt
Winemaker Frogmore Creek (Alain Rousseau) **Est.** 1998 **Cases** 240 **Vyds** 0.5 ha
Michael and Debbie Ryan bought the historic Uplands House (1823) in 1998 and decided to
plant the front paddock with chardonnay, and join the grapegrowing trend in the Coal River
Valley of southern Tasmania. The vineyard is planted with the two most suitable clones for
the area, 8127 for sparkling and the Penfold clone for their lightly wooded Chardonnay. They
have developed a partnership with another small vineyard in the valley to produce a Pinot
Noir Chardonnay that will spend at least four years on lees prior to disgorgement. The 2007
Chardonnay is a quite beautiful wine.

♀♀♀♀♀ **Chardonnay 2007** Very good green-straw colour; an elegant wine with excellent focus, seamless integration, white peach and melon fruit with oak; long finish. Gold medal Tas Wine Show '09. Screwcap. 13.8% alc. **Rating** 95 **To** 2011 $25

Upper Reach   ★★★☆
77 Memorial Avenue, Baskerville, WA 6056 **Region** Swan Valley
T (08) 9296 0078 **F** (08) 9296 0278 **www**.upperreach.com.au **Open** 7 days 11–5
Winemaker Derek Pearse **Est.** 1996 **Cases** 5000 **Vyds** 8.31 ha
This 10-ha property on the banks of the upper reaches of the Swan River was purchased by Laura Rowe and Derek Pearse in 1996. The original 4-ha vineyard has been expanded, and plantings now include chardonnay, shiraz, cabernet sauvignon, verdelho, semillon, merlot, petit verdot and muscat. All wines are estate-grown. The fish on the label, incidentally, is black bream, which can be found in the pools of the Swan River during the summer months. Exports to the UK.

♀♀♀♀♀ **Reserve Swan Valley Chardonnay 2008** Skilled winemaking captures everything this estate-grown chardonnay has to offer, but without going over the top; sweet nectarine and peach fruit is framed by barrel ferment inputs, each component balanced. Screwcap. 13.5% alc. **Rating** 90 **To** 2014 $28

♀♀♀♀ **Unwooded Chardonnay 2008** A nicely handled wine with nectarine and a little citrus providing finesse and line to the finish. Screwcap. 13% alc. **Rating** 88 **To** 2012 $17
Swan Valley Shiraz 2007 Quite striking confit fruit aromas; robust tannins give the ripe black fruit of the palate good support. Needs time. Screwcap. 14% alc. **Rating** 88 **To** 2017 $30

Valhalla Wines   ★★★
163 All Saints Road, Wahgunyah, Vic 3687 **Region** Rutherglen
T (02) 6033 1438 **F** (02) 6033 1728 **www**.valhallawines.com.au **Open** Fri–Sun & public hols 10–5, or by appt
Winemaker Anton Therkildsen **Est.** 2001 **Cases** 1400 **Vyds** 2.5 ha
This is the highly focused venture of Anton Therkildsen and wife Antoinette Del Popolo. They acquired the property in 2001, and in '02 began the planting of shiraz (1.6 ha) and durif (0.9 ha). They intend to expand the vineyard with marsanne, viognier, grenache, mourvedre and riesling, reflecting their primary interest in the wines of the Rhône Valley. For the time being, they are relying on contract-grown grapes to develop these wine styles. The straw bale winery was built in 2007, underlining their desire for sustainable viticulture and biodiversity, with minimal use of sprays and annual planting of cover crops between the rows. A worm farm and the composting of grape skins and stalks completes the picture.

♀♀♀♀ **Rutherglen Shiraz 2007** There is plenty of ripe blackberry fruit on the mid-palate, but the wine thins out on the finish for some reason. Cork. 14.3% alc. **Rating** 87 **To** 2014 $25
Rutherglen Shiraz 2006 While the fruit flavours have some confection characters, there are also spicy components to the fruit and tannins to provide contrast and relief. Cork. 14.5% alc. **Rating** 87 **To** 2014 $25
Rutherglen Grenache Shiraz Mourvedre 2007 A juicy young wine, showing red berry fruits, and a generous level of fruit on the palate; a little simple. Screwcap. 14% alc. **Rating** 87 **To** 2013 $22
Rutherglen Grenache Shiraz Mourvedre 2006 Savoury and dry; licorice and raspberry fruit, with just a touch of spice; firm on the finish. Screwcap. 14.5% alc. **Rating** 87 **To** 2013 $20

Vasse Felix ★★★★★

Cnr Caves Road/Harmans Road South, Cowaramup, WA 6284 **Region** Margaret River
T (08) 9756 5000 **F** (08) 9755 5425 **www**.vassefelix.com.au **Open** 7 days 10–5
Winemaker Virginia Willcock **Est.** 1967 **Cases** 150 000 **Vyds** 195.45 ha

Vasse Felix was the first winery to be built in the Margaret River. Owned and operated by the Holmes à Court family since 1987, the winery and vineyard have been carefully developed. Recent acquisitions of a neighbouring vineyard and property within the Wilyabrup subregion will ensure the dynamic Virginia Willcock will have the ability to craft wines of the highest calibre for many years to come, with Cabernet Sauvignon and Chardonnay leading the way. There are two ranges: at the top, Heytesbury; then a full suite of classic varietals. Exports to all major markets.

🍷🍷🍷🍷🍷 **Margaret River Semillon 2008** Intense, complex aromas reflect both the varietal fruit and partial barrel ferment in French oak; has excellent mouthfeel, the lemon and honey-accented fruit of the mid-palate drying out nicely on the herb and mineral finish. Screwcap. 11.5% alc. **Rating** 95 **To** 2018 $25
Margaret River Sauvignon Blanc Semillon 2008 Totally delicious, fruit-driven wine exploding with tropical fruit, which, however, doesn't go over the top, for the palate is svelte and streamlined. Gold WA Wine Show '08. Screwcap. 12.5% alc. **Rating** 95 **To** 2014 $25
Heytesbury Margaret River Chardonnay 2007 Bright straw-green; a powerful and aristocratic wine; upfront complexity from wild yeast ferment and 10 months in French oak gives way to an intense palate, where the nutty/creamy notes of the bouquet are seamlessly folded into piercing, citrus-tinged fruit. Screwcap. 13.5% alc. **Rating** 95 **To** 2014
Heytesbury 2005 Tightly focused and structured; particularly fine but persistent tannins add much to the texture; blackcurrant and touches of French oak complete the picture of a high-quality wine. Cabernet Sauvignon/Shiraz. High-quality cork. 14.5% alc. **Rating** 95 **To** 2020 $70
Cane Cut Margaret River Semillon 2008 Beautifully made; sweetness and acidity balanced to perfection; has a citrussy cast that could fool the unwary into guessing it is a riesling; drink while it has all this vibrancy. Screwcap. 12% alc. **Rating** 95 **To** 2010 $23
Margaret River Classic Dry White 2008 A wine of real poise and finesse; lovely depth to the generous fruit, with a slight savoury/mineral edge that offers true line and length. Screwcap. 12% alc. **Rating** 94 **To** 2014 $20

🍷🍷🍷🍷🍷 **Margaret River Chardonnay 2007** Vibrant colour; lively grapefruit aroma with a hint of oak and spice; good depth and weight, and very clean and even on the finish. Screwcap. 13.5% alc. **Rating** 90 **To** 2013 $25

🍷🍷🍷🍷 **Margaret River Shiraz 2006** Quite a cool wine, with red fruits framed by pepper and some green herbs; good weight and structure, but the fruit pulls up a little short. Screwcap. 14% alc. **Rating** 89 **To** 2012 $35
Margaret River Cabernet Merlot 2006 Relatively light developed colour; some minty overtones to the bouquet and a palate that, while flavoursome, has some sweet and sour characters from the difficult vintage. Screwcap. 14.5% alc. **Rating** 89 **To** 2012 $25
Margaret River Cabernet Sauvignon 2006 Slightly hazy colour; redcurrant and blackcurrant fruit is accompanied by nuances of earth, leaf and mint on both bouquet and palate; needs a little more structure. Screwcap. 14% alc. **Rating** 89 **To** 2014 $35
Margaret River Cabernet Merlot 2007 Has fragrant cassis aromas and flavours, but is very light-bodied; more expected of a wine such as this and a vintage such as this. Screwcap. 14.5% alc. **Rating** 87 **To** 2014

Vasse River Wines

c/- Post Office, Carbunup, WA 6280 **Region** Margaret River
T (08) 9755 1111 **F** (08) 9755 1011 **www.**vasseriver.com.au **Open** Not
Winemaker Sharna Kowalczuk, Jane Dunkley **Est.** 1993 **Cases** 7000
This is a major and rapidly growing business owned by the Credaro family; 90 ha of
chardonnay, semillon, verdelho, sauvignon blanc, cabernet sauvignon, merlot and shiraz have
been planted on the typical gravelly red loam soils of the region. The wines are released under
two labels: Vasse River for the premium and Carbunup Estate (not to be confused with
Carbunup Crest) for the lower-priced varietals. Exports to the US and Canada.

ΥΥΥΥΥ **Margaret River Sauvignon Blanc 2008** A very fresh bouquet of cut grass,
nettle and passionfruit; lean, crisp and clearly defined varietal sauvignon, with a dry,
even and poised finish. Screwcap. 12% alc. **Rating** 92 **To** 2011
Margaret River Cabernet Merlot 2007 Strong varietal cabernet personality
with cassis and cedar coming to the fore; lots of fruit on the palate, a plump
middle provides real drinkability. Screwcap. **Rating** 92 **To** 2016
Beach Head Margaret River Semillon Sauvignon Blanc 2008 Clean, crisp
and well made, showing tropical fruits, aided by a generous dollop of semillon, which
gives the palate good mouthfeel. Screwcap. 12.5% alc. **Rating** 90 **To** 2012 $15
Margaret River Shiraz 2007 Red fruits, spice and touch of earth dominate
the bouquet; the palate follows through with a generous helping of red fruits and
Asian spices on the finish. Screwcap. **Rating** 90 **To** 2016

ΥΥΥΥ **Margaret River Verdelho 2008** Plenty of personality, with fresh, clean fruit and
lively acidity on the finish; well-made, easy-drinking dry white wine. Screwcap.
13.1% alc. **Rating** 88 **To** 2011 $16
Beach Head Margaret River Chardonnay 2008 Nectarine fruit with a
touch of straw on the bouquet; vibrant and juicy on the palate, but a little one-
dimensional. Screwcap. 13.8% alc. **Rating** 87 **To** 2012

Velo Wines

755 West Tamar Highway, Legana, Tas 7277 **Region** Northern Tasmania
T (03) 6330 3677 **F** (03) 6330 3098 **Open** 7 days 10–5
Winemaker Micheal Wilson, Winemaking Tasmania **Est.** 1966 **Cases** 1800
The story behind Velo Wines is fascinating, wheels within wheels. The 0.9 ha of cabernet
sauvignon and 0.5 ha of pinot noir of the Legana Vineyard were planted in 1966 by Graham
Wiltshire, legitimately described as one of the three great pioneers of the Tasmanian wine
industry. Fifteen years ago Micheal and Mary Wilson returned to Tasmania after living in Italy
and France for a decade. Micheal had been an Olympic cyclist and joined the professional
ranks, racing in all of the major European events. Imbued with a love of wine and food, they
spent 'seven long hard years in the restaurant game'. Somehow, Micheal found time to become
a qualified viticulturist, and was vineyard manager for Moorilla Estate based at St Matthias,
and Mary spent five years working in wine wholesaling for leading distributors. In 2001 they
purchased the Legana Vineyard, planted so long ago, and have painstakingly rehabilitated the
40-year-old vines. They have built a small winery where Micheal makes the red wines, and
Julian Alcorso makes the white wines, sourced in part from 0.6 ha of estate riesling and from
grapes grown on the East Coast.

ΥΥΥΥΥ **Riesling 2007** Apple blossom and honeysuckle aromas backed by good acidity,
but the lime juice palate does dip slightly on the back-palate. Screwcap. 11.9% alc.
Rating 92 **To** 2015 $28
Pinot Noir 2007 Good colour; light- to medium-bodied, elegant and savoury
style; good length and persistence; balanced ripeness. Screwcap. 13.5% alc.
Rating 90 **To** 2013 $25

ΥΥΥΥ **Unwooded Chardonnay 2008** Complex wine, powerful bouquet suggestive
of a touch of oak – perhaps lees; also the possibility of some sweetness. Unoaked.
Screwcap. 12.5% alc. **Rating** 88 **To** 2012 $20

Veronique   ★★★☆

PO Box 599, Angaston, SA 5353 **Region** Barossa Valley
T (08) 8565 3214 **Open** Not
Winemaker Domenic Torzi **Est.** 2004 **Cases** 1500
Peter Manning, general manager of Angas Park Fruits, and wife Vicki, moved to Mt McKenzie
in the 1990s. His wine consumption soon focused on Barossa Shiraz, and he quickly became
a close drinking partner with Domenic Torzi of all things shiraz. By 2004 the Mannings
decided it was high time to produce a Barossa shiraz of their own, and, with the help of Torzi,
sourced grapes from three outstanding blocks. The vineyards also include mataro and grenache
(thoroughly excusable in the context) and sauvignon blanc.

Victory Point Wines   ★★★★☆

4 Holben Road, Cowaramup, WA 6284 **Region** Margaret River
T (08) 9381 5765 **F** (08) 9388 2449 **www**.victorypointwines.com **Open** By appt
Winemaker Keith Mugford, Ian Bell (Contract) **Est.** 1997 **Cases** 2500 **Vyds** 14.8 ha
Judith and Gary Berson (the latter a partner in the Perth office of a national law firm) have
set their aims high. With viticultural advice from Keith and Clare Mugford of Moss Wood,
they have established their vineyard without irrigation, emulating those of the Margaret River
pioneers (including Moss Wood). The plantings comprise 4.5 ha chardonnay, the remainder
the Bordeaux varieties, with cabernet sauvignon (6 ha), merlot (2 ha), cabernet franc (1 ha),
malbec (0.6 ha) and petit verdot (0.5 ha).

ՊՊՊՊՊ **Margaret River Chardonnay 2008** A distinguished blend of Mendoza and
the four Dijon clones provides a long and tightly focused palate; fruit and oak
seamlessly welded. Screwcap. 13.5% alc. **Rating** 94 **To** 2016 $45

ՊՊՊՊ **Margaret River Cabernet Sauvignon Cabernet Franc Petit Verdot
Malbec Merlot 2006** A valiant attempt to defeat the vintage climate; while light
in colour, the wine has balance to the light-bodied, savoury palate, which has some
red fruit elements. Screwcap. 13.3% alc. **Rating** 88 **To** 2012 $40

Viking Wines   ★★★★

RSD 108 Seppeltsfield Road, Marananga, SA 5355 **Region** Barossa Valley
T (08) 8562 3842 **F** (08) 8562 4266 **www**.vikingwines.com **Open** 7 days 11–5
Winemaker Rolf Binder, Kym Teusner (Contract) **Est.** 1995 **Cases** 1500
With 50-year-old, dry-grown and near-organic vineyards yielding 2.5–3.7 tonnes per hectare,
Viking Wines was 'discovered' by Robert Parker with inevitable consequences for the price
of its top Shiraz. There are 5 ha of shiraz and 3 ha of cabernet sauvignon. The Odin's Honour
wines (made by sister company Todd-Viking Wines) also come from old (20–100 years)
dry-grown vines around Marananga and Greenock. Exports to the US, the UK, Singapore
and France.

ՊՊՊՊՊ **Grand Barossa Valley Shiraz 2006** Bright colour; an oak dominant bouquet,
with ripe blackberry and mocha aromas; the coffee note continues on the palate,
with generous sweet fruit on the finish. Screwcap. 14.5% alc. **Rating** 93 **To** 2016

 ## Vinaceous   ★★★

49 Bennett Street, East Perth, WA 6004 (postal) **Region** Various
T (08) 9221 4666 **F** (08) 9221 5699 **www**.vinaceous.com.au **Open** Not
Winemaker Gavin Berry, Michael Kerrigan **Est.** 2007 **Cases** 5130
This is the somewhat quirky venture of wine marketer Nick Stacy (West Cape Howe),
Michael Kerrigan (winemaker/partner Hay Shed Hill) and Gavin Berry (winemaker/partner
West Cape Howe). The brand is primarily directed to the US market, which took 90% of
the four wines in the first release, the remaining 10% shared between Australia, Singapore and
Ireland. The wines are not primarily sourced, as one might expect, from Western Australia,
but variously from McLaren Vale, Barossa Valley and the Limestone Coast, with a Verdelho,
and the possibility of a Reserve Shiraz, from WA. Divine Light Verdelho, Snake Charmer

Shiraz, Red Right Hand Shiraz Grenache Tempranillo and Raconteur Cabernet Sauvignon, coupled with ornate, turn-of-the-19th-century graphics, gives the flavour of the wines and their export focus.

♟♟♟♟ **Divine Light Verdelho 2008** Quite a green and zesty style, with tingling acidity, providing a lively wine, made for a hot summer's day. Screwcap. 13% alc. **Rating** 88 **To** 2014 $25
Red Right Hand Shiraz Grenache Tempranillo 2007 A very lifted bouquet, with sage and dried red and black fruit; plush and sweet-fruited, yet with a bitterness that provides contrast to the rich fruits. Screwcap. 14% alc. **Rating** 88 **To** 2013 $25
Red Right Hand Shiraz Grenache Tempranillo 2006 Fragrant red fruits, then a light- to medium-bodied palate with spiced red fruit flavours; a blend of convenience or conviction? Screwcap. 14.5% alc. **Rating** 87 **To** 2013 $25
Raconteur Cabernet Sauvignon 2007 Bright colour; a hint of mint frames the red and black fruits; clean and quite firm on the finish. Screwcap. 14.5% alc. **Rating** 87 **To** 2012 $25

Vincognita

PO Box 778, McLaren Vale, SA 5171 **Region** Southern Fleurieu
T (08) 8370 5737 **F** (08) 8370 5737 **www.**vincognita.com.au **Open** Not
Winemaker Peter Belej, Carrie Belej (Consultant) **Est.** 1999 **Cases** 900 **Vyds** 40 ha
Vigneron-owner Peter Belej moved from Ukraine as a boy with his family, and grew up on the family vineyards at Gol Gol in NSW. After 40 years he moved to the Fleurieu Peninsula, planting 40 ha on the Nangkita Vineyard, with 14 ha of shiraz, 8 ha each of cabernet sauvignon, merlot and sauvignon blanc, 2 ha of viognier and one row of zinfandel. Daughter Carolyn (Carrie) Belej is a winemaker with Foster's, but directs the winemaking at Vincognita on a consultant basis. The estate vineyard continues to be available for purchase; after 40 years of growing grapes, Peter wants to spend more time winemaking, marketing and selling. Regardless of the outcome, the Vincognita (and Nangkita) labels are here to stay.

♟♟♟♟♟ **Nangkita Single Vineyard Madeleines Primitivo 2007** Good colour; raspberry and plum with a healthy splash of spice; very rich, almost sweet palate; the finish cleans up nicely with a slight savoury note. Screwcap. 14.5% alc. **Rating** 90 **To** 2012 $22

Vinden Estate

17 Gillards Road, Pokolbin, NSW 2320 **Region** Lower Hunter Valley
T (02) 4998 7410 **F** (02) 4998 7175 **www.**vindenestate.com.au **Open** 7 days 10–5
Winemaker Guy Vinden, John Baruzzi (Consultant) **Est.** 1998 **Cases** 4000
Sandra and Guy Vinden have a beautiful home and cellar door, landscaped gardens, and 3.6 ha of merlot, shiraz and alicante bouschet, with the Brokenback mountain range in the distance. The winemaking is done onsite, using estate-grown red grapes; semillon and chardonnay are purchased from other growers. The reds are open-fermented, hand-plunged and basket-pressed.

♟♟♟♟♟ **Basket Press Hunter Valley Shiraz 2007** Attractive, strongly regional style, with polished leather, earth and spice nuances to both bouquet and palate; medium- to full-bodied, with good line, length and balance. Screwcap. 13% alc. **Rating** 91 **To** 2017 $28
Estate Reserve Hunter Valley Verdelho 2008 Good verdelho, with an extra level of richness to the fruit salad flavours, yet finishes crisp; will mature nicely. Screwcap. 13.5% alc. **Rating** 90 **To** 2012 $23

♟♟♟♟ **Hunter Valley Alicante Bouschet 2008** Has the bright pale crimson expected of this temturier (red flesh) grape; very early picking has invested the wine with bracing natural acidity and freshness, and a dry finish. Screwcap. 10% alc. **Rating** 89 **To** 2010 $22

Hunter Valley Late Harvest Semillon 2007 Has a lively freshness, and a touch of firmness to the finish that stops it cloying; best with fresh fruit. Screwcap. 10% alc. **Rating** 89 **To** 2012 $23

Hunter Valley Chardonnay 2006 Pleasant melon and stone fruit flavours, with a touch of French oak to lift the wine out of the ruck. Screwcap. 12.7% alc. **Rating** 87 **To** 2012 $23

Vinea Marson   ★★★★☆

411 Heathcote-Rochester Road, Heathcote, Vic 3523 **Region** Heathcote
T (03) 5433 2768 **F** (03) 5433 2787 **www**.vineamarson.com **Open** By appt
Winemaker Mario Marson **Est.** 2000 **Cases** 1400 **Vyds** 6.5 ha
Owner-winemaker Mario Marson spent many years as the winemaker viticulturist with the late Dr John Middleton at the celebrated Mount Mary. He purchased the Vinea Marson property in 1999, on the eastern slopes of the Mt Camel Range, and in 2000 planted syrah and viognier, plus Italian varieties, sangiovese, nebbiolo and barbera. Since leaving Mount Mary, he has undertaken vintage work at Isole e Olena in Tuscany, worked as winemaker at Jasper Hill vineyard, and as consultant and winemaker for Stefani Estate. Exports to Sweden and China.

▲▲▲▲▲ **Syrah 2007** Vibrant colour; redcurrant and blueberry fruit, with an attractive sage component; full-flavoured, ample levels of tannin, roast meat and a splash of violets on the finish; dry, chewy and savoury. Diam. 14% alc. **Rating** 94 **To** 2018 $47

▲▲▲▲ **Sangiovese 2007** Ripe cherry bouquet with a touch of bramble; quite soft for the variety, with an attractive acid backbone providing some cut on the palate. Diam. 13.5% alc. **Rating** 87 **To** 2012 $42

Vinrock   ★★★★☆

23 George Street, Thebarton, SA 5031 (postal) **Region** McLaren Vale
T (08) 8408 8900 **F** (08) 8408 8966 **www**.vinrock.com **Open** Not
Winemaker Michael Fragos **Est.** 2004 **Cases** 6000 **Vyds** 30 ha
Owners Don Luca, Marco Iannetti and Anthony De Pizzol all have a background in the wine industry, none more than Don, a former board member of Tatachilla. He also planted the Luca Vineyard in 1999. The majority of the grapes are sold, but since 2004 limited quantities of wine have been made from the best blocks in the vineyard. Exports to Malaysia, Singapore and China.

▲▲▲▲▲ **McLaren Vale Shiraz 2007** Dense purple; medium- to full-bodied, with strong regional and varietal expression; has excellent structure and even more length; great outcome for the vintage. Screwcap. 14.7% alc. **Rating** 94 **To** 2020 $19.95

▲▲▲▲▲ **McLaren Vale Grenache 2007** Light but bright hue; juicy red fruits, offset by spicy, fine tannins, are strongly varietal; one of those wines to offer pleasure at any time over the next three–five years. Screwcap. 14.5% alc. **Rating** 90 **To** 2012 $19.95

▲▲▲▲ **McLaren Vale Cabernet Sauvignon 2007** Has good varietal character, but not much mid-palate vinosity, earthy/savoury characters on the finish breaking the line. Screwcap. 14% alc. **Rating** 87 **To** 2013 $19.95

Virgara Wines   ★★★

Lot 11 Heaslip Road, Angle Vale, SA 5117 **Region** Adelaide Plains
T (08) 8284 7688 **F** (08) 8284 7666 **www**.virgarawines.com.au **Open** Mon–Fri 9–5, w'ends & public hols 10–5
Winemaker Tony Carapetis **Est.** 2001 **Cases** 14 000 **Vyds** 91 ha
In 1962 the Virgara family – father Michael, mother Maria and 10 children ranging from 1 to 18 years old – migrated to Australia from southern Italy. Through the hard work so typical of many such families, in due course they became market gardeners on land purchased at Angle Vale (1967), and in the early '90s acquired an existing vineyard in Angle Vale. This included

25 ha of shiraz, the plantings since expanded to 91 ha of shiraz, cabernet sauvignon, grenache, malbec, merlot, riesling, sangiovese, sauvignon blanc, pinot grigio and alicante. In 2001 the Virgara brothers purchased the former Barossa Valley Estates winery, but used it only for storage and maturation, as the first wine (made in '02 from 40-year-old shiraz) was made by the Glaetzer family. The death of Domenic Virgara in a road accident led to the employment of former Palandri winemaker (and, before that, Tahbilk winemaker) Tony Carapetis, and the full commissioning of the winery. Exports to Canada, China, Thailand, Malaysia and Japan.

ȚȚȚȚ **Stone Chapel Adelaide Plains Sauvignon Blanc 2008** Bright and zesty, with a crisp palate built around citrussy acidity and mineral notes; has length and a thoroughly surprising gold medal from the Adelaide Wine Show '08. Good value. Screwcap. 12.5% alc. **Rating** 89 **To** 2010 $15

Adelaide Plains Sauvignon Blanc 2008 Well made; early picking paid off, the wine brightened by citrussy acidity on the finish. Screwcap. 12.5% alc. **Rating** 87 **To** 2010 $15

Stone Chapel Adelaide Plains Shiraz 2007 Good colour; has abundant black fruits then bitter chocolate borrowed from McLaren Vale and a lick of vanillin oak. Screwcap. 14% alc. **Rating** 87 **To** 2014 $15

Virgin Block Vineyard

Caves Road, Yallingup, WA 6282 **Region** Margaret River
T (08) 9755 2394 **F** (08) 9755 2357 **www**.virginblock.com **Open** 7 days 10–5 (peak), Wed–Sun 10–5 (offpeak)
Winemaker Bruce Dukes, Anne-Coralie Fleury (Contract) **Est.** 1995 **Cases** 2000 **Vyds** 9 ha
Virgin Block has been established on a 30-ha property, 3 km from the Indian Ocean, and is surrounded by large jarrah and marri forests. The vineyard is planted (in descending order of size) to sauvignon blanc, shiraz, semillon, cabernet sauvignon, merlot, cabernet franc and malbec.

ȚȚȚȚȚ **Margaret River Shiraz 2006** Cool and spicy, with redcurrant and blackberry offset by herbaceous elements; the palate is quite generous, but also tannic; well constructed and savoury on the finish. Screwcap. 14% alc. **Rating** 90 **To** 2014 $28

Voice of the Vine

155 Coolart Road, Tuerong, Vic 3915 **Region** Mornington Peninsula
T (03) 5979 7771 **www**.voiceofthevine.com.au **Open** First Sat of month 11–4
Winemaker Jeremy Magyar **Est.** 2000 **Cases** 3000 **Vyds** 14.2 ha
Terry and Merylyn Winters have invested substantially in their 33-ha property on the Coolart Hills, with views over Westernport Bay to French Island, Tortoise Head, Phillip Island, Gippsland and Mt Baw Baw. As well vines (predominantly five clones of pinot noir on a variety of spacings and trellises) they have established extensive botanical gardens incorporating three lakes, a bushland area and adjoining wetlands. The lagoons serve a practical purpose as well as an aesthetic one, providing irrigation from over 30 megalitres of storage. An onsite winery has been built, and Jeremy Magyar appointed full-time winemaker.

ȚȚȚȚȚ **Sauvignon Blanc 2007** Creamy oak bouquet, with ripe tropical fruit; the palate follows through with good texture and weight on the finish. Screwcap. 12% alc. **Rating** 90 **To** 2012 $23.10

Voyager Estate

Lot 1 Stevens Road, Margaret River, WA 6285 **Region** Margaret River
T (08) 9757 6354 **F** (08) 9757 6494 **www**.voyagerestate.com.au **Open** 7 days 10–5
Winemaker Cliff Royle **Est.** 1978 **Cases** 35 000 **Vyds** 125 ha
Voyager Estate has come a long way since it was acquired by Michael Wright (of the mining family) in 1991. It now has a substantial high-quality vineyard, which means it can select the best parcels of fruit for its own label, and supply surplus (but high-quality) wine to others. The Cape Dutch-style tasting room and vast rose garden are a major tourist attraction. Exports to the UK, the US and other major markets.

ŶŶŶŶŶ Margaret River Chardonnay 2007 In the top tier of Margaret River chardonnay (and hence Australia's) with stone fruit, melon and grapefruit flavours; has soaked up barrel ferment in French oak (40% new) and 12 months' maturation, leaving just a trace of nuttiness. Screwcap. 13.2% alc. **Rating** 96 To 2016 $42

Margaret River Cabernet Sauvignon Merlot 2004 Deep colour; a powerful bouquet and even more powerful palate, with layers of blackcurrant and cassis seamlessly interwoven with spicy/mocha oak, tannins strong but perfectly balanced; very good mouthfeel. Screwcap. 14.2% alc. **Rating** 96 To 2024 $60

Margaret River Sauvignon Blanc Semillon 2008 Fragrant aromas and juicy, vibrant flavours ranging across citrus, gooseberry and passionfruit; the palate is long and even, the finish enticing another mouthful. Screwcap. 12.9% alc. **Rating** 95 To 2012 $24

Margaret River Chardonnay 2006 Slightly finer and crisper than the usual Voyager Estate style, but none the worse for that. Taut grapefruit and stone fruit flavours drive the long palate, augmented by integrated French oak and citrussy acidity. Screwcap. 13.3% alc. **Rating** 95 To 2020 $42

Margaret River Cabernet Sauvignon Merlot 2005 Classic Margaret River blend, rich in flavour and powerful in structure; the luscious array of black fruits is complemented by ripe tannins and quality oak on the long finish. Screwcap. 14% alc. **Rating** 94 To 2025 $60

ŶŶŶŶŶ Margaret River Shiraz 2007 Bright hue; elegant, but complex, with distinct cool-region overtones of spice and licorice to the black fruits; the tannins and oak are well balanced and integrated. Screwcap. 14% alc. **Rating** 93 To 2020 $32

Margaret River Shiraz 2006 Aromatic red fruits on the bouquet, then an intense palate of blood plum, cherry and blackberry fruit, with a cool-grown spicy overlay; fine ripe tannins and good oak. Screwcap. 14.2% alc. **Rating** 93 To 2026 $32

Girt by Sea Margaret River Cabernet Merlot 2006 Good hue; fresh, juicy black and red berry fruits; minimal tannins and a touch of oak; convincing early-drinking style. Screwcap. 14% alc. **Rating** 92 To 2011 $24

Girt by Sea Margaret River Cabernet Merlot 2007 Attractive medium-bodied wine with obvious varietal inputs via blackcurrant, plum and redcurrant fruits; the tannins are soft, and there is a touch of vanillin oak on the finish. Screwcap. 14.2% alc. **Rating** 90 To 2014 $24

ŶŶŶŶ Margaret River Chenin Blanc 2008 A quite restrained bouquet with green apple fruit, yet a quite a luscious texture; ample fruit weight and generous persistence is the key. Screwcap. 13% alc. **Rating** 89 To 2014 $20

Wallaroo Wines   ★★★☆

196 Brooklands Road, Hall, ACT, 2618 **Region** Canberra District
T (02) 6230 2831 **F** (02) 6230 2830 **www**.wallaroowines.com.au **Open** W'ends & public hols 10–5, or by appt
Winemaker Roger Harris (Contract) **Est.** 1997 **Cases** 800 **Vyds** 10 ha
Foreign correspondent Philip Williams and his wife, media consultant Carolyn Jack, established their Wallaroo vineyard in 1997. The vineyard is planted to shiraz, cabernet sauvignon and riesling, the latter having had significant success in the Canberra Regional Wine Show. The dominant plantings are shiraz and cabernet sauvignon, and it is apparent from production that a substantial part of the grape harvest is sold. Exports to the UK.

ŶŶŶŶŶ Canberra District Riesling 2008 Floral, spicy aromas lead into a delicious palate, the fruit flavours lifted by the relatively low alcohol, ranging through lime to grapefruit. Screwcap. 11.5% alc. **Rating** 93 To 2020 $20

ŶŶŶŶ Canberra District Cabernet Sauvignon 2007 A wine pulling in several directions, the ripe fruit and some vanilla oak one way, the more savoury/earthy components the other. Screwcap. 15% alc. **Rating** 87 To 2014 $22

Wallington Wines ★★★

Eugowra Road, Canowindra, NSW 2904 **Region** Cowra
T (02) 6344 7153 **F** (02) 6344 7105 **www**.wallingtonwines.com.au **Open** By appt
Winemaker Murray Smith (Consultant), Margaret Wallington **Est.** 1992 **Cases** 1500
Vyds 17 ha
Margaret and the late Anthony Wallington began their Nyrang Creek Vineyard in 1994. Today
the plantings include chardonnay (8 ha), shiraz (2 ha), cabernet sauvignon and grenache
(1.5 ha each), and lesser amounts of petit verdot, mourvedre, tempranillo, cabernet franc,
semillon and viognier. Most of the grape production is sold. Exports to the US.

ΥΥΥΥ **Rockdell Shiraz Grenache Mourvedre 2003** Plummy fruit with a touch
of spice and cedar; well made with clear varietal character. Screwcap. 14.7% alc.
Rating 88 **To** 2012 $25

Walter Clappis Wine Co ★★★★

Rifle Range Road, McLaren Vale, SA 5171 **Region** McLaren Vale
T 0411 411 511 **F** (08) 8299 9500 **www**.hedonistwines.com.au **Open** Not
Winemaker Walter Clappis, Kimberly Clappis **Est.** 1982 **Cases** 8000 **Vyds** 32 ha
Walter Clappis (once known as Bill) has been a stalwart of the McLaren Vale wine scene for
decades. The estate plantings of shiraz (14 ha), cabernet sauvignon and merlot (8 ha each), and
tempranillo (2 ha) are the cornerstone of his new business, which also provides the home for
the separately-owned Amicus business (see separate entry).

ΥΥΥΥΥ **The Hedonist McLaren Vale Shiraz 2006** A rich, full-flavoured, medium- to
full-bodied wine with a supple texture and mouthfeel to the mix of blackberry,
dark chocolate and vanilla oak, the tannins ripe and soft. Screwcap. 14% alc.
Rating 93 **To** 2021 $19

Wandin Valley Estate ★★★★☆

Wilderness Road, Lovedale, NSW 2320 **Region** Lower Hunter Valley
T (02) 4930 7317 **F** (02) 4930 7814 **www**.wandinvalley.com.au **Open** 7 days 10–5
Winemaker Matthew Burton **Est.** 1973 **Cases** 5000 **Vyds** 8.5 ha
After over 15 years in the wine and hospitality business, owners Phillipa and James Davern
have decided to offer the property as a going concern, with vineyard, winery, accommodation,
function centre, cricket ground and restaurant in the package, aiming to keep its skilled staff as
part of the business, and ensure that all existing contracts are ongoing. Ironically, being offered
for sale just as the overall quality has increased. Exports to Denmark, Malaysia and Japan.

ΥΥΥΥΥ **Reserve Hunter Valley Chardonnay 2007** Very pale green-straw; lively and
fresh style, with as much cool-climate as Hunter Valley characteristics; light-bodied,
but very well balanced, with melon and barrel ferment notes perfectly integrated.
Screwcap. 14% alc. **Rating** 94 **To** 2015 $30

ΥΥΥΥΥ **Bridie's Reserve Hunter Valley Shiraz 2006** Strongly regional, with very
good concentration of red fruits and a hint of savoury leather, spice and roast
meats; the palate is dense but bright, and shows a nice leathery complexity on the
finish. Cork. 13.5% alc. **Rating** 92 **To** 2016 $35

ΥΥΥΥ **Reserve Hunter Valley Semillon 2008** Pale colour; tight lemon fruit bouquet;
fresh and quite racy on the palate, and very clean and focused. Screwcap. 10% alc.
Rating 88 **To** 2015 $20
Hunter Valley Verdelho 2008 Attractive juicy fruit flavours come through
strongly on the back-palate and finish, lifting the wine out of the ruck. Screwcap.
13.5% alc. **Rating** 88 **To** 2012 $18
Single Vineyard Hunter Valley Semillon 2008 A pungent, almost sweaty
character showing its zesty lemon fruit; good flavour for an early-drinking Hunter
style. Screwcap. 11% alc. **Rating** 87 **To** 2011 $20

Wangolina Station ★★★★

Cnr Southern Ports Highway/Limestone Coast Road, Kingston SE, SA 5275
Region Mount Benson
T (08) 8768 6187 **F** (08) 8768 6149 **www**.wangolina.com.au **Open** 7 days 10–5
Winemaker Anita Goode **Est.** 2001 **Cases** 4500 **Vyds** 13 ha
Four generations of the Goode family have been graziers at Wangolina Station, but now Anita
Goode has broken with tradition by becoming a vigneron. She has planted sauvignon blanc
(5 ha), shiraz (3 ha), cabernet sauvignon and semillon (2 ha each), and pinot gris (1 ha).

ŸŸŸŸŸ **Mount Benson Semillon 2008** Barrel fermentation immediately obvious on
the bouquet, but the oak yields to the vibrant lemony/grassy fruit on the long
palate. Impressive. Screwcap. 12.5% alc. **Rating** 93 **To** 2015 $18
Mount Benson Cabernet Sauvignon Shiraz 2007 Rich and full-bodied,
with layers of blackcurrant and blackberry fruit supported by substantial, but
balanced, tannins. Will be long lived. Value. Screwcap. 14.5% alc. **Rating** 90
To 2022 $18
Mount Benson Semillon Sauvignon Blanc 2008 Fresh and crisp with a hint
of snow pea on the bouquet and palate; fine and evenly balanced with vibrant
acidity on the finish. Screwcap. 12.5% alc. **Rating** 90 **To** 2011 $16
Mount Benson Cabernet Sauvignon 2007 Some spicy/earthy overtones to
the black fruits on the bouquet; a supple medium-bodied palate with juicy cassis/
blackcurrant fruit and more of the spice of the bouquet; good tannin. Screwcap.
14.5% alc. **Rating** 90 **To** 2015 $24

ŸŸŸŸ **Mount Benson Shiraz 2007** A relatively soft, medium-bodied wine with
plum and black fruits, and a gentle waft of oak. Screwcap. 14% alc. **Rating** 87
To 2012 $20

Wanted Man

School House Lane, Heathcote, Vic 3523 **Region** Heathcote
T (03) 9362 0186 **F** (03) 9689 4490 **www**.wantedman.com.au **Open** Not
Winemaker Andrew Clarke, Peter Bartholomew **Est.** 1996 **Cases** 1800 **Vyds** 10.3 ha
The Wanted Man vineyard was planted in 1996, and has been managed by Andrew Clarke
since 2000, producing Jinks Creek's Heathcote Shiraz. That wine was sufficiently impressive
to lead Andrew and partner Peter Bartholomew (a Melbourne restaurateur) to purchase the
vineyard in 2006, and give it its own identity. The vineyard has 6 ha of shiraz, 1.5 ha each of
marsanne and roussanne, 1 ha of viognier and 0.3 ha of dolcetto. The quirky Ned Kelly label
is the work of Mark Knight, cartoonist for the *Herald Sun*. Exports to the UK, Denmark
and France.

ŸŸŸŸŸ **Single Vineyard Heathcote Shiraz 2007** Vibrant colour; essency core of
blue fruit, sage, bay leaf and a distinctly ironstone character; the palate is densely
textured, the weight continues from start to finish; seriously dark, deep and dense,
with a mouthful of ripe tannins to leave you in little doubt of the intent. Cork.
14% alc. **Rating** 94 **To** 2018 $69.50

ŸŸŸŸŸ **Single Vineyard Heathcote Shiraz Viognier 2006** Fresh bouquet of
redcurrant, blueberry, bay leaf and a splash of spice from the oak; a full-bodied
palate, the fruit taking a back seat to the structure, as the tannins are gravelly and
firm. Diam. 14% alc. **Rating** 92 **To** 2020 $59.50
Single Vineyard Heathcote Marsanne Viognier 2008 Vibrant hue;
honeysuckle, straw and a little spice on the bouquet; round, soft and fleshy on
entry, there is a mineral backbone that provides drive through to the finish.
Screwcap. 13% alc. **Rating** 91 **To** 2012 $34

ŸŸŸŸ **Single Vineyard Heathcote Shiraz Dolcetto 2006** Bright colour; jubey
blackberry and blueberry bouquet with a touch of mint; the palate is juicy and
vibrant, with good acidity and a bit of grip; a question over the price though.
Diam. 13.8% alc. **Rating** 88 **To** 2014 $59.50

Warburn Estate

700 Kidman Way, Griffith, NSW 2680 **Region** Riverina
T (02) 6963 8300 **www**.warburnestate.com.au **Open** Mon–Fri 9–5, Sat 10–4
Winemaker Sam Trimboli, Moreno Chiappin, Carmelo D'Aquino **Est.** 1969
Cases 1.25 million
Warburn Estate, doubtless drawn in part by the success of Casella's yellowtail, has seen its production soar. It draws on 1000 ha of vineyards, and produces an encyclopaedic range of wines exported to all major markets. The wines tasted are a tiny part of its large number of wines.

♀♀♀♀♀ **1164 Family Reserve Barossa Valley Shiraz 2004** Holding hue well; a fresh bouquet with clean berry fruit; the palate is quite luscious even though the aftertaste is dry. Screwcap. 14.5% alc. **Rating** 90 **To** 2012 $17

♀♀♀♀ **Stephendale Winemakers Reserve Barossa Cabernet Sauvignon 2006** Clean and bright, with lots of sweet red fruits and some spicy oak; warm and rich on the rather simple finish. Screwcap. 14% alc. **Rating** 88 **To** 2012 $10

Warrabilla

6152 Murray Valley Highway, Rutherglen, Vic 3685 **Region** Rutherglen
T (02) 6035 7242 **F** (02) 6035 7298 **www**.warrabillawines.com.au **Open** 7 days 10–5
Winemaker Andrew Sutherland Smith **Est.** 1990 **Cases** 10 000 **Vyds** 18.4 ha
Andrew Sutherland Smith and wife Carol have built a formidable reputation for their wines, headed by the Reserve trio of Durif, Cabernet Sauvignon and Shiraz, quintessential examples of Rutherglen red wine at its best. Their vineyard has been extended with the planting of some riesling and zinfandel. Andrew spent 15 years with All Saints, McWilliam's, Yellowglen, Fairfield and Chambers before setting up Warrabilla, and his accumulated experience shines through in the wines.

♀♀♀♀♀ **Reserve Cabernet Sauvignon 2006** Elegant in body, although the decision to use 100% American oak (rather than a mix of French and American) is quixotic; has some tension and length between cassis fruit and (doubtless adjusted) acidity. Diam. 14.5% alc. **Rating** 94 **To** 2030 $22
Reserve Durif 2007 Saturated purple; has that unique structure of the Warrabillas, with fruit that is so dense it does not admit light and shade; however, the dark chocolate, licorice, maraschino cherry and prime fruit flavours are good. Heavily stained Diam. 16.4% alc. **Rating** 94 **To** 2013 $22

♀♀♀♀♀ **Reserve Cabernet Sauvignon 2007** Crimson-purple; thick, chewy texture and structure although, as usual, the tannins are ripe and soft; juicy blackcurrant fruit has largely absorbed the French and American oak. Diam. 15.6% alc. **Rating** 92 **To** 2017 $22
Reserve Shiraz 2007 Unique wine; the saturated colour, the alcohol and the fruit all suggest it should be a forbidden drink for the next 10 years, but it doesn't work that way. What you do need is a roasted ox. Diam. 16.6% alc. **Rating** 91 **To** 2017 $22
Reserve Marsanne 2008 An unusually rich and succulent Marsanne, particularly when so young; authentic honeysuckle and peach flavours backed by the grainy acidity of the variety. Watch this space. Diam. 14% alc. **Rating** 90 **To** 2015 $18

♀♀♀♀ **Brimin Series Durif 2007** Dense purple-crimson; super-luscious prune and plum jam flavours inevitably enhanced by the alcohol; a love it or leave it style – love it at a winter barbecue. Very good value. Diam. 15.5% alc. **Rating** 89 **To** 2015 $18
Reserve Riesling 2008 At the opposite end of the alcohol universe to Warrabilla's reds; while the bouquet is somewhat closed, the palate is lively, the residual sugar nicely balanced by lime juice acidity. Screwcap. 11.5% alc. **Rating** 89 **To** 2014 $18

Warramate ★★★★★

27 Maddens Lane, Gruyere, Vic 3770 **Region** Yarra Valley
T (03) 5964 9219 **F** (03) 5964 9572 **www**.warramatewines.com.au **Open** 7 days 10–6
Winemaker David Church **Est.** 1970 **Cases** 2000 **Vyds** 6.6 ha
A long-established and perfectly situated winery reaping the full benefits of its 39-year-old vines; recent plantings have increased production. All the wines are well made, the Shiraz providing further proof (if such be needed) of the suitability of the variety to the region; has moved to another level since son David Church took the full mantle of winemaker.

🍷🍷🍷🍷🍷 White Label Yarra Valley Shiraz 2007 Crimson-purple colour, far better than the Black Label; a harmonious bouquet and palate, with black cherry, plum and blackberry fruit enhanced by some spicy notes, the tannins and oak good. Screwcap. 13.5% alc. **Rating** 94 **To** 2020 $45

Black Label Yarra Valley Cabernet Sauvignon 2007 Deep purple-crimson; pure varietal expression, with vibrant, almost juicy, cassis and blackcurrant fruit, and no shortage of tannin support. Screwcap. 13.5% alc. **Rating** 94 **To** 2020 $20

🍷🍷🍷🍷½ White Label Yarra Valley Riesling 2008 Very pale-straw; bright, lively and crisp, with citrus, apple, herb and mineral flavours; good line, length and balance. Screwcap. 12.5% alc. **Rating** 91 **To** 2016 $25

🍷🍷🍷🍷 White Label Yarra Valley Pinot Noir 2007 Good colour; a ripe, rich style, with sweet black and red fruits on the bouquet and mid-palate, tied up by a savoury finish. Good value, and will develop. Screwcap. 13.5% alc. **Rating** 89 **To** 2013 $20

Black Label Yarra Valley Shiraz 2007 A light- to medium-bodied palate with spicy/foresty notes tracking the bouquet; has good balance and length in a minor scale. Screwcap. 13.5% alc. **Rating** 89 **To** 2014 $20

White Label Yarra Valley Cabernet Merlot 2006 A medium-bodied wine with dominant red fruit/cassis flavours; the tannins are fine, the finish quite juicy. Screwcap. 13.5% alc. **Rating** 89 **To** 2015 $35

Warraroong Estate ★★★★★

247 Wilderness Road, Lovedale, NSW 2321 **Region** Lower Hunter Valley
T (02) 4930 7594 **www**.warraroongestate.com **Open** Thurs–Mon 10–5
Winemaker Andrew Thomas **Est.** 1978 **Cases** 3000 **Vyds** 7.4 ha
'Warraroong' is an Aboriginal word for 'hillside', reflecting the southwesterly aspect of the property, which looks back toward the Brokenback Range and Watagan Mountains. The label design is from a painting by Aboriginal artist Kia Kiro who, while from the NT, is now living and working in the Hunter Valley. The vineyard is owned by Bob Bradley and Linda Abrahams, with a support team under the direction of Bob. The plantings are chardonnay (2 ha), shiraz and verdelho (1.2 ha each), chenin blanc, sauvignon blanc and semillon (1 ha each). The quality of the current range of wines is outstanding. Exports to Japan.

🍷🍷🍷🍷🍷 Hunter Valley Semillon 2006 Glorious green-straw; even at this low alcohol the wine is a flavour powerhouse through the length of its palate, yet is still in its infancy; offers a combination of lime sherbet and a hint of stone fruit. Screwcap. 9.6% alc. **Rating** 96 **To** 2017 $40

Hunter Valley Semillon 2005 Still brilliantly fresh and lively, with piercing thrust and great vitality to the long palate and lingering aftertaste; the flavours cross over into Riesling territory, but with more lemon than lime. Screwcap. 11.3% alc. **Rating** 96 **To** 2015 $50

Hunter Valley Semillon 2008 Intense and highly focused, with a cornucopia of fruit aromas and flavours starting to manifest themselves; the balance and line of the palate guarantee a great future for the wine, as prior vintages show. Screwcap. 10.4% alc. **Rating** 94 **To** 2018 $28

Hunter Valley Semillon 2007 Deliciously fresh, crisp and lively; amazingly pure and pointed and (unusually) seems to have become even more focused than it was when first tasted in August '07, the multi-layered fruit still very much in evidence. Screwcap. 11.8% alc. **Rating** 94 **To** 2017 $28

Hunter Valley Chardonnay 2007 A wine of considerable finesse, and with as many cool-region characters as warm region; nectarine fruit is brightened by fine citrussy acidity and framed by subtle French oak; excellent length. Screwcap. 13.5% alc. **Rating** 94 **To** 2012 $25

ᵺᵺᵺᵺᵺ **Claremont Chardonnay Methode Champenoise 2002** Good mousse; exceptionally fine and delicate for the Hunter Valley, particularly given five years on lees; a Peter Pan, with no hint of full maturity yet. Cork. 10.9% alc. **Rating** 92 **To** 2013 $50

Hunter Valley Verdelho 2008 A lively and star-bright wine with as much citrus as fruit salad in its expressive makeup; definitely an all-purpose white. Screwcap. 12.8% alc. **Rating** 90 **To** 2011 $25

ᵺᵺᵺᵺ **Long Lunch White 2008** Bright, light yellow-green; a very crisp wine with lemon zest/sherbet flavours underlined by pronounced acidity. Seafood and summer style. Screwcap. 12.8% alc. **Rating** 89 **To** 2012 $20

Long Lunch Red 2007 A supple medium-bodied red for a long and good lunch; the blend of Shiraz/Malbec provides a deliciously fruity wine, ready now or over the next few years. Screwcap. 13.6% alc. **Rating** 89 **To** 2012 $25

Liqueur Hunter Valley Verdelho NV Fresh and lively; elegant packaging directed at cellar door trade. Cork. 19% alc. **Rating** 87 **To** 2010 $25

Warrego Wines ★★★

9 Seminary Road, Marburg, Qld 4306 **Region** Queensland Coastal
T (07) 5464 4400 **F** (07) 5464 4800 **www**.warregowines.com.au **Open** 7 days 10–5
Winemaker Kevin Watson **Est.** 2000 **Cases** 2500 **Vyds** 0.2 ha

Kevin Watson completed his wine science degree at CSU, and the primary purpose of his business is custom winemaking for the many small growers in the region, including all the clients of Peter Scudamore-Smith MW. In 2001, the Marburg Custom Crush company developed a state-of-the-art winery (as the cliché goes), cellar door and restaurant. $500 000 in government funding, local business investment and significant investment from China provided the funds, and the complex opened in 2002. Since then, the business has expanded further with a public share raising. The 2500-case own-brand Warrego wines come from grapes purchased in various regions, and a tiny amount of estate-grown viognier (0.2 ha). Ten cents from each bottle sold goes to the Australian Koala Foundation. Warrego is Qld's only certified organic winery. Exports to Canada.

ᵺᵺᵺᵺ **Coalface Chardonnay 2008** Bright straw-green; clean and crisp, with a streak of citrus running through the stone fruit and melon fruit; no oak evident. Screwcap. 13% alc. **Rating** 87 **To** 2012 $18.50

Fiona's Folly No Preservative Added Chardonnay Viognier 2008 Clever winemaking technology used to produce this appealingly fruity, low-alcohol wine, which is only slightly sweet. Screwcap. 8.5% alc. **Rating** 87 **To** 2009 $15.50

Brigalow Shiraz 2007 Firm red and black fruits are a little one-dimensional, but the palate does have length, sustained by light, savoury tannins. Screwcap. 14% alc. **Rating** 87 **To** 2013 $16.50

Rum Distillery Tawny Port NV Extremely dense and luscious, with some dark chocolate fruit; surprisingly good. Cork. 17.5% alc. **Rating** 87 **To** 2010 $25

Warrenmang Vineyard & Resort ★★★★☆

Mountain Creek Road, Moonambel, Vic 3478 **Region** Pyrenees
T (03) 5467 2233 **F** (03) 5467 2309 **www**.warrenmang.com.au **Open** 7 days 10–5
Winemaker Sean Schwager **Est.** 1974 **Cases** 14 000 **Vyds** 32.1 ha

Luigi and Athelie Bazzani continue to watch over Warrenmang; a new, partially underground, barrel room with earthen walls has been completed, and production has increased over the past two years. International distribution was put in place in 2007, and Warrenmang now exports to over a dozen countries. However, after 30 years at the helm, the Bazzanis do have the combined winery and holiday complex on the market.

♀♀♀♀♀ Torchio Aged Pressings NV A blend of pressings of Shiraz (62%)/Cabernet Sauvignon (33%)/Dolcetto (5%) assembled from barrels of 2006 vintage with some 'reserve' barrels of the best vintages over the past 10 years. It is neither fearsomely tannic or alcoholic, rather a medium- to full-bodied wine with licorice, blackberry and blackcurrant fruit flavours. Cork. 14% alc. **Rating** 94 **To** 2019 $60

♀♀♀♀♀ Black Puma Shiraz 2006 A dark and savoury bouquet with bay leaf, blackberry essence and plenty of hot tar; the palate is loaded with sweet fruit, gravelly tannins and ample toasty oak, handled with ease by the level of fruit. Cork. 15% alc. **Rating** 92 **To** 2018 $80

♀♀♀♀ Pyrenees Sauvignon Blanc 2008 Tropical fruit with a touch of straw; the palate has good texture and weight, with vibrant acidity on the tropical fruit finish. Screwcap. 12.8% alc. **Rating** 89 **To** 2012 $20
Estate Pyrenees Chardonnay 2008 Deep colour; a restrained, yet ripe, bouquet of peach and straw; thickly textured with grilled nuts and toasty fruit on the soft finish. Screwcap. 12% alc. **Rating** 89 **To** 2012 $20
Estate Pyrenees Shiraz 2006 Full-bodied and very ripe, the alcohol evident on both bouquet and palate, seemingly warping the flavours on the finish. Some great material here for the taking. Cork. 16% alc. **Rating** 89 **To** 2016 $60
Grand Pyrenees 2006 Showing a little toasty development; blackcurrant confit with a fairly healthy dose of new oak; the palate is soft, fleshy and full, but a little clipped on the finish. Cabernet Franc/Cabernet Sauvignon/Merlot/Shiraz. Screwcap. 14.5% alc. **Rating** 88 **To** 2013 $35

Water Wheel ★★★

Bridgewater-on-Loddon, Bridgewater, Vic 3516 **Region** Bendigo
T (03) 5437 3060 **F** (03) 5437 3082 **www.**waterwheelwine.com **Open** Mon–Fri 9–5, w'ends & public hols 12–4
Winemaker Peter Cumming, Bill Trevaskis **Est.** 1972 **Cases** 45 000 **Vyds** 134 ha
Peter Cumming, with more than two decades of winemaking under his belt, has quietly built on the reputation of Water Wheel year by year. The winery is owned by the Cumming family, which has farmed in the Bendigo region for 50+ years, with horticulture and viticulture special areas of interest. The wines are of remarkably consistent quality and modest prices. Exports to the UK, the US and other major markets.

♀♀♀♀ Bendigo Shiraz 2007 An ever-dependable wine, although caught in the rising tide of alcohol levels; has black fruits with a slightly savoury edge. Screwcap. 15.5% alc. **Rating** 88 **To** 2015 $19
Memsie Bendigo Shiraz Cabernet Sauvignon Malbec Petit Verdot 2007 Quite bright colour and fruit; there is a little spice and generous sweet fruit on the mid-palate; an even finish. Screwcap. 14.5% alc. **Rating** 88 **To** 2014 $13
Bendigo Sauvignon Blanc 2008 Quite ripe, with candied fruit aromas and flavour; a touch of guava on the palate, with reasonable length; a little smoky on the finish. Screwcap. 13.5% alc. **Rating** 87 **To** 2011 $15
Bendigo Chardonnay 2008 No frills style; peachy fruit, a touch of vanilla (American) oak, and balanced acidity adding length. Screwcap. 14% alc. **Rating** 87 **To** 2011 $19

Watershed Wines ★★★★★

Cnr Bussell Highway/Darch Road, Margaret River, WA 6285 **Region** Margaret River
T (08) 9758 8633 **F** (08) 9757 3999 **www.**watershedwines.com.au **Open** 7 days 10–5
Winemaker Severine Logan **Est.** 2002 **Cases** 90 000 **Vyds** 187 ha

Watershed Wines has been established by a syndicate of investors, and no expense has been spared in establishing the substantial vineyard and building a striking cellar door, and a 200-seat café and restaurant. Situated towards the southern end of the Margaret River region, its neighbours include Voyager Estate and Leeuwin Estate. Exports to the UK, the US and other major markets.

ΨΨΨΨΨ Awakening Margaret River Cabernet Sauvignon 2007 Dense crimson-purple; super-luscious and rich blackcurrant fruit perfectly balanced by fine, persistent tannins and quality oak. Must have gone perilously close to winning the Jimmy Watson Trophy '09. Screwcap. 13.5% alc. **Rating** 96 **To** 2027 $54.95
Awakening Single Block A1 Margaret River Chardonnay 2008 Green-gold; has the intensity, energy and drive of the unoaked version, but with several more layers of character from barrel ferment via wild yeasts; has the discipline to develop over a decade. Screwcap. 13.5% alc. **Rating** 95 **To** 2018 $39.95
Senses Margaret River Sauvignon Blanc 2008 The complex bouquet reflects 50% barrel fermentation and lees-stirring for four months; the palate throws the emphasis onto the crisp and lively citrus, grass and passionfruit flavours, which underpin the wine and drive the long finish. Gold medal Sydney Wine Show '09. Screwcap. 12.5% alc. **Rating** 94 **To** 2012 $24
Senses Margaret River Cabernet Merlot 2007 Bright crimson-purple; a very rich, multilayered palate charged with blackcurrant, licorice and cassis fruit flavours supported by firm tannins and quality French oak. Screwcap. 13.5% alc. **Rating** 94 **To** 2020 $24.95

ΨΨΨΨ♀ Awakening Margaret River Chardonnay 2007 Bright, tangy/citrussy grapefruit overtones to stone fruit; fruit-forward; minimal oak; good length. Screwcap. 14% alc. **Rating** 93 **To** 2012 $39.95
Senses Margaret River Shiraz 2007 Strong crimson; a powerful, medium- to full-bodied palate, which is driven by its spicy black fruits more than tannins or oak; has good balance and length. Screwcap. 14% alc. **Rating** 92 **To** 2020 $24.95
Senses Margaret River Shiraz 2005 Good hue; vibrant, fresh, spicy red fruits; a faint touch of mocha oak sweetening. Screwcap. 14% alc. **Rating** 92 **To** 2015 $24.95
Shades Cabernet Franc 2007 Very good colour, once again WA achieves more with this variety than others; red fruits and cedar; good length. Screwcap. 13.5% alc. **Rating** 92 **To** 2013 $16.95

ΨΨΨΨ Shades Margaret River Merlot 2007 Light crimson; appealing red fruits on the bouquet, the palate enriched with fine tannins running through its length; good example of merlot. Screwcap. 14% alc. **Rating** 89 **To** 2012 $17.95
Shades Margaret River Sauvignon Blanc Semillon 2008 Easy style, with gooseberry and passionfruit leading the way, and a touch of herb from the semillon. Screwcap. 12% alc. **Rating** 89 **To** 2010 $17.95
Shades Margaret River Rose 2008 Fragrant red berry aromas, then a palate with just a touch of sweetness to the strawberry fruit; clever winemaking. Screwcap. 14% alc. **Rating** 89 **To** 2010 $17.95
Shades Margaret River Shiraz Merlot Cabernet 2007 Light, bright red colour; a fresh and lively palate of predominantly red fruits, made in an early-drinking style. Screwcap. 13.5% alc. **Rating** 88 **To** 2010 $16.95

Waterton Vineyards   ★★★☆

PO Box 125, Beaconsfield, Tas 7270 **Region** Northern Tasmania
T (03) 6394 7214 **F** (03) 6394 7614 **www**.watertonhall.com.au **Open** Not
Winemaker Winemaking Tasmania (Julian Alcorso) **Est.** 2006 **Cases** 300 **Vyds** 2 ha
Jennifer Baird and Peter Cameron purchased this remarkable property in 2002. Waterton Hall was built in the 1850s and modified extensively by well-known neo-gothic architect Alexander North in 1910. The property was owned by the Catholic church from 1949–96, variously used as a school, a boys home and retreat. Following its sale the new owners

planted 1 ha of riesling at the end of the 1990s, and then Jennifer and Peter extended the vineyard with 1 ha of shiraz, electing to sell the riesling until 2006, when part was made under the Waterton label. The plans are to use the existing buildings to provide a restaurant, accommodation and function facilities.

ŸŸŸŸŸ **Dessert Riesling 2007** A vibrant Mosel spatlese style; has thrust and energy, and excellent sugar/acid balance. Screwcap. 9.9% alc. **Rating** 91 **To** 2013 $32

ŸŸŸŸ **Shiraz 2007** Very good colour; firm, medium-bodied dark fruits; should evolve well over the next few years. Screwcap. 14% alc. **Rating** 89 **To** 2014 $34.50
Riesling 2008 Citrus, apple, lime on bouquet and palate; some thrust built around acidity; sure to develop well. Screwcap. 11.6% alc. **Rating** 88 **To** 2017 $23.50

Watson Wine Group

PO Box 6243, Halifax Street, Adelaide, SA 5000 **Region** Coonawarra
T (08) 8338 3200 **F** (08) 8338 3244 **www**.rexwatsonwines.com **Open** Not
Winemaker Michelle Heagney **Est.** 1997 **Cases** 80 000 **Vyds** 349.7 ha
Rex Watson started in the Australian wine industry in 1991 and began growing wine grapes in Coonawarra in '97. In 1999 he began planting the most significant modern vineyard development in Coonawarra. In less than five years this was built into a venture that now controls and manages almost 350 ha over three vineyards, all close to the historic township of Coonawarra and well within the Coonawarra GI. Exports to the US, Canada, Sweden, Russia, Singapore, Malaysia, India, Sri Lanka, Taiwan, China and NZ.

ŸŸŸŸŸ **Coonawarra Premium Vineyards Reserve Cabernet Sauvignon 2007** Cassis and mint bouquet; good flavour, with a generous core of sweet fruit. Screwcap. 15.5% alc. **Rating** 90 **To** 2014 $28.95

ŸŸŸŸ **Coonawarra Premium Vineyards Cabernet Sauvignon 2006** A dark berry bouquet with spiced plum; the palate is generous and medium-bodied, with red fruits drawing out on the finish. Screwcap. 13.5% alc. **Rating** 89 **To** 2013 $19.95
Rex Watson Coonawarra Cabernet Sauvignon 2007 Clean redcurrant and mint bouquet; fine and juicy, straight forward fruit palate. Screwcap. 14.7% alc. **Rating** 87 **To** 2012 $16.95

Wattle Ridge Vineyard

Loc 11950 Boyup-Greenbushes Road, Greenbushes, WA 6254 **Region** Blackwood Valley
T (08) 9764 3594 **www**.wattleridgewines.com.au **Open** Thurs–Mon 11–5
Winemaker Contract **Est.** 1997 **Cases** 1500 **Vyds** 6.25 ha
James and Vicky Henderson's Nelson Vineyard is planted to verdelho, merlot and cabernet sauvignon. The wines are sold by mail order and through the cellar door, which also offers light meals, crafts and local produce. Exports to the UK, Singapore and Japan.

ŸŸŸŸ **Two Tinsmiths Spring Gully Cabernet Sauvignon 2007** Blackcurrant and blackberry fruit aromas on the fore-palate, then a break in the line before tannins and vanillin oak appear on the finish. Screwcap. 14.3% alc. **Rating** 87 **To** 2014 $16

Waurn Ponds Estate

Nicol Drive North, Waurn Ponds, Vic 3217 **Region** Geelong
T (03) 5227 2143 **www**.waurnpondsestate.com.au **Open** Mon–Fri 10–4
Winemaker Duncan MacGillivray **Est.** 2001 **Cases** 4500
A somewhat unusual venture, owned by Deakin University, but managed by winemaker Duncan MacGillivray. Two ha each of chardonnay, pinot noir, cabernet sauvignon and shiraz, and 1 ha each of viognier, riesling, sauvignon blanc, merlot and petit verdot were planted in 2002. Grapes from the early vintages were sold to other Geelong wineries, notably Scotchmans Hill, but from 2005, encouraged by the quality of the grapes, increasing quantities have been retained for wines under the Waurn Ponds Estate label.

🍷🍷🍷🍷🍷 **Reserve Chardonnay 2007** Bright straw-green; an elegant and stylish wine, with stone fruit, cashew and oak inputs well balanced; lacks the intensity for top points, but nonetheless well made. Cork. 13% alc. **Rating** 91 **To** 2013 $30

🍷🍷🍷🍷 **Classic Dry White 2007** A shotgun blend of convenience, perhaps, but does add life and freshness to the quite considerable fruit assemblage. Excellent value. Chardonnay/Sauvignon Blanc/Riesling. Cork. 12.5% alc. **Rating** 89 **To** 2010 $11

Wayawu Estate

1070 Bellarine Highway, Wallington, Vic 3221 **Region** Geelong
T (03) 5250 4457 **www**.wayawawinerybb.com.au **Open** Tues–Sun 10–5
Winemaker John Henry, Stephanie Henry **Est.** 2004 **Cases** 100 **Vyds** 0.5 ha
In 2004 John and Stephanie Henry planted 0.5 ha of shiraz, with four different clones and the results so far have been impressive. The name comes from northeast Arnhem Land, and means 'where the land touches the Milky Way'. The Henrys have been given permission by Arnhem Land artist, Nami Maymuru-White, to reproduce one of her paintings of the Milky Way on their label.

🍷🍷🍷🍷🍷 **Harry's Reserve Shiraz 2007** A powerful wine that in part belies its cool-region origins; savoury black fruits, licorice and spice are the building blocks for the medium-bodied palate; finishes with firm tannins. Diam. 14% alc. **Rating** 91 **To** 2020 $25

Wedgetail Estate ★★★★★

40 Hildebrand Road, Cottles Bridge, Vic 3099 **Region** Yarra Valley
T (03) 9714 8661 **F** (03) 9714 8676 **www**.wedgetailestate.com.au **Open** W'ends & public hols 12–5, or by appt (closed from 25 Dec, reopens Australia Day w'end)
Winemaker Guy Lamothe **Est.** 1994 **Cases** 1500 **Vyds** 5.5 ha
Canadian-born photographer Guy Lamothe and partner Dena Ashbolt started making wine in the basement of their Carlton home in the 1980s. The idea of their own vineyard started to take hold, and the search for a property began. Then, in their words, 'one Sunday, when we were "just out for a drive", we drove past our current home. The slopes are amazing, true goat terrain, and it is on these steep slopes that in 1994 we planted our first block of pinot noir.' While the vines were growing Lamothe enrolled in the winegrowing course at CSU, having already gained practical experience working in the Yarra Valley (Tarrawarra), the Mornington Peninsula and Meursault (Burgundy). The net result has been truly exceptional wine, but none was made in 2007 after the devastating frosts of October '06, and the vineyard is still recovering; hence no samples for this edition. Exports to the UK, Canada, Singapore, Hong Kong and China.

Wehl's Mount Benson Vineyards ★★★★

Wrights Bay Road, Mount Benson, SA 5275 **Region** Mount Benson
T (08) 8768 6251 **F** (08) 8678 6251 **www**.wehlsmtbensonvineyards.com.au
Open 7 days 10–4
Winemaker Contract **Est.** 1989 **Cases** 2500 **Vyds** 20 ha
Peter and Leah Wehl were the first to plant vines in the Mount Benson area, beginning the establishment of their vineyard, planted to cabernet sauvignon, shiraz, sauvignon blanc and merlot, in 1989. While primarily grapegrowers, they have moved into winemaking via contract makers, and have increased the range of wines available.

🍷🍷🍷🍷🍷 **Cabernet Sauvignon Merlot 2006** Good colour; a medium- to full-bodied and intense wine; inward looking at its splendid blackcurrant and mulberry fruit, yet the palate is so perfectly balanced it is certain to bloom within a few years, and then live on for another decade. Screwcap. 14% alc. **Rating** 94 **To** 2021 $18.50

🍷🍷🍷🍷 **Sauvignon Blanc 2008** A clean, gently fruity bouquet is brought to life by the punchy capsicum, gooseberry and citrus palate, bolstered by good acidity. Early picking the correct decision. Screwcap. 12.5% alc. **Rating** 89 **To** 2010 $16.50

Cabernet Sauvignon 2006 Appealing earthy/spicy aromas are followed by a rude shock, as the intense palate has distinct raw edges to the tannins; fining could have worked wonders. Screwcap. 14% alc. **Rating** 89 **To** 2016 $19.50

Wendouree

Wendouree Road, Clare, SA 5453 **Region** Clare Valley
T (08) 8842 2896 **Open** By appt
Winemaker Tony Brady **Est.** 1895 **Cases** 2000 **Vyds** 9.52 ha
An iron fist in a velvet glove best describes these extraordinary wines. They are fashioned with passion and precision from the very old vineyard (shiraz, cabernet sauvignon, malbec, mataro and muscat of alexandria) with its unique terroir by Tony and Lita Brady, who rightly see themselves as custodians of a priceless treasure. The 100-year-old stone winery is virtually unchanged from the day it was built; this is in every sense a treasure beyond price. I should explain, I buy three wines from Wendouree every year, always including the Shiraz. This is the only way I am able to provide tasting notes, and it's almost inevitably a last-minute exercise as I suddenly realise there are no notes in place. Moreover, Wendouree has never made any comment about its wines, and I realise that the change in style away from full-bodied to medium-bodied seems a permanent fixture of the landscape, not a one-off result of a given vintage. The best news of all is that I may actually get to drink some of the Wendourees I have bought over the past 10 years before I die, and not have to rely on my few remaining bottles from the 1970s (and rather more from the '80s and '90s). The Lord moves in mysterious ways.

▼▼▼▼▼ Shiraz 2006 Purple-crimson; much better clarity than the Malbec; strong black berry and licorice aromas lead directly into a firm, though medium-bodied, palate; has the energy, thrust and length missing from the Malbec, yet is exceptionally elegant, reflecting its low alcohol. Is one of those rare wines that get better sip by sip (or mouthful). Postscript: I wrote those words before referring back to the identical comment made about the '05. Cork. 13% alc. **Rating** 97 **To** 2026

▼▼▼▼▽ Malbec 2006 Opaque purple-crimson, very slightly hazy; strong plum jam varietal expression on the bouquet; an unexpectedly fresh medium-bodied palate; very fine tannins. Stained corks in both '06 Wendouree wines a worry. 13.5% alc. **Rating** 93 **To** 2018

Wenzel Family Wines

'Glenrowan', Step Road, Langhorne Creek, SA 5255 **Region** Langhorne Creek
T (08) 8537 3035 **F** (08) 8537 3435 **www.**langhornewine.com.au **Open** By appt
Winemaker Greg Follett (Contract) **Est.** 2000 **Cases** 460 **Vyds** 53 ha
The Wenzel family left the Hartz Mountains in Germany in 1846 for Australia, and settled in Langhorne Creek in 1853. Six generations later Dale and Lisa Wenzel run two vineyards, with chardonnay, merlot, shiraz, cabernet sauvignon and petit verdot. Most of the grapes are sold to other makers; 'The Old Man's' label is a respectful tribute to Oscar (and Hazel) Wenzel who planted the first vines in 1968.

▼▼▼▼▽ The Old Man's Langhorne Creek Cabernet Sauvignon 2004 Good colour for age; attractive mouthfeel and flavour to the supple blackcurrant fruits, complexed by spicy touches and a little oak, finishing with soft tannins. Cork. 13.8% alc. **Rating** 90 **To** 2014 $20

Were Estate

Cnr Wildberry Road/Johnson Road, Wilyabrup, WA 6280 **Region** Margaret River
T (08) 9755 6273 **F** (08) 9755 6195 **www.**wereestate.com.au **Open** 7 days 10.30–5
Winemaker Clive Otto (Contract) **Est.** 1998 **Cases** 4300 **Vyds** 9.72 ha
Owners Diane and Gordon Davies say, 'We are different. We're original, we're bold, we're innovative.' This is all reflected in the design of the unusual back labels, incorporating pictures of the innumerable pairs of braces that real estate agent Gordon Davies wears at work in

Perth; in the early move to screwcaps for both white and red wines; and, for that matter, in the underground trickle irrigation system (plus a move towards to organic methods) in their Margaret River vineyard which can be controlled from Perth. Exports to Hong Kong, China and Singapore.

⟡⟡⟡⟡⟡ **Margaret River Sauvignon Blanc 2008** Lifted herbal/grassy aromas; similar flavours with touches of gooseberry and passionfruit; has very good thrust and length. Gold WA Wine Show '08. Screwcap. 12.8% alc. **Rating** 94 **To** 2011 $22
Single Vineyard Estate Margaret River Chardonnay 2007 Sophisticated winemaking has balanced the nectarine and melon fruit with enough French oak to provide complexity and balance, but still allowing the fruit to drive the wine. Screwcap. 14% alc. **Rating** 94 **To** 2014 $30

⟡⟡⟡⟡⟡ **Margaret River Semillon Sauvignon Blanc 2008** Some bottling SO_2 evident early in its life, but should quickly disappear; well balanced and integrated varietal fruit inputs to the zesty and quite long palate. Screwcap. 13.2% alc. **Rating** 90 **To** 2012 $19

West Cape Howe Wines ★★★★★

678 South Coast Highway, Denmark, WA 6333 **Region** Denmark
T (08) 9848 2959 **www**.westcapehowewines.com.au **Open** 7 days 10–5
Winemaker Gavin Berry, Dave Cleary, Imogen Casey **Est.** 1997 **Cases** 55 000 **Vyds** 317 ha
After a highly successful seven years, West Cape Howe founders Brenden and Kylie Smith moved on, selling the business to a partnership including Gavin Berry (until 2004, senior winemaker at Plantagenet) and viticulturist Rob Quenby. As well as existing fruit sources, West Cape Howe now has the 80-ha Lansdale Vineyard, planted in 1989, as its primary fruit source. In March '09 it purchased the 7700-tonne capacity Goundrey winery and 237-ha Goundrey estate vineyards from CWA; the grapes from these plantings will be purchased by CWA for years to come. The move vastly increases West Cape Howe's business base, and facilitates contract-winemaking to generate cash flow. Exports to the UK, the US and other major markets.

⟡⟡⟡⟡⟡ **Styx Gully Great Southern Chardonnay 2007** Grapefruit dominates the bouquet, with the delicate presence of oak and a hint of toast providing complexity; the palate is fresh and lively, with good acidity and true depth to the fruit on the finish; long and harmonious and the flavour builds for a surprisingly long time. Screwcap. 13% alc. **Rating** 95 **To** 2015 $24
Styx Gully Great Southern Chardonnay 2008 Bright green-gold; citrus, melon and nectarine chase each other across the vibrant palate, oak defining the perimeter of the playing field. Great value. Screwcap. 12.5% alc. **Rating** 94 **To** 2015 $24
Great Southern Sauvignon Blanc 2008 Fresh citrus and passionfruit aromas lead into a very lively, long and intense palate with a mix of citrus, herb and gooseberry flavours. Screwcap. 12% alc. **Rating** 94 **To** 2011 $19.95

⟡⟡⟡⟡⟡ **Two Steps Great Southern Shiraz Viognier 2007** Crimson-red; an aromatic red fruit bouquet leads into a spicy, tangy and vibrant medium-bodied palate, with fine-grained tannins on the finish. Screwcap. 14% alc. **Rating** 93 **To** 2017 $24
Cabernet Merlot 2007 Powerful medium- to full-bodied wine with an abundance of blackcurrant and cassis fruit backed by ripe tannins. Long life ahead. Value. Screwcap. 13.5% alc. **Rating** 92 **To** 2022 $16
Semillon Sauvignon Blanc 2008 Clean fresh aromas of lemongrass and tropical fruits lead into a palate with good intensity and an emphatic finish. Screwcap. 12% alc. **Rating** 91 **To** 2012 $16
Viognier 2008 A fragrant bouquet of apricot and orange blossom; pleasing mouthfeel from a generous mid-palate followed by cleansing acidity on the finish. Better than many. Screwcap. 13% alc. **Rating** 90 **To** 2011 $20

♟♟♟♟ **Great Southern Riesling 2008** Strongly structured wine, with a spine of mineral to the apple, lemon and lime fruit; will develop very well. Screwcap. 11.5% alc. **Rating** 89 **To** 2018 $19.95

Unwooded Chardonnay 2008 The cool-climate background invests the wine with abundant peach and nectarine fruit flavour; balanced finish. Screwcap. 13% alc. **Rating** 89 **To** 2012 $16

Shiraz 2007 Enticing aromas of spicy black fruits and toasty French oak lead into a medium-bodied palate, with highly focused red and black cherry fruit; superfine tannins on the long finish. Screwcap. 14% alc. **Rating** 89 **To** 2015 $16

Westend Estate Wines   ★★★★

1283 Brayne Road, Griffith, NSW 2680 **Region** Riverina
T (02) 6969 0800 **www**.westendestate.com **Open** Mon–Fri 8.30–5, w'ends 10–4
Winemaker William Calabria, Bryan Currie **Est.** 1945 **Cases** 300 000 **Vyds** 52 ha
Along with a number of Riverina producers, Westend Estate has made a successful move to lift both the quality and the packaging of its wines. Its leading 3 Bridges range, which has an impressive array of gold medals to its credit since being first released in 1997, is anchored in part on estate vineyards. Bill Calabria has been involved in the Australian wine industry for more than 40 years, and is understandably proud of the achievements both of Westend and the Riverina wine industry as a whole. It is moving with the times, increasing its plantings of durif, and introducing aglianico, nero d'Avola, and st macaire (a problematic variety not recognised by the ultimate authority of such matters, Jancis Robinson, who says it is a small town in the Bordeaux region). These new plantings have paralleled an increase in Westend wine production. Equally importantly, it is casting its net over Hilltops and the Canberra District, premium regions not too far from home. Exports to Canada, Denmark, Belgium, Sweden, The Netherlands, Germany, Peru, India, Malaysia, Hong Kong and China.

♟♟♟♟♟ Cool Climate Series Canberra District Riesling 2008 Bright straw-green; citrus and mineral aromas lead into a palate that gains considerable intensity on the way through to the finish and aftertaste. Good value. Screwcap. 12.5% alc. Rating 91 To 2016 $14.95

Cool Climate Series Hilltops Shiraz 2008 Deep purple hue; well-made, medium-bodied wine that has good typicity for Hilltops; the ripe blackberry fruit has an embroidery of spice; good balance and length. Screwcap. 14.5% alc. Rating 91 To 2018 $14.95

3 Bridges Winemakers Selection Chardonnay 2006 Quality wine; complex, nutty/melon/fig/white peach aromas and flavours are offset by citrussy acidity on the finish. Screwcap. 14.5% alc. **Rating** 91 **To** 2010 $21.99

3 Bridges Golden Mist Botrytis 2006 Bright yellow-gold, as it should be rising three years since vintage; luscious peach/butterscotch flavours supported by good acidity. A tried and true style. Screwcap. 10.5% alc. **Rating** 91 **To** 2012 $21.95

Richland Cabernet Sauvignon 2007 Bright and vibrant red berry fruit bouquet, intermingled with just a little char; really juicy on the palate; harmonious and full of character on the finish. Screwcap. 14% alc. **Rating** 90 **To** 2014 $10.99

♟♟♟♟ Cool Climate Series Canberra District King Valley Semillon Sauvignon Blanc 2008 A successful marriage by any measure, the grassy, citrus and tropical components all evident yet seamlessly woven together. Value. Screwcap. 13% alc. Rating 89 To 2011 $14.95

Richland Shiraz 2007 Has well above average fruit weight and expression for its price point; supple mouthfeel for the medium-bodied palate ranging through blackberry and plum. Screwcap. 14.5% alc. **Rating** 89 **To** 2012 $10.99

3 Bridges Winemakers Selection Cabernet Sauvignon 2006 Given its Riverina origin, this is an impressive wine, with clear varietal flavours in a black fruit range, sweetness offset by more savoury notes on the finish. Cork. 14.5% alc. **Rating** 89 **To** 2012 $21.99

3 Bridges Golden Mist Botrytis 2007 Heavily botrytised with apricot jam and a touch of caramel on the bouquet; very sweet, but good flavour and depth to the palate. Screwcap. 12.5% alc. **Rating** 88 **To** 2012 $22.95

Outback Cabernet Merlot 2007 Has an abundance of blackcurrant and mulberry fruit, the palate well-balanced, oak nowhere to be seen. Value plus. Screwcap. 14% alc. **Rating** 87 **To** 2012 $8.95

Richland Pinot Grigio 2008 Clean and vibrant apple and pear fruit, with a little sweetness to add a little richness to the palate. Screwcap. 12% alc. **Rating** 87 **To** 2010 $10.99

Cool Climate Series Hilltops Tempranillo 2008 Youthful purple; has flavour and varietal character, but seems to have been rushed to bottle too soon. Screwcap. 14.5% alc. **Rating** 87 **To** 2011 $14.95

Western Range Wines

1995 Chittering Road, Lower Chittering, WA 6084 **Region** Perth Hills
T (08) 9571 8800 **www**.westernrangewines.com.au **Open** Wed–Sun 10–5
Winemaker Ryan Sudano **Est.** 2001 **Cases** 25 000 **Vyds** 125 ha
Between the mid-1990s and 2001, several prominent West Australians, including Marilyn Corderory, Malcolm McCusker, and Terry and Kevin Prindiville, established 125 ha of vines (under separate ownerships) in the Perth Hills, planted with a kaleidoscopic range of varieties. The next step was to join forces to build a substantial winery. This is a separate venture, but takes the grapes from the individual vineyards and markets the wine under the Western Range brand. The wines are made and sold at four levels: Lot 88, Goyamin Pool, Julimar and Julimar Organic. The label designs are clear and attractive. Exports to Canada, France, Switzerland, Poland, Russia, China and Japan.

🍷🍷🍷🍷🍷 Julimar Perth Hills Shiraz Viognier 2007 Focused red fruit bouquet with a touch of mineral complexity; fine and lively with precise fruit, a splash of oak, and plentiful fine-grained tannins; long finish. Screwcap. 14.5% alc. Rating 94 To 2015 $28.95

🍷🍷🍷🍷🍷 Limited Release Perth Hills Chardonnay 2008 Spiced peach and grapefruit on the bouquet; a toasty and rich palate, with a creamy texture, and fine lemon fruit on the long finish. Screwcap. 14% alc. Rating 92 To 2014 $38.50

🍷🍷🍷🍷 Limited Release Perth Hills Shiraz 2007 A bit of reduction on opening; a slightly meaty character with a splash of red fruit providing light; the palate is very tannic, and the fruit struggles a little to overcome the extraction, but the flavours are varietal and generous on the finish. Screwcap. 14.5% alc. Rating 89 To 2018 $38.50

Lot 88 Shiraz Grenache 2005 Has a distinctly earthy overcoat for the body of red fruits; strong grenache influence; 70/30. Screwcap. 14% alc. **Rating** 89 **To** 2013 $14.95

Westgate Vineyard

180 Westgate Road, Armstrong, Vic 3377 **Region** Grampians
T (03) 5356 2394 **www**.westgatevineyard.com.au **Open** At Garden Gully
Winemaker Bruce Dalkin **Est.** 1997 **Cases** 500 **Vyds** 14 ha
Westgate has been in the Dalkin family ownership since the 1860s, the present owners Bruce and Robyn being the sixth-generation owners of the property, which today focuses on grape production, a small winery and 4-star accommodation. The vineyards have been progressively established since 1969, including a key holding of 12 ha of shiraz (plus 2 ha of riesling). Most of the grapes are sold to Mount Langi Ghiran and others, but a small amount of high-quality wine is made under the Westgate Vineyard label.

🍷🍷🍷🍷 Shiraz 2006 Purple colour; an inky bouquet, with a distinct iodine character framing the complex blackberry fruit; quite rich on the palate, with toasty oak evident on the finish. Screwcap. 13.5% alc. Rating 93 To 2014 $30

Westlake Vineyards ★★★★★

Diagonal Road, Koounga, SA 5355 **Region** Barossa Valley
T (08) 8565 6249 **F** (08) 8565 6208 **www**.westlakevineyards.com.au **Open** By appt
Winemaker Darren Westlake **Est.** 1999 **Cases** 300 **Vyds** 31 ha

Darren and Suzanne Westlake tend 19 ha of shiraz, 6.5 ha of cabernet sauvignon, 2 ha of viognier, and smaller plantings of petit verdot, durif, mataro and grenache planted on two properties in the Koonunga area of the Barossa Valley. The soil is red-brown earth over tight, heavy red clay with scatterings of ironstone and quartz, and the vines yield between 2.5 and 7.5 tonnes per ha, dropping to a miserable 1 tonne per ha in 2007. They, and they alone (other than with some help in the pruning season), work in the vineyards, and have a long list of high-profile winemakers queued up to buy the grapes, leaving only a small amount for production under the Westlake label. Suzanne is a sixth-generation descendant of Johann George who came to SA from Prussia in 1838, while the 717 Convicts label draws on the history of Darren's ancestor Edward Westlake, who was transported to Australia in 1788.

🍷🍷🍷🍷🍷 **Eleazar Barossa Valley Shiraz 2006** Deeper, more purple colour than Albert's Block; a more savoury, denser wine, with blackberry and licorice, and tannins to match; carries its heavy alcohol load without flinching. High-quality cork. 15.5% alc. **Rating** 95 **To** 2026 **$55**

Albert's Block Barossa Valley Shiraz 2006 An immaculately balanced wine, with a flood of seductive black fruits, dark chocolate, ripe tannins and oak all effortlessly combining on the palate. High-quality cork. 15% alc. **Rating** 94 **To** 2021 **$28**

🍷🍷🍷🍷 **717 Convicts The Warden Barossa Valley Shiraz 2005** The black and red fruit flavours have confit/stewed elements, the sweetness augmented by the oak; hardly needs to be said there is an abundance of overall flavours and the tannins are ripe. Cork. 15% alc. **Rating** 89 **To** 2015 **$50**

Whicher Ridge ★★★★

PO Box 328, Cowaramup, WA 6284 **Region** Geographe
T (08) 9753 1394 **F** (08) 9753 1394 **www**.whicherridge.com.au **Open** Not
Winemaker Cathy Howard **Est.** 2004 **Cases** 750 **Vyds** 5 ha

Whicher Ridge may be a recent arrival on the wine scene, but it is hard to imagine a husband and wife team with such an ideal blend of viticultural and winemaking experience accumulated over a collective 40-plus years. Cathy Howard (nee Spratt) has been a winemaker for 16 years at Orlando and St Hallett in the Barossa Valley, and at Watershed Wines in Margaret River. She now has her own winemaking consulting business covering the southwest region of WA, as well as making the Whicher Ridge wines. Neil Howard's career as a viticulturist spans more than 25 years, beginning in the Pyrenees region with Taltarni Vineyards and Blue Pyrenees Estate, before moving to Mount Avoca as vineyard manager for 12 years. When he moved to the west, he managed the Sandalford Wines vineyard in Margaret River for several years, then developed and managed a number of smaller vineyards through the region. He started the planning, development and planting of Whicher Ridge's Odyssey Creek Vineyard at Chapman Hill in 2004. Here the Howards have 2.5 ha of sauvignon blanc, 1.8 ha of cabernet sauvignon and 0.7 ha of viognier. They have chosen the Frankland River subregion of the Great Southern to supply shiraz and riesling, and also intend to buy grapes from Margaret River.

🍷🍷🍷🍷½ **Shiraz 2007** Excellent colour; very well balanced and composed, with black cherry and blackberry fruit supported by fine tannins and good oak. Screwcap. 14.1% alc. **Rating** 93 **To** 2017 **$28**

Whispering Brook ★★★½

Hill Street, Broke, NSW 2330 **Region** Lower Hunter Valley
T (02) 9818 4126 **www**.whispering-brook.com **Open** W'ends 11–5, Fri by appt
Winemaker Nick Patterson, Susan Frazier **Est.** 2000 **Cases** 1000 **Vyds** 3 ha

Susan Frazier and Adam Bell say the choice of Whispering Brook was the result of a five-year search to find the ideal viticultural site (while studying for wine science degrees at CSU). Some may wonder whether the Broke subregion of the Hunter Valley needed such persistent effort to locate, but the property does in fact have a combination of terra rossa loam soils on which the reds are planted, and sandy flats for the white grapes. The partners have also established an olive grove and accommodation for 6–14 guests in the large house set in the vineyard. Exports to the UK, Japan, Thailand and Cambodia.

Whispering Hills

580 Warburton Highway, Seville, Vic 3139 **Region** Yarra Valley
T (03) 5964 2822 **F** (03) 5964 2064 **www**.whisperinghills.com.au **Open** 7 days 10–6
Winemaker Murray Lyons **Est.** 1985 **Cases** 1500
Whispering Hills is owned and operated by the Lyons family (Murray, Marie and Audrey). Murray (with a degree in viticulture and oenology from CSU) concentrates on the vineyard and winemaking, Marie (with a background in sales and marketing) and Audrey take care of the cellar door and distribution of the wines. The 3.5-ha vineyard was established in 1985 (riesling, chardonnay and cabernet sauvignon), with further plantings in '96, and some grafting in '03. Exports to Japan.

ŢŢŢŢŢ **Darcy James Yarra Valley Cabernet Sauvignon 2006** Lifted red berry fruit, with a light seasoning of oak; medium-bodied and elegantly structured, with warm and ripe dark fruits on the finish. Screwcap. 13.5% alc. **Rating** 90 **To** 2014 $35

ŢŢŢŢ **Quartz Block Shiraz 2007** Colour a little dull; plum and fruitcake spice with a savoury dried herb edge to the fruit; soft and fleshy, the emphasis is more on the savoury than the fruit elements. Screwcap. 14% alc. **Rating** 88 **To** 2014 $26

Whisson Lake

Lot 2, Gully Road, Carey Gully, SA 5144 **Region** Adelaide Hills
T 0421 739 789 **F** (08) 8390 3822 **www**.whissonlake.com **Open** By appt
Winemaker Tom Munro **Est.** 1985 **Cases** 250 **Vyds** 5 ha
In 1985 Mark Whisson and Bruce Lake planted the vertigo-inducing, east-facing slope of Mt Carey to 5 ha of pinot noir. The Whisson Lake vineyard rises to over 600 m above sea level and is situated within the Piccadilly Valley appellation of the Adelaide Hills. The majority of the vineyard's small crop is sold to some of SA's most prestigious winemakers but a few tonnes are held back each year to create the flagship White Label and entry level Pinot Gaz. In 2003 Bill Bissett joined the Whisson Lake partnership, and in '08 Tom Munro was taken on to lead sales.

ŢŢŢŢŢ **Piccadilly Valley Pinot Noir 2007** Light, clear colour; while there is an overall savoury/foresty character typical of Whisson Lake there is a light-bodied, but clear, centre of small red fruits, and the wine has good length. Drink while the red fruit is still there. Cork. 13.5% alc. **Rating** 90 **To** 2011 $30

ŢŢŢŢ **Piccadilly Valley Pinot Noir 2005** Marked colour change towards brick; a complex wine with a long palate; the savoury characters persist and dominate, notwithstanding high baumé/alcohol. A conundrum. Cork. 14.5% alc. **Rating** 87 **To** 2011 $35
Pinot Gaz 2005 Shares many things with the standard Pinot, although the colour is fresher, the flavours likewise; a screwcap v cork battle, the screwcap winning hands down if this (Pinot Gaz) started as a lesser wine. 14.5% alc. **Rating** 87 **To** 2012 $15

Whistler Wines

Seppeltsfield Road, Marananga, SA 5355 **Region** Barossa Valley
T (08) 8562 4942 **F** (08) 8562 4943 **www**.whistlerwines.com **Open** 7 days 10.30–5
Winemaker Troy Kalleske, Christa Deans **Est.** 1999 **Cases** 7500 **Vyds** 14 ha

Brothers Martin and Chris Pfeiffer and their families have created one of the Barossa's hidden secrets: both the vines and the cellar door are tucked away from the view of those travelling along Seppeltsfield Road. Martin has 25 years' viticultural experience with Southcorp, and Chris brings marketing skills from many years as a publisher. The wines are estate-grown from 5.5 ha shiraz (planted in 1994), 2 ha merlot and 1.5 semillon ('97), and 4 ha of grenache, mourvedre and riesling (2001). Exports to Canada, Denmark, Taiwan and Hong Kong.

ΨΨΨΨΨ **Barossa Shiraz 2006** Bright colour; a lusciously rich array of blackberry, dark chocolate, licorice and spice; good tannins and oak management. Screwcap. 15% alc. **Rating** 93 **To** 2021 $28

The Reserve Barossa Shiraz 2006 Slightly more developed colour than the varietal, part higher pH and perhaps cork; very concentrated full-bodied palate, with masses of black fruit and savoury tannins achieved at the expense of a warming afterglow of alcohol; 166 cases made. ProCork. 15.5% alc. **Rating** 92 **To** 2026 $60

Barossa Cabernet Merlot 2005 Still fresh, with appealing cassis and raspberry fruit on a relatively light-bodied palate; no green or bitter edges. Screwcap. 14.5% alc. **Rating** 90 **To** 2014 $20

ΨΨΨΨ **Barossa Riesling 2008** A generous and rich mix of citrus and tropical/pineapple fruit is made for early consumption, although sustained by some mineral notes on the finish. Screwcap. 12.5% alc. **Rating** 89 **To** 2013 $20

Barossa Audrey May 2008 Glowing yellow-green; tighter, crisper and fresher than the Reserve Semillon, the 10% sauvignon blanc seemingly having a major impact. Semillon/Sauvignon Blanc. Screwcap. 12.5% alc. **Rating** 89 **To** 2011 $17

The Reserve Barossa Semillon 2008 Shows all the signs of some skin contact, with bright but deep yellow-green colour already evident, and a flavoursome, but soft, palate. Definitely a drink-me-quick proposition. Screwcap. 12.5% alc. **Rating** 87 **To** 2009 $20

Hubert Irving 2006 A licorice allsorts blend of Merlot/Grenache/Cabernet Sauvignon/Mataro/Shiraz, which works quite well, although inevitably falls in varietal no mans land. Screwcap. 14.5% alc. **Rating** 87 **To** 2014 $17

Barossa Cabernet Sauvignon 2006 An austere style, the tannins not entirely ripe; this apart, has good weight and length. Screwcap. 14% alc. **Rating** 87 **To** 2013 $25

White Rock Vineyard   ★★★★☆

1171 Railton Road, Kimberley, Tas 7304 (postal) **Region** Northern Tasmania
T (03) 6497 2156 **F** (03) 6497 2156 **Open** At Lake Barrington Estate
Winemaker Winemaking Tasmania (Julian Alcorso), Phil Dolan **Est.** 1992 **Cases** 150
Phil and Robin Dolan have established White Rock Vineyard in the northwest region of Tasmania, which, while having 13 wineries and vineyards, is one of the least known parts of the island. Kimberley is 25 km south of Devonport in the sheltered valley of the Mersey River. The Dolans have planted 2.4 ha of pinot noir, chardonnay, riesling and pinot gris, the lion's share going to the first two varieties. It has been a low-profile operation not only because of its location, but because most of the grapes are sold, with only Riesling, Pinot Noir and Chardonnay being made and sold through local restaurants and the cellar door at Lake Barrington Estate.

ΨΨΨΨΨ **Riesling 2008** Bright green-straw; relatively abundant tropical fruit; pushes through on a long palate; good balance. Screwcap. 12.5% alc. **Rating** 94 **To** 2015 $22

ΨΨΨΨΨ **Pinot Noir 2008** Crimson-purple; crammed to the gills with plum and black cherry fruit and appropriate tannins; will greatly benefit from five or so years in bottle. Screwcap. 13.5% alc. **Rating** 91 **To** 2015 $24

ΨΨΨΨ **Chardonnay 2008** Big, ripe flavour-packed wine; thoroughly commercial style, with fruit sweetness, not residual sugar. Unoaked. Screwcap. 13% alc. **Rating** 87 **To** 2010 $20

Whitfield Estate

198 McIntyre Road, Scotsdale, Denmark, WA 6333 **Region** Great Southern
T (08) 9840 9016 **F** (08) 9840 9016 **www**.whitfieldestate.com.au **Open** 7 days 10–5
Winemaker West Cape Howe, Matilda's Estate **Est.** 1994 **Cases** 1000 **Vyds** 4.8 ha
Graham and Kelly Howard acquired the Whitfield Estate vineyard (planted in 1994) in 2005.
The estate plantings are of chardonnay and shiraz, the bulk of which is sold to West Cape
Howe, who contract-make the remaining production for Whitfield Estate. Limited quantities
of other varieties are purchased from other growers in the region. A café, called Picnic in the
Paddock, was opened in 2008.

♀♀♀♀ **Shiraz 2007** Good colour; bright blueberry and redcurrant fruit; medium-bodied
with a little spice to conclude. Screwcap. 13.5% alc. **Rating** 87 **To** 2013 $18

Wicks Estate Wines

21 Franklin Street, Adelaide, SA 5000 (postal) **Region** Adelaide Hills
T (08) 8212 0004 **F** (08) 8212 0007 **www**.wicksestate.com.au **Open** Not
Winemaker Tim Knappstein, Leigh Ratzmer **Est.** 2000 **Cases** 10 000 **Vyds** 38.8 ha
Tim and Simon Wicks had a long-term involvement with orchard and nursery operations at
Highbury in the Adelaide Hills prior to purchasing the 54-ha property at Woodside in 1999.
They promptly planted fractionally less than 40 ha of chardonnay, riesling, sauvignon blanc,
shiraz, merlot and cabernet sauvignon, following this with the construction of a state-of-the-
art winery in early 2004. Exports to the UK, the US, China and Malaysia.

♀♀♀♀♀ **Adelaide Hills Rose 2008** Bright colour, with a real vinous edge to the red
fruits on the bouquet; good flavour, and quite dry with a savoury finish. Screwcap.
12.5% alc. **Rating** 90 **To** 2012 $15

♀♀♀♀ **Adelaide Hills Riesling 2008** A slightly Germanic, mineral style; ripe on
entry, but tightens and fines up on the finish. Screwcap. 12.5% alc. **Rating** 87
To 2012 $15
Adelaide Hills Sauvignon Blanc 2008 A mix of nettle and tropical aromas,
followed by a full-flavoured palate. Made for early drinking. Screwcap. 13% alc.
Rating 87 **To** 2009 $17

wightwick

323 Slatey Creek Road North, Invermay, Vic 3352 **Region** Ballarat
T (03) 5332 4443 **F** (03) 5332 8944 **www**.wightwick.com.au **Open** By appt
Winemaker Simon Wightwick **Est.** 1996 **Cases** 260 **Vyds** 2.41 ha
wightwick might best be described as an angel on a pinhead exercise. Keith and Ann
Wightwick planted the tiny estate vineyard to 0.12 ha of chardonnay and 0.29 ha of pinot noir
in 1996. In 2003 they purchased a 20-year-old vineyard at Cottlesbridge (1.5 ha chardonnay
and 0.5 ha cabernet sauvignon); most of the grapes from this vineyard are sold to other
producers, a small amount of cabernet sauvignon being retained for the wightwick label. Son
Simon works as a viticulturist and winemaker in the Yarra Valley, and looks after the vineyards
on weekends (using organic principles) and the micro-winemaking during vintage. The Pinot
Noir is hand-plunged, basket-pressed, with racking via gravity, and minimal fining.

♀♀♀♀♀ **Yarra Valley Cabernet Sauvignon 2006** Bright colour; essence of cassis on the
bouquet, with cigar box and and a little black olive for complexity; the palate is
full, firm and quite fine, with lingering dry tannin providing backbone and focus.
Screwcap. 13.5% alc. **Rating** 94 **To** 2016 $29

♀♀♀♀♀ **Ballarat Chardonnay 2006** Ripe nectarine and a touch of spice; focused and
fresh, with real poise, texture and weight; a dry and minerally finish. Screwcap.
13.3% alc. **Rating** 93 **To** 2014 $28
Ballarat Pinot Noir 2006 Slight haze; ripe redcurrant and dark cherry bouquet,
with charry oak providing a bit of spice; the palate is quite fleshy, then a little
grippy edge of bramble and undergrowth to the finish. Screwcap. 13.6% alc.
Rating 90 **To** 2013 $31

Wignalls Wines

448 Chester Pass Road (Highway 1), Albany, WA 6330 **Region** Albany
T (08) 9841 2848 **F** (08) 9842 9003 **www.**wignallswines.com.au **Open** 7 days 11–4
Winemaker Rob Wignall, Michael Perkins **Est.** 1982 **Cases** 9000 **Vyds** 18.5 ha
While the estate vineyards have a diverse range of sauvignon blanc, semillon, chardonnay, pinot noir, merlot, shiraz, cabernet franc and cabernet sauvignon, founder Bill Wignall was one of the early movers with pinot noir, producing wines that, by the standards of their time, were well in front of anything else coming out of WA (and up with the then limited amounts being made in Vic and Tasmania). The star dimmed, problems in the vineyard and with contract winemaking, both playing a role. The establishment of an onsite winery in 1998, and the assumption of the winemaking role by son Rob led to a significant increase in both the style and range of the wines made. Exports to the UK, Denmark, Japan and Taiwan.

ŦŦŦŦ♀ **Albany Shiraz 2007** A very attractive medium-bodied blend of spicy red cherry and plummy licorice flavours sustained by silky tannins and subtle oak. Value. Screwcap. 14.5% alc. **Rating** 93 **To** 2017 $21
Albany Pinot Noir 2008 Strong colour; continues the resurgence with Wignalls' pinots, with luscious plum fruit on the round and supple palate; would it have been better if picked a little earlier? Screwcap. 15% alc. **Rating** 93 **To** 2015 $31
Great Southern Unwooded Chardonnay 2008 A fragrant and delicious crossover between chardonnay and sauvignon blanc showing, once again, how well unwooded chardonnays work with good quality, cool-grown grapes. Screwcap. 14% alc. **Rating** 91 **To** 2012 $16.80
Albany Chardonnay 2008 Bright green-gold; tangy, complex barrel ferment aromas, then a neatly balanced package, perhaps a little too neatly, or a fraction too ripe. Screwcap. 15% alc. **Rating** 90 **To** 2015 $31

ŦŦŦŦ **Albany Sauvignon Blanc 2008** Flows evenly across the palate, the flavour building progressively, but not into unacceptable phenolics. Screwcap. 12.5% alc. **Rating** 89 **To** 2010 $19

Wild Dog Winery

Warragul-Korrumburra Road, Warragul, Vic 3820 **Region** Gippsland
T (03) 5623 1117 **F** (03) 5623 6402 **www.**wilddogwinery.com **Open** 7 days 10–5
Winemaker Mal Stewart, Folkert Janssen **Est.** 1982 **Cases** 5000 **Vyds** 14.2 ha
An aptly named winery that produces somewhat rustic wines from the estate vineyards; even the Farringtons (the founders) say that the 'Shiraz comes with a bite', but they also point out that there is minimal handling, fining and filtration. Following the acquisition of Wild Dog by Gary and Judy Surman, Mal Stewart was appointed winemaker with a far-ranging brief to build on the legacy of the previous owners, and is now assisted by Folkert Janssen. Upgrading of the vineyard has resulted in new plantings, and the grafting over of vines, the estate plantings now mainly devoted to shiraz (4 ha), chardonnay (3.5 ha), pinot noir (2 ha), riesling (1.5 ha), cabernet sauvignon (1.5 ha) with smaller blocks of cabernet franc, merlot, semillon, sauvignon blanc, viognier and pinot gris. The payback came at the Gippsland Wine Show '08 when Wild Dog Winery won four trophies (and attendant gold medals). As the tasting notes indicate, there is much to be confident about. Exports to China and Japan.

ŦŦŦŦ♀ **Gippsland Riesling 2008** Vibrant colour; focused lemon bouquet with a gentle splash of tropical fruit; fine and precise, there is real personality, with a focused line to conclude. Screwcap. 12% alc. **Rating** 92 **To** 2015 $21
Gippsland Shiraz 2007 Good colour and concentration; a cool style with a touch of fresh herbs and abundant red fruit; a warm and generous palate with fine tannin structure and noticeable, but not intrusive, oak on the finish. Screwcap. 14% alc. **Rating** 90 **To** 2014 $23

ŦŦŦŦ **Gippsland Wild Rose 2008** Bright cherry fruit with a dab of spice; good concentration and lively, almost racy, acidity on the finish. Screwcap. 13% alc. **Rating** 88 **To** 2012 $21

Gippsland Cabernet Sauvignon 2007 Good colour; cassis mixed with a touch of capsicum; good depth to the fruit, with a slight bitterness to the finish, which lends a slight European character. Screwcap. 13.5% alc. **Rating** 88 **To** 2012 $23

Wildwood

St John's Lane, Wildwood, Bulla, Vic 3428 **Region** Sunbury
T (03) 9307 1118 **F** (03) 9331 1590 **www**.wildwoodvineyards.com.au **Open** 7 days 10–5
Winemaker Dr Wayne Stott **Est.** 1983 **Cases** 800
Wildwood is just 4 km past Melbourne airport, at an altitude of 130 m in the Oaklands Valley, which provides unexpected views back to Port Phillip Bay and the Melbourne skyline. Plastic surgeon Dr Wayne Stott has taken what is very much a part-time activity rather more seriously than most by completing the wine science degree at CSU.

ΨΨΨΨΨ **Shiraz 2007** Good colour; a fragrant and spicy bouquet leads into a fresh medium-bodied palate; again with notes of spice and pepper to the black cherry and plum flavours; fine tannins to close. Screwcap. 13% alc. **Rating** 92 **To** 2017 $35

Will Taylor Wines

1B Victoria Avenue, Unley Park, SA 5061 **Region** Southeast Australia
T (08) 8271 6122 **F** (08) 8271 6122 **Open** By appt
Winemaker Various contract **Est.** 1997 **Cases** 1500
Will Taylor is a partner in the leading Adelaide law firm Finlaysons, and specialises in wine law. He and Suzanne Taylor have established a classic negociant wine business, having wines contract-made to their specifications. Moreover, they choose what they consider the best regions for each variety; thus Clare Valley Riesling, Adelaide Hills Sauvignon Blanc, Hunter Valley Semillon and Yarra Valley Pinot Noir. Exports to Canada, Hong Kong, China and Singapore.

Willespie ★★★★

555 Harmans Mill Road, Wilyabrup via Cowaramup, WA 6284 **Region** Margaret River
T (08) 9755 6248 **F** (08) 9755 6210 **www**.willespie.com.au **Open** 7 days 10.30–5
Winemaker Nathan Schultz **Est.** 1976 **Cases** 7000 **Vyds** 22 ha
Willespie has produced many attractive white wines over the years, typically in brisk, herbaceous Margaret River style; all are fruit- rather than oak-driven. The wines have had such success that the Squance family (which founded and owns Willespie) has increased winery capacity, drawing upon an additional 22 ha of estate vineyards now in bearing. Exports to the UK, Japan and Singapore.

ΨΨΨΨΨ **Old School Barrel Fermented Margaret River Semillon 2007** A lifted green nettle bouquet with some riper tropical fruit beneath; good texture, with a lively and quite vivacious personality. Diam. 12.5% alc. **Rating** 90 **To** 2012 $25
Verdelho 2008 Shows the unusually tangy and crisp style of '08 Verdelhos to full advantage, the palate incisive and long; good seafood style. Screwcap. 13.5% alc. **Rating** 90 **To** 2010 $19.50

ΨΨΨΨ **Margaret River Sauvignon Blanc 2008** Green nettle and citrus bouquet; pure, focused and very fresh on the palate, the amount of nettle will be a matter of personal taste. Screwcap. 12% alc. **Rating** 89 **To** 2011 $19.50
Old School Margaret River Shiraz 2000 Browning, but still lively; moved into savoury, leather and undergrowth character; the palate is still fleshy and fine. Cork. 14.5% alc. **Rating** 87 **To** 2012 $45

Willow Bridge Estate

Gardin Court Drive, Dardanup, WA 6236 **Region** Geographe
T (08) 9728 0055 **F** (08) 9728 0066 **www**.willowbridge.com.au **Open** 7 days 11–5
Winemaker David Crawford **Est.** 1997 **Cases** 40 000 **Vyds** 59 ha

The Dewar family has followed a fast track in developing Willow Bridge Estate since acquiring the spectacular 180-ha hillside property in the Ferguson Valley: chardonnay, semillon, sauvignon blanc, shiraz and cabernet sauvignon were planted, with tempranillo added in 2000. The winery is capable of handling the 1200–1500 tonnes from the estate plantings. Not too many wineries in Australia better the price/value ratio of the mid-range wines of Willow Bridge. Exports to the UK, the US and other major markets.

ŶŶŶŶŶ **Shiraz 2007** Bright colour; juicy red cherry and plum fruits ripple through the medium-bodied palate, enhanced by spicy French oak; then fine tannins on a long finish. Screwcap. 13% alc. **Rating** 94 **To** 2017 $15.50
Black Dog Shiraz 2007 Fragrant and perfumed with some new oak; the palate has power and persistence, with a core of red fruit and spice running through to the long finish. Screwcap. 14.5% alc. **Rating** 94 **To** 2015 $60

ŶŶŶŶŶ **Gravel Pit Reserve Ferguson Valley Shiraz Viognier 2007** The colour is bright, although not especially deep; an aromatic bouquet has a distinct touch of apricot ex the viognier, the palate a mix of sweet red fruits and more savoury components. Screwcap. 14% alc. **Rating** 90 **To** 2016 $30

ŶŶŶŶ **Reserve Wild Ferment Pemberton Sauvignon Blanc 2008** A lifted bouquet of tropical fruit and a gunflint smokiness; a rich palate, with fine acid and a little grip on the finish. Screwcap. 13% alc. **Rating** 89 **To** 2011 $22
Sauvignon Blanc Semillon 2008 Well constructed and balanced, with contrasting white peach and mineral/herb notes; good length. Screwcap. 12.5% alc. **Rating** 89 **To** 2011 $15.50
Rose 2008 Lively, bright and fresh red fruits with a tangy/zesty streak of citrussy acidity. Screwcap. 12.5% alc. **Rating** 89 **To** 2010 $15.50
Solana Reserve Geographe Tempranillo 2007 Crimson-purple; bright and zesty, with the faintly citrussy acidity that is part and parcel of many Australian tempranillos; has good length. Screwcap. 13.5% alc. **Rating** 89 **To** 2014 $22
Unwooded Chardonnay 2008 Pale colour; nectarine and a touch tropical fruit, then a sweet, ripe nectarine palate. Screwcap. 12.5% alc. **Rating** 87 **To** 2011 $16.50

Willow Creek Vineyard ★★★★★

166 Balnarring Road, Merricks North, Vic 3926 **Region** Mornington Peninsula
T (03) 5989 7448 **F** (03) 5989 7584 **www**.willow-creek.com.au **Open** 7 days 10–5
Winemaker Geraldine McFaul **Est.** 1989 **Cases** 7000
Willow Creek Vineyard is a significant presence in the Mornington Peninsula, with 12 ha of vines planted to cabernet sauvignon, chardonnay, pinot noir and sauvignon blanc. The grape intake is supplemented by purchasing small, quality parcels from local growers. The Willow Creek wines rank with the best from the Peninsula, the arrival of Geraldine McFaul as winemaker promising a continuation in (if not bettering) the quality of the wines.

ŶŶŶŶŶ **Aquitania Mornington Peninsula Cabernet Sauvignon 2006** A highly focused wine, with a tightly woven structure surrounding cassis and blackcurrant fruit, which has largely absorbed the impact of 22 months in new French oak; long, lingering finish. Cork. 14% alc. **Rating** 94 **To** 2021 $65

Wills Domain ★★★★★

Cnr Brash Road/Abbey Farm Road, Yallingup, WA 6281 **Region** Margaret River
T (08) 9755 2327 **F** (08) 9756 6072 **www**.willsdomain.com.au **Open** 7 days 10–5
Winemaker Naturaliste Vintners (Bruce Dukes) **Est.** 1985 **Cases** 7500 **Vyds** 20.8 ha
When Michelle and Darren Haunold purchased the original Wills Domain vineyard in 2000, they were adding another chapter to a family history of winemaking stretching back to 1383 in modern day Austria. Remarkable though that may be, the more remarkable is that 32-year-old Darren, who lost the use of his legs in a car accident when he was 13, runs the estate (including part of the pruning) from his wheelchair. Prior to the Haunold's purchase of the property, the grapes were all sold to local winemakers, but since '01 they have been made

for the Wills Domain label, and the vineyard holdings of chardonnay, semillon, sauvignon blanc, shiraz, cabernet sauvignon, merlot, petit verdot, malbec and cabernet franc have been expanded. Exports to the UK, the US, Singapore, Malaysia, Indonesia and Hong Kong.

♟♟♟♟♟ **Margaret River Semillon Sauvignon Blanc 2008** A restrained and elegant bouquet; grapefruit and gooseberry framed by a touch of straw; the palate is lithe and lively, with racy acidity drawing out the long and even finish. Screwcap. 13% alc. **Rating** 94 **To** 2014 $21.50

Margaret River Chardonnay 2007 Grapefruit aromas mingle gently with toasty oak and a complex mineral core; ample depth to the fruit; real grace, and overall complexity on the finish; very well made. Screwcap. 14% alc. **Rating** 94 **To** 2015 $45

Margaret River Cabernet Sauvignon Merlot 2007 Lifted herb and spice nuances to the blackcurrant fruit of the bouquet yield to a supple, juicy palate of blackcurrant and cassis, finishing with silky tannins. Screwcap. 14% alc. **Rating** 94 **To** 2017 $27.50

Reserve Margaret River Cabernet Sauvignon 2007 A stylish, fragrant bouquet with blackcurrant and cedary oak, then a tightly focused and very correct palate; cabernet fruit leaves the oak and tannins in its wake. Screwcap. 14% alc. **Rating** 94 **To** 2022 $45

♟♟♟♟♀ **Margaret River Shiraz 2006** Youthful vibrant colour; red fruits, dried herbs and smoky oak appear on the bouquet; the palate is medium-bodied with fine red fruits coming to the fore, the gravelly tannins providing extra interest on the savoury finish. Screwcap. 14% alc. **Rating** 93 **To** 2018 $23.50

Margaret River Cabernet Sauvignon Merlot 2006 Clean and focused, with cassis, cedar and a little oaky complexity in the background; good texture and fine-grained tannins show the quality of wine being produced at this estate. Screwcap. 13.5% alc. **Rating** 93 **To** 2016 $23.50

Margaret River Semillon 2006 Showing a little toasty complexity, and plenty of life; a hint of nettle and fresh, lively acidity and fruit on the ample finish. Screwcap. 13% alc. **Rating** 92 **To** 2014 $23.50

Margaret River Shiraz 2007 Good colour; the aromatic bouquet attests to the touch of viognier in the wine; the light- to medium-bodied palate has spicy fruits and gently savoury tannins, the oak well-integrated. Screwcap. 13.5% alc. **Rating** 90 **To** 2015 $27.50

♟♟♟♟ **Margaret River Rose 2008** Clean and vibrant, with defined red fruits, a touch of mineral complexity, and bright, clean acid on the finish. Screwcap. 13.5% alc. **Rating** 89 **To** 2012 $19.50

Willunga Creek Wines   ★★★☆

Lot 361 Delabole Road, Willunga, SA 5172 **Region** McLaren Vale
T (08) 8556 2244 **www**.willungacreekwines.com.au **Open** W'ends 10–5, or by appt
Winemaker Goe De Fabio, Phil Christiansen **Est.** 2002 **Cases** 3000
David and Julie Cheesley purchased the property in the early 1990s, planting 6 ha each of shiraz and cabernet sauvignon in '94, adding 0.5 ha of merlot in 2000. The vines are planted on terraced sloping hills, the wind exposure helping the Cheesley's organic management of the vineyard. The Willunga name and the Black Duck brand come from the Aboriginal word 'willangga', which means black duck. The cellar door is a refurbished circa 1850 building in the town of Willunga. Exports to the UK, South Korea and Japan.

♟♟♟♟♀ **Black Duck McLaren Vale Merlot 2006** Has a mix of savoury (varietal) and bitter chocolate (regional) influences, taking the wine away from simple fruit, and allowing its fine texture to express itself. Diam. 14.5% alc. **Rating** 90 **To** 2014 $25

Willy Bay

PO Box 193, Inglewood, WA 6932 **Region** Geographe
T (08) 9271 9890 **F** (08) 9271 7771 **www**.willybay.com.au **Open** Not
Winemaker Peter Stanlake **Est.** 2003 **Cases** 700 **Vyds** 11 ha
Willy Bay Wines is jointly owned and run by the Siciliano and Edwards families, who have
established 6.5 ha of shiraz, 2.8 ha of cabernet sauvignon and 1.7 ha of chardonnay. Some of
the wine names are borrowed from cricket (I suppose I am meant to know why, but don't)
and there may well be dissent about the umpire's (my) ratings for this year's wines.

ŸŸŸŸ **Middle Stump Geographe Shiraz 2007** A complex wine, with abundant
blackberry and plum fruit framed by vanillin (American) oak, alcohol-derived
sweetness limiting the freshness of the finish and aftertaste. Screwcap. 15% alc.
Rating 89 **To** 2015 $28
Reverse Swing Geographe Cabernet Sauvignon 2006 Bright, but light,
hue; cassis, mint and leaf aromas and flavours, in part reflecting the vintage.
Screwcap. 13.5% alc. **Rating** 87 **To** 2013 $22

Wilson Vineyard

Polish Hill River, Sevenhill via Clare, SA 5453 **Region** Clare Valley
T (08) 8843 4310 **www**.wilsonvineyard.com.au **Open** W'ends 10–4
Winemaker Dr John Wilson, Daniel Wilson **Est.** 1974 **Cases** 4000
After working at the shoulder of his father John for many years, Daniel Wilson took over
responsibility for the winemaking in 2003. The Wilson Vineyard of today is a far cry from that
of 10 years ago, taking its place in the upper echelon of the Clare Valley.

ŸŸŸŸŸ **Polish Hill River Riesling 2008** Bright straw-green; has the tension and thrust
the DJW lacks, with a compelling mix of lime, apple and mineral on the very long
palate, which also has great line. Screwcap. 13.6% alc. **Rating** 94 **To** 2016 $22
Museum Polish Hill River Riesling 2004 Gleaming green-gold; has gained
enormous complexity, with a pungent bouquet of lime, toast and a touch of
kerosene; the palate, too, is little short of majestic. Now or within five years.
Screwcap. 12.5% alc. **Rating** 94 **To** 2014 $33

ŸŸŸŸ **DJW Clare Valley Riesling 2008** A generous wine from the opening stanza to
the last; a hint of toast on the bouquet and ripe citrus fruit on the palate; doesn't
grip the senses like it usually does. Screwcap. 13.2% alc. **Rating** 89 **To** 2014 $19.50

Wimbaliri Wines

3180 Barton Highway, Murrumbateman, NSW 2582 **Region** Canberra District
T (02) 6227 5921 **Open** 7 days 11–5
Winemaker John Andersen **Est.** 1988 **Cases** 600 **Vyds** 2.2 ha
John and Margaret Andersen moved to the Canberra District in 1987 and began establishing
their vineyard at Murrumbateman in '88; the property borders highly regarded Canberra
producers Doonkuna and Clonakilla. The vineyard is close-planted with chardonnay, pinot
noir, shiraz, cabernet sauvignon and merlot (plus a few vines of cabernet franc).

Winbirra Vineyard ★★★★☆

173 Point Leo Road, Red Hill South, Vic 3937 **Region** Mornington Peninsula
T (03) 5989 2109 **F** (03) 5989 2109 **www**.winbirra.com.au **Open** W'ends &
public hols 11–5, or by appt
Winemaker Sandro Mosele (Contract) **Est.** 1990 **Cases** 1500 **Vyds** 4.1 ha
Winbirra is a small, family-owned and run vineyard that has been producing grapes since
1990, between then and '97 selling the grapes to local winemakers. Since 1997 the wine
has been made and sold under the Winbirra label. Plantings include pinot gris and viognier
(1.3 ha each), pinot noir (1 ha) and smaller amounts of pinot meunier and shiraz.

🍷🍷🍷🍷🍷 **The Brigadier Mornington Peninsula Pinot Noir 2007** Good colour; a substantial wine focused on ripe cherry and plum fruit supported by a fine web of tannins; the line is seamless, the flavours lush and true to the variety. Years to go. Diam. 13.5% alc. **Rating** 93 **To** 2014 $55

Le Marechal Mornington Peninsula Viognier 2008 A luscious viognier, with apricot and musk perfume and flavours, then (mercifully) finishing with crisp, citrussy acidity. Screwcap. 14.5% alc. **Rating** 91 **To** 2012 $35

Mimi's Mornington Peninsula Pinot Gris 2008 Has an extra degree of varietal fruit, with abundant ripe pear and some honeysuckle; doesn't rely on sugar, such sweetness as there is coming from the alcohol. Screwcap. 14.6% alc. **Rating** 90 **To** 2011 $25

Winburndale ★★★☆

116 Saint Anthony's Creek Road, Bathurst, NSW 2795 **Region** Central Ranges Zone
T (02) 6337 3134 **F** (02) 6337 3106 **www**.winburndalewines.com.au **Open** By appt
Winemaker Mark Renzaglia, David Lowe (Consultant) **Est.** 1998 **Cases** 3500 **Vyds** 10.4 ha

Michael Burleigh and family acquired the 200-ha Winburndale property in 1998: 160 ha is forest, to be kept as a nature reserve; three separate vineyards have been planted under the direction of viticulturist Mark Renzaglia. The winery paddock has shiraz facing due west at an altitude of 800–820 m; the south paddock, with north and northwest aspects, varying from 790–810 m, has chardonnay, shiraz and cabernet sauvignon. The home paddock is the most level, with a slight north aspect, and has merlot. The name derives from Lachlan Macquarie's exploration of the Blue Mountains in 1815. Exports to the US and Denmark.

🍷🍷🍷🍷🍷 **Solitary Shiraz 2006** Plum and dark cherry fruit with a touch of spice; quite fresh on the palate, with even tannin and fruit richness on the long and balanced finish. Screwcap. 15% alc. **Rating** 90 **To** 2014 $30

🍷🍷🍷🍷 **Alluvial Chardonnay 2006** Rich, ripe and very toasty, with fleshy fruit and upfront appeal; no need for patience. Screwcap. 13% alc. **Rating** 87 **To** 2012 $25

Windance Wines ★★★★★

2764 Caves Road, Yallingup, WA 6282 **Region** Margaret River
T (08) 9755 2293 **F** (08) 9755 2293 **www**.windance.com.au **Open** 7 days 10–5
Winemaker Damon Eastaugh, Liz Reed **Est.** 1998 **Cases** 3500 **Vyds** 7.5 ha

Drew and Rosemary Brent-White own this family business, situated 5 km south of Yallingup. Cabernet sauvignon, shiraz, sauvignon blanc, semillon and merlot have been established, incorporating sustainable land management and organic farming practices where possible. The wines are exclusively estate-grown, pricing fairly reflecting quality.

🍷🍷🍷🍷🍷 **Reserve Margaret River Shiraz 2007** Fragrant mulberry spice and red fruit aromas; the medium-bodied palate is generous and long, with exceptional balance, texture and mouthfeel. Gold WA Wine Show '08. Screwcap. 14.5% alc. **Rating** 95 **To** 2016 $40

Margaret River Shiraz 2007 Good clarity and hue; vibrant fruits in a red and black cherry spectrum; balanced tannin and oak, with a long, convincing finish. Top Gold WA Wine Show '08. Screwcap. 14.2% alc. **Rating** 95 **To** 2015 $31.50

Reserve Margaret River Cabernet Sauvignon 2007 Manages to combine intensity with elegance; red and black fruits accelerate through the palate and into the finish and aftertaste. Has great presence. Screwcap. 14.9% alc. **Rating** 94 **To** 2016 $45

Windowrie Estate ★★★☆

Windowrie Road, Canowindra, NSW 2804 **Region** Cowra
T (02) 6344 3234 **www**.windowrie.com **Open** At the Mill, Vaux Street, Cowra
Winemaker Folkert Jansen **Est.** 1988 **Cases** 20 000

Windowrie Estate was established by the O'Dea family in 1988 on a substantial grazing property at Canowindra, 30 km north of Cowra and in the same viticultural region. A portion of the grapes from the 116-ha vineyard are sold to other makers, but increasing quantities are being made for the Windowrie Estate and The Mill labels; the Chardonnays have enjoyed show success. The cellar door is in a flour mill built in 1861 from local granite. It ceased operations in 1905 and lay unoccupied for 91 years until restored by the O'Dea family. Exports to the UK, Ireland, Canada, Denmark, Holland, Japan and China.

ΤΤΤΤΥ **Pig in the House Shiraz 2007** Good colour; fresh red and black cherry fruit with some plum; attractive, lively wine, one of the best reds from Cowra; received no oak maturation or influence. Cork. 13.5% alc. **Rating** 90 **To** 2011 $22

ΤΤΤΤ **The Mill Central Ranges Cabernet Merlot 2007** Good colour; an attractive wine, particularly given its origins, with an abundance of juicy red and black fruits, and just enough tannins; clever adoption of Central Ranges Zone not Cowra region. Diam. 13.5% alc. **Rating** 89 **To** 2013 $14.99
The Mill Central Ranges Chardonnay 2007 Generously flavoured and upholstered, although not much finesse; honest varietal fruit and balanced oak. Screwcap. 14.5% alc. **Rating** 87 **To** 2010 $14.95
The Mill Cowra Verdelho 2008 Pleasant light- to medium-bodied fruit salad flavours; gold medal at a NZ International Wine Show '08 decidedly curious. Screwcap. 14.5% alc. **Rating** 87 **To** 2009 $14.99
The Mill Central Ranges Shiraz 2007 Has substance and structure to its blackberry fruit, due in part to the increasing maturity of the vines in this region, previously known best for its chardonnay. Cork. 13.5% alc. **Rating** 87 **To** 2013 $14.99
Pig in the House Cabernet Sauvignon 2006 Not in the same class as the Pig in the House Shiraz, but nonetheless is better than many cabernets from Cowra; has length and some finesse; subtle oak. Cork. 14% alc. **Rating** 87 **To** 2011 $22

Windows Margaret River   ★★★★
4 Quininup Road, Yallingup, WA 6282 (postal) **Region** Margaret River
T (08) 9755 2719 **F** (08) 9755 2719 **www**.windowsmargaretriver.com **Open** Not
Winemaker Chris Davies, Navneet Singh, Mick Scott (Consultant) **Est.** 1996 **Cases** 7000
Vyds 6 ha
Len and Barbara Davies progressively established their vineyard (cabernet sauvignon, shiraz, chenin blanc, chardonnay, semillon, sauvignon blanc, and merlot), initially selling the grapes. In 2006 the decision was taken to move to winemaking. Son Chris makes the red wines, Navneet Singh the whites, with Mick Scott filling an overall consulting role. It has been rewarded with considerable show success for its consistently good, enticingly priced wines. Exports to Canada, Malaysia and Singapore.

ΤΤΤΤΥ **Semillon 2008** Skilled winemaking has introduced subtle barrel ferment characters to a wine rich in fruit flavours, yet retaining finesse and elegance. Drink now or in 10 years' time. Screwcap. 12.7% alc. **Rating** 93 **To** 2018 $19.95
Sauvignon Blanc 2008 Bright straw-green; has light but fresh and precise aromas and flavours of tropical and citrus fruits; elegant wine. Screwcap. 12.7% alc. **Rating** 92 **To** 2010 $19.95
Semillon Sauvignon Blanc 2008 Shares many of the attributes of the Sauvignon Blanc, perhaps with a little more structure and length from the Semillon, and slightly less tropical fruits; very good overall balance and length. Screwcap. 12.9% alc. **Rating** 92 **To** 2012 $19.95
Shiraz 2007 Very nearly gets away with its alcohol, for the flavours are complex and multilayered, ranging across blackberry, licorice, black pepper and spice, before the heat on the finish pokes through. Food is a very plausible antidote, as it is for Italian tannins. Screwcap. 15.5% alc. **Rating** 90 **To** 2020 $22

ŸŸŸŸ Cabernet Sauvignon 2007 Fragrant aromas of cassis, mint and leaf, then a juicy ripe palate, sweet fruits up front, more savoury notes on the back-palate; however, heats up on the finish. Screwcap. 15.3% alc. **Rating** 89 To 2017 $22
Reserve Margaret River Shiraz 2007 A powerful, extractive wine needing time to loosen its hold on strong, blackberry fruit. Screwcap. 15.8% alc. **Rating** 88 To 2017 $36
Reserve Cabernet Sauvignon 2007 Good colour; assertive but correct varietal character impact; black fruits; good tannins. Screwcap. 15.5% alc. **Rating** 88 To 2016 $45

Windrush Wines

Lot 350 St Werburgh's Road, Mount Barker, WA 6324 **Region** Mount Barker
T (08) 9851 1353 **www.**windrushwines.com.au **Open** Fri–Sun & public hols 10–4
Winemaker Garlands (Michael Garland), The Vintage Wineworx (Greg Jones) **Est.** 2000
Cases 760 **Vyds** 4.9 ha
In 1999 David and Caroline Picton-King decided to exchange living and working in Perth for grapegrowing and winemaking in Mount Barker. They began to convert desire into reality in 2000 when they purchased the property and planted 1.1 ha of shiraz. In 2001 and '03 they planted a total of 2.4 ha of chardonnay, and finally 1.3 ha of cabernet sauvignon in '04, with 'soft' organic management. They had been commuting from Perth every couple of weeks to plant and tend the vines up to 2004 when they moved permanently to Mount Barker. The majority of the grapes are sold to other wineries in the district, but the establishment of a cellar door and café in 2008 will see the contract-made production steadily increase over the coming years.

ŸŸŸŸŸ Mount Barker Chardonnay 2007 Well made; nectarine, melon and a drizzle of citrus fruit has subtle French oak offering support, likewise acidity. Screwcap. 13.9% alc. **Rating** 90 To 2012 $21.90

ŸŸŸŸ Mount Barker Rose 2007 Spice and red cherry shiraz fruit is freshened by crisp acidity and a pleasantly dry finish. Screwcap. 14.4% alc. **Rating** 89 To 2009 $18.90
Mount Barker Shiraz 2006 A fragrant mix of berry, mint and leaf; fresh but the mint and leaf notes are sure markers of lack of phenological ripeness. Screwcap. 12.3% alc. **Rating** 87 To 2011 $20

wine by brad

PO Box 475, Margaret River, WA 6285 **Region** Margaret River
T 0409 572 957 **F** (08) 9757 1897 **www.**winebybrad.com.au **Open** Not
Winemaker Brad Wehr **Est.** 2003 **Cases** 3000
Brad Wehr says that wine by brad 'is the result of a couple of influential winemakers and shadowy ruffians deciding there was something to be gained by putting together some pretty neat parcels of wine from the region, creating their own label, and releasing it with minimal fuss'. In 2007 a premium range was introduced under the Mantra label, from separately sourced grapes.

ŸŸŸŸŸ Margaret River Semillon Sauvignon Blanc 2008 Attractive bouquet to a very well-put-together wine, with sweet, rather than bitter, citrussy fruit; has length and drive. Gold WA Wine Show '08. Screwcap. 13% alc. **Rating** 94 To 2011 $18

ŸŸŸŸŸ Mantra Revelation Margaret River Sauvignon Blanc 2008 A quiet bouquet bursts into song with the lively, zesty palate, which has gooseberry and apple offset by crisp acidity on the long, dry finish. Screwcap. 13% alc. **Rating** 93 To 2011 $20
Mantra Muse Reserve Margaret River Chardonnay 2007 Has more complexity than Invocation, courtesy of riper grapes and a little more oak; the difference is not so much quality as a very different style. Screwcap. 13.5% alc. **Rating** 93 To 2016 $37
Mantra Invocation Margaret River Chardonnay 2007 Light straw-green; elegant, fresh melon and stone fruit flavours; the oak has been very well handled, the finish lively and fresh. Screwcap. 13% alc. **Rating** 91 To 2017 $25

Mantra Affirmation Margaret River Semillon Sauvignon Blanc 2008
Crisp and crunchy, the semillon providing the structure and much of the flavour,
all to good effect on the long finish. Screwcap. 13% alc. **Rating** 90 **To** 2011 $20

Winstead

75 Winstead Road, Bagdad, Tas 7030 **Region** Southern Tasmania
T (03) 6268 6417 **F** (03) 6268 6417 **Open** By appt
Winemaker Neil Snare **Est.** 1989 **Cases** 350
The good news about Winstead is the outstanding quality of its extremely generous and rich
Pinot Noirs, rivalling those of Freycinet for the abundance of their fruit flavour without any
sacrifice of varietal character. The bad news is that production is so limited, with only 0.8 ha
of pinot noir and 0.4 ha riesling being tended by fly-fishing devotee Neil Snare and wife
Julieanne.

ΨΨΨΨ   **Sparkling Pinot Noir 2004** Salmon-pink; still a lot of primary fruit flavours,
strawberry and small red fruits; obviously a long life ahead. **Rating** 90 **To** 2014

ΨΨΨΨ   **Instead Pinot Noir 2008** Strong deep purple; big wine; ripe fruit and quite
obvious tannins; needs time; borders on dry red. **Rating** 89 **To** 2015
Pinot Noir 2007 Much riper than the '05 Pinot, closer to the '06, with an
abundance of black cherry and plum fruit; more flavour than finesse. **Rating** 88
To 2014

Winter Creek Wine

PO Box 170, Williamstown, SA 5351 **Region** Barossa Valley
T (08) 8524 6382 **F** (08) 8524 6382 **www**.wintercreekwine.com.au **Open** By appt
Winemaker David Cross **Est.** 2000 **Cases** 2000 **Vyds** 6 ha
David and Pam Cross acquired their small vineyard at Williamstown in the cooler foothills of
the southern Barossa Valley in 2000, in time for their first vintage that year. There are 4 ha of
shiraz, and 2 ha of 70-year-old grenache. More recently they have added a Sauvignon Blanc
and a Chardonnay to the range, the grapes purchased from the Adelaide Hills.

ΨΨΨΨΨ   **Saint Urban Shiraz 2006** Dense crimson-purple; richer and deeper flavours than
the varietal; black fruits (plum and blackberry) to the fore, but lifting on the finish
with a twist of licorice and spice. Screwcap. 14% alc. **Rating** 95 **To** 2021 $45
Barossa Valley Shiraz 2006 Excellent retention of crimson-purple hue;
delicious medium- to full-bodied wine, lively red and black fruit flavours supported
by fine, but persistent, tannins. Screwcap. 14% alc. **Rating** 94 **To** 2016 $30

ΨΨΨΨΨ   **The Old Barossa Blend Grenache Shiraz 2006** Has the usual light colour of
the blend, but here the Grenache's Turkish delight flavours are given structure by
the 25% shiraz component, the union working well. Screwcap. 14% alc. **Rating** 90
To 2015 $25
Fortified Vintage Shiraz 2008 Powerful wine; in modern style spicy and
quite dry; will develop impressively over the next 10+ years. Screwcap. 20% alc.
Rating 90 **To** 2020 $25

ΨΨΨΨ   **Adelaide Hills Sauvignon Blanc 2008** Bright and crisp, although neither
bouquet or palate can decide between herbal/grassy notes and more tropical
nuances. Screwcap. 12.5% alc. **Rating** 89 **To** 2010 $18

Wirra Wirra

McMurtrie Road, McLaren Vale, SA 5171 **Region** McLaren Vale
T (08) 8323 8414 **www**.wirrawirra.com **Open** Mon–Sat 10–5, Sun & public hols 11–5
Winemaker Samantha Connew, Paul Smith **Est.** 1969 **Cases** 180 000 **Vyds** 72.74 ha
Long respected for the consistency of its white wines, Wirra Wirra has now established an
equally formidable reputation for its reds. Right across the board, the wines are of exemplary
character, quality and style, The Angelus Cabernet Sauvignon and RSW Shiraz battling with

each other for supremacy. Long may the battle continue under the direction of new managing director Andrew Kay following the retirement of highly respected Tim James, particularly in the wake of the death of the universally loved co-founder/owner Greg Trott in early 2005. In Dec '07 Wirra Wirra purchased the 20-ha Rayner Vineyard (with blocks dating back to the 1950s), which had hitherto supplied Brokenwood with the grapes for its eponymous icon Shiraz. Exports to all major markets.

▼▼▼▼▼ **Hiding Champion Adelaide Hills Sauvignon Blanc 2008** Early picking has paid big dividends, with a chorus of juicy flavours running from apple to tropical; the palate vibrant, the finish fresh. Screwcap. 12% alc. **Rating** 95 **To** 2011 $22
Chook Block Shiraz 2006 Dark and brooding with mocha, fruitcake and a seasoning of charry oak; the medium-bodied palate is loaded with sweet fruit and oak. Not a blockbuster, rather plenty of finesse. Screwcap. 14.5% alc. **Rating** 94 **To** 2016 $132

▼▼▼▼▽ **Woodhenge McLaren Vale Shiraz 2007** Blackberry, redcurrant and chocolate, with a touch of fruitcake in the background; the palate is dense and full of warm and very ripe fruit; chewy tannin and bright acidity on the finish. Screwcap. 14.5% alc. **Rating** 92 **To** 2016 $30
The Lost Watch Adelaide Hills Riesling 2008 Pale colour; lemon, lime and mineral define the bouquet; quite lean and focused on the palate, but with real persistence from start to finish. Screwcap. 12.5% alc. **Rating** 90 **To** 2016 $18
Mrs Wigley McLaren Vale Rose 2008 A bright hue, with attractive spicy notes on the bouquet; the palate shows some richness and depth, and just a little grip adding complexity and interest to the finish. Screwcap. 13% alc. **Rating** 90 **To** 2012 $18
Church Block McLaren Vale Cabernet Sauvignon Shiraz Merlot 2007 A very tight and polished style of this classic Australian blend; plenty of black fruits, spice and plenty of structure; lots on offer. Screwcap. 14.5% alc. **Rating** 90 **To** 2016 $23

▼▼▼▼ **Scrubby Rise Unwooded Chardonnay 2008** Deep colour; ripe bouquet of peach and nectarine; plenty of flavour and persistence. Screwcap. 13.5% alc. **Rating** 88 **To** 2011 $16.50
Catapult McLaren Vale Shiraz Viognier 2007 A dark mocha personality; a suggestion of florals from the viognier; sweet fruited on the palate, with dark chewy fruit persisting to the finish. Screwcap. 14.5% alc. **Rating** 88 **To** 2012 $22
Mrs Wigley Moscato 2008 Clean, grapey aromas with a touch of talc. and floral notes; good spritz, not too sweet, and finishes quite clean and dry; very refreshing. Crown Seal. 6.8% alc. **Rating** 88 **To** 2009 $18
Scrubby Rise Sauvignon Blanc Semillon Viognier 2008 Clean, crisp and dry; not particularly varietal, but well made. Screwcap. 13% alc. **Rating** 87 **To** 2010 $15

🍇 Wisdom Creek Wines   ★★★

14 Deloraine Road, Edwardstown, SA 5039 **Region** Various
T (08) 8276 3255 **F** (08) 8276 4877 **www.**wisdomcreekwines.biz **Open** Mon–Sat 10–5
Winemaker Jim Markeas **Est.** 2001 **Cases** 35 000
This is a modern version of a co-operative winery. Forty-five growers across the Adelaide Hills, Barossa Valley and Riverland, with 250 ha of grapes, supply the winery. They are also investors in the winery and have direct or indirect board representation. The directors bring together skills as grapegrowers, winemakers and international marketers and distributors. Thus the board is involved at every level, from growing to harvesting, winemaking and marketing of the portfolio. Exports to many countries: the US and the UK lead the way, but also with significant exports to Germany, Denmark and Asia.

▼▼▼▼ **Reserve Selection Adelaide Hills Sauvignon Blanc 2008** A bright, fresh low-alcohol style; minerally and citrus acidity lengthens the palate. Screwcap. 12% alc. **Rating** 87 **To** 2009 $15.20

Paragon Valley Premium Barossa Valley Shiraz 2005 Hazy colour; the super-ripe fruit does have some length, although it struggles with the alcohol. Screwcap. 15.5% alc. **Rating** 87 **To** 2015 $28

Wise Wine ★★★★★

Lot 4 Eagle Bay Road, Dunsborough, WA 6281 **Region** Margaret River
T (08) 9756 8627 **F** (08) 9756 8770 **www.**wisewine.com.au **Open** 7 days 10–5
Winemaker Jake Bacchus, Andrew Bromley **Est.** 1986 **Cases** 32 000 **Vyds** 16.6 ha
Wise Wine, headed by Perth entrepreneur Ron Wise, has been a remarkably consistent producer of high-quality wine. The vineyard adjacent to the winery in the Margaret River is supplemented by contract-grown grapes form Pemberton, Manjimup and Frankland. The estate plantings are (in descending order of size) shiraz, cabernet sauvignon, chardonnay, sauvignon blanc, merlot, verdelho, cabernet franc and zinfandel. Exports to the UK, the US and other major markets.

ΨΨΨΨΨ Eagle Bay Margaret River Semillon Sauvignon Blanc 2008 A great example of a barrel-fermented Semillon/Sauvignon Blanc that, despite fermentation in new French oak, is primarily driven by long and incisive citrus and gooseberry fruit, finishing with cleansing acidity. Screwcap. 13% alc. **Rating** 95 **To** 2015 $35

Eagle Bay Margaret River Shiraz 2007 Deep crimson-purple; a panoply of spice, plum, blackberry and cherry aromas and flavours, with an excellently complex, savoury finish. Much more intensity than the '05. Screwcap. 14.5% alc. **Rating** 95 **To** 2017 $30

Reserve Pemberton Chardonnay 2007 There is, indeed, a touch of custard apple to the bouquet, as suggested by the back label; the palate is complex, with some creamy/nutty overtones to the nectarine and citrus fruit; very good length. Screwcap. 14.5% alc. **Rating** 94 **To** 2017 $35

Shiraz 2007 Densely coloured; intense, spicy blackberry fruit aromas lead into a striking, full-bodied palate, with deep fruit and licorice supported by ripe tannins. Will be very long lived. Screwcap. 14.5% alc. **Rating** 94 **To** 2022 $19

Eagle Bay Margaret River Shiraz 2006 Deep, dark and concentrated; a very attractive cool and spicy perfume; medium-bodied, savoury and with lovely gravelly tannins rounding out a long, fresh and harmonious finish. Screwcap. 14.5% alc. **Rating** 94 **To** 2018 $30

Lot 80 Margaret River Cabernet Sauvignon 2007 Classic Margaret River cabernet; rippling layers of cassis, black cherry, blackcurrant, fine, but persistent, tannins and integrated oak. Screwcap. 14% alc. **Rating** 94 **To** 2020 $28

ΨΨΨΨΨ Eagle Bay Pemberton Chardonnay 2007 Has the typical finesse of the Wise Wine style; grapefruit and nectarine drive the palate, with its clear focus and brisk acidity. Screwcap. 14.5% alc. **Rating** 93 **To** 2016 $55

Rose 2008 Vivid, fuchsia-crimson; bright fresh red fruits, highly flavoured but without any sweetness; good length; crisp and vibrant. **Rating** 91 **To** 2010 $19

Semillon Sauvignon Blanc 2008 Tropical fruits in a gooseberry/passionfruit/kiwi fruit and guava range say more about ripe sauvignon blanc than semillon, but this is no bad thing. Screwcap. 13% alc. **Rating** 90 **To** 2011 $19

ΨΨΨΨ Pemberton Sauvignon Blanc 2008 Generous wine, with abundant fruit flavour in the middle of the tropical range, but is somewhat four square; the finish slightly congested. Screwcap. 13% alc. **Rating** 89 **To** 2010 $28

Cabernet Merlot 2007 Has spice and cedar overtones to the red and black fruits, with unusual touches of cherry; the tannins arrive late, but are too insistent for comfort. Screwcap. 14% alc. **Rating** 87 **To** 2016 $19

Witchcliffe Estate

Wickham Road, Witchcliffe, WA 6285 **Region** Margaret River
T (08) 9757 6279 **F** (08) 9757 6279 **www**.witchcliffe-estate.com.au **Open** 7 days (summer),
Wed–Sun (winter) 11–5
Winemaker Peter Stanlake **Est.** 2003 **Cases** 2000 **Vyds** 20 ha
While the establishment date of Witchcliffe Estate is shown as 2003, 8 ha of semillon,
sauvignon blanc, chardonnay and shiraz plantings date back to the early 1990s. Tony and
Maureen Cosby acquired the 69-ha property in 2000, at which time it was best known as the
Margaret River Marron Farm. The Cosbys still farm marron on a small scale, selling them at
the farm gate and through the cellar door. It has been a very impressive start.

ŶŶŶŶŶ **Margaret River Semillon Sauvignon Blanc 2008** Combines complexity with
elegance, due in part to 20% barrel ferment, and in part to the eloquence of the
tropical sauvignon blanc component; all hangs together well; ready to go at an
appealing price. Screwcap. 12.3% alc. **Rating** 91 **To** 2009 $16.50

ŶŶŶŶ **Sauvignon Blanc 2008** Some riesling-like notes to the bouquet and palate; has
abundant overall flavour. Screwcap. 12.3% alc. **Rating** 89 **To** 2010 $20
Margaret River Chardonnay 2006 Very developed given the screwcap; perhaps
a touch of botrytis; however, generous and ready to go. 13.9% alc. **Rating** 87
To 2010 $22.50

Witches Falls Winery

79 Main Western Road, North Tamborine, Qld 4272 **Region** Granite Belt
T (07) 5545 2609 **F** (07) 5545 0189 **www**.witchesfalls.com.au **Open** 7 days 10–4
Winemaker Jon Heslop, Richard Abraham **Est.** 2004 **Cases** 6500 **Vyds** 0.4 ha
This is the venture of Jon and Kim Heslop, and former Brisbane lawyer-turned-winemaker
Richard Abraham. Richard's conversion is more recent than that of Jon Heslop, who has
12 years' experience in the wine industry, the first three as a sales rep for Orlando Wyndham,
before realising he wanted to make his own wine, rather than sell someone else's. His career
began as a cellar hand with Richmond Grove, then on to the Hunter Valley as a winemaker
at Tamburlaine; he says 'I was influenced by Rod Kemp of Lake's Folly, PJ Charteris of
Brokenwood and Andrew Thomas of Thomas Wines', which is not a bad trio. In 2004 he
moved back to Qld with his wife to establish Witches Falls Winery, and was joined in '05
by Richard, who is currently undertaking a degree in applied science (oenology) at CSU; a
degree Jon already has under his belt. The only estate planting is a small amount durif; the
other wines are made from contract-grown grapes.

ŶŶŶŶŶ **Granite Belt Marsanne 2007** Pale colour; clean and focused pear fruit, with
a touch of almond; the palate is lively, fine, fresh and as clean as a whistle, with a
refreshing twist of burnt almond on the finish. Screwcap. 12.5% alc. **Rating** 90
To 2012 $25
Prophecy Unfiltered Granite Belt Merlot 2007 Good colour; polished black
and blue fruit bouquet with a hint of spice; quite firm and minerally on the palate;
good finish. Screwcap. 14.4% alc. **Rating** 90 **To** 2014 $45
Prophecy Granite Belt Cabernet Sauvignon 2006 Black fruit bouquet, with
quite spicy tones for the variety; warm-fruited and dark with some black olive
complexity, cassis and a slight tarry note to finish. Screwcap. 14.5% alc. **Rating** 90
To 2015 $45

ŶŶŶŶ **Clare Valley Riesling 2004** Toasty and developed with a core of sweet lemon
curd at the core; quite fresh and lively, with lingering toast on the finish. Screwcap.
12.2% alc. **Rating** 89 **To** 2013 $25
Granite Belt Chardonnay 2006 Deep colour; quite savoury/struck match
bouquet; good concentration and freshness; long and toasty with varietal stone
fruit intensity on the finish. Screwcap. 13.3% alc. **Rating** 89 **To** 2013 $18
Co-Inoculated Granite Belt Verdelho 2008 Vibrant colour; lifted and smoky
tropical fruit bouquet; quite juicy on the palate; a little simple. Screwcap. 14% alc.
Rating 87 **To** 2011 $18

Witchmount Estate

557 Leakes Road, Plumpton, Vic 3335 **Region** Sunbury
T (03) 9747 1055 **F** (03) 9747 1066 **www.**witchmount.com.au **Open** Wed–Sun 10–5
Winemaker Steve Goodwin **Est.** 1991 **Cases** 10 000 **Vyds** 31 ha

Gaye and Matt Ramunno operate Witchmount Estate in conjunction with its Italian restaurant and function rooms. The vineyard is planted (in descending order) to shiraz (13.5 ha), cabernet sauvignon (7 ha), pinot gris (3 ha), chardonnay (2 ha), with lesser amounts of sauvignon blanc, merlot, tempranillo and barbera. The quality of the wines has been consistently excellent, the prices very modest. Exports to Canada and Singapore.

ΨΨΨΨΨ **Olivia's Paddock Chardonnay 2008** Greater depth of colour and more complexity to the Lowen Park, thanks to barrel ferment and lees contact, although fruit is still the cornerstone of the wine. Screwcap. 14% alc. **Rating** 92 **To** 2016 $33

ΨΨΨΨ **Pinot Gris 2008** Hints of spice and herb with more conventional pear/apple aromas; the palate, too, has good drive. Screwcap. 13.8% alc. **Rating** 89 **To** 2010 $22
Lowen Park Sauvignon Blanc 2008 Clean, well made, with light but clear varietal fruit moving from tropical to herbal flavours. Screwcap. 13.5% alc. **Rating** 88 **To** 2010 $18
Lowen Park Chardonnay 2008 Fresh and lively; some melon adds a flavour dimension to the white peach and citrus base; light-bodied wine with zero oak impact. Screwcap. 14% alc. **Rating** 88 **To** 2013 $18

Wolf Blass

Bilyara Vineyards, 97 Sturt Highway, Nuriootpa, SA 5355 **Region** Barossa Valley
T (08) 8568 7300 **F** (08) 8568 7380 **www.**wolfblass.com.au **Open** Mon–Fri 9.15–5,
w'ends & public hols 10–5
Winemaker Chris Hatcher (Chief), Mat O'Leary, Marie Clay **Est.** 1966 **Cases** 4 million

Although merged with Mildara and now under the giant umbrella of Foster's, the brands (as expected) have been left largely intact. The wines are made at all price points, ranging through Red Label, Yellow Label, Gold Label, Brown Label, Grey Label, Black Label and Platinum Label, at one price point or another covering every one of the main varietals. The pre-eminent quality of the red wines has reasserted itself over the white wines, but without in any way diminishing the attraction the latter have. All of this has occurred under the leadership of Chris Hatcher, who has harnessed the talents of the winemaking team and encouraged the changes in style. Exports to all major markets.

ΨΨΨΨΨ **Platinum Label Barossa Shiraz 2006** Strong purple-crimson; from the first whiff to the finish and aftertaste, the wine has remarkable cohesion, line and balance; there are hints of spice to the essentially black fruits, the French oak evident but seamless, the mouthfeel supple and velvety; the finish with a dry, savoury twist, is just what was needed. Screwcap. 15% alc. **Rating** 96 **To** 2030 $158
White Label Specially Aged Release Eden Valley Riesling 2002 Has continued to evolve, with a striking herb, spice and lime blossom bouquet, the palate long and immaculately balanced. Clearly deserves higher points than originally given. Screwcap. **Rating** 95 **To** 2015 $39.99
Gold Label Clare Valley Eden Valley Riesling 2008 Lime blossom aromas lead into a very lively palate with great energy and precise thrust; the zesty, minerally finish and aftertaste lengthening and refreshing. A modern evocation of the variety. Screwcap. 11.5% alc. **Rating** 94 **To** 2017 $25.99

ΨΨΨΨΨ **Grey Label McLaren Vale Shiraz 2007** Dense colour; strongly regional and unapologetically full-bodied, dark chocolate and plum fruit is surrounded by generous, barrel ferment oak; gets away (just) with its alcohol. Screwcap. 15.5% alc. **Rating** 93 **To** 2027 $40.99
Yellow Label Shiraz 2007 This wine certainly keeps delivering; bright blackberry fruit, framed by well-handled oak and spice; the palate is very fresh and lively, and has a dense core of tarry fruit; very good winemaking and value. Screwcap. 13.5% alc. **Rating** 90 **To** 2014 $16.99

Gold Label Adelaide Hills Chardonnay 2008 Vibrant hue; yellow nectarine, grapefruit and a touch of spice; full and rich, with well-balanced acidity and a drawn out nutty finish. Screwcap. 13% alc. **Rating** 90 **To** 2013 $25.99

Gold Label Adelaide Hills Shiraz Viognier 2006 Vibrant crimson colour; a quite intense bouquet of red and black fruits, with a strong spicy component; good structure and length. Screwcap. 15% alc. **Rating** 90 **To** 2016 $25.99

ҮҮҮҮ **Gold Label Mount Gambier Sauvignon Blanc 2008** Early picking and the very cool climate of Mount Gambier have resulted in a zesty, crisp and lively palate, with a lemony finish. Slightly left of centre. Screwcap. 10.5% alc. **Rating** 89 **To** 2010 $25.99

Gold Label Pinot Chardonnay 2005 Quite fine and linear citrus fruit, with a touch of toast on the bouquet; a vibrant and clean palate, with an attractive dry, slightly chalky, finish. Cork. 12% alc. **Rating** 89 **To** 2012 $25.99

Red Label Cabernet Merlot 2007 Redcurrant and a splash of cassis; plummy, soft and forward with crisp acid to clean up. Screwcap. 13.5% alc. **Rating** 87 **To** 2012 $13.99

Yellow Label Cabernet Sauvignon 2007 A clean and polished red wine, not showing great varietal definition, but certainly showing some skill in winemaking. Screwcap. 13.5% alc. **Rating** 87 **To** 2012 $16.99

Wombat Lodge ★★★☆

PO Box 460 Cowaramup, WA 6284 **Region** Margaret River
T 0418 948 125 **F** (08) 9755 6070 **www**.wombatlodgewines.com.au **Open** Not
Winemaker Ian McIntosh, Ian Bell **Est.** 1997 **Cases** 600 **Vyds** 4 ha

It pays to have a keenly developed sense of humour if you are a small winemaker committed to producing the very best possible wine regardless of cost and market constraints. The short version (and I quote) is 'Warick (sic) Gerrard, owner/consumer; Jan McIntosh, winemaker and life partner; Danny Edwards, viticulture and adopted son; 60 ha of central Wilyabrup land, two houses and 60 cows; 4 ha of spoilt vines and 600 cases of red wine.' There is a much longer version, underlining Danny's freedom to organically grow the vines with limited irrigation limiting yield and maximising quality, and Jan MacIntosh's freedom to buy as much French oak as she wishes. The outcome is four clones of cabernet sauvignon, merlot, cabernet franc, malbec and petit verdot in the 600-case make up, selling for the ludicrously low price of $120 per case plus postage.

ҮҮҮҮҮ **Margaret River Cabernet Sauvignon Merlot Petit Verdot Malbec Cabernet Franc 2007** Bright purple-red; while medium-bodied at best, has very good balance and length to the array of red and black fruits, framed by fine, savoury tannins. Absolute bargain. Screwcap. 13.5% alc. **Rating** 90 **To** 2015 $10

ҮҮҮҮ **South Point Margaret River Cabernet Sauvignon Merlot Shiraz 2005** Retains good hue; savoury/foresty components have started to emerge on both bouquet and palate, although there are some red and black fruits to provide balance. Great value. Screwcap. 13.5% alc. **Rating** 89 **To** 2012 $10

Margaret River Cabernet Sauvignon Merlot 2005 Retains good hue; has attractive red fruit flavours on the bouquet and light- to medium-bodied palate. Particularly good value. Screwcap. 13.5% alc. **Rating** 88 **To** 2012 $10

South Point Margaret River Cabernet Sauvignon Merlot Shiraz 2007 Good colour; has more weight to the palate and its flavours than the cabernet blend, but slightly less complexity and finesse; nice wine and excellent value nonetheless. Screwcap. 13.5% alc. **Rating** 88 **To** 2014 $10

Wonga Estate ★★★★☆

204 Jumping Creek Road, Wonga Park, Vic 3115 **Region** Yarra Valley
T 0417 346 953 **www**.wongaestate.com.au **Open** By appt (7 days 10–5)
Winemaker Greg Roberts **Est.** 1997 **Cases** 1000 **Vyds** 2.5 ha

Greg and Jady Roberts developed their vineyard in 1997 with a minor expansion in 2002. The wines are made at the onsite micro-winery by Greg set among the pretty bushland surroundings of Wonga Park. Limited production has not stopped the listing of the wines at an impressive array of Melbourne, Yarra Valley and Brisbane restaurants.

ΨΨΨΨΨ **Yarra Valley Chardonnay 2008** Tightly wound, washed pebble and citrus bouquet; lemon zest on entry, with fine acidity, and a very long grilled nut conclusion; inspired by Chablis? Diam. 13% alc. **Rating** 94 **To** 2014 $35

ΨΨΨΨΨ **Heathcote Shiraz 2006** Bright colour; sage, blueberry, and a touch of Asian spice; warm and inviting palate weight, with quite a lavish fruit profile; a big wine, for big-wine lovers. Diam. 14.5% alc. **Rating** 91 **To** 2016 $60

Yarra Valley Pinot Noir 2008 Bright cherry fruit bouquet with a touch of undergrowth and spice; the light-bodied palate is velvet-like and textural, good persistence on the finish. Screwcap. 13% alc. **Rating** 90 **To** 2012 $15

ΨΨΨΨ **The Fugue 2006** An interesting wine showing a split personality; weight and power from the shiraz, and lightness from the pinot; lacks identity, but medium-bodied, clean and well made. Heathcote Shiraz/Yarra Valley Pinot Noir. Diam. 14.5% alc. **Rating** 89 **To** 2014 $75

Woodlands   ★★★★★

3948 Caves Road, Wilyabrup, WA 6284 **Region** Margaret River
T (08) 9755 6226 **F** (08) 9755 6236 **www**.woodlandswines.com **Open** 7 days 10.30–5
Winemaker Stuart Watson, Andrew Watson **Est.** 1973 **Cases** 8500 **Vyds** 18.87 ha

The quality of the grapes has never been in doubt. A priceless core of 6.8 ha of cabernet sauvignon planted more than 30 years ago, joined more recently by merlot, malbec, cabernet franc, pinot noir and chardonnay. The two estate vineyards (the second on Puzey Road, called Woodlands Brook Vineyard) are, except for 1 ha of chardonnay and pinot noir, planted to the Bordeaux varieties. Whatever the shortcomings of the 1990s, these days Woodlands is producing some spectacular wines in small quantities. The larger volume Cabernet Sauvignon is also of very high quality, and Woodlands is now a major player in the top echelon of Margaret River producers. Exports to the UK and other major markets.

ΨΨΨΨΨ **Chloe Reserve Margaret River Chardonnay 2007** A striking, high-quality wine, with tremendous drive and intensity to its nectarine and grapefruit base; this is in turn given complexity by barrel ferment and extended lees contact. Screwcap. 13.5% alc. **Rating** 96 **To** 2020 $55

Reserve de la Cave Margaret River Merlot 2007 The fragrant and aromatic bouquet is all merlot with its mix of cassis, blackcurrant and a twist of black olive and spice; the fluid, silky palate flows across the mouth with perfect weight and great length. Screwcap. 13.5% alc. **Rating** 96 **To** 2020 $60

Emily Special Reserve 2007 Very good hue and clarity; a fragrant and silky wine, which effortlessly captures the bouquet and palate with its array of cassis, raspberry and a touch of black olive. Merlot/Malbec/Cabernet Sauvignon. Screwcap. 13.5% alc. **Rating** 95 **To** 2022 $30

Reserve de la Cave Margaret River Cabernet Franc 2007 Vivid crimson-purple; a penetrating, ripe bouquet is followed by a silky, luscious palate, the tannins fine and ripe, the oak restrained. Masterly making. Screwcap. 13% alc. **Rating** 95 **To** 2020 $60

Margaret River Chardonnay 2008 Yet another example of the trend to earlier picking, the fruit flavours enhanced rather than diminished, the acidity fresh, and the oak restrained, all adding up to a very good wine. Screwcap. 13.5% alc. **Rating** 94 **To** 2016 $17.50

Margaret River Cabernet Sauvignon Merlot 2007 Youthful colour, with complex black olive and cassis aromas; savoury, deep and full of red fruits on the long, fine and focused finish. Screwcap. 13.5% alc. **Rating** 94 **To** 2017 $19

Margaret 2007 Crimson-red; an austere wine taking its cue from Bordeaux, partly from the savoury black fruits and partly from the tannins; deliberately early picked. Screwcap. 13.5% alc. **Rating** 94 **To** 2020 $39.50

Reserve de la Cave Margaret River Malbec 2007 Good colour; luscious plum and raspberry jam varietal fruit on the soft, medium-bodied palate. The best single-variety malbec in Australia, however oxymoronic that judgement may be; 300 bottles made. Screwcap. 13.5% alc. **Rating** 94 **To** 2017 $60

ΨΨΨΨΦ Reserve de la Cave Margaret River Pinot Noir 2007 A brave and largely successful attempt to make a silk purse out of a sow's ear (the climate of Margaret River); has excellent texture and mouthfeel; graceful and unforced; highly perceptive winemaking; 400 bottles made. Screwcap. 13% alc. **Rating** 92 **To** 2012 $60
Margaret River Cabernet Franc Merlot 2008 Youthful crimson-purple; while early bottled, is not callow, but the fruit flavours are razor sharp and clear, with cassis and hints of tobacco, the tannins controlled. Screwcap. 13.5% alc. **Rating** 92 **To** 2017 $20

ΨΨΨΨ Robert Margaret River Cabernet Sauvignon 2006 The wet vintage has stripped the wine of its usual colour and fruit flavour; everything that could be done in the winery was done. Screwcap. 13% alc. **Rating** 87 **To** 2013 $105

Woodside Valley Estate

PO Box 332, Greenwood, WA 6924 **Region** Margaret River
T (08) 9345 4065 **F** (08) 9345 4541 **www**.woodsidevalleyestate.com.au **Open** Not
Winemaker Kevin McKay **Est.** 1998 **Cases** 1500 **Vyds** 19.4 ha
Woodside Valley has been developed by a small syndicate of investors headed by Peter Woods. In 1998 they acquired 67 ha of land at Yallingup, and have now established chardonnay, sauvignon blanc, cabernet sauvignon, shiraz, malbec and merlot. The experienced Albert Haak is consultant viticulturist, and together with Peter, took the unusual step of planting south-facing in preference to north-facing slopes. In doing so they indirectly followed in the footsteps of the French explorer Thomas Nicholas Baudin, who mounted a major scientific expedition to Australia on his ship *The Geographe*, and defied established views and tradition of the time in (correctly) asserting that the best passage for sailing ships travelling between Cape Leeuwin and Bass Strait was from west to east. Exports to the UK, the US, Singapore, China and Japan.

ΨΨΨΨΨ Le Bas Margaret River Chardonnay 2007 Glorious mouthfeel jumps out at first taste; the very attractive bouquet forgotten; has all the effortless depth of Margaret River at its best, with peach and nectarine. Diam. 13.1% alc. **Rating** 96 **To** 2017 $48

ΨΨΨΨ Baudin Margaret River Cabernet Sauvignon 2006 Light colour; varietal flavour is there, but in a green spectrum, and without structure. Cork. 13.5% alc. **Rating** 87 **To** 2012 $65

Woodstock

Douglas Gully Road, McLaren Flat, SA 5171 **Region** McLaren Vale
T (08) 8383 0156 **F** (08) 8383 0437 **www**.woodstockwine.com.au **Open** 7 days 10–5
Winemaker Scott Collett, Ben Glaetzer **Est.** 1974 **Cases** 25 000 **Vyds** 16 ha
One of the stalwarts of McLaren Vale, producing archetypal and invariably reliable full-bodied red wines, spectacular botrytis sweet whites and high-quality (14-year-old) Tawny Port. Also offers a totally charming reception-cum-restaurant, which does a roaring trade with wedding receptions. Supplements its McLaren Vale vineyards with its Wirrega Vineyard in the Limestone Coast Zone. Exports to Northern Ireland, France, Denmark, Switzerland, Malaysia, Philippines, Hong Kong, Japan and Singapore.

ΨΨΨΨΦ McLaren Vale Cabernet Sauvignon 2006 Pure cassis and black olive bouquet, with just a hint of leaf involved; the palate is generous, but offers a strict backbone of tannin and acid, providing focus and persistence. Screwcap. 14.5% alc. **Rating** 93 **To** 2015 $22

The Stocks Single Vineyard McLaren Vale Shiraz 2006 A dark bouquet of confit blackberry, prune and chocolate; the palate shows a slight undergrowth complexity, which lifts the fruit and provides texture to balance the lavish oak treatment; bright and squeaky acid on the finish. Screwcap. 15% alc. **Rating** 92 **To** 2016 $60

Woody Nook   ★★★★

506 Metricup Road, Wilyabrup, WA 6280 **Region** Margaret River
T (08) 9755 7547 **F** (08) 9755 7007 **www**.woodynook.com.au **Open** 7 days 10–4.30
Winemaker Neil Gallagher **Est.** 1982 **Cases** 5000 **Vyds** 14.23 ha
This improbably named and not terribly fashionable winery has produced some truly excellent wines over the years, featuring in such diverse competitions as Winewise, the Sheraton Wine Awards and the WA Wine Show. Cabernet Sauvignon has always been its strong point, but it has a habit of also bobbing up with excellent white wines in various guises. Since 2000 owned by Peter and Jane Bailey; Neil Gallagher continues as viticulturist, winemaker and minority shareholder. Exports to the UK, the US, Canada, Bermuda, Singapore and Hong Kong.

 Gallagher's Choice Margaret River Cabernet Sauvignon 2005 A savoury bouquet of cedar, leaf and black olive; lively and fine, with layers of flavour opening across the palate; elegant and understated. Cork. 13.5% alc. **Rating** 93 **To** 2014 $34.95

Woolybud   ★★★

Playford Highway, Parndana, SA 5220 **Region** Kangaroo Island
T (08) 8559 6110 **F** (08) 8559 6031 **Open** Not
Winemaker Dudley Partners **Est.** 1998 **Cases** 1300
The Denis family moved to their sheep-farming property, Agincourt, west of Parndana, in 1986. Like many others, the downturn in the wool industry caused them to look to diversify their farming activities, and this led to the planting of cabernet sauvignon, shiraz and sauvignon blanc, and to the subsequent release of their Woolybud wines. The wines are available by mail order.

 Kangaroo Island Cabernet Sauvignon 2006 Good concentration of dark fruit, with a distinct leathery/savoury edge to the bouquet; a solid finish. Screwcap. 13.5% alc. **Rating** 87 **To** 2014 $19.50

Woongarra Estate   ★★★★

95 Hayseys Road, Narre Warren East, Vic 3804 **Region** Port Phillip Zone
T (03) 9796 8886 **www**.woongarrawinery.com.au **Open** Thurs–Sun 9–5 by appt
Winemaker Bruce Jones, Sergio Carlei, Mal Stewart **Est.** 1992 **Cases** 850 **Vyds** 5 ha
Dr Bruce Jones, and wife Mary, purchased their 16-ha property many years ago; it falls within the Yarra Ranges Shire Council's jurisdiction but not within the Yarra Valley wine region. In 1992 they planted 1 ha of sauvignon blanc, small patches of shiraz and a few rows of semillon. Over 1 ha of sauvignon blanc and pinot noir followed in 1996 (mostly MV6, and some French clone 114 and 115), with yet more 114 and 115 pinot noir in 2000, lifting total plantings to 3.2 ha of pinot noir, 1.4 ha of sauvignon blanc and a splash of the other two varieties. Success has also come with Three Wise Men Pinot Noir (a joint venture between Woongarra and Passing Clouds – see separate entry).

 Shiraz 2006 Good colour; spicy/savoury red and black fruits with a hint of mint adding a juicy quality to the medium-bodied palate before a slightly savoury finish. Excellent value. Screwcap. 14.6% alc. **Rating** 90 **To** 2016 $15

Word of Mouth Wines   ★★★★★

Campbell's Corner, 790 Pinnacle Road, Orange, NSW 2800 **Region** Orange
T (02) 6362 3509 **www**.wordofmouthwines.com.au **Open** Tues–Sat 11–5, Sun 11–3.30
Winemaker David Lowe, Jane Wilson (Contract) **Est.** 1991 **Cases** 2000 **Vyds** 11 ha

The 1991 plantings (made by the former Donnington Vineyard) have changed over the years, and, in particular, since the business was acquired by Word of Mouth Wines in 2003. Pinot gris, viognier, riesling, chardonnay, sauvignon blanc, merlot, pinot noir and cabernet sauvignon are all in bearing, and were joined by significant plantings of petit manseng and albarino in the winter of '08.

ΨΨΨΨΨ Orange Sauvignon Blanc 2008 Voluminous aromas of grass, nettle and passionfruit lead into a remarkably intense and long palate, with an exceptional aftertaste. Orange strikes again. Outstanding bargain. Screwcap. 13.1% alc.
Rating 95 To 2011 $25
Orange Riesling 2008 Light straw-green; delicate perfumed apple blossom aromas, then a delicious change of pace to lime juice on the palate; perfect balance of acidity and a little residual sugar. Screwcap. 12.6% alc. Rating 94 To 2018 $23

ΨΨΨΨΥ Pinnacle Orange Pinot Gris 2008 A very good pinot gris that has the personality and flavour almost all lack; vibrant pear, apple and citrus aromas and flavours; has a particularly long palate and finish, grading to grapefruit. Screwcap. 13.1% alc. Rating 92 To 2011 $25
Orange Viognier 2008 The Orange climate and skilful winemaking invest the wine with a juicy vibrancy that is most appealing, but isn't especially varietal; that is a downside well worth the price, and some patience. Screwcap. 13.3% alc.
Rating 90 To 2012 $23

Wordsworth Wines

Cnr South Western Highway/Thompson Road, Harvey, WA 6220 **Region** Geographe
T (08) 9733 4576 **F** (08) 9733 4269 **www**.wordsworthwines.com.au **Open** 7 days 10–5
Winemaker Lamont's, Western Range Wines **Est.** 1997 **Cases** 5000
David Wordsworth has established a substantial business in a relatively short space of time: 27 ha of vines have been planted, with cabernet sauvignon (10 ha), shiraz (5 ha) and verdelho (4 ha) predominant, and lesser amounts of zinfandel, petit verdot, chardonnay and chenin blanc. The winery features massive jarrah beams, wrought iron and antique furniture, and the tasting room seats 80 people. The wines have had show success. Exports to the US.

ΨΨΨΨΥ Geographe Zinfandel 2006 Good, bright colour; has come through a difficult vintage with flying colours, featuring lush red fruits and a carpet of spice; in zinfandel fashion, carries its alcohol with contemptuous ease. Screwcap. 15.5% alc.
Rating 92 To 2013 $30

ΨΨΨΨ Liqueur Zinfandel NV Obviously enough, an oddity, but works better than expected; the spirit largely behind the scenes, the foreground like Cherry Ripe, the chocolate exterior quite evident. Screwcap. 18% alc. Rating 87 To 2010 $25

Wovenfield Wines

Lot 1117 Henty Road, Dardanup, WA 6236 **Region** Geographe
T (08) 9728 0317 **F** (08) 9481 3076 **www**.wovenfield.com **Open** W'ends 11–5
Winemaker Damien Hutton, Rienne Buck **Est.** 1997 **Cases** 600 **Vyds** 16 ha
Martin Buck, together with daughter Rienne, purchased an old dairy farm in 1996, and with advice from experienced local viticulturist, Phil Gumbrell, came up with a three-stage planting program. Five hectares of shiraz and semillon were planted in 1997; 7.5 ha of merlot and cabernet sauvignon in '98; and in 2002 a further 3.5-ha, northwest-facing paddock was partially planted with viognier on a trial basis, the planting extended in '05 after a successful outcome. Nor have they rested there; in 2004 1.85 ha of merlot and cabernet sauvignon were grafted over to sauvignon blanc, and a small amount of tempranillo planted. They have also formed a highly successful winemaking team, the wines made at the small winery established on the property. A new cellar door is scheduled to open in late 2009. Exports to Singapore.

ŸŸŸŸ̉ Cabernet Rose 2007 Very pale pink; the eloquent bouquet has tangy/savoury aromas unique to cabernet rose; the palate and finish are bone-dry, the restrained alcohol making this a top food style at an enticing price. Screwcap. 12.5% alc. Rating 90 To 2009 $13
Sauvignon Blanc 2008 Crisp, clean and delicate throughout, with just a hint of tropical fruit on the palate, which finishes (and lengthens) with citrussy acidity. Screwcap. 12.3% alc. **Rating** 90 **To** 2010 $18

ŸŸŸŸ Viognier 2008 There is some varietal character in the light peach and apricot flavours on the palate, and a touch of fresh ginger on the aftertaste. Screwcap. 14.3% alc. **Rating** 89 **To** 2012 $20
Single Vineyard Reserve Shiraz Viognier 2007 Attractive red-purple; the wine is fragrant, the palate with distinct spicy notes, but not quite enough fruit to balance the slightly dry tannins on the finish. Screwcap. 14.5% alc. **Rating** 88 **To** 2014 $30
Verdelho 2008 Has more structure than many, with a twist of lemon on the fruit salad core. Screwcap. 13.9% alc. **Rating** 87 **To** 2012 $15

Wright Family Wines

'Misty Glen', 293 Deasey Road, Pokolbin, NSW 2320 **Region** Lower Hunter Valley
T (02) 4998 7781 **F** (02) 4998 7768 **www**.mistyglencottage.com.au **Open** 7 days 10–4
Winemaker Contract **Est.** 1985 **Cases** 1600 **Vyds** 6.6 ha
Jim and Carol Wright purchased their property in 1985, with a small existing vineyard in need of tender loving care. This was duly given, and the semillon, chardonnay and cabernet sauvignon revived. In 2000, 1.5 ha of shiraz was planted; 1.5 ha of chambourcin was added in '02. Carol has been involved in the wine industry since the early 1970s, and is now helped by husband Jim (who retired from the coal mines in '02), and by children and grandchildren. Wines are released under the Misty Glen Cottage label.

ŸŸŸŸ Misty Glen Cottage Hunter Valley Semillon 2008 Developed green-gold; must have been heavily worked in the winery, with the possibility of botrytis also intruding; flavoursome, but finishes short. Screwcap. 10.5% alc. **Rating** 87 **To** 2012 $26.50
Misty Glen Cottage Hunter Valley Cabernet Sauvignon 2007 Sweet cassis fruit on the bouquet and early palate falls away somewhat on the finish, moving to sweetness without the fruit; doubtless has cellar door appeal. Screwcap. 13% alc. **Rating** 87 **To** 2014 $35

Wroxton Wines

Flaxman's Valley Road, Angaston, SA 5353 **Region** Eden Valley
T (08) 8565 3227 **F** (08) 8565 3312 **www**.wroxton.com.au **Open** By appt
Winemaker Henschke (Riesling), Rusden Wines (Shiraz) **Est.** 1995 **Cases** 60 **Vyds** 37.3 ha
Ian and Jo Zander are third-generation grapegrowers on the 200-ha Wroxton Grange property, which was established in 1845 in the high country of the Eden Valley. The Zander family purchased the property in 1920, and planted their first vines that year; since '73 an extensive planting program has seen the progressive establishment of riesling (15.4 ha), shiraz (10.5 ha), chardonnay (6.9 ha), semillon (2.5 ha) and traminer (2 ha). The majority of the grapes are sold, the best parcels from the mature vineyards retained to produce single-vineyard wines.

ŸŸŸŸ̉ Single Vineyard Eden Valley Riesling 2006 Bright green-straw; a potent bouquet with lime and a hint of kerosene development; the palate is full-flavoured and long. Screwcap. 12.5% alc. **Rating** 90 **To** 2015 $25

Wyndham Estate

700 Dalwood Road, Dalwood, NSW 2335 **Region** Lower Hunter Valley
T (02) 4938 3444 **www**.wyndhamestate.com **Open** 7 days 10–4.30 except public hols
Winemaker Nigel Dolan **Est.** 1828 **Cases** 1 million

This historic property is now merely a shop front for the Wyndham Estate label. The Bin wines often surprise with their quality, representing excellent value; the Show Reserve wines, likewise, can be very good. The wines come from various parts of South Eastern Australia, sometimes specified, sometimes not. The wines are all made in the Barossa Valley, as from 2009 under the vastly experienced Nigel Dolan, long-term winemaker at Saltram and thereafter Group Red Winemaker with Foster's, before moving to Wyndham Estate. It's easy to dismiss these wines with faint praise, which does no justice whatsoever to their quality and their value for money.

ΨΨΨΨ **Black Cluster Hunter Valley Shiraz 2005** Good colour; very attractive and immaculately balanced wine, showing the great vintage to full advantage; silky blackberry and black cherry fruit, satin tannins and good oak. Cork. 13.5% alc. Rating 95 To 2015 $67

George Wyndham Shiraz Cabernet 2006 Pencilly lead oak sits atop a range of fruit from cassis to blackberry, and an undertone of mineral; the palate is fleshy on entry but firms quickly, with ample levels of tannin on display; the fruit quality should see this wine have a long and fruitful future. Screwcap. 15% alc. Rating 94 To 2020 $21.60

ΨΨΨΨΨ **McLaren Vale Shiraz 2006** Rich, vibrant and full of sweet fruit, mocha and gently toasty oak; quite oaky on the palate, the fruit holds its own and delivers generous flavour on the long and even conclusion. Screwcap. 14.9% alc. Rating 93 To 2016 $37.99

George Wyndham Founder's Reserve Semillon Sauvignon Blanc 2008 It is not explained how George Wyndham, who died well over a century ago, needs a reserve wine, as he was not a Pharaoh. Nonetheless a bright and zesty wine with all the right flavours. Screwcap. 13% alc. Rating 92 To 2010 $21.60

George Wyndham Shiraz Grenache 2006 A mix of tarry and sweet fruit aromas; the palate is quite rich, and saturated with sweet red and black fruits, and a touch of oak on the finish. Follows on the multi-trophy-winning '05. Cork. 15% alc. Rating 91 To 2014 $21.60

George Wyndham Founder's Reserve Shiraz 2005 Lifted, vibrant red and black fruit aromas come through on the palate, and are joined by persistent tannins that just stay within the bounds of balance. Screwcap. 14.5% alc. Rating 90 To 2020 $20

ΨΨΨΨ **Bin 111 Verdelho 2008** A full-flavoured verdelho, with an abundance of tropical fruit salad/pineapple fruit; ready now. Screwcap. 13% alc. Rating 89 To 2010 $16

Bin 333 Pinot Noir 2007 A sign of the times, for it is clearly sourced from appropriate areas; certainly it is light-bodied, but the flavours are correct; nice entry point wine. Screwcap. 13% alc. Rating 87 To 2009 $14.95

Coonawarra Shiraz 2006 Quite minty and a little coarse on opening; blueberry fruits with plenty of mint dominate; the palate is quite fleshy with grainy tannins coming through as the fruit subsides; needs time to integrate. Screwcap. 14.9% alc. Rating 87 To 2014 $37.99

Wynns Coonawarra Estate ★★★★★

Memorial Drive, Coonawarra, SA 5263 **Region** Coonawarra
T (08) 8736 2225 **F** (08) 8736 2208 **www**.wynns.com.au **Open** 7 days 10–5
Winemaker Sue Hodder, Sarah Pidgeon **Est.** 1897 **Cases** NFP
Large-scale production has not prevented Wynns from producing excellent wines covering the full price spectrum, from the bargain basement Riesling and Shiraz through to the deluxe John Riddoch Cabernet Sauvignon and Michael Shiraz. Even with steady price increases, Wynns offers extraordinary value for money. The large investments since 2000 in rejuvenating and replanting key blocks under the direction of Allen Jenkins, and skilled winemaking by Sue Hodder, has resulted in wines of far greater finesse and elegance than most of their predecessors. Exports to the UK, the US and Canada.

ŦŦŦŦŦ **Michael Limited Release Shiraz 2005** Amazing colour, and a bouquet to match; explosive dark fruit and oak aromas jump out of the glass and assault the senses, and then caress the palate with beautiful fruit delineation and intensity; appropriate oak for the fruit is the key to this wine. Screwcap. 14.5% alc. **Rating** 97 **To** 2025 $75.99

Cabernet Sauvignon 2006 Bright red-purple; a striking and fragrant bouquet, with blackcurrant, earth and cedar aromas; the palate moves onto a different plane, with considerable tannin-derived structure that has an earthy/savoury regional profile; serious wine. Screwcap. 14% alc. **Rating** 95 **To** 2016 $31.99

The Gables Cabernet Shiraz 2006 Deep, bright colour; complex medium- to full-bodied wine with abundant blackberry and blackcurrant fruit perfectly balanced by tannins; good oak handling. Will age superbly. Cellar door special. Screwcap. 14% alc. **Rating** 95 **To** 2026 $45

ŦŦŦŦŦ **Riesling 2008** Delicate floral blossom in apple/citrus spectrum are repeated on the palate, which is fine and crisp; firm finish underwrites cellaring potential. Screwcap. 13% alc. **Rating** 93 **To** 2018 $19.99

Shiraz 2007 Good purple-red; nicely ripened plum and blackberry fruit on the bouquet leads into a well-balanced palate with good texture, and savoury/spicy tannins. Screwcap. 14% alc. **Rating** 92 **To** 2020 $19.99

Riesling 2007 Bright pale straw; flowery apple blossom aromas; a delicate, elegant palate, still evolving, and needs more time to reveal all within. Screwcap. 12% alc. **Rating** 91 **To** 2018 $13.99

Cabernet Shiraz Merlot 2007 Good colour; the wine is full of fresh, juicy red and black fruit flavours, but with enough structure from fine tannins to underwrite future development. Screwcap. 14% alc. **Rating** 90 **To** 2015 $19.99

ŦŦŦŦ **Chardonnay 2008** A full rich style, with plenty of toasty oak framing the ripe peach and fig fruit; quite lively on the palate, with tangy acidity cleaning up the finish. Screwcap. 13% alc. **Rating** 89 **To** 2012 $19.99

Xabregas ★★★★

Cnr Spencer Road/Hay River Road, Narrikup, WA 6326 **Region** Great Southern **T** (08) 9321 2366 **www.**xabregas.com.au **Open** By appt tel 0409 532 255 **Winemaker** The Vintage Wineworx (Greg Jones) **Est.** 1996 **Cases** 18 000 **Vyds** 125.14 ha In 1996 stockbrokers Terry Hogan and Eve Broadley, the major participants in the Spencer Wine Joint Venture, commenced a viticulture business that has now grown into three vineyards on sites 10 km south of Mount Barker. The varieties planted are riesling, chardonnay, sauvignon blanc, cabernet sauvignon, cabernet franc, merlot and shiraz. As well as being contract growers to Houghton, Howard Park and Forest Hill, they act as contract managers to surrounding vineyards, and are investors in the Vintage Wineworx contract winemaking facility. The wines are modestly priced. Exports to the UK, the US, Canada, China and NZ.

ŦŦŦŦŦ **Riesling 2008** Lively, crisp, fresh, minerally and citrussy; bright and incisive finish and aftertaste. Screwcap. 11.5% alc. **Rating** 93 **To** 2012 $16.99

Show Reserve Chardonnay 2007 Has well-controlled barrel ferment inputs to nectarine fruit; good line and balance. Screwcap. 13.5% alc. **Rating** 93 **To** 2013 $26.99

Show Reserve Cabernet Sauvignon 2007 Full-bodied; somewhat extractive at this point; long cellaring should help greatly, for the wine has all the right ingredients. Gold WA Wine Show '08. Screwcap. 14.5% alc. **Rating** 93 **To** 2020 $26.99

Show Reserve Shiraz 2007 Very big, solid, slightly extractive, oaky style that will calm down with age. Screwcap. 15% alc. **Rating** 90 **To** 2017 $26.99

Xanadu Wines

Boodjidup Road, Margaret River, WA 6285 **Region** Margaret River
T (08) 9758 9500 **F** (08) 9757 3389 **www**.xanaduwines.com **Open** 7 days 10–5
Winemaker Glenn Goodall **Est.** 1977 **Cases** 70 000 **Vyds** 109.5 ha
Xanadu fell prey to over-ambitious expansion and to the increasingly tight trading conditions
in 2005 as wine surpluses hit hard. The assets were acquired by the Rathbone Group,
completing the Yering Station/Mount Langi Ghiran/Parker Coonawarra Estate/Xanadu
group. The prime assets were (and are) the 110 ha of vineyards and a winery to match. The
increasing production is matched by exports to most major markets.

ŸŸŸŸŸ Dragon Margaret River Cabernet Merlot 2005 Bright colour; a fresh,
elegant medium-bodied style; nicely savoury/spicy notes frame a juicy fruit core.
Gold WA Wine Show '08. 14% alc. **Rating** 94 **To** 2018 $16

ŸŸŸŸŸ Margaret River Sauvignon Blanc Semillon 2008 A clean bouquet hints
at the flavours of citrus, stone fruit and kiwi fruit on the palate, the texture and
structure suggesting a touch of oak; good length and balance. Screwcap. 13% alc.
Rating 93 **To** 2011 $25
Margaret River Chardonnay 2007 Restrained nectarine, grapefruit and spice
bouquet; lively and focused grapefruit on the palate; clean, fresh and bright on the
finish. Screwcap. 13.5% alc. **Rating** 93 **To** 2015 $25
Margaret River Chardonnay 2006 Highly focused and precise, the nectarine
and melon fruit on the medium-bodied palate driving through to the lingering
finish. Screwcap. 13.5% alc. **Rating** 93 **To** 2016 $25
Limited Release Cabernet Sauvignon 2007 Good concentration, with highly
polished cassis fruit coming to the fore; well constructed, it ticks all the boxes but
fails to deliver the knockout blow. Screwcap. 14% alc. **Rating** 93 **To** 2015 $65
Dragon Margaret River Cabernet Sauvignon 2007 Bright, focused cassis
and cedar fruit with just a touch of black olive; the palate is ample, yet tightens up
on the finish, with plenty of fine-grained tannins coming to the fore; very good
value for money. Screwcap. 14% alc. **Rating** 92 **To** 2016 $16
Margaret River Cabernet Sauvignon 2005 Classic Margaret River cabernet,
with a mix of blackcurrant, black olive and briar, the tannins savoury but balanced;
will evolve further. Screwcap. 14% alc. **Rating** 92 **To** 2015 $25
Margaret River Sauvignon Blanc Semillon 2007 A complex wine, with very
good texture aided by a small portion of barrel ferment; the herb, grass and citrus
flavours are still in ascendancy. Screwcap. 13% alc. **Rating** 91 **To** 2010 $25
Margaret River Chardonnay 2008 Restrained grapefruit and nectarine
bouquet, complemented by a little spice; the stone fruits come out on the palate,
with a fleshy and toasty finish. Screwcap. 14% alc. **Rating** 91 **To** 2014 $25
Viognier 2008 Highly aromatic lemon zest aromas carry through onto the palate
with just a hint of phenolics. Screwcap. 14.5% alc. **Rating** 91 **To** 2011 $25
Margaret River Shiraz 2007 Dominated by pencilly oak, there is plenty of
vibrant and savoury red fruit; oaky on the palate, but time should see integration
and a resultant cohesive product. Screwcap. 14% alc. **Rating** 91 **To** 2018 $25
Dragon Margaret River Unoaked Chardonnay 2008 A fragrant bouquet
leads into a lively, fresh palate, which has considerable drive and length to the
white peach and citrus flavours; clean finish. Screwcap. 13% alc. **Rating** 90
To 2013 $16
Next of Kin Shiraz 2007 Vibrant red fruit, sage and a touch of spice; medium-
bodied with gravelly tannins and crisp acidity on the finish. Screwcap. 14% alc.
Rating 90 **To** 2015 $16
Dragon Margaret River Shiraz 2007 Pleasant medium-bodied shiraz with
good balance but not enough intensity for higher points. Screwcap. 14% alc.
Rating 90 **To** 2015 $16
Margaret River Cabernet Sauvignon 2007 Ripe, sweet and supple with
good texture; a very accessible style. Screwcap. 14% alc. **Rating** 90 **To** 2014 $25

Yabby Lake Vineyard ★★★★★

1 Garden Street, South Yarra, Vic 3141 (postal) **Region** Mornington Peninsula
T (03) 9251 5375 **F** (03) 9639 1540 **www.**yabbylake.com **Open** Not
Winemaker Tom Carson, Tod Dexter, Larry McKenna (Consultant) **Est.** 1998 **Cases** 3350
This high-profile wine business is owned by Robert and Mem Kirby (of Village Roadshow)
who have been landowners in the Mornington Peninsula for decades. In 1998 they established
Yabby Lake Vineyard, under the direction of vineyard manager Keith Harris; the vineyard is on
a north-facing slope, capturing maximum sunshine while also receiving sea breezes. The main
focus is the 21 ha of pinot noir, 10 ha of chardonnay and 5 ha of pinot gris; the 2 ha each of
shiraz and merlot take a back seat. Tod Dexter (former long-term winemaker at Stonier) and
Larry McKenna (ex Martinborough Vineyards and now the Escarpment in NZ) both have
great experience. The arrival of the hugely talented Tom Carson as Group Winemaker can
only add lustre to the winery and its wines. Robert has taken the ultimate step of opening
the Yabby Lake Cellar Door Wine Bars in China, the first in Beijing, with others planned
to follow; although whether the parlous state of the economy will slow down the roll-out
remains to be seen.

ΨΨΨΨΨ **Red Claw Mornington Peninsula Sauvignon Blanc 2008** Clean and varietal,
with defined aromas of gooseberry and a touch of nettle; good texture on the
palate, and cleansing, slightly raspy, acidity on the finish. Screwcap. 13.5% alc.
Rating 94 **To** 2012 $24
Red Claw Heathcote Shiraz 2007 Dark colour; blue and black fruits, with a
slight tarry edge to the aromas; dried herbs and black fruits marry on the palate,
oak playing a fine supporting role. Screwcap. 14% alc. **Rating** 94 **To** 2016 $26.50

ΨΨΨΨΨ **Red Claw Mornington Peninsula Pinot Gris 2008** Vibrant and fresh pear
fruit bouquet, with just a hint of vanillin oak in the background; rich and
ample on entry, with good concentration and depth on offer. Screwcap. 14% alc.
Rating 90 **To** 2012 $30

Yaccaroo Wines ★★★★☆

PO Box 201, Yankalilla, SA 5203 **Region** Southern Fleurieu
T (08) 8558 3218 **Open** Not
Winemaker Contract **Est.** 2004 **Cases** 250 **Vyds** 2 ha
Gavin and Julianne Schubert planted 2 ha of shiraz in 1998; the original intention was to
simply sell the grapes, but oversupply in the grape market has led to part of the production
being made under the Yaccaroo label.

ΨΨΨΨΨ **Southern Fleurieu Shiraz 2007** A fragrant bouquet of spice, licorice and black
fruits leads into a fresh, well-balanced and textured palate with some delicious
juicy notes of red cherry; fine tannins and subtle oak. Screwcap. 14.8% alc. **Rating**
94 **To** 2017 $18

Yalumba ★★★★★

Eden Valley Road, Angaston, SA 5353 **Region** Barossa Valley
T (08) 8561 3200 **F** (08) 8561 3393 **www.**yalumba.com **Open** 7 days 10–5
Winemaker Louisa Rose (chief), Brian Walsh, Peter Gambetta **Est.** 1849 **Cases** 950 000
Vyds 107 ha
Family-owned and run by Robert Hill Smith, Yalumba has long had a commitment to quality
and has shown great vision in its selection of vineyard sites, new varieties and brands. It has
always been a serious player at the top end of full-bodied (and full-blooded) Australian reds,
and was the pioneer in the use of screwcaps. While its estate vineyards are largely planted to
mainstream varieties, it has taken marketing ownership of Viognier. However, these days its
own brands revolve around the Y Series and a number of stand-alone brands across the length
and breadth of SA. Yalumba has been very successful in building its export base. Exports to
all major markets.

ΨΨΨΨΨ **Single Site Bartholomaeous Vineyard Eden Valley Shiraz 2006** The bouquet offers spiced redcurrant fruit, with a touch of bramble and a mere suggestion of oak; poised and precise, with fine acidity, fine-grained tannin, and a savoury edge to the fruit that is completely alluring; elegance and power, seamlessly combined. Cork. 14.5% alc. **Rating** 96 **To** 2025 $80

The Octavius Old Vine Barossa Shiraz 2005 Impenetrable colour; the concentration of old vine material is without question, and the array of dark fruit is beautifully framed by the oak; essency on the palate with generous levels of fruit simply swallowing the new oak; dark, tarry, earthy and very complex finish; the wine is massively proportioned, but superbly put together. Cork. 14.5% alc. **Rating** 96 **To** 2035 $99.95

The Reserve 2002 Very good colour for age, still showing strong red hues; intense, long and highly focused palate with a succulent mix of blackcurrant and blackberry fruit supported by cedar oak and a fine web of tannins. Cork. 14% alc. **Rating** 96 **To** 2017 $109.95

The Virgilius Eden Valley Viognier 2007 Yalumba has got the handling of this challenging variety down pat; mouthfilling yet not phenolic, with apricot and almond flavours coursing through the length of a long palate. Screwcap. 14.5% alc. **Rating** 95 **To** 2012 $49.95

Single Site Fromm Vineyard Lyndoch Shiraz 2006 Rich, dark mocha bouquet, with tar and earth, and an abundance of ripe blackberry fruit; the palate is dense and chewy, plenty of toasty oak providing a framework for the fruit to weave through; surprisingly elegant and poised on the finish; the muscle on show is quite impressive, and completely in balance. Cork. 14.5% alc. **Rating** 95 **To** 2025 $80

Single Site Fromm Vineyard Lyndoch Shiraz 2005 Very bright colour; a strong showing of abundant black fruits, with red fruit in support; plenty of oak, but the fruit swallows it with ease; the palate is generous and rich, yet lively and fine; great fruit definition being the key to this well-crafted wine. Cork. 14.5% alc. **Rating** 95 **To** 2020 $80

Hand Picked Barossa Shiraz Viognier 2006 An imposing wine of undoubted concentration and class; red fruits sit comfortably on top of darker notes, with a strong mineral element coming through the floral fruit. Cork. 14.5% alc. **Rating** 95 **To** 2020 $29.95

Tri-Centenary Vineyard Vine Vale Grenache 2005 Chock full of dark fruits, and quite slippery in texture; vibrant, pure, long and with just a little exotic spice adding a fine accent to the ample finish. Cork. 14.5% alc. **Rating** 95 **To** 2015 $75

Ringbolt Margaret River Cabernet Sauvignon 2007 A poised bouquet of cassis and cedar and a lovely note of violets; equally as attractive on the palate, the balance between fruit, acid, oak and tannin is impeccable; very long and varietal, with refreshing tannin and fruit. Cork. 14.5% alc. **Rating** 95 **To** 2020 $24.95

FDW[7c] Adelaide Hills Chardonnay 2007 A very fine, even and quite elegant style; melon and nectarine, with very fine acidity, and quite unencumbered by lavish winemaking; lovely purity. Screwcap. 13% alc. **Rating** 94 **To** 2017 $24.95

Hand Picked Barossa Shiraz Viognier 2007 Bright colour; oak sits atop the blue and black fruit on show, with an element of spice and violet; truly medium-bodied; silky texture, and a slow expansion of flavours from earth, tar, bramble and redcurrant; long, poised and very fine. Cork. 14.5% alc. **Rating** 94 **To** 2018 $29.95

The Signature Barossa Cabernet Shiraz 2005 Good bright colour; a fragrant bouquet, with a cascade of red and black fruits coursing through the medium-bodied palate, with notes of chocolate and vanilla on the finish. Cork. 14.5% alc. **Rating** 94 **To** 2015 $46.95

FDR1A Barossa Cabernet Shiraz 2004 Fragrant cedar, spice and black fruits on the bouquet, with added nuances of licorice and chocolate on the long, even flow of the palate; fine, ripe tannins. Cork. 13.5% alc. **Rating** 94 **To** 2017 $36.95

ΨΨΨΨΨ **Wild Ferment Eden Valley Chardonnay 2008** Restrained white peach and nectarine bouquet; light and airy on the palate, with weight building toward the conclusion; pure, fine and focused. Screwcap. 13.5% alc. **Rating** 93 **To** 2014 $18.95

Y Series Viognier 2008 An exotic bouquet of apricot kernel, cinnamon and some white pepper; generous and thickly textured, with good persistence and freshness on the finish; a terrific example of the variety, and very well priced; enjoy in the full flush of youth. Screwcap. 14.5% alc. **Rating** 93 **To** 2012 $12.95

Eden Valley Viognier 2007 Verges on aristocratic, with razor sharp varietal character on bouquet and palate, then quite a savoury finish. This is a rare food-style Viognier. Screwcap. 14.5% alc. **Rating** 93 **To** 2012 $22.95

Barossa Shiraz Viognier 2006 A stylish wine, with bramble notes alongside blackberry fruit and ironstone; oak comes forward on the palate, supported by mocha, leather and chocolate. Screwcap. 14% alc. **Rating** 93 **To** 2016 $19.95

Single Site Hahn Farm Vineyard Light Pass Shiraz 2006 Bright colour; an aromatic blend of red fruit, blackberry, mocha and toasty oak combine effortlessly; the palate is dense and dark on entry, with red fruit providing light on the back-palate; tannic and quite oaky, but the fruit is there to handle the extract. Cork. 14.5% alc. **Rating** 93 **To** 2025 $80

The Octavius Old Vine Barossa Shiraz 2004 Plenty of oak comes through on the bouquet, but the power of the wine is unmistakable; layered with flavour and aroma, this is built on sheer brute force. Cork. 14.5% alc. **Rating** 93 **To** 2019 $99.95

Patchwork Barossa Shiraz 2007 Bright colour; black plum and raspberry bouquet with a touch of toasty oak; the palate is very fresh and lively, pure fruit coming to the fore; quite long and luscious, a touch of sage providing interest on the finish. Screwcap. 14% alc. **Rating** 92 **To** 2018 $19.95

Patchwork Barossa Shiraz 2006 Rich wine; a mosaic of enticing fruit flavours reflecting the very different vineyard sources; lightens off fractionally on the finish. Screwcap. 14.5% alc. **Rating** 92 **To** 2016 $19.95

The Scribbler Cabernet Sauvignon Shiraz 2006 A wine showing plenty of depth, richness and generosity; dark fruits dominate, with a delicate lick of oak; clean and long on the juicy, tannic finish. Cork. 14.5% alc. **Rating** 92 **To** 2014 $19.95

Galway Vintage Traditional Shiraz 2008 Bright colour; spicy and pure blackberry fruit bouquet; very juicy palate, lively mouthfeel, and fleshy fruit on the finish. Great value. Screwcap. 14% alc. **Rating** 91 **To** 2014 $14.95

Y Series Riesling 2008 An intense bouquet with crushed citrus leaf/lemon zest aromas; the palate is refined and elegant in a light-bodied mode. Top value. Screwcap. 12% alc. **Rating** 91 **To** 2013 $12.95

Wild Ferment Eden Valley Chardonnay 2007 Vibrant depth and weight, and a little mineral complexity; the oak only starts to assert itself on the finish as the fine citrus fruit dissipates. Screwcap. 13.5% alc. **Rating** 91 **To** 2013 $18.95

Y Series Shiraz Viognier 2008 Bright purple; a lifted bouquet with stone fruit dominating the blackberry at this point; the palate switches this around, with a distinctly darker personality coming through on the finish; an alluring combination of aroma and flavour. Screwcap. 14% alc. **Rating** 91 **To** 2014 $12.95

Y Series Langhorne Creek Vermentino 2008 The voluminous, fragrant bouquet comes as the first surprise, the tangy, lively citrus and fruit salad palate, the second. And if you didn't know the price in advance, that would be the biggest surprise of all. Don't dilly dally, drink it up. Screwcap. 11.5% alc. **Rating** 90 **To** 2010 $12.95

Y Series Shiraz 2007 It is hard to imagine how much more can be expected at this price (doubtless lower still in the discount warehouses); supple and smooth black fruits on a medium-bodied palate. Screwcap. 13.5% alc. **Rating** 90 **To** 2012 $12.95

Y Series Barossa Pinot Grigio 2008 Has personality and flavour; pear and a little citrus, with a strong mineral component coming through on the palate; good texture and life on the finish. Screwcap. 12.5% alc. **Rating** 90 **To** 2010 $12.95

Organic McLaren Vale Shiraz 2005 Lifted aromas ranging through raspberry, blackberry and dark chocolate, precisely replayed on the palate; doubtless aimed at export markets. Cork. 14.5% alc. **Rating** 90 **To** 2014 $17.95

Single Site Hahn Farm Vineyard Light Pass Shiraz 2005 The oak is quite prominent, with a slight desiccated aroma to the fruit; very ripe and certainly warm-fruited, the palate is ample and quite long. Cork. 14.5% alc. **Rating** 90 **To** 2016 $80

Single Site Nursery Block Vine Vale Grenache 2006 Slightly darker personality than the Bowden Vineyard, with more pronounced savoury Provençale herb notes; medium-bodied and quite firm, with chewy/tarry tannin on the finish. Cork. 14.5% alc. **Rating** 90 **To** 2014 $75

Hand Picked Barossa Tempranillo Grenache Viognier 2007 Prominent apricot bouquet from the viognier; a more savoury and interesting wine on the palate; light-bodied with supple sweet red fruits and a touch of garrigue to finish. Screwcap. 13.5% alc. **Rating** 90 **To** 2014 $25.95

Yalumba The Menzies (Coonawarra) ★★★★☆

Riddoch Highway, Coonawarra, SA 5263 **Region** Coonawarra
T (08) 8737 3603 **F** (08) 8737 3604 **www**.yalumba.com **Open** 7 days 10–4.30
Winemaker Peter Gambetta **Est.** 2002 **Cases** 5000 **Vyds** 64 ha

Like many SA companies, S Smith & Son had been buying grapes from Coonawarra and elsewhere in the Limestone Coast Zone long before it became a landowner there. In 1993 it purchased the 20-ha vineyard that had provided the grapes previously purchased, and a year later added a nearby 16-ha block. Together, these vineyards now have 22 ha of cabernet sauvignon and 3.5 ha each of merlot and shiraz. The next step was the establishment of the 35-ha Mawson's Vineyard in the Wrattonbully region. The third step was to build The Menzies Wine Room on the first property acquired – named Menzies Vineyard – and to offer the full range of Limestone Coast wines through this striking rammed-earth tasting and function centre. Exports to all major markets.

🍷🍷🍷🍷🍷 **The Menzies Coonawarra Cabernet Sauvignon 2006** A deep and concentrated bouquet of ripe cassis fruit, earth, violets, a touch of mint and well-handled spicy oak; the palate is multi-layered, with great depth and precision; violets keep making their presence felt; the tannins are plentiful, but quite silky on the finish. Cork. **Rating** 96 **To** 2030 $46.95

🍷🍷🍷🍷 **Mawson's Bridge Block 7A Wrattonbully Sauvignon Blanc 2008** Pale colour; passionfruit and straw bouquet; clean and fresh with a lively finish. Screwcap. 11.5% alc. **Rating** 89 **To** 2011 $15.95

Wrattonbully Vineyards Tempranillo 2007 Sour cherry fruit, with plenty of acid and pronounced aromatics; not a bad effort at this burgeoning Spanish varietal. Screwcap. 13% alc. **Rating** 89 **To** 2014 $19.55

Yangarra Estate ★★★★☆

Kangarilla Road, McLaren Vale, SA 5171 **Region** McLaren Vale
T (08) 8383 7459 **F** (08) 8383 7518 **www**.yangarra.com **Open** 7 days 10–5
Winemaker Peter Fraser, Shelley Thompson **Est.** 2000 **Cases** 13 700 **Vyds** 89.3 ha

This is the Australian operation of Kendall-Jackson, one of the leading premium wine producers in California. In 2000 Kendall-Jackson acquired the 172-ha Eringa Park vineyard from Normans Wines (the oldest vines dating back to 1923). The renamed Yangarra Estate is the estate base for the operation, which has, so it would seem, remained much smaller than originally envisaged by Jess Jackson. Exports to the UK, the US and other major markets.

🍷🍷🍷🍷🍷 **High Sands McLaren Vale Grenache 2006** The bottle, the cork (indifferent) and the price all have the US written on them, but this is in fact a seriously good grenache, with great colour and mouthfeel to its perfectly ripened, deep and luscious fruit. 15.5% alc. **Rating** 96 **To** 2021 $80

🍷🍷🍷🍷½ **McLaren Vale Shiraz 2007** Dense colour; a high-quality regional style with an assemblage of black fruits, dark chocolate and a dash of licorice on the supple, medium- to full-bodied palate; extract and tannins well balanced. Screwcap. 14.5% alc. **Rating** 93 **To** 2027 $28

Old Vine McLaren Vale Grenache 2007 Uncompromisingly varietal sweet fruit from the 60-year-old vines is not overly confection-like, but nor is it in the mainstream of McLaren Vale grenache; that said, its flavour has to be respected. Screwcap. 14.5% alc. **Rating** 90 **To** 2013 $28

Cadenzia McLaren Vale Grenache Shiraz Mourvedre 2007 Very spicy/savoury and with more grenache confection from the High Sands or Old Vine 100% grenache; however, the wine has length thanks to its tannins. Screwcap. 14.5% alc. **Rating** 90 **To** 2014 $28

ŸŸŸŸ **McLaren Vale Unoaked Chardonnay 2008** Has an abundance of stone fruit and citrus/grapefruit flavours on a lively palate; something of a surprise. Screwcap. 13.5% alc. **Rating** 89 **To** 2012 $17

McLaren Vale Roussanne 2008 Glowing golden-green colour must indicate prolonged skin contact and perhaps some oak; the palate doesn't confirm or deny either, although there is a touch of sweetness from one source or another. Screwcap. 13.5% alc. **Rating** 87 **To** 2010 $28

Yarra Burn

Reynell Road, Reynella, SA 5161 **Region** Yarra Valley
T (03) 5967 1428 **F** (03) 5967 1146 **www**.yarraburn.com.au **Open** Not
Winemaker Mark O'Callaghan **Est.** 1975 **Cases** NFP **Vyds** 88 ha
The headquarters of Constellation's Yarra Valley operations centring on the large production from its Hoddles Creek vineyards. The new brand direction has taken shape; all the white and sparkling wines are sourced from the Yarra Valley, as is the Pinot Noir; the Shiraz Viognier is a blend of Yarra and Pyrenees grapes. Exports to the UK and the US.

ŸŸŸŸŸ **Bastard Hill Chardonnay 2006** Developing very slowly but gracefully, with strong Burgundian overtones to the seamless, intense palate, grapefruit and white peach to the fore. Screwcap. 13% alc. **Rating** 95 **To** 2016 $57

Bastard Hill Chardonnay 2007 Glowing yellow-green; very complex wine; some smoky notes behind layers of fruit on both bouquet and palate rippling with stone fruit, grapefruit and cashew notes; very long, persistent finish. Has the stamp of authority. Screwcap. 13% alc. **Rating** 94 **To** 2017 $55

Bastard Hill Pinot Noir 2008 Bacon bone bouquet, with cherry fruit, toasty oak and a touch of spice; surprisingly sweet-fruited palate, with drive and nerve; needs time but the precision is certainly there to suggest an interesting future. Screwcap. 13% alc. **Rating** 94 **To** 2016 $65

ŸŸŸŸŸ **Pinot Noir 2008** Light, bright colour; fresh and lively with distinct forest and spice nuances to the red fruits of the palate; good line and length. Screwcap. 12.5% alc. **Rating** 92 **To** 2013 $29.50

Viognier 2006 Brilliant green-yellow; clean, vibrant aromas then a fluid, almost silky, palate with a mix of fresh and dried fruit flavours; clean finish. Screwcap. 13.5% alc. **Rating** 91 **To** 2012 $26

Pinot Noir 2007 Bright, light, clear; a pretty wine, with good fragrance and cherry/strawberry flavours; now at or near its best. Screwcap. 12.5% alc. **Rating** 91 **To** 2011 $29.50

Cabernet Sauvignon 2006 Quite a toasty bouquet, with cassis and some warm earth character; the palate is firm, with rounded tannins and fleshy fruit on the finish. Cork. 13.2% alc. **Rating** 90 **To** 2015 $29

ŸŸŸŸ **Pinot Gris 2008** Tangy/citrussy edges travel along with the core of pear and apple; has good length. Screwcap. 13% alc. **Rating** 89 **To** 2010 $25.50

Premium Cuvee Rose NV Bright pale salmon-pink; lively strawberry, stone fruit and citrus flavours inhabit a wine ready to enjoy right now. Cork. 12.5% alc. **Rating** 89 **To** 2010 $20

Premium Cuvee Brut NV Light, fresh and crisp, made from 100% chardonnay; no claim of bottle fermentation, and somewhat short. Fully priced. Cork. 12.5% alc. **Rating** 87 **To** 2010 $20

Yarra Park Vineyard

4 Benson Drive, Yering, Vic 3770 **Region** Yarra Valley
T (03) 9739 1960 **F** (03) 9841 7522 **www**.yarrapark.com.au **Open** By appt
Winemaker Mac Forbes (Contract) **Est.** 1996 **Cases** 750 **Vyds** 2.5 ha
Stephen and Rosalind Atkinson established 1 ha each of chardonnay and cabernet sauvignon, and 0.5 ha of sauvignon blanc, between 1996 and '97. The vineyard is run on organic principles, with heavy mulching and what is technically termed Integrated Pest Management. Yields are deliberately kept low. Until 2006 the wines were made by Phil Kerney at Willow Creek in the Mornington Peninsula, but since '07 have been made by Mac Forbes. The vineyard is situated in what the Atkinsons call 'the golden mile', 1 km to the north of Mount Mary. Frost has decimated production over the years since '07.

Yarra Vale

Paynes Road, Seville, Vic 3139 **Region** Yarra Valley
T (03) 9735 1819 **F** (03) 9737 6565 **Open** Not
Winemaker Domenic Bucci **Est.** 1982 **Cases** 1500
This is the second time around for Domenic Bucci, who built the first stage of Eyton-on-Yarra (now Rochford) before being compelled to sell the business in the hard times of the early 1990s. He has established 2 ha of cabernet sauvignon and 0.5 ha of merlot, supplemented by chardonnay, which is supplied in return for his winemaking services to the grower.

ΨΨΨΨΨ **Reserve Shiraz 2005** A medium-bodied wine; attractive cool-grown fruit, the black cherry fruit complexed by spice, pepper and fine, savoury tannins. Developing slowly but well. Diam. 15.5% alc. **Rating** 91 **To** 2020 $33.10

ΨΨΨΨ **Reserve Merlot 2004** Has good varietal expression to a medium-bodied and well-balanced wine; spicy/earthy/olivaceous undertones to the cassis and blackcurrant fruit. Cork. 14.2% alc. **Rating** 89 **To** 2014 $29.80

Yarra Yarra

239 Hunts Lane, Steels Creek, Vic 3775 **Region** Yarra Valley
T (03) 5965 2380 **F** (03) 5965 2086 **www**.yarrayarravineyard.com.au **Open** By appt
Winemaker Ian Maclean **Est.** 1979 **Cases** NFP **Vyds** 9.3 ha
Despite its small production, the wines of Yarra Yarra found their way into a veritable who's who of Melbourne's best restaurants, encouraging Ian Maclean to increase the estate plantings from 2 ha to over 7 ha in 1996 and '97. Demand for the beautifully crafted wines continued to exceed supply, so the Macleans planted yet more vines and increased winery capacity. All this seemed to go up in flames as the terrible 2009 Black Saturday bushfires in Vic consumed the winery, irreplaceable museum stock from '83 to 2000, the then yet-to-be-bottled '08 Syrah and '06 and '08 Sauvignon Blanc Semillon (the '07 vintage having been destroyed by frost), and scorched or burnt 50% of the estate vineyards, the other 50% destroyed by smoke taint. In the midst of this, current bottled wine stock and the '08 Cabernet Sauvignon in another building, as well as the Maclean's house, miraculously escaped the fire. The further good news is that through a combination of gifts and sales, Ian was able to make a Sauvignon Blanc from a top-drawer Yarra grower, Semillon given by De Bortoli, Pinot Noir from grapes sold by Phillip Jones (of Bass Phillip) and Murrumbateman Syrah sourced by Tim Kirk of Clonakilla. De Bortoli, Mount Mary and Yering Station donated 24 older white wine French oak barriques, and the wines were made at Maddens Rise winery. Exports to Singapore, Malaysia and Hong Kong.

ΨΨΨΨΨ **Sauvignon Blanc Semillon 2005** Bright colour; is fully developed; a very complex wine with layers of flavour framed by texture and structure from barrel ferment through to bottle age; great length. Diam. 13% alc. **Rating** 94 **To** 2013 $40
Syrah Viognier 2006 Elegant wine, with strongly spicy/peppery overtones to the bright red berry fruit flavours; cedary oak and fine, savoury tannins complete the picture. Diam. 13.5% alc. **Rating** 94 **To** 2016 $50

The Yarra Yarra 2005 A wine that is all about texture and structure rather than fruit flavour; it is very complex, with savoury/tarry black fruits and persistent tannin support. Blink and you're in Bordeaux. Diam. 13.5% alc. **Rating** 94 To 2020 $75

Cabernets 2005 A powerful multi-faceted bouquet and multilayered plate; a certain imperious austerity to the wine, reinforced by the uncompromising tannins. Demands a minimum of a decade, twice that if possible. Diam. 13% alc. **Rating** 94 **To** 2025 $50

Yarra Yering   ★★★★★

Briarty Road, Coldstream, Vic 3770 **Region** Yarra Valley
T (03) 5964 9267 **F** (03) 5964 9239 **www.**yarrayering.com **Open** Sat 10–5, Sun 2–5 while stocks last
Winemaker Mark Haisma, Paul Bridgeman **Est.** 1969 **Cases** 6000 **Vyds** 26.37 ha
In September 2008, founder Bailey Carrodus died, and in April '09 Yarra Yering was put on the market. It was Bailey's clear wish and expectation that any purchaser would continue to manage the vineyard and winery, and hence the wine style, in much the same way as he had done for the previous 40 years. The low-yielding, unirrigated vineyards have always produced wines of extraordinary depth and intensity, and there is every reason to suppose there will be no change in the years ahead. Dry Red No 1 is a cabernet blend; Dry Red No 2 a shiraz blend; Dry Red No 3 is a blend of touriga, tinta cao, tinta amarela, roriz and sousao; Pinot Noir and Chardonnay are not hidden behind delphic numbers; Underhill Shiraz is from an adjacent vineyard purchased by Yarra Yering over a decade ago; and Portsorts is an extraordinary vintage style made from the same varieties as Dry Red No 3. Exports to the UK, the US and other major markets.

♀♀♀♀♀ **Underhill Shiraz 2006** Very high-quality cool-grown shiraz from 30+-year-old vines; spice, damson plum and blackberry fruit are seamlessly framed by French oak and exemplary tannins; surges on the long finish. Cork. 14.5% alc. **Rating** 95 To 2021 $75

Merlot 2006 Of undoubted pedigree and quality; medium-bodied; red fruits dominant on the long and silky palate, tannins seamlessly interwoven into the fabric of the wine, oak where it should be. Cork. 13.5% alc. **Rating** 95 **To** 2020 $150

Pinot Noir 2006 Good hue and clarity; a full-bodied pinot in the expected style of Yarra Yering; supple and velvety in the mouth, it has the full spectrum of plum, black cherry and spice flavours, which carry the generous amount of new oak. Long lived style. Cork. 14.5% alc. **Rating** 94 **To** 2016 $75

Dry Red No. 2 2006 A complex, fragrant bouquet foreshadows a palate with tremendous thrust and vitality to its array of spicy, ripe black fruits, which have a backbone of sweetness; imposing length. Cork. 14.5% alc. **Rating** 94 **To** 2021 $75

Dry Red No. 3 2006 Fragrant spicy/savoury/chewy aromas; a fine, long and intense palate that is no more than medium-bodied, but has exemplary sour cherry and spice flavours, and fine tannins to close. Cork. 13.5% alc. **Rating** 94 To 2016 $75

Agincourt Dry Red No. 1 2006 Has more weight and fruit richness than the standard No. 1; lovely cassis wrapped around black fruits; tannin and French oak in faultless balance. Cork. 13.5% alc. **Rating** 94 **To** 2021 $75

♀♀♀♀♀ **Viognier 2006** Bright yellow-gold; my tasting note would not be relevant; you will have to decide for yourself. The points are nominal, the price not. Cork. 15% alc. **Rating** 90 **To** 2012 $150

Chardonnay 2006 As always, marches to the tune of its own drum; verges on full-bodied, and is quite developed in colour and flavour; some obviously enjoy the baroque style. The points are a cowardly compromise. Cork. 14.5% alc. **Rating** 90 To 2012 $75

Dry Red No. 1 2006 Fairly austere early in its life, although has the expected complexity; savoury olive and briar notes dominate the finish. Happy to be proved wrong about the wine. Cork. 13.5% alc. **Rating** 90 **To** 2016 $75

Yarrabank ★★★★★

38 Melba Highway, Yarra Glen, Vic 3775 **Region** Yarra Valley
T (03) 9730 0100 **F** (03) 9739 0135 **www**.yering.com **Open** 7 days 10–5
Winemaker Michel Parisot, Willy Lunn, Darren Rathbone **Est.** 1993 **Cases** 5000 **Vyds** 4 ha
Yarrabank is a highly successful joint venture between the French Champagne house Devaux and Yering Station, established in 1993. Until 1997 the Yarrabank Cuvee Brut was made under Claude Thibaut's direction at Domaine Chandon, but thereafter the entire operation has been conducted at Yarrabank. There are 4 ha of dedicated 'estate' vineyards at Yering Station; the balance of the intake comes from other growers in the Yarra Valley and southern Vic. Wine quality has consistently been outstanding, frequently with an unmatched finesse and delicacy. Exports to all major markets.

🍷🍷🍷🍷🍷 Cuvee 2004 Fine persistent mousse; as ever, immaculately composed, structured and balanced; this is the real deal for mainland sparklings, great on its own, or with food. Cork. 12.5% alc. **Rating** 95 **To** 2013 $38

YarraLoch ★★★★★

58 Stead Street, South Melbourne, Vic 3205 **Region** Yarra Valley
T (03) 9696 1604 **F** (03) 9696 8387 **www**.yarraloch.com.au **Open** By appt
Winemaker David Bicknell, Ray Nadeson **Est.** 1998 **Cases** 4500 **Vyds** 12 ha
This is the ambitious project of successful investment banker Stephen Wood. He has taken the best possible advice, and has not hesitated to provide appropriate financial resources to a venture that has no exact parallel in the Yarra Valley or anywhere else in Australia. Twelve ha of vineyards may not seem so unusual, but in fact he has assembled three entirely different sites, 70 km apart, each matched to the needs of the variety/varieties planted on that site. The 4.4 ha of pinot noir are on the Steep Hill Vineyard, with a northeast orientation, and a shaley rock and ironstone soil. The 4 ha of cabernet sauvignon have been planted on a vineyard at Kangaroo Ground, with a dry, steep northwest-facing site and abundant sun exposure in the warmest part of the day, ensuring full ripeness. Just over 3.5 ha of merlot, shiraz, chardonnay and viognier are planted at the Upper Plenty vineyard, 50 km from Kangaroo Ground. This has an average temperature 2°C cooler and a ripening period two–three weeks later than the warmest parts of the Yarra Valley. Add the winemaking skills of Sergio Carlei, and some sophisticated (and beautiful) packaging, and you have a 5-star recipe for success.

🍷🍷🍷🍷🍷 Chardonnay 2007 Tightly wound, restrained, pear-fruit bouquet; a taut and fine palate with a little savoury complexity and very bright and focused fruit; the finish is very long and opens up with a complex array of flavours, from grilled nuts to lemon fruit. Screwcap. 12.5% alc. **Rating** 95 **To** 2016 $35
Pinot Noir 2006 Retains all of the indicia of a young wine, with a vibrant colour, bouquet and palate; the rich black cherry and plum fruit is energised by spicy/savoury tannins, oak adding to the overall appeal. Screwcap. 13.5% alc. **Rating** 94 **To** 2014 $30

🍷🍷🍷🍷 Cabernets 2006 Bright crimson; a fragrant bouquet, then a penetrating palate, opening with blackcurrant fruit before finishing in a savoury tannin mode; good acidity ensures future development. Diam. 14% alc. **Rating** 93 **To** 2020 $25
Heathcote Shiraz 2006 A wine that speaks volumes about the quality of texture; restrained aromatics give way to a palate full of dark fruit, spice and some bay leaf complexity; quite velvety, with a bright core of red fruit, finally making its way through the darker notes. Diam. 14% alc. **Rating** 92 **To** 2018 $30
Arneis 2008 Citrus zest and crushed flower aromas are followed by an equally lively and flavoursome palate; good example. Screwcap. 12.5% alc. **Rating** 90 **To** 2012 $25

🍷🍷🍷🍷 Shiraz Viognier 2006 A bit green and herbal on the bouquet, there is a firm, dry and slightly savoury element to this wine; made with a distinctly European feel. Diam. 14% alc. **Rating** 89 **To** 2014 $30

Yarraman Estate ★★★

Yarraman Road, Wybong, NSW 2333 **Region** Upper Hunter Valley
T (02) 6547 8118 **www**.yarramanestate.com **Open** Mon–Fri 9–4, w'ends 10–3
Winemaker Ian Long **Est.** 1958 **Cases** 80 000 **Vyds** 149 ha
This is the oldest winery and vineyard in the Upper Hunter, established in 1958 as Penfolds Wybong Estate. It was acquired by Rosemount in 1974, and retained until '94. Between 1999 and '01 a new winery and storage area was built; after hitting financial turbulence it was acquired by a small group of Sydney businessmen. Board changes and subsequent strengthening of the management and winemaking team have seen export markets established in the US, the UK and other major markets.

ΨΨΨΨ **Black Cypress Hunter Valley Shiraz 2005** Gentle light- to medium-bodied Hunter shiraz is approaching its peak, although there isn't too much to explain its gold medal at the Hunter Valley Wine Show '06. Screwcap. 13.5% alc. **Rating** 88 **To** 2012 $16.95
Hunter Valley Chardonnay 2006 Nicely put together, unostentatious style, with stone fruit and melon aromas and flavours. Screwcap. 14% alc. **Rating** 87 **To** 2011 $16.95
Hay Burner Chardonnay 2006 Clean and crisp, with a touch of nectarine, and vibrant zesty acidity. Screwcap. 13.5% alc. **Rating** 87 **To** 2011 $14.99
Gundagai Hunter Valley Merlot 2006 Not certain which component drives the wine, but it does have some authentic varietal character in a savoury/tangy spectrum. Screwcap. 14% alc. **Rating** 87 **To** 2012 $16.95
The Bolter Cabernet Merlot 2006 Has some surprising juicy berry/cassis flavours on the light- to medium-bodied palate, which hangs together well. Screwcap. 14% alc. **Rating** 87 **To** 2012 $9.99

Yarrambat Estate ★★★☆

45 Laurie Street, Yarrambat, Vic 3091 (postal) **Region** Yarra Valley
T (03) 9717 3710 **F** (03) 9717 3712 **www**.yarrambatestate.com.au **Open** By appt
Winemaker John Ellis (Contract) **Est.** 1995 **Cases** 1500 **Vyds** 2.6 ha
Ivan McQuilkin has chardonnay, pinot noir, cabernet sauvignon and merlot in his vineyard in the northwestern corner of the Yarra Valley, not far from the Plenty River. It is very much an alternative occupation for Ivan, whose principal activity is as an international taxation consultant to expatriate employees. While the decision to make wine was at least in part triggered by falling grape prices, hindsight proves it to have been a good one, because some of the wines have impressed. In 2006 the vineyard-grown grapes were supplemented with shiraz from Heathcote. Exports to Singapore.

ΨΨΨΨΨ **Sauvignon Blanc 2008** Clean and vibrantly crisp lemon and tropical fruit flavours run through a perfectly balanced and focused sauvignon blanc, which has revelled in its very early picking. Screwcap. 11.1% alc. **Rating** 91 **To** 2011 $13.50

ΨΨΨΨ **Chardonnay 2007** The early picking shows a consistent approach by Yarrambat, which works far better with its white wines than its reds; this has light, but lively, citrus and stone fruit, with minimal oak. Screwcap. 12.7% alc. **Rating** 89 **To** 2014 $13.50
Cabernet Sauvignon 2004 Bright crimson hue; as ever with Yarrambat, very fresh, and here that freshness has been achieved without green characters; bright red fruits and just a touch of mint. Screwcap. 13% alc. **Rating** 89 **To** 2014 $17.50
Shiraz 2005 The red fruit aromas have undertones of mint, spice and green leaf; the light- to medium-bodied palate providing more of the same. Screwcap. 14.5% alc. **Rating** 87 **To** 2012 $19.50

Yarrawood Estate ★★★★

1275 Melba Highway, Yarra Glen, Vic 3775 **Region** Yarra Valley
T (03) 9730 2003 **F** (03) 9730 1144 **www**.yarrawood.com.au **Open** 7 days 10–5
Winemaker Contract **Est.** 1997 **Cases** NFP **Vyds** 40.6 ha

Yarrawood Estate has pinot noir (10.6 ha), cabernet sauvignon (7.9 ha), chardonnay (7.2 ha), merlot (5.3 ha), shiraz (4.5 ha) and lesser amounts of sauvignon blanc, riesling and verdelho. The major part of the production is sold, and the Yarrawood Tall Tales wines are contract-made. It does, however, have a café and cellar door on the Melba Highway, 3 km north of Yarra Glen. Exports to the US, Japan, Singapore and China.

ΨΨΨΨΫ **Tall Tales Shiraz 2007** Good colour; loganberry and violet bouquet with a touch of undergrowth for complexity; quite juicy on the palate, with vibrant acidity and a crisp finish; medium-bodied, fresh and poised. Screwcap. 14% alc. **Rating** 92 **To** 2018 $20.50
Tall Tales Cabernet Sauvignon 2003 Fully developed; there is an attractive core of sweet red fruits, hints of earth and some fragrant leathery complexity. Screwcap. 13.5% alc. **Rating** 90 **To** 2014 $19

ΨΨΨΨ **Tall Tales Autumn Harvest Riesling 2007** A little botrytis and some green apple freshness combine to make a fine example of off-dry riesling. Screwcap. 12.5% alc. **Rating** 88 **To** 2012 $18.50
Tall Tales Chardonnay 2005 Clean pear and nectarine bouquet; toasty palate, with good fruit weight and intensity. Screwcap. 13.4% alc. **Rating** 87 **To** 2012 $17

Yarrh Wines

Greenwood Road, Murrumbateman, NSW 2582 **Region** Canberra District
T (02) 6227 1474 **www**.yarrhwines.com.au **Open** Sep–June w'ends & public hols 11–5
Winemaker Fiona Wholohan **Est.** 1997 **Cases** 3600 **Vyds** 6 ha
It is probably best to quickly say that Yarrh is Aboriginal for running water, and is neither onomatopoeic nor letters taken from the partners names, the partners being Fiona Wholohan, Neil McGregor and Peta and Christopher Mackenzie Davey. The vineyard was planted in three stages between 1997 and 2000, and there are now cabernet sauvignon, shiraz, sauvignon blanc, riesling, pinot noir and sangiovese (in descending order), and all of the wines are estate-grown, and competently made by Fiona. Exports to Norway and China.

ΨΨΨΨΫ **Canberra District Cabernet Sauvignon 2006** Bright colour; fragrant and clearly enunciated cassis and blackcurrant fruit on both bouquet and medium-bodied palate alike; fine tannins and subtle oak. Screwcap. 14.5% alc. **Rating** 91 **To** 2016 $20

ΨΨΨΨ **Canberra District Riesling 2008** Clean, crisp and minerally, with some lemon zest fruit aromas; light-bodied, but is well balanced. Screwcap. 11.5% alc. **Rating** 89 **To** 2013 $18
Canberra District Sauvignon Blanc 2008 Well made, matching tropical fruits with notes of fresh cut grass, herb and a little mineral; bright finish to a well-priced wine. Screwcap. 12.5% alc. **Rating** 89 **To** 2011 $16
Canberra District Shiraz 2006 A medium-bodied wine, with distinctly savoury/spicy/earthy overtones to the fruit; just a little more vinosity needed on the mid-palate. Screwcap. 14.5% alc. **Rating** 89 **To** 2014 $20
Canberra District Cabernet Shiraz 2006 Bright colour; the light- to medium-bodied palate and crisp red fruit flavours belie the alcohol; superfine tannins are a positive. Screwcap. 14.5% alc. **Rating** 88 **To** 2012 $18
Half Dry Canberra District Riesling 2008 Only marginally off-dry, which explains why the alcohol is the same as the regular wine; doesn't quite manage to pull it off, but far from unpleasant. Screwcap. 11.5% alc. **Rating** 87 **To** 2012 $18

Yarrowlumla Estates

1133 Bungendore Road, Bywong, NSW 2621 (postal) **Region** Canberra District
T (02) 6236 9108 **F** (02) 6236 9508 **www**.yarrowlumla.com.au **Open** Not
Winemaker Lark Hill **Est.** 2004 **Cases** 600 **Vyds** 1.5 ha

In 2004 Martine and Stuart Gibson-Bode, together with Gary and Dianne Gibson (Stuart's parents) purchased a vineyard that was planted to chardonnay, sauvignon blanc and merlot in 1997; since purchasing the property they have added pinot noir. The property is located in the hills above Bungendore, the Aboriginal name means 'where the cry comes back from the mountains' (echo).

ΨΨΨΨ   **Canberra District Sauvignon Blanc 2008** Tropical gooseberry fruit carries the palate over the line, but doesn't have the thrust or energy of the better sauvignon blancs. Screwcap. 12.5% alc. **Rating** 87 **To** 2009 $18

Yaxley Estate   ★★★

31 Dransfield Road, Copping, Tas 7174 **Region** Southern Tasmania
T (03) 6253 5222 **F** (03) 6253 5222 **www**.yaxleyestate.com **Open** By appt
Winemaker Frogmore Creek **Est.** 1991 **Cases** 370 **Vyds** 2.5 ha
While Yaxley Estate was established back in 1991, it was not until '98 that it offered each of the four wines from its vineyard plantings. Once again, it is the small batch-handling skills (and patience) of Frogmore Creek that have made the venture possible.

ΨΨΨΨ   **Pinot Noir 2006** A tight, but light-bodied, strongly savoury/foresty Pinot, which has length, but needs more sweet fruit. Organically grown. Screwcap. 13% alc. **Rating** 87 **To** 2012 $32

Yelland & Papps   ★★★★★

PO Box 256, Greenock, SA 5360 **Region** Barossa Valley
T (08) 8562 8434 **F** (08) 8562 8434 **www**.yellandandpapps.com **Open** By appt
Winemaker Michael Papps **Est.** 2005 **Cases** 900
Michael and Susan Papps (née Yelland) set up this venture after their marriage in 2005. Susan decided she did not want to give up her surname entirely, and thus has been able to keep her family name in the business. Michael has the technical background, having lived in the Barossa Valley for more than 20 years, working at local wineries, bottling facilities and wine technology businesses. Susan, who grew up on the Yorke Peninsula, headed to New York for a year, working and studying at the Windows of the World Wine School. The quantity of wine made is limited by the scarcity of the high-quality grapes they have managed to secure from the Greenock area for their wines.

ΨΨΨΨΨ   **Old Vine Barossa Valley Grenache 2007** Bright and welcoming colour; a vibrant and moderately spicy light- to medium-bodied wine with red fruits and no excessive confection characters; has delightful texture and structure. Top Barossa grenache. Screwcap. 14.5% alc. **Rating** 94 **To** 2015 $30
Barossa Valley Cabernet Sauvignon 2007 Deep colour; generous and bold cabernet fruit, with lush cassis perfectly balanced by French oak and soft tannins. A maximum result for the region and vintage. Screwcap. 14.5% alc. **Rating** 94 **To** 2017 $30

ΨΨΨΨΨ   **Barossa Valley Shiraz 2007** A powerful, concentrated wine with quite chunky black fruits on the mid-palate before moving to a finer and more elegant finish, with cedary oak offering assistance. Screwcap. 14.5% alc. **Rating** 93 **To** 2017 $19.95
Greenock Barossa Valley Shiraz 2007 A complex spicy/savoury wine; its black fruits more angular than the '06, less appealing on entry but, like the Barossa Valley, all the components come together on the lively spicy/savoury finish and aftertaste. Screwcap. 14.5% alc. **Rating** 93 **To** 2020 $30
Barossa Valley Grenache Rose 2008 Attractive crimson-red; full-flavoured, but supple and balanced, with attractive cherry flavours. Screwcap. 13% alc. **Rating** 91 **To** 2010 $17

Yellowglen   ★★★☆

77 Southbank Boulevard, Southbank, Vic 3006 **Region** South East Australia
T 1300 651 650 **F** (03) 9633 2002 **www**.yellowglen.com.au **Open** Not
Winemaker Charles Hargrave **Est.** 1975 **Cases** NFP

It may come as a surprise to some (it certainly did to me) that Yellowglen is the clear leader in the value share of the sparkling wine category in Australia, with 22.9%, and growing at 4.3% per annum, way in front of Jacob's Creek at 7.6%, and with zero growth. It is this dominant position (and a spread of RRP prices from $13.99 for Yellow up to $28.99 for Vintage Perle) that underpins its separate listing. Exports to the UK, the US and NZ.

ŶŶŶŶŶ **Limited Release Perle Rose NV** A light blush, with a suggestion of small red berries on the bouquet; the palate is quite dry and offers a serious style of rose for contemplation. Cork. 12% alc. **Rating** 90 **To** 2012 $28.99

ŶŶŶŶ **Vintage Bella 2008** Cleverly made low-alcohol wine with grapey muscat flavours and lemon juice finish. Hard to fault within the parameters of its style. Cork. 7.5% alc. **Rating** 87 **To** 2009 $17.99

Yering Farm ★★★★
St Huberts Road, Yering, Vic 3770 **Region** Yarra Valley
T (03) 9739 0461 **F** (03) 9739 0467 **www.**yeringfarmwines.com **Open** 7 days 10–5
Winemaker Alan Johns **Est.** 1988 **Cases** 7000 **Vyds** 12 ha
Former East Doncaster orchardist Alan Johns acquired the 40-ha Yeringa Vineyard property in 1980; the property had originally been planted by the Deschamps family in the mid-19th century and known as Yeringa Cellars. From orchardist to vigneron is not a large step, and he intuitively chose optimum vine spacing and trellis systems, with a relatively low yield per ha. The wines are largely sold through Vic restaurants and the cellar door. All are made onsite by Alan. Exports to the US, Canada and Asia.

Yering Station ★★★★★
38 Melba Highway, Yarra Glen, Vic 3775 **Region** Yarra Valley
T (03) 9730 0100 **F** (03) 9739 0135 **www.**yering.com **Open** 7 days 10–5
Winemaker Willy Lunn, Darren Rathbone **Est.** 1988 **Cases** 60 000 **Vyds** 112 ha
The historic Yering Station (or at least the portion of the property on which the cellar door sales and vineyard are established) was purchased by the Rathbone family in 1996 and is also the site of the Yarrabank joint venture with French Champagne house Devaux (see separate entry). A spectacular and very large winery has been erected that handles the Yarrabank sparkling wines and the Yering Station and Yarra Edge table wines. It immediately became one of the focal points of the Yarra Valley, particularly as the historic Chateau Yering, where luxury accommodation and fine dining are available, is next door. Yering Station's own restaurant is open every day for lunch, providing the best cuisine in the Valley. In July 2008, winemaker Tom Carson moved to take up the position of Group Winemaker/General Manager of Heathcote Estate and Yabby Lake Vineyard, with overall responsibility for winemaking at those two properties. His replacement is William (Willy) Lunn, a graduate of Adelaide University with more than 24 years' cool-climate winemaking experience around the world, including Petaluma, Shaw & Smith and Argyle Winery (Oregon). Exports to all major markets.

ŶŶŶŶŶ **Yarra Valley Cabernet Sauvignon 2006** High-quality cabernet from a vintage that was perfect for the variety; has great colour, and the cassis fruit has superb tannins to bind it together, further assisted by French oak (if assistance was needed in the first place). Screwcap. 14.5% alc. **Rating** 95 **To** 2026 $26
ED Pinot Noir Rose 2008 Salmon-pink; has similarities with the De Bortoli Rose, especially the complex fruit flavours, with some sweetness on the mid-palate before a savoury finish. Screwcap. 14% alc. **Rating** 94 **To** 2010 $21
Yarra Valley Pinot Noir 2007 Stronger colour than many from '07; likewise, more powerful than prior vintages, with tannins quite evident, although not excessive; plum and black fruits will hold the palate for the longer term. Screwcap. 13% alc. **Rating** 94 **To** 2014 $26
Yarra Valley Shiraz Viognier 2007 Deep crimson-purple; the frost and smoke-ravaged '07 vintage resulted in a journey to Heathcote to bolster the make; sensitive and experienced winemaking has produced the goods, even if the wine is more luscious than the usual more elegant style. Screwcap. 14.5% alc. **Rating** 94 **To** 2021 $26

ŶŶŶŶ♀ **Yarra Valley Chardonnay 2007** Reflects former winemaker Tom Carson's philosophy of lower alcohol and lesser oak, pushing the wine more in the direction of Chablis; stone fruits and some citrus are the drivers, perhaps a little too much so. Time will tell. Screwcap. 12.5% alc. **Rating** 93 **To** 2017 $26

Yeringberg ★★★★★

Maroondah Highway, Coldstream, Vic 3770 **Region** Yarra Valley
T (03) 9739 1453 **F** (03) 9739 0048 **www.**yeringberg.com **Open** By appt
Winemaker Guill de Pury, Sandra de Pury **Est.** 1863 **Cases** 1200 **Vyds** 3.2 ha
Makes wines for the new millennium from the low-yielding vines re-established in the heart of what was one of the most famous (and infinitely larger) vineyards of the 19th century. In the riper years, the red wines have a velvety generosity of flavour rarely encountered, yet never lose varietal character, while the long-lived Marsanne Roussanne takes students of history back to Yeringberg's fame in the 19th century. Exports to the UK, the US, Switzerland, Singapore, Japan and Hong Kong.

ŶŶŶŶŶ **Yarra Valley Chardonnay 2007** A classic wine in the fullest and best sense of the term, with a backwards glance to the 19th-century glory days of Yeringberg, and a future certainty of wonderful development over the next 20 years. Diam. 13% alc. **Rating** 96 **To** 2025 $40
Yarra Valley Pinot Noir 2006 Gently spicy/foresty/savoury nuances to the bouquet lead into a palate with energy and persistence, the flavours in tune with the bouquet; developing slowly but surely. Diam. 14% alc. **Rating** 94 **To** 2015 $60
Yarra Valley Shiraz 2006 From a 'young' block of vines planted on a bony north-facing slope; has impeccable balance and mouthfeel, so much so the length of the palate and the aftertaste came as a surprise. Cork. 14.5% alc. **Rating** 94 **To** 2018 $40
Yeringberg 2006 Good purple-crimson; a medium- to full-bodied wine, with substantial tannins framing the vibrant display of predominantly black fruits; a wine with a pedigree that demands patience. Cabernet Sauvignon/Cabernet Franc/Merlot/Malbec/Petit Verdot. Diam. 14.5% alc. **Rating** 94 **To** 2021 $60

ŶŶŶŶ♀ **Yarra Valley Chardonnay 2007** Has surprising richness and complexity for such a young wine, already with ripe stone fruit and creamy notes. Uncertain long-term future, but good now. Diam. 13% alc. **Rating** 91 **To** 2012 $40

Yilgarnia

1847 Redmond West Road, Redmond, WA 6327 **Region** Denmark
T (08) 9845 3031 **F** (08) 9845 3031 **www.**yilgarnia.com.au **Open** 7 days 11–late
Winemaker Harewood Estate (James Kellie) **Est.** 1997 **Cases** 2500 **Vyds** 11.9 ha
Melbourne-educated Peter Buxton travelled across the Nullarbor and settled on a bush block of 405 acres on the Hay River, 6 km north of Wilson Inlet. That was over 40 years ago, and for the first 10 years Peter worked for the WA Department of Agriculture in Albany. While there, he surveyed several of the early vineyards in WA, and recognised the potential of his family's property. The vineyard is planted on north-facing blocks, the geological history of which stretches back two billion years. A new cellar door opened Easter 2009.

ŶŶŶŶ♀ **Denmark Sauvignon Blanc 2008** A vibrant bouquet of guava, cut grass and pea pod; quite zesty and full of juicy ripe fruit on the palate. Screwcap. 13% alc. **Rating** 90 **To** 2011 $15.95

ŶŶŶŶ **Denmark Unwooded Chardonnay 2008** Ripe stone fruit bouquet; quite good texture, with fleshy fruit and lively acidity on the finish. Screwcap. 14.5% alc. **Rating** 88 **To** 2011 $15.95

Yuroke Vineyards

830 Craigieburn Road, Yuroke, Vic 3063 **Region** Sunbury
T (03) 9333 3308 **F** (03) 9333 3308 **Open** Sun 11–3 or by appt
Winemaker Diggers Rest (Mark Matthews) **Est.** 1997 **Cases** 1000 **Vyds** 8.2 ha
Robyn and Peter Simmie planted 5.6 ha of shiraz and 2.4 ha of pinot noir (and a few rows of cabernet, and few vines of chardonnay) in 1997 and '99. Initially, the grapes were sold to Southcorp, but are now partly vinified for the Yuroke Vineyards label. It seems that I was indirectly responsible for the plantings of pinot (in preference to cabernet sauvignon), good advice at the time, but who knows what lies in the future. Not surprisingly, Shiraz is the wine that has received most accolades.

YYYY **Rose 2008** Bright raspberry fruit; quite sweet, with vibrant fresh fruit on the finish. Screwcap. 14.2% alc. **Rating** 87 **To** 2010 $20
Pinot Noir 2008 Bright colour; a plum and beetroot bouquet; quite tannic, with dark fruit on the finish; give it a year or two. Screwcap. 13.5% alc. **Rating** 87 **To** 2013 $20
Pinot Noir 2006 Unusually deep colour heralding a robust wine with above-average tannin extract; more dry red in character than pinot. Age may partially unlock the jaws imprisoning the fruit. Screwcap. 14.5% alc. **Rating** 87 **To** 2013 $24

Z Wine

PO Box 135, Lyndoch, SA 5351 **Region** Barossa Valley
T 0411 447 986 **F** (02) 4998 7740 **www**.zwine.com.au **Open** At the Small Winemakers Centre, Chateau Tanunda
Winemaker Janelle Zerk **Est.** 1999 **Cases** 375 **Vyds** 60 ha
Z Wine is the venture of vigneron Robert Zerk, a fifth-generation family owner of the old Zerk vineyard at Lyndoch, and daughters Kristen with a degree in wine marketing from Adelaide University, and oenology graduate (with 10 vintages under her belt) Janelle. It is a minor part of the partners' lives with only a tiny part of the production from the family-owned vineyard being used; the remainder is sold to wineries in the area. Janelle has a 'real' winemaker's job elsewhere, the Z Wines being made in borrowed space. They are available at the Small Winemakers Centre at Chateau Tanunda.

YYYYY **Barossa Valley Shiraz 2006** Good colour; a dark mocha bouquet with fruitcake in support; dark blackberry fruit comes to the fore, with a supporting role of redcurrant and spice; some oak on the finish, but the fruit level is ample to swallow it with ease. Screwcap. 14% alc. **Rating** 94 **To** 2015 $45

YYYY **Riesling 2007** Straw and lemon bouquet; suggests broadness on entry, but tightens on the finish, with lime and talc. Screwcap. 11.5% alc. **Rating** 87 **To** 2014 $15

Z4 Wines

PO Box 57, Campbell, ACT 2612 **Region** Canberra District
T (02) 6248 6445 **F** (02) 6249 8482 **www**.Z4.com.au **Open** Not
Winemaker Greg Gallagher **Est.** 2007 **Cases** 600
Z4 Wines is the venture of the very energetic Bill Mason and wife Maria. The name derives from the Mason's four children, each having a Christian name starting with 'Z'. Bill has been distributing wine in Canberra since 2004, with a small but distinguished list of wineries, which he represents with considerable marketing flair.

YYYY **Zoe Canberra District Riesling 2008** Ripe lime and mineral bouquet; a lively palate, with zesty acidity, and a distinctly minerally finish. Screwcap. 11.9% alc. **Rating** 88 **To** 2014 $13.95

Zema Estate   ★★★★★

Riddoch Highway, Coonawarra, SA 5263 **Region** Coonawarra
T (08) 8736 3219 **F** (08) 8736 3280 **www**.zema.com.au **Open** 7 days 9–5
Winemaker Greg Clayfield **Est.** 1982 **Cases** 20 000 **Vyds** 61 ha
Zema is one of the last outposts of hand-pruning in Coonawarra, with members of the Zema
family tending a 61-ha vineyard progressively planted since 1982 in the heart of Coonawarra's
terra rossa soil. Winemaking practices are straightforward; if ever there was an example of
great wines being made in the vineyard, this is it. The extremely popular and equally talented
former Lindemans winemaker Greg Clayfield has joined the team, replacing long-term
winemaker Tom Simons. Exports to the UK, the US and other major markets.

♥♥♥♥♥ **Family Selection Coonawarra Shiraz 2006** Deeper colour, and altogether
more concentrated than the varietal; while luscious, carries its alcohol with ease;
the flavours ranging through plum, black cherry and bramble; has absorbed 24
months in oak. Screwcap. 15% alc. **Rating** 95 **To** 2021 $45
Coonawarra Cabernet Sauvignon 2006 Attractive medium-bodied wine,
with effortless cabernet flavours in the blackcurrant/cassis spectrum; fine, ripe
tannins and controlled oak run through the finish. Screwcap. 14% alc. **Rating** 94
To 2016 $25

♥♥♥♥♡ **Family Selection Coonawarra Cabernet Sauvignon 2006** Deeper, denser
colour than the varietal; a radically different palate, full-bodied, with lush, ripe
fruits and substantial tannins. Will emerge on top of the varietal in 10–15 years.
Screwcap. 15% alc. **Rating** 93 **To** 2026 $45
Coonawarra Shiraz 2006 Pleasant, quite elegant blackberry and spice fruit on
bouquet and palate; the tannins are balanced, as is the oak, and the wine has good
texture. Screwcap. 14.5% alc. **Rating** 90 **To** 2016 $25
Cluny Coonawarra Cabernet Merlot 2006 Fragrant red and black fruits
with some earthy nuances on the bouquet; the medium-bodied palate provides
more of the same before thinning out fractionally on the finish. Screwcap. 14% alc.
Rating 90 **To** 2014 $25

♥♥♥♥ **Coonawarra Merlot 2006** Clear-cut varietal expression with cassis and
savoury/black olive on a light- to medium-bodied palate. Screwcap. 13.5% alc.
Rating 89 **To** 2013 $25

Zig Zag Road   ★★★☆

201 Zig Zag Road, Drummond, Vic 3446 **Region** Macedon Ranges
T (03) 5423 9390 **F** (03) 5423 9390 **www**.zigzagwines.com.au **Open** Thurs–Mon 10–6
Winemaker Eric Bellchambers, Llew Knight **Est.** 1972 **Cases** 400 **Vyds** 3.2 ha
Zig Zag Road's dry-grown vines produce relatively low yields, and until 1996 the grapes were
sold to Hanging Rock Winery. In 1996 the decision was taken to manage the property on
a full-time basis, and to make the wine onsite. In 2002 Eric and Anne Bellchambers became
the third owners of this vineyard planted by Roger Aldridge in 1972. The Bellchambers have
extended the plantings of riesling and merlot, supplementing the older plantings of shiraz and
cabernet sauvignon, pinot noir.

♥♥♥♥♡ **Macedon Ranges Sparkling Shiraz 2005** Purple hue; lightly spicy with
redcurrant fruit, and a fine acid backbone; cleverly handled dosage provides a
delightful and focused wine, with real personality. Cork. 12.5% alc. **Rating** 90
To 2015 $25

♥♥♥♥ **Macedon Ranges Shiraz 2004** Good colour; lifted and fragrant, with plenty
of spice and cranberry fruit; prominent acidity is keeping the fruit together well.
Diam. 13.7% alc. **Rating** 88 **To** 2015 $22
Macedon Ranges Cabernet Sauvignon 2005 Bright colour; not a classic
cabernet, but there is a vibrancy to the fruit that is quite attractive; certainly a
matter of personal preference. Diam. 13.7% alc. **Rating** 87 **To** 2016 $22

Zilzie Wines ★★★☆

Lot 66 Kulkyne Way, Karadoc via Red Cliffs, Vic 3496 **Region** Murray Darling
T (03) 5025 8100 **F** (03) 5025 8116 **www**.zilziewines.com **Open** Not
Winemaker Mark Zeppel **Est.** 1999 **Cases** 100 000 **Vyds** 572 ha
The Forbes family has been farming Zilzie Estate since the early 1990s; it is currently run by
Ian and Ros Forbes, and sons Steven and Andrew. A diverse range of farming activities now
include grapegrowing from substantial vineyards. Having established a position as a dominant
supplier of grapes to Southcorp, Zilzie formed a wine company in 1999 and built a winery in
'00. It has a capacity of 16 000 tonnes, but is designed so that modules can be added to take
it to 35 000 tonnes. The business includes contract processing, winemaking and storage. The
recent expansion may face problems given the state of the Murray Darling Basin. Exports to
the UK, the US, Canada and Hong Kong.

♥♥♥♥♀ **Shiraz Viognier 2007** Bright, clear crimson; quite lively, full-flavoured wine,
with deep red and black fruits and soft tannins. Very good value for the vintage
and price. Screwcap. 14% alc. **Rating** 90 **To** 2013 $15

♥♥♥♥ **Cabernet Sauvignon 2007** A sturdy cabernet that rises above its theoretical
station in life, with ample varietal character and structure. Cork. 14% alc.
Rating 89 **To** 2013 $15
Bulloak Shiraz 2007 A bright and juicy young wine with mulberry and
blackberry fruit dominating the bouquet and palate; very good value. Screwcap.
14.5% alc. **Rating** 88 **To** 2012 $10
Pinot Grigio 2008 Quite fragrant and aromatic, with fruit salad and citrus notes
on the delicate palate; adventurous, low-alcohol style that works well. Screwcap.
10.5% alc. **Rating** 88 **To** 2009 $15
Selection 23 Shiraz 2007 Bright colour; well-made wine, with good varietal
expression and adequate tannin support to give structure. Very well priced.
Screwcap. 14.5% alc. **Rating** 88 **To** 2010 $11
Shiraz 2007 A particularly well put–together wine given the vintage and its
Riverland provenance; modest alcohol has not thinned the wine, nor led to any
green notes. Value. Twin top. 13.5% alc. **Rating** 88 **To** 2012 $15
Merlot 2006 Attractive, fresh and quite juicy red fruits, with lively acidity
underpinning the lively back-palate and finish. Twin top. 13.5% alc. **Rating** 88
To 2010 $15
Bulloak Chardonnay 2008 Clean and vibrant, peach and nectarine fruit;
good flavour and plenty of wine for the money. Screwcap. 13.5% alc. **Rating** 87
To 2012 $10
Sauvignon Blanc 2008 A light style on both bouquet and palate, but is very
correct and balanced. Screwcap. 13% alc. **Rating** 87 **To** 2009 $15
Merlot 2007 Nuances of savoury black olive and bracken underscore the varietal
character of a wine to match most red meats. Twin top. 13.5% alc. **Rating** 87
To 2010 $15
Sangiovese 2007 Bright clear colour; opens with cherry fruit then proceeds
to persistent tannins on the finish, but no more than expected from the variety.
Screwcap. 13% alc. **Rating** 87 **To** 2010 $15
Selection 23 Moscato 2008 If you must have this style, this is a good example;
lemon sherbet and grape fruit with good acidity to provide balance. Not sure this
is technically wine. Screwcap. 6.5% alc. **Rating** 87 **To** 2009 $10

Zimmermann Wine ★★★★☆

Lot 6/7 Newman Close, Willunga South, SA 5172 **Region** McLaren Vale
T (08) 8556 4075 **www**.zimmermann.com **Open** By appt
Winemaker Scott Rawlinson, Chris Thomas **Est.** 1998 **Cases** 1000 **Vyds** 6.5 ha
Hans and Ulrike Zimmermann have a 10-ha property in the south Willunga Hills, with a
small winter creek running through. It took a considerable time for the 6.5 ha of organically-
grown shiraz on a granite, limestone and clay soil, to come into bearing. The first commercial

wine was made in 1998, and the cellar door opened to the public, along with The Blue Grape B&B. The quality of the 2005 The Blue Grape Shiraz is very impressive, heralding a bright future. Exports to Germany, Switzerland and Austria.

ΨΨΨΨΨ **Blue Grape McLaren Vale Shiraz 2005** Elegant, lively, medium-bodied wine, with a mix of bright red cherry and blackberry fruits; balanced oak and fine-grained tannins. Trophy Best Red, 2005 and Older, McLaren Vale Wine Show '07. Cork. 14.5% alc. **Rating** 94 **To** 2015 $35

Zitta Wines ★★★

26 Dover Street, Malvern, SA 5061 (postal) **Region** Barossa Valley
T 0419 819 414 **F** (08) 8272 3735 **www**.zitta.com.au **Open** Not
Winemaker Angelo De Fazio **Est.** 2004 **Cases** 1000 **Vyds** 25.8 ha
Owner Angelo De Fazio says that all he knows about viticulture and winemaking came from his father (and generations before him). It is partly this influence that has shaped the label and brand name: Zitta is Italian for 'quiet' and the seeming reflection of the letters of the name Zitta is in fact nothing of the kind; turn the bottle upside down, and you will see it is the word Quiet. The Zitta vineyard is on a property dating back to 1864, with a few vines remaining from that time, and a block planted with cuttings taken from those vines. Shiraz dominates the plantings (22 ha), the balance made up of chardonnay, grenache and a few mourvedre vines (only a small amount of the production is retained for the Zitta Wines label). The property has two branches of the Greenock Creek running through it, and the soils reflect the ancient geological history of the site, in part with a subsoil of river pebbles reflecting the course of a long-gone river. Tradition there may be, but there is also some highly sophisticated writing and marketing in the background material and the website.

ΨΨΨΨ **Greenock Single Vineyard Barossa Valley Shiraz 2006** A powerful, somewhat rustic, wine, with an abundance of black fruit flavours along with prune, licorice and a dash of dark chocolate. Cork. 14.8% alc. **Rating** 89 **To** 2016 $38

Index

♀	Cellar door sales
ᵢᵢ	Food: lunch platters to à la carte restaurants
⊨	Accommodation: B&B cottages to luxury vineyard apartments
⌕	Music events: monthly jazz in the vineyard to spectacular yearly concerts

McLaren Vale (SA)

Mornington Peninsula (Vic)

Mount Barker (WA)

Tasmania

Tumbarumba (NSW)

The following wineries appear on www.winecompanion.com.au: